The industry's best and brightest offer praise for Ted Alspach's *Illustrator Bible*

"The Illustrator Bible is the ultimate guide to Adobe Illustrator."

—Gene Steinberg, author of *Using America Online*

"The Illustrator Bible is a great book containing a wealth of knowledge about using and applying Illustrator. Its ideas are demonstrated with plentiful examples. Ted's extensive section on Adobe and 3rd party plug-ins is terrific."

—Matt Foster, Adobe Illustrator API Engineer, Adobe Systems

"The Illustrator Bible is the one-stop answer for all Illustrator questions. This 'Bible' is mandatory for all who have faith in vectors!"

—Sandee Cohen, author of *FreeHand Visual QuickStart Guide*

"If you want to really know Illustrator inside and out, the Illustrator Bible is a must-have addition to your library."

—Steve Broback, coauthor of *Beyond the Little Mac Book* and founder of Thunder Lizard Productions

"The Illustrator Bible is a 'can't live without' guide proven to be the definitive resource for Illustrator technicians and artists alike."

—Eric Hess, Product Support Engineer, Illustrator, Streamline & Dimensions, Adobe Systems, Inc.

"Illustrator should be simple...Alspach's Illustrator Bible makes it so."

—David Blatner, author of *The QuarkXPress Book*

"The Illustrator Bible is an amazing compilation of Illustrator techniques, shortcuts, and advice. Ted's irreverent wit makes this book a good read, as well as an indispensable reference."

—Steven Frank, coauthor of *Illustrator Complete* and *KPT Studio Secrets*

"The Illustrator Bible is your guide to the full power of Illustrator."

—Ellen Ablow, Adobe Illustrator Product Manager

"When I have Illustrator questions, I call Ted Alspach. I have the feeling Ted wrote this book for me, just to get me off the phone!"

—Olav Martin Kvern, author of *Real World FreeHand*

"The Illustrator Bible tells you everything you want to know about Adobe Illustrator."

—Shankar Iyer, Adobe Illustrator Product Manager

"With an informal and humorous style, the *Illustrator Bible* introduces the reader to even the most minute details of Adobe Illustrator."

—Sharon Steuer, author of *The Illustrator Wow! Book*

The IDG Books Bible Advantage

The *Illustrator 7 Bible* is part of the Bible series brought to you by IDG Books Worldwide. We designed Bibles to meet your growing need for quick access to the most complete and accurate computer information available.

Bibles work the way you do: They focus on accomplishing specific tasks — not learning random functions. These books are not long-winded manuals or dry reference tomes. In Bibles, expert authors tell you exactly what you can do with your software and how to do it. Easy to follow, step-by-step sections; comprehensive coverage; and convenient access in language and design — it's all here.

The authors of Bibles are uniquely qualified to give you expert advice as well as insightful tips and techniques not found anywhere else. Our authors maintain close contact with end users through feedback from articles, training sessions, e-mail exchanges, user group participation, and consulting work. Because our authors know the realities of daily computer use and are directly tied to the reader, our Bibles have a strategic advantage.

Bible authors have the experience to approach a topic in the most efficient manner, and we know that you, the reader, will benefit from a "one-on-one" relationship with the author. Our research shows that readers make computer book purchases because they want expert advice on a product. Readers want to benefit from the author's experience, so the author's voice is always present in a Bible series book.

In addition, the author is free to include or recommend useful software in a Bible. The software that accompanies a Bible is not intended to be casual filler but is linked to the content, theme, or procedures of the book. We know that you will benefit from the included software.

You will find what you need in this book whether you read it from cover to cover, section by section, or simply one topic at a time. As a computer user, you deserve a comprehensive resource for answers. We at IDG Books Worldwide are proud to deliver that resource with the *Illustrator 7 Bible*.

Brenda McLaughlin
Senior Vice President and Group Publisher

Internet: YouTellUs@idgbooks.com

Illustrator 7 Bible

Ted Alspach

IDG BOOKS

IDG Books Worldwide, Inc.
An International Data Group Company

Foster City, CA ♦ Chicago, IL ♦ Indianapolis, IN ♦ Southlake, TX

Illustrator 7 Bible

Published by
IDG Books Worldwide, Inc.
An International Data Group Company
919 E. Hillsdale Blvd.
Suite 400
Foster City, CA 94404
http://www.idgbooks.com (IDG Books Worldwide Web site)
http://www.dummies.com (Dummies Press Web site)

Library of Congress Catalog Card No.: 97-70956

ISBN: 0-7645-4027-0

Printed in the United States of America

10 9 8 7 6 5 4 3 2 1

1B/RY/QX/ZX/IN

Distributed in the United States by IDG Books Worldwide, Inc.

Distributed by Macmillan Canada for Canada; by Transworld Publishers Limited in the United Kingdom; by IDG Norge Books for Norway; by IDG Sweden Books for Sweden; by Woodslane Pty. Ltd. for Australia; by Woodslane Enterprises Ltd. for New Zealand; by Longman Singapore Publishers Ltd. for Singapore, Malaysia, Thailand, and Indonesia; by Simron Pty. Ltd. for South Africa; by Toppan Company Ltd. for Japan; by Distribuidora Cuspide for Argentina; by Livraria Cultura for Brazil; by Ediciencia S.A. for Ecuador; by Addison-Wesley Publishing Company for Korea; by Ediciones ZETA S.C.R. Ltda. for Peru; by WS Computer Publishing Corporation, Inc., for the Philippines; by Unalis Corporation for Taiwan; by Contemporanea de Ediciones for Venezuela; by Computer Book & Magazine Store for Puerto Rico; by Express Computer Distributors for the Caribbean and West Indies. Authorized Sales Agent: Anthony Rudkin Associates for the Middle East and North Africa.

For general information on IDG Books Worldwide's books in the U.S., please call our Consumer Customer Service department at 800-762-2974. For reseller information, including discounts and premium sales, please call our Reseller Customer Service department at 800-434-3422.

For information on where to purchase IDG Books Worldwide's books outside the U.S., please contact our International Sales department at 415-655-3200 or fax 415-655-3295.

For information on foreign language translations, please contact our Foreign & Subsidiary Rights department at 415-655-3021 or fax 415-655-3281.

For sales inquiries and special prices for bulk quantities, please contact our Sales department at 415-655-3200 or write to the address above.

For information on using IDG Books Worldwide's books in the classroom or for ordering examination copies, please contact our Educational Sales department at 800-434-2086 or fax 817-251-8174.

For press review copies, author interviews, or other publicity information, please contact our Public Relations department at 415-655-3000 or fax 415-655-3299.

For authorization to photocopy items for corporate, personal, or educational use, please contact Copyright Clearance Center, 222 Rosewood Drive, Danvers, MA 01923, or fax 508-750-4470.

About the Author

Ted Alspach is the author of several books on desktop publishing and graphics, as well as hundreds of articles on related topics. He is a contributing editor to *Adobe Magazine.*

Ted is the owner of Bezier Inc., located in the untamed desert somewhere in the middle of Arizona, where he continues to fight the evil menace of pixel-based graphics.

Other books by Ted Alspach

Illustrator 7 Studio Secrets

Acrobat 3 Visual QuickStart Guide

*Photoshop Complete**

*KPT Studio Secrets***

Illustrator Effects Magic

Macworld Illustrator 6 Bible, 2nd Edition

The Complete Idiot's Guide to Microsoft Word for the Mac

Microsoft Bob† (I was young and foolish)

Internet E-Mail Quick Tour

The Complete Idiot's Guide to QuarkXPress

The Complete Idiot's Guide to Photoshop

*The Mac Internet Tour Guide, 2nd Edition**

Macworld Illustrator 5.0/5.5 Bible

Illustrator Filter Finesse†

*with other contributors **with Steven Frank
†with Jennifer Alspach

ABOUT IDG BOOKS WORLDWIDE

Welcome to the world of IDG Books Worldwide.

IDG Books Worldwide, Inc., is a subsidiary of International Data Group, the world's largest publisher of computer-related information and the leading global provider of information services on information technology. IDG was founded more than 25 years ago and now employs more than 8,500 people worldwide. IDG publishes more than 275 computer publications in over 75 countries (see listing below). More than 60 million people read one or more IDG publications each month.

Launched in 1990, IDG Books Worldwide is today the #1 publisher of best-selling computer books in the United States. We are proud to have received eight awards from the Computer Press Association in recognition of editorial excellence and three from *Computer Currents'* First Annual Readers' Choice Awards. Our best-selling *...For Dummies®* series has more than 30 million copies in print with translations in 30 languages. IDG Books Worldwide, through a joint venture with IDG's Hi-Tech Beijing, became the first U.S. publisher to publish a computer book in the People's Republic of China. In record time, IDG Books Worldwide has become the first choice for millions of readers around the world who want to learn how to better manage their businesses.

Our mission is simple: Every one of our books is designed to bring extra value and skill-building instructions to the reader. Our books are written by experts who understand and care about our readers. The knowledge base of our editorial staff comes from years of experience in publishing, education, and journalism — experience we use to produce books for the '90s. In short, we care about books, so we attract the best people. We devote special attention to details such as audience, interior design, use of icons, and illustrations. And because we use an efficient process of authoring, editing, and desktop publishing our books electronically, we can spend more time ensuring superior content and spend less time on the technicalities of making books.

You can count on our commitment to deliver high-quality books at competitive prices on topics you want to read about. At IDG Books Worldwide, we continue in the IDG tradition of delivering quality for more than 25 years. You'll find no better book on a subject than one from IDG Books Worldwide.

IDG BOOKS WORLDWIDE

John Kilcullen
CEO
IDG Books Worldwide, Inc.

Steven Berkowitz
President and Publisher
IDG Books Worldwide, Inc.

VIII WINNER — *Eighth Annual Computer Press Awards 1992*

IX WINNER — *Ninth Annual Computer Press Awards 1993*

COMPUTER CURRENTS 1995 READERS' CHOICE 1995

X WINNER — *Tenth Annual Computer Press Awards 1994*

XI WINNER — *Eleventh Annual Computer Press Awards 1995*

IDG Books Worldwide, Inc., is a subsidiary of International Data Group, the world's largest publisher of computer-related information and the leading global provider of information services on information technology. International Data Group publishes over 275 computer publications in over 75 countries. Sixty million people read one or more International Data Group publications each month. International Data Group's publications include: **ARGENTINA:** Buyer's Guide, Computerworld Argentina, PC World Argentina; **AUSTRALIA:** Australian Macworld, Australian PC World, Australian Reseller News, Computerworld, IT Casebook, Network World, Publish, Webmaster; **AUSTRIA:** Computerwelt Osterreich, Networks Austria, PC Tip Austria; **BANGLADESH:** PC World Bangladesh; **BELARUS:** PC World Belarus; **BELGIUM:** Data News; **BRAZIL:** Annuário de Informática, Computerworld, Connections, Macworld, PC Player, PC World, Publish, Reseller News, Supergamepower; **BULGARIA:** Computerworld Bulgaria, Network World Bulgaria, PC & MacWorld Bulgaria; **CANADA:** CIO Canada, Client/Server World, ComputerWorld Canada, InfoWorld Canada, NetworkWorld Canada, WebWorld; **CHILE:** Computerworld Chile, PC World Chile; **COLOMBIA:** Computerworld Colombia, PC World Colombia; **COSTA RICA:** PC World Centro America; **THE CZECH AND SLOVAK REPUBLICS:** Computerworld Czechoslovakia, Macworld Czech Republic, PC World Czechoslovakia; **DENMARK:** Communications World Danmark, Computerworld Danmark, Macworld Danmark, PC World Danmark, Techworld Denmark; **DOMINICAN REPUBLIC:** PC World Republica Dominicana; **ECUADOR:** PC World Ecuador; **EGYPT:** Computerworld Middle East, PC World Middle East; **EL SALVADOR:** PC World Centro America; **FINLAND:** MikroPC, Tietoverkko, Tietoviikko; **FRANCE:** Distributique, Hebdo, Info PC, Le Monde Informatique, Macworld, Reseaux & Telecoms, WebMaster France; **GERMANY:** Computer Partner, Computerwoche, Computerwoche Extra, Computerwoche FOCUS, Global Online, Macwelt, PC Welt; **GREECE:** Amiga Computing, GamePro Greece, Multimedia World; **GUATEMALA:** PC World Centro America; **HONDURAS:** PC World Centro America; **HONG KONG:** Computerworld Hong Kong, PC World Hong Kong, Publish in Asia; **HUNGARY:** ABCD CD-ROM, Computerworld Szamitastechnika, Internetto online Magazine, PC World Hungary, PC-X Magazin Hungary; **ICELAND:** Tolvuheimur PC World Island; **INDIA:** Information Communications World, Information Systems Computerworld, PC World India, Publish in Asia; **INDONESIA:** InfoKomputer PC World, Komputek Computerworld, Publish in Asia; **IRELAND:** ComputerScope, PC Live!; **ISRAEL:** Macworld Israel, People & Computers/Computerworld; **ITALY:** Computerworld Italia, Macworld Italia, Networking Italia, PC World Italia; **JAPAN:** DTP World, Macworld Japan, Nikkei Personal Computing, OS/2 World Japan, SunWorld Japan, Windows NT World, Windows World Japan; **KENYA:** PC World East African; **KOREA:** Hi-Tech Information, Macworld Korea, PC World Korea; **MACEDONIA:** PC World Macedonia; **MALAYSIA:** Computerworld Malaysia, PC World Malaysia, Publish in Asia; **MALTA:** PC World Malta; **MEXICO:** Computerworld Mexico, PC World Mexico; **MYANMAR:** PC World Myanmar; **NETHERLANDS:** Computer! Totaal, LAN Internetworking Magazine, LAN World Buyers Guide, Macworld Netherlands, Net, WebWereld; **NEW ZEALAND:** Absolute Beginners Guide and Plain & Simple Series, Computer Buyer, Computer Industry Directory, Computerworld New Zealand, MTB, Network World, PC World New Zealand; **NICARAGUA:** PC World Centro America; **NORWAY:** Computerworld Norge, CW Rapport, Datamagasinet, Financial Rapport, Kursguide Norge, Macworld Norge, Multimediaworld Norge, PC World Ekspress Norge, PC World Nettverk, PC World Norge, PC World ProduktGuide Norge; **PAKISTAN:** Computerworld Pakistan; **PANAMA:** PC World Panama; **PEOPLE'S REPUBLIC OF CHINA:** China Computer Users, China Computerworld, China InfoWorld, China Telecom World Weekly, Computer & Communication, Electronic Design China, Electronics Today, Electronics Weekly, Game Software, PC World China, Popular Computer Week, Software Weekly, Software World, Telecom World; **PERU:** Computerworld Peru, PC World Profesional Peru, PC World SoHo Peru; **PHILIPPINES:** Click!, Computerworld Philippines, PC World Philippines, Publish in Asia; **POLAND:** Computerworld Poland, Computerworld Special Report Poland, Cyber, Macworld Poland, Networld Poland, PC World Komputer; **PORTUGAL:** Cerebro/PC World, Computerworld/Correio Informático, Dealer World Portugal, Mac*In/PC*In Portugal, Multimedia World; **PUERTO RICO:** PC World Puerto Rico; **ROMANIA:** Computerworld Romania, PC World Romania, Telecom Romania; **RUSSIA:** Computerworld Russia, Mir PK, Publish, Seti; **SINGAPORE:** Computerworld Singapore, PC World Singapore, Publish in Asia; **SLOVENIA:** Monitor; **SOUTH AFRICA:** Computing SA, Network World SA, Software World SA; **SPAIN:** Communicaciones World España, Computerworld España, Dealer World España, Macworld España, PC World España; **SRI LANKA:** Infolink PC World; **SWEDEN:** CAP&Design, Computer Sweden, Corporate Computing Sweden, Internetworld Sweden, it.branschen, Macworld Sweden, MaxiData Sweden, MikroDatorn, Nätverk & Kommunikation, PC World Sweden, PCaktiv, Windows World Sweden; **SWITZERLAND:** Computerworld Schweiz, Macworld Schweiz, PCtip; **TAIWAN:** Computerworld Taiwan, Macworld Taiwan, NEW ViSiON/Publish, PC World Taiwan, Windows World Taiwan; **THAILAND:** Publish in Asia, Thai Computerworld; **TURKEY:** Computerworld Turkiye, Macworld Turkiye, Network World Turkiye, PC World Turkiye; **UKRAINE:** Computerworld Kiev, Multimedia World Ukraine, PC World Ukraine; **UNITED KINGDOM:** Acorn User UK, Amiga Action UK, Amiga Computing UK, Apple Talk UK, Computing, Macworld, Parents and Computers UK, PC Advisor, PC Home, PSX Pro, The WEB; **UNITED STATES:** Cable in the Classroom, CIO Magazine, Computerworld, DOS World, Federal Computer Week, GamePro Magazine, InfoWorld, I-Way, Macworld, Network World, PC Games, PC World, Publish, Video Event, THE WEB Magazine, and WebMaster; online webzines: JavaWorld, NetscapeWorld, and SunWorld Online; **URUGUAY:** InfoWorld Uruguay; **VENEZUELA:** Computerworld Venezuela, PC World Venezuela; and **VIETNAM:** PC World Vietnam. 3/24/97

Dedication

Dedicated to the furry creatures that allow us to share their lives:

Linus *Felis orangeris*

Murphy *Equus stubbornis*

Toulouse *Felis monstrositis*

Pyro *Felis whinyis*

Yote *Canis lazyis*

Static *Felis obnoxious*

Sage *Felis affectionis*

Credits

Acquistions Editor
Andy Cummings

Development Editor
Barbra Guerra

Technical Editor
Andrei Herasimchuk

Copy Editor
Felicity O'Meara

Project Coordinator
Debbie Stailey

Cover Art
Brad Neal
Thomas-Bradley Illustration and Design

Production Staff
Cameron Booker, Angela F. Hunckler, Brent Savage, Anne Sipahimalani, Kate Snell

Proofreaders
Melissa D. Buddendeck, Nancy L. Reinhardt, Joel K. Draper, Robert Springer

Indexer
Rebecca Plunkett

Supervisor of Graphics and Design
Shelley Lea

Production Director
Beth Jenkins

Product Marketing Manager
Melisa Duffy

Acknowledgments

Whew. As I write these acknowledgments, I'm just about finished with the total revamping of this gigantic book. And while I'm just plain exhausted, I know I'd be much more tired if it were not for the help and support of several key people. This list is by no means exhaustive, but the individuals named here are the ones most responsible for getting this book out the door.

The most important person *is* the most important person. Jennifer Alspach patiently read the pages as they churned out of the printer, giving me supportive comments, such as "you're not going to really put that in there, are you?" and constructive criticism, such as "That's the worst art you've ever created. Which is hard to believe, considering. . . ." Of course, now that Jen has written her very own Illustrator book *(Illustrator 7 Complete,* Hayden Books, 1997*),* she is now the Illustrator authority in the family. Jen's artwork appears uncredited throughout this book. If you like something and it doesn't have a © symbol next to it, I stole it from Jen.

Nancy Dunn and Andy Cummings at IDG Books Worldwide, Inc., who withstood my whining about this and that, as well as considerable delays.

All the other people at IDG Books, including Barb Guerra, who immersed herself in assembling this book quickly and in a somewhat orderly fashion; Andrei Herasimchuk, who tech-edited this book into perfection; Felicity O'Meara, who caught and corrected my grammar and spelling errors; and Debbie Stailey and her production team who brought it all together. A special thanks to Amy Thomas and Mike Roney for letting *Illustrator Studio Secrets* book take a back seat to this one.

Ellen Ablow and Shankar Ayer, the product managers at Adobe Systems who've been living and breathing Illustrator for years, for getting a stable, usable product to me early enough in development so that I could write some useful insights about it.

The pre-beta group of Illustrator experts who helped whine to Andrei, and also made sure that Illustrator was as good as it could be when the interface was finally frozen.

Thomas-Bradley Design and Illustration for the outstanding cover artwork.

Sandee Cohen for being both a friend and a backboard (for bouncing Illustrator questions and dilemmas off), and for helping me with the FreeHand user's Guide to Illustrator that appears on the CD-ROM. If you must give in to the dark side, at least take Sandee's *FreeHand Visual QuickStart* book along to keep you sane.

Diana Smedley of Extensis for giving me an exclusive to provide readers of the *Illustrator 7 Bible* with a fully functional VectorFrame SE plug-in.

Thanks to everyone at Extensis who was involved with creating VectorTools, which is sure to be the standard by which all other plug-ins are measured.

And finally, thanks to Static and Sage, the two kittens who have managed to do more typing than I during the revamping of this book. They taught me how to work with considerable distractions such as tails in front of the monitors, a rousing game of Bat the Cursor, and the always-popular "We thought it was a real mouse. Sorry."

Contents at a Glance

Part I: Introducing Illustrator

1: Illustrator Basics

2: Creating and Painting Shapes

3: Drawing and Manipulating Paths

4: Tracing, Grids, and Guides

5: Working with Illustrator Files

6: Customizing Illustrator

Part II: Putting Illustrator to Work

7: Fine-Tuning Illustrator Artwork

8: Type

9: Masks and Compound Paths

10: Blends and Gradients

11: Patterns, Graphs, and Textures

Part III: Filters and Plug-Ins

12: Illustrator's Built-In Filters and Plug-Ins

13: Using Photoshop Filters and Raster Images

14: VectorTools

15: Other Third-Party Plug-Ins

Part IV: Mastering Illustrator

16: Illustrator and the Web

17: Working with Strokes

18: Printing, Separations, and Traps

19: Using Streamline 4 and Dimensions 3 with Illustrator

20: Getting the Most out of Illustrator

Part V: Appendixes

A: Using the CD-ROM

B: Installing Illustrator

C: What's New in Illustrator 7 for Macintosh

D: What's New in Illustrator 7 for Windows

E: Shortcuts for Illustrator 7 for Macintosh

F: Shortcuts for Illustrator 7 for Windows

G: Troubleshooting

H: Resources

I: Context-Sensitive Menus

Table of Contents

Part I: Introducing Illustrator 1

Chapter 1: Illustrator Basics 3

In This Chapter
The Learning Curve 3
That Was Then, This Is Not Then 6
Techniques for Learning More 6
Mousing Around 8
Cursors 9
Keyboard Commands 9
Illustrator Terminology 10
Fonts 11
Bitmap Fonts 12
PostScript Fonts 12
TrueType Fonts 14
Fonts and Adobe Illustrator 14
Adobe Type Manager 14
Multiple Master Fonts 15
PostScript and Printing 16
What PostScript Does 17
Why PostScript Is So Cool 19
Paths 20
Anchor Points 23
Bézier Curves 25
Control Handles and Control Handle Lines 27
Clear, Cut, Copy, and Paste 30
Clear 30
Cut, Copy, and Paste 31
The Clipboard 32
Undo and Redo 33
Artwork and Preview Modes 35
Artwork Mode 35
Preview Mode 36
Illustrator's Menus 37
Using Menus Effectively 38
Palettes versus Windows 39
The Document Window 41
The Pasteboard 41
The Artboard 42

The Page Tool 42
Miscellaneous Window Stuff 42
The Toolbox 43
Summary 45

Chapter 2: Creating and Painting Shapes 47

In This Chapter 47
Shapes 47
Drawing Rectangles 50
Drawing Rectangles from Their Centers 53
Drawing a Perfect Square 54
Drawing Rounded Rectangles and Squares 54
Using the Round Corners Filter 57
Rounding Corners Backward 57
Drawing Ellipses and Circles 58
Creating Cool Shapes 63
Creating Polygons 65
Seeing Stars 66
Spiral Madness 71
Drawing Shapes at an Angle 73
Filling and Stroking Shapes 74
Fills 74
Strokes 75
Combining Strokes with Fills 77
Applying Fills and Strokes 78
Using the Swatches Palette 81
Spot/Process Swatches and Color Space Indicators 84
The Other Swatch Libraries 85
Choosing and Mixing Colors 87
The Color Ramp 90
Gamut Trouble 91
Spot Colors 91
Putting All the Color Palettes to Use 92
Dif'rent Strokes for Dif'rent Folks 93
Stroke Weight 93
Caps 94
Joins 94
Dashes 95
The Eyedropper and Paintbucket Tools 97
The Eyedropper Tool 97
The Paintbucket Tool 98
Summary 99

Chapter 3: Drawing and Manipulating Paths 101

In This Chapter 101

Drawing Paths in Illustrator 102
- About the Paintbrush Tool 103
- Drawing with the Paintbrush Tool 106
- The Calligraphic Angle 107
- Bends and Ends 108
- Variable Widths and Pressure-Sensitive Tablets 109

Drawing Loosely with the Pencil Tool 109
- Using the Pencil Tool 110
- Drawing Open Paths and Closed Paths 112
- Drawing Semistraight Segments 113
- Erasing in Real Time 114
- Jagged Paths Versus Smooth Paths 114
- Adding to an Existing Open Path 116

Precision Drawing with the Pen Tool 117
- Drawing Straight Lines 121
- Closing Paths 122
- Drawing Curves 122
- Knowing the Pen Commandments 126
- Closing Curved Paths with the Pen Tool 129
- Curved Corner Points 130
- Combination Corner Points 132
- Using the Pen Tool 133

Selection Tools 133
- Using the Selection Tool 137
- Using the Direct Selection Tool 137
- The Group Selection Tool 138

Selecting, Moving, and Deleting Entire Paths 139

Selecting, Moving, and Deleting Portions of Paths 141

Locking and Hiding Objects 142
- Locking 142
- Hiding 143
- Object Information 144

Stacking Order 144
- Pasting Objects in Front of and Behind Selected Objects 146

Grouping and Ungrouping 147
- Ungrouping 148
- Using the Group Selection Tool 148

Summary 149

Chapter 4: Tracing, Grids, and Guides 151

In This Chapter 151

A Teary Farewell to 1-Bit Templates 152
- When Is a Template Not a Template? 153

Tracing 154
- Automatically Tracing Placed Images 155

Manual Tracing 155
About Adobe Streamline 4 155
Using Layers for Tracing 156
Measuring 156
The Measure Tool 157
Sizing Up Objects with the Transform Palette 158
Changing the Measurement Units 159
Using Rulers 160
Measuring with Objects 161
Using Offset Path (for Equidistant Measuring) 161
Grids 162
Grid Color, Style, and Spacing 163
The Magically Spinning Grid 164
The Secret Power of Grids 164
Guides 165
Creating Guides 166
Moving Guides 166
Releasing Guides 167
Guide Preferences 167
Measuring for Printing 168
Stepping 168
Creating Cropmarks 169
Japanese Cropmarks and Trim Marks 171
Summary 173

Chapter 5: Working with Illustrator Files 175

In This Chapter 175
Setting Up a New Document 175
Changing the Document Setup 178
Artboard Options 179
View Options 180
Path Splitting Options 181
Using the Printer's Default Screen 183
Compatible Gradient Printing 183
Navigating the Document 183
Who's Zoomin' Who? 184
The Zoom Tools 184
Other Zooming Techniques 186
Using the Scroll Bars 187
Scrolling with the Hand Tool 188
Artwork Mode versus Preview Mode 189
Artwork (Only) Mode 189
Preview Mode 191
Preview Selection Mode 192
Combining Artwork and Preview Modes 192

Now You See It ... 193
Using Custom Views ... 194
The Window Menu ... 195
Managing Files ... 196
Saving Files ... 197
The Save As Command ... 200
Save a Copy ... 200
Reverting to the Last Saved Version ... 201
File Types ... 201
Compatibility Options ... 201
Saving as Illustrator EPS ... 203
Illustrator EPS Preview Options ... 203
Exporting ... 204
Exporting Files in PDF Format ... 204
Opening and Closing Illustrator Files ... 204
Placing Art ... 205
Placed Art Size Issues ... 206
Publish and Subscribe (Mac Only) ... 206
Document Info ... 207
Summary ... 208

Chapter 6: Customizing Illustrator ... 211

In This Chapter ... 211
Preferences ... 212
Modifying the Startup File ... 213
Changing General Preferences ... 215
The General Preferences Dialog Box ... 215
Tool Behavior ... 216
The Constrain Angle Option ... 216
The Corner Radius Option ... 217
The Curve Fitting Tolerance Option ... 218
The Auto Trace Gap Option ... 218
General Preference Options ... 218
The Snap to Point Option ... 219
The Transform Pattern Tiles Option ... 219
Use Precise Cursors Option ... 219
The Paste Remembers Layers Option ... 221
New Tool Shortcuts ... 221
The Area Select Option ... 221
The Scale Line Weight Option ... 222
Show Tool Tips ... 222
Japanese Cropmarks ... 223
Disable Warnings ... 223
Units & Undo ... 224
The Cursor Key Option ... 225

The Size/Leading Option 225
The Baseline Shift Option 225
The Tracking Option 226
The Greek Text Limit Option 226
Undo Settings 227
Guides & Grid 227
The Hyphenation Options Dialog Box 227
The Plug-Ins and Scratch Disk Preference 227
The Color Settings Dialog Box 228
Placement and Toolbox Value Preferences 229
Things You Can't Customize 231
Summary 231

Part II: Putting Illustrator to Work 233

Chapter 7: Fine-Tuning Illustrator Artwork 235

In This Chapter 235
Path Editing 237
Adding Anchor Points 238
The Add Anchor Points Function 240
Removing Anchor Points 241
Simplifying Paths by Removing Anchor Points 242
Splitting Paths 242
Dividing and Duplicating Paths 243
The Knife Tool 244
Slicing with other paths 245
Cleanup 245
Offset Path 246
Outline Path 247
Averaging Points and Joining 248
Averaging Points 249
Joining 250
Aligning and Distributing Objects 252
Converting Anchor Points 253
Converting Smooth Points 253
Converting Straight Corner Points 254
Converting Combination Corner Points 255
Converting Curved Corner Points 257
The Pathfinders 257
The Pathfinder Options Dialog Box 259
Unite 259
Intersect and Exclude 261
Minus Front and Minus Back 262

Divide 262
Outline 264
Trim 265
Merge 265
Crop 266
Hard and Soft 266
Trap 267
The Reshape Tool 269
The Twirl Tool 270
Transforming Objects 272
The Rotate Tool 274
The Scale Tool 275
The Reflect Tool 276
The Shear Tool 277
Moving 279
The Transform Palette 280
Transform Each 283
Transformation Effects 286
Creating Shadows 286
Transforming Gradients 287
Rotating into a Path 288
Making Tiles Using the Reflect Tool 289
Using Transformation Tools on Portions of Paths 290
Rotating into Kaleidoscopes 292
Transforming Patterns 293
The Select Functions 293
Select Same Fill Color 294
Select Same Paint Style 295
Select Same Stroke Color 296
Select Same Stroke Weight 296
Custom Paint Style Selections 297
Select Inverse 297
Select Masks 298
Select Stray Points 298
Layers 299
Getting Started with Layers 301
Using the Layers Palette 302
The Main Section of the Layers Palette 302
The Layers Palette Icons 304
The Layers Palette Pop-up Menu 304
Layer Advice and Strategies 306
Summary 306

Chapter 8: Type 309

In This Chapter 309
The Type Menu 310
Font 311
Size 311
Character 312
Paragraph 312
MM Design 314
The Tab Ruler Palette 314
Graphical Tabs 316
The Link Blocks Option 316
The Unlink Blocks Option 318
The Make Wrap Option 318
The Release Wrap Option 320
The Fit Headline Option 320
The Create Outlines Option 320
Type Outlines 322
Making Letters That Normally Appear in Your Worst Nightmares .. 322
Creating Logos from Type Outlines 324
Distorting Words and Phrases 325
Masking and Other Effects 326
Avoiding Font Conflicts by Creating Outlines 327
Hinting 328
Find 328
Find Font 330
Check Spelling 330
Change Case 333
Smart Punctuation 333
Rows & Columns 335
Type Areas 338
Using the Type Tools 339
The Type Tool 340
The Area Type Tool 341
The Path Type Tool 341
The Vertical Type Tools 341
Point Type 343
Area Type as a Rectangle 344
Area Type 345
Choosing the Good Shapes for Area Type 346
Outlining Areas of Area Type 346
Doing Bizarre Things with Area Type 348
Coloring Type That Is Anchored to a Path 349
Changing the Area, Not the Type 350

Area Type 351
Path Type 353
Type on the Top and Bottom of a Circle 354
Avoiding Path Type Trouble 356
Path Type 357
Selecting Type 358
Editing Type 360
Anti-Aliased Type 361
Character Attributes 362
The Character Palette 362
Font and Style Changes 363
Size Changes 364
Leading 366
Kerning and Tracking 367
Vertical and Horizontal Scale 370
The Language Barrier 370
More Multinational Options 370
Paragraph Palette 370
Alignment 373
Indentation 374
Space Before Paragraphs 374
Spacing 375
Hang Punctuation 375
Hyphenation 376
Those Unusual Options 377
Special Characters on a Mac 377
Symbol Typefaces on a Mac 378
Special Characters in Windows 379
Customizing Fonts 381
Export/Place 382
Vertical Type 383
Changing the Direction of Type 384
Path Type and Vertical Type 386
Other Type Considerations 386
Summary 387

Chapter 9: Masks and Compound Paths 389

In This Chapter 389
Compound Paths 389
Creating Compound Paths 390
Releasing Compound Paths 392
Understanding Holes 392
Overlapping Holes 393
Creating Compound Paths from Separate Sets of Paths 394

Type and Compound Paths 394
Path Directions 395
The Winding Numbers Rule, or What Happened to My Fills? 396
Reversing Path Directions 397
Using Unite to Create Compound Paths 398
Faking a Compound Path 399
Masks 399
Creating Masks 400
Masking Raster Images 401
Masking Blends and Other Masks 402
Stroking and Filling Masking Objects 402
Releasing Masks 403
Masks and Printing 404
Masks and Compound Paths 405
Using Compound Paths and Masks in an Illustration 406
Summary 410

Chapter 10: Blends and Gradients 411

In This Chapter 411
Understanding Blends and Gradients 412
Blends 415
Creating Linear Blends 416
Multiple Colors with Linear Blends 419
Nonlinear Blends 421
Masking Blends 421
New and Improved Pseudolinear Blends 424
Guidelines for Creating Color Linear Blends 425
End Paths for Linear Blends 426
Calculating the Number of Steps 427
Creating Radial Blends 430
Creating Shape Blends 431
Shape Blend #1: Computer Vents 432
Shape Blend #2: Circle to Star 433
Complex-Shape Blending 435
Shape Blend #3: Cheating 436
Creating Realism with Shape Blends 438
Airbrushing and the Magic of Stroke Blends 443
Tubular Blends 443
Spring-Tube Blends 445
Airbrushed Shadows 446
Creating Glows 448
Softening Edges 449
Neon Effects 450
Backlighting 451

Gradients 452
The Gradient Tool 452
Using Preset Gradients 453
Using the Gradient Palette 453
Shadows, Highlights, Ghosting, and Embossing 454
Expand Fill 459
Summary 459

Chapter 11: Patterns, Graphs, and Textures 461
In This Chapter 461
Patterns 461
Using the Default Patterns 463
Creating Custom Patterns 465
Pattern Backgrounds and Boundaries 467
Making Seamless Patterns 469
Symmetrical Patterns 472
Line Patterns and Grids 474
Diagonal-Line and Grid Patterns 476
Transparency and Patterns 477
Modifying Existing Patterns 477
Putting Patterns and Gradients into Patterns 477
Transforming Patterns 478
Graphs 479
The Nine Types of Graphs 483
Grouped-Column Graphs 483
Stacked-Column Graphs 484
Line Graphs 484
Area Graphs 487
Pie Graphs 487
Scatter Graphs 487
Customizing Graphs 488
Using the Graph Data Dialog Box 489
Using Marker and Column Designs 490
Texture Generation 491
Ink Pen Density 493
Ink-Pen Dispersion 493
Thickness 495
Rotation 495
Scale 497
Other Ink Pen Fill Controls 497
Summary 498

Part III: Filters and Plug-Ins 499

Chapter 12: Illustrator's Built-In Filters and Plug-Ins 501

In This Chapter 501
Filters in Illustrator 502
Filter Organization 503
Illustrator and Photoshop Filters 504
The Plug-Ins Folder 506
Third-Party Filters 506
Why You Can Apply the Last Filter but Never "Apply Last Filter" 507
The Color Filters 507
  Adjust Colors 507
  The Color Blend Filters 508
  The Convert to Filters 509
  The Invert Colors Filter 509
  The Overprint Black Plug-In 509
  The Saturate Filter 510
Manipulating Colors with the Color Filters 511
  Techniques for Creating Shadows and Highlights 511
  Creating Extruded Multiple Path Objects 512
  Creating Negatives with the Color Filters 513
The Create Filters 514
  The Fill & Stroke for Mask Filter 514
  Creating Object Mosaics 515
The Distort and Stylize Filters 524
  The Free Distort Filter 524
  The Punk and Bloat Filter 527
  Twirl Filter 530
  The Zig Zag Filter 533
The Random Mangle Filters 535
  The Roughen Filter 535
  The Scribble and Tweak Filter 539
The Stylize Filters 542
  Add Arrowheads 542
  Drop Shadow Filter 547
  The Round Corners Filters 548
  Calligraphy 550
Path Patterns 551
  Creating a Pattern for Path Patterns 553
  The Trouble with Corners 555
Summary 557

Chapter 13: Using Photoshop Filters and Raster Images 559

In This Chapter 559
Vectors versus Pixel-Based Images 559
Changing Illustrator Artwork into Pixels 560
Going to Photoshop and Back with Pixels and Paths 562
Colorizing One-Bit TIFF Images 563
Using Photoshop-Compatible Filters in Illustrator 564
Illustrator's Photoshop Plug-Ins 566
Other Third-Party Photoshop filters 566

Chapter 14: VectorTools 575

In This Chapter 575
The VectorTools Components 577
VectorBars 577
VectorLibrary 577
VectorMagicWand 577
VectorObjectStyles 577
VectorColor 578
VectorShape 578
VectorFrame 578
VectorNavigator 578
VectorTips 578
Installing and Using VectorFrame SE 579
Using VectorTools 579
VectorFrame 580
VectorBars 582
VectorMagicWand 585
VectorLibrary 586
VectorColor 587
Using Edit Curves in VectorColor 590
VectorShape 590
VectorObjectStyles 592
VectorNavigator 593
VectorTips 594
Summary 594

Chapter 15: Other Third-Party Plug-Ins 595

In This Chapter 595
Third-Party Plug-In Roundup 596
Installing and Using Third-Party Plug-Ins 598
BeInfinite InfiniteFX 599
IFX Theory 600
The IFX Filters 600

CSI Socket Set 1 601
- CSI AI Plug-In Manager 602
- CSI AI Startup Manager 603
- CSI Adjust Colors 603
- CSI Adjust Stroke 604
- CSI Select Colors 605
- CSI Select Placed Art 606
- CSI Select Strokes 606
- CSI Select Text 606
- CSI Select Similar 606
- CSI Process to Grayscale 607

CSI Socket Set 2 607
- CSI Align and Distribute 608
- CSI Align Edges 608
- CSI Align to Guide 609
- CSI Patterns to Paths 610
- CSI Reflect Each 610
- CSI Scale to Dimension 610
- CSI Scale to Fit Page 612
- CSI Step and Repeat 612

MetaCreations Vector Effects 614
- VE Commonalties 615
- KPT 3D Transform 617
- KPT ColorTweak 619
- KPT Emboss 621
- KPT Flare 622
- KPT Inset 624
- KPT Neon 624
- KPT Point Editor 626
- KPT Resize and Reposition 626
- KPT ShadowLand 627
- KPT ShatterBox 628
- KPT Sketch 630
- KPT Vector Distort 631
- KPT Warp Frame 633

hot door CADtools 1.0 634

Vertigo 3D Words 638

Alien Skin Stylist 641

Why Nobody Uses LetraSet Envelopes 642

MAPublisher 2.0 643

Kara Fonts 643

Creating Plug-Ins for Illustrator 7 646
- The Illustrator API and SDK 646
- Plug-In Types 648

Suites 648
Plug-Ins I'd Like to See 649
Fun Plug-Ins on the Illustreator 7 Bible CD_ROM 650
KPT Gradients/Patterns to Paths 651
Matt Foster's Melt & Drip Filters 651
BeInfinite Smart Remove Points 652
Ted Alspach's Doodle Jr. 653
Adobe's Plug-Ins 653
The Analog Clock 654
The Arrow Tool 657
Point and Delete 657
Summary 659

Part IV: Mastering Illustrator 661

Chapter 16: Illustrator and the Web 663

In This Chapter 663
Vector Graphics and the World Wide Web 663
Exporting to JPEG Format 664
Exporting to PNG Format 667
Exporting to GIF Format 667
The Web-Ready Swatches Palette 667
Assigning URLs to Objects 668
Creating Image Maps 669
Creating Web Page Headings with Illustrator 670
Using the Heading in a Web Page (Text-Based Editors) 672
Heading Effects 672
The PDF Situation 673
Summary 673

Chapter 17: Working with Strokes 675

In This Chapter 675
The Secret Magic of Strokes 676
Using the Stroke Charts 679
Stroking Type 684
Creating Rough Edges 686
Using Fills to Create Half-Stroked Paths 688
Workin' on the Railroad 688
The Wild River 692
The Highway 692
Putting Type into Strokes 698
Incredibly Intricate Strokes 699
Summary 700

Chapter 18: Printing, Separations, and Traps 701

In This Chapter 701
Prior to Printing 701
  Document Setup 702
  Page Setup (Macintosh) 703
Print Setup (Windows) 706
  Printing Composites 706
  Gray Colors 710
Printing Color Separations 711
  Spot Color Separation 711
  Process Color Separation 713
  How Many Colors? 714
  Combining Both Spot and Process Color Separations 717
The End of Adobe Separator 718
Using Separation Setup 718
  The Bounding Box and Bleed 719
  Changing Printer Information 720
  Changing Page Size 721
  Changing the Orientation 722
  Understanding Emulsion 724
  Setting Up the Halftone Screen 724
  Understanding Halftone Line Screens 725
  Adding Custom Line Screens 727
  The Printing Process and Saving $$ with Your Computer 728
  Changing from Positive to Negative to Positive 729
  Working with Different Colors 729
  Printing Separations 730
Printing Separations from Other Applications 730
Trapping 731
  Understanding What Trapping Does 731
  Why You Need Trapping 733
  How Much Trap? 734
  Trapping Illustrator Files Manually 735
  Trapping with Trap 736
  Complex Trapping Techniques in Illustrator 737
Summary 739

Chapter 19: Using Streamline 4 and Dimensions 3 with Illustrator 741

In This Chapter 741

Adobe Streamline ... 742
The Streamline Toolbox and Menu Items ... 743
  Streamline Tools ... 743
Using Streamline ... 745
Introducing Dimensions ... 747
  A Brief History ... 748
  Be Frightened, Be Afraid, Be Intimidated ... 748
  Why Dimensions Is the Best 3D Software for Printing ... 750
Understanding the Three-Dimensional World ... 751
  Changing from Two Dimensions to Three Dimensions ... 751
  Three-Dimensional Positioning ... 752
An Overview of Dimensions ... 753
  Tools ... 753
  The 3D Toolbox ... 755
  The 2D Toolbox ... 756
Creating Primitives ... 757
Rendering Artwork ... 760
Changing How Three-Dimensional Objects Look ... 761
  The Surface Properties Palette ... 761
  The Lighting Palette ... 766
Creating Two-Dimensional Artwork ... 768
  Using Illustrator Artwork ... 768
  Modifying 2D Artwork ... 768
  Saving 2D Artwork ... 769
  Previewing 2D Artwork ... 769
  Using the Tile and Stack Options ... 769
Extruding and Revolving 2D Artwork ... 769
  Extruding Flat Art ... 770
  Understanding Bevels ... 771
  Revolving Artwork ... 773
Manipulating 3D Artwork ... 776
  Moving Objects in Three Dimensions ... 776
  Scaling in Three Dimensions ... 778
  Rotating Objects in Three Dimensions ... 779
Views and Perspectives ... 781
  Different Viewing Options ... 781
  Getting a Better Perspective ... 782
Mapping 2D Artwork onto Three-Dimensional Surfaces ... 785
Other 3D Techniques ... 786
  Creating a Three-Dimensional Object in Illustrator ... 786
  Using Gradients to Make Bumps and Dents ... 790

Combining Dimensions Artwork with Illustrator 790
Summary 792
Answers to the Puzzle in Figure 19-31 793

Chapter 20: Getting the Most out of Illustrator 795

In This Chapter 795
What You Can Learn from Existing Artwork 795
  Taking Apart Artwork 796
  Making Your Art Easy to Understand 796
  Copyrighting Your Electronic Artwork 796
The Art in the Illustrator 7 Bible 797
  File Types 798
  Paths 798
  Labeled Palettes 799
  Color Section Artwork 800
  Using Art as Outlines for a Transparency 800
  Scanning Artwork at the Proper Resolution 801
Backgrounds for Illustrations 802
  Using Gradients for Backgrounds 802
  Using Blends and Blend Effects for Backgrounds 804
  Using Textures for Backgrounds 804
Discovering New Features on Your Own 805
  Finding New Features 806
  Knowing versus Memorizing 807
  What You Can Do to Learn More 808
  Getting Answers and Information from Adobe 808
Summary 809

Part V: Appendixes 811

Appendix A: Using the CD-ROM 813

Installing Acrobat 3.0 Reader 813
Using the Illustrator Bible Tutorial PDF 814
Installing and Using VectorFrame SE (Mac only) 816
Installing and Using Doodle Jr. (Mac Only) 816

Appendix B: Installing Illustrator 817

System Requirements for Macintosh 817
  Macintosh Computer Requirements 817
  RAM 818
  Other Attachments 818

Macintosh System Recommendations 819
CPU and FPU 819
Too Much RAM Is Never Enough 820
Installing Illustrator 7 for Macintosh 820
System Requirements for Windows 821
Windows System 821
Installing Illustrator for Windows 822

Appendix C: What's New in Illustrator 7 for Macintosh 823

New Features 823
Changes 826
Menu Changes 826
Tools 829
Palettes 830
Other Changes 832
The Top Ten List of Things You Need to Know When Using Illustrator 7 the First Time 833

Appendix D: What's New in Illustrator 7 for Windows 837

New Features 837
Palettes 843
New Tools 846
Changes 847
Menu Changes 847
Tools 852
Palettes 853
Other Changes 854
The Top Ten List of Things You Need to Know When Using Illustrator 7 for Windows for the First Time 855

Appendix E: Shortcuts for Illustrator 7 for Macintosh 859

Menu Commands 859
Tool Shortcuts 862
Color Commands 876
Other Palettes 878
Miscellaneous Commands 880
Generic Dialog Box Commands 880

Appendix F: Shortcuts for Illustrator 7 for Windows 881

Menu Commands 881
Tool Shortcuts 885
Color Commands 898
Other Palettes 900

Appendix G: Troubleshooting 903

Appendix H: Resources 909

People and Companies 909
Other Illustrator Books 912
FreeHand Books 914

Appendix I: Context-Sensitive Menus 915

What's a Context-Sensitive Menu? 915
The Context-Sensitive Menus 916
No Selection 916
Standard Path Selection 916
Group, Mask, or Compound Path Selection 917
Placed Image Selection 917
Type Selection 918
Graph Selection 918

Index 919

License Agreement 961

Installation Instructions 963

IDG Books Worldwide Registration Card ... Back of Book

Foreword by Pierre E. Bézier

Around 1960, engineers and technicians in the European car industry were divided into two groups: those who worked on mechanical parts and those who worked on car body parts.

For the mechanical group, the surfaces that could be manufactured were clearly defined with dimensions and limits — there was no place for haggling or bargaining at inspection time, and the verdict was simple: GOOD or SCRAP.

For the body-design group, things were far from being simple. From the stylist's small scale mock-up to the full-scale drawing of the "skin," to the clay model, to the final drawing, to the master model, to the stamping tools — each rendering was supposed to be in accordance with the preceding one. Designers used French curves, sweeps, and lathes (plastic splines), but small discrepancies could not be avoided at each step. These minor errors added up, to the detriment of the final product.

Although these problems had gone on for decades, people were not satisfied and still looked for a solution. They believed, as Plato said, that "Number is the expression of everything," and, as Lord William Kelvin said, that "No one can claim to have mastered a phenomenon as long as he has not been able to express it with figures."

By 1960, a small number of people believed that the computer could provide an acceptable solution to the problem of discrepancies in measurements. The aircraft industry was probably the first industry in the U.S. to use computers, but the automotive industry rapidly followed suit.

At this time, two solutions were considered. The first solution was to keep the general process of manufacturing and, with the help of computers (CRT or numerically controlled machine tools), improve one or two steps. The second solution was to forget the existing scheme and start from scratch to take full advantage of the computer's capabilities. This step entailed greater risks but also had greater advantages.

For those who chose the latter solution, the first task was to build a list of requirements that included the following:

- Creating or adopting a mathematical system that could be easily understood and operated by draftsmen, designers, and methods people. The system needed to describe space curves — not only conics and surfaces — and to provide an accurate, complete, and distortion-free definition of the curves. It needed to be easily transmitted between offices, shops, and subcontractors.

- Providing the body- and tool-drawing offices with full-scale drawing machines, controlled completely by computers that work in interactive mode, such as those capable of tracing curves at a speed of one foot per second.
- Equipping the drawing offices, not the tool shops, with rapid milling machines that could carve large portions of a car — the top, the hood, and so on — in a soft material, such as Styrofoam, urethane foam, or plaster.
- Devising the relevant software.
- Equipping the tool shops with heavy NC milling machines for manufacturing stamping units.

In 1960, the mathematical theory was based on the use of conics — nonrational polynomials with vector coefficients. Mathematical theory now includes B-splines and NURBS, but mathematicians still search for other solutions.

By the end of the '60s, some simple systems were operative, but a complete system was not fully operative until the end of the '70s. Since that time, many basic improvements in car design have been developed, including color, reflection lines, perspective viewing, animation, finite elements, crash simulation, aerodynamics, stress and strain, vibration and noise, and so on.

No doubt, the advent of CAD/CAM has been one of the most important changes that took place in the industry during the present century. Of course, it is not necessary for the lay user to master the complete theory — one can play basketball without referring to Galileo, Newton, Keppler, or Einstein — but students and engineers who take part in the development or improvement of a system will find plenty of food for thought in this book.

Pierre E. Bézier

Pierre Bézier is the creator of Bézier Curves, a unique mathematical system used for defining curves. Bézier Curves were adopted by Adobe when they created the PostScript page description language. Illustrator is very much a "front end" for PostScript, and the software would undoubtedly be quite different today if not for Bézier's (unknown at the time) contribution. Pierre Bézier lives in Paris, France.

Preface

You are holding in your hands the biggest, most thorough, and most helpful guide to Adobe Illustrator you'll find anywhere.

Gives you a bit of a rush, doesn't it?

This is the third edition of the best-selling *Illustrator Bible,* the first book I had ever written, and still my favorite (well, I'm also partial to the original version of *The Stand,* but Mr. King probably won't let me take credit for that...especially since I was only about 9 when I first read it).

The *Illustrator 7 Bible* is the book I wrote because I couldn't find the book I wanted about Adobe Illustrator. Now I have it, and believe it or not, I'm constantly using my own book for a reference. I'd love to tell the world, "sure, I know that," without putting them on hold while I search my own index for the "Reset Tracking to 0" key command (Command-Shift-X, by the way). There's just too much about Illustrator for any one person to keep in their head at one time; the *Illustrator 7 Bible* gathers all of the Illustrator information you can't remember and makes it more available and easier than most of the characters on *Melrose Place.*

If you're at your local bookstore, looking at the different Illustrator books to choose from, don't just pick this one because it weighs the most (sorry about that...I get more thank-you letters from chiropractors who've stayed in business because of this monstrosity) or because it works great as a booster seat for your two-year-old nephew. Instead, take a look-see through these pages, which are stuffed to overflowing with in-depth Illustrator information that you just won't find anywhere else. And then there's the CD-ROM — packed with chapters that didn't fit in the book, QuickTime tutorials, tons of images and software, as well as two fully functional, *free* plug-ins from Extensis and Cytopia.

What's new in this edition

Illustrator has gone through a serious makeover with Version 7. So has this book. I've chopped out several sections and stuck them on the CD-ROM to make room for two brand new chapters (covering Illustrator and the Web, and Extensis VectorTools), and reorganized the existing chapters into a leaner, meaner book. Okay, it's not any leaner, but it is meaner, in a good way.

All the new <cough, cough> features in Illustrator 7 have been covered thoroughly, although those additions are really the least of the new material. Instead, you'll find that because the Illustrator interface has changed, so has the way that you work with Adobe Illustrator, and I've spent a considerable amount of time making the transition as painless as possible for you. Because the Paint Style palette has been ripped out <sniff> and replaced by the Color palette, the Swatches palette, the Stroke palette, and a bunch of icons on the Toolbox, most of Chapter 2 (Creating and Painting Shapes) has been rewritten from scratch. The keyboard commands appendixes (Appendix E + F) have been totally redone as well, with a different slant that is sure to be helpful to both new users and Illustrator 6 users alike.

Two appendixes for keyboard commands? The reason is this: Illustrator 7 is the first version of Illustrator to be released simultaneously for Macintosh and Windows — ever. Not only that, but it's the first major upgrade to Illustrator for Windows since 1992 when Adobe released Illustrator 4. (It has since been updated to 4.1 and is compatible with Windows 95, but it's still old technology.)

To accommodate all the Illustrator for Windows users, I've included a sidebar in to summarize what's new and/or different in each chapter since Version 4.1.

There's stunning new art in the color section, as well as a handy Pantone color reference chart for process-based Pantone Colors, making the color section more of a tool than you'll find in any other similar color pages. The CD-ROM contains all of the Illustrator images you see in the book, labeled by figure number, including the images in the color section. Finally, and most importantly, in addition to the free distortion filter Doodle Jr., Extensis has graciously given me the exclusive rights to distribute a fully working version of VectorFrame, a frame-making plug-in from their VectorTools set of plug-ins (covered in Chapter 14).

Is this the Illustrator book for you?

I've been to bookstores. I've seen all those other Illustrator books that are out there. Some of them are quite good. Some of them are fairly awful. But none of them can match the *Illustrator 7 Bible* for thoroughness, usefulness, or completeness. I've left no vector-based stone unturned.

Here's some more reasons why the *Illustrator 7 Bible* is the best overall book on Illustrator:

The most complete coverage of Illustrator. This book isn't big because I wanted to hog all of the retail book space to myself (of course, that's not a bad idea) but because I've included every possible thing you'd ever want to know about Illustrator 7. From learning the basics of drawing to creating outstanding special effects with vectors and rasters, it's all here.

Fun, original, different artwork to illustrate the techniques and capabilities of Illustrator. When I say *different,* I'm not talking about the type of "art" where there's a naked guy in a room sitting on a stool reciting the first few lines of the Declaration of Independence over and over and over again (that's supposedly "performance art," heh), but instead, I mean that each technique is created with a different piece of artwork. Some of it is simple and some of it is complex, with each piece showing not only a particular feature but other Illustrator capabilities as well.

Clean artwork without those annoying jaggies. This is *vector* software. When you think of vectors, you probably think of smooth, flowing paths that don't look like someone filled in a bunch of squares on a sheet of graph paper. So instead of using screen shots for paths shown in this book, each path was painstakingly drawn in Illustrator. I think you'll appreciate the difference.

Top-notch technical prowess. Once again, the *Illustrator 7 Bible* has gotten the best possible person to do a technical review of the book. The past edition was technically reviewed by Eric Gibson, the lead technical support engineer for Illustrator. This edition has been tech-edited by Andrei Herasimchuk, who designed and implemented the new Illustrator interface and was behind such useful new features as the visible transformation origin point. No one is more familiar with the inner workings of Illustrator, and Andrei has done an exceptional job to ensure that this book is as accurate as possible.

Perfect for Teaching. If you know Illustrator inside and out, you'll find the *Illustrator 7 Bible* the best teaching tool available for Illustrator, with examples and explanations that perfectly complement a teaching environment. Most computer training companies teaching Illustrator use this book, as do schools and universities.

The most in-depth coverage of filters and plug-ins. Filters and plug-ins are an integral part of Adobe Illustrator, so I've devoted an entire section of the book to covering native filters and third-party plug-ins such as Extensis VectorTools. There's even a section on how you can make your own plug-ins.

Real-world examples and advice. Illustrator doesn't exist in a vacuum. Instead, it is often used in conjunction with other programs, in a variety of different environments and situations. Some people use Illustrator to create logos, others create full-page advertisements, and still others create entire billboards with Illustrator. Throughout this book, various real-world situations and examples are presented that truly add to your understanding of each topic.

A CD-ROM with artwork and exclusive plug-ins. The CD-ROM contains Illustrator artwork from this book, as well as several software and plug-in demo files. In addition, Doodle Jr. and VectorFrame are included free on the CD-ROM. As if that weren't enough, fully functional plug-ins from Adobe that they don't want anyone to know about are on the CD-ROM for your use in Illustrator 7.

The best information for upgrading from previous versions: Appendixes E (Shortcuts for Macintosh) and F (Shortcuts for Windows) indicate different and new shortcuts. Appendixes C (What's New in Illustrator 7 for Macintosh) and D (What's New in Illustrator 7 for Windows) list each and every new feature, as well as changed features, with cross references to supporting material throughout the book.

You don't need to be an artist, a computer geek, or anything else to learn Illustrator with this book. No matter what your level of Illustrator experience — from the person who calls tech support for help getting the #$@&#!! shrinkwrap off the box to the person who puts the frustrated party on hold at Adobe — you'll undoubtedly find new things to try, and learn more about Illustrator along the way.

How to get the most out of this book

There are a few things you might want to be aware of before you dive too deeply into the mysteries of Vector-based graphics, Adobe style:

Versions. When you see the word *Illustrator,* it refers to all versions of Illustrator. When I stick a number after the word Illustrator, it's relevant to that version only. Version numbers in the software industry change faster than time slots for *Murder One,* so Version 7.0 may become Version 7.0.1, 7.1, 7.2, or some other number before you know it. When I'm talking about Version 7, I'll be referring to 7.*x*, where *x* is any number at all. When Adobe releases Version 8 or the next major upgrade, there will be a new version of this book to help you through it.

Menu and keyboard commands. To indicate that you need to choose a command from a menu, I write something like MenuName⇨Command. For instance, File⇨Save. If there is a command nested in a submenu, it is MenuName⇨Submenu⇨Command, like Filter⇨Distort⇨Roughen. If a command has a keyboard command, I mention that as well for both Macintosh and Windows versions. For instance, Save uses "Command-S," on the Mac, which I'll put here as ⌘-S (the ⌘ corresponds to the ⌘ symbol on your keyboard). The other Mac keys are spelled out — Option, Shift, Control, and so forth. Save uses "Control+S" in Windows (corresponds to the Ctrl key on your Windows keyboard).

This is not a novel. As much as I'd like you to discover plot intricacies, subtle characterizations, and moral fabric woven into the story, none of those things exist in this book (if they do, be sure to let me know about them). There are two really good ways to use this book:

1. Look up what you're interested in the Table of Contents or the Index, and refer to that section. Rinse and repeat as necessary.
2. Slowly, calmly work your way through the entire book, trying out examples (the funky Steps that are almost everywhere) and techniques as you run across them. The book is designed to be read this way, each chapter building on the previous chapter.

Have fun. This book is a pretty straightforward, serious tome, although I have managed to include many bad puns (rotate the image as far as you're *inclined* to) and terrible jokes — *How many FreeHand users does it take to draw a light bulb? Three. One at the computer, one on the phone talking to Macromedia tech support, and the other back at the computer store, trying to exchange the software for Illustrator.* Of course, I show you how to draw a realistic-looking light bulb in Chapter 10, with an abbreviated version in the color section.

What's a computer book without icons?

Nonexistent, for the most part. I'm not exactly Dr. Icon, but I've included five throughout this edition that may make reading this book a little more enjoyable and helpful.

These icons indicate some sort of power user secret you absolutely need to know to be able to illustrate with the big kids.

Did you know that the second edition of this book was the best-selling book on Illustrator 6? Interesting tidbits like this are noted by this icon. Sort of like having Cliff from Cheers rambling on about something every few pages. Slightly interesting, but they won't increase your Illustrator skills. Just something I thought you might want to know.

Danger Will Robinson!!! If Robby the Robot used Illustrator, he'd be reading about all the nasty things that can happen and how to avoid them.

These are little gems of information packed into a chatlike sidebar. Toulouse is my screen name on America Online, where I moderated the Illustrator SIG chat, back when they wanted people online. You have to ask yourself what in the world was I doing between the ages of 2 and 12....

These icons indicate what's brand new in this version of Illustrator.

What's inside the book

Part I: Introducing Illustrator. This section has me pointing out points and helping you get a handle on paths. You learn how to color things, how to uncolor things, and how to delete the things when you don't like their color. I even show you how to customize Illustrator to work better and faster.

Part II: Putting Illustrator to Work. This section puts *you* to work learning about type and how to fine-tune those paths you drew in Part 1. Part II also contains a healthy dose of the hard stuff — like compound paths, masks, blends, gradients, patterns, and graphs.

Part III: Filters and Plug-Ins. Here's where the fun begins, as you start distorting and coloring using the native Illustrator filters and plug-ins. Then there's a whole chapter on VectorTools (Chapter 14), one on other third party filters and plug-ins like CADtools, VectorEffects, and Stylist, and another on Photoshop Filters.

Part IV: Mastering Illustrator. This is the section that contains the nitty gritty — and I don't mean the band. Hot topics such as using Illustrator on the Web, printing, and techniques for creating fantastic graphics are presented.

Part V: Appendixes. The nine appendixes contain information on installing Illustrator, using the CD-ROM, what's new in Illustrator 7, shortcuts, context-sensitive menus, and troubleshooting. There's also a handy guide to all sorts of useful Illustrator resources.

Yo, Ted!

Send any comments you might have about the book to:

IB7@bezier.com

(IB7 is my own personal mis-ordered acronym for the *Illustrator 7 Bible.*)

I get tons of e-mail from my loyal, intelligent readers, and I try to answer each and every message. However, due to time constraints, it may appear that I'm blowing you off. Please be assured that I do respond to e-mail when I can, although there are times when I'm holed up with a deadline of some sort for weeks and just can't respond. Either that or I'm perpetually napping....

And while you're in cyberspace, stop by VectorVille, the world's only Web site dedicated to vector graphics, at:

http://www.bezier.com/vectorville

You can even visit the Bézier, Inc., home page at:

www.bezier.com

Help make Illustrator better

Okay, you know by now that I just love Illustrator. But there are always things that can be done to make the program more user-friendly, more functional, and just plain better.

If you have such an idea, please send an e-mail to:

suggestions@adobe.com

Send me a copy of your e-mail, too (IB7@bezier.com). I'd love to know what features you want to see in future versions, and if and when they're implemented.

Adobe does listen to its users, and the more readers that ask for a feature, the more likely that feature will get into a future version of Illustrator. The Illustrator product managers are eager for any and all suggestions.

Help make VectorTools better

You've also figured out that I really really *like* VectorTools (*love* is such a strong word). If you can think of a way to make an existing component better, or if you have a plug-in you'd like to see implemented, send an e-mail to:

suggestions@extensis.com

Copy me on it as well (IB7@bezier.com).

Introducing Illustrator

The first time you run Adobe Illustrator, you may be overwhelmed by the number of tools and palettes that you have to choose from. And then there are those menus. Fifty tools, thirteen palettes (more if you count all those swatch palettes), and seven menus (containing more than two hundred menu items). It's almost enough to drive you to pixels. And if that weren't bad enough, each Illustrator session starts with an artist's nightmare: a giant white virtual canvas staring him or her in the face.

Part I dispels the apprehension and fear of learning Illustrator. This part includes such basic concepts as drawing, painting, and how Illustrator works with files. I've included samples and interactive lessons throughout so that you can try out the concepts that are being introduced.

CHAPTER 1

Illustrator Basics

In This Chapter

- The length of time it takes to learn a PostScript drawing program
- How to learn faster
- Outline theory
- Pierre Bézier and his curves
- Basic editing functions: Cut, Copy, Paste, and Clear
- Undoing and redoing
- Working in Preview mode
- Using palettes and windows

Not too long ago, artists and illustrators worked by hand, not on computers. It may seem hard to believe, but artists spent hours and hours with T squares, rulers, French curves, and type galleys from their local typesetters.

Now, of course, artists and artist wanna-bes spend hours and hours with their computer, a mouse, a monitor, and on-screen type that they've set themselves. Some traditional artists are still out there . . . although they seem to be a dying breed. Eventually, most serious computer artists come face to face with Illustrator, the king of PostScript drawing programs. And they're frightened by what they see.

Windows Update

Most of the Illustrator fundamentals remain the same, with such common Illustrator objects as paths, points, and handles working just like they always have. Most of the changes addressed in this chapter are cosmetic and interface-based.

What's Missing	What Replaces It
Most dialog boxes	A plethora of palettes
The old toolbox	A brand new toolbox with loads of additional tools

What's New

Multiple Master palette, for manipulating Multiple Master fonts within Illustrator

Fill types now include gradients

Unlimited Undos and Redos

The Learning Curve

Quite a few years ago, I was setting type with PageMaker at the service bureau where I worked. I noticed that the specs called for type to be set at a 15° angle. In those days, type at any angle on the computer was a big deal because none of the desktop publishing programs at the time had that capability. PageMaker 3 had more options and menus than almost any other software currently on the market, and I spent considerable time searching for "rotate" or something similar. No such luck. I got so desperate that when I spied the manual out of the corner of my eye, I began to reach for it.

"What troubles you, young Skywalker?" asked my boss.

Out of instinct, I punched ⌘-S on my keyboard. (The boss, a former soldier, had this thing about saving often; his method of enforcement was a lightning-fast flick of my Mac's power switch.) "I can't find where you rotate type in PageMaker," I replied sheepishly.

He nodded. And then he spoke two simple, forceful words: "Adobe Illustrator."

Thus began my journey into the land of Illustrator, and my subsequent PageMaker productivity slide.

Figuring out how to rotate type wasn't too difficult, but then I started playing with some of the other tools and features of the software. Confusion ensued. Hours of staring at an Illustrator document and wondering "Why?" took up most of my time in those days. I didn't understand Fills and Strokes, I didn't understand how to make things certain colors, and I didn't understand why what I drew was so different from what I printed (see Figure 1-1).

Figure 1-1: Artwork as it appears in Artwork mode (left) and the printed result (right)

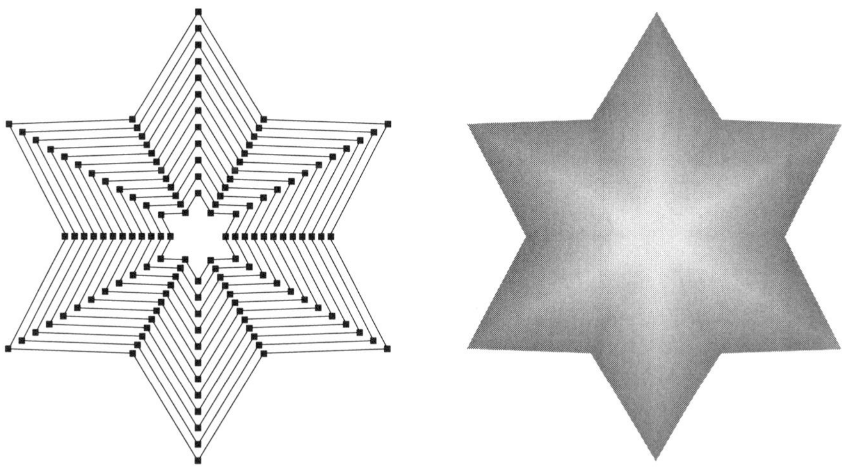

Even my boss couldn't help me much with Illustrator; questions to him resulted in a knowing nod and the now-customary tilt and swivel of his head toward the Illustrator manual. I went through the tutorial three times, but when I tried to mask anything but those darn fish, it wouldn't work. I was convinced that the Pen tool was Satan's pitchfork in disguise. Patterns made about as much sense as differential equations (those I'll *never* understand, much to my math-teaching mother's chagrin). Then there were things like flatness (huh?), miter limits (yeah, right), and splitting paths (I wouldn't know a clue if I was sitting on one) — all subjects that might as well have been written in a third-century Chinese dialect.

I had never used or seen software as *different* as Illustrator.

That Was Then, This Is Not Then

The version of Illustrator I was introduced to was Illustrator 88, an incredible improvement over Illustrator 1.1, but still not a user-friendly piece of software. Version 3, introduced in 1990, was a little better, but most of its improvements were in functionality, not user interface. In the summer of 1993, Illustrator 5 was introduced, with a full load of not just new features but better ways for people to access those features.

Finally, in 1997, Illustrator 7 arrived in all its glory. But there's still a problem with Illustrator — although the program is now easier for beginners to understand, most of the intermediate and advanced areas of Illustrator are still beyond the scope of the majority of users.

Techniques for Learning More

There are a number of ways you can get to know Illustrator faster than the average Joe D. Designer:

- **Playing, the right way:** I used to hate the term *playing,* which has been typically used to describe trying out new features and areas of the software you aren't familiar with. Normally, the word is said in a negative way, although if done correctly, it can be the most important and valuable time spent while learning software. When playing with Illustrator, follow these rules for the most effective playtime:
    - Create something that you want to keep, like a business card, a new logo (especially if your company currently has a hokey one designed in the '70s by the owner), a letterhead, or a graphic masterpiece.
    - Even if you don't like what you're doing, *don't* delete it. It may look awful, but it could be a starting point for another illustration in the future. Save it.
    - Print everything. After an hour of playing, you will (1) feel better about the time your coworkers and boss think you spent playing with new software and (2) have a file of stuff you did that you can review in the future. I love going back to artwork I did three months before and remembering a feature I used for that art that I've just plain forgotten about since then. (Imagine if you had years' worth of this stuff — you'd have a treasure chest full of Illustrator experiments at your fingertips that could save you lots of time and effort in the future.) Or, if you'd like to take the high-tech route, save the paper and add the Illustrator files to your favorite Fetch catalog.

- Don't do real-life projects during playtime. Real-life projects consist of two possible things: artwork you are doing for someone else, which has to be perfect, and artwork you are doing for yourself, which — surprise! — also has to be perfect. Either way, you will invariably delete quite often, and hardly ever print anything but the final product. Try to separate real life from playtime. (I'm currently just trying to distinguish what exactly *is* real life, so you're already a step ahead of me.)
- Don't do too much in one sitting. The more you do at one time, the more you'll forget. More than a couple hours of play at one time starts becoming detrimental.

- **Dissect existing illustrations:** "How'd they do that?" You can figure out all but the most complex artwork by opening it up in Illustrator and selecting different pieces. You can discover techniques that you probably would never have come across on your own.

POWER TIP

The *Illustrator 7 Bible* CD-ROM contains much of the artwork that you see here in the book. Just open up the folder called Artwork, and find the chapter and figure number you're looking at. You can see how the artwork that graces these pages was created by dissecting and examining it.

- **Talk to other Illustrator users:** By talking to other users, you can discover ways they approach similar illustrations or learn of their pitfalls before they become yours. One of the best places to do this is at the frequent Illustrator Conferences sponsored by Thunder Lizard Productions (1-800-221-3806), where hundreds of top-notch Illustrator users gather for several days of talks and seminars about every aspect of Illustrator. Another great place to "talk Illustrator" is at the weekly Illustrator Special Interest Group chat on America Online, each Tuesday night at 9 p.m. EST in the Mac Graphics conference room (keyword "Illustrator").
- **Attempt the impossible:** If you successfully use Illustrator to create a replica of the ceiling of the Sistine Chapel, including the proper shading and discoloration associated with aging, you will undoubtedly master the software in the process. Realistically, if you try something that you believe is beyond either your skills or the capabilities of the software, you may be surprised at what you know and what Illustrator can do with you in the driver's seat. And, in the process, you'll probably also come up with new techniques and procedures for creating similar, simpler artwork.
- **Visit the Vectorville website at http://www.bezier.com/vectorville:** This is the unofficial vector capital of the online world, with tons of insider information on Illustrator, VectorTools, and other vector products. You find tips, transcripts of the AOL Illustrator chats, demo software, reviews of plug-ins and other vector software.

- **Read the entire *Illustrator 7 Bible:*** Just because you never understood masking before, and never thought you would need it in the future, doesn't mean that nothing else in the chapter on masking is going to be of interest to you. Throughout this book, I've tried to show new and exciting ways of doing everything, from the basics of drawing a line and creating a simple closed shape to reversing gradients and accessing the Convert Direction Point tool while using a pressure-sensitive brush.
- **Watch the CD-ROM tutorials:** If you think a tutorial on basic pattern creating is too elementary, you just might miss out on that new way of creating a cloverleaf in a few simple steps. Most of the tutorials on the CD included with this book show more tricks on side topics than they do on their main subject.

POWER TIP

The *Illustrator 7 Bible* CD-ROM tutorials are arranged in the same order as this book, with each section corresponding to a book chapter.

Mousing Around

Illustrator requires the use of a mouse for selecting items, pulling down menus, moving objects, and clicking buttons. Learning to use the mouse efficiently requires a great deal of patience, practice, and persistence (the three-*p*s, which is where American Indians might have lived but for that H&R Block). In most programs, you can master using the mouse quickly, but using the mouse with Illustrator's Pen tool takes those *p*'s to a new extreme. If you're unfamiliar with using a mouse, a fun way to get used to working with one is by playing a mouse-driven game, such as *Eric's Ultimate Solitaire* from Delta Tao. After several hours of play (providing you don't get fired by your employer or kicked out of the house by your irritated spouse), you'll become Master of Your Mousepad, King of Your Klicker, and so on.

You use the mouse to perform five basic functions in Illustrator:

- **Pointing,** which is moving the cursor around the screen by moving the mouse around your mousepad.
- **Clicking,** which is pressing and releasing the mouse button in one step. Clicking is used to select points, paths, and objects, and to make windows active. Windows users: *Clicking* means left-button clicking, as you'd expect.
- **Dragging,** which is pressing the mouse button and keeping it pressed while you move the mouse. You drag the cursor to pull down menus, select contiguous characters of text, move objects, and create marquees.
- **Double-clicking,** which is quickly pressing and releasing the mouse button twice in the same location. Double-clicking is used to select a word of text, select a text field with a value in it, access a dialog box for a tool, and run Illustrator (by double-clicking its icon in the Finder).

- **Control-clicking [right-clicking],** which displays a context-sensitive menu when you press Control and click. Windows users: Simply press the right mouse button.

Cursors

When I refer to a cursor, I don't mean someone whose favorite phrase is "@#&*%!!" — although this is a popular saying for people who are using Illustrator for the first time.

The cursor is the little icon (usually an arrow) that moves in the same direction as the mouse. (If the cursor seems to be moving in the opposite direction from the mouse, check to make sure that the mouse isn't upside down, or, heaven forbid, that you aren't upside down.)

In Illustrator, the cursor often takes the form of a tool that you are using. When the computer is busy — doing whatever it is a computer does when it is busy (computing, probably) — an ugly little watch takes its place. Figure 1-2 shows many of the standard cursors that appear in Adobe Illustrator.

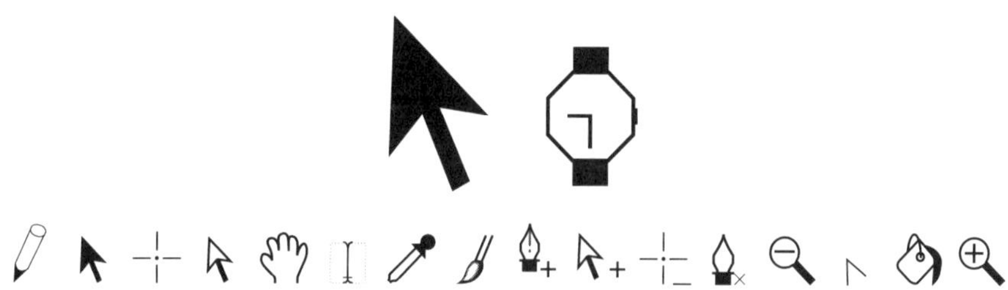

Figure 1-2: An assortment of cursors from Illustrator

Keyboard Commands

Keyboard commands are shortcuts for common activities that you perform in Illustrator. Ninety percent of the shortcuts use the Command key (the one with the cloverleaf symbol ⌘ and the on a Macintosh; the Ctrl key in Windows) in combination with other keys.

Many of the Illustrator menu items have keyboard shortcuts listed next to their names. Pressing the key combination does the same thing as choosing that menu item from the menu. Some menu items do not have keyboard commands; usually, you have to choose those items from the menu.

On a Macintosh, common keys that are used with the Command key are the Option key (located handily next to the Command key) and the Shift key. The Control key had been used in Versions 5, 5.5, and 6, but Illustrator 7 uses the Control key only to simulate the right mouse button that Windows users have. You hold down these keys while you press another key or click the mouse. Figure 1-3 shows these four modifier keys.

Figure 1-3: The four keyboard modifier keys for Macintosh

On a Windows system, the Ctrl key is used along with the Alt and Shift keys. If you press certain combinations of these keys while pressing another key or clicking the mouse, special things happen.

A complete listing of key commands for Macintosh and Windows systems can be found in Appendixes E and F, respectively.

Keyboard commands are as important to an Illustrator artist as the mouse is, and with a little practice, you can learn them quickly. Besides, many keyboard commands are the same from program to program, which will make you an instant expert in software that you haven't even used yet!

Illustrator Terminology

The language of Illustrator users sounds kinda funny to normal people and FreeHand users.

Sometimes Illustrator users, in their enthusiasm, start spouting off all manner of ungodly terms, such as *RAM, Pantone colors, megabytes, PostScript Level 3, dpi,* and *Option[Alt+7]-clicking.* Then there are the power users, who are into *megahertz, gigabytes, Bézier curves, line screens,* and *⌘-Option-Shift-clicking* [Ctrl+Alt+Shift+clicking]. In this book, such terms are discussed as they come up.

A word of advice: Don't use Illustrator language in front of people who have never used (or never plan to use) Illustrator. You might get put away in one of those places where the walls are soft and so is the food, as should anyone who spouts off, "Thank God for RGB support in 7.0!" at the drop of a bitmapped hat.

Fonts

Fonts are a big deal to Illustrator users.

For the seasoned graphic artist, the thousands of typefaces that are available for the Mac provide a typesetting heaven on earth. For a newcomer to Illustrator and typesetting, fonts can be overwhelming. Illustrator ships with about 300 Adobe PostScript Type 1 fonts; others are available for purchase at costs that range from about $2 per face to hundreds of dollars for a family.

Fonts for the Macintosh come in various formats, each format having advantages and disadvantages over other formats. Fonts fall into the following categories:

- Bitmap fonts, also known as screen fonts
- PostScript fonts, also called Type 1 or Type 3
- TrueType fonts

ASK TOULOUSE

Commanding Attention

Mrs. C: Do you know the"Illustrator Alphabet" commands?

Toulouse: Sure. A is for Select All, B is for Paste Behind, C is for Copy, D is for Transform Again.

Mrs. C: Wait, D is for Transform Again? What happened to T?

Toulouse: T is for the Character palette.

Mrs. C: Oh.

Toulouse: O is for Open.

Mrs. C: I see.

Toulouse: I shows and hides the color palette, C, as I said before, is for Copy.

Mrs. C: You and...

Toulouse: Hide. New Document.

Mrs. C: Why...

Toulouse: Preview and Artwork toggle.

Mrs. C: Heyyyyyyy!

Toulouse: What, are you Fonzie? You know, I know the Command-Shift alphabet as well.

Mrs. C: Sometimes I really wish *Brooklyn Bridge* would've stayed on the air.

Bitmap Fonts

A bitmap font is a font that is made up of a series of dots inside a grid pattern. Bitmap fonts were the original fonts for computers, and they worked well both on-screen and on the dot-matrix printers that were prevalent at the time they were introduced.

Each character in a bitmap font has a certain number of square black dots that define its shape. Some bitmap fonts include different point sizes, with the smaller point sizes having fewer dots than the larger point sizes. The larger the point size of the bitmap fonts, the more detail is available, and the better the letter looks.

A problem arises when a point size is specified for which no corresponding bitmap font is available. Then dots from the point size that is closest to the specified size are scaled to the new size. The result is usually large, blocky-looking letters. The larger the size specified, the larger the "blocks," as shown in Figure 1-4.

Figure 1-4: Different point size of bitmapped type

Because bitmap fonts were originally designed for a computer screen, the dots in a bitmap font are set at 72 *dpi* (dots per inch). When you print a bitmap font on a laser printer, which has a resolution of at least 300 dpi, the letters look blocky, even when their sizes are supported by the typeface. A typical viewer of such a font might be heard to say, "bitmapped . . . too jaggy . . . must find outline font."

PostScript Fonts

PostScript fonts are the most popular font format (see Figure 1-5), but they also are the most confusing and frustrating fonts to use because they have two parts: the screen fonts (which are really bitmap fonts) and the printer fonts.

Figure 1-5: Three PostScript typefaces

In order for the computer to recognize a PostScript font in the different programs you use, its corresponding screen font must be installed. If the printer font is installed but the screen font is not installed, you can't use the font at all. Screen fonts for PostScript fonts are usually in little suitcases. Double-clicking the suitcases reveals the bitmap fonts inside the suitcase, and each point size has its own file. Double-clicking a bitmap font displays a screen with that font in that point size and a sentence that contains all the letters in the alphabet. This makes for sentences that are pretty bizarre. Nothing like reading "How razorback-jumping frogs can level six piqued gymnasts!"

Printer fonts are needed, as their name implies, for printing. Printer fonts consist of outlined shapes that get filled with as many dots as the printer can stuff into that particular shape. Because these printer fonts are mathematical outlines, and not a certain number of dots, they make characters look good at any point size. In fact, PostScript printer fonts are *device independent,* meaning that the quality of the type depends on the dpi of the printer (which is device dependent). The higher the dpi, the smoother the curves and diagonal lines look. If printer fonts are missing, the printer either uses the corresponding bitmap font or substitutes another font whose printer font is available (usually Courier . . . ick).

PostScript fonts were developed by Adobe, which, just by coincidence, created the PostScript page description language, which is also, just by coincidence, based on outlines instead of dots. Adobe also created typefaces in PostScript format, called Type 1 format. They released a set of specifications for third-party manufacturers to use in creating other fonts, called Type 3 fonts. Type 3 fonts have one advantage over Type 1 fonts in that the outlines of these fonts can be Stroked, not just Filled, and they can be filled with various shades of gray instead of just black. However, Type 1 fonts are easier to program and to test, and they also have *hinting* (a method for adjusting type for better viewability at small point sizes at low resolutions). Then Adobe released the specifications for Type 1 fonts, and third-party manufacturers have been creating fonts in the Type 1 format ever since.

Things wouldn't be so bad if printer fonts were needed only for printing, but they are also needed for drawing good fonts on the screen at any point size. If a control panel called Adobe Type Manager (ATM) is installed, the screen font information is supplemented by the printer font outline. (Illustrator's built-in font engine replaces the need for ATM; that's what CoolType lib is.)

Since the rise of desktop publishing, the standard in fonts has been PostScript. In 1990, Apple developed a new font format, called TrueType, and then licensed it to Microsoft.

TrueType Fonts

The greatest advantage of TrueType fonts is that they have only one component. There's no separate screen font and printer font, just the TrueType font. Actually, many TrueType fonts do include screen fonts because hand-tuned screen fonts at small sizes tend to look better than Filled outlines at screen resolution. The difference is that both the TrueType font and the bitmap are contained in the same suitcase. Believe me, when you are used to finding two of everything, this idea of one font, one file, and so on, is a godsend. The quality of TrueType fonts is comparable, if not better, to that of PostScript typefaces. Apple includes TrueType fonts with every new computer it sells. There are some potential quality advantages to TrueType fonts, such as the Quadratic curves used to draw TrueType outlines and the supposedly superior hint capability.

Why, you ask, haven't the high-quality type vendors (like Lino, ITC, and so forth) jumped on the TrueType bandwagon? My sources tell me that TrueType fonts are harder to engineer and draw. The comparison is this: TrueType font-creation environment feels more like an engineering environment, and the Type 1 environment feels more like a design environment. Obviously, we are talking about the high end here. A program like Fontographer uses the same interface to create both TrueType and Type 1 fonts. But the high-end folks go in and hand-tune everything to the *n*th degree, and the difference shows.

Battles between the two formats are still raging, but PostScript appears to be winning the war. In this case, competition isn't really better for the consumer, just confusing.

Fonts and Adobe Illustrator

Adobe makes PostScript. Adobe makes Illustrator. What type of fonts should you use? Although PostScript is the obvious answer, Illustrator also supports the use of TrueType fonts. One thing that Illustrator does *not* support, however, is having two fonts with the same name, one in PostScript and one in TrueType. If this event should occur, you may end up with some strange results, such as invisible type.

Make sure that you have only one type of font format per typeface.

Adobe Type Manager

Adobe Type Manager (ATM) is to computer screens what PostScript is to printers. ATM is a sort of link between the screen fonts and the printer fonts. If the point size that you choose is unavailable for a certain typeface, the screen font references the printer font for its outline and fills the outline with dots. The result is a smooth character, whatever the point size on-screen.

Because of screen-resolution limitations (72 dpi), type smaller than 8 points can be hard to read, even with ATM. When type gets below this size, many software applications use *greeking,* which changes small type into gray bars, saving the application a great deal of processing time. (They figure that if you can't read it anyway, no reason exists to put all those dots in the right places.) And remember that in the smaller point sizes, it is better to have the hand-tuned bitmap font installed.

If you start up a Macintosh with extensions off (by pressing Shift until the "Welcome To Macintosh" screen appears), ATM will be disabled, and you can see bitmap fonts in all their glory (this isn't recommended for those with weak stomachs). Oddly enough, the fonts will still print correctly to a PostScript printer, which doesn't use ATM to generate font outlines.

TrueType automatically renders type at various point sizes without the use of ATM.

ATM 4.0 is automatically installed with Adobe Illustrator. The most important new feature in 4.0 is that type can be set to appear anti-aliased (smooth-edged). You can turn on and off the Smooth Type option in the ATM 4.0 control panel (located in your Control Panels folder).

Multiple Master Fonts

Multiple Master fonts, again from Adobe, provide an impressive, if not somewhat complex, way to vary typestyles. Normally, a typeface may come in several weights, such as bold, regular, light, and black. But what if you want a weight that is between bold and black? Usually, you're out of luck.

The theory behind Multiple Master fonts is that a font has two extremes — black and light, for example. Multiple Master technology creates any number of in-betweens that range from one extreme to the other. Multiple Masters don't stop with weights, though. They also work to step between regular and oblique, wide and condensed, and serif or sans serif.

Multiple Master font capabilities are built into many high-end graphics applications, such as Illustrator, Adobe PageMaker, and QuarkXPress.

Illustrator 7 contains a special Palette for adjusting multiple master fonts.

PostScript and Printing

Up until the mid-'80s, computer graphics were, well, crusty. Blocky. Jagged. Rough. If we saw graphics that were done on computers in 1981 and printed to a black-and-white printer, we'd laugh so hard we couldn't breathe, stopping the laughter only when we realized . . . that we couldn't breathe. Of course, in 1981, the world was gaga over the capabilities of computers and computer graphics. Those same pictures were admired, and the average person was generally amazed (the average designer, on the other hand, shuddered and prayed that this whole computer thing wouldn't catch on).

Desktop publishing was pushed to a level of professionalism in 1985 by a cute little software package called PageMaker. With PageMaker, you could do typesetting *and* layout on the computer screen, seeing everything on the screen just as it would eventually be printed. Well, almost. Aldus was the company that created PageMaker. In 1994, Adobe swallowed Aldus, and now PageMaker is "made" by Adobe as well.

The worst acronym this planet has ever seen was coined at this time: *WYSIWYG,* pronounced the way it reads (wizzy-wig), and standing for "what you see is what you get." Oddly, a more accurate term would have been *WYSISSTWYGIYGIAL,* (pronounced wizzys-twiggy-guyal), meaning "what you see is somewhat similar to what you get if you get it at all." The screen representation was poor, and the likelihood that anything remotely complex would actually print was even poorer. Figure 1-6 shows a common response to these silly acronyms.

Figure 1-6: What you see here is just another unnecessary acronym

Problems aside, PageMaker would not have been a success if the laser printer hadn't handily arrived on the scene. Even so, there were problems inherent with laser printers too: at 300 dpi, there were 90,000 dots in every square inch. A typical $8^{1}/_{2}$ x 11-inch page of type had 8.5 *million* dots to put down. Computers were finally powerful enough to handle this huge amount of dots, but the time it took to print made computers pretty much useless for any real work.

Several systems were developed to improve the printing process, and the one standout was PostScript from Adobe Systems. Apple licensed PostScript from Adobe for use on its first Laser-Writer, and a star was born. Installed on every laser printer were two things from Adobe: the PostScript page description language, and the Adobe Base fonts, including Times, Helvetica, Courier, and Symbol.

PostScript became fundamental to Apple Macintosh computers and laser printers and became the standard. In order to use PostScript, Apple had to pay licensing fees to Adobe for every laser printer it sold. Fonts were PostScript, and if there ever was a standard in graphics, the closest thing to it was PostScript (commonly called *EPS,* for Encapsulated PostScript).

Today, the majority of fonts for both Macintosh and Windows systems are PostScript, and almost all graphics and desktop-publishing software can read PostScript in some form. However, technically speaking (I'm supposed to speak technically, aren't I?), there are actually a greater number of TrueType fonts available.

What PostScript Does

A typical graphic object in painting software is based on a certain number of pixels that are a certain color. If you make that graphic larger, the pixels get larger, giving a rough, jagged effect to the art (see Figure 1-7). To prevent these *jaggies,* two things can be done: make sure that there are enough dots per inch in the image so that when enlarged, the dots are too small to appear jagged; or define graphics by mathematical equations instead of by dots.

PostScript is a mathematical solution to high-resolution imaging. Areas, or *shapes,* are defined, and then these shapes are either *Filled* or *Stroked* with a percentage of color. The shapes are made up of paths, and the paths are defined by a number of points along the path *(Anchor Points)* and controls off those points (*Control Handles,* sometimes called *curve handles* or *direction points*) that control the shape of the curve. Figure 1-8 shows a PostScript outline around a bitmapped image and the enlarged outline Filled with black.

Figure 1-7: A bitmap image at normal size (left) and enlarged by 300%

Figure 1-8: A PostScript outline surrounds the original bitmapping image

Because the Anchor Points and Control Handles have real locations on a page, mathematical processes can be used to create the shapes based on these points. The mathematical equation for Bézier curves is quite detailed (at least for someone who fears math, like me).

PostScript is not just math, though. It is actually a programming language, and more specifically, a *page description language*. Like BASIC, Pascal, and C, PostScript is made of lines of code that are used to describe artwork.

Fortunately, the average user never has to use PostScript code, but instead uses a simplified interface, like Illustrator. Software that has the capability to save files in PostScript or to print to a PostScript printer writes this PostScript code for you. Printers that are equipped with PostScript then take that PostScript code and convert it to dots on a printed page.

Why PostScript Is So Cool

Obviously, the facts that most applications can handle EPS files and that most printers can print PostScript are a great benefit to users, but the strength of PostScript is not really in its widespread use.

If you create a 1-inch circle in Photoshop or any other pixel-based drawing software and then enlarge that same circle in any application, the circle will begin to lose detail. A 300-dpi circle at twice its original size becomes 150 dpi. This makes those jagged edges more apparent than ever.

If you create a 1-inch circle in Illustrator, you can enlarge it to *any size possible* without losing one iota of resolution. The Illustrator circle stays perfectly smooth, even enlarged to 200 percent. In fact, the resolution of that circle depends on the laser printer or imagesetter that prints it. That means that a perfect 1-inch circle has the potential to be a perfect 2-foot circle (providing you can find a printer or imagesetter that can print a 2 x 2-foot circle).

But scaling objects is only the beginning. You can distort, stretch, rotate, skew, and flip objects created in Illustrator to your heart's content, and still the object will print to the resolution of the output device (see Figure 1-9).

Capital *S*?

Al's Diner: So, what's up with that capital *S* in the middle of PostScript?

Toulouse: I believe it was a creative way to establish a trademark, considering the word Postscript is quite common. Adobe's pretty conservative about that sort of thing, normally. They didn't do "IllusTrator" or "PhotoShop" or "StreamLine" or "DimeNsions" or "PreMiere."

Al's Diner: That's the best you could come up with?

Toulouse: Oh, and the name of your restaurant was thought up by a team of marketing whizzes?

Al's Diner: What about PageMaker?

Toulouse: Aldus did that. It's too late to change it, really.

Figure 1-9: The original PostScript mouse (we'll call him "Theme") is in the upper-left corner. The other mice are, appropriately, "Variations on a Theme."

Here's an example: A company wants its tiny logo on a 3-foot wide poster. If you use conventional methods, the edges will become fuzzy and gross looking, pretty much unacceptable to your client. Your other conventional option is to redraw the logo at a larger size or to trace the blown-up version — a time-consuming proposition either way.

The Illustrator solution? Scan the logo, trace it either in Adobe Streamline or with the Auto Trace tool, touch it up, and build your design around it. Afterward, output the illustration on a printer that can handle that size poster. There is no loss of quality; instead, the enlarged version from Illustrator will often look better than the scanned original.

Paths

The most basic element in Illustrator is a *path*. A path in Illustrator must have at least two Anchor Points, and there will be a line segment between those two Anchor Points (see Figure 1-10). Conceptually, there is no limit to how many Anchor Points or segments can be in any one path. Depending on the type of Anchor Points that are on either end of a line segment, the segment may be straight or curved. A path really must have two Anchor Points because without two Anchor Points, there is no place to draw a path segment (the line between the points). A single Anchor Point will never print anything.

There are three major types of paths:

- **Open paths** are paths that have two distinct End Points, with any number of Anchor Points in between.
- **Closed paths** are paths that are continuous. There are no End Points and no start or end to a closed path — it just continues around and around.

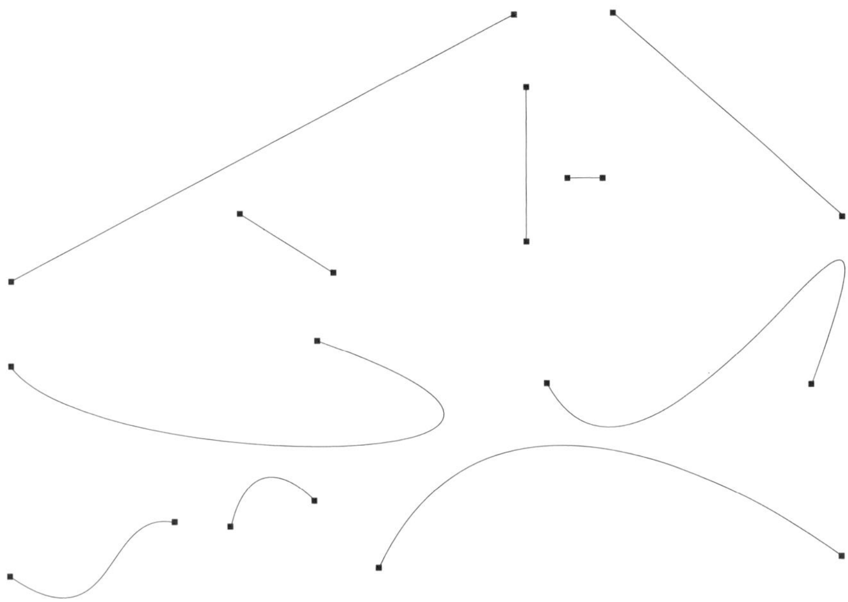

Figure 1-10: Paths consisting of two Anchor Points with a line segment between them

- **Compound paths** are paths that are made up of two or more open or closed paths. (For a detailed look at compound paths, see Chapter 11.)

When you are working in Illustrator in Artwork mode (View⇨Artwork), only paths are visible. In Preview mode (View⇨Preview), Fills and Strokes applied to paths are visible. Unless a path is selected in Preview mode, that path (Anchor Points and line segments) isn't visible.

Paths in Illustrator can be Filled with color, a pattern, or a gradient. Closed paths always use the color to Fill the *inside* of the shape they form (see Figure 1-11).

Open paths also can be Filled; the Fill goes straight across the two End Points of the path to enclose the object. Figure 1-12 displays how different types of open paths are Filled. Filling an open path is usually not desirable, although in some circumstances it may be necessary.

CAUTION

Filled two-dimensional line mistake: In PostScript, when a Fill is specified but there are only two dimensions to an object (a straight line), it prints (rasterizes) at one "device pixel." At 100% on-screen, the Filled line looks exactly like a 1-point Stroked line (72 dpi = 1 device pixel = $^1/_{72}$ inch, 1 point = $^1/_{72}$ inch). When you zoom in to 200% the Stroked line scales by 200%, but the Filled line stays the same (1 device pixel or $^1/_{72}$ inch). When you print this line to a laser printer, one device pixel is as tiny as $^1/_{300}$ or $^1/_{600}$ inch. By the time you print to a typical Imagesetter, one device pixel will be $^1/_{2,570}$ inch, making it too small to be visible in most situations.

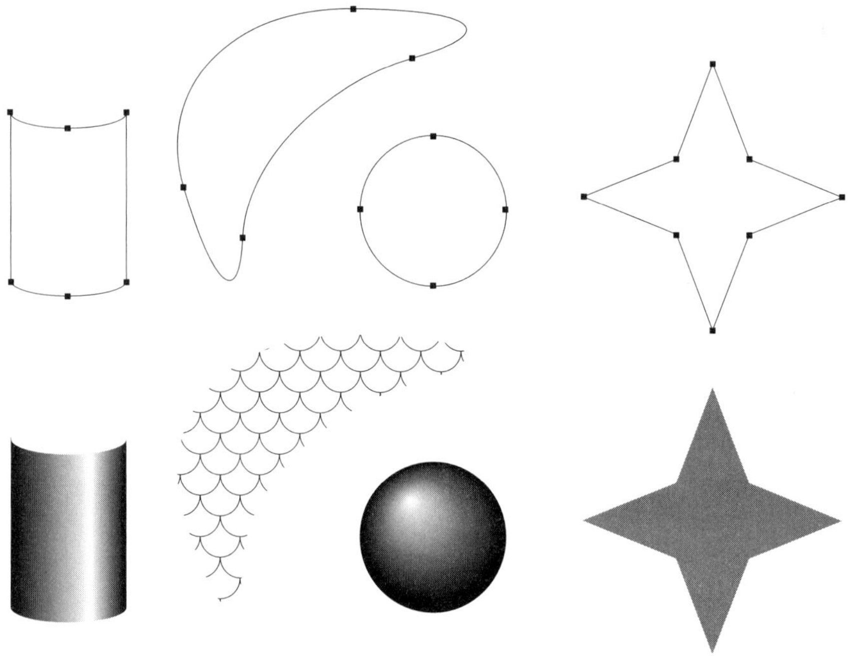

Figure 1-11: Closed paths with different Fills: the top row is how they appear in Artwork mode (⌘-Y) [Ctrl+Y], while the bottom row shows what they look like in Preview mode (⌘-Y) [Ctrl+Y]

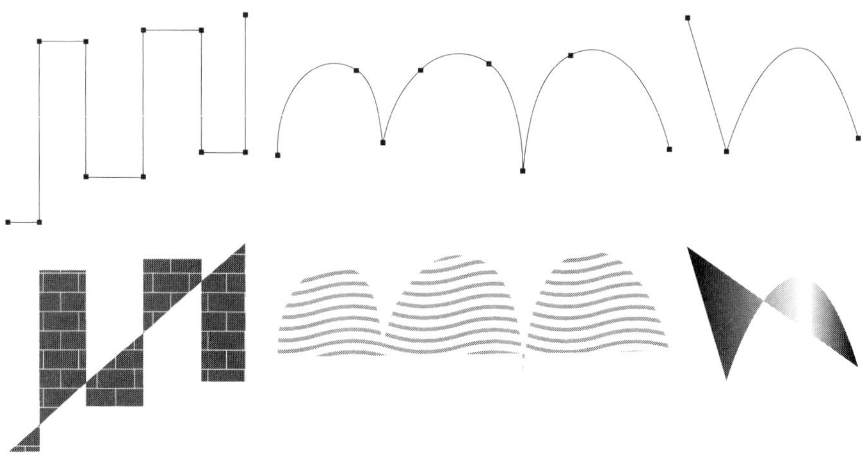

Figure 1-12: Open paths with different Fills: the top row is how they appear in Artwork mode, while the bottom row shows what they look like in Preview mode

Besides Filling paths, you can also Stroke paths with any tint of any color or a pattern. These Strokes can be any weight (thickness), and the width of the Stroke is equally distributed over each side of the path. Open paths have ends on the Strokes; these ends can be either cropped, rounded, or extended past the end of the Stroke by half the width of the Stroke. Several different paths with Strokes are shown in Figure 1-13.

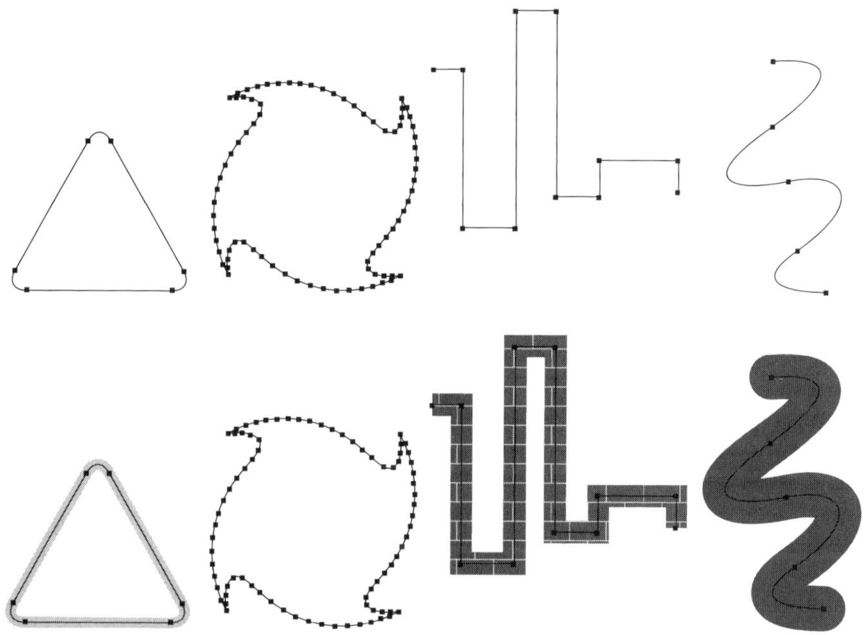

Figure 1-13: Various paths with different Strokes applied to them (sans Gary Coleman)

CAUTION

A single point is also considered a path, but in Illustrator, single points can have no printable qualities. This isn't readily noticeable because you can assign a Fill or Stroke color to a single point, although it can't be seen in Preview mode or when printed. When the document is color separated, it will cause a separation of the color to print even if nothing else on that page is using that same color, and the separation will be blank. If you think you may have individual Anchor Points floating around your illustration, you can select all of them at once by choosing Filter⇨Select⇨Select Stray Points and then delete them.

Fills and Strokes in Illustrator can be colors or an opaque white, which knocks out any color underneath. Fills and Strokes may also be *transparent,* in which case the Stroke or Fill will not be opaque. Transparency in Illustrator is commonly referred to as a Fill or Stroke of None.

Anchor Points

Paths are made up of a series of points and the line segments between these points. These points are commonly called *Anchor Points* because they anchor the path; paths *always* pass through or end at Anchor Points. There are two classes of Anchor Points:

- **Smooth Points** are Anchor Points that have a curved path flowing smoothly through them; most of the time you don't know where a Smooth Point is unless the path is selected. Smooth Points keep the path from changing direction abruptly. There are two linked *Control Handles* on every smooth point.
- **Corner Points** are a class of Anchor Points in which the path changes direction noticeably at those specific points. There are three different corner points:
  - *Straight Corner Points* are Anchor Points where two straight line segments meet at a distinct angle. There are no Control Handles on this type of Anchor Point.
  - *Curved Corner Points* are points where two curved line segments meet and abruptly change direction. There are two *independent Control Handles* on each Curved Corner Point.
  - *Combination Corner Points* are the meeting places for straight and curved line segments. There is one independent Control Handle on a Combination Corner Point.

Figure 1-14 shows the different types of Anchor Points in Illustrator.

Anchor Points, Control Handles, and Control Handle Lines do not appear on the printed output of your artwork. In fact, they only appear in Illustrator and Photoshop, never on artwork imported into other applications.

Figure 1-14: The different types of Anchor Points in Illustrator

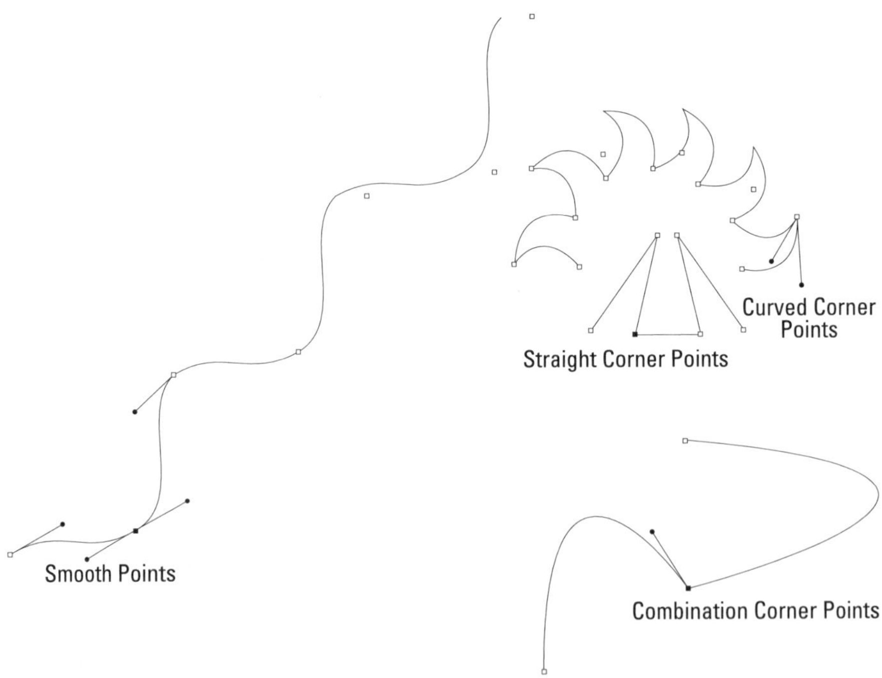

Bézier Curves

Not knowing all that much about geometry (or maybe not remembering that much . . . it was eighth grade, after all), I find the very concept of creating curves by using math frightening. But most of the curve creation in Illustrator takes place behind the scenes in the PostScript language code we almost never see.

PostScript curves are based on *Bézier* curves (pronounced *bez-ee-ay*), which were created by Pierre Bézier (see Figure 1-15) in the early '70s as a way of controlling mechanical cutting devices, commonly known as Numerical Control. Bézier (see the Foreword) worked for Renault (the car manufacturer) in France, and his mission was to streamline the process by which machines were controlled.

A mathematician and engineer, Bézier developed a method for creating curves using four points for every curved segment. Two of these points lay at either end of the segment (we call them Anchor Points in Illustrator), and two points just floated around the curve segment, controlling the shape of the curve (Control Handles). Using these four points, a person could conceivably create any curve; using multiple sets of these curves, one could create any possible shape. The two PostScriptateers, John Warnock and Chuck Geschke of Adobe, decided that Bézier curves were the best method for creating curves for a page-description language, and suddenly those curves became a fundamental part of high-end graphic design.

Bézier curves are anything but intuitive. I believe that Bézier curves represent the most significant stumbling block in learning to use Illustrator well. After you've mastered the concept and use of these curves, everything about Illustrator suddenly becomes easier and friendlier. Don't try to ignore them, because they won't go away. You'll find it easier in the long run to try to understand how they work.

You already know half of what a Bézier curve is: two Anchor Points. Here comes the hard part (brace yourself).

Figure 1-15: Pierre Bézier, who laid the groundwork for PostScript and, thus, Illustrator

Control Handles and Control Handle Lines

If an Anchor Point has a Control Handle coming out of it, the next segment will be curved. No Control Handle, no curve. Couldn't be simpler.

Control Handles are connected to Anchor Points with *Control Handle Lines*. Figure 1-16 shows what happens when an Anchor Point with no Control Handle and an Anchor Point with a Control Handle are connected to another Anchor Point.

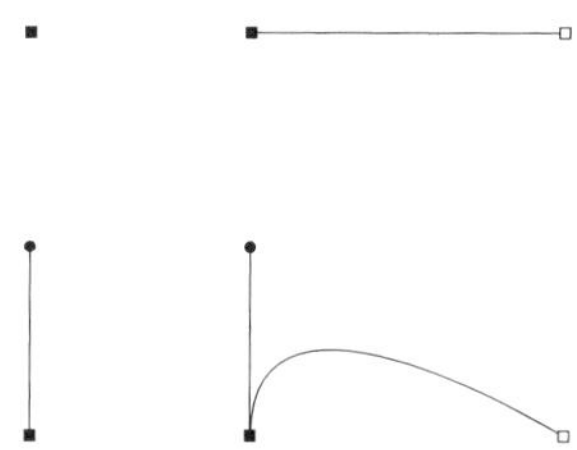

Figure 1-16: An Anchor Point without a Control Handle (top left) and an Anchor Point with a Control Handle (bottom left) are connected to new Anchor Points, resulting in a straight line segment (top right) and a curved line segment (bottom right)

The Control Handle Lines themselves really have no function other than to show you which Anchor points the Control Handles are attached to. You cannot select a Control Handle Line. The only way to move a Control Handle Line or change the length of a Control Handle Line is by moving its corresponding Control Handle. Figure 1-17 displays how Control Handles and Lines work with curves and Anchor Points.

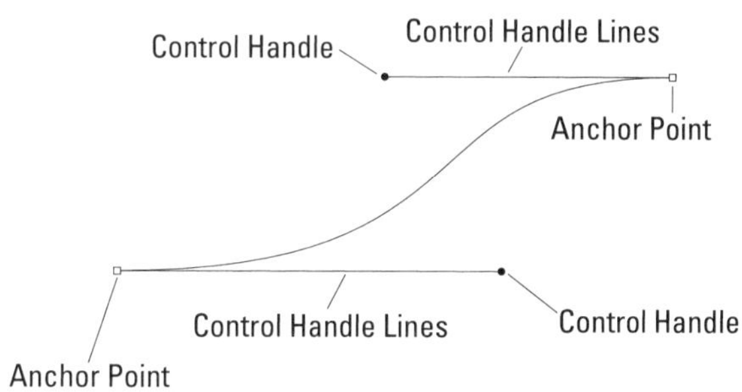

Figure 1-17: Anchor Points, Control Handles, and Control Handle Lines along a path

The basic concept concerning Control Handles is that Control Handles act as magnets, pulling the curve toward them (see Figure 1-18). This presents an interesting problem because there are usually two Control Handles per curved line segment. Just as you might suspect, the Control Handle exerts the greatest amount of force on the half of the curved segment nearest to it. If there is only one Control Handle, then the segment is curved more on the side of the segment with the Control Handle than the side with no Control Handle.

The greater the distance between a Control Handle and its corresponding Anchor Point, the farther the curve (on that end of the curve segment) will pull away from an imaginary straight segment between the two points (see Figure 1-19). If the Control Handles on either end of the segment are on different sides of the curved segment, the curved segment will be somewhat S-shaped, as the bottom path in Figure 1-19 shows. If the Control Handles on the ends of the curved segment are on the same side, the curve will be somewhat U-shaped, as shown in the top path of Figure 1-19.

Control Handle Lines coming out of an Anchor Point are always *tangent* to the curved segment where it touches the Anchor Point, regardless of whether the Anchor Point is a Smooth Point, a Curved Corner Point, or a Combination Corner Point. By tangent, I'm referring to the angle of both the Control Handle Line and the angle of the curved segment as it crosses the Anchor Point (see Figure 1-20).

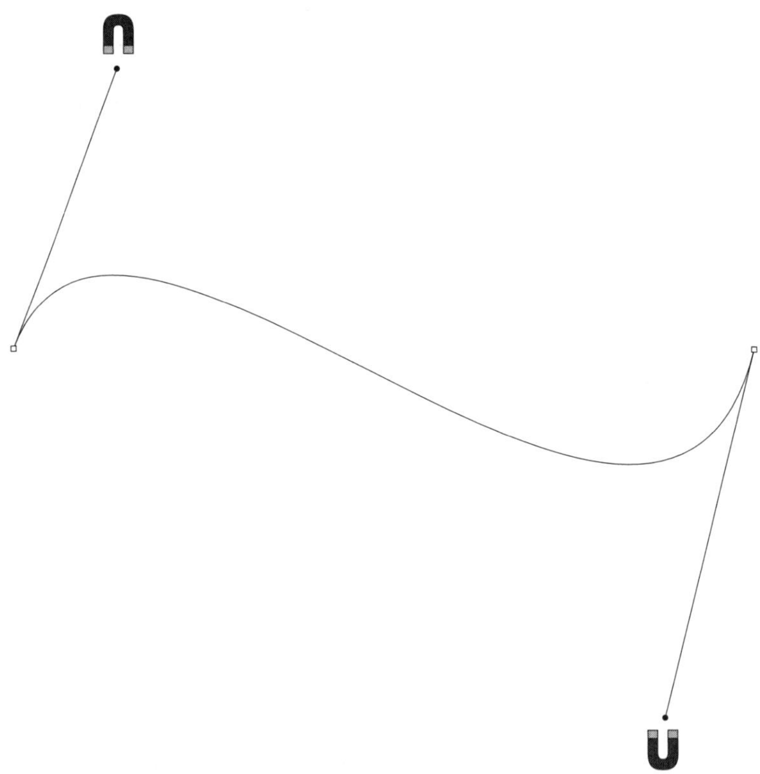

Figure 1-18: Control Handles act as magnets, pulling the curve toward them

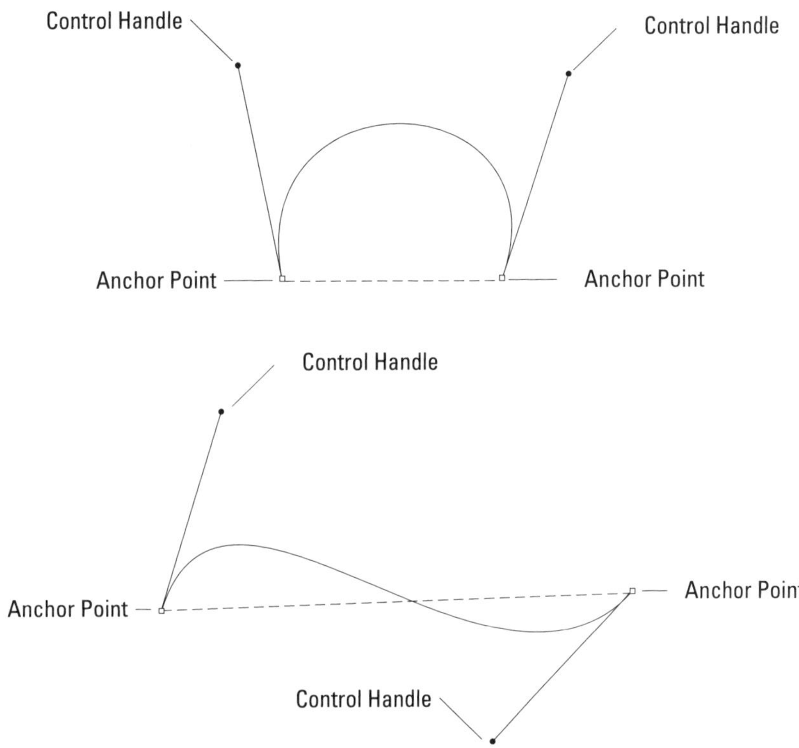

Figure 1-19: Control Handles pull the line segment away from the straight line that would normally exist between them. The bottom path is an *S* shape because the Control Handles are being pulled in opposite directions

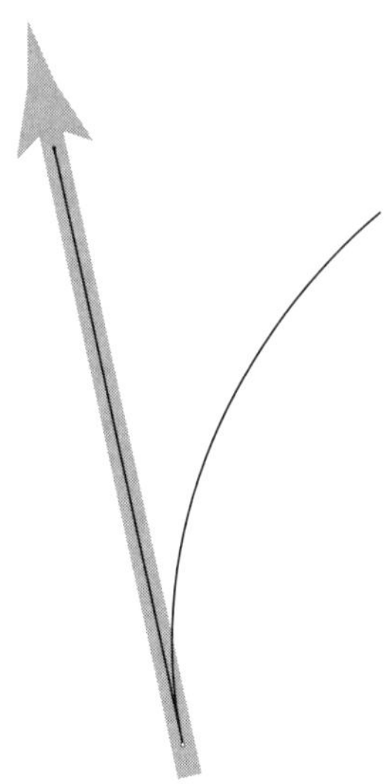

Figure 1-20: Control Handle Lines run tangent to the path where the path meets the Anchor Point

Curves Are Tough

Potsie: I'm having trouble with curves.

Toulouse: What kind of trouble?

Potsie: Moving the Control Handles around is really difficult.

Toulouse: You know, there's an easier way. . . but it's not quite as accurate.

Potsie: Tell me! At this rate I'll never finish my drawing of Jennie Piccolo.

Toulouse: Wow. Lots of curves there. Looks like you might need to add a few extra Anchor Points....

Potsie: (blush)

Toulouse: To adjust the curves without moving the Control Handles, just click the curve and drag it.

Potsie: Wow!

Toulouse: Keep in mind that you're changing both Control Handles at once with that, and it's very imprecise. Sort of like your occasional musical outbursts.

Potsie: Was I really that bad?

Toulouse: Ever notice the lack of work after the series ended?

In Chapter 3, you learn how to use the Pen tool for drawing with Anchor Points, Control Handles, and Control Handle Lines. Rules are also given to help you determine the placement, length, and angle of the various points and Control Handle Lines that are encountered using this tool.

Clear, Cut, Copy, and Paste

In most software, including Illustrator, many of the most basic functions of the Edit menu work the same way. If you have used the Edit menu in QuarkXPress or Microsoft Word, for example, you should have no trouble using the same functions in Illustrator because the menu options are located in the same place in each program.

Clear

The most simplistic of these commands is Clear, which in Illustrator works almost exactly like the Delete key on the keyboard. When something is selected, choosing Clear will delete, or get rid of, what is selected.

You're probably asking yourself, "If the Delete key does the same thing, why do we need Clear?" or "Why didn't they just call the Clear command *Delete?*" Ah, the makers of Illustrator are a step ahead of you in this respect. Note that I said "almost" the same way; there actually is a subtle yet important difference in what the Clear command does and what the Delete key does, due to Illustrator's abundant usage of palettes in Version 7.0.

If you are working on a palette and (1) have just typed a value in an editable text field; (2) tabbed down or up to an editable text field, highlighting text; or (3) dragged across text in an editable text field, highlighting text; the Delete key (1) deletes the last character typed; or (2) and (3) deletes the highlighted characters. In all these situations, the Clear command deletes anything that is selected in the document.

Cut, Copy, and Paste

The Cut, Copy, and Paste commands in Illustrator are very handy. Copying and cutting selected objects places them onto something called the Clipboard, a temporary holding place for objects that have been cut or copied. After an object is on the Clipboard, it may be pasted into (1) the center of the same document, (2) the same location as the cut or copied object, or (3) another document in Illustrator, Photoshop, Dimensions, or Streamline.

Choosing Cut (⌘-X) [Ctrl+X] from the Edit menu deletes the selected objects and copies them to the Clipboard, where they are stored until another object is cut or copied or the computer is shut down or restarted. Quitting Illustrator *does not* remove objects from the Clipboard. Cut is not available when no object is selected.

Choosing Copy (⌘-C) [Ctrl+C] from the Edit menu works like Cut, but it doesn't delete the selected objects. Instead, it just copies them to the Clipboard, at which time you can choose Paste and slap another copy onto your document.

Choosing Paste (⌘-V) [Ctrl+V] from the Edit menu places any objects on the Clipboard into the center of the document window. If type is selected with the Type tool or copied from another application to the Pasteboard, either a Rectangle type, Area type, Path type, or Point type area must be selected with the Type tool. Paste is not available if nothing is in the Clipboard or if the contents of the Clipboard were copied there from another application.

Now, the really cool part: Just because you've pasted the object somewhere doesn't mean it isn't in the Clipboard anymore; it is! You can paste again and again, and keep on pasting until you just get plain bored, or until your page is an indecipherable mess, whichever comes first. However, the most important rule to remember about Cut, Copy, and Paste is that whatever is currently in the Clipboard will be replaced by anything that subsequently gets cut or copied to the Clipboard.

Cut, Copy, and Paste also work with text that you type in a document. Using the Type tools, you can select type, cut or copy it, and then paste it. When you're pasting type, it will go wherever your blinking text cursor is located. If you have type selected (highlighted) and you choose Paste, the type that was selected is replaced by whatever you had on the Clipboard.

You can cut or copy as much or as little of an illustration as you choose; you are only limited by your hard disk space. A good rule of thumb is that if you ever get a message saying you can't cut or copy because you are out of hard disk space, it is time to start throwing out stuff on your hard drive that you don't need or simply get a bigger hard drive.

Thanks to the Adobe PostScript capability on the Clipboard, Illustrator can copy paths to other Adobe software, including Dimensions, Streamline, and Photoshop. Paths created in those packages can be pasted into Illustrator. With Photoshop, you have the option of pasting your Clipboard contents as rasterized pixels instead of as paths.

With Illustrator 7 and Photoshop 3.0.4 and later, you have the ability to drag Illustrator artwork from an Illustrator document right into a Photoshop document. In addition, because Adobe goes both ways, you can drag a Photoshop selection from any Photoshop document right into an Illustrator document.

The Clipboard

You can view the contents of the Clipboard by going under the Edit menu to Show Clipboard. Unfortunately, the only thing you'll usually see in Illustrator is (1) the PostScript logo with the number of objects you have selected and the layers those objects are on or (2) copied text. In order to see text in the Clipboard, you must copy it using the Type tools. Type that is cut or copied using the selection tools does not appear as type, but instead as an *object.* When you view type, it usually does not look like the type you selected; the words are there, but the font and style information isn't. Instead, the type is displayed in Geneva, at either 12 points or 9 points, depending on what you have copied prior to copying your text.

Selecting Show Clipboard from the Edit menu opens a window that shows the current contents of the Clipboard. You can keep this window open and put it anywhere on the screen, but it will always be behind all palettes and the active document once you click within any of the palettes or the document. When a portion of the Clipboard is visible behind the palettes or document window, clicking the visible part of it brings it back to the front (of course, you can also just select Show Clipboard from the Edit menu again).

You can't do anything to the Clipboard by displaying the Clipboard window. You may only resize the window and move it around on your screen for the sole purpose of displaying what you have copied last. The Clipboard can be resized with the box in the lower-right corner, toggled between the current size and the full screen with the box in the upper-right corner, and closed with the box in the upper-right corner. The only way the contents of the Clipboard window can be altered is when something is cut or copied. Figure 1-21 shows two examples of how the Clipboard can look when different things are copied.

Selecting Hide Clipboard from the Edit menu hides the Clipboard. This option is available only if the Clipboard window is *active* — that is, in front of all open documents.

Figure 1-21: The Clipboard when several objects on different layers have been copied or cut (left), and the Clipboard when text selected in a type tool has been copied or cut (right)

Undo and Redo

In most applications, you can undo the last thing done by choosing Undo from the Edit menu. That works in Illustrator, but Adobe has taken the undo concept just a little further: You can keep undoing in Illustrator up to 200 times, providing your system has enough memory and you have enough patience. After you have undone, you can redo by choosing Redo, right below Undo in the Edit menu. And, guess what — you can redo up to 200 times as well.

Choosing Undo (⌘-Z) [Ctrl+Z] from the Edit menu undoes the last activity that was performed on the document. Successive undos undo more and more activities, until (1) the document is at the point where it was opened or created or (2) you have reached the undo limit, set in the Units and Undo Preferences dialog box (File⇨Preferences⇨Units and Undo).

The Undoables

Not Opie: I think my Undo command is broken.

Toulouse: Uh-oh. Are you sure it's not set to 0 in your preferences?

Not Opie: Yeah, it's set to 10. Most of the time it undoes fine, but every once in a while...

Toulouse: What types of things can't you undo?

Not Opie: Well, my receding hairline, for one thing. Why do you think I'm *behind* the camera now? I can't undo my saves, either.

Toulouse: Ah-ha! Saving has no impact on Undo or Redo. Saving is not considered to be an option that can be undone, or done again, so its very existence is ignored by Undo and Redo. After you save, you'll undo the last thing you did before you saved.

Not Opie: Oh. Well, I can't undo my zooms or scrolls either.

Toulouse: Two more things that Illustrator ignores when it comes to undoing and redoing. Sorry.

Not Opie: Anything else I should look out for?

(continued)

The default number of undos in Illustrator is 10. To change the number of undos, go to the Units and Undo Preferences dialog box (File➪Preferences➪Units and Undo) and type in the number of undos that you want. You *can* set the undo levels to 0, but I wouldn't recommend it; this will disallow any undo or redo operations. If you *do* set the number of undos too low and later realize you want to undo more actions, the cold, hard truth of the Undo levels box will raise its ugly head: You can't increase the number of undos after you have run out of them.

CAUTION: Undos are the chief source of Illustrator's occasional memory woes. All those undos are being kept track of in the Illustrator RAM partition; when it fills up, you'll be presented with a dialog box to get rid of the oldest undos. Never do this. Instead, click the Cancel button and manually change the number of undos to a smaller amount and try again. This way you can control the number of undos Illustrator has available at all times.

Choosing Redo (⌘-Shift-Z) [Ctrl+Shift+Z] from the Edit menu redoes the last undo. You can continue to redo undos until (1) you are back to the point where you started undoing or (2) you perform another activity, at which time you can no longer redo any previous undos.

If you undo a couple of times and then *do* something, you won't be able to redo. You have to undo the last thing you did and then actually do everything again. In other words, all the steps that you undid are gone.

It is fine to use the Undo feature to go back and check out what you did, but after you have used multiple undos, don't do anything if you want to redo back to where you started undoing from. Got that???

Artwork and Preview Modes

Ah . . . Gone are the days of working blind, having to wait to see what you were illustrating until you chose Preview and then not being able to work again until you chose Artwork. I'm being sarcastic, of course. FreeHand has enabled artists to work in Preview for many a year (since 1989, to be exact), and Adobe finally included this capability for Windows users in 1992, and Macintosh owners in 1993.

Artwork Mode

Many artists who have used Illustrator in the older versions (1.1, 88, and 3.2) actually *like* working in Artwork mode because it's faster, you can see every path in the document (and select those same paths), and the Anchor Points and Control Handles stand out more. Artwork mode is much closer to what the printer sees: paths that define the edges of the objects you are working with.

Artwork mode seems to be a misnomer. *Wireframe* mode would be more descriptive — or maybe *Paths* mode. The only thing visible in Artwork mode is the paths that make up the objects, and all paths are always visible.

Since Illustrator 5, Artwork mode has worked slower than in previous versions. The reason? Layers could be colored via the Layers Palette, and selected points and paths reflected those colors. To give that little extra boost of speed back to Artwork mode, install the Artwork View Speedup Plug-In from the Extra Plug-Ins folder in your Illustrator folder (by placing it in the Plug-Ins folder). When installed, all points and paths will be black, not their layer colors. This

(continued)

Toulouse: Undo and Redo only work on actions that actually change your document. Zooming and scrolling don't affect your document. Neither does changing tools or selecting or deselecting things.

Not Opie: I guess my hairline doesn't affect my documents either...(sigh!).

speed difference is determined by the difference in redraw times between 1-bit (black and white) and 8-bit (256 colors) color.

Preview Mode

In Preview mode, you see on-screen what your illustration really looks like when it prints (with the exception of displayed paths, which don't print). Figure 1-22 shows Illustrator art in both Artwork and Preview modes.

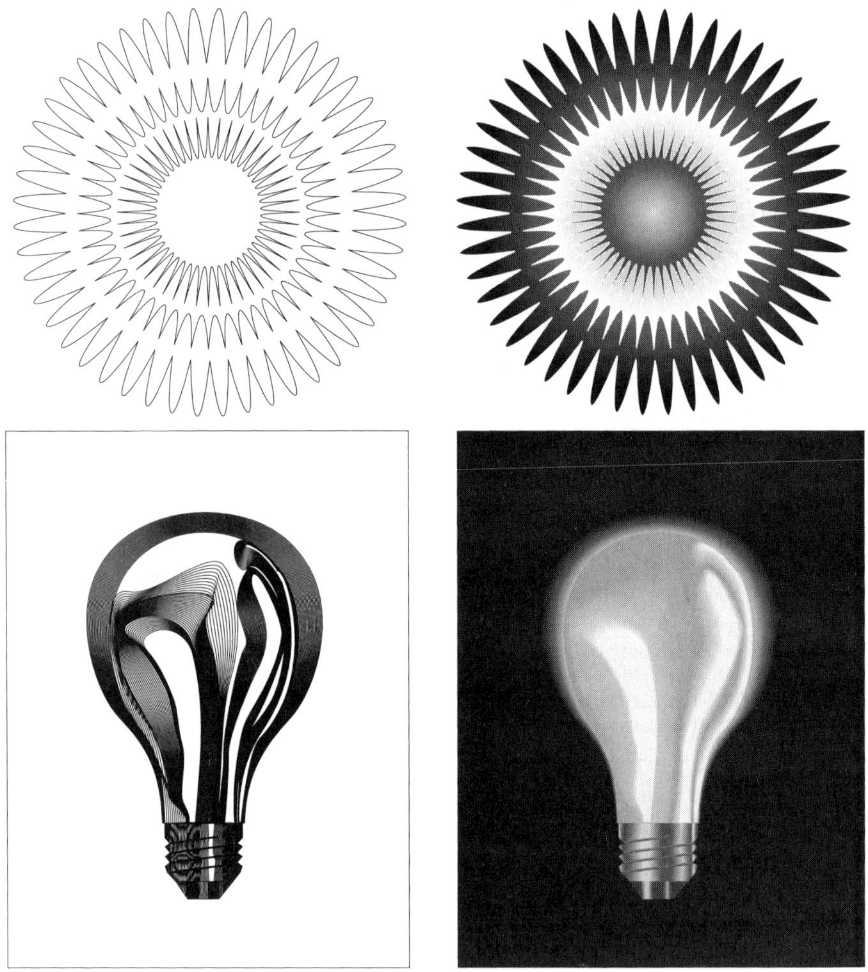

Figure 1-22: Art from Illustrator shown in Artwork mode (left) and Preview mode (right)

Illustrator can't show overprinting when previewing. To see overprinting, open, paste, or drag the artwork to Photoshop.

Instead of selecting a path by clicking it, you can select entire paths by clicking the inside of those paths in a Filled area. It becomes a little more difficult to select certain points on paths because the Strokes on those paths are also visible. Sometimes, there is so much stuff on your screen in Preview that you don't know what to click. The option that allows this is called Area Select, a check box (turned on by default) in the General Preferences dialog box (⌘-K) [Ctrl+K].

The inside of a compound path is considered a Fill for Area Select functionality. It may look trasparent, but you can't directly select an object appearing behind the transparent portion of a compound path. When Area Select is on, clicking the transparent portion of a compound path results in the compound path being selected.

The major drawback to Preview mode is not the inability to select paths or parts of paths, but the amount of time it takes for certain types of Fills and blends to redraw accurately on your screen. The first time a slow redraw takes place in your document, you hardly notice it; you are too busy looking at how that object appears now that it has, say, a pattern Fill. After that, though, you may not be working with that object but others, and you still have to wait for that pattern-filled object to completely redraw every time you change views, move that object, or move something in front of that object.

Fortunately, Illustrator has a saving grace that makes this slowness almost acceptable. Whenever the screen is in this redraw mode, you can do other things. While your patterned, Filled object is redrawing, for example, Illustrator lets you go to the Type menu to change typefaces you've selected; when you are done selecting the type, the image finishes redrawing. This process is called *interruptable redraw,* and it is a godsend for Illustrator users.

You can quickly toggle between Artwork and Preview modes by pressing ⌘-Y [Ctrl+Y].

Illustrator's Menus

Adobe's main products — Illustrator, Photoshop, PageMaker, Premiere, Dimensions, and Streamline — all have a fairly consistent interface, including menus, palettes, and dialog boxes. It appears that Adobe has listened carefully to their end users and made certain that Illustrator is not so *different* anymore in almost all respects.

Some general rules apply to Illustrator menus:

- To select a menu item, pull down to that item and release the mouse button (Macintosh) or click on that item (Windows). If the cursor is not on that item, but it is still highlighted, the command will not take effect.
- Whenever an *ellipsis* appears (three little dots that look like . . .), choosing that menu item brings up a dialog box where you must verify the current information by clicking an OK button, or enter more information and then click OK. If there is no ellipsis, the action you select takes place right away.
- Anytime there is a *key command* listed on the right side — usually the Command (⌘) symbol and a character for Macintosh, Ctrl plus a character for Windows, sometimes the ⌘ symbol [Ctrl] and other modifier keys and a character — instead of using the mouse to pull down this menu, you can type this key command. Using key commands for menu items works just like clicking the menu bar and pulling down to that item.
- If you see a little *triangle* next to a menu item, it means there is a *pop-up menu* associated with it. Items in the pop-up menu can be chosen by pulling over to the menu and then pulling up or down to select the menu item needed. Pop-up menus usually appear on the right side of the menu, but due to space limitations on your monitor, they may appear on the left side for certain menus.

Using Menus Effectively

If you can never remember what is on which menu, and you are constantly holding down the mouse button and slowly running along the menu bar, reading every menu item, looking for a certain command, you have a disease. Every year millions of people become afflicted with Menu Bar Scanning Syndrome (MBSS): the need to continually search and hunt for special menu items that they just can't remember the locations of. MBSS is a disease that can be treated fairly easily, but it wastes valuable production time, costing companies billions of dollars a year. Don't be surprised if the next time you flip to *60 Minutes,* Steve Kroft is doing an inside investigation into the mysteries of MBSS.

MBSS is deadly not only because it wastes time, but because the user is forced to read every single menu and pop-up menu. Sure, in the File menu you *know* that Document Setup is where to go to change the size of the page, but as you work your way over, things begin to get a little fuzzy. By the time you get to the Filter menu, your mind is mush. You see the Distort category and figure that all the pop-up menu items in there are legal functions. If you can manage to get to the Windows menu, thewordswouldjustruntogether, making no sense whatsoever. If Figure 1-23 looks familiar, then you're probably one of the millions of afflicted computer users.

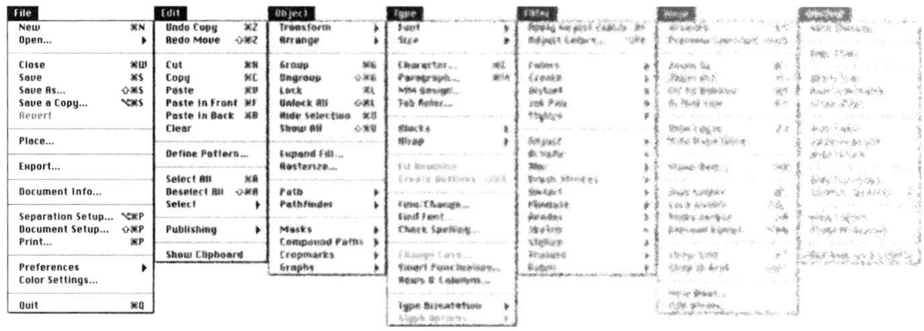

Figure 1-23: MBSS in the later stages

You can help prevent MBSS by doing three things:

- **Memorize what is in each menu.** This is the hardest thing to do, but a few hours spent memorizing each menu item and where it goes will eventually prevent countless MBSS-related searches. Make sentences out of the first letter of each menu item, if it helps. The File menu is either, "New, Open, Close, Save, Save As, Save a Copy, Revert, Place, Export, Document Info, Document Setup, Print, Preferences, Color Settings, Quit" or "Nine Old Cats See Some Silly Senior Retired People Eating Damp Danish Pieces of Pruned Cauliflower Quiche." (I know, I know. You're not supposed to eat Pruned Cauliflower Quiche when its damp. That's why the Senior Retired People are *Silly*.)
- **Use the menus as little as possible.** Instead, memorize key commands. Most of the menu items have them (if you don't include the Filter menu, more than half do), so now you only need to go up to the menu bar when a menu item doesn't have a key command.
- **Create buttons for menu commands with VectorTools' VectorBars.** VectorBars can be a serious time-saver if used properly. See Chapter 14, "VectorTools," for more info on using Extensis VectorTools.

Palettes versus Windows

If there is a trend in graphics programs, it's the trend toward using palettes for everything possible. It started becoming noticeable with Fractal Design Painter, which has 12 palettes that can be on the screen at the same time. QuarkXPress soon followed with a half-dozen palettes, and Photoshop has scads of them. Illustrator 7 has even more palettes than Version 5, all of which can remain open while you work on your document (providing you can still see your document through all those palettes!).

Technically speaking, a palette is a window. Everything on the Mac and in Windows is a window except (I think) the desktop. Movable Modeless Windows (palettes) are a variation on windows.

In many respects, palettes are like windows. They have a title bar that can be clicked and dragged to move the palette. There is usually a close box in the upper-left corner of the palette, and in the upper-right corner there is often an auto-resize box, which makes the palette smaller or larger than its original size. Occasionally, a manual resize box is located in the lower-right corner for dragging the palette to a new size. Options for hiding and showing palettes are even located under the Window menu. Figure 1-24 shows the Character palette with all its parts labeled.

Figure 1-24: The Character palette

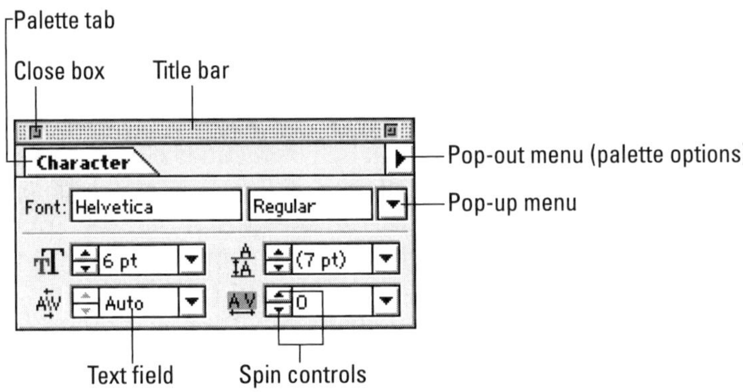

Palettes are unlike windows in several ways. Palettes seldom have scroll bars, although the Layers palette is an exception. When you hop from one program to another, palettes automatically hide, while windows remain visible.

Unlike windows, palettes are never really active. Instead, the one you are working in is in the front, and if it has editable text fields, one is highlighted, or a blinking text cursor appears. To bring a palette to the forefront — bring it into focus — simply click it anywhere.

Palettes in Illustrator 7 can be linked together in different ways called tabbing and docking. Each palette (except for the toolbox) has a tab on it. Clicking the tab of a palette brings it to the front. Dragging a tab from one palette to another moves that palette into another palette. Dragging a tab out of a palette makes the palette separate from the previous palette. Palettes can be docked together by dragging the tab of one palette to the bottom of another palette; when the bottom of the other palette darkens, releasing the mouse button will "dock" the moved palette to the bottom of the other palette. Now when the other palette is moved, the docked palette will move with it.

The Document Window

Illustrator no longer requires that you resize your document window if you have a monitor that is a different resolution than 640 x 480. Instead, the Illustrator window automatically resizes to match the resolution of your monitor.

The Pasteboard

Probably the worst thing that can possibly happen when you are using Illustrator is for you to lose everything you've worked on. "Where'd it all go?" you cry, along with the expected vulgarities. You can make this happen very easily in Illustrator, just by clicking a few times on the gray parts of the scroll bars at the bottom of the document window. When you click those gray parts, you are moving about half the width (or height) of your window with every click, and three clicks later, your page and everything on it is no longer in front of you. Instead, you see the Pasteboard, a vast expanse of white nothingness.

The Pasteboard measures 120 x 120 inches, which works out to 100 square feet of drawing space. At actual size, you only see a very small section of the Pasteboard. A little letter-size document looks extremely tiny on a Pasteboard that is this big. If you get lost on the Pasteboard, a quick way back is by choosing View⇨Actual Size. This puts your page in the center of the window at 100% view, at which time you should be able to see at least part of your drawing. To see the whole page quickly, choose View⇨Fit In Window, which resizes your page down to where you can see the entire page.

This assumes, of course, that you have actually drawn artwork on the defined page. I used to get frantic calls from people who had double-clicked the Zoom tool and all their artwork would disappear. It took me a while to figure out that they had drawn their artwork way off on the side of the Pasteboard.

VectorTools to the rescue again! VectorNavigator is a floating palette that shows you all of the artwork in the document and where you are in relation to that artwork. You can even move around your document by clicking in the VectorNavigator preview. See Chapter 14 for more on VectorTools and VectorNavigator.

The Artboard

In the center of the Pasteboard is a black-bordered box called the Artboard. The Artboard represents the largest area that will actually print out of Illustrator. If you are taking your Illustrator artwork into another application, such as Photoshop or QuarkXPress, the size of the Artboard is irrelevant; your entire illustration appears in most other software applications even if that artwork is larger than the Artboard.

The dotted lines on the Artboard represent which area will print and the size of your printer's paper, referencing the printer options you have chosen in Page Setup for this information. There are two sets of dotted lines on the Artboard, although you can normally only see the inside line. The inside line represents what will actually print; the outside line is the size of the paper you have chosen in Page Setup.

The dimensions of the Artboard can be changed by choosing File➪Document Setup and typing in different values in the width and height text fields of the Document Setup dialog box.

The Page Tool

The Page tool changes how much of your document will print by moving the printable area of the document, without moving any of the printable objects in the document. Clicking and dragging the lower-left corner of the page relocates the page to the place where you release the mouse button.

This tool is useful when your document is larger than the biggest image area your printer can print. The tool enables you to *tile* several pages to create one large page out of several sheets of paper. *Tiling* is the process whereby the image consists of several pieces of paper, arranged in a grid formation. A portion of the image is on each page, and when fitted together, the image can be viewed in its entirety. This is really only good for rough laser prints, as there will be $^{1}/_{4}$ inch around the edge of each paper that will need to be manually trimmed.

Miscellaneous Window Stuff

Illustrator windows act like windows in most other programs. The close box is in the upper-left corner, and the manual resize box is in the lower-right corner. The box in the upper-right corner toggles between your current window size and full-screen size.

The title bar at the top of the window is used to move the window around your screen. On the title bar is the name of the document (if you have not yet saved your document, the name of the document is Untitled Art 1, with the number changing for each new document you create). Next to the title of the document is the current viewing zoom percentage relative to actual size.

The scroll bars on the right side of the window let you see what is above and below the current viewing area. The scroll bars at the bottom of the window control panning from side to side. The arrows on each scroll bar let you see just a bit more with every click; holding down the mouse on an arrow slowly scrolls to other parts of the document. Dragging the *elevator box* in the scroll bar takes you to another part of the document, relative to the direction you are dragging. Clicking at either side of the elevator box in either bar changes your view by chunks of about half the width or height of your window.

In the lower-left corner is the status bar, which tells you all sorts of neat information you just can't get anywhere else. The default is usually set to display the name of the tool you are working with.

The Toolbox

The Illustrator 7 toolbox has undergone some dramatic changes since Version 6:

- The toolbox now incorporates the (Version 6) Plug-in Tools palette tools. There is no longer any need for a Plug-in Tools palette, as the toolbox can grow as additional tools are added to it (via plug-ins such as VectorTools Magic Wand).
- The tools have been dramatically reorganized (see Figure 1-25).
- Color controls (for Fill, Stroke, None, Gradient, and Solid) have been added to match the Photoshop toolbox.
- Viewing controls have been added to the bottom of the toolbox.
- All tools can be accessed through the keyboard.
- And perhaps the most startling (and welcome) change: the Freehand tool has been renamed the Pencil tool, removing any mention of a certain competing product.

Figure 1-25: The Illustrator 7 toolbox

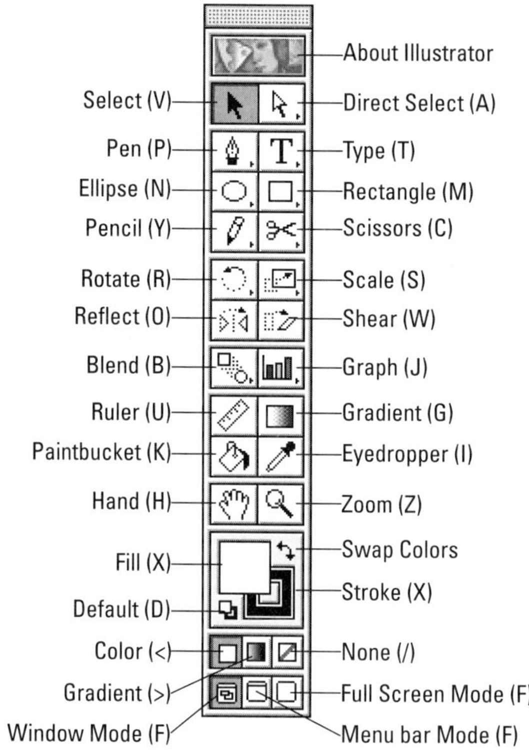

The toolbox appears on top of your document window, covering up part of your illustration in the upper-left corner. The toolbox has no close box; to close it you must choose Window⇨Hide Tools. To show the toolbox, choose Window⇨Show Tools; it will appear. You can also press the Tab key (which hides *all* palettes, not just the toolbox).

The toolbox has two columns of tools, with the tools in each section related to each other. The viewing tools — the Hand tool and the Zoom tool, for example — are next to each other. The transformation tools — Scale, Rotate, Reflect, and Shear — are in one section together. However, the middle two sets of tools are more miscellaneous groupings than anything else.

To choose a tool, click the one you want to use in the toolbox and release the mouse button. You can use this tool until you click another. You can also choose tools by pressing a key on the keyboard; for instance, pressing the P key selects the Pen tool. The keys to press for each tool are listed in Figure 1-25.

Many tools have additional *pop-up* tools — tools that appear only when you click and hold down the mouse on the default tool. The default tools that have pop-ups are located in the right column and are indicated with a little triangle in the upper-right corner of the tool. To select a pop-up tool, click and hold on a tool with a triangle until the pop-up tools appear; then drag to the pop-up tool you want. The new pop-up tool replaces the default tool in that tool slot.

NEW IN 7

These tools from the Illustrator 6 plug-in tools palette are now included in the Illustrator 7 toolbox:

- The Star, Spiral, and Polygon tools are located in the slot with the Ellipse tool.
- The Twirl tool is located in the Rotate tool slot.
- The Knife tool is located in the Scissors tool slot.

Summary

- Illustrator seems difficult to learn at first, but with this book and a bit of dedication, it can be mastered.
- Illustrator works best with PostScript fonts.
- Illustrator can be interpreted as a good front end for the PostScript page description language.
- There are four types of Anchor Points: Straight Corner Points, Smooth Points, Curved Corner Points, and Combination Corner Points.
- Curved paths in Illustrator are created with Bézier curves, named after the French mathematician Pierre Bézier.
- Curved segments are controlled by manipulating Control Handles, which extend from Anchor Points at either end of the segment.
- Illustrator has virtually unlimited available undos and redos.

ASK TOULOUSE

Where's That Tool?

The Fonz: I can't find the Convert Direction Point tool.

Toulouse: It's to the right of the Pen tool.

The Fonz: I can't find my Pen tool, either.

Toulouse: Are you sure you're using Illustrator?

The Fonz: Heeeeyyyyyy....

Toulouse: Just kidding. Someone (maybe Chachi?) might have been using another tool in that slot.

The Fonz: Is there any way to reset all the tools back to the original ones?

Toulouse: Sure. Just ⌘-Shift [Ctrl+Shift]-double-click on any tool to reset all of them.

Creating and Painting Shapes

2 CHAPTER

In This Chapter

- How to draw basic ellipses and rectangles
- How to create polygons, stars, and spirals
- How to color paths with Fills and Strokes
- All about the Color, Swatches, and Stroke palettes
- How to define paint styles
- How to use the Paintbucket and Eyedropper tools

Technically, the name of this section should really be "Placing, Sizing, and Colorizing Preformatted Open and Closed Paths," but then no one would read it. And this is an important chapter because it introduces many concepts that are built upon in later chapters.

Shapes

Drawing the most basic shapes — rectangles, ovals, polygons, and stars — is precisely what a computer is for. Try drawing a perfect oval by hand. Troublesome, isn't it? How about a square that doesn't have ink bubbles or splotches at the corners? How about a nine-point star? Yuck. Drawing these objects and then coloring them in Illustrator is so easy and so basic that after a few weeks of using Illustrator, you'll never be able to draw a shape by hand again without wincing, maybe even shuddering. Figure 2-1 compares shapes drawn by hand with those drawn by a computer.

Getting rid of the shape you've drawn is even easier than creating it in the first place (delete it by pressing the Delete or Backspace key). And after the shape is created, it can be moved, rotated, scaled, and manipulated in any way you like.

Windows Update

While the creation of shapes is quite similar to 4.1, the painting of shapes is totally different. Fortunately, it's almost as different for Macintosh users as it is for Windows users.

What's Missing	What Replaces It
Paint Style dialog box	Color palette, Stroke palette, Swatches palette, and Attributes palette
Freehand tool	Pencil tool (same tool, different name)
Freehand tolerance	Curve Fitting Tolerance

Spiral tool: For drawing Spirals (hard, if not impossible to do, otherwise)

Polygon tool: For drawing any-sided shapes

Star tool: For drawing all sorts of stars

Gradient palette: For creating multicolor gradients

Paintbrush tool: For drawing filled brushstrokes

Paintbucket and Eyedropper tools: For sucking colors from and applying colors to objects

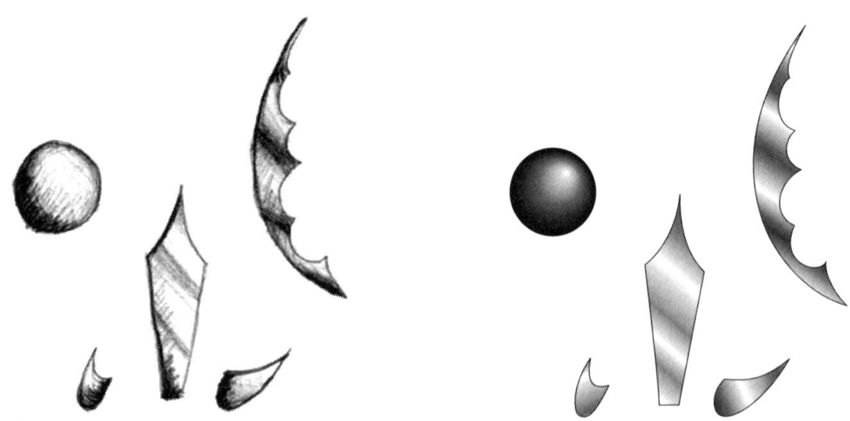

Shapes drawn by hand   Shapes drawn by computer

Figure 2-1: Hand-drawn shapes and their computer-drawn counterparts

The true power of object-oriented drawing programs is exemplified in Illustrator. No matter what you draw, you can adjust and move each piece of the drawing independently until it's just right. Don't like the sun so high in your background? Pull it down and tuck it in just a bit behind those mountains. Is the tree too small for the house in your illustration? Scale it up a bit. This feature is great not only for artists, but also for your pesky client (or boss) who demands that everything be moved except that darned tree. Figure 2-2 shows an illustration drawn one way and then modified in a matter of seconds by moving and transforming existing elements.

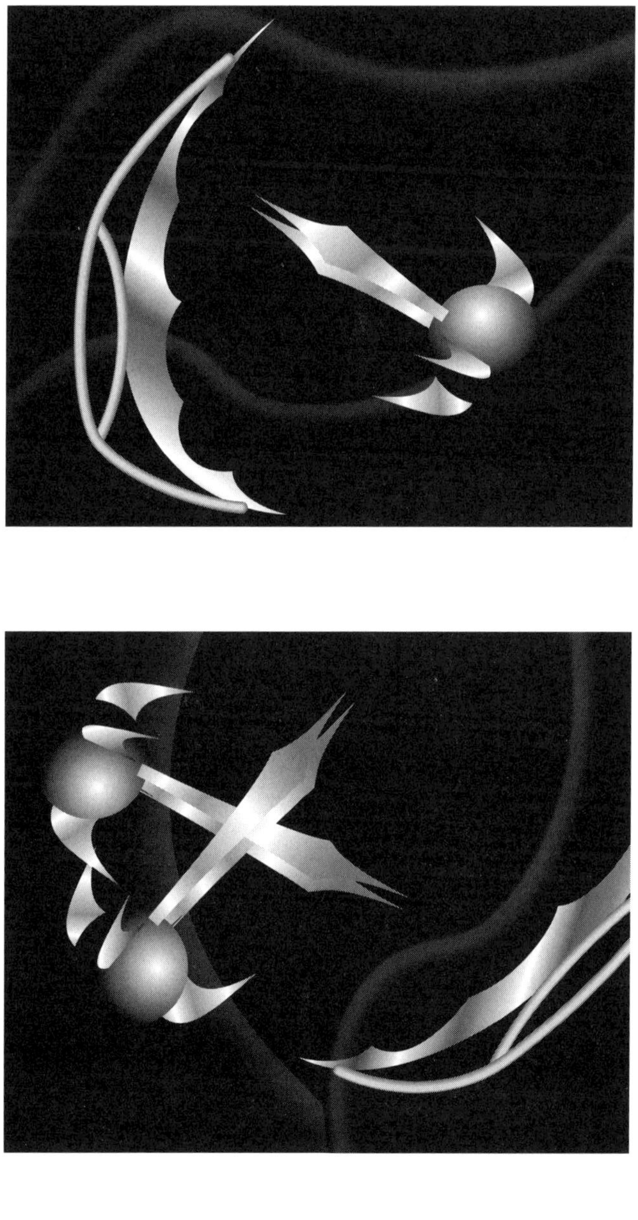

Figure 2-2: Illustrator objects moved from one drawing to the next

Traditional bitmap paint applications do not have the capability to move pieces of a drawing (with the exception of the use of layers in software such as Photoshop 4 and Painter 5). After an image is moved in a bitmap program, a *hole* appears in the place where the section used to be. And if there is anything under the section where the image was moved to, that information is gone when the section is replaced with the new image.

Drawing Rectangles

The most basic shape you can draw is a rectangle. The following steps, and the illustration of these steps in Figure 2-3, explain how to draw a simple rectangle.

STEPS:	**Drawing a Rectangle**
Step 1.	Select the Rectangle tool (highlighted in the toolbox in Figure 2-3) by clicking it in the toolbox (or by pressing the letter M on the keyboard).
Step 2.	Click to set the origin and hold down the mouse button.
Step 3.	Drag diagonally (down and to the right) to the size you desire.
Step 4.	Release the mouse button. A rectangle is created. The farther the distance from the initial click until the point where you release the mouse button, the larger the rectangle.

After you release the mouse button, a white rectangle outlined in black appears with four blue points in the corners and one blue point in the center (if you are in Preview mode, the default viewing mode). The edge of the rectangle has thin blue lines surrounding it. The blue points in the corners are *Straight Corner Anchor Points.* The blue point in the center is the *Center Point.* The blue lines are *Straight Line Segments* that connect the Anchor Points of the rectangle. The blue points and blue lines together are considered a *path.* In Artwork mode, the rectangle has no Fill or Stroke, and the points and path appear black.

If you aren't sure what View mode you're in, display the View menu by clicking View and keeping the mouse button down. If the top item of the menu reads Artwork, you're in Preview mode. If it reads Preview, you're in Artwork mode. If this seems a little backward, choosing that menu item will change the viewing mode to the one you choose. So when you're in Preview mode, and you see and choose Artwork, you're switched to Artwork mode.

Figure 2-3: Steps for drawing a rectangle

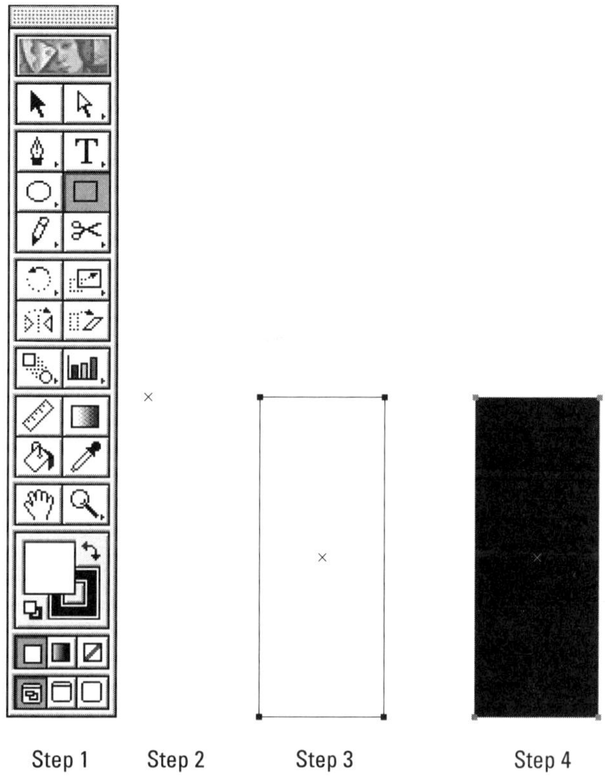

The initial click you make with the Rectangle tool is called the *origin point.* While you drag a figure, the origin point never moves; however, the rest of the rectangle is fluid, changing shape as you drag in different directions and to different distances with your mouse. Dragging horizontally with almost no vertical movement results in a long, flat rectangle. Dragging vertically with very little horizontal movement creates a rectangle that is tall and thin. Dragging at a 45° angle (diagonally) results in a squared rectangle.

Rectangles can be drawn from any corner by clicking and dragging in the opposite direction of where you want that corner to be. For instance, to draw a rectangle from the lower-right corner, click and drag up and to the left. As long as you have the Rectangle tool, dragging with it in the document window produces a new rectangle.

If you need to draw a rectangle that is an exact size, instead of dragging with the Rectangle tool, just click it once and release where you want the upper-left corner to be. The Rectangle dialog box appears, as shown in Figure 2-4. Type in the width and height, click OK, and the rectangle draws itself, becoming precisely the size that you specified.

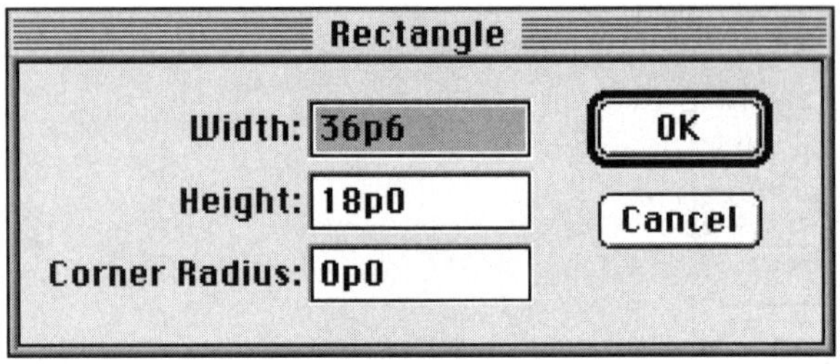

Figure 2-4: The Rectangle dialog box, used for specifying exact dimensions of a rectangle

The third text field in the Rectangle dialog box is for the size of the corner radius. This option makes the corners of the rectangle curved, although leaving the setting at a value of 0 keeps the corners straight. Rectangles whose sizes are specified in the Rectangle size dialog box are always drawn from the upper-left corner unless you press the Option [Alt] key while drawing (see the next section, "Drawing Rectangles from Their Centers"). The largest rectangle you can draw is only 10 feet by 10 feet. It's a wonder you can get anything done at all with these limitations. . . .

When the Rectangle dialog box appears, values are usually already inside the text fields. Those numbers correspond to the size of the rectangle you last drew. To create another rectangle the same size, just click OK (or press Return or Enter). To make the rectangle a different size, replace the values with your own measurements. If a text field is highlighted, typing replaces the text in the text field and deletes what had been highlighted. To highlight the next field in a dialog box, press the Tab key. You can also highlight the preceding field in a dialog box by pressing Shift-Tab. If you'd like to highlight any text field instantly, double-click the value, or click the label next to that value. To accept the options in the dialog box, click OK or press Return or Enter.

When you first run Illustrator, all measurements are set to points. This means that the values inside the Rectangle dialog box appear in so many points (12 points in a pica). You can work in inches in three ways. The first way, before you bring up the Rectangle dialog box, is to choose File⇨Preferences⇨Units & Undo and choose inches as the measurement system. All dialog boxes in all new documents will then express their measurements in inches, not points. The second way is to choose File⇨Document Setup and choose inches in the Ruler Units pop-up menu, which will change the units to inches in that document *only.* The third way is to type either the inch symbol (") or **in** after the number, even though the text fields show points. Illustrator does conversions from points to inches and centimeters (and vice versa) on the fly, so after you enter a point value, the program converts the points into inches as soon as you press the Tab key. This little feature can be an excellent way for you to become more comfortable with points and picas.

To get out of the Rectangle dialog box without drawing a rectangle, click the Cancel button (or just press ⌘-Period [esc]). Anything you have typed in that dialog box is then forgotten; the next time the dialog box is opened, it still has the size of the previously drawn rectangle inside it.

STEPS: Creating a Basic Drop Shadow Box

Step 1. Using the Rectangle tool, draw a rectangle that is about 1 inch wide by 1 inch tall. Change the Fill color of the rectangle to 100% Black by clicking the Fill square in the toolbox, and then choosing Black in the Color palette. Change the Stroke to Black by clicking the Stroke icon in the toolbox and then choosing Black in the Color palette.

Step 2. Choose the Selection tool and drag up and to the right just a little while holding down the Option [Alt] key. (The farther you drag, the greater the depth of the drop shadow.)

Step 3. After you release the mouse button, you should have two overlapping rectangles. Change the fill color of the rectangle on top to 50% gray by clicking the Fill square in the toolbox, and then clicking on 50% Black in the Color palette. Change the Stroke to Black by clicking the Stroke icon in the toolbox and then choosing Black in the Color palette. Your illustration should now look like Figure 2-5.

Figure 2-5: A basic drop shadow box

Drawing Rectangles from Their Centers

Instead of drawing a rectangle from a corner, you can also draw one from its center. Rectangles are often placed on top of or under certain other objects, and there needs to be an even amount of space between the rectangle and the object it is surrounding. Drawing from the corner forces you to "eyeball" the space around the object, while drawing from the center of the other object ensures that space surrounding the object is the same.

To draw a rectangle from its center, hold down the Option [Alt] key, click, and drag. The origin point is now the center of the rectangle. The farther you drag in one direction, the farther the edges of the rectangle go out in the opposite direction. Drawing from the center of a rectangle lets you draw a rectangle twice as big as the one you can draw if you drag from a corner. As long as the Option [Alt] key is pressed, the rectangle continues to be drawn from its center. If you release the

Option [Alt] key before you release the mouse button, the origin of the rectangle changes back to a corner. You can press and release the Option [Alt] key at any time while drawing, toggling back and forth between drawing a corner rectangle and a centered rectangle.

If you click without dragging when the Option [Alt] key is pressed, the Rectangle dialog box appears. The center of the rectangle is now where you clicked (normally, the corner of the rectangle is where you click). Unlike manually drawing (dragging) centered rectangles, the values you enter for the width and height are the actual width and height of the rectangle. The value is *not* doubled, as it is when you are dragging a centered rectangle.

You can also draw a rectangle from its center by selecting the Centered Rectangle tool from the right of the Rectangle tool. Drawing with the Centered Rectangle tool automatically draws a rectangle from its center. Now the Option [Alt] key toggles from drawing from the middle to drawing from the corner. So if you keep the Option [Alt] key pressed until after you release the mouse button, the rectangle is drawn from the corner, not the center.

Drawing a Perfect Square

Few things in life really are perfect, but squares in Illustrator are pretty darn close.

When drawing, you can force Illustrator to create perfect squares by holding down the Shift key as you draw. When you press the Shift key while drawing a rectangle, it constrains to a square. (In review of your fourth-grade math class, the difference between a square and a rectangle is that a square is a rectangle with four sides of exactly the same length.) You can also use the Rectangle dialog box to draw a perfect square by entering equal values for the width and height.

To draw a square from its center, hold down the Option [Alt] and Shift keys while drawing. Make sure that *both* keys are still pressed when the mouse button is released. If you are using the Centered Rectangle tool (it has a little + in it) and you press Option[Alt]-Shift, the square is drawn from a corner.

Drawing Rounded Rectangles and Squares

Sometimes, straight corners just aren't good enough. That's when it's time to create a rectangle with *rounded corners.* Why? Maybe you want your rectangles to look less "computery." A tiny bit of corner rounding (2 or 3 points) may be just what you need.

To draw a rectangle with rounded corners, choose the Rounded Rectangle tool, a pop-up tool that appears when you click on the Rectangle tool in the toolbox and drag to the right. Click and drag with this tool as if you were drawing a standard rectangle; the only difference is that this rectangle has rounded corners. The point at which you clicked is where the corner would be — if there were a corner. Of course, with rounded corners, there is no real corner, so the computer uses an imaginary point, called the *origin point,* as its on-screen corner reference.

The *corner radius* in Illustrator is the length from that imaginary corner (the origin point) to where the curve begins, as shown in Figure 2-6. The larger the value you enter in the Corner radius field of the Rectangle dialog box, the farther the rectangle starts from the imaginary corner, and the bigger the curve is. For example, if you set the corner radius at 1 inch, the edge of the rectangle would start curving 1 inch from where a real corner would normally appear.

Figure 2-6: The corner radius

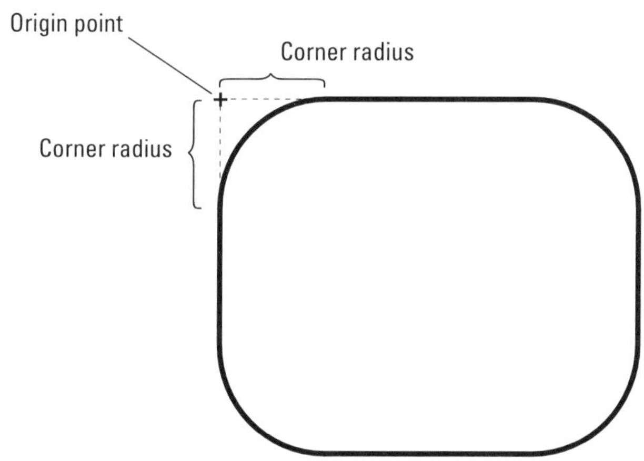

To draw a rounded rectangle from the center, press the Option [Alt] key and keep it pressed until you release the mouse button. To draw a rounded square, hold the Shift key while dragging and do not release it until after you release the mouse button. Drawing a rounded square from its center requires that you press both the Option [Alt] and Shift keys until you release the mouse button.

The *roundness* of the corners is determined by either the corner radius used by the most recent rounded-corner rectangle drawn or the radius set in the General Preferences dialog box (File⇨Preferences⇨General or ⌘-K [Ctrl+K]). The corner radius in the General Preferences dialog box changes each time you change the radius with the Rounded Rectangle tool. To change the radius of the next rounded rectangle to be drawn, go to the General Preferences dialog box and enter the new corner radius value. All rounded rectangles are now drawn with this new corner radius until this value is changed.

The corner radius can also be changed by clicking once with the Rounded Rectangle tool anywhere in the document, which displays the Rectangle dialog box. Changing the value in the Corner radius field box not only changes the current rounded rectangle's corner radius, but also changes the radius in the General Preferences box. This corner radius is used for all subsequently drawn rounded rectangles until the radius value is changed again.

CAUTION

If the corner radius is more than one-half the length of either the length or width of the rectangle, the rectangle will appear to have perfectly round ends on at least two sides. If the corner radius is more than one-half the length of both the length or width of the rectangle, then the rectangle will be a circle!

How the Corner Radius *Really* Works

For all you geometry buffs, this is the real way that this whole corner radius business works: The width of any circle is called the *diameter* of that circle. Half the diameter is the *radius* of the circle, as shown in the following figure.

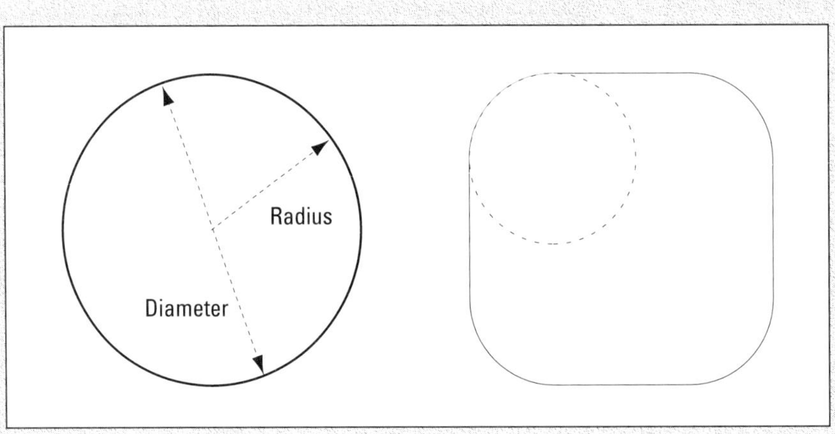

If you create a circle with a radius of 1 inch, the circle actually has a diameter of 2 inches. Put this 2-inch circle into the corner of the rectangle, as in the figure above, and the curve of the circle matches the curve of the rounded rectangle that has a corner radius of 1 inch. Huh?

To realistically determine the way a round corner will look, use the method that measures the distance from the imaginary corner to the place where the curve starts.

You are limited to a maximum of a 4,320-point corner radius, which works out to 5 feet. The largest rectangle you can create has a 10-foot length (the size of the Illustrator Pasteboard). So a 10-foot square with a 5-foot radius is another circle. (Those clever engineers. . . .)

Artificial Intelligence in Illustrator: If you are in the Rectangle dialog box and enter a value of 0 in the Corner Radius field, the Rounded Rectangle tool is replaced by the standard Rectangle tool in the toolbox. If you enter a value greater than 0, the Rounded Rectangle tool takes over that slot in the toolbox.

Using the Round Corners Filter

If you have an existing rectangle with straight corners and you'd like to make the corners round, neither of the preceding methods will work. Instead, you must choose Filter⇨Stylize⇨Round Corners and enter the value of the corner radius you would like for the existing rectangle in the dialog box that appears. Using this filter allows you to change straight-corner rectangles to rounded-corner rectangles, not rounded-corner rectangles to straight-corner rectangles. Using this filter on rectangles that already have rounded corners isn't recommended, as it will usually result in an unsightly (ugly) distortion.

Furthermore, this filter cannot change corners that have been rounded with either the Rounded Rectangle tool or by previous use of the Round Corners dialog box. Using this dialog box affects corners that are *not* round. Figure 2-7 shows the Round Corners filter applied to various rectangles and the results.

Figure 2-7: Rounded corners on rectangles

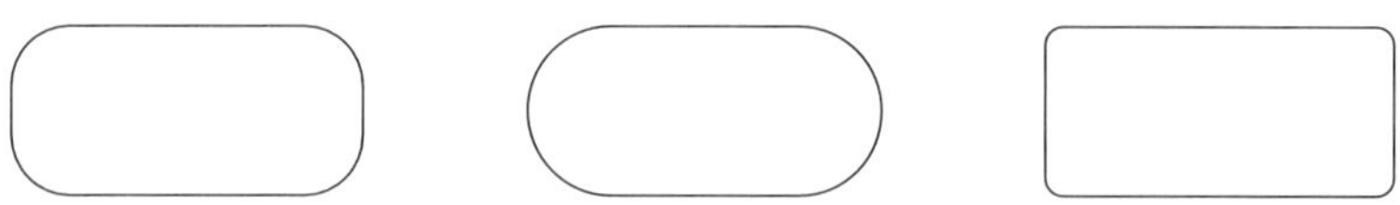

Rounding Corners Backward

What if you want your corners to round inward instead of out? Well, it would seem that you are initially out of luck, for Illustrator doesn't provide any way for you to enter a negative value for a corner radius. Instead, you need to manipulate the corners manually. The following steps, and the illustration of these steps in Figure 2-8, explain how to create a reverse rounded-corner rectangle.

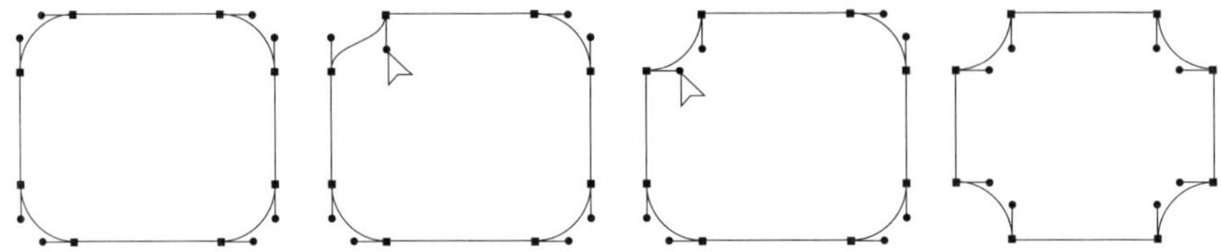

Figure 2-8: Steps for creating "backward" rounded corners on a rectangle

STEPS: Creating a Reverse Rounded-Corner Rectangle

Step 1. Choose File➪Preferences➪General and set the Corner radius to .25". Draw a rounded rectangle that is about 3 inches wide by 1inch tall.

Step 2. Select the topmost point on the left side of the rounded rectangle with the Direct Selection tool (hollow arrow). One Control Handle appears, sticking out to the left.

Step 3. Using the Rotate tool, click the Anchor Point once to set the origin. Click the Control Handle again and drag it down below the Anchor Point. Press the Shift key to ensure that the Control Handle Line is perfectly vertical and then release the mouse button.

Step 4. Select the second point from the top on the left side with the Direct Selection tool. A Control Handle appears, sticking straight up out of this Anchor Point.

Step 5. Using the Rotate tool, click the Anchor Point once to set the origin. Click the Control Handle again and drag it to the right of the Anchor Point. Press the Shift key to ensure that the Control Handle line is perfectly horizontal and then release the mouse button.

Step 6. Repeat these steps for each of the corners. After you get the hang of it, the points start flying into position almost by themselves.

Drawing Ellipses and Circles

Drawing ellipses and circles is *almost* as easy as drawing rectangles and squares. You can create a wide variety of ellipses and circles in Illustrator.

To draw an ellipse (what Illustrator calls ovals), choose the Ellipse tool, click, and drag diagonally. The outline of an ellipse forms, and when you release the mouse button, the ellipse itself appears on-screen. Ellipses, like rectangles, have four Anchor Points, but the Anchor Points on an ellipse are at the top, bottom, left, and right of the ellipse.

Drawing an ellipse is harder than drawing a rectangle because the point of origin on an ellipse is outside the ellipse. With a rectangle, the point of origin corresponds to either a corner of the rectangle, which also happens to be an Anchor Point, or the center of the rectangle. On an ellipse, there are no corners. This means that clicking and dragging does not align the top or bottom, or left or right, but one of the 45° curves to the origin point (an *arc*). Figure 2-9 shows that the top of the curve extends above the origin point, the bottom of the curve extends below the origin point, the right edge extends to the right of the origin point, and the left edge extends to the left of the origin point. (More detailed — and largely unnecessary — math is available at the end of this section.)

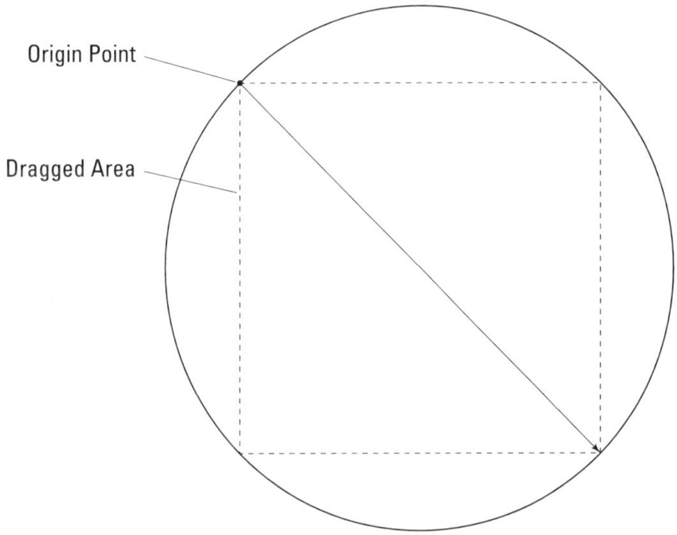

Figure 2-9: The curves of an ellipse extend beyond the boundaries of the dragged area

Drawing an ellipse from its "corner" is a difficult task when the top, bottom, left, and right edges of the oval need to be at a specific location. On the other hand, tracing elliptical objects is easier because clicking and dragging on the edge of an existing elliptical object results in a close-to-perfect match, as shown in Figure 2-10.

Figure 2-10: Tracing a dimmed EPS image with the Rectangle and Ellipse tools

For easier tracing of circles, change the Constrain Angle value (File➪General Preferences) to 45°. Now you can place the cursor on the top, bottom, or sides of the circle, and drag horizontally or vertically for a perfect fit. This technique doesn't work for ellipses because the ellipse will be angled at 45° if drawn this way.

STEPS: Tracing an EPS Image with Basic Shapes

Step 1. Place the Snowman file from the Artwork folder on the *Illustrator 7 Bible* CD-ROM. Choose Window➪Show Layers. In the Layers palette, double-click Layer 1 and check the Dim placed images option.

Step 2. Use the Rectangle tool to trace the frame of the picture, the walls, and the pieces of the snowman's arms. Place the cursor in a corner of the object to be traced and drag toward the opposite corner. Use the Rotate tool to rotate the arms. For the hat, choose File➪Preferences➪General (⌘-K) [Ctrl+K] and change the Constrain Angle to 14°. Trace the hat and brim at this angle and then change the Constrain Angle back to 0°.

Step 3. Use the Ellipse tool in the same way as the Rectangle tool to trace the snowman circles, eyes, nose, mouth, snowballs, and snow drifts. If you can't see an entire circle, as is the case with most of the snow drifts and the bottom section of the snowman, just estimate.

To draw from the center of an ellipse, press the Option [Alt] key and drag. As long as you are holding down the Option [Alt] key when you release the mouse button, the ellipse uses the initial click as the origin point and is drawn from the center.

To change the Ellipse tool so that it *always* draws ovals from the center, select the Centered Ellipse Tool (an ellipse with a plus sign in its center) from the Ellipse tool slot. Double-clicking the tool again transforms it back to the standard Ellipse tool.

Clicking without dragging with the Ellipse tool brings up the Ellipse dialog box, where you can enter any value for the width and height of your ellipse. The ellipse is drawn from the upper-left arc. Entering identical values results in a circle. Option[Alt]-clicking brings up the same dialog box, but the ellipse is now drawn from the center instead of the left arc.

To draw a perfect circle, hold down the Shift key as you drag. The oval now has equal width and height, making it a circle. Make sure that you keep pressing the Shift key until you release the mouse button; otherwise, the ellipse loses its equal proportions. To draw a circle from the center with the Ellipse tool, hold down both the Option [Alt] and Shift keys and drag diagonally.

Ellipses are drawn from the upper-left corner and extend about 20 percent of the total height above the origin point and about 20 percent of the total width to the left of the origin point. It's not just a coincidence that the right edge and bottom also extend 20 percent past the release point. The way this works out in mathematics (numerophobics should skip ahead to the next paragraph now) is that the height and width of the ellipse will be the square root of 2 (about 1.414) times the height and width of the box that is dragged from corner to corner.

Only rectangles and ellipses were used to create the illustration in Figure 2-11. Through a creative use of Fills, the illustration comes alive.

Figure 2-11: An illustration drawn with only rectangles and ellipses

STEPS: Drawing the Juggler with Rectangles and Ellipses

Step 1. Change the Paint Style to a Fill of None and a Stroke of 1 point black.

Step 2. Using the Ellipse tool, drag to create the juggler's body and then his head, as shown in Figure 2-12.

Figure 2-12: Ellipses and circles

Step 3. To tilt back the juggler's head, select the head oval and double-click the Rotate tool. Then enter a value of 30°, which angles the head back.

Step 4. Next, create one of the rings by pressing the Shift key and dragging to create a perfect circle.

Step 5. Duplicate the circles by pressing the Option [Alt] key and dragging one of the circles to a new location. As long as the Option [Alt] key is pressed when you release the mouse button, the circle is duplicated rather than moved.

Step 6. Draw a much smaller circle for one of the balls the juggler is balancing on his head. Option[Alt]-copy the balls in the same way you copied the rings.

Step 7. Option[Alt]-copy two more ball-sized circles to create hands, the white area of the eye, and the mouth.

Step 8. Choose File➪General Preferences (⌘-K) [Ctrl+K] and change the Constrain Angle to 45°.

Step 9. Using the Rectangle tool, create first the top part of the hat and then the rim of the hat, as shown in Figure 2-13. The pieces will automatically be angled at 45°.

Step 10. Change the Constrain Angle back to 0° and draw both arms. They may need to be rotated individually, depending on the location of the rings.

Step 11. Draw the rectangular background and choose Object➪Arrange➪Send to Back (⌘-Shift-[) [Ctrl+Shift+[].

Step 12. Select individual paths and Fill them with different colors and gradients.

Creating Cool Shapes

Although it is just loads of fun to create more and more ovals, rectangles, and rounded rectangles, sooner or later you're gonna get bored. There are other, dare I say, *more interesting* shapes that you can create automatically by using some of the additional shape tools that come with Illustrator. Most of them are located in the Oval tool slot in the toolbox (see Figure 2-14).

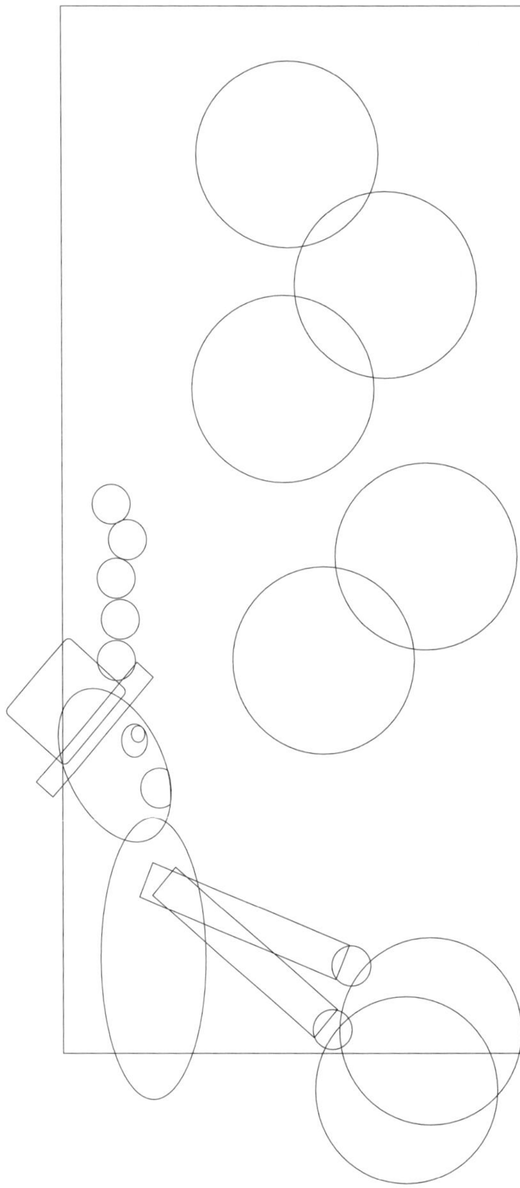

Figure 2-13: Rectangles are added to the illustration

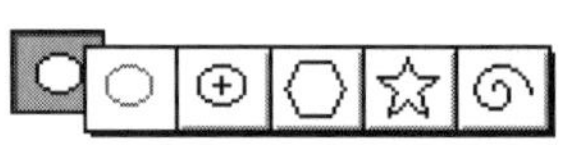

Figure 2-14: The Ellipse tool slot and its tools

The tools that were in the Plug-In Tools palette in Version 6 (and were only filters in Versions 5.0 and 5.5) have been incorporated into the main toolbox in Version 7. They've been placed in tool slots which are for the most part logical. The Plug-In Tools palette was conceived out of need in Version 6 anyway, not by any grand design; all tools should reside within one area to reduce clutter.

Creating Polygons

To create a polygon, select the Polygon tool (to the right of the Ellipse tool in the Ellipse tool slot, and shown in Figure 2-15) and click and drag in a document. As you drag, the polygon will grow from its center and get larger and larger.

Figure 2-15: The Polygon tool

To specify the number of sides for your polygon *before* you draw the polygon, Option[Alt]-click with the Polygon tool. That will bring up the Polygon tool dialog box (shown in Figure 2-16), where you can specify both the number of sides and the size of the polygon.

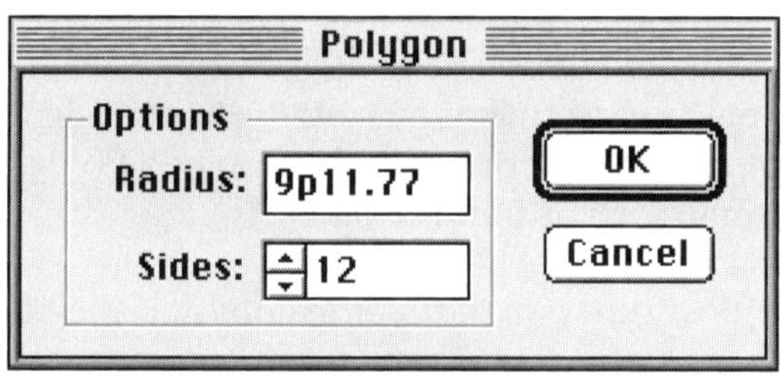

Figure 2-16: The Polygon dialog box

The radius is the distance from the center of the polygon to the corners of the polygon. For even-sided shapes (4, 6, 8, 10 sides, and so on), the radius is half the width of the object, from one corner to the opposite corner. For odd-sided shapes, the radius is *not* half the width of the object, but instead, can *only* be measured by going from one corner point to the center.

All polygons created with the Polygon tool are equilateral polygons. I looked up *equilateral,* just to make sure I wasn't spouting off multisyllabic (heh) words to sound impressive, and it means "sides of the same length." So every polygon you create has sides that are all the same. That's why every four-sided polygon you create is a square, and each six-sided object a perfect hexagon. You might find the

Square capabilities of the Polygon tool useful (no, really); it can save you a step when you want to draw a square at an angle. That's something that can't be done with the Rectangle tool unless you (1) change the Constrain Angle in General Preferences prior to drawing the square; or (2) use the Rotate tool on the square after it is drawn. I've found it helpful on several occasions.

While drawing a polygon, you can change the number of sides on the fly. To increase the number of sides, press the up arrow. To decrease the number of sides, press the down arrow. Figure 2-17 shows different polygons drawn with the Polygon tool.

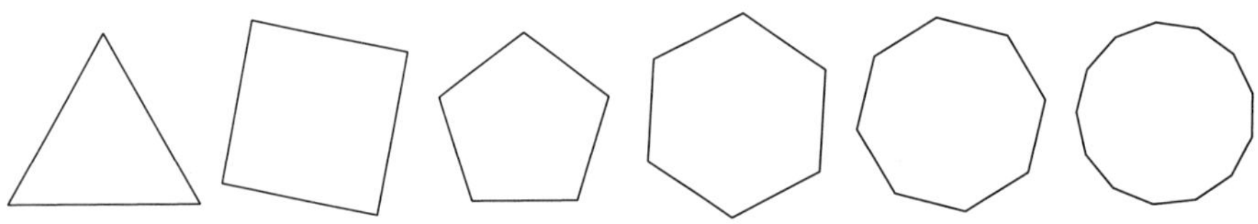

Figure 2-17: Polygons drawn with the Polygon tool

If you press the Shift key while dragging, the polygon you're creating is upright; it aligns to the current Constrain Angle (usually 0°). This means that if you're creating a triangle and you press Shift, the triangle has one side that is perfectly horizontal (the bottom). That is, unless you have a different Constrain Angle, in which case that edge of the triangle aligns to that angle.

Press the Spacebar to move your polygon around when dragging with the Polygon tool. You can do this at any time during the creation of a Polygon; when you release the Spacebar, the tool functions as before.

POWER TIP

Possibly the niftiest function of the Polygon (and the Star and Spiral tools) is the wonderful Spaz function that comes from using the tilde (~) key. Press it when you're drawing and you'll see several shapes appear rapidly. All sorts of questionable designs can be created by Spazzing, as shown in Figure 2-18.

Seeing Stars

To create stars, choose the Star tool from its hiding place next to the Polygon tool in the Ellipse tool slot and drag in the document. As you drag, a star is born. . . . Several stars are shown in Figure 2-19.

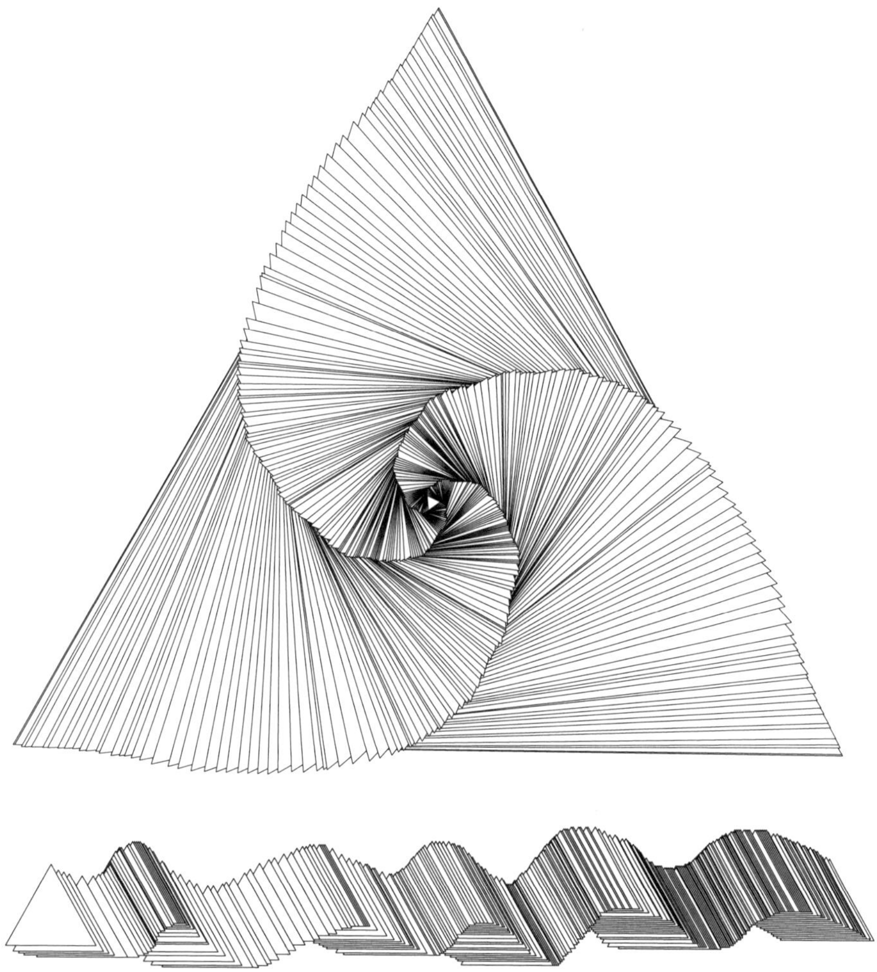

Figure 2-18: Spazzing triangles with the Polygon tool. Funky? Yes. Art? Doubtful.

Figure 2-19: Stars

Stars have several of the same controls as Polygons when they're being drawn: Shift aligns the star to the constrain angle, the Spacebar moves the star around, and the tilde key makes millions of duplicates. The up and down arrows work a bit differently, however. Instead of adding and removing sides, the arrows add and remove entire points. So they're actually adding two sides, in a way. Stars have to have an even number of sides, or they're not really stars, they're the pointy lumps you doodled during your Poly Sci classes as a sophomore.

The Star tool adds two additional keys for other functions. Pressing the Option [Alt] key makes every other side align with each other. It's hard to describe, but these stars look "perfect." Adobe refers to them as *fixed* stars, but I'm not aware of any neutering or spaying taking place when the Option [Alt] key is pressed ("It's the responsible thing to do; press the Option [Alt] key when you draw stars"). These fixed stars are shown in Figure 2-20. In case it's keeping you up at night, the Option [Alt] key has no effect on stars with four points, and it turns three-pointed stars into triangles.

Figure 2-20: Fixed Stars drawn while the Option [Alt] key is pressed

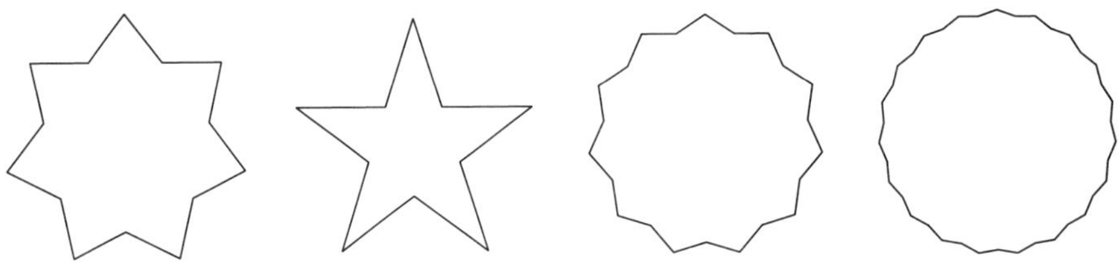

Stars can come in all shapes, not just the fixed and standard shapes. These shapes are created by pressing the ⌘ [Ctrl] key when you drag. When the ⌘ [Ctrl] key is held down, the outer points are extended only; the interior points remain fixed in place. Figure 2-21 shows the same star (points, rotation, size) with points extended differently.

You can also specifically design a star by clicking with the Star tool to display the Star dialog box, where you can enter the number of points and both the first and second radius of the points.

Figure 2-21: These stars are the same except for the difference in the distance between the inner points and outer points

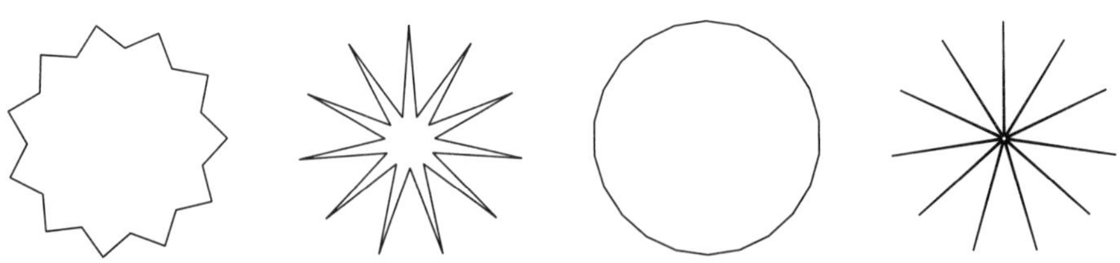

Of course, all of these stars created with the star tool consist of regular-looking stars. For a more dramatic looking starburst, follow these steps.

STEPS: Creating an Irregular Starburst

Step 1. Create a star with about 30 sides. Make it look something like the one shown in Figure 2-22.

Figure 2-22: A star about to become a starburst

Step 2. Choose Filter⇨Distort⇨Roughen.

Step 3. In the Roughen dialog box (Figure 2-23), change the Size to 5%, and the Detail to 0 (keeping the Detail at 0 won't let Roughen add any anchor points. Check the Corner checkbox (so we don't have curves on our starburst), and click OK. You can also check the Preview checkbox; each time you check and uncheck it, a new random preview results; clicking OK uses the Roughen preview you see on-screen. My result appears in Figure 2-24.

(continued)

STEPS: *(continued)*

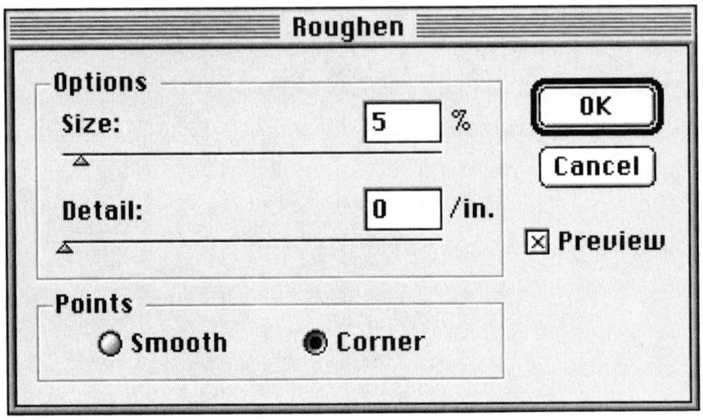

Figure 2-23: The Roughen dialog box, set up for changing a star into a starburst

Figure 2-24: The resulting starburst

Step 4. Add any extras, like a drop shadow, text, and so on. My end result is shown in Figure 2-25.

Figure 2-25: The final, ready-for-stamping-on-the-front-of-the-book starburst

Spiral Madness

If there's one really good thing to say about being able to draw spirals with the Spiral tool in Illustrator, it's that it was hellish to create them before a Spiral tool (or filter) existed. If there's another good thing to say, I haven't quite figured it out yet. The thing to say, that is . . . not the Spiral tool.

The Spiral tool (located at the far right end of the Ellipse slot tools) makes spirals. All sorts of spirals. What would you use a spiral for? Well, I used the Spiral tool to create a simulated Lucy and the Rugrats' "Live Dinner LP," which included such classics as "Eat It Before It Dies," "Watch Out, Tomcat," and the Top Ten hit "No

Control (I'm in Heat)." Of course, the path was exceedingly long and refused to print on most imagesetters. Other than that, I've created lots of art for this and other Illustrator books using spirals. I'm still waiting for a practical use to rear its twisted, spun head. Figure 2-26 shows several useless spirals I've manufactured with the Spiral tool.

Figure 2-26: Spirals

CAUTION: Spirals beg to be stroked, not filled. Putting just a fill on a spiral makes it look like a circle you drew in that Poly Sci class: lumpy and not quite round.

Here's a rundown of keys you can press while spiraling out of control with the Spiral tool:

- **Tilde (~):** It duplicates here as well, but don't do it with spirals. The mess is usually disastrous on all but the most windless spirals.
- **Shift:** This keeps the spiral aligned to the Constrain Angle. Actually, it keeps the protruding line segment of the spiral aligned to a 45° variant of the Constrain Angle.
- **Option [Alt]:** Pressing this key makes the spiral grow by adding or removing line segments (winds) to the spiral's outermost edge. Dragging away from the origin (where you initially clicked) adds segments; dragging toward the origin removes segments.
- **⌘ [Ctrl]:** Pressing the ⌘ [Ctrl] key while dragging changes the decay of the spiral. Dragging away from the origin decreases the decay %, making the space between winds larger toward the outer edge of the spiral. Dragging toward the origin increases the decay %, making the space between winds similar from inside to outside. A decay of 100% results in a perfect circle. The decay can never be less than 5%.
- **Spacebar:** Pressing the Spacebar lets you move the spiral around the screen.

If you click in your document with the Spiral tool, the Spiral dialog box (see Figure 2-27) appears, and you can enter specific values for a spiral. Handy for all those times your client or boss wants that 82.5% decay spiral.

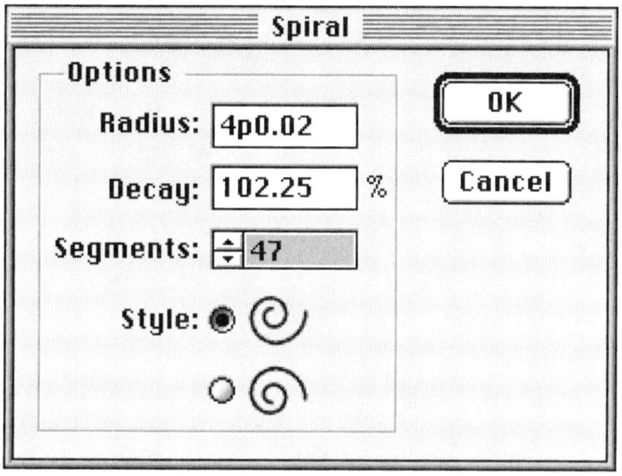

Figure 2-27: The Spiral dialog box

Drawing Shapes at an Angle

Normally, when you draw a shape with a tool, it appears to be oriented with the document and the document window. For instance, the bottom of a rectangle is parallel to the bottom of the document window.

But what if you want to draw shapes that are all angled at 45° on the page? Well, one possibility is to rotate them after they are drawn using the Transform Each command or the Rotate tool. Better than this alternative, however, is to set up your document so that every new shape is automatically angled.

The angle of the shapes is dependent on the *constrain angle*. Normally, the constrain angle is 0°, where all shapes appear to align evenly with the borders of the document. To change the constrain angle, choose File➪Preferences➪General and enter a new value in the Constrain Angle text field inside the General Preferences dialog box.

When you are done drawing these angled shapes, make sure that you change the Constrain Angle setting back to 0°, or all new shapes will be created at the altered constrain angle.

The constrain angle affects not only shapes, but other objects created in Illustrator, such as type. In addition, dragging objects with the Shift key pressed will constrain them to the current constrain angle, or a 45° or 90° variation of it.

The Constrain Angle is much easier to see if you have Grids turned on (choose View➪Show Grids, or press ⌘-" [Ctrl+"]). The grid shown on the page is always aligned to the Constrain Angle.

Filling and Stroking Shapes

One of the most powerful capabilities of Illustrator is its capability to color objects. In Adobe Illustrator, you can color both the Fill and the Stroke of the paths you have created.

Fills

The *Fill* of an object is the color inside the shape. If a path is closed, the Fill exists only on the inside of the path. If the path is open (meaning that it has two End Points), the Fill exists between an imaginary line drawn from End Point to End Point and the path itself. Fills in open paths can provide some very interesting results when the path crosses itself, or the imaginary line crosses the path. Figure 2-28 shows an example of Fills in open and closed paths and how the paths appear in Artwork mode. For text, the Fill is the color of the text. Fills do not appear in Artwork mode, only in Preview mode. Depending on the complexity of the path and the type of Fill, Illustrator may refuse to preview the Fill and will automatically switch to Artwork mode.

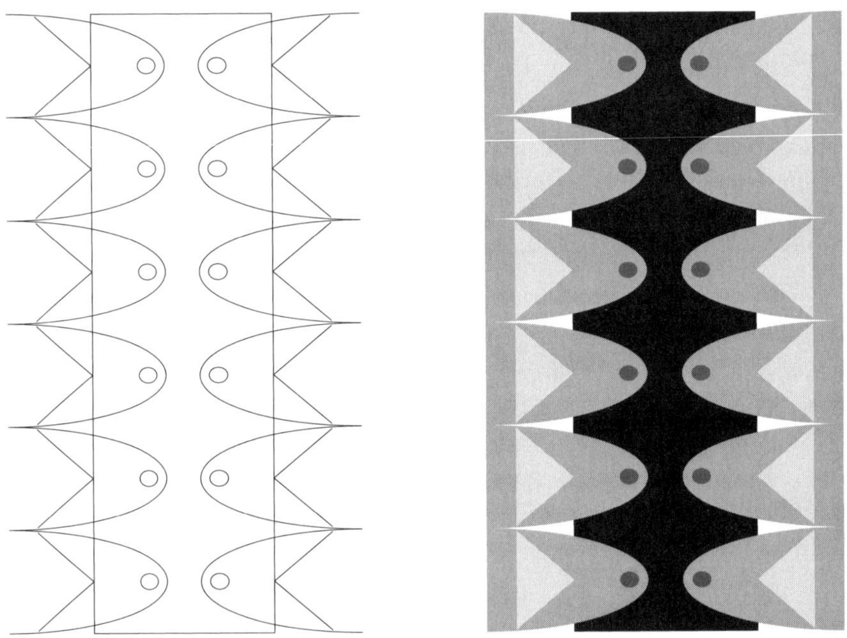

Figure 2-28: Open and closed paths in both Artwork mode (left) and Preview mode (right)

The Fill color options include White, Black, Tints, Process Colors, Spot Colors, Patterns, and Gradients. The Fill option for an object can also be set to None, where the Fill is transparent. This lets you see behind a path to what is underneath it when the Stroke of an object is the visible part.

Strokes

The *Stroke* of an object is made up of three parts: its color, weight, and style. Strokes appear where there are paths, or around the edges of type. Like Fills, any one path or object may have only one type of Stroke on it; the color, weight, and style of the Stroke are consistent throughout the length of the path or the entire text object. (Individual characters in a text object can have different Strokes if they are selected with the Type tool when the Stroke attributes are applied.)

The Stroke color options are White, Black, Tints, Process Colors, Spot Colors, Patterns, and None (the Stroke is off). When the Stroke color option is set to None, then the object is said to have no Stroke. Strokes cannot display patterns in Preview mode, nor can they have gradients applied to them.

The weight of a Stroke is how thick it is. On a path, the Stroke is centered on that path, with half the thickness of the Stroke on one side of the path and half the thickness on the other side of the path. Strokes can be anywhere from 0 to 1,000 points thick.

The style of a Stroke consists of several parts, including the cap style, join style, miter limit, and dash pattern. The *cap style* is the way that the ends of a Stroke look and can be either butt cap, rounded cap, or projected cap. The *join style* is the way that Corner Points on paths appear when stroked and can be either mitered join, rounded join, or beveled join. Figure 2-29 shows examples of the cap styles and join styles.

The *miter limit* is the length at which miter joins are cropped. If a path has a thick stroke and there is a tight angle (like those that appear on some stars with a tiny inner radius and a large outer one), the point at which the outside edges of the stroke would meet might be ridiculously far from where the points are set. Using a miter limit tells Illustrator that if the meeting point of the outside edges is more than so many times the thickness of the stroke, to crop it off at the point.

Figure 2-29: The three different cap and join styles for strokes

Normally, the *dash pattern* for a Stroke is solid, but various dash patterns can be created for different effects. Figure 2-30 shows different miter limits on different corners.

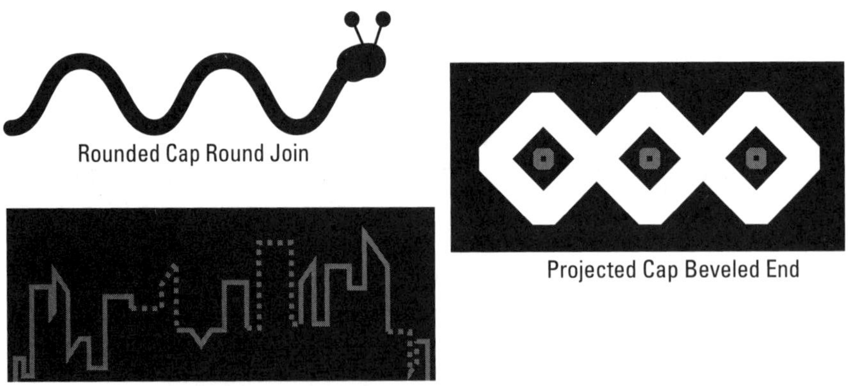

Figure 2-30: "Whatcha talkin' about, Willis?" A sampling of all the different cap styles, join styles, miter limits, and dash patterns for strokes

Combining Strokes with Fills

Many times, paths in Illustrator require both Fills and Strokes. When you give both a Fill and a Stroke to a single path, the Stroke knocks out the Fill at the edges of the path by one half the weight of the Stroke. Figure 2-31 demonstrates this.

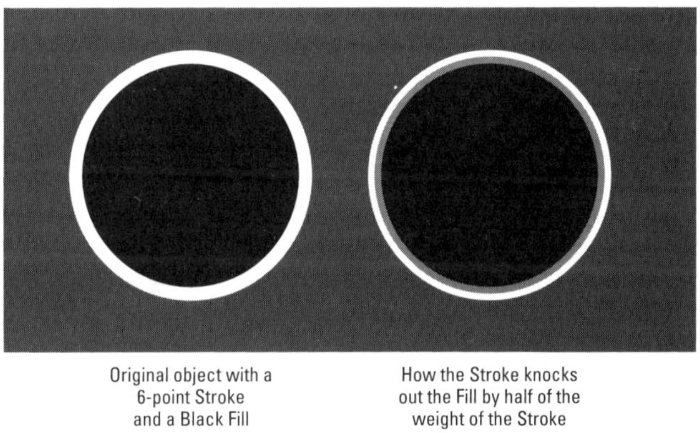

Figure 2-31: A Stroke knocks out a Fill by one-half the weight of the stroke

If knocking out the fill of a path presents a problem for your design, you can correct this problem by copying the path and pasting it in front, removing the frontmost path's Stroke. The Filled path, on top of the Stroked path, will knock out the "inner" half of the Stroke. This technique is discussed in detail in Chapter 17.

Preference Practical Jokes: Part 27

Apollo: I want to play a practical joke on my buddy Boomer.

Toulouse: Good man. I've got a great Illustrator one for you. Change the General Preference setting called Constrain Angle to 180 degrees.

Apollo: What'll that do?

Toulouse: At first, everything will seem perfectly normal. But then....

Apollo: His computer'll explode, right?

Toulouse: Not quite. Actually, everything will work normally except type, which will appear upside down. All the time.

Apollo: Ha! That's great.

Toulouse: There's a worse one, you know.

Apollo: Would Boomer get really mad at this one?

Toulouse: Depends. For a really good joke that probably won't discover until he prints, set the Constrain Angle to .2 degrees.

Apollo: And that'll do....

Toulouse: It'll make everything off by just a fraction. Could wreck his day, however ...and thus yours.

Apollo: Noted.

Applying Fills and Strokes

The toolbox contains two icons, one for Fill and one for Stroke, located in the Paint Style section of the toolbox (see Figure 2-32).

Figure 2-32: The Paint Style section of the toolbox

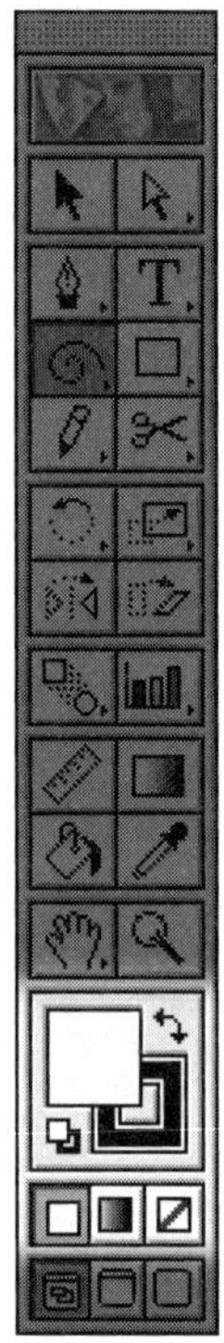

By default, the Fill is set to White and the Stroke is set to 1 pt. Black. In fact, at any time you can reset to the default Fill and Stroke by clicking the Default Fill and Stroke icon in the lower-left corner of the Paint Style section.

POWER TIP: You can quickly reset the fill and stroke colors to their default by pressing the D key.

You can quickly swap between the colors in the Fill and Stroke icons by clicking the Swap Fill and Stroke icon located in the upper-right of the Paint Style section.

ASK TOULOUSE

The Color Purple

Cassiopeia: How can I make a purple color with the CMYK sliders?

Toulouse: Try 50% Cyan and 100% Magenta.

Cassiopeia: Wow, that was easy. How'd you know that?

Toulouse: Well, I sorta cheated. All the sliders in the Color palette are interactive.

Cassiopeia: They provide a real-to-life multimedia experience?

Toulouse: Not exactly. But the sliders change color relative to what the current color is. For instance, when I set Magenta to 100%, I looked at the other sliders, and saw there was purple in the middle of the Cyan slider bar. So I dragged the Cyan slider to 50% and voilà!

Cassiopeia: Voilà, indeed. You know, someone should stick that in a book somewhere....

Toulouse: Good idea....

When you first start Illustrator, the Fill icon is in front of the Stroke icon. This means that any changes made in the Color or Swatch palettes affect the Fill. When the Fill icon is in front of the Stroke icon, the Fill is said to be in *focus*. You can change the focus to the Stroke by either clicking the Stroke icon or by pressing the X key. Figure 2-33 shows the focus on the Stroke and the focus on the Fill. When the focus is on the Stroke, changes made in the Color or Swatch palettes affect the Stroke, not the Fill.

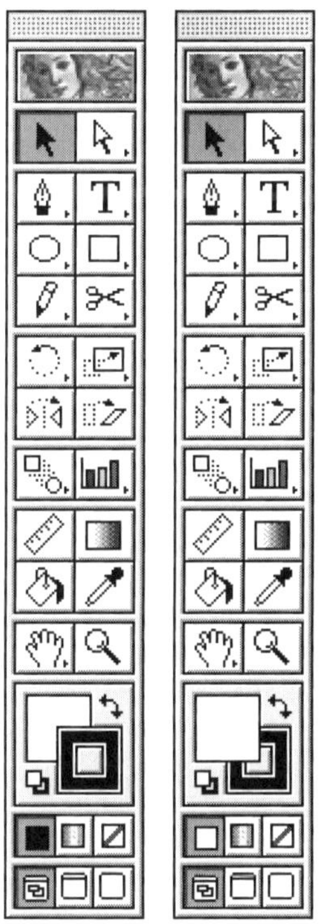

Figure 2-33: Focus on the Stroke (left) and focus on the Fill (right)

Use the X key. It's right down by the modifier keys (where your left hand should be anyway), and it's extremely handy, not to mention easier and faster than clicking on the Stroke or Fill icons to change focus.

Tinting Process Colors

Starbuck: Why isn't there a tint control for Process Colors?

Toulouse: That would be too confusing; you'd have a 50% tint of 20% cyan, 50% magenta and 10% black, which would really be 10% Cyan, 25% Magenta, and 5% Black.

Starbuck: So, I have to do all that math each time I want to change a process tint?

Toulouse: You can, but there's a shortcut....

Starbuck: I thought all the letters on the keyboard were used up, but go ahead, tell me.

Toulouse: All you do is press Shift before you drag a slider, and all the sliders with values move along with the one you're dragging.

Starbuck: Wow! Great! Wait, it goes too fast, much too hard to control....

Toulouse: When adjusting the tint this way, be sure to move the slider with the largest percentage, as it gives you more control. The other sliders will move proportionately with that one.

R.I.P. Paint Style Palette 1993-1997

The Paint Style palette (shown in Figure 2-34) debuted in the Summer of 1993 with Illustrator 5, to well-received reviews and customer appreciation. An odd combination of Swatches, Mixing, and Strokes, it served thousands of designers during its four-year lifespan. Created by Bruce Hodge of Adobe Systems (who also gave gradients to Illustrator and several components to Extensis VectorTools), it teemed with efficiency for the power user.

The untimely death of this most unusual of any applications' palettes was due as much to its integration of various functions and varying display capabilities as it was to new technology. Although Macintosh Illustrator users would never admit to it, the combination of four different display modes was awkward at best, and at full size it was much too large for its own good.

The Paint Style palette is survived by the Swatches palette, the Color palette, the Stroke palette, and the Stroke and Fill icons on the Toolbox, all happily living in Illustrator 7. It will be remembered for all the good Illustrations it inspired and the countless workhorse duties it performed during its all-too-short time in our Macs.

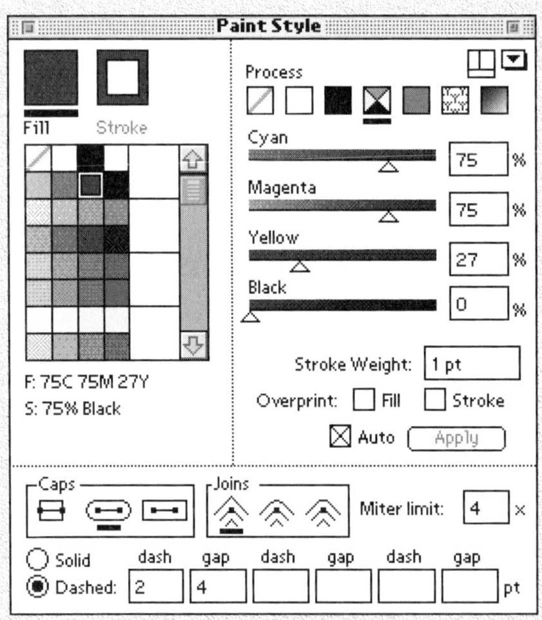

Figure 2-34: The Paint Style Palette during its peak of popularity in Illustrator 6

The Fill and Stroke icons change in appearance to match the current Fill and Stroke. For instance, if you have a green Fill and an orange Stroke, the Fill icon is green and the Stroke icon is orange, and you obviously slept through the color lectures in your design classes. The Fill icon displays a gradient or pattern if that is the current Fill.

The three icons at the bottom of the Paint Style section are used to determine the type of Fill or Stroke:

- **Color:** This icon is used when the Fill or Stroke is a solid color or a pattern. Press the comma key (, or <) on the keyboard to quickly push the color icon.
- **Gradient:** This icon is used when the Fill contains a gradient. Strokes cannot be colored with gradients; clicking this icon when the Stroke icon is in focus changes the Fill to gradient and changes the focus to Fill as well. Press the period key (. or >) to quickly push the gradient icon.
- **None:** This creates an empty Fill or no Stroke. Fills of None are entirely transparent. Strokes of None are neither colored nor have any Stroke weight. Press the forward slash key (/) to quickly push the None icon.

Oddly enough, you don't need to determine the type of Fill when switching between color and gradient by using the color and gradient icons; you can simply click the appropriate swatch in the Swatches palette to change the Fill type. There is, however, no swatch for None, so to change the Fill or Stroke to None you must either click the icon or press the forward slash (/) key. Get used to the forward slash key; it will save you loads of time when changing colors for objects. I'll often do a quick combination of X and / keys to change focus and apply None to the Stroke or Fill.

Using the Swatches Palette

View the Swatches palette (see Figure 2-35) by choosing Window⇨Show Swatches, or press F5. By default, the Swatches palette contains and displays several commonly used colors, patterns and gradients. Change the display by clicking on the icons along the bottom of the palette.

Figure 2-35: The Swatches palette

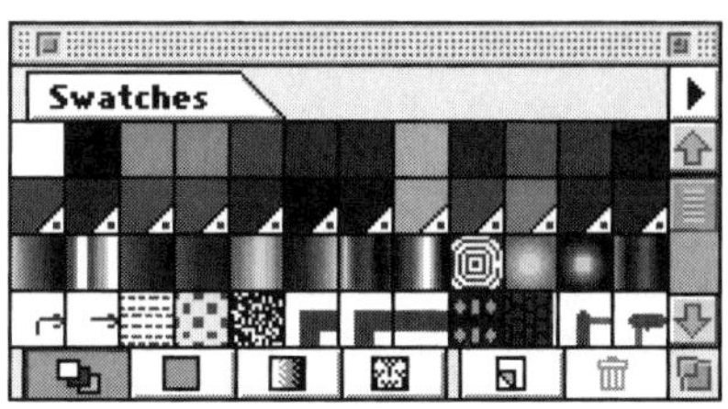

- **Show All Swatches:** This displays all color, gradient, and pattern swatches.
- **Show Color Swatches:** This displays only the color swatches.
- **Show Gradient Swatches:** This displays only the gradient swatches.
- **Show Pattern Swatches:** This displays only the pattern swatches.

You can also view the swatches in either small or large squares, or view all the swatches in a list, with names if they have them (see Figure 2-36). Change the view mode by selecting the appropriate option from the Swatches pop-up menu.

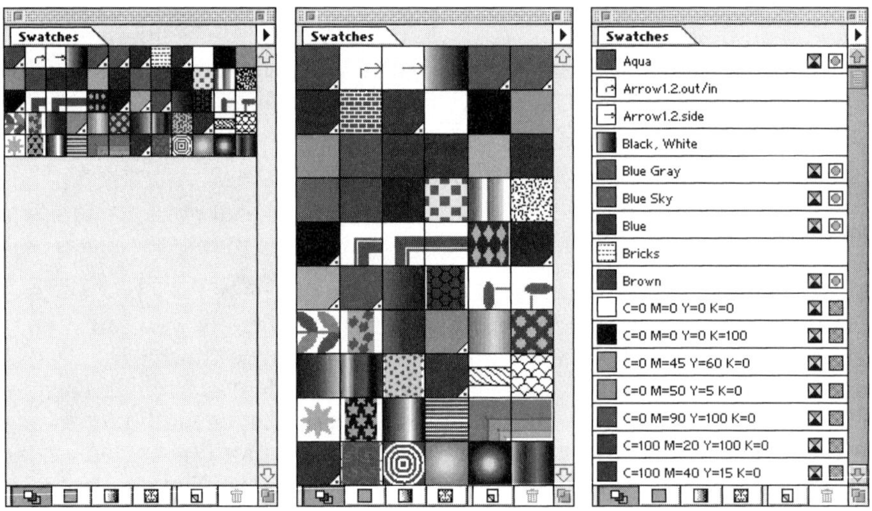

Figure 2-36: The Swatches palette displayed with small swatches (left), large swatches (middle), and in Name view (right)

Create a new swatch based on the current paint style (shown in the Paint Style section of the toolbox) by clicking the New Swatch icon along the bottom of the Swatches palette. If you press Option [Alt] when creating a new swatch, the New Swatch dialog box appears, enabling you to initially name the swatch and set its color mode to either process (CMYK) or spot. You can also create a new swatch by choosing New Swatch from the Swatches palette pop-up menu.

Double-clicking a swatch displays the Swatch Options (shown in Figure 2-37) for that swatch. The Swatch Options dialog box lets you change the name of the swatch (primarily for use in Name view mode), and to set the color mode of the swatch to either process or spot.

In addition, you can select one or more swatches to edit, duplicate, or remove them from the Swatches palette. Click on a swatch to select it; a frame appears on the selected swatch. When a swatch is selected, choosing Swatch Options from the Swatch menu also displays the Swatch Options for the selected swatch.

Regardless of the view mode (Small, Large, or Name), ⌘-Option-clicking [Ctrl+Alt+clicking] the Swatches palette makes the palette respond to key-board entry for selecting swatches. For instance, if you wanted to use the swatch called PrenatalGoo you would ⌘-Option-click [Ctrl+Alt+click] in the Swatches palette and then type the first few letters of the swatch name; in this case the letters *P-R-E* should do it. When you stop typing, the swatch whose name is closest to the one you typed highlights, and pressing the Enter key makes that the active (selected) swatch in the Swatches palette. This is extremely useful for selecting Pantone colors in the huge Pantone Swatches palettes.

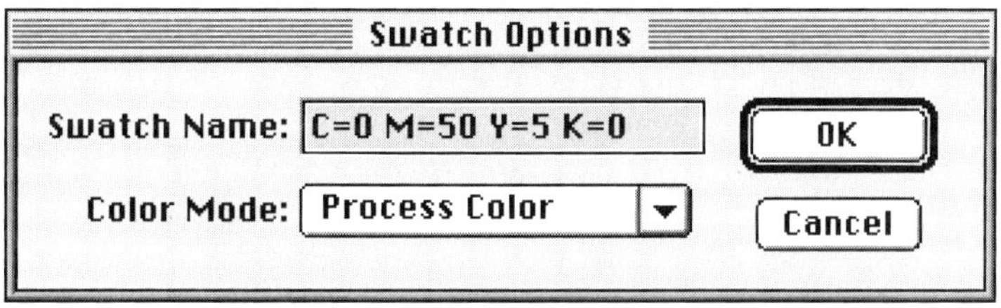

Figure 2-37: The Swatch Options dialog box

Choosing Duplicate from the pop-up menu duplicates the selected swatch(es). You can also drag a selected swatch to the New Swatch icon (the little piece of paper) to duplicate the swatch. If you press Option [Alt] while duplicating a swatch, the New Swatch dialog box appears; this is really the same as the Swatch Options dialog box (but the swatch is new, so the box has a different name).

To delete a swatch, select the swatch and click the Trash icon or choose Delete from the Swatches palette pop-up menu. A warning dialog box (see Figure 2-38) appears, asking if you're sure if you want to delete the swatch. Click OK to delete the swatch, keeping in mind that you *cannot* undo swatch deletion. This box provides a check box that can prevent the dialog box from appearing when you click the trash can icon or select Delete from the pop-up menu. However, *don't* check this box. It's actually one of the few useful warnings in Illustrator, allowing you one last chance in case you clicked or selected the wrong icon or option accidentally. You can avoid the dialog box in other ways instead. Press the Option [Alt] key when clicking the Trash icon or selecting Delete from the pop-up menu, and the swatch is deleted with no message. In addition, if you drag the swatch to the Trash icon the swatch will be deleted without any warning message.

You can select more than one swatch by pressing the ⌘ [Ctrl] key and clicking additional swatches. If you press the Shift key and click additional swatches, a contiguous (connected) set of the swatches is selected, from where you initially clicked to where you Shift-clicked. Deselect individual swatches by ⌘ [Ctrl]-clicking selected swatches. Deselect all the swatches by clicking an empty area of the Swatches palette. By selecting multiple swatches, you can duplicate and delete several swatches at once.

Figure 2-38: The Warning dialog box that appears when you attempt to delete a swatch

The Swatches pop-up menu (shown in Figure 2-39) has other functionality as well. Choosing Select All Unused selects the swatches in the Swatches palette that aren't being used in the current document. You can then delete those swatches if necessary. Sort by Name organizes the swatches (regardless of which viewing mode the swatch palette is in) alphabetically. Sort by Kind sorts the swatches to appear starting with color, then gradients, then patterns.

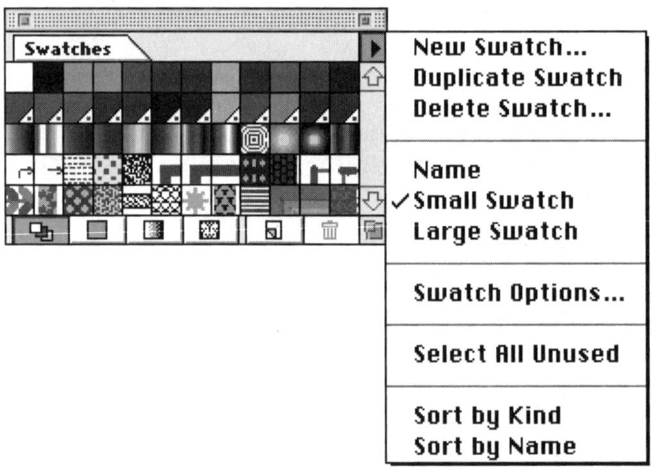

Figure 2-39: The Swatches palette pop-up menu

If you want to sort the swatches manually, you can do so by selecting any number of swatches and dragging them to a new location within the swatches palette.

Spot/Process Swatches and Color Space Indicators

You can tell the difference between spot colors and process colors in Small Swatch and Large Swatch viewing modes by looking at the lower-right corner of the swatch. A white triangle with a dot in it indicates that the color is a spot color. Figure 2-40 shows process and spot colors in both viewing modes.

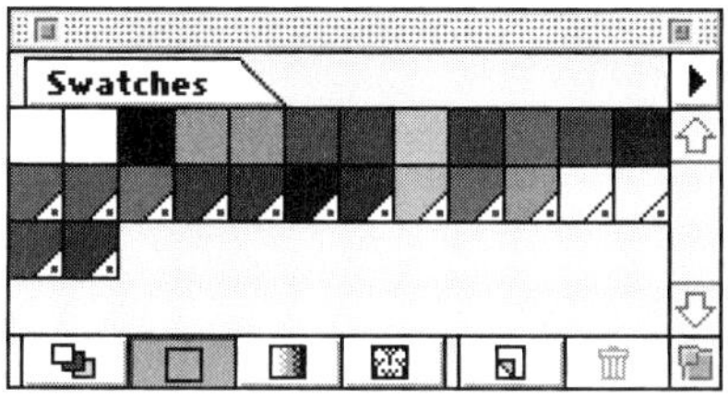

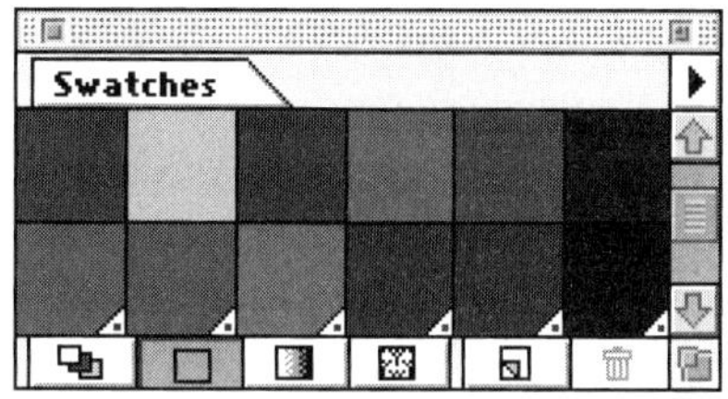

Figure 2-40: Process and spot colors in Small Swatch viewing mode (left) and Large Swatch viewing mode (right)

In Name viewing mode, both the colorspace (grayscale, RGB, or CMYK) and Process/Spot status are indicated to the right of the color chip and name. Figure 2-41 shows colors of different color spaces and Process/Spot status.

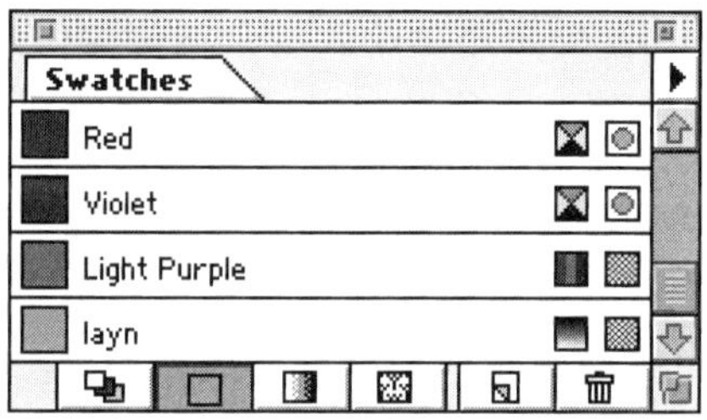

Figure 2-41: The Name viewing mode shows both the color space and Process/Spot status of each swatch

The Other Swatch Libraries

Several other default Swatch Library palettes in addition to the standard one are accessible from the Swatch Libraries submenu of the Window menu (see Figure 2-42). You can also create a new Swatch Library palette from any Illustrator document.

To view one of the other default Swatches palettes, choose it from the Swatch Libraries submenu. You cannot edit these Swatch libraries; you can only add swatches from these libraries to your main Swatches palette.

To add a swatch (or several selected swatches) to your main Swatches palette, select the swatches to be added and choose Add to Swatches from the library's pop-up menu, or drag the swatch(es) to the main Swatches palette. Fortunately, the main Swatches palette is saved with your document; this way you can customize a palette for a specific document, or edit the Adobe Illustrator Startup document's Swatches palette to use a certain set of colors in each new document you create. (Using and abusing the startup document is covered in Chapter 6.)

Otherwise, these swatch libraries work the same way as your main Swatches palette; you can choose colors for Fill and Stroke, sort the swatches by Kind or Name, and view the swatches by Name, Small, or Large. Figure 2-43 shows several swatch libraries in different views.

Figure 2-42: The Window menu and Swatch Libraries submenu

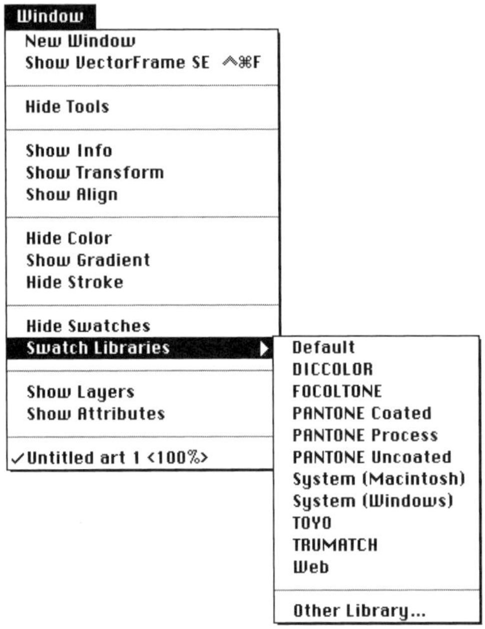

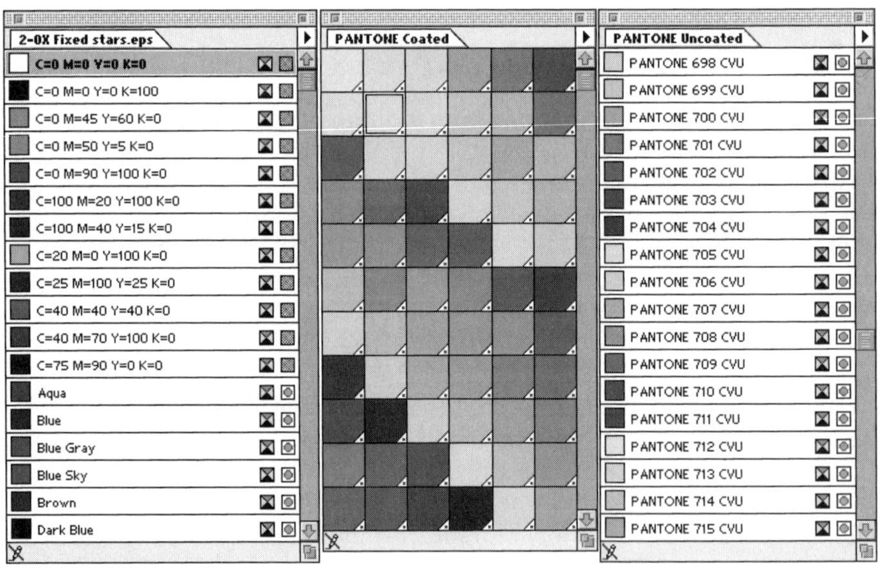

Figure 2-43: Three swatch libraries

Choosing and Mixing Colors

You can create any color to be used in an illustration by defining it in the Color palette (shown in Figure 2-44). The Color palette provides basic color selection via the Color Ramp along the bottom of the palette, and more precise control via sliders and percentage entries in grayscale, RGB, CYMK, HSB, and spot color spaces.

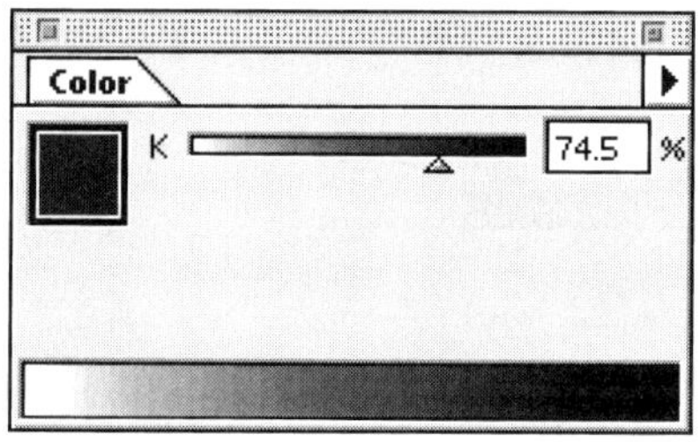

Figure 2-44: The Color palette

The Color palette has a pop-up menu that enables you to display options and to choose from the available color spaces. The "options" are really the color mixing sliders; I've never found a reason to hide them. In fact, the sliders take up such a small amount of space that once they're in view, you'll probably never hide them either.

The color space options let you switch between

- **Grayscale:** White to black with all shades of gray in between (see Figure 2-45).

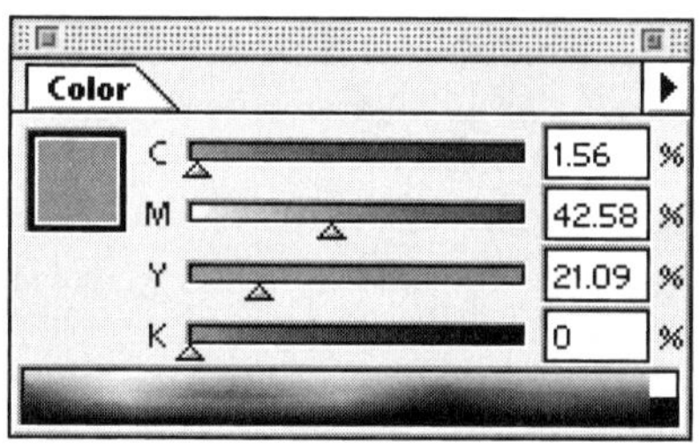

Figure 2-45: The Color palette displaying grayscale color space

- **RGB:** Red, green, and blue. This is the color space used by computer monitors, and it's perfect for multimedia and Web page graphics (see Figure 2-46). You can enter RGB values as percentages or as values from 0 to 255. Double-click to the right of the text fields to change the RGB measurement system from percentages to the numeric 0 to 255 system and back.

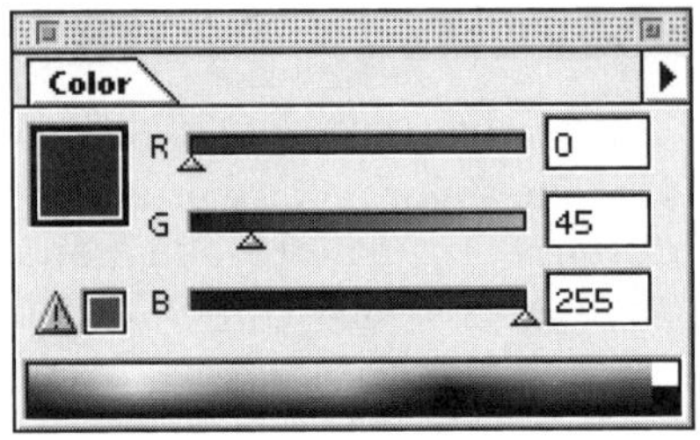

Figure 2-46: The Color palette displaying RGB color space

- **HSB:** Hue, Saturation, Brightness. This RGB-derived color space is best for adjusting RGB colors in brightness and saturation (see Figure 2-47).

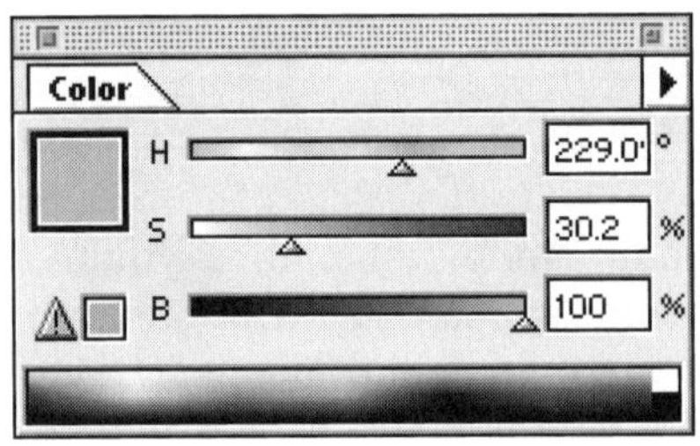

Figure 2-47: The Color palette displaying HSB color space

- **CMYK:** Cyan, magenta, yellow, and black. These are considered typical printing process colors (although Illustrator calls any colors *process* that aren't spot). (See Figure 2-48.)

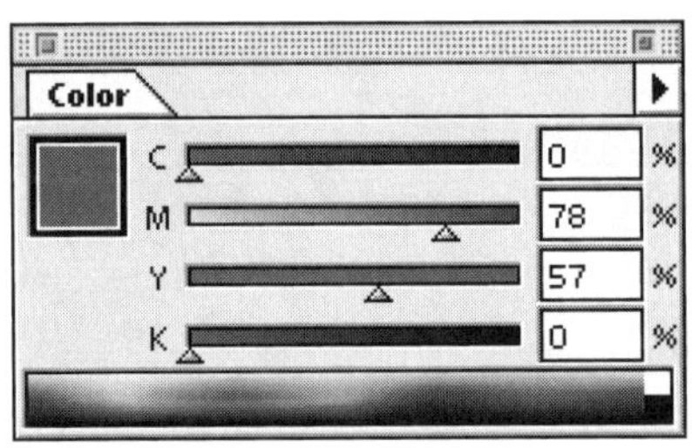

Figure 2-48: The Color palette displaying CMYK color space

- **Tint:** This isn't really an option in the pop-up menu, but if you select a spot color swatch (or choose a spot color with the Eyedropper tool), the color palette goes into a sort of tint colorspace, where you can tint the color from 100% to 0% of that color (see Figure 2-49).

When you change color spaces, the Color Ramp along the bottom of the palette changes as well to show the colors in that color space.

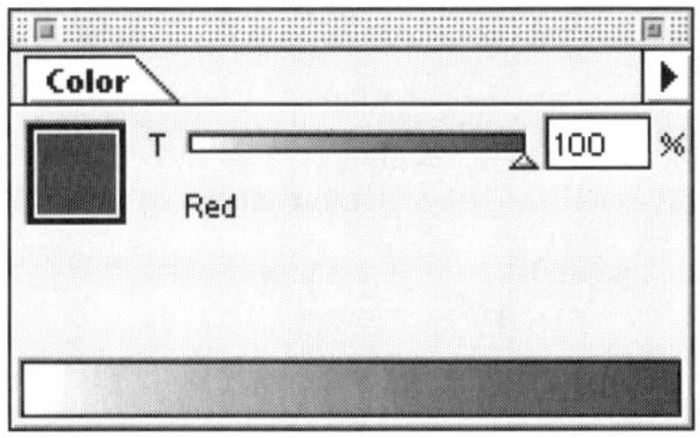

Figure 2-49: The Color palette displaying tint color space for the color red

Shift-click the Color Ramp to cycle through the color spaces; this is much faster than choosing a color space from the pop-up menu.

As you drag the sliders, the other sliders will change in color. This gives you a sort of preview for what would happen if you were to drag along the sliders. The icon to the left of the sliders shows (1) the current color and (2) whether you're adjusting the Fill (solid box) or Stroke (box with a hole). Instead of dragging, you can also just simply click a different location along the slider to change its value.

Press the Shift key to adjust RGB and CMYK sliders proportionately. This is a great way to tint process colors. Shift-drag the slider with the largest value for the most control. When you release the mouse button, the new color will be a tint of the original.

You can also change the slider values by typing in values for each of the individual color channels (Cyan is a color channel in CMYK, for instance). Press the Tab key to highlight the next text field, or Shift-Tab to highlight the previous text field.

Quickly highlight the text fields by clicking to the right of the text field, or by clicking the name of the text field on the other side of the slider.

Most of Illustrator's palette's text fields are mathematically adept. You can add, subtract, multiply and divide in them. This is useful when entering color percentages in the text fields of the Color palette. To add 5% to the current value, type +5 after the current value. To subtract 5%, type -5 after the current value. To divide the current value by 2, type /2 after the current value. To multiple the current value by 2, type *2 after the current value.

Press Shift-Return/Enter after entering values to rehighlight the current text field. In this way you can type in different values without ever having to reselect the text field.

The Color Ramp

The Color Ramp enables you to quickly pick a color from the current color space. When you rest your cursor above the Color Ramp area, the cursor changes into an eyedropper. Figure 2-50 shows the Color Ramps for Grayscale, RGB (which is the same as HSB), CMYK, and Spot colors.

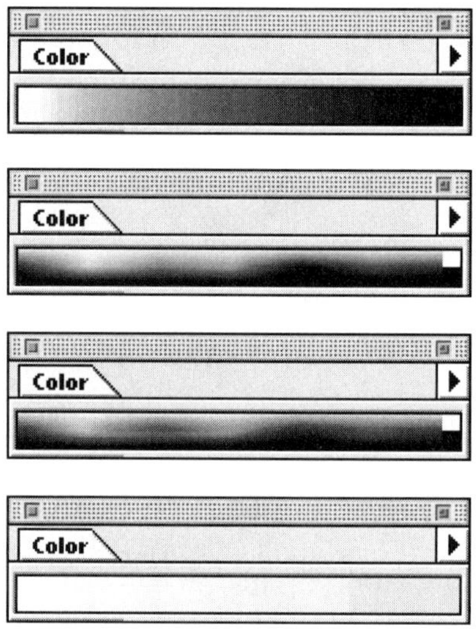

Figure 2-50: Color Ramps from top to bottom: grayscale, RGB, CYMK, and spot

Click any portion of the Color Ramp to select that color. The RGB (and HSB) and CMYK Color Ramps have large rectangles of black and white to make choosing them easier. The grayscale and spot ramps have large areas for both 0% and 100% to make selecting those percentages easier. You can also drag over the Color Ramp, watching the large square in the top of the Color palette (if Options are showing) to see the color you're dragging over. If Options aren't shown, look at the active Fill/Stroke icon in the toolbox to see the color you're currently positioned over (this *only* works when the mouse button is pressed as you pass across the Color Ramp).

You can press the X key while dragging around the Color Ramp to switch between the Fill and Stroke focus. This way you can quickly select colors for both Fill and Stroke with *one* mouse-click! If the Fill is in focus, click and drag through the Color Ramp to the appropriate color. Then, with the mouse button still pressed, press the X key; you'll now be picking a color for the Stroke. Want to change the Fill again? Just press X, keeping the mouse button down.

Here's a super-cool power tip: Option[Alt]-clicking anywhere on the Color Ramp affects the opposite attribute! For instance, if Stroke is in focus on the toolbox, Option[Alt]-clicking on the Color Ramp changes the Fill color, not the stroke. Be aware, however, that Option[Alt]-clicking on a swatch in the Swatches palette does *not* affect the opposite attribute; this only works on the Color Ramp (and the color box in the Color palette).

Gamut Trouble

If you choose certain colors in the RGB or HSB color spaces, a little icon will appear in the lower left of the Color palette (see Figure 2-51). This icon is indicating that the current color is out of gamut with CMYK color space. This issue is only important if you'll be printing the document using CMYK process colors. If you'll be using the image on-screen, such as in Web or multimedia publishing, it doesn't matter if the color is in gamut or not.

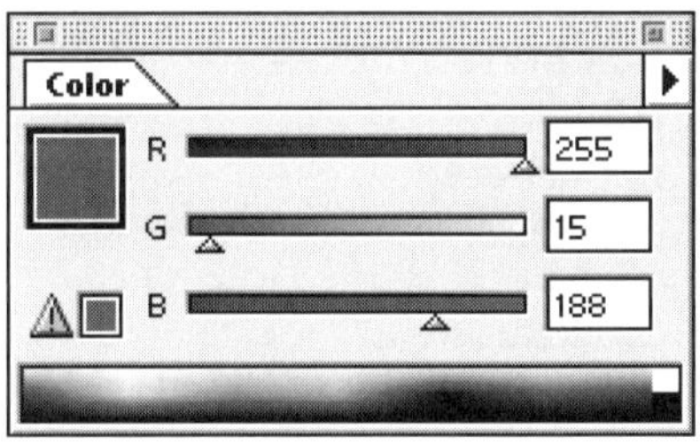

Figure 2-51: The Out of Gamut indicator appears when the current color can not be accurately converted into CMYK values

The best way to reset the current color to CMYK color space is to click the Out of Gamut icon. The RGB or HSB values change so that the resulting color is well within CMYK color space. Another way to change the current color to CMYK color space is to choose CMYK from the Color palette pop-up menu.

POWER TIP: If you want to change the color space of several objects — or perhaps your entire document — to CMYK, select the objects to be changed and choose Filter⇨Colors⇨Convert to CMYK. There are also filters for changing the color space to grayscale and RGB.

Spot Colors

Spot colors are colors in Illustrator that aren't separated into process colors (cyan, magenta, yellow and black) when printed. Instead, they are printed on a different separation. A commercial printer uses a special ink (commonly Pantone) for this spot color.

You can use as many spot colors in an illustration as you would like, though it isn't usually practical or desirable to have more than four in one document (because CMYK printing can duplicate most colors, process colors are often a better choice than four spot colors). Illustrator's default Swatch libraries (choose Window➪Swatch Libraries➪Your Library) contain mostly spot colors that you can choose from, or you can create your own. To create your own Spot color, create a new swatch with the appearance (using the color sliders) you want. Then change the Swatch type from Process to Spot in the Swatch Options dialog box (access Swatch Options by double-clicking the swatch). When you use that swatch as a Fill or Stroke, it will be considered a spot color when it comes time to print.

Spot colors are indicated in the Swatches palette in Small and Large Swatch views by a white triangle containing a black dot in the lower right of the spot color swatch. Name view shows a square with a circle inside of it (a "spot") on the right edge of the swatch listing.

You can convert any spot color to a standard CMYK color (the color, not the swatch) by selecting the spot color and then changing the color space in the Color palette to CMYK. You can even change the color space to grayscale, RGB or HSB in this way. This only works on the selected paths; the swatch itself is not affected.

Putting All the Color Palettes to Use

Now you know how the palettes work, but how do you change the color of paths to what's in the palettes? The easiest thing to do is to select the path you want to change the Fill or Stroke (or both) of, change the focus (if necessary) of the Fill/Stroke icons, and select a color from either the Color or Swatches palette. Press X to change the color for the other (Fill or Stroke).

The key here is *selecting*. If you have the paths selected, any changes you make will affect those selected paths.

When you create a new path, it will be the Fill and Stroke that are currently displayed in the Paint Style section of the toolbox.

To apply colors to text, you can either select an entire text area with a Selection tool, or select individual characters with a Type tool.

Selecting Type with a Selection tool can cause type paths and type areas to be Filled and Stroked as well as the type; you can use the Group Selection tool to deselect the associated paths, or better yet, just use the Type tool and drag across the characters you want to select.

Dif'rent Strokes for Dif'rent Folks

The Stroke palette (shown in Figure 2-52) contains everything you need to control the way your stroke looks . . . except its color. To change the color of a stroke, the Stroke icon must be active (in front of the Fill icon, in focus). Then you can select a swatch from the Swatches palette or choose a color from the Color palette.

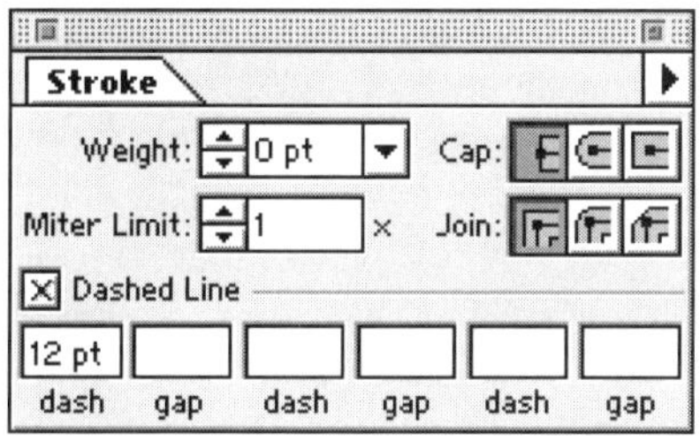

Figure 2-52: The Stroke palette

Instead of changing the color of the Stroke, the Stroke palette lets you change the thickness of the Stroke, the caps and joins, and the dash pattern of the Stroke.

Stroke Weight

The thickness of the Stroke is called the Stroke Weight, which you can change by either selecting a preset weight from the Weight pop-up menu, or by typing in a value in the Weight text field. The Weight of a stroke is always evenly divided between each side of the path it is applied to. So a 1-point Stroke has $^{1}/_{2}$ point on each side of the path.

Use mathematical operations in the Stroke weight palette! You can mathematically change the current Stroke Weight by adding, subtracting, multiplying or dividing. Just place the appropriate symbol (+ for add, - for subtract, * for multiply, and / for divide) after the current value, and then the number you want to perform the operation by.

Strokes can never be wider than 1,000 pts. A Stroke with a weight of 0 can exist in Illustrator, though I wouldn't recommend that you choose such a value. Instead, set the Stroke to None. If you do set a weight of 0, the path will have a stroke as thick as one device pixel of the output device. For a 300-dpi laser printer, that would be a healthy quarter point thick. For a typical 1,270-dpi imagesetter, that would be about $^{1}/_{17th}$ point, or a fourth of a quarter point; much to small to use for most purposes. Because a stroke of 0 will change to match the output device (it will appear one pixel thick on screen, appearing to be a 1 pt. stroke), the potential changes in thickness can drastically change the way an image looks. Be very careful if you choose to venture into this area of Illustrator.

Caps

There are three different Cap styles that can be applied to strokes. Caps apply only to End Points on open paths. You can choose a Cap style for a closed path (with no end points), but nothing will happen; if the path is cut into an open path, that Cap style go into effect.

The Cap styles are shown in Figure 2-53.

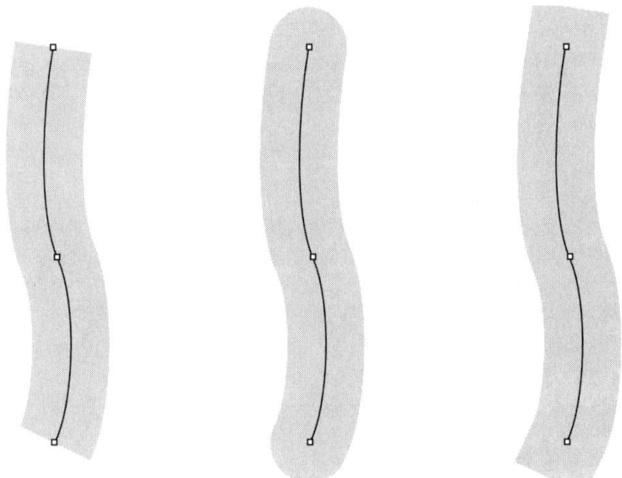

Figure 2-53: Butt Caps (left), Round Caps (middle), and Projected Caps (right)

- **Butt Caps** chop the stroke off perpendicularly at the end of the path, in addition to being good ammo for Illustrator bathroom humor.
- **Rounded Caps** are smooth, rounded ends that resemble a half circle. These caps protrude from the End Point 1/2 the Stroke Weight.
- **Projected Caps** project from the endpoint 1/2 the Stroke Weight and appear perpendicular to the direction of the path at its End Point.

Joins

Three different Join types can be applied to paths. Joins only affect Corner points, including Straight Corner points, Curved Corner points, and Combination Corner points.

The three Join styles are shown in Figure 2-54.

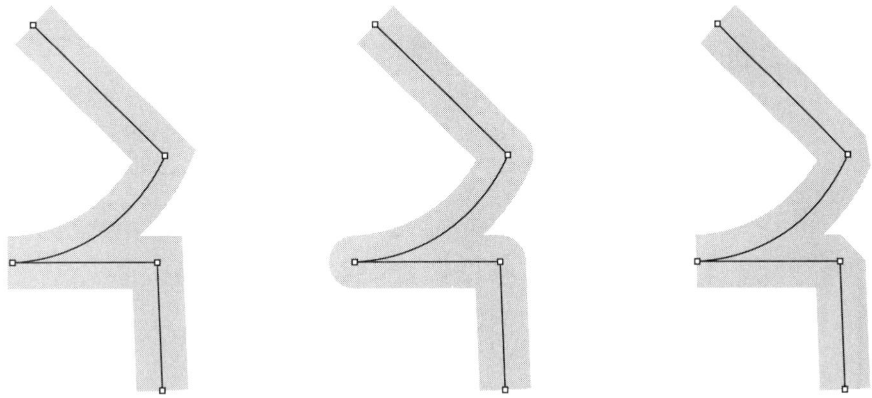

Figure 2-54: Mitered Joins (left), Rounded Joins (middle), and Beveled Joins (right)

- **Mitered Joins** cause the outer edges of the stroke to meet at a point. This Join type is the only one affected by the miter limit.
- **Rounded Joins** round off the outside edge of corners.
- **Beveled Joins** are cropped off before the angle can reach a corner.

In all cases, Join types only affect outside corners. Inside corners always appear mitered.

The Miter Limit option controls how far a corner can extend past the edge of the path. This is important for tight corners of paths with large Weights, as the place where the outside edges would meet in a corner could be really far away from the original edges of the paths. The number in the Miter Limit controls how many times the width of the stroke the Miter can extend beyond the point. The default is 4, which is good for the majority of applications.

Dashes

The bottom of the Stroke palette controls if and how dashed strokes should appear. Checking the Dashed Line box allows you to enter different values for up to three dash and gap lengths. Figure 2-55 shows different Stroked paths with their Dashed Line settings.

Chapter 17 provides four pages of Stroke dash charts, and several projects for utilizing strokes to their fullest.

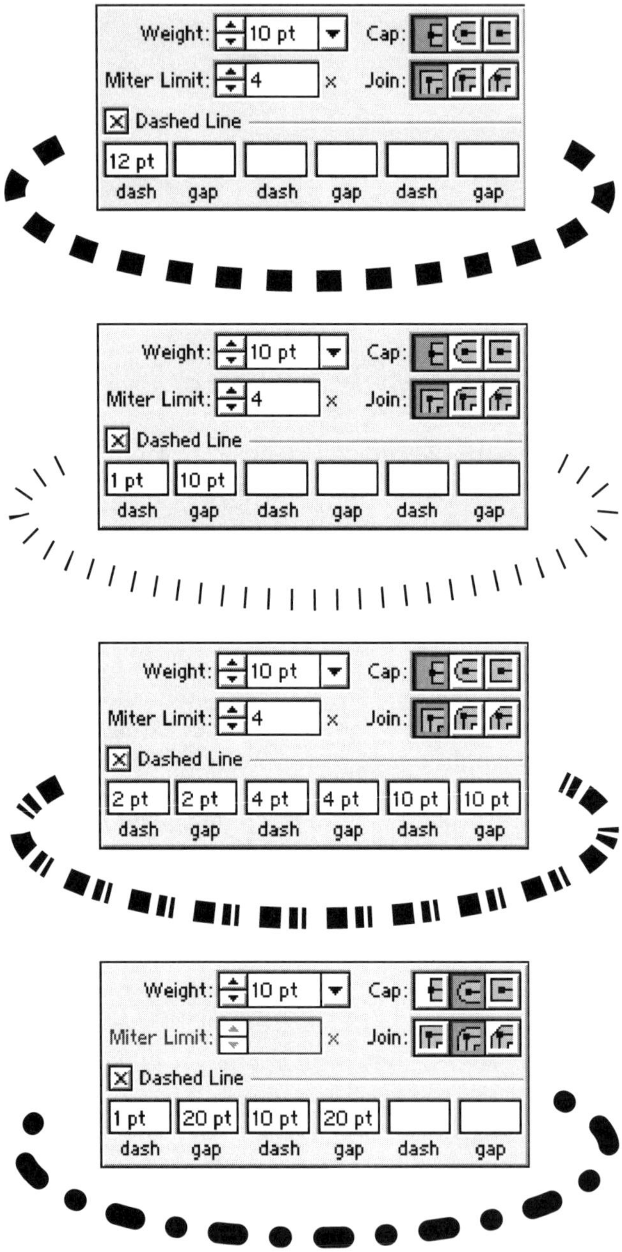

Figure 2-55: Dashed lines and their settings

The Eyedropper and Paintbucket Tools

The Eyedropper and Paintbucket tools are lifesavers for those of us who are constantly using up notes to jot down what the percentages of CMYK (cyan, magenta, yellow, and black) are in one path so that we can apply those same amounts to another path. Double-clicking either tool brings up the Paintbucket/Eyedropper dialog box (shown in Figure 2-56), where you can select or deselect multiple options regarding paint style information.

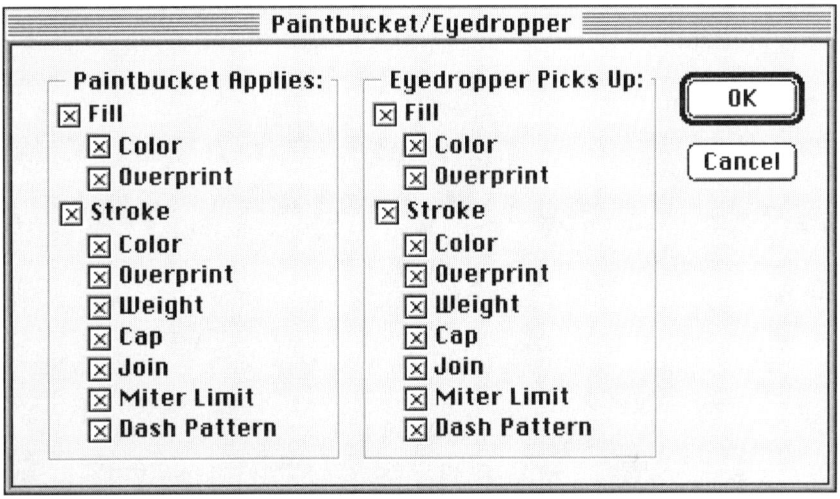

Figure 2-56: The Paintbucket/ Eyedropper dialog box

The Eyedropper Tool

The Eyedropper tool, shown with the Paintbucket tool in Figure 2-57, samples paint style information from a path or a placed image and stores it in the Paint Style fill and stroke boxes (on the toolbox), without selecting that path. The information stays there until you change the information in the color palette, select another path with different paint style information, or click any other path or placed image with a different paint style.

Figure 2-57: The Paintbucket and Eyedropper tools

Why Use the Eyedropper and Paintbucket Tools?

Baltazar: Why should I use the Paintbucket and Eyedropper tools? It seems like a lot of work.

Toulouse: One reason is that you can be assured that your colors are consistent throughout the illustration. So if you used a custom color somewhere, you don't try to duplicate it with a CMYK mix somewhere else, for instance. And you don't have to select the objects you're clicking with the Paintbucket tool.

Baltazar: What's all this nonsense about sampling colors from pixel-based images?

Toulouse: You can sample colors from any placed image. And that's not all.

Baltazar: It's not?

Toulouse: You can sample colors right on your desktop or from within a Photoshop document that's open in the background.

Baltazar: Wow. Does the Eyedropper sample an average color, like that "other" Illustration program?

Toulouse: No, it samples the exact pixel you click on.

Pressing the Shift key when the Eyedropper tool is active allows it to do *Direct Sucking*. Direct Sucking is used to pull colors from anywhere, including such areas as palettes, window edges, and from within gradients.

If you have paths selected when you click with the Eyedropper tool, all selected objects in the document are changed to the paint style of the path that you clicked on. If you hold down the Option [Alt] key and click the Eyedropper tool, it toggles to the Paintbucket tool.

The Paintbucket Tool

The Paintbucket tool is used for applying the current paint style to both paths and 1-bit TIFF images.

Holding down the Shift key when clicking a path fills the Paintbucket tool with the current paint style and also selects that path. If the path was already selected, a Shift-click deselects it. Pressing the Option [Alt] key toggles from the Paintbucket tool to the Eyedropper tool.

Summary

- Illustrator provides basic drawing capabilities by allowing you to quickly draw basic objects with specialized tools, like the Rectangle, Ellipse, Star, Polygon, and Spiral tools.
- The toolbox contains Fill and Stroke icons; choose one to change the color attributes of it.
- The Swatches palette is used to store and apply commonly used colors.
- Pantone colors can be accessed by choosing Window⇨Swatch Libraries⇨Pantone.
- The Color palette enables you to choose colors from a Color Ramp and to mix colors using interactive sliders.
- Change the color space from grayscale to CMYK to RGB to HSB by selecting one from the Color pop-up menu.
- The Stroke palette is used to change the stroke weight, cap and join style, and Dash pattern.
- Paths can be colored quickly by using the Eyedropper tool (to sample colors from paths or placed images) and the Paint-bucket tool (to apply those sampled colors).

Baltazar: Thanks for the info. I won't tell the Cylons, honest.

Toulouse: Oh, sure, rat out your race but keep quiet about graphics applications.... I believe you.

CHAPTER 3

Drawing and Manipulating Paths

In This Chapter

- Drawing with the Paintbrush tool
- Drawing with the Pencil tool
- Using the Pen tool
- Learning the laws of the Pen tool
- Selecting, moving, and deleting entire paths
- Selecting, moving, and deleting portions of paths
- Understanding the concept of foreground and background
- Grouping and ungrouping paths
- Using the Group Selection tool

The most effective (and challenging) way to create paths is to draw them with one of the drawing tools. The Paintbrush tool, the Pencil tool, and the Pen tool are Illustrator's primary drawing tools. These tools are shown in Figure 3-1.

NEW IN 7

Illustrator 7 provides keyboard shortcuts for accessing the three drawing tools: Pencil, Paintbrush, and Pen. Press Y for the Pencil, press Y again for the Paintbrush (and again to toggle back to the Pencil), and press P to access the Pen tool. Unlike the modifier keyboard commands (Command, Shift, and Option [Ctrl and Shift and Alt]), pressing a letter to select a tool changes that tool until you select another tool either with the keyboard or by clicking on it.

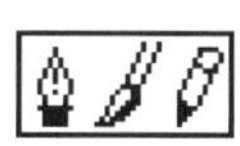

Figure 3-1: Illustrator's drawing tools

Windows Update

Two of the three primary drawing tools remain almost exactly as they were before, with the Paintbrush tool being the sole addition since version 4.

What's Missing	What Replaces It
Freehand tool	Pencil tool
Freehand tolerance	Curve Fitting Tolerance
Path direction options in the Paint dialog box	Path direction options in the Attributes palette

What's New

The Paintbrush tool for drawing filled freeform paths

The Attributes palette for setting notes, URLs, and other object-specific attributes

Drawing Paths in Illustrator

Using the Paintbrush tool is the easiest way to create paths, but also the most limiting unless you use it with a pressure-sensitive tablet. The Pencil tool is simple to use to create paths, but the results can be questionable. The Pen tool is the most difficult to use, but the results from it can be better than from either the Paintbrush or the Pencil tool.

Each drawing tool does something better than the others, as well as having its own limitations. However tempting it may be, don't ignore any one of these tools because you think that another tool can perform the same function.

If I were a gambling man, I'd bet that the one tool that you want to avoid is the Pen tool. Unfortunately, mastering Illustrator becomes impossible if you avoid learning how to use this tool. Hey, I won't kid you — mastering the Pen tool is like mastering calculus: It makes no sense at first and even less sense when people explain it to you. But, as with calculus, the more you use the Pen tool, the more you like it, and the more technically amazing things you can do with it. (Personally, I think the Pen tool is easier to learn than calculus, and fortunately, this shaky analogy ends here.)

Understanding how the Pen tool works helps you understand not only how Illustrator works but also how PostScript and many other tools in other programs work. Adobe Photoshop also has a Pen tool, which is virtually identical to Illustrator's Pen tool; so by understanding and using the Pen tool in Illustrator, you've already learned one of the most difficult tools to use in Photoshop.

Figure 3-2 was drawn with a combination of all three drawing tools. Throughout this chapter, I'll explain how the various parts of this illustration were drawn and how they were manipulated to produce the final drawing.

Figure 3-2: This illustration was drawn using a combination of the Paintbrush, Pencil, and Pen tools

About the Paintbrush Tool

The Paintbrush tool is more similar to the Rectangle and Ellipse tools than it is like the Pen or Pencil tool because it draws closed paths, and closed paths only.

The Paintbrush tool is similar to paintbrush-type tools in painting programs; the Paintbrush has a certain width, and you can paint with this Paintbrush at this width anywhere in your document. The big difference between paint programs' paintbrushes and Illustrator's paintbrush is that when you finish drawing with Illustrator's Paintbrush tool, a filled, outlined path has been created.

To use the Paintbrush tool, just choose the tool and start drawing. A freeform path appears wherever you drag. That's all there is to it. Kinda. Figure 3-3 shows a drawing that was created with the Paintbrush tool set to a variable width with a pressure-sensitive stylus.

Figure 3-3: A drawing created with the Paintbrush tool

Drawing with the Paintbrush tool is a bit more complicated than I just explained. The most important consideration is the width of the paintbrush stroke. The paintbrush stroke can be as narrow as 0 points and as wide as 1,296 points (that's 18 inches to you and me).

Although 0 is the smallest width, a paintbrush stroke drawn with a width of 0 points actually has a width bigger than 0 points. To change the paintbrush stroke width (the default is 9 points), double-click the Paintbrush on the toolbox and enter a number in the Width text field.

The terms *Stroke* in Illustrator and *paintbrush strokes* drawn with the Paintbrush tool are entirely different critters. In fact, paintbrush strokes are usually Filled, not Stroked. Paintbrush strokes are made of paths that surround the edges of the stroke, and the width of the paintbrush stroke is the distance between the path on either side of the paintbrush stroke. Paintbrush strokes created with the Paintbrush tool on the tool palette are always closed paths. After you release the mouse button, several Anchor Points appear. These Anchor Points and their corresponding Control Handles shape the path.

Results achieved with the Paintbrush tool vary depending on two very important characteristics: your artistic ability and your ability to control the mouse. If you can't draw with a pencil or other forms of traditional media, there is very little possibility that using a mouse will turn you into a Michelangelo (the artist, not the turtle). If Michelangelo'd had to use a mouse to draw, he probably would have become a philosopher or sunk so low as to be an editor for a Mac magazine, constantly complaining about the inefficient means by which cursors are controlled.

A mouse is *not* an intuitive drawing tool, and not being able to draw in the first place makes it even more difficult to draw with the Paintbrush tool. So if artists have trouble with the mouse, what's the point of having the Paintbrush tool at all? Well, instead of a mouse, you can use several types of alternative drawing devices. The best of these is a pressure-sensitive tablet. Trackballs with locking buttons are also good for drawing with the Paintbrush tool (this allows more control over the direction and speed of the paintbrush).

When you're drawing with any of the tools in Illustrator, dragging off the edge of the window causes the window to scroll, which creates a frightening effect for the uninitiated. If you don't want the window to remain where it scrolled to, don't let go of the mouse button, but instead just drag in the opposite direction until the window returns to the original position. To scroll the other way while still using a tool, drag off the other side of the window.

To help you draw more precisely, you have the option of changing the cursor shape from the cute little brush into a crosshair. Press the Caps Lock key (to engage it), and the cursor changes into the crosshair with a dot in the center. Press the Caps Lock key again (to release it), and the cursor returns to the brush shape. The dot at the center of the crosshair is the center of any paintbrush stroke drawn with the Paintbrush tool. Normally, when the cursor is in the shape of a paintbrush, the tip is the center of the paintbrush stroke. Some people find it easier to draw when the paintbrush cursor is replaced with the precise crosshair.

Problems with Corners and the Paintbrush Tool

Gabe: I'm having trouble with the Paintbrush tool... I'm getting....

Toulouse: Overlapping paths whenever you make a sharp corner?

Gabe: Yeah! How'd you guess?

Toulouse: Unfortunately, it's a common problem when using the Paintbrush tool. Paths at sharp turns and corners overlap each other, sometimes extensively.

Gabe: You know, I didn't even notice it before, and I've been using Illustrator forever.

Toulouse: That's because if the paintbrush stroke is just Filled, this usually isn't much of a problem. But if you give the paintbrush stroke a regular Stroke, the Stroke goes into the middle of the paintbrush stroke and looks, well, bad.

Gabe: You're telling me. Any way around it?

Toulouse: Sure. Use the Unite filter on individual paintbrush strokes that have overlapping pieces.

(continued)

(continued)

Gabe: You know, we haven't gotten that far in the book...to filters, that is.

Toulouse: In Illustrator 7, Unite isn't a filter, but instead is merely one of the Pathfinder functions. To use the Unite function on paintbrush strokes, draw your paintbrush stroke with the Paintbrush tool and then immediately select Object⇨Pathfinder⇨Unite. All the overlapping paths magically disappear. Make sure that only one path is selected when you apply the Unite function, or any intersecting paintbrush strokes will be joined.

The best and, at the same time, the most limiting capability of the Paintbrush tool is its consistency of width. If you make the width 18 points, the paintbrush creates a paintbrush stroke that is 18 points wide for the length you draw it. No other tool in Illustrator can be this precise, even the Pen tool with all its precision capabilities. Unfortunately, the Shift key doesn't constrain the Paintbrush tool to 45° angles like it does for most of the other tools.

Drawing with the Paintbrush Tool

In this section, you will create the grass and the horse outlines previously shown in Figure 3-2. Both can be drawn with or without a pressure-sensitive tablet (discussed in detail in "Variable Widths and Pressure-Sensitive Tablets," later in this chapter), although you can achieve better effects if you use a tablet.

STEPS: Drawing the Horse and Tall Grass Outlines

Step 1. Choose the Paintbrush tool from the Pencil tool slot, and double-click the Paintbrush tool. Set the width to 3 points. If the Variable option can be checked (it can if you have a pressure-sensitive tablet), make the minimum 1 point and the maximum 10 points. Change your Paint Style to a Fill of Black and a Stroke of None.

Step 2. Using the Paintbrush tool, draw each piece of the basic shape of the horses, as shown in Figure 3-4. The more individual pieces you draw, the easier it is to use the Paintbrush tool. Long strokes are difficult to produce and aren't as appealing as shorter strokes. Don't worry about filling in the horses with color at this point. You are using the Paintbrush tool only to create the smoothly flowing outlines of the horses. If you make a mistake while drawing, choose Edit⇨Undo (⌘-Z) [Ctrl+Z].

Step 3. To draw the tall blades of grass, just draw a few select blade outlines to create a clump of grass. For the best effects, drag the Anchor Points from the base of the clump up and outward with the Scale tool and the Option [Alt] key pressed.

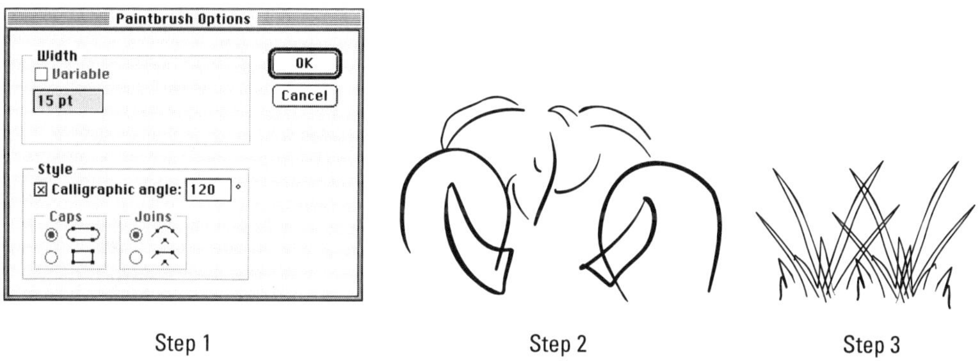

Figure 3-4: Horse and grass outlines created with the Paintbrush tool

The Calligraphic Angle

Double-clicking the Paintbrush tool brings up the Paintbrush dialog box, in which the little Calligraphic check box appears. If this box is checked, the Paintbrush tool no longer creates paintbrush strokes with even widths; instead, it creates paintbrush strokes that vary according to the angle that they are drawn.

When the Calligraphic box is checked, another box appears where you can set the angle of the Calligraphic paintbrush. The angle you should choose depends on what is going to be drawn. To mimic hand-drawn lettering in a calligraphic style, the angle should be set to 45° (or if you're left-handed, it should be set to –45°).

You can also use the Calligraphy filter in the Stylize submenu of the Filters menu. However, the result achieved with the Paintbrush tool and the Calligraphic option is much better than any possible result obtained from using the filter.

Bends and Ends

You can specify how the *joins* and *caps* appear when drawing paintbrush strokes.

Caps are the way the ends of each paintbrush stroke should appear — either rounded (the default) or straight. If you choose Straight, the ends appear perpendicular to the direction of the paintbrush stroke at its ends — which can be a little disconcerting because the ends appear rounded while you are drawing the paintbrush stroke, but are promptly cut off after the mouse button is released.

Joins can be made round (default) or straight. When the joins are set to Straight, the width of the paintbrush is usually much less at the point where the corner is straightened out.

The difference between the types of paintbrush stroke caps and joins is shown in Figure 3-5.

Figure 3-5: The different types of caps and joins used with paintbrush strokes

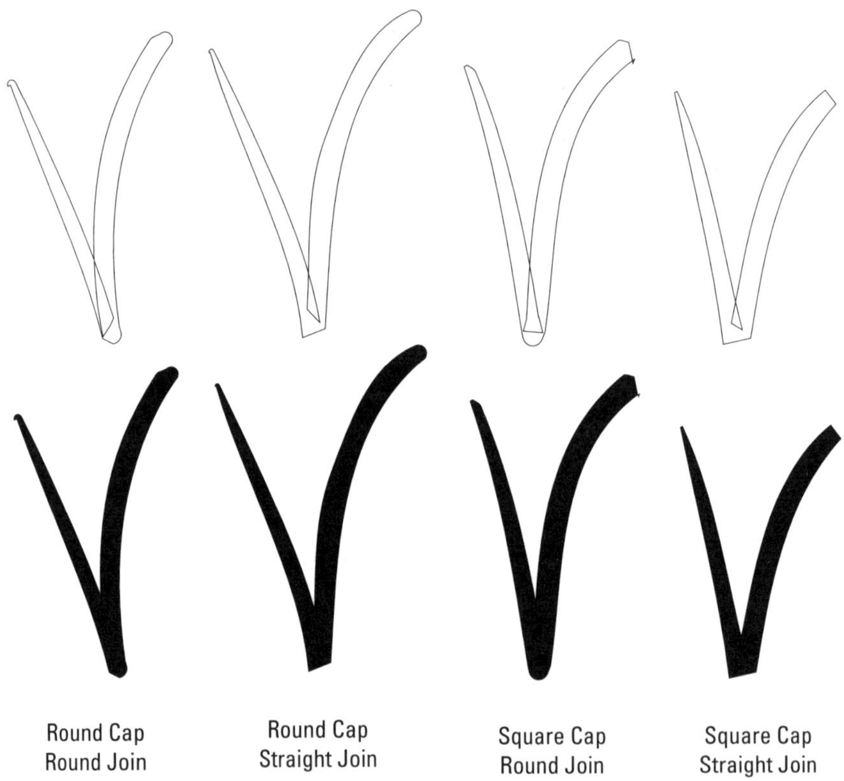

Variable Widths and Pressure-Sensitive Tablets

If you have a pressure-sensitive tablet — a Wacom (pronounced "walk 'em") tablet, some call them, because a large majority tend to be made by Wacom — you can select the Variable check box in the Paintbrush dialog box (accessed by double-clicking the Paintbrush tool). If you don't have a pressure-sensitive tablet, this option is grayed out (unselectable).

A *pressure-sensitive tablet* is a flat, rectangular device over which you pass a special stylus. The more pressure exerted by the stylus on the tablet, the wider a paintbrush stroke will be, providing the Variable option in the Paintbrush dialog box is checked. When using the Variable option, try to set the minimum and maximum widths fairly close to get the most realistic paintbrush look for your drawings.

After you check the Variable option, two new text fields appear, giving you an option to specify the minimum and maximum width of the paintbrush stroke as it is drawn. The minimum width is as narrow as the stroke can appear when you are pressing the pen as lightly as possible; the maximum width is as wide as the stroke can appear when you are pressing the pen as hard as possible.

Drawing Loosely with the Pencil Tool

The Pencil tool initially seems to be a primitive version of the Paintbrush tool. Like the Paintbrush tool, the Pencil tool draws a freeform path wherever the cursor is dragged, but instead of creating a closed path that is a certain width, the result is a single path following approximately the route you've taken with the cursor. You can get the resulting path to follow your cursor-drawn line exactly by lowering the curve-fitting tolerance.

When you need to draw rough edges or realistic illustrations that don't look "computery," the Pencil tool is the tool to use. It draws a path wherever you drag the tool with the mouse, creating Smooth Points and corner Anchor Points relative to how you draw. Although the Pen tool is the tool to use to get precise, super-straight lines, it is difficult to use. The Pencil tool is much easier to use, but it draws lines that are far from perfect.

The Pencil tool has the unique capability to make the lines you draw with the cursor look . . . well . . . good. A swooping, uneven, jagged line that looks terrible as it is being

Ask Toulouse

Keeping Lawyers Out of Work

Arnold: Okay, something's wrong. What happened to the Freehand tool?

Toulouse: It has been magically transformed into the Pencil tool.

Arnold: What's the difference between the old Freehand tool and the new Pencil tool?

Toulouse: As far as functionality, nothing. It's exactly the same as the Freehand tool from previous versions.

Arnold: Then why the name change?

Toulouse: This is kinda embarrassing.

Arnold: Oh, good.

Toulouse: I sent e-mail to the Illustrator 7 product managers stating that is was awfully odd for Illustrator to have a Freehand tool when their chief competition doesn't have an Illustrator tool. "How about naming it the pencil, like in Photoshop," I said.

Arnold: You have to be kidding.

Toulouse: The moral here is that you *can* make a difference, however inconsequential.

drawn can be instantly transformed into a beautifully curved piece of artwork reminiscent of lines drawn traditionally with a French curve.

Still, the Pencil tool has some limitations. The main limitation is that, unlike the Pen tool, it is an *imprecise* path-drawing tool. It is difficult to draw a straight line with the Pencil tool. It is even more difficult to draw a shape with precise curves. The location of a path drawn with the Pencil tool is directly relevant to the direction and speed that the cursor is moving.

Using the Pencil Tool

Before you use the Pencil tool for the first time, it's a good idea to change the Paint Style attributes to a Fill of None and a Stroke of Black, 1 point. Having a Fill other than None while drawing with the Pencil tool often results in bizarre-looking shapes.

To use the Pencil tool, select it from the toolbox, click in the document window, and begin dragging the mouse. As you drag, you see a series of dots following the cursor. These dots show the approximate location of the path you have drawn. After you release the mouse button, the path of dots is transformed into a path with Anchor Points, all with Control Handle Lines and Control Handles shooting off from them. The faster you draw with the Pencil tool, the fewer points are created. The slower you draw, the more points are used to define the path.

STEPS: Drawing Grass and a Tree with the Pencil Tool

Step 1. Choose File⇨Preferences⇨General (⌘-K) [Ctrl+K] and set the Pencil tolerance setting to 2, which allows for detail in the paths without making all the segments straight lines. Set the Fill to C100 Y70 and a Stroke of Black, 1 point using the Color and Stroke palettes.

Step 2. You can create the short grass by drawing three different clumps of grass (see the top of Figure 3-6) and then duplicating the clumps to create the appearance of random blades. To do this, select the Pencil tool and drag up and down to create the blades; then drag across under the blades to connect the bottom to form a closed path. Repeat this procedure to create three or four clumps of different sizes. Be sure to change the Fill color to a slightly different greenish color each time.

Step 3. Using the Selection tool, click the clumps of grass and Option[Alt]-drag them side by side, overlapping them slightly. (Pressing the Option [Alt] key duplicates the dragged clumps.) Repeat this process until there are enough clumps to resemble a grassy area.

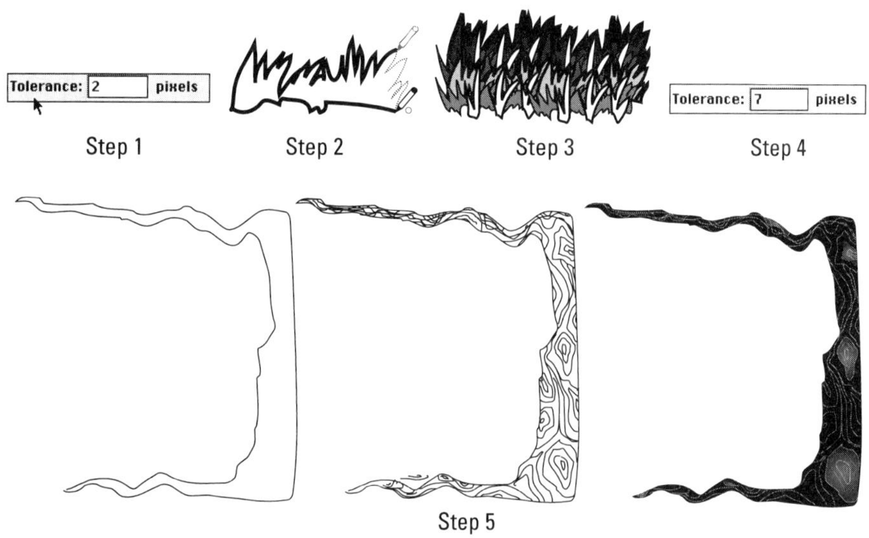

Figure 3-6: Clumps of grass and tree bark created with the Pencil tool

Step 4. To create the tree, first change the Pencil tolerance setting to 7 in the General Preferences dialog box (⌘-K) [Ctrl+K]. Drag with the Pencil tool to create the outline of the tree branch, trunk, and roots. Connect the ends of the path to close it and change the Fill to a dark brown (C75 M100 Y100 K25), keeping the Stroke set to black.

Step 5. To create the textured areas of the bark on the tree, change the Fill to None and the Stroke to a dark shade of gray. Drag along the contours of the tree, which creates circles and wavy patterns.

Every Anchor Point created with the Pencil tool has two Control Handles shooting out of it; this means that Straight Corner Points cannot be drawn with the Pencil tool. This lack of Straight Corner Points makes constructing precise objects not only difficult, but impossible. Also, though they may appear to exist at first glance, smooth Anchor Points are also not created with the Pencil tool, which can be especially deceiving when the Curve Fitting Tolerance option is set to a high number, and all the Anchor Points look like they have to be Smooth Points. This is *not* the case. In fact, most Anchor Points created with the Pencil tool — except for its End Points — are *Curved Corner Points,* which are Anchor Points with two independent Control Handles shooting out. If the Curve Fitting Tolerance setting is high enough, you'll get Smooth Points as well. (See "Jagged Paths versus Smooth Paths," later in this chapter for more information.)

Normally, the Pencil tool resembles a little pencil when you are drawing, which is far better than having to draw with the little squiggle that appears in the toolbox. The line of dots that is drawn comes directly from the point (tip) of the pencil cursor. Pressing the Caps Lock key (engaging it) changes the cursor from the pencil shape to a crosshair, which looks suspiciously like the crosshair from the Paintbrush tool. The line of points comes from the dot in the center of the crosshair.

If you like using the crosshair cursors all the time, but get really mad that every time you start typing you forget to take off the Caps Lock key, you've got short-term memory problems. To fix this, you might need brain surgery. Fortunately, you can set your cursors to *always* be crosshair style just by going to General Preferences (⌘-K) [Ctrl+K] and checking the Use Precise Cursors checkbox. When this option is checked, the Caps Lock key changes the cursor back to the regular tool.

Drawing Open Paths and Closed Paths

You can draw both open and closed paths with the Pencil tool. An *open path* has two separate, distinct End Points. A *closed path* has no End Points. To change an open path into a closed path, the End Points must be joined together. (Joining is discussed in Chapter 7.)

Paths in Illustrator may cross themselves (no, not to protect against vampires). When these paths cross, the Fills may look a little unusual. Strokes look normal; they just overlap where paths cross.

To create an open path, draw a path with the Pencil tool, but make sure that the beginning and end of the path are two separate points at different locations. Open paths with Fills may look a little bizarre because Illustrator automatically fills in between the End Points on the path, even if the imaginary line between the End Points crosses the path itself. Figure 3-7 shows both open and closed paths drawn with the Pencil tool.

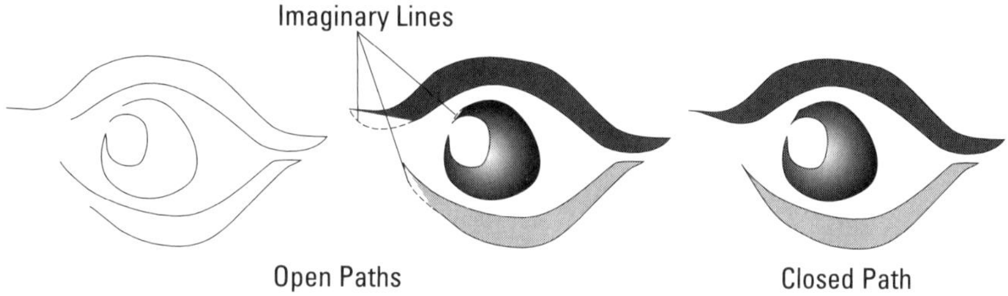

Figure 3-7: Paths drawn with the Pencil tool

To create a closed path, end your path at the same place that you started the path. When the pencil cursor is directly over the location where the line begins, the eraser end of the pencil (at the opposite end from the tip) turns black, and a little circle appears to the lower right of the pencil. This change means that the path is a closed path if you release the mouse button when that particular cursor is showing.

Drawing Semistraight Segments

You can draw semistraight segments — that is, segments that look straight but, upon closer inspection, are really just a teeny bit curved — with the Pencil tool. To draw these segments, start drawing with the Pencil tool and press the ⌘ [Ctrl] key at the point where you want the semistraight segment to begin. The cursor changes to an eraser (see the next section for details on erasing). Keep dragging to where you want the semistraight segment to end and release the ⌘ [Ctrl] key to continue drawing with the Pencil tool.

Notice that the dots that normally appear along the path that the Pencil tool takes do not appear between the area where you first pressed the ⌘ [Ctrl] key and where you released the ⌘ [Ctrl] key; this is normal. After you are done drawing, release the mouse button, and a semistraight line segment appears between the locations where you pressed and then released the ⌘ [Ctrl] key. Upon further inspection with the Direct Selection tool, you will notice that Control Handles extend out from the Anchor Points on either side of the semistraight segment.

One of the important things to remember in this process is that you should never release the mouse button while pressing the ⌘ [Ctrl] key. You can create as many semistraight segments in a path drawn with the Pencil tool as you like by pressing and holding the ⌘ [Ctrl] key for each of them. Keep in mind, however, that when drawing multiple semistraight segments, there must be some movement of the mouse between drawing the semistraight segments. After you press the ⌘ [Ctrl] key, move the mouse, and then release the ⌘ [Ctrl] key, you *must* move the mouse before you press the ⌘ [Ctrl] key again to create a new segment. If the mouse is not moved between ⌘ [Ctrl]-key presses, only one segment is drawn, from the location where the ⌘ [Ctrl] key is initially pressed to the location where it is ultimately released.

A problem with drawing semistraight segments is that it is difficult to see exactly where to place the End Point of the segment because the cursor looks like a huge eraser (the type you were given in first grade that you needed two hands to hold onto and use properly and that always seemed to take the varnish right off the desk after they tore through that wonderful Grade Triple Z paper that still had tree bark in it). If you press the Caps Lock key before the ⌘ [Ctrl] key, the big fat eraser cursor becomes the suave dotted crosshair cursor.

Of course, it is my belief that the ⌘ [Ctrl] key was never intended to be used with the Pencil tool to draw these semistraight lines. In fact, the only real reason the ⌘ [Ctrl] key does anything like this at all is because it is used for erasing.

Erasing in Real Time

The Pencil tool has a capability not found in any of Illustrator's other tools: the capability to erase itself right away while being drawn. Some people think they are erasing when they draw a rectangle or ellipse and then decide they don't want the figure, so they make it so tiny that it seems to disappear. Of course, the shape isn't erased; instead, a tiny rectangle or ellipse is created, which is visible only in Artwork mode and on final output. The Paintbrush tool doesn't erase, nor does the Pen tool.

To erase a path as it is being drawn with the Pencil tool, press the ⌘ [Ctrl] key (that's right, the ⌘ [Ctrl] key again) and while still pressing the mouse button, retrace over the line of dots that you just drew. The dots that the cursor, now an eraser shape, passes over are deleted. After you release the ⌘ [Ctrl] key (still pressing the mouse button), the dots again begin to form wherever the cursor is being dragged. While the ⌘ [Ctrl] key is pressed, the cursor appears as an eraser — a big ugly eraser, but an eraser nonetheless. If the Caps Lock key was engaged first, the cursor appears not as an eraser but as a dotted crosshair, which I find much easier to use than the big fat eraser when I'm drawing semistraight segments.

Erasing works *only* if you haven't let go of the mouse button yet. Releasing the mouse button results in a path with points that can't be erased with the ⌘ [Ctrl] key and the Pencil tool; you can only delete selected Anchor Points.

Jagged Paths versus Smooth Paths

Because drawing nice-looking paths with the Pencil tool and a mouse is just a tad difficult and frustrating ("Really?" you ask sarcastically), Illustrator provides a way to determine how rough or smooth your path will be *before* you draw it.

Normally, paths that appear from the dotted lines created with the Pencil tool are fairly similar to those dotted lines in direction and curves and such. When lines are being drawn, though, human error can cause all sorts of little bumps and *skiddles* (a skiddle is a little round misdrawn section resembling a small fruit-flavored candy) to appear, making the path look lumpy. In some cases, lumpy is good. More often than not, though, lumpy is an undesirable state for your illustrations.

The smoothness of the resulting paths drawn with the Pencil tool relies on the Curve Fitting Tolerance option in the General Preferences dialog box (⌘-K) [Ctrl+K], which determines how jagged or smooth each section will appear from the dotted line to the path.

Curve-fitting tolerance is a value between 0 and 10 that determines the smoothness of the paths drawn, with 0 being rough, and 10 being really smooth. To change the curve-fitting tolerance, choose File⇨Preferences⇨General (⌘-K) [Ctrl+K] and enter a number between 0 and 10 in the curve-fitting tolerance text field. Figure 3-8 shows the same clump of grass created with different curve-fitting tolerance settings. After the number is changed, the new setting affects all paths drawn *after* the new value has been entered. Previously drawn curve-fitting paths are not affected by a change in the curve-fitting tolerance setting. The default value is 2, which is a good all-around value, supplying partially smooth curves and some detail.

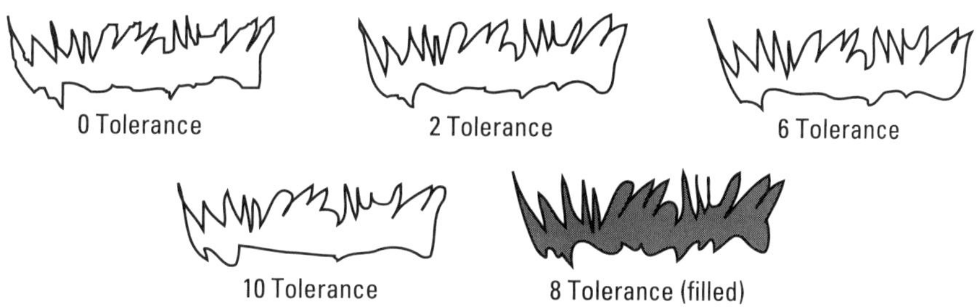

Figure 3-8: The result of different Curve Fitting Tolerance values

At a curve-fitting tolerance setting of 0, paths appear jagged and rough. Also, many more Anchor Points are present, although there are still no Straight Corner Points. A setting of 0 is great for creating some photo-realistic illustrations of complex, detailed objects, such as tree leaves and textures. When the setting is this low, the resulting path follows the dotted line as closely as possible.

When the Curve Fitting Tolerance option is set to 10, paths created with the Pencil tool appear extremely smooth. The smallest number of Anchor Points are used, and the curve of the line appears to be very graceful. Because so few Anchor Points are used, much detail is lost, and the path wavers from the original dotted line of the Pencil tool by a significant amount. Even though it appears that all the Anchor Points are Smooth Points, they are actually Curved Corner Points, with two independent Control Handles.

Because the Curve Fitting Tolerance setting is changed in the General Preferences dialog box, it retains its current value until it is changed, even if you quit Illustrator or restart the entire system.

Curve Fitting Tolerance affects the way the Auto Trace tool (discussed in more detail in the next chapter) works in the same way as it affects the Pencil tool (higher numbers for smooth paths with few Anchor Points and lower numbers for jagged paths with many Anchor Points).

Adding to an Existing Open Path

To continue drawing on an existing path (which could have been drawn with the Pen tool or the Pencil tool), the existing path must first be an open path with two distinct End Points. After you pass your drawing tool over one end of the path with the Pencil tool, the pencil cursor changes into a pencil with a black eraser. This action means that if you click and drag, you can now extend the path with the Pencil tool. If the Caps Lock key is engaged, the cursor looks like a crosshair with a hollow box in the center.

Although you are continuing with the same path, you may not erase that part of the path that was in place before you added to it. You may, however, press the ⌘ [Ctrl] key and erase any part of the dotted line that appears from the new segment you are drawing.

So far, all the points in paths drawn with the Pencil tool have been Curved Corner Points. This changes when you add to an existing path with the Pencil tool. The point that connects the existing path to the newly drawn path is a Smooth Point. No matter which way you drag, the point always is a Smooth Point. However, you can force a Curved Corner Point in place of the Smooth Point by pressing the Option [Alt] key while clicking the end of the existing path.

If you drag to the other open end of the existing path, you have the opportunity to make the path into a closed path. This point will also be a Smooth Point — unless you press the Option [Alt] key, at which time it changes into a Curved Corner Point.

You can add on only to End Points on an existing path. Anchor Points that are within paths cannot be connected to new (or existing, for that matter) segments. If you attempt to draw from an Anchor Point that is not an End Point, you create an End Point for the path you are drawing that is overlapping but not connected to the Anchor Point you clicked above.

CAUTION

Illustrator's pencil cursor changes the eraser to black whenever the pencil tip passes over any Anchor Point, not just End Points on open paths. This change can be a little confusing at first, so try to remember that you *absolutely cannot* add a new path to an existing path on an Anchor Point that is not an End Point.

Precision Drawing with the Pen Tool

The Pen tool is the most powerful tool in Illustrator's arsenal because you are dealing more directly with Bézier curves than with any other tool. It's one thing to adjust paths, Anchor Points, and Control Handles with the Direct Selection tool, but using the Pen tool to create paths out of nothing is dumbfounding.

For the first several months of my experience using Illustrator, I avoided the Pen tool like the plague. Then I slowly worked up to where I could draw straight lines with it comfortably, and finally curved segments. Even after I had been drawing curved segments for a while, I really didn't understand how the tool worked, and I was missing out on a lot of its capabilities because of that lack of knowledge. The manuals for Illustrator really weren't very clear on how to use the Pen tool, and no one I knew could do any better. To learn how to use it, I forced myself to use the Pen tool to draw objects that I could've just traced with the Auto Trace tool.

While practicing with the Pen tool, I necessarily learned about the four types of Anchor Points — Smooth Points, Straight Corner Points, Curved Corner Points, and Combination Corner Points — because the key to using the Pen tool is understanding how Anchor Points work (see Figure 3-8).

ASK TOULOUSE

Why Use the Pen Tool?

Vinnie: Why should I use the Pen tool instead of the other drawing tools?

Toulouse: The Pen draws paths *exactly* where you want them.

Vinnie: Yeah...that's it?

Toulouse: The Pen tool also draws curves.

Vinnie: I thought that's what the Pencil tool was for.

Toulouse: Yes, but the Pen draws *precise, perfect* curves.

Vinnie: Like the Ellipse tool.

Toulouse: Ah, here's a difference: the Pen draws curves one line segment at a time.

Vinnie: It sounds like a lot of work.

Toulouse: No, you just click and drag for each point. Once you get the hang of it, you'll be amazed that you ever used Illustrator without it.

The Pen tool draws points one at a time. The first click of the Pen tool produces one Anchor Point. The second click (usually in a different location) creates a second Anchor Point that is joined to the first Anchor Point by a line segment. Clicking without dragging produces a Straight Corner Point.

After you get the hang of it, the Pen tool isn't so bad. Go ahead, ask anyone who has been using Illustrator for, say, two years or longer. They like the Pen tool. I use the Pen tool more than the Paintbrush, Auto Trace, and Pencil tools combined.

I have approached this tool delicately because, although it is a little frustrating and confusing to use well, it is the most important tool to learn, and this is the one section of this book that you should really read well. (On the enclosed CD-ROM, there are several examples that should help to clarify the Pen tool's use.)

In our sample illustration from Figure 3-2, the weeds in the upper-right corner were created with the Pen tool. The weeds are composed entirely out of straight lines and were duplicated in clumps, just as the long and short grasses were. Figure 3-9 shows the process used for creating the mass of weeds in the illustration.

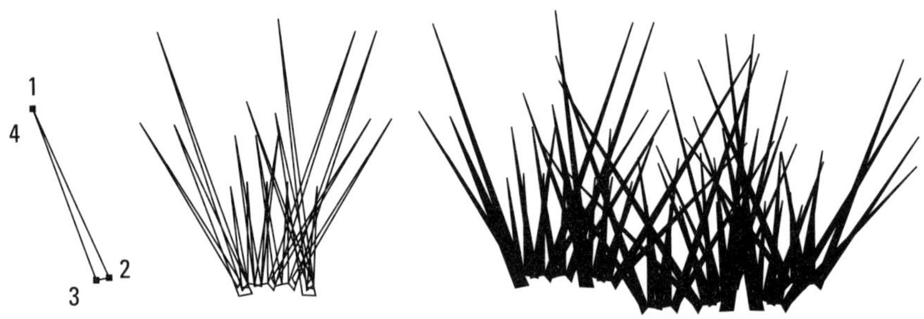

Figure 3-9: A clump of weeds as drawn with the Pen tool

STEPS: Drawing Weeds with the Pen Tool

Step 1. Change the Paint Style to a Fill of Black and a Stroke of None. Using the Pen tool, click (don't drag!) at the top of the first weed (1). Then click lower at the bottom right of the first weed (2). Click to the right (3) and click back at the start point (4) to complete the weed. When the last weed in the clump has been finished, click the first Anchor Point to close the path.

Step 2. Repeat Step 1 to create additional weeds, making clumps of them like the one in Figure 3-9.

Step 3. With the Selection tool, Option[Alt]-drag the clumps a few times to create a mass of weeds.

CAUTION: When drawing straight lines with the Pen tool, never drag with the mouse while pressing the button. Doing so results in at least one curved segment.

The Pen tool draws precise lines, both curved and straight. With a little practice and with using the tips given in these pages, you can master the tool. In the process, you will understand Illustrator much better than is possible otherwise.

It would be really simple if the Pen tool did *all* the work, but you do have to do some of the labor involved in creating curves and straight lines yourself. Actually, using the Pen tool is easier than I have been letting on. All you have to do is place Anchor Points where you want the path to go.

Okay, I've oversimplified it just a bit. Drawing with the Pen tool isn't *just* placing Anchor Points. The first obstacle is to figure out where the heck those Anchor Points are going to go. Two drawings with the same number of Anchor Points can look totally different depending on where they're placed. You have to think ahead to determine what the path will look like before you draw it.

Points should always be located where there is a change in the path. That change can be a different curve or a corner. The three changes to look for are

- A corner of any type
- The point where a curve changes from clockwise to counterclockwise or vice versa
- The point where a curve changes *intensity:* from tight to loose or loose to tight (by far, the hardest change to judge)

The second obstacle is to decide what type of Anchor Point you want to use. Remember, there are four different Anchor Points to choose from when drawing with the Pen tool:

- **Smooth Points** are Anchor Points with two connected Control Handles sticking out, resulting in a path that moves smoothly through the Anchor Point. Changing the angle of one Control Handle changes the angle of the other Control Handle. Changing the length of the Control Handle Line does not affect the other Control Handle. A Smooth Point guides the path along its journey but doesn't severely or suddenly alter that path's direction.
- **Straight Corner Points** are Anchor Points where two line segments meet in a corner. The line segments are not curved where they reach the Anchor Point, and there are no Control Handles. Straight Corner Points usually, but not always, distinctly change the direction of the path at the location where it passes through the Anchor Point.

- **Curved Corner Points** are Anchor Points where two different curved segments meet in a corner. There are two Control Handles coming out of a Curved Corner Point, but the Control Handles are independent of each other. Moving one Control Handle does not affect the other.
- **Combination Corner Points** are Anchor Points where two segments meet, one curved and one straight. There is one Control Handle on a Combination Corner Point. That Control Handle affects only the curved segment, not the straight segment.

If the path is smoothly curving, you use a Smooth Point. If there is a corner, use one of the Corner Points.

Figure 3-10 shows each of the Anchor Point types.

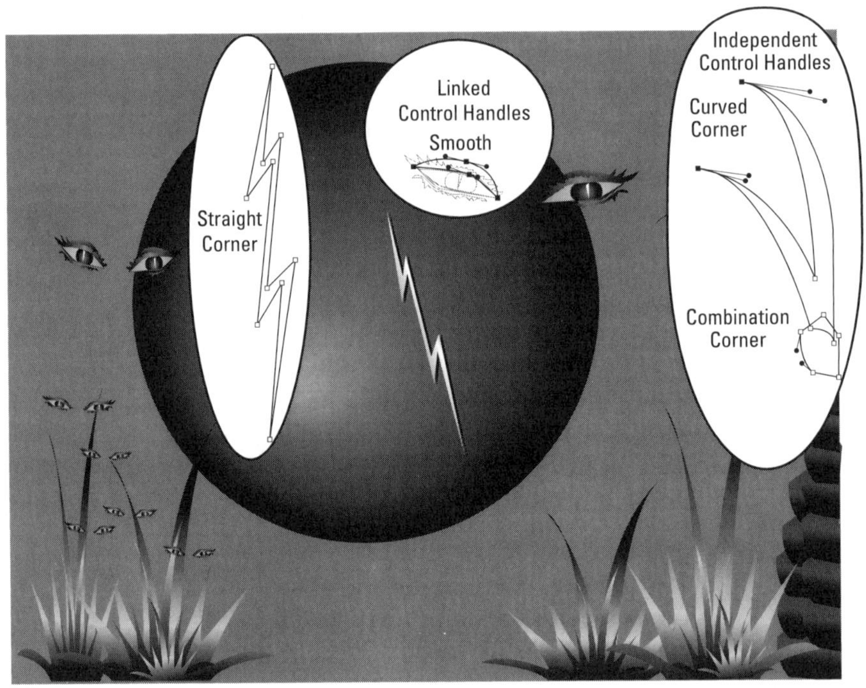

Figure 3-10: The four types of Anchor Points

The third obstacle arises when you decide that the Anchor Point should be anything but a Straight Corner Point. All the other Anchor Points have Control Handles, you see. The obstacle is figuring out how to drag the Control Handles, how far to drag them, and in which direction to drag them.

Drawing Straight Lines

The easiest way to start learning to use the Pen tool is by drawing straight lines. The lightning bolt in Figure 3-11 was created entirely with straight lines. The great thing about straight lines drawn with the Pen tool is that there are no Control Handles to worry about or fuss over.

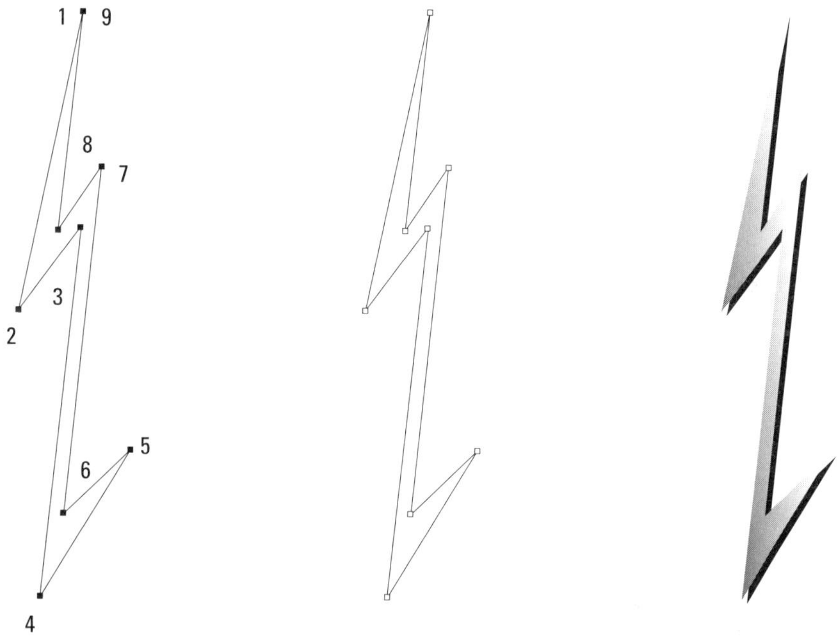

Figure 3-11: Straight lines drawn with the Pen tool

To draw the lightning bolt in Figure 3-11, click at each number with the Pen tool in order. Before you click at number 9, the Pen tool changes to a pen cursor with a little circle in the lower-right corner. This change signifies that the path is going to close when you click this point.

The simplest straight line is a line drawn with only two Anchor Points. To draw a line like this, select the Pen tool and click and release where you want the first End Point (the beginning of the line) to appear. Then click and release where you want the second End Point (the end of the line) to appear. A line appears between the two points. Too easy, isn't it?

Hold down the Shift key to keep the line constrained to a 45° angle (0, 45, 90, and zoom).

To draw another separate line, first click the Pen tool in the toolbox or hold down the ⌘ [Ctrl] key and click. Either action tells Illustrator that you are done drawing the first line. Clicking and releasing again in one spot and then another draws a second line with two End Points. Be careful not to drag when clicking the Pen tool to form straight lines.

Paths drawn with the Pen tool, like the Pencil tool, may cross themselves. The only strange result you may see involves the Fills for objects whose paths cross. In open paths created with the Pen tool, Fills may look unusual because of the imaginary line between the two End Points and any paths that the imaginary line crosses.

Closing Paths

If you want to create a closed path (one with no End Points), return to the first Anchor Point in that segment and click. As the Pen tool crosses over the beginning Anchor Point, the cursor changes to a pen with a circle in the lower-right corner. After you have created a closed path, there is no need to click the Pen tool again. Instead, the next click of the Pen tool in the document automatically begins a new path.

You must have at least three Anchor Points to create a closed path with straight lines. You can change the identity of one of these points to a different type of Anchor Point by curving one of the segments and giving the closed path some substance.

Drawing Curves

Initially, the worst thing about drawing curves with the Pen tool is that the whole process is rather disorienting. You actually have to think differently to grasp what the Pen tool is doing. The difference that you notice right away between drawing straight lines and drawing curves is that to draw a curve, you need to drag with the Pen tool; whereas, when drawing straight lines, you click and release.

The most basic of curves is the bump (a curved segment between just two points). A bump was used to create a path to fill the horses' rears (previously shown in Figure 3-2). Use the following steps to create the bump that is illustrated in Figure 3-12.

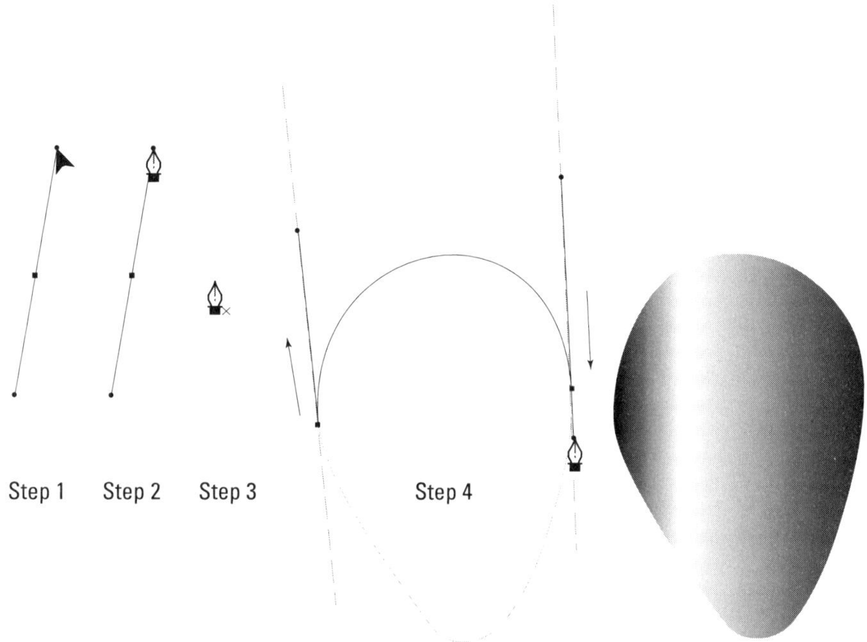

Figure 3-12: The four steps for creating a basic bump curve

STEPS: Creating a Basic Curve

Step 1. Click with the Pen tool and drag up about 1/2 inch. You'll see an Anchor Point and a Control Handle Line extending from it as you drag.

Step 2. When you release the mouse button, you see the Anchor Point and a line extending to where you dragged, with a Control Handle at its end.

Step 3. Position the cursor about 1 inch to the right of the place you first clicked.

Step 4. Click with the mouse and drag down about 1/2 inch. As you drag, you see a curve forming that resembles a bump. When you release the mouse, the curve is Filled with the current Fill color. You see the Control Handle you just dragged.

Before you try to draw another curve, remember that the Pen tool is still in a mode that continues the current path; it does not start a new one. To start a new path, choose Deselect All (⌘-Shift-A) [Ctrl+Shift+A] or hold down ⌘ [Ctrl] and click an empty area on-screen. The next time you use the Pen tool, you will draw a separate path.

To create an S shape, one more step is needed. The steps for creating the S shape are illustrated in Figure 3-13.

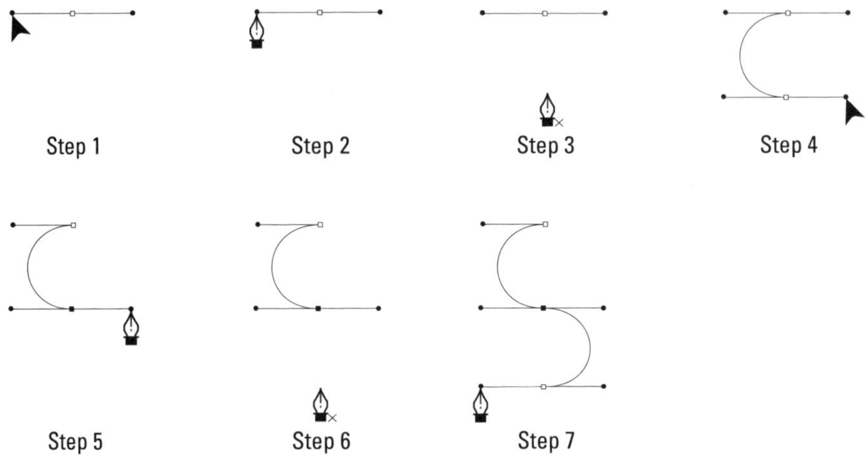

Figure 3-13: The seven steps to creating a basic S curve

STEPS: Creating a Basic S Curve

Step 1. Click and drag with the Pen tool about 1/2 inch to the left.

Step 2. Release the mouse button. You should see the Anchor Point and the Control Handle that you just drew, with a Control Handle Line between them.

Step 3. Position the cursor about 1 inch below where you first clicked.

Step 4. Click and drag to the right about 1/2 inch.

Step 5. Release the mouse button.

Step 6. Position the cursor about 1/2 inch below the last point you clicked.

Step 7. Click and drag to the left, about 1/2 inch. Now you have an S shape. To make the S look more like a real S, change the Fill to None and the Stroke to Black, 1 pt.

All the Anchor Points we have created in these two examples are Smooth Points. The Control Handles were dragged in the direction of the next curve to be drawn, and the lengths of the Control Handle Lines on either side of the Anchor Point were equal.

The lengths of the Control Handle Lines on either side of the Smooth Point do not have to be the same. Instead, a Smooth Point may have both long and short Control Handle Lines coming out of it. The length of the Control Handle Line affects the curve, as shown on the S curve in Figure 3-14.

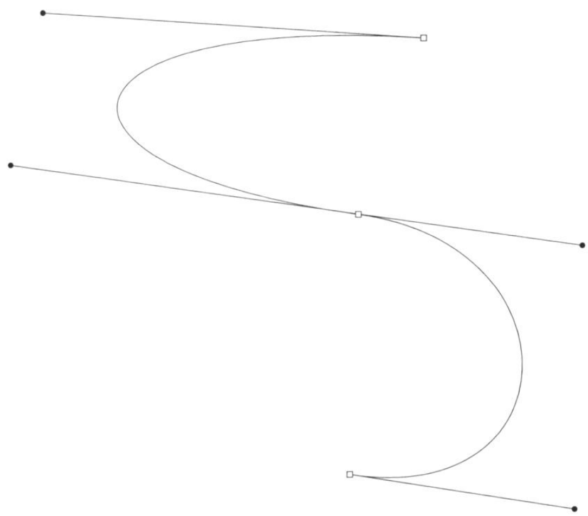

Figure 3-14: The length of the Control Handle Lines controls the shape of the curve

To create a Smooth Point with two Control Handle Lines of different lengths, first create a Smooth Point along a path. Go back to this point after it has been created and click and drag it again using the Direct Selection tool. You can adjust the angle for both Control Handle Lines and the length for the new Control Handle Line that you are dragging. Note that as you are dragging out this Control Handle Line, the other Control Handle Line wobbles to the angle that you are dragging. This happens because on any Smooth Point, the Control Handle Lines *must* be at the same angle, and as you drag out the new Control Handle Line, you are changing the angle for both Control Handle Lines simultaneously.

Making Bad Waves with the Pen

Boom-Boom Washington: I'm having loads of trouble with my paths and the Pen tool.

Toulouse: What sort of trouble? Lines not connecting? Lumps everywhere? Pen running out of ink?

Boom-Boom Washington: Actually, I'm getting the "wave" thing happening, except my waves have....

Toulouse: ...Curved tips. I've been there. It isn't pretty.

Boom-Boom Washington: Wow, it's like you're in my head, looking out....

Toulouse: The wave effect you're describing usually happens when you click and drag with the Pen tool....

Boom-Boom Washington: Uh-huh....

Toulouse: And then let go, and the next click is right on top of the Control Handle you've dragged out. You drag out again, the next click is on the handle you've dragged out...and so on.

Boom-Boom Washington: So...how do I prevent it?

(continued)

(continued)

Toulouse: Just remember that each time you drag, you're setting the location of the Control Handle, not the path itself. Don't click the Control Handle, click far away from it.

Boom-Boom Washington: Like, if the first click is right in the middle of the page, the next click should be in, what, Jersey?

Toulouse: Not quite that far away. Now I know why you were 28 and still in 11th grade....

Knowing the Pen Commandments

The Pen Commandments are laws to live by — or, at least, to draw by — as shown dramatically in Figure 3-15.

The commandments are

- **Thou shalt drag approximately one-third of the length of the next curved segment.** What this means, as shown at the bottom of Figure 3-16, is that the Control Handle you drag from the Anchor Point should be about one-third of the distance between this Anchor Point and the next one you click. (This technique takes some planning ahead.) In fact, you have to be aware of where the next Anchor Point is going to be located before you can determine the length of the Control Handle Line you are dragging. Dragging by one-third is always an approximation — a little more or a little less doesn't hurt and, in fact, is sometimes quite necessary. You might run into trouble when the Control Handle Line is more than half or less than one-quarter of the next segment.

  If your Control Handle Line is too long or too short, chances are the line will curve erratically. Remember not to drag where the next point will be placed, just one-third of that distance.

- **Thou shalt remember that Control Handle Lines are always tangent to the curved segment they are guiding.** Tangent? Well, a simpler way of putting this commandment may be that Control Handle Lines go in the same direction as the curve and that they are always outside of the curve, as previously shown in Step 4 of Figure 3-13. Don't get the outside of the curve and the outside of the shape you are drawing confused — they may well be two different things. If your Control

Figure 3-15: The Pen Commandments

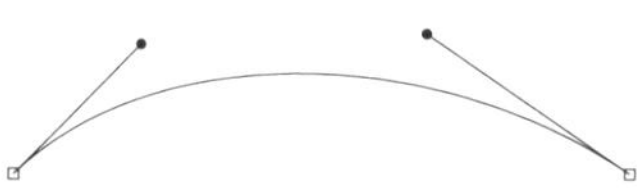

Figure 3-16: Handles used for curving segments should be approximately one-third of the length of the curved segment

Handle lies inside the curve you are drawing, it will be too short and overpowered by the next Anchor Point. Control Handles *pull* the curve toward themselves; this makes them naturally curve out toward the Control Handle Lines. If you fight this natural pull, your illustrations can look loopy and silly.

- **Thou shalt always drag the Control Handle in the direction that you want the curve to travel at that Anchor Point.** Once again, the Control Handle pulls the curve toward itself by its very nature; doing otherwise will certainly cause some trouble. If you drag backward toward the preceding segment, you will create a little curved spike that sticks out from the Anchor Point. This commandment applies *only* to Smooth Points, as shown in Step 4 of Figure 3-13. If the Anchor Point is to be a Curved Corner Point, then the initial drag should be in the direction the curve was traveling, and the next drag (an Option-drag) should go in the direction that the curve is going to travel. If the Anchor Point is a Combination Curve Point and the next segment is straight, then the dragging motion should be in the direction that the curve was traveling; then the Anchor Point should be clicked and released. If the Combination Curve Point's next segment is curved, the first click should be clicked and released, and the second click should be dragged in the direction of the next curve.

- **Thou shalt use as few Anchor Points as possible.** If your illustration calls for smooth, flowing curves, use very few Anchor Points. If, on the other hand, your illustration should be rough and gritty, use more Anchor Points. The fewer Anchor Points you have, the smoother the final result, as demonstrated in Figure 3-17. When there are only a few Anchor Points on a path, changing its shape is easier and faster. More Anchor Points mean a bigger file and longer printing times, as well. If you're not sure if you need more Anchor Points, don't add them. You can always add them later with the Add Anchor Point tool.

Figure 3-17: The path on the left was created with 12 Anchor Points; the one on the right, with 60

- **Thou shalt place Anchor Points at the beginning of each "different" curve.** Anchor Points should be used as *transitional* points, where the curve either changes direction or increases or decreases in size dramatically. If it looks as though the curve will change from one type of curve to another, then the location to place an Anchor Point is in the middle of that transitional section. The top drawing in Figure 3-18 shows good locations to place Anchor Points on a curved path.

- **Thou shalt not overcompensate for a previously misdrawn curve.** If you really screw up on the last Anchor Point you've drawn, don't panic and try to undo the mistake by dragging in the wrong direction or by dragging the Control Handle out to some ridiculous length. Doing either of these two things may temporarily fix the preceding curve but usually wrecks the next curve, causing you to have to overcompensate yet again. The results of just minor overcompensation are shown in the bottom drawing in Figure 3-18.

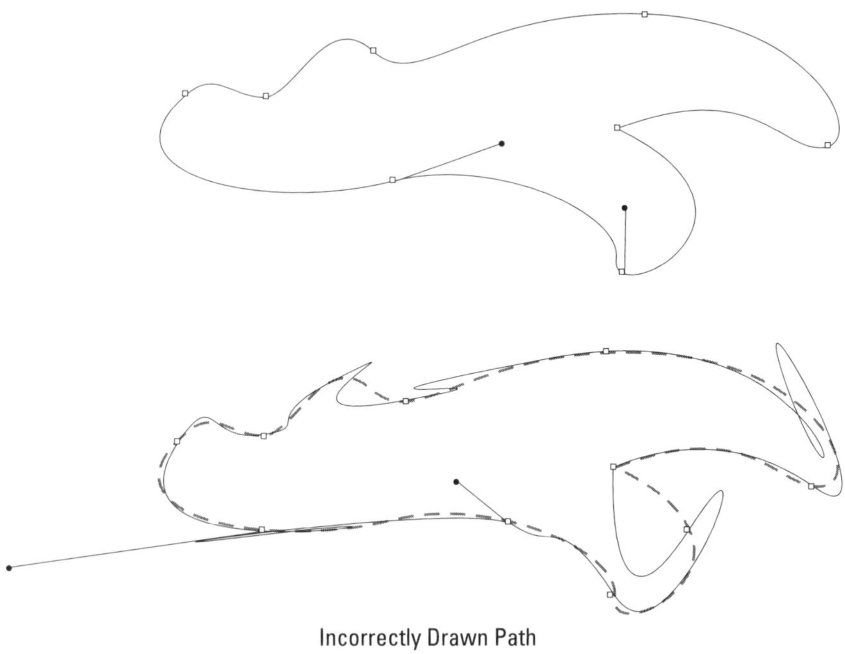

Figure 3-18: The Anchor Points on the top path are placed where the curve changes. The path at the top was drawn correctly; the one on the bottom was drawn by overcompensating for previously misdrawn curves.

Closing Curved Paths with the Pen Tool

The majority of the paths you draw with the Pen tool will be closed paths, not the open ones we've drawn so far. Like open curved paths, any closed curved path must have at least two Anchor Points, just as paths with Straight Corner Points need three distinct points to create a closed path.

When the Pen tool is placed over the starting point of the path you've drawn, a little circle appears to the right of the pen shape. This is an indicator that the path will become a closed path if you click this Anchor Point.

Points on a Path to Make a Figure 8

How few points does it take to create a basic curved shape? This is a good test of your abilities. The following infinity shape was drawn with the least number of Anchor Points possible.

The number of points used to draw this shape was a number something less than infinity.

After you've tried to do this a few times, look ahead a couple of pages to see some of the different ways it can be done.

Of course, to ensure that the initial Anchor Point remains a Smooth Point, you need to click and drag on the initial Anchor Point. Simply clicking produces a Combination Corner Point, which only has one Control Handle associated with it.

Curved Corner Points

Curved Corner Points are points where two different, usually distinct, curved segments meet at an Anchor Point. Because the two curves meet this way, a Smooth Point does not provide the means for their joining correctly. Instead, a Smooth Point would make the two different curves blend into each other smoothly.

The main difference between a Curved Corner Point and a Smooth Point is that a Smooth Point has two linked Control Handles on their ends; a Curved Corner Point has two *independent* Control Handles. As the word indicates, the Control Handles and their associated Control Handle Lines move independently of each other, enabling two different, distinct types of curves to come from the same Anchor Point.

To create a Curved Corner Point, create a Smooth Point in a path and then Option [Alt]-drag the Control Handle you just drew. As you Option[Alt]-drag the Control Handle, you are breaking the Control Handles independently. The next segment will curve as controlled by this Control Handle, not by the original one.

The clumps of grass in Figure 3-2 were created by using Curved Corner Points. The process is explained in the following steps.

STEPS: Creating Paths with Curved Corner Points

Step 1. As shown in Figure 3-19, click the first point (1) and drag up and to the left. Try to duplicate the locations of all the points for the best results.

Step 2. Click at (2) and drag left and down just a little bit, which creates the curved segment between (1) and (2). You won't see the Control Handle you are dragging on the figure on the right because Step 3 replaces it.

Step 3. To create the first Curved Corner Point, Option[Alt]-click on (2) and drag up and to the right.

Step 4. Click at (3) and drag to the lower right.

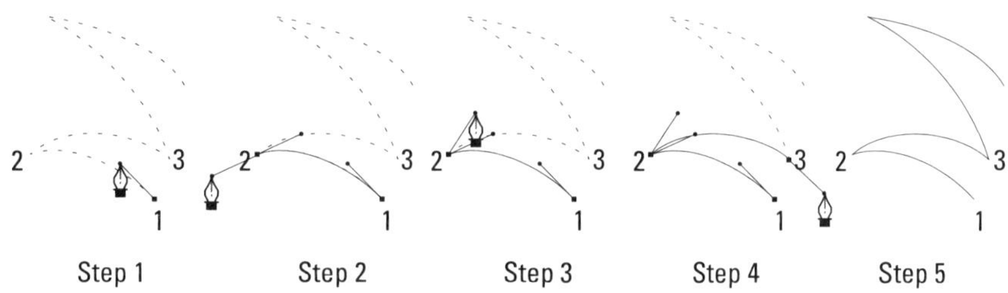

Figure 3-19: How to create paths with Curved Corner Points

Step 5. Continue to Option[Alt]-drag Control Handles when drawing a new segment, effectively creating independent Control Handles until you have created a clump of grass.

Step 6. Option[Alt]-copy and transform the clumps to create several clumps of grass.

When creating Curved Corner Points, you can press the Option[Alt] key (to create independent points) all the time, not just when starting a new segment.

Points on a Path to Make a Figure 8: The Answers

There are several ways to make a figure 8, as shown by the following figures.

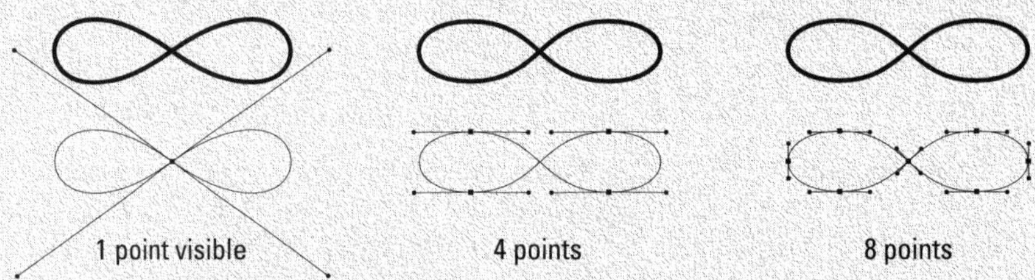

Compare these figures to the one you've drawn.

Your score is as follows:

1 visible point (really 2 overlapping): PenMaster

2 points, both visible: Lots of Pentential

3–4 points: ApPentice

6 or more points: The sword is still mightier

Combination Corner Points

A Combination Corner Point is a point where a curved segment and a straight segment meet each other. At this Corner Point, there is one Control Handle coming from the Anchor Point from the side where the curved segment is located and, on the other side, there is no Control Handle, indicating a straight segment.

To create a Combination Corner Point with the Pen tool, draw a few curved segments and then go back to the last Anchor Point. There should be two linked Control Handles displayed at this point. Simply click once on the Anchor Point, and one of the two Control Handles will disappear. The next segment then starts out straight.

POWER TIP: You can change existing Smooth and Curved Corner Points into Combination Corner Points simply by dragging one of the Control Handles into the Anchor Points.

Using the Pen Tool

In the sample illustration that was shown in Figure 3-2, the Pen tool was used not only to draw the spiky weeds, but also to draw the horses on the hill and the Fill shapes for the hill. The horse outlines and the blade outlines were created with the Paintbrush tool.

To Fill the hillside, click where the left edge of the hill should begin and drag down and to the right about 1/2 inch. Next, click at the top of the hill and drag just a tiny bit (less than 1/4 inch) to the right. Click again at about halfway down the hill and drag at about the same angle as the hill. Click again at the base of the hill and drag to the right 1 inch. Click without dragging on the far side of the illustration. To finish off the hillside Fill, click the lower-right and lower-left corners and then click the starting point. Fill the path with a gradient that complements a hillside and change the Stroke to None.

To create the horse Fill shape, create a path with the Pen tool by using mostly Smooth Points that go right through the center of the horse outlines. Make separate shapes for the head area, manes, body area, and the tails. Fill the paths with gradients or solid colors and choose a Stroke of None.

To create the long grass blade Fills, use the Pen tool to draw paths that go right through the center of the blades of grass. Create separate paths for each blade, and Fill the blades with a green linear gradient.

Selection Tools

If there is one group of tools in Illustrator you absolutely *must* have, it is the set of three selection tools. As in most applications, to alter something (move, transform, and so on), you must first select it. When you draw a new path or when you paste in Illustrator, the program automatically selects the object you're working on; however, as soon as you draw another path, the preceding object is deselected and Illustrator automatically selects the object with the new path. The selection tools allow you to select paths and perform additional manipulations on them. Illustrator has three selection tools: the Selection tool, the Direct Selection tool, and the Group Selection tool, as shown in Figure 3-20.

Figure 3-20: The Selection tools. The Group Selection tool is accessed by clicking and holding on the Direct Selection tool slot in the toolbox.

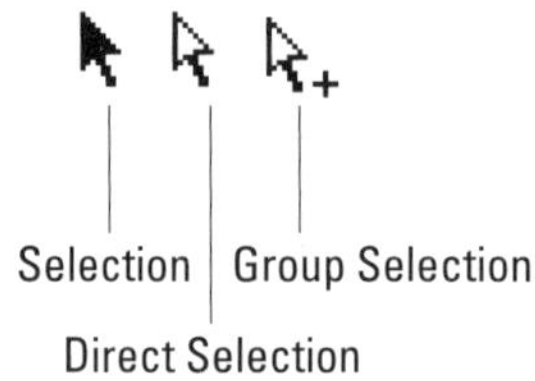

There are several different ways to make selections in Illustrator, depending on what you wish to change:

- **InterPath selecting:** *InterPath selecting* means that at least one point or segment within a path is selected, usually with the Direct Selection tool. InterPath selecting is used to adjust individual points, segments, and series of points.

  Even though just a portion of the path is selected, many changes will affect the entire path — not just the selected points. For example, most of the attributes available in the Object menu (including Pathfinder, Masking, and Compound Paths) affect the entire path even when only a point or segment is selected.

  InterPath selecting also allows you to use most of the functions in the Arrange menu, such as hiding, locking, or grouping. But these options lock, hide, or group the entire path.

  Selected Anchor Points on InterPath selected paths are solid squares; unselected points are hollow squares. Selected segments are indicated by visible Control Handles and Control Handle Lines on either side of the segment if the selected segment is curved. If the selected segment is not curved, no indication that the segment is selected appears on-screen. If you delete a segment or point, the entire remaining path becomes selected at the second level.

  Figure 3-21 shows InterPath selection.

Figure 3-21: InterPath selection on paths

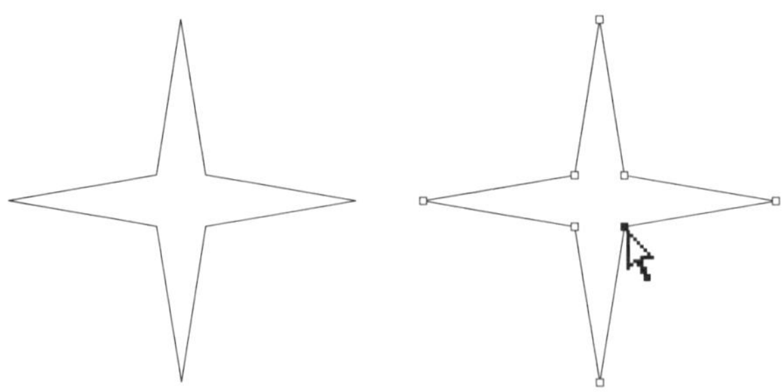

- **Path selecting:** *Path selecting* means that all points and segments on a path are selected. When a path is clicked by using the Group Selection tool or the Selection tool, the entire path is automatically selected. (Drawing a marquee entirely around a path with the Direct Selection tool also selects the entire path.)

  All the capabilities from InterPath selecting are available, such as the entire Object menu and the Arrange menu and most of the functions in the Filter menu.

  After you select a path, the entire path is affected by moving, transforming, cutting, copying and pasting, and deleting. An example of Path selecting is shown in Figure 3-22.

Figure 3-22: Path selection

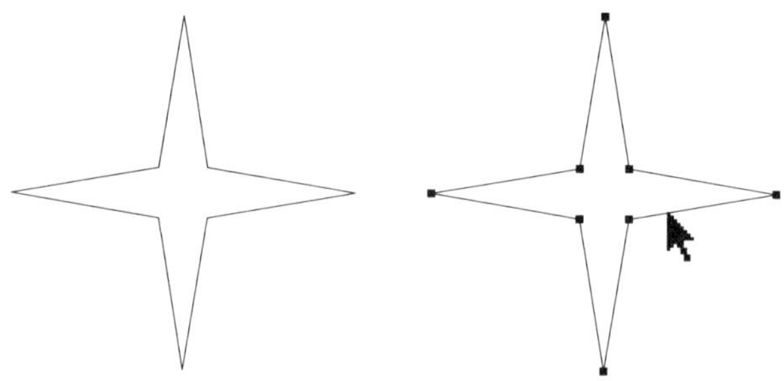

- **Group selecting:** You can select and affect any series of grouped paths as if they were a single object using *Group selecting*. All paths in the group are affected in the same way as paths that you select with Path selecting. The Selection tool selects entire grouped paths at once. If you use the Group Selection tool instead, you need a series of clicks to select a group of paths. Refer to Figure 3-23 to see what you can accomplish with Group selecting.

Figure 3-23: Group selection

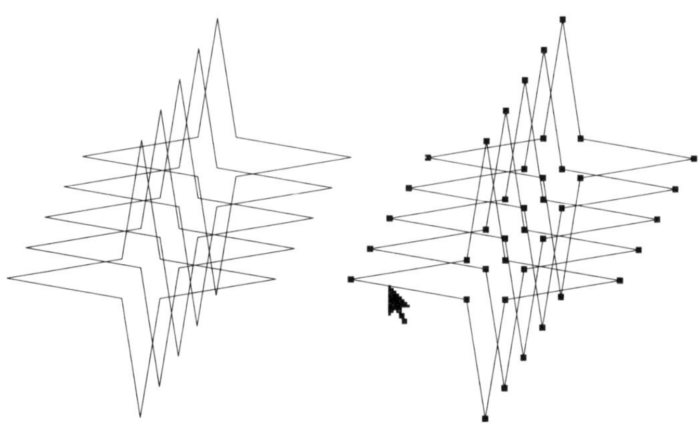

- **InterGroup selecting:** You can select and affect groups of paths within other groups by using *InterGroup selecting.* All paths in the group are affected in the same way as paths that you select with Path selection. Use the Group Selection tool to select a group of paths at once. Each successive click on the same path selects another set of grouped paths that the initial path is within. InterGroup selecting is demonstrated in Figure 3-24.

Figure 3-24: InterGroup selection

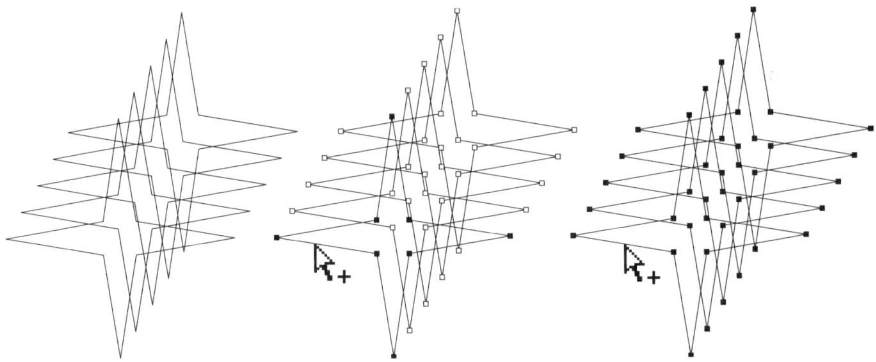

To select everything in your document that hasn't been hidden or locked, choose Edit➪Select All (⌘-A) [Ctrl+A], which selects all the points and segments on every path in the document. You can also select everything in the document by drawing a marquee around all the paths with any selection tool.

Normally, after you select something new, everything that you have previously selected becomes *deselected.* To continue to select additional points, paths, or segments, you must hold down the Shift key while clicking.

The Shift key normally works as a toggle when used with a selection tool, selecting anything that is not selected and deselecting anything that is currently selected. Each selection tool works with the Shift key a little differently, as described in the following sections.

POWER TIP

To deselect everything that is selected, click a part of the document that is empty (where you can see the Pasteboard or Artboard) without using the Shift key. You also can deselect everything by choosing Edit➪Deselect All (⌘-Shift-A) [Ctrl+Shift+A].

You can use the selection tools for manually moving selected points, segments, and paths. Personally, the thought of manual labor terrifies me, but when I do something *manually* in Illustrator, I am usually referring to the process of dragging or clicking with the mouse. You use *automatic* or *computer-assisted manipulations* when you type in specific values in Transform palette, for example. The next few sections cover the selection tools and their functions.

Using the Selection Tool

The Selection tool selects entire paths or complete groups at one time. You can't select just one point or a few points on a path with the Selection tool. Instead, the entire path on which that point lies is selected (all the Anchor Points turn black). Drawing a marquee (clicking and dragging as a box forms behind the cursor) around parts of paths or entire paths also selects those entire paths.

Using the Direct Selection Tool

To select individual points, line segments, or a series of specific points within a path, you need to use the Direct Selection tool. It is the *only* tool that enables you to select something less than an entire path. You can also draw a marquee over a portion of a path to select only those points and segments within the area of the marquee. If the marquee surrounds an entire path, the entire path is selected. Individual points or a series of points on different paths can also be selected by drawing a marquee around just those points.

NEW IN 7: With Illustrator 7, you can permanently switch to the Direct Selection tool by pressing A on the keyboard. Press A again to choose the Group Selection tool. Another press of the A key takes you back to the Direct Selection tool.

The Shift key is used with the Direct Selection tool to select additional points or segments or to deselect previously selected points. If only one segment or point on a path is selected and you Shift-click on that segment or point with the Direct Selection tool, the entire path is deselected.

Too Many Selection Tools?

Marcia: I'm getting mouse wrist because of all these different selection tools.

Toulouse: How so?

Marcia: It's such a pain to keep going up to the toolbox to select different selection tools. And then there are the other tools as well....

Toulouse: You use the toolbox to access the selection tools?

Marcia: No, I have them flown in from Hackensack when I wanna use them. Of *course* I use the toolbox.

Toulouse: Actually, you can use the keyboard to jump around each of the selection tools.

Marcia: I have a keyboard. Tell me more.

Toulouse: No matter what tool is selected in the toolbox, pressing ⌘ [Ctrl] will toggle to the Selection tool.

Marcia: Wow! This is great!

Toulouse: You can toggle between the regular Selection tool and the Direct Selection tool by pressing ⌘-tab [Ctrl+tab].

Marcia: No kidding.

Toulouse: When you have the Direct Selection tool, press Option, and you'll access the Group Selection tool!

Marcia: You should really write a book on this stuff....

If you press the Shift key, the Selection tool works as a toggle between selecting and deselecting paths. While you hold down the Shift key and click on paths that are not selected, they become selected. When paths that are selected are Shift-clicked, they become deselected. The Shift key can be used in this way to add to or subtract from a series of selected paths.

Selecting items with the Direct Selection tool can be a little intimidating because Anchor Points show up as *solid* when selected and *hollow* when deselected. Furthermore, a selected segment does not have any Anchor Points selected; instead, any Control Handles and Control Handle Lines associated with that segment become selected. If there are no Control Handles associated with a segment, such as a segment that is in between two Straight Corner Points, then it is difficult to tell which segment is selected.

After you select a point or series of points, those selected points can be manipulated in a number of ways, including being moved and transformed (via the transformation tools) and having certain filters applied to them. Individual segments and series of segments can be selected and modified in the same way points are transformed.

The Group Selection Tool

The Group Selection tool is driven by a very cool concept: it first selects a path, then the group that the path is in, then the group that the other group with the path is in, and so on.

For the Group Selection tool to work properly, the first path or paths can be chosen by either clicking them or drawing a marquee around them. To select the group that a particular path is in, however, requires you to click one of the initially selected paths. To select the next group also requires a click; if you drag at any point, only the paths you drag over are selected.

This process may seem a little fuzzy at first, but it will get easier the more you use the Group Selection tool. Remember, the first time you select something with the Group Selection tool, you select only the paths you click or drag over. The next time you click an already-selected path, all the paths in its group will be selected.

CAUTION

Still confused about how the Shift key selects and deselects paths? I can make it worse. The Shift key is an odd duck when used with the Group Selection tool. What happens when you click an unselected path with this tool while holding down the Shift key? The path is selected. But what happens when you click a selected path? The process deselects *just one path.* What makes more sense to me is if you would click again with the Shift key, and it then would deselect the entire group. Nope. Ain't gonna happen. The Shift key works as a toggle on the one path you are clicking: selecting it, deselecting it, and so on.

Dragging a marquee around paths with the Group Selection tool works only for the first series of clicks; dragging another marquee, even over the already-selected paths, just reselects those paths.

If you have selected several paths at once, clicking a selected path selects only the group that the selected path is in. If other selected paths are in different groups, those groups are not selected until you click those paths with the Group Selection tool. However, clicking multiple times on any of the paths in the selected group continues to select "up" in the group that the selected path is part of.

The Group Selection tool is the most useful when dealing with graphs and blends, but it can be used in a number of other situations to greatly enhance your control of what is and is not selected. People who are always ungrouping and regrouping paths (groupies) can greatly benefit from using the Group Selection tool. In fact, proper use of this tool prevents you from ever having to ungroup and regroup objects for workflow reasons.

POWER TIP: You can access the Group Selection tool when the Direct Selection tool is selected by holding down the Option key. If the Direct Selection tool is not chosen, then select it by holding down the ⌘ [Ctrl] key (you may have to press ⌘-tab [Ctrl+tab] to toggle from the Selection tool to the Direct Selection tool) and pressing the Option [Alt] key at the same time.

Selecting, Moving, and Deleting Entire Paths

Usually, the best way to select a path that is not currently selected is by clicking it with the regular Selection tool, which highlights all the points on the path and enables you to move, transform, or delete that entire path.

To select more than one path, you can use a number of different methods. The most basic method is to hold down the Shift key and click the successive paths with the Selection tool, selecting one more path with each Shift-click. Shift-clicking a selected path with the Selection tool deselects that particular path. Drawing a marquee around paths with the Selection tool selects all paths that at least partially fall into the area drawn by the marquee. When drawing a marquee, be sure to place the cursor in an area where there is nothing. Finding an empty spot may be difficult to do in Preview mode because Fills from various paths may cover any white space available. Drawing a marquee with the Selection tool when the Shift key is depressed selects nonselected paths and deselects currently selected paths.

If paths are part of either a compound path or a group, all other paths in that compound path or group are also selected.

To move a path, click the path and drag (in one motion) with the Selection tool. To move several paths, select the paths and then click an already-selected path with the regular Selection tool or the Direct Selection tool and drag.

CAUTION If you have been selecting multiple paths by using the Shift key, be sure to release it before clicking and dragging on the selection. If the Shift key is still pressed, the clicked path becomes deselected, and no paths move. If this does happen, just Shift-click the paths that were deselected and drag.

To delete an entire path, select it with the Selection tool and press the Delete key. To delete multiple paths, select them and press the Delete key.

Often, many objects need to be moved and duplicated at the same time. To duplicate paths when moving them, hold down the Option [Alt] key while the mouse button is released.

The short grass, long grass, and silhouetted horses can be duplicated the same way, by choosing one and dragging it to the left or right and pressing Option [Alt] while the mouse button is released.

Choosing Select All (⌘-A [Ctrl+A] or ⌘-period [Ctrl+period] when the screen is not redrawing) from the Edit menu selects all paths in the active document. If a type tool is selected and there is an insertion point in the text, all the type in that story will be selected.

Choosing Select None (⌘-Shift-A) [Ctrl+Shift+A] from the Edit menu deselects all selected objects. Select None does *not* work with type selected with a type tool although I'm told that it may work in a 7.x release.

Selecting, Moving, and Deleting Portions of Paths

To select just a portion of a path, you *must* use the Direct Selection tool. To select an Anchor Point or a line segment, simply click it. To select several individual points or paths, click the points or paths to be selected while holding down the Shift key. Series of points and paths can be selected by dragging a marquee across the paths that are to be selected.

Individual points that are selected become solid squares. If these points are Smooth, Curved Corner, or Combination Corner Points, Control Handles appear from the selected Anchor Point.

Line segments that have at least one Anchor Point that is either a Smooth, Curved Corner, or Combination Corner Point may display a Control Handle Line and Control Handle coming out from that Anchor Point. Samples of each of these selected types of Anchor Points are shown in Figure 3-25.

To move these selected points or paths, release the Shift key and click a selected path or point and drag.

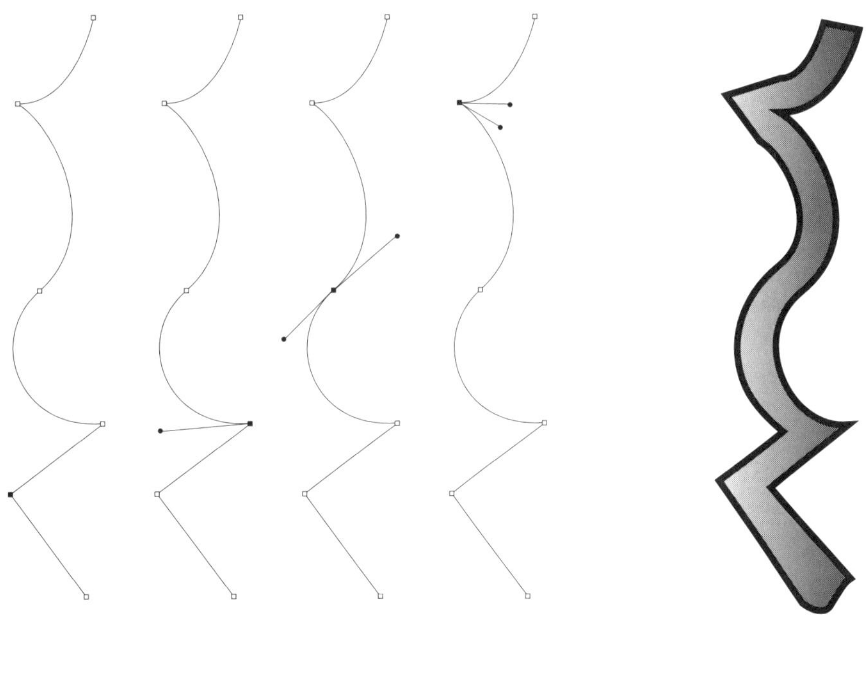

Figure 3-25: The four different types of Anchor Points when selected

Illustrator doesn't tell you when a straight line segment is selected or which one is selected. The first time you click a straight line segment, all the Anchor Points on the path appear as hollow squares, which is just telling you that something on that path is selected. Selected points turn black, and curved line segments have one or more Control Handles and Control Handle Lines sticking out from the ending Anchor Points, but straight line segments don't do anything when selected. The inventive side of you may think that you can get around this problem by dragging the selected segments to a new location or by copying and pasting them and then undoing — but this solution doesn't work because of Illustrator's habit of selecting all points on paths when undoing operations on those paths.

POWER TIP

When you run into this problem of not knowing if a straight segment is selected, do the following: Instead of moving, copying, or pasting, simply whack the good ol' Delete key, and whatever disappears is what you had selected. Now when you undo, just the segments that were selected before the deletion are still selected, not the entire path.

To delete points and segments, select them as described previously and then press Delete. Remember that line segments exist only when there is one point on either side of the segment. Even if the line segment is not selected, if one of its Anchor Points is deleted, the line segment is deleted as well. A path is made up of points, and those points are connected via segments. If the points are gone, the paths disappear along with them. But if you delete all the segments, all the points can still remain.

Portions of paths can be duplicated when pressing the Option [Alt] key while the mouse button is being released. Duplicating segments also duplicates the Anchor Points on either side of that segment.

Locking and Hiding Objects

All objects in Illustrator can be locked or hidden — including guides. Locking and hiding work about the same, and the results are only marginally different. In a way, Hiding is an "invisible lock."

Locking

To lock an object, select it and choose Object⇨Lock (⌘-L) [Ctrl+L]. The selected object is not only locked but also deselected. In fact, an object is unselectable when locked. Locked objects cannot be moved or changed, but they are always visible and will always print (locked objects cannot be hidden). Because a locked object can't be selected, it can't be changed, and in Illustrator, as in most Macintosh applications, objects can be modified only when selected.

A locked object remains locked when the document is saved and closed. As a result, locked objects are still locked the next time the document is opened. Locked objects print with no indication as to whether they are locked or not.

Holding down Option and choosing Object⇨Lock or typing ⌘-Option-L [Ctrl+Alt+L] locks all the objects that are not selected.

To change a locked object, choose Object⇨Unlock (⌘-Shift-L) [Ctrl+Shift+L], unlocking (and selecting) all objects. There is no way to unlock just a few objects locked with the Lock command.

A tricky way to invisibly "copyright" your illustration is to create a small text box in a far corner of the pasteboard with your copyright information in it, color the text white, and lock the text box. No one will know it is there, and it can't be easily selected. In fact, it'll even print if it is placed on top of a background in another program.

I like to lock objects under the following circumstances:

- When the document is full of complex artwork, so I can do a Select All and not have to wait forever for the selection to finish
- When I don't want to accidentally move or change certain artwork
- When I can't easily select paths that are under other paths (in which case, I lock the ones on top)
- When I have to fit an illustration into a certain area (in which case, I'll create a box of that size and lock it so I have an instant boundary to work with)

Hiding

Sometimes, you don't want to see certain objects on your document page — perhaps because they obstruct your view of other objects or they take a long time to redraw. In these cases, it's a good idea to hide the objects in question. To do so, select them and then choose Object⇨Hide Selection (⌘-U) [Ctrl+U].

Hidden objects are invisible and unselectable; they still exist in the document, but they do not print. When a document is reopened, hidden objects reappear.

Holding down Option [Alt] and choosing Object⇨Hide Selection or typing ⌘-Option-U [Ctrl+Alt+U] hides all the objects that are *not* selected.

To show (and select) all hidden objects, choose Object⇨Show All (⌘-Shift-U) [Ctrl+Shift+U]. Think of it as "unhide." There is no way to show just a few of the hidden objects when using the Show All command.

Object Information

Choosing Window Show⇨Attributes (F11) brings up the Attributes palette. In this palette, notes can be added to any selected object, the path direction can be reversed (if the object is part of a compound path), the center point of the object can be made to display or hide, and the flatness characteristics (output dpi) can be changed. At least one object must be selected in order to choose Attributes.

Another useful way to "copyprotect" your artwork is to select all the objects, and then go to the Attributes palette and enter your copyright information within the palette.

The Attributes palette also allows you to set a URL for an selected object or objects. This feature is discussed in more detail in Chapter 16: "Illustrator and the Web."

Stacking Order

One of the crucial concepts that you'll need to understand in the world of Adobe Illustrator is that of stacking order. This concept is not the same as the layer concept that is discussed in Chapter 7, but it is rather the forward/backward relationship between objects within each layer.

After you create the first object in Illustrator, the next object is created *above* the first object, or on top of it. The third object is created above both the first and second objects. This cycle continues indefinitely, with objects being stacked on top of one another.

A great deal of planning goes into creating an illustration so that the object you draw first is on the bottom of the pile, and the last thing you draw ends up on the top. To make your life much more pleasant, Illustrator has the capability to move objects up and down (forward or backward) through the stack of objects. In fact, Illustrator's method of moving objects up and down is so simplistic and basic that it is also quite limiting.

You can change the stacking order of objects in Illustrator relative to foreground and background either all the way to the bottom or all the way to the top, or you can move objects up or down through the stacking order. Figure 3-26 shows the same illustration after various objects were moved in the stacking order.

Figure 3-26: The original art (left) and after the stacking order of various pieces has changed (right)

To move an object to the front, choose Object➪Arrange➪Bring To Front (⌘-Shift-]) [Ctrl+Shift+]]. The selected object is brought forward so that it is in front of every other object (but only in that layer — Chapter 7 explains how layers work). If more than one object is selected, the topmost object of the selected group will be at the very top and the bottommost object of the selected group will be beneath all the other selected objects — but all the selected objects will be on top of all the nonselected objects. Bring To Front is not available when no objects are selected. Multiple-selected paths and grouped paths still retain their front/back position relative to each other.

To move an object to the back, choose Object➪Arrange➪Send To Back (⌘- Shift-[) [Ctrl+Shift+[]. The selected object is sent to the back so that it is behind every other object. Send To Back is not available when there are no objects selected. Multiple selected paths and grouped paths still retain their front/back position relative to each other.

Illustrator 7 enables you to move selected objects through the stacking order one object at a time, forward or backward. To move selected objects forward one object at a time, choose Object➪Arrange➪Bring Forward (Command-]) [Ctrl+]]. To move selected objects backward one object at a time, choose Object➪Arrange➪Send Backward (Command-[) [Ctrl+[].

Individual characters in a string of text work in a similar manner to their object cousins when it comes to front/back placement. The first character typed is placed at the bottom of the text block, and the last character typed is placed at the top, as shown in Figure 3-27. To move individual characters forward or backward, you must first choose Type⇨Create Outlines (⌘-Shift-O) [Ctrl+Shift+O] and select the outline of the character you wish to arrange.

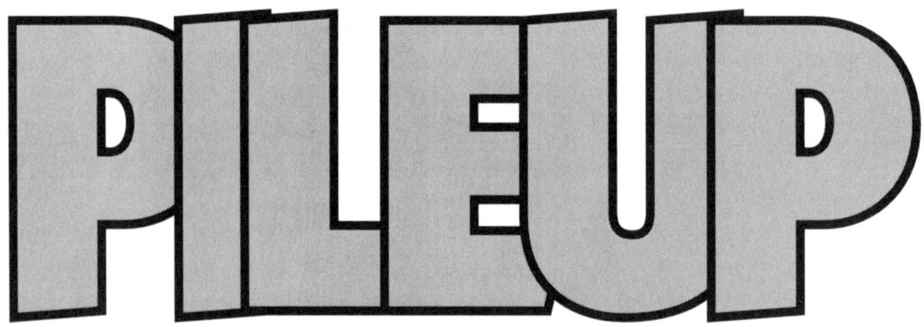

Figure 3-27: Text characters that overlap each other

Try as you might, you cannot change the forward/backward relationship of Strokes and Fills. Strokes are always in front of Fills for the same path. To get the Fill to cover or overlap the Stroke, you must copy the path, use the Paste In Front command (choose Edit⇨Paste In Front or press ⌘-F [Ctrl+F]), and then remove the stroke from the path you just pasted.

Pasting Objects in Front of and Behind Selected Objects

Choosing Paste In Front (⌘-F) [Ctrl+F] from the Edit menu pastes any objects on the Clipboard on top of any selected objects, or on the top of the current layer if no objects are selected.

Choosing Paste In Back (⌘-B) [Ctrl+B] from the Edit menu pastes any objects on the Clipboard behind any selected objects, or on the bottom of the current layer if no objects are selected.

In addition, both Paste In Front and Paste In Back paste objects *in the same* location as the copied object, even from document to document. If the documents are different sizes, Illustrator pastes them in the same location relative to the center of each document. If the Clipboard is empty, or if type selected with a type tool is on the Clipboard, these options are not available.

Copied items in Illustrator always retain their layer name and related layer information. When you copy an item that is on layer "X-Flies" and paste that item in another document that contains an X-Flies layer, the item will appear on the X-Flies layer. If the document doesn't contain that layer, a new layer will be created with that name, and the item will appear on that layer. This only works if the Paste Remembers Layers option is checked in the Layers palette. Chapter 7 contains more information on layers.

Grouping and Ungrouping

Grouping is the process of putting together a series of objects that need to remain spatially constant in relationship to one another. Groups can be made up of as little as one path, and they may contain an unlimited number of objects.

To group objects together, they should first be selected with any of the selection tools. After you select the objects, choose Object➪Group (⌘-G) [Ctrl+G] to make the separate objects stay together when selected.

Selecting any object in a group with the regular Selection tool selects all the objects in that group and makes all the points in a path solid (selected). To see how the Group Selection tool works with selecting groups, see "Using the Group Selection Tool," at the end of this chapter.

Not only can several objects be grouped together, but groups can be grouped together to form a group of groups, in which there is a hierarchical series of grouped groups. In addition, groups can be grouped to individual objects or to several other objects.

After a set of objects or groups is grouped together, grouping it again produces no effect. The computer does not beep at you, display a dialog box, or otherwise indicate that the objects or groups you are attempting to group together are already grouped. Of course, it never hurts to choose Object➪Group (⌘-G) [Ctrl+G] again if you are not sure if they are grouped. If they weren't grouped before, they now are, and if they were grouped before, nothing unusual or unexpected happens. If you choose Group again after the selected objects have already been grouped, nothing happens.

In our example illustration shown in Figure 3-2, the objects will be much easier to manipulate if they are grouped. Group the short grass together as one group, the long grass as one group, the horse outlines and Fills as one group, and the hillside outline and Fills as one group. The tree outline and bark detail should be one group as well.

POWER TIP: If you are having trouble selecting all the objects for each type in a group, choose Object⇨Select⇨Same Paint Style after one object is selected. This process usually (but not always) selects all the objects of one type.

Grouping similar areas is helpful for moving entire areas forward or backward as well as for doing any type of horizontal or vertical movement or transformation upon a set of objects.

Grouping is also helpful for controlling blends.

Ungrouping

To ungroup groups (separate them into standalone paths and objects), choose Object⇨Ungroup (⌘-Shift-G) [Ctrl+Shift+G], and any selected groups become ungrouped. Ungrouping, like grouping, works on one set of groups at a time. For example, if you have two groups that are grouped together, ungrouping that group results in the two original groups. (Don't worry, I'm just as confused as you are in this area. It makes my head do the "Linda Blair.") If Ungroup is chosen again, those two groups will also become ungrouped.

POWER TIP: When you absolutely do not want anything in a group grouped with anything else — and you suspect that there may be several minigroups within the group you have selected — simply press ⌘-Shift-G [Ctrl+Shift+G] several times. You do not need to select the subgroups individually to ungroup them. To get rid of all the groups in your illustration, choose Edit⇨Select All (⌘-A) [Ctrl+A] and then proceed to ungroup (⌘-Shift-G) [Ctrl+Shift+G] several times. To remove certain objects from a group or compound path, select just these objects, cut, and Paste In Front (or Paste In Back).

When you're ungrouping, groups must be selected with either the Group Selection tool or the regular Selection tool.

Using the Group Selection Tool

The Group Selection tool is used primarily to select groups within other groups or individual paths within groups. To access the Group Selection tool, click the Direct Selection tool in the toolbox and drag to the right to the Group Selection tool. Clicking once with the Group Selection tool on any path selects that particular path. Clicking again with the Group Selection tool on the same path selects the group that path is in. Clicking yet again selects the group that the previously selected group is in.

To move a path that is part of a group, do not ungroup the path; instead, select the path with the Group Selection tool and move it.

If you select a path in a group with the Group Selection tool and then click the same path again to move it, the group that path is in will be selected instead. To avoid this problem, either select and move at one time or use the Direct Selection tool for moving.

If several different paths are selected with the Group Selection tool either by dragging a marquee or Shift-clicking, clicking again on a selected path or object selects the group that object is in. If that object's group is already selected, then the group that the selected group is in will be selected.

The Group Selection tool also selects compound paths. One click selects an individual path within the compound path, and the second click selects the entire compound path.

Using the Shift key with the Group Selection tool on selected paths or objects deselects just one path at a time. Shift-clicking a path that has just been deselected reselects that path; it does not deselect the group that path is in.

For quick access to the Group Selection tool, press the Option [Alt] key when the Direct Selection Tool is the active tool. But release the Option [Alt] key before the mouse button is released, or you'll have a duplicated path or object. The Direct Selection tool can be selected by pressing the ⌘ [Ctrl] key (⌘-tab [Ctrl+tab] toggles between the Direct Selection and regular Selection tools). Pressing the ⌘ [Ctrl] and Option [Alt] keys together can be used to access the Group Selection tool, no matter which tool is selected in the toolbox!

Summary

- Use a pressure-sensitive tablet with the Paintbrush tool for the best results.
- The Paintbrush tool creates closed paths.
- To get rid of overlapping inside corners within paintbrush strokes, apply the Unite filter to the paintbrush strokes.
- The Pencil tool creates single paths that are open or closed.
- Erase Pencil tool paths while you're drawing them by pressing ⌘ [Ctrl] and retracing your path.

- Control the roughness of Pencil-tool-generated paths by setting the curve-fitting tolerance *before* you draw with the Pencil tool.
- The Pen tool is the most powerful tool in Illustrator, enabling you to create perfectly formed curves and straight paths.
- Clicking with the Pen tool creates straight line segments; dragging with the Pen tool creates curved segments.
- Keep the distance of Control Handle Lines to about one-third of the length of the affected curved line segment for the best results.
- The Selection tool selects entire paths or groups with one click.
- The Direct Selection tool selects individual points, segments, or portions of paths that are surrounded with a drag marquee.
- Quickly duplicate objects in Illustrator by dragging them and then releasing the mouse button while pressing the Option [Alt] key.
- Locking objects prevents paths from being selected or altered in any way.
- Lock selected objects by pressing ⌘-L [Ctrl+L] or lock unselected objects by pressing ⌘-Option-L [Ctrl+Alt+L]; unlock all locked objects by pressing ⌘-Shift-L [Ctrl+Shift+L].
- Group paths together by selecting more than one path and pressing ⌘-G [Ctrl+G]; ungroup selected groups by pressing ⌘-Shift-G [Ctrl+Shift+G].
- Use the Group Selection tool to select paths and groups within other groups.

CHAPTER 4

Tracing, Grids, and Guides

In This Chapter

- How to use "Templates" for Tracing
- Creating high-quality traceable images
- Manual tracing versus automatic tracing
- Measuring by using the Measure tool
- Measuring by using circles and using the Offset Path filter
- Using the New Grid feature
- Creating and using guides
- How to measure for printing

It's often much easier to create artwork in Illustrator by starting with something to trace, whether it's a logo, a floorplan, or your cousin Fred's disproportionate profile. Even the best artists use some form of template when they draw, to keep proportions consistent, to get angles just right, and for other reasons that help them to achieve the best possible result.

This chapter discusses different methods and techniques for tracing different types of artwork within Illustrator (and even outside of Illustrator). Don't think of this as cheating, but instead, a way to do better, faster, and more accurate artwork.

Okay, it's cheating just a little bit....

Windows Update

Tracing has gone through a major overhaul, with the elimination of templates and a souped-up Auto Trace tool. While guides are about the same as before, grids have been added.

What's Missing	What Replaces It
Templates	Placed images dimmed via the Layers palette

What's New

The Auto Trace tool can now trace any placed image, and distinguishes colors.

Grids can be placed behind illustrations.

A Teary Farewell to 1-Bit Templates

Version 7 of Adobe Illustrator no longer uses templates. Instead, to do tracing, either manually or automatically (using the Auto Trace tool), you can use any image just by placing it into Illustrator.

Templates from older versions of Illustrator consisted of 1-bit PICT or PAINT images (black and white only) that were limited to certain sizes. They looked ghastly onscreen, and getting the right pixels to appear black (gray, actually) was always a tedious process in Photoshop.

A few things are different, now that placed images are considered templates by Illustrator.

There is no Hide/Show Template option. Instead, templates are placed image objects that can be selected and hidden (⌘-U) [Ctrl+U]. However, I recommend setting up a special layer just for your placed image if you'll be using it as a template.

Templates will print. This is usually a bad thing. If your image is on its own, separate layer, however, you can turn layer printing off for that layer in the Layer Options dialog box.

Images must be dimmed manually. Templates of the past were always gray, making it easy to spot your paths, points, and handles. Placed images can be any color. However, you can dim them by choosing the Dim Images option in that layer's Layer Options dialog box.

Templates can move. Using a placed image as a template gives you both the freedom and the problem of being able to move it. The plus side to this is that you can position the image in the best place to trace it; the minus side is that it can be easy to bump accidentally. Lock the image, or even better, lock the image layer.

When Is a Template Not a Template?

The best Illustrator templates were never really templates; they were placed files that you locked into place. You can dim any placed image (see Figure 4-1) by using the following steps:

Figure 4-1: The original image (left) and after dimming (right)

STEPS: Dimming an Image for Tracing

Step 1. Place an image into the document by choosing File➪Place and selecting the image. You can also Rasterize any vector artwork by selecting it and choosing Object➪Rasterize.

(continued)

STEPS: *(continued)*

Step 2. Move the image into the proper position and transform it if necessary.

Step 3. Open the Layers palette by choosing Window⇨Show Layers (F7). In the Layers palette, double-click Layer 1. In the Layer Options dialog box, select the Dim Images checkbox and then click OK.

Dimming an image in Illustrator used to cause severe performance problems in your documents. Oddly enough, it was the dimming of the image, and not the image itself, that caused the performance hit. This is no longer a problem in Illustrator 7.

Placed images work well as templates because their resolution is independent of the Illustrator document. You can scale placed images up or down, *changing their on-screen resolution* as you change their size. For instance, if you scale a 72-dpi image down to one-fourth of its imported size (making the dpi of the placed image 4 x 72 dpi, or 288 dpi), you may zoom in on the image in Illustrator at 400%. At 400%, the placed EPS image still has a 72-dpi resolution because one-fourth of 288 dpi is 72 dpi. The more the placed image's dpi is increased by scaling it down, the more you may zoom in to see the details of the image. If the placed image's dpi is already higher than 72, you'll be able to zoom in to a certain amount and retain quite a bit of detail automatically.

Another plus: A placed image "template" is a full-color template that keeps all the shading and colors and enables you to see all the fine details easily.

Tracing

Now that you've got your template (placed image) all set up, you're ready to trace it — or so you would think. There are lots of different ways to go about tracing, and I've included the "best of the best" techniques in this section to help you muddle through this mess.

You can trace templates in two ways: manually and automatically. Manually tracing consists of using the Pencil and Pen tools to tediously trace the edges of a template — often a very time-consuming task. Using the Auto Trace tool, though, speeds up the process.

Automatically Tracing Placed Images

The Auto Trace tool (hidden in the same slot as the Blend tool) can be used for basic tracing of placed images, both black and white and full color. However, the results obtained by using this tool are usually less than satisfactory, requiring a great deal of time-consuming cleanup.

To use the Auto Trace tool, click the edge of a colored area of a placed image; the Auto Trace tool attempts to trace the edge of a solid area and applies the current Paint Style to it.

POWER TIP: Always use the Auto Trace tool from the outside in. This makes sure that bigger paths around the outside don't overlap the inside paths.

The Curve Fitting Tolerance setting in the General Preferences dialog box (⌘-K) [Ctrl+K] directly affects the Auto Trace tool in much the same way that it affects the Pencil tool — the higher the number, the less precise the tracing. A Curve Fitting Tolerance setting of 2 or 3 works pretty well for automatically tracing templates, but neither setting enables the Auto Trace tool to follow the ridges created from the template's diagonal and curved edges.

Manual Tracing

Most designers prefer manually tracing templates. Using the Pen and Pencil tools provides illustrators with a level of precision not found with the Auto Trace tool. Furthermore, illustrators may add detail, remove oddities, and change curves, angles, and the like to their satisfaction (as opposed to an image that has been automatically traced, which gives it a more final appearance with less editability).

I've found that a combination of manual and automatic tracing works quite nicely for drawing fairly basic illustrations, especially those with type and straight lines. Automatically trace the basic shapes first and then use the path editing tools to add or remove Anchor Points and move paths so that the image has a consistent look. After fixing the traced section, use the Pen and Pencil tools to draw in the intricate shapes.

About Adobe Streamline 4

Adobe Streamline is the Auto Trace tool on a natural high (actually, it's more like a coke rush, I'm told, but I hate to equate software to drugs . . . though both can be addicting and expensive). Anyway, Streamline can automatically trace full-color images, *retaining their color* automatically.

Adobe Streamline is so cool that I've given it its own chapter, along with its big cousin Adobe Dimensions, later in the book. It takes tracing images to a whole 'nother plane, like . . . [yet another unsavory reference, this time deleted by a savory editor]. Streamline's tools, features, and interface are discussed in Chapter 19.

Using Layers for Tracing

You can use layers for more than just dimming images for tracing.

One of the unsung features of Illustrator's layers (more features are sung in Chapter 7) is the capability to show some layers in Preview mode, and others in Artwork mode.

This is great for tracing because now you can take any placed image, put it on a layer that is shown in Preview mode, lock that layer (so the "template" isn't moved), and then create a new layer *above* the existing one and set it to Artwork view. Not only will you be able to see the placed image in color, but the paths you draw will be outlines with the placed image visible below them.

You can also use layers to turn off the printing for placed images used as templates. Lock the template layer so you don't move it accidentally, and then use the Hide Layer function (in the Layers palette) to hide the artwork when you don't want to view it. Finally, when you're done with the template, remove it quickly by deleting the layer it is on.

Measuring

You can measure distances in Illustrator in four ways:

- Use the Measure tool
- Use the rulers along the side of the document window
- Place objects whose dimensions are known against the edges
- Eyeball it (popular since the first artist painted his recollections of the preceding day's battle with the saber-toothed animals of his time)

The Measure Tool

The fastest way to obtain a precise, exact measurement in Illustrator is to use the Measure tool (shown in Figure 4-2). As soon as you click an object with the Measure tool, the Info palette appears, showing the distance between the location first clicked and the next location clicked or the distance between where the tool was first clicked and where the mouse was released after dragging.

Figure 4-2: The Measure tool

If the Snap to point option in the General Preferences dialog box (⌘-K) is checked, the Measure tool automatically snaps to nearby paths and points.

As soon as the Measure tool measures a distance, it routes that information to the Move dialog box, shown in Figure 4-3. The next time you open the Move dialog box (by choosing Object➪Transform➪Move, double-clicking the Selection tool), it will hold the values sent by the Measure tool.

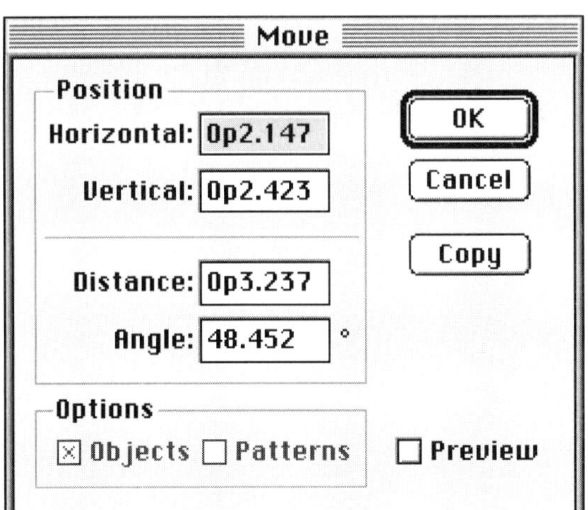

Figure 4-3: The Move dialog box

Measuring Trouble

Jack: You know, my measurements never seem accurate.

Toulouse: Really? How far are they off?

Jack: It varies. Sometimes they'll be right on, other times they'll be half the size, twice as big.... Once they were 1/16 the actual size!

Toulouse: I hate to ask this, but what are you using to measure your on-screen objects?

Jack: The rulers on the monitor, of course.

Toulouse: Well, that's very weird. I've always found those rulers to be quite accurate.

Jack: You've used my computer?

Toulouse: No, but I have rulers on my system too.

Jack: But how do you know they're the same as mine?

Toulouse: You know, I'm thinking there's a lack of communication somewhere here....

Jack: The real problem was getting them to stay in place.

Toulouse: Huh?

(continued)

(continued)

Jack: Yeah, I ended up hot-gluing each ruler to the edges of the monitor. Duct tape would've been my next choice.

Toulouse: You know, there are rulers *within* Illustrator.

Jack: Yer kidding me.

Toulouse: Command-R [Ctrl+R]. Check it out.

Know anything about PostScript? Well, one thing you absolutely have to know is that pages in PostScript are always measured from the lower-left corner of the page. That means moving something along the *Y* axis with a positive number will move it up, not down. It's a math thing. Your geometry teacher would've thought that's the way to measure things, while the rest of the world thinks it's stupid.

If you hold down the Shift key, you can constrain the movement of the measuring line to the following:

- In Preview mode, the measuring line defines a 45° or 90° angle if no paths or Filled parts of paths are under the cursor.
- In Artwork mode, your cursor snaps to the paths.
- In Preview mode, the cursor snaps to any Filled part of any path.

Sizing Up Objects with the Transform Palette

The Transform palette (choose Window⇨Show Transform) shows the height, width, and location of any select path or paths, as illustrated in Figure 4-4.

Figure 4-4: The Transform palette

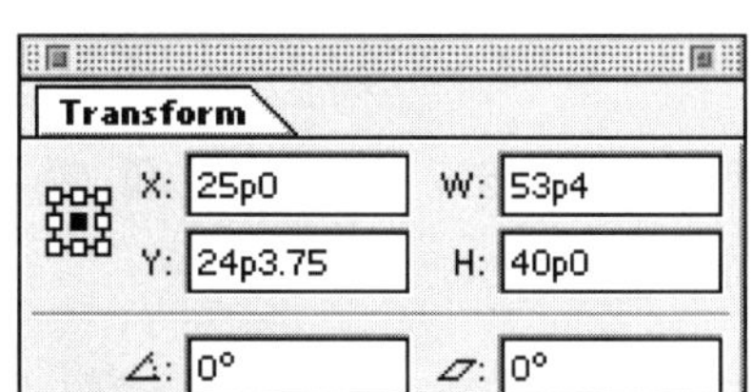

X and *Y* show the location of the object on the page, measured (as always) from the lower-left corner.

W is the width of the selected object (or the total width of the selected objects when more than one is selected), while *H* is the height or total height of the selected object or objects.

All these measurements will be in points — unless, of course, you know how to change the measurement units, which, coincidentally, is the topic of my next section.

Changing the Measurement Units

When you first use Illustrator, you'll be faced with points. That's great for type and numbering star tips, but when was the last time your art director said, "I'd like you to design a 360 x 288 ad and make the logo at least 144 high." (Or your grandmother said to you, "Gosh, you must be at least 5,600 tall, maybe taller. You've grown at least 100 since the last time I saw you. And does your mother let you wear *that* to school?!")

Points don't work for everything, so Adobe lets us change the measurement units to picas, inches, centimeters, or millimeters. The way to choose this is to temporarily indicate a different unit of measurement each time you enter a value, by appending a character or two to the end of your numerical value. For instance, to enter two inches you'd type **2 inch, 2 in,** or **2".** To enter two millimeters, you'd enter **2 mm.** To enter 2 points you'd enter **2 pt** or **p 2.** You can enter picas by putting a *p* after the number, such as **2p** for 2 picas. You can also combine picas and points by sticking a *p* between them, as in **2p6** for two picas, six points. For centimeters, type 2 cm.

Illustrator 7 adds two new measurement systems, both based on previously existing systems (from Versions 6 and before). Centimeters is one such system (there are 100 centimeters in a meter, and 10 millimeters in a centimeter, if you live in the U.S. and have not yet been metricized). The other system, which is much more significant to Illustrator users, is the pica/point system. When the pica measurement system is selected in the Units and Undo Preferences, measurements are displayed using the common (common to typesetters and designers, anyway) system of picas followed by points. So a distance of three picas and six points is displayed as 3p6. Such a measurement would be displayed as 42 pts. using the Point System.

A quick refresher on measurement units and their relations:

1"	=	6p	=	72 pts.	=	25.4 mm	=	2.54 cm
.17"	=	1p	=	12 pts.	=	4.2 mm	=	.42 cm
.01"	=	p1	=	1 pts.	=	.35 mm	=	.035 cm
.04"	=	p2.83	=	2.83 pts.	=	1 mm	=	.1 cm
.39	=	2p4.35	=	28.35 pts.	=	10 mm	=	1 cm

To permanently alter your measurement units, choose File➪Preferences➪Units and Undo and change the Measurement Units pop-up menu to the measurement system you want.

Using Rulers

You can toggle rulers on and off by choosing View➪Show/Hide Rulers (⌘-R) [Ctrl+R]. Normally, the rulers measure up and across from the document's lower-left corner; however, you can alter this orientation by dragging the ruler origin (where the zeros are) from its position in the upper-left corner, between where the two rulers meet. Because rulers take up valuable on-screen real estate, it's usually a good idea to leave them turned off unless you are constantly measuring things or you want to display your illustration at a higher magnification. Rulers are easy to show and hide: just press ⌘-R [Ctrl+R] when you want to see them; press ⌘-R [Ctrl+R] again to lose them.

If you change the ruler origin to the middle of the document page, try to move it back to a corner when you are finished. When you zoom in, rulers may be your only indicator of your location within the document.

Finally, you can double-click in the origin box of the rulers and the origin resets to the lower-left corner, where it belongs.

Rulers now appear along the top and left edges of the document window (they used to appear inexplicably at the bottom and right of the document window). The rulers now show the measurement systems of picas and centimeters, if you're using one of those two systems. However, the rulers still measure from the lower-left corner of the document.

One of the rulers' nicest features is the display of dotted lines corresponding to the cursor's position. And yet, at times, measuring with rulers works no better than eyeballing: although the process requires precision, you are limited by the rulers' hash marks in pinpointing the cursor's exact position. The rulers are best suited for measuring when the document is at a very high zoom level.

Measuring with Objects

Using objects to compare distances can be more effective than using either the Measure tool or the rulers, especially when you need to place objects precisely — for example, when you want several objects to be the same distance from one another.

If you place a circle adjacent to an object (so that the objects' edges touch), you know that the second object is placed correctly when it's aligned to the circle's other side. (A circle is the object most commonly used because the diameter is constant.)

You can use other objects for measuring, including the following:

- Squares — when you need to measure horizontal and vertical distances
- Rectangles — when the horizontal and vertical distances are different
- Lines — when the distance applies to only one direction

To enable better precision, turn the measuring object into a guide. (Guides are discussed in more detail later in this chapter.)

Using Offset Path (for Equidistant Measuring)

Sometimes, you may want to place several objects the same distance from a central object. Using any of the previously mentioned measuring techniques can be time-consuming and even inaccurate, especially when you deal with complex images. Illustrator's Offset Path (see Figure 4-5), however, enables you to automatically align objects equidistantly from a central object.

More Measuring Woes

Furley: This isn't working. I'm no mathematician.

Toulouse: Trouble with rulers?

Furley: Yeah. I want to place objects at certain distances from the edges of different pieces of artwork.

Toulouse: Why's that a problem?

Furley: Well, my object is at about 2.3" across the page, and 6.7" from the bottom. I can't work this way.

Toulouse: You can reset the way the rulers measure, so you can measure from the top left of any artwork on the page.

Furley: Without doing the math?

Toulouse: No math. Just drag the origin (that's where the rulers meet at the top left of the page) to where you want to measure from.

Furley: Wow! This is great! I haven't been this excited since Stanley took off for his own show! Which then bombed, of course, leaving me on a top 10 show.

Toulouse: If I recall, wasn't the ratings high point *before* you came on the show?

Furley: I've never really done the math....

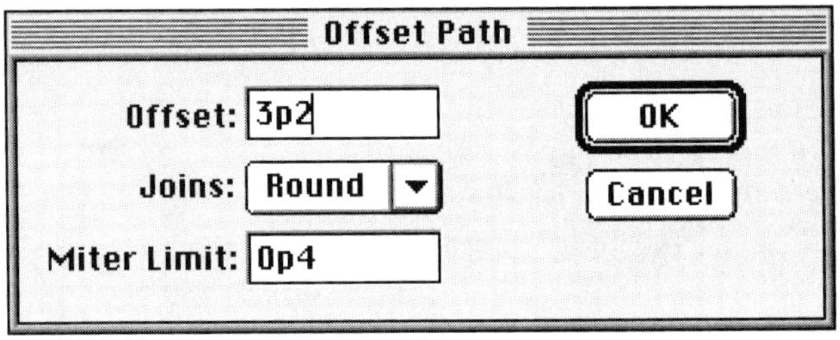

Figure 4-5: The Offset Path dialog box

First, select the central object. Then choose Object➪Path➪Offset Path and enter the desired distance (in points, millimeters, or inches) in the Offset text field. After the new path is created, check the corner areas to see whether there are any overlapping areas that appear as loops. If so, use Unite to eliminate these unsightly aberrations by choosing Object➪Pathfinder➪Unite. Change the new path into a guide and align your objects to this guide.

Grids

Of all the nifty new features, enhancements, and changes in Illustrator 7, there is nothing I've found more useful on a day-to-day basis than the new Grid feature. Grids act as a framework for your artwork, providing an easy method for aligning and positioning images. Figure 4-6 shows an Illustrator document that has grids turned on.

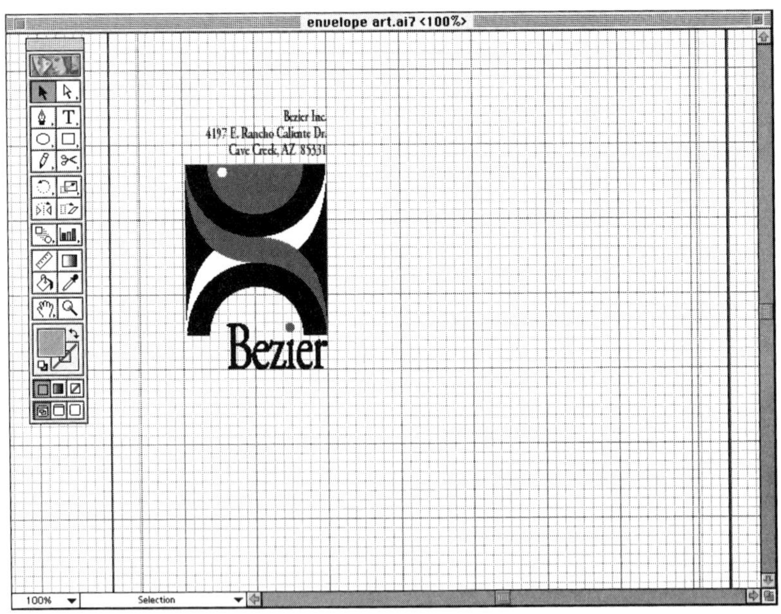

Figure 4-6: A document with Illustrator's Grid function turned on

Display grids by choosing View⇨Show Grid (⌘-") [Ctrl+"]. Once grids are displayed, you can automatically snap to the grid points by turning on the Snap to feature: choose View⇨Snap to Grid (⌘-Shift-") [Ctrl+Shift+"]. Turn off grids by choosing View⇨Hide Grid (⌘-") [Ctrl+"].

Grids start from the origin of your document (usually the lower-left corner). If you want to change the position of the grid, you can do so by dragging the origin point (at the Origin Marker where the rulers meet) to the new starting position for the grid. Reset the grid position (and the ruler origin) by double-clicking the Origin Marker.

POWER TIP: If you would like grids to be displayed in each new document, open your Adobe Illustrator Startup file in your Illustrator Plug-Ins folder and turn on grids in that document. Then save the Startup file. All new documents will have grids displayed when you first create them.

Grid Color, Style, and Spacing

You can customize the way grids look by changing the Grid preferences. Choose File⇨Preferences⇨Guides & Grid, and the Guides & Grid Preferences dialog box (Figure 4-7) appears. Here you can change the grid color and spacing. Pick a new color from the list of colors, or choose Other to use the color picker to pick a new color for your grids. Because I'm just too darn picky, I pick cyan, and then go to the color picker and lighten it substantially. The result is non-repro-blue-looking lines that make my grid resemble graph paper (which I've always thought should be called grid paper, anyway).

You can also choose between lines and dots as the grid style. I prefer to use lines for my grid, as dots can turn an already busy-looking page into one with all sorts of, well, dots all over the place.

To change the space between the major (darker) gridlines, enter a value in the Gridline Every text field. To create subdivisions (minor) between the dark values, enter a number of how many sections should be created between the main lines. If you enter 1 as the value, no subdivisions are created. Because you're defining the number of divisions, not the number of lines, entering a 2 will create one line between the two main lines. The standard 1-inch gridline with eight subdivisions creates $^1/_8$-inch squares.

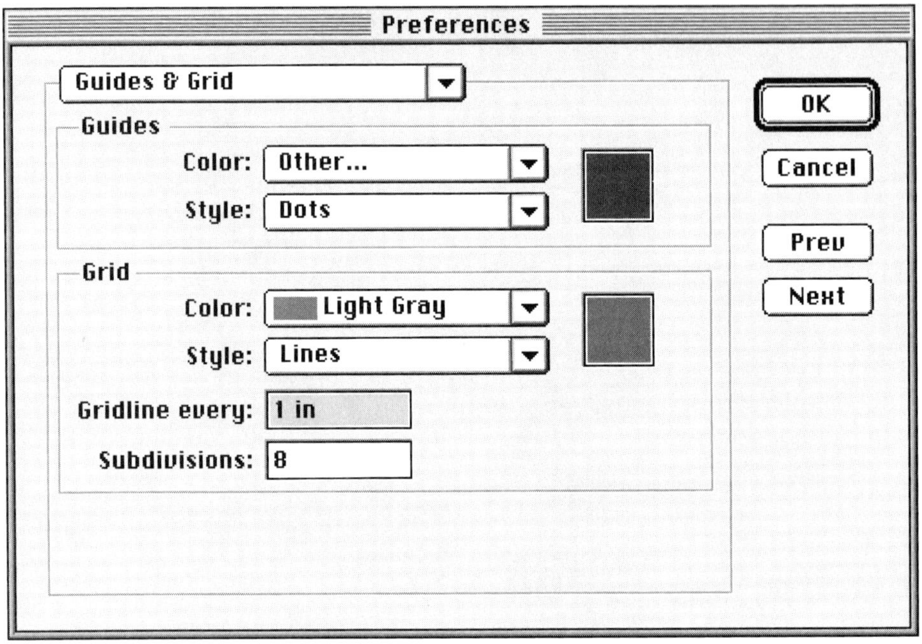

Figure 4-7: The Guides & Grid Preferences dialog box

The Magically Spinning Grid

Your grid doesn't have to consist of just vertical and horizontal lines, however. You can rotate the grid to any angle you like by changing the Constrain Angle in General Preferences (⌘-K) [Ctrl+K]. Figure 4-8 shows a grid set at an angle of 6.275°. This is perfect for working with angled artwork; even if only a portion of the artwork is at an angle, the Constrain Angle can be set temporarily to the angle of the artwork.

The Secret Power of Grids

If what I've listed above were all that grids could do, I'd be way happy. After all, this is a feature that makes Illustrator closer to CAD programs without losing any of its wonderful design capabilities. But the one, secret feature of grids that Adobe doesn't want you to know about (actually, I'm sure they don't really care either way) is this: Grids are the perfect transparency indicator layer.

Figure 4-8: A grid rotated to 6.275°

What the heck am I talking about? Well, because Illustrator's paper color (the document and the artboard) is always white, it can be hard to tell if paths are Filled with white, Filled with None, or are the hole part of a compound path. Displaying the grid ends the confusion instantly. Objects with a white Fill don't display the grid behind them; objects with a Fill of None or that are simply a hole in a compound path show the grid through their openings. Even if you aren't going to use the grid for alignment or snap-to, the transparency indicator feature is a great way to know *exactly* what's going on with questionably filled paths. Figure 4-9 shows objects with Fills of white and None on a grid background.

Guides

Guides are teeny, tiny little people who show you around Illustrator. The more of them you make, the easier it is to use the program. (Uh huh . . . I know, let you know when the shuttle lands . . . Sigh.)

Okay, actually, *guides* are dotted lines that help you align artwork. Guides do not print, and they are saved with documents. In Illustrator and most desktop-publishing software, guides are straight lines extending from one edge of a document to the other. But in Illustrator, you can also turn *any* path into a guide (see the following section).

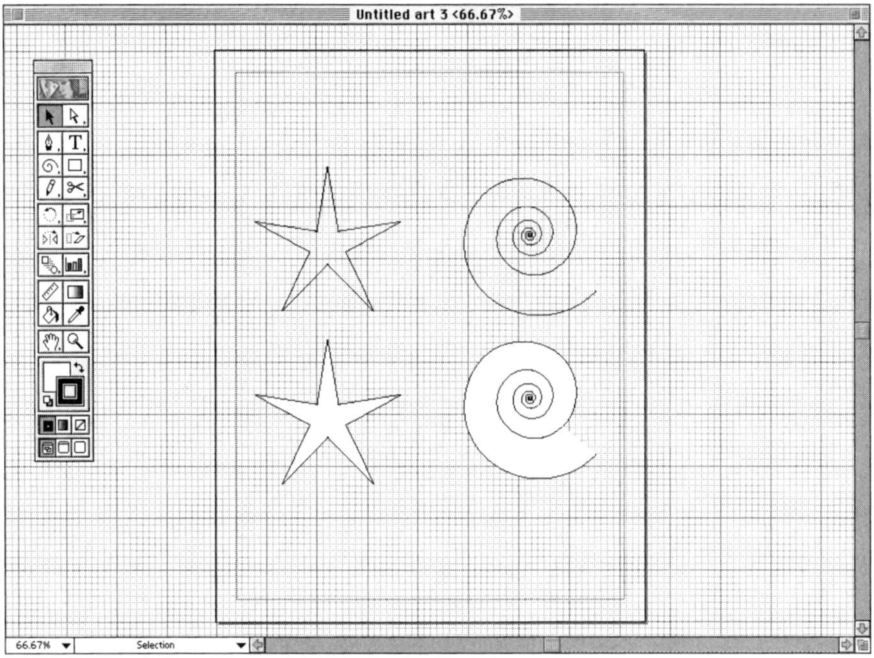

Figure 4-9: The top objects have a Fill of None, the bottom objects have a Fill of white

Creating Guides

You can create guides in two ways: by pulling them out from the rulers and by transforming paths into guides.

To pull a guide from a ruler, first make the vertical and horizontal rulers visible by choosing View⇨Show Rulers (⌘-R) [Ctrl+R]. To create guides that span the entire Pasteboard, click the vertical or horizontal ruler and drag out.

To transform an existing path into a guide, select the path and choose View⇨Make Guides (⌘-5) [Ctrl+5].

POWER TIP: And now a word about the Magic Rotating Guide (possibly the coolest tip you'll ever learn): When you drag a guide out from the vertical ruler, hold down Option [Alt], and the vertical guide becomes a horizontal guide. And vice versa.

Moving Guides

Moving an unlocked guide is simple — click it and drag. If guides are locked, unlock them by choosing View⇨Lock.

If you aren't sure whether the guides in your document are locked or unlocked, click and hold on the View menu. If you see a check mark next to Lock Guides, the guides are locked (and all new guides will also be locked). To unlock all the document's guides, choose View➪Lock Guide; to lock guides again, choose View➪Lock Guide (yes, it's a toggle).

All guides in a document have a special status of "lockedness," where all guides are either locked or unlocked. Weirdly enough, however, guides can be locked and unlocked individually as well by selecting them and choosing Object➪Lock (⌘-L) [Ctrl+L] and Object➪Unlock All (⌘-Shift-L) [Ctrl+Shift+ L].

Releasing Guides

To release a guide, or change it into a path, select the guide and choose View➪Release Guides (⌘-Option-5) [Ctrl+Alt+5].

To release multiple guides: First, make sure that the guides are unlocked; in other words, make sure that there's no check mark next to Lock Guides in the View menu. Then select the guides (in the same way you select multiple paths: either drag a marquee around the guides or Shift-click each guide) and choose View➪Release Guides (⌘-5) [Ctrl+5].

Selecting *all* guides — even those that are currently paths — by dragging a marquee or Shift-clicking can be a chore. Here's another way: Make sure that the guides are not locked and choose Edit➪Select All (⌘-A) [Ctrl+Alt]. Then select View➪Release (⌘-Option-6) [Ctrl+Alt+6]. This releases all guides and, more importantly, selects all paths that were formerly guides (all other paths and objects are deselected). Then choose View➪Make Guides (⌘-5) [Ctrl+5] and all guides become guides again and are selected.

For the most part, guides behave exactly like their path counterparts. As long as guides are unlocked, you may select them, hide them, group them, and even paint them (although paint attributes will not be visible on-screen or on a printout until the guides are converted back into paths).

Guide Preferences

In the Guide Preferences (choose File➪Preferences➪Guides & Grid), you can change the style and the color of the guides. Choose a color from the pop-up menu or select Other to choose a color from the color picker. Unlike with grids, I like to use a darker, more vibrant color than a watered-down cyan. No matter which color you choose, keep it different from the Grid color and a contrasting color to colors you're using in your document.

Picas Picas

Chrissy: I'm about to get fired.

Toulouse: I thought you had a stake in the Thighmaster thing....

Chrissy: No, things I print don't measure correctly.

Toulouse: How so?

Chrissy: Well, picas don't equal picas.

Toulouse: Actually, that's a common occurrence. But you're not doing anything wrong.

Chrissy: Pardon me for asking, but why the hell does it happen?

Toulouse: Well, when you measure, you're probably using one of those pica sticks, right?

Chrissy: Sure. It's *the* weapon of the graphic artist.

Toulouse: Okay. The problem is that until just recently, most pica sticks were *traditional picas,* which aren't the same as new *picas,* sometimes called *Adobe picas.*

Chrissy: And traditional picas are different from Adobe picas?

(continued)

Guide Style can be set to either dots or lines; which you choose is a matter of preference. However, you might want to pick the opposite of what you've chosen for grids, to further differentiate the two.

Measuring for Printing

Thinking ahead to the time your job will be printed is always a good thing, and one of the most important areas of printing is both the placement and sizing of your artwork within the Illustrator document. This section deals with production-oriented issues you might face while using Illustrator to create printable pieces.

Stepping

Oftentimes, you'll create something that's quite small and need to have several copies of the artwork on the page at once. Setting up your artwork for optimal spacing and printing is referred to as *stepping.*

Illustrator doesn't do stepping automatically, but it does provide the tools you need to step your artwork.

POWER TIP: The best way to do step and repeat actions is with CSI's Socket Set 2, which includes a Step and Repeat filter with lots of flexibility. See Chapter 15 for a complete description of this amazing third-party filter.

STEPS: Creating Stepped Artwork

Step 1. Make sure the Control palette is open. Then select the finished artwork and open the Move dialog box (double-click the Selection tool).

Step 2. Enter the width of the art in the Horizontal field. Enter **0** (zero) in the Vertical field. Click the Copy button (or press Option-Return).

Step 3. Choose Object⇨Transform⇨Transform Again (⌘-D) [Ctrl+D] to create another duplicate of the artwork. Press ⌘-D [Ctrl+D] until there are the right number of pieces across the page.

Step 4. Select the entire row of artwork, and open the Move dialog box again.

Step 5. Enter **0** (zero) in the Horizontal field, and enter the height of the art in the Vertical field. Click the Copy button (or press Option-Return).

Step 6. Choose Object⇨Transform⇨Transform Again (⌘-D) [Ctrl+D] to create another duplicate of the row of artwork. Press ⌘-D [Ctrl+D] until there are the right number of pieces down the page, as shown in Figure 4-10.

(continued)

Toulouse: Um, yeah...See, there are 72.27 points in an inch using traditional points and picas, and there are 72 points in an inch using Adobe points and picas. So picas, which are 12 points, are different sizes between the two systems.

Chrissy: So, which programs use Adobe picas, and which ones use traditional picas?

Toulouse: Actually, by default, most software uses Adobe picas and points. Some programs, like QuarkXPress, let you switch between them.

Chrissy: How confusing.

Toulouse: It is. You know, step by step....

Creating Cropmarks

Cropmarks are little lines that are designed to help you cut (or crop) along the edges of your illustration after the document has been printed (see Figure 4-11). Crops (that's the slang term; if you're even half cool you won't say "cropmarks") don't intrude on the edges of the artwork, but instead are offset a bit from the corners of where the edges are.

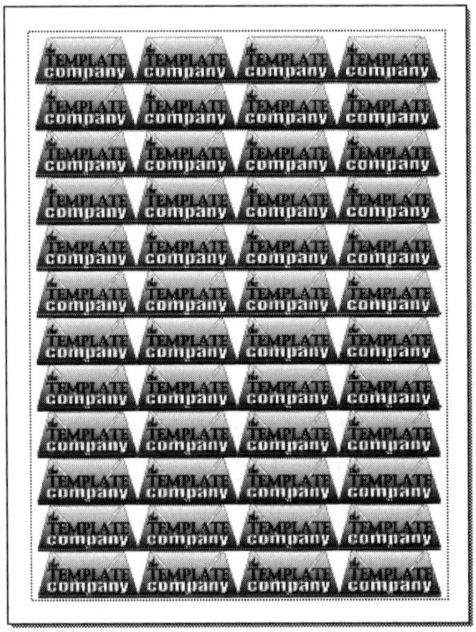

Figure 4-10: Artwork that has been stepped and repeated on a page

Figure 4-11: Cropmarks show where the edges of the artwork are

Unfortunately, you can only create one set of cropmarks per document. Making multiple cropmarks by drawing them yourself or using the Trim Marks filter (Filter⇨Create⇨Trim Marks) isn't enough for color separations; black cropmarks that you create by drawing may be 100% of process colors but will not contain any other spot colors you may have in your illustration. (This problem is the result of a serious limitation in Illustrator: the program does not allow you to choose "registration" as a color, which would print on every different color plate.) Trim marks created with the Trim Marks filter are 100% black.

Here's a workaround: Choose the cropmarks and/or trim marks you created and Stroke them with 100% of all four process colors when you are printing out four-color separations. If you are printing out spot-color separations, you must copy the cropmarks, choose Edit⇨Paste in Front (⌘-F) [Ctrl+F] or

Edit⇨Paste in Back (⌘-B) [Ctrl+B], and then color the Stroke of the crops with the spot color you are using, choosing the Overprint Strokes option in the Paint Style palette. Additional cropmarks need to be pasted in front or pasted in back for every additional color separation in your document.

To transform a selected rectangle drawn with the rectangle tool into cropmarks, choose Object⇨Cropmarks⇨Make.

CAUTION

The rectangle can only be modified prior to becoming cropmarks by moving it or resizing it via the Scale tool. If any transformation is done to the rectangle, a message appears saying that you can only make cropmarks out of a single rectangle. If a rectangle is drawn with a Constrain Angle set to an angle other than 0°, 90°, 180°, or 270° (–90°), you will not be able to make cropmarks out of that rectangle.

If you choose Object⇨Cropmarks⇨Make when nothing is selected, cropmarks will appear around the edge of the single full page. If Tile Imageable Areas is enabled in Document Setup, the cropmarks will appear only around the first page. If crops are set to the size of the page and the page is moved with the Page tool, or if the document has been resized with the Document Setup dialog box, the cropmarks *will not move*.

To release selected cropmarks, choose Object⇨Cropmarks⇨Release. If the cropmarks were created from a rectangle, then that rectangle is an editable path that can be resized and changed back into cropmarks, deleted, or modified. Any rectangle that has been changed back from being a set of cropmarks will have a Fill and Stroke of None.

BY THE WAY

You cannot choose Object⇨Cropmarks⇨Release when no cropmarks are in your document. In addition, Object⇨Cropmarks⇨Release does not release trim marks made with the Filter⇨Create⇨Trim Marks command.

Japanese Cropmarks and Trim Marks

Instead of using standard cropmarks, you can choose to use Japanese cropmarks, which are different looking, yet seemingly no more functional than regular cropmarks. If you check the General Preference setting Japanese Cropmarks, both cropmarks and trim marks will take on the characteristics of Japanese cropmarks (shown in Figure 4-12).

Figure 4-12: Japanese cropmarks

You can create a document that has both traditional and Japanese trim marks. To do so, select the object you would like traditional trim marks on and apply the Create Trim Marks filter (Filter⇨Create⇨Trim Marks). Then check the Japanese Cropmarks check box in General Preferences (File⇨Preferences⇨General, ⌘-K) [Ctrl+K], select the next object, and reapply the filter (just press ⌘-Shift-E [Ctrl+E]). The second set of trim marks will be Japanese.

After checking with several local printers and designers (in the United States), most of them said that they would be able to use the Japanese cropmarks as well as traditional ones. Each of them, however, expressed concern that they might be more prone to trim or measure incorrectly with Japanese cropmarks because of their unfamiliarity with them.

Summary

- Templates are used in Illustrator to make your drawing easier and more precise.
- The Auto Trace tool works with any placed bitmap image.
- Manual tracing will usually generate better results than using the Auto Trace tool.
- The Measure tool provides a quick way to measure distances in your Illustrator documents.
- Measurements generated by the Measure tool will appear in the Move dialog box the next time you open it.
- Guides can be created from any object by selecting the object and pressing ⌘-5 [Ctrl+5].
- You can quickly create document high/wide guides by dragging out from the rulers.
- Use the Copy button within the Move dialog box to step and repeat artwork.

CHAPTER 5

Working with Illustrator Files

In This Chapter

- Setting up and viewing documents
- Managing files
- Opening and saving Illustrator files
- Placing and exporting files

Setting Up a New Document

Illustrator has a way of working that is unique, at least in the world of desktop publishing and graphics. As soon as you run the program, an empty document window appears, ready for you to begin drawing. No hassles. Just an instant drawing area. A new document window that is ready to use is shown in Figure 5-1.

Choosing New (⌘-N) [Ctrl+N] from the File menu when you're already *in* Illustrator creates a brand new document and makes that new document the *active* document. In previous versions of Illustrator, users were hit with an evil dialog box, where they had to indicate which template they wanted to use. Because most users did not normally use templates, this command was altered to instantly create a new document with no questions asked.

Windows Update

Illustrator 7 is more cross-platform than ever, and that means that it can now work with more file types than ever before.

What's Missing	What Replaces It
Opening Templates	Placing images and dimming them via the Layers palette

What's New

A multitude of exporting options and file formats (Choose File⇨Export)

Save A Copy [Ctrl+Alt+S] to save the current state of your work while continuing to work on the original file

Support for placing almost all image and text formats (up from just EPS files in Version 4)

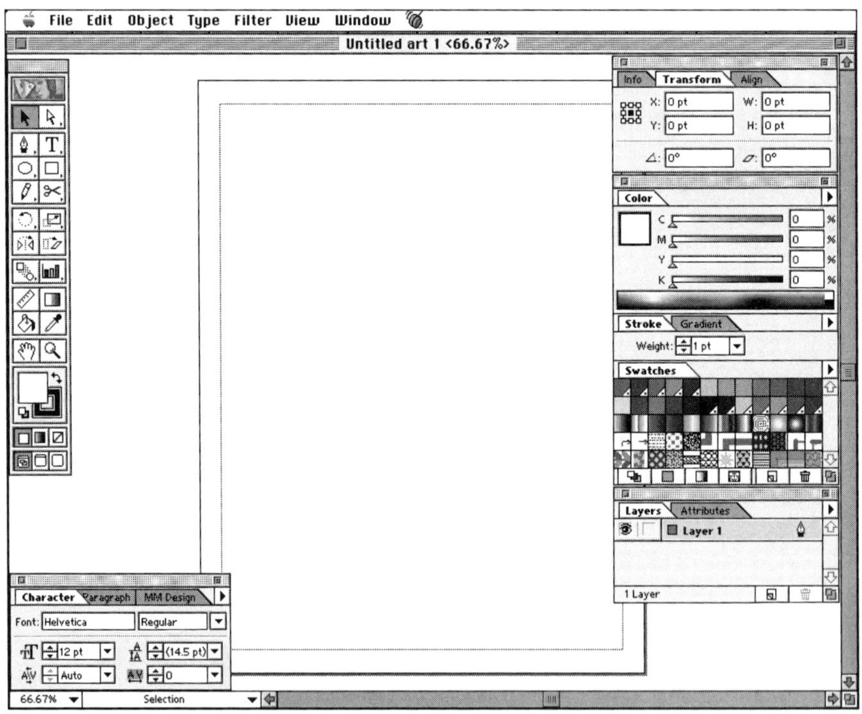

Figure 5-1: The new document window that appears when you first run Illustrator

The Dark Ages

Creating a new document hasn't always been easy. Back in the days of Illustrator 88, and even Illustrator 3 to some extent, creating new illustrations was rather annoying. Choosing New Document brought up a dialog box that politely yet sternly asked you to choose a template to trace in Illustrator. Most of the time, though, you didn't want a template, so you had to click the little None button in the dialog box. If you pressed Return, Illustrator would attempt to open a template.

Illustrator 3 was a little more flexible. It let you create a new document without having to deal with the dialog box that asked you to choose a template. You could either press ⌘-Option-N [Ctrl+Alt+N] or hold down the Option [Alt] key when you chose File⇨New. If you forgot about the Option [Alt] key, you had another chance. Pressing ⌘-N [Ctrl+N] when you were in the dialog box would send the box away and create a new document with no template — as long as you didn't have Directory Assistance, Super Boomerang, or any other utilities that created a new folder open when you pressed ⌘-N [Ctrl+N].

Adobe slowly seemed to realize that you didn't want or need a template to do everything, and now, fortunately, template-forcing is a thing of the past.

In fact, templates have been removed entirely, giving you the one option of placing an image on the background layer.

Many other graphics and desktop-publishing programs, including PageMaker, Photoshop, and QuarkXPress, all ask you to set up your document size before the document is created. When you create a new Illustrator document, it defaults to the size of the startup document that is located in the Plug-Ins folder (see Chapter 6 for more information on altering the start-up document). By default, this document is 8.5 x 11 inches, and it is in the *portrait* orientation (meaning that the width is less than the height). The document window initially shows up at Fit in Window size. In the title bar at the top of the window, you see Untitled Art 1 <100%> (or whatever percent the document is displayed at). As soon as you save the document, the title bar contains the name of the document.

You cannot change the way that some things appear when you first start Illustrator. For example, the Selection tool is always selected in the toolbox. Another unchangeable item is the initial Paint Style that you begin drawing with: a Fill of white and a Stroke of 1 pt. Black. The character attributes are always the same: 12-point Helvetica, Auto leading, Flush left alignment. In addition, the initial layer color is always light blue (a color that is just dark enough so that it doesn't conflict with cyan).

Changing the Document Setup

To change almost anything about the document structure and how you work with that document, you need to go to the Document Setup dialog box (see Figure 5-2) by choosing File⇨Document Setup or pressing ⌘-Shift-P [Ctrl+Shift+P]. In this dialog box, you can change the size of the Artboard, define how and when paths are split, change the ruler units, and change the way that printable page edges, patterns, and placed images are viewed.

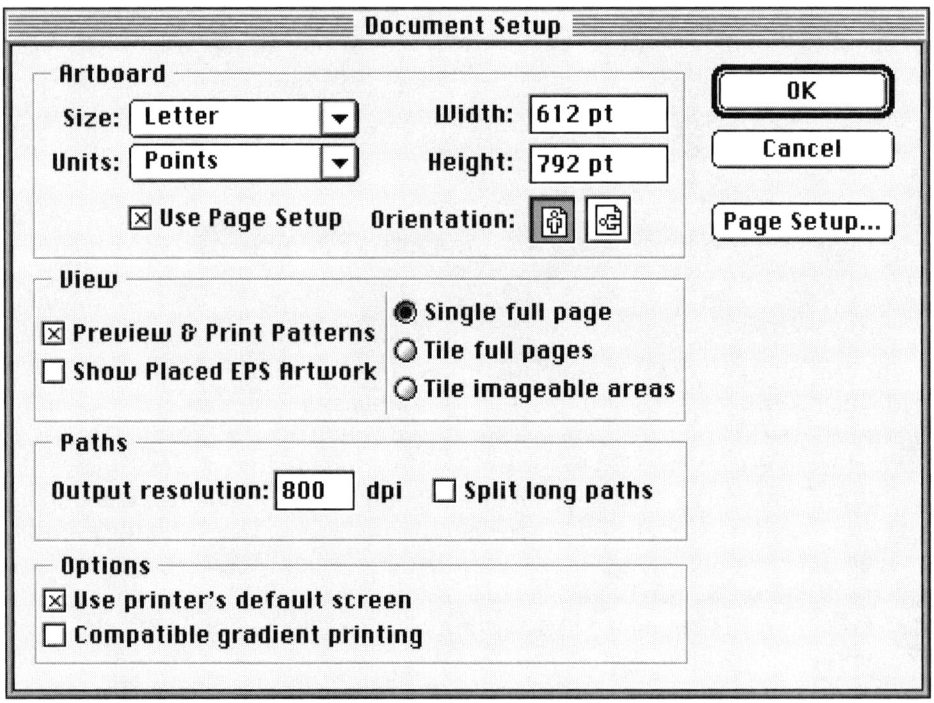

Figure 5-2: The Document Setup dialog box

The following sections describe the various options that are available in the Document Setup dialog box. Any changes that you make to these options are saved with the document.

Page Setup is now accessible through Document Setup. See Chapter 20 for more on Page Setup.

Artboard Options

In Illustrator, the *Artboard* defines the maximum drawing area that can be printed. The Artboard is useful as a guide for where the objects on a page belong. In older versions of Illustrator, the maximum printable size was 11 x 17 inches; in Version 6, it is 120 x 120 inches or 10 square feet (provided that you can find a printer that prints that big).

Illustrator's separation setup ignores the Artboard and places cropmarks around the entire imagable area. The imagable area, according to this dialog box, is only the area where artwork exists. It may be within the Artboard, but it also may extend onto the Pasteboard. When you export an illustration to another program, such as QuarkXPress, the Artboard is ignored entirely.

You can view a document in inches, points and picas, or centimeters. The measurement units affect the numbers on the rulers and the locations of the hash marks on those same rulers. The measurement system also changes the way measurements are displayed in the Info palette and in all dialog boxes where you enter a measurement (other than a percentage).

The measurement system is changed in either the Units + Undo Preferences dialog box (choose File⇨Preferences⇨Units + Undo) for all documents, or in the Document Setup dialog box (choose File⇨Document Setup, or press ⌘-Shift-P [Ctrl+Shift+P]) for the currently active document.

To choose the size of the Artboard, you select from one of the following preset sizes in the Size pop-up menu:

- **Letter** is 8.5 x 11 inches.
- **Legal** is 8.5 x 14 inches.
- **Tabloid** is 11 x 17 inches.
- **A4** is 8.268 x 11.693 inches (21 x 29.7 centimeters).
- **A3** is 11.693 x 16.535 inches (29.7 x 42 centimeters).

180

Multiple Pages in Illustrator?

Kate: I think my Illustrator is broken.

Toulouse: I doubt it, but why do you think that's the case?

Kate: I can't put anything on page 2.

Toulouse: That might be because there is no page 2.

Kate: Ha, ha, ha. Okay, so how do I create page 2?

Toulouse: Look, this isn't Word or XPress. There is no page 2.

Kate: Really?

Toulouse: Really. But you can kinda fudge it.

Kate: I'm trying to lose weight...I put on some pounds after the Scarecrow gig ended.

Toulouse: Sorry to hear that. You can set up Illustrator to have either one or nine pages.

Kate: One or nine? Oh, that makes sense.

Toulouse: Good. Now, to get nine pages, go into Document Setup, and select the Tile imageable areas option.

Kate: And where are pages 2 through 9?

(continued)

- **B5** is 7.165 x 10 inches (18.2 x 25.4 centimeters).
- **B4** is 10.118 x 14.331 inches (55.7 x 36.4 centimeters).
- **Custom** is whatever size you type in the Dimensions text fields.

A4, A3, B5, and B4 are European paper sizes.

To define the orientation of your Artboard, you choose one of the two Orientation pages. On the left is the Portrait orientation, where the lesser of the two dimensions goes across the page from left to right, and the greater of the two dimensions goes from top to bottom. On the right is the Landscape orientation, where the greater of the two dimensions goes across the page from left to right, and the lesser of the two dimensions goes from top to bottom.

If you check the Use Page Setup box, then the Artboard will default to the page size and orientation that is selected in the Page Setup dialog box.

View Options

You can control how certain things in Illustrator are viewed by checking the appropriate boxes:

- The **Preview & Print Patterns** option displays patterns that are used as Fills in objects when Illustrator is in Preview mode or selected objects that are Filled with patterns when Illustrator is in Preview Selection mode. Illustrator will also print patterns when this option is checked. If this option is not checked, it affects only the way that Illustrator sees and prints the pattern objects; it does not affect how other applications see and print them. Choosing this option can dramatically increase screen redraw times (Preview mode) and printing times. If this checkbox is not checked, patterns will not print or preview in Illustrator, but they will print in other software.

- The **Show Placed EPS Artwork** option displays placed EPS images. When the checkbox is not checked, placed artwork is represented as a box with an *X* inside it.
- The **Single full page** option creates one Page Setup size outline on the page.
- The **Tile full pages** option creates as many page outlines (from Page Setup) as will completely print. For example, if the Artboard is landscape, 11 x 17 inches, and the selected page size in Page Setup is portrait, 8.5 x 11 inches, then two page outlines appear side by side in the document.
- The **Tile imageable areas** option creates a grid on the document, with the size of each *block* equal to the page size that is chosen in the Page Setup dialog box. Little page numbers appear in the lower-left corner of each block, representing the pages you entered in the page *x* to page *x* fields in the Print dialog box.

To move the page outlines, select the Page tool and click and drag in the Artboard. The click-point of the page is always the lower-left corner.

(continued)

Toulouse: Zoom out a few times, and you'll see all nine pages.

Kate: All I see is a big grid thing that divides my artboard into nine sections.

Toulouse: That's it!

Kate: You're kidding me.

Toulouse: Nope. And when you print, you can pick which pages to print. They're numbered 1, 2, and 3; then 4, 5, and 6; then 7, 8, and 9. So you normally start on page 5.

Kate: I think I'll wait for Illustrator 8.

Path Splitting Options

Robbie the Robot would be screaming his metal head off if Will Robinson ever thought about clicking the Split long paths check box. The checkbox looks friendly enough, but the results of checking it can be deadly. If you are quick enough, you can always undo the split paths function, but the actual splitting of paths doesn't always happen when and where you expect it to happen.

Instead, it happens only when you save or print a document. This feature presents some very interesting problems. First, if you save the document and close it right after you save it, the paths are split permanently, and you cannot undo the damage the next time you open the document. Second, after you print a document, saving and closing it is a very natural thing to do. But once again, you cannot get it back to normal. Another problem arises when you are working in Preview mode: if you forget whether you checked the option, sometimes you can't easily determine whether paths have been split.

The Split long paths function tries to fix paths that are too long or too complex for your laser printer to handle. By entering the final output resolution for the Illustrator document, you can ensure that it will have a better chance of printing than if paths were not split. Every curve in Illustrator is made of tiny straight segments. The higher the resolution of the output device, the more straight segments are needed to create the curve. The processing power of the laser printer limits how many little straight segments can be in one path. If you exceed that limit, Illustrator chops away at the paths, splitting them into several smaller sections. Because this problem occurs more with high-resolution devices, the greater the number you enter in the Output resolution field, the more paths will be split. Figure 5-3 shows an original document and several examples of path splitting.

The only reason to use the Split long paths function is if a document fails to print because of a PostScript error (usually a Limitcheck error). But instead of just checking the Split long paths check box, first make a copy of the entire document

Figure 5-3: A document before and after path splitting at different output resolutions

(doing a Save As with another name will do this quickly) and then split paths in the new document. Then the original file will not contain split paths. Split paths are extremely difficult to reassemble, and the results from split paths can be horrifying. Please use caution when you split paths.

Using the Printer's Default Screen

For gradients on low-resolution printers (600 dpi or less) when composite printing only, Illustrator uses a dither pattern called Adobe Screens (not to be confused with Adobe Accurate Screens) when Use Printer Default Screen is unchecked. This increases the apparent levels of gray by fracturing the halftone cells.

You'll notice when you first open a document that the Use Printer Default Screens check box is checked. But, the first time you Fill an object with a gradient, it automatically unchecks itself. Illustrator assumes when you use gradients that you want Adobe Screens turned on — if you don't want it on, you have to manually turn Use Printer Default Screen back on. When checking Use Printer Default Screens, you're just disabling Adobe Screens; you are *not* telling Illustrator to image the file at the printer's default line screen. Output software can still set the printer's line screen for the Illustrator file.

Compatible Gradient Printing

Checking this option allows gradients created with Illustrator to be printed on older PostScript Level 1 printers and PostScript clone printers. However, checking this option when printing to a PostScript Level 2 printer can dramatically slow down print processing time.

If you aren't sure if your printer can handle gradients properly, create a document with about 20 ellipses that are filled with gradients. If the document prints, you shouldn't have any trouble. If the document prints and there are empty or solid areas where there should be a gradient, you'll need to check this option when printing documents with gradients.

Navigating the Document

Being able to move through a document easily is a key skill in Illustrator. You rarely can fit the entire illustration in the document window at a magnification where you can see much of the detail of the image. Usually, you are zooming in, zooming out, or moving off to the side or above or below to focus in on certain areas of the document.

Who's Zoomin' Who?

The most basic of navigational concepts in Illustrator is the ability to zoom to different magnification levels. Illustrator's magnification levels work like a magnifying glass. In the real world, you use a magnifying glass to see details that aren't readily visible without it. In the Illustrator world, you use the different magnification levels to see details that aren't readily visible at 100% view. The magnification levels of Illustrator do not affect the illustration. If you zoom in to 200% and print, the illustration will be printed at the same size as it would if the view were 100%. It will *not* print twice as large.

The Zoom Tools

You use the two Zoom tools, Zoom In and Zoom Out, to magnify a certain area of artwork and then return to the standard view.

To use the Zoom In tool, select it in the toolbox, press Z or press ⌘-Spacebar [Ctrl+Spacebar]. Either way, the Zoom In tool should appear. It looks like a magnifying glass with a plus sign in it. Clicking any spot in the illustration enlarges that part of the illustration to the next magnification level. Seventeen different Zoom levels are available in Illustrator. The highest magnification level is 1600%, which shows the illustration at 16 times the size of its original measurements. Of course, the Zoom In feature is not without its pitfall: The more you zoom in on an illustration, the less of that illustration you see at one time.

Where you click with the Zoom In tool is very important. Clicking the center of the window enlarges the illustration to the next magnification level, but the edges (top, bottom, left, and right) are cropped off as the magnification increases. Clicking the upper-right corner crops off mostly the lower-left edges, and so

Zooming Out Wrong?

Charlie: You know, that marquee thing just isn't happening here.

Toulouse: I bet Joan Collins sabotaged your system.

Charlie: Uh, wrong show. Anyway, I drag and... nothing!

Toulouse: It doesn't zoom in? Maybe I should be calling you Blake?

Charlie: No, and no, it doesn't zoom out!

Toulouse: Well, it's supposed to zoom in, not out. I guess then it's only half broke.

Charlie: I thought the Zoom Out tool zoomed out. Hence the name.

Toulouse: You aren't trying to draw a marquee with the Zoom Out tool, are you?

Charlie: Sure. Is that a problem?

Toulouse: The Zoom Out tool doesn't work by drawing a marquee. You have to click with it. Drawing with a marquee is the same as clicking.

Charlie: But what if I want to zoom out really far, right away?

(continued)

forth. If you are interested in seeing a particular part of the illustration close up, click that part at each magnification level to ensure that it remains in the window.

If you zoom in too far, you can use the Zoom Out tool to zoom out again. To access the Zoom Out tool, press Option while you click with the Zoom tool or press ⌘-Option-Spacebar [Ctrl+Alt+Spacebar]. Clicking with the Zoom Out tool reduces the magnification level to the next lowest level. You can zoom out to 6.25%, or 1/16 actual size.

When you use the Zoom tools, you change the size of everything in the document, not just the illustration. You change the size of all paths, objects, the Artboard, the Pasteboard, and the Page Setup boundaries relative to the current magnification level. However, the points and paths retain their shape and thickness at all times.

If you need to zoom in quite a bit, you can zoom in more easily by using the Zoom In tool to draw a marquee (by clicking and dragging diagonally) around the objects that you want to magnify. The area that is surrounded will magnify as much as possible so that everything inside the box just fits in the window that you have open, as shown in Figure 5-4. Dragging a box with the Zoom Out tool does nothing special; it works the same as if you had just clicked with the Zoom Out tool.

POWER TIP: You can move a zoom marquee around *while you're drawing it* by pressing the Spacebar after you've drawn the marquee but before you release the mouse button.

(continued)

Toulouse: Double-click on the Hand tool to make the page fit in your window. Is that small enough?

Charlie: No...I want it smaller.

Toulouse: You can quickly go to 6.25% by Option-clicking the Zoom tool.

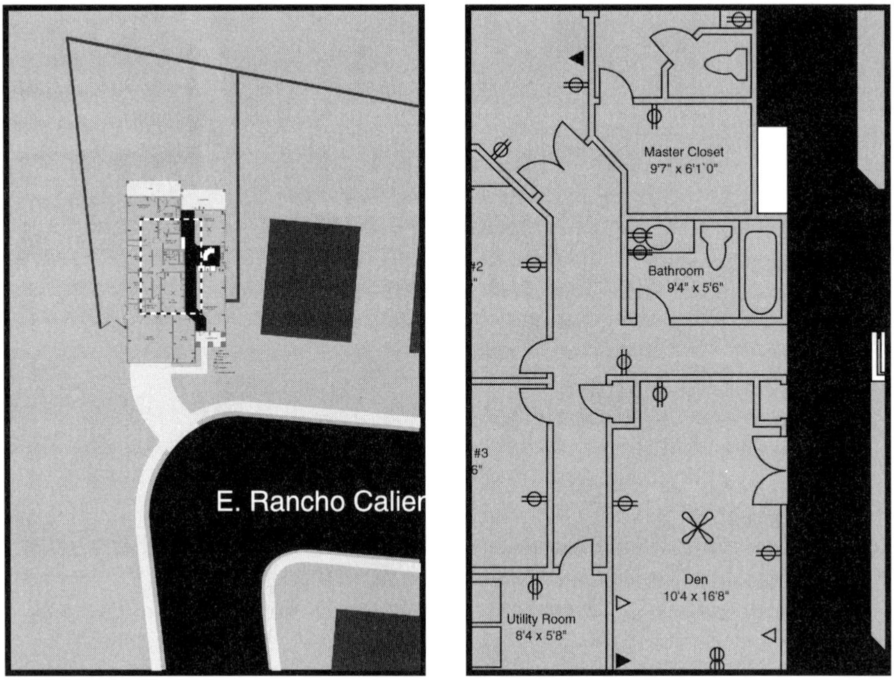

Figure 5-4: Zooming in to a certain area in the original image (left) results in the magnification and placement of the image on the right

Other Zooming Techniques

You also can zoom in and zoom out by using commands in the View menu. Choose View⇨Zoom In (⌘-+) [Ctrl++] to zoom in one level at a time until the magnification level is 1600%. The Zoom In feature zooms from the center out. Choose View⇨Zoom Out (⌘- -) [Ctrl+-] to zoom out one level at a time until the magnification level is 6.25%.

You can use two different methods to automatically zoom to 100%. The first method is to double-click the Zoom tool in the toolbox. This action changes the view to 100% instantly. A better way to zoom in to 100% is to choose View⇨Actual Size (⌘-1) [Ctrl+1], which not only changes the magnification level to 100% but also centers the page. At this view, an 8.5 x 11-inch piece of paper should fit squarely over an 8.5 x 11-inch document on your Illustrator screen. The accuracy of the fit depends on the pixels-per-inch of your monitor.

Choosing Actual Size also centers the document in your window (this is unlike double-clicking the Zoom tool, which resizes the page to 100% but brings the current center at the smaller or larger size to the center when resizing).

You can choose from two different methods to change the document view to the Fit in Window size. Fit in Window instantly changes the magnification level of the document so that the entire Artboard (not necessarily the artwork, if it isn't located on the page) fits in the window and is centered in it. One way to automatically change to the Fit in Window view is to choose View➪Fit in Window (⌘-0). Another way is to double-click the Hand tool.

To instantly zoom in to 1600%, draw a tiny marquee with the Zoom In tool. At actual size, the marquee must be smaller than 1/2 x 1/2 inches for the magnification level to go instantly to 1600%. It may be necessary to draw more than one marquee if the current magnification level is lower than 100%.

You can never undo any type of magnification level change. Choosing Edit➪Undo after zooming will undo the last change you made to the document before you changed the magnification level.

Using the Scroll Bars

Sometimes after you zoom in to a high magnification, part of the drawing that you want to see is outside the window area. Instead of zooming in and out, you can use one of two different scrolling techniques to move around inside the document.

The scroll bar on the right side of the document window controls where you are vertically in the document. Clicking the up arrow displays what is above the window's boundaries by pushing everything in the window *down* in little increments. Clicking the down arrow displays what is below the window's boundaries by pushing the document *up* in little increments. Dragging the thumbnail up displays what is above the window's boundaries proportionately by whatever distance that you drag. Dragging the little elevator box down displays what is below the window's boundaries proportionately by whatever distance that you drag. Clicking on the gray bar above the little elevator box between the arrows displays what is above the window's boundaries in big chunks. Clicking the gray bar below the little elevator box between the arrows displays what is below the window's boundaries in big chunks.

The gray area of the right scroll bar is proportionate to the size of the Pasteboard. If the little elevator box is at the top of the scroll bar, then you are viewing the top edge of the 120" x 120" Pasteboard. If it is centered, you are viewing the vertical center of the Pasteboard.

The scroll bar on the bottom of the document window controls where you are in the document horizontally. Clicking the left arrow displays what is to the left of the window's boundaries by pushing everything in the window *right* in little increments. Clicking the right arrow displays what is to the right of the window's boundaries by pushing the document *left* in little increments. Dragging the little elevator box left displays what is to the left of the window's boundaries by whatever distance proportionately that you drag. Dragging the little elevator box right displays what is to the right of the window boundaries by whatever distance proportionately that you drag. Clicking the gray bar between the arrows that is to the left of the little elevator box displays what is to the left of the window's boundaries in big chunks. Clicking the gray bar between the arrows that is to the right of the little elevator box displays what is to the right of the window's boundaries in big chunks.

Scrolling with the Hand Tool

The Hand tool improves upon the scroll bars. Instead of being limited to only horizontal and vertical movement, you can use the Hand tool to scroll in both directions simultaneously. It is especially useful for finding your way around a document when you are at a high magnification level. The higher the magnification level, the more you will end up using the Hand tool.

To use the Hand tool, either select it in the toolbox, press H, or press and hold the Spacebar. (If you are currently using the Type tool, press ⌘-Spacebar [Ctrl+ Spacebar] and then release ⌘ [Ctrl] , keeping the Spacebar pressed.) Clicking and dragging the page will move the document around inside the document window.

POWER TIP

When you click with the document, be sure to click the side that you want to see. Clicking at the top of the document and dragging down enables you to scroll down through almost an entire document at a height of one window. Clicking in the center and dragging enables you to scroll through only half a window size at a time. If the window of the document does not take up the entire screen space, you can continue to drag right off the window into the empty screen space. Just be sure that you first click within the document that you want to scroll.

The best thing about the Hand tool is that it works *live*. As you drag, the document moves under "your Hand." If you don't like where it is going, you can drag it back, still live. The second best thing is that to access it requires only one keystroke, a press of the Spacebar.

CAUTION

You cannot use Undo (⌘-Z) [Ctrl+Z] to reverse scrolling that you have done with the scroll bars and the Hand tool.

VectorTools VectorNavigator — included in the fully functional demo mode on this book's CD-ROM — provides a much better way to scroll around your document. The Navigator palette displays a little red rectangle that shows what portion of your document is displayed in the main document window. You can move the red rectangle around within the palette, which moves the viewing area of your document window. VectorTools is discussed in depth in Chapter 14.

Artwork Mode versus Preview Mode

In the old days, everyone worked in Artwork mode. You could occasionally check work in progress to see what the illustration would look like by switching to Preview mode. Usually the preview was not quite what you had in mind while you were in Artwork mode, so it was back to Artwork mode to fix everything, and then to Preview again to check. . . .

Illustrator 7 enables you to work in both Artwork and Preview modes. The mode that you are in when documents are printing does not matter. Illustrator Fills and Strokes all paths and objects with the colors that are defined in the document, even if the document is in Artwork mode and those colors aren't visible. Saving the document while you are in Artwork mode does not affect anything in the document, but the next time you open it, it will be in Artwork mode. The same thing applies to Preview and Preview Selection modes: Whatever mode you are in is saved with the artwork.

You cannot undo a Preview or Artwork mode change (going from Preview Selection to Artwork, for example). If you make a Preview or Artwork mode change and then close your document, Illustrator asks you if you want to save changes, which in this case only refers to the view change.

Artwork (Only) Mode

To change the current document to Artwork mode, choose View⇨Artwork (⌘-Y) [Ctrl+Y]. In Artwork mode, the illustration disappears and is replaced on-screen by outlines of all the Filled and Stroked paths. Text that has yet to be converted into outlines looks fine, although it is always black. Depending on your choice in the Document Setup dialog box (choose File⇨Document Setup or press ⌘-Shift-P) [Ctrl+Shift+P], a placed image is displayed as a box with an *X* in it (if Show placed images is not checked) or as a black-and-white-only image, surrounded by a box with an *X* in it (if Show placed images is checked).

Artwork Shmartwork

Farrah: You know how you keep saying Artwork mode is so wonderful?

Toulouse: Well, it is.

Farrah: Then how come I still can't select certain paths?

Toulouse: Can you see the path you want to select?

Farrah: Sure, it's right next to the path that I keep selecting accidentally.

Toulouse: There's a couple things you can do.

Farrah: Great. And number one is....

Toulouse: First, you could zoom in really close, so the paths appear further apart. This allows for easier selecting.

Farrah: Makes sense. What if I don't feel like zooming in?

Toulouse: You know, I'm really not that surprised that you got dumped by the "fall guy."

Farrah: I dumped *him,* you know.

(continued)

Working with a drawing in Artwork mode can be significantly faster than working with it in Preview mode. In more complex drawings, the difference between Artwork mode and Preview mode is significant; on very slow computers, working in Preview mode is next to impossible.

Artwork mode enables you to see every path that isn't directly overlapping another path; in Preview mode, many paths can be hidden. In addition, invisible masks are normally visible as paths in Artwork mode.

Placed artwork is displayed in black and white only, and templates are grayer than before. The main advantage to working in Artwork mode is the speed increase over Preview mode. The speed that you gain is even greater when the artwork contains gradients, patterns, placed artwork, and blends. In addition, you can select paths that were hidden by the Fills of other objects.

If you have installed a Plug-In called Artwork Speedup (originally located in the Utilities folder), your Anchor Points, Control Handle points, and Control Handle Lines are black in Artwork mode.

Artwork mode can take some getting used to. To select paths in Artwork mode, you must click the paths or draw a marquee across them.

Artwork mode can be better than Preview because it's faster, and also because your brain can learn to know what the drawing looks like from seeing just the outlines, which show *all* of the paths, including masks (masking paths cannot be viewed in Preview).

Preview Mode

Choosing View⇨Preview (⌘-Y) [Ctrl+Y] changes the view to Preview mode. In Preview mode, the document looks just the way it will look when you print it.…sort of. Patterns in strokes and patterns in type show as gray areas, and you can't view overprinting.

In Preview mode, the color that you see on the screen represents only marginally what the actual output will be because of the differences between the way computer monitors work (red, green, and blue colors — the more of each color, the brighter each pixel appears) and the way printing works (Cyan, Magenta, Yellow, and Black colors — the more of each color, the darker each area appears). Monitor manufacturers make a number of calibration tools that decrease the difference between what you see on the monitor and the actual output. You can also use software solutions. One software solution, CIE calibration, is right in Adobe Illustrator (choose File⇨Color Setting).

In Preview mode, you can see which objects overlap, which objects are in front and in back, where gradations begin and end, and how patterns are set up.

Sometimes previewing complex drawings on-screen can take a long time. Usually this problem occurs when you are displaying paths with patterns or a great number of blends. To stop an illustration from being redrawn in Preview mode, press ⌘-period [Ctrl+period] to change the document to Artwork mode. If the redrawing has been completed before you press ⌘-period [Ctrl+period], everything is selected. Objects that were unselected are selected. This can be especially frustrating when you have spent a good deal of time selecting certain objects, but you didn't group these objects together. The selection or deselection of objects cannot be undone.

(continued)

Toulouse: Yeah, I can see that. Anyway, you could also select the path that keeps being selected and then press Shift and drag a marquee around both paths. That'll select the unselected path and deselect the selected path.

Farrah: That's it?

Toulouse: Since you asked, you could also lock the path you keep selecting, then the next click would select the other path.

Preview Selection Mode

To change to Preview Selection mode, choose View⇨Preview Selection (⌘-Shift-Y) [Ctrl+Shift+Y] to display all selected objects in Preview mode and all unselected objects in Artwork mode. Figure 5-5 shows an illustration in Preview Selection mode.

Figure 5-5: An image in Preview Selection mode

The Preview Selection mode can be useful in a complex illustration when you need to adjust a few object colors and want to see the results without waiting a long time. You can cancel redrawing in progress and return to Artwork mode by pressing ⌘-period [Ctrl+period]. You can even create new paths and adjust existing ones while in Preview Selection mode.

Combining Artwork and Preview Modes

Using the Layers palette, you can easily combine Artwork and Preview or Artwork and Preview Selection modes. You can force individual layers to display in Preview mode while other layers remain in Artwork mode. This feature can be useful when you have a layer with a placed image, gradients, or patterns (or all three) that would normally slow down the work flow. You can place those images on their own layer and set that layer to Artwork mode.

You also can view the same artwork in both Preview mode and Artwork mode at the same time by creating a new window for the current document. Choose Window⇨New Window to create a window that is the same size as the original window. You can manipulate these two windows so that they are next to each other, and each window can have different viewing characteristics. One window can be in Preview mode, and the other one can be in Artwork mode. One window can be at Fit in Window size, and you can zoom the other to any percentage.

Using multiple windows to show Artwork and Preview modes of the same drawing simultaneously was used mainly when Illustrator did not enable artists to edit and create in Preview mode. This function is no longer as helpful as it was before, but you can still use it to preview an illustration when you want to select artwork that is hidden by Fills and Strokes of other artwork in Preview mode. In addition, two windows can be used for viewing the entire artwork at a small size, while editing a blown-up version in another.

Now You See It

Illustrator also provides options that enable you to show and hide various parts of an illustration:

- **Show Rulers** (choose View⇨Show Rulers or press ⌘-R [Ctrl+R]) displays rulers (in the current measurement system) on the left side of the document and on the top of the document window. By default, all rulers measure up and to the right from the lower-left corner of the Artboard.

  If you're confused about why the rulers in Illustrator are on the right side of the document window — but they measure up from the lower-left corner — you're not alone. Undoubtedly the Adobe engineers themselves are confused on this topic, so they set up the rulers this way to confuse the general public. Of course, in previous versions the rulers were on bottom and right edges.

  To change the measurement system that is displayed on the rulers, choose File⇨Document Setup (⌘-Shift-P) [Ctrl+Shift+P] and select the new measurement system. A quick way to instantly change ruler unit measurement systems is by pressing ⌘-Ctrl-U (Mac only), which cycles through the three measurement systems.

To change the origin of the rulers (0 across, 0 up), drag from the box where the rulers meet to the new intersection point.

Pressing ⌘-R [Ctrl+R] toggles between showing and hiding rulers. If rulers are showing, the menu item is Hide Rulers. If rulers are displayed when you save the document, they will be displayed the next time you open it. If rulers are not showing when you save the document, the rulers will be hidden the next time you open the document.

- **Show Page Tiling** (choose View➪Show Page Tiling) shows the outlines of the page guides from the Page Setup and Document Setup dialog boxes. When Page Tiling is visible, the menu item changes to Hide Page Tiling. The condition of Page Tiling is saved with the file.
- **Hide Edges** (choose View➪Hide Edges or press ⌘-H) [Ctrl+H] does not show paths, Anchor Points, Control Handles, or Control Handle Lines when it is selected in Preview mode and does not show Anchor Points, Control Handles, or Control Handle Lines in Artwork mode. When edges are hidden, the menu item reads Show Edges. Pressing ⌘-H [Ctrl+H] toggles between showing and hiding edges. Edges are always visible when you open a file, regardless of whether they were visible or hidden when you saved it.

  Be careful to note when you have this feature enabled, as it can appear to the unwary that they are unable to select anything just because Hide Edges has been activated.
- **Show Guides** (choose View➪Show Guides or press ⌘-; [Ctrl+;]) shows all guides in your artwork, whether you created them by using rulers or by transforming paths into guides. Show Guides does not show guides that were hidden with the Hide (⌘-U) [Ctrl+U] command. The alternate, Hide Guides, hides all guides in the document. Whether you save a document with guides visible or hidden, they are always visible when you open a document.

Remember when this function is on so that you don't unwittingly pull guide after guide onto your document, wondering why they don't show up. Or you may choose Make Guides and wonder if you accidentally chose Hide instead because paths changed into guides when Hide Guides is on simply disappear.

Using Custom Views

Illustrator has a special feature called *custom views* that enables you to save special views of an illustration. Custom views contain view information, including magnification, location, and whether the illustration is in Artwork or Preview mode. If you have various layers in Preview mode and others in Artwork mode, custom views can also save that information. However, custom views do not record whether templates, rulers, page tiling, edges, or guides are showing or hidden.

To create a new view, set up the document in the way that you would like to save the view. Then choose View⇨New View and name the view in the New View dialog box. Each of the first 10 views that you create is given a key command of ⌘-Option Shift-1 [Ctrl+Alt+Shift+1], and so on. You can create up to 25 custom views, but the last 15 will not have a key command. Custom views are saved with a document as long as you save it in Illustrator 7 format later.

If you find yourself continually going to a certain part of a document, zooming in or out, and changing back and forth between Preview and Artwork mode, that document is a prime candidate for creating custom views. Custom views are helpful when you show clients artwork that you created in Illustrator. Instead of fumbling around in the client's presence, you can, for example, instantly show the detail in a logo if you have preset the zoom factor and position and saved the image in a custom view.

The Window Menu

The Window menu (see Figure 5-6) contains the various options for displaying the different palettes available in Illustrator, as well as any documents that are currently open:

- **New Window** creates a new window that displays the current document, usually at a different viewing percentage or in a different mode. This new window is initially the same size and has the same viewing options as the existing, frontmost window, but the viewing options can be changed without affecting the other window.
- **Hide/Show Tools** hides the toolbox from view. If the toolbox is hidden, this command reads Show Tools.
- **Hide/Show Info** (F8) hides the Info palette from view. If the Info palette is hidden, this command reads Show Info. The Info palette appears automatically when the Measure tool is used.
- **Hide/Show Transform** hides the Transform palette.
- **Hide/Show Align** hides the Align palette if it is displayed. If the Align palette is hidden, this command reads Show Align.
- **Hide/Show Color** (F6 or ⌘-I [Ctrl+I]) hides the Color palette from view. If the Color palette is hidden, this command reads Show Color.
- **Hide/Show Gradient** (F9) hides the Gradient palette from view. If the Gradient palette is hidden, this command reads Show Gradient. The Gradient palette also appears automatically when the Gradient tool is clicked or if the Gradient icon in the toolbox is clicked (in the paint style section of the toolbox).

- **Hide/Show Attributes** (F11) hides the Attributes palette.
- **Hide/Show Stroke** (F10) hides the Stroke palette.
- **Hide/Show Swatches** (F5) hides the Swatches palette.
- **Swatch Libraries** displays a submenu of swatch palettes that contain specialized color sets. Chapter 2 contains a list of these palettes and uses for them.
- **Hide/Show Layers** (F7) hides the Layers palette.
- **Hide/Show Layers** (F7) hides the Layers palette from view. If the Layers palette is hidden, this command reads Show Layers.
- **Untitled Art 1** and all other titles below this dotted line are referencing the open Illustrator documents and duplicate document windows. A check mark appears in front of the title of the active document or window.

Figure 5-6: The Window menu

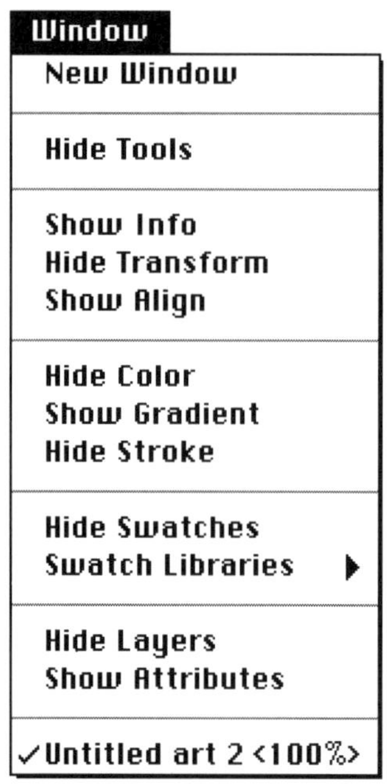

Managing Files

Controlling how files are saved in Illustrator can be a little daunting at first. Although you have many different options for saving file types, you need to follow one basic rule: Save as an EPS with a color preview if you are going to take the file into other applications. This type of file is not the smallest file type, but it is compatible with most software.

Opening files in Illustrator is fairly simple. Illustrator can open and manipulate only files that were created in Illustrator, Streamline, or Dimensions and files that were saved in an Illustrator format. It can open raster files, but they will be pixel-based.

Files placed in Illustrator can be almost any raster file format. PostScript files that are printed to disk usually can't be placed in Illustrator, although PostScript Level One files can be opened in Illustrator.

Other important file issues: Illustrator opens pixel files as a new Illustrator document with the pixels inside. Arbitrary PostScript Level One files can be opened with the built-in PostScript Interpreter. Illustrator files can be saved directly into pixel formats.

Saving Files

Saving Illustrator documents is the most important Illustrator activity you do. Saving often prevents damage to your computer — by keeping you from picking it up and sending it flying across the room. Saving often makes your life less stressful, and backing up your saved files helps you sleep better.

The amount of space that a saved Illustrator file takes up on a hard drive depends on two things: the complexity of the drawing and the Preview option (if any) that you've selected. Tiny Illustrator files take up the smallest amount, about 10K or so. The biggest illustrations are limited only by your storage space, but they can regularly exceed 2MB. As a practice, when you are working on a drawing, save it to the hard drive, not to a floppy disk or a removable cartridge. Hard drives are faster and much more reliable. If you need to place a file on a floppy disk, zip, or Syquest cartridge, copy it there in the Finder by dragging the icon of the file from the hard drive to the disk or cartridge.

The Unopenable File

Bosley: Well, I did as you asked, saving and all. But now I'm screwed.

Toulouse: You forgot the name of the file?

Bosley: No, I'm getting an error, something about operators making illegal calls to Texas.

Toulouse: Ah, the ole Illegal Operand 'TZ' error.

Bosley: That's it. It won't let me open my document.

Toulouse: There's a way to fix that.

Bosley: Cool. What causes it?

Toulouse: If you use a certain symbol in the first font after the Symbol font, you'll get this error. Usually the degree sign.

Bosley: Ick. But I can fix it, right?

Toulouse: Sure. Open the Illustrator document in a word processor.

Bosley: I can do that?

Toulouse: Yes, but you want to open it as a text file, not as a graphic.

Bosley: Done. What a mess.

(continued)

(continued)

Toulouse: Find the line: "/_Symbol_/Symbol 0 0 0 TZ" and add a "[" to the beginning of the line so it looks like this: "[/_Symbol_/ Symbol 0 0 0 TZ." Save the document and open it in Illustrator. Voilà.

Because Illustrator 7 uses *virtual memory* (the hard drive as RAM), you may want to keep additional hard drive space available, especially if you plan on working with lots of embedded images.

You should only save the file to another disk if you run out of room on the hard drive. To ensure that you never run out of room, always keep at least 10 percent of the hard drive space free. A hard drive that is too full can cause many problems that are more serious than being unable to save a file.

To save a file, choose File⇨Save (⌘-S) [Ctrl+S]. If you have previously saved the file, then updating the existing file with the changes that you have made takes just a fraction of a second. If you have not yet saved the file, the Save As dialog box appears, as shown in Figure 5-7.

STEPS: Saving Illustrator Documents

Step 1. Decide how you are going to save the file. Choose the correct Preview and Compatibility options for the file. (See the descriptions in the "Illustrator EPS Preview Options" and "Compatibility Options" sections, later in this chapter.)

Step 2. Decide where you are going to save the file and make sure that the name of the folder that you want to save it in is at the top of the file list window. Saving your working files in a location other than the Illustrator folder is a good habit. Otherwise, you can have trouble figuring out which files are yours, which files are tutorial files, and so on.

Step 3. Name the file something distinctive so that if you look for it six months from now you will recognize it. Avoid using Untitled Art 1, Untitled Art 2, and so on.

The names are nondescriptive, and besides, you can too easily accidentally replace the file at a later date with a file of the same name. For the same reasons, do not use Document 1, Document 2, and so on (QuarkXPress's default names). Also avoid using Test1 (if I had a nickel for every Test1 or Test2 I've seen on people's hard drives, I'd have . . . well, I'd have a lot of nickels), stuff, #$*&!! (insert your favorite four-letter word here), picture, drawing, or your first name.

A file name can have up to 31 characters, and you can use all the letters, numbers, and special characters (except a colon [:]), so make the most of them and describe the file.

Figure 5-7: The Save As dialog box

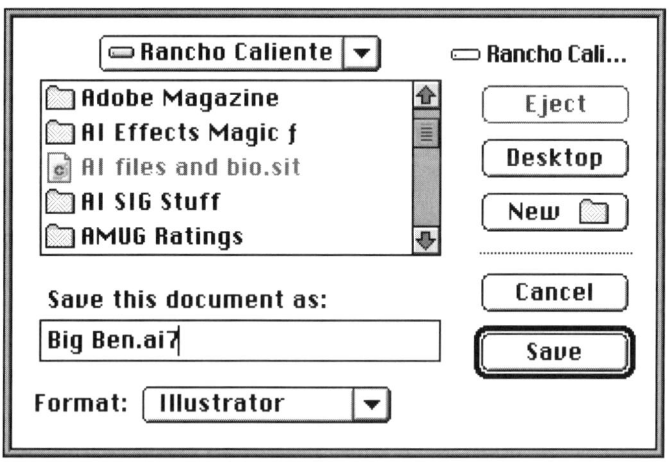

When Should I Save?

You really can't save too often. Whenever I put off saving for "just a few minutes," that's when the system locks up, crashes, or gives me a Type 1 error. Depending on your work habits, you may need to save more frequently than other people do. Here are some golden rules about when to save:

- Save as soon as you create a new file. Get it out of the way. The toughest part of saving is deciding how and where you are going to save the file and naming it. If you get those things out of the way in the beginning, pressing ⌘-S [Ctrl+S] later is fairly painless.

(continued)

(continued)

- Save before you print. For some reason, PrintMonitor and PostScript errors can crash a system faster than almost anything else.
- Save before you switch to another application. Jostling stuff around in a computer's RAM is an open invitation for the whole system to poop out.
- Save right after you do something that you never want to have to do again — such as getting the kerning "just right" on a logo or matching all of the colors in your gradients so that they meet seamlessly.
- Save after you use a filter that takes more than a few seconds to complete.
- Save before you create a new document or go to another document.
- Save at least every 15 minutes.

The Save As Command

The Save As command (⌘+Shift+S) [Ctrl+Shift+S] enables you to save multiple versions of the document at different stages of progress. If you choose Save As and do not rename the file or change the save location, you are prompted to replace the existing file. If you choose Replace, the file that you saved before is erased and replaced with the new file that you are saving. Most disk and trash recovery utilities cannot recover a file that you delete this way.

The Save As command is also useful for changing the Preview and Compatibility options (which are described in the "Illustrator EPS Preview Options" and "Compatibility Options" sections, later in this chapter). If you have saved in Omit Header Preview and want to change to Color Preview, choose File⇨Save As, don't change the file name or file location, and choose Color from the Preview pop-up menu.

Save a Copy

The Save a Copy command (⌘-Option-S) [Ctrl+Alt+S] saves a copy of your document at its current state without affecting your document or its name. Here's the scoop: Let's say you've designed a fairly nice logo — Whittles Logo — for Dr. Whittles, the plastic surgeon down the street. Dr. Whittles is pretty conservative, but his patients aren't. You need to show him both a basic logo and the same logo that is somehow spruced up. Once you've created the basic logo, you can Save a

Copy as *Basic Logo* and continue working on *Whittles Logo*. The next time you press ⌘-S [Ctrl+S], you'll save your changes to *Whittles Logo,* and it won't affect *Basic Logo* at all.

Reverting to the Last Saved Version

Choosing File⇨Revert is an option that automatically closes the document and opens the last saved version of it. This option will be grayed out if the file has not been saved yet. When it is selected, a dialog box appears, asking you to confirm that you *do* want to revert to the last saved version of the document.

CAUTION A Revert action cannot be undone, and you won't be able to redo anything you've done up to that point with the document.

File Types

You can save and export Illustrator 7 files in several ways. Actually, you can save and export them in almost 30 different formats…though some formats just don't make any sense.

Saving an Illustrator file with the wrong options can dramatically affect whether that file can be opened or placed in other software, as well as what features are included with the file when it is reopened in Illustrator. For example, saving the file as anything but EPS makes it virtually useless to every piece of software but Illustrator (although PageMaker, Photoshop, and a few other Adobe products can read Illustrator native format). Saving a document as an older version of Illustrator may alter the document if the older version was missing features you used in your document.

As a rule, unless you're going to take your Illustrator document into another program, you can save it as Illustrator without any problems. This keeps the file size down and makes saving and opening the file much quicker.

Compatibility Options

Illustrator is one of the few software programs that is almost fully backward-compatible. If you open a file in Illustrator 88 that you created in Illustrator 7, it looks almost exactly the same. Most software packages are forward-compatible for one major version, but Illustrator is a novelty in that you can open an Illustrator 1.1 file in Version 7 of the software, even though more than ten years have passed between those product versions.

There are a number of reasons to save illustrations in older versions of Illustrator. The following list provides information about saving files in each version:

- **Illustrator 7** saves the file in a cross-platform (Mac and Windows) Illustrator 7 format. Illustrator 7 supports several bitmap file formats that Illustrator 6 could not. In addition, RGB color is not supported in previous versions of Illustrator.
- **Illustrator 6** saves the file in the Illustrator 6 format. The major file structure difference between Illustrator 6 and Illustrator 5.x is Illustrator 6's capability to import almost any type of raster image, while 5.x only supported EPS images. Other, not-so-obvious changes have to do with advanced object labels that plug-in developers use to achieve all sorts of effects.
- **Illustrator 5** saves the file in the Illustrator 5 format, which includes both Illustrator 5.0 and 5.5. The features added to Version 5.5 do not affect file content. Thus, files created in Version 5.5 have the same structure as files created in Version 5.0.
- **Illustrator 4** saves the file in the Illustrator 4 format, which is a version that is available only for Windows users. Saving a file in the Illustrator 4 format ensures that Illustrator 4 for Windows will open that Illustrator file. Gradients, views, layers, and custom Artboard sizes are not supported by the Illustrator 4 format. Technically speaking, there is really no difference between the Illustrator 3 and 4 formats.
- **Illustrator 3** saves the file in the Illustrator 3 format. In fact, you can use the Illustrator 3 format for a lot of cheating — doing things that Illustrator normally doesn't enable you to do. For example, technically, you can't put gradients or masks into patterns. But if you save a gradient as an Illustrator 3 file and reopen it in Illustrator 7, the gradient becomes a blend, which you can use in a pattern (although Illustrator's Expand feature is quicker for this sort of thing).
- **Illustrator 88** saves the file in the Illustrator 88 format, which, for about four years (1988 to 1991), was the Illustrator standard. Much clip art has been created and saved in the Illustrator 88 format. The main problem with saving in the Illustrator 88 format is that type changes occurred between Illustrator 88 and Illustrator 3. Illustrator 88 cannot handle type on a curve (called path type which it turns into individual segments), and it doesn't deal correctly with compound paths (type converted to outlines are made up of several compound paths, one for each character).
- **Illustrator 1.1** saves the file in the oldest of Adobe Illustrator formats, Version 1.1. Saving in the Illustrator 1.1 format is useful when you want to take files into older versions of Freehand and many other older draw programs. Illustrator 1.1 format doesn't support custom colors or masks.

Saving as Illustrator EPS

If you do have to place your Illustrator document in another program, like QuarkXPress, you need to save the file as Illustrator EPS. After you select the Illustrator EPS option in the Save As box and name the file, clicking the Save button brings up yet another dialog box, shown in Figure 5-8.

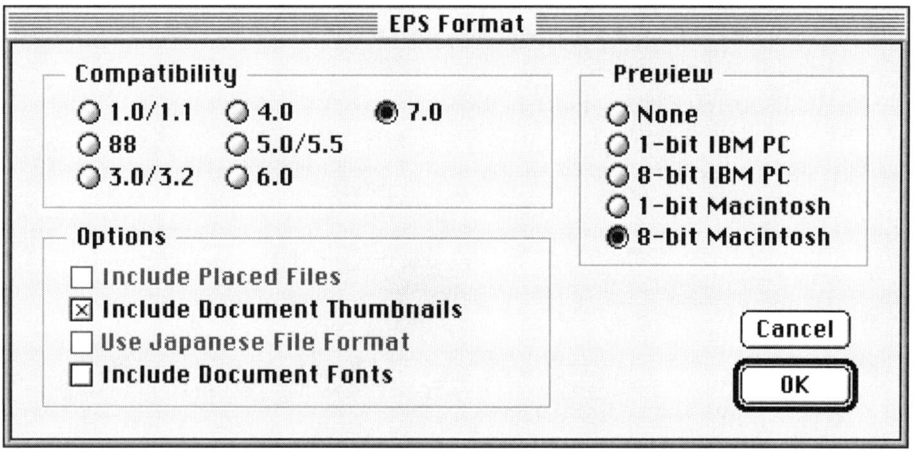

Figure 5-8: The EPS Format dialog box

The multiple options that are available when saving a file as an Illustrator EPS are discussed in the following section.

Illustrator EPS Preview Options

The following options in Illustrator 7 affect the way that other software programs see Illustrator files when they are saved as Illustrator EPS files:

- **None** lets most software programs recognize the Illustrator document as an EPS file, but instead of viewing it in their software, you see a box with an *X* in it. Usually, this box is the same size as the illustration and includes any stray Anchor Points or Control Handles. The file will print fine from other software.
- **1-bit Macintosh IBM PC** saves the EPS file with a PICT file preview as part of the EPS file. A PICT image is embedded within the EPS file (technically, a PICT resource); you do not have two separate files. Page-layout and other software displays this illustration in a black-and-white preview with no shades of gray in it. This file may take up substantially more space than the Include EPSF Header file requires because of the PICT file. The larger the illustration measures, the more storage space the PICT file uses.

- **8-bit Macintosh IBM PC** saves the file with a color preview that is an embedded PICT image. Page-layout and other software displays this file in 8-bit color (256 colors) when you place it in a document. An Illustrator file that you save with a color preview takes up more file space than a file saved with any other option.
- **1-bit IBM PC** saves the file with a preview for IBM systems. Page-layout or other software for PCs that can import EPS files can preview illustrations that you save with this option.

Exporting

Adobe Illustrator 7 allows you to export to several different file formats, most of them bitmap formats such as TIFF, JPEG, and PICT. You can also export in PDF format so that Illustrator documents can be read in Adobe Acrobat Reader.

Exporting Files in PDF Format

The PDF format option saves files in Adobe Acrobat-compatible Portable Document Format. An Illustrator document saved as a PDF file will become a page when opened in Acrobat. Saving your Illustrator file this way removes several Illustrator attributes, like layers, gradients, patterns, and path type.

Acrobat Reader is free on most online services and is provided on the CD-ROM that comes with this book.

Opening and Closing Illustrator Files

You can open any Illustrator file from any version of Illustrator in Illustrator 7. Regardless of which Preview options you select, Illustrator 7 can still open the file. When you choose File⇨Open or press ⌘-O [Ctrl+O], the Open dialog box appears and asks you to find an Illustrator file. Find the file and double-click it to have it open into a document window on the screen.

To close the active Illustrator file, choose File⇨Close (⌘-W) [Ctrl+W]. The active document is the one that is in front of all other documents and has a title bar with lines on it and text in black. Nonactive documents don't display any lines in their title bar, and the text in the title bar is gray. Closing an Illustrator document does not close Illustrator; it continues running until you choose Quit.

If you saved the file prior to closing it, it just disappears. If you have modified the file since the last time you saved it, a box appears, asking whether you want to save changes before closing. If you press Return or Enter to save the file, it is updated. If you have not saved the file at all, the Save As dialog box appears so that you can name the file, choose a location for it, and choose Preview and Compatibility options for the file. If you click the Don't Save button (D while the dialog box is showing), then any changes that you made to the document since you last saved it (or if you have never saved it, all the changes you made since you created it) are lost. Clicking Cancel (⌘-period [Ctrl+period] or Esc) takes you back to the drawing, where you can continue to work on it.

Placing Art

Files that you can place or import into Illustrator are EPS (Encapsulated PostScript), TIFF (Tagged Image File Format), and most other bitmap file formats. To place files, choose File⇨Place. A standard Open dialog box appears. Only files that can be placed show up in the file window. Because text files are also placed, be sure the file you've chosen is indeed an image document.

After you place art into Illustrator, you can transform it (move, scale, rotate, reflect, and shear it) in any way.

The quality of placed art is as good as the original; if the original file was bitmapped (created or saved in a paint program such as Photoshop), then the quality will lessen as the file is scaled up, and the quality will increase as the file is scaled down. If the file was in PostScript outline format (created in Illustrator or FreeHand, EPS only), then the quality will stay consistent as the file changes in size.

You can use placed raster images for tracing, but the Auto Trace tool does not recognize EPS and does not automatically surround it.

Illustrator shows placed art differently in Artwork mode and in Preview mode. In Artwork mode, placed art is in black and white, or just shows up as a box with an X inside of it.

When you save a document with placed art in it with a preview, you can link the placed art to Illustrator or include it in the Illustrator file. Normally, including the placed art within the Illustrator file is the better choice. This method prevents the two files from being separated; if you have one and not the other, you are out of luck. But you may want to link the file instead of including it for two reasons. First, placed art can be huge and may make your Illustrator file too large. Second, if you need to make changes to a placed art file that you have included in an Illustrator file that you have saved with a preview, you have to replace the placed art in the preview file with the new version. If you have linked the placed art, instead of including it, it is automatically updated when you make changes.

You may want to replace placed art with new versions or completely different artwork. Illustrator has made this process painless. If placed artwork is selected, a dialog box appears asking if you would like to replace current artwork or place new artwork, not changing the selected artwork.

POWER TIP: The really cool part about changing placed art this way is that if you have placed artwork that has been transformed, the artwork you exchange with it via the Place Art command will have the exact same transformation attributes! For example, if you scale down placed artwork to 50% and rotate it 45°, artwork that is exchanged with that artwork is also scaled down 50% and rotated 45°.

You can dim placed art by checking the Dim Images checkbox in the Layer Options dialog box on the Layers palette. If you dim placed art, then a ghost of the image appears instead of the solid image. This feature makes manually tracing placed art easy. Dimming placed art does not affect its printed output.

Placed Art Size Issues

Be careful when importing artwork other than EPS images into Illustrator, as TIFF and most other bitmap formats increase the size of your document dramatically. The reason for this is that the image information for TIFFs and other formats is stored within the Illustrator document, and is not linked to the document in the way Placed EPS image are. Making the issue even stickier, duplicating TIFFs within Illustrator increases the document size by the size of that TIFF once again.

Publish and Subscribe (Mac Only)

Publish and Subscribe is a convenient way to keep various elements in different documents current by updating affected documents when other related documents are changed.

The Edit menu contains the following Publish and Subscribe options:

- The **Publishing** option displays a category with four submenu items, all related to System 7's Publish and Subscribe feature. Publish and Subscribe allows certain users to publish documents that are subscribed to by others. As the Publisher changes its edition, the Subscriber receives updated information about that edition. You may neither publish nor subscribe text only, but you may publish and subscribe to entire type objects (such as a Area type or Path type).
- The **Create Publisher** option creates an edition file that other users can subscribe to (by choosing Subscribe in their application). The edition includes any selected objects at the time Create Publisher is chosen. After the edition is created, a light gray border appears around the edition's objects when one or more of those objects is selected. After you have created an edition using the Create Publisher command, it is updated every time you save the file that contains the edition. An edition border is a fixed size and cannot be changed.
- The **Subscribe To** option lets your document subscribe to an edition. A dark gray border appears around editions you have subscribed to if that edition is selected. Your document is updated instantly whenever the edition is updated, even if your document is open.
- The **Publisher Options** give you the ability to manually update the edition, even without saving your file. You can also choose to Unpublish your edition at this point.
- The **Show Borders** option always shows the borders of both the edition files you have published (light gray) and the edition files to which you have subscribed (darker gray).
- The **Hide Borders** option reverses the Show Borders option.

Document Info

You can use this feature in any document by choosing File⇨Document Info. A dialog box (shown in Figure 5-9) appears with a pop-up menu at the top.

The pop-up menu consists of seven different ways to view information about the active document:

- The first option, **Document,** shows the document setup of the active document. All the relevant options from the Document Setup dialog box are shown, along with the name of the file.

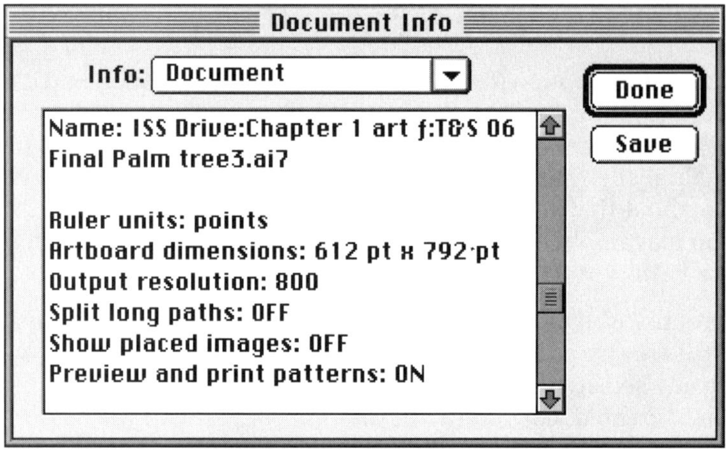

Figure 5-9: The Document Info dialog box

- The second option is **Objects,** which lists how many paths, masks, compound paths, custom colors, patterns, gradients, fonts, and placed EPS artwork are used in the document. This can be used as a rudimentary guide to how long a file may take to print.
- The remaining options show the names of any enclosed custom colors, patterns, gradients, and fonts. The final option, **Embedded Images,** lists not only the name of the placed art but the disk path that tells Illustrator where to find it.

If you have anything selected, the Selection Info dialog box will contain only information about these selected objects.

Along the right side of the Document Info dialog box are two buttons: The Save button creates a TeachText format file with all eight categories of information about the document, while the Done button closes the dialog box.

TeachText format cannot be read in Illustrator. To view the saved Document Info file, you must double-click the file name or open it within a word processor.

Summary

- When you launch Illustrator, a new document automatically appears.
- New documents are based on the start-up file size and attributes, and are created as soon as you choose New Document from the File menu.

- The current document setup can be modified in the Document Setup dialog box, accessed by pressing ⌘-Shift-P [Ctrl+Shift+P] or by choosing File⇨Document Setup.
- You can automatically use the current Page Setup as your artwork size by selecting the "Use Page Setup" checkbox in the Document Setup dialog box.
- Path splitting is useful if you have several long paths, and are getting PostScript Limitcheck errors when printing.
- You can quickly change ruler measurement systems by pressing ⌘-Ctrl-U (Mac only) to cycle through the Inches, Points, Picas, Millimeters, and Centimeters options.
- Zoom in by pressing ⌘-Spacebar [Ctrl+spacebar] to access the Zoom In tool, and then drag a marquee around the area you wish to zoom into.
- You can zoom out rapidly by pressing ⌘-Option-Spacebar [Ctrl+Alt+Spacebar] and clicking.
- Pan around your document by pressing the Spacebar to access the Hand tool and then dragging the document around within its window.
- Artwork mode can be useful when drawing a complex piece of artwork, enabling Illustrator to operate quicker than in Preview mode, and letting you select points and paths that might have otherwise been obscured.
- Preview Selection mode is handy for when you'd like to see just a portion of your illustration without having to wait for the entire document to redraw.
- Using various options in the View menu, you can specify which elements you'd like to view and which ones you'd like to hide.
- The Window menu enables you to show and hide all the different palettes in Illustrator, as well as letting you arrange document windows.
- Unless you'll be taking files into another application, save them as Illustrator 7 files.
- If you'll be taking files into another application, you probably want to save them as EPS, with an 8-bit preview.
- You can place any EPS image, bitmap, text or vector file, by using the Place command, located in the File menu.

Customizing Illustrator

6 CHAPTER

In This Chapter

- Personalizing Illustrator
- Modifying the Adobe Illustrator Startup file
- Setting preferences that affect all documents
- Setting document-specific preferences

Under the Apple menu () on a Macintosh and under the Help menu in Windows, you'll find a few useful items of information.

About Illustrator displays a dialog box with the user information and scrolling credits for everyone, absolutely everyone, who had any teeny tiny little thing to do with Illustrator. If nothing else, you'll become aware of the large numbers of people who are involved in creating the software.

About Plug-Ins displays a submenu that lists all the installed Plug-Ins. Choosing one of the items in the Plug-Ins submenu displays who made the Plug-In, and occasionally some useful or interesting information about that Plug-In.

On a Macintosh, About this Computer (in the Finder, while Illustrator is running under System 7.6) displays how much memory is allocated to Illustrator, and how much Illustrator is actually using of that allocated amount.

POWER TIP

You can also determine how much memory is used and is currently available by clicking on the Status bar at the lower left of the Document window and selecting the Free Memory option from the pop-up menu. This displays how much memory is free both in megabytes and as a percentage of the total amount of memory.

Windows Update

Illustrator can be customized in many more ways than in Version 4, with expanded preferences and an easier-to-use startup file.

What's New

Additional preferences can be accessed through either the Preferences submenu or within the General Preferences dialog box (via a pop-up menu).

Adding items to the startup file (colors, patterns, gradients) is now done by adding to the Swatch palette only.

Japanese cropmarks can be used instead of traditional ones through an option in preferences.

Preferences

No two illustrators work the same. To accommodate the vast differences in styles, techniques, and habits, Illustrator provides many settings that each user can change to personalize the software.

Illustrator provides four major ways to change preferences. The most dramatic and difficult changes are to a small file called Adobe Illustrator Startup. The startup file changes how new documents appear and which custom colors, patterns, and gradients are available.

You can also control how Illustrator works by accessing the Preferences submenu (choose File⇨Preferences). You make most of these changes in the General Preferences dialog box, which you access by choosing File⇨Preferences⇨General (⌘-K) [Ctrl+K].

A third way to make changes is by changing preferences relative to each document. You usually make these changes in the Document Setup dialog box, but a few other options are available. There is more information on document-specific preferences later in this chapter.

The fourth way that you can customize preferences happens pretty much automatically. When you quit Illustrator, it remembers many of the current settings until the next time you run it. These settings include palette placements and values in toolbox settings.

Illustrator has a few settings that you cannot customize. These features can really get under your skin because most of them seem like things that you should be able to customize. See the "Things You Can't Customize" section, later in this chapter, for a list of these settings.

Modifying the Startup File

When you first run Illustrator, the program looks to the Illustrator startup file to check a number of preferences. Those preferences include window size and placement, as well as custom colors, gradients, patterns, zoom levels, tiling options, and graph designs.

New documents (like the one created automatically when you first run the program) have all the attributes of the startup file. Opened documents have all the gradients, custom colors, patterns, and graph designs of the startup file.

STEPS: Changing the Startup File

Step 1. Open the startup file. The start-up file, called Adobe Illustrator Startup, is located in the Plug-Ins folder in the Adobe Illustrator folder. The file is an Adobe Illustrator 7 document, so double-clicking the file opens Illustrator, as well.

Step 2. Figure 6-1 shows what the file looks like. Each square in the document contains a pattern, gradient, named color, or color swatch square. Remove any square that contains patterns, gradients, or custom colors that you don't use. Then go to the Swatches Palette and delete those same patterns, gradients, and colors.

If you delete a pattern, custom color, or gradient from the startup file, it is gone. Kaput. The only way to get it back is to replace the startup file from the original disks or CD-ROM.

Step 3. To add something to the startup file, add the color, pattern, or gradient to the Swatches palette.

To add a graph design, create the graph design and apply it to a graph. Place the graph in the startup file.

(continued)

STEPS: *(continued)*

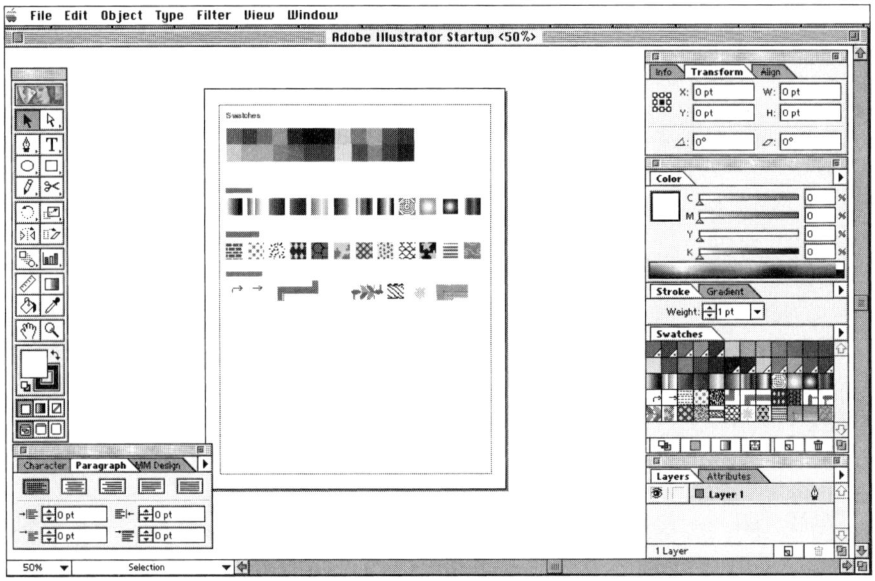

Figure 6-1: The Adobe Illustrator Startup document

Step 4. To change the window size, just save the startup file with the window size that you want new documents to have.

Step 5. To change the color swatches on the Swatches palette, add, replace, or delete color swatches while the startup file is open and then save the startup file.

If you delete the Adobe Illustrator Startup file, most patterns, gradients, and custom colors will not be available until you create a new startup file or place the original startup file from the disks or CD-ROM in the Plug-Ins folder.

To check whether changes that you made in the startup file will work, quit Illustrator and run the program again. You cannot tell whether the changes are in place until you quit and then reopen Illustrator.

You can change not only the window size of new documents, but also the viewing percentage. Most people like documents to fit in the window when it is created. For a 13-inch screen, use 50%; for a 16- or 17-inch screen, use 66%.

Changing General Preferences

The preferences in the General Preference dialog box are preferences that affect the way the entire program works, regardless of which document you pull up. To alter application preferences, access the Preferences submenu (choose File⇨Preferences).

Within the Preferences dialog box, a number of different preference panels can be selected from the pop-up menu at the top of the dialog box. You can go through each of the preference panels one by one by clicking the Next and Previous buttons, or simply choose a preference panel from the Preferences submenu. The preference panels are General, Keyboard Increments, Units & Undo, Guides & Grid, Hyphenation Options, and Plug-Ins & Scratch Disk.

In most programs, "Preferences" is logically located on the Edit menu, not on the File menu. General Preferences, unlike everything else on the File menu, deals with the entire program rather than with a specific document.

The General Preferences Dialog Box

The General portion of the Preferences dialog box (choose File⇨Preferences⇨General or press ⌘-K [Ctrl+K]) contains most of the *personalized* customizing options for Illustrator. The options in this box affect keyboard increments, measuring units, and the way that objects are drawn. These options are considered personalized options because they are specific to the way that each person uses the program. Few people have the same preference settings as others have (unless they never change the defaults). The General Preferences dialog box is shown in Figure 6-2.

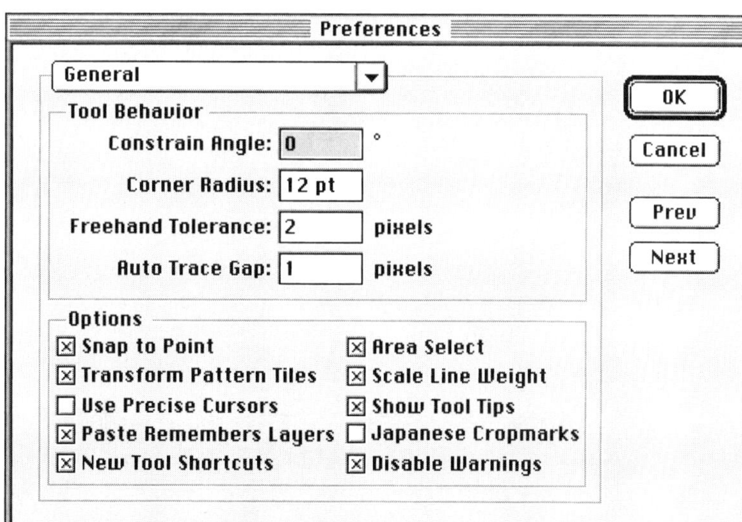

Figure 6-2: The General Preferences dialog box

Tool Behavior

The Tool Behavior options control how most of Illustrator's tools work. Some tools have their own options, accessed by a double-click on that tool.

The Constrain Angle Option

The Constrain Angle option controls the angle on which all objects are aligned. Rectangles are always drawn "flat," aligning themselves to the bottom, top, and sides of the document window. When you press the Shift key, lines that you draw with the Pen tool and objects that you move will align to the Constrain Angle, or 45°, 90°, 135°, or 180°, plus or minus the constraining angle.

The Constrain Angle also affects how the four transformation tools transform objects. The Scale tool can be very hard to use when the Constrain Angle is not 0°, and the Shear tool becomes even more difficult to use than normal at different Constrain Angles. Pressing Shift when you are using the Rotate tool constrains the rotational angle to 45° increments added to the Constrain Angle. Chapter 7 discusses the Rotate tool and other transformational tools.

In Illustrator, 0° is a horizontal line, and 90° is a vertical line. Figure 6-3 shows Illustrator angles.

Figure 6-3: Angles in Illustrator

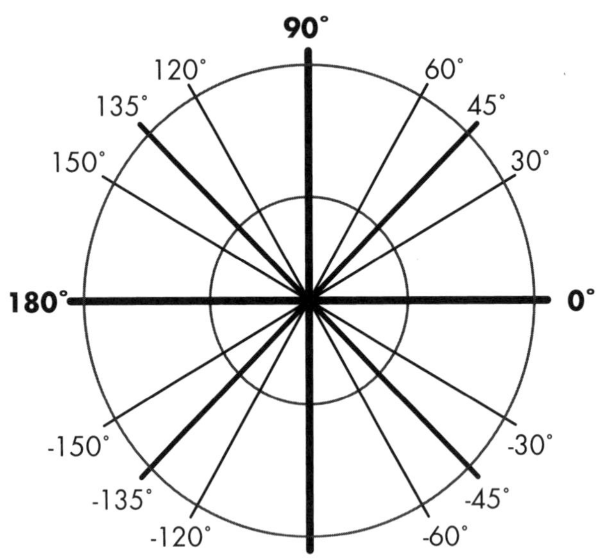

If you set the Constrain Angle at 20°, objects are constrained to movements of 20°, 65°, 110°, 155°, and 200°. Constrain Angles of 90°, 180°, and –90° (270°) affect only type, patterns, gradients, and graphs; everything else works normally.

When Option[Alt]-copying objects, you can use the Shift key in conjunction with a Constrain Angle to duplicate objects at a specific angle. Option[Alt]-copy means to press the Option [Alt] key while dragging an object and then release the mouse button before releasing the Option [Alt] key to produce a duplicate of the object at the new location.

The Corner Radius Option

The Corner radius option affects the size of the curved corners on a rounded rectangle. For a complete explanation of the corner radius and rounded rectangles, see Chapter 2.

The corner radius value changes each time you enter a new value in the Rectangle dialog box. This dialog box appears when you click the Rectangle or Rounded Rectangle tools without dragging in a document. If, for example, you create one rounded rectangle with a rounded-corner radius of 24 points, all rounded rectangles that you create from that point forward will have a radius of 24 points. The only ways to change the corner radius are to click a Rectangle tool without dragging in a document and then enter a new value in the Rectangle dialog box or to enter a new value in the Corner radius text field in the General Preferences dialog box.

The real advantage to changing the corner radius in the General Preferences box is that the corner radius will affect manually created (dragged with the Rounded Rectangle tool) rounded rectangles immediately. Changing the corner radius in the Rectangle dialog box requires that you know the exact dimensions of the rectangle or that you draw a rectangle by entering information in the Rectangle dialog box (clicking with the Rectangle tool without dragging) and specifying the corner radius. You must then delete the original rectangle in order to draw a rounded rectangle with the correct corner radius manually.

CAUTION: Because you can change the Corner Radius setting easily, be sure to check it before you draw a series of rounded rectangles manually. There is no easy or automatic way to change the corner radius on existing rounded rectangles.

If you use 0 point as the Corner radius setting, the corners are not rounded at all. If you click with the Rounded Rectangle tool and enter 0 pt. as the corner radius, the Corner radius setting in the General Preferences dialog box changes to 0 point.

The Curve Fitting Tolerance Option

The Curve Fitting Tolerance setting controls how accurate the paths that Illustrator creates are when you compare them to the area dragged with the Pencil tool and to any templates being traced with the Auto Trace tool. Chapter 3 discusses Curve Fitting Tolerance settings and resulting paths.

The lower the Curve Fitting Tolerance setting, the more exact the resulting path. A higher setting results in smoother, less accurate paths. You can enter a value from 0 to 10, in increments of $^{1}/_{100}$ point (two decimal places).

The Curve Fitting Tolerance number is relative to the number of pixels on the screen that the resulting path may vary. A tolerance of 10 means that the resulting path may vary up to 10 pixels from the location of the actual dragged or traced area.

The Auto Trace Gap Option

When you use the Auto Trace tool to trace a placed image, the tool may encounter gaps, or white space, between solid areas. The Auto Trace gap option enables you to specify that if the Auto Trace tool runs into a white-space gap of 1 or 2 pixels, it can jump over the gap and continue tracing on the other side of it.

A value of 0 prevents the Auto Trace tool from tracing over gaps. If you use a value of 1, the Auto Trace tool traces over gaps that are up to 1 pixel wide. If you use a value of 2 (the highest allowed), it traces over gaps that are 2 pixels wide. The Auto Trace gap setting not only goes over gaps, it also adheres less closely to the original template.

I usually use a setting of 0 because when I trace any image in Illustrator, I examine it closely in Photoshop to make sure that it does not have any gaps. I can then be sure that the resulting paths will not be misshapen because of image-tracing inaccuracies.

General Preference Options

The 12 checkboxes in the Options section of General Preferences is Illustrator's version of the *Battlestar Galactica* ragtag fleet of unwieldy spacefaring craft. Some are quite powerful, others seem like they aren't capable of transferring millions of people across the galaxy, much less defending themselves against the evil menace of the Cylon empire. Okay, that wasn't the best analogy. The fact is, there is no other place in Illustrator where so many totally unrelated options share the same dialog box, and I had to come up with a snazzy introduction. . . .

The Snap to Point Option

You turn on the Snap to Point feature in Illustrator to automatically align a point that you are dragging with another point that already exists within the illustration. As soon as the cursor is within 2 screen pixels of an anchor point, the cursor becomes hollow. If you release the mouse button when the cursor is hollow, the new point precisely overlaps the existing point.

CAUTION

Be sure to click and drag a *point* when you are dragging and using the Snap to Point feature, or you may unintentionally align part of a line segment with the existing point.

I usually keep this feature on to make sure that my points always align; the only trouble that I have is accidentally clicking and dragging segments rather than points.

Never assume that Snap to Point is on, unless you know that you have not changed it. Watch for those hollow arrows, and if you don't see them, check the General Preferences box to see whether the feature is turned on.

The Transform Pattern Tiles Option

Check the Transform Pattern Tiles option if you want patterns in paths to be moved, scaled, rotated, sheared, and reflected when you use the transformation tools. When this option is checked, pulling up a transformation dialog box (either Move, Rotate, Scale, Reflect, or Shear) automatically checks the Pattern checkbox. When the option is not checked, the Pattern checkbox is not checked in the transformation dialog box. This option controls whether selected patterns are transformed when the transform palette is used.

I usually keep the Transform pattern tiles box checked, which sets all patterns to automatically transform and move with the objects that are being transformed and moved. This feature is especially useful when you want to create perspective in objects because the transformations of patterns can enhance the intended perspective.

Use Precise Cursors Option

Precise cursors are cursors that appear as a variation of a crosshair instead of in the shape of a tool. Figure 6-4 shows cursors that are different when the Use Precise Cursors feature is on.

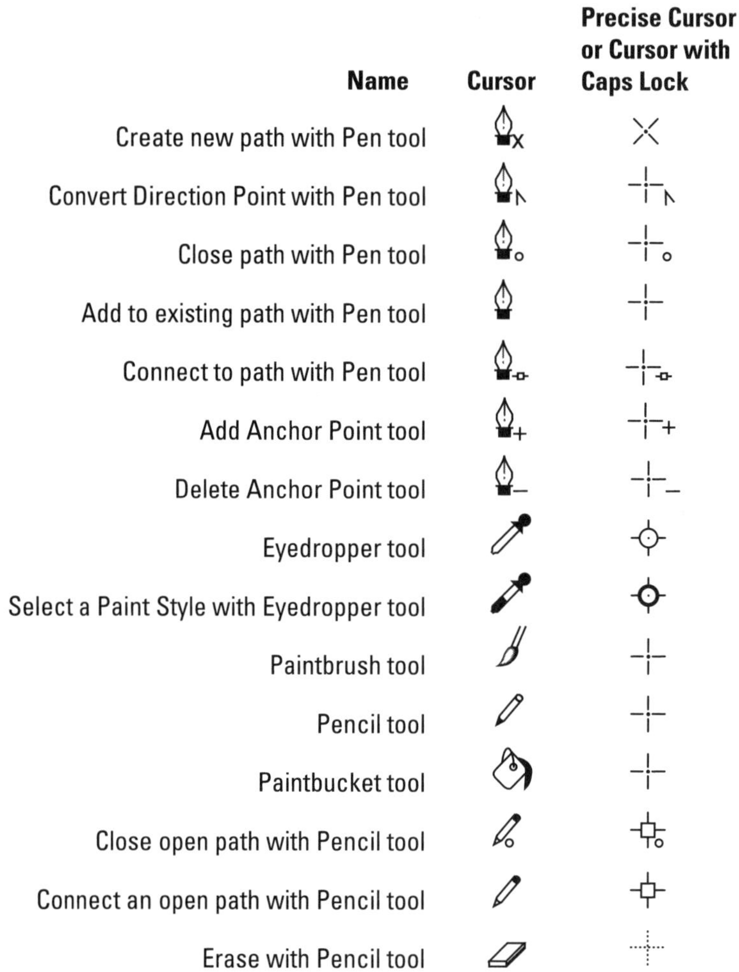

Figure 6-4: The regular cursors are on the left, the precise cursors are on the right

The Caps Lock key toggles between standard cursors and precise cursors. When the Use precise cursors option is checked, the Caps Lock key makes the cursors standard. When the Use precise cursors option is not checked, Caps Lock activates the precise cursors.

I usually keep this option on and rarely engage the Caps Lock button to change the cursors back to normal. In particular, I've found the precise cursor for the Brush tool to be quite useful, seeing as how the standard Brush cursor is one giant amorphous blob.

The Paste Remembers Layers Option

Checking the Paste remembers layers checkbox causes all objects to be pasted on the layer that they were copied from, regardless of which layer is currently active. Unchecking this box causes objects on the Clipboard to be pasted in the current layer.

This option is available in the Layers palette as well, and if it is on, a checkmark appears next to Paste Remembers Layers in the pop-up menu. When you turn the Paste Remembers Layers menu item on or off, the preference setting changes in the General Preferences dialog box.

CAUTION One of the unheralded super features of the Paste remembers layers option is what happens when you paste in another document that doesn't contain that particular layer. A new layer with the same name as the one you copied the items from is created automatically. This is also a good way to quickly copy layers to another document . . . just delete the items after you've pasted them, and the new layers will remain.

New Tool Shortcuts

NEW IN 7 When this check box is checked, all the keyboard commands in the Macintosh version of Illustrator 7 have a corresponding, nearly identical keyboard command in the Windows version of Illustrator 7. When this check box is unchecked, several keyboard commands match those of Illustrator 6. Keyboard commands that have changed are listed in Appendixes E and F. The majority of commands that are different due to checking or unchecking this check box involved the Control key, which is only available on the Macintosh (the Windows Ctrl key is the equivalent of the Macintosh ⌘ key).

The Area Select Option

When the Area Select feature is on, you can select an object in Preview mode by clicking the object's Fill. If the Area Select feature is off, you select an object the same way that you select it in Artwork and Preview Selection mode: by clicking paths or Anchor Points of objects. The Area Select feature has no effect on selecting objects in Preview Selection mode, but after you select them, you can move them by clicking a Filled area.

I have yet to have a good reason to turn this option off. The only reason that I can imagine for turning off this feature is if, for a particular illustration, I need to select specific paths from several overlapping, Filled objects. To be honest, I think that selecting individual paths in Preview would still be difficult because you can't see most of them.

CAUTION

The Area Select feature does not enable you to select paths by clicking Strokes, unless you click the center of the Stroke where the path is (in which case you would be clicking the path anyway). In addition, you can't select "through" a compound path; instead, clicking in the empty areas of a compound path will result in selecting the compound path itself.

The Scale Line Weight Option

When the Scale Line Weight feature is on, it automatically increases and reduces line weights relative to an object when you uniformly scale that object manually. For example, if a path has a Stroke weight of 1 point and you reduce the path uniformly by 50 percent, the Stroke weight changes to .5 point.

POWER TIP

Scaling objects nonuniformly (without the Shift key pressed) does not change the Stroke weight on an object, regardless of whether the Scale line weight feature is on or off.

If an object is scaled uniformly throughout the Scale dialog box, the Scale Line Weight option in the Scale dialog box will default to checked if the Scale Line Weight check box is checked in the General Preferences dialog box.

BY THE WAY

Unlike the Corner radius option, checking or unchecking the check box in the Scale dialog box for Scale Line Weight has no effect on the corresponding check box in the General Preferences dialog box.

Show Tool Tips

NEW IN 7

This option displays little pop-up names for each of the tools if you rest your cursor above them for one second. It's a great idea to keep this option on, as not only do you see the name of the tool, but also the key to press to access that tool.

Japanese Cropmarks

The Japanese Cropmarks setting, when checked, will change the standard cropmarks usually created with Objects⇨Cropmarks⇨Make (⌘-7) [Ctrl+7] to Japanese cropmarks (see Figure 6-5).

Figure 6-5: Standard cropmarks (top) and Japanese cropmarks (bottom)

Disable Warnings

This tiny little check box has the graphics community sending letters of thanks to Adobe. Version 6.0.1 of Illustrator allowed you to turn off some of the warnings, but it had to be done by editing the preference file, a task that most users found daunting at best. The warnings I'm referring to are those handy little messages that appear when you've clicked in the wrong spot with the wrong tool. For instance, clicking with the Scissors tool off a path would result in an ugly, overly long essay on the evils of clicking in empty space. Clicking with the Convert Direction Point tool brought up a dialog box condemning you for trying to convert something that wasn't a suitable Anchor Point. The first few times, the messages were helpful reminders.

Years later, they've become an annoying thorn in the side of experienced Illustrator users. Checking this box turns off the messages; instead of a nagging dialog box, a simple system beep noise is produced. This noise is still a bit annoying, but it does let you know you've clicked in an unacceptable portion of the document.

Units & Undo

The General pop-up menu in the Units Section changes the measurement system for the current document and all future new documents. This change affects most of the ways that dialog boxes, the Info palette, and the rulers display measurements.

Illustrator 7 contains five different measurement units: inches, picas, points, millimeters, and centimeters. The ⌘-Control-U command (Macintosh only) toggles between all five units, and each unit can be selected from the General pop-up menu.

Changing the General units in the Units & Undo Preferences dialog box changes the Ruler units in the Document Setup dialog box (choose File➪Document Setup or press ⌘-Shift-P [Ctrl+Shift+P]).

Being aware of which measurement system you are working in is important. When you enter a measurement in a dialog box, any numbers that are not measurement-system-specific are applied to the current unit of measurement. For example, if you want to move something 1 inch and you open the Move dialog box (choose Object➪Transform➪Move, double-click the Selection tool), you need to add either the inch symbol (") or the abbreviation *in* after you type a 1 in the dialog box if the measurement system is not inches. If the measurement system is points and picas, entering just a 1 moves the object one point, not one inch. If the measurement system is inches already, entering just the number 1 is fine.

Usually the measurement system is indicated by a corresponding letter or letters: *in* for inch, *pt* for points, and *cm* for centimeters.

I use the points/picas system for several reasons. First, using points and picas is easier because you can specify smaller increments exactly (ever try to figure out what $^{1}/_{12}$ inch is in decimals?). Second, type is measured in points, not inches. Third, points and picas are the standard in measuring systems for designers and printers.

The default measurement is points and picas, so if you ever toss your preferences file or reinstall Illustrator, be aware that you might have to change the measurement system.

The Cursor Key Option

The increment that you specify in this setting controls how far an object moves when you select it and press the keyboard arrows.

I have this increment set to .5 point because this is the smallest amount that I usually need to move things. I make my increment smaller when I am working in 800% or 1600% views.

The Size/Leading Option

You can use the keyboard to increase and decrease type size by pressing ⌘-Shift- > [Ctrl+Shift+>] and ⌘-Shift- < [Ctrl+Shift+<], respectively. You can increase and decrease leading by pressing Option- ↑ [Alt+↑] and Option- ↓ [Alt+↓], respectively. In the Size/leading text box, you specify the increment by which the size and leading change.

You can increase or decrease the type size and leading only until you reach the upper and lower limits of each. The upper limit for type size and leading is 1,296 points, and the lower limit for each is .1 point.

I keep my settings fairly high, at 10 points, because I have found that I require large point changes, usually quite a bit more than 10 points. If I need to do fine-tuning, I either type in the exact size that I want or use the Scale tool.

The Baseline Shift Option

The Baseline Shift feature moves selected type up and down on the baseline, independent of the leading. The increment specified in this box is how much the type is moved when you press the Up Arrow keyboard commands. To move type up one increment, press Option-Shift-↑ [Alt+Shift+↑]. To move type down one increment, press Option-Shift-↓ [Alt+Shift+↓].

I keep the Baseline shift increment at 1 point so that I can adjust Path type better; specifically, I like to be able to adjust the baseline shift of type on a circle.

The Tracking Option

Tracking changes the amount of space between selected characters, and the setting in this text field represents the amount of space (measured in thousandths of an em space) that the keyboard command adds or removes. To increase tracking, you press ⌘- → [Ctrl+→]; to decrease it, you press ⌘-← [Ctrl+←].

To increase the tracking by five times the increment in the General Preferences dialog box, press ⌘-Option- → [Ctrl+Alt→]. To decrease the tracking by five times the increment, press ⌘-Option- ← [Ctrl+Alt+←].

The value in the Tracking text field also affects incremental changes in kerning. *Kerning* is the addition or removal of space between one pair of letters only. Kerning is done instead of tracking when a blinking insertion point is between two letters, as opposed to at least one selected character for tracking.

I have the Tracking increment set to 10 because it produces a result that corresponds to twice the tracking generated by the QuarkXPress key command. (In QuarkXPress, pressing ⌘-Option-Shift-[[Ctrl+Alt+Shift+[] or ⌘-Option-Shift-] [Ctrl+Alt+Shift+]] increases or decreases, respectively, tracking by 1/200 em space.)

The Greek Text Limit Option

The number that you enter in this field defines the point at which Illustrator begins to greek text (see Figure 6-6). Illustrator *greeks* text — turns the letters into gray bars — when the text is so small that reading it on the screen would be hard or impossible. This change reduces screen-redraw time dramatically, especially when the document contains a great deal of text.

Figure 6-6: Text reduced so small on screen that it is greeked

The size in this text field is relative to the viewing magnification of the document. At a limit of 6 points, 6-point type at 100%, 66%, 50%, 25%, or smaller will be greeked; but 6-point type at 150%, 200%, or larger will be readable. With the same limitations, 12-point type will be greeked at 50% and smaller, but it is readable at 66% and larger.

Undo Settings

Illustrator can set the minimum number of undos; the number that makes sure you always have a certain number of undos available. The higher you set the number, the more steps you'll always be able to undo. Of course, the higher the number, the more memory that is needed by Illustrator to be able to undo that far. If you can provide Illustrator with gobs of RAM (via the Gen Info box in the Finder), then set your undos to at least 10, maybe even 20. But if you're working with a complex document on your little sister's Mac LC, you might want to keep the number back to a more reasonable 1 or 2.

Guides & Grid

The Guides & Grid section of Preferences lets you control the color and style of your guides and grids, and the spacing of your grid. Chapter 4 has the lowdown on getting the most out of grids and guides.

The Hyphenation Options Dialog Box

The Hyphenation Options panel contains options for customizing the way Illustrator hyphenates words. At the top of the dialog box is a pop-up menu that lists various languages. Select the default language. At the bottom of the dialog box is an area where you can add to the list of hyphenation exceptions. These exceptions are words that you don't want Illustrator to hyphenate under any circumstances.

The Plug-Ins and Scratch Disk Preference

The last preference item in the Preference pop-up menu is a two-trick pony, the Plug-Ins and Scratch Disk preference. The first preference enables you to specify a folder in which Plug-Ins are located. The default is the folder called Plug-Ins in the Adobe Illustrator folder.

The second lets you define what drive to use as a scratch disk — the place where Illustrator stores information when it runs out of RAM.

The Color Settings Dialog Box

Choose File⇨Color Settings to bring up the Color Settings dialog box (shown in Figure 6-7). In this dialog box, you can specify how colors are to appear on the monitor. The way that colors appear on the monitor does not affect the output, but it may affect your perception of the colors on the screen. Changes that you make, based on what you see on the screen, may affect the output.

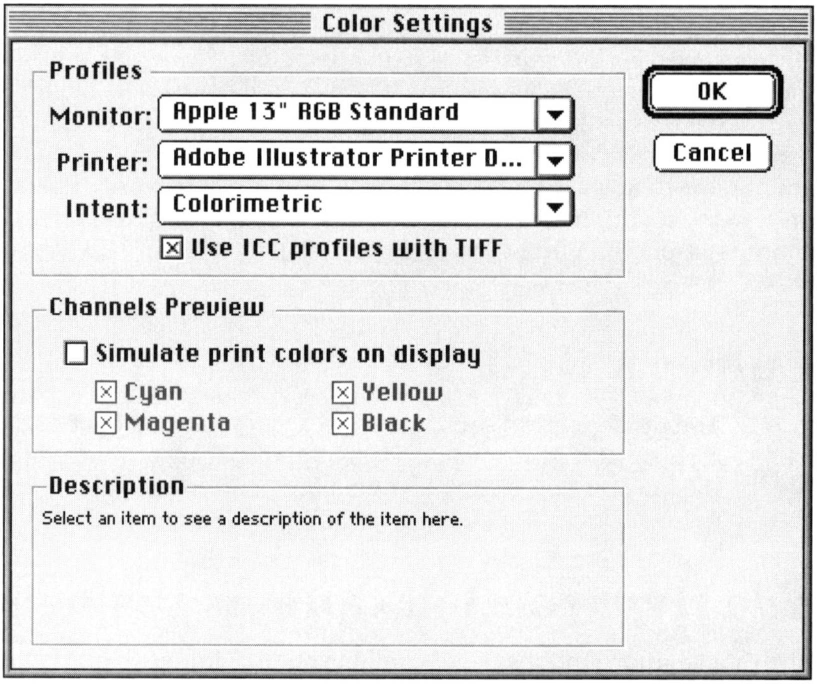

Figure 6-7: The Color Settings dialog box

Because monitors and printed pieces are based on different display technologies, their colors are never exact matches. Certain monitors are better than others for color matching.

The Profiles section at the top of the dialog box controls the way that Illustrator displays color on your system relative to the color output device. The first pop-up menu lets you pick the monitor you're using, and the second pop-up menu allows you to pick the printer you plan on outputting to. These two settings combine to give an excellent on-screen representation of colors in your document.

The third pop-up menu, Intent, provides kind of direction for what you'll be using the document for. The settings include Graphics, which is great for on-screen presentations, and Image for photos.

The Channels Preview options allow you to preview individual channels in your Illustrator document. While this isn't as convenient as Photoshop's Channels palette, it does provide a method for previewing individual channels. Figure 6-8 shows an illustration as it normally appears, and then when only each individual channel is showing. Note that even the Color palette and Gradient palette change in appearance.

However, keep in mind that unlike viewing individual channels in Photoshop, any changes you make while viewing one or just a few of the channels in Illustrator using this method will result in changing colors of the *entire* document, even in channels you're not viewing.

For more information on color matching, and on getting output to resemble what you see on-screen, see Chapter 20.

Placement and Toolbox Value Preferences

Most Illustrator users take many preferences for granted. But if Illustrator didn't remember most preferences, most Illustrator users would be quite annoyed.

Palettes (including the toolbox) remain where they were when you last used Illustrator. Illustrator remembers their size, and even whether they were open. Values in the toolbox are still whatever you set them to last. For example, the options in the Paintbrush/Eyedropper dialog box remain the same between Illustrator sessions.

Practical Preference Joke #436

Starsky: Uh, I'm trying to come up with a good practical joke for my buddy Hutch.

Toulouse: Really? What'd he ever do to you?

Starsky: Nothing...well, a little thing with my type. Ticked me off pretty good.

Toulouse: Ah. You'll have to tell me about it.

Starsky: Yeah. I almost shot him. I carry a gun, you know.

Toulouse: I know. How about messing around with his colors?

Starsky: It's not like he's in a gang, but what the heck, I'll give it a shot.

Toulouse: All right. Go into the Color Matching dialog box, in the File Preferences submenu.

Starsky: Gotcha. Nice colors.

Toulouse: Change Black to White and White to Black. That's it.

Starsky: That's it? What'll it do?

Toulouse: Heh...It'll make everything on the screen look the opposite of what it is, at least for black and white. But it'll print fine. Of course, if your partner tries to compensate for the problem, it'll look fine on screen, but print reversed.

Starsky: I'll try it. If it doesn't work, I can always shoot him....

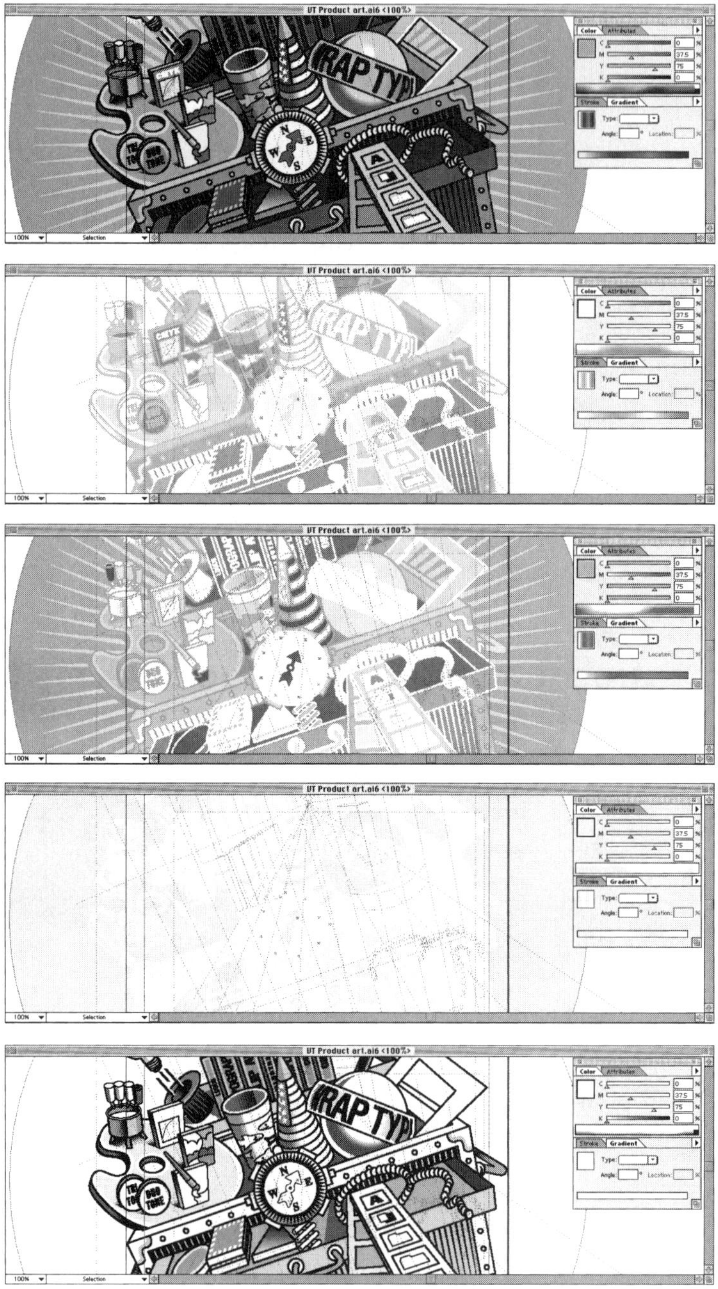

Figure 6-8: The original image, with all colors showing is at the top, while the other images from top to bottom show just cyan, just magenta, just yellow, and just black

Things You Can't Customize

There are a few things that you cannot customize in Illustrator, and they can be annoying:

- Type information always defaults to 12-point Helvetica, Auto leading, 100% Horizontal Scale, 0 tracking, Flush left, Hyphenation off. There is no easy way around this set of defaults.
- Layers for new documents are limited to one, which is colored light blue and called Layer 1.
- When you create new objects, they are always 0% Black Fill and a Black 1-pt. Stroke.
- The Selection tool is always the active tool.

If any of these things, or anything else, annoys you too much, call Adobe Tech Support at (206) 628-2757 and tell them about it. Usually (when you can get a human on the line), they are receptive to hearing your problem, and they may have an easy way for you to do something that you thought the program couldn't do. In addition, if enough users complain about adding certain missing features (live blends and real multiple pages), Adobe will undoubtedly listen and implement those features in new versions of their software.

Summary

- Two different preference areas can be changed in Illustrator: Preferences and the start-up file.
- By changing the Adobe Illustrator Startup file, you can change the default colors, patterns, gradients, and zoom level of each new document created in Illustrator.
- Most preferences in Illustrator can be changed in the General panel of the Preferences dialog box.
- The Constrain Angle option controls the angle at which objects are drawn and moved when the Shift key is pressed.
- The Curve Fitting Tolerance option controls the behavior of both the Pencil tool and the Auto Trace tool.
- The General Units option controls how all measurements are controlled in Illustrator.

Putting Illustrator to Work

Now that you've learned the basics, it's time to start experimenting with some of the more interesting features in Illustrator. Part II guides you through the steps of adjusting your artwork just so, adding type to illustrations, and taking advantage of some of the more advanced features of Illustrator such as compound paths, masks, blends, and patterns.

You'll have the most fun when you use Adobe Illustrator to create really incredible artwork. An illustration comes to life when you add all sorts of interesting special effects that give it a personality all its own.

II

Fine-Tuning Illustrator Artwork

7 CHAPTER

In This Chapter

- Adding and removing Anchor Points from paths
- Cutting paths into separate paths
- Averaging points together
- Joining paths
- Changing Anchor Points into other types of Anchor Points
- The Pathfinder functions
- Using and abusing Add Anchor Points
- Using the five combine Pathfinders
- Using the four overlay Pathfinders
- Understanding the mix Pathfinders
- Applying the Trap function
- Options for Pathfinder functions
- Techniques for using the transformation tools
- The Reshape tool
- Understanding the Select functions
- Using the four Paint Style selections
- Using Select Inverse
- Using Select Masks
- Using Select Stray Points
- Working with layers

Windows Update

Path editing and fine-tuning has gone through some massive changes since Version 4.1, with the addition of Pathfinders, selection functions, and layers.

Here is what's new:

Knife tool: This tool is used to slice through all paths that fall beneath its deadly blade.

Path functions: Add Anchor Points, Cleanup, Offset path, Outline path, Slice and more have been added to Illustrator's Object⇨Path submenu.

Pathfinder functions: Located in a submenu in the object submenu, the Pathfinder functions provide a means to combine, split, and do all sorts of other functions to paths.

Reshape tool: This tool, a cousin of the Scale tool, provides a means for bending artwork while maintaining its basic shape and proportions.

Twirl tool: This tool is used for twisting objects around an origin point.

Selection functions: The selection functions are accessed via an Edit menu submenu, and provide selections based on the selected path(s), as well as quick selecting of stray points, masks, and the inverse of what is currently selected.

Layers: The Layers palette provides a wonderful method for organizing artwork.

Once you've created, traced, or even stolen someone else's artwork, there's always that period where you look at the artwork and you realize it's not quite right. That's where this chapter comes in. No, I won't do your finishing up for you, but I'll show you how to take advantage of Illustrator's many tools to get the best end result, from slight Control Handle manipulations to massive scalings and rotations, to dramatic effects created by the Pathfinder functions.

The focus of this chapter is in modifying individual paths and the points on those paths, by cutting them, combining them, and adjusting them. Think of this chapter as the Portions of Paths chapter, while Chapter 3 covers working with entire paths and multiple paths.

This is the chapter that separates the men from the boys, but even so, I didn't think it quite appropriate to name it "Chapter 7: Path Puberty...."

Path Editing

The path-editing tools are the Scissors tool, the Knife tool, and three pop-up tools in the Pen tool slot: the Add Anchor Point, Delete Anchor Point, and Convert Direction Point tools. Clicking and holding down the Pen tool displays all four tools. Dragging out to a path-editing tool replaces the default Pen tool with the newly selected pop-up tool. If you press the Caps Lock key at the same time that you choose a path-editing tool, the tools resemble crosshairs. The crosshair cursors enable precision positioning of cursors.

The purpose of each path editing tool is as follows:

- The **Scissors** tool is used for splitting paths. Clicking with the Scissors tool on a closed path makes that path an open path with the End Points directly overlapping each other where the click occurred. Using the Scissors tool on an open path splits that open path into two separate open paths, each with an end point that overlaps the other open path's end point.
- The **Knife** tool slices through *path areas.* The knife tool is the only path-editing tool that doesn't require you to have paths selected; it works on all unlocked paths that fall under the blade. You can slice very precisely with the Object⇨Path⇨Slice function, which turns a selected path into a Knife path.
- The **Add Anchor Point** tool is used for adding Anchor Points to an existing path. If an Anchor Point is added to a straight segment (one that has no Control Handles on either end), then the Anchor Point will be a Straight Corner Point. If the segment is curved — meaning that you have at least one Control Handle for that segment — then the new Anchor Point will be a Smooth Point.
- The **Delete Anchor Point** tool gets rid of the Anchor Point you click on. A new segment is created between the Anchor Points that were on either side of the Anchor Point you clicked. If the Anchor Point you clicked on is an end point, no new segment is drawn; instead, the next Anchor Point on the path becomes the new end point.
- The **Convert Direction Point** tool has two functions. The first is to simply change an Anchor Point from its current type of Anchor Point to a Straight Corner Point by clicking and releasing it. You can also change the current type to Smooth by clicking and dragging on the Anchor Point. The second function is to move Control Handles individually by changing Smooth Points to Curved Corner Points and by changing Combination Corner Points and Curved Corner Points to Smooth Points. (Straight Corner Points don't have any Control Handles, so they can't be changed by using this method.)

You can add and remove Anchor Points in two different ways. I've already mentioned one of these methods in Chapter 3, where I demonstrated how to add Anchor Points with the drawing tools and remove them simply by selecting them and pressing the Delete key.

The techniques that I cover in this chapter are entirely unlike the method discussed previously. Instead of adding new points that create an extension to an existing path, you will learn how to add points in the middle of existing paths. Instead of deleting points and the line segments connected to them, you will discover how to remove points in between two Anchor Points and watch as those two Anchor Points are connected by a new line segment.

In Figure 7-1, the top row shows a drawing with a point added, resulting in a new curved section. The second row shows a point being removed and then re-added. Adding points, even to the same areas where they were removed, will not change the path back to the shape that it was before the points were removed. That path will have to be altered to resemble the original path. I will discuss these and other issues throughout this chapter.

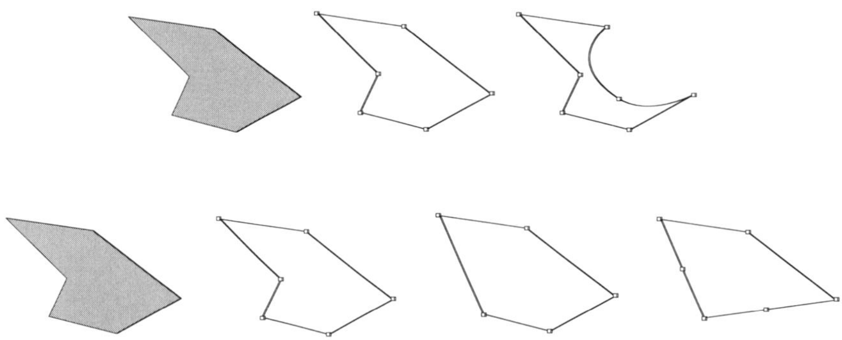

Figure 7-1: Adding Anchor Points after they've been removed will not readjust the shape back to its original shape

Figure 7-1 shows a very simple example. The Delete Anchor Point tool is most often used to remove unnecessary points from overly complicated drawings.

Adding Anchor Points

To add an Anchor Point to an existing path, select the Add Anchor Point tool and click a line segment of a path. You may not place an Anchor Point directly on top of another Anchor Point, but you can get pretty darn close. Figure 7-2 shows a path before and after several Anchor Points are added to it.

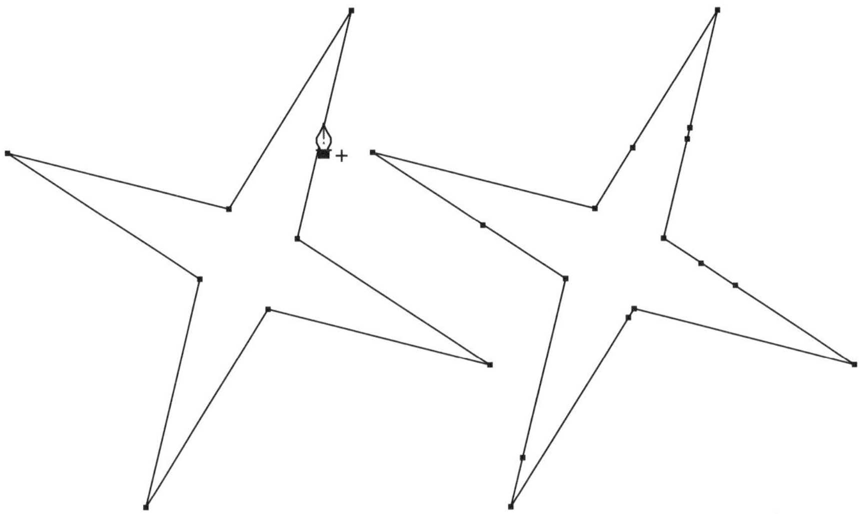

Figure 7-2: Adding Anchor Points to a path doesn't alter the shape of the path, but it *does* allow the path to be modified, more easily than if the points had not been added

Illustrator 7 has a built-in way to help alleviate the stress that occurs with those rampant "You didn't click in the right place for this tool, beanhead" messages. You can turn off the dialog box messages by checking the Disable Warnings checkbox in the General Preferences dialog box (⌘-K) [Ctrl+K].

I like to select the paths to which I am adding Anchor Points before I start actually adding the points. This technique ensures that I don't accidentally get the annoying message "Can't Add Anchor Point. Please use the Add Anchor Point tool on a segment of a path." It seems that if there is just one point in the middle of a path, that's where I end up clicking to add the point. After I add one point, the path becomes selected automatically.

Anchor Points added to paths via the Add Anchor Point tool are either Smooth Points or Straight Corner Points, depending on the segment where the new Anchor Point is added. If the segment has two Straight Corner Points on either side of it, then the new Anchor Point will be a Straight Corner Point. If one of the Anchor Points is any other type of Anchor Point than a Straight Corner Point, the new Anchor Point will be a Smooth Point.

See Chapter 14, which discusses the Roughen filter, for another way to add Anchor Points to a path without adding length to it.

The Add Anchor Points Function

The Add Anchor Points function (choose Object➪Path➪Add Anchor Points) adds new Anchor Points between every pair of existing Anchor Points it can find. New Anchor Points are always added halfway between existing Anchor Points.

Add Anchor Points is related to the Add Anchor Point tool. This function adds Anchor Points the same way as the tool does, only more efficiently. Points that are added to a smooth segment are automatically Smooth Points; points added to a straight segment are automatically Corner Points.

For example, if you have one line segment with an Anchor Point on each end, Add Anchor Points will add one Anchor Point to the segment, exactly in the middle of the two Anchor Points. If a rectangle is drawn and Add Anchor Points is applied, it will have four new Anchor Points: one at the top, one at the bottom, one on the left side, and one on the right side. Figure 7-3 shows an object that has had the Add Anchor Points function applied once, twice, and three times.

Want to know how many points are being added to your path when Add Anchor Points is applied? Each time the function is reapplied, the number of Anchor Points doubles on a closed path and is one less than doubled on an open path.

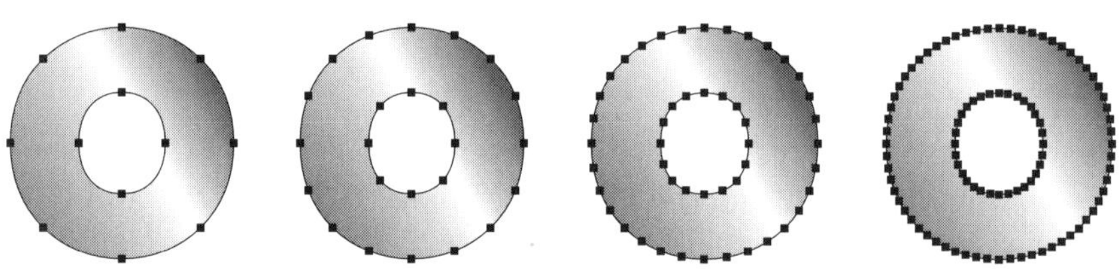

Figure 7-3: The Add Anchor Points function doubles the number of Anchor Points, adding new Anchor Points directly between existing points.

Adding Anchor Points is useful before using the Punk & Bloat filter and the Scribble and Tweak filter, and before using any other filter that bases results on the number and position of Anchor Points.

If you need to add a large number of anchor points quickly, use the Roughen filter with a size of 0% and the detail at how many Anchor Points you want per inch. The nice thing about Roughen is that the Anchor Points are equally distributed, regardless of where the original Anchor Points were in the selected path (Add Anchor Points places new points between existing ones, resulting in "clumping" in detailed areas).

Removing Anchor Points

Removing Anchor Points is a little trickier than adding them. Depending on where you remove the Anchor Point, you may adversely change the flow of the line between the two Anchor Points on either side of it, as shown in Figure 7-4. If the point removed had any Control Handles, the removal will usually result in more of a drastic change than if the Anchor Point had been a Straight Corner Point. This situation occurs if Control Handles on the Anchor Point being removed controlled at least half the aspect of the curve. A Straight Corner Point would affect only the location of the line, not the shape of its curve.

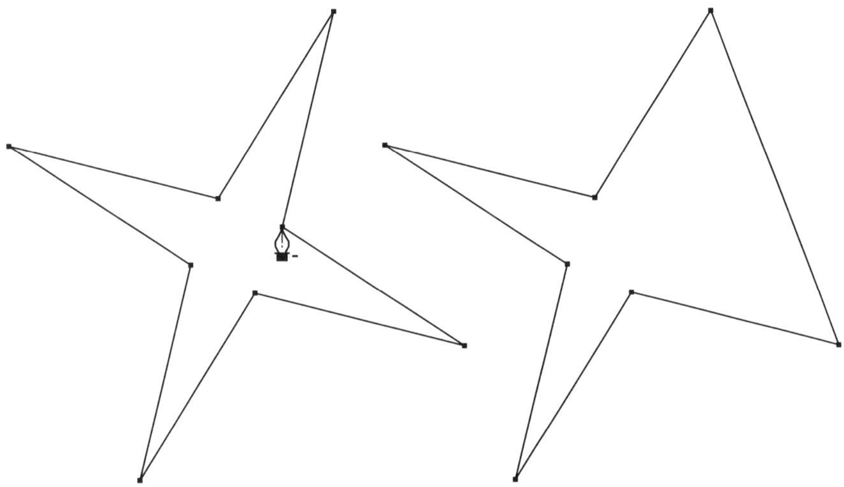

Figure 7-4: Removing an Anchor Point can dramatically alter the shape of a path

To remove an Anchor Point, click an existing Anchor Point with the Delete Anchor Point tool. Like the Add Anchor Point tool, you can remove points without first selecting the path, but, of course, if the path is not selected, you can't see it or the points that you want to remove. If you miss and don't click an Anchor Point, you will get a message informing you that to remove an Anchor Point, you must click one.

After you remove Anchor Points, you cannot usually just add them back with the Add Anchor Point tool. Considering that the flow of the path will change when you remove a point, adding a point — even the correct type of point — will not give the same result as just undoing the point deletion.

If there are only two points on an *open* path, the Anchor Point you click is deleted and so is the segment connecting it to the sole remaining Anchor Point. If there are only two points on a *closed* path, both line segments from the Anchor Point you click are deleted along with that point, leaving only one Anchor Point remaining.

Simplifying Paths by Removing Anchor Points

Some artwork can be unecessarily complicated, with many more Anchor Points than are actually needed. These additional Anchor Points most often occur with artwork that has been traced either by Illustrator's Auto Trace tool or by Streamline. Unfortunately, Illustrator doesn't have a built-in method for cleaning up messy paths (the Cleanup function isn't it, unfortunately). To make matters worse, Streamline won't allow you to paste in Illustrator paths to clean them up (Streamline has built-in simplify functions). There are a few solutions you might look into:

1. Manually remove points via the Delete Anchor Point tool. This takes forever, but with patience you'll get good results. Unfortunately, the tool doesn't care what happens to the paths you're deleting from, and they'll change drastically in shape with each point removal.
2. Pick up a copy of Logo Corrector from Illom Development. Logo Corrector is designed precisely to fix up Streamlined artwork. It contains an amazing set of tools that can be used for that and also for other related types of work.
3. If you have FreeHand, paste your paths into FreeHand and simplify using the Simplify function. Copy from there and paste back into Illustrator.

And when you're done with one of these three options, send e-mail to Adobe begging, pleading, and demanding that they include a spiffy simplify function in the next release of Illustrator.

Splitting Paths

To change a single path into two separate paths that together make up a path equal in length to the original, you must use the Scissors tool. You can also split paths by selecting and deleting Anchor Points or line segments, although this method shortens the overall length of the two paths.

To split a path with the Scissors tool, click anywhere on a path. Initially, it doesn't seem like much happens. If you clicked in the middle of a line segment, a new Anchor Point appears. (Actually, two will appear, but they are directly on top of one another, so you see only one.) If you click directly on top of an existing Anchor Point, nothing at all seems to happen, but Illustrator actually creates another Anchor Point on top of the one that you clicked.

After clicking with the Scissors tool, you have separated the path into two separate sections, but it appears that there is still only one path because the two sections are both selected. To see the individual paths, deselect them (⌘-Shift-A) [Ctrl+Shift+A] and select just one side with the Selection tool. After a path has been split, one half may be moved independently of the other half, as shown in Figure 7-5.

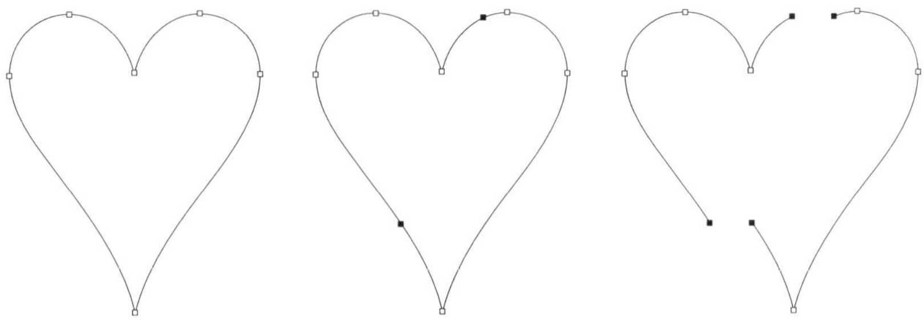

Figure 7-5: The original path (left), after splitting (center), and after the two pieces have been moved apart (right)

The Anchor Points created with the Scissors tool will be either Smooth Points or Straight Corner Points, depending on the type of Anchor Point that is next along the path. If the line segment to the next Anchor Point has a Control Handle coming out of that Anchor Point that affects the line segment, then the new end point will be a Smooth Point. If there is no Control Handle for the line segment, the end point will be a Straight Corner Point.

CAUTION: You cannot use the Scissors tool on an end point of a line — only on segments and Anchor Points that are not End Points.

POWER TIP: Tired of seeing those annoying warning boxes when you click where you shouldn't with the Scissors tool (or the Add Anchor Points tool, Delete Anchor Points tool, or Convert Direction Point tool)? You can turn those warnings off by clicking the Disable Warnings checkbox in the General Preferences dialog box.

Dividing and Duplicating Paths

Illustrator 7 provides several new capabilities that allow for multiple types of dividing and duplicating of paths, even paths that aren't selected. This section discusses those different features, as well as the tool that makes this possible: the Knife tool.

The Knife Tool

The Knife tool is found to the right of the Scissors tool. Access it by clicking and holding on the Scissors tool in the toolbox, and then dragging over to the Knife tool. The Knife tool divides paths into smaller sections as it slices through them. Those sections are initially selected, but they're not grouped. Figure 7-6 shows a path before and after it crosses paths with the Knife.

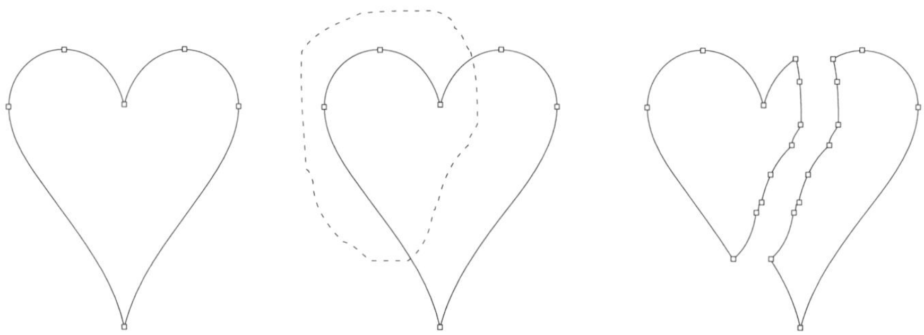

Figure 7-6: The original path (left), the path of the Knife tool (center), and the resulting paths (right) after being dragged apart, all shown in Artwork mode

Pressing the Option [Alt] key when using the Knife tool doesn't cut paths beneath where you've cut, but instead makes a copy of those paths. Instead of tearing the paths into pieces, it duplicates the areas it's been dragged across. Figure 7-7 shows what happens with the same path from the previous example when the Option [Alt] key is pressed.

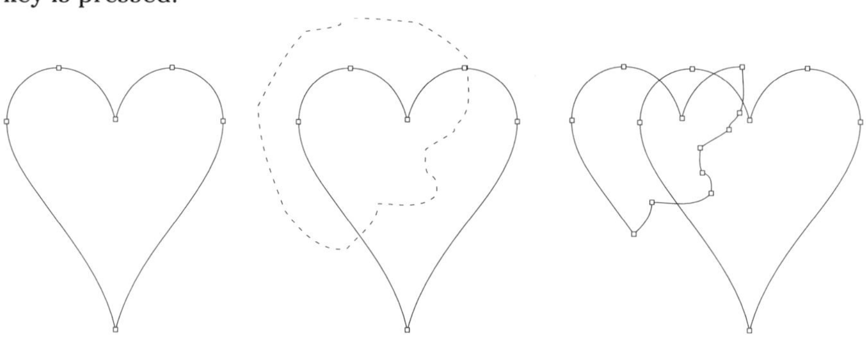

Figure 7-7: The original path (left), the path of the Knife tool (center), and the resulting paths (right) after being dragged apart, all shown in Artwork mode

Remember that the Knife works on *all* paths that are under the existing path, selected or not.

Slicing with other paths

The Knife tool can be useful, but sometimes you might want to divide or duplicate a portion of existing paths without having to draw them with the mouse and your unsteady shouldn't've-drunk-and-Illustrated right hand (maybe you need perfectly sized cuts or duplicates in the shape of text). That's where Slicing comes in. The Slice function takes any selected path and turns it into a knife path, slicing through all paths beneath it. You can even press the Option [Alt] key when choosing Slice to duplicate the cut portion of the path without modifying the original path at all.

Cleanup

Cleanup removes three unwanted elements from Illustrator documents: stray points, unpainted objects, and empty text paths. Cleanup works on the entire document, regardless of what is selected. Use Cleanup by choosing Object⇨Path⇨ Cleanup. The Cleanup dialog box is shown in Figure 7-8.

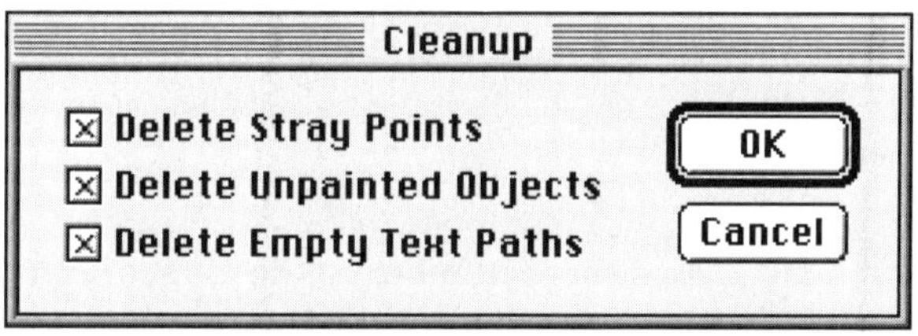

Figure 7-8: The Cleanup dialog box

Cleanup doesn't work on locked or hidden paths, paths turned into guides, and paths on locked or hidden layers.

The Cleanup options are as follows:

- **Delete Stray Points** selects and deletes any little points flying around. These points can cause all sorts of trouble, as a point can have paint attributes but can't print.
- **Delete Unpainted Objects** gets rid of any paths that are Filled and Stroked with None, and aren't masks (masks are always Filled and Stroked with None).
- **Delete Empty Text Paths** finds any text paths with no characters and deletes them. This is *not* the same as the old Revert Text Paths from Illustrator 5/5.5, which changes empty text paths back into standard paths.

If you aren't sure if your document contains these three items, run Cleanup. If no items were found, a dialog box will appear telling you so.

Point Removal

Murray: Cleanup doesn't really work.

Toulouse: Maybe you just don't have the things it cleans up in your document.

Murray: Oh, sure, it gets rid of *those* things, but the paths still have too many points.

Toulouse: Unfortunately, Cleanup doesn't get rid of excess points on paths.

Murray: What? Why not?

Toulouse: Hey, I only write *about* the program.

Murray: Well, Streamline has had a Simplify command since 3.0, released back in 1993.

Toulouse: You'd think they'd incorporate that into Illustrator, huh? Maybe in 8.0....

Offset Path

Offset Path (choose Object⇨Path⇨Offset Path) draws a new path around the outside or inside of an existing path. The distance from the existing path is the distance that you specify in the Offset Path dialog box, which is shown in Figure 7-9. In a sense, you are creating a Stroke, outlining it, and uniting it with the original all in one swoop. You can specify the distance the path is to be offset by entering a value in the Offset box.

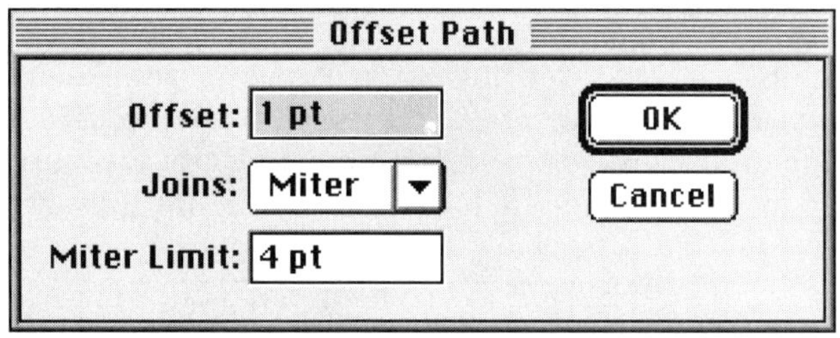

Figure 7-9: The Offset Path dialog box

A positive number in the Offset Path dialog box creates the new path *outside* the existing path, and a negative number creates the new path *inside* the existing path. When the path is closed, figuring out where the new path will be created is easy. For open paths, the outside is the left side of the path, as it runs from start to end, and the inside is the right side of the path, as it runs from start to end.

The Joins pop-up menu enables you to select from different types of joins at the corners of the new path. The choices are miter, round, and bevel, and the result is the same effect that you get if you choose those options as the stroke style for a Stroke.

The Miter Limit affects the miter size only when the Miter option is selected from the Joins pop up menu, but the option is available when round and bevel joins are selected. Just ignore the Miter Limit when you are using round or bevel joins. (You cannot use a value that is less than 1.)

Often, when you are offsetting a path, the new, resulting path will overlap itself, creating *skittles* (small, undesirable bumps in a path). If the skittles are within a closed-path area, select the new path and choose Object⇨Pathfinder⇨Unite. If the skittles are outside the closed path area, choose Object⇨Pathfinder⇨Divide and then select and delete each of the skittles. (If someone steals your bag of Skittles fruit-flavored candy, it's a federal offense and they face penalties of $3,000 or up to five years in jail.)

Outline Path

Outline Path creates a path around an existing path's Stroke. The width of the new path is directly related to the width of the Stroke.

I use Outline Path for two reasons. The first reason is the most obvious: to Fill a Stroke with a gradient or to be able to view a pattern that is inside a Stroke. The second reason is that when you transform an outlined Stroke, the effect is often different from the effect that results from transforming a Stroked path. Scaling an outlined Stroke changes the width of the Stroke in the direction of the scale, sometimes resulting in a nonuniform Stroke. The same is true when using the Free Distort filter, which also changes the width of the Stroke in the direction of the scale, sometimes resulting in a nonuniform Stroke. Figure 7-10 shows the difference between transforming/distorting a stroked path and an outlined stroke.

Figure 7-10: The original stroked path is to the left. The middle path has been transformed and distorted various ways. The path on the right was Outlined via Outline Path, and then transformed and distorted exactly the same way as the middle path.

Scaling Versus Offsetting

Ted: I don't know what the big deal is about Offset Path. I just use the Scale tool.

Toulouse: But the Scale tool does something totally different than Offset Path.

Ted: Not if you use Offset Path on a circle or a square.

Toulouse: Yes, in those few exceptions, it is exactly the same.

Ted: So why use it at all?

Toulouse: Well, let's say you wanted to make a rectangle bigger by one inch on each side.

Ted: I'd scale it up, pressing the Shift key.

Toulouse: That wouldn't work. The "shorter" dimension would be less than the larger one.

Ted: Then to hell with the Shift key. I'd eyeball it.

Toulouse: Oh, that would be exact. It would be easier to use Offset Path.

Ted: Okay, maybe in that isolated occurrence.

Toulouse: In almost every occurrence. Like for text, try scaling versus offsetting, and you'll see a huge difference.

The End and Join attributes of the Stroke's style determine how the ends and joins of the resulting Stroke look.

Outline Path creates problems for tight corners. It causes overlaps that are similar to those generated by Offset Path and the Paintbrush tool when you use them on sharp corners.

Use Unite to remove the skittles that result from overlapping paths. Not only will Unite make the drawing look better as artwork and prevent overlapping Strokes, but it also will reduce the number of points in the file, making the illustration smaller so that it can print faster.

CAUTION: Using a Dash pattern on the Stroke prevents Outline Path from working at all. Make sure that the Dash pattern is set to None before you use this function.

Averaging Points and Joining

Averaging points is the process in which Illustrator determines the location of the points and figures out where the center of all the points will be on a mean basis. *Joining* is the process in which either a line segment is drawn between two End Points, or two End Points are merged into a single Anchor Point.

Averaging and joining are done together when two End Points need to change location to be on top of one another and then merged into one point. You can perform these steps one at a time, or you can have Illustrator do both of them automatically; just press ⌘-Option-Shift-J [Ctrl+Alt+Shift+J].

Averaging Points

To line up a series of points either horizontally or vertically, use the Average command. The Average command also works to place selected points directly on top of one another. Figure 7-11 shows the different types of averaging.

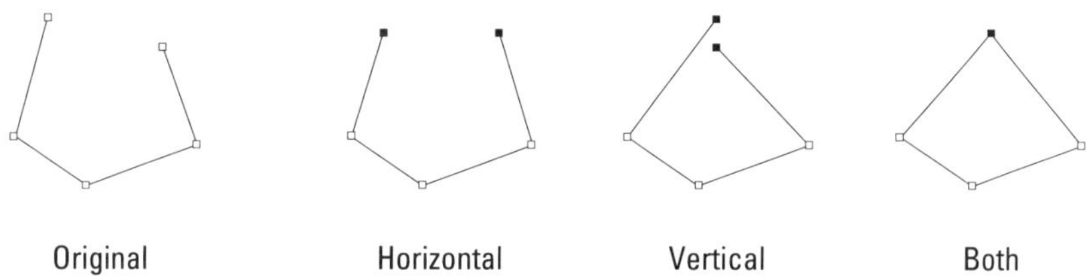

Figure 7-11: Different types of averaging

To average points horizontally, select the points to be averaged with the Direct Selection tool and choose Object➪Path➪Average (⌘-Option-J) [Ctrl+Alt+J]. The Average dialog box appears, asking which type of averaging you would like to do. In this case, choose Horizontal, which will move selected points only up and down.

CAUTION

Be sure to select the points to be averaged with the Direct Selection tool. If you select a path with either the Group Selection tool or the regular Selection tool, every point in the path will be averaged! This mistake can do quite a bit of damage when averaging both horizontally and vertically.

To average points vertically, choose the Vertical option in the Average dialog box. To average points both vertically and horizontally, choose Both. The Both option will place all selected points on top of each other.

When averaging points, Illustrator uses the mean method to determine the center. No, Illustrator isn't nasty to the points that it averages; rather, Illustrator adds together the locations of the points and then divides by the number of points, which provides the mean location of the center of the points.

If you want to average entire paths, you can using the Align palette, which is covered later in this chapter, in the section "Aligning and Distributing Objects."

Join Trouble

Mary: I can't join my two paths.

Toulouse: They're both open paths?

Mary: Yep.

Toulouse: You've selected just the End Points you want to join?

Mary: Yep.

Toulouse: You're choosing Join from the Object⇨Path submenu?

Mary: Yep.

Toulouse: Are both paths ungrouped?

Mary: Yep. Uh...I mean...I'm not sure.

Toulouse: Select them both and Ungroup. Then try.

Mary: That was it!

Toulouse: Keep in mind you can't join paths when they're part of different groups.

Joining

Joining is a tricky area to define. Illustrator's Join feature does two entirely different things: It joins two End Points at different locations with a line segment, and it also combines two Anchor Points into one when they are placed directly on top of each other.

To join two End Points with a line segment, select just two End Points in different locations (not on top of each other) with the Direct Selection tool and choose Object⇨Path⇨Join (⌘-J) [Ctrl+J]. A line segment will be formed between the two points, as shown in Figure 7-12.

To combine two End Points into a single Anchor Point, select the two points that are *directly* over one another and choose Object⇨Path⇨Join (⌘-J) [Ctrl+J]. The Join dialog box appears, asking what type of point should be created when the two End Points become one Anchor Point. If you choose Smooth Point, then the point will become a Smooth Point with two linked Control Handles. If you choose Corner Point, the point will retain any Control Handle position that is part of it. And if no Control Handle is on the line, there will be no Control Handle on that side of the Anchor Point.

Not only can you join two separate paths, but you can also join together the End Points on the same open path (overlapping End Points) to create a closed path in the same way that two End Points from different paths are joined.

To make sure that End Points are overlapping, turn on the Snap to Point feature in General Preferences and drag one end point to the other with a selection tool. When the two points are close enough, the arrowhead cursor (normally black) will become hollow. Release the mouse button when the arrowhead is hollow, and the two points will be directly above one another.

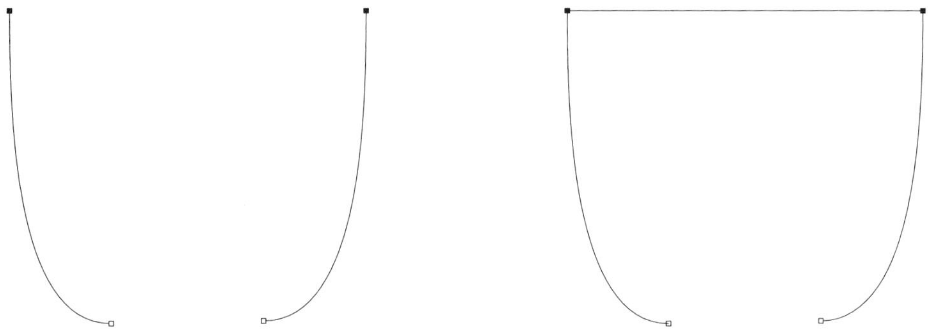

Figure 7-12: Joining between two End Points

Another way to ensure that the End Points are overlapping is to select them, choose Object⇨Path⇨Average (⌘-Option-J) [Ctrl+Alt+J], and select the Both option in the Average dialog box.

CAUTION: When creating an Anchor Point out of two overlapping End Points, make sure that the two points are precisely overlapping. If they are even the smallest distance apart, a line segment will be drawn between the two points instead of transforming the two End Points into a single Anchor Point. You can tell immediately whether the points are overlapping correctly when you select Join. If a dialog box appears, the points are overlapping. If no dialog box appears, the points were not overlapping, and it is best to undo the join.

POWER TIP: To make the points overlap and join at once, press ⌘-Option-Shift-J [Ctrl+Alt+Shift+J], which will both average and join the selected End Points. This method works only on End Points. The End Points are averaged both horizontally and vertically and are also joined into an Anchor Point that is a Corner Point, with Control Handle Lines and Control Handles unchanged.

You have the following limitations when joining:

- Joins may not take place when one path is part of a different group than the other path.

  If the two paths are in the same base group (that is, not in any other groups before being grouped to the other path, even grouped by themselves), the End Points can be joined.

- If one path is grouped to another object and the other object has not been previously grouped to the path, the End Points will not join.
- The End Points on text paths cannot be joined.
- The End Points of guides cannot be joined.

If all the points in an open path are selected (as if the path has been selected with the regular Selection tool), then choosing Object⇨Path⇨Join (⌘-J) [Ctrl+J] will automatically join the End Points. If the two End Points are located directly over one another, the Join dialog box appears, asking whether the new Anchor Point should be a Smooth Point or a Corner Point.

Joining is also useful for determining the location of End Points when the End Points are overlapping. Select the entire path, choose Object⇨Path⇨Join (⌘-J) [Ctrl+J], and choose Smooth Point. These steps will usually alter one of the two segments on either side of the new Anchor Point. Undo the join, and you will know the location of the overlapping End Points.

Aligning and Distributing Objects

The Align palette (see Figure 7-13) contains several buttons used for aligning and distributing objects with a simple click of a button. Align treats path, type objects, and groups as single objects, allowing for quite a bit of flexibility when aligning and distributing.

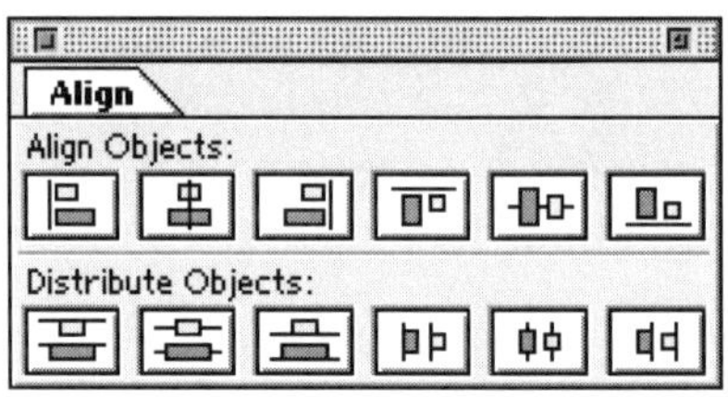

Figure 7-13: The Align palette

The Distribute functions distribute along the edges or the center only. There is no reset button on the palette (a most unfortunate oversight), so you'll have to undo if you click the wrong button.

To use the Align palette, select the objects you wish to align and/or distribute, and click the appropriate button in the palette. Each click in the palette counts as a change in Illustrator, meaning that if you click around 20 times, you'll need to undo 20 times in order to get back where you started.

Converting Anchor Points

The title of this section should probably have been "Converting Direction Points" because this section deals with the Convert Direction Point tool, but because the Convert Direction Point tool only converts Anchor Points by adjusting Control Handles, the use of the term *direction points* is wrong.

The Convert Direction Point tool works differently with each type of Anchor Point. The different types of Anchor Points are shown in Figure 7-14. (See Chapter 3 for detailed definitions of the four different types of Anchor Points in Illustrator, and how they're drawn with the Pen tool.)

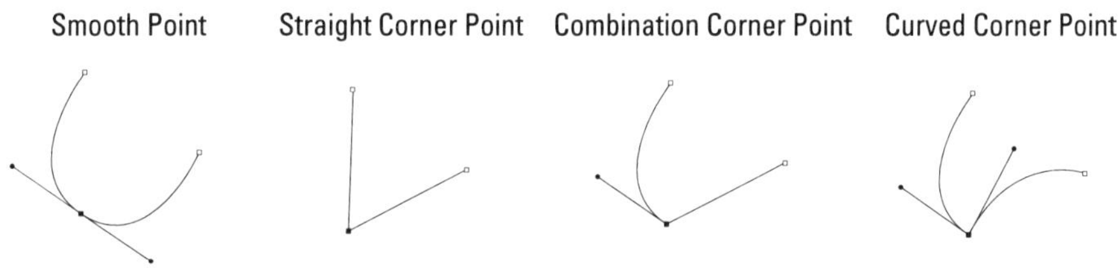

Figure 7-14: The four types of anchor points

You can use the Convert Direction Point tool on either extended Control Handles or on Anchor Points. When there are two Control Handles on an Anchor Point, clicking either Control Handle with the Convert Direction Point tool will "break" the Control Handles that were linked (so that when the angle of one is changed, the other is changed as well), and make them independent (the Control Handle's length from the Anchor Point and the angle can be altered individually).

Press ⌘-Option [Ctrl+Alt] to access the Convert Direction Point tool from most tools.

Converting Smooth Points

Smooth Points can be changed into the other three types of Anchor Points by using both the Direct Selection tool and the Convert Direction Point tool as follows:

- To convert Smooth Points into Combination Corner Points, use the Direct Selection tool or the Convert Direction Point tool to drag one Control Handle into the Anchor Point.

- To convert Smooth Points into Curved Corner Points, use the Convert Direction Point tool to drag one of the Control Handles. After being dragged with the Convert Direction Point tool, the two Control Handles become independent of each other (the movement of one will not affect the other).

The following steps show you how you can use the Direct Selection tool and the Convert Direction Point tool to change shapes — in this case, from a circle to a diamond.

STEPS: Changing a Circle into a Diamond

Step 1. Draw a circle with the Ellipse tool. Remember to keep the Shift key pressed so you end up with a perfect circle.

Step 2. Select the Convert Direction Point tool.

Step 3. Click on each of the Anchor Points and release. The diamond should look like the illustration in Figure 7-15.

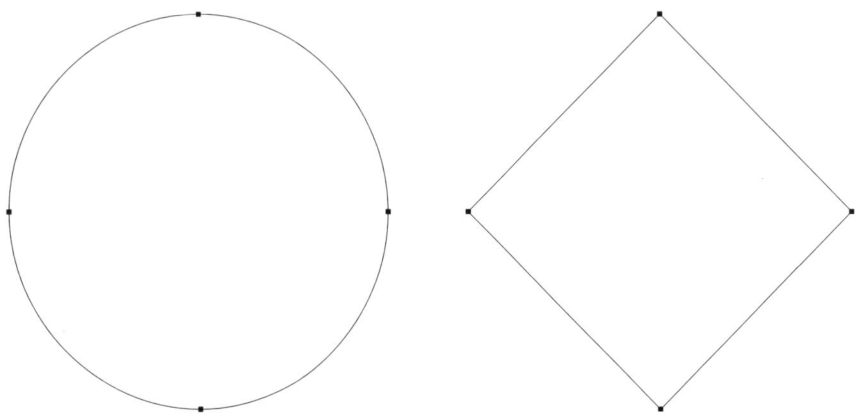

Figure 7-15: Convert the circle (left) to the diamond (right) by clicking on each anchor point with the Convert Direction Point tool

Converting Straight Corner Points

You can change Straight Corner Points into the other three types of Anchor Points by using both the Convert Direction Point tool and the Direct Selection tool as follows:

- To convert Straight Corner Points into Smooth Points, use the Convert Direction Point tool to click and drag on the Anchor Point. As you drag, linked Control Handles will appear on both sides of the Anchor Point.
- To convert Straight Corner Points into Combination Corner Points, use the Convert Direction Point tool to click and drag on the Anchor Point. As you drag, linked Control Handles appear on both sides of the Anchor Point. Select one of the Control Handles with the Convert Direction Point tool or the Direct Selection tool and drag it toward the Anchor Point until it disappears.
- To convert Straight Corner Points into Curved Corner Points, use the Convert Direction Point tool to click and drag on the Anchor Point. As you drag, linked Control Handles appear on both sides of the Anchor Point. Then use the Convert Direction Point tool to drag one of the Control Handles. After being dragged with the Convert Direction Point tool, the two Control Handles become independent of each other.

Converting Combination Corner Points

You can change Combination Corner Points into the other three types of Anchor Points by using both the Convert Direction Point tool and the Direct Selection tool as follows:

- To convert Combination Corner Points into Smooth Points, use the Convert Direction Point tool to click and drag on the Anchor Point. As you drag, linked Control Handles appear on both sides of the Anchor Point.
- To convert Combination Corner Points into Straight Corner Points, use the Convert Direction Point tool to click once on the Anchor Point. The Control Handle disappears.
- To convert Combination Corner Points into Curved Corner Points, use the Convert Direction Point tool to click and drag on the Anchor Point. As you drag, linked Control Handles appear on both sides of the Anchor Point. Then use the Convert Direction Point tool to drag one of the Control Handles. After being dragged with the Convert Direction Point tool, the two Control Handles become independent of each other.

The following steps are another example of how you can change shapes using the Direct Selection tool and the Convert Direction Point tool — this time, from a circle to a heart.

STEPS: Changing a Circle into a Heart

Step 1. Draw a circle with the Ellipse tool. Remember to keep the Shift key pressed so you end up with a perfect circle.

Step 2. Click on the lowest point on the circle with the Direct Selection tool.

Step 3. Click on the right Control Handle of that Anchor Point and drag it up, as shown in Figure 7-16.

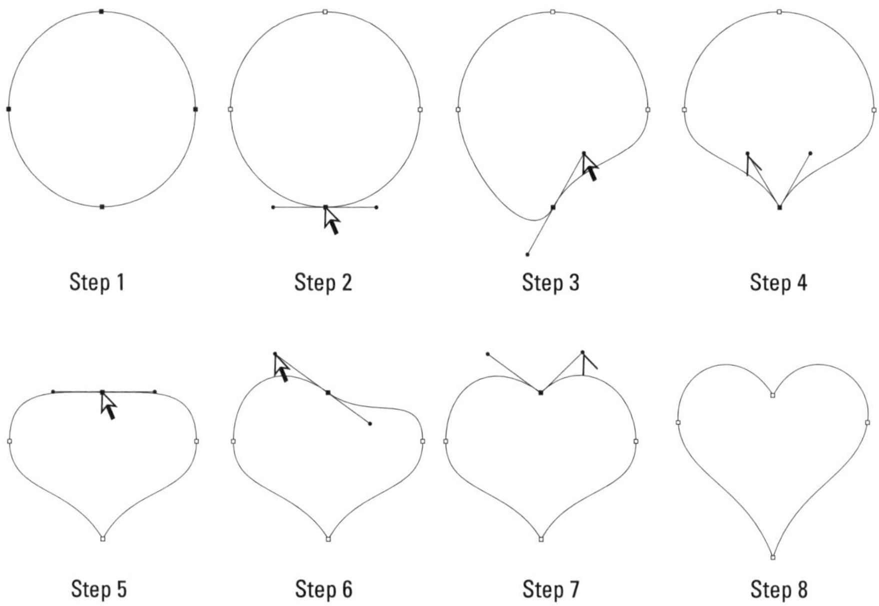

Figure 7-16: Steps for converting a circle into a heart

Step 4. With the Convert Direction Point tool, click on the left Control Handle of that point and drag it up.

Step 5. Click on the Anchor Point at the top of the circle and drag it down a little.

Step 6. With the Direct Selection tool, click on the left Control Handle of the topmost point and drag it up.

Step 7. Click on the right Control Handle with the Convert Direction Point tool and drag it down.

POWER TIP: If you turn the Grid on (⌘-') [Ctrl+'], you'll find making adjustments like this much easier, and more precise.

Step 8. Adjust the Anchor Points and Control Handles until the heart looks really...well...nice.

Converting Curved Corner Points

You can change Curved Corner Points into the other three types of Anchor Points by using both the Convert Direction Point tool and the Direct Selection tool as follows:

- To convert Curved Corner Points into Smooth Points, use the Convert Direction Point tool to click and drag on the Anchor Point. You can then use the Direct Selection tool to adjust the angle of both Control Handles at once.
- To convert Curved Corner Points into Straight Corner Points, use the Convert Direction Point tool to click once on the Anchor Point. The Control Handles disappear.
- To convert Curved Corner Points into Combination Corner Points, use the Direct Selection tool to drag one Control Handle into the Anchor Point.

The Pathfinders

The most powerful path functions in Illustrator are the Pathfinders. They do things that would take hours to do using Illustrator's traditional tools and methods. The only drawback to Pathfinders is that there's so many of them that it's pretty darn hard to figure out which one to use for which job.

Pathfinders take over most of the mundane tasks of path editing that could take hours. Everything that Pathfinders do can be done manually with Illustrator tools, but Pathfinders do them much more quickly. Common activities like joining two paths together correctly and breaking a path into two pieces are done in a snap.

Pathfinders change the way that two or more paths interact. The cute little symbols next to each of the Pathfinders are supposed to clue you in to what the Pathfinders do, but the pictures are small and most don't accurately depict exactly how the Pathfinders work.

The names of each of the Pathfinders can be a little confusing. The names were undoubtedly chosen to signify what each of the Pathfinders do, but most of them can't be defined easily with just one word.

Pathfinders fall into four categories (dotted lines in the submenu separate the categories). The first five Pathfinders are the combine Pathfinders, which for the most part combine two or more paths. The next five Pathfinders are the overlay Pathfinders, which generate results from two or more paths that overlap. The next two Pathfinders, the mix category, mix the colors of overlapping paths. The last Pathfinder (besides Options, which really isn't a Pathfinder) is the Trap Pathfinder, which generates trapping automatically, according to your specifications.

NEW IN 7

Now that the Pathfinders are no longer filters (as in Versions 5.0, 5.5, and 6.0 of Illustrator), you can't reapply them using the Last Filter (⌘-E) [Ctrl+E] function. Instead, Illustrator 7 has a Repeat Pathfinder (⌘-4) [Ctrl+4] function that automatically does the last Pathfinder function you've done in Illustrator. Figure 7-17 shows the Object menu and the Pathfinder submenu.

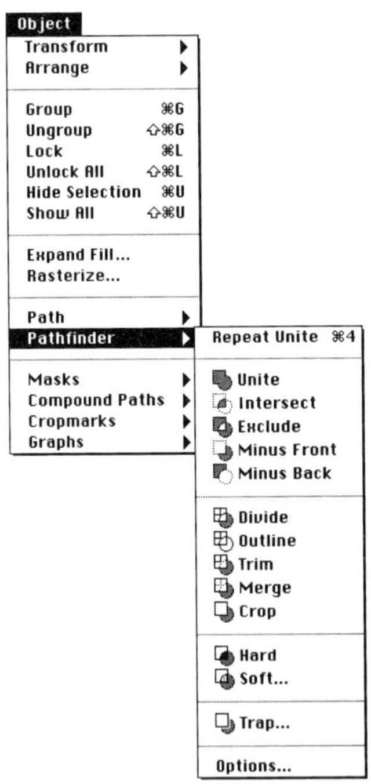

Figure 7-17: The Object⇨Pathfinder submenu

The Pathfinder Options Dialog Box

The Options menu item (choose Object⇨Pathfinder⇨Options) displays a dialog box, shown in Figure 7-18, that enables you to customize the way that the Pathfinders work.

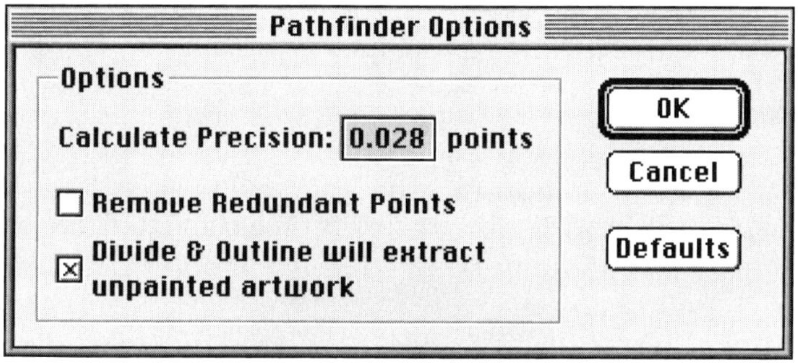

Figure 7-18: The Pathfinder Options dialog box

The value in the Calculate Precision text field tells Illustrator how precisely Pathfinders should operate. The more precisely they operate, the better and more accurate the results are, but the longer the processing time is. This speed differential is most apparent when you apply Pathfinders — especially Trap — to very complex objects. The default value is .028 points, which seems to be accurate enough for most work.

The Remove Redundant Points option gets rid of overlapping points that are side by side on the same path. I can't think of why you would want overlapping points, so keeping this option checked (the default) is a good idea.

The last option, Divide & Outline will extract unpainted artwork, if checked, and automatically deletes unpainted artwork. Checking this option keeps you from having to remove all those paths that Divide always seems to produce that are Filled and Stroked with None.

Usually, the defaults in the Pathfinder Options dialog box are the best options for most situations. If you change the options, be aware that the Pathfinder Options dialog box will reset to the defaults when you quit Illustrator.

Unite

Unite unites the selected objects if they are overlapping. A new path outlines all the previously selected objects. There are no paths where the original paths intersected. The new object takes the Paint Style attributes of the topmost object. If any objects are within other objects, those objects will be assimilated. If there are "holes" in the object, the holes will become reversed out of a compound path.

You'll find that Unite is one Pathfinder you'll use often. Play with combining various paths for a while so you know what to expect, and you will develop a sense of when using Unite is a better option than doing the same tasks manually.

Unite combines two or more paths into one path, as described in the following steps.

STEPS: Using Unite

Step 1. Create and select the artwork that you want to apply Unite to. In the example in Figure 7-19, the artwork is type converted into outlines.

Figure 7-19: Using Unite

Pathfinders work only with paths. You have to convert type into outlined paths, and you cannot use EPS images.

Step 2. Choose Object⇨Pathfinder⇨Unite. Any overlapping artwork is united into one path.

The color of the united path is always the color of the path that was the topmost selected path before you used Unite.

When you use Unite, paths that don't overlap but are outside of other paths become part of a group. Illustrator draws paths between End Points of open paths before it unites those paths with other paths. Compound paths remain compound paths.

Intersect and Exclude

These two Pathfinders are opposites. Using one results in the opposite of what you get from using the other. Kind of the "Punk & Bloat" of the Pathfinder variety.

Intersect creates only the intersection of the selected paths. Any part of a selected path that does not intersect is deleted. If two paths are intersecting and selected, only the area that intersects between the two paths will remain. If three or more paths are selected, all must intersect at a common area for the function to produce results. If the paths selected do not intersect at all, nothing will happen. If one selected path is contained within all the other selected paths, the result will be that contained path. The resulting path will have the Paint Style attributes of the topmost path.

Exclude is pretty much the opposite of Intersect. Choosing Exclude deletes the intersecting areas, grouping together the outside pieces. If you are having trouble making a compound path, try using Exclude; any path within another path will be reversed, creating a compound path automatically.

After you select two or more paths and Object⇨Pathfinder⇨Intersect, only the overlapping portions of the paths remain. If you select three paths, the only area that remains will be the area where all three selected paths overlap each other.

If you use Exclude, only the areas that don't overlap will remain. Exclude follows the Winding Number rule, which is discussed in Chapter 9.

The color of the intersected or excluded path is always the color of the path that was the topmost selected path before you used Intersect or Exclude.

Style Sheets with Unite

Phyllis: So, is that all Unite is good for?

Toulouse: You mean joining abutting and overlapping paths?

Phyllis: Yeah. That's it?

Toulouse: Actually, no. You can use Unite to create compound paths.

Phyllis: That's interesting.

Toulouse: You can also use Unite to create pseudo style sheets.

Phyllis: How so?

Toulouse: If you want several paths to have the same paint style, and it might change in the future, unite them. Make sure the topmost path is the color you want it to be.

Phyllis: And that works as a style sheet?

Toulouse: Sorta. By selecting any of those paths and changing the paint style, all the paths will change to that paint style. Of course, if you want real style sheets, you can use Alien Skin's full-featured Stylist plug-in, or VectorTools' Vector Object Style.

Minus Front and Minus Back

Each of these Pathfinders works on the principle that one path, either the frontmost or backmost of the paths selected, will have all the other overlapping paths subtracted from it.

Minus Front subtracts all the selected paths in front of the backmost selected path from the backmost selected path. With two objects, it is quite simple: the object in front is deleted, and the area where the object in front was located is also deleted. It gets a little more confusing when you have more objects, but the function performs the same operation on all of them, all at once to all the selected paths. If the area to be subtracted is totally within the path it will subtract *from,* then a compound path results.

Minus Back is the opposite of Minus Front: it subtracts all the selected paths behind the frontmost selected path from the frontmost selected path. With two objects, it is also quite simple: the object in the back is deleted, and the area where the object in back was placed is also deleted. It gets a little more confusing when you have more objects, but it does the same thing, all at once to all the selected paths. If the area to be subtracted is totally within the path it will subtract *from,* then a compound path results.

When you apply Minus Front, the color of the remaining path is the color of the backmost path before you applied it. When you apply Minus Back, the color of the remaining path is the color of the frontmost path before you applied it.

Figure 7-20 shows the same paths with several different Pathfinders applied to them.

Divide

Divide (choose Object⇨Pathfinder⇨Divide) checks to see where the selected paths overlap and then creates new paths at all intersections where the paths crossed, creating new paths if necessary. Fills are kept, but any Strokes are changed to None. In the process, Divide also groups the pieces of the Fill together. Divide also keeps sections their original colors; the illustration appears to look the same unless it previously had Strokes. To keep the Strokes, copy before using Divide, and then Paste in Back (⌘-B) [Ctrl+B].

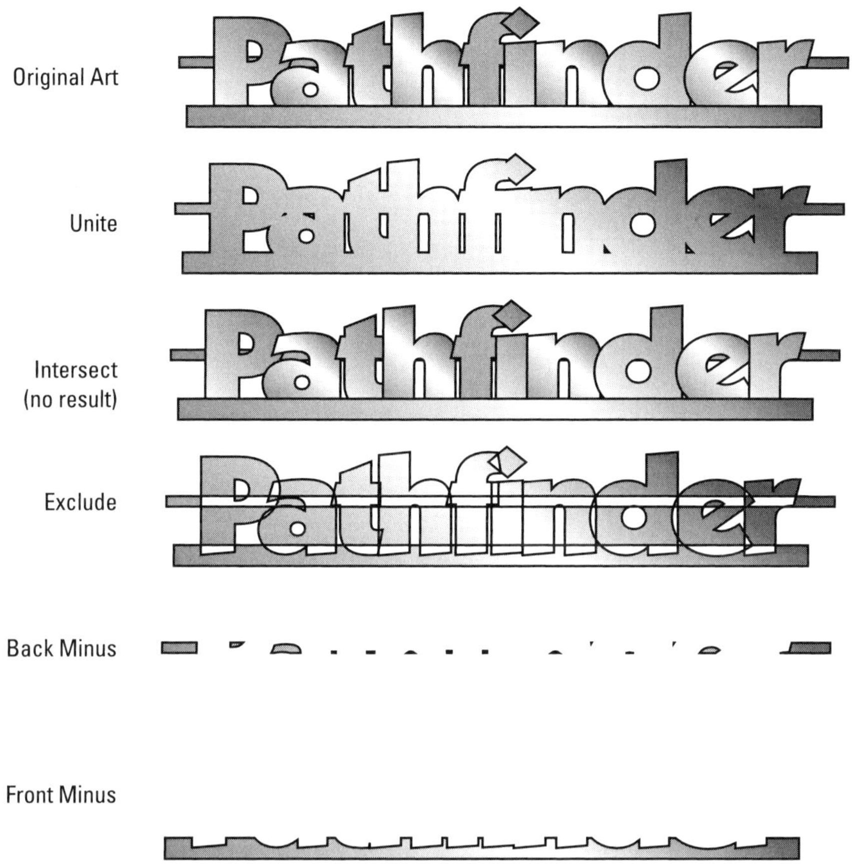

Figure 7-20: Selected paths, with different Pathfinders applied to them

Simply put, Divide divides overlaying paths into individual closed paths, as illustrated in Figure 7-21 and described in the following steps.

STEPS: Using Divide

Step 1. Create the artwork that you want to divide into sections.

Step 2. Create a path or paths where you want to divide the object.

If the division lines consist of more than one path, you do not need to make those paths into a compound path, though it doesn't hurt.

(continued)

STEPS: *(continued)*

Step 3. Select all paths, both artwork and dividing paths, and choose Object⇨Pathfinder⇨Divide.

Step 4. If you wish to move the pieces apart, you first have to ungroup them (Divide groups them automatically).

Figure 7-21: Using Divide

Outline

Outline creates small sections of paths wherever paths cross and color the Strokes, using the Fill of the path they were part of and giving the Strokes a weight of 1 point. Outline is useful for spot trapping as it will automatically create the sections needed that have to be chosen for overprinting, although many times the colors will be incorrect.

Outline creates smaller path pieces than Divide does; but instead of making each section a closed path, each path maintains its individuality, becoming separate from adjoining paths. The result of outlining is several small Stroke pieces. Instead of maintaining the Fill color of each piece, each piece is Filled with None and Stroked with the Fill color.

Divide and Outline completely ignores the Stroke color.

Trim

Trim removes sections of paths that are overlapped by other paths. Frontmost paths are the only ones that will remain. This Pathfinder is very useful for cleaning up complex overlapping illustrations, although it can take a bit of time to complete.

I'll often use Trim if I want to use a piece of artwork for one portion of the Soft Pathfinder (described later). This removes overlapping paths, which would otherwise change in color when Soft is applied.

Merge

Merge combines overlapping paths that have the exact same Fill applied to them. Even if the Fill is different by as little as 1 percent, Merge will create two separate paths. This Pathfinder is much more efficient than Unite for making areas of the same color into one object.

Figure 7-22 and the following steps describe how to use Merge.

STEPS: Using Merge

Step 1. Create the artwork that you want to use Merge for.

Step 2. Select the artwork to be merged and choose Object➪Pathfinder➪Merge. All paths that were overlapped are removed, leaving only the paths that had nothing in front of them. All adjacent areas that contained identical colors are united.

Trim Your Blends

Garrett: What can Trim do for me?

Toulouse: First of all, you can trim your blends.

Garrett: Why? Are they overgrowing into the neighbor's yard?

Toulouse: Heh. Actually, it removes overlapping paths, allowing you to use Soft and Hard with a blend.

Garrett: And why would I want to do that?

Toulouse: I've trimmed blends to use them for shadowing or applying highlights to objects.

Figure 7-22: Using Merge

Crop

Crop works in much the same way as masks work, except that anything outside the cropped area is deleted, not just masked. To use Crop, bring the object that you wish to use as a cropper (ugh! you can call it a maskette if it makes you feel better) to the front, select all the paths you wish to crop with it and the cropper itself, and choose Object⇨Pathfinder⇨Crop. Everything outside the cropper will be deleted. The objects that were cropped are grouped together in the shape of the crop.

Unlike masks, there is no outside shape after a crop is made. The cropper used to crop the image is deleted when Crop is chosen.

Hard and Soft

The two "mix" Pathfinders simulate transparency or shadows between two or more paths. Hard combines the colors at their full amount, while Soft enables you to specify the amount of color from each path that shows up in the intersecting paths.

Hard adds the values of overlapping path Fills. The more objects that are overlapping, the darker the Fill. Each section that overlaps is a new path, just like what happens when you choose Divide. Any Strokes are changed to none and ignored.

Soft adds colors together based on a percentage that you enter into the Mix Soft dialog box.

Figure 7-23 and the following steps describe how to use Soft.

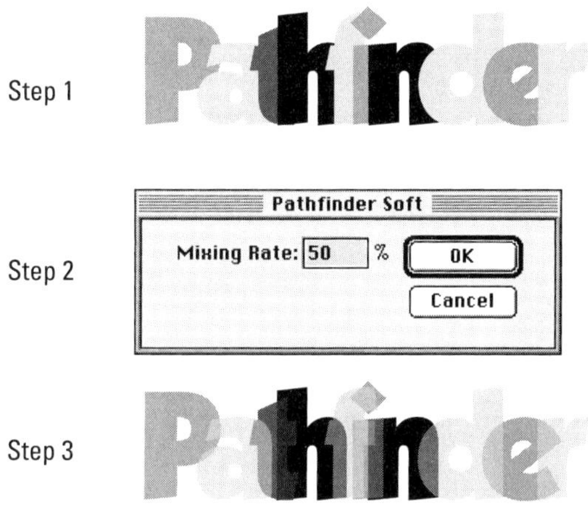

Figure 7-23: Using Soft

STEPS: Using Soft

Step 1. Create and select the overlapping paths that you want to use Soft for.

Step 2. Choose Object⇨Pathfinder⇨Soft. The Pathfinder Soft dialog box appears. Enter the amount that you want the colors to mix.

How the colors mix depends not only on the mixing rate percentage, but also on the drawing order of the objects.

Step 3. Click OK.

Soft can be a little difficult to understand at first. Soft determines how much of the background color will bleed through the foreground color. If each of the colors is at 100% and you use a setting of 50% for the function, the background color will be 33.3%, and the foreground color will be 66.6% (50% of 66.6% = 33.3%, and 33.3% + 66.6% = 100%).

Trap

Trap takes some of the drudgery away from trapping. The only limitation for Trap is that it doesn't work well on extremely complex illustrations, due to time and memory constraints. The other concern with Trap is that it leaves your illustrations pseudo-uneditable. It doesn't affect the existing paths, but if you do much editing, you'll have to delete the trap paths and retrap.

Strokes Are Gone

Ida: My Strokes are gone!

Toulouse: Yikes! What happened?

Ida: I was just Pathfindering around, and suddenly...no more Strokes.

Toulouse: Almost all Pathfinders zap your Strokes into oblivion.

Ida: I'd rather they didn't. What if I want to use strokes from the paths *before* they're chopped up into little pieces?

Toulouse: The best thing to do is to copy the paths before you apply Pathfinders, and then Paste in Front.

Ida: But they'll cover up the new Pathfindered paths!

Toulouse: To see the paths underneath, change the Fill of the Paste in Front paths to None. Keep the Strokes as they are.

Soft and Hard create the same path sections as Divide creates.

Prior to trapping, I create a layer called *Traps*. Immediately after trapping, I move all the trap objects to the Traps layer. This keeps the traps together, in case I need to redo, adjust, or delete them.

Trap automatically creates a trap between abutting shapes of different colors. You set the amount (width) of trap in a dialog box that appears after choosing Trap.

STEPS: Using Trap

Step 1. Create and select the artwork that you want to trap.

If the artwork is overly complex, you may want to select only a small portion of the artwork before you continue.

Step 2. Choose Object⇨Pathfinder⇨Trap. In the Trap dialog box, enter the width of the trap in the Thickness text field. The default is 0.25 points.

Enter the amount that you want the height of the trap to differ from the width. Entering 400% (the maximum) widens the horizontal thickness of the Stroke to four times the amount set in the Thickness text field and leaves the vertical thickness the same. Changing this value allows for different paper-stretching errors.

The Tint reduction setting determines how much the lighter of the two colors is tinted on that area.

Checking the Traps with Process Color checkbox converts spot colors to process equivalents only in the resulting trap path that is generated from Trap.

Checking the Reverse Traps check box converts any traps along the object that are Filled with 100% Black but no other colors to be less black and more of the lighter abutting color.

Step 3. Click OK. Figure 7-24 shows these three steps as well as the trap as a separate piece below the original object.

Figure 7-24: Using Trap

All traps generated by Trap result in Filled paths, not Strokes, and are automatically set to overprint in the Attributes palette.

The Reshape Tool

The Reshape tool (see Figure 7-25) is a new tool that moves curved points relative to each other. It will also create a new point if it is clicked on a line segment with no curve. Once you start using this tool, you might be inclined (whoops, that's a Rotate tool joke) to think of it as a rubber band or stretch tool. It seems that the tool turns paths into elastic material while it's being used.

To use the Reshape tool on any path, just click where you want to bend the path and drag. To use the Reshape tool on several paths at once, use the Reshape tool to select the points you wish to move. At least one point (that's not a Straight Corner point) must be selected on each path. Then drag on a Reshape-selected point; all the curved points will be moved as well.

Trapping to Placed Images

Rhoda: Can I trap to placed images?

Toulouse: Oops. Heh. Well, not really.

Rhoda: You're kidding me.

Toulouse: No, I wouldn't kid you about that.

Rhoda: Why can't I?

Toulouse: Think of it this way: When you bring in a placed image, it's this little self-contained image. It knocks out everything in its path (pun intended).

Rhoda: Anything I can do?

Toulouse: You might want to have your printer do it manually with the film separations.

Figure 7-25:
The Reshape tool

The Twirl Tool

Have you ever wanted to twist your artwork around its middle, continuously until you can't make out what the original artwork was? Me neither. But to humor someone at Adobe, the Twirl tool was incorporated into Illustrator, hiding to the right of the Rotate tool.

To use the Twirl tool, click and drag either left or right. Any selected artwork will spin around the center of the combined objects. Figure 7-26 shows artwork before and after twirling.

Figure 7-26: Artwork before (left) and after (right) twirling with the Twirl tool

You can twirl around any origin simply by clicking to set an origin point and then dragging. The artwork will twirl around the origin point you set. I took the original artwork from Figure 7-26 and twirled it around a couple of different origins (not the center) to get the funhouse effect shown in Figure 7-27.

POWER TIP: To twirl a specific amount, Option[Alt]-click at the origin point you wish to twirl around.

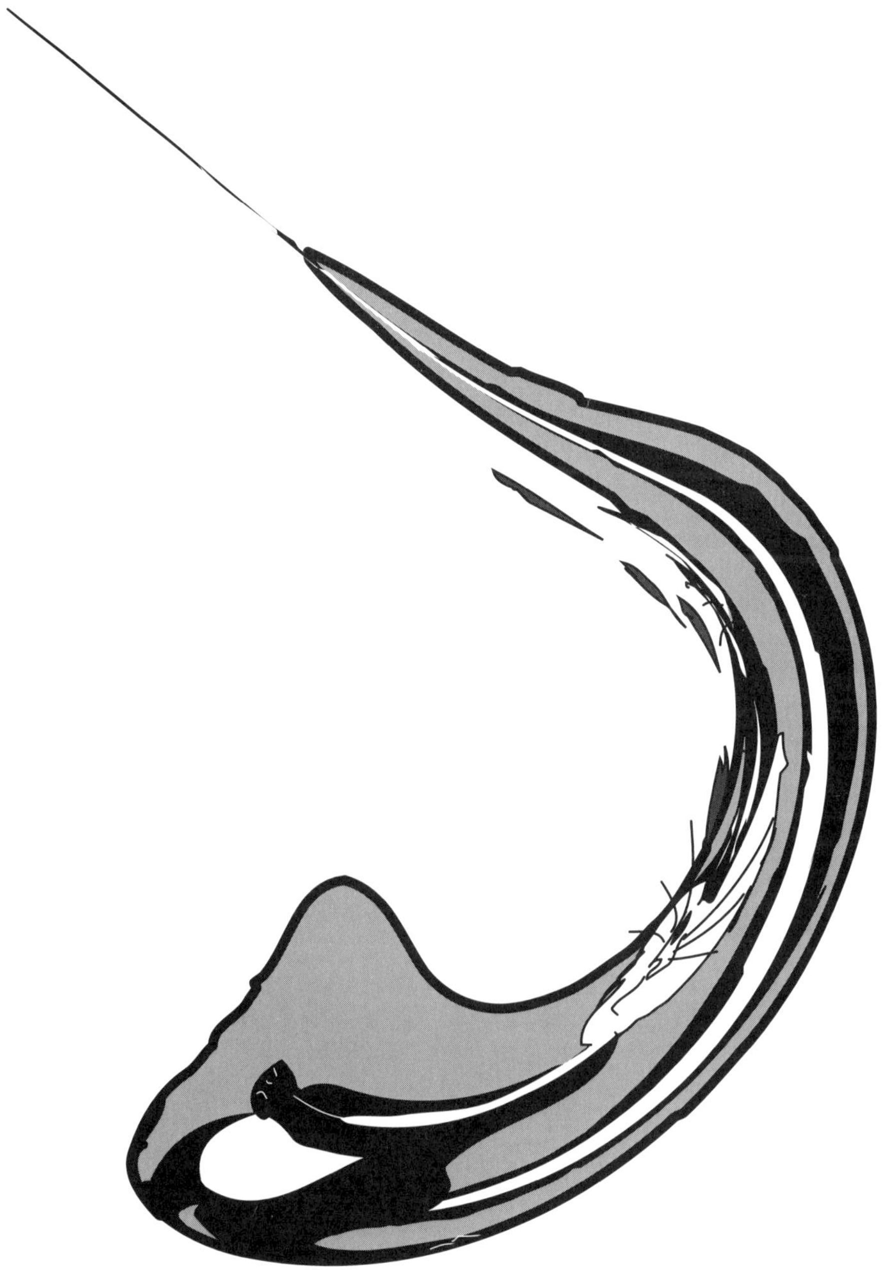

Figure 7-27: Funhouse twirling, achieved by twirling around different origin points

Transforming Objects

PostScript has the capability to transform any PostScript object by scaling it, rotating it, reflecting it, and shearing it. Illustrator takes this power and enhances it by providing you the flexibility of using certain tools, each of which does one of those transformations.

The following four tools in the Illustrator toolbox (shown in Figure 7-28) have been a staple of PostScript drawing applications for years because they address four fundamental functions: the Rotate tool, the Scale tool, the Reflect tool, and the Shear tool. Before any of these tools can be used, one or more objects (including paths, points, and segments) must be selected. The selected paths are the paths that are transformed.

Figure 7-28: The four transformation tools

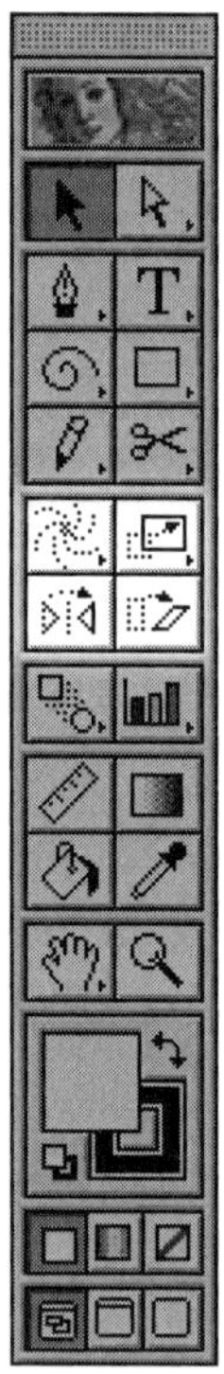

There are five ways to transform selected objects:

- Click with the transformation tool to set an origin point and then drag from a different location. (This is called a *manual transformation*.)
- Click and drag in one motion to transform the object from its center point (or last origin point).

- Option[Alt]-click to set the origin and then enter exact information in the tool's transformation dialog box. (This method is more precise than manually transforming.)
- Double-click a transformation tool to set the origin in the center of the selected object; then you can enter information in the tool's transformation dialog box.
- Use the Transform palette (where all four transformation functions are located together).

All the transformation tools work on a relative basis. For instance, if an object is scaled by 150% and then is scaled again by 150%, the object is now 225% of its original size (150% × 150% = 225%). If the object is initially scaled to 150% of its original size, and you want to take it back to that original size, you must do the math and figure out what percentage is needed to resize it — in this case, 66.7% (100% ÷ 150% = 66.7%). Entering 100% in the Scale dialog box leaves the selected objects unchanged.

Illustrator 7 automatically creates a visible origin point (shown in Figure 7-29) when you are using a transformation tool. Because the origin is in the center of the selection if you just drag with the transformation tool, the origin point is visible as soon as you select the transformation tool. If you click without dragging to set the origin, it shows up at that location until the origin is reset. Having the origin point visible (as a blue crosshair) makes the transformation tools much more usable and functional.

Figure 7-29: The origin point that appears when using any of the transformation tools

When manually transforming objects, you can make a copy of the selected object (and thus leave the original untransformed) by holding down the Option[Alt] key before and after releasing the mouse button. In a transformation dialog box, you can make a copy by clicking the Copy button, pressing Option[Alt]-Return, or Option[Alt]-clicking OK.

If the Patterns checkbox is available (you must have a pattern in one of the selected paths for this option not to be grayed out) inside any of the transformation dialog boxes, you can check its option box to transform your pattern along with the object. You can also transform the pattern only, leaving the object untransformed, by unchecking the Objects box.

You can manually transform just patterns (and not the objects themselves) by pressing the tilde (~) key while using any of the transformation tools (including the Selection tool for moving).

Manually transforming objects is fairly simple if you keep in mind that the first place you click (the point of origin) and the second place should be a fair distance apart. The further your second click is from the point of origin, the more control you have when dragging to transform. The Shear tool is an exception — although it does matter where you click — because you can lose control of your shape anywhere.

All the transformation tools perform certain operations that rely on the Constrain Angle setting as a point of reference. Normally, this setting is set to 0°, which makes your Illustrator world act normally. You can change the setting by choosing File⇨Preferences⇨General (⌘-K) [Ctrl+K] and entering a new value.

You can access each of the Transformation dialog boxes from the Object⇨Transform submenu (see Figure 7-30).

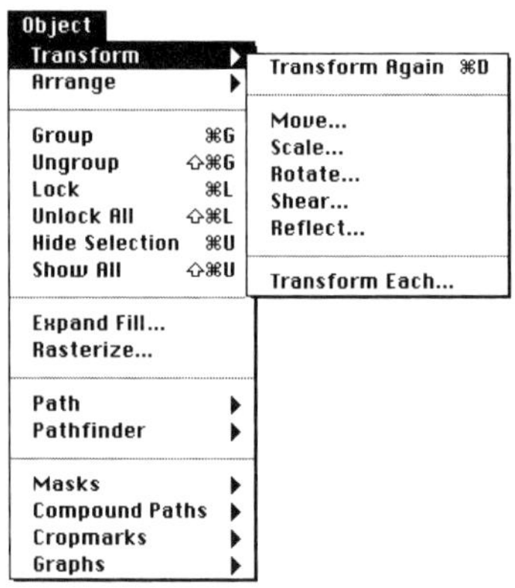

Figure 7-30: The Transformation submenu as it appears in the Object menu

The Rotate Tool

The Rotate tool rotates selected objects within a document. Double-clicking the Rotate tool displays the Rotate dialog box, where the precise angle of the selected item's rotation can be entered in the Angle box. The object rotates around its origin, which by default is located at the center of the object's bounding box. A positive number between 0 and 180 rotates the object counterclockwise that many degrees. A negative number between 0 and –180 rotates the selected object clockwise. The Rotate tool works on a standard 360° circle of rotation, although it is usually easier to type in numbers between 0 and 180 or 0 and –180 than numbers like 270, which is the same as –90°.

Holding down the Option [Alt] key and clicking somewhere in the document also brings up the Rotate dialog box (see Figure 7-31); however, the object now rotates around the point where the Rotate tool was clicked. This point can be on or off the selected object. Be careful because it is quite easy to rotate an object right out of your viewing area! Illustrator has many precautions, however, that prevent you from transforming or moving an object off the Pasteboard.

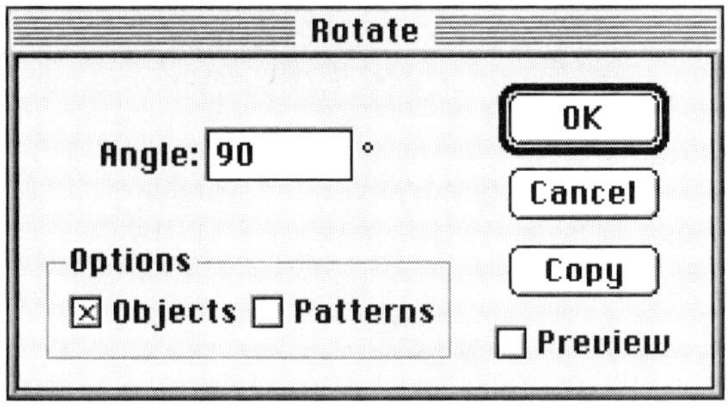

Figure 7-31: The Rotate dialog box

Click once to set the origin point from where the object's center of rotation should be and then click fairly far from the origin and drag in a circle. The selected object spins along with the cursor. To constrain the angle to 45° increments as you are dragging, hold down the Shift key. This angle is dependent on the Constrain Angle box (File⇨Preferences⇨General or ⌘-K [Ctrl+K]), and is in 45° increments plus the angle in this box. Figure 7-32 shows an illustration before and after being rotated.

Figure 7-32: An Illustration before (left) and after (right) being rotated

The Scale Tool

The Scale tool resizes objects both proportionally and nonproportionally. You can also use the Scale tool to flip objects, but without the precision of the Reflect tool. (It is impossible to keep both the size and proportions of an object constant while flipping and scaling.)

Double-clicking on the Scale tool brings up the Scale dialog box, shown in Figure 7-33. All selected objects are scaled from its origin, which by default is located at the center of the object's bounding box. If the Uniform option is chosen in the pop-up menu, numbers typed into the text field result in proportionately scaled objects (where the width and height of the object remain proportional to each other). Numbers less than 100% shrink the object; numbers greater than 100% enlarge it. When the Uniform option is chosen, you may also check the box called Scale line weight (this option is grayed out if nonproportional scaling is used).

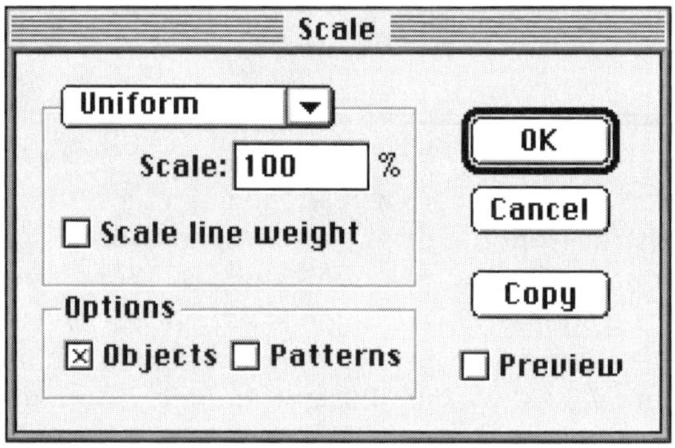

Figure 7-33: The Scale dialog box

Nonproportional scaling resizes the horizontal and vertical dimensions of the selected objects separately, distorting the image. The way nonproportional scaling works is related to the Constrain Angle box (File⇨Preferences⇨General or ⌘-K [Ctrl+K]), where the angle set there is the horizontal scaling, and the vertical scaling is 90° from that angle.

Pressing the Option [Alt] key and clicking in the document window also brings up the Scale dialog box, but now the objects are scaled from the location in the document that was Option[Alt]-clicked.

Manual resizing is achieved by clicking your point of origin and then clicking away and dragging to scale. If you cross the horizontal or vertical axis of the point of origin, the selected object flips over in that direction. Holding down the Shift key constrains the objects to equal proportions (if the cursor is dragged at approximately 45° from the point of origin) or constrains the scaling to either horizontal or vertical scaling only (providing the cursor is being dragged along at about a 90° angle from the point of origin relative to the constrain angle).

The Reflect Tool

The Reflect tool makes a mirror image of the selected objects, reflected across an axis of reflection. Double-clicking on the Reflect tool reflects selected objects across an axis of reflection that runs through the center of the selected objects. In the Reflect dialog box, you can enter the axis of rotation. If you want to rotate the object along either the horizontal or vertical axis, click the appropriate button.

Option[Alt]-clicking in the document window also brings up the Reflect dialog box, but the axis of reflection is now not in the center of the selected object, but in the location in the document where you Option[Alt]-clicked.

Manual reflecting is done by clicking once to set the origin point (the center of the axis of reflection) and again somewhere along the axis of reflection. If you click and drag after setting your origin point, you can rotate the axis of reflection and see what your objects look like reflected across various axes. The Shift key constrains the axis of reflection to 90° angles, relative to the constrain angle (File⇨Preferences⇨General or ⌘-K [Ctrl+K]). Holding down the Option [Alt] key during the release of the click leaves a copy of the original object. Figure 7-34 shows an illustration before and after being reflected.

Figure 7-34: An illustration before (left) and after (right) being reflected across the vertical axis

The Shear Tool

This tool should actually be called the "Swear" tool because it causes more cursing (no, not cursoring; that's different) than any other tool (except perhaps for the mighty Pen tool). Another good name for the Shear tool (one that I have heard many people use) is the "Stupid" tool because that's usually how you feel when trying to get good results from its use. It's a terrifying feeling to see the artwork you spent an hour touching up until it's just right go zinging off the screen, seemingly all by itself.

The Shear tool is rightfully distrusted because using it manually is usually a quick lesson in futility. Double-clicking on the Shear tool brings up the Shear dialog box, shown in Figure 7-35, which is much more controllable. Double-clicking causes the origin to be in the center of the selected object. The Angle box is simple enough; in its text box, you enter the angle amount the object should shear. Any amount over 75° or less than –75° renders the object into an indecipherable mess, because at this angle or higher the art has been "flattened." The Shear tool reverses the positive-numbers-are-counterclockwise rule: To shear an object clockwise, enter a positive number; to shear counterclockwise, enter a negative number. The Axis Angle box is for shearing an object along a specified axis.

Figure 7-35: The Shear dialog box

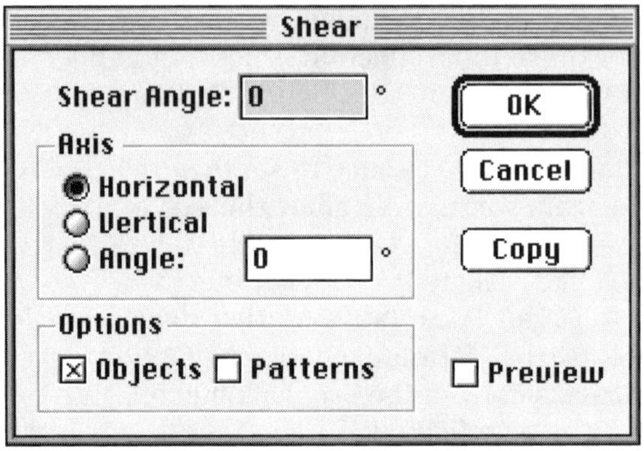

Option[Alt]-clicking in the document window also brings up the Shear dialog box, with the origin of the shear being the location of the preceding Option[Alt]-click.

Manual shearing is something else again because you are doing two things at once: changing both the angle of shearing (the distance from the beginning of the second click until it is released) and the angle of the axis of shearing (the angle the mouse is dragged during the second click). Usually, it's best to start your second click fairly far away from the point of origin. Holding down the Shift key constrains the axis of shearing to a 45° angle, relative to the constraining angle. Figure 7-36 shows an illustration before and after being sheared.

Figure 7-36: An illustration before (left) and after (right) being sheared

Moving

The most common way to move an object is to use a selection tool and drag the selected points, segments, and paths from one location to another.

The precise way to move an object is to use the Move dialog box (see Figure 7-37) or the Transform palette (see the following section). Select the object you want to move and then choose Object➪Transform➪Move. The Move dialog box appears, and you can enter the appropriate values in either the horizontal or vertical text fields. If you want to move an object diagonally, enter a number in the Distance text field and then enter the angle of movement direction in the Angle text field.

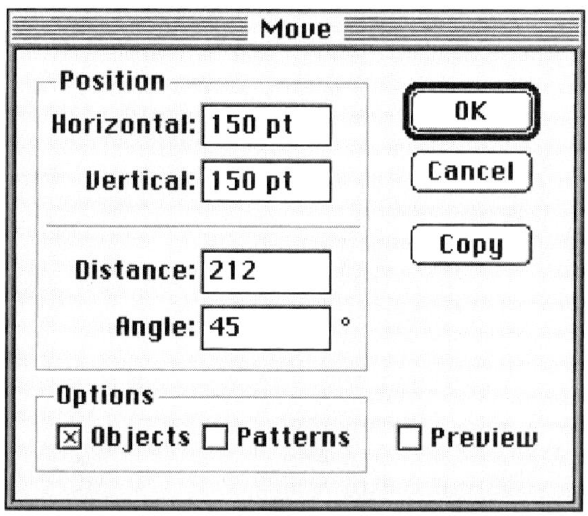

Figure 7-37: The Move dialog box

Any selected object (except for text selected with a type tool) can be moved via the Move dialog box, including individual Anchor Points and line segments.

By default, the Move dialog box contains the distance and angle that you last moved an object, whether manually (with a Selection tool) or in the Move dialog box. If you have used the Measure tool prior to using the Move dialog box, the numbers in the Move dialog box correspond to the numbers that appeared in the Info palette when you used the Measure tool.

Double-clicking on the Selection tool in the toolbox displays the Move dialog box.

In the Move dialog box, positive numbers in the horizontal text field move an object from left to right, while negative numbers move an object from right to left. Positive numbers in the vertical text field move an object from bottom to top, while negative numbers move an object from top to bottom. Negative numbers in the Distance text field move an object in the opposite direction of the Angle text field. The Angle text field works a bit differently. Negative numbers in the Angle text field move the angle in the opposite direction from 0° (so entering –45° is the same as entering 315° and entering –180° is the same as entering 180°).

The measurement system in the Move dialog box matches the system set in the General Preferences dialog box. To enter a measurement different from the current measurement system, use the following indicators:

- **For inches:** 1" or 1in (one inch)
- **For picas:** 1p or 1pica (one pica)
- **For points:** 1pt or 0p1 (one point)
- **For picas/points:** 1p1 (one pica, one point)
- **For millimeters :** 1mm (one millimeter)
- **For centimeters:** 1cm (one centimeter)

The Horizontal and Vertical text fields are linked to the Distance and Angle text fields; when one of the fields is changed, the others are altered accordingly.

Pressing the Copy button duplicates selected objects in the direction and distance indicated, just as holding down Option [Alt] when dragging duplicates the selected objects.

POWER TIP: The Move dialog box is a great place to enter everything via the keyboard. Press Tab to move from text field to text field, press Return to push the OK button, and press ⌘-Period [Esc] to push the Cancel button. Pressing Option[Alt]-Enter or pressing Option [Alt] while clicking OK pushes the Copy button. The same is true for all the transformation dialog boxes.

The Transform Palette

Imagine, if you will, a palette that combines four of Illustrator's five transformation capabilities into one place. Then take a look at Figure 7-38, which shows Illustrator's Transform palette in all its glory.

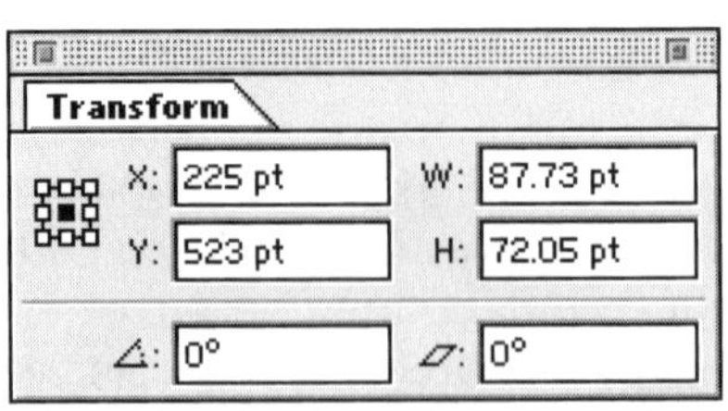

Figure 7-38: The Transform palette

The Transform palette provides a way to Move, Scale, Rotate, and Shear selected artwork. There's no reflect option (you'll need to use the tool or the transform submenu option to reflect artwork). Instead of manually setting an origin point or transforming from the center by default, the Transform palette gives you nine "fixed" origin points based on the bounding box of the selected objects (the bounding box is the imaginary box that is just the right size to contain all selected objects). Choose an origin point before entering values in the palette, and the transformations will originate from the corner, center of a side, or the center of selected objects.

The text fields in the Transform palette are as follows:

- **X:** This is the horizontal location of the artwork, measured from the left edge of the document (or horizontal ruler origin if it has been moved from the left edge).
- **Y:** This is the vertical location of the artwork, measured from the bottom edge of the document (or vertical ruler origin if it has been moved from the bottom edge).
- **W:** This is the width of the artwork's bounding box.
- **H:** This is the height of the artwork's bounding box.
- **Rotation:** This field lets you apply a rotation to the selected artwork.
- **Shear:** This field lets you apply a shear to the selected artwork.

To use the palette, type the new value you'd like to use in any field, and then press Enter. If you have another value to enter, press the Tab key to go to the next text field (or Shift-Tab to go back a field). Pressing Option [Alt] when you press Enter or Tab creates a duplicate of the selected artwork with the transformations you specified.

For Scaling, you can enter either absolute measurements (the size in inches, picas, and so on, that you want the artwork to be), or by percentage by adding the % symbol after your value. You can also force Illustrator to scale uniformly, regardless if you're using absolute measurements or percentages, by pressing ⌘ [Ctrl] when you press the Enter or Tab keys.

Okay, time for me to 'fess up. I'm not a big fan of the Transform palette, and here's why:

- **No Reflect option:** Couldn't we have a button enabling us to enter a negative scale value to reflect across the horizontal/vertical axis?
- **Each option:** Transform Each is hard to get to, and this would've provided an easy way to do these transformations.
- **No Random option:** Transformations are perfect for random values, as evidenced by Transform Each's Random check box.
- **No Keyboard commands to highlight the text fields:** Even the transformation tools can be accessed by pressing keys on the keyboard.

- **After rotating and shearing, the value reverts back to 0° instantly:** I'd like the values here to show how far the art has been transformed since it was created. There are a few technical issues to work out here (groups? compound paths? portions of paths? Objects pasted?) but I'm sure Adobe can figure them out. . . .
- **No keyboard command to show/hide the palette:** This is a chicken-and-egg dilemma.
- **No automated repeat function:** A text field for number of duplicates would be handy (I hate pressing ⌘-D [Ctrl+D] thirty-four times when I want to duplicate/rotate an object around a circle at 10° increments).
- **No Apply at once feature like Transform Each has.**
- **No floating origin point:** I have to use one of the nine presets — and there's no way to change them automatically or revert to center using the keyboard.

Okay, sure, many of the things I don't like about the Transform palette are wish-list features, not missing functionality. But if I'm going to have this palette sucking up valuable screen real estate, I want something back for it. Most of Illustrator's other palettes are worthy of taking up chunks of pixels; the Transform palette isn't.

The comments above are here for two reasons. First, because I think you as a reader should know that while I love Illustrator (my program of choice were I to be stuck on a desert island with a computer, remember), there are a few things I don't like, or that I feel could be improved. The second reason is to show a sample of the types of communication that Adobe and other software companies use to determine what features take priority for implementation in the future. If instead of listing what I don't like and would like to see in the next version of Illustrator, I just said "I don't like the transformation palette," Adobe would just shrug and ignore me. But their concern is to make the best software they can, and that means addressing their customers' needs. If you have suggestions or ideas for Adobe (or for third-party plug-in developers such as Extensis), make sure you're both as concise and descriptive as possible.

This actually has worked for me personally in the past. In the 5.0/5.5 edition of this book, I commented that Punk and Bloat should be one filter, as should be Scribble and Tweak, and that it would be nice to have all the Each filters together, and several other filter suggestions. In addition to publishing these suggestions in the *Illustrator 7 Bible* and *Illustrator Filter Finesse,* I forwarded them along to Adobe and posted them on AOL and Internet message boards. Other Illustrator users commented with most agreeing, and Adobe took notice. Many of these suggestions were incorporated into Illustrator 6. These were little things, but Adobe has made big changes based on direct user input as well.

Transform Each

Transform Each provides a way to do several transformations in one shot, but that's only the beginning. The unique thing about Transform Each is that each selected object is transformed independently, as opposed to having all the selected objects transformed together. Figure 7-39 shows the difference between "normal" rotating and scaling, and the Rotate and Scale functions in Transform Each.

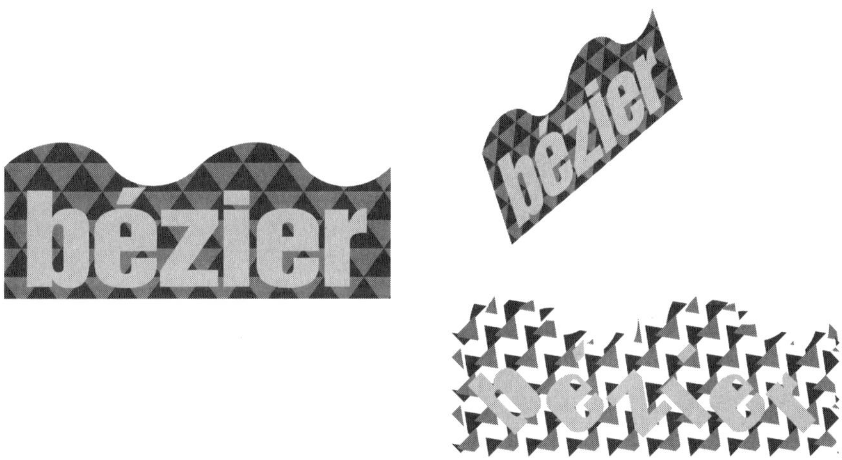

Figure 7-39: An illustration (left) after being rotated and scaled, and then after using the same values with the Rotate and Scale functions within Transform Each

To access the Transform Each dialog box (see Figure 7-40), choose Object➪Transform➪Transform Each. In the dialog box, use the sliders/dial or type in values for each of the transformations. The Random checkbox on the right side of the dialog box gives each object selected a random value that falls within the default (100% for Scale, 0 for Move and Rotate) and the value set by the slider/dial.

Figure 7-40: The Transform Each dialog box

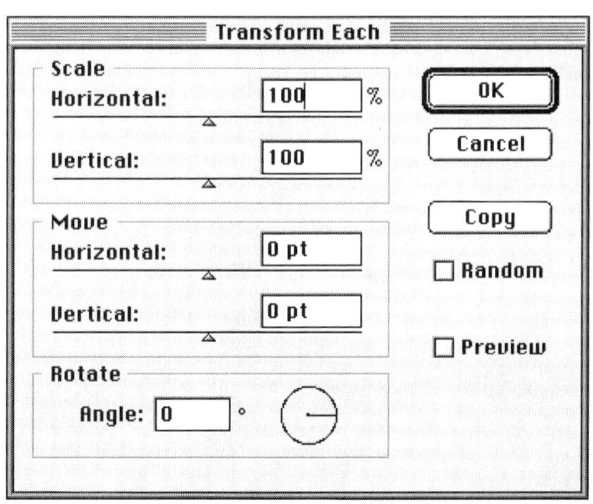

But of all things, the randomize function of Transform Each is its most powerful asset. Checking the Random checkbox can turn a grid into a distinct random texture, as shown in Figure 7-41.

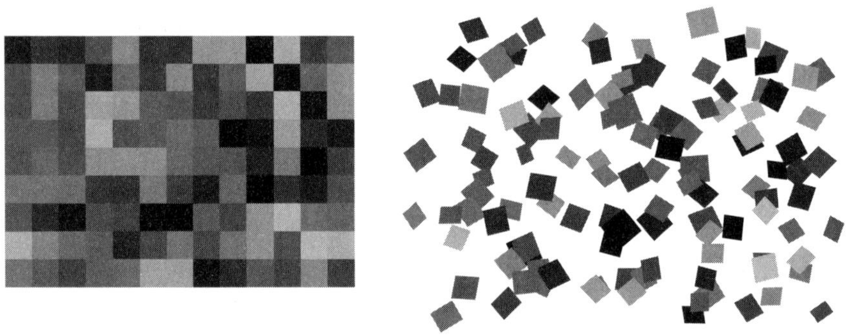

Figure 7-41: Transform Each's Random function applied to a checkerboard of colored squares

STEPS: Creating a Flower with Transform Each

Step 1. Create a rectangle (like the one shown in Figure 7-41) and fill it with the Purple, Red, Yellow gradient.

Step 2. Use the Direct Selection tool to move the upper-right point down and the lower-right point up.

Step 3. Add a color stop to the gradient (in the Gradient palette) that's black.

Step 4. Expand the Gradient (Choose Object⇨Expand) using 100 blend steps. Choose Object⇨Pathfinder⇨Crop. This will crop the blend along the angles you defined in Step 2.

Step 5. In the Align palette, choose the Align Vertically button (second from the left, top row).

Step 6. Horizontally Scale the objects until they resemble those shown in Step 6 of Figure 7-42.

Step 7. Choose Filter⇨Distort⇨Zig Zag, and enter 10%, 2 segments, and Smooth.

Step 8. Choose Filter⇨Distort⇨Scribble and Tweak, and Scribble at 5% Horizontal, 5% vertical, with all options checked.

Step 9. Choose Object⇨Transform⇨Transform Each, enter a rotation of 180°, and check the Random box. This will rotate the objects anywhere between 0° and 180°.

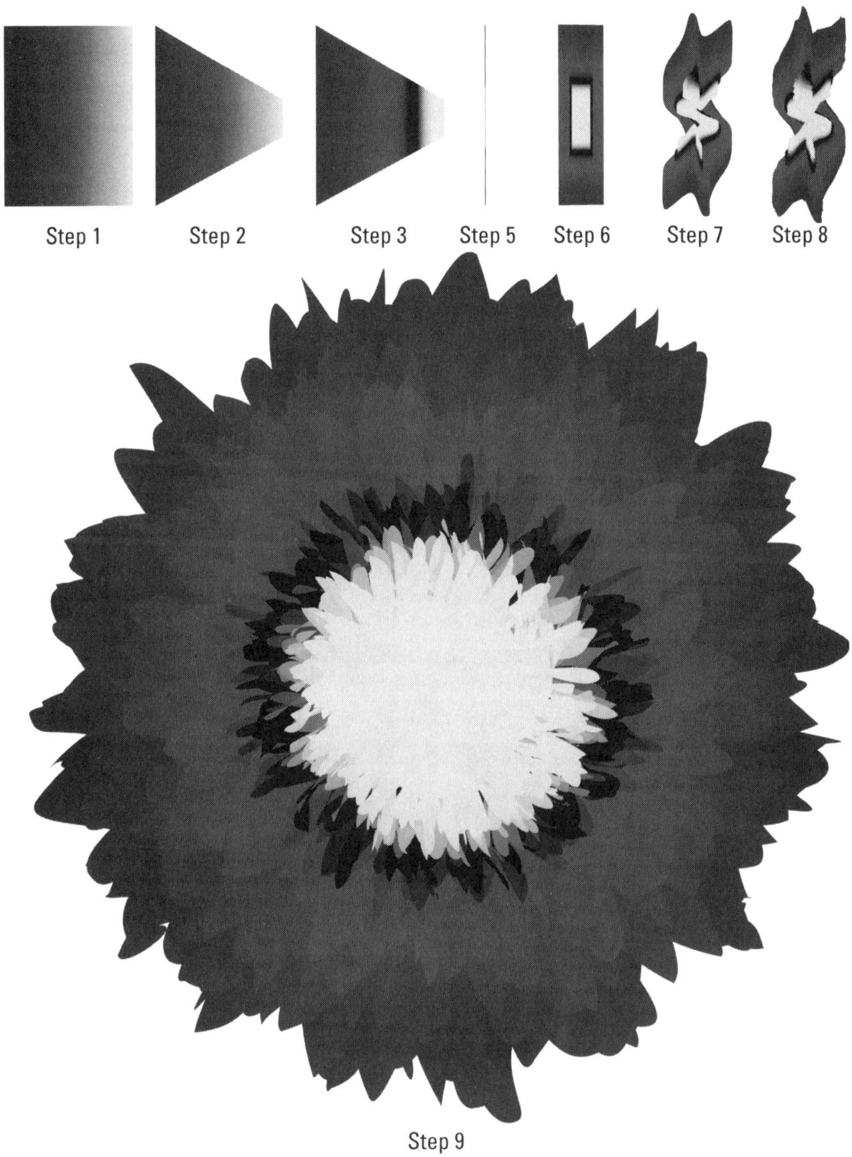

Figure 7-42: Steps for creating a flower using Transform Each

Transformation Effects

The transformation tools open up a world of possibilities within Illustrator. The following tips and ideas should give you a head start in exploring the amazing power of transformations.

Choosing Transform Again (⌘-D) [Ctrl+D] from the Transform submenu of the Object menu redoes the last transformation that was done to a selected object. Transformations include Move, Rotate, Scale, Reflect, Shear, and Transform Each. Transform Again also makes a transformed copy if a copy was made either manually or by clicking the Copy button in the prior transformation dialog box.

Transform Again remembers the last transformation, no matter what else you do, and it can apply that same transformation to other objects, or reapply it to the existing transformed objects.

Creating Shadows

You can create all sorts of shadows by using the Scale, Reflect, and Shear tools, as shown in the illustrations in Figure 7-43.

Figure 7-43: Creating shadows with the transformation tools

STEPS: Creating a Shadow with Transformation Tools

Step 1. Select the path where you want apply the shadow and click the bottom of the path once with the Reflect tool. This action sets the origin of reflection at the base of the image. Drag down while pressing the Shift key. The image flips over, creating a mirror image under the original. Press the Option [Alt] key (keeping the Shift key pressed) before and during the release of the mouse button.

Step 2. Using the Shear tool, click the base of the reflected copy to set the origin. Click and drag left or right at the other side of the reflection to set the angle of the reflection.

Step 3. Using the Scale tool, click once again on the base of the reflected copy to set the origin. Click and drag up or down at the other side of the reflection.

Step 4. Color the shadow darker than its background.

To create a shadow for type, you must first vertically scale a copy of the type. Hold down the Option [Alt] key when you release the mouse button to make the copy, and hold down the Shift key to constrain the scaling to vertical as you drag the mouse up or down. Setting the origin of the scale to the baseline of the type helps, as does using all caps or type with no descenders.

Send the copy to the back (⌘-Shift-[) [Ctrl+Shift+[] and shear the shadow off to one side or the other, once again setting the origin at the baseline of the type. Holding down Shift as you shear prevents the baseline of the copy from angling up or down.

If you want the shadow in front of the type (making it appear as if the light source is coming from behind the type), use the Reflect tool to flip the copy of the type across the baseline of the type.

Transforming Gradients

You can transform gradients in the same way that you transform objects that are colored by gradients. All of the transformation tools affect gradients, but the best effects are achieved by scaling and shearing gradients, especially radial gradients, as shown in Figure 7-44.

To create an effect similar to that of Figure 7-44, create a radial gradient inside a circle with no Stroke. (Use a circle so that no portions of it are cropped outside of the shape when it is distorted.) Scale and shear the circle with the radial gradient, and the radial gradient becomes scaled and sheared as well.

Figure 7-44: Transforming a Gradient

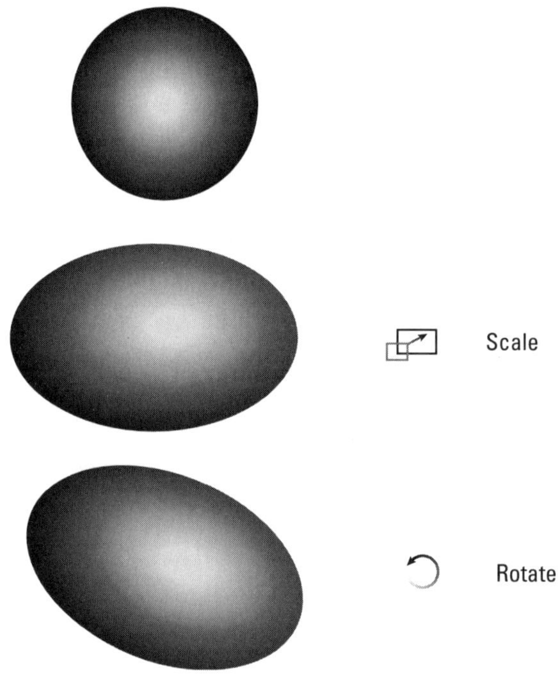

Rotating into a Path

Clever use of the Rotate tool can create a realistic, winding path by duplicating the same object at different rotational intervals, rotated from different origins.

Start by creating an object of some sort. (The illustration in Figure 7-45 uses paw prints.) Select the objects (I've found it best to group them together) and choose the Rotate tool. Click to set an origin a little distance from the side of the object. Click the other side of the object and drag. As you drag, you see the outline of the shape of the object that you are dragging. When the object is a good distance away, press the Option [Alt] key (to copy) and release the mouse button; then release the Option [Alt] key. A copy of the object appears. Press ⌘-D [Ctrl+D] (Transform Again) to create *another* object the same distance away.

After using the Transform Again command (⌘-D) [Ctrl+D] a few times, click with the Rotate tool on the other side of the object to set another origin. Click and drag the outline of the object about the same distance; then press the Option [Alt] key and release the mouse button. Use the Transform Again command a few more times.

The farther you click from the objects to set the origin, the smaller the curve of the path of objects. Clicking right next to the objects causes them to turn sharply.

Figure 7-45: Paw prints that have been rotated into a path

Making Tiles Using the Reflect Tool

You can make symmetrical tiles with the Reflect tool. You can use a set of four differently positioned yet identical objects to create artwork with a floor-tile look, as shown in Figure 7-46.

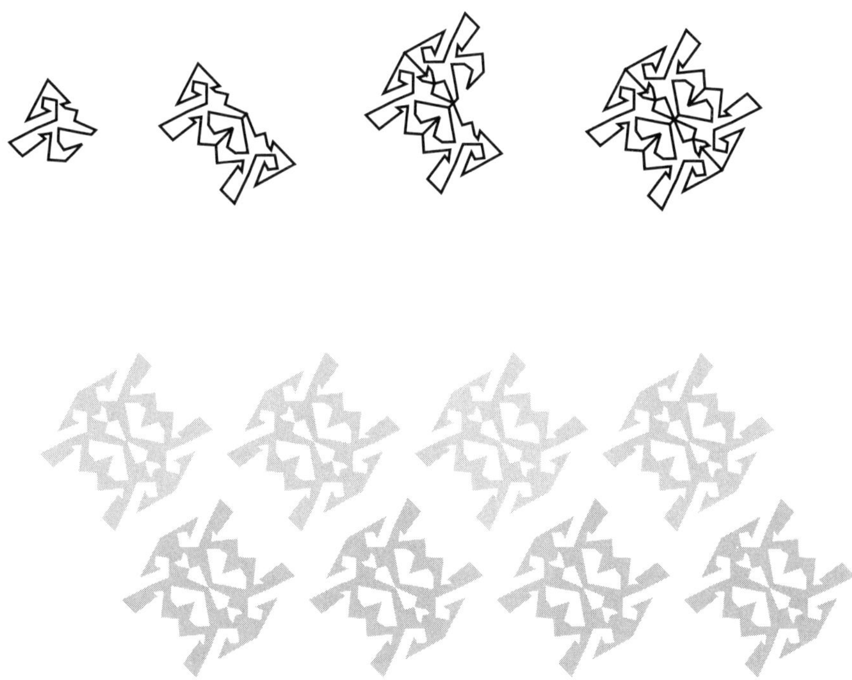

Figure 7-46: Creating tiles with the Reflect tool

STEPS: Creating Symmetrical Tiles with the Reflect Tool

Step 1. Create the path (or paths) that you will make into the symmetrical tile. Group the artwork together.

Step 2. Take the Reflect tool and click off to the right of it to set the origin. Click and drag on the left edge of the object and drag to the right while pressing the Shift and Option [Alt] keys. (Using the Shift key reflects the image at only 45° angles.) When the object has been reflected to the right side, let go of the mouse button, still pressing the Option [Alt] key. Release the Option [Alt] key. You now have two versions of the object.

Step 3. Select the original and reflected object and reflect again, this time across the bottom of the objects. There are now four objects, each mirrored a little differently, that make up a tile. You can now use this tile to create symmetrical patterns.

Using Transformation Tools on Portions of Paths

When using the transformation tools, you don't need to select an entire path. Instead, try experimenting with other effects by selecting single Anchor Points, line segments, and combinations of selected Anchor Points and segments. Another idea is to select portions of paths on different objects.

When you're working with portions of paths, one of the most useful transformation tool procedures is to select a Smooth Point with the Direct Selection tool and then choose a transformation tool.

You can achieve precise control with the Rotate tool. Click the center of the Anchor Point and drag around the Anchor Point. Both Control Handles move, but the distance from the Control Handles to the Anchor Point remains the same. This task is very difficult to perform with just the Direct Selection tool, which you can also use to accomplish the same task.

You can accomplish the exact lengthening of Control Handle Lines by using the Scale tool. Click the Anchor Point to set the origin and then drag out from one of the Control Handles. Both Control Handles will grow from the Anchor Point in equal proportions.

When working on a Smooth Point, you can use the Reflect tool to switch lengths and angles between the two Control Handles.

The following are some more portion-of-path transformation ideas:

- Select all the points in an open path except for the End Points and use all the different transformation tools on the selected areas.
- Select the bottommost or topmost Anchor Point in text converted to outlines, and scale, rotate, and shear for interesting effects.
- Select two Anchor Points on a rectangle, and scale and skew copies into a cube.

STEPS: Creating Spirographs

Step 1. Create a star with lots of points, and a fairly tight inner radius (see Figure 7-47).

Step 2. Select just the middle points with the Direct Selection tool.

Step 3. Use the Rotate tool to "twist" the inner points around.

Step 4. Use the Scale tool to invert the inner points outside of the outer ones.

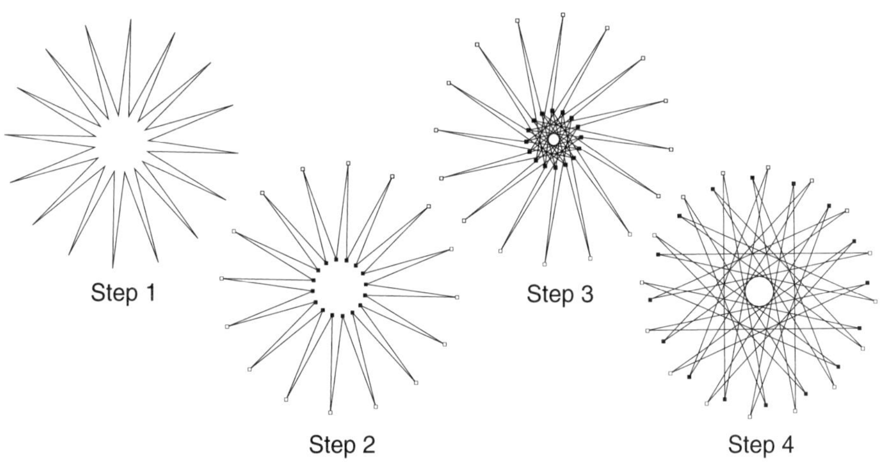

Figure 7-47: Steps for creating a spirograph

Rotating into Kaleidoscopes

By rotating and duplicating objects that have strokes, you can make kaleidoscopic illustrations, such as the one in Figure 7-48. You may have trouble working with the last two or three objects, but this section shows you how to work through any difficulties.

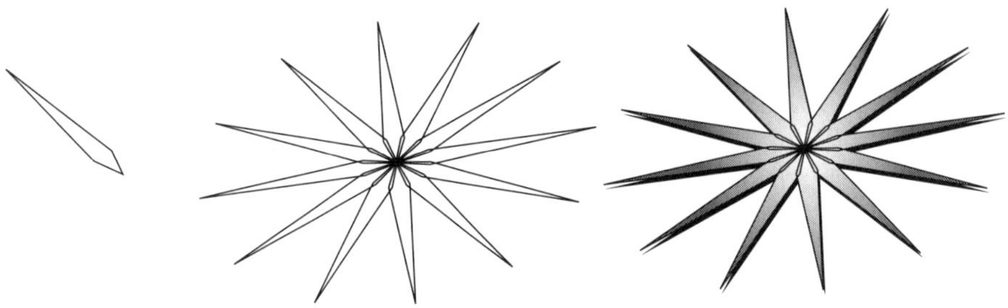

Figure 7-48: Objects that have been rotated into kaleidoscopes

First, select the object that you wish to rotate and duplicate. Choose the Rotate tool and Option[Alt]-click at one end or corner of the object. In the Rotate dialog box, enter an angle that goes into 360 evenly, such as 18 (20 × 18 = 360), and press the Copy button (Option[Alt]-Return). Choose Transform Again (⌘-D) [Ctrl+D] until the object circles around the origin back to the beginning.

The trouble that you might run into here is that if the objects have a Fill and they overlap at all, the last object looks as if it's on the top, and the original object looks as if it's on the bottom, which destroys the perspective of the kaleidoscope. So either the original or the last object has to be fixed. It is generally easier to fix the original (bottommost) object.

Start by selecting the bottommost (original) object. Copy (⌘-C) [Ctrl+C] it and paste it in front (⌘-F) [Ctrl+F]. Then create two breaks in the path of the object with the Scissors tool, one on either side of the area where the two objects overlap. Remove that portion of the path by deselecting all (⌘-Shift-A) [Ctrl+Shift+A] and selecting it, and then delete just that portion. Many times this step alone fixes the path. If there is a Fill and a Stroke, however, your problems may not work out quite so easily. Copy the remaining piece of the copied object, choose Paste in Front (⌘-F) [Ctrl+F] again, and change the Fill to None. This procedure corrects any Stroke deficiencies from the first copy.

Transforming Patterns

The option in all transformation dialog boxes (and the Move dialog box) to apply transformations to patterns can produce some very interesting results, as shown in Figure 7-49.

Figure 7-49: A pattern that has been scaled up inside text and rotated

One of the most interesting effects results from using patterns that have transparent Fills. Select an object that has a pattern Fill and double-click a transformation tool. Enter a value, check the Pattern tiles box, uncheck the Objects box, and then click Copy. A new object (which is unchanged) will overlap the original object, but the pattern in the new object will have changed. If desired, use the Transform Again command (⌘-D) [Ctrl+D] to create additional copies with patterns that have been transformed even more.

POWER TIP: You can transform just patterns "live" by pressing the Tilde (~) key while dragging with any transformation tool (including the Selection tool for moving).

The Select Functions

Illustrator 7 has several special select functions (they were filters in Illustrator 5/6). The Select functions are used for selecting paths with common or specific attributes. The Select functions make mundane, repetitive tasks easy to accomplish by doing all the nasty work for you.

To choose the Select functions, choose Edit⇨Select and the appropriate selection function from that submenu (shown in Figure 7-50).

Figure 7-50: The Select submenu is found in the Edit menu

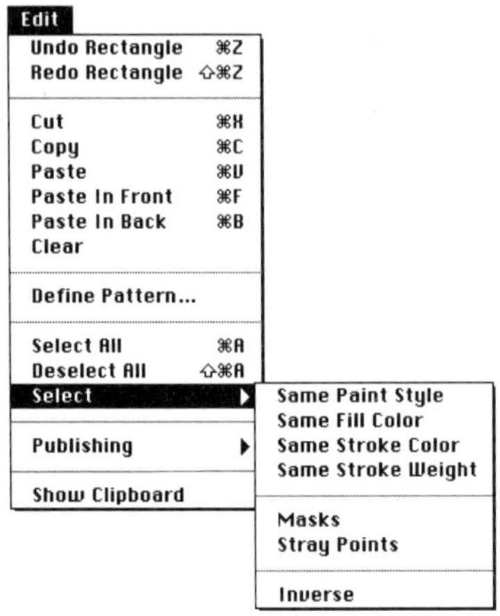

Four selection functions use the Paint Style attributes of currently selected objects to select additional objects. Using these functions makes object selection quick and intuitive. The main limitation of these functions is that they are limited to four categories of comparison, each of which must be used independently of the others. This limitation causes problems in selecting objects that share more than one attribute, such as objects that have the same Stroke color and the same Stroke weight.

The Select Inverse function is perfect for selecting all paths that aren't selected. You can use this selection function to instantly select paths that are hidden, guides, and other objects that are hard to select.

The Select Masks function makes the process of manipulating masks much easier by showing you where masks are in the document.

The Select Stray Points function selects all isolated Anchor Points. Individual Anchor Points don't print or preview, and you can see them in Preview mode only when they are selected. After you cut portions of line segments, stray points often appear; and often these individual points interfere with connecting other segments. You can't use this selection function enough.

Select Same Fill Color

Same Fill Color (Edit➪Select➪Same Fill Color) selects objects that have the same Fill color as the currently selected object. This function selects objects regardless of their Stroke color, Stroke weight, or Stroke pattern. You cannot select objects with different Fills for Same Fill Color to work, but you may select two objects that have the same Fill.

Same Fill Color considers different tints of spot colors to be the same color. This function works in two ways. First, if you select one object with any tint value of a spot color, then Same Fill Color will select all other objects with the same spot color, regardless of the tint. Second, you can select more than one object, no matter what tint each object contains, provided that the selected objects have the same spot color.

To be selected with Same Fill Color, process color Fills have to have the same values as the original. Even single colors, such as yellow, have to be the same percentage. Same Fill Color considers 100% Yellow and 50% Yellow to be two separate colors.

If you use spot colors often, Select Same Fill Color is extremely useful. It enables you to instantly select all objects that are Filled with the spot color, regardless of the tint of the selected object or the tints of the objects to be selected.

Same Fill Color also selects objects that are Filled with the same gradient, regardless of the angle or the starting or ending point of the gradient. This function does not, however, select objects that have the same pattern Fill.

Select Same Paint Style

Same Paint Style (Edit⇨Select⇨Same Paint Style) selects objects that have almost exactly the same paint style as the paint style of the selected object. The following information has to be the same:

- The Fill color (as defined in the preceding section, "Select Same Fill Color")
- The Stroke color
- The Stroke weight

Selecting More Than One Color

Archie: How can I select all occurrences of two different Fill colors?

Toulouse: You'll need to use Same Fill Color.

Archie: I tried that, but it doesn't work.

Toulouse: Do it this way: Select a representative of the first color, and then run the function.

Archie: Okay, but now I'm stuck.

Toulouse: Not really. Lock those objects with ⌘-L [Ctrl+L], then select a representative of the second Fill color, and run Same Fill Color again.

Archie: I'm still stuck.

Toulouse: Ah...here's the tricky part. Lock those objects as well.

Archie: Excuse me for noticing, but now I *can't* select those objects. They're all locked.

Toulouse: Just Unlock All (⌘-Shift-L) [Ctrl+Shift+L], and they'll all be selected!

Archie: You know, I really don't think these different colors should be mixed....

Some things in the object's Paint Style that don't matter (that is, they don't prevent Same Paint Style from selecting an object) are any of the Stroke style attributes and the overprinting options.

CAUTION

Don't select objects with more than one paint style if you select more than one object. If you have different paint styles (as defined previously) selected, no objects will be selected by the selection function. The best thing to do with Same Paint Style, as with Same Fill Color, is to select only one object.

If you have a spot color selected, the Select functions will select all other occurrences of that spot color, regardless of the tint. This can be troublesome.

BY THE WAY

Extensis VectorTools has a VectorMagicWand, which works like the Select Same Paint Style function, except that you can select *similar* paths to the original clicked-on path. The tool appears in the middle of the toolbox, and is invaluable.

Select Same Stroke Color

Same Stroke Color (Edit⇨Select⇨Same Stroke Color) selects objects that have the same Stroke color, regardless of the Stroke weight or style and regardless of the type of Fill.

The color limitations that are defined in the "Select Same Fill Color" section, earlier in the chapter, also apply to Same Stroke Color.

Although you can choose a pattern for a Stroke that makes the Stroke look gray, Same Stroke Color does not select other objects that have the same Stroke pattern.

Select Same Stroke Weight

Illustrator's Same Stroke Weight function (Edit⇨Select⇨Same Stroke Weight) selects objects that have the same Stroke weight, regardless of the Stroke color, the style, or the Fill color.

Even if the Stroke is a pattern, other paths that have the same Stroke weight as the patterned Stroke will be selected when you use Same Stroke Weight.

Don't select more than one Stroke weight if you select more than one object. If you select different Stroke weights, no paths will be selected. The best thing to do with Same Stroke Weight, as with Same Fill Color and Same Paint Style, is to select only one object.

Custom Paint Style Selections

Unfortunately, you cannot do multiple-type selections with any of the special selection functions. You cannot, for example, select at one time all of the objects that have the same Stroke color and Fill color, but have different Stroke weights.

The Lock Unselected command (press Option [Alt] and Object⇨Lock or ⌘-Option-L [Ctrl+Alt+L]) is the key to specifying multiple selection criteria. The following instructions describe how to perform multiple-type selections in a few steps.

STEPS: Selecting Objects That Have Same Stroke and Fill Colors

Step 1. Select a representative object that has the Stroke and Fill color that you want.

Step 2. Choose Edit⇨Select⇨Same Fill Color. All objects that have the same Fill color as the original object will be selected, regardless of their Stroke color.

Step 3. This step is the key step. Press Option [Alt] and choose Arrange⇨Lock (⌘-Option-L) [Ctrl+Alt+L] to lock any objects that are not selected. The only objects that you can modify or select now are the ones that have the same Fill color.

Step 4. Deselect All (⌘-Shift-A) [Ctrl+Shift+A] and select the original object, which has both the Fill color and the Stroke color that you want to select.

Step 5. Choose Edit⇨Select⇨Same Stroke Color. Only objects that have the same Stroke and Fill colors will be selected.

Select Inverse

Select Inverse (Edit⇨Select⇨Select Inverse) quickly selects all objects that are not currently selected. For example, if one object is selected and the document contains 15 other objects, the 15 objects will become selected, and the one object that was selected originally will become deselected.

CAUTION: Select Inverse does not cause locked or hidden objects to be selected and does not select guides unless guides are not locked. Objects on layers that are locked or hidden will not be selected either.

Inverse on Specific Layers

Miguel: I want to select the inverse of the objects I selected that are just on specific layers.

Toulouse: You've already selected the inverse objects of the ones you want?

Miguel: Yep. How do I select just the inverse on certain layers only?

Toulouse: Easy. Run the Select Inverse function.

Miguel: Uh, there's lots of paths selected that *aren't* on those layers.

Toulouse: Then just lock all the layers you don't want paths selected on. Anything on a locked layer will deselect.

Select Inverse is useful because selecting a few objects is usually quicker than selecting most objects. After you select the few objects, Select Inverse does all the nasty work of selecting everything else.

When no objects are selected, Select Inverse selects all the objects, just as Edit⇨Select All (⌘-A) [Ctrl+A] would. When all objects are selected, Select Inverse deselects all the objects, just as Edit⇨Deselect All (⌘-Shift-A) [Ctrl+Shift+A] would.

Select Masks

Select Masks (Edit⇨Select⇨Select Masks) selects all the objects that are currently being used as masks. The only masks in the document that are not selected are the masks that are locked or hidden and the masks that are on layers that are locked or hidden.

CAUTION

Select Masks does not select Fills and Strokes that were created with the Fill and Stroke Mask filter (Filter⇨Create⇨Fill & Stroke for Mask). These separate paths are the same size as the masks, but they are not masks.

See Chapter 9 for detailed information on creating and using masks and using the Fill & Stroke for Mask filter.

Use Select Masks before you select the Fill & Stroke for Mask filter. Knowing whether the path that you have selected is really a mask can be difficult, but by using Select Masks you can be sure that the selected objects are indeed masks.

Select Stray Points

Select Stray Points (Edit⇨Select⇨Select Stray Points) selects Anchor Points in the document.

Individual Anchor Points are nasty beasts, because although they don't show up in preview or printing, they contain Fills and Strokes that can cause separation software to print additional blank color separations that aren't needed.

Stray points can be created in various ways:

- Clicking once with the Pen tool creates a single Anchor Point.
- Deleting a line segment on a path that has two points by selecting the line segment with the Direct Selection tool and pressing Delete will leave behind the two Anchor Points.
- Using the Scissors tool to cut a path, and while deleting one side or another of the path, not selecting the points turns these points into stray points.
- Ungrouping an oval or rectangle in Version 3.2 or an older version of Illustrator, and then deleting just the frame of the shape leaves the center point in the document.

Bringing an Illustrator 4 or older document that has still-grouped rectangles or ovals into Version 7 automatically deletes the center point and turns on the Show Center Point option in the Attributes palette (choose Window⇨Show Attributes or press F11).

Be careful not to think that center points of object are stray points — they aren't, and you cannot select them without selecting the object they belong to. Center points of objects are visible when the Show Center Point option is chosen in the Attributes palette. Selecting the center point of an object selects the entire object, and deleting the center point deletes the entire object.

Layers

The layering feature of Illustrator provides an easy and powerful way to separate artwork into individual sections. A layer is a separate section of the document that is on its own level, above, under, or in between other layers, but never on the same level as another layer. You can view these sections separately, locked, hidden, and rearranged around each other. Figure 7-51 shows objects that have been layered, along with a snazzy poem.

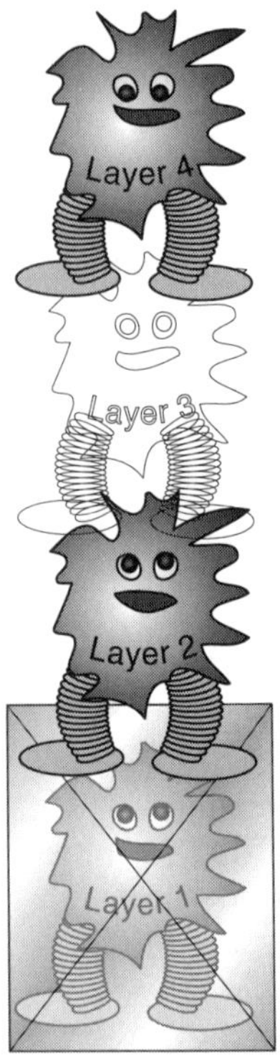

The Paths and Points and Handles
All of them wearing open-toed sandals
Had a dilemma, a confusing vector problem
That stumped even the most brightest of them
(Editors noted that this rhyming was sad
"It's unbalanced and ugly and just plain bad")

W'ever objects would meet, yet stay separated
They'd still be intermingled and some even dated
Groups were formed with a hierarchical slant
"We paths stick together" was their war cry and chant
Yet that wasn't enough, grouping groups was confusing
After keeping score for a while, the users were losing

Adobe Techs fielded support calls by the hundred zillions
So busy their Sega scores never made it to the millions
Suddenly the engineers assigned to make vectors better
Thought "We'll make layers, and make them to the letter"
Layers were magic and frosting and sugar and spice
The things of calories, tooth decay, and Disney mice

Vector objects rejoiced and cheered and screamed in glee,
"This is how life in a PostScript application should be"
Layers could be moved and previewed and printed
They could be colored and of course the fonts were still hinted
When the Paths and Points and Handles heard this great news
They ditched those open-toed sandals and bought leather dress shoes....

Figure 7-51: A layers Seussian story

You create, control, and manipulate layers by using the Layers palette. Each layer can have its own color, and that color will show up when all paths and points of objects are selected.

You can create as many layers as you want, up to the limitations of application memory. To make sure that the Adobe people were on the up-and-up about this, I created 5,000 layers in one document. It worked without ever questioning my need for 5,000 layers. Why would you need 5,000 layers? I hope you wouldn't. But you shouldn't have any fears that you will not be able to create enough layers for an illustration. Of course, having all those layers to work with slowed the operation of Illustrator to a crawl. I had to click the mouse button and hold on the menu bar for about 3 seconds before the menu appeared. Suffice it to say, the more layers you create after a certain point (several hundred), the slower Illustrator runs.

Getting Started with Layers

After you realize that you need to use layers, what do you do? The only way to manipulate, create, and delete layers is by using the Layers palette.

STEPS: Creating and Customizing New Layers

Step 1. If the Layers palette is not showing, choose Window⇨Show Layers (F7). When you open the Layers palette for the first time in a new document, you see only Layer 1 listed.

Step 2. To create a new layer, Option[Alt]-click the New Layer icon at the bottom of the palette (it looks like a piece of paper with the corner folded over). You can also click the triangle in the upper-right of the palette to display a pop-up menu. Drag over to the first item, New Layer, to display the New Layer dialog box.

Step 3. In the Layer Options dialog box, the name of the new layer, Layer 2, is highlighted. To change this name, type a new name, and it will replace the generic name.

Step 4. The options below the name affect how the layer works and is viewed. The first option is the color of the paths and points when objects on that layer are selected. Choose one of the preset colors from the pop-up menu or select the Other option to use a Custom Color.

Each time you create a new layer, a different color (going in order from the list) is applied to that layer.

Step 5. Select any of the options that you want for this layer. Show makes the objects in the layer visible. Print enables you to print objects that are on this layer. Preview makes the objects on this layer preview. Lock prevents objects on this layer from being selected and prevents any objects from being put on this layer. Dim Placed Images dims any placed images on the layer, making them about 80 percent lighter than normal.

Step 6. Click OK after you have chosen all the options you want. The new layer appears above the existing layer in the Layers palette. If you want the objects on the new layer to appear below the objects on the existing layer, click the name of the new layer and drag it under Layer 1.

Step 7. To modify the existing layer, double-click it. You see the Layer Options dialog box again. Make the changes and choose the options that you want for this layer and then click OK.

The Layer Options dialog box can be easily bypassed when creating new layers. Clicking on the New Layer icon (without pressing Option [Alt]) or pressing Option [Alt] while choosing New Layer from the Layer palette pop-up menu will create a new layer with the default naming scheme. You can always double-click on that layer to access the Layer Options for that layer.

Using the Layers Palette

The Layers palette (shown in Figure 7-52) is the control center where all layer-related activities take place. Most activities take place on the main section of the Layers palette, which is always visible when the Layers palette is on-screen. Other activities take place in the pop-up menu that appears when you press the triangle in the upper right of the palette.

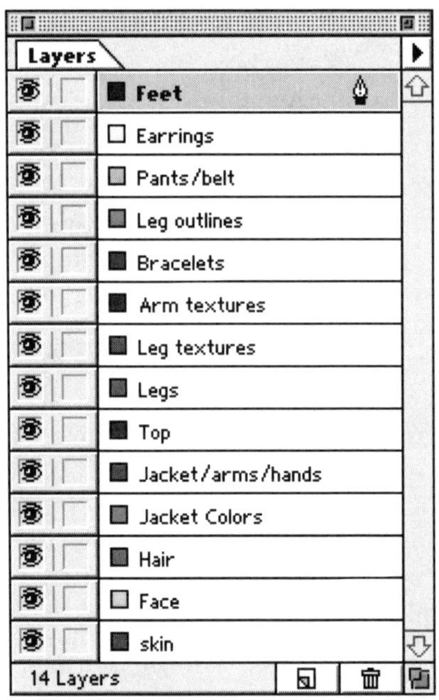

Figure 7-52: The Layers palette

The Main Section of the Layers Palette

Clicking the Close box in the upper-left corner closes the Layers palette. Another way to close the Layers palette is to choose Window⇨Hide Layers (F7).To bring the Layers palette back to the screen, choose Window⇨Show Layers (F7).

Clicking the Collapse box in the upper-right corner of the Layers palette resizes the palette to be collapsed, and then toggles to the previous height.

The left column controls how each layer is viewed. Solid eyes represent a layer that is in Preview mode. Hollow eyes mean that the layer is in Artwork mode. No eye means that the layer is hidden. Clicking a solid or hollow eye toggles it from showing to hidden. Clicking in the Show/Hide Column when no eye is present shows the layer. ⌘[Ctrl]-clicking the eye changes it from solid (Preview mode) to hollow (Artwork mode). Option[Alt]-clicking an eye shows or hides all other layers.

The right column is the Lock/Unlock column. The pencils with slashes through them in this column signify whether each layer is locked or unlocked. An empty column means that the layer is not locked. A pencil with a red slash means that the layer is locked from use. A pencil with a gray slash means that the layer is hidden, and that when the layer is shown it will be locked. You can move items to hidden layers as long as those layers are not locked, but you cannot change anything that is already on a hidden layer.

The column in the center of the palette lists the names of all the layers in the document. When no documents are open, no layers are listed. If one layer has a pen to the right of it, it is the active layer. All new objects are created on the active layer. Select more than one layer by Shift-clicking each layer to be selected. To deselect a layer, Shift-click it while it is selected. One layer must always be selected. If a pen with a slash through it is in that column, then that layer is active, and it is locked.

The layer at the top of the column is the layer that is on top of all the other layers. The layer at the bottom of the column is at the bottom of all the other layers. To move a layer or layers, click it and drag it up or down. As you drag, a dark horizontal line indicates where the layer(s) will be placed when you release the mouse button.

You can undo all layer changes as they happen by choosing Edit⇨Undo (⌘-Z) [Ctrl+Z] right afterward.

To the right of the layer names is the object status of the layer. If a square appears in that column, at least one object on that layer is selected.

STEPS: Moving Objects from Layer to Layer

Step 1. Select the objects that you want to move from one layer to another. If the objects are on one layer, group them together so that you can reselect them easily.

Do not group objects from different layers together, or all objects will be placed on the topmost layer.

(continued)

STEPS: *(continued)*

Step 2. Open the Layers palette by choosing Window⇨Show Layers (F7). A square should appear next to one of the layers. The square represents the selected objects.

If you select objects on more than one layer, a square appears on each of the layers that has a selected object.

Step 3. Drag the square from its current layer to the target layer. The objects do not move left, right, up, or down, but now they may be in front of or behind other objects, depending on the layer that they are now upon.

The Layers Palette Icons

There are two icons along the bottom of the Layers palette that make layer manipulation much easier than ever before. The first icon (a little piece of paper) is the New Layer icon. The second icon is the trash icon.

Clicking the New Layer icon creates a new layer instantly, without the New Layer dialog box appearing. Option[Alt]-clicking the New Layer icon creates a new layer by way of the New Layer dialog box. Dragging a layer or layers to the New Layer icon duplicates those layers, *and everything on them.*

Clicking the trash icon deletes the selected layers. If there is art on a layer that is about to be deleted, a dialog box will appear to make sure that you really want to delete that layer. Option[Alt]-clicking the trash icon deletes selected layers without a warning dialog box, whether or not art is on the selected layers. You can also drag a layer or layers to the trash icon; the layers will be deleted without a warning dialog box.

The Layers Palette Pop-up Menu

Clicking the triangle in the upper-right of the Layers palette displays a pop-up menu that shows different options that are available relative to the selected layers.

The first option, New Layer, creates a new layer at the top of the list. When New Layer is selected, the New Layer dialog box appears, which is the same as the Layer Options dialog box, except for the title. When a new layer is created with Illustrator, it is automatically assigned the next color in the color list.

If you press the Option [Alt] key before you click the pop-up menu triangle, the first menu item will read New Layer Above First Layer, or New Layer Above whatever the name of the active layer is.

The second menu item is Duplicate, which duplicates selected layers, along with any objects that are on those layers. You can also duplicate select layers by dragging them to the New Layer icon at the bottom of the Layers palette.

The next option is Delete, which deletes the layer and any artwork on the layer. If the layer to be deleted contains artwork, a dialog box warns you that you are about to delete it. If several layers are selected, the entry reads Delete Layers, and all selected layers are deleted. You can undo layer deletions.

The fourth menu item is Layer Options for Layer 1 (or Layer Options for whatever the name of the active layer is) — the menu item reads Layers Options if more than one layer is selected. Selecting Layer Options displays the Layer Options dialog box, in which you can choose a number of different options. If more than one layer is selected, the layer options affects all selected layers.

Double-clicking a layer name also brings up the Layer Options dialog box.

The next three options are different ways of changing the locking and viewing options. The first option reads either Show All Layers (if one or more is hidden), or Hide Other Layers (if all are visible). Hide Other layers hides all the layers but the selected ones. This is like pressing the Option [Alt] key and clicking the column to the left of the selected layers. The second option is either Preview all layers (if one or more is set to Artwork view) or Artwork Others, which changes all unselected layers to Artwork view. The third option is either Unlock All Layers (If any layers are locked) or Lock Others, which locks all layers but the selected ones. The third option can be done on the palette by Option[Alt]-clicking the selected layers' Lock/ Unlock column.

Checking the Paste Remembers Layers option causes all objects to be pasted on the layer they were copied from, regardless of which layer is currently active. Unchecking this menu item causes objects on the Clipboard to be pasted on the current layer.

The last item in the Layers Palette pop-up menu is Merge Layers, which combines selected layers into one. This was a feature that was sorely lacking from previous versions of Illustrator. Merge Layers does two important things: First, it places art that you want on the same layer together in one step. Second, it eliminates all those empty layers automatically. When you've finished an Illustration, if you know you won't need separate layers anymore, it's a great idea to go ahead and select all your layers and Merge them into one.

Layer Advice and Strategies

Layers take up RAM and computer power, and the more layers you have, the slower your system will be.

Create layers when you believe that they will help you organize an illustration better. Even setting up one additional layer can dramatically ease selection and moving problems. One of the best uses for layers is for tracing placed images. To learn exactly how to perform this procedure, see Chapter 4.

Use vivid, distinct colors for each layer. Using the same colors for all layers makes you miss out on half the power of layers. By choosing Select All (⌘-A) [Ctrl+A], you can quickly see which objects are on which layers, just by the color of the paths and points.

Summary

- Path editing is done in Illustrator by using the Direct Selection, Scissors, and Convert Direction Point tools.
- Adding Anchor Points alone never changes the shape of a path.
- Adding Anchor Points doubles the number of points on selected paths.
- Use Add Anchor Points before using the Punk and Bloat filter or the Scribble and Tweak filter.
- Cleanup deletes unwanted path types from your entire document.
- Offset Path moves a path inward or outward by the number of points you specify.
- Outline Path creates a Filled path in the same location as a Stroke, at the size of the width of the Stroke.
- The Pathfinder functions are path-specific.
- Unite joins together abutting and overlapping paths.
- Intersect creates paths where all the selected paths overlap, deleting the rest of the paths.
- Exclude creates paths only where there is no overlap.

- Back Minus and Front Minus subtract from the backmost or frontmost paths.
- Trap creates trapping in the amount you specify between abutting or overlapping paths.
- Removing Anchor Points can drastically change the shape of a path.
- Paths can be split one at a time with the Scissors tool.
- You can slice through paths with the Knife tool.
- Quickly make duplicates of certain sections of paths by pressing Option [Alt] when using the Knife tool.
- Selected points can be aligned using the Average command.
- Any two selected End Points can be joined by using the Join command.
- Entire objects can be aligned by using the Align palette.
- The Convert Direction Point tool changes the Anchor Point type.
- The five major types of PostScript transformations are represented by four tools, Rotate, Scale, Reflect, and Shear, and the Move dialog box.
- Transform Each incorporates the Move, Scale, and Rotate functions that work on selected objects independently.
- The Select functions aid in selecting objects.
- Same Fill Color selects objects with the same Fill color as the currently selected object.
- Same Paint Style selects objects with the same paint style as the currently selected object.
- Inverse selects everything that isn't selected, and deselects everything that is selected.
- Select Masks selects all paths used as masking paths.
- Layers can be used to effectively separate different sections of your artwork.

CHAPTER 8

Type

In This Chapter

- Using Vertical type
- Methods of entering type in a document
- Creating Point type
- Creating Rectangle type
- Placing type within areas
- Creating type on a path
- Selecting type and changing type attributes
- Importing type
- Converting type into editable outlines
- Designing with the Type tool
- Using Special characters
- Avoiding type compatibility problems
- Creating custom fonts

Type is a huge part of Illustrator. In previous versions of this book, I split type between several different chapters in different areas. But for the *Illustrator 7 Bible,* I've packed this one chapter full of everything I could about type, to the point where this version of the *Illustrator Bible* is a little type-heavy, and severely off balance.

But then, when I talk to Illustrator users, from vets to those who are wet behind the ears, and even those users who have just started using Illustrator, they all tell me one thing: "Yer really tall, Ted." And a lot of them tell me that the main thing they use Illustrator for is manipulating type. So here's what could be the most important chapter in the book (and, by last count, it's the biggest).

Windows Update

Most of the general type tools and controls give the same results as Version 4.1; however, the locations of these tools and controls have been moved all over the place. Tabs and Vertical Type are the most significant changes to Type in Illustrator 7.

What's Missing	What Replaces It
Type dialog box	Many Paragraph controls, such as Alignment and Spacing
Character Palette	Similar controls in the Paragraph palette

What's New

Vertical Type capabilities, through the new Vertical Type tools

Tabs and the new Tab palette

Anti-aliased type on-screen

The Type Menu

The Type menu, shown in Figure 8-1, contains all of Illustrator's type controls (with the exception of the Type tools). No longer is the Font menu a separate menu on the menu bar; it is now incorporated into a submenu in the Type menu.

Most of the Type options can be changed in the Character palette (choose Type⇨Character or press ⌘-T [Ctrl+T]) or the Paragraph palette (choose Type⇨Paragraph or press ⌘-M [Ctrl+M]), which are discussed later in this chapter.

Type is set in Illustrator in *stories.* A story is a set of continuous, linked text. When the term *paragraph* is mentioned, it is usually referring to the characters that are between Returns. If there are no Returns in a story, then that story is said to have one paragraph. Returns end paragraphs and begin new ones. There is always exactly one more paragraph in a story than there are Returns.

The following sections describe each of the Type menu options.

Figure 8-1: The Type Menu

Font

Font displays a submenu with all the fonts that are currently installed on the computer you are using. Pressing ⌘-Option-Shift-F [Ctrl+Alt+Shift+F] or ⌘-Option-Shift-M [Ctrl+Alt+Shift+M] automatically highlights the Font field on the Character palette and shows or notes the palette as well. A check mark appears next to the font that is currently selected. If no check mark appears next to any of the fonts, more than one font is currently selected.

If you are wondering why the folks at Adobe chose such an odd combination of keys and commands, you probably don't use QuarkXPress too much. Quark's key command for highlighting the font field in its measurement palette is ⌘-Option-Shift-M [Ctrl+Alt+Shift+M].

Size

Type Size displays a submenu with "Other" and various point sizes listed. When Other is chosen, the Character palette appears with the Size field highlighted. You can type any point size from .1 to 1,296 in this field.

Type created in Illustrator may be scaled to any size, but to go beyond the size limits, you must convert the type into outline paths by using the Create Outlines command (⌘-Shift-O) [Ctrl+Shift+O].

A check mark appears next to the point size that is currently selected. If the point size currently selected does not correspond to a point size in the Size submenu, a check mark appears next to the Other menu item. Point size for type is measured from the top of the ascenders (like the top of a capital letter *T*) to the bottom of the descenders (like the bottom of a lowercase *g*). If no check mark appears next to any of the sizes, more than one size is currently selected (even if the different sizes are all Other sizes).

You can also increase and decrease the point size of type by using the keyboard shortcuts ⌘-Shift-> [Ctrl+Shift+>], which increases the point size by the amount specified in Keyboard Increments Preferences, and ⌘-Shift-< [Ctrl+Shift+<], which decreases the point size by the amount specified in Keyboard Increments Preferences.

Yet another way to change point size is to use the Scale tool. Using the Scale tool to change point size lets you change to any size; that size is displayed in the Character palette as soon as you are done scaling. Once again, keep in mind that the limit in scaling type is 1,296 points, and you cannot exceed that even with the Scale tool (unless the type has been converted to outlined paths).

Character

Character (⌘-T) [Ctrl+T] brings up the Character palette with the Font field highlighted. In the Character palette, you can change fonts, styles, point size, leading, baseline shift, horizontal scale, and tracking/kerning values, all at one time!

When you choose the Show Options item from the Character palette's pop-up menu, the Horizontal and Vertical Scaling controls and the Baseline shift control are available (see Figure 8-2). Choosing the Multinational Options displays the Multinational Options at the very bottom of the palette.

If the Character palette is currently open, choosing the Character option or pressing ⌘-T [Ctrl+T] will close (hide) it.

Paragraph

Paragraph (⌘-Shift-M) [Ctrl+Shift+M] displays the Paragraph palette with the Left Indentation field highlighted (see Figure 8-3). You can use this palette to change the left, right, and first line indents, and change the alignment by clicking different alignment boxes. In addition, Space Before Paragraph, Hang Punctuation, Auto Hyphenate, Repeated Character Processing, and Line Breaking are available. In the bottom part of the palette (choose Show Options from the pop-up menu of the palette to see the bottom part), you can set spacing limitations and guidelines.

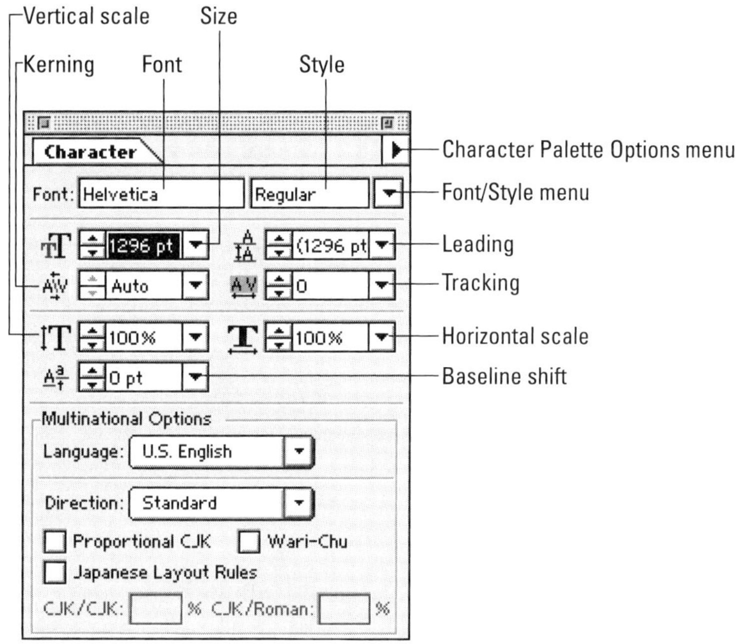

Figure 8-2: The Character palette, expanded to show both Options and Multinational Options

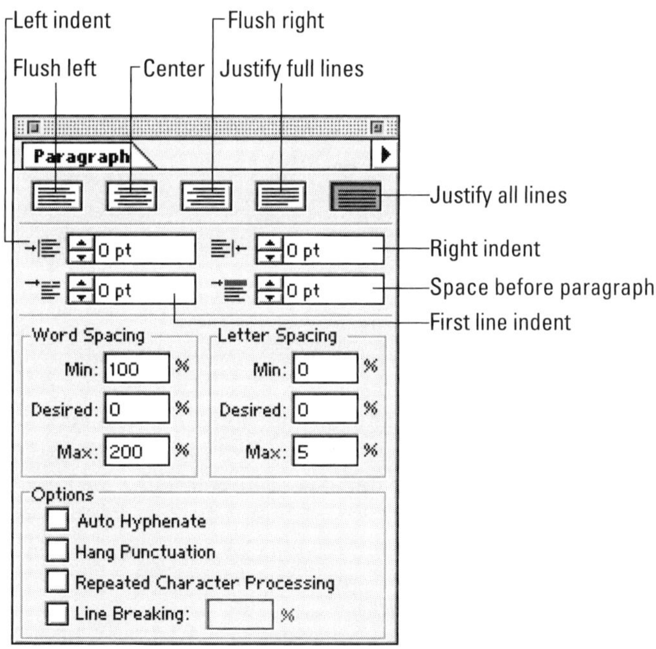

Figure 8-3: The Paragraph palette

If the Paragraph palette is currently open, choosing the Paragraph command will close (hide) it.

Choosing Hyphenation Options from the pop-up menu displays the Hyphenation Options dialog box (see Figure 8-4), where you can specify the number of letters before and after hyphens, and how many consecutive hyphens can appear in a row.

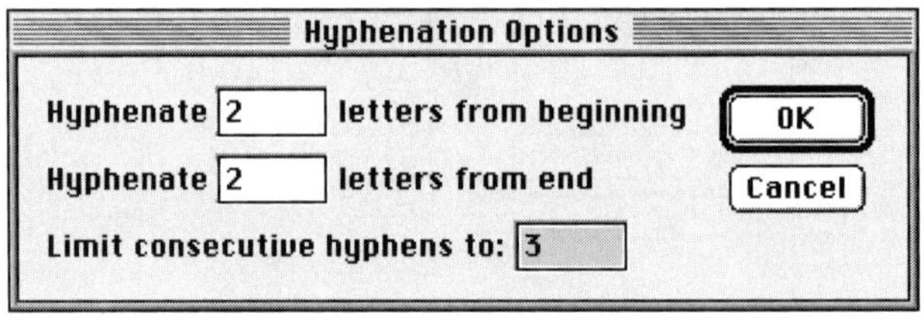

Figure 8-4: The Hyphenation Options dialog box

MM Design

Choosing Type⇨MM Design displays the Multiple Master Design palette, where you can create variations of any installed Multiple Master fonts (see Figure 8-5). Multiple Master fonts are flexible fonts that can be modified in real time within Illustrator. These fonts are changed along several different "axes," such as weight, serif, italics, and width. The Multiple Master Design palette enables you to modify the axis available for each font.

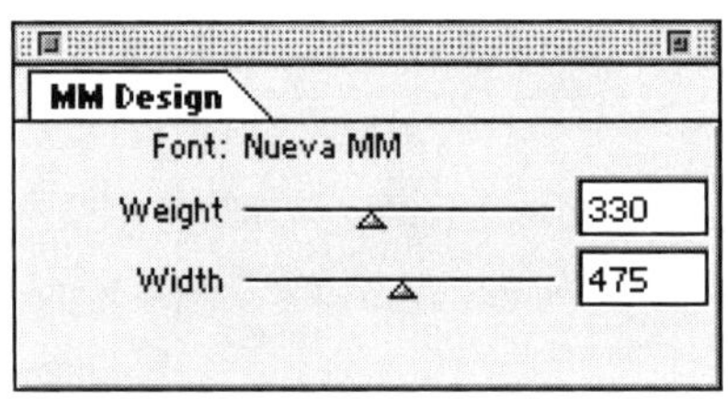

Figure 8-5: The Multiple Master Design palette when Nueva MM is selected, a Multiple Master font with two axes (Weight and Width)

The Tab Ruler Palette

The Tab Ruler palette is used to set tabs the same way you would in your word-processing or page-layout software. To access the Tab Ruler palette, choose Type⇨Tab Ruler. The Tab Ruler palette is shown in Figure 8-6.

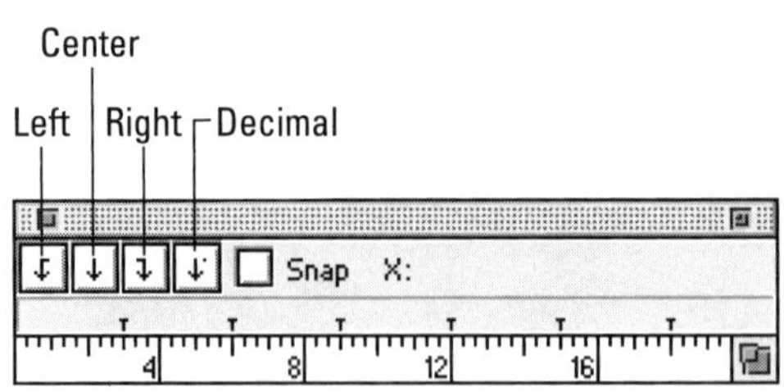

Figure 8-6: The Tab Ruler palette

To set tabs for type, select the type and choose Type⇨Tab Ruler. The Tab Ruler palette appears above the type you have selected and automatically assumes the width of the type area.

To change the width of the Tab Ruler palette, click and drag on the Extend Tab Ruler button in the lower-right corner of the palette. The Tab Ruler palette can be made wider or thinner, but not taller. To reset the Tab Ruler palette back to the exact size of the type area, click on the Alignment box in the upper-right corner of the palette.

POWER TIP: The Alignment box will move the Tab Ruler palette to make it flush left with the type and move it up or down so that it is right above the selected text area.

Before you set any tabs, tabs are automatically set at every half inch. These are called *Auto tab stops.* Once you set a tab, all the Auto tab stops to the left of the tab you have set disappear. The Auto tab stops work like left-justified tabs.

If the Snap option box is checked, tab stops correspond to ruler tick marks.

The measurement system shown on the ruler is the same system that is used by the rest of the document and can be changed in the Preferences dialog box.

To set a tab, select a tab from the four Tab Style buttons on the upper left of the Tab Ruler palette and click on the ruler below to set exactly where you would like the new tab. Once the tab has been set, you can move it by dragging it along the ruler or remove it by dragging it off the top or bottom edge of the ruler.

There are four types of tabs you can set:

- **Left-justified tabs** make type align to the right side of the tab, with the leftmost character aligning with the tab stop.
- **Center-justified tabs** make type align to the center of the tab, with the center character aligning with the tab stop.
- **Right-justified tabs** make type align to the left side of the tab, with the rightmost character aligning with the tab stop.
- **Decimal-justified tabs** make type align to the left side of the tab, with a decimal or the rightmost character aligning with the tab stop.

To change a tab from one style to another, select a tab stop and click on the Tab style button that you wish to change to. To deselect all tabs, click in the area to the right of the Tab position box. It is a good idea to get in the habit of deselecting tabs after they are set so that defining a new tab style for the next tab stop does not change the tab stop that was just set.

There is no way to create dot leader tabs automatically by using the Tab Ruler palette. We may have to wait for Version 8 of Illustrator for this feature to be incorporated. As always, if you think this feature or any other feature that Illustrator lacks would be useful, send Adobe a note (a “feature request”) and it *will* be considered.

Graphical Tabs

Graphical tabs are tabs that flow around objects (paths) in Illustrator automatically. The following steps show you how to use graphical tabs.

STEPS: Creating Graphical Tabs

Step 1. Create a rectangle type area and type in five words separated by tabs. (Yes, each word will be set at 1/2" apart — we’ll fix that shortly.) Press Return after the last word entered.

Step 2. Select All (⌘-A) [Ctrl+A] and Copy (⌘-C) [Ctrl+C]. Then click the last line of type (it should be blank) and paste it a few times (⌘-V, ⌘-V, ⌘-V, ⌘-V) [Ctrl+V, Ctrl+V, Ctrl+V, Ctrl+V].

Step 3. Using the Pencil tool, draw a series of four straight or curved vertical lines that extend above the top and below the bottom of the type area. Select the lines and the type area and choose Type➪Wrap➪Make. The type should be tabbed to the lines that you drew.

Tabs will tab to the other side of text wrap objects. Play with this a little, and you’ll discover that this method is much more flexible than standard word processing tab stops.

The Link Blocks Option

The Link Blocks option (Type➪Blocks➪Link) links text from one area or rectangle to another, continuing a story from one area or rectangle to another (see Figure 8-7). Linked blocks act like groups, enabling you to use the regular Selection tool and click on just one area in order to select all areas. (Individual blocks can still be selected with the Direct Selection tool.) Whenever more text is available than can fit into a text area, a tiny little plus sign in a box appears, alerting you that there is more text in the box than you see.

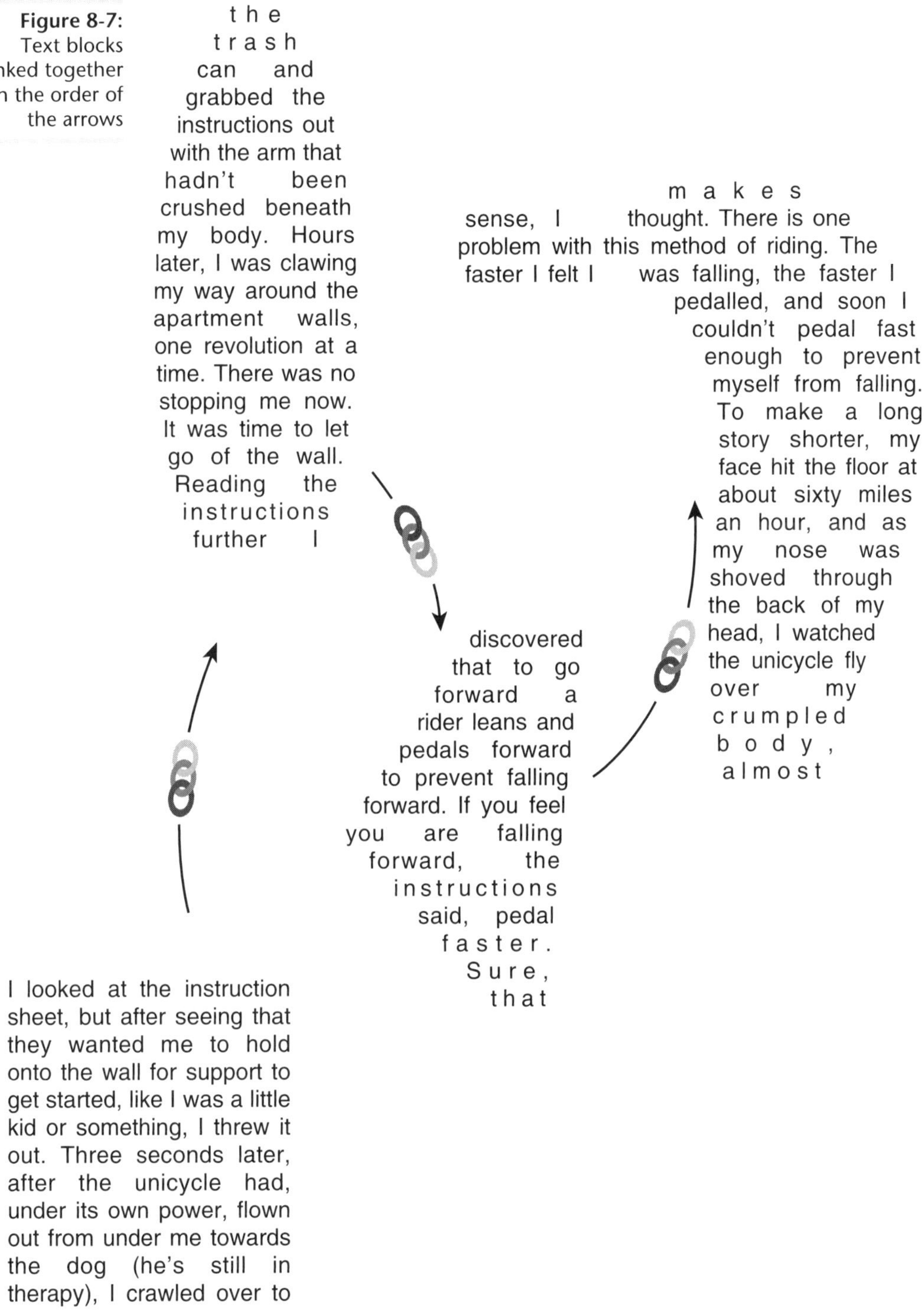

Figure 8-7: Text blocks linked together in the order of the arrows

To use Link Blocks, select a text area or rectangle and any other shapes, even text rectangles and areas, and choose Link Blocks. Text will flow from the backmost shape to the frontmost in any group of linked blocks, so be careful to order your boxes correctly when setting up linked text. In fact, if you send a box to the back, that will be where the text starts from, going to the next box forward, and then the next, and so on. You cannot select Link Blocks if at least one text area and one other path or text area is not selected.

The Unlink Blocks Option

The Unlink Blocks option (Type⇨Blocks⇨Unlink) destroys the links made with the Link Blocks command. Blocks can only be unlinked when all boxes linked together are chosen. This is done quite easily with the regular Selection tool. When blocks are unlinked, the text inside them is split into several stories, one for each block. If the boxes are later relinked with the Link Blocks command, they will be separated by paragraph returns.

The Make Wrap Option

The Make Wrap option wraps text around any paths, as shown in Figure 8-8. To use Make Wrap, select both the type and the paths you want the type to wrap around. The paths that the type wraps around must be in front of the type in order for them to wrap around the paths. Choose Type Wrap⇨Make. The objects then act like a grouped object; you can use the regular Selection tool to select all objects in a Make Wrap area.

Make Wrap only works with Area type and Rectangle type (the option is dimmed for Path type and Point type).

Make Wrap works in levels: you can Make Wrap with one type area or rectangle to a path and then Make Wrap again with the same type area or rectangle to another path, and the type will wrap around both paths.

CAUTION Remember that Make Wrap only wraps around paths; regardless of how thick the Stroke on your path is, the wrap will not change. This can cause the wrapping object to run into the text if the object has a heavy Stroke.

Additional objects can be used to wrap. Just place them in front of the type area, select both the type area and the new wrapping object, and choose Type⇨Make Wrap.

Figure 8-8: Text wrapped around different objects

Text wrapping objects need no Fill or Stroke, but they do need to be closed. If you want to use an existing path and that path is not closed, simply copy the path, choose Edit⇨Paste In Front (⌘-F) [Ctrl+F], and change the Fill and Stroke to None.

The Release Wrap Option

The Release Wrap (Choose Type⇨Wrap⇨Release) option releases any text wraps that are selected, all at one time. Release Wrap does *not* release wraps in the order that they were created. Because paths wrapped to type areas and rectangles do not lose or change attributes when they become wrapped paths, those paths retain their original Paint Style attributes when released.

The Fit Headline Option

The Fit Headline option is designed to automatically increase the weight and width of type using Multiple Master fonts in order to fit type perfectly from the left side of a type area or rectangle to the right side of that same type area or rectangle. Of course, for this to work, you must have Multiple Master typefaces. Personally, I think this feature would have been great if it just increased the point size of any type, Multiple Master or not, so that the type fit from left to right.

If you don't have Multiple Master typefaces, you can still use Fit Headline. Although the command only increases the tracking of the type until it is justified, it actually does a lot better job than the Justify All Lines command (in the Paragraph palette), which only puts space between words.

The Create Outlines Option

After your type is set (and spelled correctly), choose Type⇨Create Outlines (⌘-Shift-O) [Ctrl+Shift+O] and the type selected is converted into *editable paths* (see Figure 8-9). To convert type to outlines, the type needs to be selected with a selection tool, not a type tool. Each letter is its own compound path, and each path can be edited with the Direct Selection tool.

Create Outlines only works with Type 1 PostScript and TrueType fonts, not bitmapped or Type 3 PostScript fonts. You must have both the screen and printer fonts for those fonts.

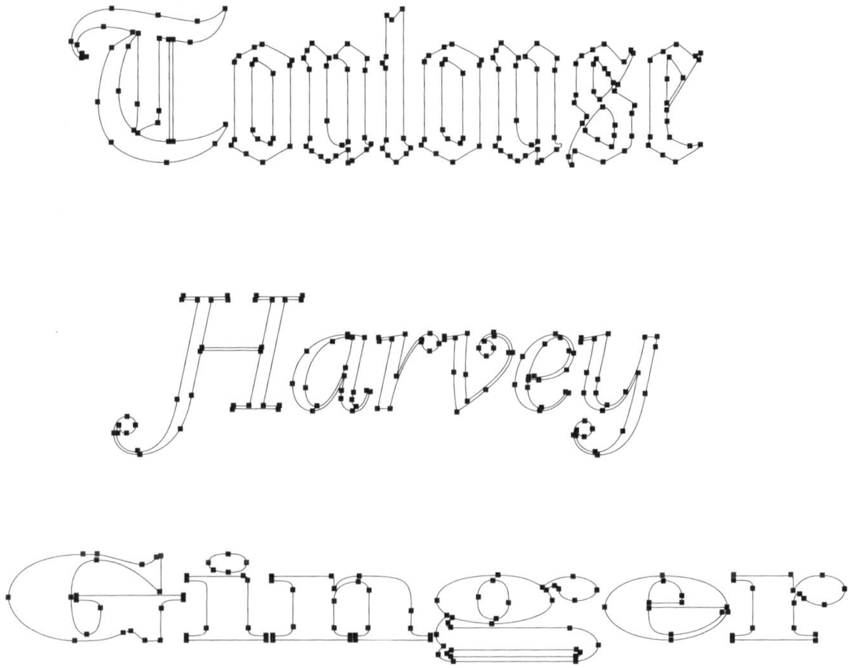

Figure 8-9: Type converted into outlines with the Create Outlines command

TrueType combines the screen and printer fonts into one file — if you can select a TrueType font in Illustrator, you can create outlines from it.

When type has been converted to outlines, you can apply gradients to its Fill, as well as apply patterns to its Fill that you can preview on-screen. (Patterns can be applied to nonoutline type, but you cannot see those patterns in the type on-screen; instead, the type becomes a dingy gray color.)

CAUTION

While you can undo Create Outlines, be forewarned that there is no way to convert back to type in case you made a spelling error or wish to change the font or any other type attributes.

All forms of type, including Point type, Path type, Area type, and Rectangle type, may be converted to outlines.

POWER TIP

Creating outlines out of type is also very useful when you want to send the file to be output and the person doing the output does not have the font you are using. Simply use the Create Outlines option before you send the file, and it will print just fine.

Type Outlines

The process of creating editable type outlines has many uses, the main one that I have seen being the ability to distort mild-mannered characters into grotesque letters. More practical uses for editable type outlines include the following: making type-based logos unique, arcing type (where one side is flat and the other is curved), special effects and masking, and avoiding font compatibility problems.

To change type from being editable text into an Illustrator path (for that is what an editable type outline really is), select the type with a selection tool, not a type tool. Choose Type➪Create Outlines or press ⌘-Shift-O [Ctrl+Shift+O], and the type changes into paths that you can edit. Figure 8-10 shows the "CHO" logo before and after being converted into outlines.

CAUTION: After type has been changed into Illustrator paths using Create Outlines, the only way back is to use the Undo command (⌘-Z) [Ctrl+Z]. There is no "Convert from Paths to Type" function. Type cannot be edited in Outline mode. This means that if you misspell somthing, it will remain misspelled.

Initially, when type is converted into outlines, individual characters are turned into compound paths. This ensures that holes in letters such as in a lowercase *a*, *b*, or *d* are see-through, and not just White-Filled paths placed on top of the original objects. (See Chapter 11 for an in-depth discussion of compound paths.)

Making Letters That Normally Appear in Your Worst Nightmares

After letters have been turned into outlines, there is nothing stopping you from distorting them into shapes that only resemble letters in the most simplistic sense of the word, and even then it takes some imagination.

The results of letter distortion usually aren't all that eye-pleasing, but they can be *fun.* Few things in life are as pleasing as taking a boring letter *Q* and twisting it into "the letter that time forgot." Or fiddling around with your boss's name until the letters look as evil as he does. Or adding pointed ears and whiskers to a random array of letters and numbers and printing out several sheets of them with the words "Mutant kittens for sale." Some of these samples are shown in Figure 8-11.

When modifying existing letters, use the Direct Selection tool. Select the points or segments you wish to move, and drag them around to your heart's content. This can be great practice for adjusting paths, and you might accidentally stumble onto some really cool designs.

Figure 8-10: Type that has been converted to outlines and united via the Unite function

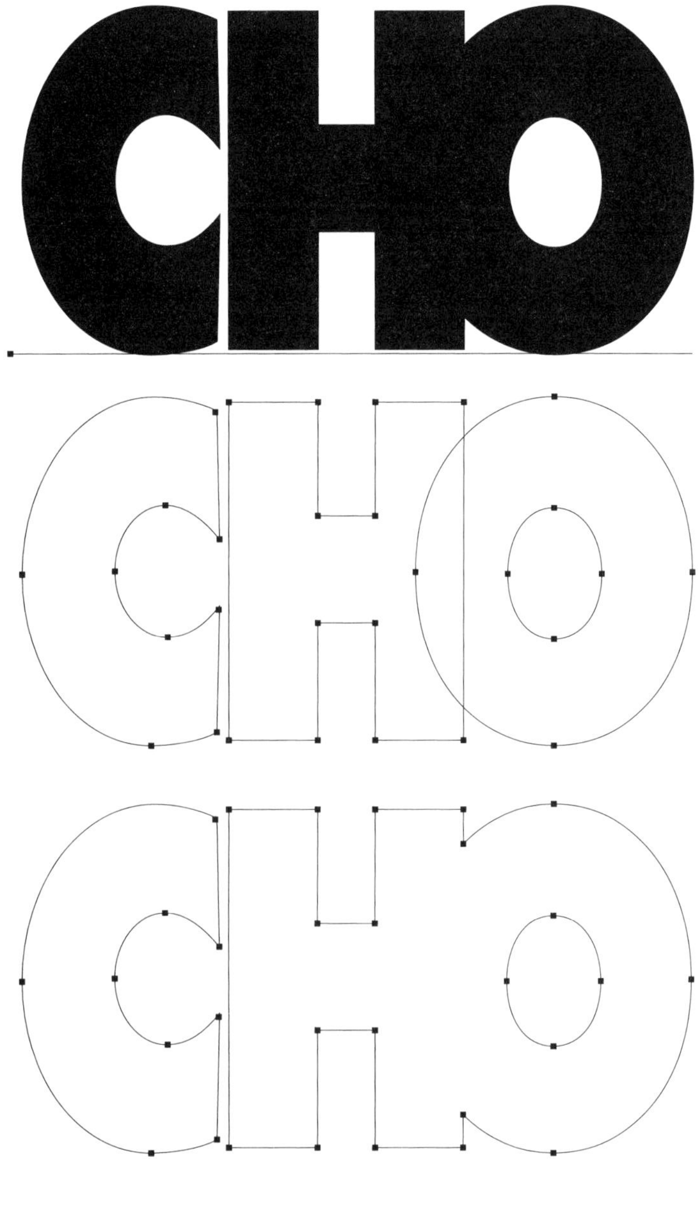

Figure 8-11: Fun with type outlines

Creating Logos from Type Outlines

Type outlines provide you with the flexibility to manipulate letters to turn an ordinary, boring, letters-only logo into a distinct symbol embodying the company's image.

Outlines are flexible enough that there really are no limits to what can be done with something as simple as a word of type.

The examples in Figure 8-12 show some logos that have been "touched up" by changing them into outlines and moving around the paths that comprise them.

Figure 8-12: Type converted to outlines, edited, and ready to be used for logos

Distorting Words and Phrases

The difference between arced words and type on a circle is that the letters in type on a circle are rotated individually, making each letter line up with one part of the circle; the letters in arced type are not rotated, but instead either the top or bottom of them is stretched to fit to a circular curve, as in the examples shown on the right side of Figure 8-12.

Arcing type is easier and creates better results when the type is created as all capital letters, especially when the tops of the letters are being curved to fit a circle.

To arc type, first convert it into outlines, and then create an oval or circle above or below the outlines. As an example, the following steps arc type using the circle-below method.

STEPS: Arcing Type by Creating a Circle Below Outlines

Step 1. Make sure that the tip of the top of the circle touches the center letters in the word so that these letters don't need to be changed. Always adjust the horizontal scaling prior to aligning the circle to the outlined type, as this prevents unnecessary adjustments.

Step 2. Using the Scale tool, scale the first letter vertically only (hold down the Shift key) and drag until either the left or right side is even with the path of the circle. Do the same for the remaining letters.

Step 3. After the letters are the correct approximate height, use the Direct Selection tool to adjust the bottoms of the letters to fit the curve well. This can take some time and a bit of practice to get the technique correct, but the results can be outstanding.

The best way to arc type is by using a third-party filter, such as the KPT Warp Frame filter in the KPT Vector Effects set of filters.

Arcing curved letters is much more difficult than arcing straight ones, and arcing letters with serifs is slightly more difficult than arcing letters that are sans serif.

Arcing letters just on one side of a curve can be started easily by selecting just those letters on that half and using the Free Distort filter (choose Filter⇨Distort⇨Free Distort). This does the scaling even more accurately than using the Scale tool because the letters aren't just scaled proportionately but angled automatically as well.

Masking and Other Effects

After type has been converted into outlines, it can then be used as a mask or Filled with gradients or patterns, as shown in Figure 8-13. (Standard type cannot be used as a mask, Filled with gradients, or Filled with patterns.)

Figure 8-13: Type that has been converted to outlines and is now Filled with a pattern (left) and used as a masking path (right)

In order for words to work as a single mask, they must first be changed into a compound path. Usually, individual letters of converted type are changed into individual compound paths, whether the letter has a hole in it or not. In order for masks to work properly, you must select the entire word or words you want to use as a mask and then choose Object⇨Compound Paths⇨Make (⌘-6) [Ctrl+6]. This changes all the selected letters into one compound path.

In some third-party (nonAdobe) and shareware typefaces, making a compound path out of a series of letters can produce results where the holes are not transparent at all. This issue is usually one of path direction, which can be corrected by selecting the inner shape (the hole) and changing the direction with the path direction buttons on the Attributes palette.

After the words are a compound path, place them in front of the objects to be masked, select both the words and the masked objects, and then choose Object⇨Masks⇨Make (⌘-5) [Ctrl+5].

Avoiding Font Conflicts by Creating Outlines

If you ever give your files to a service bureau or to clients, you've probably already run into some font compatibility problems. A font compatibility problem usually means that the place you gave your file doesn't have a typeface that you've used within your Illustrator document.

This is a problem that there is no great solution to, and if nothing else, the trouble seems to be worsening as more font manufacturers spring up — TrueType fonts being the Windows standard, and PostScript Type 1 fonts being the Mac standard. And then there are shareware typefaces, some of which resemble Adobe originals to an uncanny degree of accuracy. All this leads to a great deal of confusion and frustration for the average Illustrator user.

Masking Type Mishaps

Kim: I can't get masking with text to work right.

Toulouse: What's happening?

Kim: Well, only the last letter in the word I'm using as a mask is working like a mask. The other letters disappear.

Toulouse: Did you make a compound path out of all the letters in your word *before* you masked?

Kim: Uh, no. That's bad, huh?

Toulouse: Actually, yes. What's happening now is that the last letter in the word, which is in front of all the other objects that are selected, is trying to mask everything else that's selected.

Kim: Ah. Including the other letters.

Toulouse: Exactly. Illustrator has to see the word as *one* path, which is what making a compound path out of the entire word does.

Kim: So to fix it?

Toulouse: First, release the mask, select just the letters, and make them a compound. Then select everything and click Make Mask.

But there is a way around this problem, at least most of the time. Convert your typefaces into outlines *before* you send them to other people with other systems — they don't need your typefaces for the letters to print correctly. In fact, converted letters aren't really considered type anymore, just outlines.

Save your file before converting the text to outlines and then save as a different file name after converting the text to outlines. This will allow you to do text editing later on the original file, if necessary.

CAUTION

Converting typefaces to outlines removes the hinting system that Adobe has implemented. This hinting system makes small letters on low-resolution (less than 600 dpi) devices print more accurately, controlling the placement and visibility of serifs and other small, thin strokes in characters. Type at small point sizes looks quite different on laser printers, although it retains its shape and consistency when it is output to an imagesetter or an output scanner system.

Hinting

Most Type 1 fonts have *hinting* built into them. Hinting is a method for adjusting type at small point sizes, especially at low resolutions. While hinting is built into several fonts, when those fonts are converted into paths via the Create Outlines command, the hinting functionality is gone. This is part of the reason that type converted to outlines can look heavier than otherwise.

Creating outlines shouldn't cause that much of a problem when the type will be output to an imagesetter, because the high resolution of the imagesetter makes up for the loss of hinting. However, very small type — 4 pts. or less — could be adversely affected.

Find

Find/Change feature (Type➪Find/Change) uses the Find/Change dialog box that is shown in Figure 8-14 to search for and, if necessary, replace certain letters, words, or character combinations.

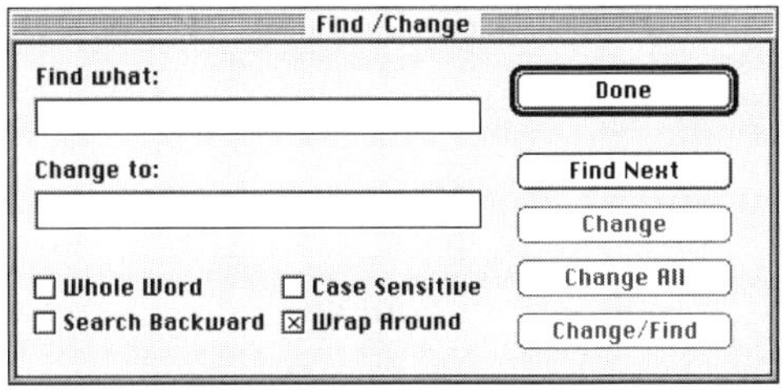

Figure 8-14: The Find/Change dialog box

STEPS: Finding and Replacing Text

Step 1. Choose Type⇨Find/Change. The Find/Change dialog box appears.

Step 2. Type the word, phrase, or characters that you want to find in the Find What text field.

You do not need to select areas of type with the Selection or Type tools. All that is necessary is that the document that you want to search be the open and active document.

Step 3. Check the appropriate options:

- **Whole Word:** Tells Illustrator that the characters you type in the Find What box are an entire word, not part of a word.
- **Case Sensitive:** Selects the characters only if they have the same uppercase and lowercase attributes as the characters you type in the Find What text field.
- **Search Backward:** Tells Illustrator to look before the current word for the next instance of the characters, instead of using the default, which is to look after the current word.
- **Wrap Around:** Keeps Illustrator going through all the text blocks and makes Illustrator continue looking and finding the next occurrence throughout each text block. When it reaches the last text block, it starts where it originally began and continues finding the word or characters that you specified in the Find What box.

Step 4. Click the Find Next button to find the first occurrence of the word or characters.

Step 5. In the Replace with box, type the word or characters that you want to use to replace the text that Illustrator found.

Step 6. Click the Replace button to replace the selected text. Click the Replace button and then the Find button to replace the selected text and automatically highlight the next matching word or characters. Click the Replace All button to replace all occurrences of the word or characters throughout the document.

CAUTION: Illustrator cannot find words or characters that you have converted to outlines.

Find Font

Find Font looks for certain fonts in a document and replaces them with fonts you specify.

Select type with either a selection tool or with a type tool. Then choose Type⇨Find Font. The Find Font dialog box appears, as shown in Figure 8-15.

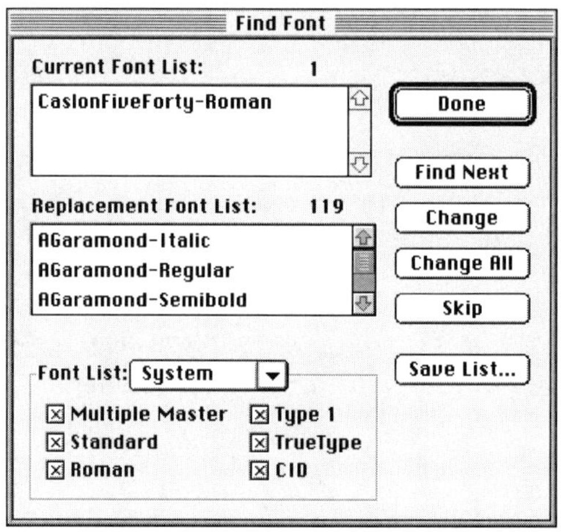

Figure 8-15: The Find Font box

To change all occurrences of a certain font to another font, select the font to be changed in the top window, titled Current List. Then select a font in the Replacement Font List window and click the Change All button. To change one particular instance, click the Change button. To find the next occurrence of that font, select Find Next. The Skip button skips over the currently selected text and finds the next occurrence of that font.

Pressing the Save List button enables you to save your font list as a text file. After the fonts are found, you have to select type with the Type tool, no matter how it was selected before Find Font was used.

Check Spelling

Check Spelling checks all text in a document to see if it is spelled (and capitalized) correctly. To use this feature, choose Type⇨Check Spelling. The Check Spelling dialog box appears, as shown in Figure 8-16.

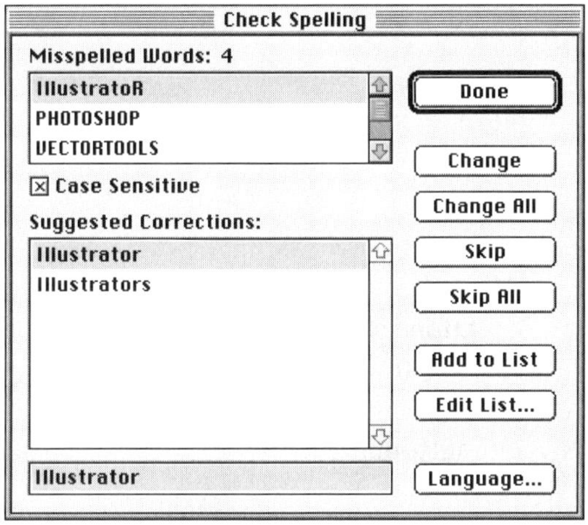

Figure 8-16: The Check Spelling dialog box

If all words are spelled correctly, a congratulatory message appears telling you that your spelling is "excellent."

If you have any misspelled words or words that are not in the spelling dictionaries, those words are listed at the top of the Check Spelling dialog box in the Misspelled Words window. Selecting a word in this list displays similar words below in the window titled Suggested Corrections.

If the Case Sensitive option is checked, the capitalization of words must match the words in the spell checker's dictionary, or they will appear as misspelled words.

The Add to List button is used when you would like to add the selected "misspelled" word to your custom dictionary. Clicking the Edit List button displays the Learned Words dialog box, showing you which words are currently in the user dictionary. The Learned Words dialog box enables you to add, remove, or change entries in the user dictionary.

STEPS: Adding Words to the User Dictionary

Step 1. To add a new entry to the user dictionary, select the Edit List button in the Check Spelling dialog box, which displays the Learned Words dialog box.

Step 2. Type in the word that you would like to add to the user dictionary. Click the Add button, and the word is added to the list of words in the user dictionary.

Capitalization is very important when adding words, so be sure to place initial caps on proper nouns and to use correct capitalization on all words that require it.

(continued)

STEPS: ***(continued)***

If the word you are trying to add exists in the user dictionary or the main dictionary, a dialog box appears telling you that it is already a dictionary entry.

Step 3. Repeat Step 2 until all the words have been added.

Step 4. If at any time you make a mistake, you may change the spelling of an entered word by selecting it in the window above, typing in the correct spelling, and then clicking the Change button. If you wish to delete an entry that exists in the Learned Words window, select that word and click the Remove button.

Step 5. When you are finished, click the Done button.

The user dictionary words are saved in a file called "AI User Dictionary," which is stored in the Plug-Ins folder. The file is in Text-compatible format, but the character that separates the words is indistinguishable (it appears as an open rectangle, the symbol for a symbol that is not available in that typeface), so there is no way to add words to the dictionary by using any word processor.

CAUTION

Be careful not to delete or remove the AI User Dictionary file when reinstalling the software or moving the files in the Plug-Ins folder. Doing so causes Illustrator to create a new user dictionary file with no words in it. There is no way to combine two different user dictionary files.

While you're checking your spelling in the Check Spelling dialog box, clicking the Change button replaces the misspelled word with the highlighted word in the Suggested Corrections list. Clicking the Change All button replaces all misspelled occurrences of that word throughout the entire document with the correctly spelled word.

Clicking the Skip button ignores that occurrence of the misspelled word. Clicking Skip All skips all occurrences of that word in the document.

Clicking the Language button uses a dictionary for the language you specify. Illustrator supplies dictionaries for the United States and the United Kingdom, both located in the Plug-In filters files.

Clicking the Done button closes the Check Spelling dialog box.

Change Case

Change Case converts selected text to a variety of case options. To use this filter, select type with a type tool and then choose Type➪Change Case. The Change Case dialog box appears, as shown in Figure 8-17.

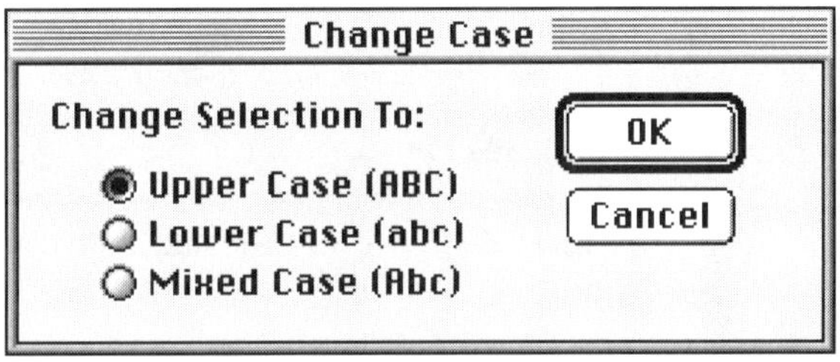

Figure 8-17: The Change Case dialog box

Type *must* be selected with the Type tool (characters must be highlighted) to use the Change Case feature. If type is selected with a Selection tool, then the filter will not work, and a dialog box stating this is displayed.

The three Change Case options affect only letters, not numbers, symbols, or punctuation. The options are as follows:

- **UPPER CASE** converts all selected letters into uppercase, regardless if any letters were uppercase or lowercase.
- **lower case** converts all selected letters into lowercase, regardless if any letters were uppercase or lowercase. It also doesn't matter if the letters were originally uppercase because they were typed with the Caps Lock key engaged, or if the uppercase letters were uppercase because of a style format.
- **Mixed Case** converts all selected words into lowercase, with the first letter of each word becoming uppercase, regardless if any letters were originally uppercase or lowercase. It also doesn't matter if the letters were originally uppercase because they were typed with the Caps Lock key engaged, or if the uppercase letters were uppercase because of a style format. The Mixed Case option separates words by making *any* character that is between letters end one word and begin another. At the time of this writing, even apostrophes in contractions caused words like "don't" and "can't" to display as "Don'T" and "Can'T."

Smart Punctuation

The Smart Punctuation filter looks for certain fonts in a document and replaces them with fonts you specify. To use this filter, select type with either a selection tool or with a type tool. Then choose Type➪Smart Punctuation. The Smart Punctuation dialog box appears, as shown in Figure 8-18.

But My Insertion Point Is Waaayyy Over There

Hawkeye: My insertion point is possessed.

Toulouse: Possessed, eh?

Hawkeye: When I enter text using the Text tool, my cursor floats 2 to 6 spaces to the right of its actual position in the line of text.

Toulouse: This usually happens when you have both TrueType and Type 1 versions of the same fonts installed.

Hawkeye: How can I fix it?

Toulouse: Just remove one or the other. I'd recommend keeping the PostScript Type 1 version.

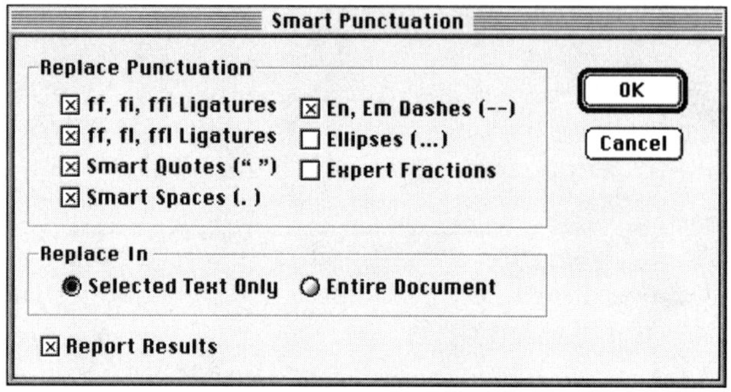

Figure 8-18: The Smart Punctuation dialog box

The Smart Punctuation filter works after the fact, making changes to text already in the Illustrator document. There are no settings, for instance, to convert quotes to curved quotes as you are typing them. The types of punctuation to be changed are determined by a set of checkboxes in the Smart Punctuation dialog box. A checked box means that Illustrator will look for these certain instances and, if it finds them, correct them with the proper punctuation.

The first two options are used for replacing ff, fi (or fl), and ffi (or ffl) with *ligatures*. Ligatures are characters that represent several characters with one character that is designed to let those characters appear nicer when placed next to each other. Most fonts have fi and fl ligatures, which look like ﬁ and ﬂ, respectively.

The remaining Smart Punctuation options work as follows:

- **Smart Quotes** replaces straight quotes (" " and ' ') with curly quotes, known as typesetter's quotes or printer's quotes (“ ” and ‘ ’).
- **Smart Spaces** replaces multiple spaces after a period with one space. (In typesetting, there should only be one space following a period.)
- **En, Em Dashes** replaces hyphens (-) with en dashes (–) and double hyphens (- -) with em dashes (—).

- **Ellipses** replaces three periods (...) with an ellipsis (…).
- **Expert Fractions** replaces fractions with expert fractions if you have the expert fractions available in the font family you are using. Adobe sells "Expert Collection" fonts that contain these fractions. If you do *not* have expert fractions, your fractions remain unchanged.

Checking the Report Results box displays a dialog box when the filter is finished, telling you how many of the punctuation changes were made, divided into several categories.

Rows & Columns

Rows & Columns divides rectangular paths (text or standard Illustrator rectangles) into even sections.

To use Rows & Columns, select a path and choose Type⇨Rows & Columns. The Rows & Columns dialog box appears, as shown in Figure 8-19.

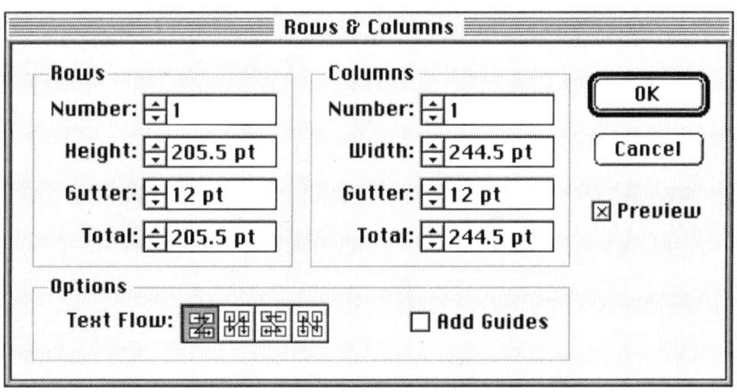

Figure 8-19: The Rows & Columns dialog box

Any text path, open or closed, can be selected and divided into rows and columns, with one catch: The object will become a rectangular shape, the size of the original path's *bounding box* (the smallest box that could completely contain the path). There is no way to divide a nonrectangular path automatically. See the steps later in this section for a way to do this without Illustrator knowing about it.

The left side of the Rows & Columns dialog box determines the width of the columns. The right side determines the height of the rows. At the bottom of the dialog box is a Preview checkbox; checking this displays changes as you make them in the Rows & Columns dialog box.

All measurements in the Rows & Columns dialog box are displayed in the current measurement system.

The first text field is the Number of Rows that the original path will be divided into. The second text field, Height, is the height of each of the rows. The Height must be less than the Total (the fourth field) divided by the number of rows. The third text field on the left is Gutter, which is the space between rows. The Total is how high the entire rectangle is.

As the Row Height is increased, the Gutter decreases. When Row Height is decreased, the Gutter increases. Likewise, as the Gutter is increased, the Height decreases. When the Gutter is decreased, the Height increases.

In the Column section, Number determines how many columns the selected path will be cut into. Below that, the Width text field determines the width of the columns. The Width must be less than the Total (fourth field) divided by the number of columns. The third text field is Gutter, which is the space between columns. The Total value is how wide the entire rectangle is.

As the Column Width is increased, the Gutter will decrease. When Column Width is decreased, the Gutter increases. Likewise, as the Gutter is increased, the Column Width decreases. When the Gutter is decreased, the Column Width increases.

Remember that using the Rows & Columns feature actually divides the selected rectangle into several pieces.

The Text Flow options determine the direction of text as it flows from one section to the next. You may choose between text that starts along the top row and flows from left to right, and then goes to the next lowest row, flowing from left to right, and so on. The second option is to have text start in the left column, flowing from top to bottom, and then to the next column to the right, flowing from top to bottom. The third option causes text to flow from the upper right to the upper left to the lower right to the lower left. The fourth (rightmost) option flows the text from the upper right to the lower right to the upper left to the lower left.

The Add Guides checkbox creates guides that extend off each edge of the page. These guides align with the edges of each of the boxes created from the Rows & Columns feature.

The following steps describe how to create rows and columns in a nonrectangular object.

STEPS: Creating Rows and Columns in a Nonrectangular Object

1. Create the object that you wish to divide into rows and columns. (In Figure 8-20, I used type converted into outlines and made the entire word one compound path.)

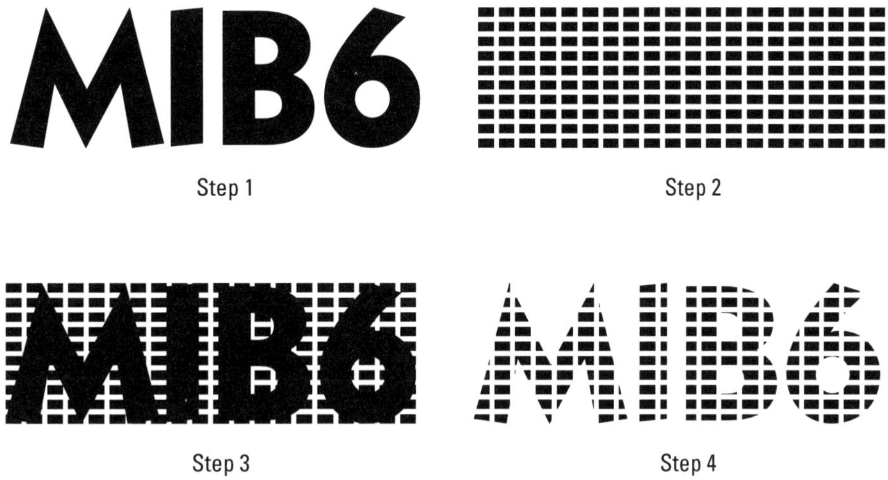

Figure 8-20: Steps for creating nonrectangular columns and rows

Step 2. Copy the object to the Clipboard (choose Edit⇨Copy, or press ⌘-C [Ctrl+C]).

Step 3. Choose Type⇨Rows & Columns and divide the object into the number of rows and columns desired. Click OK. The object becomes rectangular.

Step 4. Paste in Front. The original object appears in front of the rectangle that is divided into rows and columns.

Step 5. Select all objects and choose Object⇨Pathfinder⇨Crop. The result is a nonrectangular shape that has been divided into rows and columns.

These steps show how to create angled rows and columns.

STEPS: Creating Angled Rows and Columns

Step 1. Create an oversized object that will become the rows and columns.

Step 2. Choose Type⇨Rows & Columns and divide the object into the rows and columns, but this time specify the size of the rows and columns, not how many you want. Click OK.

Step 3. Rotate the columns and rows you have just created.

(continued)

STEPS: *(continued)*

Step 4. Create the object that will contain the angled rows and columns, and place it in front of the rows and columns. (In Figure 8-21, I used a plain rectangle.)

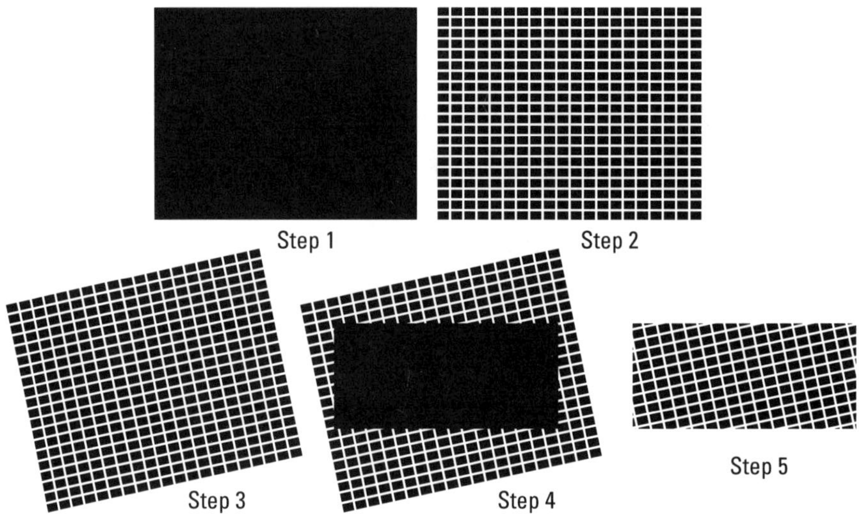

Figure 8-21: Steps for creating angled rows and columns (with outlined sections for easier viewing)

Step 5. Select all objects and choose Object➪Pathfinder➪Crop. The result is an object with angled rows and columns within it.

Type Areas

In order for type to exist in Illustrator, there must first be a *type area* defined. Type can never be outside these areas because type is treated very differently from any other object in Illustrator.

There are three different kinds of type areas: Point type, Area type, and Path type. Point type exists around a single point clicked with the standard Type tool. Area type is type that flows within a specific open or closed path. Path type is type whose baseline is attached to a specific open or closed path.

Figure 8-22 shows the same sentence as Point type, Rectangle type, Area type, and Path type.

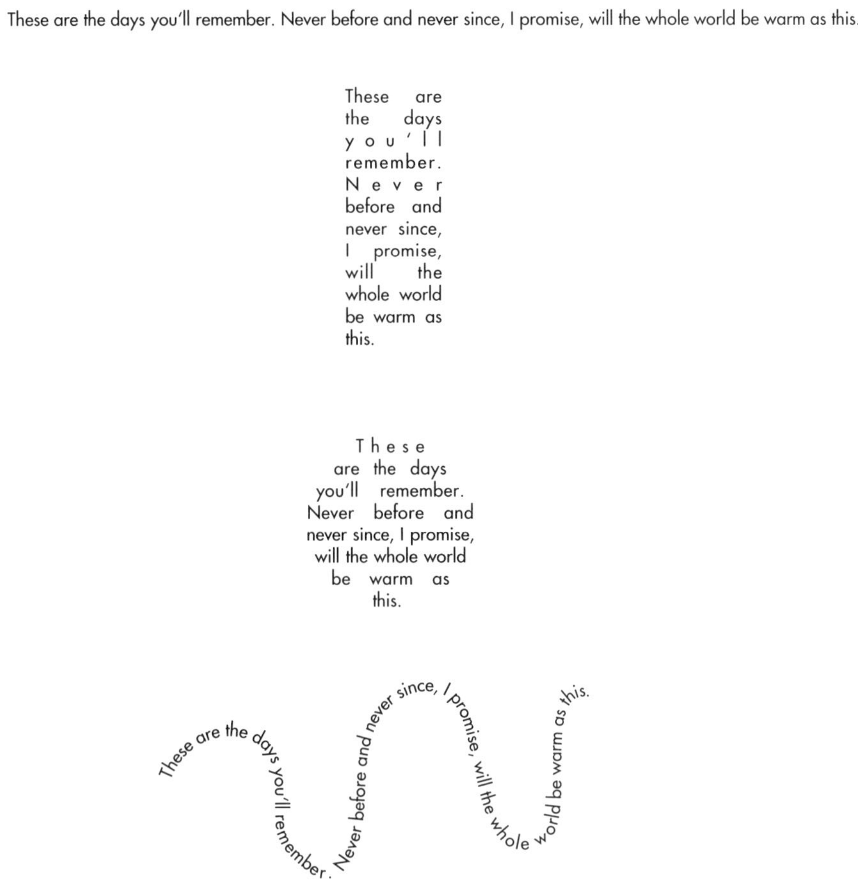

Figure 8-22: The same sentence as it appears in Point type, Rectangle type Area type, and Path type

Using the Type Tools

Initially, the six type tools are used to create type, and then later they can be used to edit that very same type. The default tool is the standard Type tool, which creates both Point type and Area type. The pop-up tools (shown in Figure 8-23) are the Area Type tool, the Path Type tool, the Vertical Type tool, the Vertical Area Type Tool, and the Vertical Path Type tool. (All of these tools are explained in detail in the following sections.) Each of the type tools displays a different cursor.

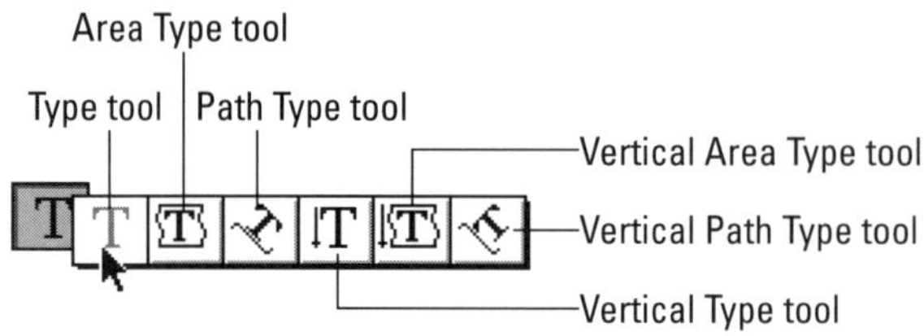

Figure 8-23: The Type tools

You can select type in Illustrator with the Selection tool, in which case *all* the type in the story is modified (a *story* is a contiguous set of type in either Point type, Rectangle type, Area type, or Path type).

You select type with a type tool by dragging across either characters or lines — every character from the initial click until the release of the mouse button is selected. Double-clicking with a type tool selects the entire word you clicked, including the space after it. Triple-clicking (clicking three times in the same place) selects an entire paragraph.

You can enter new type into an existing story by clicking with a type tool where you want the new type to begin and then typing. If type is highlighted when you begin typing, the highlighted type is replaced with the new type.

Vertical Type is new for Illustrator 7. While the primary reason for this capability's inclusion is for Japanese type (commonly referred to as Kanji) compatibility, Vertical Type can have a number of specialized uses as well. The following sections that discuss the different types of type blocks (point, rectangle, area, and path) address both normal (horizontal) type and the new vertical type capabilities.

The Type Tool

With the Type tool, you can do everything you need to do with type. Clicking in any empty part of your document creates Point type, an Anchor Point to which the type aligns. Type created as Point type does not wrap automatically; instead, you must manually press the Return key and start typing the next line. Point type is usually used for creating smaller portions of type, like labels and headlines.

Clicking and dragging with the Type tool creates Area type — type that is bordered by a box, which you create when you click and drag the Type tool.

As the Type tool passes over a closed path, it changes automatically into the Area Type tool. Clicking a closed path results in type that fills the shape of the area you clicked. Holding down the Option [Alt] key as you pass over a closed path changes the tool into the Path Type tool. This intelligent switching of type tools by Illustrator keeps you from having to choose different type tools when you want a different kind of type.

If the Type tool crosses over an open path, it becomes the Path Type tool. Clicking an open path places type *on the path,* with the baseline of the type aligning along the curves and angles of the path. Holding down the Option [Alt] key when the Type tool is over an open path changes it into the Area Type tool.

The Type tool can be toggled to the Vertical Type tool by pressing the Shift key. In fact, pressing the Shift key with the Area Type and Path Type tools automatically toggles those tools to their Vertical Type counterparts. This holds true even if you press Shift along with the Option [Alt] key (when toggling between Area Type and Path Type tools).

The Area Type Tool

The Area Type tool is used for Filling closed or open paths with type. Even compound paths can be Filled in Illustrator.

You can toggle between the Area Type tool and the Path Type tool by pressing the Option [Alt] key.

The Path Type Tool

The Path Type tool is used for running type along any path in Illustrator. This is a great tool for putting type on the edges of a circle.

You can toggle between the Path Type tool and the Area Type tool by pressing the Option [Alt] key.

The Vertical Type Tools

Vertical Type? I was a little confused when I saw this new tool (and its Area and Path counterparts). The easiest way to understand how the Vertical Type tools work is by example. Figure 8-24 shows the same line of type created with the regular Type tool and the Vertical Type tool. For the most part, the Vertical Type tool works like the regular Type tool, but instead of placing characters side by side, characters are placed from top to bottom. Because this area of Illustrator can be a little unusual, I've added a section later in this chapter that directly addresses Vertical Type and related issues.

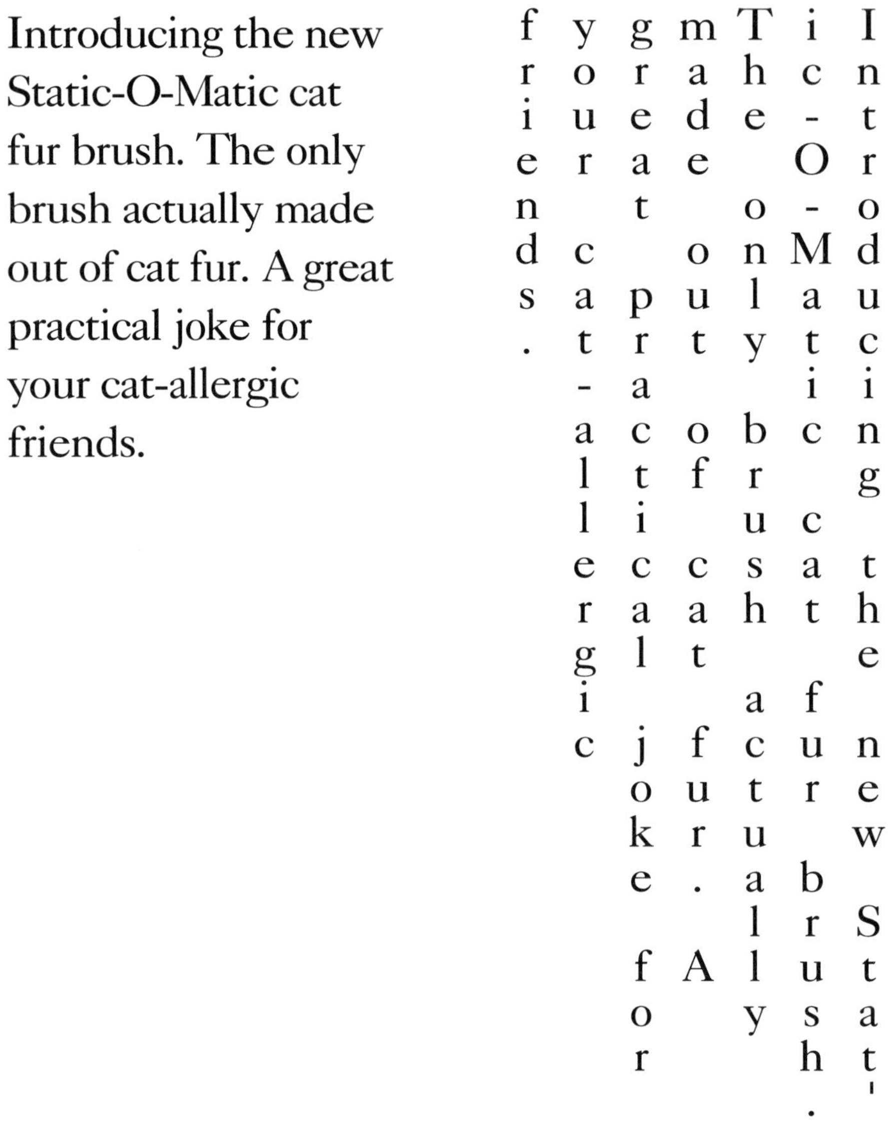

Figure 8-24: Horizontal and Vertical type

Point Type

To create type with a single point defining its location, use the Type tool and click a single location within the document window where there are no paths. A blinking *insertion point* appears, signifying that type will appear where that point is located (see Figure 8-25). When you type on the keyboard, text will now appear in the document at that insertion point. Type cannot be entered when a selection tool is being used. Type selected with a selection tool appears at the bottom of Figure 8-25.

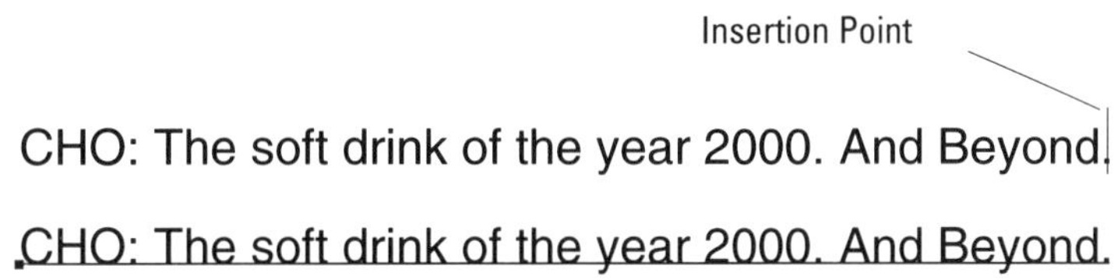

Figure 8-25: Point type with an insertion point at the end of the line, and the same line of type selected with a selection tool

When the Illustrator program is first launched, text defaults into the following values: 12 Helvetica, Flush left, Auto Leading on, Spacing 0, Baseline Shift 0, Tracking/Kerning 0, Horizontal Scale 100%, Auto Kerning on, no indentation or paragraph spacing. There is no method within Illustrator to automatically change this default upon startup of the program.

Point type that is flush left has its left side flush against the vertical location of the point initially clicked. Centered type is centered left to right on the vertical location of the point. Flush right type has its right edge flush with the vertical location of the point. Point type cannot be justified with either of the two methods available.

When creating Point type, keep in mind that only hard Returns forces a new line of text to be created. If no Returns are used, text eventually runs right off the document. When importing text used as Point type, be sure that the text contains these hard Returns, or the text will run into oblivion. Hard Returns can be added after importing, but it may be difficult to do so.

Area Type as a Rectangle

There are two ways to create Rectangle type (see Figure 8-26). The easiest way is by clicking and dragging the Type tool diagonally, which creates a rectangle as you drag. The blinking insertion point appears in the top row of text, with its horizontal location dependent on the text alignment choice. Choosing flush right forces the insertion point to appear in the upper-right corner; centered puts the insertion point in the center of the row; and flush left, or one of the justification methods, makes the insertion point appear in the upper-left corner.

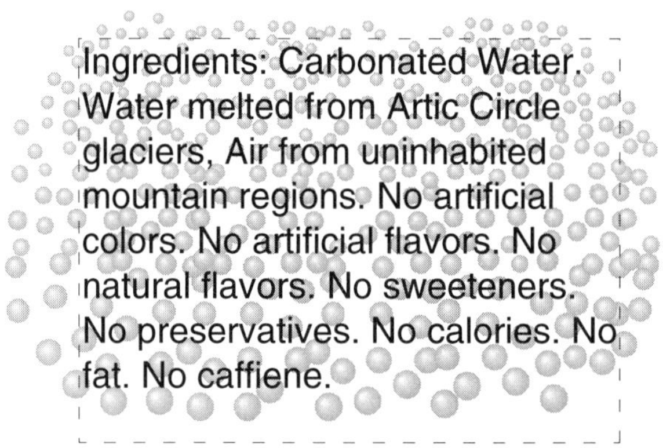

Figure 8-26: Area Type (The dotted line is the border of the rectangle.)

If you press the Shift key while drawing the rectangle, the rectangle is constrained to a perfect square. There is no need to drag from upper left to lower right — you can drag from any corner to its opposite — whichever way is most convenient.

To create type in a rectangle of specific proportions, draw a rectangle with the Rectangle tool by clicking once in the document window. The Rectangle Size dialog box appears, where you can enter the information needed. Then choose the Area Type tool and click the edge of the rectangle. The type will fill the rectangle as you type.

STEPS: Creating Rectangle Type in an Area of Specific Proportions

Step 1. Using the Rectangle tool, click without dragging to get the Rectangle dialog box. Enter the exact dimensions of the type area.

Step 2. Choose the Type tool and click the Type cursor on the edge of the rectangle. Any type entered into this box will be constrained to that particular rectangle.

> **CAUTION:** Once a rectangle has been used as a type rectangle, it is always a type rectangle, even if the text is removed.

If you need to create a Rectangle type area that is a precise size but don't want to draw a rectangle first, open the Info palette by choosing Window⇨Show Info (press F8) and as you drag the type cursor, watch the information in the Info palette, which will display the dimensions of the type area. When the W field is the width you want, and the H field is the height you want, release the mouse button.

Area Type

The capability of placing type within any area is one of the cooler features of Illustrator, right up there with the fact that the program comes in a hip, '90s-looking box.

To create type within an area, first create the path that will be the area that confines the type. The path can be closed or open and any size. Keep in mind that the area of the path should be close to the size needed for the amount of text (at the point size that it needs to fit). After the path has been created, choose the Area Type tool and position the type cursor over the edge of the path and click.

The type in Figure 8-27 has been flowed into the outline of the CHO logo. Using text wraps, the type exists only inside the letters yet reads across all of them.

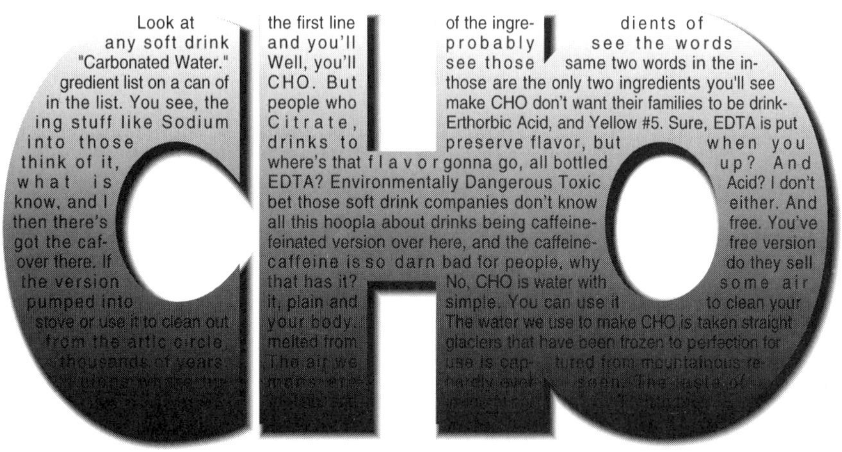

Figure 8-27: Area type created so that the text flows inside the outlines of the word "CHO"

Choosing the Good Shapes for Area Type

What exactly constitutes a "good" shape to be used for Area type? As a rule of thumb, gently curved shapes are better than harsh, jagged ones. Type tends to flow better into the larger lumps created by smoothly curving paths.

Try to avoid creating paths with wild or tight curves. Other designs that can cause problems are "hourglass" shapes or any closed path that has an area where the sides are almost touching. Figure 8-28 shows how type flows into a smoothly curved area and how it has trouble flowing into a sharp, spiky shape.

Figure 8-28: Type flows much better into a smoothly curved area (left) than a sharp, spiky one

Try to make the top and bottom boundaries of the path have less "bumpiness" than the sides. This will reduce the number of times that type jumps from one area across another.

For the best results with Area type, make the type small and Force justify it (⌘-Shift-F) [Ctrl+Shift+F]. This will ensure that the type flows up against the edges of the path.

Outlining Areas of Area Type

Placing a Stroke on the path surrounding Area type can be a great visual effect, but doing so and getting good results can be a bit tricky.

If the Stroke is thicker than a point or two, and you don't want the type to run into the edges of the Stroke, there are a few things you can do.

The fastest way to do this (although it requires a bit of math) is to copy the Stroked path that contains the type and paste it in front. Fill the shape with the background color and a Stroke equal to twice the amount of white space you would like between the Stroke and the text. Then hide the path and the type, and select the original path. Delete the text from this path and use the following formula to calculate the correct Stroke width:

(Desired Width + White Space size) × 2 = Bottom layer Stroke weight

For example, if you want a Stroke that is 6 points wide on a shape and has 3 points of white space between the Stroke and the text, the bottom shape will have a Stroke of (6 + 3) × 2 = 18. The top layer will have a "white" Stroke of 6, with a Fill the same color as the Stroke.

The second way to do this is by using the Offset Path filter. This is better for two reasons: First, it requires much less math, and second, you don't have to worry about background color (especially if the background is a bunch of other objects or a placed raster image). Of course, there is a catch: The path cannot be turned into a text area boundary before Offset Path is applied to it.

STEPS: Creating Inset Type Areas with Offset Path

Step 1. Create a path for your Area type with any drawing tool. Close the path for the best results when using Offset Path.

Step 2. Do not make the path into a type area by clicking the path with a type tool at this point. Select the path you wish to use for Area type with the Selection tool and then choose Object⇨Path⇨Offset Path.

Step 3. Determine the distance that you wish your text to be from the edge of the real path. If there is a Stroke on the edge of the real path, add half the width of the Stroke to your distance. In the Offset field, enter this distance in negative form. For example, if you want the distance from the edge of the path to be 6 points and the width of the Stroke is 10 points, you would enter **–11** points in the Offset field (6+10/2).

Step 4. After you click OK, a new path is created inside the original. Click on this path with the Area Type tool; the text appears "inside" the edge, with a buffer (see Figure 8-29).

Figure 8-29: Steps to create Area type with a buffer between the type and the edge

Doing Bizarre Things with Area Type

Probably the most overlooked rule when it comes to manipulating Area type and the paths that create the type boundaries is the simple fact that the path and the type are treated equally, unless the path is chosen with the Direct Selection (or Group Selection) tool. Area type is selected when there is an underline under all the characters in the area.

When using the transformation tools, be sure that if you don't want to change any of the characteristics of the type, you select just the path. Use the Group Selection tool to click once on the deselected path, and only the path is selected, not the type.

If the type is selected as well as the path, then the transformations will affect both the type and the path. Figure 8-30 shows transformations taking place to both type and its surrounding path as opposed to transformations taking place to just the surrounding path.

Figure 8-30: The original (left) after both the type and the path have been transformed (top right) and after only the path has been transformed (bottom right)

Coloring Type That Is Anchored to a Path

When type is anchored to a path, either as Area type or Path type, there are some important considerations to think of before Filling and Stroking the type.

First, if just the type or just the path is selected with the regular Selection tool, the other (path or type) is selected as well. Do you want to put a Stroke along that path that surrounds your type? If you select the path with the regular Selection tool, then the type is selected as well, and each character in the type area will have the same Stroke you meant to apply to the path.

For changing just the path's Paint Style attributes, be sure to use the Direct Selection tool to select the path. If no underlines appear under the text, then the text is *not* selected. To change all of the text, you must choose a type tool, click within the text area, and then use the Select All command (⌘-A) [Ctrl+A]. Only then will just the text be affected.

Changing the Area, Not the Type

Many times, you'll need to adjust the path that makes up the area of the Area type, like scaling that path up or down so that the text flows better. The trick here is to make sure the entire path is selected without selecting any of the characters. To do this, deselect the type and select the path with the Group Selection tool (the hollow arrow with the plus sign).

Now any changes you make will only affect the path, so you can scale it, rotate it, or change its Paint Style attributes without directly affecting the text within it. Figure 8-31 shows a path that has been transformed, allowing the text inside to flow differently.

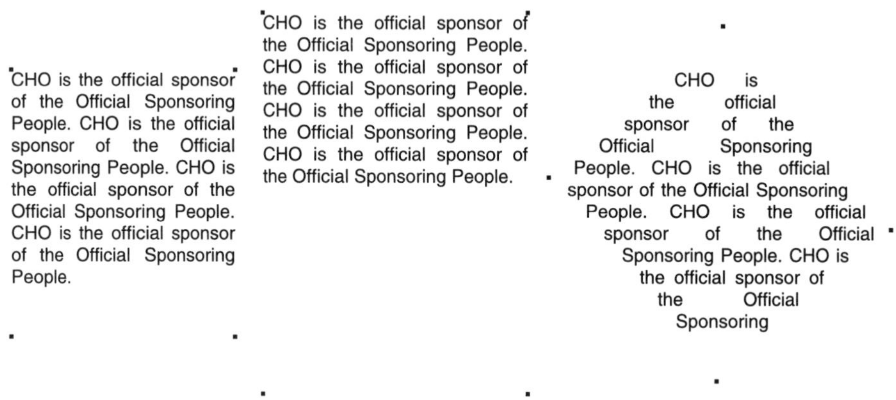

Figure 8-31: Changing the size (middle) and rotation (right) of the original path (left) only affects the text flow, not the text itself

Type Color and the Color of Type

There is a difference between the *color of type* and *types color.* Type can be painted in Illustrator to be any one of millions of different shades, which determines the color we normally think of.

The color of type, on the other hand, is the way the type appears in the document and is more indicative of the light or dark attributes of the text. The actual red-green-blue colors of the type do work into this appearance, but many times, the weight of the type and the tracking and kerning have a much more profound effect on color.

To easily see the color of type, unfocus your eyes as you look at your document, or turn the page upside down. This works better on a printed area than on-screen, but you can still get the gist of the way it will appear when viewing it on your monitor. Dark and light areas become much more apparent when you can't read the actual words on the path. This method of unfocusing your eyes to look at a page also works well when trying to see the "look" of a page and how it was designed. Many times, unfocusing or turning the page upside down will emphasize the fact that you don't have enough white space or that all the copy seems to blend together.

Heavy type weights, such as boldface, heavy, and black, make type appear darker on a page. Type kerned and tracked very tightly also seems to give the type a darker feel.

The x-height of type (the height to which the lowercase letters, such as an *x*, rise) is another factor that determines the color of type. Certain italic versions of typefaces can make the text seem lighter, although a few make text look darker because of the additional area that the thin strokes of the italic type covers.

Combined with red-green-blue colors, type can be made to stand out by appearing darker, or blend into the page when lighter. When you add smartly placed images near the type, your page can come alive with color.

Area Type

All sorts of nifty things can be done with type that has been flowed into areas — from unusual column designs to fascinating shapes.

A publication can be livened up quite easily by using nonrectangular columns. *Mondo 2000* magazine uses curved columns that are easy to read and lend a futuristic, hip look to the publication. Angled and curved columns are simple to create in Illustrator by creating the shape of the column and flowing Area type from one shape to the next.

Traditionally, forcing type into an irregular (nonrectangular) area was quite a task. The typesetter had to set several individual lines of type, each specced by the art director or client to be a certain specific length so that when all the text was put together, the text formed the shape (see Figure 8-32). This is probably the main reason the world has not seen too much of this, except in overly zealous art students' portfolios.

Figure 8-32: The subject matter fit into related shape

For example, you can give a report on toxic waste in New Jersey more impact by shaping the text into the form of a hypodermic needle. Or you can make a seasonal ad in the shape of a Christmas tree. Look at some of the Absolut Vodka ads to see what they've done to flow text into that all-too-familiar bottle.

Path Type

The unique thing about type on a path is that when the path is not visible, the type *becomes* the path, as shown in Figure 8-33. This can produce some really fascinating results, especially when combined with various fonts of different weights, styles, colors, and special characters.

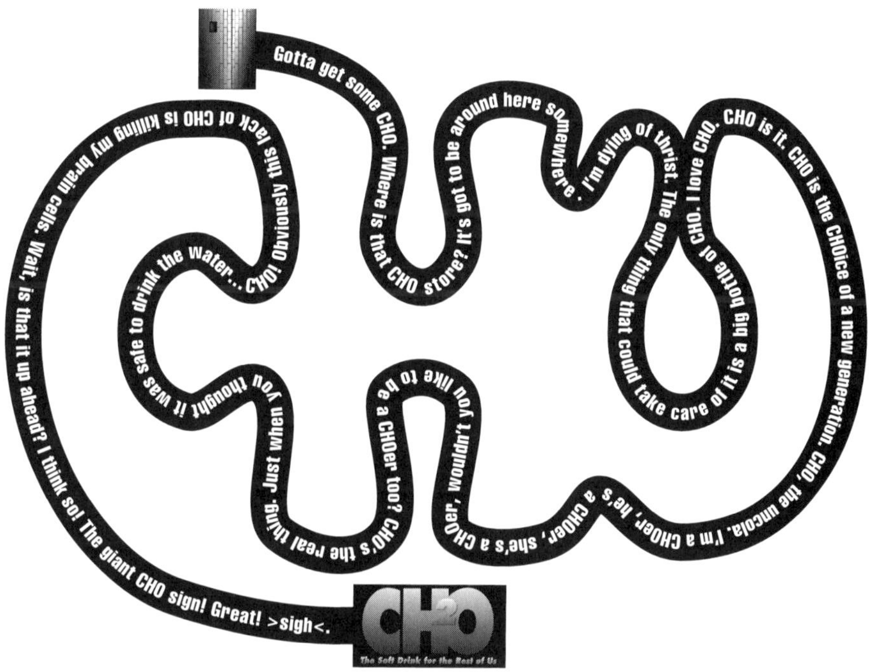

Figure 8-33: Type, when set on a path, can actually *become* the path

To create Path type, first create a path in your document. Then click the path with the Path Type tool to create an insertion point along the path. This works whether the path is a closed path or an open path.

Type aligns to the insertion point; if the type is set to flush left, the left edge of the type aligns to the location where the Path Type tool was first clicked. Unlike Point type, where a hard Return sent the type to the next line, hard Returns work just like spaces.

You can flow Path type along the path to which it is aligned by clicking the Insertion bar (which resembles a little I-beam) with any selection tool and dragging along the path. If the I-bar is dragged to the other side of the path, then the type flips over in the direction of the bar. For this reason, it is a good idea to click the topmost part of the Insertion bar before dragging.

As with other objects in Illustrator that can be moved by dragging, pressing the Option [Alt] key before releasing the mouse causes the object being dragged to duplicate instead of just move. This works with the Type I-bar, as well.

If you would like the type you are dragging to appear below the path but not get flipped upside down and change direction, use baseline shift (found in the Character palette) to raise and lower the type to your liking. The key commands for baseline shift are Option-Shift-↑ [Alt+Shift+↑] and Option-Shift-↓[Alt+Shift+↓] to move up and down by increments set in the Keyboard Increments Preferences dialog box. These commands are particularly useful when adjusting Path type.

Even though there are six different type tools, you only need to choose one. If you have the standard Type tool, it changes into the Area Type tool when you pass over a closed path and changes into a Path Type tool when the cursor passes over an open path. And you can access the Vertical types versions of these tools by pressing shift.

Type on the Top and Bottom of a Circle

Everyone's doing it. Peer pressure is going to make you succumb as well. If you can put type on the top and the bottom of a circle so that it runs along the same path, you are quite the designer, or so thinks the average guy on the street. The simple "Type On A Circle" shown in Figure 8-34 can be created quite easily.

Follow these steps (which are also illustrated in Figure 8-35 at the end of this procedure), and with a little practice, you can create type on a circle in less than 15 seconds. Pretty impressive to even those who understand how it's done.

STEPS: Creating Type on the Top and Bottom of a Circle

Step 1. Draw a circle with the Ellipse tool (hold down the Shift key to make sure it is a perfect circle). Then choose the Path Type tool and click the top center of the circle. The blinking insertion point appears at that point on the circle.

Step 2. Type the text that is to appear at the top of the circle and press ⌘-Shift-C [Ctrl+Shift+C], which centers the type at the top of the circle.

Step 3. Choose the Selection tool and click the top of the I-bar marker, dragging it down to the bottom center of the circle. Before letting go of the mouse button, center the type, making sure that it is readable from left to right,

(continued)

Figure 8-34: Type on the top and bottom of a circle

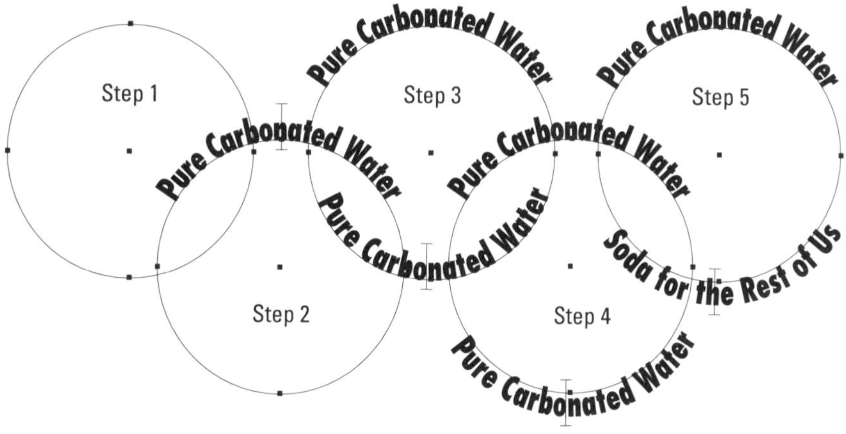

Figure 8-35: Steps for creating type on the top and bottom of a circle

STEPS: *(continued)*

and press the Option key. When you do release the mouse button, there will be type along the top and the bottom of the circle, but the type on the bottom will be inside the circle.

The key here is that the Option [Alt] key is pressed. The Option [Alt] key duplicates the text and circle, moving them both to a new location in the process. If the Option [Alt] key were not pressed, the type would have just moved to the bottom of the circle.

Step 4. Select the bottom text with the Type tool and slowly scoot the type down below the baseline by pressing Option-Shift-↓ [Alt+Shift+↓]. This pushes the type down the baseline in the increments set in the General Preferences dialog box (the default is 2). Keep pressing the key combination until the type is vertically positioned to mimic the type on the top of the circle.

Step 5. Select the text along the bottom of the circle with the Type tool. Type in the text that is to appear at the bottom of the circle. It replaces the selected text.

You're finished. Amazing, isn't it? Just remember that you now have *two* circles with type on them, not one circle with two type paths (that can't happen).

Avoiding Path Type Trouble

The most common trouble with Path type usually occurs when the path has either corner Anchor Points or very sharp curves. Letters will often *crash* (run into one another) when this occurs.

Besides the most obvious way to avoid this problem, which is to not use paths with corner Anchor Points and sharp curves, the areas where the letters crash can sometimes be kerned apart until they aren't touching anymore.

When kerning Path type, be sure to kern from the flush side first. For instance, if the type is flush left, start your kerning from the left side and work to the right. If you start on the wrong end, the letters you kern apart will move along the path until they aren't in an area that needs kerning, but instead, other letters will appear there.

Another method of fixing crashed letters is to tweak the path with the Direct Selection tool. Careful adjusting of both Anchor Points and Control Handles can easily fix crashes and letters that have huge amounts of space between them.

If the path that is the base of the letters doesn't need to be directly under the letters, use the baseline shift keyboard commands (Option-Shift-↓ [Alt+Shift+↓] and Option-Shift-↑ [Alt+Shift+↑]) to move the type until the path runs through the center of the text. This can automatically fix the spacing problems encountered by text that crashes over sharp turns and corners.

Path Type

One of the most desirable effects with Path type (and, in my opinion, much cooler than type on a circle) is Path type that is reversed, as shown in Figure 8-36.

STEPS: Creating Reversed Path Type

Step 1. Create the path you want to use for the Path type. In my example, I used a rounded rectangle. Your path can be open or closed.

Step 2. Click the path with the Path Type tool and type in the text for the path. Type with no descenders works better than type with descenders.

Step 3. Vertically center the type on the path by adjusting the baseline shift (Option-Shift-↑ or -↓ [Alt+Shift+↑ or+↓]). If there are descenders, make sure the type is centered from ascender to descender.

Step 4. Select the type with a type tool and change the Fill to White. Select the path with the Direct Selection tool and change the Fill to None and the Stroke of the path to Black. Make the weight of the Stroke just greater than the point size of the type.

Trouble with Path Type

Trisha: I'm having all sorts of trouble with Path type.

Toulouse: Aren't we all. Anything in particular?

Trisha: Well, for starters, I'm having a dickens of a time trying to move the little I-bar marker along the path.

Toulouse: The key to moving the I-bar marker is to click right at the top of it.

Trisha: Thanks. Also, it seems to flip over all the time.

Toulouse: Actually, grabbing the I-bar at the top will fix this as well.

Trisha: How come sometimes my type is below the path and sometimes above, but it reads the right way?

Toulouse: This usually happens after you've done something like type on a circle, where you've last changed the baseline shift to something less than 0. Change the baseline shift back to 0 and all will be well.

Figure 8-36: Steps for creating type reversed on a path

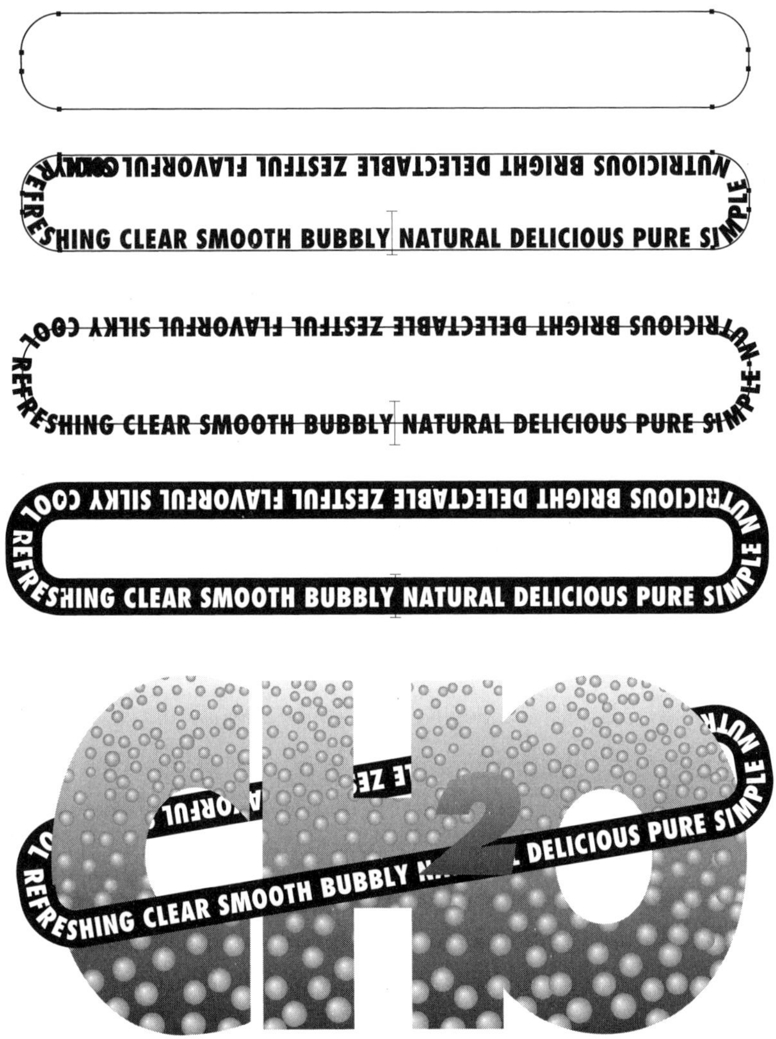

Selecting Type

Before you can make changes to text, you must first select it. There are two ways of selecting type: you can select type areas with a selection tool, which selects every character in the type area, or you can select characters individually or in groups with any of the type tools.

To select the entire type area or multiple type areas, click the baseline of a line of type within the type area you want to select. Any changes made in the Type menu, Font menu, Character palette, or Paragraph palette affect every character in the selected type areas.

If there are blank fields in any of the palettes or no check marks next to some of the menu items (for instance, no font is checked) when type areas are selected, that means that there are different options for each of those fields or menu items within the type area (for instance, Helvetica for some characters, Times for others). Changing a blank field or unchecked menu item after a type area is selected affects all characters in that area.

To select characters within a type area, you must use a type tool. As you near text that has been typed in the document, the dotted lines surrounding the cursor disappear. The *hot point* of the type cursor is the place where the short horizontal bar crosses the vertical bar (see Figure 8-37). It is this hot point that you should use when clicking with the type cursor.

Figure 8-37:
The hot point of the type cursor

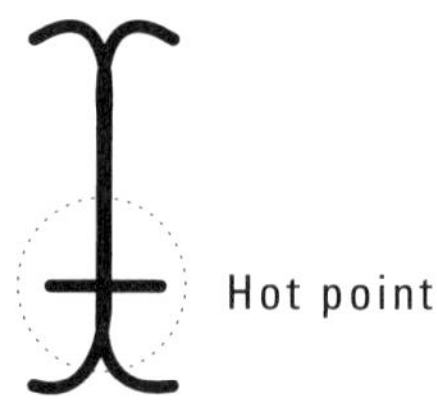

To select an individual character, drag across the character to be selected. As a character is selected, it is reversed. To select more than one character, drag left or right across multiple characters; all characters from the location you originally clicked to the current location of the cursor are highlighted. If you drag up with the cursor over straight text, you select all the characters to the left and all the characters to the right of the cursor's current location. Dragging down does the reverse. The more lines you drag up or down, the more lines are selected.

To select one word at a time (and the space that follows it), double-click the word to be selected. The word and the space after it are reversed. The reason that the space following the word is selected is mainly due to the times you copy, cut, and paste words from within sentences. For example, to remove the word *Lazy* in the phrase "The Lazy Boy," you double-click the word *Lazy* and press Delete. The phrase is then "The Boy," which only has one space where the word *Lazy* used to be. To select several words, double-click and drag the Type cursor across the words you want to select. Each word you touch with the cursor is selected, from the location initially double-clicked to the current location. Dragging to the previous or next line selects additional lines, with at least a word on the first line double-clicked and one word on the dragged-to line.

For the nimble-fingered clickers, you may also click three times to select a paragraph. Triple-click anywhere inside the paragraph and the entire paragraph is selected, including the hard Return at the end of the paragraph (if there is one). Triple-clicking and dragging selects successive paragraphs if the cursor is moved up or down while the mouse button is still pressed following the third click.

To select all the text within a type area with a type tool, click once in the type area and choose Edit⇨Select All (⌘-A) [Ctrl+A]. All the text in the type area is reversed. As in most programs, text can only be selected in contiguous blocks. There is no way to select two words in two different locations of the same type area without selecting all the text between them.

Type can also be selected through the use of the Shift key. Click one spot (we'll call it the beginning) and then Shift-click another spot. The characters between the beginning and the Shift-click are selected. Successive Shift-clicks select characters from the beginning to the current location of the most recent Shift-click.

Editing Type

Text editing features in Illustrator are available on a limited scale. By clicking once within a type area, a blinking insertion point appears. If you begin typing, characters appear where the blinking insertion point is. If you press Delete, you will delete the previous character (if there is one).

The arrow keys on your keyboard move the blinking insertion point around in the direction of the arrow. The right arrow moves the insertion point one character to the right, and the left arrow moves the insertion point one character to the left. The up arrow moves the insertion point to the previous line; the down arrow moves the insertion point to the next line.

Pressing the ⌘ [Ctrl] key speeds up the movement of the insertion point. ⌘-← [Ctrl+←] or -→ [Ctrl+→] moves the insertion point to the preceding or next word, and ⌘-↑ [Ctrl+↑]or -↓ [Ctrl+↓] moves the insertion point to the preceding or next paragraph.

Pressing the Shift key while moving the insertion point around with the arrows selects all the characters that the insertion point passes over. This works for the ⌘-arrow [Ctrl+arrow] movements as well.

When you select characters with a type tool, typing anything deletes the selected characters and replaces them with what is currently being typed. Pressing the Delete key when characters are selected deletes all the selected characters. If you paste type (⌘-V) [Ctrl+V] when characters are selected, the selected characters are replaced with the pasted characters.

Anti-Aliased Type

Pixel-based software has always had the capability to display anti-aliased type on screen, but Illustrator 7 is the first vector program to provide this capability. The main difference between anti-aliased type in Photoshop (or another pixel-based program) and Illustrator is that when you choose anti-alias in Photoshop, the text itself is anti-aliased. It both appears on-screen and when printed as anti-aliased type. In Illustrator, however, the anti-aliasing only takes place on screen; printed text will appear sharp as ever.

So the obvious question is "Why bother?" Well, think back to the late '80s, before Adobe Type Manager. All type shown on screens had to be at the installed point sizes (usually 10, 12, 14, 18 and 24) or it looked terrible. Bigger and smaller type looked especially atrocious. Of course, this type printed wondrously, which was what was really important. Anyway, along came Adobe Type Manager, which made Type 1 PostScript fonts (at that time there was no TrueType) render perfectly on-screen. That was a huge jump forward in display capabilities. Now, however, the next huge jump is here.

Anti-aliased type (for on-screen display purposes only) looks amazingly better than standard type that has either black or white pixels. Part of the problem is that the resolution of a computer monitor is quite low; an average of 72 pixels per inch results in small type that is inherently ugly, regardless of the font. Anti-aliasing makes type edges look softer and enhances readability — at least it does at larger and very small point sizes. At on-screen sizes between 9 and 14 points, the effect is negligible.

You can turn on anti-aliasing within Illustrator by checking the Anti-aliased option in the Keyboard Increments dialog box (don't ask me why it got stuck there when it has nothing whatsoever to do with keyboard increments).

Character Attributes

The easiest way to change the attributes of characters is by using the Character palette, shown in Figure 8-38. Many of the changes in the Character palette are available as options in the Type menu. As a rule, if you have more than one change to make, it is better to do it in the Character palette than the menu, if just for the simple fact that everything you need will be in one place.

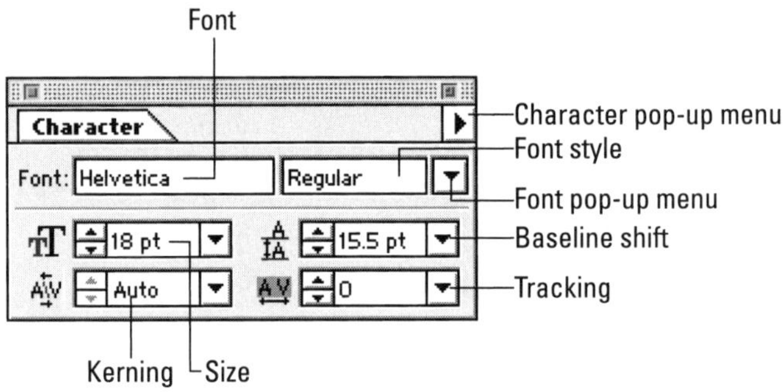

Figure 8-38: The Character palette

Character-attribute changes affect only the letters that are selected, with the exception of leading (explained later), which should really be in the Paragraph palette.

You can change several character attributes by increments. The increments are set in the Keyboard Increments Preferences dialog box (choose File➪Preferences➪Keyboard Increments). Increments can be changed for point size, leading, baseline shift, and tracking/kerning values. Where appropriate, the key commands for each attribute change are listed in the following sections.

The Character Palette

The Character palette can be displayed in three different modes: Standard, With Options, or Multinational. Choose Show Options from the Character palette pop-up menu to display the Options section (which includes Horizontal Scaling, Vertical Scaling, and Baseline Shift). Choose Show Multinational to display the Multinational options: the language, character direction, and several different Kanji options. You can display both Options and the Multinational options at the same time (which some would consider four total modes, but that's getting a bit picky, don't you think?). The Character palette remembers which mode the palette was in the last time it was displayed and shows that view the next time you display it.

The Tab key can be used to tab across the different text fields. When in partial display palette mode, the Tab key works only in the partial palette; when the last field (Tracking/Kerning) is selected, the Tab key then goes back to the Font field. If a field in the lower part of the palette is highlighted when the palette is closed, the Font field will be highlighted. When the palette is in full view, tabbing past the last field (Baseline Shift) highlights the Font field as well. In addition to the Tab key tabbing forward through the text fields, pressing Shift-Tab tabs backward through the text fields.

Choosing Edit⇨Undo (⌘-Z) [Ctrl+Z] does *not* undo items typed in the Character palette while you are still in the text field. To undo something, you must first move along (tab) to the next field and then undo, and then Shift-Tab back. Canceling (Ecs) does not cancel what you have typed but instead highlights the text (if a type tool is selected).

All of the text fields in the Character palette have both pop-up menus with common values in them for quick access, and they also have cute little up and down arrows to the left of each field. These arrows increase (up) and decrease (down) the values of each of the currently selected text field. Pressing the Shift key while clicking on the little arrow buttons makes the change with each press even greater.

You can use the keyboard to press these buttons. When the field is highlighted, press the Up arrow on your keyboard to press the up arrow button; press the down arrow on your keyboard to press the down arrow button. Press Shift at the same time to jump the value to a greater amount.

Font and Style Changes

The first field on the Character palette (in the upper-left corner) is the Font family field. When you type the first couple of letters of the font you want to use, Illustrator fills in the rest of the name for you. What happens if you type in a font that you don't have? Illustrator just ignores you, for the most part. In a nice touch, you don't get silly dialog boxes appearing telling you that there is no such typeface (à la QuarkXPress), but instead, the blinking insertion point remains in the same location until a letter that works is typed.

Let's say you wanted to use the font TypoCity, but it isn't installed. You've highlighted the font field, and you start typing the name of the font. As you type the letter *T* the first font that starts with *T* is displayed, maybe Times. You type a *y* and discover, to your horror, that nothing happens. The blinking cursor remains between the *T* and the *i* in Times. You can verify that the font is indeed not installed by clicking on the pop-up font menu on the Character palette. The Font field can be automatically highlighted (and the Character palette displayed if it is not) by pressing either ⌘-Option-Shift-F [Ctrl+Alt+Shift+F], or ⌘-Option-Shift-M [Ctrl+Alt+Shift+F].

The field in the upper right, next to the Font field, is the Style field of the font family. The same rules as entering text for the Font field apply here. Type in the first couple of letters of the style, and Illustrator fills in the rest for you. Only if you have the font style installed on your system will you be able to type it in. Illustrator is very strict when it comes to bold and italic versions of typefaces. If there is not a specific type style for what you want, you will *not* be able to type it in, unlike with most software, which has "bold" and "italic" checkboxes.

For every text field, the information entered may be applied by either tabbing to the next or preceding text field, or by pressing Enter or Return.

To the right of the font and style text fields is a little pop-up menu triangle that, when pressed, displays a list of all the typefaces installed on your system. The families are displayed in the main list, and arrows show which families have different styles. To select a font, drag the cursor over it until it is highlighted. To select a specific style of a font family, drag the cursor to the font family name, and then drag to the right to select the style name. The fields to the pop-up menu's left are updated instantly.

Size Changes

The field directly below the Font field is the Size field. Type in the desired point size (from .1 point to 1,296 points in increments of 1/10,000 point) and any selected characters increase or decrease to that particular point size. Next to the Size field is a pop-up menu triangle, which lists the standard point sizes available. Point size for type is always measured from the top of the ascenders to the bottom of the descenders. Type point size can be increased and decreased from the keyboard by typing ⌘-Shift-> [Ctrl+Shift+>] to increase and ⌘-Shift-< [Ctrl+Shift+<]to decrease the point size by the increment specified in the General Preferences dialog box.

The keyboard commands for increasing and decreasing typographic attributes, such as point size, leading, baseline shift, and tracking, are more than just another way to change those attributes. Instead, they are invaluable for making changes when the selected type has more than one different value of that attribute within it. For example, if some of the characters have a point size of 10 and some of them have a point size of 20, using the keyboard command (with an increment set to 2 points) changes the type to 12 and 22 points. This would be tedious to do separately, especially if there are multiple sizes or just a few sizes scattered widely about.

Measuring Type

So, you've finally mastered this whole silly point/pica concept, you know that there are 72 points in an inch, and you think you're ready to conquer the world. And you are, as long as no one asks you to spec type.

At 72 points, the letter I is about 50 points tall. In inches that would be just under $^3/_4$". To get better results for specially sized capital letters, a good rule of thumb is that every 100 points is about a 1-inch capital letter. This works for most typefaces, and only for the first several inches, but it is a good start to getting capital letters that are sized pretty accurately.

Curves in capital letters are yet another wrench thrown into the equation. In many typefaces, the bottom and top of the letter O go beneath the baseline and above the ascender height of most squared letters (see the following figure). Serifs on certain typefaces may also cross these lines.

Type is measured from the top of the ascenders (like the top of a capital *T*) to the bottom of the descender (like the bottom of a lowercase *j*) as shown in the figure. So when people tell you they want a capital *I* that is 1 -inch high, you can't just say, "Oh, there are 72 points in an inch, so I will create a 72-point *I* for them."

Leading

Next to the Size field is the Leading text field. Enter the desired leading value (between .1 of a point and 1,296 points, in increments of $^{1}/_{1000}$ point). To the right of the leading field is a pop-up menu triangle, from which common leading values can be chosen. In Illustrator, leading is measured from the baseline of the current line up to the baseline of the preceding line, as shown in Figure 8-39. The distance between these two baselines is the amount of leading.

Figure 8-39: Leading is measured from baseline to baseline. The 23-point leading was set by selecting the second line and changing the leading. The 14.5-point leading was set by selecting the third and fourth lines and changing the leading.

CAUTION

Unlike in most other programs, leading actually works on an entire line at once, not just on individual paragraphs. So if one letter in a 12-line paragraph is selected, and the leading for that character is changed, the distance between only that line and the line above it is changed to reflect the new leading value.

If the Leading field is changed from the number that displays there by default, the auto leading entry in the leading menu becomes unchecked. Auto leading box, when checked, makes the leading exactly 120% of the point size. This is just great when the type is 10 points because the leading is 12 points, a common point size-to-leading relationship. But as point size goes up, leading should become proportionately less, until, at around 72 points, it is less than the point size. Instead, when Auto leading is checked, 72-point type has 86.5-point leading. That's a lot of unsightly white space.

Leading increments can be set in the General Preferences dialog box (⌘-K) [Ctrl+K]. Press Option-↑ [Alt+↑] to increase the leading (which pushes lines farther apart) and Option-↓ [Alt+↓] to decrease the leading.

Kerning and Tracking

Kerning is the amount of space between any specific pair of letters. Kerning values can only be changed when there is a blinking insertion point between two characters.

Tracking is the amount of space between all the letters currently selected. If the type area is selected with a selection tool, then it refers to all the space between all the characters in the entire type area. If characters are selected with a type tool, tracking only affects the space between the specific letters selected.

Although they are related, and appear to do basically the same thing, tracking and kerning actually work quite independently of each other. They only *look* like they are affecting each other; they never actually change the amount of one if the other is altered. The Kerning field appears directly below the point size of the type, while the Tracking field appears below the leading (see Figure 8-40).

The Kerning field often reads Auto instead of a value when several letters are selected. If Auto appears in that field, the kerning built into the font is used automatically. Choosing a different value (only 0 can be chosen if several letters are selected, but any number can be entered if a blinking insertion point appears between the letters) overrides the Auto setting and uses the value you type in. Auto kerning works by reading the kerning values of the typeface that were embedded by the type designer when the typeface was originally created. The space between letters is normally defined by the typeface designer; different typefaces look like they have different amounts of space between letters. There are usually a couple hundred preset kerning pairs for common Adobe typefaces, although the expert sets have quite a few more. When Auto kerning is in effect, those preset kerning values can be seen by clicking between kerned letter pairs (capital *T* with most vowels is a good one to check) and reading the value in the Kerning field. If Auto kerning is being used, the value will be shown in parentheses. Different typefaces have different kerning pairs, and kerning pairs don't only change from typeface to typeface, but even from weight to weight and style to style.

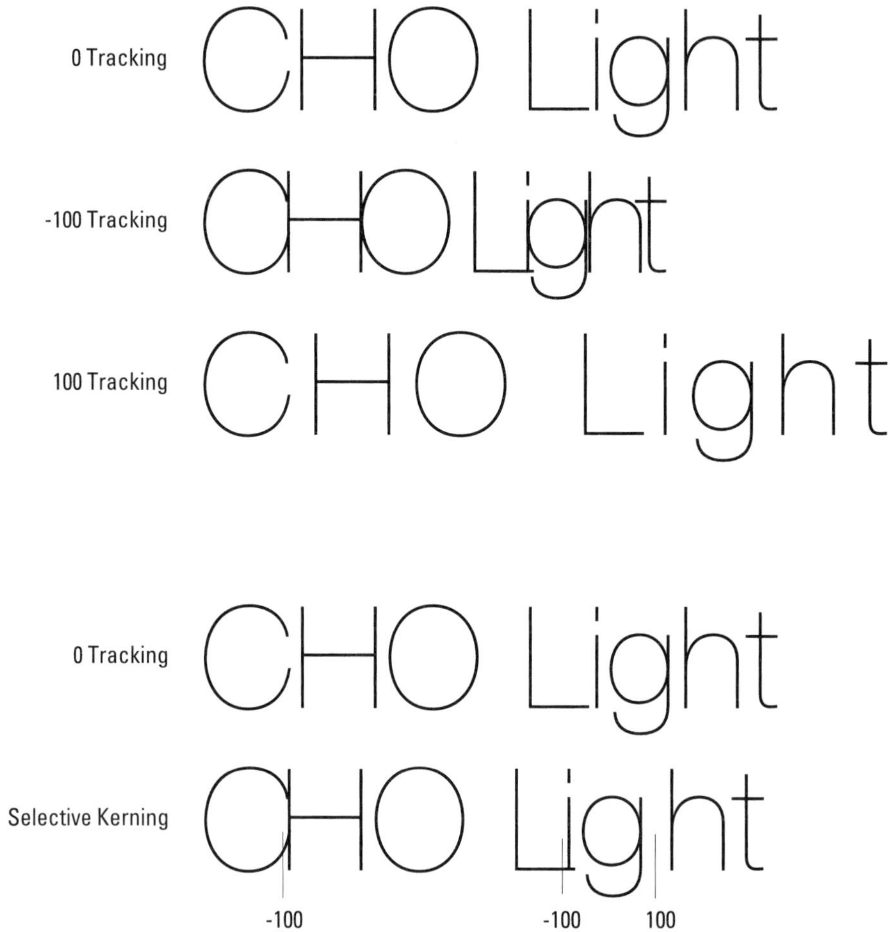

Figure 8-40: Examples of tracking and kerning

For example, a kerning pair of the letters *AV* in Adobe Garamond, when Auto kerning is on, is set to (-80). If you type in a value of -150, that value will override the Auto kerning, turning it off and using your new value of -50. Figure 8-41 shows the slight difference between a kerning of (-80) and -150.

To increase or decrease the kerning or tracking by the increments specified in the Keyboard Increments Preferences dialog box, press Option-← [Alt +←] or Option-→ [Alt +→]. To increase or decrease the tracking or kerning by a factor of five times the amount in the General Preferences dialog box, press ⌘-Option-← [Alt +←] or ⌘-Option-→ [Alt +→].

Figure 8-41: The left letters are using Auto kerning (-80). The right letters are using -150 kerning

To quickly reset the tracking of selected characters to 0, press ⌘-Shift-Q [Ctrl+Shift+Q]. Sneaky, huh?

Kerning and tracking values are based on $^{1}/_{1,000}$ *em space*. An em space is the width of two numbers (think of two zeros — they tend to be the widest-looking numbers) at that particular point size.

The values entered for tracking and kerning must be between –1,000 and 10,000. A value of –1,000 will result in stacked letters. A value of 10,000 will make enough space between letters for 10 em spaces, or 20 numbers. That's a *lot* of space.

Different software works with kerning and tracking differently. In those programs that *do* offer numerical tracking, it is usually represented in some form of a fraction of an em space, but the denominator varies from software to software. In QuarkXPress, for example, tracking and kerning is measured in $^{1}/_{200}$ of an em space. Check the documentation that came with your software to determine the denominator in other software. This can get a little confusing when going from program to program, although the transformation from QuarkXPress to Illustrator is quite simple: to get the same tracking and kerning values in Quark that you used in Illustrator, divide the number you used in Illustrator by 5 ($^{1,000}/_{200}$=5).

The bottom portion of the Character palette contains the Baseline Shift field, which, unlike leading, moves individual characters up and down relative to their baseline (from leading). Positive numbers move the selected characters up, and negative numbers move the characters down by the amount specified. The maximum amount of Baseline Shift is 1,296 points in either direction. Baseline shift is especially useful for Path type. Baseline shift can be changed via the keyboard by pressing Option-Shift-↑ [Alt+Shift+↑] to increase and Option-Shift-↓ [Alt+Shift+↓] to decrease the baseline shift in the increment specified in the General Preferences dialog box.

Vertical and Horizontal Scale

Also in the Options section of the Character palette is the Horizontal scale field. Horizontal scale controls the width of the type, causing it to become expanded or condensed horizontally. Values from 1% to 10,000% can be entered in this field. Like most other fields in the Character palette, the values entered are absolute values, so whatever the horizontal scale is, changing it back to 100% returns the type to its original proportions.

POWER TIP: You can quickly reset the Horizontal Scale value to 100% by pressing ⌘-Shift-X [Ctrl+Shift+X].

The Language Barrier

If you're reading a translation of the *Illustrator 7 Bible* in a language other than English, I'd like to welcome you by saying hello in your native language: "Hello." Okay, I'm probably not fooling you here; through the magic of translators who speak several languages much more fluently than I do "Westernized East Coast American English," my current language of choice, this book is translated into other languages without one iota of input from me.

If your language of choice is not English, you'll be interested in the Language option along the bottom of the Character palette. It allows you to change to your language of choice, so that things like the Spelling dictionary and hyphenation dictionary work for words you'll be typing.

More Multinational Options

The other options along the bottom of the Character palette are specifically designed for Kanji character operations, with the exception of the Direction pop-up menu, which can be used with Roman characters to achieve various effects. The Direction pop-up menu is discussed later in this chapter in the Vertical Type section.

Paragraph Palette

Some changes that can be made to text affect entire paragraphs at the same time. Paragraph attributes include alignment, indentation, space before paragraphs, hanging punctuation, hyphenation, spacing, repeated Character Processing, and Line Breaking.

You can change paragraph attributes if you first select a type area using a selection tool, in which case, the changes affect every paragraph within the entire type area. If you use the Type tool to select one or more characters, changes made to paragraph attributes affect the entire paragraphs of each of the selected characters.

Type the Right Way

Although at first it seems quite simple to outline characters of type using a 1-pt. Stroke in the Stroke palette, just slapping on a Stroke of a weight that seems to look good on the screen and changing the Fill to None or White is technically incorrect.

The right way to outline type is only a little bit more involved. First, select the type that you want outlined and give the type a Stroke that is twice the weight you want on the printed piece. Then Copy, Paste in Front, and give the new type a Stroke of None and a Fill of White. The White Fill knocks out the inside half of the Stroke, leaving the Stroke one-half the width you specified, which is what you really want.

The following Figure shows both the right way and the wrong way to outline type. The top line is the original type. The middle line is outlined the wrong way with a 1-point Stroke and a Fill of White. The bottom part of the figure shows "100% Natural" outlined correctly, first with a white Fill and no Stroke, and then with a 2-point Stroke.

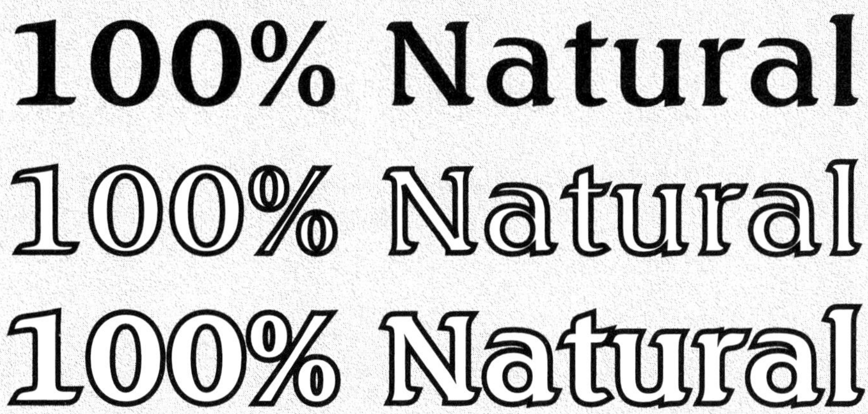

(continued)

(continued)

"Serif preservation," as it's known to a select few, requires a teeny bit of math, but it's worth the effort. The white area inside the Stroke is exactly the size of the character when done this way, as opposed to being smaller by half the width of the Stroke when done normally.

Paragraph attributes include alignment, indentation, leading before paragraphs (other programs usually refer to this as space between paragraphs), hanging punctuation, hyphenation, and spacing.

To display the Paragraph palette (see Figure 8-42) using menu commands, choose Type⇨Paragraph. To display the Paragraph palette with key command, press ⌘-M [Ctrl+M].

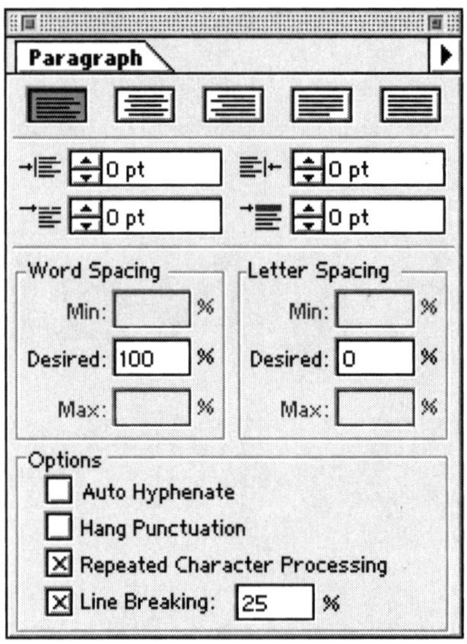

Figure 8-42: The Paragraph palette

Pressing Tab tabs forward through the text fields, and Shift-Tab tabs backward through the same text fields. Press Enter or Return to apply the changes that were made.

The bottom part of the Paragraph palette contains information that doesn't get changed too often, so for the most part, it doesn't need to be displayed. If you wish to display it, choose Show Options from the Paragraph palette pop-up menu.

Alignment

There are five different types of paragraph alignment (see Figure 8-43). Each of them is represented by a graphical representation of what multiple lines of type look like when that particular alignment is applied.

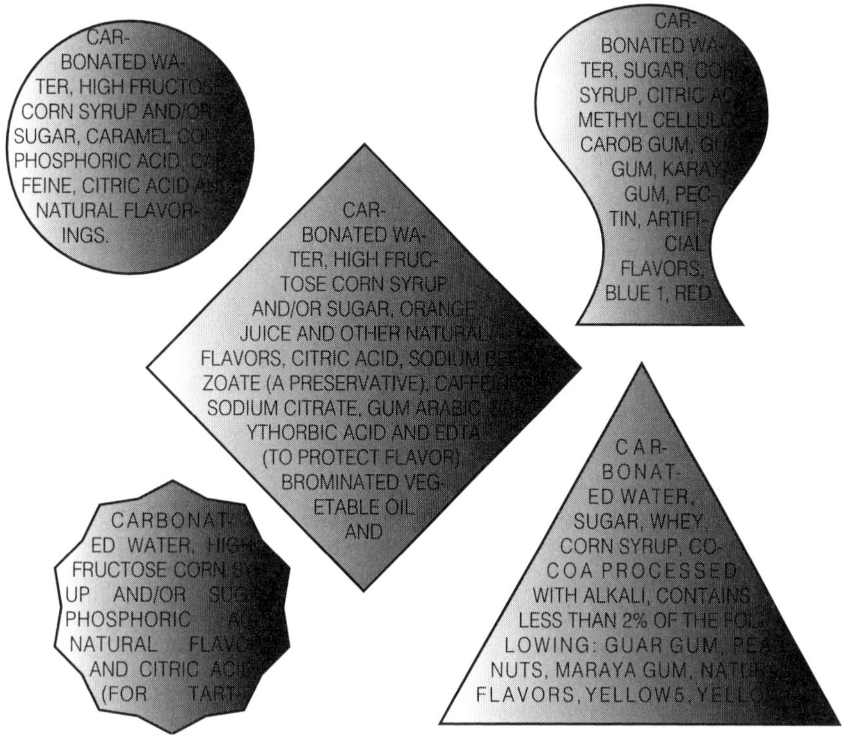

Figure 8-43: The five different types of alignment: Flush Left, Flush Right, Centered, Justify Full Lines, and Justify All Lines

The first alignment type is the most common: Flush Left, which experienced typesetters often refer to as *ragged right* due to the uneven right side of the text. You can also apply this type of alignment by pressing ⌘-Shift-L [Ctrl+Shift+L].

The next type of alignment is Centered, where all lines of type in the paragraph are centered relative to each other, to the point clicked, or to the location of the I-bar in Path type. You can also apply this type of alignment by pressing ⌘-Shift-C [Ctrl+Shift+C].

The middle alignment choice is Flush Right, in which type has a smooth, even right side and an uneven left side (no, ragged left isn't really a correct term). You can also apply this type of alignment by pressing ⌘-Shift-R [Ctrl+Shift+R].

The fourth type of alignment is Justified (Illustrator calls them Justify Full Lines), where both the left and right sides appear smooth and even. Extra space is added between letters and words, as defined in the "Spacing" section later in this chapter. The last line in a justified paragraph appears to be flush left. You can also apply this type of alignment by pressing ⌘-Shift-J [Ctrl+Shift+J].

The last alignment is called Justify All Lines (commonly called Force Justify), which is the same as Justify except that the last line of every paragraph is justified along with the other lines of the paragraph. This can create some really *awful* looking paragraphs, and is done mainly for artistic emphasis, not as a proper way to justify type. Justify All Lines is particularly useful for stretching a single line of type across a certain width. You can also apply this type of alignment by pressing ⌘-Shift-B [Ctrl+Shift+B].

Justification only works on Area type. Illustrator will not allow you to select Justify or Justify All Lines for Path type or Point type.

Indentation

Paragraphs can be indented within the Paragraph palette by choosing different amounts of indentation for the left edge, right edge, and first line of each paragraph. The maximum indentation for all three fields is 1,296 points, and the minimum is –1,296 points.

Using indents is a great way to offset type, such as quotes, that have smaller margins than the rest of the type surrounding the quote. Changing the indentation values is also useful for creating hanging indents, such as numbered or bulleted text.

To create hanging indents easily, make the Left Indent as large as the width of a bullet or a number and a space, and then make the First Line value the negative value of that. If the left indent were 2 picas, the first line would be –2 picas. This creates great hanging indents every time.

Space Before Paragraphs

Illustrator lets you place additional space between paragraphs by entering a number in the Space Before Paragraphs text field. This measurement is added to the leading to determine the distance from baseline to baseline before the selected paragraphs. You can also enter a negative number to decrease space between paragraphs, if necessary. Values for Space Before Paragraphs can be between –1,296 and 1,296 points.

Spacing

Illustrator enables you to control the spacing of letters and words in text by editing the Spacing fields in the middle of the Paragraph palette (see Figure 8-44).

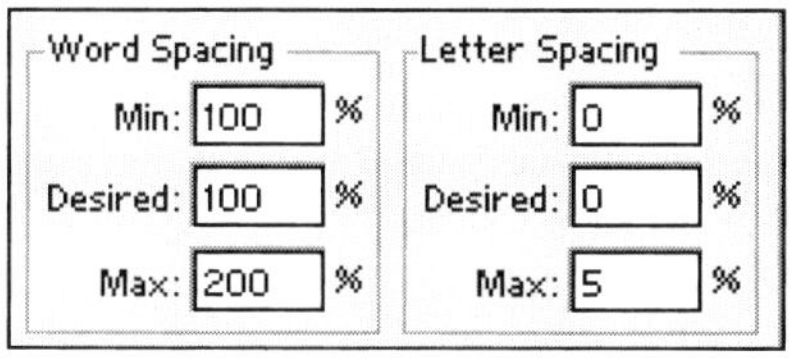

Figure 8-44: The Spacing section of the Paragraph palette

Spacing affects the space between letters and words regardless of the alignment, although Justified text has even more spacing control than Flush Left, Flush Right, and Centered text.

When Flush Left, Flush Right, and Centered alignment are chosen, the only text fields that can be changed are the Desired fields for Letter spacing and Word spacing.

You can enter values between 0% and 1,000% for Word Spacing. The Minimum must be less than the amount in the Desired box, and the Maximum must be more than the amount in the Desired box. At 100%, the word space is normal; at less than 100%, the word space is reduced; and at a number greater than 100%, the word space is increased.

The values for Letter Spacing must be between –50% and 500%. The Minimum must be less than the amount in the Desired box, and the Maximum must be more than the amount in the Desired box. At 0%, the letter space is normal; at less than 0%, the letter space is reduced; and at a number greater than 0%, the letter space is increased.

The Minimum and Maximum boxes in the Word Spacing and Letter Spacing areas are mainly used to control where the extra space goes and where it is removed from when stretching out and compressing the lines of text.

Hang Punctuation

If Hang Punctuation is checked, punctuation at the left edge of a Flush Left, Justified, or Justified Last Line paragraph appears outside the type area, as shown in Figure 8-45. Punctuation on the right edge of a Flush Right, Justified, or Justified Last Line paragraph also appears outside the type area. Strangely enough, Illustrator is one of the few programs that supports this very hip feature.

Figure 8-45: When the Hang Punctuation box is checked, quotes, periods, commas, and hyphens fall outside the boundary of the type area

"I watch it for the subtle nuances in plot, for the rich and dramatic char-acterizations of the title characters, and for a refreshingly accurate por-trayal of pre-medieval times."

Jennifer Alspach, on why she's hooked on *Xena: Warrior Princess*

Hyphenation

Hyphenation? In a drawing program? I couldn't believe it either, but there it was staring me in the face. A nice addition to Illustrator's text-handling capabilities, hyphenation works in the background, silently hyphenating when necessary.

To use Illustrator's hyphenation, you must check the Auto Hyphenate box in the lower-left of the Paragraph palette. After this is checked for selected text, that text hyphenates fairly well.

Hyphenation in Illustrator works from a set of hyphenation rules that you define in the Hyphenation Options dialog box (shown in Figure 8-46). View the Hyphenation dialog box by choosing Hyphenation from the Paragraph pop-up menu. Here you can specify how many letters must fall before the hyphen can appear and how many letters must fall after the hyphen. You can also limit the number of hyphens in a row to avoid the "ladder look" of multiple hyphens.

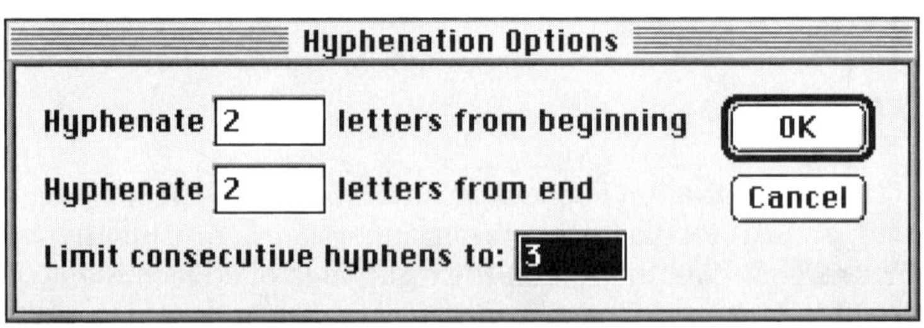

Figure 8-46: The Hyphenation Options dialog box

When you need to hyphenate a word at a place where Illustrator doesn't seem to want to hyphenate it, you can create a discretionary hyphen. A discretionary hyphen is created by placing the blinking insertion point where the word should break and typing ⌘-Shift-Hyphen [Ctrl+Shift+Hyphen]. This causes the word to hyphenate at a certain part of the word only if that word has to be hyphenated. If the word doesn't have to be hyphenated, no hyphen appears. This is much better than just typing a normal hyphen, which works temporarily; but if the manually hyphenated word is moved from the edge of the line, the hyphen remains within it.

Those Unusual Options

Repeated Character Processing and Line Breaking % are two options that are only relevant to Kanji typefaces. They aren't available when a standard Roman typeface is being used.

Special Characters on a Mac

On a Macintosh, many special characters are available besides the standard letters, numbers, and symbols that appear on your keyboard. To show you these special characters, Apple's system software includes a desk accessory called KeyCaps, which displays the keyboard you are using and shows what each character will look like in the typeface you choose.

There are essentially four sets of characters in each font. The first set is reached by normal typing of the keyboard keys, which include numbers, lowercase letters, and a few symbols. The second set is

I Can't Select My Type!

Winchester: This is really annoying. Every time I select my type, nothing happens.

Toulouse: Nothing's supposed to happen. Selecting doesn't "do" anything.

Winchester: I know that, but my type isn't being selected.

Toulouse: Have you talked to Frank?

Winchester: Yes, but I don't have any other text areas in the document. It can't be that.

Toulouse: Well, it might be....

Winchester: And the really spooky thing is, that sometimes, when the type isn't selected, I can change the font, and other type attributes.

Toulouse: Actually, the type is selected....You just can't see it.

Winchester: I've been meaning to update my eyeglasses prescription.

Toulouse: Actually, you probably have the Hide Edges option selected in the View menu.

Winchester: Whaddaya know, it *is* selected. But what does that have to do with my type?

Toulouse: Hide Edges doesn't just hide path edges and points, it hides the selection area when text is selected.

(continued)

(continued)

Winchester: That's silly.

Toulouse: Maybe, but it's a good way to change attributes of a few characters in a text story without having to see them in reverse.

reached by pressing the Shift key prior to pressing the keyboard key and includes capital letters and symbols that appear on the top half of the keyboard keys. The third set is reached by pressing the Option key before pressing a keyboard key. This set consists primarily of the common special symbols, such as a bullet (•), the cents symbol (¢), an ellipsis (…), and the pi symbol (π). The fourth set of characters can only be reached when both the Option and Shift keys are pressed before a keyboard key is pressed and includes less common symbols, like f ligatures (fi, fl), the double dagger (‡), and the Apple symbol ().

While almost all typefaces have the first and second sets, many typefaces do not contain very many characters in the third and fourth sets. The list in Figure 8-47 shows the common symbols and their keyboard equivalents, but not all typefaces have all the symbols, and some of the symbols in some of the typefaces may have different keyboard commands.

Symbol Typefaces on a Mac

There are several symbol typefaces available that contain symbols in place of letters and numbers. The most popular of these is the Symbol typeface, which has Greek letters and mathematical operands and symbols. The next most popular symbol font would have to be Zapf Dingbats, which contains a wide variety of different symbols, as shown in Figure 8-48.

Some other typefaces that contain primarily symbols are Carta, the map symbol typeface; Bill's Dingbats, a shareware set of symbols that nicely complements Zapf Dingbats; and Mathematical Pi, a math font containing math symbols.

Figure 8-47: The standard keyboard set for most fonts on a Mac

1st set	2nd set + Shift	3rd set + Option	4th set +Option–Shift
`	~	`	`
1	!	¡	⁄
2	@	™	¤
3	#	£	‹
4	$	¢	›
5	%	∞	ﬁ
6	^	§	ﬂ
7	&	¶	‡
8	*	•	°
9	(	ª	·
0	)	º	‚
-	_	–	—
=	+	≠	±
q	Q	œ	Œ
w	W	∑	„
e	E	´	
r	R	®	‰
t	T	†	ˇ
y	Y	¥	Á
u	U	¨	¨
i	I	ˆ	ˆ
o	O	ø	Ø
p	P	π	∏
[	{	“	”
]	}	‘	’
\			«	»
a	A	å	Å
s	S	ß	Í
d	D	∂	Î
f	F	ƒ	Ï
g	G	©	˝
h	H	˙	Ó
j	J	∆	Ô
k	K	˚	
l	L	¬	Ò
;	:	…	Ú
'	"	æ	Æ
z	Z	Ω	¸
x	X	≈	˛
c	C	ç	Ç
v	V	√	◊
b	B	∫	ı
n	N	˜	˜
m	M	µ	Â
,	<	≤	¯
.	>	≥	˘
/	?	÷	¿

One of the great things about Symbol typefaces is that individual characters can be turned into outline characters and edited to create different illustrations.

Special Characters in Windows

To access special characters on a Windows system, you usually have to enter a code where you want the special character to be. Codes can be entered in Illustrator by pressing and holding Alt, and then typing in the four-digit code for that

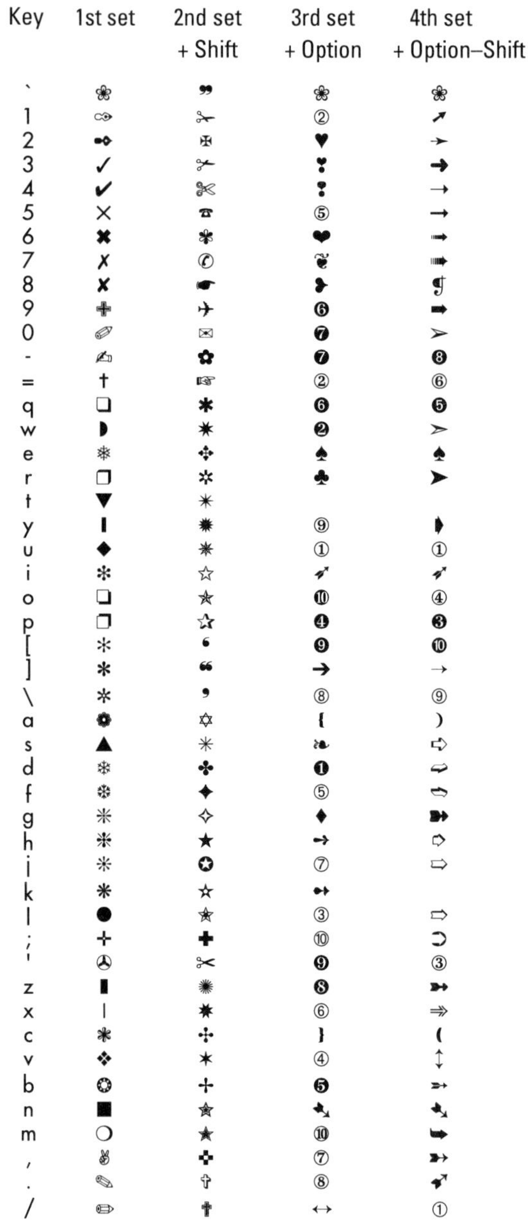

Figure 8-48: The character set of Zapf Dingbats

character. Figure 8-49 shows all the hidden special characters (ones that aren't shown on the keyboard), and the code needed to type them.

To access a bullet, for instance, you would press Alt, type **0149,** and then release the Alt key. A bullet appears where your text cursor last was.

Figure 8-49: The hidden special characters and their corresponding four-digit ANSI codes

Char	Code	Char	Code	Char	Code
ƒ	0131	-	0173	×	0215
„	0132	®	0174	Ø	0216
…	0133	¯	0175	Ù	0217
†	0134	°	0176	Ú	0218
‡	0135	±	0177	Û	0219
ˆ	0136	²	0178	Ü	0220
‰	0137	³	0179	Ý	0221
Š	0138	´	0180	ß	0222
‹	0139	µ	0181	à	0223
Œ	0140	¶	0182	à	0224
	0141	·	0183	á	0225
	0142	¸	0184	â	0226
	0143	¹	0185	ã	0227
	0144	º	0186	ä	0228
‘	0145	»	0187	å	0229
’	0146	¼	0188	æ	0230
“	0147	½	0189	ç	0231
”	0148	¾	0190	è	0232
•	0149	¿	0191	é	0233
–	0150	À	0192	ê	0234
—	0151	Á	0193	ë	0235
˜	0152	Â	0194	ì	0236
™	0153	Ã	0195	í	0237
š	0154	Ä	0196	î	0238
›	0155	Å	0197	ï	0239
œ	0156	Æ	0198	ð	0240
	0157	Ç	0199	ñ	0241
	0158	È	0200	ò	0242
Ÿ	0159	É	0201	ó	0243
	0160	Ê	0202	ô	0244
¡	0161	Ë	0203	õ	0245
¢	0162	Ì	0204	ö	0246
£	0163	Í	0205	÷	0247
¤	0164	Î	0206	ø	0248
¥	0165	Ï	0207	ù	0249
¦	0166	Ð	0208	ú	0250
§	0167	Ñ	0209	û	0251
¨	0168	Ò	0210	ü	0252
©	0169	Ó	0211	ý	0253
ª	0170	Ô	0212	þ	0254
«	0171	Õ	0213	ÿ	0255
¬	0172	Ö	0214		

Customizing Fonts

Typefaces can be created and modified right on your computer, with tools very similar to the ones in Adobe Illustrator. Creating fonts is, in a way, the reverse process of outlining existing fonts because you are taking outlines and turning them into characters in typefaces. Figure 8-50 shows two of the most popular shareware fonts created through a combination of Illustrator and Fontographer: Lefty Casual and Ransom Note.

Figure 8-50: Lefty Casual and Ransom Note

By taking existing typefaces, you can customize the characters, creating a unique typeface. In a typeface you create, all the special characters can be ones you've designed especially for that face.

CAUTION

Check with the original typeface manufacturer before customizing, to ensure that you will not be violating any copyright laws for that particular font vendor.

Macromedia Fontographer is the most popular font-creation software currently available, boasting Multiple Master capabilities and very precise Bézier control tools.

Export/Place

To export text, select the text you want to export and choose File➪Export. A Save dialog box appears, asking in what format and where you want to save the text.

You can save text in most of the common formats, and you can import it back into Illustrator with the Place command (choose File➪Place when a text area is active with a Type tool). Word-processing software, page-layout software, or any other software that can read text files can open and use text that you saved in Illustrator.

Vertical Type

Vertical Type is a fascinating new capability in Illustrator 7. If you use Kanji characters, you'll find it invaluable. But even if you don't, you might find some interesting uses for setting type vertically, instead of horizontally.

There are two ways to make your type appear vertical instead of horizontal. You can create type using any of the three Vertical Type tools, or you can convert horizontal type into Vertical Type with the Type➪Type Orientation➪Vertical. Figure 8-51 shows Rectangle Type both horizontally and vertically. Note that Vertical type takes up a great deal more space than Horizontal type.

Figure 8-51: Horizontal type (left) and the same type reoriented to Vertical

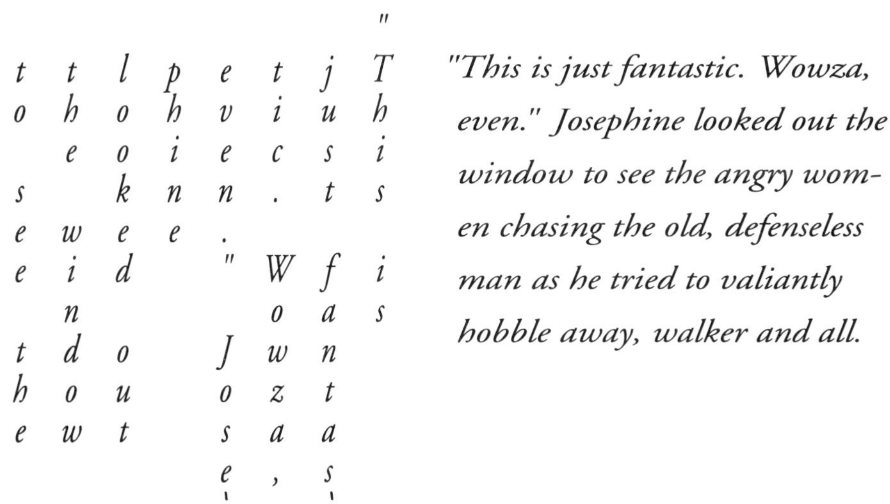

Most of Illustrator's standard character and paragraph palette changes work with vertical type, but not always in ways you would expect. For instance, type is set on a centerline, not a baseline. The centerline runs vertically through the center of each character. The following is a list of differences in the way each of the major functions works:

- **Font:** Same
- **Size:** Same
- **Leading:** Changes the amount of space between the vertical "lines" of type, measured from centerline to centerline.
- **Kerning/Tracking:** Changes the amount of vertical space between each character. Because very few Roman characters have both ascenders and descenders, tracking and kerning substantially can really help get rid of the excess white space between characters that makes Vertical Type so hard to read.

- **Vertical Scale:** Changes the width (horizontal scale) of the characters.
- **Horizontal Scale:** Changes the height (vertical scale) of the characters.
- **Baseline Shift:** Moves the type left (negative values) and right (positive values) along the centerline.
- **Flush Left:** Words are Flush Top.
- **Center:** Words are vertically centered.
- **Flush Right:** Words are Flush Bottom.
- **Justify Full Lines:** Words on full (vertical) lines are justified from top to bottom.
- **Justify All Lines:** All lines are vertically justified.
- **Left Indent:** Top Indent. Positive numbers move the text down, negative numbers move the text up.
- **Right Indent:** Bottom Indent, with numbers working like Left Indent.
- **First Line Indent:** The Rightmost Line Indent. Once again, positive numbers move the text down, negative numbers move the text up.
- **Space Before Paragraph:** Paragraphs go from right to left, so this control increases the space to the right of the selected paragraph(s).
- **Auto Hyphenate:** Hyphenates words the same way as Horizontal type, but the hyphens appear at the bottom of each line.
- **Hang Punctuation:** Punctuation is hung above and below the text area.
- **Tab Ruler:** Appears to the right of text areas in vertical form.
- **Create Outlines:** Same.

Changing the Direction of Type

Direction and Orientation are two totally different things. The Orientation is a text area control; changing it affects the entire text area. The Direction control is a character-based control, which can affect all characters or one character. It is this one control that really makes Vertical Type worth using.

There are three options in the Direction pop-up menu (located in the Character palette):

- **Standard:** This keeps characters in the direction that is the default of the type area. This is usually displayed so that each character is "right side up."
- **Rotated:** This rotates characters -90° (see Figure 8-52).

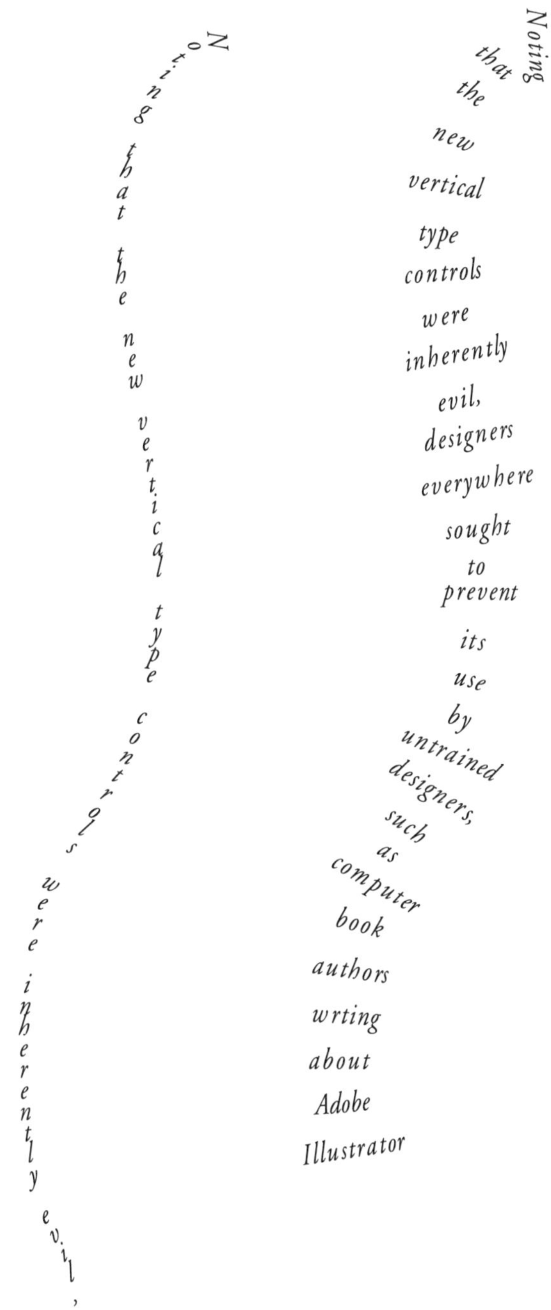

Figure 8-52: Vertical type on a curved path as it normally appears (left) and when each word has Kumi direction applied to it

- **Kumi:** This "direction" affects selected characters, grouping selected characters onto one horizontal line. In Figure 8-52, I've selected each word separately and applied the Kumi direction to them. In addition, I increased the leading so that the columns of text would be easier to read.

Path Type and Vertical Type

Type on a path takes on new life when you use Vertical Type. That, combined with the capability to group characters (words, and so forth) together along the chain of text provides additional text capabilities that can't be found anywhere else.

Figure 8-53 shows type on a path with and without Kumi Character Direction adjustments.

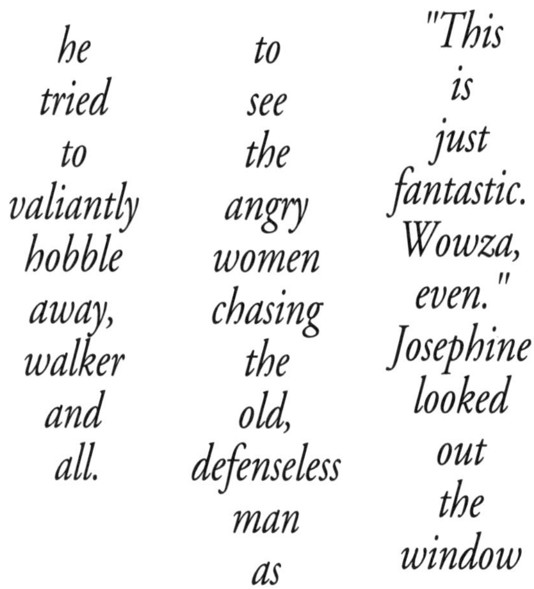

Figure 8-53: Vertical Type which has been rotated using the Direction pop-up menu

Other Type Considerations

When you're using type in Illustrator, there are a number of things to keep in mind to get good results:

- Make sure that the person you are sending the Illustrator file to has the same fonts you have. It isn't enough just to have the same name of a font; you'll need the exact font that was created by the same manufacturer.

- Try not to mix TrueType fonts with PostScript fonts. This usually ends up confusing everyone involved.
- If the person you are sending Illustrator files to does *not* have your typeface, select the type in that font and choose Type⇨Create Outlines (⌘-Shift-O) [Ctrl+Shift+O].
- When you're printing an Illustrator file that has been placed in other software, missing typestyles may go unnoticed until after the job has printed. Be doubly sure that the person outputting the file has all the fonts in the embedded Illustrator file.

Summary

- Most of the options used to control type can be found in the Type menu.
- There are four different ways to put type on a page: Point type, Rectangle type, Area type, and Path type.
- Point type has one point as its "anchor," and the type is aligned to that point.
- Rectangle type exists within a rectangle drawn with the Type tool.
- Area type is type that exists within the confines of any path.
- Path type is type that runs along the edge of a path.
- Type can be selected all at once by clicking the path (or point) of the type with the Selection tool.
- Individual characters, words, and paragraphs can be selected by using any of the type tools.
- The Character palette (accessed by pressing ⌘-T [Ctrl+T]) contains all the character-specific information about selected type, and can be used to change that information.
- There are no "styles" in Illustrator with regard to type; instead, you must select the exact font you wish to use.
- Tracking and kerning remove or add space between groups or pairs of letters, respectively.
- The Paragraph palette (accessed by pressing ⌘-M) [Ctrl+M] contains all the paragraph-specific information about selected type and can be used to change that information.

- Type can be set to wrap around selected paths by using the Text Wrapping feature.
- Type can be set to jump from text block to text block by linking text blocks together.
- The Tab Ruler palette is used to set tabs for text areas.
- If you have both the screen font and the printer font of a Type 1 typeface, or if you have a TrueType font installed, you can convert the font into outlines via the Create Outlines command.
- Once type has been changed to outlines, you may use those outlines as a mask, or Fill those outlines with gradients or patterns.
- Many special characters can be accessed in each font on a Mac by pressing the Option key.

Masks and Compound Paths

CHAPTER 9

In This Chapter

- Understanding compound paths
- The difference between a Fill of None and a hole
- How paths travel in directions, and reversing those directions
- Type and compound paths
- Faking a compound path
- Understanding masks
- Putting Strokes and Fills on masks
- Printing problems with masks
- Compound masks: an output nightmare

Compound Paths

Compound paths are one of the least-understood areas of Illustrator, but after you understand a few simple guidelines and rules, manipulating and using them correctly is simple.

Compound paths are paths made up of two or more open or closed paths. Where the paths cross or every other Fill area exists there is a hole, which is transparent. You can specify which paths create the holes by changing the direction of the paths via the Reverse option in Object⇨Attributes. The general rule is that holes are formed by paths traveling in the opposite direction of any adjoining paths. Compound paths can be fun or frustrating, depending on the location of Pluto relative to Saturn, Jupiter, and Mickey.

Creating Compound Paths

You can create compound paths of all sorts by following the steps below. It's a good idea to make sure that none of the paths are currently compound paths or grouped paths before creating a new compound path.

STEPS: Creating a Compound Path

Step 1. Create all the paths that you need for the compound path, including the outside path and the holes.

Step 2. Select all the paths and choose Object➪Compound Paths➪Make (⌘-8) [Ctrl+8]. The paths are now treated as one path by Illustrator. When you click one of the paths with the Selection tool, the other paths in the compound path are selected as well. Fill the object with any Fill. (I used a custom radial gradient for the illustration in Figure 9-1.)

Figure 9-1: The frame of this window is a compound path with several holes in it

Step 3. Place the compound path over any other object. (I used a placed EPS image for this example.) The inner paths act like holes that enable you to see the object underneath.

Figure 9-2 shows these three steps.

Figure 9-2: The steps in creating a compound path

You can select individual paths by clicking them once with the Group Selection tool. As always, you can select points and segments within each path by using the Direct Selection tool.

Clicking only once with the Group Selection tool on paths that you wish to select is important. Clicking those paths more than once with the Group Selection tool will select all the other paths in the compound path. To click (for moving or copying purposes) the selected individual paths after they have been clicked by the Group Selection tool once, click them with the Direct Selection tool.

CAUTION Paths belonging to different groups cannot be made into a compound path unless all paths in all the groups are selected.

When you create a compound path, it takes on the Paint Style attributes of the bottommost path of all the paths that were selected and have become part of that compound path.

You can create a compound path that is only one path, though there are very few reasons to do so. If the singular compound path is selected as part of a larger compound path (with either the Direct Selection tool or Group Selection tool), the path directions may be altered. If you aren't sure whether an individual path is a compound path, select the path and choose Object⇨Compound Path. If the Release option is available, the path is a compound path; if it is not available, the path is not a compound path.

Compound paths do not work in a hierarchical process as groups do. If a path is part of a compound path, it is part of that compound path only. If a compound path becomes part of another compound path, the paths in the original compound path are compounded only with the new compound path.

CAUTION You cannot blend between multiple-path compound paths. Only the individual paths that you click with the Blend tool are blended. You can blend each of the paths in a compound path separately; however, the blend step paths will not be compound paths.

Blending Compounds

Mindy: I can't blend my compound paths right.

Toulouse: Actually, the Blend tool only works with a single path at a time.

Mindy: So I'm out of luck?

Toulouse: Not really. There's two different options available.

Mindy: And they are...?

Toulouse: Well, what are you trying to do with the blend?

Mindy: I'm trying to make zooming text.

Toulouse: Ah. Well, instead of blending, you could use KPT Vector Effects. Some of the filters, ShadowLand specifically, does some amazing things with compound blends.

Mindy: Okay. The other way?

Toulouse: Change your compounds to "fake compounds," making them consist of truly one path.

Mindy: How could I do that?

Toulouse: It involves quite a bit of splitting paths and joining. But there's a catch.

Mindy: As long as it doesn't involve stalking....

Toulouse: No...actually, you just can't use Strokes, which would appear in the seams.

Mindy: Sounds fair, I'll try it.

Releasing Compound Paths

When you want to release a compound path, select the path and choose Object➪Compound Path➪Release (⌘-Option-8) [Ctrl+Alt+8]. The path changes into regular paths.

If any of the paths appeared as holes, they are, instead, filled with the Fill of the rest of the compound path. The results might be a little confusing because these holes then seem to blend right into the outer shape of the compound paths, as shown in Figure 9-3.

If the compound path that you are releasing contains other compound paths, they are released as well because Illustrator doesn't recognize compound paths that are within other compound paths.

Understanding Holes

Holes for donuts, Life Savers, and rings are quite simple to create. Just select two circles, one smaller than, and totally within, a larger circle, and choose Compound Path➪Make (⌘-8) [Ctrl+8]. The inside circle is then a hole.

A compound path considers every path within it to lie along the borders of the compound path. Path edges within an object appear to you to be on the inside of an object, but they appear to Illustrator to be just another edge of the path.

With this concept in mind, you can create a compound path that has several holes, such as a slice of Swiss cheese or a snowflake. Just create the outermost paths and the paths that will be holes, select all the paths, and then select Object➪Compound Path➪Make.

You aren't limited to one set of holes. You can create a compound path with a hole that has an object inside it with a hole. In that hole can be an object with a hole, and so on.

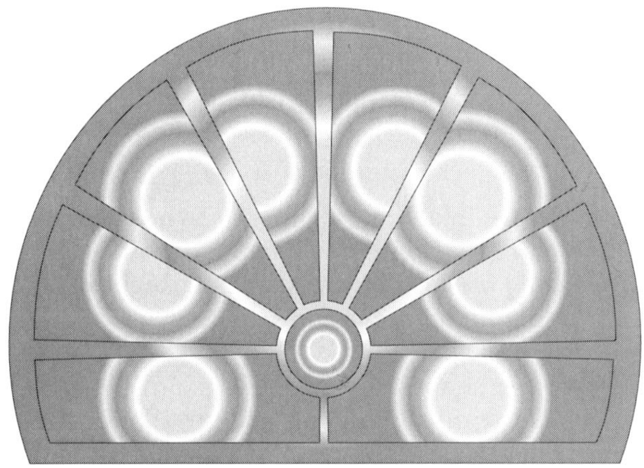

Figure 9-3: The compound path from Figure 9-1, after you release the path. The circles are the radial gradients that the compound path uses.

Overlapping Holes

Holes, if they really are paths that are supposed to be empty areas of an object, should not overlap. If anything, you can combine multiple holes that are overlapping into one larger hole, possibly by using Unite.

If holes within a compound path do overlap, the result is a solid area with the same Fill color as the rest of the object. If multiple holes overlap, the results can be quite unusual, as shown in Figure 9-4. (See "Reversing Path Directions," later in this chapter, to learn more about multiple overlapping holes.)

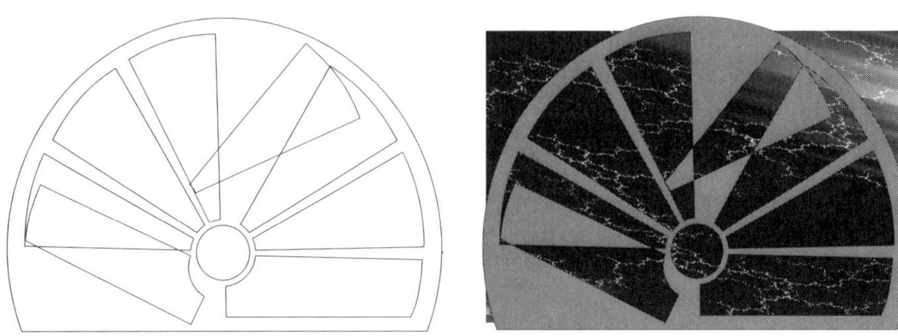

Figure 9-4: Overlapping holes in compound paths, in Artwork mode (left) and Preview mode (right)

In most cases, you will get the desired results with holes only if the outermost path contains all the holes. As a rule, Illustrator uses the topmost objects to "poke" holes out of the bottommost objects. If you want holes to overlap, make sure that the holes are above the outside border.

Creating Compound Paths from Separate Sets of Paths

Compound paths are very flexible. You can choose two sets of paths, each with an outline and a hole, and make them into one compound path. This technique is especially useful for making masks, but you also can use it to alleviate the repetition of creating several compound paths and selecting one of them at a time.

For example, if you have two shapes, a square and a circle, and want a round hole in each of them, you draw two smaller circles and put them into place. After you position the two shapes in the correct locations, you select them and the round paths inside each of them, and then you choose Object⇨Compound Path⇨Make (⌘-8) [Ctrl+8]. Each of the objects now has a hole, and they act as if they are grouped.

To move separate objects that are part of the same compound path, select each object with the Group Selection tool, which selects an entire path at a time, and then move them. Remember that once they're selected, you should use the Direct Selection tool to move the selected portions of a compound path.

Type and Compound Paths

You have been using compound paths as long as you have been using computer PostScript typefaces. All PostScript typefaces are made of characters that are compound paths. Letters that have holes, such as uppercase *B, D,* and *P* and lowercase *a, b,* and *d,* benefit from being compound paths. When you place them in front of other objects, you can see through the empty areas to objects behind them that are visible in those holes.

Each character in a PostScript typeface is a compound path. When you convert characters to editable outlines in Illustrator, each character is still a compound path. If you release the compound paths, the characters with empty areas appear to fill with the same color as the rest of the character, as shown in Figure 9-5, because the holes are no longer knocked out of the letters.

Power Tip: Many times, type is used as a mask, but all the letters used in the mask need to be one compound path. Simply select all the letters and choose Object➪Compound Path➪Make (⌘-8) [Ctrl+8]. This action creates a compound path in which all of the letters form the compound path. Usually, all the holes stay the same as they were as separate compound paths.

Figure 9-5: Type as it normally appears after you convert it to outlines (top) and after you release compound paths (bottom)

Any letters that overlap in a word that you make into a compound path can change path directions and thus affect the "emptiness" of some paths. If letters have to overlap, use Unite on them first and then select all the letters and choose Object➪Compound Path➪ Make (⌘-8) [Ctrl+8].

Path Directions

Each path in Illustrator has a direction. For paths that you draw with the Pen or Pencil tool, the direction of the path is the direction in which you draw the path. When Illustrator creates an oval or a rectangle, the direction of the path is counter-clockwise.

Power Tip: If you're curious about which way a path travels, click any spot of the path with the Scissors tool and then choose Filter➪Stylize➪Add Arrowheads. In the Add Arrowheads dialog box, make sure that the End button is selected and click OK. An arrowhead appears, going in the direction of the path. (Figure 9-6 shows several paths and arrowheads appearing for each path.) If the path is Filled and not Stroked, you see only half the arrowhead in Preview mode. Choose the Undo command twice (once for the arrowhead and once for the path splitting) to go back to where you started.

Paths have directions for one purpose (one purpose that you need to know about, anyway), and that is to determine what the solid areas of a compound path will be and what the empty areas will be. The individual paths in a compound path that create holes from solid paths go in opposite directions.

Create a large circle and put a smaller circle within it. Both circles are traveling in the same direction — counterclockwise. Select both of them and choose Object⇨Compound Path⇨Make (⌘-8) [Ctrl+8]. The outside circle changes its direction to clockwise so that the two circles can work together to form a doughnut-like shape.

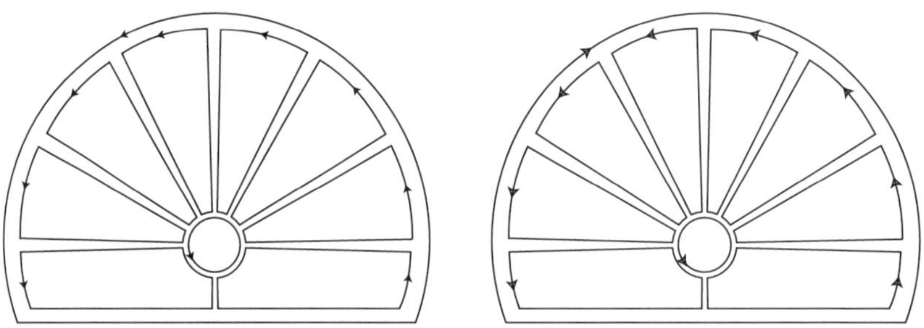

Figure 9-6: The paths on the left are individual paths. The paths on the right make up a compound path. The arrows represent the direction of the paths. Notice that the only difference in direction is on the outermost path.

If two smaller circles are inside the larger circle, they still punch holes in the larger circle because both of them are traveling in the same direction. But what happens when the two inside circles are overlapping? The area where they overlap is inside the empty areas, but both holes go in the same direction. The intersection of the two holes is solid because of the winding path rule.

The Winding Numbers Rule, or What Happened to My Fills?

Understanding the Winding Numbers Rule is helpful when you are dealing with compound paths. The Winding Numbers Rule counts surrounded areas, starting with 0 (outside the outermost edge) and working its way in. Any area with an odd number is Filled, and any area with an even number (such as 0, the outside of the path) is empty, or a hole.

You can apply this rule to most compound paths — although taking the time to diagram the paths you've drawn and place little numbers in them to figure out what is going to be Filled and what isn't is usually more time consuming than doing it wrong, undoing it, and doing it right. I've done the work for you in Figure 9-7.

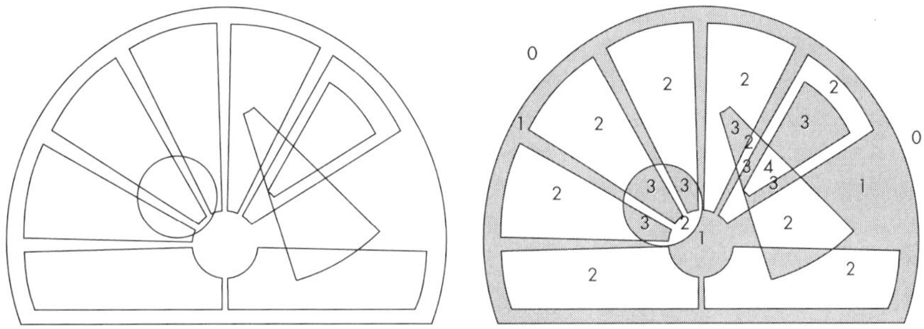

Figure 9-7: As the paths wind in from the outside, odd-numbered areas are Filled and even areas are empty

Reversing Path Directions

To change the direction of a path, select just the path that you need to use the Group Selection tool and choose Window⇨Show Attributes (F11). In the Attributes palette box (see Figure 9-8), click the other (not darkened) direction button.

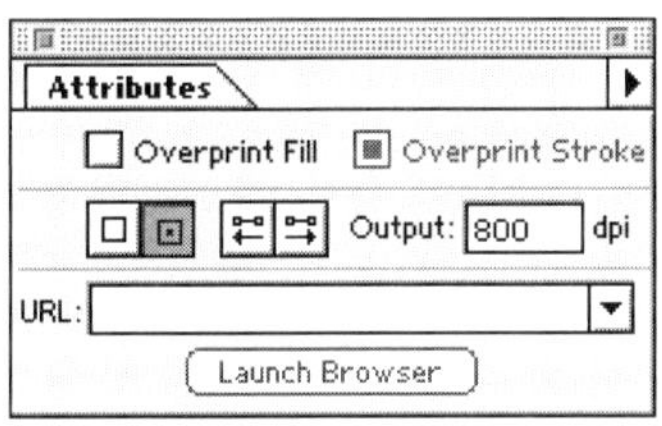

Figure 9-8: Attributes

When paths are changed into compound paths, their direction may change. The strange thing about this is that the Reverse Path Direction button is usually on for objects that are traveling counterclockwise. The outermost path does not change direction from counterclockwise to clockwise until more than one overlapping path is made into a compound path. The paths that make up the holes don't change direction. They're still counterclockwise, but when you look at their Attributes, Reverse Path Direction is on.

One thing that is consistent when dealing with path directions is that holes must travel in the opposite direction from the outside path. As a result, if the Reverse Path Direction button is on for the holes, it is not on for the outside path. That

Can't Make a Compound

Mork: I can't make a compound out of my selected paths!

Toulouse: That often happens when one or more of the paths is already a compound path.

Mork: Huh. How would I find out if that's the case?

Toulouse: Well, you can check and fix it at the same time. First, select the paths you'd like to make into a compound path.

Mork: Got it.

Toulouse: Then, go under Object to Compound Path and hold.

Mork: Okay.

Toulouse: Is Release gray or black?

Mork: Black.

Toulouse: That means at least one of the selected paths is already a compound. Drag over to release.

Mork: Done.

Toulouse: Then choose Object⇨Compound Paths⇨Make.

Mork: It worked!

Toulouse: And what did you learn this week...?

scenario is the normal one when you create compound paths with holes. You can, if you so desire, check the Reverse Path Direction button for the outside path and uncheck it for the inside paths. The resulting image will have the same holes as produced by the reverse. Figure 9-9 shows a compound path and its path directions before and after four of the paths were reversed.

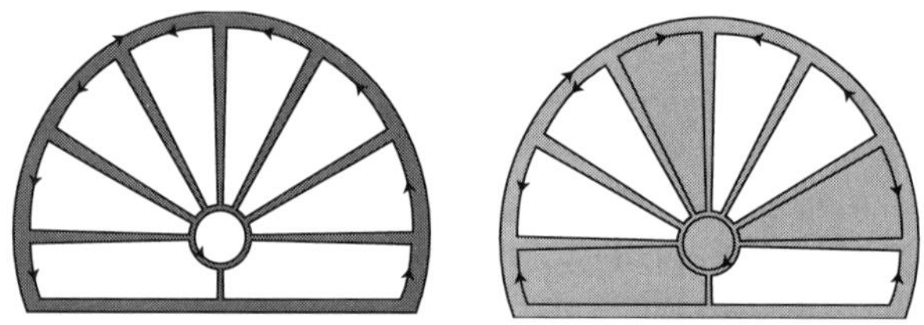

Figure 9-9: Reversing the direction of the four paths in the illustration on the left Fills these holes

CAUTION

Never, never, never attempt to change path direction when all paths of a compound path are selected. Clicking once on either button will make all the paths in the compound path go in the same direction at this point, meaning that no holes will appear.

Using Unite to Create Compound Paths

Another way to make compound paths is by using Unite. Unite works a little differently from the Make Compound Path command. All the selected paths become a single compound path, but none of the path directions are reversed. This means that no holes will be created when Unite is applied.

Unite is quite useful for creating compound paths when there are overlapping pieces of paths that you don't want to create holes between accidentally, such as text converted to outlines.

In addition, Unite removes any overlapping path areas where Filled areas or holes are, so if you Stroke the object, you'll get a much better result than you would if the object were just a plain compound path.

Faking a Compound Path

At times, using a compound path just doesn't work. You may need to cheat a little. Except in the most extreme circumstances, you can fake compound paths, but you need to make quite an effort.

If the background is part of a gradient, select the hole and the object that is painted with the gradient, apply the gradient, and use the Gradient Vector tool to make the gradient spread across both objects in exactly the same way. This trick can fool even the experts.

POWER TIP: One way to fake a compound path is by selecting the background, making a copy of it, making the hole a mask of the background area, and grouping the mask to the copy of the background.

Masks

In Illustrator, you use masks to mask out parts of underlying objects that you don't want to see. The shape of the mask is defined by a path that you draw in Illustrator. Anything outside the mask is hidden from view in Preview mode and does not print.

Masks are objects that *mask* out everything but the paths made up by the mask (see Figure 9-10). Masks can be open, closed, or compound paths. The masking object is the object whose paths make up the mask, and this object must be in front of all the objects that are being masked.

Figure 9-10: An object, its mask, and the resulting masked object

You can make masks from any path, including compound paths and text. You can use masks to view portions of multiple objects, individual objects, and placed EPS images.

Creating Masks

In order for you to create a mask, the masking object (the path that is in the shape of the mask) has to be in front of the objects that you want it to mask. You select the masking object and the objects that you want to mask. Then you choose Object⇨Mask⇨Make (⌘-7) [Ctrl+7]. In Preview mode, any areas of the objects that were outside the mask vanish, but the parts of the objects that are inside the mask remain the same. Figure 9-11 shows an illustration with masks and without them.

Figure 9-11: The image on the left uses masks to hide portions of objects. The image on the right is the result of releasing those masks.

Masks are much easier to use and understand in Preview mode than in Artwork mode.

If you want to mask an object that is not currently being masked, you need to select the new object and all the objects in the mask, including the masking object. You then choose Object⇨Mask⇨Make (⌘-7) [Ctrl+7]. The mask then applies to the new object as well as to the objects that were previously masked. The new object, like all others being masked, must be behind the masking object.

Like compound paths, masking does not work in hierarchical levels. Each time you add an object to a mask, the old mask that didn't have that object is released, and a new mask is made that contains all of the original mask objects as well as the new object. Releasing a mask affects every object in the mask, as described in "Releasing Masks," later in this chapter.

Usually, grouping all the objects in a mask is a good idea, but group them only after you have created the mask. Having the objects grouped facilitates moving the mask and its objects and selecting them when you want to add other objects to the mask.

Masking Raster Images

There are two different ways to mask raster images. The first method is done in Photoshop by creating a *clipping path* and saving it as an EPS image. The second method is to use a mask in Illustrator.

The two methods have their strengths and weaknesses, with the best solution being a combination of both methods. The main advantage to creating a clipping path in Photoshop is that the path can be adjusted while viewing the image clearly at 16:1. (Viewing an image at 1600% in Illustrator displays chunky, unrecognizable blocks of color.) In this manner, the path can be precisely positioned over the correct pixels so that the right ones are selected to be masked. One disadvantage to using Photoshop's clipping path is that the Path tool and path-editing controls in Photoshop are a limited version of Illustrator's Pen tool and path-editing controls, making it more difficult to create and edit a path. The second disadvantage to using a clipping path is that compound paths in Photoshop adhere to one of two different Fill rules, which control the way holes appear for differing path directions. Illustrator is much more flexible in this respect because you are able to change the path direction of each individual path with the Reverse Path Direction check box in the Attributes palette.

The best solution is to create the clipping path in Photoshop, and then, when the clipping path is selected, choose File➪Export➪Paths to Illustrator, which saves an Illustrator-compatible file with the clipping path intact. Save the Photoshop image as an EPS and place it in Illustrator (File➪Place). Then open the Illustrator file (that was created by Paths to Illustrator) and copy the path to the document with the raster image. The path is sized to fit directly onto the raster image.

Copying the selected path in Photoshop enables you to paste it directly in Illustrator, even if you can run only one of those programs at a time. Just copy, quit Photoshop, run Illustrator, and paste it into the Illustrator document. This works when going from Illustrator to Photoshop (paths only) as well.

Masking Blends and Other Masks

You can mask objects that are masking other objects. Just make sure that you select all the objects in each mask and that, as with other objects, they are behind the path that you want to use for a masking object. You also can mask blends, as described in Chapter 12.

Stroking and Filling Masking Objects

Creating a basic mask requires four steps.

STEPS: Creating a Mask and Stroking It

Step 1. Select the path that you want to use as a mask and bring it to the front.

Step 2. Select the mask and any objects that you want to mask and then choose Object⇨Masks⇨Make (⌘-7) [Ctrl+7]. Group the masked objects with the mask for easier selecting in the future.

Step 3. Using the Group Selection tool, select the mask. Then change the Stroke to 1-point Black. Nothing happens in Preview mode.

Step 4. Choose Filters⇨Create⇨Stroke & Fill for Mask. A dialog box appears; click OK. The mask now has a 1-point Black Stroke. The result should resemble Step 4 in Figure 9-12.

You cannot Stroke or Fill masking objects. Any Paint Style attributes that you applied to the masking object prior to transforming it into a mask are replaced by a Fill and Stroke of None. If you release the mask, the path that was the masking object continues to have a Fill and Stroke of None. You can, however, use two other methods to create a Stroke or Fill on a duplicate path of the masking object:

- The first method is to copy the masking object before you turn it into a masking object so that you can paste the copy onto the mask after you create it. To save a step, you can Fill and Stroke the masking object before you copy it. After you create the mask, choose Edit⇨Paste in Front (⌘-F) [Ctrl+F] to put a Stroke on the mask (remove the Fill or it will obscure all the objects that you are masking). Choose Edit⇨Paste in Back (⌘-B) [Ctrl+B] and Arrange⇨Send to Back (⌘-Shift-[) [Ctrl+Shift+[] if you want the object to have a Fill. If the object in the back has a Stroke, the masking object will obscure half of it; the other objects in the mask may obscure other parts of it. If you want both a Stroke and a Fill, you need to paste two copies, one in front and one in back, to see both the Fill and Stroke accurately.

- The second method is to select the masking object and then from the Paint Style palette, choose the Paint Style attributes that you want for the masking object (it won't change in color, but you can change the attributes). Then choose Filter⇨Create⇨Fill & Stroke for Mask to create two more copies of the mask. Finally, paste the Filled copy behind the mask's objects and the Stroked copy in front of the masking object.

Figure 9-12: Steps for creating a Stroked mask

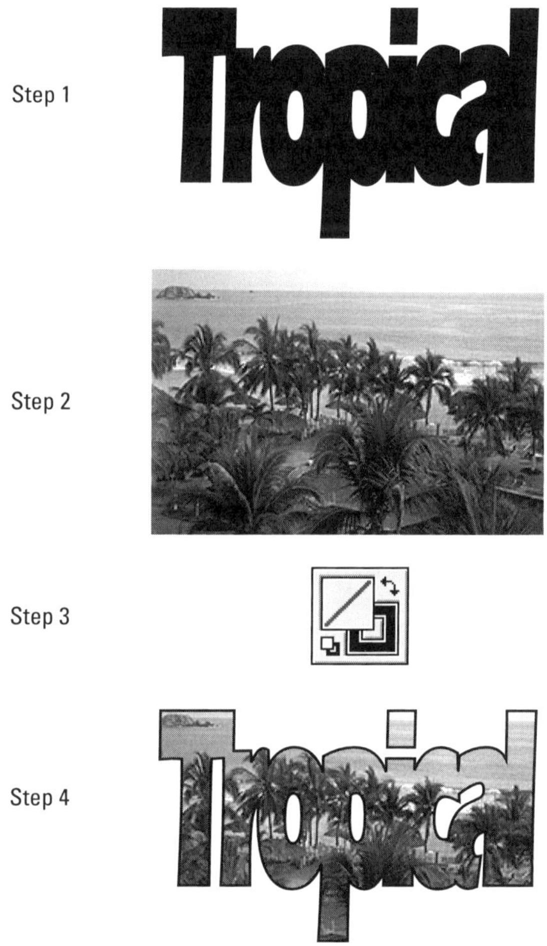

Releasing Masks

To release a mask, first select the masking object (you may select other objects as well). Then choose Object⇨Mask⇨Release (⌘-Option-7) [Ctrl+Alt+7], and the masking object no longer is a mask.

Masking vs. Cropping

Mearth: Should I mask, or should I crop?

Toulouse: You mean with the Pathfinder Crop filter?

Mearth: No, I'm considering a career change in the direction of shucking corn.

Toulouse: I take it you're being sarcastic.

Mearth: Harumph.

Toulouse: It really depends. Cropping has two serious advantages over masking.

Mearth: And those are…?

Toulouse: First, unnecessary paths are deleted, and second, potential printing problems that might occur when a mask is being used are eliminated.

Mearth: So I should crop.

Toulouse: Actually, there's more in favor of masking.

Mearth: Aha!

Toulouse: Yep. Masking allows you to edit the artwork in the future.

Mearth: That's a big one.

Toulouse: Real big. You can change the shape, size, whatever, of the mask and the masked objects.

Mearth: Good points.

Toulouse: And, you can mask raster images and non-outlined text.

Mearth: I'm sold.

If you aren't sure which object is the masking object or if you are having trouble selecting the masking object, choose Edit⇨Select All (⌘-A) [Ctrl+A] and choose Object⇨Mask⇨Release (⌘-Option-7) [Ctrl+Alt+7]. Of course, this action releases any other masks that are in the document — unless they were separate masks that were being masked by other masks — got that?

To release all the masks in the document, even those masks that are being masked by other masks, Select All (⌘-A) [Ctrl+A] and choose Release Mask repeatedly. Usually, three Release Masks gets everything, unless you went mask-happy in that particular document. You can also use the Select⇨Masks option to check if there are any remaining masks.

Masks and Printing

As a rule, PostScript printers don't care too much for masks. They care even less for masks that mask other masks. And they really don't like masks that are compound paths.

Unfortunately, because of the way that Illustrator works, every part of every object in a mask is sent to the printer, even if only a tiny piece of an object will be used. In addition, controlling where objects are sliced by the masking object requires a great deal of computing power and memory. You can have a problem, for example, when you have more stuff to mask than the printer can handle.

More important than any other issue involved with masks and printing is the length and complexity of the masking path.

The more objects in a mask, the more complex it is. The more Anchor Points, the more complex it is. The more direction points coming off those Anchor Points, the more complex the mask is. In other words, your printer would enjoy a mask if the masking object were a rectangle and no objects were being masked.

CAUTION

Masks are usually incredibly complex. This complexity causes many problems for printers (especially ones equipped with PostScript Level 1 and PostScript clones) and quite often results in PostScript printing errors. In addition, be careful not to go mask-crazy (using hundreds of masks), or your document may never see toner.

Masks and Compound Paths

Creating masks from compound paths is especially useful when you are working with text and want several separate letters to mask a placed EPS image or a series of pictures that you created in Illustrator.

The reason that you need to transform separate objects into compound paths is that a masking object can only be one path. The topmost object of the selected objects becomes the masking object, and the others become objects within the mask. Creating a compound path from several paths makes the masking feature treat all the objects as one path and makes a masking object out of the entire compound path.

You can use compound paths for masking when you are working with objects that need to have holes as well as when you are working with text and other separate objects. Figure 9-13 was created by making one compound path from all of the parts of the window frame and using that compound path as a mask for the space scene.

Figure 9-13: Creating a compound path out of all of the parts of the window frame made the window frame a mask for the space scene

Using Compound Paths and Masks in an Illustration

I used several compound paths and masks to achieve the effects in Figure 9-14. The compound paths are the word *Tropical* and the large strips of film across the lower half of the illustration. The masks are the word *Tropical,* the binocular shape, and the outside frame of the poster.

The first set of steps explains how to create the strip of film and place the island pictures into the film. You do not use masks in this process. I make this point so that you don't think that you always have to use masks, especially when another method is easier.

STEPS: Creating Complex Compound Paths

Step 1. To create the film shape, draw a long, horizontal rectangle with the Rectangle tool and place five rounded-corner rectangles inside the long rectangle.

Step 2. To create the sprocket holes in the film, place a right-side-up triangle next to an upside-down triangle and continue placing triangles until you have a row of triangles across the top of the film.

Step 3. After you group all the triangles together, Option[Alt]-copy them (drag the triangles with the Option [Alt] key pressed, releasing the mouse button before releasing the Option [Alt] key) to create a second row of triangles along the bottom of the film.

Step 4. Select all the pieces of the film and choose Object⇨Compound Paths⇨Make (⌘-8) [Ctrl+8]. Fill the compound path with a dark purple color that is not quite black.

Step 5. This part looks as if you use a mask, but you don't need to do any masking here. Instead, place one image, size it so that it just covers the hole, and Option-copy it across the remaining holes. Select each image in turn, choose File⇨Place Art, and select a different image for each square. To complete the effect, simply bring the strip of film to the front.

Step 6. Before you place the film into the poster, group the images and the film and rotate them slightly. Grouping them prevents the hassle of selecting each one later if you need to move or transform them.

Figure 9-15 illustrates each of these steps.

Figure 9-14: This poster was created by using several different compound paths and masks

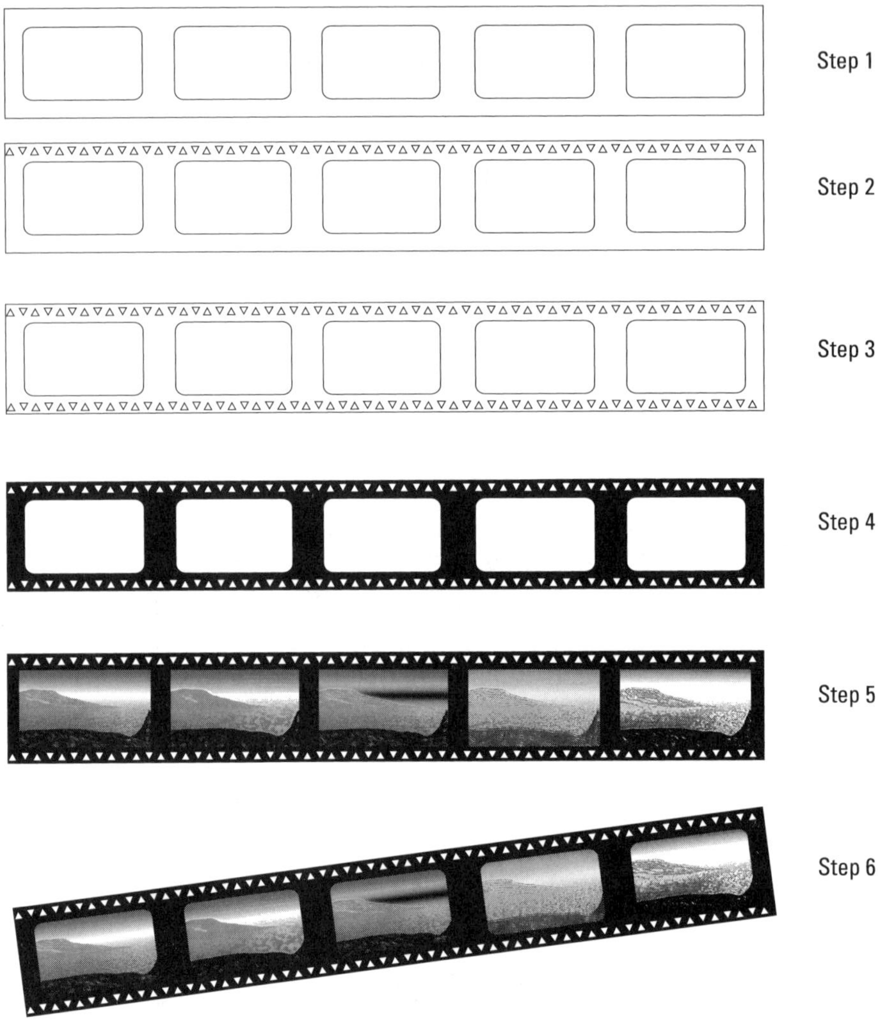

Figure 9-15: Steps for creating a complex compound path to achieve a masking effect

Instead of making the film a compound path, you could mask each of the photos and place each masked photo on top of the film. The method described in the preceding steps makes changing photos easier and takes less of a toll on the output device.

The next set of steps describes how to use the word *Tropical* to show the tropical island.

STEPS: Using Slightly Altered Images with Masks

Step 1. Place an image in the document and create a masking path for the top of it. Before you make the objects into a mask, select the image and choose Edit⇨Copy (⌘-C) [Ctrl+C]. (You use this copy in Step 3.)

Step 2. Select both the masking path and the image and choose Object⇨Mask⇨Make (⌘-7) [Ctrl+7].

You can use the outline of the masking path as a shadow by Option-copying it before you perform Steps 1 and 2. Change the Fill in the copy to Black and place the copy below and to the right of the original.

Step 3. Choose Edit⇨Paste in Back (⌘-B) [Ctrl+B] to position the image directly underneath the original image. Choose File⇨Place Art and substitute a slightly varied version of the original image. The letters stand out decisively, as the third image in Figure 9-16 shows. The image behind the word Tropical has been changed in Photoshop by using a Mosaic filter.

Figure 9-16: Using dissimilar raster images as masked objects makes the word *Tropical* stand out in the image

Summary

- Compound paths are one or more paths that Illustrator treats as a single path.
- Compound paths give you the ability to put holes in your paths.
- Changing the direction of a path via the Attributes palette can change the holes in the compound path.
- Each character of type converted to outlines consists of a compound path.
- Masks are paths that overlay other Illustrator objects, showing the objects only through the masking path.
- When using text outlines as a mask, make sure all the paths making up the text outlines are a single compound path.

Blends and Gradients

10 CHAPTER

In This Chapter

- Comparing blends to gradients
- Creating blends of color
- Creating shape blends
- Understanding complex shape blends
- Using blends created in dimensions
- The magic of stroke blending
- Creating airbrush effects
- Understanding radial and linear gradients
- Creating gradients
- Using the Gradient Vector tool
- Using the Gradient palette
- Using gradients in software that doesn't like gradients

In Illustrator, a blend is a series of paths that Illustrator creates based on two other paths. The series of paths transforms from the first path into the second path, changing Fill and Stroke attributes as it moves. Gradients are Fills that change from one color to another in either linear or radial form.

Windows Update

Gradients are entirely new to Illustrator 7, and users of Version 4.1 will find them much easier to use than blends for basic linear and radial vignettes. The Gradient Vector tool is also new. This tool allows you to change the direction, length, and highlight of gradients in objects.

Understanding Blends and Gradients

Blends and gradients, at first glance, seem to do the same things but in different ways — so why have both? The Blend tool, moreover, seems to be much harder to use than the Gradient Vector tool. On the surface, it seems that more can be done with gradients than with blends. Blends are limited to two colors; gradients can have tons of colors. Blends take a long time to redraw; gradients take a fraction of the time.

After all, if gradients are so much easier to use and produce so much better results, is it really necessary to have a Blend tool? I've been asked this question quite often by students, clients, and the occasional passerby, and they seem to have a good point at first. Upon further study, however, it becomes apparent that blends are quite different from gradients, both in form and function.

Gradients are used only as Fills for paths. Gradients can be either linear or radial, meaning that color can change from side to side, top to bottom, or from the center to the outside. Every gradient can have as many distinct colors in it as you can create, limited only by RAM.

Blends, on the other hand, are series of transformed paths between two *end paths.* The paths between the end paths mutate from one end path into the other. All the attributes of the end paths change throughout the transformed paths, including shape, size, and all Paint Style attributes. The major drawback is that you can only blend two colors at a time. Of course, you can blend between 34 different pairs of end paths, but that would be a little time-consuming, especially when you can use gradients to make the task much easier and quicker.

To summarize, gradients are an easier way to create blends that change only in color, not in shape or size. Figure 10-1 shows how you can use blends and gradients to create a similar result.

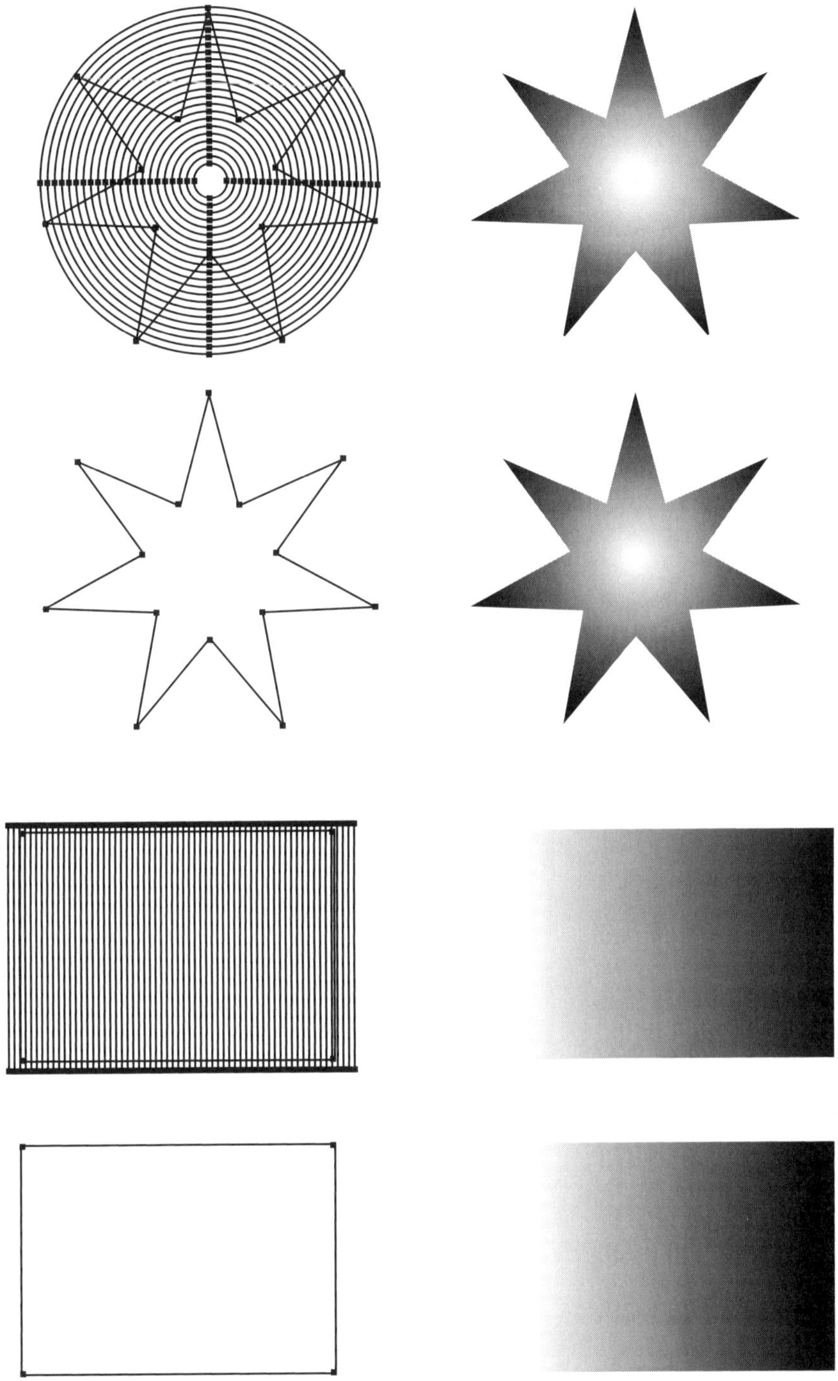

Figure 10-1: Each example uses a blend or a gradient. The left side shows the image in Artwork mode; the right side shows the Preview mode.

If you keep in mind that gradients work only with color, not with shapes, you should already have an idea of when to use which function. Linear and radial gradients usually look better than their blended counterparts because the quality is better and more colors can be added and manipulated. Changes to color are also more easily accomplished with gradients than with blends. In addition, changes to angles and the placements of the gradients are much easier to make than analogous position changes with blends.

One drawback to using gradients is their "computery" look. Gradients are exact blends that are even from start to finish. Of course, with a little practice, additional colors or tints can be added, and the midpoint balance between two adjacent colors can be offset, giving the blend a more natural look. In general, though, realistic effects aren't all that easy to achieve with gradients.

Blends, on the other hand, can be incredibly flexible when it comes to creating photo-realistic changes in color, if you plan ahead. Changes to blends aren't really changes at all; instead, they are deletions of the transformed objects and changes in the attributes of the end paths. If you know what you want, blending colors can take on an incredibly realistic look by changing the shapes of the blend's end paths just slightly.

But even more useful than creating realistic changes in color is blending's capability to transform shapes from one shape to another, as shown in the examples in Figure 10-2. With a bit of practice (and the information in this chapter), you can transform any illustration into another illustration. There is a limit to the complexity of the illustrations that can be transformed, but the limit is due more to the time it takes to create the blends than to limitations inherent in Illustrator.

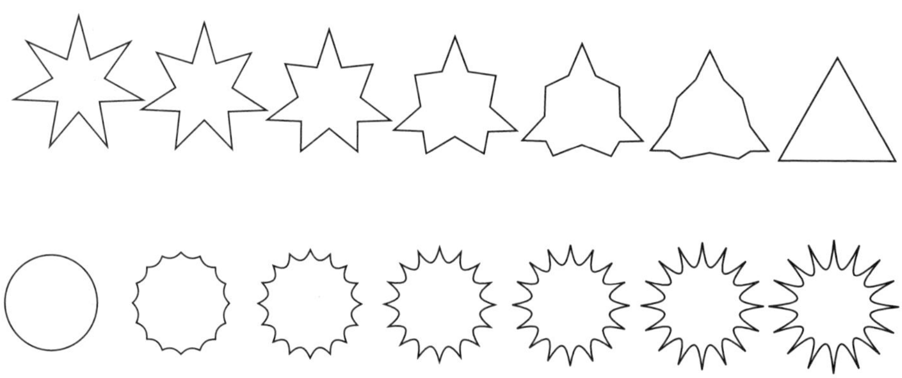

Figure 10-2: Blending to transform a shape

Because blends work on both Stroke and Fill attributes of objects, some really exciting effects can be created that aren't possible by using any other technique, electronic or traditional.

Blends

In past versions of Illustrator, blends were used predominantly for what gradients are used for now: to blend between different colors, normally just two different colors. But some artists took it upon themselves to stretch the capabilities of the Blend tool to create fantastic effects that amazed even the creators of the tool.

Originally, Adobe marketed the Blend tool (new to Version 88) as a tool with the primary purpose of transforming shapes, not blending colors. Yeah, that's cool, designers said, but instead they used the tool for blending colors to create what were known as vignettes, or what traditional artists called gradients.

The Blend tool creates in-between steps in the area between two paths, where the paint style and shape of one path transform themselves into the paint style and shape of the second path.

For the most part, the blending function really hasn't changed since Version 88 was released more than nine years ago. Unfortunately, Adobe (or Macromedia, which has a similar tool in FreeHand) never emphasized the incredible variations of effects that can be achieved with the Blend tool. In combination with some of the filters available in Illustrator, some pretty amazing effects are now possible.

> The most noticeable change to the way the Blend tool works was in Version 3, when Illustrator began to calculate blend steps automatically and put the best number relative to color changes in the Steps field. This change was an indication that Adobe realized more people were using the blending function for color blends than shape blends. In Version 5 of Illustrator, instead of making the Blend tool better, Adobe opted to create the Gradient feature, which does what most people were using the Blend tool for in previous versions. Once again, the emphasis on the Blend tool is on shape transformation, rather than as a way to create gradients.

Although any blend takes into account both color and shape, in this chapter I treat color and shape separately because people using the Blend tool are often trying to obtain *either* a color effect *or* a shape effect, rather than both at once.

The Blend tool is the tool used to create blends, which are a group of paths (commonly referred to as *blend steps*) that change in shape and color as each path is created closer to the opposite *end path.*

STEPS: Creating a Basic Blend

Step 1. Using the Rectangle tool, create a small (1-inch) vertical rectangle. With the Selection tool, Option[Alt]-copy the path a few inches to the side. Press Shift as you drag horizontally to constrain the movement of the path.

Step 2. On the left rectangle, change the Fill to Black and the Stroke to None. Change the right rectangle to a Fill of White and a Stroke of None.

Step 3. Select both paths and choose the Blend tool (press the B key). Click the top-left point of the left path and then the top-left point of the right path. This step tells Illustrator to blend between these two paths, and it uses the two Anchor Points as reference. The Blend dialog box appears after the second click.

Step 4. Click OK in the Blend dialog box. A mass of paths is created between the two end paths, all of them selected. Press ⌘-Shift-A [Ctrl+Shift+A] to deselect all selected paths. The blend is made up of a total of 256 paths, including the two end paths. Each path is a slightly different tint of black.

You must use the Blend tool to click one point on each of two different paths, and those points must have been previously selected. Both paths must be open paths or closed paths. If the paths are open paths, only End Points can be clicked.

CAUTION: You should always click the corresponding points on both end paths. Figure 10-3 shows what can happen when opposite points are selected.

Before you click any paths, the cursor looks like a crosshair. After the first click of the Blend tool, the cursor looks like a crosshair with three dots after it. After the second point has been clicked, the Blend dialog box appears.

Creating Linear Blends

Color blends are made by creating two end paths, usually identical in shape and size, giving each path different Paint Style attributes, and creating a series of steps between them with the Blend tool. The more end paths that are created, the more colors you can create. Figure 10-4 shows the steps needed to create a basic linear blend.

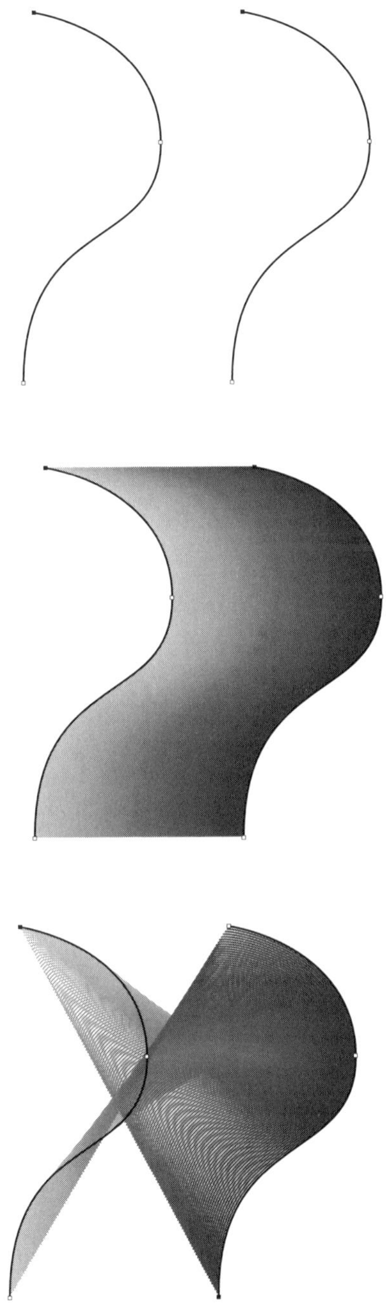

Figure 10-3: Selecting the correct points (middle) and the wrong points (bottom) to create a blend

Figure 10-4: The steps needed to create a linear blend

The examples in this chapter are easier to understand when you are working in Preview mode.

STEPS: Creating a Basic Linear Blend

Step 1. Draw a vertical path with the Pen tool. Give it a Fill of None and a Stroke of 2 points Black.

Step 2. Option[Alt]-copy the path to the right. Give the new path a Stroke of 2 points White.

Step 3. Select both paths. With the Blend tool, click the top point on the left path and then the top point on the right path. When the Blend dialog box appears, click OK.

Step 4. Deselect all (⌘-Shift-A) [Ctrl+Shift+A] to see the result.

Whenever you create a blend that you think is final, stop and select the blend steps (which are already grouped together) and the two end paths, and group them all together. This step makes selecting the entire blend easier in the future, especially if you use the Group Selection tool.

Multiple Colors with Linear Blends

To create linear blends that have multiple colors, you must create intermediate end paths, one for each additional color within the blend.

STEPS: Creating Multiple Color Blends

Step 1. Create two end paths at the edges of where you want the entire blend to begin and end. Don't worry about colors at this time.

Step 2. Select the two end paths and click the top point in each of them. In the Step field in the Blend dialog box, enter the number of additional colors you will be adding to the blend and click OK. For instance, if you want a blend to go Blue, Yellow, Red, Black, Green, you would enter **3** in the Step field because there are three colors between the two end colors. For my example, I entered 3 to create three evenly spaced paths between the two end paths.

Step 3. Ungroup the newly created Strokes, color each of the Strokes of the paths differently, and give them a weight of 2 points. Select the first two paths and blend them together.

Step 4. Select the next pair and blend the next pair together. Continue blending until all the paths have been blended together. The result should look like the blend of colors at the bottom of Figure 10-5.

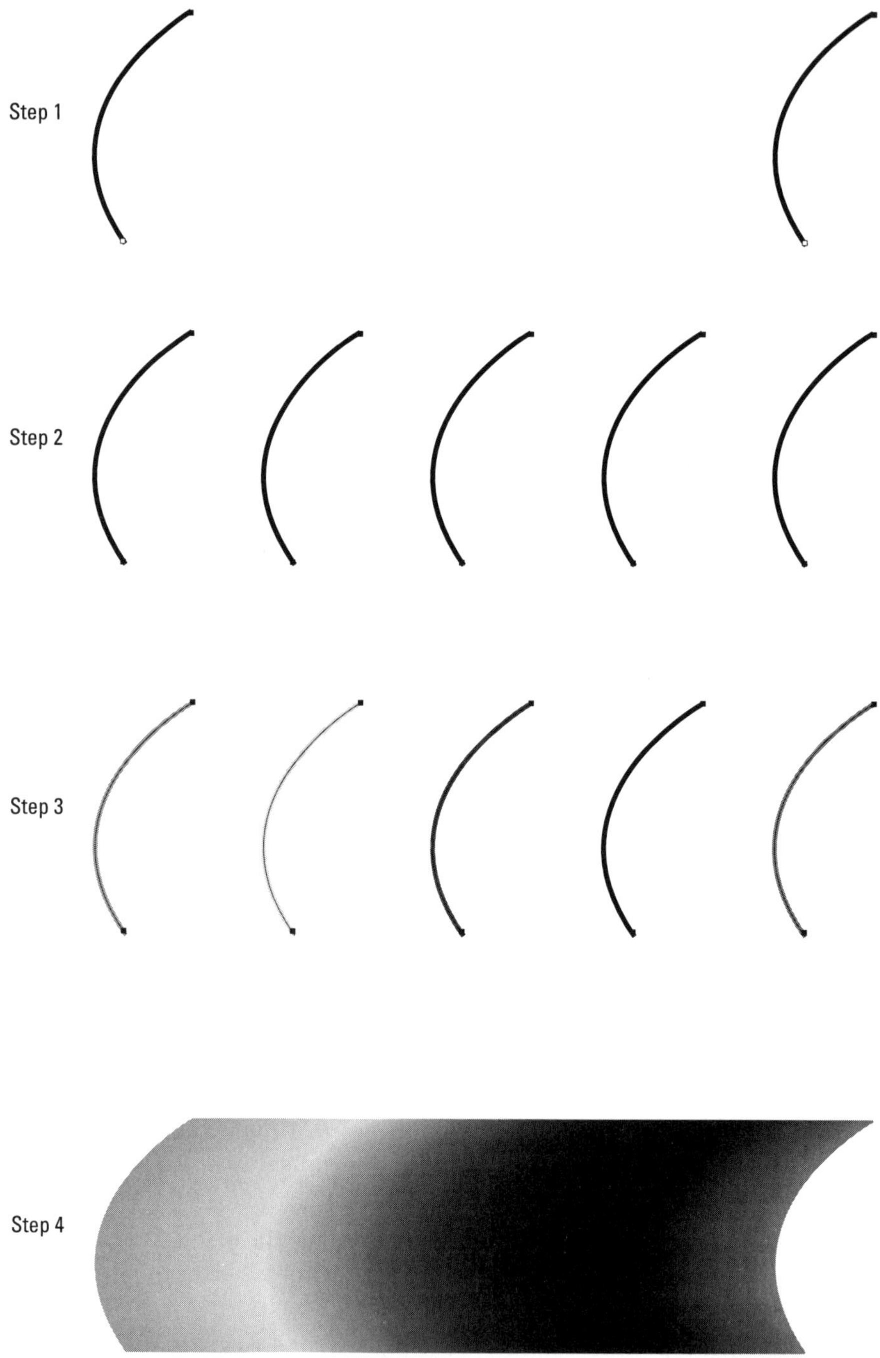

Figure 10-5: The steps to create a multiple-color linear blend

Group all the end paths to all the blends after creating them. This step makes selecting the multiple color blend easy with the Group Selection tool.

Nonlinear Blends

End paths created with two End Points that make up blends don't have to be just horizontal or vertical. And when you create multiple color blends, the intermediate end paths don't have to be aligned in the same way as the end paths are aligned.

Careful setup of intermediate blends can create many interesting effects, such as circular and wavy appearances, all created with straight paths.

End paths that cross usually produce undesirable effects. If carefully constructed, however, the resulting blends can be quite intriguing. Blending crossed end paths creates the appearance of a three-dimensional blend, where one of the end paths blends "up" into the other.

To create nonlinear blends, set up the end paths and either rotate them or change their orientation by using the Direct Selection tool on one of the End Points. Then blend from one end path to the intermediate end paths and then to the other end path. Figure 10-6 shows two examples of nonlinear blends.

Masking Blends

Blends by themselves are great, but when masked by other paths, they can really take on a life of their own. To illustrate this concept, use the following steps to create a color wheel (see Figure 10-7).

STEPS: Creating a Color Wheel

Step 1. Using the Pen tool, draw a straight segment and give it a 2-point Green (100% Cyan, 100% Yellow) Stroke and a Fill of None in the Paint Style palette.

Step 2. Choose the Rotate tool, press Option [Alt], and click one End Point of the path to set the origin. Type in **60°** for the angle in the Rotate dialog box and press the Copy button (Option[Alt]-Return). This procedure creates a copy of the Stroke at a 60° angle, with one End Point directly on top of one of the existing ones.

(continued)

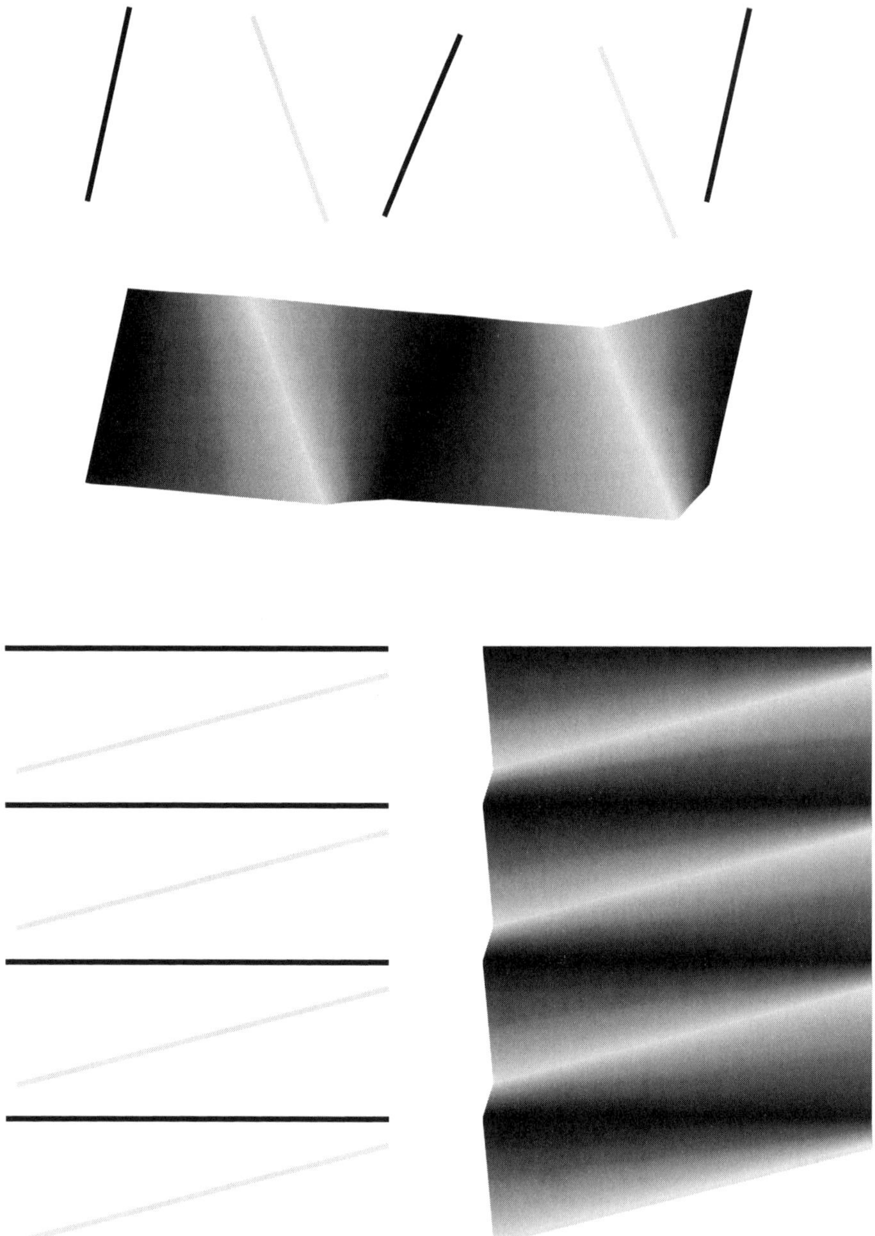

Figure 10-6: Blending end paths together to create a nonlinear blend

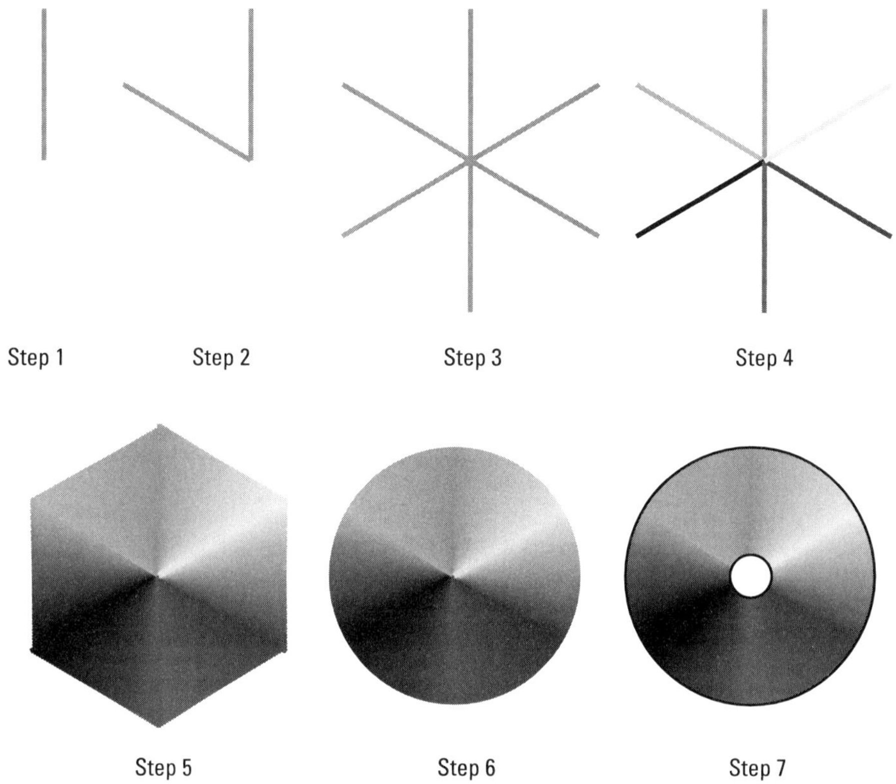

Figure 10-7: Creating a black-and-white color wheel

STEPS: *(continued)*

Step 3. Choose Object⇨Transform⇨Transform Again (⌘-D) [Ctrl+D]. Another Stroke is created at a 60° angle from the second. Continue to choose Transform Again until there are six Strokes. Each of these Strokes is used as an end path.

Step 4. Color each Stroke as follows, moving clockwise: 1. Green (100% Cyan, 100% Yellow); 2. Yellow (100% Yellow); 3. Red (100% Magenta, 100% Yellow); 4. Magenta (100% Magenta); 5. Blue (100% Cyan, 100% Magenta); 6. Cyan (100% Cyan).

Step 5. Blend each pair of end paths together, a pair at a time. Click the outermost points to get the best results. When you are finished blending all the end paths together, the result is a beautifully colored hexagon. Because of the shape, the end paths really stand out as points on the hexagon.

(continued)

STEPS: *(continued)*

Step 6. To complete the illusion of a perfect color wheel, the blend needs to be in the shape of a circle. Using the Ellipse tool, draw a circle so that the edges are just inside the flat sides of the hexagon, with its center corresponding to the center of the hexagon. This process is easiest to do by Option[Alt]-clicking with the Ellipse tool at the center of the hexagon and pressing the Shift key as the oval is being drawn. Select the circle, the blend steps, and the end paths, and choose Object⇨Masks⇨Make (⌘-7) [Ctrl+7].

Step 7. For a more realistic color-wheel effect (one that resembles Apple's color wheel), create a Black Stroke on the mask and a small circle at the center that has a Fill of White and a Stroke of Black.

POWER TIP: Blends can be masked with any object. For some really great effects, mask your blends with text (converted to outlines).

New and Improved Pseudolinear Blends

There is very little difference in the end product of straight-line linear blends and linear gradients. Both are very "computery" looking, but gradients are easier to create. The important thing about blends is that the end paths of linear blends *don't have to be straight lines.* This blend capability makes all the difference in the world and is why using linear blends takes on a really cool aspect.

If you use a smoothly curving line, the blend takes on a fluidity and life of its own, gently caressing the objects it is behind, next to, or masked by. The curves (especially if the end paths are masked off) are not always visible to the eye, and this creates an effect that is both realistic and surreal, giving depth to your illustration in a way that flat linear blends can't.

Instead of smoothly curving lines, try broken, jagged paths, which can add fierce highlights to a blend. Once again, this type of blend is even more effective when the end paths are masked off. Figure 10-8 shows two examples of masked pseudolinear blends.

CAUTION: When using end paths that have more than two Anchor Points, be sure to click the same End Point on each path. Clicking an Anchor Point that is not an End Point results in a dialog box telling you to . . . click an End Point. If you click different End Points, the result resembles an X shape, which is usually undesirable (as previously shown in Figure 10-3).

Figure 10-8: Masked pseudolinear blends

Guidelines for Creating Color Linear Blends

Although the preceding procedure should have gone nice and smoothly with no problems, you should follow these guidelines when creating blends to get good results each time you print:

- For linear blends, use rectangles with only four Anchor Points. If you use a shape with any more Anchor Points or if you use a curved shape with any paths that aren't perfectly straight, you get extra information that isn't needed to create the blend, and printing takes much longer than usual. You *can* use basic 2-point paths, but printing could take longer than if you use rectangles.

Twisted Blends

Daphne: My blends are really strange.

Toulouse: How so?

Daphne: Well, they keep bunching up and twisting.

Toulouse: What are you blending from and to?

Daphne: Two different paths.

Toulouse: But they have the same number of points, right?

Daphne: Uh...heh....

Toulouse: You need either (1) the same number of points on your end paths or (2) the same number of points selected on those end paths.

Daphne: Or they'll twist. Gotcha.

- When creating linear blends, use one rectangle per end path and color the Fills of the paths, not the Strokes. Coloring the Strokes may appear to work, but it usually results in a moiré pattern when printed. Make sure that the Stroke is set to None, regardless of what the Fill is.
- Don't change the number that appears in the Steps text field in the Blend dialog box. Making the number higher creates additional paths that can't be printed; making the number lower can result in banding when printed (see the "Avoiding Banding" sidebar, later in this chapter).

End Paths for Linear Blends

In the previous linear blend example, I used lines with Stroke weights to create the blend. You can also use rectangles with Fills and no Strokes and achieve pretty much the same printed result. Figure 10-9 shows both lines and rectangles used for end paths.

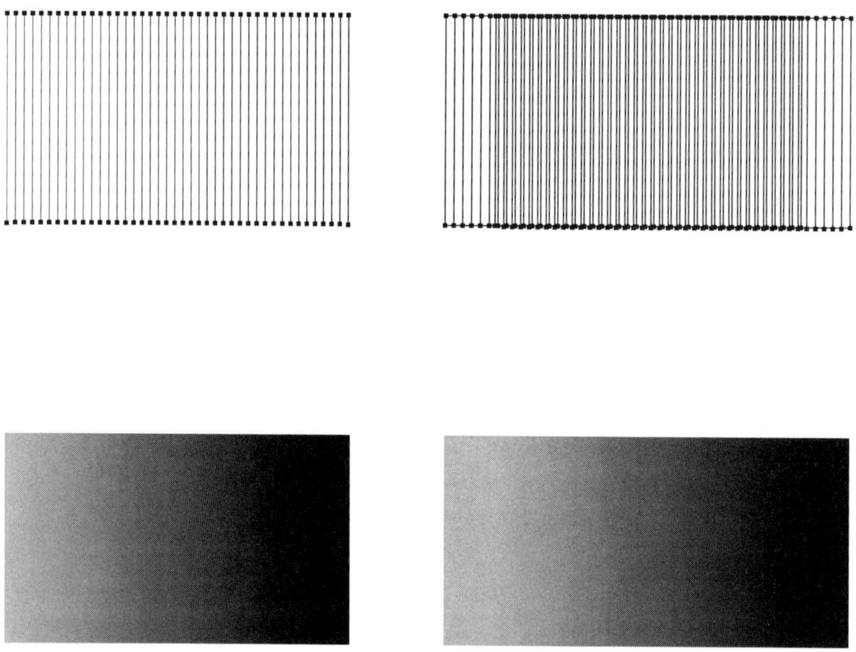

Figure 10-9: Lines (left) and rectangles (right) used for end paths in both artwork and final output

There is no good reason to use a rectangle as an end path instead of a single line with two End Points (at least, none that I can dig up). In fact, lines are better than rectangles for three reasons: First, lines use half as much information as rectangles because there are two Anchor Points on a line while there are four on a rectangle. Second, the width of a line (Stroke weight) is much easier to change after the blend has been created (just select the lines and enter a new weight in the Paint Style palette) than the width of rectangles (you would have to use the Scale Each filter). Third, creating a linear blend with lines (Strokes) creates a thick mess of paths, but creating a linear blend with rectangles creates a thicker mess, so much so that it is difficult to select specific rectangles.

An open path cannot be blended with a closed path and vice versa. Open paths can be blended to other open paths, as long as you click an End Point on each with the Blend tool. Closed paths can be blended with another closed path.

Calculating the Number of Steps

Whenever you create a blend, Illustrator provides a default value in the Steps text field that assumes you are going to be printing your illustration to an Imagesetter or other high-resolution device capable of printing all 256 levels of gray that PostScript allows.

The formula Illustrator uses is quite simple. It takes the largest change that any one color goes through from end path to end path and multiplies that percentage by 256. The formula looks like this: 256 × largest color change % = the number of steps to be created.

For instance, using our linear blend example, the difference in tint values is 100% (100% – 0% = 100%). Multiply 100% by 256, and you get 256. Because the total number of grays must be 256 or fewer, only 254 were created. When added to the two ends, there are 256 tints.

In the second example, where the first line was changed to a 10% Stroke, the difference in tint values is 10% (10% – 0% = 10%). 10% × 256 is 26, the number of steps Illustrator calculates.

In a process color example, if the first end path is 20% Cyan, 100% Magenta, and 40% Yellow, and the second end path is 60% Cyan, 50% Magenta, and 0% Yellow, the largest difference in any one color is Cyan (100% – 50% = 50%). 50% × 256 is 128, the number of steps created.

Avoiding Banding

The graphic artist's worst nightmare: Smooth blends and gradations turn into large chunks of tints, as shown in the accompanying figure, and suddenly get darker or lighter instead of staying nice and smooth. *Banding*, as this nightmare is called, is an area of a blend where the difference from one tint to the next changes abruptly and displays a defining line showing the difference between the two tints. Individual tints appear as solid areas called *bands*.

Avoiding banding is easier when you know what is causing it. Usually one of three things in Illustrator is the cause: too few blend steps, too much of a distance between end paths, or too little variation in the colors of the end paths. Preventing banding due to any of these causes depends on the line screen setting and the capability of your printer to print it.

These causes pretty much make sense. Take the linear blend example in a previous section. If there are only three intermediate steps between end paths, there will be only five colors in the blend, thus creating five bands. If the end paths are each on one side of a 17-inch span, each blend step created would take up the 5 points of width of the Stroke, making each shade of gray 5 points wide, a noticeable size. If the color on the left were 10% Black instead of 100% Black, there would be only 26 color steps between the two end paths.

So to avoid banding, use the recommended number of steps over a short area with a great variation of color.

If you find it hard to fix the banding problem and the blend is made of process colors, try adding a small amount of an unused color (Black, for instance) to cover up the banding breaks. A 5 percent to 30 percent change over distances may provide just enough dots to hide those bands. Keeping this in mind, there is more chance for banding if you use the same tints for different process colors. Alter the tint values for one of the colors at one of the end paths just a little, and this alteration will stagger the bands enough to remove them from sight.

See "Calculating the Number of Steps" earlier in this chapter for more information on banding.

But, of course, not everything you create is output on an Imagesetter. Your laser printer, for example, cannot print out 256 grays, unless the line screen is set extremely low. To determine how many grays your laser printer can produce, you need to know both the dpi and the line screen. In some software packages, you can specify the line screen, but unless the printer is a high-end model, it is usually difficult to specify or change the dpi. Use the following formula to find out how many grays your printer can produce:

```
(dpi/line screen) x (dpi/line screen) = number of grays
```

For a 300-dpi printer with a typical (for 300 dpi) line screen of 53, the formula looks like this:

```
(300/53) x (300/53) = 5.66 x 5.66 = 32
```

A 400-dpi printer at a line screen of 71 has the following formula:

```
(400/65) x (400/65) = 6.15 x 6.14 = 38
```

A 600-dpi printer at 75 lines per inch uses this formula:

```
(600/75) x (600/75) = 8 x 8 = 64
```

Sometimes you may want to reduce the number of blend steps in a blend from the default because either your printer can't display that many grays or the distance from one end path to another is extremely small (see "Airbrushing and the Magic of Stroke Blends," later in this chapter).

When reducing the number of blends, start by dividing the default by 2 and then continue dividing by 2 until you have a number of steps that you are comfortable with. If you aren't sure how many steps you need, do a quick test of just that blend with different numbers of steps specified and print it out. If you are going to an Imagesetter, don't divide by 2 more than twice, or banding (oh no!) can occur.

Creating Radial Blends

To create a radial blend, make a circle about 2 inches in diameter, Filled with 100% Black. Make a smaller circle inside the larger circle and Fill it with White. Select both shapes, click the point at the top of the larger circle, and then click the point at the top of the smaller circle. Click OK in the Blend dialog box and deselect.

Radial blends can be created with objects other than circles. In Figure 10-10, the radial blend was created with a star.

As with most other blends, when blending from two identically shaped end paths, always click the Anchor Point in the same position on each object. Figure 10-10 shows the difference between clicking the Anchor Points in the same position and clicking those that are not in the same position.

One of the nice things about creating radial blends manually (not using the gradient feature) is that by changing the location and the size of the inner object, the gradient can be made to look vastly different. The larger the inner object, the smaller the blended area.

The Gradient feature enables you to change the highlight point on a radial Gradient without changing the source, or angle, of the highlight.

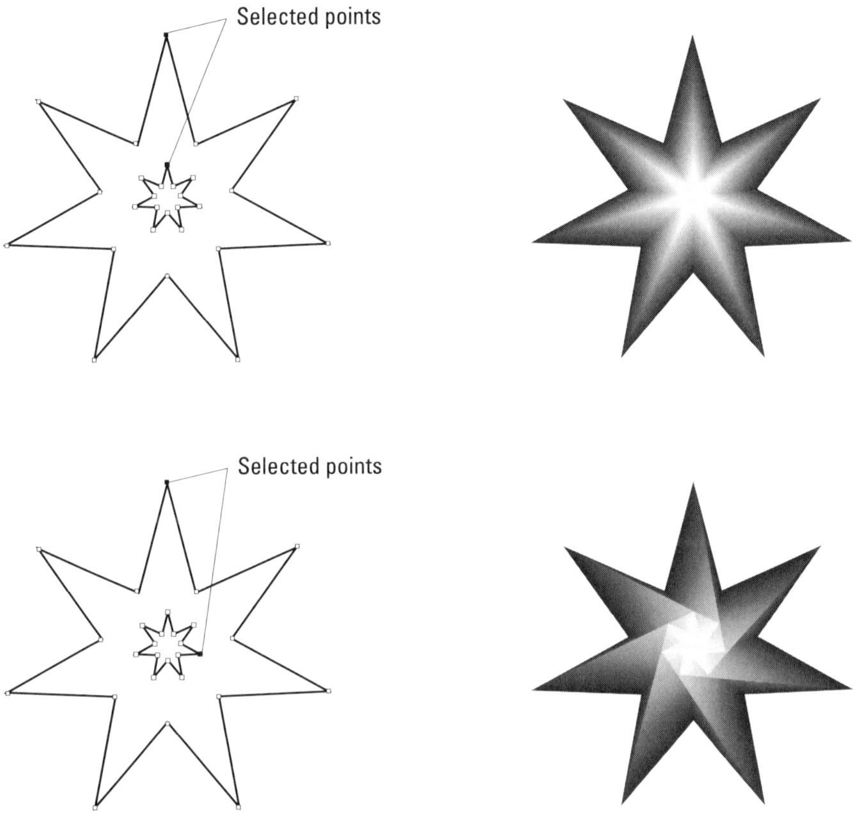

Figure 10-10: Each example uses a blend or a gradient. The left side shows the image in Artwork mode; the right side shows the Preview mode.

Creating Shape Blends

The difference between color blends and shape blends is in their emphasis. Color blends emphasize a color change; shape blends emphasize blending between different shapes.

There are a number of things to keep in mind when creating the end paths that form a shape blend. Both paths must be either open or closed. If open, only End Points can be clicked to blend between the two paths. If the shapes also change color, be sure to follow the guidelines in the preceding section related to color blends.

For best results, both paths should have the same number of Anchor Points selected before blending, and the selected points should be in a relatively similar location. Illustrator pairs up points on end paths and the segments between them so that when it creates the blend steps, the lines are in about the same position.

Shape Blend #1: Computer Vents

Look on the side of your monitor or on the side of a computer or hard drive case. You will undoubtedly see vents or simulated vents used for design purposes running back along these items. This type of blend (changing the angle of straight lines) is the most basic of shape blends and is rather easy to create, so I've added an extra tip at the end of this section to make these blends more realistic. Figure 10-11 shows the process for creating computer vents.

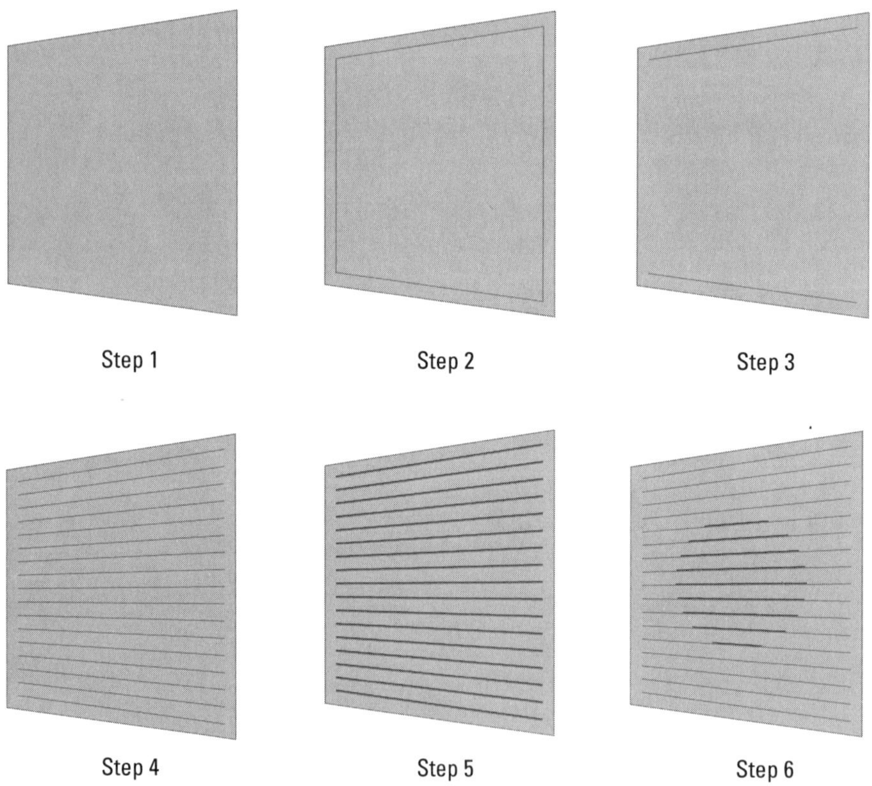

Figure 10-11: A computer vent blend

STEPS: Creating Computer Vents

Step 1. Draw a rectangular shape that has been distorted to appear like the side of your monitor (use the Pen tool). Choose a Fill of 25% Black and a Stroke of 1/2 point, 50% Black.

Step 2. Select the shape and double-click the Scale tool. Enter 90% in the Uniform field of the Scale dialog box and click Copy (Option[Alt]-Return).

Step 3. With the Direct Selection tool, select and delete the two vertical segments of the shape. Select both of the horizontal segments and change the Fill to None.

Step 4. Blend the two paths together with 15 steps. One side of a monitor is now complete.

Step 5. Select all the paths and copy them up 1/2 point by using the Copy button in the Move dialog box. Group the paths and change the Stroke to 75% gray.

Step 6. Draw a circle over the center of the group and select the group and the circle. Choose Object⇨Masks⇨Make, and you have a "real" vent in the simulated one.

Shape Blend #2: Circle to Star

The preceding blend slowly transformed one path to another, but the paths were basically the same. The real power of the Blend tool is evident when it is used to generate intermediate paths between two totally different, distinct paths, as in the following example.

STEPS: Blending a Circle to a Star

Step 1. Create a 1-inch circle with the Ellipse tool. Create a 5-point star by clicking with the Star tool and entering **5** in the Points text field. Enter **.19"** in the First Radius text field and **.5"** in the Second Radius text field.

Step 2. Fill both shapes with a color (I used light gray) and give each of them a 2-point Stroke of another color. Change the view to Fit In Window (⌘-0) [Ctrl+0] and place the two objects as far apart on-screen as possible.

(continued)

STEPS: ***(continued)***

Step 3. Choose the Direct Selection tool and select the entire circle. Press the Shift key and click four points on the star that closely match the four on the circle. If you accidentally click a point that you decide should not be selected, just click it again with the Direct Selection tool. As long as the Shift key is pressed, the tool deselects only that point while all the other points remain selected.

Step 4. After four points are selected on both the circle and the star, blend them together with the Blend tool. Click the corresponding points on each, such as the topmost point, and enter **7** in the Steps dialog box.

Step 5. To see what happens if a different number of points are selected on each path, select both paths with the Selection tool. Click the topmost point of the circle with the Blend tool and then click the topmost point of the star. In the Blend dialog box, enter **7** in the Steps text field and then click OK. The star appears to work its way out of a growth on the circle. Figure 10-12 shows the difference between blending without corresponding Anchor Points selected and with corresponding Anchor Points selected.

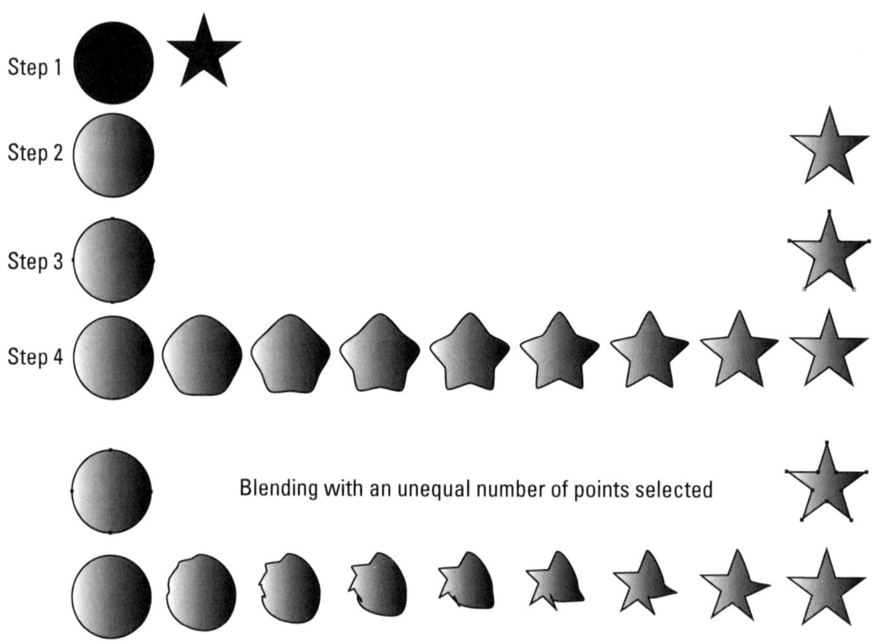

Figure 10-12: The difference between selecting the same number of Anchor Points on each path in a shape blend (top) and selecting a different number of Anchor Points on each path (bottom)

Another way to get a smooth transformation between two paths with different numbers of Anchor Points is to add Anchor Points strategically to the path with fewer points. By selecting both of the paths with the Selection tool, you can get results that are similar to selecting similarly positioned points. The results can actually be better when Anchor Points are added because they can be added in positions that correspond to the Anchor Points on the other path.

Complex-Shape Blending

Whenever a shape is complex (that is, it isn't a perfectly symmetrical shape, such as a circle or a star), a number of things may have to be done to create realistic and eye-pleasing effects. Figure 10-13 shows a complex-shape blend.

Figure 10-13: Complex shape blending

One thing you can do to make the blend better is to add or remove Anchor Points from the end paths. Even if the same number of points are selected and those points are in similar areas on each path, the results can be anything but acceptable.

The Add Anchor Point and Delete Anchor Point tools become quite useful here. By adding points in strategic locations, you can often fool Illustrator into creating an accurate blend; otherwise, the blend steps can resemble a total disaster.

CAUTION: As a general rule, it is less disturbing to the composition of the graphic to add Anchor Points than to remove them. On most paths, removing any Anchor Points changes the shape of the path dramatically.

Another method of getting the paths to blend more accurately is to shorten them by splitting a long, complex path into one or two smaller sections that aren't nearly as complex. After the blends are finished — each path has to be blended separately and can't all be done at once — it takes just a few seconds to go through and Average and Join (⌘-Option-Shift-J) [Ctrl+Alt+Shift+J] the End Points of the paths back together.

And then there is the third method of blending paths, which is described in the next section.

Shape Blend #3: Cheating

There are times when blending together two different shapes produces results that end up being just plain grotesque no matter what you do with the Anchor Points. In these cases, a little fixing (which I will call "cheating") is in order: the more blend steps you need, the more you benefit from this method.

To get more aesthetically pleasing results from shape blending, it is sometimes easier to create one or more intermediate (middle) end paths. Instead of blending from end to end, you blend from end to middle and then middle to end. Keep in mind that the middle should contain aspects of both end paths. Figure 10-14 shows how a blend would naturally appear (Steps 1 and 2) and how it appears after cheating (Steps 3 through 7).

Remember, cheating is apparent only to you. The client or your boss will never know from seeing the final output that the results were forced. Surprisingly, many illustrators actually feel guilty about creating another end path by using this method. If you can't live with yourself, by all means continue trying to select just the right points. However, I'll let you in on a secret: Adobe cheats too. In one of the original ads for Illustrator 88 and in the accompanying videotape (watch it and check for the poor splicing!), you see an *S* transformed into a swan. Of course, in

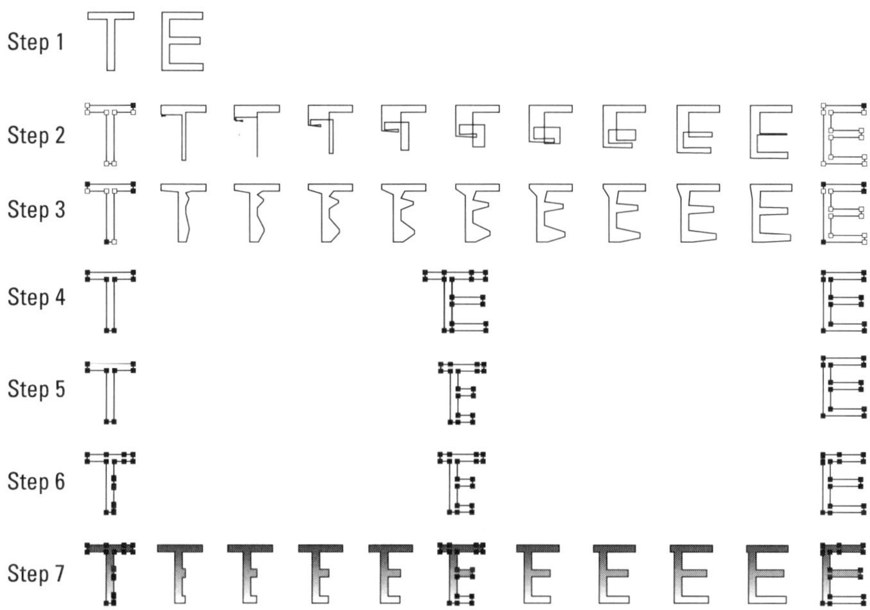

Figure 10-14: Blending a *T* to an *E* without cheating (Steps 1 and 2) and with cheating (Steps 3 through 7)

Adobe's case, it was misrepresenting the capabilities of the Blend tool by making it look as if the tool automatically made eye-pleasing middle paths when, in reality, the "blended" paths were only loosely based on the real blends.

STEPS: Creating Complex Shape Blends by Cheating

Step 1. In this example, create a text area with a 100-point T and E in any font, (a sans serif font, such as Helvetica, is easier than a serif one, such as Times). Select the type with a Selection tool and choose Type⇨Create Outlines (⌘-Shift-O) [Ctrl+Shift+O]. You are blending between these two letters. Change the Fill to None and the Stroke to 1-point Black.

Step 2. Choose View⇨Fit in Window (⌘-0) [Ctrl+0] and put each letter on either side of the document. Select both of them with the regular Selection tool and then blend them together with ten steps by choosing the upper-right point in each object. The results are quite ugly. A common shape-blending problem, called *blend arcing,* occurs when you choose very few or no Anchor Points on either the top or bottom of end paths. In this case, you selected an Anchor Point along the top and no Anchor Points along the bottom, so the blend arc formed along the bottom of the letters.

(continued)

STEPS: *(continued)*

Step 3. Undo the blend. A better blending effect can be achieved by selecting the two upper-right points, the upper-left point, and the lower-left point of the *T* and the *E* (previously shown in Figure 10-14), but then the blend takes on an ugly, lumpy look.

Step 4. Undo the blend again. The best thing to do in this case is to create an intermediate end path. Copy the *E* and *T* and place them over the top of each other between the two original letters.

Step 5. Select the overlapping letters and choose Object⇨Pathfinder⇨Unite. The two paths merge into one. Bring in the horizontal bars about halfway by using the Direct Selection tool.

Step 6. Select both the *T* and the merged letters. Make sure that there are corresponding points for each path by adding Anchor Points to the *T* with the Add Anchor Point tool. Both paths should have the same number of Anchor Points. Add corresponding Anchor Points to the *E,* as well.

Step 7. Blend the *T* to the merged path with the Blend tool by clicking the lower-right point of each and creating four steps. Blend the *E* to the merged path by clicking the lower-right point of each and creating four steps. The transformation should be almost perfect. If necessary, individual points can be touched up with the Direct Selection tool.

POWER TIP

Some really interesting effects can be achieved by using the Rotate tool or the Rotate Portion of the Transform Each filter, which makes the paths appear to spin as they are transforming from one shape into another. Using these tools also serves to mask any anomalies in the blend steps.

Creating Realism with Shape Blends

To create a realistic effect with shape blends, the paths used to create the blends need to resemble objects you see in life. Take a look around you and try to find any solid-colored object — doesn't the color appear to change from one part of the object to another? Shadows and reflections are everywhere. Colors change gradually from light to dark, not in straight lines but in smooth, rounded curves.

Blends can be used to simulate reflections and shadows. Reflections are usually created with shape blends; shadows are usually created with Stroke blends.

In the following example, I show you how to simulate reflections with shape blends. This procedure is a little tricky for any artist because a reflection is determined by the environment. The artwork you create will be viewed in any number of environments, so the reflections have to compensate for these differences. Fortunately, unless you are creating a mirror angled directly at the viewer (impossible, even if you know who the viewer is in advance), you can get the person seeing the artwork to perceive reflection without really being aware of it.

The chromelike type in the word DON'T in Figure 10-15 was created by masking shape blends designed to look like a reflective surface.

STEPS: Creating Muted Reflective Surfaces in Type

Step 1. Type the word or words you want to use for masking the reflective surface. The typeface and the word itself have an impact on how the finished artwork is perceived. I chose the word *DON'T* and the typeface Madrone. I also did a great deal of tracking and kerning so that all the letters touched, which makes the word look like one piece of material. In addition, I used baseline shift to move the apostrophe up several points.

Step 2. Choose Type➪Create Outlines (⌘-Shift-O) [Ctrl+Shift+O]. Choose a Fill of White for the text and a Stroke of Black. At this point, most of the serifs on the letters overlap.

Step 3. Select all the letters and choose Object➪Pathfinder➪Unite. This command gets rid of any unsightly seams between the letters. Create a rectangle and place it behind the letters.

(continued)

Complex Realistic Blends

Freddy: My blends aren't... well, they look fake.

Toulouse: So, they don't look like real blends?

Freddy: No, they don't look *real.*

Toulouse: An important key to getting shape blends to look really good is to blend from the background color of the shape to the first blend, or to make that first blend the background color.

Freddy: What'll that do?

Toulouse: That'll flow the blend smoothly into the background, so you can't tell exactly where the blend starts and stops.

STEPS: *(continued)*

Step 4. Set the Curve Fitting Tolerance option to 2 in the General Preferences dialog box (Object⇨Preferences⇨General, ⌘-K [Ctrl+K]). Using the Pencil tool, draw a horizontal line from left to right across the rectangle. With a low Curve Fitting Tolerance setting, this step should result in a path with many points.

Step 5. Option[Alt]-copy several paths from the original down to the bottom of the rectangle. An easy way to copy the paths is to Option[Alt]-drag down just a bit and then choose Object⇨Transform⇨Transform Again (⌘-D) [Ctrl+D] several times. In my example, I created five more paths. With the Direct Selection tool, randomly move around individual Anchor Points and direction points on each path, but try to avoid overlapping paths. I left the third and fourth paths virtually identical and kept them close together so that there would be a swift change in color that brings out a "shine." Color the Stroke of each path differently, going from dark to light to dark. In my example, I went from dark to light to dark to light and back to dark again.

Step 6. Blend the Stroked paths together and mask them with the type outlines. In my example, I did this step twice. The first time, I created the front piece; the second time, I used lighter-color Strokes for a highlight, which I offset slightly up and to the left and placed behind the original type.

In the preceding steps, I Option[Alt]-copied the path not only because it was easy, but also to ensure that the end paths in the blends would have the same points in the same locations. This technique is much more effective than adding or deleting points from one path or another.

POWER TIP

With slight transformations, you can use the same reflection blend for other objects in the same illustration, and no one will be the wiser. A method that I often use is to reflect the original, scale it to 200%, and then use only a portion of the blend in the next mask.

In the next example, I use shape blends to create the glowing surface of a light bulb (see Figure 10-16). The key to achieving this effect successfully is to draw the light bulb first and then use a copy of exactly the same path for the highlights. The relative locations of Anchor Points stay the same, and the number of Anchor Points never changes.

Figure 10-15: Steps for creating type with a reflective surface

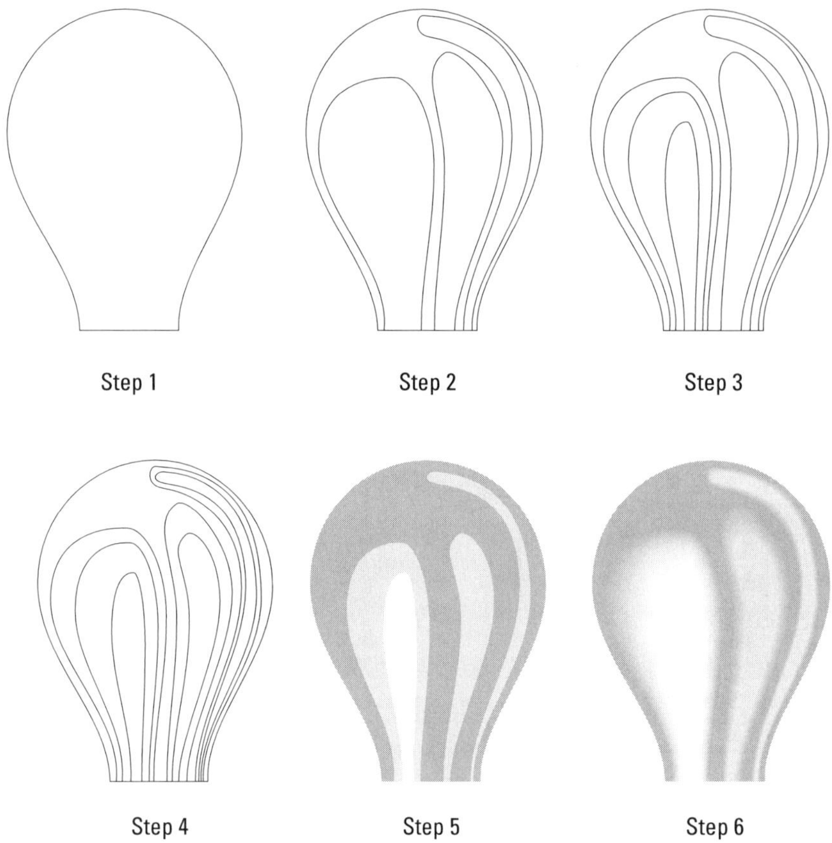

Figure 10-16: Steps for creating real surfaces of a light bulb

STEPS: Blending to Simulate Real Surfaces

Step 1. Draw a light bulb. Take your time and get it exactly the way you want it, because this path is the basis for everything else in this example. Fill the light bulb with 30% Magenta, 80% Yellow, and a Stroke of None. The first four steps in Figure 10-16 show the light bulb in Artwork mode.

Step 2. Option[Alt]-scale the light bulb down just a little bit, setting the origin on the base of the bulb. Option[Alt]-scale two more copies of the light bulb. Use the Direct Selection tool to change the shape of the paths until they resemble the paths in Step 2 of Figure 10-16. These paths are the basis for blends within the light bulb. Don't change the color of these paths.

Step 3. Option[Alt]-scale down three copies of the path on the left and shape them to resemble the paths in Figure 10-16. While your paths do not have to be exactly like the ones in the picture, be sure that each smaller path does not overlap the larger path. Color the paths as follows, from inside out: Color the first (inside) path as 5% Magenta, 10% Yellow; the next path as 10% Magenta, 30% Yellow and the last path as 15% Magenta, 40% Yellow. The outermost path should still be 30% Magenta, 80% Yellow.

Step 4. Option[Alt]-scale one copy of each of the other two outermost paths and reshape them. Color the new paths 5% Magenta and 10% Yellow.

Step 5. The paths should be in the correct top-to-bottom order, but if they are not, fix them. To see if they are in the correct order, go to Preview mode. If the smaller paths are not visible, then send the outer paths to the back.

Step 6. Blend the paths together by selecting similar Anchor Point locations on each step.

Airbrushing and the Magic of Stroke Blends

After wading through all the technical mumbo-jumbo about blending information, you are ready to enjoy your newfound blending powers. Blending can create effects that are usually reserved for bitmap graphics software, such as Fractal Design Painter and Adobe Photoshop, but without the limitation of pixels.

Most of the effects described in this section are created by blending identical overlapping paths together and varying their Stroke weights and colors. This technique can provide some of the best effects that Illustrator has to offer.

Usually, the bottommost Stroke has a heavier weight than the topmost Stroke, and as the color changes from bottom Stroke to top Stroke, the colors appear to blend in from the outside.

Tubular Blends

Creating tubular blends with the Blend tool is quite often easier than creating any other type of Stroke blend for one simple reason: The two paths, while identical, are not placed *directly* over each other, but instead are offset just slightly, giving the tube a three-dimensional appearance.

STEPS: Creating Tubular Blends

Step 1. Draw a path with the Pencil tool. Smooth curves work better than corners, so make the Curve-Fitting Tolerance high (7 to 10) in the General Preferences dialog box before drawing the curves. Change the Fill to None and the Stroke to 50% Yellow, with a weight of 1/4 point in the Paint Style palette. The path may cross itself.

Step 2. Copy the path and Paste In Back (⌘-B) [Ctrl+B]. Offset the copy about 1/2 point up and to the right by selecting Object⇨Transform⇨Move and entering the appropriate values in the text fields. Change the stroke on the copy to 50% Yellow and 100% Black and a weight of 4 points.

Step 3. Blend the two paths together. Create a Black rectangle and send it to the back. The result should look similar to the tube in Figure 10-17.

Figure 10-17: Steps for creating Tubular blends

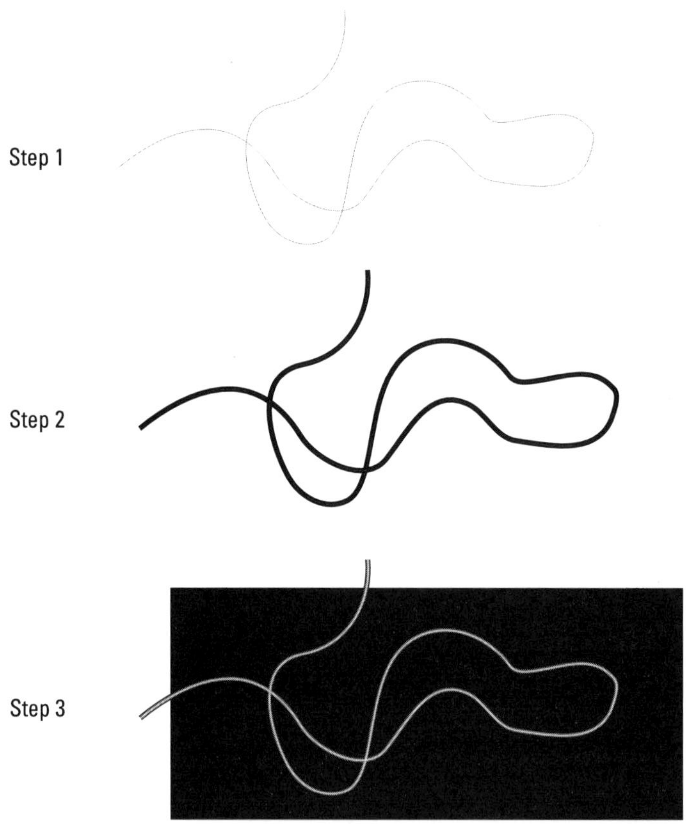

When you're creating Stroke blends, the number of steps usually doesn't need to exceed 100. If the default is more than 100, divide it by 2 (as explained in the section, "Calculating the Number of Steps," earlier in this chapter) until the number is less than 100.

In order to see the End Points better on Stroke-blend end paths, draw a tiny marquee around one of the ends with the Zoom tool. If you still can't see the End Points, switch to Artwork mode while creating the blend.

To create a Stroke blend that has more shine to it, make the Stroke lighter and thinner and do not offset it as far as in the preceding example.

To create a color Stroke blend that has more depth, make two end paths and color the bottom darker and wider and the top lighter and thinner. Then blend the paths together with one step between the end paths. Add a bit of Black (20% to 40%) to the bottommost Stroke and then blend from the bottom to the middle and from the middle to the top. The extra Black usually creates a much more realistic appearance of depth than using just two colors, and it keeps Black from being in the upper-half of the tube.

Try not to use White as your topmost path when creating tubes, because White not only looks bad, but can also cause problems when you print. The more subtle your color change, the more realistic your results. If necessary, you can always add highlights of much lighter colors after the Stroke has been blended.

There are many shapes besides free-flowing tubes that benefit from this type of Stroke effect, including stars, spirals, and line drawings. Objects that appear in everyday life that can be created with tubelike Stroke blends include wires, rods, paper clips, hangers, antennas, pins, and needles. The next section explains how to make one of the most confusing types of objects with blends — the spring tube.

Spring-Tube Blends

To create the curly section of a telephone cord (a spring tube), use the Spiral Tool to create a spiral with two winds and get rid of the inner spiral. Select the outer spiral and go through the steps to create a tube. Make this particular tube look like a section of a telephone cord, as shown in Figure 10-18.

After the spring tube has been created, group the entire tube together and Option[Alt]-copy it down until one side of the spiral lines up with the other side of the spiral. Choose Object⇨Transform⇨Transform Again (⌘-D) [Ctrl+D] until the telephone cord is the desired length. To curve the phone cord, draw a marquee around one of the ends with the Direct Selection tool and move it, if necessary. Then use the Rotate tool to change the direction of the curve. Option[Alt]-copy the next section and rotate that section into place.

Figure 10-18: A telephone cord created with tubular blends

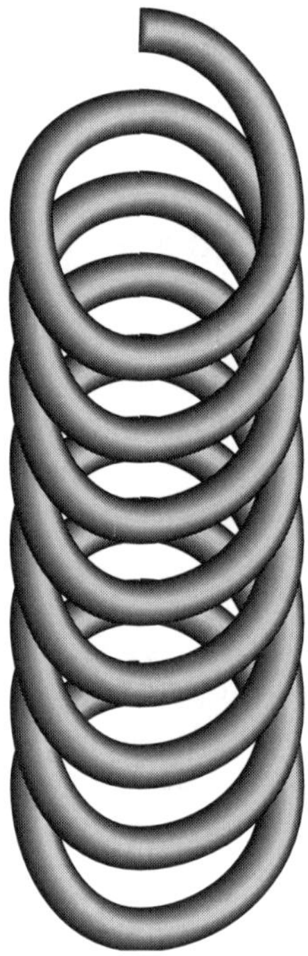

For quicker but less effective changes in direction, select a small section of the telephone cord and just rotate that section.

Airbrushed Shadows

To create a realistic shadow effect, the edges of an object must be a little fuzzy. The amount of fuzziness on the edges of the path is relative to the distance of the object from its shadow and the strength of the light source. These two areas also affect how dark the shadow is.

To make really cool shadows, you can use either Pathfinder Soft, which can be used to darken areas, or the Color Adjust filter, which can be used to change the types of color in a selected area. The Drop Shadow filter creates hard-edged shadows, which are usually good only for creating text shadows quickly.

A second way to create cool shadows is to use Stroke blends. Stroke blends can allow the shadows to fade smoothly into the background with a Gaussian Blur-like effect. You can combine Stroke blends with Pathfinder Soft for even better effects. For information on using Pathfinder Soft to create shadows, see Chapter 7.

STEPS: Creating Airbrushed Shadows

Step 1. Create a path (or copy it from an original object) for which you want to create a shadow. At this point, you may want to hide the object from which the shadow is being made so that it doesn't get in your way, especially if this object is right above where the shadow will be. Fill the shadowed path with the color you want the shadow to be and then make the Stroke the same color, with a 1/2-point Stroke weight.

Step 2. Copy the shadow, choose Edit⇨Paste In Back (⌘-B) [Ctrl+B], and then change the Stroke color to whatever the background color is (usually White, unless something else is under the shadow). Make the Stroke weight twice the distance you want the shadow to fade out to. In my example, I made the Stroke 12 points.

Step 3. The hard part now is blending these two paths together (because they overlap each other). The easiest way to fix this problem is to offset the two paths by 1/2 point and then zoom in to 1600% and blend them together. The shadow slowly fades in from the background color to the shadow color. Show the hidden objects (you may have to bring them to the front), and your shadow effect has been created (see Figure 10-19).

Figure 10-19: Airbrushed shadows with linear blends

Clicking Trouble

Shaggy: I can't handle it any more. No pun intended.

Toulouse: What's your point? Pun intended.

Shaggy: Everytime I click to blend I miss and I have to start over again.

Toulouse: Have you tried zooming in?

Shaggy: Uh, no. But the points don't get any bigger on-screen then, do they?

Toulouse: No, but the paths they're on get further and further apart.

Shaggy: Big deal.

Toulouse: That makes them easier to click on.

Shaggy: Zoinks!

Toulouse: Exactly. Be careful not to overlap shadows. Because all the steps of a blend are grouped together, the steps should all be above or behind neighboring blends.

Creating Glows

Glows are very similar to soft-edged shadows, but instead of a dark area fading into the background, a lighter area fades into the background. Using the light bulb from Figure 12-16, you now can create a glow for that light bulb by using Stroke blending.

STEPS: Creating Glows with Stroke Blends

Step 1. Select the edge of the object on which you want to create the glow. In my example, I use the light bulb shown in Figure 10-16. Copy the edge, Paste In Back (⌘-B) [Ctrl+B], and press ⌘-Option-L [Ctrl+Alt+L]. These steps lock everything that is not selected. Give the copied edge a Stroke of 6% Magenta and 62% Yellow and a Weight of 1 point.

Step 2. Draw a Black rectangle around the outside edge of the object and send it to the back. Copy the edge of the light bulb and Paste
In Back (⌘-B) [Ctrl+B] again. Change the Stroke to 6% Magenta, 60% Yellow, and 100% Black and make the Stroke about 40 points wide. Move this path about 1/2 point to the right and up.

Step 3. Blend the two edge paths together, which creates the glow of the light bulb (see Figure 10-20). The larger the Weight of the second copied path from Step 2, the bigger the glow.

When creating glows, make the initial glow area (around the edge of the object) *lighter* than the object edges if there are bright highlights in the object. Make the initial glow *darker* than the edges if the edges of the object are the brightest part of the object.

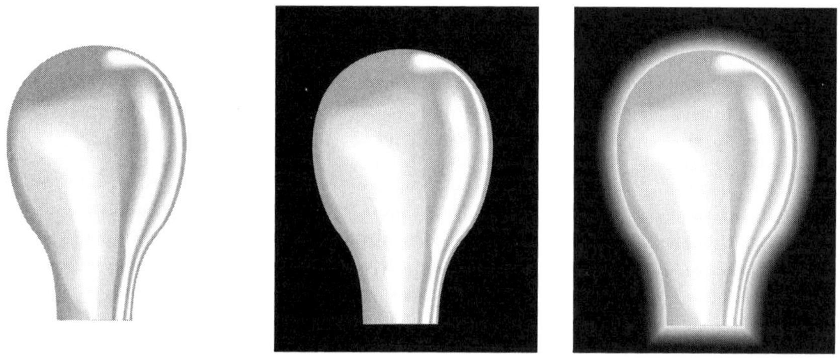

Figure 10-20: Creating a glow around the light bulb

Softening Edges

Edges of objects can be softened in a manner very similar to that of creating shadows. The reason that edges are softened is to remove the hard, computerlike edges from objects in your illustration. Softening edges can be done to an extreme measure so that the object appears out of focus, or just a tiny bit for an almost imperceptible change.

When determining how much of a distance should be softened, look at the whole illustration, not just that one piece. Usually, the softening area is no more than 1 or 2 points (unless the object is being blurred).

To soften edges on an object, select the object, copy, and hide the original object. Choose Edit⇨Paste in Back (⌘-B) [Ctrl+B] and then make the Stroke on the object .1 point, the same color as the Fill. Copy again, Paste in Back, make the Stroke the color of the background, and make the Weight 2 points (which makes the softening edge 1-point thick).

When softening objects, rather than moving the entire path in the background, try moving one Anchor Point out just far enough to be able to click it. Blend the two paths together and then show the original object (it may have to be brought to the front).

To blur an object, just make the bottom layer Stroke extremely wide (12 to 20 points or more, depending on the size of the illustration) and blend as described in the preceding paragraphs.

Neon Effects

To create neon effects with Stroke blends, you need to create two distinct parts. Part one is the neon tubing, which by itself is nice, but it doesn't really have a neon effect. The second part is the tubing's reflection off the background, which usually appears as a glowing area. These two separate blends give the illusion of lit neon.

Neon effects work much better when the background is very dark, though some interesting effects can be achieved with light backgrounds.

STEPS: Creating Neon Tubing

Step 1. To make the tubing, create a path that will be the neon. In Figure 10-21, I used two paths: a candle and a flame. Give the Stroke of the paths a Weight of 4 and color them 100% Yellow. Make sure that the Fill is set to None. Change the cap of the Stroke to round and the join of the Stroke to curved.

Step 2. Create a rectangle that is larger than the area of the path. Send it to the back and set the Fill to Black.

Step 3. Select the neon path, copy it, and choose Edit⇨Paste in Front (⌘-F) [Ctrl+F]. Offset the copy by .25 point and change the Weight of the copy to .25 point. Hold down the Shift key and change the color of the Stroke by dragging the sliders to the left to make the color lighter. Do not make the copy White, but make it noticeably lighter than the neon color.

Step 4. Blend the two paths together and then group the two end paths with the blend. This is the neon tube part of the illustration. Hide this tube.

Step 5. To create the reflected area of the background, choose Edit⇨Paste in Back (⌘-B) [Ctrl+B]. This step pastes a copy of the original path behind the bottom part of the existing neon tube. Give the path a Stroke of 4 and change the color to 100% Yellow and 75% Black.

Step 6. Copy the Stroke and Paste in Back (⌘-B) [Ctrl+B] again, changing the color of the Stroke to the same as the background and then making the weight of the Stroke 24 points. Offset this copy by .25 point and blend the two together.

Step 7. Choose View Object⇨Show All (⌘-Shift-U) [Ctrl+Shift+U]. Your result should now look similar to Figure 10-21.

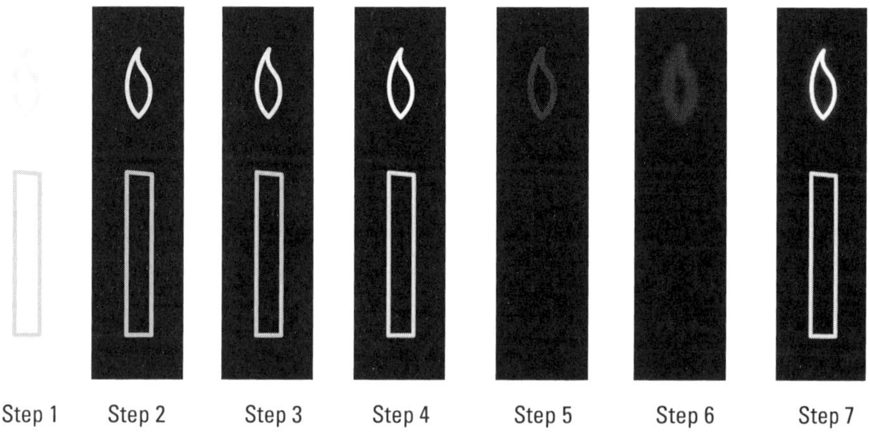

Figure 10-21: Neon candles

Try crossing paths with neon or, for an even more realistic look, create "unlit" portions of neon by using darker shading with no reflective glow.

Backlighting

Backlighting effects can be accomplished by simply creating a glow for an object and then placing that same object on top of the glow. By making the topmost object Filled with Black or another dark color, a backlit effect is produced, as shown in Figure 10-22.

Figure 10-22: Backlighting the word *dark*

Gradients

The Gradient feature has no rivals. It is by far the most powerful gradient-creating mechanism available for PostScript drawing programs. Gradients in Adobe Illustrator can have 32 different colors, from end to end in a linear gradient, and from center to outside in a radial Gradient. Gradients can consist of custom colors, process colors, or just plain Black and White. The midpoint of two adjacent colors can be adjusted smoothly and easily toward either color. The Gradient palette can be made available at all times because it is a floating palette, and can be accessed or viewed by pressing F9. And, for what they do, gradients are easier to use than blends.

You can apply gradients only to the Fills of paths, not to Strokes or text objects. Gradients cannot be used in patterns, either.

Checking the Compatible Gradients checkbox in the Document Setup box prevents most gradient problems from occurring. When you're printing to PostScript Level 1 printers, checking this box speeds up gradient printing dramatically. Compatible gradients bypass a high-level imaging system within Illustrator that older printers and printers without genuine Adobe PostScript (commonly referred to as "PostScript clones") cannot understand. Checking this box may cause documents to print slower on printers that would ordinarily be able to print those documents.

The Gradient Tool

You use the Gradient tool to change the angle and the starting and ending points for a linear gradient as well as the location of the center and edges of a radial gradient. The tool is also used to offset the highlight on a radial gradient.

Unlike blends, which can be created only with the Blend tool, gradients can survive quite nicely without the Gradient tool. Gradients are created with the Gradient palette and applied from the Gradient or tool palette. Double-clicking the Gradient tool displays the Gradient palette.

To use the Gradient tool, you must select at least one path that is Filled with a Gradient. Dragging with the Gradient Vector tool on linear gradients changes the angle and the length of the gradient as well as the start and end points. Dragging with the Gradient tool on radial gradients determines the start position and end position of the gradient. Clicking with the Gradient tool resets the highlight to a new location.

Using Preset Gradients

To choose a preset gradient, select a path and make sure the Fill box is active in the toolbox. On the right side of the Paint palette, click the seventh box along the top, which is the Gradient Fill box. The eight default Gradient presets appear below the row of boxes. None of the options is selected until you click one of them.

Do you think it's strange that Illustrator doesn't have a preset radial fill that goes from White to Black? You're not alone. This is one of the great mysteries of modern times, right up there with "Why is the # symbol on a phone called the *pound* key?"

These preset gradients appear in Illustrator because they exist in the Illustrator start-up file, which is discussed in Chapter 6.

Using the Gradient Palette

The Gradient palette, if nothing else, is really *neat* looking, with all sorts of nifty little controls at your disposal for creating and modifying gradients, as shown in Figure 10-23.

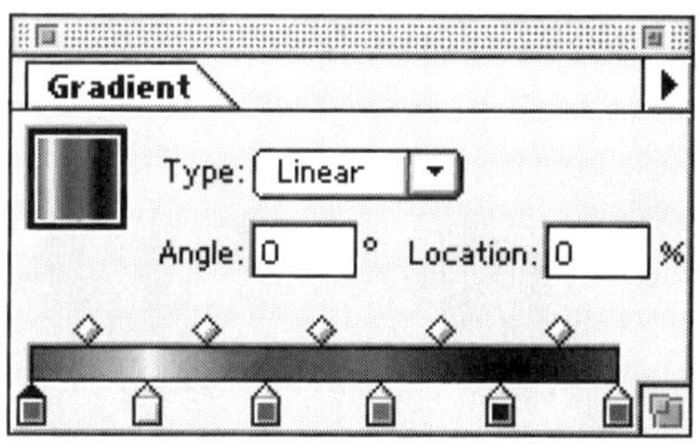

Figure 10-23: The Gradient palette

The bottom of the Gradient palette is where you control what colors are in the gradient and where the colors are in relation to one another.

To add a new color to the bar, click below the bar where you want the new color to appear. Then change the settings in the Color palette to create the color you want for that *color stop*. You can enter up to 32 color stops between the two end colors. When a color stop is selected, entering a different percentage in the text field on the right changes the color stop's position.

You can sample a color to the Gradient palette by Shift-clicking with the Eyedropper anywhere on the screen.

The diamonds above the color bar show where the midpoint between two color stops is. By moving the midpoint left or right, you alter the halfway color between two color stops. When a diamond is selected, entering a different percentage in the text field on the right changes the diamond's position.

STEPS: Using Custom Gradients to Create a Cityscape

Step 1. Draw a series of vertical rectangles, some overlapping, with their bases horizontally even. In my example (Figure 10-24), I angled the top of one of the rectangles.

Step 2. Fill the rectangles with the Black & White Gradient (by clicking it in the Swatches Palette) and be sure that the Gradient angle in the Gradient palette is 0°.

Step 3. In the Swatches palette, duplicate the Black & White Gradient and name the copy "Buildings." In the Gradient Palette, enter a new color stop at 31% across and make the color 70% Black. Change the color of the leftmost color stop to 85% Black. Apply the Gradient "Buildings" to the rectangles.

Step 4. Draw a rectangle and send it behind the buildings. Change the fill to the Black & White Gradient and change the Gradient angle to 90°.

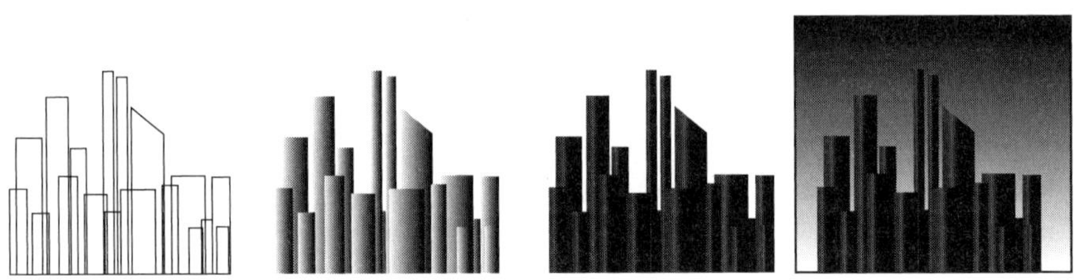

Step 1 Step 2 Step 3 Step 4

Figure 10-24: A cityscape created from rectangles and gradients

For added dramatic impact in a cityscape, copy the buildings one by one and Paste in Front (⌘-F) [Ctrl+F]. Fill the front copies with a Custom pattern of lights with a transparent background.

Shadows, Highlights, Ghosting, and Embossing

You can use gradients to simulate special effects by either duplicating and altering a gradient or by using the Gradient Vector tool on similar gradients.

You can simulate ghosting by using the Gradient Vector tool to slightly alter the starting and ending locations of the gradient.

STEPS: Creating Ghosting Effects with Gradients

Step 1. Ghosting effects are easiest to see on text, so create a rectangle and then create large text on top of the rectangle.

Step 2. Convert the type into outlines and position the type outline just to the right and below the center of the rectangle.

Step 3. Select both the type and rectangle and apply a Gradient Fill to them. For Figure 10-25, I used the Red & Yellow Gradient at 90°.

Step 4. Move the type to the center of the rectangle. The type appears to be ghosted there, as in Figure 10-25.

Figure 10-25: Ghosting with gradients

Embossed gradient images are created by offsetting two copies of the original graduated image. In one offset image, the gradient is lightened; in the other, the gradient is darkened.

STEPS: Embossing Text

Step 1. Create text and convert it to outlines.

Step 2. Select the outlined type and choose Object➪Pathfinder➪Unite. Draw a rectangle around the type and send it to the back.

Step 3. Select both the type outline and the rectangle and Fill them with a Gradient. Use a process gradient for this example. Drag the Gradient Vector tool across the rectangle (keeping both objects selected) to set the gradient length and angle.

Step 4. In the Swatches palette, select the gradient used for both the rectangle and type outlines, and make two duplicates of it. Make one duplicate lighter by selecting each color stop and moving it to the left. Create one gradient darker than the original by moving each color stop to the right.

Step 5. Using the Move dialog box, create a copy of the path that's offset a few points up and to the left. Create another copy offset a few points down and to the right.

Step 6. Fill the upper-left path with the lighter gradient you created and the lower-right path with the darker one you made.

Step 7. Select the middle type path and choose Object➪Arrange➪Bring to Front (⌘-Shift-]) [Ctrl+Shift+]]. The type appears embossed, as shown in Figure 10-26.

To make embossed images seem sunken rather than raised, make the lighter image below and to the right and the darker image above and to the left. To make the image seem further raised or recessed, increase the distance between the original path and the offset images.

You can simulate shadows by creating darker gradients based on an existing Gradient. You create the new, darker Gradient in a path that is the same shape as the object causing the shadow.

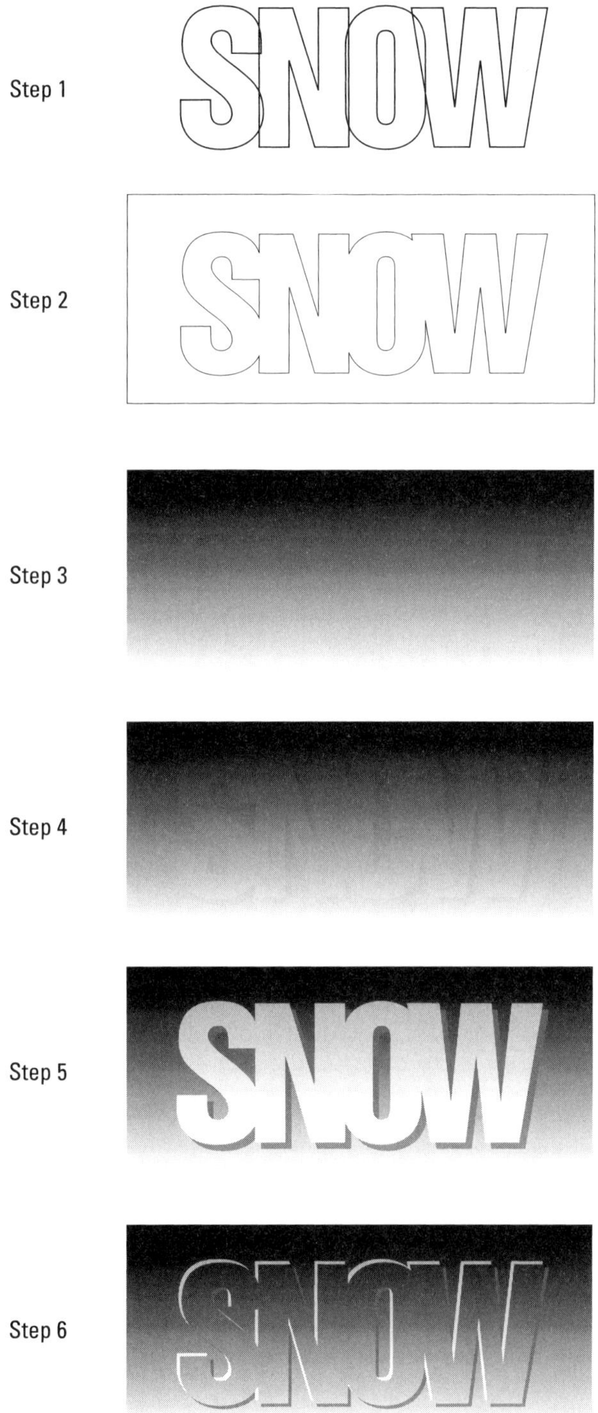

Figure 10-26: Steps for making embossed type

STEPS: Creating Shadows with Gradients

Step 1. For this example, use the cityscape created in Figure 10-24. Create a rectangle at the bottom of the city and give it a blend from light to dark. Send the rectangle behind the city. Duplicate the Gradient and add some Black to the color stops in the duplicate.

Step 2. Select the city and choose the Reflect tool. Reflect a copy of the city across the base of the city.

Step 3. Unite the reflected city buildings with Unite (Object⇨Pathfinder⇨Unite). Fill the united city with the darker Gradient.

Step 4. Select both the background and the city, and draw the Gradient tool across both paths. The shadow is automatically created.

Step 5. Using the Scale and Rotate tools, adjust the shadow to more accurately resemble the light source. The result should resemble Figure 10-27.

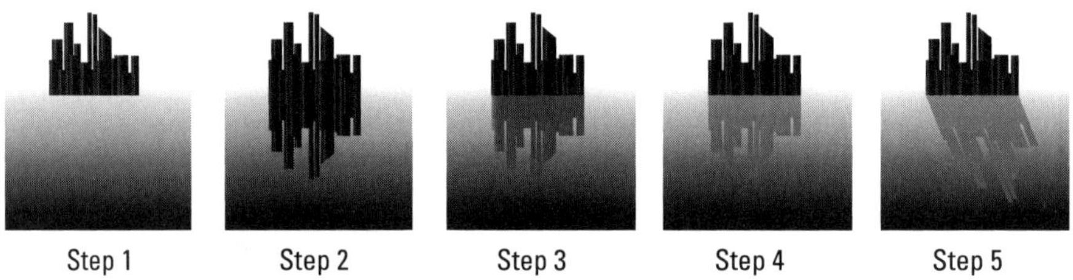

Figure 10-27: Creating a shadow on a gradient

Taking Gradients Where Gradients Fear to Go

Many pieces of software accept Illustrator files but don't care for gradients very much. Dimensions 3 just ignores gradients. And even Illustrator says "uh-uh" when you try to use a gradient in a pattern.

The solution to this problem is to use the Expand feature, described in the next section. Expand converts gradients into blends automatically.

After expanding, select the blends and choose Object⇨Pathfinder⇨Merge, which gets rid of the overlapping areas always present with blends in Illustrator.

In addition, gradients cannot be used in Strokes of paths. To get around this limitation, select the path, make the Stroke the correct weight, and choose Object⇨Path⇨Outline Path. The Stroke is transformed into a closed path, which can then be Filled with a gradient.

Before using Outline Path, be sure that the weight of the Stroke on the path to be outlined is the correct weight; otherwise, there is no way short of undoing the whole thing to convert outlined Strokes back into a single path.

Expand Fill

In Illustrator, you can automatically change gradients into blends by selecting the Gradient you wish to change, and then choosing Expand (Object⇨Expand). A dialog box appears like the one shown in Figure 10-28.

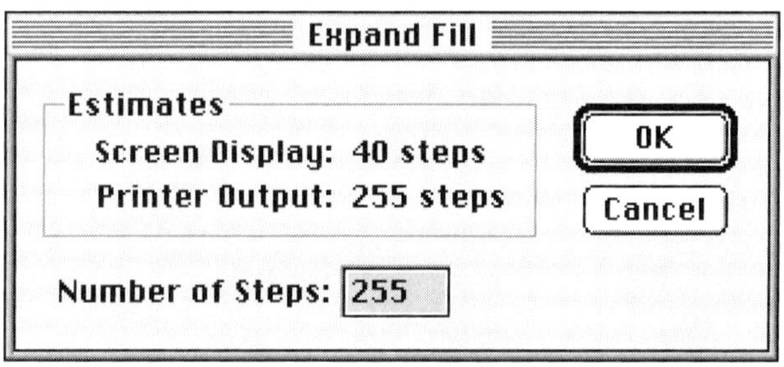

Figure 10-28: The Expand Fill dialog box

In the dialog box, you can specify how many blend steps there should be in the blend.

Summary

- Blends and gradients may resemble each other on the surface, but they are both quite different in their capabilities and functionality.
- Blends can be created between any two open or closed paths.
- Blends can be masked so that a blend can be used as a Fill.

- Shape blends can be created to transform from one shape to another.
- Blends can be used to create smooth airbrushing effects.
- Gradients can be much easier to use than blends.
- You can quickly turn gradients into blends by selecting the gradient and applying the Expand option.

CHAPTER 11

Patterns, Graphs, and Textures

In This Chapter

- Using the default patterns
- Creating your own patterns
- Making patterns seamless
- Understanding how transparency works with patterns
- Modifying existing patterns
- Putting patterns and gradients into patterns
- Transforming patterns
- Creating graphs
- Entering information into graphs
- Working with different types of graphs
- Modifying existing graphs
- Using marker and column designs

Patterns

"The Perfect Pattern is one in which you cannot determine the borders of its tiles," so saith the Chinese *Book of Patterns*. If that is the case, you can use Adobe Illustrator to create perfect patterns.

The Pattern function in Illustrator is twofold. First, you can Fill or Stroke any path with a pattern, although Strokes are not visible on-screen. Second, you can edit existing patterns or create new ones from Illustrator objects. The real strength of Illustrator's pattern features is that you can create patterns as well as apply them on-screen in almost any way imaginable.

Windows Update

Illustrator 7 has totally overhauled the way Windows users deal with patterns, refined the graph-making process, and added the fantastic Ink Pen filter.

What's New

Patterns are now created by dragging the artwork for a pattern into the Swatches palette (or by using the Edit Pattern command).

You no longer need a background rectangle to create a pattern.

A few new graph types have been added, including a Radar Graph.

The Ink Pen filter has been added, which is useful for adding textures to flat artwork.

A pattern in Illustrator is a series of objects within a rectangle that is commonly referred to as a pattern tile. When you choose a pattern in the Swatches palette, the selected pattern is repeated on each of the four sides of the rectangle as well as in the four corners, as shown in Figure 11-1.

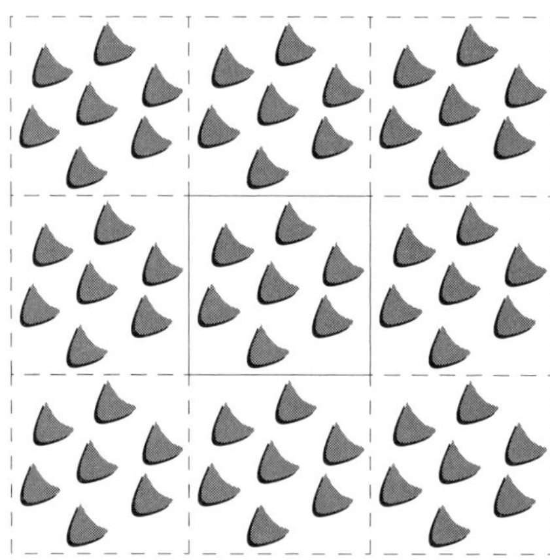

Figure 11-1: The area inside the solid rectangular outline in the center of the figure is the original pattern tile. The dotted-line rectangles represent additional pattern tiles that are aligned with the original to create the pattern and fill up the object.

Illustrator places the pattern tiles together for you. After you apply a pattern to an object, you can use any of the transformation tools to transform it, and you can move within the object by using the Move command. You can move and transform patterns with or without the objects they are within.

Tile patterns can have a background color, or they can be transparent. Transparent patterns can overlay other objects, including objects Filled with patterns.

Using the Default Patterns

There are 24 ready-made patterns available all the time in Illustrator. Of these 24, 13 were designed to be used as fill patterns, while 11 were designed for path pattern usage. Path patterns are covered in Chapter 17.

Figure 11-2 shows the thirteen fill patterns and their names.

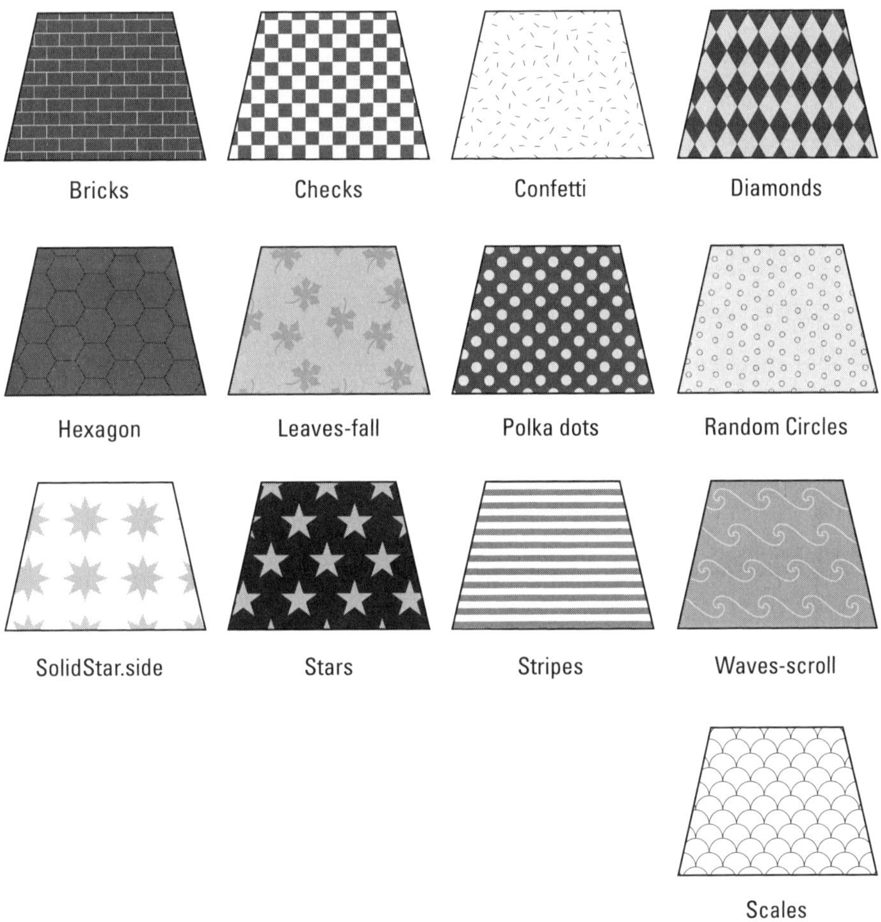

Figure 11-2: The default fill patterns

To Fill a path with a pattern, select that path, make sure the fill icon is active, then click on the corresponding pattern swatch in the swatches palette. The path will be filled with the pattern indicated.

While there are only 13 different default fill patterns, each of them can take on a whole new perspective if you use the various transformation functions — move, rotate, scale, reflect, and skew — on them. Figure 11-3 shows what appears to be several hundred patterns; it's really only the same 13 patterns with various transformations applied.

Figure 11-3: These patterns were created using only the original 13 patterns, with various transformations applied to them

In Preview mode, patterns that are applied to Fills appear, but patterns that are applied to Strokes do not. Instead of the latter patterns, you see a Gray Stroke. When you print the illustration, however, patterns will appear in strokes. If you want to see a pattern in a Stroke on-screen, apply the Outline Path filter (Object⇨Path⇨Outline Path) to convert a Stroke into outlines and Fill the outlines with the pattern.

Patterns used as Strokes can send your printer to a crashing halt. A Pattern-Filled object has the object's path to figure out where to put the pattern when it is printed. The Stroke command in PostScript is a one-shot command that follows the path with thickness and a line join attribute. With a pattern in a Stroke, the PostScript interpreter must figure out where the Stroke should be and then Fill it with a pattern.

If you see just a gray area in place of the pattern, you may not have the Preview and Print Patterns option selected in the Document Setup dialog box. This option is usually on by default.

In addition to the default patterns, you can choose from an incredibly wide variety of patterns that are in the Collector's Edition folder on the Illustrator CD-ROM. This folder contains borders and clip art as well as patterns. Open the pattern file to see large blocks that contain the patterns as well as the art that was used to create the patterns.

The default patterns are stored in the Adobe Illustrator Startup file. To learn how to modify the start-up file to have a specific set of patterns available every time you use Illustrator, see Chapter 6.

Creating Custom Patterns

In addition to using the patterns provided with Illustrator, you can create custom patterns by following the steps shown in Figure 11-4.

STEPS: Creating a Basic Pattern Tile

Step 1. Create the artwork you would like to appear in the pattern tile. For this example, I created a bunch of different stars.

Step 2. Select the artwork.

Step 3. Drag it into the swatches palette.

Figure 11-4 also shows the artwork applied as the fill of another shape; the pattern was scaled down dramatically when placed in the larger star shape.

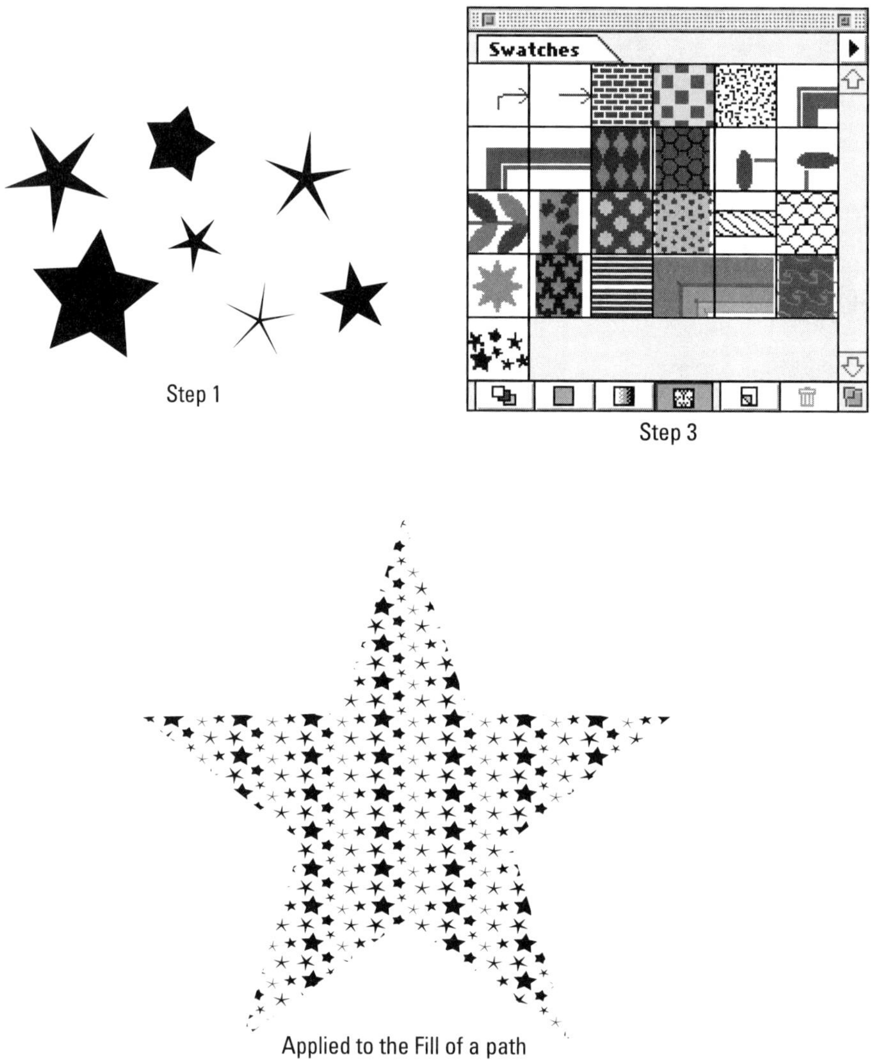

Figure 11-4: Steps for creating a basic pattern tile

The old Pattern dialog box is gone. Don't look for it, as you won't be able to find anything even close to resembling the classic Illustrator pattern definition box. Instead, Adobe has opted for the much more clever method of using the Swatches palette as the home for all patterns.

Of course, creating patterns, while pretty easy initially, can actually be a little more time-consuming for specialty patterns. Patterns that need to appear symmetrical, random, or seamless require special steps. The following sections show different methods for creating these special pattern types.

Patterns in Illustrator 7

With the removal of the pattern dialog box from previous versions of Illustrator, getting used to the new system can take a bit of adjustment. Once you get the hang of it, you'll love the new way of creating patterns. Until then, here are the changes to keep in mind as you work with patterns in Illustrator 7:

- **No more Pattern dialog box.** Patterns are now kept in the Swatches palette which is used to both create and apply patterns.
- **Create patterns by dragging pattern elements to the Swatches palette.** Select all the items to be in the pattern (including the boundary box if you have one), and drag them into the Swatches palette. A new swatch will be created that contains that pattern.
- **Apply patterns by clicking on the pattern swatch when a path is selected.** Make sure the appropriate Fill/Stroke icon is active.
- **Access existing patterns by dragging the swatch to your document.** Instead of the old Paste button in the Patterns dialog box, you simply (and logically) drag the pattern swatch to your document.
- **Duplicate patterns by dragging pattern swatches to the New Swatch icon.**
- **Delete patterns by dragging pattern swatches to the Delete icon.**
- **Name or Rename patterns by double-clicking on them.**

Pattern Backgrounds and Boundaries

Any pattern tile you create can have the color background you specify, simply by making a rectangle to the size of the tile and placing it behind the objects in the pattern. When the pattern is created, just select the background with the pattern objects, and the background of the pattern will be colored automatically.

If you don't create a background rectangle, Illustrator uses the *bounding box* of the selected objects to determine the size of the pattern tile. The bounding box is a rectangle that is the exact size of all the selected paths in their current positions.

Use Extensis VectorFrame (a full version — VectorFrame SE — is included on the *Illustrator 7 Bible* CD-ROM) to quickly view the bounding box. Change the offset to 0, select the objects, and click the Apply button in the VectorFrame palette. VectorFrame uses the bounding box to calculate where the frame should be.

But what happens if you want the edge of the pattern tile to be somewhere inside the bounding box? Illustrator provides a way for you to define a boundary box to define pattern tiles that consist of objects that extend beyond the pattern edges. Create a boundary box by creating a Rectangle with the Rectangle tool, Fill it with None, and make it the backmost object in the pattern tile.

To quickly make a boundary box for a pattern tile that is to have a background, make the background rectangle the size of the tile (with any objects in front sticking out if necessary), copy and Paste In Back, and whack the good ole Slash (/) key to set the Fill to None. Make sure you select both the background rectangle and the boundary box along with your other pattern elements when creating a pattern.

Why Patterns Aren't Always Seamless

In order for patterns to appear seamless, the edges of the pattern cannot be apparent. Avoiding this problem sounds rather easy: You just avoid creating any objects that touch the edges of a background rectangle. Well, that technique will do it, but when you use such a pattern, the pattern tiles become evident because of the lack of any objects along the borders.

So, then, you do want objects to cross the edges of the pattern rectangle. The catch is that those objects cannot appear to be broken. Doing an illustration the wrong way can help you understand this principle.

Start by drawing a background rectangle with a Fill of None. Draw a 1-point Black Stroked wavy path from left to right, overlapping both edges. Draw a circle, Filled with 50% Gray, that overlaps the bottom of the rectangle. Select all the objects and define the pattern.

When you Fill an object with the new pattern, the edges of the pattern are very noticeable because the wavy path and the circle are both cut at the edges of the pattern boundary.

Making Seamless Patterns

In order to make patterns seamless, you need to remember that objects that lie across the edge of the pattern border will be cut into two sections, the outside section of which will be invisible. You also need to make sure that lines that stretch from one edge of a pattern border to the other side connect to another line on the opposite edge of the boundary. The second problem is more difficult to deal with than the first one. To make a line match well from one side to the other, you usually have to move one or both of the ends up or down slightly.

Use the following steps to fix objects that get sliced apart at the edges of the pattern tile boundary.

STEPS: Making Seamless Patterns, Part 1

Step 1. Create the boundary (always the backmost rectangle) and the pattern tile objects. The objects may overlap any of the edges, including the corners. In the example that I created (see Figure 11-5), the stones overlap all four sides as well as one of the corners. I created a background rectangle so that you can see the boundary clearly.

Step 2. Select all of the objects, including the pattern boundary, and group them. Click the upper-left corner of the pattern and drag to the right until the arrow pointer is directly over the upper-right corner (it will turn hollow at this point indicating it is snapping into place). Press Option [Alt] and release the mouse button. A copy of the tile will be created to the right of the original.

(continued)

Changing Pattern Color

Julie: I can't change the color of the background of my pattern.

Toulouse: There are two ways you can do this.

Julie: Tell me the easiest way first.

Toulouse: Okay, the first way is to Duplicate the pattern, and change the color.

Julie: Take me through it step by step.

Toulouse: First, drag the pattern swatch out of the Swatches palette and onto the document.

Julie: What does that do?

Toulouse: It puts a copy of the original pattern tile artwork in your document.

Julie: Cool.

Toulouse: Then select the background rectangle of the pattern and change its Fill color. Select the background and the rest of the pattern and drag them into the swatches palette. You'll have another pattern with a different background color.

Julie: And the other way?

(continued)

(continued)

Toulouse: If you'll be changing colors all the time, or you want to use a gradient or another pattern for your background....

Julie: I thought you couldn't do that with patterns.

Toulouse: That's why you need to know this workaround.

Julie: Gotcha.

Toulouse: Go ahead and drag the Pattern swatch like before, but this time, make the background rectangle Filled with None.

Julie: Ahhhhh....

Toulouse: Yes, now the new pattern won't have any background, and you can paste a background behind the copy of the path that has the pattern.

STEPS: ***(continued)***

Step 3. Repeat the process in Step 2 until all four sides have copies of the pattern up against them.

Step 4. Select all five sections and ungroup them. Select the boundary rectangles on the four copied sections and delete them.

Step 5. Delete all the paths (stones, in the example) that don't cross the border of the rectangle.

Step 6. Look at the corners of the rectangle. If an object overlaps any of the corners at all, it should overlap the other three corners. If it doesn't overlap the other three (as in the upper-right corner in the example), Option[Alt]-copy (drag the selected object, pressing the Option [Alt] key, and release the mouse button before the Option [Alt] key) that piece and the boundary to cover the empty corners. Move the boundary with a corner as before so that the piece lines up perfectly. Delete the rectangle after you finish.

Step 7. Look for any overlapping pieces of art in the artwork, including areas of objects that are too close for your liking. Move any pieces of art that are not overlapping a boundary.

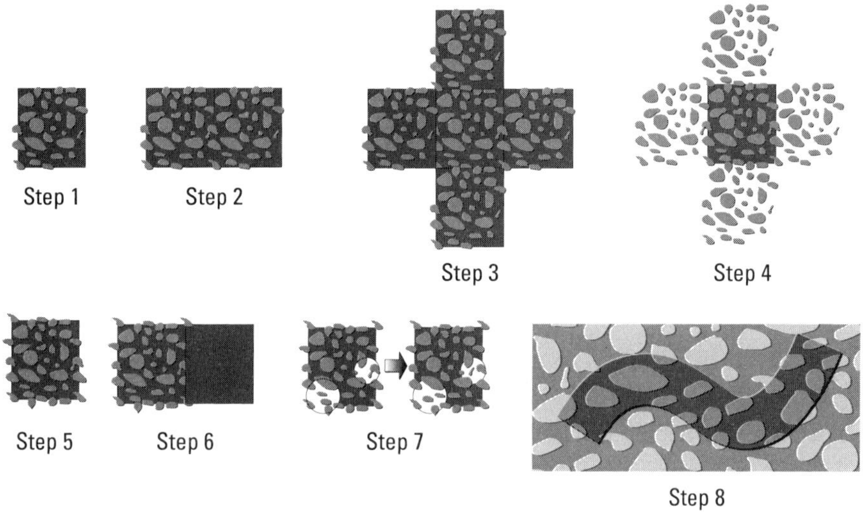

Figure 11-5: Steps for creating a seamless pattern

Step 8. Make the boundary and objects into a pattern by dragging them into the Swatch palette. Apply it to a shape and check the seams to make sure that it is correct. (If I am even the least bit doubtful that a pattern may be showing seams, I zoom in to 1600% to examine the questionable area.)

If you deleted the original pattern artwork, drag the pattern swatch to your document to place a copy of the original artwork on the screen.

To fix lines that cross the edges of the pattern tile boundary, you need to adjust both the lines and the boundary rectangle itself.

STEPS: Making Seamless Patterns, Part 2

Step 1. Create the artwork that you will use in the pattern.

Step 2. Option[Alt]-copy all of the artwork to the right. At a few points inside the original tile boundary, use the Scissors tool to cut along each path in order to prevent any change to the location and angle of the lines as they meet the opposite edge. You must cut the paths inside the original boundary, not outside. Join the paths together, moving only the End Point of the path in the original tile boundary.

(continued)

STEPS: *(continued)*

Step 3. Option[Alt]-copy both the original and the copied artwork down. Use the Scissors tool to cut along the inside bottom edge of the tile boundary and join the pieces, moving only the End Point of the paths inside the original tile boundary.

Step 4. Using the Scissors tool again, click about $^{1}/_{2}$ inch down the outside right and bottom edges of the tile boundary. Select all paths that do not go into the tile boundary and delete them.

Step 5. Select the tile boundary rectangle and move it $^{1}/_{8}$ inch down and to the right. Make sure that no new paths are overlapped on the top and left edges; if they are, do not move the rectangle so far.

Step 6. If you plan to use a blended line or a series of lines placed on top of each other, you may want to join the ends of the paths outside the rectangle to make blends merge together and keep layers of paths separate. I joined such ends in the example; if I hadn't, the pattern edges would not have lined up directly.

Step 7. Add any other elements of the pattern and change the background color if necessary. In the example, I added meatballs and a sauce-color background. Select all the elements and make them into a pattern.

Step 8. Fill a path with the pattern. Three variations on the pattern appear at the top of Figure 11-6.

Symmetrical Patterns

You can easily create symmetrical patterns in Illustrator. The key to creating them is to draw the boundary box after you create the rest of the objects, drawing outward from the center point of one of the objects.

When you are creating symmetrical patterns, the main difficulty is judging the space between the objects in the pattern. Objects always seem too close together or too far apart, especially in patterns that have different amounts of space between the objects horizontally and vertically.

POWER TIP

To have an equal amount of space from the center of one object to the center of the next object both vertically and horizontally, use a square as the pattern tile boundary.

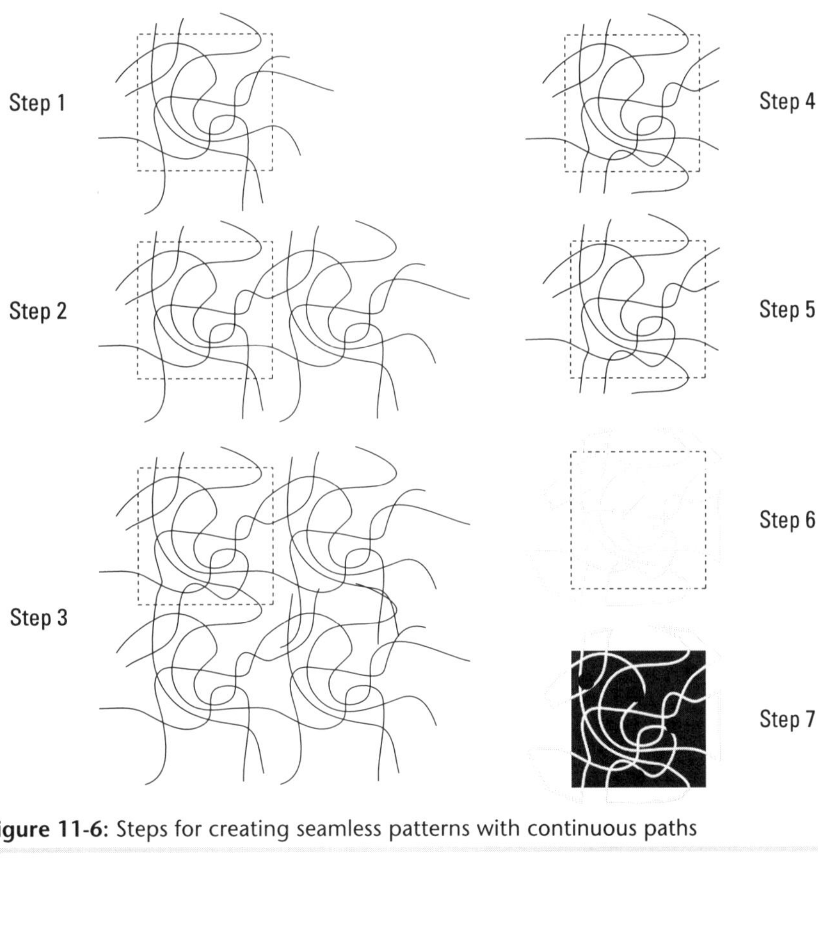

Figure 11-6: Steps for creating seamless patterns with continuous paths

Using the method described in the following steps (and illustrated in Figure 11-7), you can visually adjust the amount of space between objects before you make the objects a pattern.

STEPS: Making Symmetrical Patterns

Step 1. Create the artwork to use in the pattern.

Step 2. Draw a rectangle from the center of the object so that the object is in the upper-left corner of the rectangle.

Step 3. Option[Alt]-copy the object and the rectangle across and down. Delete the extra rectangles.

Step 4. Using the Direct Selection tool, drag to select the objects on the right and Shift-drag (move the object with the Shift key pressed, releasing the mouse button before the Shift key) them left or right to change the horizontal spacing.

Step 5. Drag the Direct Selection tool to select the objects on the bottom and Shift-drag up or down to adjust the vertical spacing.

Step 6. Move the rectangle so that it surrounds only the initial object and delete the other three objects.

Step 7. Make the objects into a pattern and fill a path with it. The pattern is the background for Figure 11-7.

Line Patterns and Grids

Using lines and grids for patterns is ideal because they are so easy to create. The key in both types of patterns is the size of the bounding rectangle.

To create a line pattern with horizontal 1-point lines that are aligned on every $^1/_2$ inch, do the following: Draw a rectangle that is exactly $^1/_2$-inch tall, at any width, with a Fill and Stroke of None. Draw a horizontal line from outside the left edge of the rectangle to outside the right edge of the rectangle, with a Fill of None and a Stroke of 1 point.

Figure 11-7: Creating perfectly symmetrical patterns

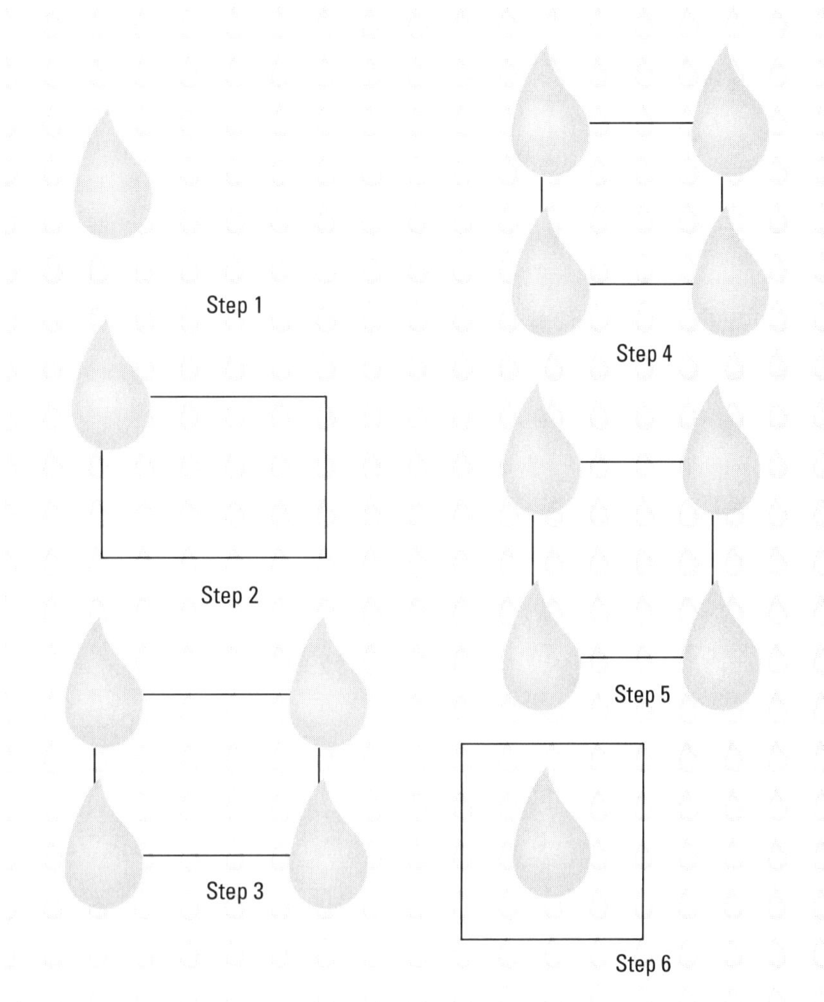

Creating grids is even easier than creating evenly spaced lines. Create a rectangle that is the size of the grid holes (for a quarter-inch grid, the rectangle would be 1/4 x 1/4 inch) and apply a Stroke to the object. Make the Stroke the weight that you want the grid lines to be. Make that rectangle into a pattern. That's it. You now have a pattern grid that is as precise as possible.

Patterns to Paths

Isaac: Is there an easy way to convert patterns to paths that really works?

Toulouse: Well, there are several options. The Expand option in the Object menu, KPT Gradients/Patterns to Paths (included on the *Illustrator 7 Bible* CD-ROM) and CSI Patterns to Paths.

Isaac: Which works the best?

Toulouse: Well, CSI gives you the option of keeping any transformations that were done to the patterns before they're converted.

Isaac: I sometimes get bad results with patterns to paths.

Toulouse: Actually, because of the way Illustrator patterns work, the patterns are always offset a little bit.

Isaac: Any way to fix this?

Toulouse: Just manually. :(

Make a pattern out of the two objects. The new pattern consists of 1-point horizontal Strokes that are spaced 1/2 inch apart.

You can use this technique with vertical lines, as well. Just make the bounding rectangle the width of the distance from line to line.

If you want the space between gridlines to be an exact measurement, make the rectangle bigger by the stroke weight. A quarter-inch grid (18 points) with 1-point grid lines requires a rectangle that is 19 points by 19 points. Remember that four of these grids don't equal an inch; instead, they equal 4 points more than an inch.

Diagonal-Line and Grid Patterns

Creating diagonal-line and grid patterns can be difficult if you try to make a rectangle; draw a path at an angle, and then use the rectangle with the path in it as a pattern. Joining diagonal lines at the edges of the pattern is nearly impossible.

A better method is to create line and grid patterns in horizontal or vertical alignment and apply the pattern to a path, and then double-click the Rotate tool. In the Rotate dialog box, enter the angle to change the lines and uncheck the Object checkbox. The pattern will rotate to the desired angle inside the path.

Using this technique is also a great way to avoid making several patterns when you need line patterns that are set at different angles. Just make one horizontal line pattern and rotate the patterns within the paths.

Transparency and Patterns

To make the background of a pattern transparent, don't use a background rectangle. Only the objects in the pattern will be opaque.

To make the objects in a pattern transparent, make the background rectangle and the other objects into a compound path. Select the compound path and make the objects into a pattern. You can achieve some fascinating effects by using the transformation tools to make transformed copies of patterns on top of themselves.

CAUTION: When you make the bounding rectangle part of a compound path, it is no longer a rectangle, and you cannot use it as the bounding rectangle. Always copy the rectangle before you make the objects and the rectangle into a compound path.

Another way to achieve interesting effects is by making a copy of the object behind the original. Select the object, choose Edit⇨Copy (⌘-C) [Ctrl+C], and then choose Edit⇨Paste In Back (⌘-B) [Ctrl+B]. Change the Fill in the copy of the object to a solid or a gradient or change it to another Pattern. Chapter 17 describes a technique for creating a hollow honeycomb effect.

Modifying Existing Patterns

To change an existing pattern, drag the pattern swatch to your document. A copy of the original artwork will be placed in the document.

Select individual parts with any of the selection tools and change Fill & Stroke attributes or change the shape of any of the objects with selection or transformation tools.

After modifying the artwork, select all the pattern-related objects and drag them to the Swatches palette on top of the original version to replace the old swatch.

Putting Patterns and Gradients into Patterns

Under normal circumstances, you cannot put gradients into patterns or patterns into other patterns. But if Illustrator doesn't think of the objects as patterns or gradients, you can put patterns and gradients into patterns.

Pattern Printing Problems

Stubing: Why does it take so long to print patterns?

Toulouse: Well, if you think of what patterns actually are, you'll know.

Stubing: If I knew, would I be asking?

Toulouse: It's just that patterns are really bunches of masked sections of — get this — Type 3 fonts. The masks are rectangles.

Stubing: Which means...?

Toulouse: Masks can always cause printing problems, as can Type 3 fonts, but if you do complex transformations to complex patterns, you're asking for trouble.

To put a pattern into another pattern, drag the pattern that you want to put into the new pattern from the Swatches palette to your document. Group the pattern artwork and Option[Alt]-copy several squares. Draw a rectangle around the squares and add any additional artwork for the new pattern. Select the artwork and drag to the Swatches palette.

Including gradients in patterns is not quite so simple. First, create the object in the shape of the gradient and Fill it with the Gradient. Expand the gradient with the Object⇨Expand command. You can then use the blended object in any pattern.

CAUTION

When you transform gradients into blends via Expand for placement in a pattern, check for masked areas. You cannot use masks in patterns, so you need to release the mask before you incorporate the blend into the pattern. Also, try to keep the number of blend steps to a minimum.

BY THE WAY

Technical overkill: Patterns in Illustrator are actually saved as Type 3 fonts into your Illustrator file. Remember how long it takes some of those fancy Berthold fonts to print? Imagine stuffing hundreds of colored, tinted, twisted, turned objects into a font. . . .

Transforming Patterns

After you create patterns and place them within paths, they may be too big or at the wrong angle, or they may start in an awkward location. You can use the transformation tools and the Move command to resolve these problems.

To transform a pattern inside a path, select the path and double-click the transformation tool that corresponds to the change that you want to make to the pattern. In the transformation tool's dialog box, uncheck the Object checkbox. The Pattern Tiles and Objects checkboxes are grayed out if the selected object does not contain a pattern.

Any changes that you make in the transformation tool's dialog box when only the Pattern checkbox is checked affect only the pattern, not the outside shape. The default (which cannot be changed) is for both checkboxes to remain checked always.

If you are using any of the transformation tools manually, the pattern inside the selected object will transform with the object only if the Transform pattern tiles option in the General Preferences dialog box is checked.

To move a pattern within a path, choose Arrange⇨Transform⇨Move (double-click on the Selection tool). The Move dialog box also contains Pattern and Objects checkboxes. If you uncheck the Objects checkbox, only the pattern will be moved.

Graphs

The Graphs feature seems to be one of the most underused features in Illustrator.

All the graph tools work in a manner similar to that of the shape creation tools: Click and drag to set the size of the graph, or click to display the Graph Size dialog box and then enter the size information. If you press the Shift key while you drag, the graph is constrained to a perfect square (or circle, if it's a pie graph). If you press the Option [Alt] key while you drag, you drag from the center of the graph out. If you Option[Alt]-click, the graph you create is centered at the point you Option[Alt]-clicked. That's it. That's all you have to do to use the graph tools. Neat, huh?

Double-clicking on the Graph tool brings up the Graph Type dialog box, shown in Figure 11-8. Choosing a different graph type at this point and clicking OK changes the tool to represent the type of graph you selected. You can choose from nine graph types; the column graph is the default.

One of the most exciting things about graphs in Illustrator is their fluidity. Not only can you create graphs easily, but after you create them, you can change them easily. In addition, if the data that you used to create a graph changes, you can enter the new data and have it show up in the graph instantaneously.

Figure 11-9 and the steps that follow describe the basics of creating and modifying a graph. The type of graph in this example is a grouped column graph, which is commonly used to compare quantities over time or between different categories.

Figure 11-8: The Graph Type dialog box

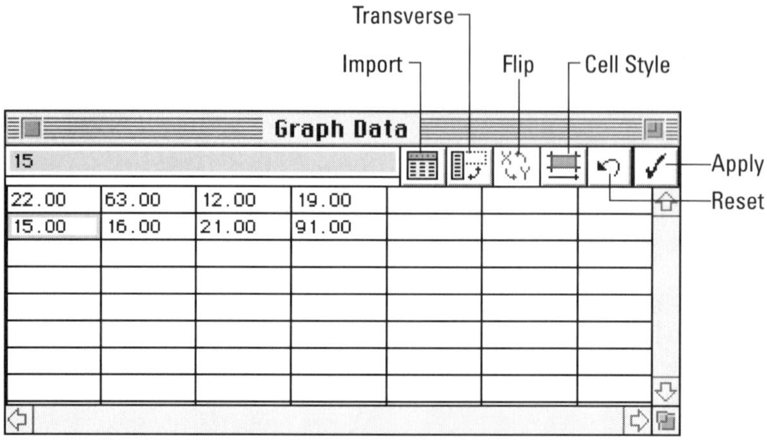

Figure 11-9: The basic steps for creating a graph in Illustrator

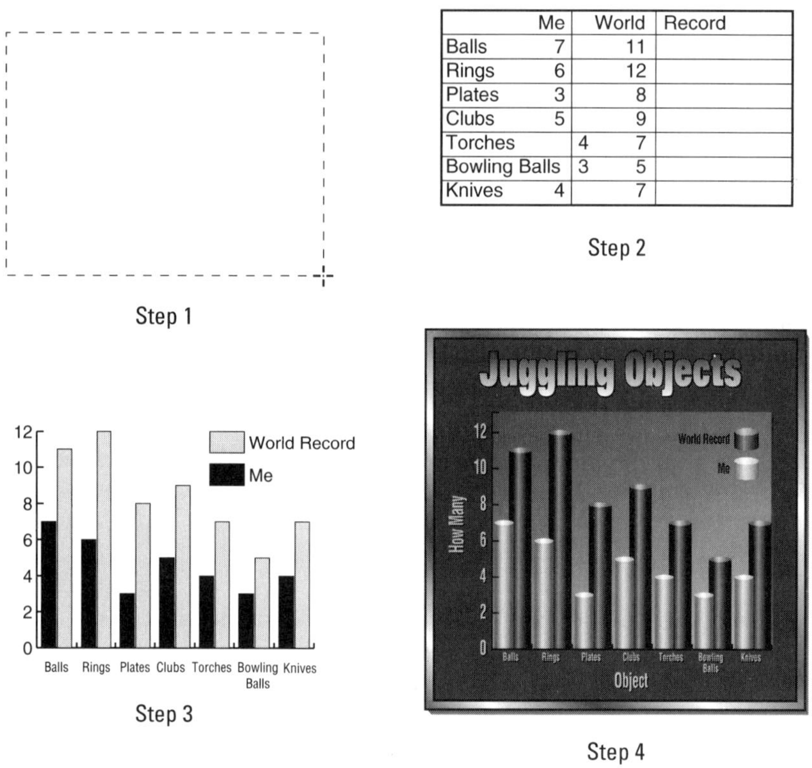

STEPS: Creating a Graph

Step 1. Select the Graph tool and click and drag to form a rectangular area, similarly to the way that you use the Rectangle tool. The size of the rectangle that you create will be the size of the graph.

Step 2. As soon as you release the mouse button, the Graph Data dialog box appears. Information that you enter in the Graph Data dialog box becomes formatted into graph form.

The top row in the Graph Data dialog box worksheet area should contain the labels for comparison within the same set. In the example, I compared how many things I can juggle to what the current world records are for juggling those particular objects. The items in the top row appear as *legends* outside the graph area.

In the leftmost column, you can enter labels that appear at the bottom of the grouped column graph as *categories*. I entered the types of objects that are to be compared in the graph.

In the remaining *cells*, enter the pertinent information.

Step 3. Close the window to have all the data that you entered used in the graph. The graph appears, and it should look something like the one in Step 3 of Figure 11-9.

Step 4. After I created the graph, I edited it by changing the paint style of the bars and legends, adding a background, changing the point sizes and font of the type in the graph, and adding the lightened circles at the top of each bar and legend to make the elements in the graph look more three-dimensional.

When to Use Graphs

Graphs are most useful when they show numerical information that would normally take several paragraphs to explain or that can't be expressed easily in words. Furthermore, you can express numerical information easily in graphs, and using graphs makes finding and understanding information easier than when the same information is in lines of text.

Numbers are fascinating concepts that most people have a good grasp of, but you can overlook their significance, especially when you are comparing different numbers. The numbers 2 and 9 are the same size when you type them; however, when you use them in a graph, they can represent a drastic difference.

(continued)

(continued)

Of course, although graphs are normally used to educate and inform, they are also suited very well for misinforming. Stretching or crushing a graph can cause a great difference in the way the information appears. Even worse is the ability to stretch or compress information in one part of the graph. The figure shows the same information in two radically different graphs.

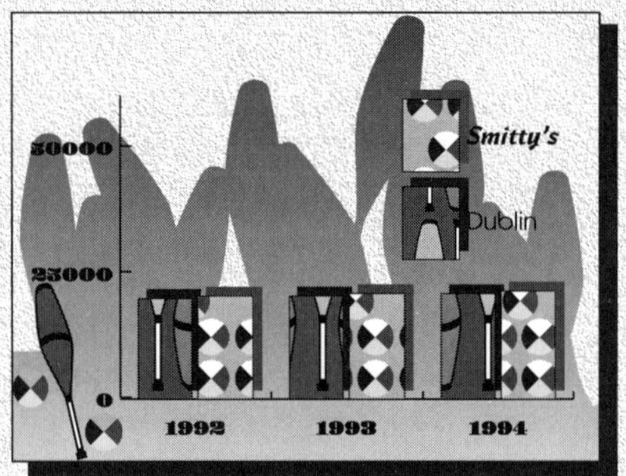

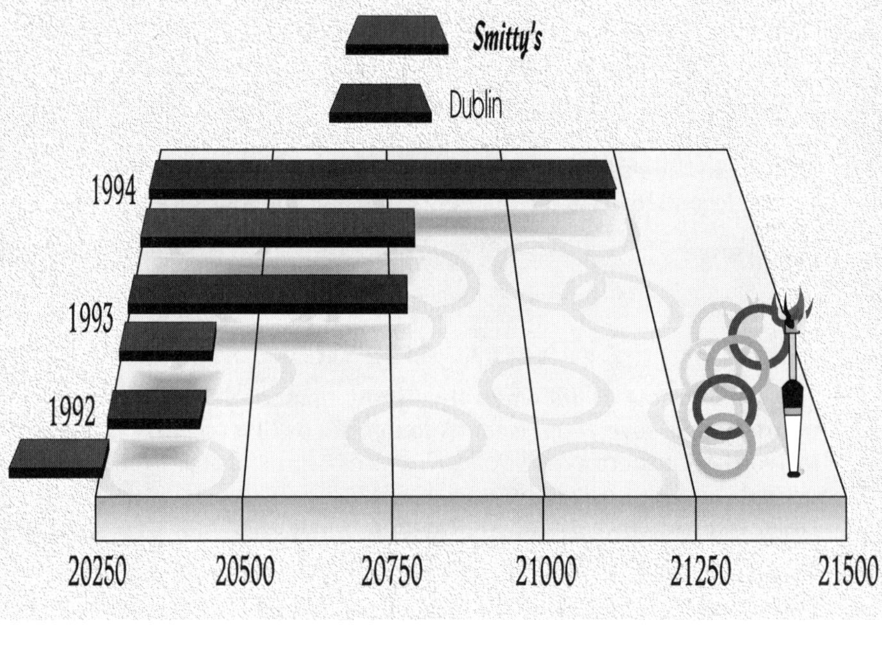

The information for the top graph, created by the Smitty's people, shows them to be even with their competitors. The text for the numbers, the column drop shadows, and the distracting images cause the data to make less impact on the reader than it does in the graph below. Dublin's graph indicates that Dublin is doing substantially better than Smitty's. The vast difference in the length of the bars is one way to show the difference, as is the numbering scheme, which starts at 20250, making the first Smitty's bar appear to be a negative number.

The Nine Types of Graphs

You can choose from nine different types of graphs in Illustrator. Each type gives a specific kind of information to the reader. Certain graphs are better for comparisons, others for growth, and so on. The following sections describe the graphs, explain how to create them, and tell how you can use them.

Grouped-Column Graphs

You primarily use grouped-column graphs to show how something changes over time. Often, they are referred to as bar graphs because the columns that make up the graphs resemble bars.

Step 3 of Figure 11-9 showed a grouped-column graph as created in Illustrator. This graph contains seven categories, and each of the seven categories is represented by two different totals. The height of the bars represents the number in each case, with higher bars representing higher values.

The real strength of a grouped-column graph is that it provides for the direct comparison of different types of statistics in the same graph. In the sample graph, the number of rings that I can juggle is compared to the bowling ball juggling world record by the height of the bars.

Both column and cluster width are two customizable options for grouped-column graphs and stacked-column graphs. Column width refers to the width of individual columns, with 100% being wide enough to butt up against other columns in the cluster. Cluster width refers to how much of the available cluster space is taken up by the columns in the cluster. At 80% (the default), 20% of the available space is empty, leaving room between clusters.

You can widen columns and clusters to 1,000% of their size and condense them to 1% of the width of the original column or cluster.

Stacked-Column Graphs

Stacked-column graphs are good graphs for presenting the total of a category and the contributing portions of each category. In Figure 11-10, I used objects once again as categories and split each object into the number of those objects being juggled. The total of the time it takes (in weeks) to learn to juggle that number of objects is the height of the object's bar. The time for each number of objects juggled represents a certain portion of the entire time, reflected in each of the smaller sections of the bars.

CAUTION: To get the labels on the legends to read numbers only, I had to put quotation marks (" ") around each of the numbers. If I had not used quotation marks, the numbers would have been considered data, not labels.

This graph shows the same amount of information as the grouped-column graph, but the information is organized differently. The stacked-column graph is designed to display a total of all the legends, and the grouped-column graph is designed to aid comparison of all individual legends in each category.

Line Graphs

Line graphs (also known as line charts) show trends over time. They are especially useful for determining progress and identifying radical changes. For example, the line graph in Figure 11-11 shows the average income of three street performers on successive weeks throughout the summer.

The Mark Data Points option in the Line graphs area of the Graph Style dialog box (Object⇨Graphs⇨Style) forces data points to appear as squares. If this box is not checked, the data points are visible only as direction changes in lines between the data points.

If the Connect Data Points option is checked, lines will be drawn between each pair of data points.

The Draw Filled Lines option and the corresponding text box for line width create a line that is Filled with the data point legend color and is outlined with Black. The Fill Lines option changes the line from a single path with a Stroke weight into a Filled path with a Black Stroke.

	"3"	"4"	"5"	"6"	"7"	"8"	"9"	
Balls	1	6	28	32	40	38	72	
Rings	2	8	42	10	35	14	34	
Clubs	4	38	50	75	140			

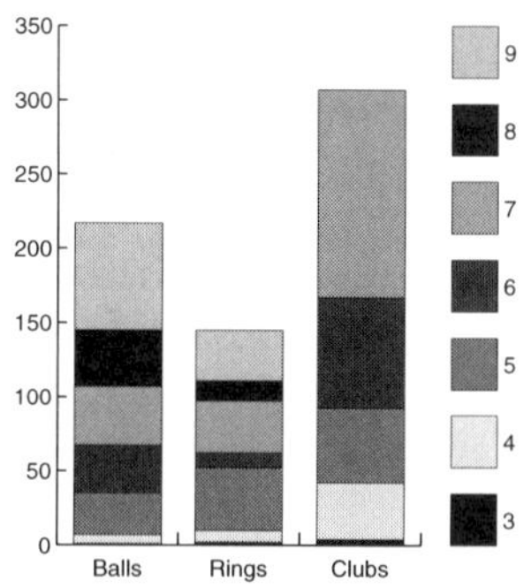

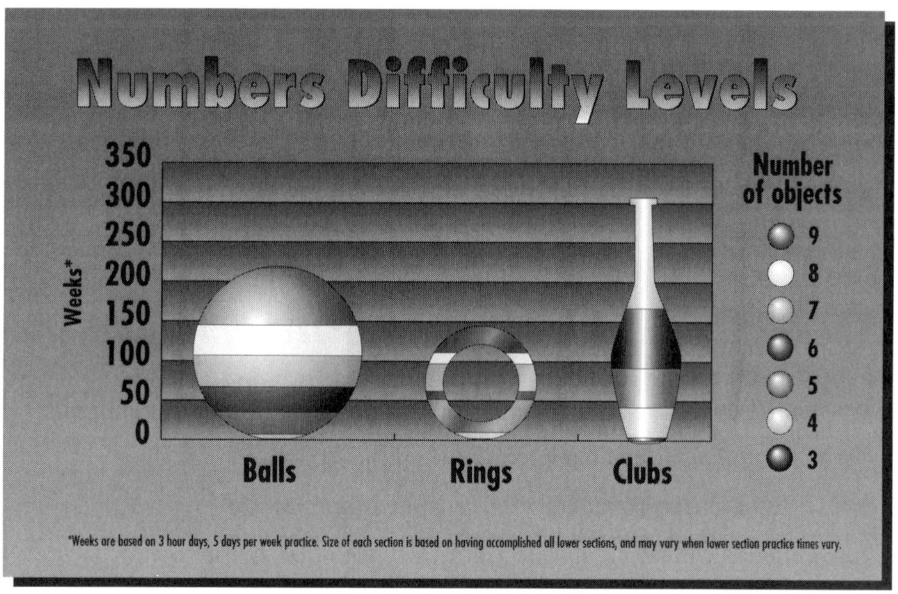

Figure 11-10: Data for a stacked-column graph, how the graph appears when it is first created in Illustrator, and the graph after it is altered

The Edge to Edge lines option stretches the lines out to the left and right edges of the graph. Although the result is technically incorrect, you can achieve better visual impact by using this feature.

	Animated Suspension	The Flying Linguini	Disoriented Convolution
May	300	220	145
	240	190	120
	260	260	140
	320	300	200
June	380	360	150
	400	350	195
	395	320	230
	435	420	190
July	520	190	200
	600	290	195
	440	405	240
	380	340	150
August	300	210	200
	275	250	240
	360	280	230
	300	290	210
September	420	280	170
	220	140	110

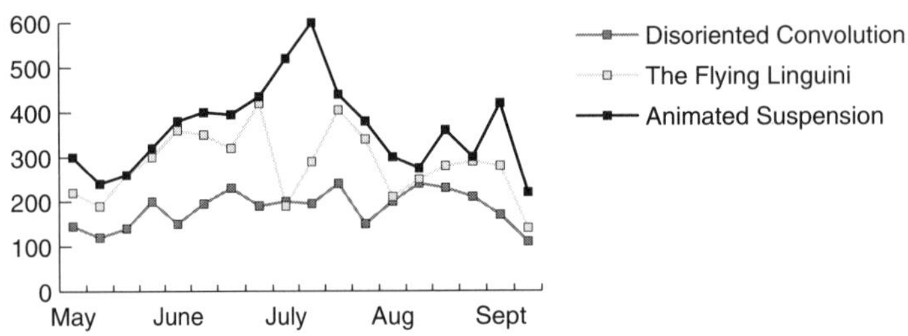

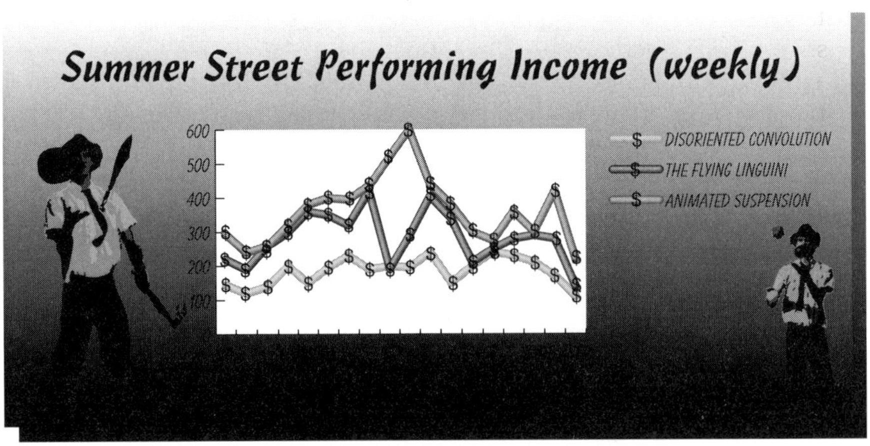

Figure 11-11: Line graph data (top), the graph as it first appears in Illustrator (center), and the graph after it has been redesigned (bottom)

Area Graphs

Upon first glance, area graphs may appear to be just like line graphs that are Filled. Like line graphs, area graphs show data points that are connected, but area graphs are stacked upon each other to show the total area of the legend subject in the graph.

Pie Graphs

Pie graphs are great for comparing percentages of the portions of a whole. In Figure 11-12, pie graphs show how much of a juggling performance was spent doing particular activities. The higher the percentage for a certain activity, the larger its wedge.

When you create pie graphs, you can remove the individual wedges from the central pie with the Group Selection tool to achieve an exploding pie effect.

The Legends in wedges option is the only option in the Graph Style dialog box that is specifically for pie graphs. If Legends in wedges is selected, the name of each wedge will be centered within that wedge. Illustrator doesn't do a very good job of placing the legend names, many times overlapping neighboring names. In addition, the letters in the legend names are black, which can make reading some of the names difficult or impossible.

Scatter Graphs

Scatter graphs, which are primarily used for scientific charting purposes, are quite different from all the other types of graphs. Each data point is given a location by *x-y* coordinates instead of by category and label. The points are connected, as are the points in line graphs, but the line created by the data point locations can cross itself and does not go in any specific direction. Scatter graphs have the same customization options as line graphs.

Graph Trouble

Doc: Sometimes my data values change when I close a document and open it later.

Toulouse: Really?

Doc: Yeah, it's very annoying.

Toulouse: I'm just fooling with you. That's a problem within Illustrator.

Doc: What can I do to fix it?

Toulouse: The best thing to do is to change the graph into plain Illustrator artwork.

Doc: Done. Wait. How do I do that?

Toulouse: Select the graph and ungroup it.

Doc: But I get a message saying it won't work as a graph anymore.

Toulouse: That's the downfall, unfortunately.

	Passing knives around a small child	Begging for Money	Juggling a Bowling Ball, Torch, and Razor Sharp Machete	Riding a 12' Unicycle	Eating Fire	Spinning 10 Basketballs	Juggling 5 Torches
Disoriented Convolution	12	15	1	3	4	4	2
Animated Suspension	7	2	3	12	8	5	3
The Flying Linguini	10	7	2	6	7	2	8

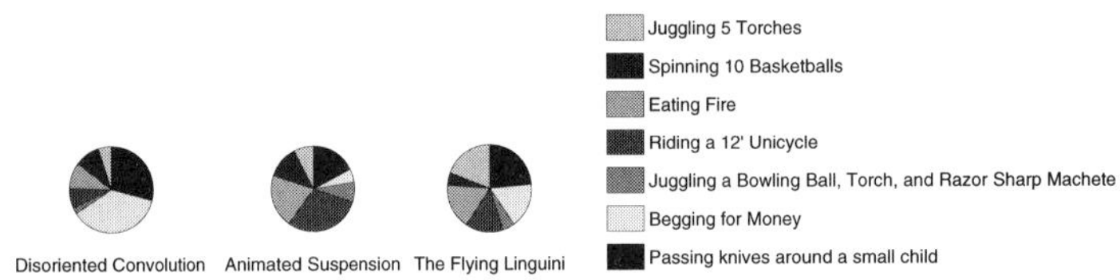

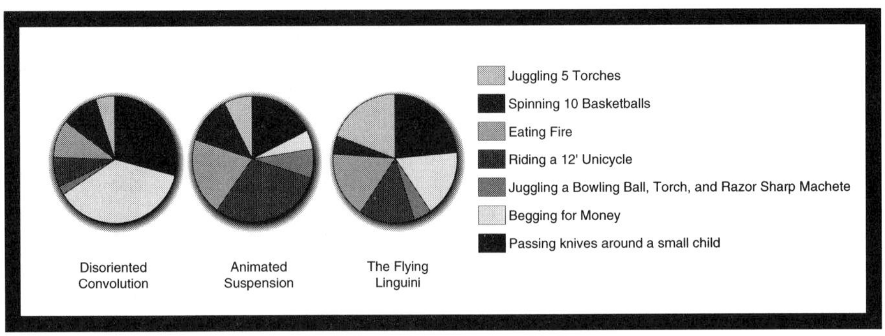

Figure 11-12: Pie graphs showing how much time each performer spent on certain activities, constructed from the data above

Customizing Graphs

When a graph is selected and the Graph Type dialog box is displayed, a number of options become available for most graphs:

- The Left or Right axis options display the vertical values on either the left side (the default) or the right side. The Same axis both sides option puts the same axis on both sides. Clicking the Left or Right button displays options for customizing axes.
- Checking the Drop shadow option places a black shadow behind the graph objects. The shadow is offset up and to the right.
- The Legends across top option makes existing legends (if any) appear across the top of the graph, instead of being grouped together on the right side of the graph.
- The First row in front option places overlapping rows in order from left to right, wherever columns, clusters, or other objects overlap.

Each type of graph has its own customization options. The preceding sections that describe each type of graph explain those options.

To make visually striking graphs, use a combination of graph types. Simply use the Group Selection tool to select all the objects that are one legend type and then choose Object⇨Graphs⇨Graph Type and enter the new graph type for that legend.

Using the Graph Data Dialog Box

You can change the numbers and the text in the Graph Data dialog box (Figure 11-13) at any time by selecting the graph and Object⇨Graphs⇨Data. Illustrator will re-create the graph to reflect the changes you make. If you have moved some of the graph objects around, they may revert to their original locations when Illustrator re-creates the graph. If a number does not have quotation marks around it, Illustrator assumes that you want the number to be entered as a value in the graph.

Figure 11-13: The Graph Data dialog box

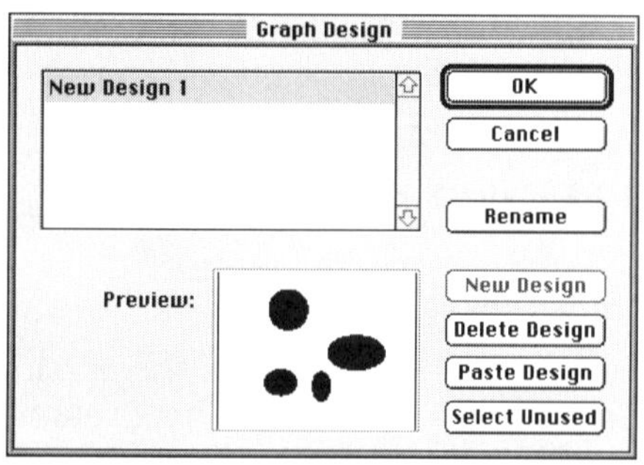

Make sure that the graph is never ungrouped, at least not until you have finished making all graph data and graph style changes. If you ungroup the graph, you will not be able to use any of the graph options to change the ex-graph because it will be just a set of paths and text in Illustrator's view.

You can import graph data in tab-delimited word processing files. Tab-delimited files are text and numbers that are separated by tabs and returns. To import data from another file, click the Import button or click the Import button while you are in the Graph Data dialog box.

Illustrator is not really a graphing or spreadsheet program, so many of the usual controls for arranging data in such programs are not available, including inserting rows and columns and creating formulas.

The Cut, Copy, and Paste functions work within the Graph Data dialog box, so you can move and duplicate information on a very basic level.

One very useful feature in the Graph Data dialog box is the Transverse button. This function switches the *x* and *y* axes of the data, reversing everything that you have entered.

Using Marker and Column Designs

The most exciting part about the graphing functions in Illustrator is the capability to give column, line, and area graphs special icons to indicate values on the graphs.

On line and area graphs, marker designs are created, which you can use in place of the standard markers. For each value in the graph, the marker design is placed, adding visual impact to the graph.

Column designs are created for grouped-column graphs and stacked-column graphs. The strength of using column designs is most evident in grouped-column graphs, where images are placed side by side (see Figure 11-14).

STEPS: Creating and Using a Column Design

Step 1. Create the graphic object in Illustrator.

Step 2. Draw a rectangle around the border of the object. Illustrator uses this border to determine the area of the object relative to the values entered for the graph.

Step 3. Draw a horizontal line across the rectangle at a good place for the image to stretch. Make the horizontal line into a guide (View⇨Make Guide or press ⌘-5 [Ctrl+5]).

(Step 3 is necessary only if you use the column design as a sliding design.)

Step 4. Select the rectangle, object, and guide, and choose Object⇨Graphs⇨ Design. Click the New button to make the selected object appear in the window. Name the design and click the OK button.

Step 5. Select just one legend type by clicking twice on the legend graphic with the Group Selection tool. Choose Object⇨Graphs⇨Design and select the design from the list. Choose the column design type (see Figure 11-13 for examples of each type). Repeat this step for each legend.

You can combine column-design types by selecting a different type for each legend.

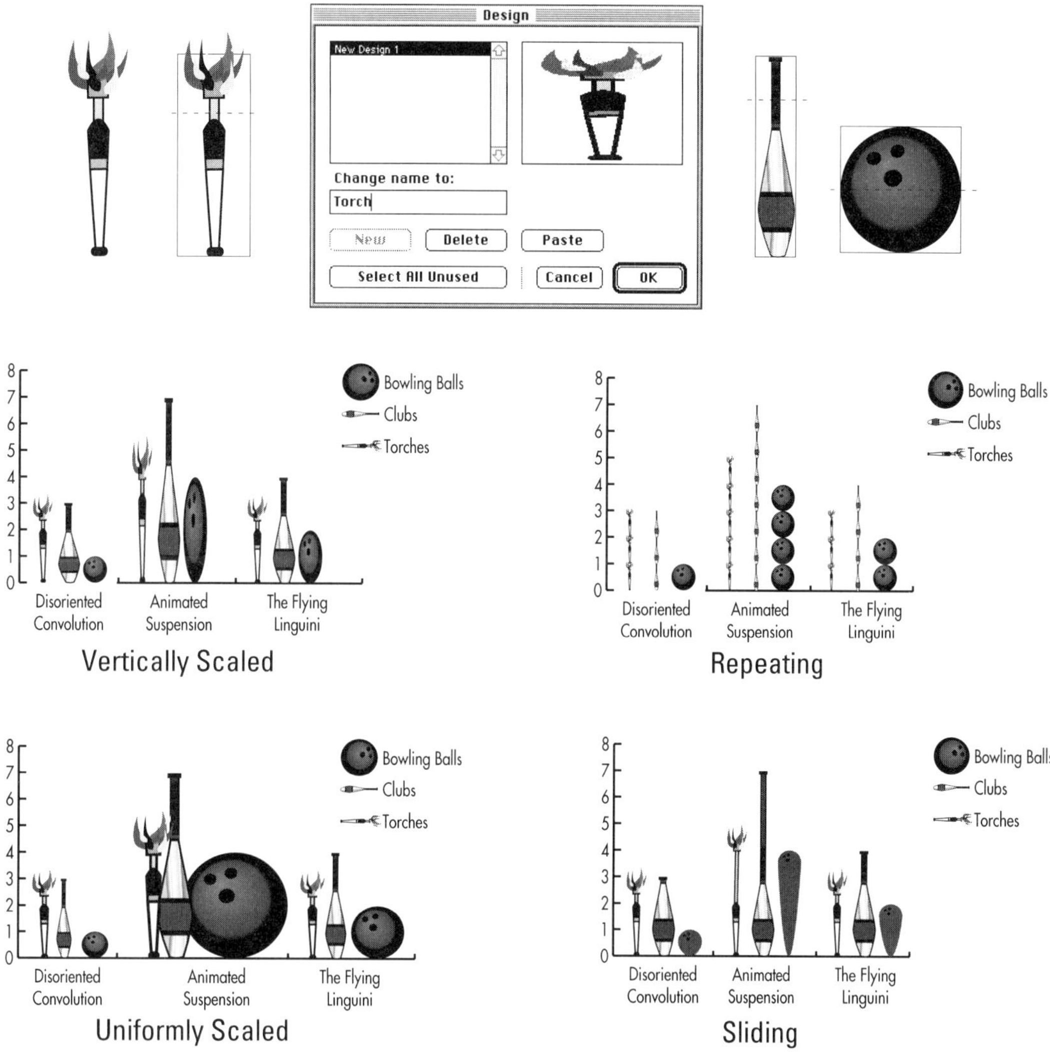

Figure 11-14: Creating a column design and using it in four different grouped column graphs

Texture Generation

One of the niftiest features in Illustrator is a filter called Ink Pen. Ink Pen takes basic Illustrator paths and turns them into random textures that you can control and manipulate through a variety of options.

To create a texture, select any path or paths and choose Filter⇨Ink Pen⇨Hatches. The Ink Pen Hatches dialog box will appear, as shown in Figure 11-15.

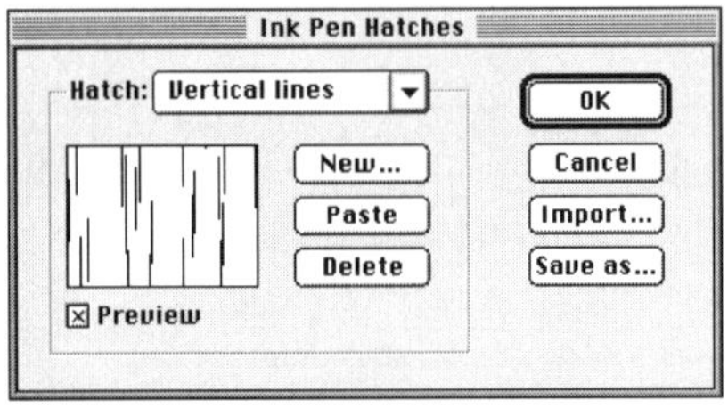

Figure 11-15: The Ink Pen Hatches dialog box

Click the New button and name your hatch. Click OK, and you'll be able to use that hatch as an Ink Pen Fill.

After the hatch has been created, you're ready to apply it as a Fill for any selected path. To do so, select the path you wish to fill and choose Filter⇨Ink Pen⇨Effects. The Ink Pen Effects dialog box appears, as shown in Figure 11-16.

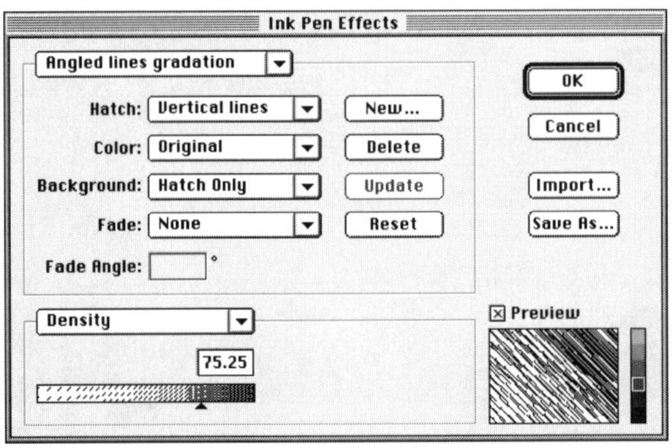

Figure 11-16: The Ink Pen Effects dialog box

Inside the Ink Pen Effects dialog box, you have an infinite amount of combinations of various properties to apply to the hatch style. The effects are listed, with figures showing the effects of various property settings chosen from the pop-up menu.

The texture that is created is actually a grouped mask of several paths. This enables you to change the paint attributes of the texture after it has been applied. In addition, you can then modify the individual paths just like you would any other path in Illustrator.

Remember that the paths you use in a hatch style can have both Fills and Strokes, but the thickness property only affects Stroke width.

Ink Pen Density

Density is how closely packed together the elements of the hatch style are. The closer together the pieces, the darker or thicker the texture will appear. You can adjust the density by dragging the Density slider to the left and right; left is less dense, right is more dense. Figure 11-17 shows various amounts of density.

Ink-Pen Dispersion

Dispersion controls how evenly the texture elements are spread within the Fill. Setting the dispersion to None results in a pattern-tile appearance that is very uniform, while increasing it randomizes the location and grouping of the pieces of the hatch style. Figure 11-18 shows various settings of the Dispersion slider.

Each of the lower four settings in the Ink Pen Fill dialog box has different ways of creating each parameter. For instance, instead of a Constant dispersion, you can choose from Linear, Symmetrical, Reflected, or Random dispersion. Each of the other properties (with the exception of density) has these same controls.

The Ink Pen Fill options work as follows:

- **Constant** keeps the setting the same throughout the entire Fill shape.
- **Linear** changes the amount of the effect across the Fill shape. The angle at which this is applied is changed in each effect section, either by moving the angle indicator or by entering a different angle in the Rotate field. There are two sliders to adjust, controlling the maximum and minimum amount of the effect.
- **Reflect** increases and decreases the amount of the effect (somewhat like a double-linear effect). The angle and minimum and maximum amounts are controlled in the same way as Linear.

Ink Pen Color Change

Gopher: I want to change the color of my hatch style.

Toulouse: After it's applied or before?

Gopher: Before, since I'm using the Fade to White option.

Toulouse: Okay. Open the Ink Pen Hatches dialog box.

Gopher: Done.

Toulouse: Then select the hatch style you wish to recolor.

Gopher: Done again.

Toulouse: Then click the Paste button.

Gopher: Paste does what?

Toulouse: Paste puts a copy of the hatch art in your document. Then change the color, go back to Ink Pen Hatches, click New, and name your new hatch something else.

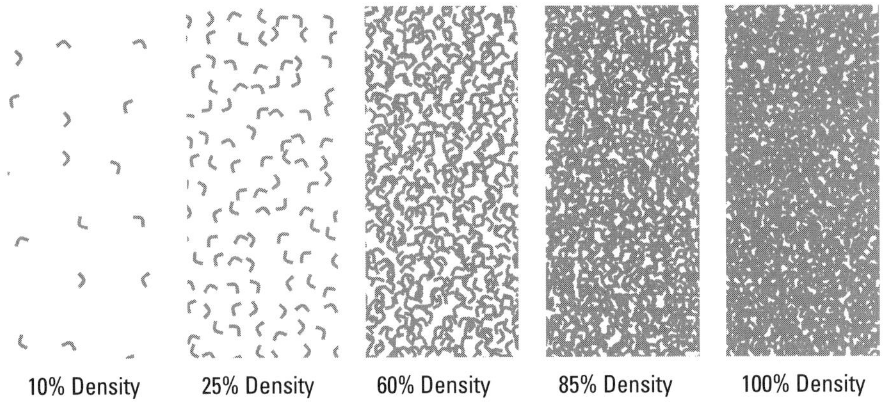

Figure 11-17: Different amounts of density for a hatch style

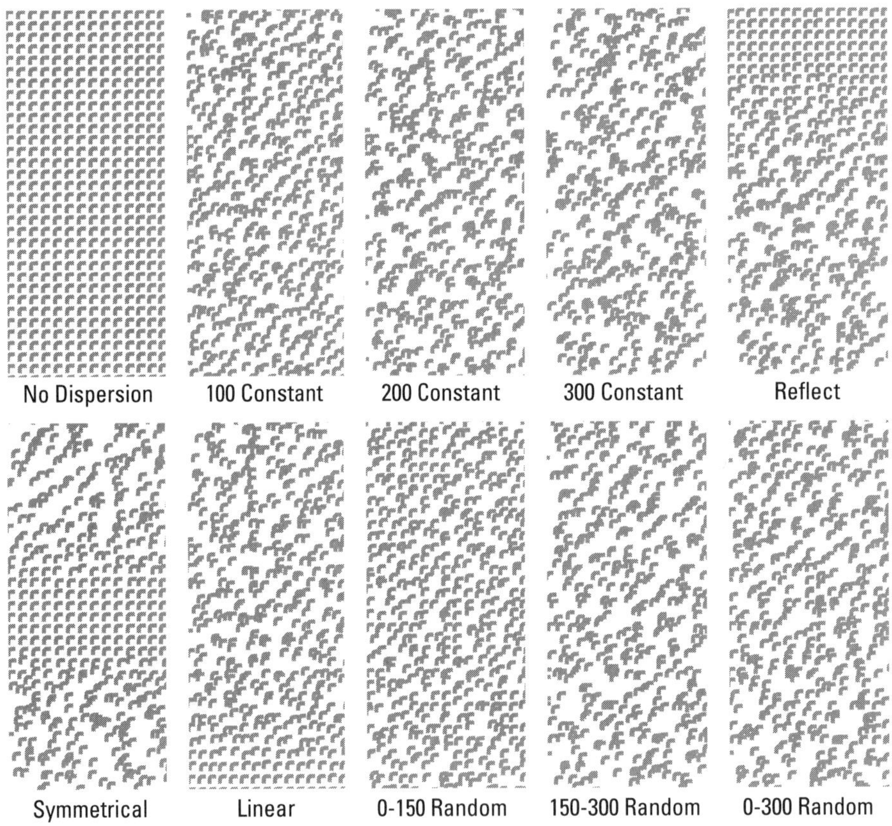

Figure 11-18: Different amounts of dispersion for a hatch style

- **Symmetrical** creates a symmetric pattern of the effect. The angle and amounts are adjusted in the same way as they are in Linear and Reflect.
- **Random** generates random amounts of the effect, between the minimum and maximum amount that you specify.

Thickness

Thickness controls the Stroke thickness of the paths in the hatch style. Some of the variations of Stroke thickness are shown in Figure 11-19.

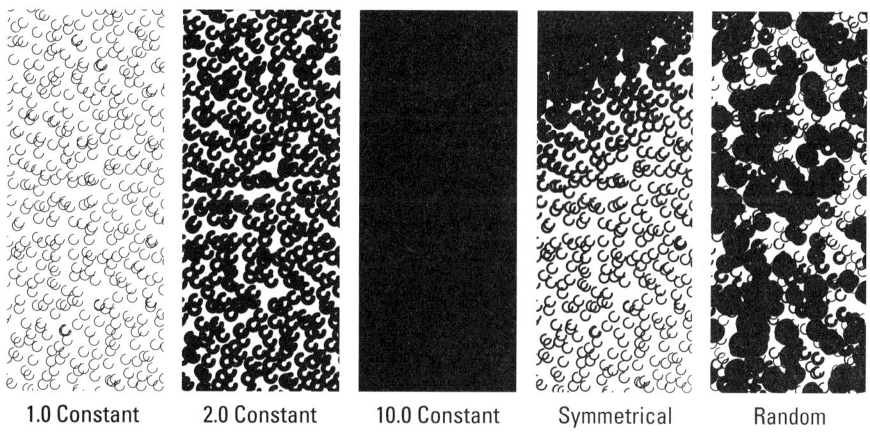

Figure 11-19: Different thickness settings for a hatch style

Rotation

Rotation controls the angle of the pieces in the hatch style. A constant amount of rotation rotates each of the pieces in the hatch style the same amount. Other rotation options vary the amount of rotation, as shown in Figure 11-20.

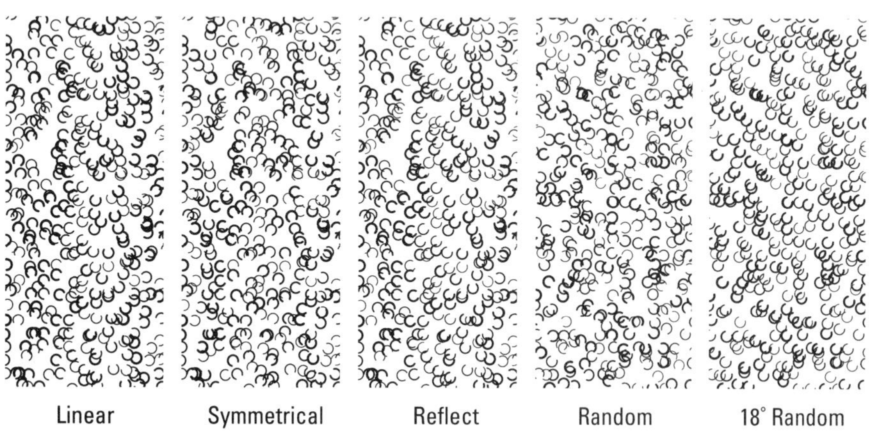

Figure 11-20: Different settings for the Rotation property

STEPS: Creating Symmetrical Textures

Step 1. Start by creating the path you wish to Fill with the symmetrical texture.

Step 2. With the path selected, choose Object⇨Ink Pen Effects, and select the hatch style to use.

Step 3. Change the Rotation property setting to Linear, making the left and right sliders the same (for example 90, 90). Click the OK button to apply the texture to the path.

Step 4. Select the path and rotate-copy the path 180°, so that it overlaps itself. The texture will be symmetrical.

Step 5. To finish up, you might want to place a gradient behind the image, as I did in Figure 11-21.

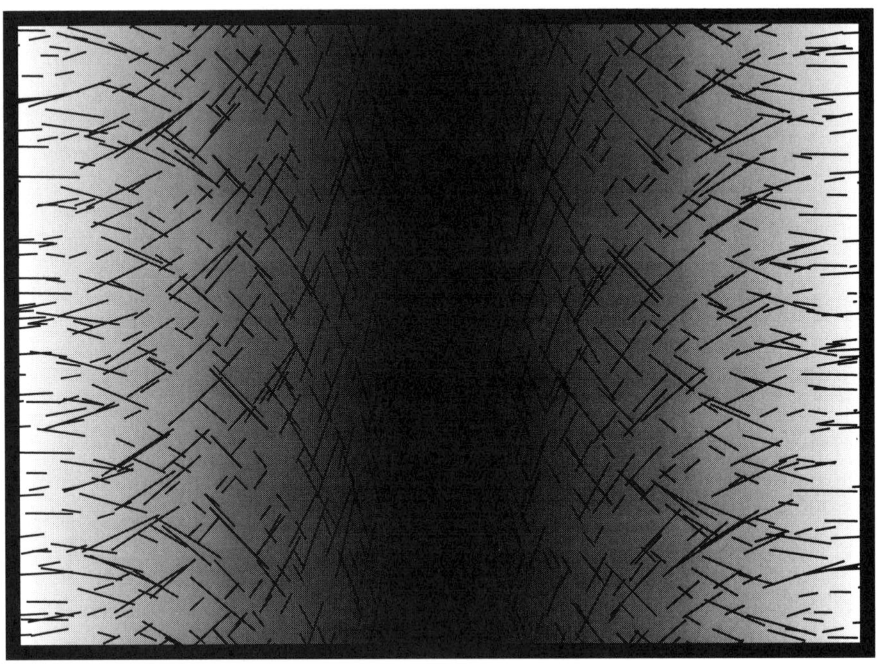

Figure 11-21: A symmetrical texture. Don't stare at this too long, or it starts to look really gross.

Scale

The Scale property changes the size of the hatch style pieces. It does *not* change the Stroke weight, however, just the size of the paths. Figure 11-22 shows sample scale settings.

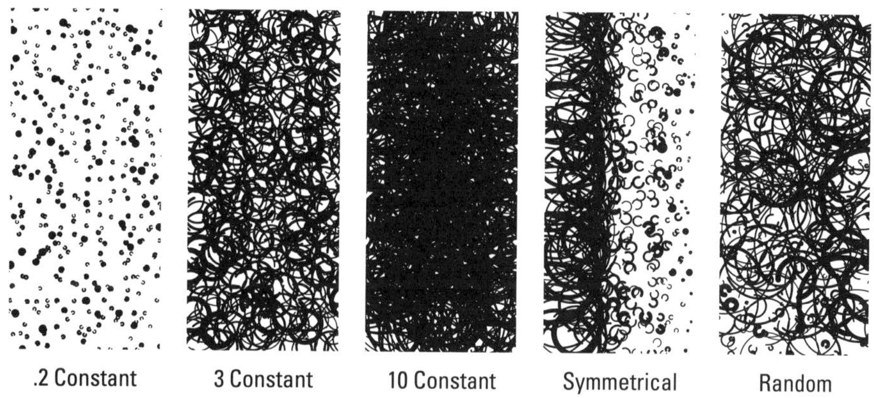

Figure 11-22: Different settings for the Scale property

POWER TIP

If you are going to be using "lines" that you'd like to scale uniformly (instead of just the length changing, you'd like the width to change as well), then create thin rectangles instead of single paths. That way, the width of the rectangle increases with its length. However, the Thickness property then has no effect on the hatch style.

Other Ink Pen Fill Controls

Several other controls determine how your Fill interacts with the background. These controls are located in the lower right of the Ink Pen Fill dialog box.

Select the hatch style you'd like to use in the Hatch pop-up menu. The hatch color can be Original (the color of the original paths when they were created as a hatch) or the color of the Fill of the selected path. The Background color of the original object can be the color of the original path or a Retain Fill by changing the Background pop-up menu. The Fade pop-up controls the fade of the hatch style. The Fade Angle option controls the angle of the fade.

Figure 11-23 shows two examples of the Fade to White option with the background (a gradient) and no background.

Figure 11-23: Fade to White with a gradient background and no background

Summary

- Patterns are a type of Fill that provides texture to any path.
- Several default patterns are supplied with Illustrator, and these patterns can be transformed in the same ways that other Illustrator objects can be transformed.
- Almost anything in Illustrator can be used as a pattern, with the exception of masks, gradients, placed images, and other patterns.
- Diagonal-line patterns can be created by creating a horizontal-line pattern and then rotating it by using the rotate tool while the pattern is filling a path.
- Graphs can be created in Illustrator just by entering the data.
- After a graph has been created, it can be adjusted and manipulated like any other path-based object.
- Textures can be created with the Ink Pen Effects command.

Filters and Plug-Ins

III

The Filter menu in Illustrator is unlike any menu in any other program. It can be remotely compared with the Filter menu in Photoshop, although Illustrator contains many of the Photoshop filters anyway. However, the comparison falls short because Illustrator is a *vector* program, and the filters and plug-ins do much more than modify colors and shapes.

Part III takes you on a journey of discovery into all the filters and plug-ins that exist for Illustrator, from the built-in filters to the fantastic third-party plug-ins from vendors such as Extensis (VectorTools), MetaCreations (Vector Effects), and hot door (CADtools).

Illustrator's Built-In Filters and Plug-Ins

CHAPTER 12

In This Chapter

- An overview of filters and plug-ins
- Filters in Illustrator compared to filters in Photoshop
- Moving and using the Plug-Ins folder
- Using filter combinations
- The mysterious Last Filter option
- How color filters work
- Using color filters to create highlights and shadows
- Adding and subtracting colors from multiple paths
- Blending colors without changing path shapes
- Changing raster images into vector object mosaics
- Creating fills and strokes for Masks
- How the Distort and Stylize filters work
- Perspectives with Free Distort
- Rippling paths with the Zig Zag filter
- Randomizing paths with Roughen, and Scribble and Tweak
- Adding arrowheads to open paths
- Using the Round Corners filter to soften harsh angles
- Applying patterns to the edges of paths with Path Patterns

Adobe introduced Illustrator filters back in Version 5.0. Most users of Illustrator expected Photoshop-type filters and were a little disappointed with the Illustrator filters. Actually, the only filters that are like Photoshop filters are the Distort filters and a few of the Stylize filters.

The plug-ins and filters included with Illustrator are nice, but it's the third-party plug-ins and filters that really make the concept of filters and plug-ins exciting. Plug-ins like Extensis VectorTools and MetaCreations VectorEffects give Illustrator capabilities that Illustrator users have wanted and dreamed about for years.

Windows Update

All of the filters in this section...heck, all filters...are new to Illustrator 7 for Windows. Being able to use filters on vector objects was one of the most innovative changes to Illustrator, and Windows users will find most of them invaluable. The toughest part of all these new filters is how to keep what they do straight; this chapter will help immensely in that area.

Filters in Illustrator

Instead of just changing the appearance of images, most of the filters in Illustrator perform tasks that took hours to do manually in previous versions of Illustrator. In a way, most of these filters work as intelligent macros, and they enable you to produce a variety of effects.

Some filters, such as the Zig Zag filter, seem to perform quite simple tasks. In reality, however, these filters are complex, math-based programs that accomplish certain tasks faster than the fastest illustrator could dream of performing without them.

So why are all these functions in the Filter menu, and not just functions within the software? Because none of them are really integrated into Illustrator; instead, each filter is an individual file called a *plug-in,* which resides in the Plug-Ins folder. For a filter to be available, the plug-in must be in the Plug-Ins folder.

Adobe, in its marketing wisdom, initially pushed two filters with grungelike names: Punk and Bloat. To be honest, I rarely use either of these filters, though I was quite intrigued the first time I saw them demonstrated. Cool names, little functionality. The same thing applies to the Twirl filter, which produces some really amazing

Where Did All the Filters Go?

Not only are there no new filters in Illustrator 7, but the Filter menu has been dramatically parsed down to only a few Illustrator-specific categories as well. It's not that any functions were taken away, but many of the functions were moved from the Filter menu to other menus in Illustrator.

To help make this clearer, you'll need a little background story. In 1993, when Illustrator 5.0 (the first version to support plug-ins) was introduced, Adobe thought that any add-on functionality created from plug-ins should be placed in the Filter menu (as was the practice in Photoshop 2.5). While most of the new plug-in-based enhancements really weren't filters in a Photoshop sense of the word, they thought that because Illustrator was such a different product from Photoshop, these new features really could be considered "vector filters."

By the time Illustrator 6.0 was released, that thought had changed substantially. The Illustrator engineers changed the API (Application Programming Interface) to let plug-ins be not just in the Filter menu, but also in any menu, or as a palette, or as a tool. Adobe started moving some things that were filters to tools (Spiral, Twirl, Polygon, Star), and others to palettes (align). With Illustrator 7, the only functions left in the Filter menu fall into the categories of Colors, Create (still not really filters), Distort, Ink Pen, and Stylize.

Select, Pathfinder, and Object "filters" have been moved to the Edit and Object menus.

effects. But once again, I don't use it very much (but I do use it more than the Punk and Bloat brothers). Yet I understand Adobe's marketing: I certainly wasn't that excited at first about the Select filters (now functions on the Edit menu) in comparison to these and other Distort filters.

Filter Organization

Illustrator 7 includes many of the Photoshop filters that ship with Photoshop 4. All the Photoshop (pixel-based) filters are set up to appear at the bottom of the Filter menu, while the vector-based filters appear at the top of the menu. (See Figure 12-1.)

What Are Filters?

Johnny: Now, how are filters in Illustrator different from the things I use to make sure all those little black things don't get in my coffee?

Toulouse: Filters in Illustrator do all sorts of amazing things that would be really difficult or time-consuming to normally do in Illustrator.

Johnny: That's nice, but then why have all the hard ways to do things in Illustrator, if you've got these filters hanging around?

Toulouse: A good example is the Roughen filter. It adds points to paths and then randomly moves them around.

Johnny: Wouldn't the easy thing be to just draw the paths using the Pencil tool with a low Curve Fitting Tolerance? Seems like you could avoid the Roughen filter all together that way.

Toulouse: Ah, but what if you want to roughen existing artwork? The Roughen filter does this in just a few seconds.

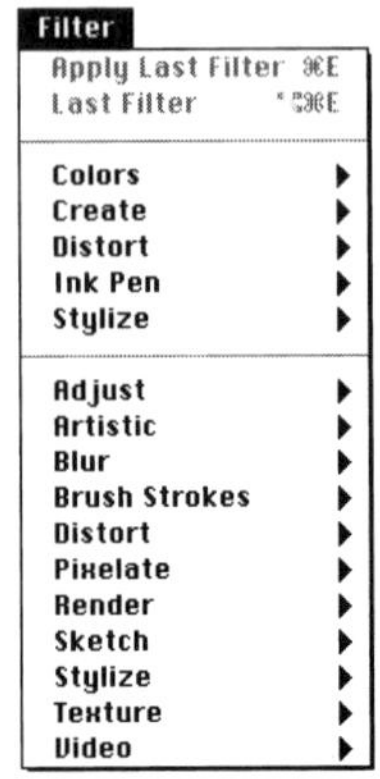

Figure 12-1: The Filter menu

Illustrator and Photoshop Filters

The filters in Illustrator have to be different from the filters in Photoshop because Illustrator deals with vector-based images and Photoshop works with bitmapped graphics. Many electronic artists use Photoshop as a staple of their graphics work. For them, the word *filter* conjures up thoughts of blurring and sharpening, as well as some of the fantastic effects that they can achieve by using filters from third parties, such as Kai's Power Tools or Alien Skin Eye Candy.

The very term *filters* is based in photography terminology for special lenses that are attached to cameras to achieve special effects. Photoshop's filters are based on this concept, and they take it quite a bit further, creating controls for variety and exactness that a camera lens could never match.

For this reason, filter isn't really the best term for the manipulations that Illustrator performs when you choose a filter. The following list compares some of the Illustrator filters with their Photoshop counterparts that perform similar functions:

- Illustrator: Filter➪Create➪Object Mosaic
  Photoshop: Filter➪Stylize➪Mosaic

  The Mosaic filters take bitmap images and reduce the number of colored areas to large, single-colored squares.

  These two filters produce results that are the most alike of any of the Illustrator and Photoshop filters. The dialog boxes are a little different, but the results are functionally the same. One big difference is that stylizing a mosaic in Photoshop is a fairly fast procedure, but creating an object mosaic in Illustrator is a complex task that eats up tons of RAM and can take up to ten minutes to complete.

- Illustrator: Filter➪Distort➪Twirl
  Photoshop: Filter➪Distort➪Twirl

  Twirling spins an object or picture more in the center than around the edges.

- Illustrator: Filter➪Distort➪Free Distort
  Photoshop: Image➪Effects➪Distort

  Distorting gives you the ability to move the four corners of a selected object/picture to any new location, changing the perspective or just plain mangling the original object/picture.

  A boon for Illustrator users, the Free Distort filter makes tedious perspective gridwork a thing of the past. Photoshop's Distort feature is not a filter per se but rather part of the Image control subsection.

Some features that you would expect to do the same thing in each program are not the same:

- Illustrator: Filter➪Colors➪Invert Colors
  Photoshop: Image➪Map➪Invert

  Illustrator's Invert Colors filter is annoying because you expect a negative image but don't get it. Instead, you get Cyan, Magenta, and Yellow values that have been subtracted from 100, and a Black value that is untouched. Photoshop's Invert command creates a true negative, and it is a feature, not a filter.

- Illustrator: Filter➪Colors➪Saturate
  Photoshop: Image➪Adjust➪Hue/Saturation

  The saturation filter in Illustrator increases/decreases the CMYK values for selected objects. In Photoshop, the color intensity is increased. Saturation in Illustrator is a misnomer, at least when compared to the functionality of Saturation in most other software packages.

The Plug-Ins Folder

All of the filters in Illustrator are in the Filter menu because a file with the same name as the filter is in the Plug-Ins folder. If the filter's file is not in the Plug-Ins folder, the filter will not appear in the Filter menu.

The Plug-Ins folder is put inside the first level of the Adobe Illustrator folder when Illustrator is installed. If you move the folder, you need to tell Illustrator where it is located.

STEPS: Relocating the Plug-Ins Folder

Step 1. In the Finder, with Illustrator not running, move or copy the Plug-Ins folder to the desired location.

Step 2. Double-click the Illustrator icon.

Step 3. Choose File⇨Preferences⇨Plug-Ins & Scratch Disk.

Step 4. In the Plug-Ins dialog box, click the Choose button, find the Plug-Ins folder, and click the Select button at the bottom of the dialog box.

Step 5. Quit Illustrator and double-click the Illustrator icon to restart Illustrator. The new Plug-Ins folder location is now used.

Third-Party Filters

Several companies are currently producing third-party filters for Illustrator. In fact, companies such as Extensis, Alien Skin, MetaCreations, and hotdoor are producing high-profile filter sets for Illustrator.

Because Illustrator filters are taking off like wildfire, I've included two chapters on third-party filters plug-ins, Chapter 14: "VectorTools," and Chapter 15: "Other Third-Party Filters." For additional information on Illustrator filters, pick up a copy of *Illustrator Filter Finesse,* which contains all sorts of Illustrator filter information that I couldn't squeeze into this book.

Why You Can Apply the Last Filter but Never "Apply Last Filter"

Whenever you start up Illustrator, the top menu item in the Filter menu reads "Apply Last Filter," but it is grayed out. This causes some confusion initially. After you use a filter, its name appears where the menu once listed "Apply Last Filter." Thereafter, the name of the last filter that you used appears at the top of the menu. The key command for reapplying the last filter is ⌘-E [Ctrl+E].

To return to the last filter's dialog box, select Filter⇨*[Name of Last Filter]*, located right below the Apply Last Filter option, or press ⌘-Option-E [Ctrl+Alt+E].

The Color Filters

The color filters in the Color submenu of the Filter menu really take Illustrator's color capabilities to the next level in many ways. Unfortunately, they fall far short of Photoshop's color cababilities, but they're making good headway.

Extensis VectorTools VectorColor provides many of the color capabilities that Adobe left out. VectorColor contains Edit Curves (like Photoshop's Curves), Brightness/Contrast, Multitone (duotones, tritones, and so forth), and even a Randomize function. VectorColor is discussed in Chapter 14.

Adjust Colors

Adjust Colors increases and decreases process color Fills in each color component. The percentages entered in Adjust Colors are absolute changes, meaning that a 10% decrease of Cyan when Cyan is 100% results in 90%, and a 10% decrease of Cyan when Cyan is 50% results in 40%, not 45%. If the increase makes the tint of a color greater than 100%, it stays at 100%, but other colors may still increase, if they are not yet at 100%. If the decrease makes the tint of a color less than 0%, that color remains at 0%, but other colors may still decrease, as long as they are not yet at 0%. For example, a 25% increase to both Yellow and Magenta to a path with 80% Yellow and 50% Magenta results in the colors being 100% Yellow and 75% Magenta. Reapplying this filter results in 100% Yellow and 100% Magenta. Reapplying this filter at this point results in no change at all.

The Adjust Colors filter is shown in Figure 12-2.

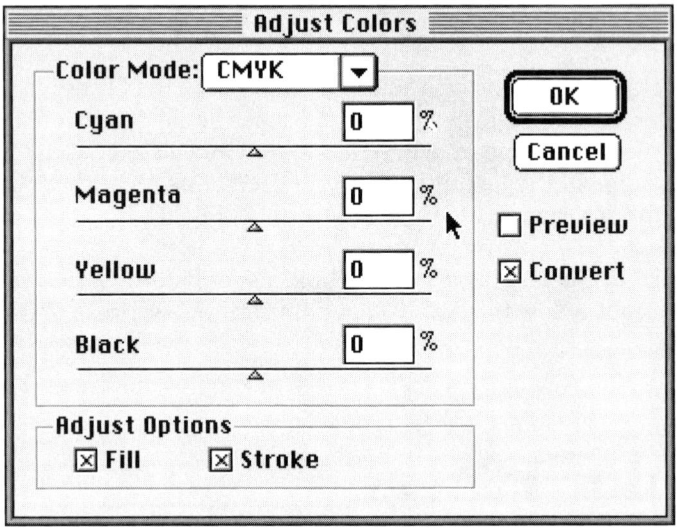

Figure 12-2: The Adjust Colors dialog box

At the bottom of the Adjust Colors filter dialog box are several options. The Preview checkbox lets you see the changes that have been applied so far. The checkbox automatically converts custom and Illustrator Black-based colors to process equivalents.

You can adjust colors using any color model, even if your selected paths are a different model. Click the Convert checkbox and choose a different model.

The Color Blend Filters

Blend Front To Back, Blend Horizontally, and Blend Vertically blend the colors of at least three objects whose ending objects are both process tints or both Black tints. The Blend filters do not work with custom colors, patterns, or gradients. Using the Blend filters is very similar to using the Blend tool, but instead of making different shape *and* color blends, the Blend filters create new colors inside the between objects automatically. If the ending paths' colors are different color *types,* the Blend filters will produce undesirable results.

The main difference between each of these filters is how they determine what the end paths are, and in what direction the blend flows.

The Convert to Filters

The three Convert to filters, Convert to CMYK, Convert to Grayscale, and Convert to RGB, allow you to change the color model of selected paths with a simple menu selection. In addition to switching between Grayscale, CMYK and RGB, the Convert to filters change custom colors to those color models as well.

The Invert Colors Filter

Invert Colors works in strange and mysterious ways on selected paths. Whatever the color of the path, Invert Colors takes the first three colors in the Paint palette (Cyan, Magenta, Yellow) and subtracts them from 100. If the original color was a shade of Red (for example, where Cyan = 0%, Magenta = 100%, and Yellow = 100%), then Invert Colors makes the new color Cyan = 100%, Magenta = 0%, and Yellow = 0%.

CAUTION: The percentage of Black is not affected by Invert colors. Therefore, this is *not* the same as getting a negative image.

Although Invert works poorly with CMYK images, it works perfectly with both Grayscale and RGB images.

STEPS: Getting the Proper Inverse of a CMYK image

Step 1. Select the art you wish to invert.

Step 2. Choose Filter⇨Color⇨Convert to RGB.

Step 3. Choose Filter⇨Color⇨Invert Colors.

Step 4. Choose Filter⇨Color⇨Convert to CMYK.

CAUTION: When using the steps above, be aware that slight differences may result from changing the color mode of your artwork.

The Overprint Black Plug-In

The Overprint Black Plug-In is placed in the Optional Plug-Ins folder when Illustrator is installed. In order for it to be used, it needs to be moved to the Plug-Ins folder.

Choosing Filter⇨Color⇨Overprint Black displays the Overprint Black dialog box (shown in Figure 12-3), which enables you to apply overprinting of black to selected paths. A number of options can be selected, including whether to add or remove overprinting from the selected objects. Another option lets you specify the amount of black percentage that is the minimum that will be used to overprint.

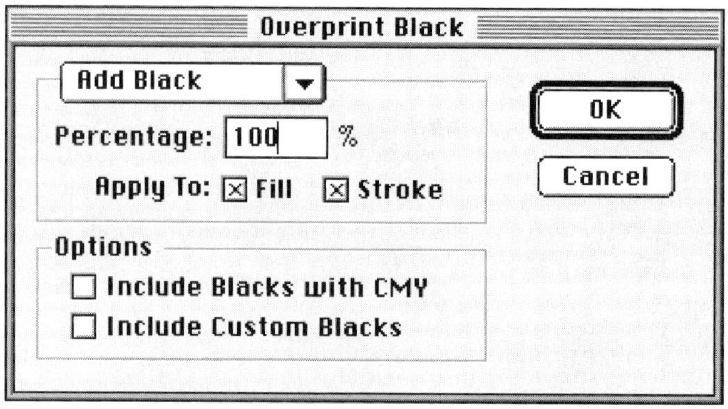

Figure 12-3: The Overprint Black dialog box

You can specify where the overprint affects Fills or Strokes or both. The other options determine whether black will overprint when combined with CMY or when part of a custom color.

The Overprint Black filter adds overprinting only to selected objects that are not currently overprinted when the Add button is selected, and it removes overprinting from objects that currently have overprinting when the Remove button is selected. In no circumstances does it remove overprinting when the Add button is selected, even if the overprinting object does not fall within the parameters of the settings of the Overprint dialog box.

The Saturate Filter

Saturate adds or subtracts equal amounts of color to the selected objects. This filter does not correspond in any way to saturation changes made by Photoshop; instead, the color added is proportional to each color in a path. Using Saturate works in much the same way as holding the Shift key down and dragging a triangle to the right in the Color palette. Saturate does not work with patterns or gradients.

The Saturate dialog box (shown in Figure 12-4) enables you to saturate or desaturate, depending on the direction the slider is dragged. The Preview checkbox in this dialog box is quite helpful, letting you see what is happening to the paths in real time.

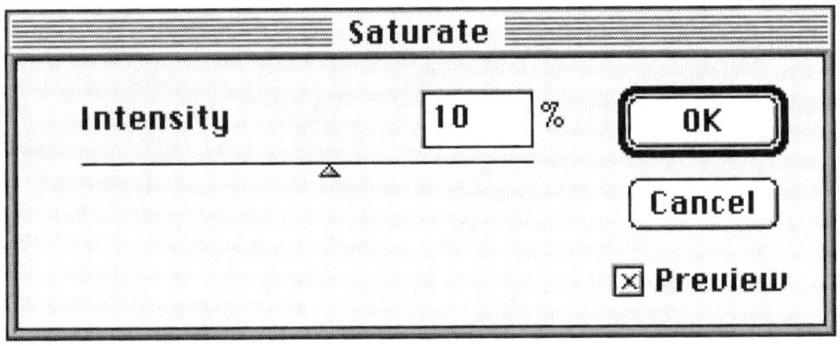

Figure 12-4: The Saturate dialog box

Manipulating Colors with the Color Filters

The color filters provide automated ways of changing colors for a variety of objects. Most of the filters work on paths that are Filled with black or a process color, and some of them work on the Strokes of the paths as well. The following sections describe various uses for the color filters.

Techniques for Creating Shadows and Highlights

You can easily use color filters to create shadows and highlights for black and process-color paths.

You create most shadows by simply creating a copy of the object and placing it under, and slightly offset from, the original. You can darken the copy in a number of ways, but the easiest way is to use the Adjust Colors filter.

You create highlights in the same way as you create shadows, but instead of darkening the copy, you lighten it.

STEPS: Creating Shadows and Highlights with the Adjust Colors Filter

Step 1. Create an object that has several colors in it. Group the individual elements in the object.

Step 2. Copy the object and choose Edit⇨Paste in Back (⌘-B) [Ctrl+B]. Offset the copy down and to the right.

(continued)

STEPS: *(continued)*

Step 3. Choose Filter⇨Colors⇨Adjust Colors. To darken the shadowed copy evenly, add 20% to Cyan, Magenta, and Yellow, and 40% to Black.

Step 4. To create the highlight, choose Edit⇨Paste in Back (⌘-B) [Ctrl+B] again and decrease all four process colors by 40% if the background is dark or 20% if the background is light. My background is dark, so I reduced the color in the highlight by 40% of each color.

Figure 12-5 shows the four steps that you follow to create shadows and highlights.

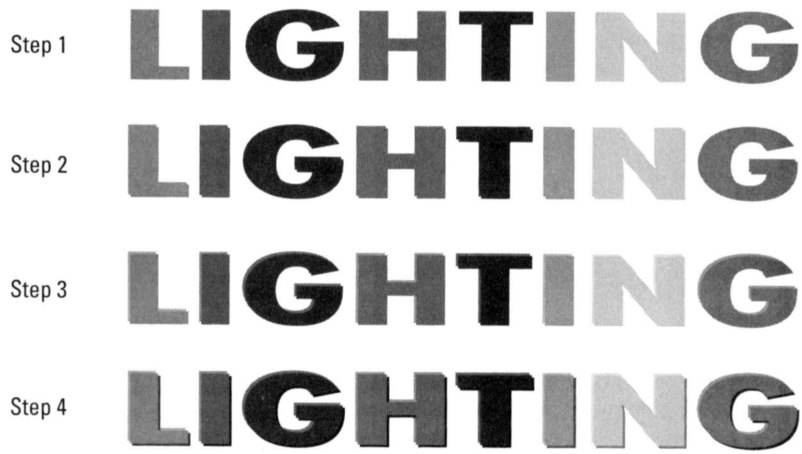

Figure 12-5: Steps for creating highlights and shadows on text

Creating Extruded Multiple Path Objects

You can normally make objects appear to be beveled by blending two objects together. If the objects contain multiple paths, however, you have to blend each of the paths separately. And if the objects contain compound paths, the blends that you create will not share the compound attributes of the original objects.

You can use the Blend Front To Back filter to make objects appear to be extruded, as described in the following steps.

STEPS: Creating Extruded Multiple Path Objects

Step 1. Release any compound paths in the object and group all the paths in the object together.

Step 2. In the Move dialog box (choose Object⇨Transform⇨Move), enter **.25 pt** in the Horizontal text field and **.1 pt** in the Vertical text field. Click the Copy button (or press Option-Return).

Step 3. Choose Arrange⇨Transform Again (⌘-D) [Ctrl+D] until the object has been duplicated far enough to appear 3D. Copy the final duplicate object. (It should still be selected.)

Step 4. Change the color of the final duplicate object to be the color of the frontmost part of the blend. In my example, I made the final duplicate object black and left the rest of the objects red. (The color insert shows the result.)

Step 5. Select all the objects and choose Filter⇨Colors⇨Blend Front to Back.

Step 6. Choose Edit⇨Paste In Front (⌘-F) [Ctrl+F] and give a different color to the object just pasted. In the example, I used yellow. Choose Object⇨Compound Path⇨Make (⌘-8) [Ctrl+8] and then Object⇨Arrange⇨Hide (⌘-U) [Ctrl+U].

Step 7. Continue to select each grouped object, making each group a compound path and then hiding it, until all the paths are hidden.

Step 8. After you have hidden all the paths, choose Arrange⇨Show All (⌘-Shift-U) [Ctrl+Shift+U] and then group all the paths together.

CAUTION: Do not make all the paths one compound path, or the color information for each path will be lost.

POWER TIP: Actually, you can automate the whole process described in the preceding steps by using the KPT Vector Effects' ShadowLand filter, which includes all sorts of shadowing effects, including a useful one for zooming.

Creating Negatives with the Color Filters

You can produce negative images in Illustrator almost automatically by using the Invert Colors filter. For a process color, the Invert Colors filter subtracts the tints of Cyan, Magenta, and Yellow from 100% and leaves Black as is. On an object that is Filled or Stroked with black only, the filter subtracts the tint of black from 100%.

To get around the way that this filter works when creating negatives, select all the objects that you want to reverse. Next, choose Filter⇨Colors⇨Invert Colors, select each path, and check whether the paths have a process color Fill that contains black. If you find any Fills that contain black, manually change black to the correct value.

POWER TIP: After you check a path to see whether it is a process color that contains black, hide that path. Using this method can help you be sure that you have checked every path, and you do not have to worry about wasting time by rechecking paths.

The Create Filters

There used to be bunches of create filters, back in Version 5.5 of Illustrator. In Illustrator 7, the category is all but extinct, with only Create Fill & Stroke for Mask and Object Mosaic being the remaining stragglers. The Star, Spiral, and Polygon filters have been replaced with tools.

As with most filters, you can manually perform the functions that the two create filters do, but using the filters is much easier.

The Fill & Stroke for Mask Filter

Fill & Stroke for Mask takes any selected masks and copies them. The mask is then seemingly given the current Fill & Stroke attributes. But because masks cannot be Filled or Stroked, this filter at first glance seems to be working some really great magic.

Of course, Fill & Stroke for Mask really doesn't do anything all that spectacular. After it copies the mask, it does a Paste Behind for the Fill (this object is made into the bottommost part of the mask). If a Stroke is specified, the filter also does a Paste in Front for the Stroke — but this path is not masked and is not part of the masking object. Before choosing Fill & Stroke for Mask, make sure that you have only the mask you want to Fill & Stroke selected, and that you have chosen the proper Paint Style attributes for the mask.

POWER TIP: It's a good idea to get into the habit of grouping the new Stroke and Fill paths to the mask. To do so, you have to group everything that is part of the mask. Of course, the Group Selection tool enables you to move anything necessary, even if everything is grouped together.

When you turn a masking path into a mask, any Fill & Stroke attributes that the masking path had before it was a mask are removed, and you cannot give it any attributes. If you select a masking path, the tool palette shows a Fill & Stroke of None. (Creating masks is discussed in Chapter 9.)

STEPS: Adding a Stroke and Fill to a Mask

Step 1. Create a mask and masked object.

Step 2. Select the masking path and choose the Stroke and Fill that you want to give to the masking path. As you choose and apply the Fill and Stroke, the mask will not show these changes.

Step 3. Choose Filter⇨Create⇨Fill & Stroke for Mask. The masking path will have the Fill & Stroke that you requested.

The Fill & Stroke for Mask filter creates two copies of the original masking path. It places the first copy under all of the masked items and Fills it with the Fill that you chose before you applied the filter. It places the second copy above the mask and gives it the Stroke that you specified.

CAUTION

If either the Fill or Stroke for the masking object is set to None before you activate the filter, a dialog box appears, telling you that the Fill & Stroke for Mask filter applies the current Fill & Stroke to the mask. Whenever this message appears, I always look at my tool palette to make sure that I did indeed select the mask before I made changes.

POWER TIP

Group the masking objects, the masking path, the Filled masking path, and the Stroked masking path to ensure that all the objects in the mask stay together.

Creating Object Mosaics

The Object Mosaic filter creates a series of tiles out of a placed bitmap image, as shown in Figure 12-6. Any size or color image may be used. When an image is converted through the Object Mosaic filter, it becomes a series of rectangles, each Filled with a different color.

In the Object Mosaic dialog box (see Figure 12-7), you can specify the number of tiles that the image is made up of and the space between the tiles. You also can specify a different size for the entire object mosaic.

Figure 12-6: An original TIFF image (left) and the image after Object Mosaic has been applied

Figure 12-7: The Object Mosaic dialog box

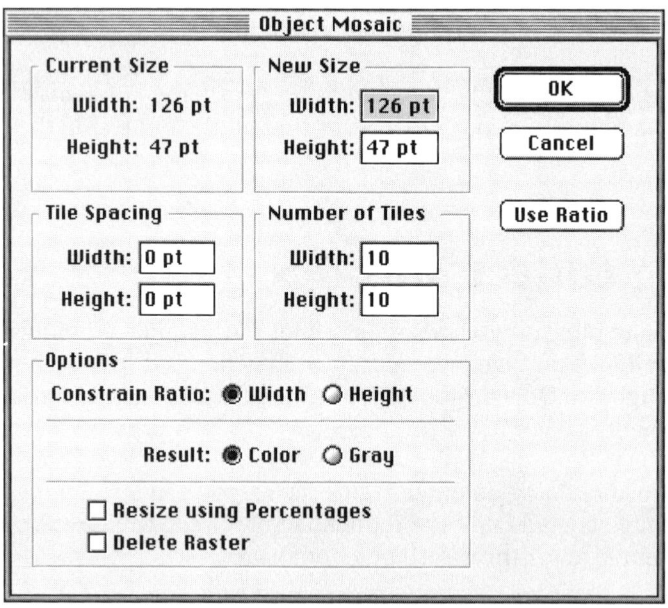

CAUTION

Be careful with Object Mosaic, for this filter, unlike almost any other, will run out of memory if the source image or number of tiles is too large. This is the one filter in Illustrator that does almost exactly what its counterpart in Photoshop does.

The more rectangles, the more detail in the mosaic. Bitmapped images are mosaics of a sort, with each pixel equal to 1 square.

POWER TIP

If you need to apply Object Mosaic to an illustration you've created in Illustrator, you can rasterize it using the Object⇨Rasterize command. Do this at a low resolution (72 dpi works great for me), and then apply Object Mosaic to the rasterized image.

Use the following steps to create a fairly simple and basic mosaic in Illustrator.

STEPS: Creating a Mosaic

Step 1. Create a TIFF file and place it in Illustrator. You do not need to use a high-resolution TIFF file. The Illustrator object mosaic looks just as good when you convert a 72-dpi TIFF file as when you convert a 300-dpi TIFF file.

Step 2. Choose Filters⇨Create⇨Object Mosaic. In the Object Mosaic dialog box, enter the size that you want the mosaic to be and also the number of tiles across and down. Click the Use Ratio button to keep the same proportions as in the original image.

Step 3. Click OK when you are satisfied with the information that you have entered in the Object Mosaic dialog box. Figure 12-8 shows the results that are produced by entering three different tile widths and heights into the Number of Tiles boxes.

CAUTION

The number of tiles that Illustrator can produce is strictly limited and is directly related to the amount of RAM allocated to Illustrator. Exceeding the limit causes Illustrator to create only a portion of the tiles.

You can create some very exciting effects with the Object Mosaic filter when you use it in conjunction with other filters. The best ones to use with it are Round Corners, all of the Distort filters, and most of the color filters, as well as the Transform Each function. In the following example, I combined the Object Mosaic filter with the Round Corners filter and the Transform Each function.

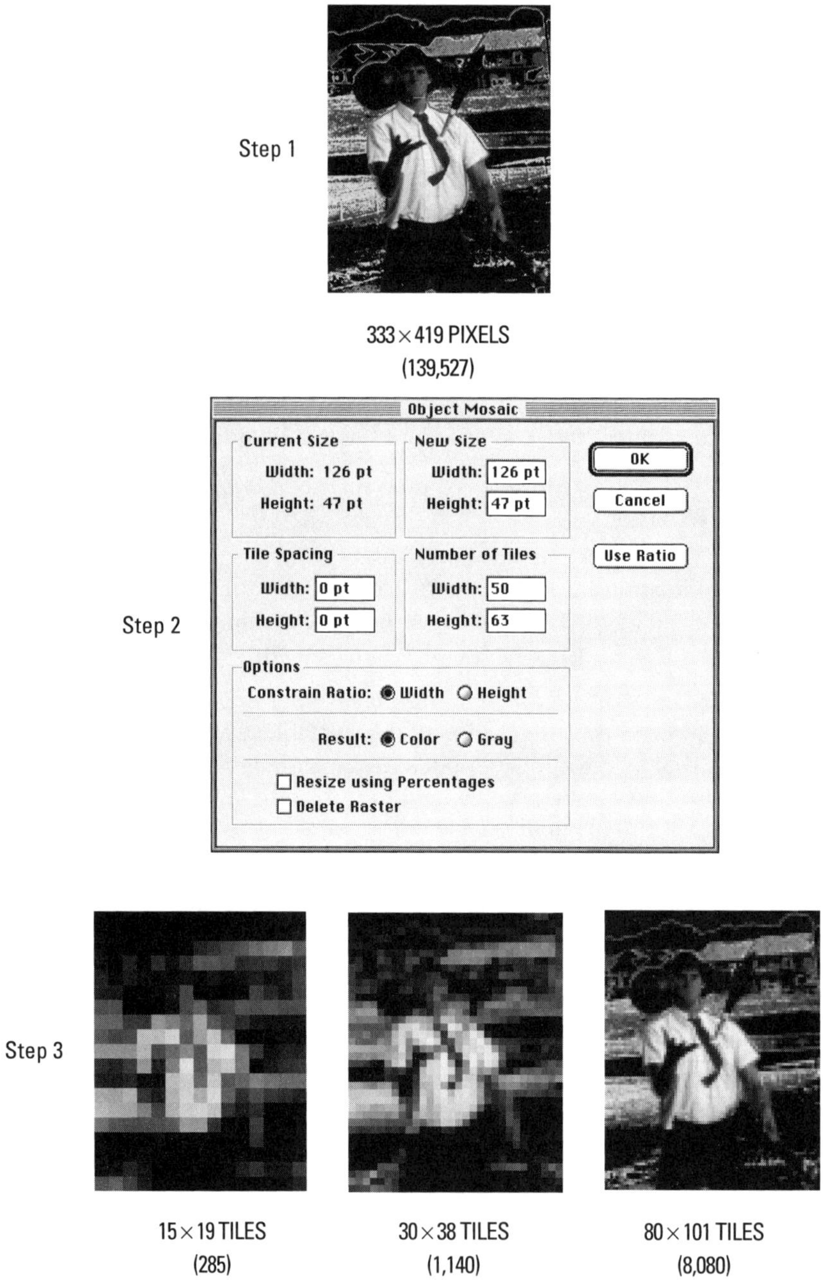

Figure 12-8: Steps for creating object mosaics

STEPS: Creating a Seurat-Like Illustration

Step 1. Create an object mosaic with an average number of tiles (between 1,600 and 10,000 tiles, which would be from 40 x 40 to 100 x 100). In the example shown in Figure 12-9, I used an object mosaic with 50 x 63 tiles, or 3,150 tiles total.

Step 2. Select all the mosaic tiles and choose Filters⇨Stylize⇨Round Corners. In the Round Corners dialog box, enter a large number. I usually enter at least 10 points. As long as the tiles are not larger than 20 points wide, the Round Corners filter turns all the tiles into circles.

Step 3. Copy all the tiles and choose Edit⇨Paste in Front (⌘-F) [Ctrl+F]. Select all the tiles (the image now has 6,300 tiles) and choose Object⇨Transform⇨Transform Each. In the Move section of the dialog box, enter **5** in both text fields and check the Random checkbox. Click OK. If you want less white space between all the circles, choose Edit⇨Paste in Front (⌘-F) [Ctrl+F] again and then choose Arrange⇨Transform Again (⌘-D) [Ctrl+D]. The results should look similar to Step 3 in Figure 12-9.

The tiles created with the Object Mosaic filter are placed on the page from top left to bottom right. The top-left tile is underneath all the other tiles (in the back), and the bottom-right tile is on top of all the other tiles (in the front). The tiles are butted up against each other, so none of them overlap.

Because of the way that these tiles overlap, you can create a tiled or shingled roof quite easily, providing the original image is upside down. The following steps describe this process in detail.

STEPS: Creating a Tiled Roof

Step 1. Create a TIFF file to be used as the roof. In the example shown in Figure 12-10, I created the name of a restaurant. Then I rasterized it in Illustrator.

Step 2. In Illustrator, rotate the image 135° clockwise. Choose Filter⇨Create⇨Object Mosaic. Make the number of tiles across about 50 or more, and click the Use Ratio button.

Step 3. Rotate the entire mosaic by 135°. Using the Selection tool, draw a marquee around any white squares above, below, to the left, and to the right of the roof area to select them. Delete all white squares. Because the squares are white, you may need to switch to Artwork mode to see them all.

(continued)

Figure 12-9: Creating a Seurat-like effect with the Object Mosaic filter

Step 1

Step 2

Step 3

STEPS: ***(continued)***

It may seem strange that the mosaic gets rotated twice, but there is a method to this seemingly mad busywork. By placing the upper-left tiles on the bottom and the lower-right tiles on the top, the image is rotated first so that the lower parts of the image are turned into squares.

By the way, if I hadn't helped put shingles on a roof recently (you have to work from the bottom up), I would never have been able to figure this out. So I guess that this is one of those "real life" examples, huh?

Step 4. Select the remaining tiles and group them. Choose Object Path⇨Add Anchor Points to add one Anchor Point to every side of every square in the mosaic. Choose Filter⇨Stylize⇨Punk and Bloat to make all the points on each square come out a little.

Step 5. To round off the points and make the squares smoother, choose Filter⇨Stylize⇨Round Corners, and enter **10 pt** in the text field. Choose Object⇨Transform⇨Transform Each and enter **150** in both the Width and Height fields of the Scale section of the Transform Each dialog box. Because the squares were scaled up, they now overlap.

Step 6. Choose Object⇨Transform⇨Transform Each, and enter 45° in the Rotate section. In the Color and Stroke palettes, give each tile a black Stroke of .25 point. Depending on the size of the tiles, the Stroke weight may vary.

Step 7. Use the Free Distort filter (choose Filter⇨Distort⇨Free Distort) to change the shape of the roof to be more . . . well . . . rooflike.

Figure 12-10: Creating a tiled roof with the Object Mosaic filter

The following steps describe how to make the tiles in a mosaic overlap with no white space between them. This technique can easily create a background image or a funky illustration, as shown in the steps and used in context in Figure 12-11.

Figure 12-11: Steps for creating random overlapping tiles with no white space

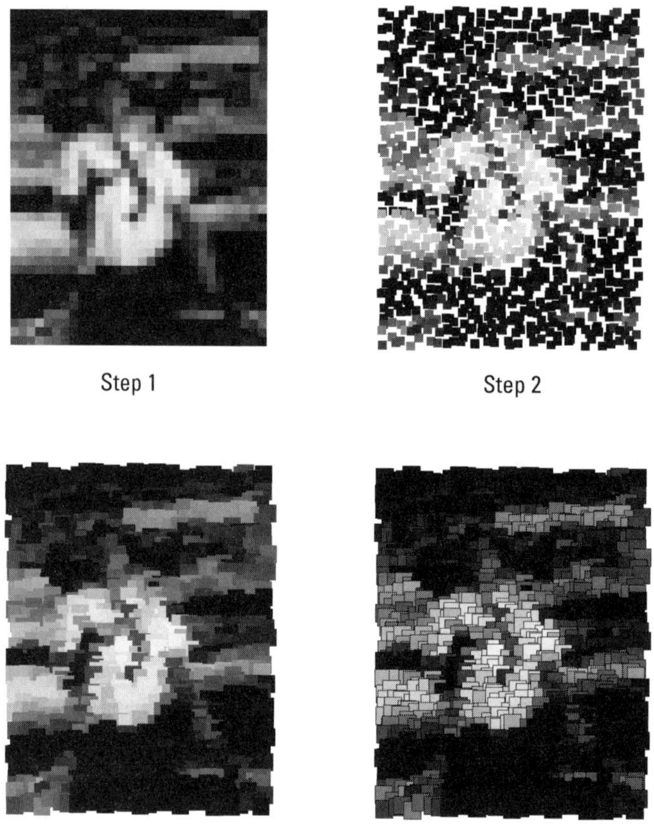

Step 1 Step 2 Step 3 Step 4

STEPS: Creating Random Overlapping Tiles with No White Space

Step 1. Create an Object Mosaic from a raster image.

Step 2. Choose Object⇨Transform⇨Transform Each, and enter the amount of movement for the tiles in the Move section. Check the Random checkbox. Measure one tile with the Measure tool. The tiles that I created for the example shown in Figure 12-11 are 3.3 points across, and the move distance that I used is 3.3 points. The most white space between any two tiles is 6.6 points.

Step 3. Select Object⇨Transform⇨Transform Each. Enter the percentage that the tile must be scaled up to eliminate the white space in the Scale area. In this example, I entered 200%.

Step 4. To see the edges of the tiles more easily, place a .25-point 100% Black Stroke on them.

By using the Object Mosaic filter in combination with the color blend filters, color sets can be created very easily. These color sets can be sampled for inclusion into the Swatch palette.

STEPS: Creating Color Sets with the Mosaic Filter

Step 1. Create an Object Mosaic from any image, making the total number of tiles equal to the number of different tiles that you want in the color set.

Step 2. Change the colors of the tiles that mark the beginning and end of each color set. In the example (Figure 12-12), I used primary colors and white as the beginning and end of each color set.

Step 3. Select one range of color and choose Filter⇨Color⇨Blend Front to Back to blend the colors from the upper-left tiles toward the lower-right tiles. Repeat this step for each range of colors.

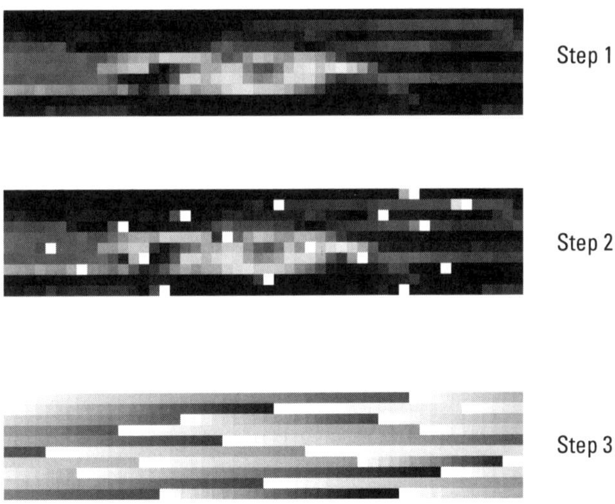

Figure 12-12: Using the Object Mosaic filter to create color sets

The Distort and Stylize Filters

The following pages describe the Distort and Stylize filters (found in the Distort and Stylize submenus of the Filter menu), and provide tips and techniques for getting the most out of them.

The Free Distort Filter

Choosing Filter⇨Distort⇨Free Distort displays the Free Distort dialog box, where you control how much you want to distort the selected paths. Within this dialog box is a representative sample of the selected artwork surrounded by four corner handles. You adjust and move the four handles to change the shape of the object.

Reshaping artwork was very time-consuming in older versions of Illustrator. You used the Scale tool on individual points and segments, scaling a little more for each successive row of points. Before Illustrator 5.0 was released, the only widely used software that could distort freely was Broderbund's TypeStyler, but its exceedingly clunky and awkward interface and its requirement that artwork be in a font (with all colors removed) made the process cumbersome at best.

If the Preview box is checked, you see what the image looks like as it is distorted. To distort the selected paths, click and drag the four corner points of the box surrounding the artwork (see Figure 12-13). Those handles can be pulled anywhere, including right out of the dialog box onto the document — and even off the document!

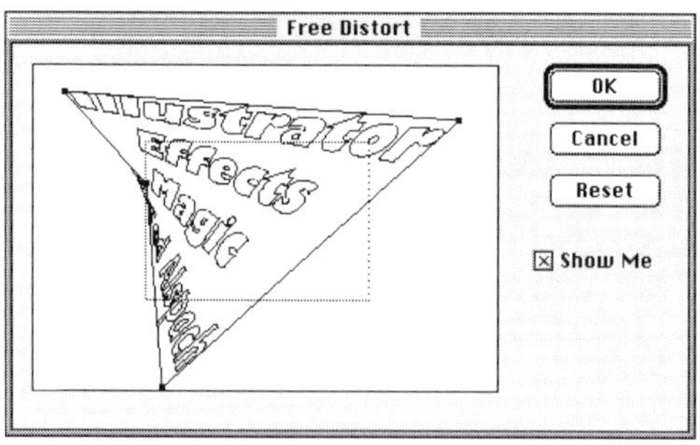

Figure 12-13: Distorting an image in the Free Distort dialog box

If you pull the handles too far, you have to click the Reset button to get your handles back. Doing so resets the image to its original shape.

If you think that Free Distort is too limiting, take a look at VectorShape, part of VectorTools, described in Chapter 14.

Text can be distorted using Free Distort, but it must first be converted into outlines.

STEPS: Using the Free Distort Filter

Step 1. Create the artwork that you want to distort. In the example in Figure 12-14, I used text converted to outlines.

Before you can distort text in the Free Distort dialog box, you have to convert it to outlines. Although you can distort Rectangle type, Path type, and Area type without converting it to outlines, only the paths that the type is in or on will be distorted.

The Free Distort filter does not work with placed images or with type that has not been converted to outlines. Nor does the Free Distort filter affect patterns or gradients that are being used as Fills.

Step 2. Choose Filter⇨Distort⇨Free Distort. The Free Distort dialog box appears, containing a line art (Artwork view only) view of the selected paths that you want to distort.

If the artwork is very complex, you may want to uncheck the Preview checkbox. A rectangle will appear instead of the complex artwork. For this example, I found that adjusting the rectangle without seeing the artwork was much easier because the artwork contained several hundred compound paths that Illustrator had to redraw.

Step 3. Move the handles around until the artwork is reshaped to your liking. If you don't have Preview checked while you are moving the handles around, click it to preview the reshaped artwork when you think the handles are in a good position. Then if you realize that the artwork doesn't look the way you want it to look, you can make changes without having to choose the Undo command and select the filter again.

Step 4. Click the OK button to have the reshaped artwork appear in the document. If the artwork is complex, you may want to group everything that was distorted. Or if you are really conscientious, you may have grouped everything already.

Step 5. Add any finishing touches by coloring the distorted artwork. I placed a black background behind the distorted text and then Filled the text with the Black & White Gradient. I used the Gradient Vector tool to drag upwards, starting in the bottom-middle of the last paragraph and dragging up to the top line of type.

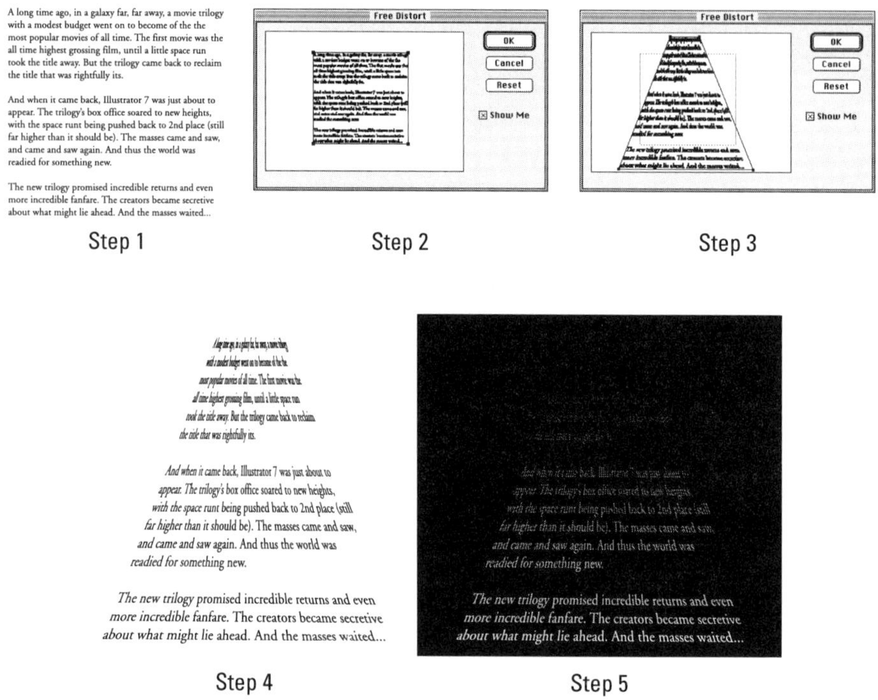

Figure 12-14: Steps for using the Free Distort filter

You can use the Free Distort filter to create artwork that twists. In the Free Distort dialog box, simply create an *X* pattern with the rectangle. To do so, switch the handles on one edge of the rectangle. Depending on the type of twist, the artwork will turn upside down or become reversed. By combining different twists, you can produce ribbonlike effects. For example, Figure 12-15 shows a banner that has two different twists.

Figure 12-15: A double twist in the Free Distort dialog box produced this flipping, twisting banner

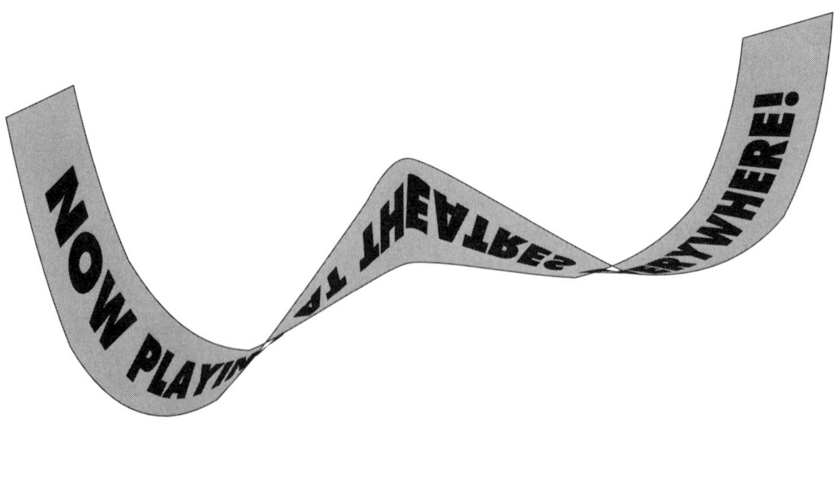

After you use the Free Distort filter, the handle positions are remembered in the dialog box. If you use the filter again during the same Illustrator session, those settings are immediately applied to the artwork. Press the Reset button to return the handles (and the artwork) back to their original positions.

You can pull the handles in the Free Distort dialog box right out of the dialog box and stretch them as far as the monitor is wide or tall. The catch in this maneuver is that when you release the mouse button on a handle that you have dragged outside the dialog box, you can no longer select that handle. The only way to recover the handle is to click the Reset button, which resets all the handles to their original positions without significantly changing the previously distorted image.

The Punk and Bloat Filter

Although the Punk and Bloat filter undoubtedly has the coolest sounding name that Illustrator has to offer, this filter also is one of the least practical. But Illustrator is a fun program, right? And these filters make it lots of fun.

Punking makes objects appear to have pointy tips sticking out everywhere, and bloating creates lumps outside of objects. Punking and bloating are inverses of each other; a negative punk is a bloat, and a negative bloat is a punk. If you are bewildered by these functions, stop reading right here. The following information spoils everything.

I Can't Get Punked Stuff Back to Normal

Squiggy: After I punk, I can never get the paths back to normal.

Toulouse: Undo doesn't work?

Squiggy: Sure, but I like changing things I've saved, closed, and reopened.

Toulouse: Undo won't work in that case.

Squiggy: So, I'm trying to bloat the paths I punked, since Bloat is the opposite of Punk.

Toulouse: It just doesn't work that way.

Squiggy: Why?

Toulouse: Punk and Bloat change each Anchor Point into a Curved Corner Point. Each point has two independent handles, and those handles are moved with Punk and Bloat.

Squiggy: Wouldn't bloating punked paths move the handles back to where they started from?

Toulouse: No, because originally, many of those points didn't have handles at all.

Squiggy: Anything else that can be done?

Toulouse: Redraw, or, if you have the patience, edit each of the points. Unless you added Anchor Points before punking.

Selecting Punk and Bloat opens the Punk and Bloat dialog box, where you may specify a percentage that you want the selected paths to be punked or bloated by either typing in the amount or dragging a slider.

Bloating causes the segments between Anchor Points to expand outwards. The higher the percentage, the more bloated the selection. You can bloat from –200% up to 200%. Punk is the inverse of Bloat. While Bloat makes rounded, bubblelike extrusions appear on the surface of your object, Punk makes tall spikes appear on its path. When you drag toward Punk, you can enter how much you want to punk the drawing. Punk amounts can range from –200% to 200%. The number of spikes is based on the number of Anchor Points in your drawing. Figure 12-16 shows several punked and bloated objects.

Figure 12-16: Punked and bloated objects

The Punk and Bloat filter moves Anchor Points in one direction and creates two independent direction points on either side of each Anchor Point. The direction points are moved in the opposite direction of the Anchor Points, and the direction of movement is always toward or away from the center of the object.

The distance moved is the only thing that you control when you use the Punk and Bloat filter. Entering a percentage moves the points that percentage.

POWER TIP: Nothing about the Punk and Bloat filter is random. Everything about it is 100% controllable and, to some extent, predictable.

STEPS: Using the Punk and Bloat Filter

Step 1. Create and select the artwork that you want to punk, as shown in Figure 12-17.

Step 2. Add Anchor Points or use the Roughen filter at 0% to create additional Anchor Points if necessary. I chose Object⇨Add Anchor Points twice, increasing the number of Anchor Points from 4 to 16.

Step 3. Choose Filter⇨Stylize⇨Punk and Bloat. In the dialog box, enter the amount that you want to punk or bloat the object, or drag the slider in the appropriate direction.

Step 4. Check to see whether the result is what you intended.

Step 5. Add other artwork to the punked or bloated object.

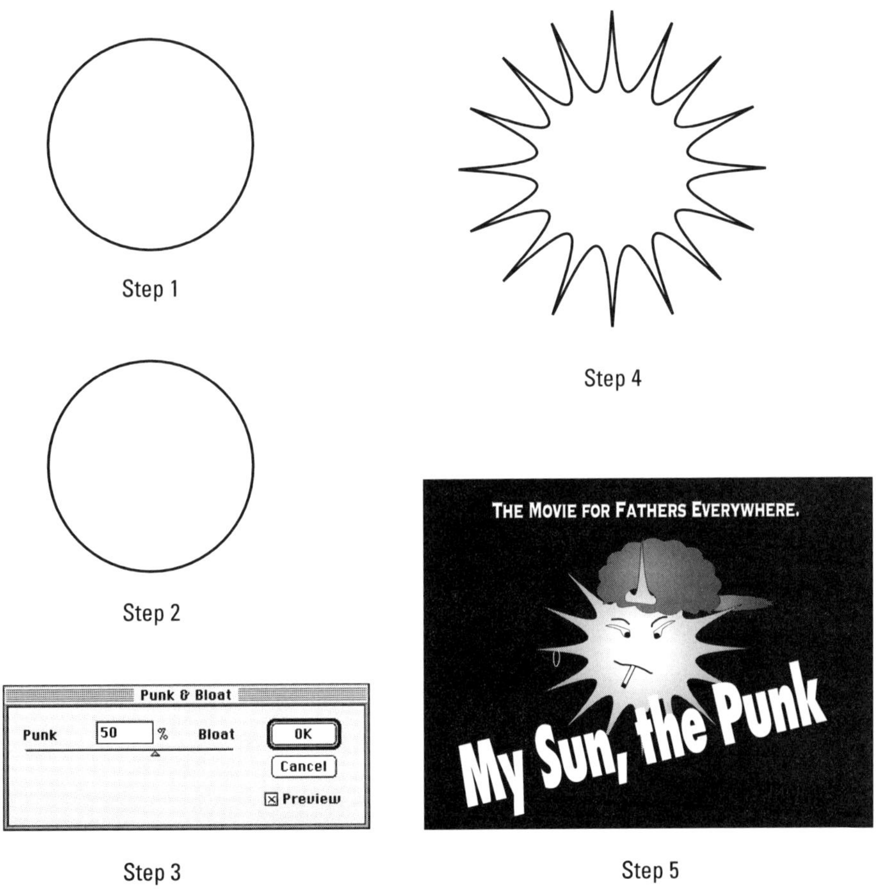

Figure 12-17: Steps for punking and bloating

Twirl Filter

Like the Free Distort filter, the Twirl filter reshapes objects in ways that would be time-consuming and tedious if you were using conventional Illustrator methods. The Twirl filter moves the innermost points a certain number of degrees around a circle. The farther away the points are from the center of the circle, the less they move; and the points at the outermost edges of the object hardly rotate at all.

In Illustrator 7, there is both a Twirl filter and a Twirl tool, found in the Plug-In Tools palette. The Twirl filter is described here, while the Twirl tool is discussed in Chapter 7.

Selecting Twirl displays the Twirl dialog box, where you specify how much the selected objects will spin. You can set the twirl angle from –4,000° up to 4,000°. The very center of the selected objects rotate the degree specified, while the objects on the edges rotate around the center very little. Positive values rotate the selected paths clockwise; negative values rotate the selected paths counterclockwise. Figure 12-18 shows an object before and after being twirled.

Figure 12-18: The original paths (left) are twirled (right)

Unlike previous versions of Twirl, adding more Anchor Points to your path doesn't necessarily result in a better effect. I used to apply Add Anchor Points several times or add Anchor Points via the Roughen filter before applying the Twirl filter. Now, however, the Twirl filter is "smart" and curves paths automatically.

The Twirl filter can twirl single paths or multiple paths. When it twirls multiple paths, the twirling takes place from the center of the entire group of objects, not from within each object.

STEPS: Using the Twirl Filter

Step 1. Create the artwork that you want to use with the Twirl filter. In the example in Figure 12-19, I created a star with several points and a tiny first (inner) radius. Then I selected the center points with the Direct Selection tool and dragged them down and to the left.

The constraints on the Twirl filter are similar to the constraints on the Free Distort filter. You cannot twirl placed images, type that has not been converted to outlines, or patterns and gradients that are used as Fills.

Step 2. Choose Filter⇨Distort⇨Twirl to see the Twirl dialog box. Enter the number of degrees that you want to twirl objects. In the example, I used 300°.

Entering a positive number in the Angle text field twirls the object clockwise; entering a negative number twirls the object counterclockwise. This setting works the opposite way from how the degree setting for the Rotate tool works.

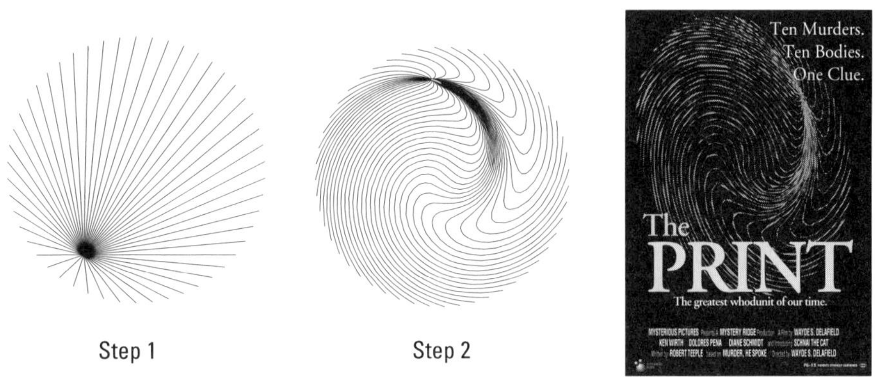

Figure 12-19: Steps for twirling artwork

I wanted the twirled artwork in the example to resemble a fingerprint, so I used the Scale and Rotate tools, and then the Scribble and Tweak filter (see the section "The Scribble and Tweak Filter," later in this chapter) to achieve the desired effect. After scribbling the artwork just .5% horizontally and vertically, I added the background and the accompanying text. A larger version of the resulting poster is in the color section of this book. You can twirl paths up to 4,000° in both directions (4,000 and –4,000). The Twirl filter by itself enables you to create many different effects. By moving different objects to different positions, the Twirl filter can produce entirely different results. For example, you can use the following steps to create an arc in an illustration.

STEPS: Creating Arced Illustrations with Twirl and Free Distort

Step 1. Create the type that you want to arc and convert it to outlines.

Step 2. Make a copy of the type to the left of the original type and place an object between the two areas of type. Then place the same object at either end of the words. At this point, the illustration looks like Step 2 of Figure 12-20.

Step 3. Select the objects and choose Filter⇨Twirl. In the Twirl dialog box, enter 90° and click OK.

Step 4. Delete all the portions of the path except for the one shown.

Step 5. Select the remaining portion and choose Filter⇨Distort⇨Free Distort. Move the handles so that the paths resemble the lower part of an arc.

Step 6. Click OK.

. Create the rtwork to be used s a chip.

2. Rotate the chip.

3. Vertically scale the chip.

4. Option[Alt]-copy the entire chip up to the thickness of a real chip.

. Hide the top ortion's original rtwork, and delete ne bottom art. Only eep the bottom dges. Connect the aths using Join.

6. Show the top portion's original artwork.

7. Replace flat areas with gradients.

8. Option[Alt]-copy to create additional chips.

doodle jr.

Generate textures quickly and easily with doodle jr., applying it to blends of any shape and size. This text texture was created by taking a 50-step blend (from red to red, oddly enough) and applying doodle jr.'s "scramble colors" feature and a large amount of doodle. Access the scramble colors feature by clicking on the doodle jr. logo in the dialog box.

doodle jr. is included FREE on the enclosed *Illustrator 7 Bible* CD-ROM!

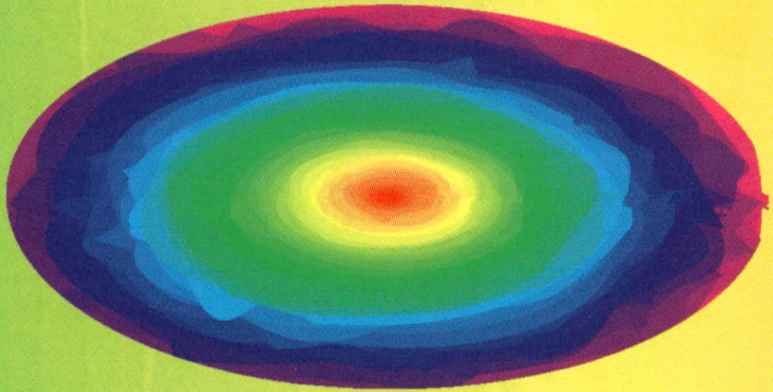

Different levels of detail were used on these blends to create these different, glass-like effects.

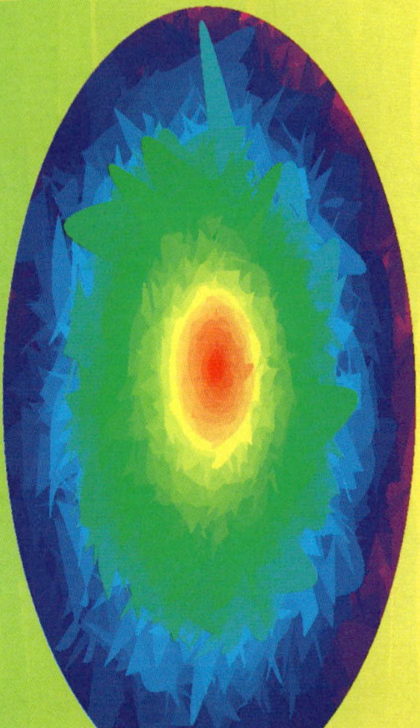

Original Artwork

After doodling around with doodle jr.

Subtle textural changes can be made with doodle jr. on gradients converted to blends, like the one used in the background of this page. Here the original gradient was placed behind the resulting texture.

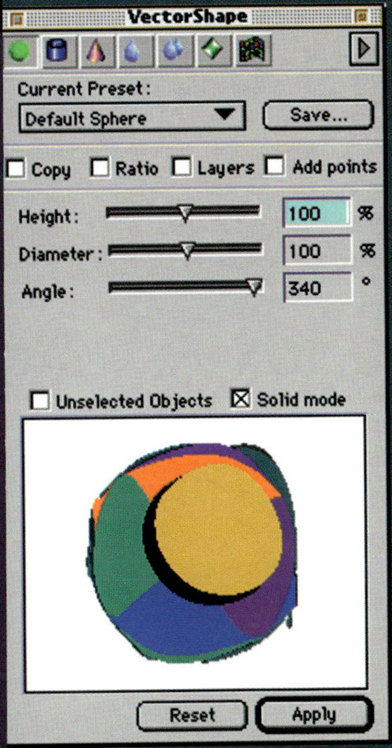

Smurtle

It's hard to believe, but the image at the bottom (called "Smurtle" for obvious reasons) was originally the image to the left. It was changed into a Smurtle by applying VectorTools VectorShape's Sphere setting several times in a row. Afterwards, additional gradients were added to create the illusion of shadows.

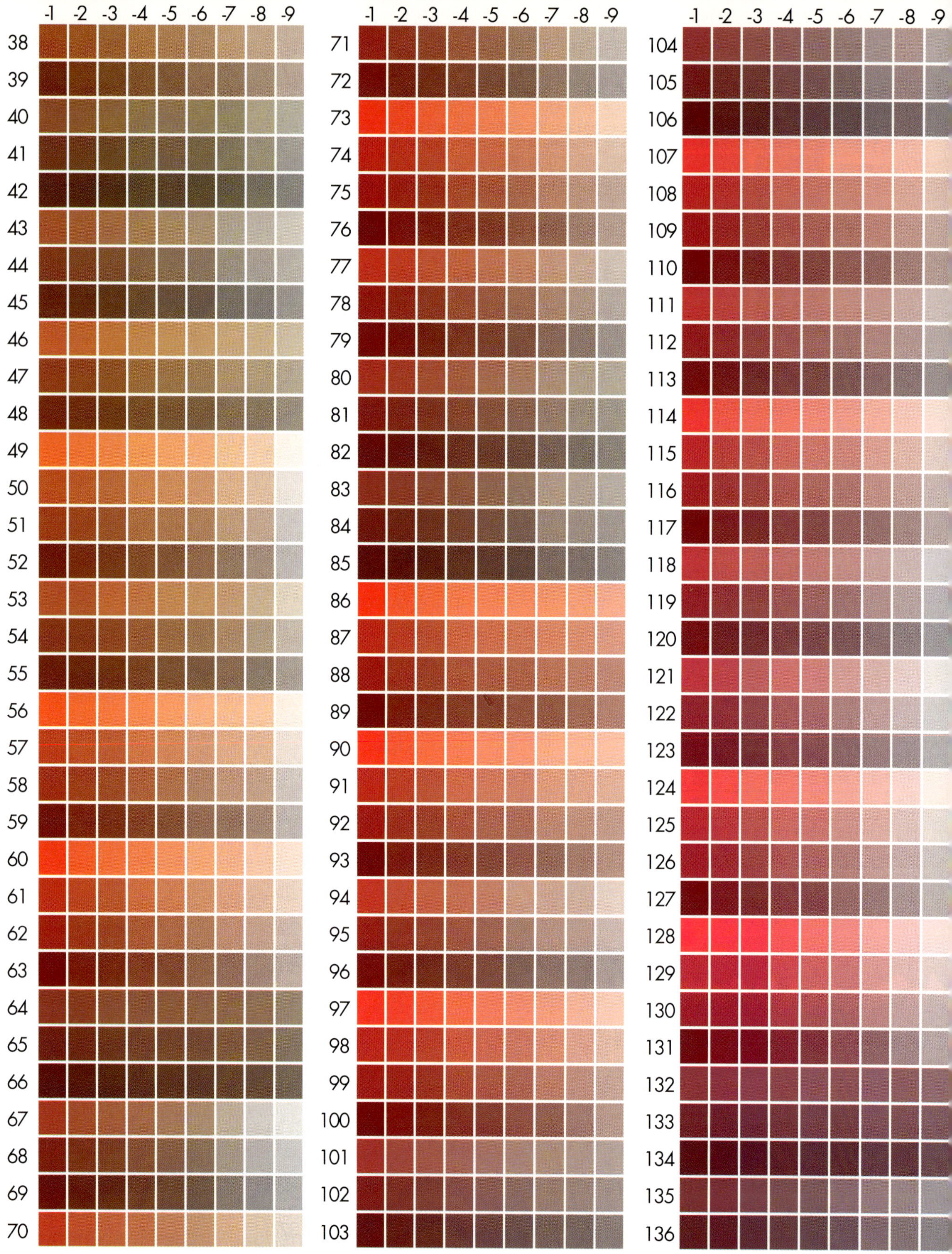
-1 -2 -3 -4 -5 -6 -7 -8 -9
38
39
40
41
42
43
44
45
46
47
48
49
50
51
52
53
54
55
56
57
58
59
60
61
62
63
64
65
66
67
68
69
70
-1 -2 -3 -4 -5 -6 -7 -8 -9
71
72
73
74
75
76
77
78
79
80
81
82
83
84
85
86
87
88
89
90
91
92
93
94
95
96
97
98
99
100
101
102
103
-1 -2 -3 -4 -5 -6 -7 -8 -9
104
105
106
107
108
109
110
111
112
113
114
115
116
117
118
119
120
121
122
123
124
125
126
127
128
129
130
131
132
133
134
135
136

-1 -2 -3 -4 -5 -6 -7 -8 -9
37
38
39
40
41
42
43
44
45
46
47
48
49
50
51
52
53
54
55
56
57
58
59
60
61
62
163
164
165
166
167
168
169
-1 -2 -3 -4 -5 -6 -7 -8 -9
170
171
172
173
174
175
176
177
178
179
180
181
182
183
184
185
186
187
188
189
190
191
192
193
194
195
196
197
198
199
200
201
202
-1 -2 -3 -4 -5 -6 -7 -8 -9
203
204
205
206
207
208
209
210
211
212
213
214
215
216
217
218
219
220
221
222
223
224
225
226
227
228
229
230
231
232
233
234
235

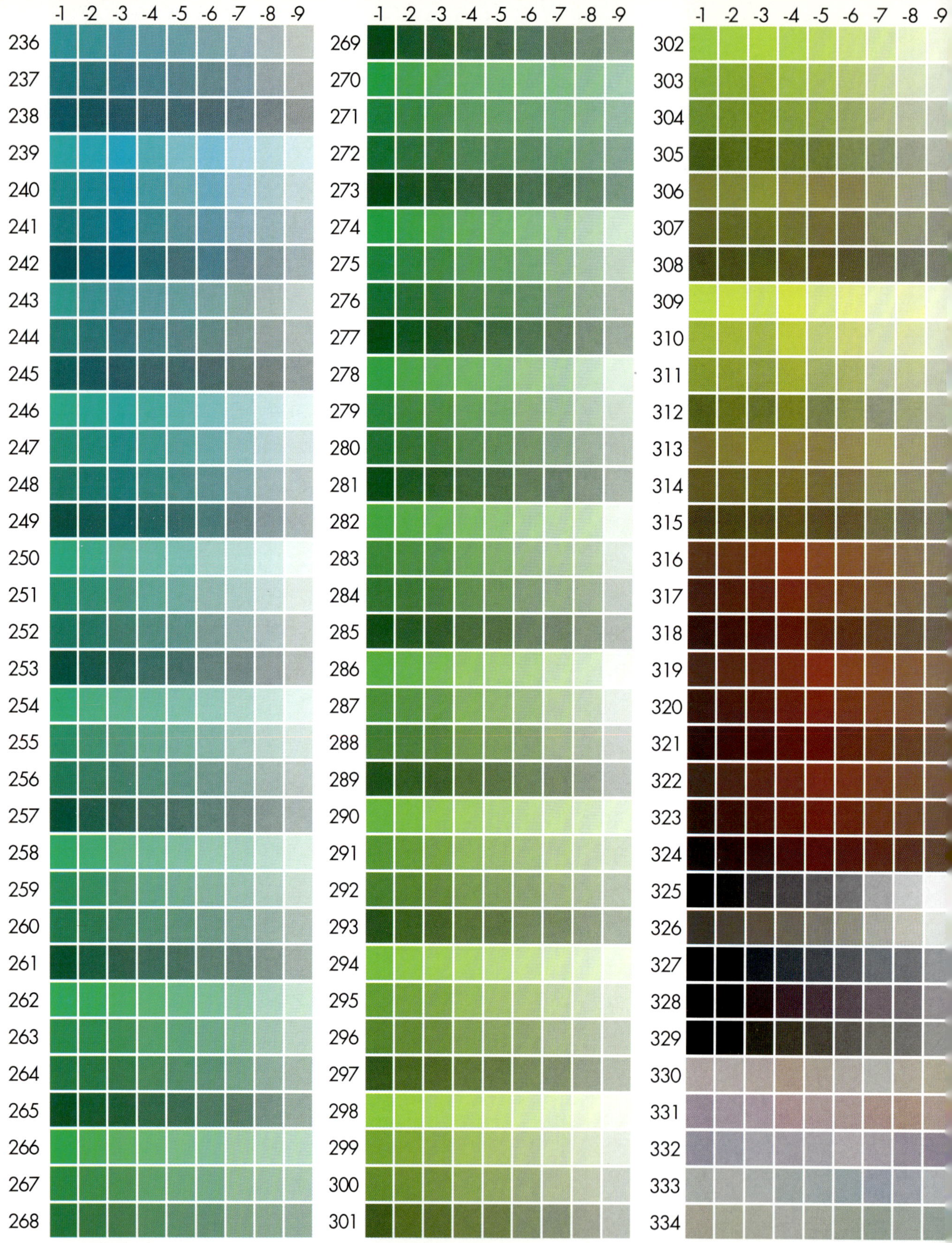
-1 -2 -3 -4 -5 -6 -7 -8 -9
236
237
238
239
240
241
242
243
244
245
246
247
248
249
250
251
252
253
254
255
256
257
258
259
260
261
262
263
264
265
266
267
268
-1 -2 -3 -4 -5 -6 -7 -8 -9
269
270
271
272
273
274
275
276
277
278
279
280
281
282
283
284
285
286
287
288
289
290
291
292
293
294
295
296
297
298
299
300
301
-1 -2 -3 -4 -5 -6 -7 -8 -9
302
303
304
305
306
307
308
309
310
311
312
313
314
315
316
317
318
319
320
321
322
323
324
325
326
327
328
329
330
331
332
333
334

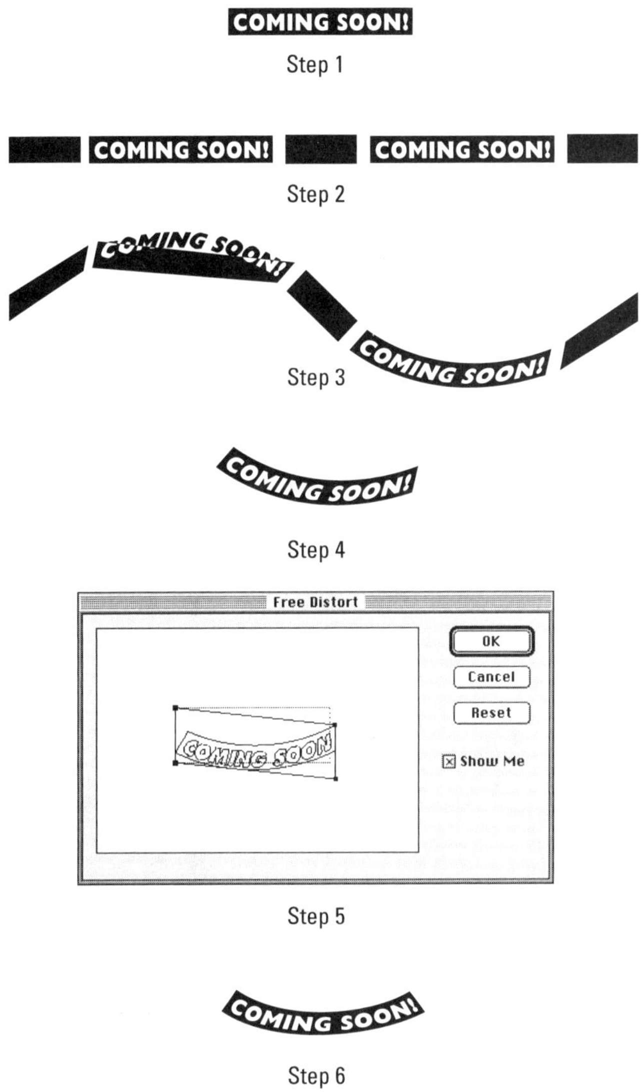

Figure 12-20: Steps for creating arced illustrations with the Twirl filter

The Zig Zag Filter

The Zig Zag filter changes normally straight paths into zigzagged versions of those paths. When you first select Zig Zag, the Zig Zag dialog box appears, shown in Figure 12-21.

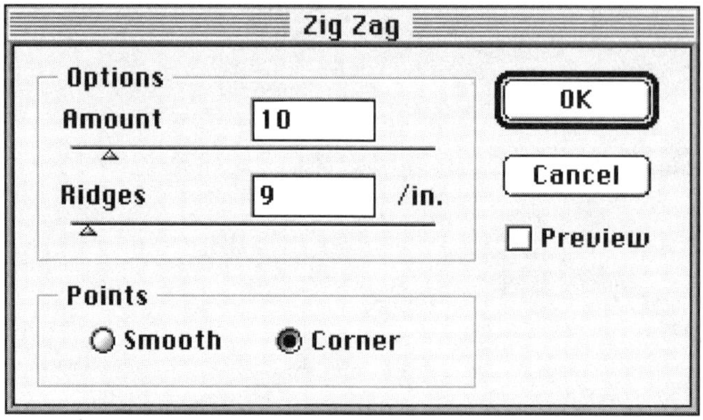

Figure 12-21: The Zig Zag dialog box

The dialog box allows you to specify various parameters of the zigzag effect, including the Amount, which is how large each zigzag is, and the number of Ridges, which is how many zigzags there are. In addition, you can specify if you'd like the zigzags to be curved (choose Smooth) or pointed (choose Corner). Like most of the other Illustrator 6 filters, Zig Zag has a handy Preview checkbox. Figure 12-22 shows an example of zigzagged artwork.

Figure 12-22: Zigzagged art

CAUTION: Don't keep the Preview checkbox checked while you're changing values in the Zig Zag dialog box. Instead, change your settings first, and *then* click the Preview checkbox. This prevents massive slowdowns that can occur when the Preview checkbox is checked.

The Random Mangle Filters

The two Random Mangle filters — Roughen, and Scribble and Tweak — both do similar things to paths. Roughen adds Anchor Points and then moves them randomly by a percentage that you define. Scribble and Tweak randomly moves existing Anchor Points and Control Handles by a percentage or by an absolute measurement that you define.

Because the mangle filters work randomly, you get different results when you apply the same settings of the same filter to two separate, identical objects. In fact, the results will probably never be duplicated. The mangle filters are a good reason by themselves for having the Undo command, so you can apply the filter, undo, and reapply until you achieve the desired effect.

Using the keyboard, you can continually reapply any filter that works randomly and get different results. Select the object and apply the filter by dragging the mouse to the menu item and entering the values. If you don't like the result, press ⌘-Z [Ctrl+Z] (Undo) and ⌘-E [Ctrl+E] (reapply last filter).

One important limitation of the mangle filters is that they work on entire paths, even if only part of the path is selected. The best way to get around this limitation is to use the Scissors tool to cut the path into different sections.

The Roughen Filter

The Roughen filter does two things at once. First, it adds Anchor Points until the selection has the number of points per inch that you defined. Second, it randomly moves all the points around, changing them into Straight Corner Points or Smooth Points, whichever you specified.

Not the Same Effect

Carmine: You know, what I really hate about Illustrator is the inconsistency.

Toulouse: What's inconsistent?

Carmine: The Roughen filter, for one.

Toulouse: It's supposed to be inconsistent. After all, it does random stuff.

Carmine: But let's say I want to duplicate a roughen effect.

Toulouse: I think you're out of luck.

Carmine: How does Illustrator come up with the random values? Surely there's a chart somewhere....

Toulouse: Actually, most "random" numbers are generated based on the time and date. Because this always changes, you'll get a different "result" each time.

Carmine: So if I went back in time to when I applied the Roughen filter the first time, it would be the same.

Toulouse: Well, you'd have to do it at the exact moment when you applied it before. Which would be almost as hard as traveling back in time in the first place.

Carmine: I could change my system clock, couldn't I?

Toulouse: Yes, but still, we're talking fractions of a second. The odds are you won't be able to do it right, unfortunately.

Selecting Roughen opens the Roughen dialog box (see Figure 12-23), where you can enter information to roughen up the illustration — literally.

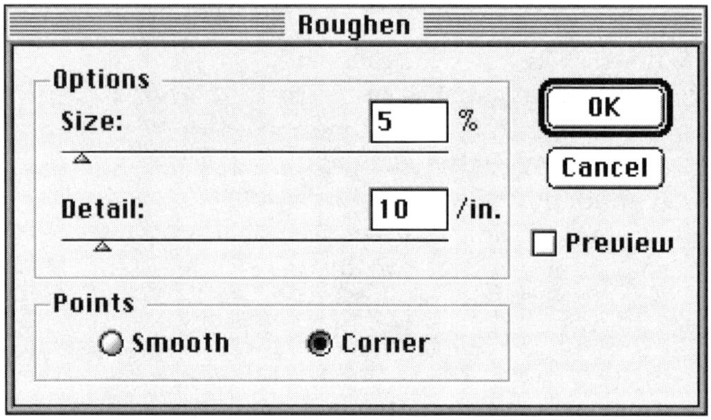

Figure 12-23: The Roughen dialog box

Three options are available here:

- **Size:** How far points may move when roughed relative to the width or height (whichever is greater) of the selected path.
- **Detail:** How many points are moved. For example, if you have a 1 x 1 inch square, the number of points added would be 36. (4 inches at the top, bottom, left, right and at 10 points per inch equals 40 points. There are already 4 points on a rectangle, so you only need 36 more points.)
- **Smooth or Corner:** If Smooth, all the Anchor Points added will be Smooth Points. If Corner, all the points added will be Straight Corner Points.

Roughen never takes away points when roughening a path.

The Roughen filter can be used as a very hip version of the Add Anchor Points filter. If the Size box is set to 0%, all points added will be added along the existing path all at once. Instead of going to Add Anchor Points again and again, just try entering a value of 25 into the Segments/Inch field of the Roughen filter. You have instant multiple Add Anchor Points. This is a great technique for Scribble and Tweak, or anything else where you need a bunch of Anchor Points fast.

Using the Roughen filter on a path is fairly straightforward, but using it on a portion of artwork is not. Figure 12-24 and the following steps take you through setting up artwork so that only a portion of the artwork is affected by the Roughen filter.

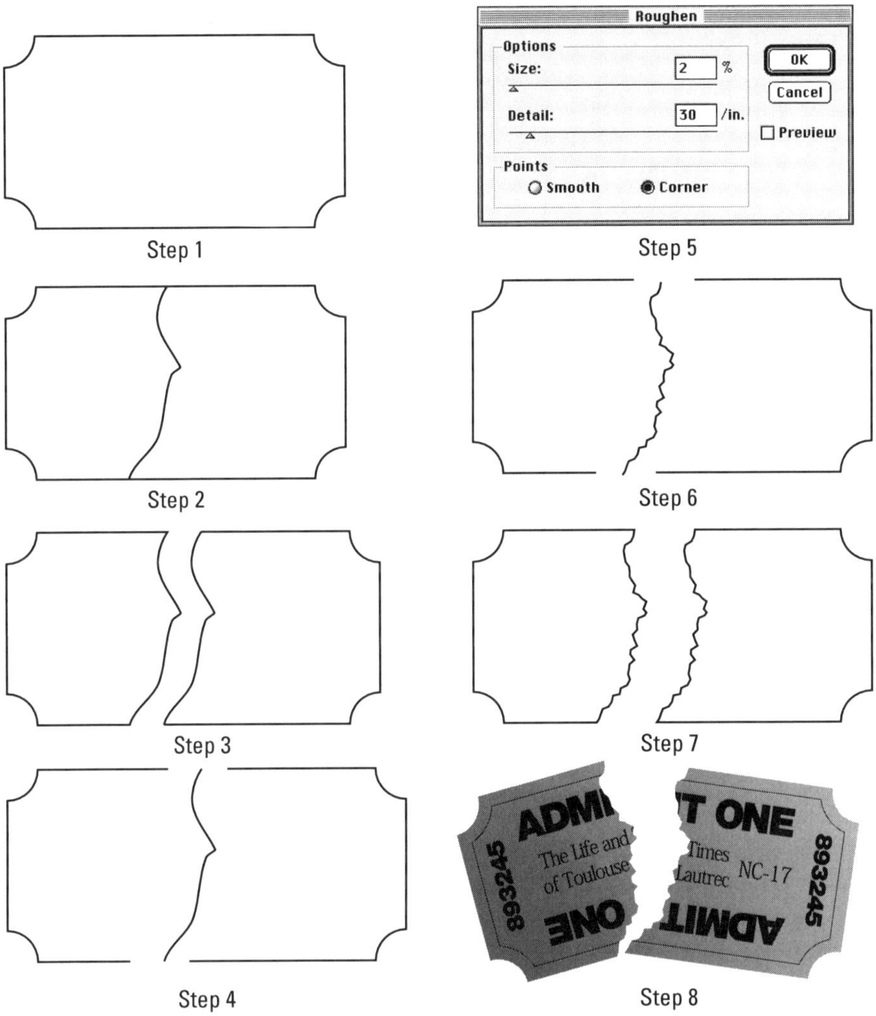

Figure 12-24: Steps for creating a tear in a path

STEPS: Creating a Tear with the Roughen Filter

Step 1. Create the artwork that you want to tear.

Step 2. Select the Pen tool and click from one edge of the artwork to another, crossing the path that you want to tear. If you don't want the tear to be straight, click additional points to change direction. If you want a curved tear, make the path curved. Connect the path by continuing around the outside of the artwork.

(continued)

STEPS: *(continued)*

Step 3. Select the artwork and the path. Choose Object➪Pathfinder➪Divide. Ungroup (⌘-Shift-G) [Ctrl+Shift+G] and choose Edit➪Deselect All (⌘-Shift-A) [Ctrl+Shift+A]. Select the paths on one side of the tear and drag them away from the remaining paths.

Step 4. Using the Scissors tool, click the ends of the tear on one side of the split path. Drag the cut section away from the rest of the path. On the other half of the tear, cut that tear away and delete it as well.

Step 5. Choose Filter➪Distort➪Roughen to see the Roughen dialog box. In the Size text field, enter the percentage that you want the Anchor Points to be moved. In the example, I used 2% to move the points just slightly.

Next, determine how many points you want to add to the tear. I chose 30 points per inch. Then decide on the type of roughen: Rounded or Jagged. A Rounded roughen produces Smooth Points with Control Handles that stick out a very small amount from the Anchor Point, and a Jagged roughen has only Straight Corner Points.

Step 6. Click OK and check the newly roughened path to ensure that it is roughened correctly. If it isn't, or if you don't like the random movement of the anchor Points, choose Edit➪Undo (⌘-Z) [Ctrl+Z] and select the Filter dialog box again (press Option [Alt] and choose Filter➪Distort➪Roughen). Continue undoing and roughening until the artwork is the way you want it or just adjust the Anchor Points with the Direct Selection tool.

Step 7. Option[Alt]-copy the roughened path to the edge of the path that it was torn from. The best way to perform this task is to click on an end point with the Selection tool and drag to the end point of the existing path with the Option [Alt] key pressed. Average and join the points (⌘-Option-Shift-J) [Ctrl+Alt+Shift+J]. Move the original roughened path to the other side of the path and average and join both points.

I usually zoom in, sometimes all the way to 1600%, to make sure that the two points are directly on top of each other and that only two points are selected.

Step 8. Add any other artwork to the torn paths. In the example, I rotated each of the sides a small amount.

The Roughen filter has a secret function that very few people know about: You can use it to add Anchor Points to paths. Simply enter **0%** in the first text field, and the points that are added will not be moved at all. This method is especially useful as a substitute for Add Anchor Points when some of the paths in a compound path don't need as many additional Anchor Points as others. The Roughen filter evens out the number of points for each of the paths in a compound path.

If you want roughened edges to be *really* rounded, don't choose the Rounded option in the Roughen dialog box. Instead, choose the Jagged option and then choose Filter⇨Stylize⇨Round Corners. The Round Corners option changes only Straight Corner Points, so it will change all the points in the Jagged roughened object to smooth curves.

If you choose the Rounded option in the Roughen dialog box, the Round Corners filter has no effect on the roughened object.

The Scribble and Tweak Filter

Although it sounds like characters from *Animaniacs,* the Scribble and Tweak filter, as is true for most filters, creates effects that would take an unrealistically long amount of time to do manually.

One important thing needs to be made clear right away: The Scribble and Tweak filter does one thing. The only difference between scribbling and tweaking is in the way that you enter the amount of random movement. When Scribble is selected, you'll enter percentages that are based on the size of the object's bounding box, but when Tweak is selected, points are moved based on absolute measurements that you enter.

Because of the measuring system that Tweak uses, I have found that selecting the Tweak option is much easier than using the Scribble option most of the time. Having to enter percentages when Scribble is selected can be very confusing, especially because you have to be concerned with both horizontal and vertical proportions.

Selecting Scribble and Tweak displays the Scribble and Tweak dialog box. When the Scribble option is selected, you define the amount of scribble, including how much horizontal and vertical scribble and which points are moved (Anchor Points, In Control Points, or Out Control Points).

No Anchor Points are added with the Scribble dialog box.

For Scribble, horizontal and vertical percentages correspond to the movement of the selected points. If 0% is entered in either field, no movement will occur in that direction. The percentage is based on the width or height of the shape, whichever is longer. If Anchor Points is checked, then all Anchor Points on the selected path are moved in a random distance corresponding to the amounts set in the Horizontal and Vertical text fields. If "In" or "Out" Control Points is checked, then those points are moved the specified distance as well. The *"In" Control Points* are the points on one side of the Anchor Point, while *"Out" Control Points* refers to the points on the other side of the Anchor Point.

Selecting Tweak displays the Tweak options. Instead of specifying a distance based on percentage, the Tweak option lets you enter the distance in real measurements (like picas or inches), in whatever unit your measurement system is currently using. All Tweak options have the same effects as the Scribble options.

STEPS: Using the Scribble and Tweak Filter

Step 1. Create the artwork that you want to use with the filter.

The Scribble and Tweak filter does not work with type that has not been converted to outlines or with placed images. Nor does it affect patterns or gradients that are being used as Fills.

Step 2. Choose Filter⇨Distort⇨Scribble and Tweak.

I use the Scribble option when I am not sure of the size of the selected artwork, or when I can determine only that I want points moved a certain portion of the whole, but cannot determine an absolute measurement.

In the Scribble and Tweak dialog box, enter the amount that you want points to be moved, both horizontally and vertically. Moving the points a large amount usually results in overlapping, crisscrossing paths that aren't very attractive.

Check the options that correspond to the points that you want to move randomly. Checking the Anchor Points checkbox moves Anchor Points randomly. Checking the "In" or "Out" Control Points checkboxes moves the Control Handles.

The "In" Control Points are the Control Handles that affect the segment that precedes the Anchor Point relative to the path direction. The "Out" Control Points are the Control Handles that affect the segment that appears after each Anchor Point relative the path direction. (Path direction is explained in Chapter 9.)

Step 3. Click OK. If the artwork isn't what you expected, choose Edit⇨Undo (⌘-Z) [Ctrl+Z] and then either reapply the filter (⌘-E) [Ctrl+E] or press Option and enter new values in the dialog box (choose Filter⇨Distort⇨Scribble and Tweak).

Step 4. Add any further artwork to the completed object.

Figure 12-25 shows these four steps. At the bottom of the figure are eight different versions of the artwork. Each version has the same settings, but the points have been moved randomly eight different times.

Figure 12-25: Steps for using the Scribble and Tweak filter

The percentages that you enter in the Scribble dialog box move points relative to the size of the bounding box.

The bounding box is an invisible box that surrounds each object. If the bounding box is 5 inches wide and 2 inches tall and you enter a percentage of 10% for width and height in the Scribble dialog box, the filter moves the points randomly up to .5 inches horizontally and .2 inches vertically in either direction.

CAUTION: The most important thing to remember when you are entering horizontal and vertical percentages when the Scribble option is checked is that the height and width of any object are usually different. As a result, entering the same percentage in each box usually causes different amounts of movement for each dimension.

The Stylize Filters

The Stylize filters are used for a variety of functions, kind of a catch-all for filters that really couldn't go anywhere else. Add Arrowheads puts arrowheads (all sorts!) onto the ends of open paths. Calligraphy changes the selection into something that could have been drawn with a calligraphy pen. Drop Shadow adds a darkened shadow to the selected path. Path Pattern takes paths you've created and applies them to paths, instead of to Fills and Strokes. Round Corners seems better suited to the Distort submenu, but Adobe has chosen to put it here.

The five Stylize filters fall into two different categories. The first category contains the Add Arrowheads, Drop Shadows, and Path Patterns filters. All of these filters create additional objects that are based on existing objects.

The Stylize filters in the second category work in much the same way as the Distort filters. The Calligraphy filter distorts the path, giving it a calligraphic appearance. The Round Corners filter removes Corner Points and replaces them with Smooth Points.

Add Arrowheads

The Add Arrowheads filter is a boon to technical artists, sign makers, and anyone else in need of a quick arrow. The number one complaint about the Add Arrowheads filter is that Illustrator offers too many arrowheads to choose from. Some complaint.

Choosing Filter⇨Stylize⇨Add Arrowheads adds an arrowhead (or two) to any selected open paths. If more than one path is selected, arrowheads are added to each open path. To use Add Arrowheads, select an open path and choose Add Arrowheads. The Add Arrowheads dialog box appears, as shown in Figure 12-26. In this box, you can pick which of the 27 different arrowheads you want to stick on the end of your path. Scale refers to the size of the arrowhead relative to the Stroke weight of the path; you may enter any number between 1% and 1000% in this box. Choosing Start places the arrowhead on the beginning of the path (where you first clicked to draw it), choosing End places the arrowhead on the ending of the path (where you last clicked to draw it), and choosing Start and End places the same arrowhead on both the beginning and ending of the path. Reapplying this filter to the same paths will continue to put arrowheads on top of arrowheads.

Figure 12-26: The Add Arrowheads dialog box

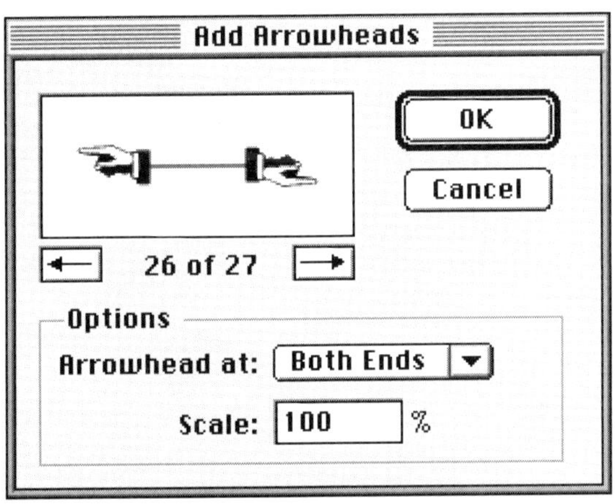

CAUTION: Add Arrowheads does *not* work on closed paths.

Arrowheads are grouped to the paths that were selected when they were created; it is sometimes necessary to rotate the arrowhead by either ungrouping it or choosing it with the Direct Selection tool.

The size of the arrowheads is based on the width of the Stroke, but you can alter each arrowhead's dimensions in the Scale text field in the Add Arrowheads dialog box. Figure 12-27 and the steps that follow show you how to create and customize arrowheads.

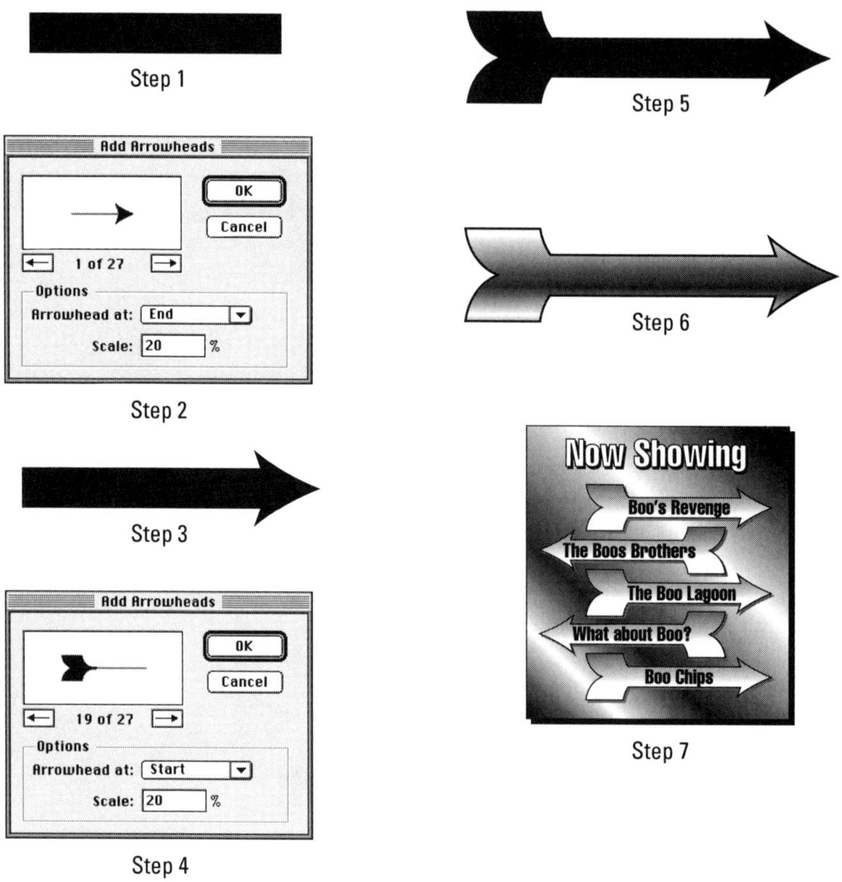

Figure 12-27: Steps for creating and customizing an arrowhead by using the Add Arrowheads filter

STEPS: Creating a Customized Arrow

Step 1. Use the Pen or Freehand tool to create an open path. Set the width of the path to the width that you want it to be with an arrowhead attached to it.

You have to use an open path. Nothing happens when you select a closed path and apply the Add Arrowheads filter.

Even if you want just the arrowhead, and not the path, you still have to create a path first. You can delete the path after the arrowhead appears.

Step 2. Choose Filter⇨Stylize⇨Add Arrowheads. The Add Arrowheads dialog box appears. Enter the size of the arrowhead (100% = normal size). Pick the end of the path where you want the arrowhead to appear. If you want the arrowhead on both ends of the path, click the Start and End option.

If you drew the path yourself with either the Pen or Freehand tool, the path direction is the direction that you drew the path. Closed paths that were created with the Rectangle or Oval tools or the Create filters and were then cut usually go in a counterclockwise direction.

Pick an arrowhead from the 27 options. Figure 12-28 shows all the arrowheads.

Press down and hold on the directional arrows to flip through the arrowheads quickly. After arrowhead #27, you see arrowhead #1.

Step 3. Click OK. The path now has an arrowhead. Whenever arrowheads are created, they are grouped to the path. You have to use the Group Selection tool to select individual pieces of the arrow, or choose Arrange⇨Ungroup (⌘-Shift-G) [Ctrl+Shift+G].

Step 4. To add a different arrowhead to the other end of the path, select the path, press Option [Alt], and choose Filter⇨Stylize⇨Add Arrowheads. Change the buttons to indicate that the new arrowhead should go at the other end of the path and select the type of arrowhead.

Step 5. Click OK. Make sure that the arrowhead is correct. If it isn't, choose Edit⇨Undo (⌘-Z) [Ctrl+Z], press Option [Alt], and choose Filter⇨Stylize⇨Add Arrowheads. Then add a different arrowhead.

Step 6. To make the arrowheads and path into one path, select the path and choose Object⇨Path⇨Outline Path. Then select both the new outlined path and the arrowheads and choose Object⇨Pathfinder⇨Unite.

Now you can Fill the new arrow object with anything, including gradients, and Stroke the entire object at once.

Step 7. Add any other artwork that you want to the arrow.

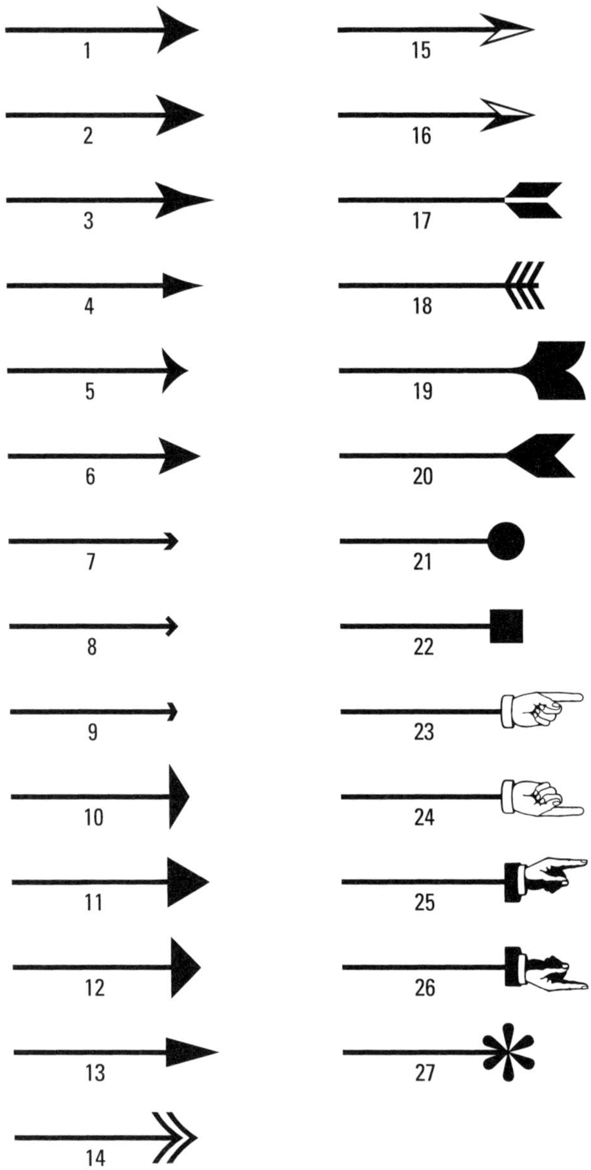

Figure 12-28: The arrowheads that are available in the Add Arrowheads dialog box

Drop Shadow Filter

The Drop Shadow filter makes creating drop shadows for most paths a relatively simple task.

Unlike most other filters, selecting Drop Shadow affects both Stroke *and* Fill. In the Drop Shadow dialog box (see Figure 12-29), you may specify the offset of the drop shadow by entering values for how far across the drop shadow should move (X Offset) and how far up or down it should move (Y Offset). Positive numbers move the shadow to the right and down; negative numbers move the shadow to the left and up.

Figure 12-29: The Drop Shadow dialog box

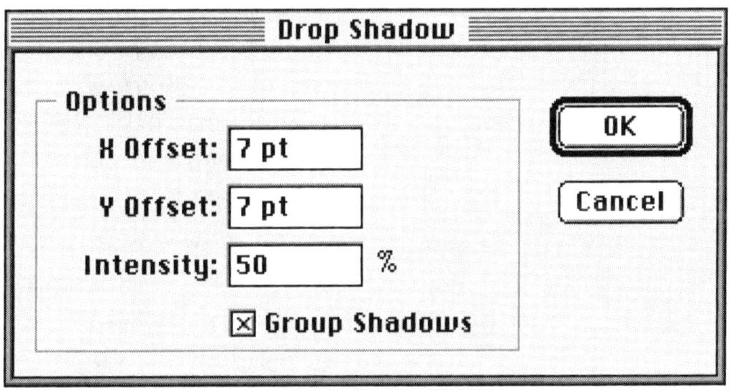

The general rule in drop shadowing is that the more offset the drop shadow is, the higher the original object looks. To make an object look as if it is floating far above the page, enter high offset values.

The percentage entered in Intensity is how much black is added to the Fill and Stroke colors. Intensity does not affect any of the other custom or process colors. If you check Group Shadows, the drop shadow is grouped to the original object, which is a good idea, because you shouldn't just leave your shadow lying around.

STEPS: Creating a Drop Shadow

Step 1. Create and select the artwork that you want to give a drop shadow to.

Step 2. Choose Filter⇨Stylize⇨Drop Shadow. The Drop Shadow dialog box appears, as shown in Figure 12-29.

Step 3. Enter the amount that you want the drop shadow to be offset. A positive value in the X Offset text field puts the shadow to the right of the object; a negative value in the X Offset text field puts the shadow to the left of

(continued)

Extra Points?

Laverne: I keep getting extra points after I apply Round Corners.

Toulouse: That's what Round Corners does. It replaces most corner points with two Smooth Points.

Laverne: But I only want one point there.

Toulouse: Well, you could change each point individually to a Smooth Point.

Laverne: How long would that take?

Toulouse: Let's see ... if you had 20 paths, each with 15 anchor points....

Laverne: I have a Cray handy, to help you figure this out.

Toulouse: That would be 300 Anchor Points. If you take 3 seconds on each, and 3 seconds to find the next po4int....

Laverne: The Cray is smoking. Too tough.

Toulouse: ... it would take you half an hour of constant clicking.

Laverne: Isn't that a kd lang tune?

STEPS: ***(continued)***

the object. A positive value in the Y Offset text field puts the shadow below the object; a negative value in the Y Offset text field puts the shadow above the object.

The larger the offset amounts, the higher up the object appears to float above the original object.

The value that you enter in the Intensity field determines how much black will be added to the shadow to make it appear darker. If you check the Group Shadows box, the shadow is grouped to the original object.

Step 4. Click OK. If the shadow isn't what you want, use the Undo command (⌘-Z) [Ctrl+Z], press Option [Alt], choose Filter⇨Stylize⇨Drop Shadow, and create a new drop shadow.

The Round Corners Filters

You can use the Round Corners filter to create round corners just like (snap your fingers) that. This filter works on any path that has corner points, but the best results seem to be on polygons and stars.

Selecting Round Corners changes all types of corner points to Smooth Points. In the Round Corners dialog box, you specify what the radius of the Round Corners should be. The larger the number you enter for the radius, the bigger the curve.

CAUTION: Don't apply the Round Corners filter to a rounded rectangle to make the corners more rounded. Instead of making the corners rounder, the flat sides of the rounded rectangle will curve slightly.

STEPS: Using the Round Corners Filter

Step 1. Select the artwork that will have its corners rounded. I used type converted to outlines in the example in Figure 12-30.

Step 2. Choose Filter⇨Stylize⇨Round Corners. The Round Corners dialog box appears. Enter the amount that you want the corners to be rounded.

I wanted my corners rounded as much as possible, so I entered **100 pt** in the dialog box. Entering a large number usually ensures that all points will become as curved as possible.

Step 3. Click OK.

Step 4. Add other artwork to the final rounded artwork.

Figure 12-30: Using the Round Corners filter

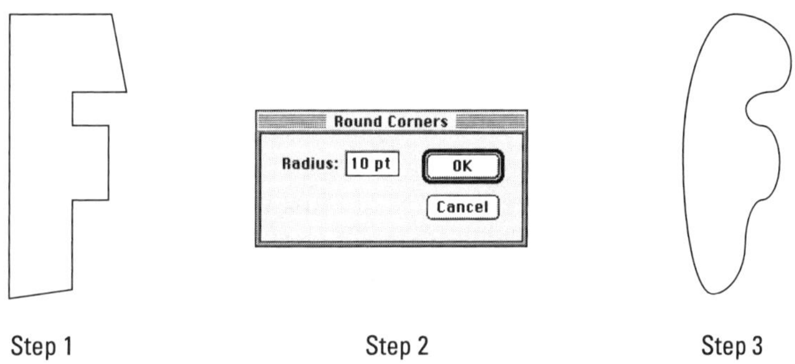

You can use the Round Corners filter to smooth out overly bumpy edges. Using the Round Corners filter with Roughen can produce very smooth, flowing areas.

Calligraphy

For those of us who are not blessed with the skill of calligraphy, Adobe has provided the Calligraphy filter. You can use it to turn any path into calligraphic art, although the results usually end up looking more like what your dog might draw with a calligraphy pen strapped to his tail when he's *really* happy.

Choosing Calligraphy opens the Calligraphy dialog box, where you specify the width and angle of the pen you want to use. Calligraphy works with paths, not Fills or Strokes, and is entirely dependent on the shape of the path for its results.

Drawing with the Paintbrush tool over the same area with the same settings will have a similar effect as using the Calligraphy filter, but the results will be slightly better with the Paintbrush tool.

The maximum thickness of the calligraphic line is called *pen width,* and pen angle is the angle at which the pen is at its thickest.

Although you can turn any path into calligraphy, text converted to outlines and then "calligraphied" looks just plain nasty. If you've ever seen a calligrapher draw letters, you appreciate how wonderful calligraphic type looks. But because type outlines are just that — outlines — the result that you get from using the Calligraphy filter with text doesn't look like calligraphy at all. Instead, it looks like a giant mess. And no, script type isn't any better.

Why would you want to turn artwork into calligraphy? Well, the folks at Adobe were hardpressed to come up with an answer (never heard so much hemmin' 'n' hawin' in my life), but I've found one thing that it's good for: creating pictures of cookie cutters.

STEPS: Creating Cookie Cutters with the Calligraphy Filter

Step 1. Create the artwork that you want to use with the Calligraphy filter and select it. I used a pig shape for the example in Figure 12-31.

Corners can look bad with the Calligraphy filter. If the artwork has too many corners, use the Round Corners filter to change the corners into curved areas.

Step 2. Choose Filter⇨Stylize⇨Calligraphy and enter the width and the angle of the calligraphic stroke.

Step 3. Click OK.

Step 4. To give the cookie cutter a metallic look, I applied a silver gradient to it and put it on a dark background, as I did in the example.

Figure 12-31: Creating a cookie cutter with the Calligraphy filter

Path Patterns

When I first saw the Path Patterns feature demonstrated, I was stunned, awed, and confused. How could this work? How was it possible? Before I get into the technical concepts and rules regarding path patterns, let's get rid of the misconceptions you might have regarding this feature.

First, this may not seem like a big deal. After all, Illustrator has supported patterns as a Stroke attribute since Illustrator 88, when patterns were introduced. Even now, in Illustrator 6, you can still select a pattern for your Stroke, and it'll (usually) print just fine. Of course, patterns on Strokes are *tiled,* meaning they stack up on top of each other, like the pattern on the left in Figure 12-32.

Second, you don't have to do anything special for basic path patterns. As you can see in Figure 12-32, I used one of the default patterns (Tablecloth) for both the standard Stroked pattern and the path pattern on the left. You may want to design patterns especially for the Path Patterns feature (as explained in the next section), but you don't have to.

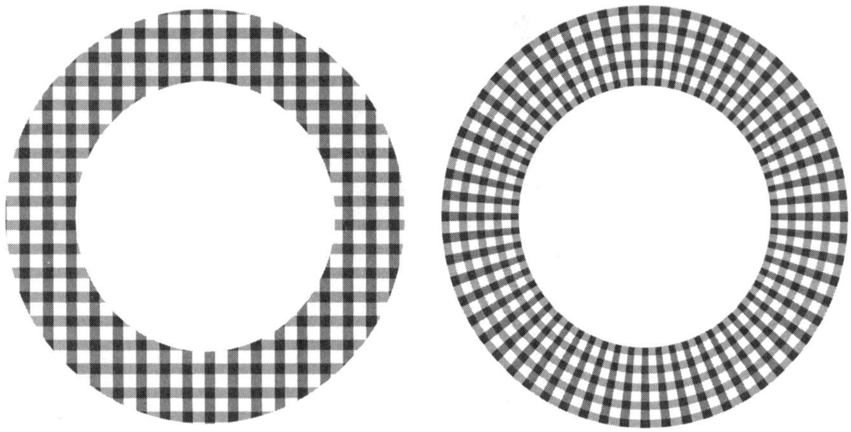

Figure 12-32: The circle on the left has the Tablecloth pattern on its Stroke, while the circle on the right has the Tablecloth pattern applied to it as a path pattern

Third, unlike patterns used as Strokes, path patterns are both viewable on-screen and fully editable after they've been applied. The Path patterns feature creates paths, not pattern tiles.

STEPS: Using Path Patterns

Step 1. To use Path Patterns, first select the path you'd like the pattern applied to.

Step 2. Choose Filter⇨Stylize⇨Path Pattern. The Path Pattern dialog box appears.

Step 3. In the Path Pattern dialog box, select the pattern you'd like to apply to your path and click OK. The path now contains the pattern.

Figure 12-33 illustrates these three steps. Of course, there's a lot more depth, but those are the basics you'll need to get started.

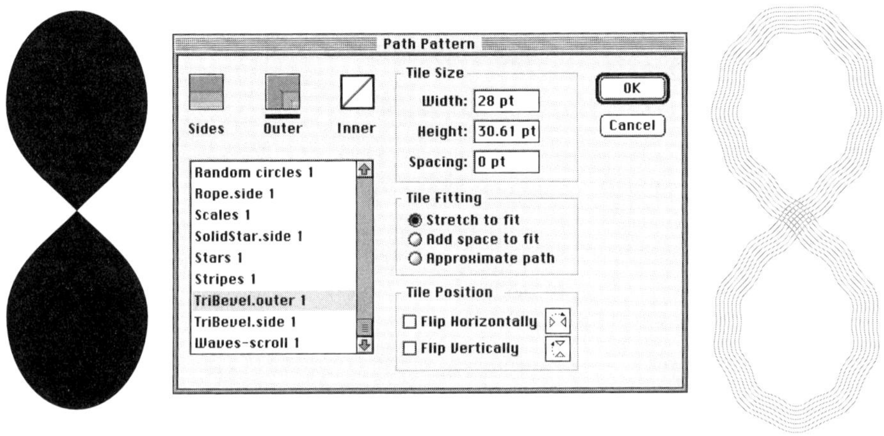

Figure 12-33: Steps for placing a pattern on a path

Creating a Pattern for Path Patterns

You might want to create a special pattern for the Path Patterns feature. In this example, I'll show you how to create a metal tube pattern quickly.

Think linearly when creating patterns for use with Path Patterns. You're always going to be concerned with how the patterns line up left and right, and will have little concern for how they work top and bottom.

STEPS: Creating and Applying a Tube Pattern for Path Patterns

Step 1. Draw a horizontal line with the Pen tool. Use the Shift key to ensure that it is perfectly horizontal. Give the path a Fill of None, and a stroke of 6-point Black.

Step 2. Copy the line and Paste in Front (⌘-F) [Ctrl+F]. Change the weight to 4 points, and change Stroke color to 75% Black.

Step 3. Paste in Front again and change the weight to 2 points, and the Stroke color to 50% Black.

Step 4. Paste in Front again and change the weight to .5 points, and the Stroke color to 25% Black.

(continued)

STEPS: *(continued)*

Step 5. Select all the overlapping paths and make two duplicates using Option[Alt]-Copy.

Step 6. Create a rectangle surrounding the paths you've drawn that is flush against the left and right side. Send it to the back (⌘-Shift-[) [Ctrl+Shift+[] and change the color to a stroke and fill of none. Figure 12-34 shows a good location for that rectangle; the edges of the rectangle are shown only so you can see it.

Step 7. Select the lines and the rectangle and drag them into the Swatch palette. Double-click the new swatch and name the pattern.

Step 8. Draw the path you'd like to apply the path pattern to. For this example, use a path with no corners, just smooth curves. (I'll explain corners a little later.)

Step 9. Select the path and choose Filter⇨Stylize⇨Path Pattern. Select the Tubes pattern, and keep the corners at None. (None is found at the top of the list of patterns.) For my example, I changed the height of the pattern to 12 points, so it could fit into the space allotted.

Step 10. Click OK. The pattern is now on the path.

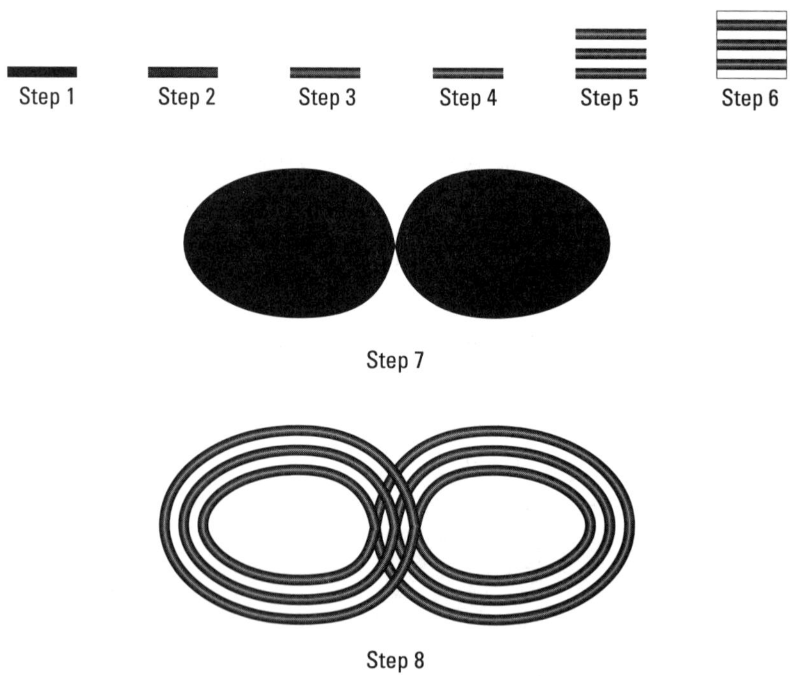

Figure 12-34: The steps for creating and applying a pattern to a curved path

The Trouble with Corners

Unfortunately, corners cause a whole slew of problems with path patterns. Figure 12-35 shows what happens to a path with corners when our tube pattern is applied to it as a path. In order to get around this, you can create pattern tiles that will be used just for corners. To show how this is done, we'll create corners for our tube pattern from Figure 12-34.

Figure 12-35: Corners can be problematic with path patterns

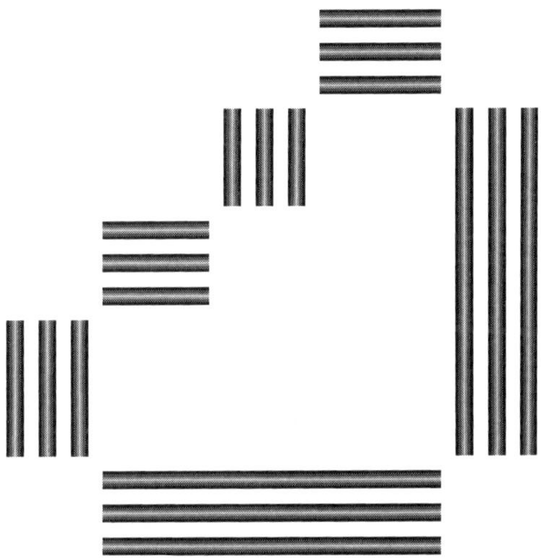

STEPS: Creating Corners for Path Patterns

Step 1. First, paste a copy of the pattern in the document dragging the pattern swatch to the document.

Step 2. Next, you need to rearrange the pattern tile so you can easily create corners. I've moved mine around, and copied and rotated one of them to create both an inside and outside border in Figure 12-36.

Step 3. Create the corner pieces. For the outside corner, I've created a basic corner piece, but for the inside, I've jazzed it up a little. No matter what you do, make sure the corner pieces match the artwork.

Step 4. Rotate the lower corner (the inside corner) 180°.

Step 5. Create bounding boxes for the pattern corners. They must be perfect squares, the width and height of the original pattern height.

(continued)

STEPS: *(continued)*

Step 6. Make each of the corners a pattern using the Define Pattern command on the Edit menu. Designate which is the outside and which is the inside corner.

Step 7. Create a path with corners (and curves, if desired). The corners do not have to be right angles, but avoid very sharp (acute) angles if possible.

Step 8. Select the path and apply the Path Pattern filter to it. Specify the corners with the tiles you've just created.

Step 9. Click OK. You now have corners.

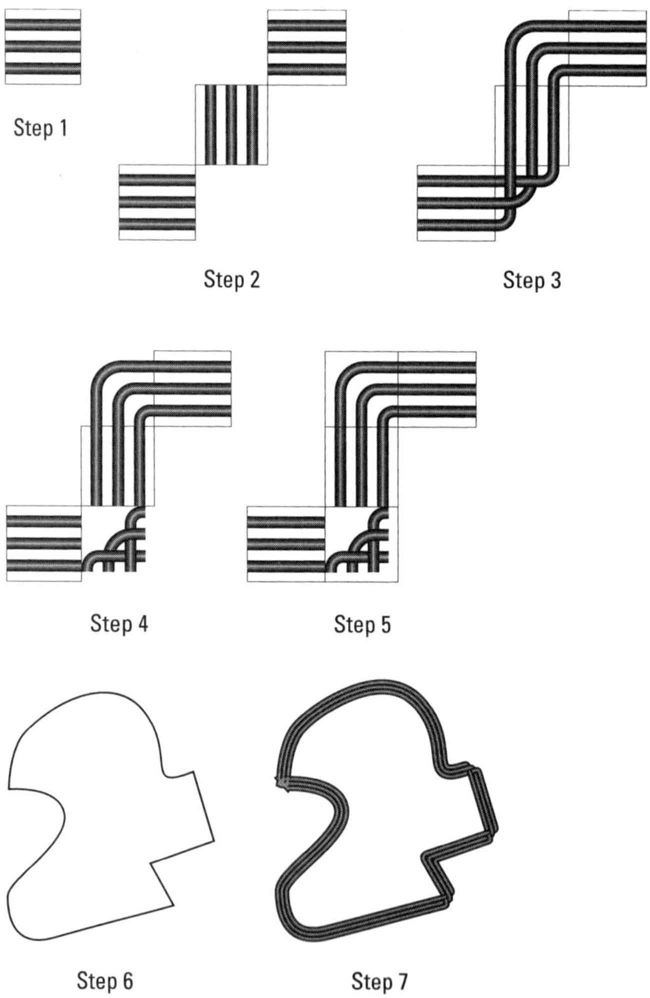

Figure 12-36: Steps for creating corner tiles for path patterns

CAUTION Unlike standard patterns, path patterns do not always properly mask out edges that lie outside the bounding rectangle.

Summary

- Filters add extra functionality to Illustrator through commands in the Filter menu.
- Several filters from previous versions of Illustrator have been combined into other menus, or changed into tools or palettes.
- To use a filter, select the artwork you wish to "filterize" and select the filter from the Filter menu.
- The hardest thing about filters is knowing what they do, and when and how to use them; the filters themselves are pretty simple.
- Third-party companies have developed several filter sets for Illustrator, and more are on the way.
- You can reapply the last filter quickly by pressing ⌘-E [Ctrl+E].
- Access the last filter's dialog box by pressing ⌘-Option-E [Ctrl+Alt+E].
- Adjust Colors adds and subtracts various amounts of process colors from multiple colored objects.
- The color blend filters look at two opposite paths and blend between the two colors.
- Saturate increases or decreases the amount of color in selected paths.
- The Fill & Stroke for Mask filter provides a quick method for putting Fills behind and Strokes on top of masking objects.
- The Object Mosaic filter takes TIFF files and square streamlines them into Illustrator paths.
- The Distort and Stylize filters work by moving points around in selected paths.
- Free Distort lets you add perspective to your artwork.
- Punk and Bloat create spiked and bubbled effects, respectively.
- There are two ways to twirl artwork: with the Twirl filter or with the Twirl tool.

- Twirling adds Anchor Points as needed when twirling.
- Zig Zag creates even wavy or spiky paths.
- Roughen can be used to intelligently add Anchor Points.
- Scribble and Tweak are used to move existing points and Control Handles randomly.
- Add Arrowheads creates arrowheads on the ends of open paths.
- Drop Shadow creates instant drop shadows.
- Round Corners changes Straight Corner Points into Smooth Points.
- Path Patterns applies patterns to paths automatically.

Using Photoshop Filters and Raster Images

13 CHAPTER

In This Chapter

- How pixel-based images work in Illustrator
- The difference between pixels and vectors
- Working with Photoshop and Illustrator concurrently
- Using Photoshop filters in Illustrator
- A look at some of the Photoshop filters available

When I first learned that Illustrator would support Photoshop filters, all the wrong thoughts entered my brain. "Great, now I'll be able to Gaussian Blur my shadows without having to turn them into pixels first!" and "Wow, I wonder what'll happen with blends and some of the Distort filters."

Of course, I was misled (those silly press releases again, I'm sure). Photoshop filters work only on *pixel-based* images, not vector images (paths and such). Fortunately, however, there is a command for making paths into pixel-based images (Rasterize). So, it's an extra step . . . but it still works.

Vectors versus Pixel-Based Images

I covered this (sorta) back in Chapter One, but I'll go into a little more depth here. Illustrator, when it originally was formed, was a pure vector piece of software. There was nary a pixel to be found round these parts. But with Version 7, the border has been crossed, and Illustrator is just this side of the pixel border (which is nowhere near as smooth as the vector border).

Windows Update

Illustrator 4.1 could only use placed EPS raster images (and pict templates). Illustrator 7 can use virtually *any* file format for raster images. In addition, Photoshop filters can be applied to any *embedded* raster images (not to linked raster images).

When you think vectors, think Illustrator's paths. Illustrator's paths consist of outlines. Sure, they're outlines that can be Filled with various colors and gradients, but they're outlines still. And it is the manipulation of these outlines that is the essence of Illustrator. Outlines can be resized and transformed in almost any way imaginable. And when you create a curve in Illustrator, it's really a curve, not a jagged mass of pixels. Vector-based images can be stretched bigger, and look better for it (except for blends and gradients if they're scaled up too large).

When you think pixels, think Photoshop's little teeny tiny squares of color. Squares that don't ever change position, that you don't add or delete. The only thing you change about pixels is their color. Pixels can only be square, and they take up space regardless if they're "empty" (Filled with white or another background color) or "filled." Pixels exist on an immobile grid. Enlarging a pixel-based image results in giant, ugly squares of color.

Okay, I'm not a pixel person. If I were to be reincarnated as an electronic drawing tool, it wouldn't be as a Painter piece of chalk, but instead as Illustrator's Pen tool or Direct Selection tool. I'm a believer in vectors. Some say it's an obsession, but I'm too busy staring at Control Handles to pay attention to that nonsense.

Fortunately, my mind is not so closed that I ignore the importance of pixels, nor their place in our electronic graphics society. In fact, I wrote the best-selling *The Complete Idiot's Guide to Photoshop* just to prove that point (yes, the working title was "Ted's Guide to Photoshop" and . . . ha, ha, ha, . . . they changed the title on me).

So I'm glad there are pixels in Illustrator. After all, you can do things to pixels in Illustrator that you *can't* do in Photoshop. Ah, now I've got your attention.

Changing Illustrator Artwork into Pixels

There are several ways to turn Illustrator art into pixels, but the best way is to use the Rasterize command, which transforms any selected artwork into pixel-based artwork, at the resolution you specify.

STEPS: Changing Illustrator Artwork into Pixels Without Ever Leaving Illustrator

Step 1. Create your artwork in Illustrator.

Step 2. Select the artwork and choose Object⇨Rasterize. The Rasterize dialog box appears. Enter the ppi (pixels per inch) and click OK.

Step 3. Your artwork has been rasterized.

Figure 13-1 illustrates these three steps.

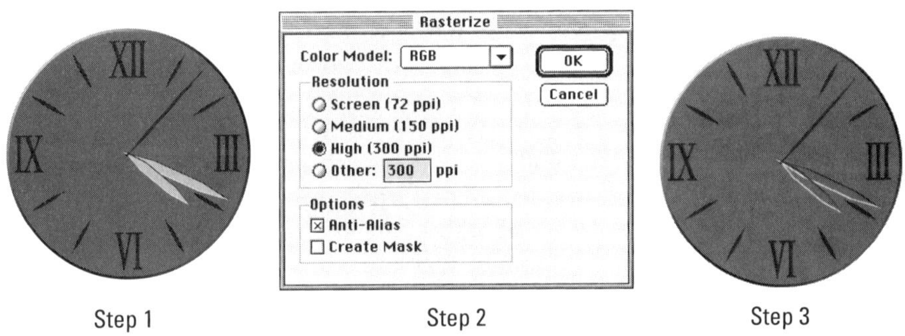

Figure 13-1: Steps for rasterizing artwork

A funky little checkbox in the Rasterize dialog box asks if you'd like to make a mask of your artwork. This can be a good thing to do for such items where sharp edges are important, like for text. Checking the Create Mask option creates an automatic mask around the edges of the artwork, and masks the image. In addition to keeping the edges nice and straight (because they're paths, not pixels), this masks off the areas of "white" or "empty" pixels, making those areas appear transparent.

As an Illustrator user, you might not be all that familiar with having to decide resolution, as you would in Photoshop. The quick rule of thumb is that the resolution of pixel-based images should be $1^1/_2$ to 2 times the line screen that the piece will be printed at. So if you'll be using a line screen of 133, your ppi should be between 199 and 266. It doesn't hurt to go higher than 2 times the line screen, but it is unnecessary. Since the math is easier, plan on using double the line screen for the resolution.

All in the Details

Steve: So why should I use vectors instead of pixels?

Toulouse: It really depends on what you're doing.

Steve: Let's say I was creating a new four-color logo.

Toulouse: Vectors, probably. That way the logo can be resized without any loss in quality.

Steve: When would I use pixels?

Toulouse: Pixels are good for the abstract things, like blurriness, subtle color changes, and the like.

Steve: So, for anything that needs to be photorealistic, you would use pixels.

Toulouse: Not necessarily. Take a look at what some of the premier design studios are doing, like Thomas-Bradley Design, and you'll see that it's hard to tell the difference between pixels and vectors.

Steve: So why do they use vectors then?

Toulouse: File size, transformability, and precision you can't get from pixels.

Going to Photoshop and Back with Pixels and Paths

Even with its new pixel capabilities, Illustrator is no Photoshop. There are tools and features in Photoshop that are invaluable for adjusting pixel-based artwork. Adobe recognizes this, so it has provided several methods for moving pixels to Photoshop from Illustrator, and from Illustrator to Photoshop.

The most rudimentary way, which has existed for several versions of both software packages, is to save art in a format the other program can read, and then to open or place the art in the other program. To place Illustrator art into Photoshop, save the art in Illustrator format, then open the art in Photoshop. To place Photoshop art into Illustrator, save in Photoshop as a format that Illustrator can read, like TIFF, and then in Illustrator choose File⇨Place and select the file.

The next way is through Adobe's wonderful PostScript on the Clipboard process, which allows for transferring artwork between Adobe software by simply copying in one program and pasting in another. To place Illustrator art in Photoshop, copy the art in Illustrator, switch to Photoshop, and paste in any document. To place Photoshop art in Illustrator, copy the art in Photoshop, switch to Illustrator, and paste in any document.

The easiest way to move art between these programs is to drag it from one program to the other. To drag art from Illustrator to Photoshop, select the art in Illustrator and drag it out of the Illustrator window onto a Photoshop window. To drag art from Photoshop to Illustrator, select the art in Photoshop and drag it out of the Photoshop window onto an Illustrator window.

CAUTION

You must have a window from the "to" application showing when you start dragging for drag-and-drop to work between programs.

You can also move just paths between the two programs. When opening or pasting Illustrator art in Photoshop, click the Paste As Paths option in the dialog box that appears, as shown in Figure 13-2. Instead of Filled and Stroked paths appearing in Photoshop, paths appear, which can be manipulated by the Path tools on the Paths palette.

Figure 13-2: The Paste dialog box

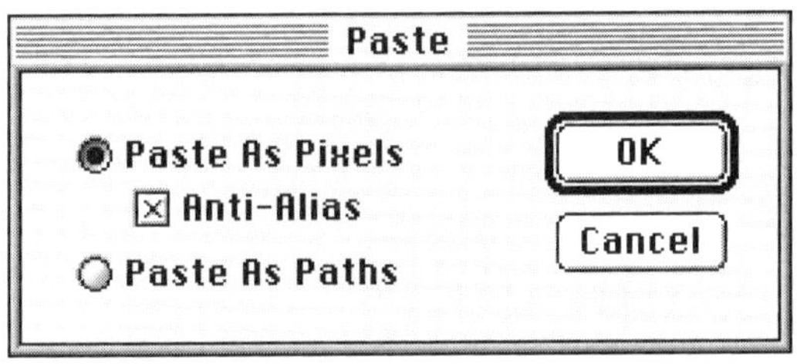

To place paths from Photoshop into Illustrator, select the paths in Photoshop with the Path Selection tool and copy, then paste in Illustrator.

Colorizing One-Bit TIFF Images

One-bit TIFF images (black and white only) can be colored in Illustrator. This effectively turns the black pixels into the color you specify.

To color a 1-bit TIFF image, select the imported image, and change the Fill color to the desired color.

Figure 13-3 and the steps that follow show how to color portions of a 1-bit image.

Figure 13-3: Steps for giving a 1-bit image multiple colors

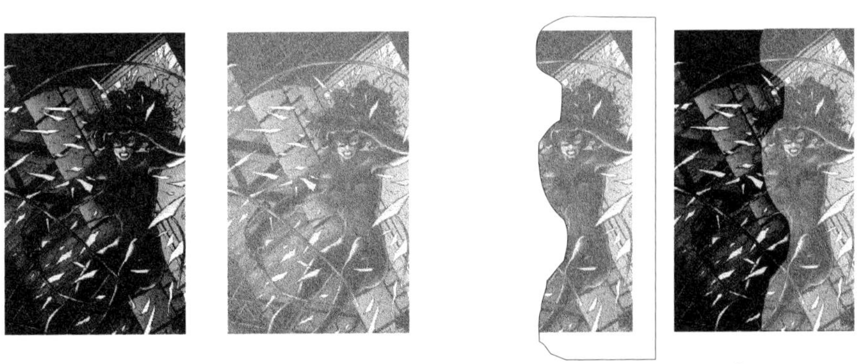

Step 1 Step 2 Step 3 Step 4

You can create an unlimited number of colors in a 1-bit image by creating additional copies and applying different masks to each one.

STEPS: Coloring a One-Bit Image with More Than One Color

Step 1. Select the imported image you wish to color, and apply a color to it by changing the Fill on the Color palette.

Step 2. Copy the image, and paint the copy with a different color.

Step 3. Create a mask over the portion of the copied object that should be the different color. Group the mask with the copied image.

Step 4. Realign the copied image or mask with the original image.

Using Photoshop-Compatible Filters in Illustrator

By themselves, these filters are really neat, but because such a large number of Illustrator users have Photoshop, are they necessary?

For starters, these filters make things a bit easier than before, especially for doing things such as creating drop shadows and other special effects. Instead of having to allocate memory to Photoshop, you can do filter operations right in Illustrator.

But here's the very cool thing, the one thing that Illustrator has over Photoshop when it comes to applying filters. It's so special that I've decided to offset it with one of those wonderful little "Power Tip" icons. . . .

Because Illustrator has multiple undos, you can apply several different filters to an imported image, and undo all of them in turn. Photoshop *can't* do that.

Photoshop filters work only on pixel-based images. If you'd like to apply a Photoshop filter to your Illustrator artwork, you have to first select it and choose Object⇨Rasterize to turn it into a pixel-based image.

Figure 13-4 and the steps that follow describe how to apply a Photoshop filter to an image.

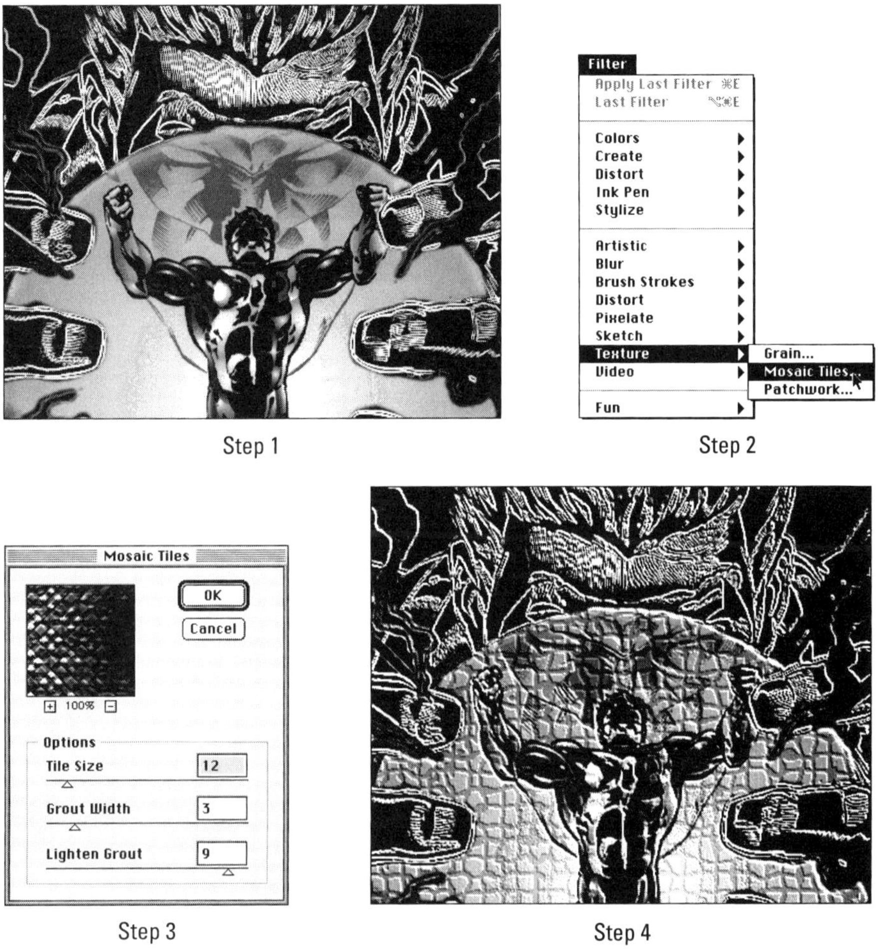

Figure 13-4: Steps for applying Photoshop filters in Illustrator

STEPS: Applying Photoshop Filters in Illustrator

Step 1. Select the pixel-based image in Illustrator that you'd like to apply the Photoshop filter to.

Step 2. Choose Filter⇨*Name of Photoshop filter submenu*⇨*Name of filter.* This could be, for instance, Filter⇨Texture⇨Mosaic Tiles.

Step 3. In the Filter dialog box (if there is one), adjust the settings and values.

Step 4. Click OK in the Filter dialog box to produce the effect.

One big limitation of using Photoshop filters in Illustrator is that you can't make any selections *within* the pixel-based image. A way around this is to create a copy of the image, apply the filter, and then mask the area you'd like that effect applied to.

Illustrator's Photoshop Plug-Ins

All the Photoshop plug-ins that were originally Aldus Gallery Effects (way back in the days before Adobe snarfed up Aldus) are included in Illustrator. They're sectioned off from the vector filters, appearing below them (the logic being that you won't be using them as much as Illustrator filters, so why let them get in the way).

The plug-ins are primarily special effect plug-ins, so I've included the following images to show both the filter, the settings, and the result on the originally vector-based artwork (shown in Figure 13-5).

Figure 13-5: The original vector artwork

Other Third-Party Photoshop filters

There are several Photoshop filter sets created by third parties, including Kai's Power Tools, KPT Convolver, CSI PhotoLab, and Alien Skin Eye Candy.

For Illustrator use, I've found KPT Convolver to be the most useful, as it has Gaussian Blur, Unsharp Mask, and other filter effects not otherwise available from Photoshop. In addition, for high-end color correction, CSI PhotoLab is indispensible.

Figure 13-6: Art Filters

Figure 13-7: Blur Filters

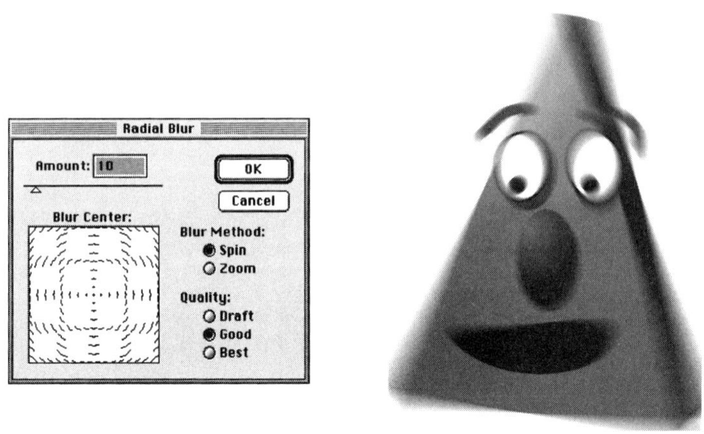

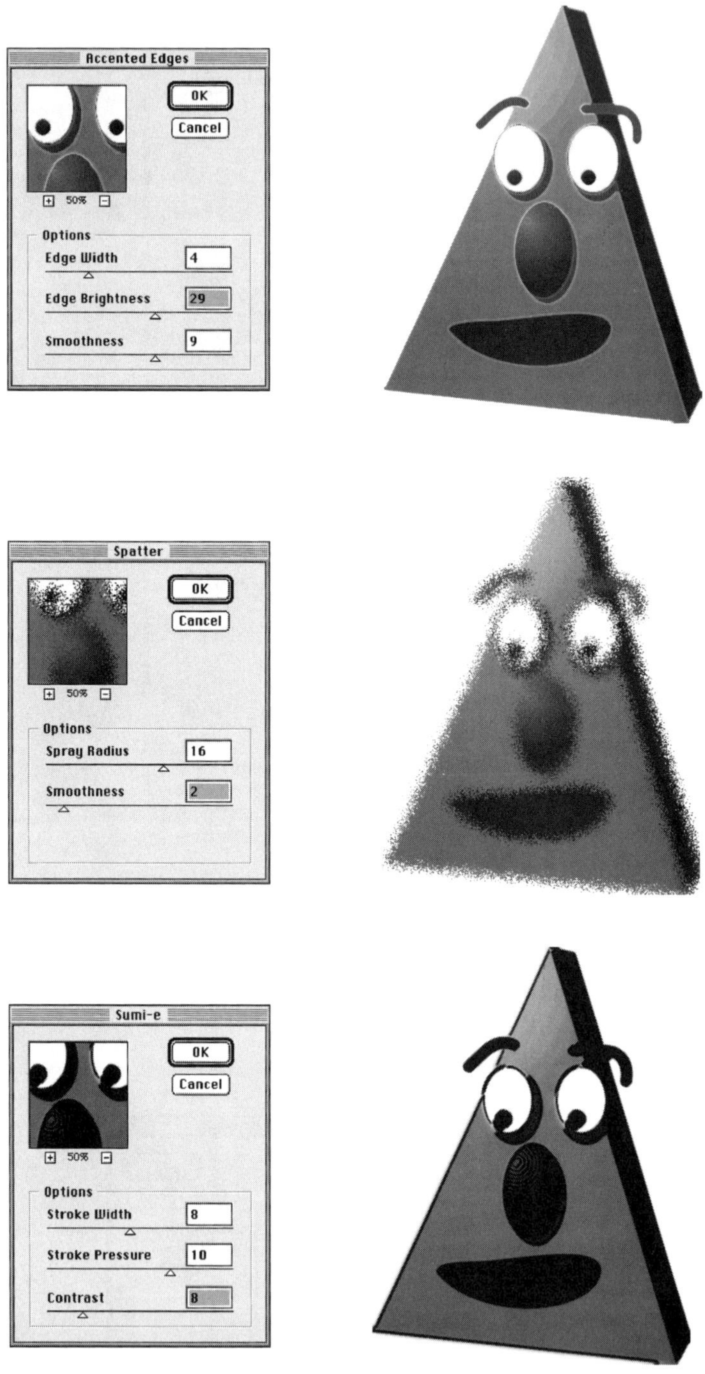

Figure 13-8: Brush Stroke Filters

Figure 13-9: Distort Filters

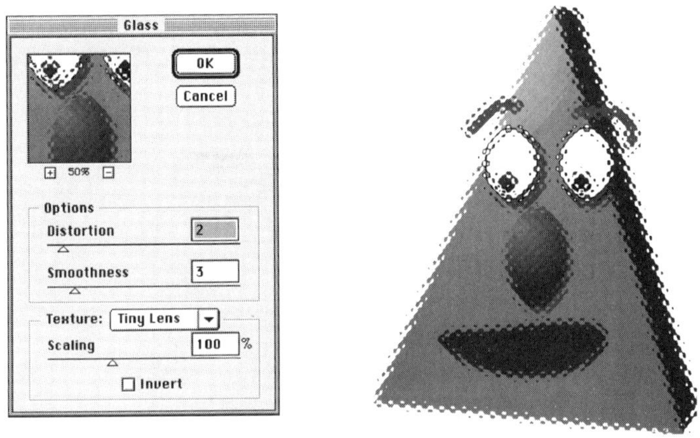

Figure 13-10: Pixelate Filters

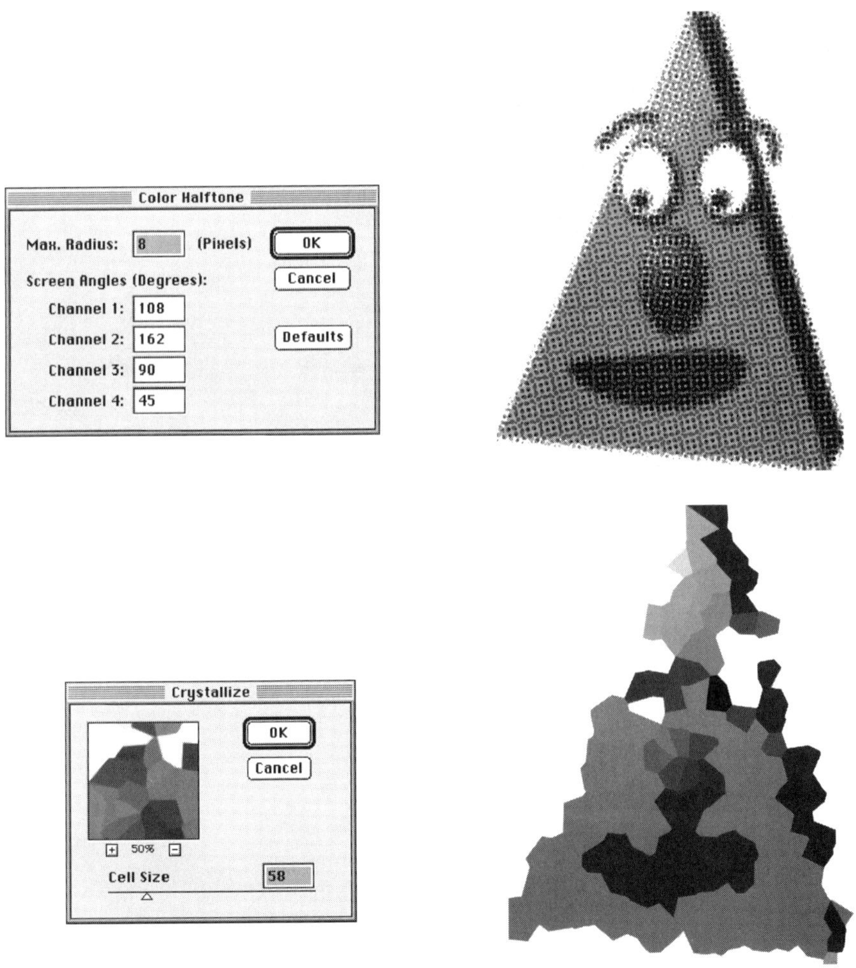

Figure 13-10: Pixelate Filters (continued)

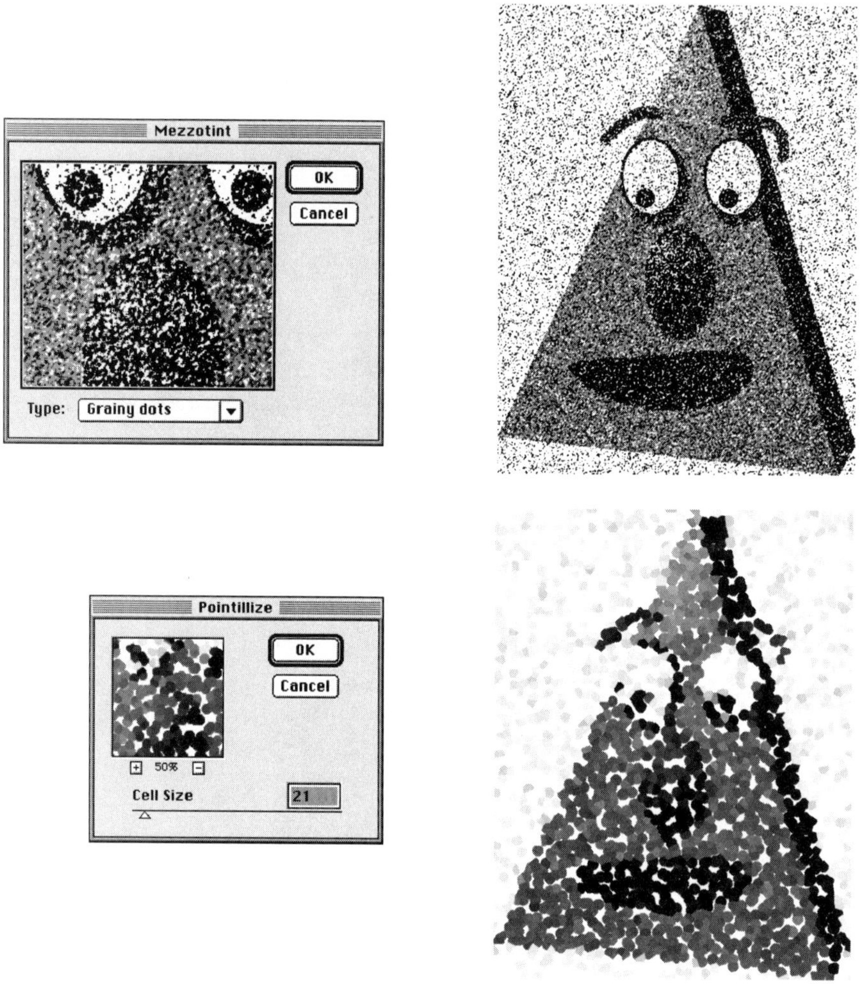

Figure 13-11:
Sketch Filters

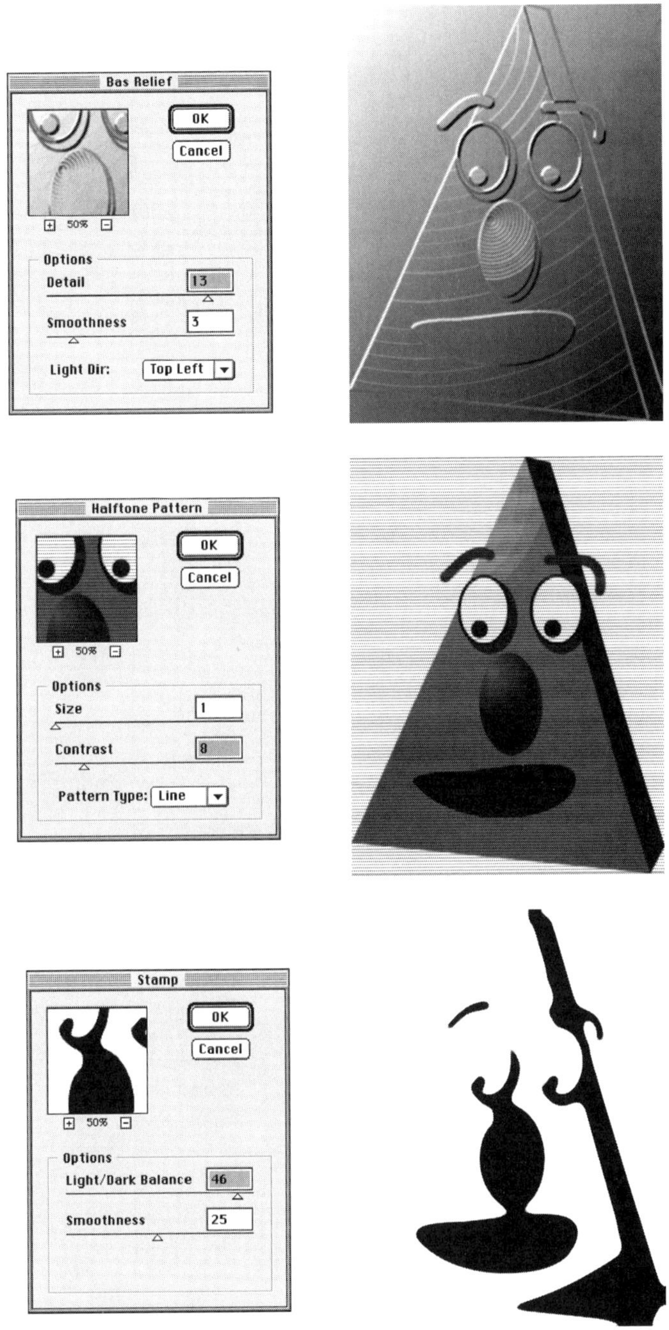

Figure 13-12: Texture Filters

Summary

- Pixel-based artwork can be incorporated into Illustrator by importing it.
- The quickest way to move images between Illustrator and Photoshop is to drag-and-drop them between windows in each program.
- Paths can also be taken back and forth between the two programs.
- One-bit images can be colorized by selecting the image and changing the Fill color in the Color palette.
- Photoshop filters appear in the Filter menu alongside Illustrator filters.

The Plug-Ins Folder Has Folders in It?

Oscar: Why does the Plug-Ins folder seem to have other folders inside of it?

Toulouse: To help keep your plug-ins organized. There's lots of them there, you know.

Oscar: What if I want to use all my Photoshop Plug-Ins in Illustrator?

Toulouse: The easiest way to do this is to make an alias of your Photoshop Plug-Ins folder....

Oscar: Okay.

Toulouse: ...and then drop it in your Illustrator Plug-Ins folder. All your Photoshop Plug-Ins will be available in Illustrator.

VectorTools

14 CHAPTER

In This Chapter

- Why VectorTools is a revolutionary set of plug-ins
- How to use the free VectorFrame SE (on the *Illustrator 7 Bible* CD-ROM)
- Tips and techniques for using each of the nine VectorTools plug-ins

When Extensis told me they'd be updating their Illustrator plug-ins package, DrawTools, I was thrilled. The package contained some amazingly powerful tools, but the interface was definitely substandard. I was hoping for a few new features in addition to increased ease of use — maybe palette-based color and shape controls and a few other goodies thrown in.

But when I finally learned what was going to be in VectorTools, I was blown away. The color and shape components *were* palletized and upgraded and are a dramatic improvement over the DrawTools versions. But they were no longer the core of the package. Instead, *seven* new fully functional components were to be added, from the basic and handy VectorTips to the incredibly powerful VectorObjectStyles and VectorLibrary. This package is every illustrator's dream come true.

Before you read more of my enthusiastic ramblings, be aware that I begged, pleaded, attempted to blackmail, and finally succeeded in coercing Extensis to let me do the Illustrator tips and tricks that appear in the product. So, in a way, I'm very proud of the one plug-in, Tips and Tricks. However, I consider it the least of the nine (count 'em, nine!) plug-in components.

POWER TIP

As a purchaser of the *Illustrator 7 Bible,* you happen to be getting one of the plug-ins, fully functional, for free (VectorFrame), and also a 30-day fully functional trial set of VectorTools (see Figure 14-1), both located on the *Illustrator 7 Bible* CD-ROM. That's why I've taken the liberty of providing an entire chapter to discuss using some of VectorTools' most useful and impressive features.

Windows Update

VectorTools was not available for Windows at the time this book went to press. Extensis and Adobe have confirmed that there will be a version of VectorTools for Windows Illustrator users, but they did not say when it would be available. The VectorFrame SE plug-in on the *Illustrator 7 Bible* CD-ROM is Mac-only, unfortunately. Although this chapter is only relevant to Mac users at this time, once VectorTools for Windows ships, most of the information in this chapter should be applicable.

Figure 14-1: VectorTools

The VectorTools Components

There are a total of eleven components in VectorTools, but two of them are for FreeHand users only (don't worry; two of the remaining nine are for Illustrator users only as well). Illustrator users don't need VectorCaps, which is similar to (though more powerful than) Illustrator's built-in Change Case function. FreeHand users also get a nifty plug-in called VectorTypeStyles, which is used for applying quick character-based formatting. Of course, those plug-ins pale in comparison to the two exclusive Illustrator plug-ins: VectorBars, which provides Extensis's toolbar technology to Illustrator users, and VectorObjectStyles, fully functional Object Style Sheets in Illustrator.

Here's the complete list, with a brief description of each:

VectorBars

VectorBars brings toolbars to Adobe Illustrator — Full-color buttons, fully customizable floating palettes, or edge-of-the-screen bars. Buttons can be assigned a menu command, keyboard command, or even used to open a file or folder.

VectorLibrary

VectorLibrary is a floating palette that contains Illustrator artwork. You can add artwork to the library, drag it from the library to your document, and export the library to share with other Illustrator users.

VectorMagicWand

VectorMagicWand is a MagicWand tool that is used to select paths based on how much alike they are to the path you click. You can adjust the type and amount of similarity in such areas as Fill and Stroke Color, Stroke weight, and object size.

VectorObjectStyles

VectorObjectsStyles bring object-based style sheets to Illustrator. By styling objects, you can make drastic changes to your entire document with one click, and also maintain consistency throughout your document(s).

VectorColor

VectorColor offers Photoshop-quality color control in Adobe Illustrator. Instead of playing around with the sliders on the Color Palette, you can adjust path fills and strokes using the VectorColor Palette, which features Curves, Brightness and Contrast, Multitone (duotones, and so on), Grayscale, and Randomize.

VectorShape

The other lone holdover from DrawTools has been significantly upgraded as well, now based on a palette instead of a dialog box. Your 2D artwork can be wrapped around all sorts of 3D objects, including Spheres, Waves, Cylinders, Cones, and Water. There's even a FreeDistort function that adds curving capabilities to Illustrator's Free Distort filter.

VectorFrame

Included free on the *Illustrator 7 Bible* CD-ROM, VectorFrame applies frames to selected objects. You can specify the frame style, the offset from the edges of the object, and if it should frame individual objects, groups, or all at once.

VectorNavigator

VectorNavigator brings document navigation (à la Photoshop's Navigator palette) to Adobe Illustrator. A floating palette displays all of the art in the image, indicating what portion you're currently zoomed into. By dragging the palette around, you can instantly zip around your document.

VectorTips

VectorTips is a collection of hundreds of useful, indispensable tips for Adobe Illustrator. Written by Ted Alspach (Hey! That's me!), they can be set to appear at Illustrator's launch for a "tip of the day" or be used to search for a better, faster way to solve any problem you might be having with Illustrator.

Installing and Using VectorFrame SE

While a fully functional trial version of VectorTools is included on the CD-ROM that accompanies this book, it will only work for 30 days before expiring. The VectorFrame SE plug-in we've included on the CD-ROM, on the other hand, is completely self sufficient, and won't expire. Ever.

If you're planning on buying VectorTools or already have it, then you can ignore the instructions in this section and use VectorFrame with the free trial or as a fully functional package. The only difference is that with the SE plug-in (on the CD-ROM included with this book), it is chosen from the window menu.

POWER TIP: If you have both VectorFrame SE and VectorFrame installed, you now have a total of ten presets to work with. Preset 1 in SE is different from the regular preset 1, so you now have twice as many options.

To install VectorFrame SE, find it inside the VectorFrame SE folder on the *Illustrator 7 Bible* CD-ROM. Drag it into your Adobe Illustrator Plug-ins folder. Restart Illustrator, and VectorFrame SE is now accessible in the window menu. To display the VectorFrame palette, select it from the window menu.

Using VectorTools

The following sections contain the basics and several ideas and uses for various VectorTools components.

When VectorTools is installed, Illustrator gets an additional menu tacked on to the end of its menu bar, right after the window menu. This menu is called "VectorTools," and is shown in Figure 14-2. Even though keyboard commands don't appear in the menu, each component can be accessed using a keyboard command, which is also indicated in the figure.

Figure 14-2: The VectorTools menu and the keyboard commands which correspond to each component (Mac only)

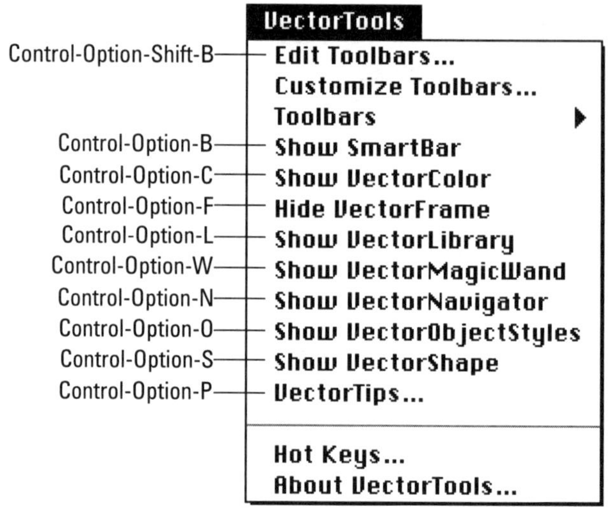

VectorFrame

VectorFrame is a floating palette (shown in Figure 14-3) that provides a quick and easy method for applying frames quickly to selected paths and placed images.

Figure 14-3: The VectorFrame palette

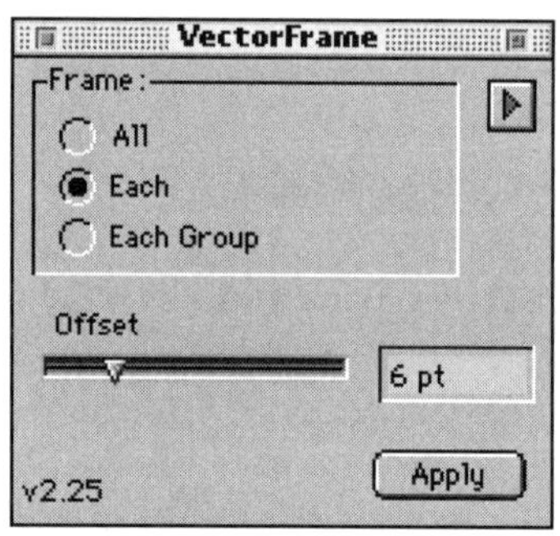

STEPS: Framing Several Placed Images at Once

Step 1. Create a document with several placed images (see Figure 14-4).

Step 2. In the VectorFrame palette, click the Apply button, set the Offset to 0, and choose the Each option.

Step 3. Change the Paint Style to a fill of None and a stroke of 10 pt. Black.

Step 4. Hold the Option [Alt] key and press the Apply button again. This creates a frame on the active frames.

Step 5. Change the Frame options to All, and drag the slider to the right until the frame is away from the edge of the framed images (see Figure 14-5).

Step 6. Change the background color to complement the placed images.

There are five static presets available in VectorFrame. Each of these presets is for Fill and Stroke attributes. To set a preset, change the Paint Style of the Fill and Stroke to the desired settings. Then choose Set Preset # from the VectorFrame pop-up menu.

POWER TIP: Apply a frame to a frame by pressing Option-Apply [Alt+Apply].

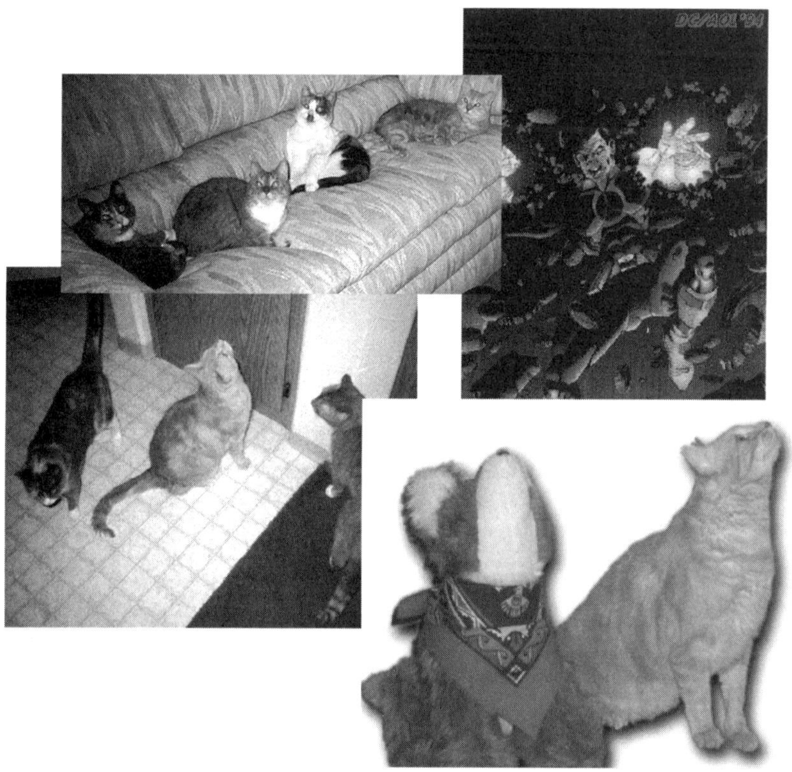

Figure 14-4: An Illustrator document with several placed images

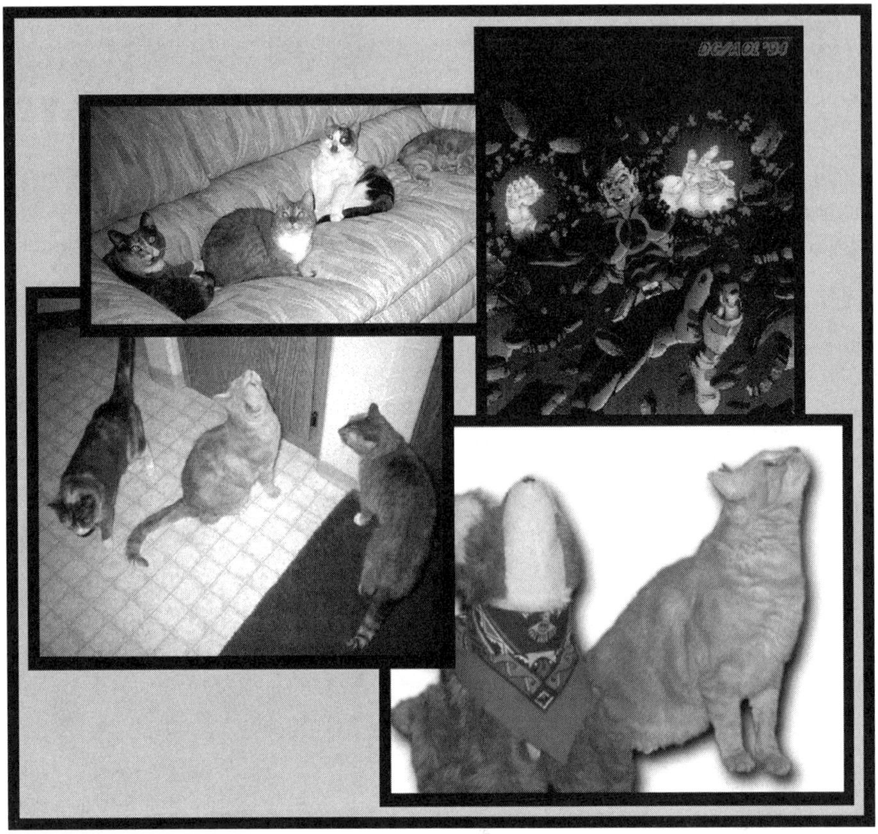

Figure 14-5: After frames have been applied to this Illustrator image

VectorBars

I've never been a big fan of toolbars. But Extensis takes the concept several steps further, allowing me to create buttons for virtually every function within Illustrator. Any menu item or keyboard command can have a button applied to it. These buttons are placed on toolbars that can be floating palettes, embedded in any side of your screen. Extensis supplies several prefabricated bars ready for your use (see Figure 14-6). Fortunately, only a few appear by default, and you can choose to hide and show them by choosing an option from the VectorBars submenu (in the VectorTools menu).

POWER TIP: Move buttons from bar to bar by ⌘-dragging [Ctrl+dragging] them. Insert or remove space between buttons by ⌘-dragging [Ctrl+dragging] them along the bar. Remove buttons by ⌘-dragging [Ctrl+dragging] them off their current bar.

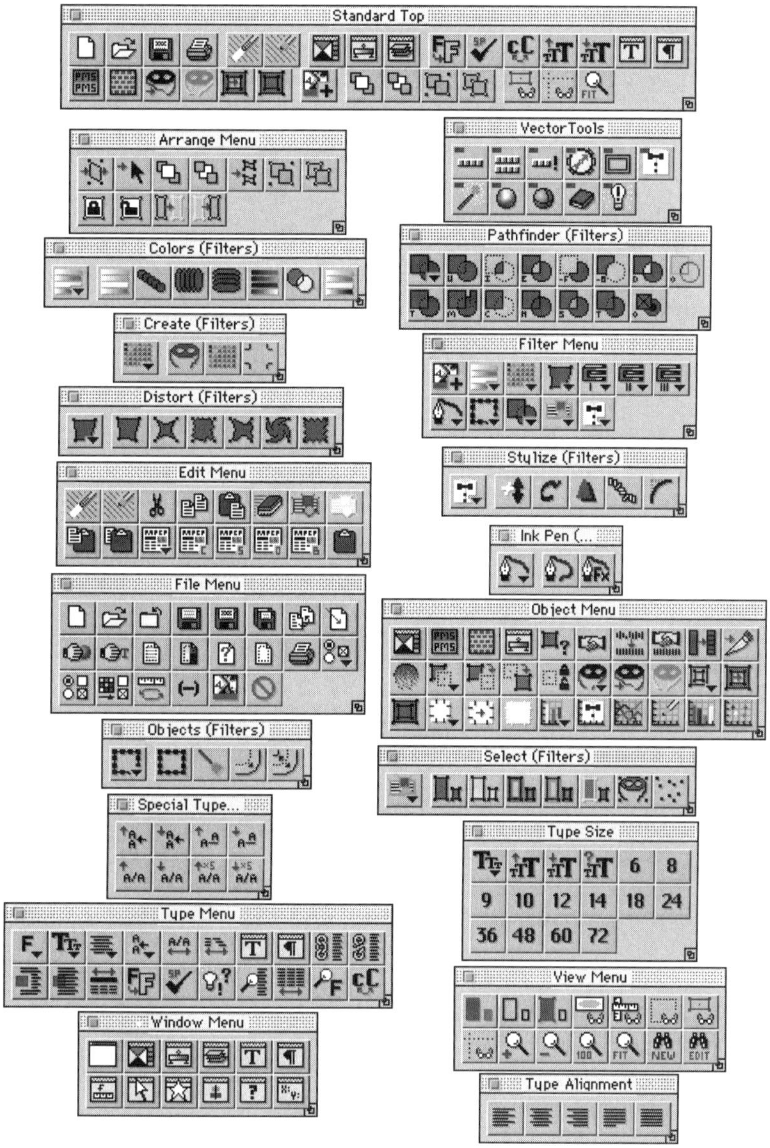

Figure 14-6: Every VectorBar Extensis has to offer — Wow!

I've created a toolbar that contains the menu items I access the most. In my case, it's my job to know keyboard commands, so none of my buttons have corresponding keyboard commands; that doesn't mean that a button that can be accessed with a keyboard command is useless; rather, it can help free up your brain for additional, more important information (like your spouse's birthday, which can be significantly more important than ⌘-Option-Shift-M).

My toolbar, shown in Figure 14-7, contains the following buttons:

Invert Colors: This command is indispensable for inverting the colors of selected objects. It doesn't work as well as swapping the curve in VectorColor, but it does the job for nonblack process fills and strokes.

Saturate Colors: The poor man's version of real saturation/desaturation, but it does the job in a pinch.

Roughen: Not only perfect for evenly adding anchor points (see Chapter 7), but also for converting the point type without dramatically altering the shape of the selected path(s).

Ink Pen Effects: Once you start filling with Ink Pen Effects, it's hard to stop. I'm at a point now where I'd like to have an Ink Pen swatch on the Swatches palette.

Trim Marks: One click for trim marks is much better than Filter⇨Create⇨Trim Marks. And I use it for almost everything I get printed.

Round Corners: For smoothing out computery-looking shapes, and for smoothing roughened paths.

Keyboard Increments Preferences: This is the one Preference I'm in all the time, second only to General Preferences.

Divide, Unite, Crop, Merge, Inverse: The Pathfinder functions I use all the time. Unite used to be the most common. Now it's Divide. Maybe I'm more mature now?

Show/Hide Transform: This button makes it more usable (and allows me to have it tabbed with Info, which has a key command). Besides, Andrei (the interface designer and the *Illustrator 7 Bible* tech editor) says that the more I use it, the more I'll like it.

Show/Hide Tools: There's no way to do this except via the menu command. Having a button right next to the toolbox is almost as good as a close box, or better, considering it shows as well as hides.

Show/Hide Tab Palette: Hard to believe there's no key command for this, isn't it?

Show/Hide Page Tiling: This is one of those "half the time I love it/half the time I hate it" options that I'm always fumbling around the View menu for.

Transform Each: By far the dialog box I use the most that has no keyboard command.

Select Inverse: Sure, I can Shift-drag around the entire document, but one click on a button is infinitely easier.

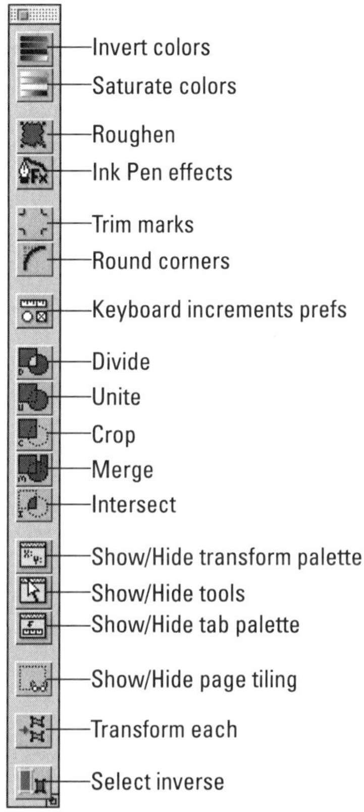

Figure 14-7: The custom toolbar I use each and every day with Illustrator 7

VectorMagicWand

This amazing plug-in gives you Photoshop's Magic Wand tool with a few extra surprises. The Magic Wand is accessible from the Illustrator toolbox, right below the Selection and Direct Selection tools. Double-clicking the Magic Wand displays the VectorMagicWand palette (see Figure 14-8), where you can set the amount of tolerance for four different attributes. Yes, there are six sliders, but there are really only four attributes. I'll get to that in a moment.

To use the VectorMagicWand, select the tool and click any path in the document. Other paths that fall within the tolerance settings will be selected along with the path you clicked.

Shift-click to keep the selected paths selected when clicking. Option-click to subtract from the set of currently selected paths.

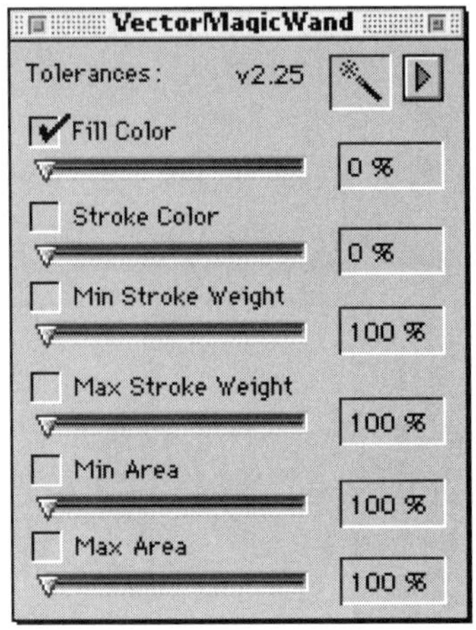

Figure 14-8: The VectorMagicWand palette

The tolerance settings are

- **Fill Color:** This is how different the fill color can be to be selected.
- **Stroke Color:** This is how different the stroke color can be to be selected.
- **Min Stroke Weight:** This is how much smaller the stroke weight can be to be selected.
- **Max Stroke Weight:** This is how much larger the stroke weight can be to be selected.
- **Min Area:** This is how much smaller the path can be to be selected.
- **Max Area:** This is how much larger the path can be to be selected.

At the settings of 0, 0, 100, 100, 100, 100, only paths that are filled and stroked with the same color, have the same stroke weight, and are exactly the same size are selected. Changing any of those values starts to increase the number of objects that can be selected.

VectorLibrary

VectorLibrary is a handy place to store often-used objects. You can place text, images, graphics, paths, and more into the library, give it a name for easy retrieval, and then sometime in the future pull the objects from the library. The VectorLibrary palette is shown in Figure 14-9.

Figure 14-9: The VectorLibrary palette

You can change views from thumbnail (the default) to list view by clicking the view icon (the rightmost one) on the VectorLibrary palette.

Using the pop-up menu on the VectorLibrary palette, you can import and export library items to give to other users of VectorLibrary.

VectorColor

VectorColor provides Photoshop-style color control in Illustrator and FreeHand.

Show the VectorColor palette by choosing VectorColor from the VectorTools menu. The VectorColor palette (see Figure 14-10) appears.

Change the Color mode by clicking one of the five mode buttons along the top of the palette. The five modes are, in order, Brightness/Contrast, Grayscale, Randomize, Multitone, and Edit Curves.

Save presets in Multitone and Edit Curves by using the Save button in each of those panels. Apply presets in Multitone and Edit Curves by choosing a preset from the Preset pop-up menu.

Choose the Auto-Apply option to have Illustrator display each change as you make it. If Auto-Apply is not checked, then click the Apply button to make changes to selected artwork.

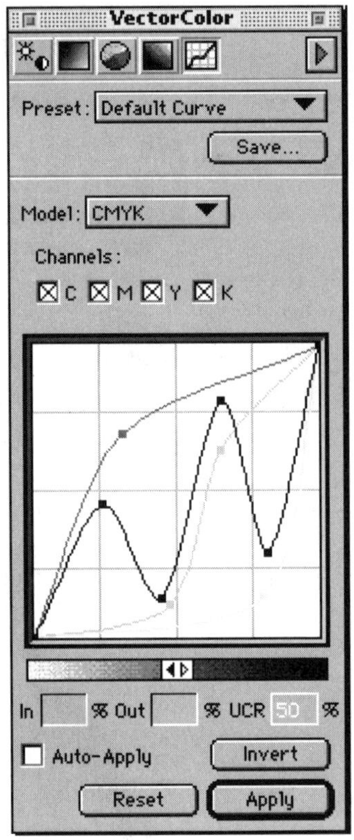

Figure 14-10: The VectorColor palette

STEPS: Using Multitone to Recolor a Full Color Image

Step 1. Open the document that contains the artwork you wish to recolor into one or two spot colors.

Step 2. Select the artwork to be recolored.

Step 3. Click the Multitone button in the VectorColor palette.

Step 4. Add the color(s) you want to use in your illustration.

Step 5. Remove Black if you don't want that as one of your colors.

Step 6. With Auto-Apply engaged, Use the ⌘ key to adjust the colors with steps, making an inverse step for the colors you don't want in that brightness level.

Using this technique, you can create an image that appears to have several colors in it, instead of the limited number that would be available using Illustrator's standard tools.

STEPS: Randomizing within a Colorspace to Maintain Spot Colors

Step 1. Select the art you wish to randomize.

Step 2. Fill and/or stroke the art with a named spot color.

Step 3. In VectorColor Randomize, make sure the Use Existing Colorspace option is checked.

Step 4. Click the Apply button on the Randomize panel.

Step 5. In my example (see Figure 14-11), I used Curves to darken the midtones of the randomized stars so that the brighter ones would pop more.

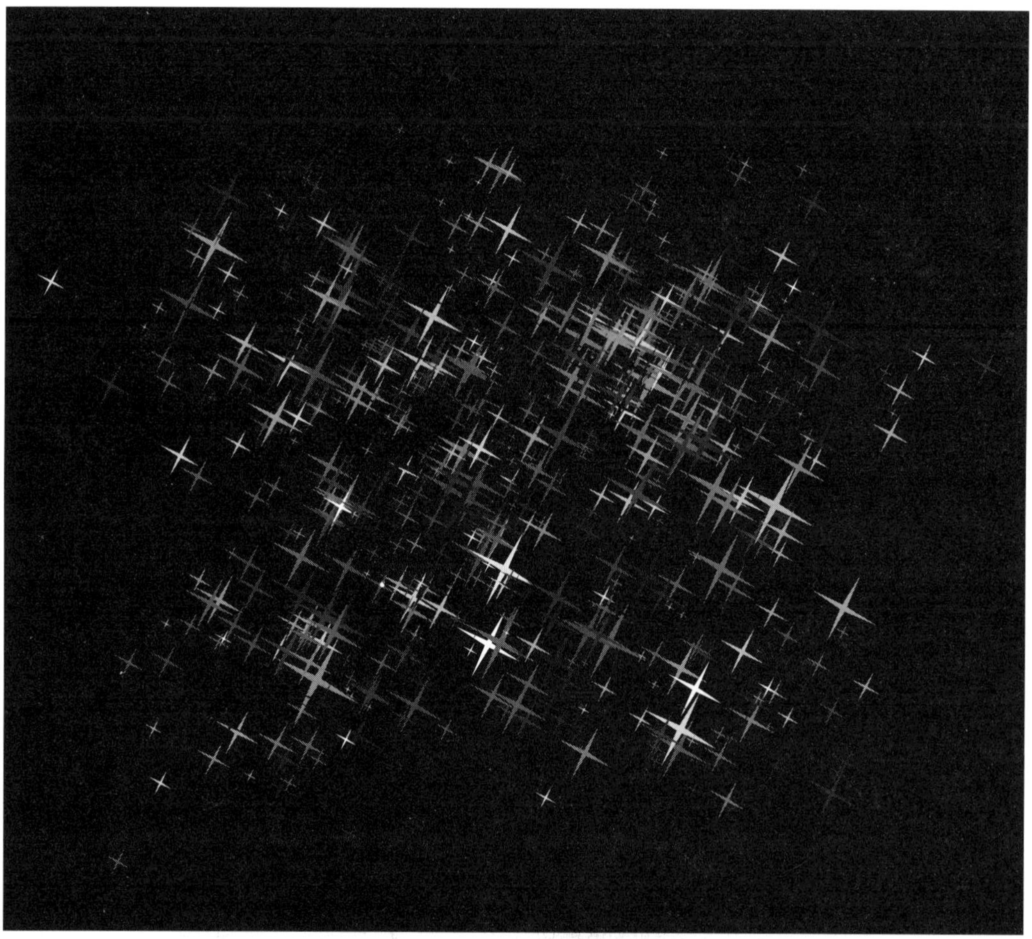

Figure 14-11: The stars in this background were randomized using the Use Existing Colorspace setting, ensuring that only the Brightness was randomized

Using Edit Curves in VectorColor

Click the Edit Curves button (far right) on the VectorColor palette and choose a color model (CMYK, RGB, and so on) from the Model pop-up menu.

Adjust the existing curve by dragging any visible points on that curve. Add a point to a curve by Shift-clicking the curve where you would like to add a point. Remove a point from a curve by Option[Alt]-clicking the point along a curve you'd like to remove.

Click the Invert button to swap curve positions along the *x-y* axes.

VectorShape

VectorShape lets you apply 3D effects to 2D artwork.

Show the VectorShape palette (see Figure 14-12) by choosing VectorShape from the VectorTools menu.

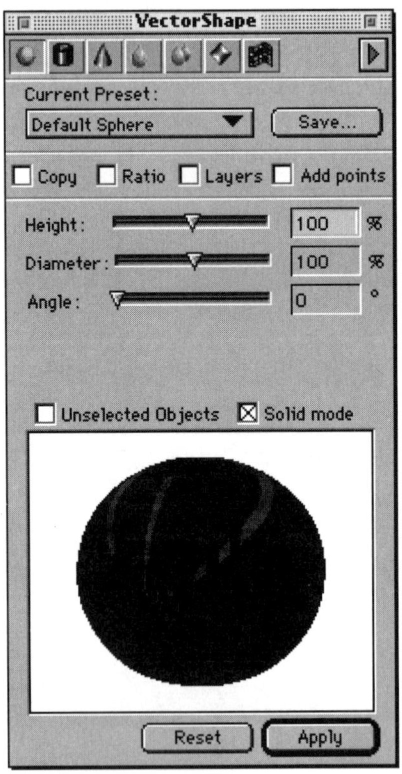

Figure 14-12: The VectorShape palette

Select the shape to wrap with by clicking one of the buttons along the top of the palette. The buttons, in order, are Sphere, Cylinder, Cone, Water, Wave, Diamond, and Free Projection.

Save a Preset by clicking the Save button. Apply a preset by choosing one from the Preset pop-up menu.

POWER TIP: After applying one VectorShape shape, reapply it or apply another shape. The results can be quite unusual. Figure 14-13 was created by applying the Sphere and Cone shapes to a grid.

Figure 14-13: The original art (left) and after VectorShaping (right)

Check the Solid mode check box to see a full-color preview of the selected art in the preview window. Check the Unselected Objects check box to view unselected objects in the preview window.

Click the Apply button to apply the current settings to the selected artwork.

VectorObjectStyles

VectorObjectStyles provides object-based style sheets to Adobe Illustrator users. Although not as advanced as Alien Skin Stylist's approach, the palette (see Figure 14-14) is easy to use and takes up a tiny amount of screen real estate.

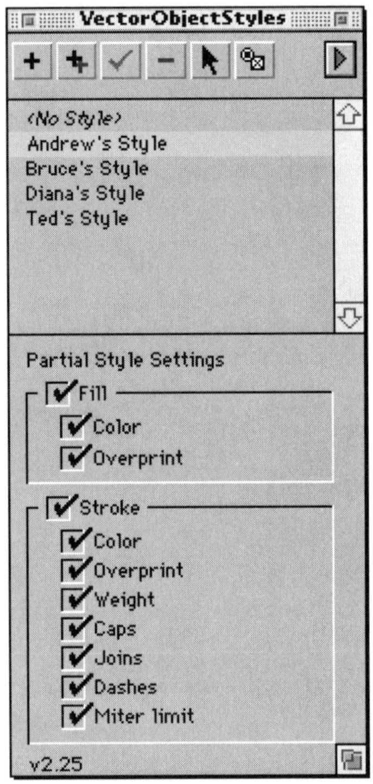

Figure 14-14: The VectorObjectStyles palette

Show the VectorObjectStyles palette by choosing VectorObjectStyles from the VectorTools menu.

Apply an existing style to selected objects by clicking the name of that style in the VectorObjectStyles palette. Create a new style by selecting an object with that style and clicking the New Style button in the VectorObjectsStyles palette. Redefine an existing style by selecting a style, making Paint Style changes, and then clicking the Redefine button.

Import and export styles by choosing the appropriate menu item from the VectorObjectStyles palette's pop-up menu. Apply partial styles by clicking the Partial Style button and unchecking undesired attributes.

The color insert shows an illustration designed with the help of VectorObjectStyles.

VectorNavigator

VectorNavigator (see Figure 14-15) provides both a complete display of all the artwork in your document and a method for easily navigating your document.

Figure 14-15: The VectorNavigator palette

Display VectorNavigator by choosing VectorNavigator from the VectorTools menu.

Resize the VectorNavigator palette by clicking in the lower right of the palette and dragging. The red rectangle (see Figure 14-16) shows the current view in your document window relative to your artwork. Change your document position by dragging the red rectangle around the VectorNavigator preview area.

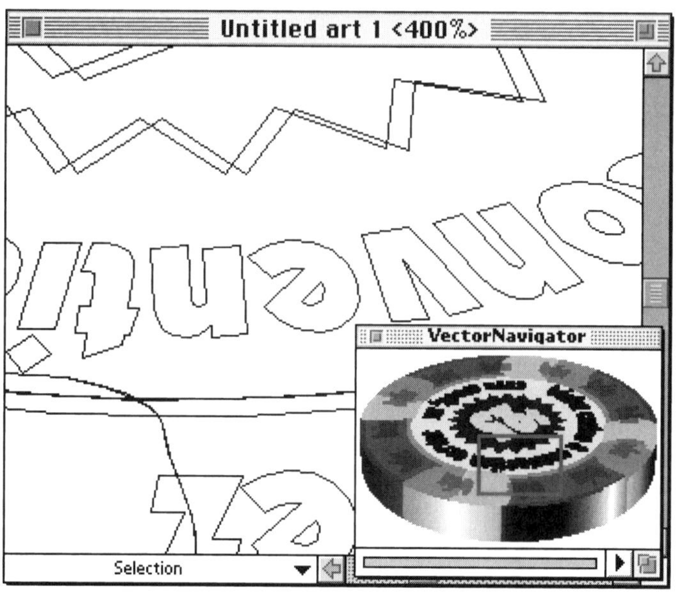

Figure 14-16: VectorNavigator shows the location of your current document view with a red rectangle

Set the VectorNavigator palette to always preview by choosing Always Preview from the Navigator pop-up menu.

VectorTips

These are the incredibly useful tips that, yes, I provided for VectorTools. Figure 14-17 shows just one of many pearls of wisdom.

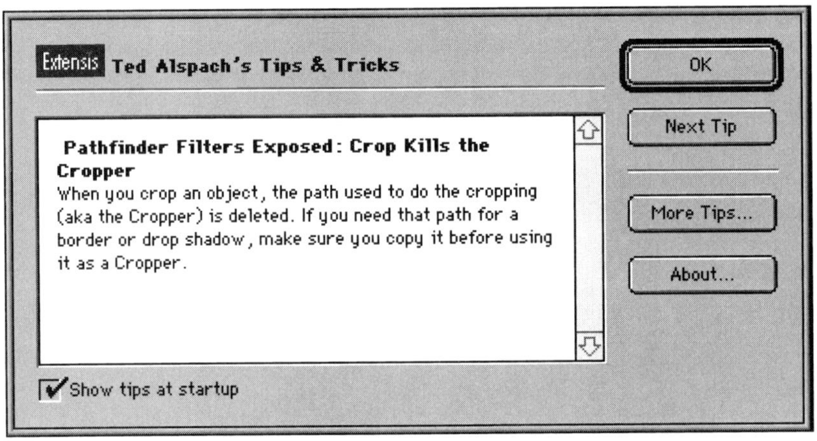

Figure 14-17: A typical VectorTip

Summary

- VectorTools is a dramatic upgrade to Extensis DrawTools
- VectorToolbars can provide you with one-click shortcuts for a number of common tasks
- VectorColor brings Photoshop-style color controls to Adobe Illustrator
- VectorFrame automatically creates frames on selected artwork by framing individual objects, groups, or all selected objects at once.
- VectorNavigator provides a resizable preview which can be used to navigate around your document.

Other Third-Party Plug-Ins

CHAPTER 15

In This Chapter

- What's available from third parties
- An in-depth look at MetaCreations Vector Effects
- All about CSI Socket Sets
- BeInfinite's IFX distortion filters
- Other plug-in manufacturers
- Creating your own plug-ins
- Why VectorTools has its own chapter
- Why most people avoid Letraset Envelopes
- Text and object style sheets with Alien Skin's Stylist
- Beyond drafting with hot door CADtools
- Vertigo 3D Words for effects that *can't* be done any other way.
- MAPublisher 2.0
- Kara Fonts (which aren't plug-ins...)
- Illom Development's Illustrator plug-ins
- Ted Alspach's Doodle Jr. (Free on the *Illustrator 7 Bible* CD-ROM)
- The exclusive Adobe plug-ins on the *Illustrator 7 Bible* CD-ROM
- Other *Illustrator 7 Bible* CD-ROM plug-ins
- How the Illustrator API works

Yeah, I know, by the time you've gone to two parties, you're already pretty well sloshed, and usually it's not worth the effort to not pass out at that point. When we're talking software, though, "third-party" usually refers to a software publisher who produces an add-on for another package. All the companies that make filters and plug-ins for Illustrator are considered third-party publishers.

In 1994 three different filter packages were announced: Letraset Envelopes, BeInfinite FX (which has the distinction of being the first U.S. third-party filter set for Illustrator), and Sree's Cool Tools, which was later purchased from the developer, Sreekant Kotay, by MetaCreations, tweaked, and published as KPT Vector Effects. But none of these actually shipped in the U.S. until 1995.

The year 1995 was the Year of the Adobe Plug-in. Sure, ever since Adobe Illustrator 5.0, released back in 1993, Illustrator has had the ability to add Plug-In filters from other manufacturers, but 1995 was when the third parties started taking off big-time. In addition, FreeHand 5.0 was released early that year and supported Illustrator-style Plug-Ins by making them usable from within FreeHand (as "Xtras," a slightly tacky moniker that Macromedia uses for all its products).

KPT Vector Effects and Extensis DrawTools were the big guns that shipped in 1995. In 1996, Alien Skin Stylist appeared for creating styles in Illustrator (a feature that is still missing from Version 7). Finally, 1997 looks to be a boom year for Illustrator users; not only is there a new version of Illustrator, but also, Extensis has released the most innovative software plug-in package yet: Extensis VectorTools, covered in Chapter 14.

Other plug-in manufacturers have created plug-ins specifically for Illustrator 7, such as hotdoor, Vertigo, and Illom Development.

The other plug-ins and filters are covered in this chapter.

Third-Party Plug-In Roundup

To make this whole third-party business a little clearer, the following is a summary of the third-party plug-in sets available (or soon to be available) at this writing:

- **BeInfinite InfiniteFX:** This filter set contains more than 50 distortion filters, all enclosed in a matching dialog box setup. In addition, all effects can be combined with a 3D rotation capability that is integrated into the filter interface.

- **CSI Socket Sets:** The Socket Set filters are production-oriented filters that enhance Illustrator's current capabilities. Socket Set 1 includes a powerful Adjust Colors filter, as well as powerful selection filters and more. Socket Set 2 contains a Process to Grayscale filter, several Alignment filters, and more.
- **Vector Effects:** This comprehensive filter set from MetaCreations, the maker of Kai's Power Tools, consists of several special-effects-oriented filters. Some of the highlights include KPT 3D Transform, which rotates and extrudes artwork in 3D; KPT ShatterBox, which fragments selected artwork into user-defined pieces; and KPT Warp Frame, an envelope-distortion filter.
- **Letraset Envelopes:** This one-shot filter is an envelope-distortion filter, with several presets.
- **Extensis VectorTools:** These plug-ins (discussed in Chapter 14) contain color management, selection, 3D-effects plug-ins, and more.
- **Alien Skin Stylist:** This is a plug-in for creating and managing object and text styles, as well as creating complex constructions out of multiple stroked paths.
- **CADtools:** This is an amazing set of actual *tools* that turn Illustrator into high-powered drafting and CAD software. Many of the tools can be used for other things besides CAD drawing, making this one of the most exciting plug-in sets to appear for Illustrator.
- **Vertigo 3D Words:** This is a one-shot plug-in that makes 3D words. The amazing thing about this plug-in is that the words are set onto paths that curve around in 3D space . . . something no other plug-in (or Dimensions) can do.
- **MAPublisher 2.0:** This is a set of tools for map making. Cartographers will have a field day with the 38 filters in the package.
- **Kara Fonts:** These aren't plug-ins, but I wasn't sure where else to stick them, so for now, they'll be here. Instead, they're a unique set of fonts that are gradient-based.
- **Illom Development's plug-ins:** These weren't in finished form at the time of this writing, but the maker of LogoCorrector has some really snazzy tools for Illustrator users, including a Lasso for selecting and a point magnet.
- **Ted Alspach's Doodle Jr.:** This is included on the *Illustrator 7 Bible* CD-ROM for free, courtesy of Cytopia. Doodle Jr. is an all-in-one distortion filter and color randomizer that can produce amazing effects and outstanding textures.

Windows Update

Third party plug-ins are *entirely* new to Illustrator for Windows, although not that many plug-in manufacturers have committed to doing Windows versions of their plug-ins.

As of this writing, there are two shipping plug-in sets for Windows: hot door CADtools and Vertigo 3D Words. Extensis has committed to doing VectorTools for Windows (although it is uncertain whether that will be the current version, 2.0, or a future version), and many other publishers are cracking the whip on their engineers to get working on Windows versions.

As with most things in the software world, economics is at the forefront. While Illustrator 4 was a well-selling product, it was dwarfed by CorelDRAW. Many software publishers of third-party filters are waiting to see how Illustrator is received by the press and the public before committing to a Windows product. Hopefully this point will be moot in the near future, as PC publications were raving about Illustrator 7 for Windows way before it shipped (*PC Computing* magazine gave it a 5 out of 5). By the time Illustrator reaches Version 8, most of the good plug-ins should be available for both platforms.

Contact information for the third-party publishers is provided in Appendix H, and most of the filter sets have demos provided on the *Illustrator 7 Bible* CD-ROM.

Installing and Using Third-Party Plug-Ins

Many of the big plug-in sets — such as VectorTools and VectorEffects — come with an installer that automatically places plug-ins in the Illustrator Plug-In folder. Other packages require that you copy the plug-in(s) to the Illustrator Plug-Ins folder manually. All come with a Read Me file with specific instructions.

So far, with all the plug-ins I have installed from almost every publisher listed in this chapter, I've not run into any conflicts between plug-in sets. That doesn't mean there won't be any, but I haven't experienced it yet. If a conflict *would* arise, be aware that some serious problems can occur — from Illustrator not being able to start up, to unexpected random crashes. If you start to experience problems after loading a set of plug-ins, check with the plug-in manufacturer about possible incompatibilities.

Third-party plug-ins can appear *anywhere* in Illustrator. Modal dialog box filters, such as VectorEffects and InfiniteFX, always appear at the bottom of the Filter menu.

BeInfinite InfiniteFX

This set of filters is united through a common dialog box, shown in Figure 15-1 for the Waves Oceanic filter.

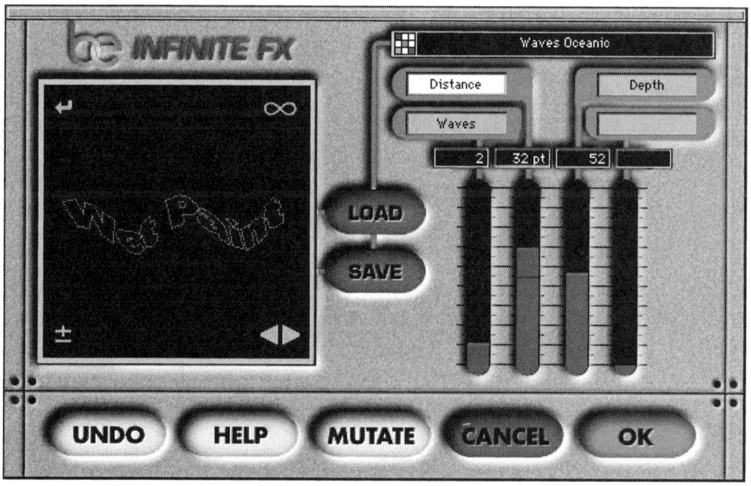

Figure 15-1: The InfiniteFX dialog box (with Waves Oceanic filter shown)

The common dialog box makes using the IFX filters much easier — once you've used one filter, you know how to use the rest. All of the filters have the 3D rotation window, which enables you to spin your artwork around in 3D by clicking and dragging on the art. Many of the filters also have sliders as well, which let you adjust the degree of each effect and other parameters.

The Zoom In button (shown in Figure 15-1 as "±") lets you zoom in on the artwork, the Zoom Out button lets you zoom out. Clicking the Reset button removes all effects from the artwork (including slider adjustments and 3D rotation). The Preview Image Cycle through arrows allow for viewing proxy images in place of the selected artwork frame. This is useful when the artwork is extremely complex, or consists of a blend or other artwork that doesn't show up well as frames.

IFX Theory

The IFX filters are primarily distortion filters, which means that they adjust and manipulate existing paths by altering Anchor Points and Control Handles. IFX does not add Anchor Points to selected paths, so sometimes you might want to add points before applying an IFX filter. Fortunately, IFX has included a filter called Smart Add Points, which adds points based on a tolerance setting similar in function to how the Curve Fitting Tolerance setting (in General Preferences) works. Personally, I'd use Roughen at 0% to add Anchor Points.

Many of the IFX filters are variations or inverses of other IFX filters. Some are quite obvious (Wiggle Horizontal versus Wiggle Vertical) while others are a little more subtle (Waves Oceanic versus Waves Atmospheric).

Several IFX filters have a Depth slider, which only affects artwork in 3D mode. If you don't rotate the artwork with the 3D trackball (the Preview window), the Depth slider has no effect. This isn't at all obvious, and it even prompted me to call the publisher and ask about it (the publisher was kind enough not to ask if I'd read the manual, which describes the depth slider and the effects relevant to the 3D rotation trackball).

The Pure Transformation filter is just that; the only thing you can do to artwork is rotate it with the 3D rotation trackball.

The IFX Filters

Figure 15-2 shows an illustration before and after having various IFX filters applied to it. Not all the filters are shown, but instead, a sampling of the filters is represented.

In addition to the filters in IFX, BeInfinite has included Smart Remove Points, a special functionality filter, on the *Illustrator 7 Bible* CD-ROM. This filter actually cleans up artwork paths that have ridiculously high numbers of points, such as streamlined artwork, or artwork to which you've applied Add Anchor Points. To use Smart Remove Points, drop it in your Plug-Ins folder and restart Illustrator. Then select the artwork from which you wish to remove points, and select the filter. No settings, no problems, no mess, and no extra points.

Figure 15-2: IFX filter effects

CSI Socket Set 1

The CSI Socket Set filters are two sets of filters that are primarily production-enhancing filters (sort of 180° from what BeInfinite's IFX filters do). The two Socket Set filter sets can dramatically increase your Illustrator efficiency by automating common Illustrator functions and adding helpful new capabilities.

Cytopia Software has not commited to creating a version of Socket Sets for Illustrator 7 at the time of this writing. Some of the Socket Set plug-ins may not work properly with Illustrator 7, so be careful if you load those plug-ins in your copy of Illustrator. The following descriptions are based on using them in Illustrator 6, but the majority of information should hold true for Illustrator 7.

CSI AI Plug-In Manager

This Plug-In enables you to select which Plug-Ins will load when Illustrator starts up. It works two ways. You can select the Plug-Ins from within Illustrator by choosing Filter⇨Other⇨CSI AI Plug-In Manager, and select the Plug-Ins to load or not load from there; or you can press the Spacebar when Illustrator is starting up and select Plug-Ins then.

In addition, you can create different sets of Plug-Ins by using the pop-up menu at the top of the dialog box shown in Figure 15-3.

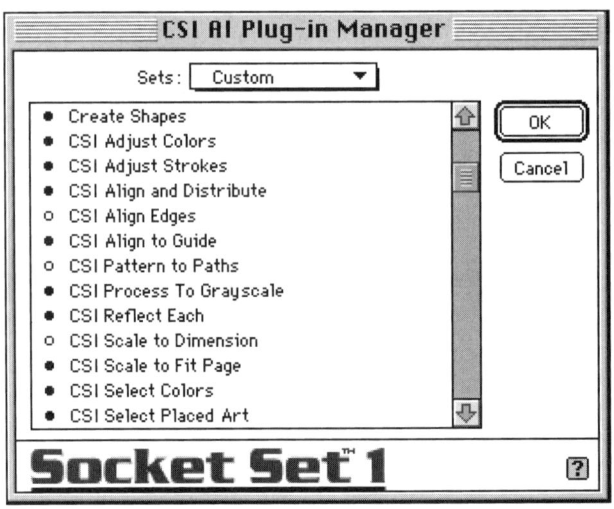

Figure 15-3: The CSI AI Plug-In Manager dialog box

Plug-Ins take up very little memory and just a fraction of a second to load, so don't think you're getting some great power boost by not loading all your Plug-Ins. Instead, Plug-In Manager is good for Plug-Ins that change the way Illustrator works, like the Artwork Speedup Plug-In that ships with Illustrator.

When CSI AI Plug-In Manager is used the first time, it creates a folder called "Plug-Ins (disabled)." Plug-Ins you opt not to install are placed there (only Plug-Ins in the Plug-Ins folder that are in the Illustrator folder are installed). In addition, Plug-In Manager does not recognize Plug-Ins that are *not* in one of these two folders.

CSI AI Startup Manager

This Plug-In lets you pick which document to use as a start-up file when Illustrator is launched. Start-up files are discussed in Chapter 6.

Like CSI AI Plug-In Manager, this Plug-In affects the way that Illustrator runs when it starts up. So making any changes won't affect Illustrator until it is restarted.

To switch the start-up files for Illustrator, press ⌘ until the Startup Manager dialog box appears.

CSI Adjust Colors

The CSI Adjust Colors filter takes Adobe's Adjust Colors filter a few steps further, making it truly useful. Utilizing sliders and an apply button, you can manipulate Strokes, Fills, or both by altering any of the four process colors or even custom colors. The dialog box for CSI Adjust Colors is shown in Figure 15-4.

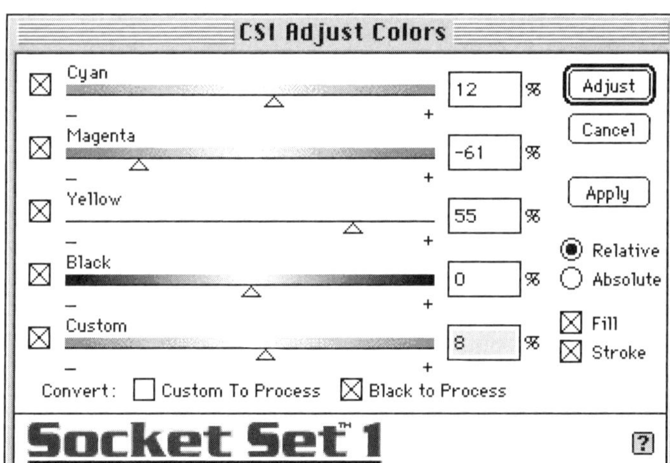

Figure 15-4: The CSI Adjust Colors dialog box

If the Absolute button is checked, you can change values to a precise amount. For instance, if you want all selected paths to have 40% black, in addition to any amounts of cyan, magenta and yellow, change the Black slider to 40% (+) and check the Absolute button.

If the Relative button is checked, the amounts in the dialog box (the ones that are checked) are added or subtracted to the current values.

Pressing Option and the Cancel button in all CSI dialog boxes undoes any Applies that have been executed.

But the real power of CSI Adjust colors is its custom color control. Using the Custom slider at the bottom of the dialog box, you can increase or decrease the tint of custom colors using the Relative or Absolute buttons. When you have several Pantone or other custom colors in a document, this feature is incredibly handy.

CSI Adjust Stroke

The CSI Adjust Stroke filter could almost be called Scale Strokes (but then, I guess it would sound like you're petting a Gila Monster). The unique thing about this filter is that it increases or decreases the Stroke of selected paths by the number of points you specify, regardless of the different Stroke weights that are selected.

As an example, let's start with one path with a 1-point Stroke, another path with a 10-point Stroke, and one with a Stroke of 4.5 points. If you apply CSI Adjust Strokes to the paths and increase by 3 points, the paths would be 4 points, 13 point, and 7.5 points, respectively.

Figure 15-5 shows the effects of this filter.

Figure 15-5: Type before (top) and after (bottom) Adjust Strokes

CSI Select Colors

The CSI Select filters aren't just souped-up versions of the Adobe Select filters; they raise color selection capability to an entirely new plateau. When the Select Colors filter is selected from the Select submenu of the Filter menu, you won't see anything right away, as the filter creates a database of each and every colorable object in your document. When the filter does open, it'll look something like the dialog box shown in Figure 15-6.

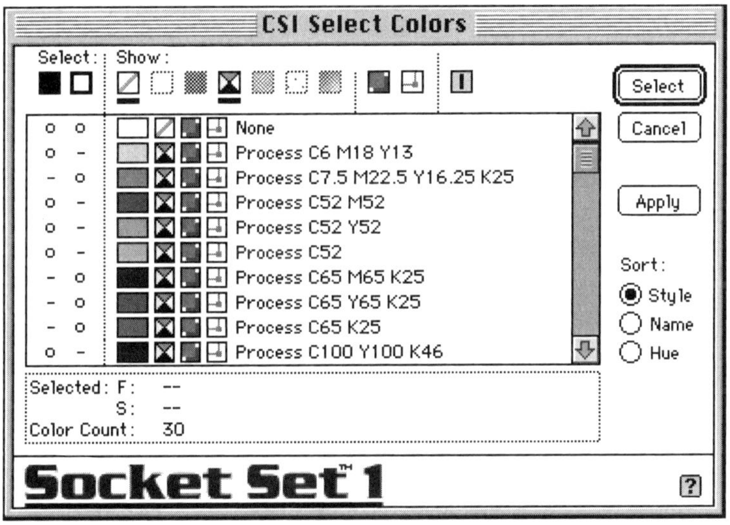

Figure 15-6: The CSI Select Colors dialog box

A complete list of every colorable object in the document appears, with several options. When you click any of the open circles to the left of an item in the list, all the items with that attribute are selected. The bottom of the dialog box displays the different colors currently selected.

CAUTION: Because CSI Select Colors creates a list of every object in your document, you might not want to use it when you have a document overflowing with paths. Check the number of paths with Document Info (File⇨Document Info) and if the number is less than three or four thousand, you can use the filter without fear. But even at those amounts, it'll take quite a while for the list to be generated in the filter, and it'll take even longer to navigate through that list.

Clicking the Apply button selects objects in the artwork window. Change the sort list by clicking on the appropriate button to make selecting easier. A nice feature of the CSI Select filters is that they all work the same way; once you've used one of them, the others are easy to figure out.

CSI Select Placed Art

You use this filter to select placed art within the document. When activated, the filter generates a list of all the placed images in the document. You can pick any number of the placed images (by file name) quickly and easily this way.

CSI Select Strokes

The CSI Select Strokes filter also generates a list of objects, but this list consists of paths with Strokes. Strokes can be selected by weight, Stroke attributes, or color.

CSI Select Text

The CSI Select Text filter selects text objects based on size, color, and font. When selected, the dialog box looks something like the one in Figure 15-7.

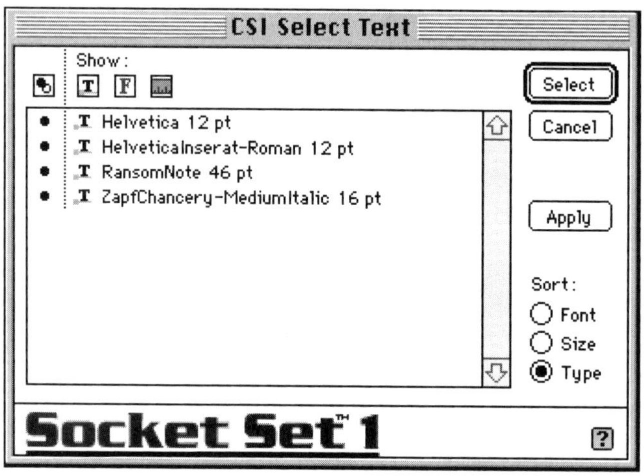

Figure 15-7: The CSI Select Text dialog box

CSI Select Similar

The CSI Select Similar filter selects paths that are similar to the currently selected paths. To use the filter, select a path that has a Fill or Stroke (or both) that is similar to all the paths you want to select. Then choose Filter⇨Select⇨CSI Select Similar. The CSI Select Similar dialog box appears, as shown in Figure 15-8.

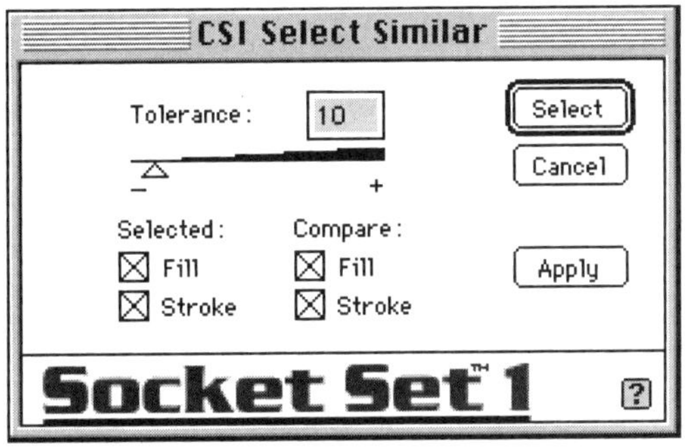

Figure 15-8: The CSI Select Similar dialog box

To get the full effect of CSI Select Similar, change the viewing mode to Preview Selection (⌘-Shift-Y) [Ctrl+Shift+Y] before entering the filter dialog box.

The higher the tolerance setting, the more paths that will be selected. Clicking the Apply button shows what paths will be selected when you click OK.

CSI Process to Grayscale

This filter used to be without a doubt one of the most-used filters on my computer. In fact, I couldn't imagine how I created Illustrator artwork without it before. Now, however, the same functionality is available as an Illustrator Color filter. CSI Process to Grayscale takes selected paths that have process color Fills and Strokes and changes them to grayscale. When you apply the filter (Filter⇨Color⇨CSI Process to Grayscale), you won't see a dialog box; instead, all process colors are instantly converted into grayscale.

CSI Socket Set 2

CSI Socket Set 2 contains object-based filters, once again making Illustrator easier to use by adding formerly nonexistent capabilities. The filters follow the same dialog box format as the CSI Socket Set 1 filters.

CSI Socket Sets

George: Toulouse, what do you think of the CSI Socket Sets?

Toulouse: I've found them indispensable.

George: So, you can't use Illustrator without them, right?

Toulouse: No, the packaging doesn't fit in my trash can.

George: They're not slipping you enough cash, are they?

Toulouse: Actually, once you start using the Socket Set filters, they become part of your everyday Illustrator usage. I've saved hundreds of hours by using them.

George: Well, that's good to hear.

Toulouse: Tell Cytopia to make out the check to....

CSI Align and Distribute

The CSI Align and Distribute filter takes selected objects and aligns and/or distributes them horizontally or vertically. This filter has more functionality than the Align palette capabilities of Illustrator.

To use CSI Align and Distribute, select the objects you wish to manipulate and choose Filter⇨Objects⇨CSI Align and Distribute. The dialog box shown in Figure 15-9 appears.

Selecting Each Other at the top of the dialog box keeps the objects aligned and distributed relative to each other. Selecting the Imageable Area option moves the objects to the outermost area of the dotted line inside your page. This provides a fixed location for the selected objects to gravitate to.

CSI Align Edges

From the name, you'd think that CSI Align Edges was really a limited version of CSI Align and Distribute. Instead, CSI Align Edges allows you to designate one of the selected objects as a stationary object that all the other objects will be aligned to. The dialog box for CSI Align Edges is shown in Figure 15-10.

After selecting the location of the stationary object from the choices on the left side (you may have to cancel and reposition the stationary object for this to work correctly), decide how you want the other selected objects to align to the stationary one.

If you choose Top/Bottom, all selected objects align their tops to the bottom of the stationary object. If you choose Left/Right, the selected objects align their left edges to the stationary object's right edge, and so forth.

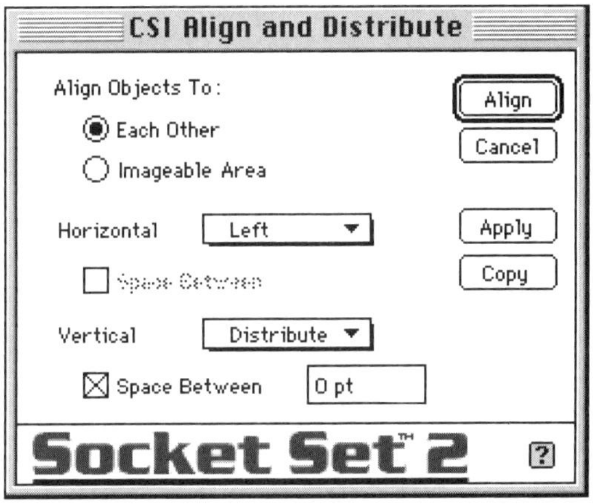

Figure 15-9: The CSI Align and Distribute dialog box

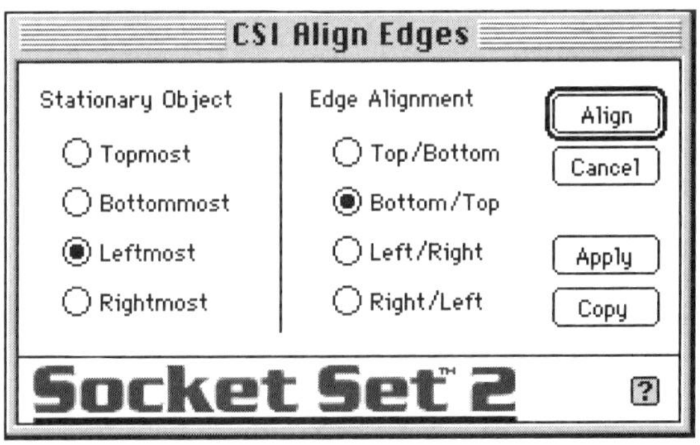

Figure 15-10: The CSI Align Edges dialog box

CSI Align to Guide

The CSI Align to Guide filter aligns objects up to guides. This only works correctly with guides that are pulled from the rulers, though it also works (sort of) with guides created with a 2-Anchor Point line. The dialog box that pops up when you choose Filter⇨Objects⇨CSI Align to Guide is shown in Figure 15-11.

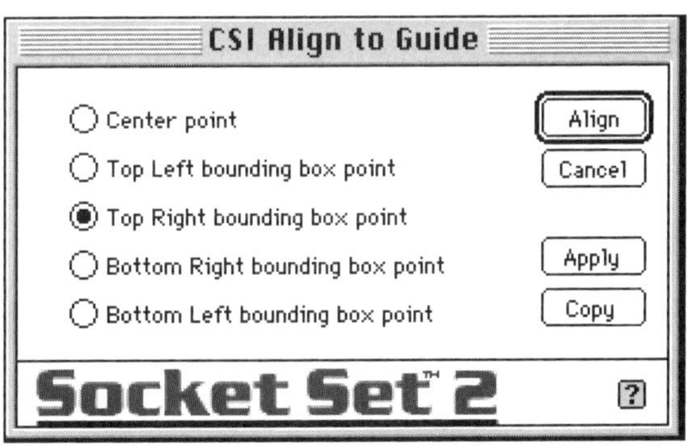

Figure 15-11: The CSI Align to Guide dialog box

The only option in the dialog box is what corner of the selected object's bounding box to align to the guide (or the center point of the object).

CSI Patterns to Paths

This incredibly useful filter takes pattern-filled objects and converts them into masked paths with better results than Illustrator's Expand function. To use the filter, select a pattern-filled object and choose Filter⇨Objects⇨CSI Patterns to Paths.

Unfortunately, because of the way in which Illustrator generates patterns, the result isn't perfect. Instead, there are several overlapping paths where pattern tiles meet.

STEPS: Getting Rid of Extra Paths from Converted Patterns

Step 1. Apply CSI Patterns to Paths to the pattern-filled path.

Step 2. With the paths selected, choose Object⇨Masks⇨Release (⌘-Option-7) [Ctrl+Alt+7].

Step 3. Ungroup (⌘-Shift-G) [Ctrl+Shift+G].

Step 4. Select just the mask that was the original path, and lock it (⌘-L) [Ctrl+L].

Step 5. Select all the remaining paths and choose Object⇨Pathfinder⇨Merge.

Step 6. Unlock All (⌘-Shift-L) [Ctrl+Shift+L].

Step 7. Select All and choose Object⇨Masks⇨Make (⌘-7) [Ctrl+7].

CSI Reflect Each

This filter is a welcome addition to the capabilities of Illustrator's Transform Each command. Just like the name says, this filter reflects individual objects across their centers. The options for reflecting are shown in Figure 15-12.

CSI Scale to Dimension

Have you ever wanted to scale artwork to fit within a certain area? For instance, artwork in the *Illustrator 7 Bible* has a maximum width of about 34 picas. A good bit of the art in the book was scaled up or down to this width using CSI Scale to Dimension.

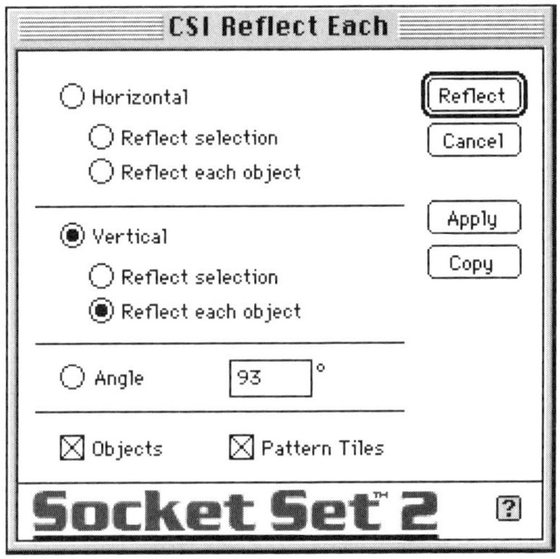

Figure 15-12: The CSI Reflect Each dialog box

To use CSI Scale to Dimension, select the objects you wish to scale, and choose Filter⇨Objects⇨CSI Scale to Dimension. The dialog box shown in Figure 15-13 appears.

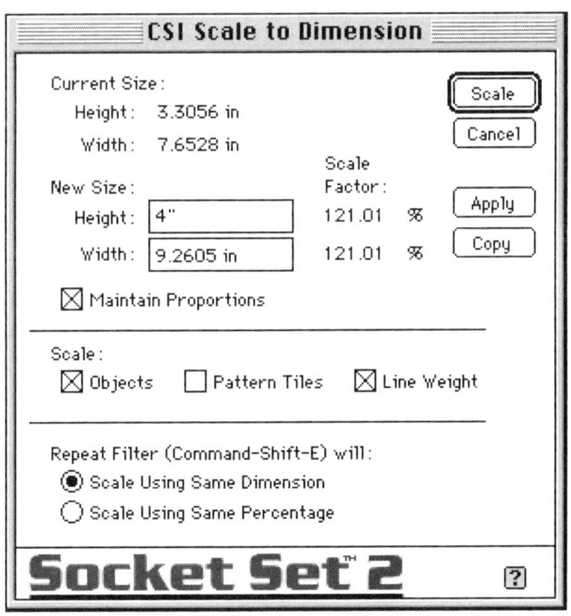

Figure 15-13: The CSI Scale to Dimension dialog box

Set the width, height, or both to which you wish to scale the artwork. Note that in order to enter *both* height and width, you must uncheck the Maintain Proportions checkbox. Take advantage of the Apply button to make sure the result is what you want, and then click OK if it works. Remember that you can always press Option[Alt] and the Cancel button to undo an Apply.

Hidden (sort of) at the bottom of the CSI Scale to Dimension dialog box is a very powerful option. You have the choice between scaling to the same percentage or to the same size when the filter is repeated with ⌘-E [Ctrl+E].

Try using CSI Scale to Dimension with a hunk of type to get a headline to fit in a space perfectly.

CSI Scale to Fit Page

This is a quickie filter (see the few options in Figure 15-14) that quickly resizes the selected artwork to the page size. Your main option is whether to scale proportionately or nonproportionately.

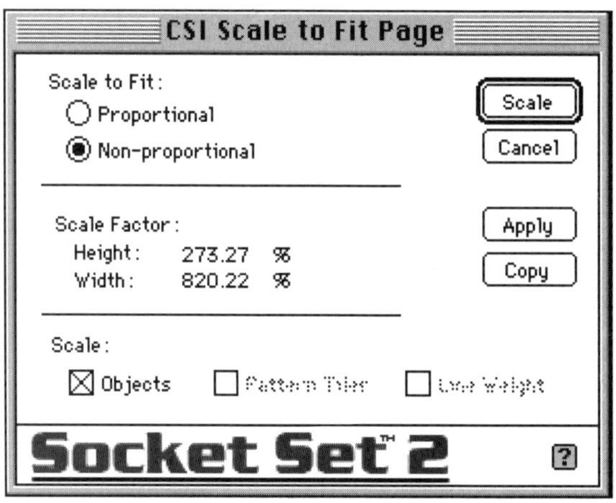

Figure 15-14: The CSI Scale to Fit Page dialog box

I've used this filter to fill up a page quickly right before I print out posters and signs.

CSI Step and Repeat

This filter automatically creates rows and columns consisting of series of the selected objects. To use the filter, select any object you wish to have repeated (and stepped), and choose Filter⇨Objects⇨CSI Step and Repeat. The dialog box shown in Figure 15-15 appears.

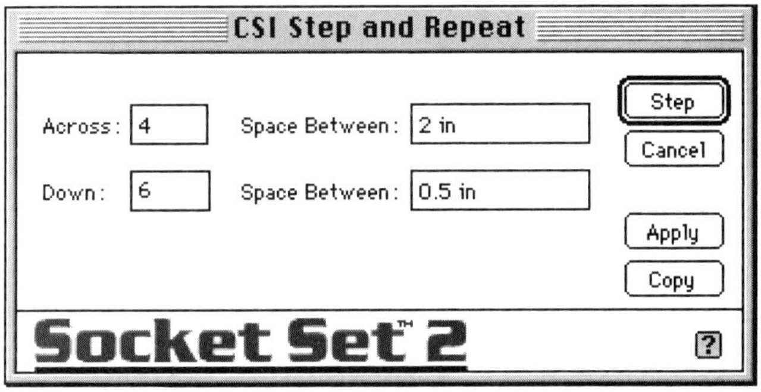

Figure 15-15: The CSI Step and Repeat dialog box

Figure out how many objects you want across and down, and enter those numbers. The original object is always in the upper left; new objects generated with CSI Step and Repeat will appear to the right and below the original object. Then enter the amount of space you want between the objects. Click Apply to make sure you're getting the correct result first, then click OK.

POWER TIP: You can make objects overlap each other by entering negative values in the Space Between text fields.

STEPS: Creating a Grid with CSI Step and Repeat

Step 1. Draw a rectangle the exact size of one of the grid squares. For instance, if you wanted a $^1/_4$" grid (like in the example in Figure 15-16), you would create a rectangle $^1/_4$" × $^1/_4$" wide. Make sure the rectangle has *no Stroke* at this point (see the following Power Tip).

Step 2. With the rectangle selected, choose Filter⇨Objects⇨CSI Step and Repeat. In the dialog box, enter the number of grid squares you want across and down (for a quarter-inch grid, multiply what you'd like the finished size to be by 4).

Step 3. After applying the Step and Repeat filter, all the squares are selected. Change the Stroke of all of them to the thickness you'd like the lines of the grid to be. Because the squares overlap perfectly at their edges, the Strokes where the squares meet will overlap, keeping the Stroke weight consistent.

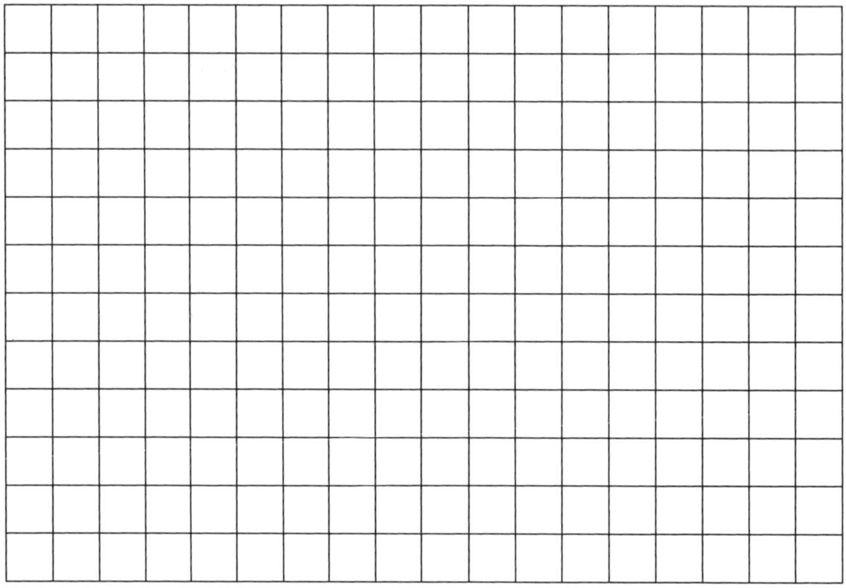

Figure 15-16: A quarter-inch grid is created by stepping and repeating a quarter-inch rectangle

CSI Step and Repeat is smarter than I am. If you have Stroked objects, Step and Repeat will figure the width of the Stroke into the distance between the objects. So if you have a rectangle with a 2-point Stroke, Step and Repeat puts an extra 2 points between objects you've specified at 0 distance apart.

MetaCreations Vector Effects

Kai's Power Tools took the Photoshop world by storm a few years ago, and KPT Vector Effects have now had the same impact on Illustrator users. Sporting a scaled-down-from-the-typical-unusual-Kai-interface, Vector Effects (referred to as "Vex") is still different enough to get noticed, and friendly enough to be quite useful.

By themselves, Vex filters are a force to be reckoned with. But double them with Illustrator's capabilities, and suddenly there's oodles of options that never existed before. Because Vex is so big, the *Illustrator 7 Bible* CD-ROM can give you only a brief summary and a few examples of its incredible capabilities. For a more detailed overview of the amazing capabilities of Vex, pick up a copy of *Illustrator Filter Finesse* (Ted and Jennifer Alspach, Random House Electronic Publishing, 1995), which covers filters from several manufacturers.

Vector Effects, while residing in the Filter menu, are not really filters. Of course, most of the Plug-Ins in Illustrator aren't filters, either, but MetaTools is adamant about this. At MetaCreations, calling Vector Effects "filters" is a good way to lose a bit of job security, if you know what I mean. MetaCreations insists on calling them Plug-In Application Extensions, which is about as silly as Kai not quite understanding this craving we Illustrator users have for numeric input. . . .

Most of the Vex filters are special-effects oriented, making the creation of nifty stuff a no-brainer. A few others are more production oriented, but those select few filters help to round out the package. All of the filters are found in the Filters menu, in a submenu called KPT Vector Effects.

KPT has even included a special filter (included on the *Illustrator 7 Bible* CD-ROM) called KPT Gradients/ Patterns to Paths, which converts both selected gradients and patterns to paths, allowing special effects and techniques to take place that otherwise wouldn't have been possible. This filter works better (and faster) than the Expand function of Illustrator.

VE Commonalties

Vector Effects have several different interfaces, but most of them share at least a half dozen features. These are discussed below:

- **The Options menu:** Many of the filters have an Options menu, accessible by clicking the umbrella with a triangle in it. In this menu are options for preferences, a Reset command, and various other filter-specific options.

Superstitious MetaTools

Weezy: How many filters are in Vector Effects?

Toulouse: Twelve, plus a bonus one. And they're not filters, they're *Plug-In Application Extensions.*

Weezy: So there's thirteen Plug-what you said.

Toulouse: No, twelve and a bonus extension. It's a marketing thing, I'm sure.

Weezy: Sounds to me like they're superstitious over at MetaCreations.

Toulouse: Nah. If they were *really* superstitious, they wouldn't have named the product Vector Effects. Count the letters.

Weezy: Grife! Wonder if they noticed that the package weighs three ounces less than a pound. . . .

Toulouse: And then there's the engineer's name....

Weezy: Sreekant Kotay? Thirteen again.

Toulouse: And they've just changed the name of the company to ... MetaCreations.

Weezy: My word.

Toulouse: I'm surprised they don't have a black cat for their logo.

- **Zoom and Pan:** You can quickly Zoom and Pan using the keyboard shortcuts from Illustrator (⌘-Spacebar [Ctrl+Spacebar] to Zoom in, ⌘-Spacebar-Option [Ctrl+Spacebar+Alt] to Zoom out, and Spacebar to Pan). Or you can click the buttons at the top of the Preview window. You can also draw a Zoom marquee to Zoom into a precise location.
- **Balloon Help:** Clicking the ? in the lower left will toggle Balloon Help on and off, which is quite useful when you're initially fumbling around.
- **Sliders:** There are sliders all over the place in each dialog box (and there are others, undoubtedly just a bit different, on parallel worlds). Access them by clicking the black box with white letters and dragging left or right.

  Pressing the Caps Lock key turns on interactive preview, where the preview changes while you are dragging the sliders, not just when you release them.

- **Presets:** You can use presets for certain filters by clicking the triangle at the bottom of the screen, and scrolling to the filter you want to use. Press Spacebar before clicking to view graphical presets, or just choose that option from the Preferences dialog box. When in Graphical Preview mode, you can also view the particular effect on the selected artwork by pressing ⌘ [Ctrl] when a preset is highlighted. If Caps Lock is pressed, all presets will display the effect on the artwork automatically.
- **Preset control:** If you create a particularly smashing effect in an extension dialog box that supports presets, like ShatterBox, you can store that preset for future use by clicking on the little + at the bottom of the dialog box. Delete the current preset by clicking –. At the bottom of the list of (nongraphical) presets, you can access the Presets Manager, which lets you import and export presets to and from each extension.
- **Cancel and OK:** The Cancel button is a circle with a slash through it. OK is a check mark.
- **Numeric control:** Each of the interfaces has an option to show exact measurements or percentages in numeric form. Check the option in the Preferences menu to see the numbers when you adjust a slider. The numbers shown below the sliders tell you (left) what the value was originally and (right) what you're changing it to. You can also access the numbers and change them individually by ⌘-clicking [Ctrl+clicking] on the slider and typing in a new number or using the arrows (or arrow keys) to nudge the amount.

The following pages discuss the filters briefly and show off some of the groovy things you can do with them (yes, groovy).

KPT 3D Transform

This is the most powerful of all the Vector Effects filters, in that it contains a fairly advanced 3D engine, and produces truly astounding effects. It's quick, it's relatively easy to use, and the resulting paths it generates are really impressive.

KPT 3D Transform takes selected paths and extrudes, bevels, and rotates them in 3D space. The 3D Transform dialog box is shown in Figure 15-17.

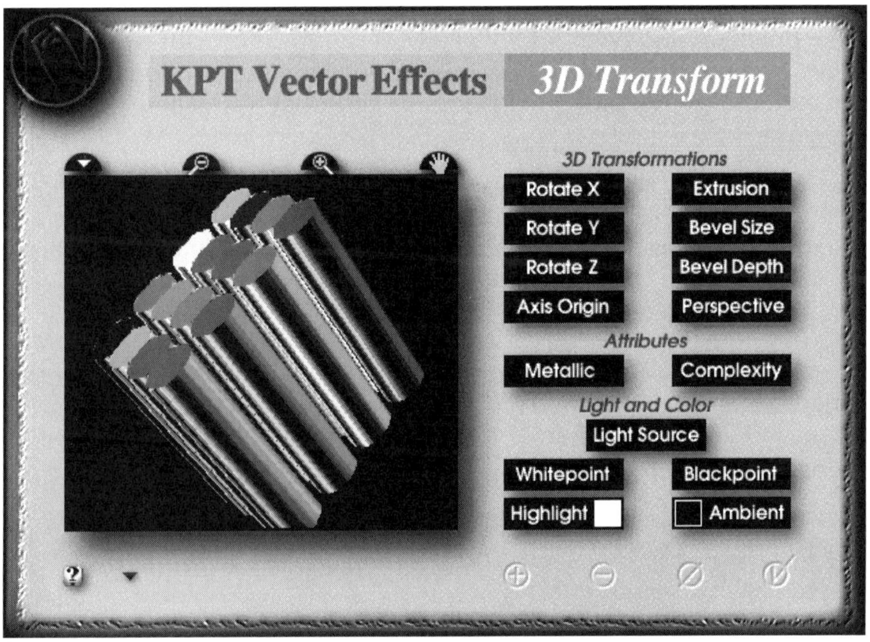

Figure 15-17: The KPT 3D Transform dialog box

STEPS: Creating Metallic-Looking Text

Step 1. Type your text in a font that has lots of curves. (The Metallic setting in KPT 3D Transform works better with curves than with straight edges.) Convert the text to outlines using Type⇨Create Outlines (⌘-Shift-O) [Ctrl+Shift+O].

Step 2. Fill the outlines with a slight cyan/magenta mix (no more than 20% of either).

(continued)

STEPS: ***(continued)***

Step 3. With the outlines selected, choose Filters⇨KPT Vector Effects⇨KPT 3D Transform.

Step 4. In the 3D Transform dialog box, select Full Preview from the Options menu (the little triangle in a half-circle the upper left of the Preview window). Engage the Caps Lock key; this shows all the changes you make immediately, even while you're dragging sliders.

If you don't have a Power Mac, you might want to stick with either the Rough or Wireframe Preview modes (both found in the Options menu). Experiment with the different settings to find what works best with your system.

Step 5. Adjust the Rotate sliders by dragging them left or right, watching the preview as you do so. Once the outlines have been rotated the way you want them, drag the Metallic slider to the right about a quarter of the way.

Step 6. Next, drag the Extrude slider to the right, to give the outlines depth.

Step 7. If you want to give the outlines beveled edges, drag the Bevel Size slider to the right just a bit. Be careful not to drag too far, as the bevels on nearby letters might intersect. To prevent this intersection in the future, increase the tracking of the text before you convert it to outlines.

Step 8. Click the check mark in the lower right of the dialog box. This is the iconic version of the OK button. That means you can press Return or Enter as well.

After you've extruded the outlines, you might want to make the front of the letters metallic-looking as well. To do this, select the front panels and change the Fill to a gradient. Figure 15-18 illustrates the final product.

KPT 3D Transform has all sorts of amazing capabilities deep within itself that you can play with, including perspective adjustments, the ability to change the source and color of lighting, and much more.

Figure 15-18: Metallic text created with KPT 3D Transform

KPT ColorTweak

The ColorTweak filter enables you to make changes to the color of the Fills and Strokes of selected artwork. Instead of the common ways of manipulating color through adjusting cyan, magenta, yellow, and black, KPT ColorTweak lets you do all sorts of different adjustments to colors. You can change the hue, saturation, brightness, contrast, and grayscale levels, *and* play with the CMYK levels.

But what really sets ColorTweak apart from all the other color-adjustment filters (besides the fact that it's a *Plug-In Application Extension*) is the Randomize option in the Options menu. When the Randomize option is turned on, all the sliders being used generate random values and apply them to the selected paths.

STEPS: Generating Textures with KPT ColorTweak

Step 1. Create a mish-mash pattern of paths, like the one shown in Figure 15-19. I used the Roughen filters and PathFinder Divide to create the paths shown here.

Step 2. Select the paths and Fill them with a color (no Stroke) that represents the overall tone you'd like the texture to be.

Step 3. With the paths still selected, choose Filters⇨KPT Vector Effects⇨KPT ColorTweak.

(continued)

STEPS: ***(continued)***

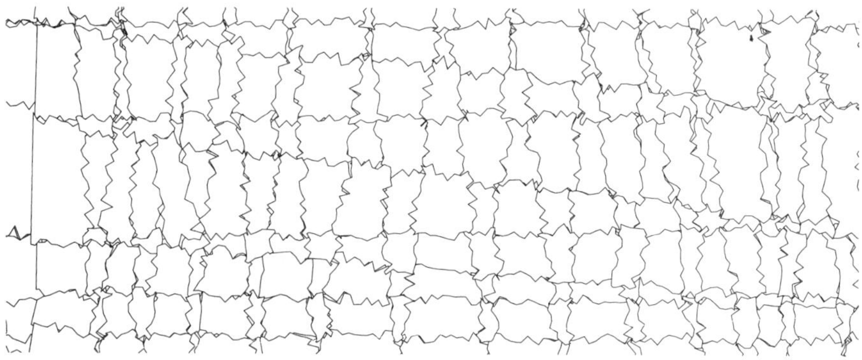

Figure 15-19: A mass of shapes

Step 4. In the ColorTweak dialog box, shown in Figure 15-20, select the Randomize option from the Options menu (accessed by clicking and holding the little triangle in the upper left of the previous window).

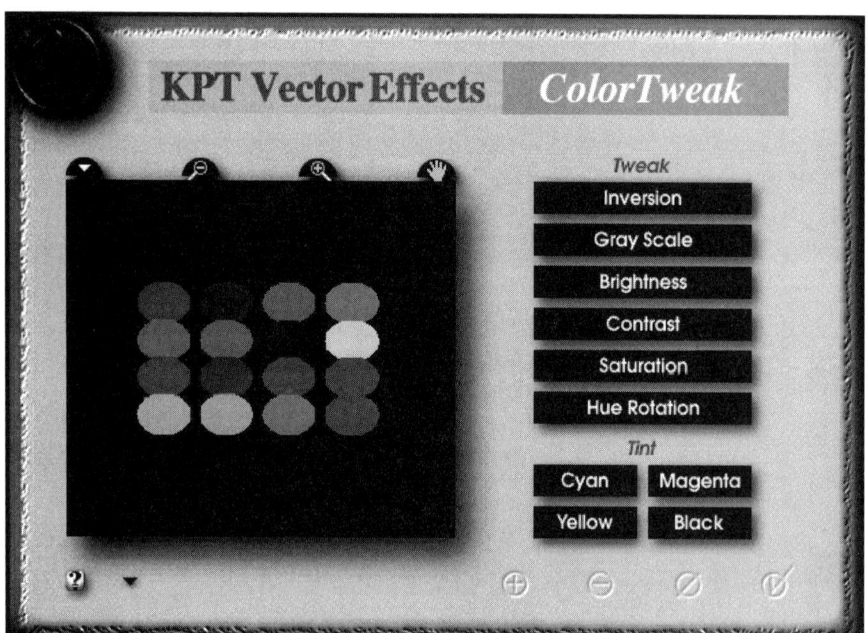

Figure 15-20: The Color Tweak dialog box

Step 5. Adjust the Brightness slider to the right about 10%.

Step 6. Click the check mark to exit the box.

Step 7. Choose Filters⇨KPT Vector Effects⇨KPT ColorTweak again, pull the Brightness slider to the left about 10%, and click the check mark. The texture I created is shown in Figure 15-21.

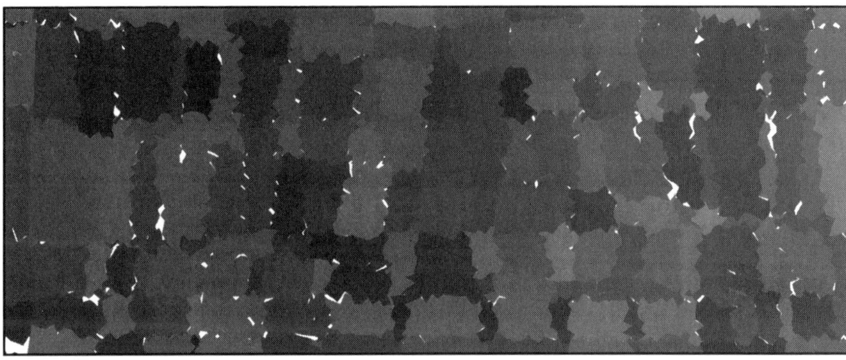

Figure 15-21: The final texture

ColorTweak works differently with Process Colors from with way it does with Custom Colors. For instance, you can't change the Hue of a Custom Color. For the best results, change your custom colors to process *before* you use ColorTweak.

KPT Emboss

The Emboss filter is a one-shot filter that does what it does, and what it does it does quite well. Of course, I'm referring to embossing, which is making artwork look like it's indented or pushed out from the surface of the surrounding artwork. Figure 15-22 shows an example of embossed artwork created with KPT Emboss.

For Figure 15-22, I changed the original artwork from color to grayscale first, to simulate various levels of depth.

There are all sorts of secret things hidden within Vector Effects. For instance, clicking on the Kai logo (when in Background mode) will display a preview as big as your monitor. Try pressing different keys when clicking there — of course, doing so may feel like a game, or as if you're being watched. . . .

Figure 15-22: Embossed art

KPT Flare

This filter seems so basic and almost trivial when you first look at it that it might not receive a second glance. Well, I'm telling you to look again, and be amazed. Sure, the filter creates flares on artwork, but it doesn't stop there. The glow from the halo is actually blended into the background of the artwork. This makes the power of the filter and the complexity of the artwork go beyond anything similar you could do previously in Illustrator.

The KPT Flare dialog box, shown in Figure 15-23, has controls for adjusting the size, number of spikes, and halo size of a flare. In addition, you can add more than one flare to your artwork.

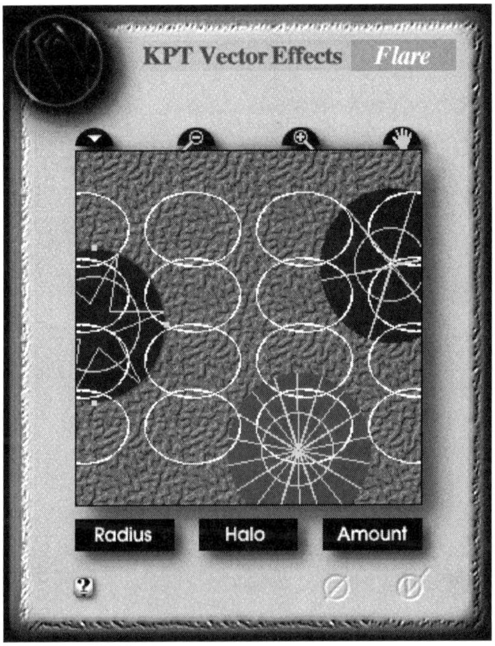

Figure 15-23: The KPT Flare dialog box

STEPS: Adding Several Flares

Step 1. Select the artwork you wish to apply the flares to. Select as few paths as possible to reduce flare-generation time.

Step 2. Choose Filters⇨KPT Vector Effects⇨KPT Flare.

Step 3. Click the middle of the flare to move it; click a handle to resize it. Add spikes with the Amount slider. Change the size of the halo with the Halo slider. Change the inside radius with the Radius slider.

Try using a negative value in the Radius slider for some jazzy, multilength starburst effects.

(continued)

KPT Flare

Florence: I'm having trouble with KPT Flare. It takes forever just to create one flare on my artwork.

Toulouse: What does the artwork consist of?

Florence: Well, it's a Victorian Impressionist statement on the nobility of the ruling class, with a hint of cynicism that reflects the political influences of the time.

Toulouse: Gee. What I meant was, how many paths are in the artwork? You can always check that by selecting Document Info from the File menu.

Florence: Let's see ... 8,912 paths.

Toulouse: Well, that's the problem right there. KPT Flare interacts with each of the selected paths in order to create its halo. The more paths you've selected, the longer it'll take.

Florence: But I really want to use a flare here.

Toulouse: One thing you can do, if you don't mind the halo being behind some of the artwork, is to create a background (or select one if it's already there), and put the flare onto that. Then you can select the "flare," sans the halo, and put it in the front.

Florence: And if I want the halo in the front?

Toulouse: Select as few paths as possible, or problems might ... er ... flare up.

STEPS: *(continued)*

Step 4. Add additional sliders by selecting New Flare from the Options menu. You can also duplicate the current flare by selecting Duplicate Flare. To delete a flare, click it and press the Delete key.

Step 5. After you've added as many flares as you'd like, click the check mark at the bottom right of the dialog box.

Figure 15-24 illustrates some of the effects you can create with this filter.

Figure 15-24: Three different flares applied to artwork at once

KPT Inset

The Inset filter is a better way of insetting or offsetting paths than the Offset Path filter from Adobe is. The best part of this filter is the Preview option, which enables you to see just how far you're moving the path. Inset also has a Copy option, so you can make a duplicate of the selected paths.

POWER TIP: Use Inset to thicken or thin characters of type that have been converted to outlines, as in Figure 15-25.

KPT Neon

You'll see a set of steps for creating neon tubing back in the Blends chapter. You'll also see that it's a lot of work to create neon tubes that way.

Insettedness

Insettedness

Figure 15-25: The original type (top) and after having its weight increased with Inset (bottom)

KPT Neon is easy, painless, and fun. And the results are nothing short of stunning. The KPT Neon dialog box is shown in Figure 15-26. Note that there are only two sliders to move: Brightness and Amount.

Figure 15-26: The Neon dialog box

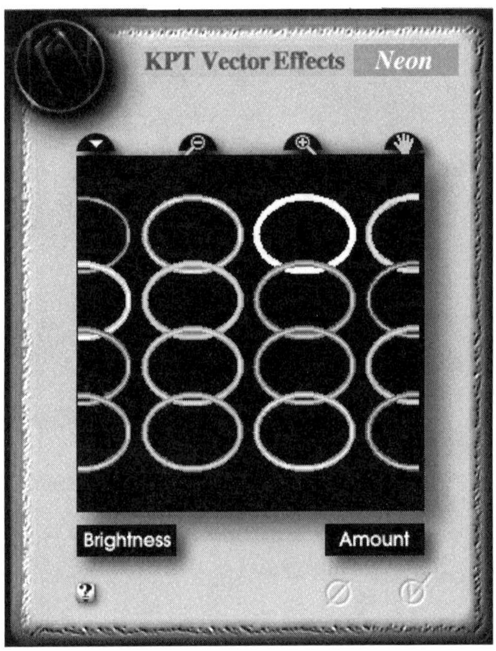

Brightness controls the brightest point of the neon tubing. Amount controls the thickness of the tubes. Easy, huh? Well, you do have to remember one thing: the neon tubes only appear on paths. That means neon text you create will consist of tubes that surround the letters, not just a tube shaped in the form of the letter.

KPT Point Editor

This filter provides a way to position and move both points and their handles to exact locations. To use the filter, select a path whose points you wish to edit, and choose Filter⇨KPT Vector Effects⇨KPT Point Editor. The Point Editor dialog box, shown in Figure 15-27, then appears.

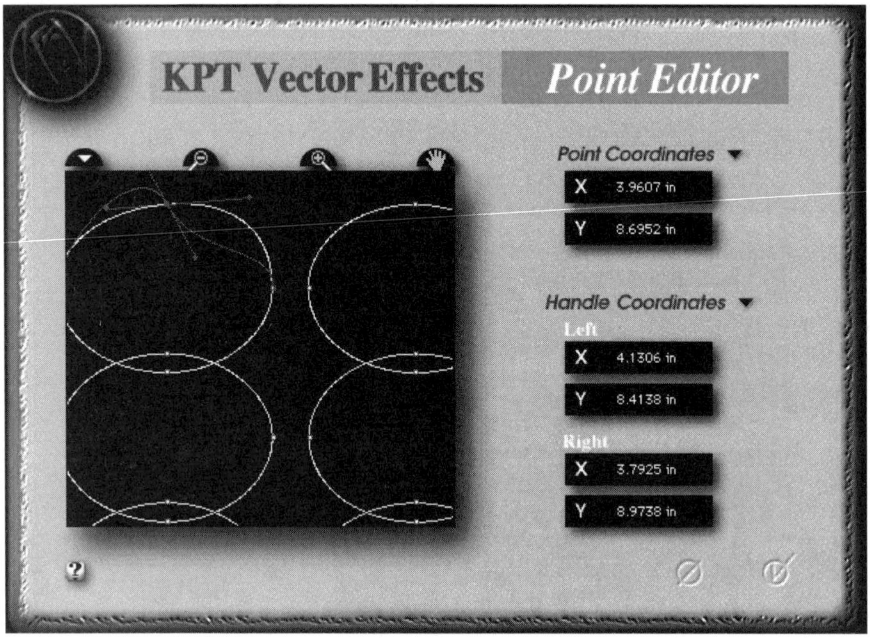

Figure 15-27: The KPT Point Editor dialog box

Select a point in the Preview window (zoom in if you can't see the point you wish to edit) and enter the new coordinates for it. If you wish to move the point by a certain amount, change the Point Coordinates menu (click the small triangle on the right) to Relative and enter the distance to be moved.

You can also select and adjust any handles on the path the same way. While in the dialog box, you can adjust as many points and handles as you'd like; when you're all done, all of them will be affected.

KPT Resize and Reposition

This filter lets you move and scale selected artwork at the same time. In addition to entering a percentage for scaling, you can actually enter the new dimensions of the artwork, and KPT Resize and Reposition figures out the rest for you.

KPT ShadowLand

ShadowLand creates special-effects shadows for selected paths. More than just that, it's a place to play with shadows and shadow effects. Traditionally, creating shadows in Illustrator has always been very difficult. But with ShadowLand, the process is quite enjoyable. To get started using ShadowLand, I'd suggest taking text and converting it to outlines, and then choosing Filter⇨KPT Vector Effects⇨KPT ShadowLand. The KPT ShadowLand dialog box is shown in Figure 15-28.

There are three major types of shadow effects to create in ShadowLand:

- **Zoom Shadow** creates a zooming shadow from one color (the default is 50% of selected paths) to the background color (the default is white). You can control the scaling, rotation, and steps associated with the shadow.
- **Soft Shadow** gives Gaussian blurred edges to the shadow, making the shadow smaller by the amount it's blurred.
- **Halosity** is like the opposite of Soft Shadow; it too gives a Gaussian blur to the shadow edges, but the blur expands the size of the shadow, rather than contracting.

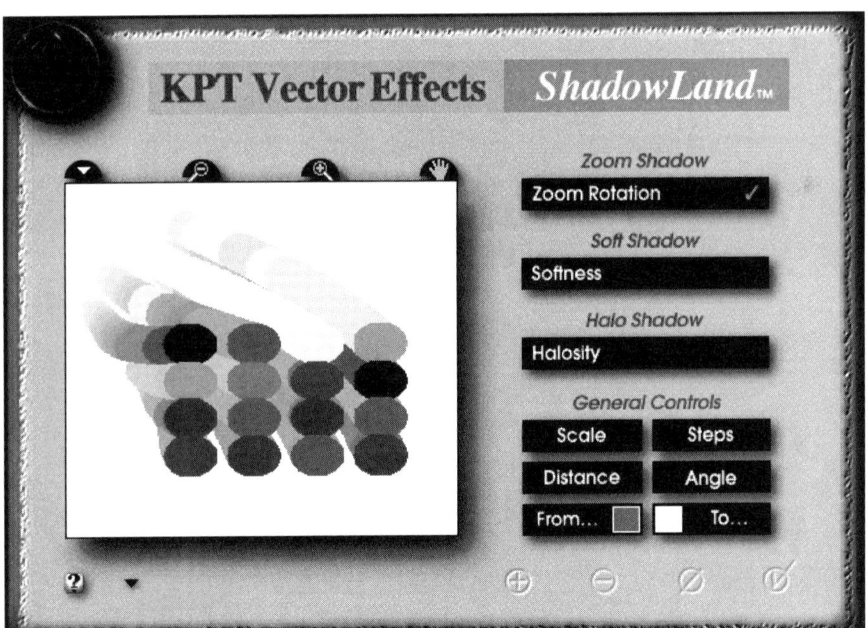

Figure 15-28: The KPT ShadowLand dialog box

Figure 15-29 shows each of these effects applied to text.

Figure 15-29: Zoom Shadow, Soft Shadow, and Halosity

Zoom shadow is the most powerful of the three shadow types, and with it you can create all sorts of un-shadowlike effects. For instance, the logo in Figure 15-30 was created with Zoom Shadow, with the Connect setting steps turned off.

Figure 15-30: Zoom Shadow created the spinning curve behind the original logo

KPT ShatterBox

This is an amazing effects generator that automatically splits your artwork into hundreds or thousands of little pieces.

FreeHand Bashing Guideline #1824: KPT ShatterBox doesn't work in FreeHand. Create something funky with the extension and then show it to your green-with-envy FreeHand-user pals.

STEPS: Using KPT ShatterBox

Step 1. Select the path or paths you wish to shatter.

Step 2. Choose Filter⇨KPT Vector Effects⇨KPT ShatterBox.

Step 3. Drag one of the three main sliders (shown in Figure 15-31) to the right. Watch the preview and stop when you think enough lines are crossing the image.

Step 4. Click the check mark in the lower right of the dialog box to make ShatterBox start shattering away.

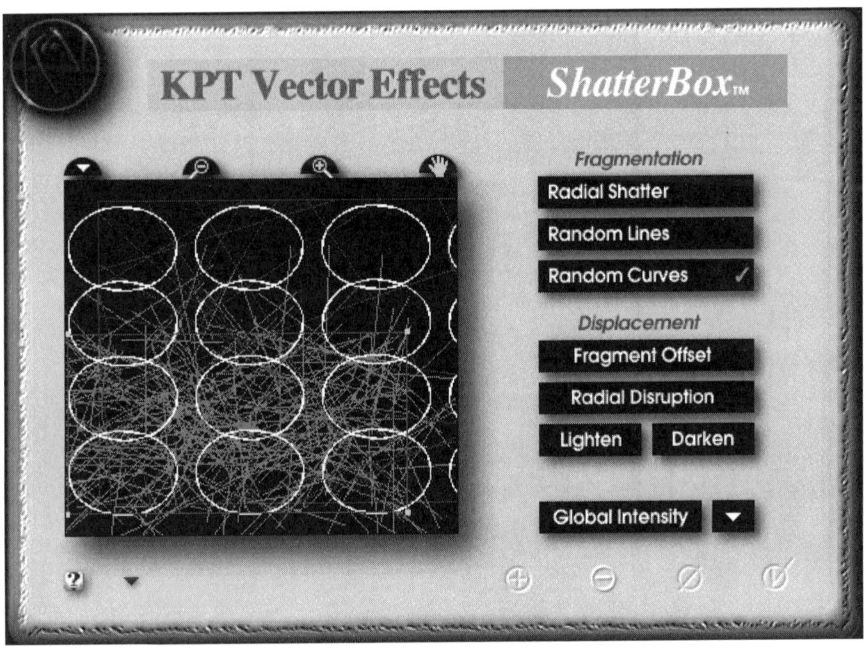

Figure 15-31: The ShatterBox dialog box

ShatterBox is a slow filter to use, depending on the number of Impacts and the complexity of each, as well as the number and complexity of selected paths.

STEPS: Applying the South Phoenix (Shots Fired) Preset in ShatterBox

Step 1. Select the art you wish to use with ShatterBox.

Step 2. Choose Filter⇨KPT Vector Effects⇨ShatterBox.

Step 3. Click the Preset button and choose Preset Manager from the list. Click Import and find the "Shots Fired" preset on the *Illustrator 7 Bible* CD-ROM (in the Presets *f* folder).

Step 4. Click the check mark in the lower right to use the effect. The effect should look something like the one in Figure 15-32.

Figure 15-32: Bullet holes created with ShatterBox

KPT Sketch

The Sketch filter takes paths and gives them a (surprise!) sketchy look. It does this by moving the points and handles on the paths in the amount you specify, and by adding another path on top of the original with a Stroke, not a Fill.

There are only two sliders in the dialog box: Stroke and Amount. Stroke controls the width of the duplicated path Stroke, while Amount determines how much the paths are moved. Figure 15-33 shows several applications of the Sketch filter on artwork.

Figure 15-33: The Sketch filter was applied to the original artwork several times with a low Stroke setting and a low Amount setting

The Sketch filter has three settings: Color Stroke, Pen Stroke, and Width Stroke. The Color Stroke option creates a darker stroke than the original color of the path. Pen Stroke creates a black Stroke. Width Stroke creates a Stroke the exact color of the original artwork.

One thing that KPT Sketch *doesn't* do is to add or subtract points during the sketching. In order to add points, you might want to apply the Roughen filter first, specifying somewhere around 5 to 10 points per inch and 0%. This will dramatically change the type of sketching that occurs, so experiment with different amounts of points added before coming up with a final design.

KPT Vector Distort

Vector Distort applies distortion effects to artwork, but doesn't require that you add points first, or that you pronounce its unsightly acronym. Through some wizardry of mathematics, Vector Distort adds points only where necessary. This makes effects like "swirl" look much better than does Adobe's Twirl tool.

Figure 15-34 shows some of the different effects in KPT Vector Distort applied to the same artwork.

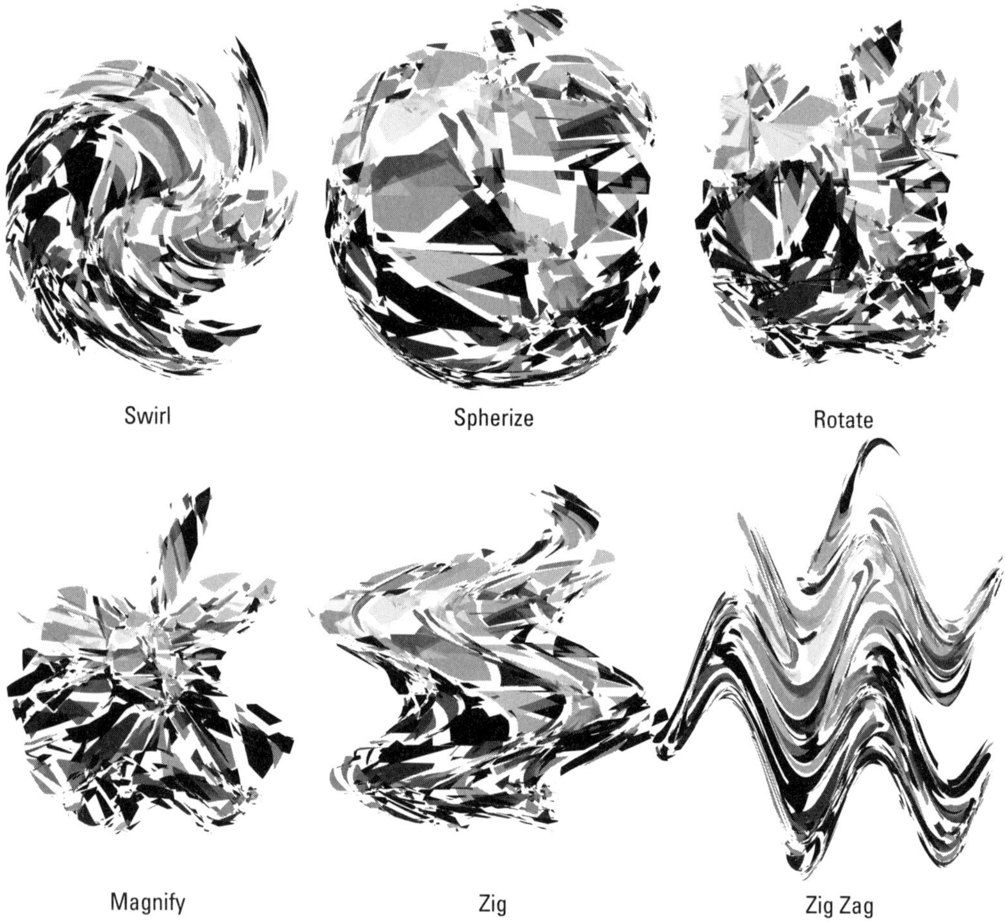

Figure 15-34: KPT Vector Distort effects

Within the Vector Distort dialog box (shown in Figure 15-35), you can use anywhere from one to several *influences*, which are the different types of effects listed on the sliders. To create a new influence, select the New Influence option from the Options menu. You can change the type of influence by clicking it and dragging a different slider. Each of the different types of influences has a different color, so you can quickly see what type of influence you're using.

You can access many of the distortion effects by pressing a number key on the keyboard:

- 1 = Swirl
- 2 = Spherize
- 3 = Zig Zag

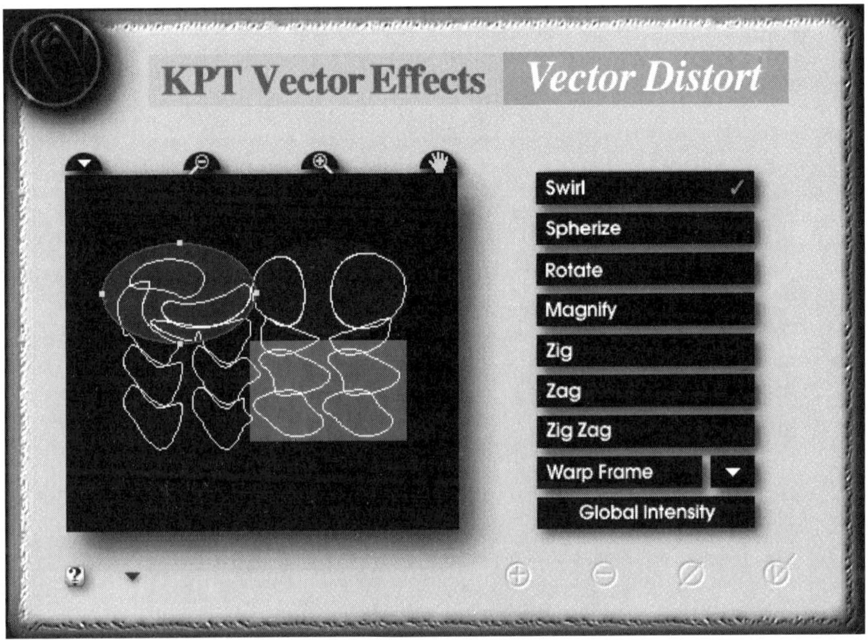

Figure 15-35: The Vector Distort dialog box

- 4 = Zig
- 5 = Zag
- 6 = Rotate

POWER TIP: Using the keyboard, there's a double-secret distortion effect you can access, that no one knows about! (Actually, I had to tell the engineer, and he was really surprised, which might cause the average software user to lose a bit of sleep.) Pressing 7 activates the Scale function, in which you change the size of paths within the sphere of influence. To use this, the amount must be set in another influence first; then when 7 is pressed, scaling takes place there. Wow! The amazing thing about Scale is that it scales just the influenced portion of the path.

KPT Warp Frame

Warp Frame is a powerful distortion envelope for Illustrator, similar to Letraset Envelopes (described later). With it, selected paths are warped into a different shape from the basic bounding box rectangle they normally have.

The best way to get started with Warp Frame is to start applying some of the presets, which you access by pressing the little triangle at the bottom of the dialog box (shown in Figure 15-36).

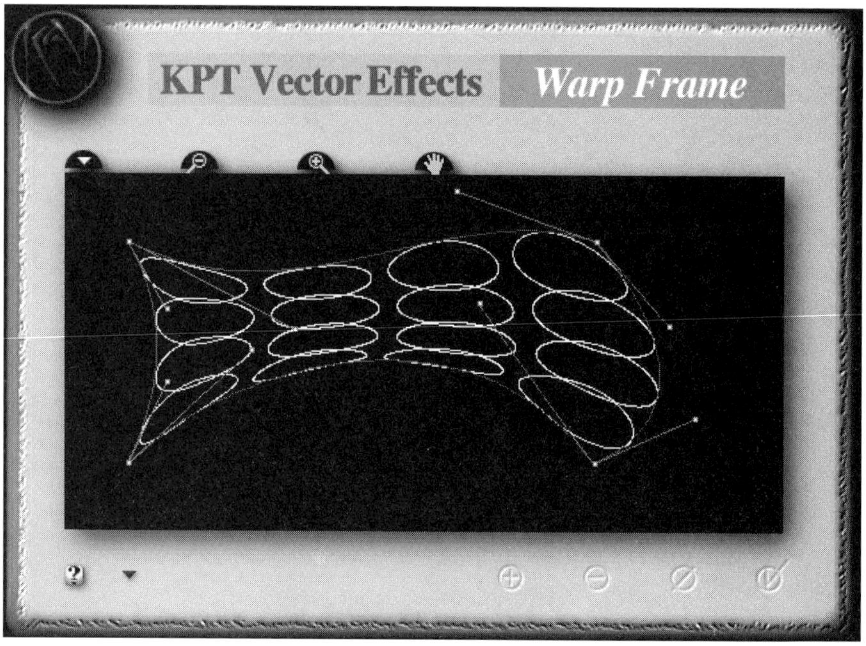

Figure 15-36: The Warp Frame dialog box

After a preset has been applied, you can click the points and handles around the edges of the envelope frame and drag them, changing the shape of the paths within. To start again from scratch (even if there's no itch), choose Reset All from the Options menu.

hot door CADtools 1.0

This product was just about ready to ship as the *Illustrator 7 Bible* was going to press, so we've managed to squeeze in a few tidbits about it here.

CADtools is an impressive set of Illustrator 7-only tools that transform Illustrator into CAD-capable software. The creation tools include wall, arc, fillet, chamfer, and trim. Measuring/dimensioning tools include angle, arc length, horizontal, vertical, radius, diameter, Bézier curvature, and more. Figure 15-37 shows the tools that CADtools adds to your Illustrator toolbox.

Figure 15-37: The impressive slate of CADtools

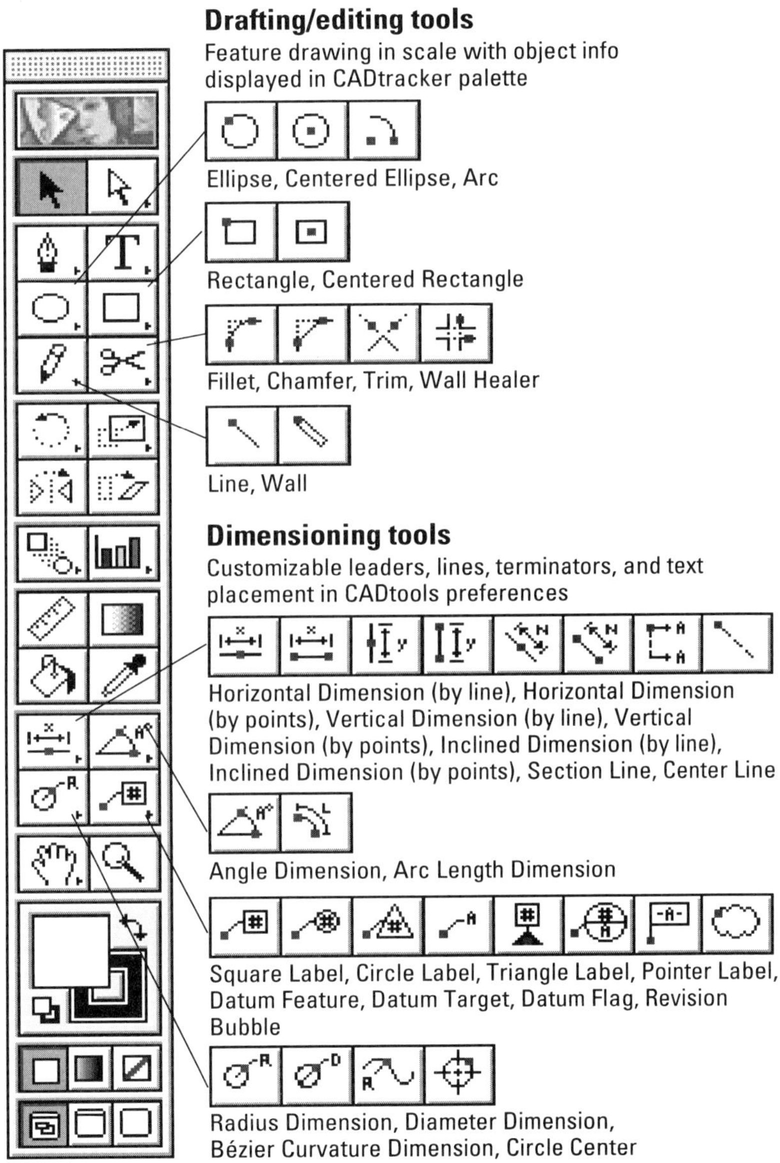

In addition, a floating palette displays all the dimensioning information, and another displays tips on using each of the tools. Figure 15-38 shows a completed drawing with CADtools used throughout.

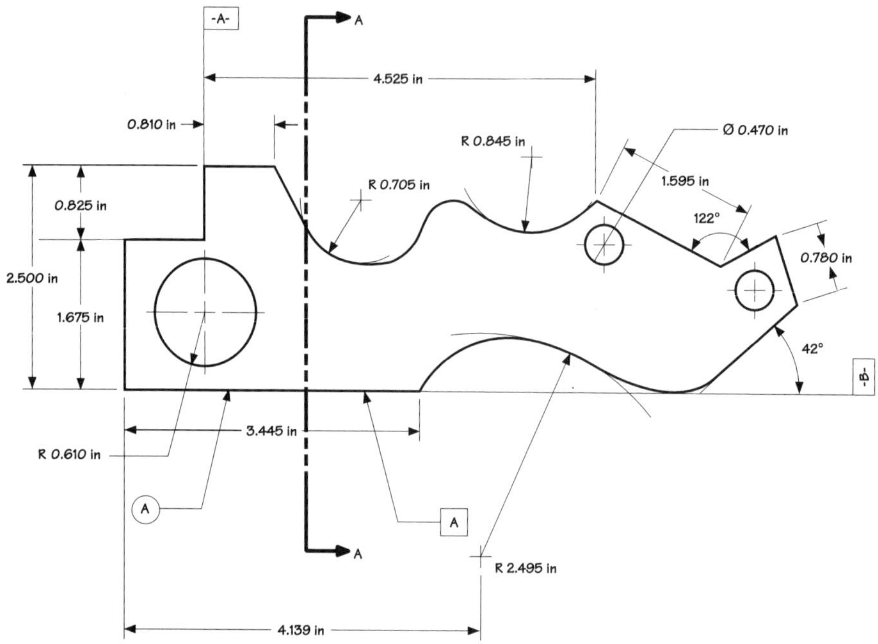

Figure 15-38: A CADtools-based drawing

I managed to put CADtools to use for a "real life" test with a beta version, however, and was pleasantly surprised to discover not only how how useful the plug-ins are, but also the wide variety of options and preferences (so many preferences, in fact, that CADtools has its own multilevel dialog box just for those preferences). Figure 15-39 shows one of the drawings that was CADtools enhanced that I used to help me as I designed a basketball court for my backyard patio (you can see the full color illustrations and a picture of the completed court in the color section of the *Illustrator 7 Bible*). Having printouts of this illustration handy as I was marking off the court to be painted was tremendously helpful.

One of the features I found exceedingly helpful was CADtools' automatic scaling feature. It allowed me to draw in "actual size," which would normally be quite difficult because the basic key of a basketball court is 12' wide, which is 2' wider than Illustrator's entire artboard. I set the scale to $^{1}/_{96}$ (where $^{1}/_{8}$"=1'), and from that point on I was able to draw real sizes. Using CADtools drawing tools, I could make the top of the key a circle that was exactly 12' in diameter.

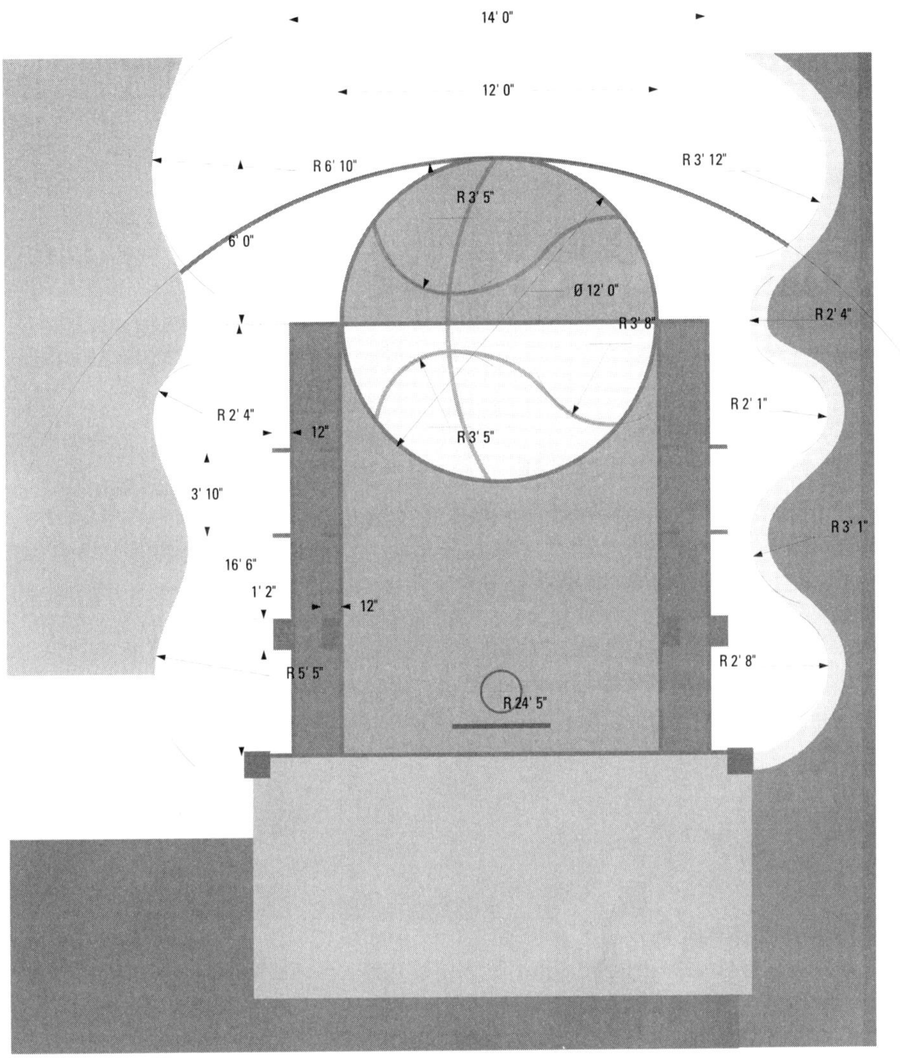

Figure 15-39: I used CADtools at 1/96 scale to produce one of many drawings used to create a basketball court on my backyard patio

If there's one feature that by itself is worth the price of the package, it is the Bezier Curvature Dimension tool. This handy tool gives you the radius of any portion of a curve, even drawing the curve radii at that point automatically. I used it to figure out the curves of the seams of the basketball image used at the top of the key.

One other thing worth mentioning (because you can't see this from a static image), is that most of CADtools' tools are 100% interactive. This means that as you're clicking and dragging, the information, labels, values, etc. all appear on screen (with no flicker) and are modified as you move the mouse around. Try out the aforementioned Bezier Curverature Dimension tool and you'll see what I mean.

Vertigo 3D Words

Text effects are always fun to do, but with Vertigo 3D Words, text can take on a life of its own. The simple interface and straighforward options make using 3D Words pretty easy, but the results can be spectacular.

The interface of 3D Words consists of a floating palette shown in Figure 15-40, which oddly enough isn't resizeable or actually interactive in the way most palettes are. Instead, it's like a dialog box that you can have up all of the time. (Although it is much too big for my taste and my monitors.)

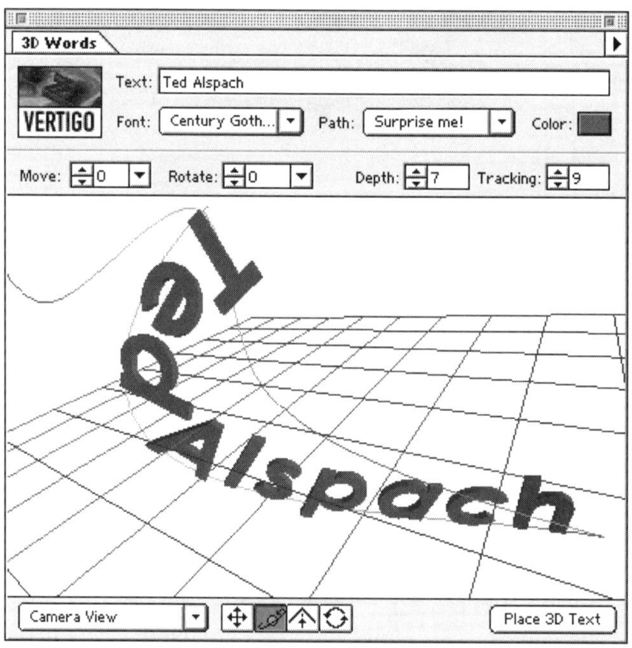

Figure 15-40: Hey! I know him! The Vertigo 3D palette, with some example text on a path

To use 3D Words, type in some text in the text field and press Enter. The text appears on the path. Using the controls in the palette, you can modify the:

- **Font:** Just what you'd expect here. One font per text string.
- **Path:** This is a big pop-up menu full of true 3D paths for you to select from.
- **Color:** What color the string of text will be.
- **Move:** This moves the text along the path, sort of sliding it (similar to grabbing the I-bar of text-on-a-path in Illustrator).
- **Rotate:** This "twists" the text on the path. 0° text is upright, -90° is text lying on its back.
- **Depth:** The Depth control determines how extruded the text is.
- **Tracking:** Just like Illustrator's tracking, this option adds (or removes) space between letters.
- **Camera View:** This allows you to pick from one of several preset camera views.

There are four buttons along the bottom of the palette that allow you to (in order) move, revolve, scale, and rotate the entire path in the viewing window.

After you have the settings just the way you like them, go ahead and click the Place 3D Text button, and the text will appear in Illustrator. An example of placed text is shown in Figure 15-41 (after some finessing and duplication via the Scale tool and VectorColor).

POWER TIP: The Surprise me! setting in the Path pop-up menu is just that; a different 3D path every time you select it. To keep getting different paths, you'll have to select another option, then go back to Surprise me!

Figure 15-42 shows additional VectorColor manipulation of the text generated by 3D Words. Of importance is that each "block" of color you see along the extruded sides is fairly large (there's no "complexity" setting as in KPT 3D Transform).

Figure 15-41: Shameless self promotion via Vertigo 3D Words

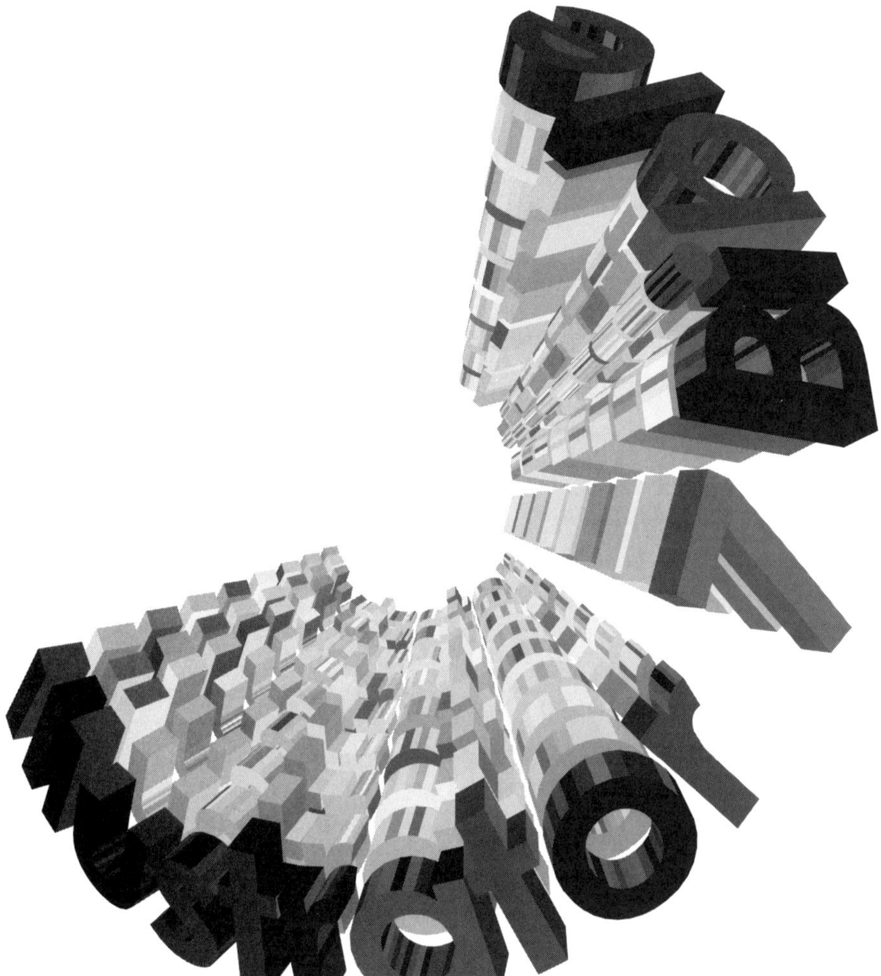

Figure 15-42: A little randomizing never hurt anyone. Well, not too badly, at least.

Alien Skin Stylist

Everyone always complains about there not being any styles in Illustrator. Before VectorTools could come out with its VectorObjectStyles, Alien Skin pioneered Illustrator style sheets with Stylist. Stylist (shown in Figure 15-43) combines both object styles and text styles together for one-click-styling.

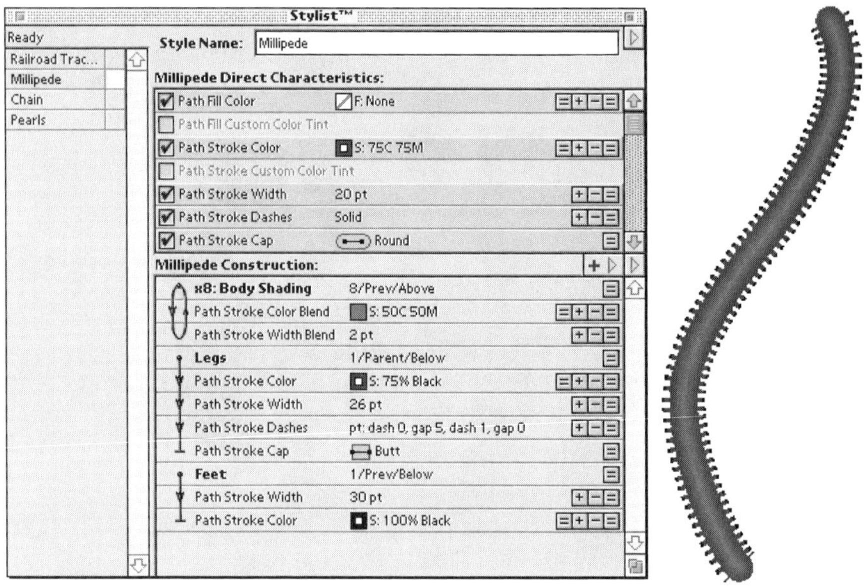

Figure 15-43: Alien Skin Stylist

If you've ever used style sheets in Word or PageMaker, you probably know that a "style" is a set of characteristics all grouped together. In Illustrator, however, styles aren't just text characteristics. Instead, they're also paint style characteristics. This means that you can create a style that contains a gradient fill, a black stroke of 2 pts (with a dash pattern of 1,2,6,10), Helvetica Bold Italic, 48 pts with tracking of -20 and a horizontal scale of 92%. To apply all these attributes, you select the object, then select the style in the Stylist palette. Voilà! Your object now has all those attributes.

In addition to creating, editing and applying styles, Stylist also lets you create complex constructions, which are linked styles that are applied to a single path, resulting in several paths. The "centipede" in figure 15-43 is an example of a complex construction. In fact, many of the examples in the stroke chapter of the *Illustrator 7 Bible* could be created using Stylist.

Why Nobody Uses LetraSet Envelopes

Envelopes were one of the first plug-ins available for Illustrator 5. Unfortunately, they were plagued by bugs and limitations, which to my knowledge have never been addressed. LetraSet Envelopes are sort of a limited KPT WarpFrame, with a smaller preview window and less options. You might be able to see where I'm going with this: when you can get all of VectorEffects (twelve other components besides WarpFrame), why would you want Envelopes? If you only need basic enveloping capabilities, you can achieve them in VectorTools VectorShape as well.

Hopefully LetraSet will build a stronger product around Envelopes in the future.

MAPublisher 2.0

Here's an exciting product that does for the map-making industry what CADtools does for drafting. There are dozens of components, including a handy grid generator, that make map-making as easy as possible with Illustrator. Even if you're not a map maker, the variety of tools in MAPublisher can come in handy.

Kara Fonts

Kare Fonts aren't plug-ins. They're not really fonts, either, though. But they *seem* like plug-ins, so I've included a brief discussion of them here. One thing many people take for granted is that fonts are flat. Sure, you can extrude them with different software, but even then, the faces of those fonts are flat. Yuck.

Kara Fonts use Illustrator gradients to produce some heavily textured, 3D-looking fonts, like the ones shown in Figure 15-44.

To use Kara Fonts, you actually run a little application (which *would* be more logical as a plug-in than an entire application) where you pick a font and enter text, shown in Figure 15-45. Then you copy the text to the clipboard and paste into an Illustrator document.

Because the fonts consist of named gradients, you can quickly recolor an existing block of text just by Option[Alt]-dragging a new gradient on top of the one used in the font! And of course, what is generated are Illustrator paths, so they can be altered in any way. Figure 15-46 shows some text after some scaling has been applied to it.

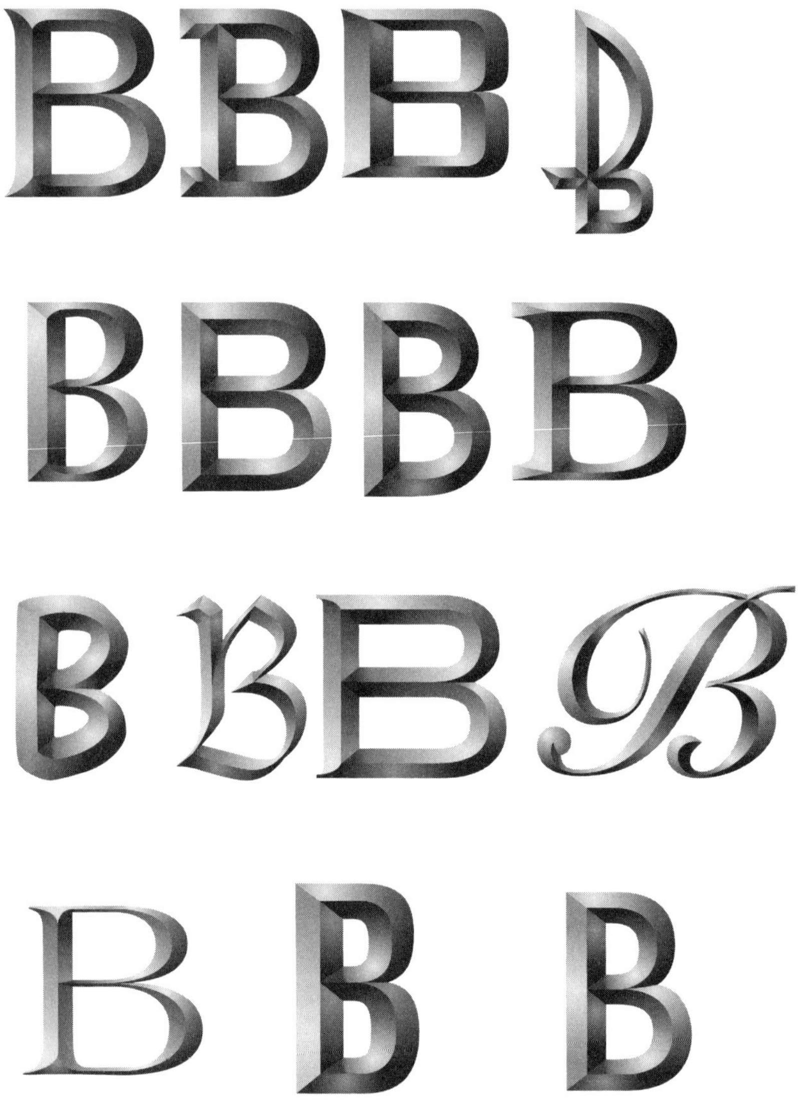

Figure 15-44: Some of the fonts that Kara Fonts can create

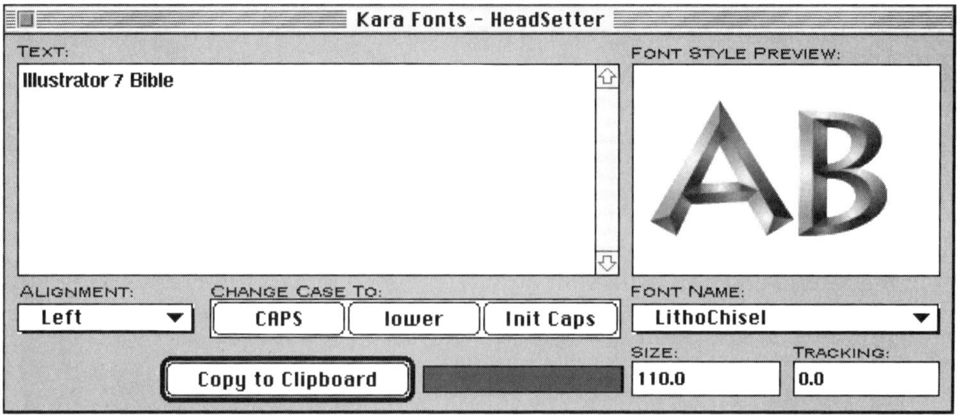

Figure 15-45: The Kara Fonts-HeadSetter application window

Figure 15-46: After some tweaking and the addition of a drop shadow, I'm ready for even more shameless promotion

Creating Plug-Ins for Illustrator 7

Much of this section is based on an article I wrote for the Adobe Technical Journal that appeared in Spring 1997.

While this section is focused towards potential plug-in developers, casual readers might find it interesting to discover what exactly can be done in Illustrator via an add-on plug-in. The little pieces of software are quite amazing indeed.

The Illustrator API and SDK

Illustrator 7's API is one of the most advanced API's (Application Program Interface) for any software, allowing plug-in developers to add features by creating modal-based functions, floating palettes, and even tools anywhere within Illustrator. The sad thing, in my opinion, is that up until this point, no software developer (with the exception of Extensis VectorTools and hotdoor CADtools) has really taken advantage of all of these fantastic capabilities.

Maybe you're asking yourself, why bother with a plug-in when I can just create an application that does what I want? Why bother spending the time to learn the API? For starters, creating a plug-in within Illustrator allows you to take advantage of Illustrator's file importing/exporting options (Illustrator supports all of Photoshop's pixel formats, as well as Illustrator native, EPS and PDF files), as well as printing issues. You don't need to worry about coding all of that boring stuff, but instead you get to dig into the meaty stuff that's really fun to create — and use. The Illustrator API makes it easy to perform almost all of Illustrator's functions and features through simple calls.

Even better, the SDK (Software Developer's Kit) can be found on the Illustrator 7 CD-ROM, with plenty of sample plug-ins and source code. A more recent (post shipping) version of the SDK is available from Adobe's Web site.

To create a plug-in for Illustrator you must have a basic knowledge of C programming, and you must own a compiler of some sort. For what little programming I've done, I wouldn't know where to start, but all my programmer/engineer buddies tell me Metrowerks CodeWarrior is the only coding software you'll ever need.

To learn programming, you might want to take a class or read one of the excellent books available on the subject, such as *Programming Starter Kit for Macintosh* (Hayden Books, 1995) by Jim Trudeau. Be aware, however, that programming can be an obsessive line of work. Just ask any Mountain Dew addicted, pale-skinned, three-glasses-prescription-changes-in-the-last-year engineer.

How Extensis VectorTools uses the Illustrator API

Extensis is shipping a brand new collection of plug-ins for Illustrator, VectorTools 2.0 (see Chapter 14). With the exception of Extensis' trademark toolbars and tips, tricks and techniques dialog box, the other seven plug-ins for Illustrator were created using the Illustrator API. While VectorTools doesn't take full advantage of the 7.0 API (the components were developed using the 6.0 API, which is similar), it does show some of its powerful capabilities, including palettes and tools. Some of the more interesting plug-ins (from a developer's point of view):

VectorLibrary is a floating palette that stores Illustrator objects. Using the Macintosh drag manager, the API allows objects to be dragged in and out of the palette without negatively affecting the artwork in the document.

VectorFrame is another floating palette that provides an interactive slider that places frames on selected objects. The slider adjusts the frame (an Illustrator path) in real time.

VectorObjectStyles applies tagged styles to Illustrator paths. Each object in Illustrator can be tagged using the Illustrator API.

VectorNavigator is a floating palette with two functions. First, it shows the entire existing illustration within the palette, scaled to the size of the palette, with a red rectangle showing what is currently displayed within the document window. Second, it allows the user to move around within the document by dragging the red rectangle around the palette.

VectorMagicWand is clearly the most impressive (both technologically and otherwise) of the set. The plug-in creates a tool that is added to the Illustrator Toolbox. This tool is used for selecting paths that are similar to the path that is being clicked on with the tool. The amount of similarity is controlled by several sliders on a floating palette (which can be shown/hidden either via menu or by double-clicking on the tool). In addition, the palette contains a button that is used to select and deselect the MagicWand tool.

Plug-In Types

There are three major plug-in types in Illustrator: menu selectable modal dialogs, floating palettes, and tools.

- **Modal Dialogs** are the standard filter type of plug-ins common to Photoshop. The user selects a menu item, and a dialog box appears. MetaTools' Vector Effects, CSI Socket Sets and BeInfinite's InfiniteFX use modal dialog boxes for their plug-ins. Versions 5.0 and 5.5 of Illustrator only supported modal dialog box-based plug-ins, and they were only accessible via a submenu off of the Filter menu. Versions 6 and 7 support putting menu items in *any* menu, not just the Filter menu.
- **Floating Palettes** are fully supported by Illustrator 7. If you use the API to create a palette in Illustrator, the palette is treated as a standard Illustrator palette, following the behavior of other palettes in Illustrator, including snapping to the edges of other palettes, snapping to the document window, and snapping to the edges of the screen. Palettes you create via the API are also hidden and shown automatically when the user presses the Tab key.
- **Tools** are plug-ins that add tools to the Toolbox. Tools can interact with Illustrator objects in various ways. The Spiral, Polygon, Star and Twirl tools were originally modal-based plug-ins (in Versions 5.0 and 5.5 of Illustrator), now transformed into tools with added functionality (double-clicking on the tools displays a dialog box that is eerily similar to the original filters).

Suites

One of the most useful API innovations is that of suites. Illustrator 7 has several integrated suites that provide loads of additional functionality. The two suites that you might find especially helpful are the Path Construction Suite and the Shape Construction Suite. These two suites assist in creating and adjusting paths, and are especially helpful with distortion filters.

The most striking difference between the 5.0/5.5 distortion filter Twirl and its 6.0/7.0 counterpart (besides the fact that it is also a tool) is the way it works. Twirling a star in Versions 5.0/5.5 resulted in a twirling of points only; the path shape was only affected in that the line segments followed the path. The Illustrator 6/7 Twirl filter (and tool) uses the Shape Construction Suite to adjust the entire path, not just the selected points, resulting in a smooth twirling effect, as shown here.

The capabilities of each suite are documented in the SDK.

Plug-Ins I'd Like to See

There are all sorts of plug-ins that could be created for Illustrator, now that it has such a powerful API. Here are a few ideas of undeveloped plug-ins that Illustrator users have been clamoring for:

- **3D Transformation Tool, Find/Replace, Live Blends, an Arc Tool:** FreeHand (that *other* Illustrator program) has these features and many others that could be included in Illustrator using the Illustrator API. Of course, FreeHand is a little feature-heavy, but the best place to start is the competition.
- **Levels color controls:** I use Levels in Photoshop as much (or more) than curves. Levels is perfect for quick "watermarking" of images.
- **Layers Management:** Many Layer-based functions could be automated or enhanced, such as automatic layer creation, layer sorting and layer linking.
- **Enhanced Previewing:** A plug-in could create a viewing mode that shows anti-aliasing, overprinting, and individual separations.
- **Animation Plug-in:** Adobe Dimensions does basic key sequencing for animation, but Illustrator provides the tools that would allow a developer to create animation that could be viewed within Illustrator (like the SDK clock, shown later in this chapter). The animated frames could be exported as QuickTime, GIF Animation, or sequential PICS.
- **Simulated Animation:** A plug-in that takes a selection and applies virtual animation to it by creating a series of more transparent copies along a path.
- **Spotlight/Lighting Effects Tool:** A tool that could shine a spotlight on the artwork, creating both a reflected light surface and a drop shadow.
- **Random Movement and Distortion:** A plug-in that scatters paths and points based on specific criteria.
- **A Better Blend Tool/Plug-In:** The current Blend tool works, but forces you to choose paths with similarly selected points, and then to click on those points. A new, better Blend tool/function could blend between several paths (not just the current limitation of two), not require specific points to be selected, and intelligently create the proper number of in between steps.
- **Illustrator Document Viewer:** A plug-in that cycles through custom views, multiple documents, and more using a simple VCR style palette; mouse clicks could be used to advance through images like a slide show.
- **Blur and Blur Tool:** Blurring can be done with vector objects, it just isn't that easy. A plug-in that automatically blurred would be a tremendous boon.

- **Real Transparency:** Objects in Illustrator can be set to overprint, but you never know what they'll look like until you print separations. And the Hard and Soft Pathfinder filters break paths up into little pieces.
- **3D Path Splines:** VectorEffects extrudes, Dimensions both extrudes and revolves. However, there is no tool that allows paths to be constructed in three dimensions, or to be displayed that way.
- **A Stippling Tool:** A tool to create stippling effects in Illustrator, with varying intensity and color amounts.
- **Path Generator:** A plug-in that automatically generates random paths based on specific criteria. Perfect for backgrounds, random objects, and more.
- **Mosaic Creation:** A plug-in to create mosaic tiles from vector artwork; the current Object Mosaic is quite limited.
- **Area Tool:** Illustrator's Measure tool is fine for measuring distance. An Area tool would measure the area within several clicked points or selected paths.

Many of these potential plug-ins can be done using little more than the tools provided with the Illustrator API. Other plug-ins would require a higher level of complexity. But most, if not all of them, are doable.

If you have plug-in ideas that you'd like to see developed, or if you've created a plug-in that you need marketed, contact the Adobe Developer's Association, which works with up-and-coming programmers to help them realize their plug-in goals. In addition, you may want to check with any of the existing plug-in developers, such as Adobe or Extensis, who may be interested in licensing your technology for inclusion in a future product.

Fun Plug-Ins on the Illustrator 7 Bible CD-ROM

The *Illustrator 7 Bible* CD-ROM contains a boatload of free, fully functional plug-ins for your use in Illustrator 7 (most for Macintosh only). Some of these are freeware (like Matt Foster's Melt and Drip filters) and some are exclusive to the *Illustrator 7 Bible* (Ted Alspach's Doodle Jr., VectorFrame SE, and the Adobe plug-ins). The following sections describe the plug-ins and some uses for them.

KPT Gradients/Patterns to Paths

This handy filter takes paths filled with gradients or patterns, and converts the gradients to blends and the patterns to paths. This provides you with the capability to do some truly amazing effects that wouldn't be possible otherwise.

Matt Foster's Melt & Drip Filters

Matt Foster is one of the amazingly talented engineers at Adobe systems. He designed the Melt & Drip filters to show off some of the capabilities of the Illustrator Plug-In interface, to help potential programmers in writing their own filters for Illustrator. Little did he know I'd find all sorts of amazing uses for it. Melt & Drip filters affect selected paths. The dialog box for Melt is shown in Figure 15-47.

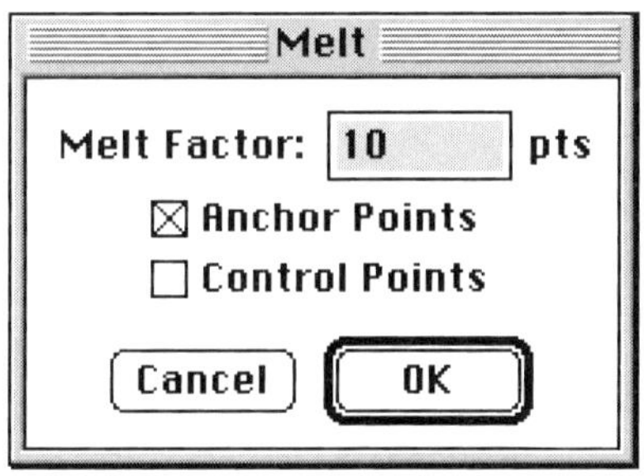

Figure 15-47: The Melt dialog box

Following are a few images that show how text can be manipulated with Melt & Drip to get various effects. Instead of the common Steps format, I've condensed the explanations to save space. For all the Figures, first create type and then convert to outlines.

To achieve the effect in Figure 15-48, apply Add Anchor Points three times. Apply Drip at 20 points, with both the Anchor and Control points check boxes checked. Apply Rounded Corners at 100 points. Apply Unite. Select the bottommost points and scale them down with the Scale tool.

To achieve the effect in Figure 15-49, apply Add Anchor Points three times. Rotate the words 90°. Apply Melt at 10 points, with both the Anchor and Control points checkboxes checked. Rotate 180°. Reapply Melt (just press ⌘-E [Ctrl+E]) at the same settings. Apply Rounded Corners at 100. Rotate 90° (back to regular position). Apply Unite.

Figure 15-48: The original outlined path, and after Dripping

Figure 15-49: The original outlined path, and after Melting

To achieve the effect in Figure 15-50, apply Add Anchor Points once. Apply Round Corners at 100. Apply Add Anchor Points twice. Apply Twirl at 90°. Apply Melt at 10, checking on the Control Points checkbox. Apply Twirl at –95°. Rotate with the Rotate Tool back to horizontal. Apply Drip at 20, with both the Anchor and Control points checkboxes checked. Apply Unite.

Figure 15-50: The original outlined path, and after Melting and Dripping

BeInfinite Smart Remove Points

This filter removes unnecessary points from paths. It's a useful tool for cleaning up artwork created with Streamline or the AutoTrace tool.

Ted Alspach's Doodle Jr.

This filter (Figure 15-51) was designed to take advantage of some of the normally unseen path-manipulation capabilities of the Illustrator API. By playing with the various controls, you can distort and reshape artwork dramatically.

Figure 15-50: Doodle Jr. is a new distortion filter that lets you reshape your work

A hidden feature of Doodle Jr.: Click the Doodle Jr. logo, and the selected objects are randomized.

To use Doodle Jr., copy it to your Illustrator Plug-Ins folder and restart Illustrator. The filter appears in a new Filter menu submenu called Fun.

Adobe's Plug-Ins

I managed to twist Adobe's arm a little so that they would let me include three plug-ins that aren't quite ready for prime time. These plug-ins may or may not ever make it into Illustrator, so I'm giving you a pseudo-sneak preview.

One of the reasons these otherwise useful plug-ins are not included with Illustrator is because they have not ever been tested properly by anyone other than the original engineer and a few red-eyed Illustrator users. There may very well be problems with the plug-ins (I haven't found any, but then again, I'm not a Q/A person). That said, if you experience problems with Illustrator with these plug-ins installed, *take them out.* Neither I nor Adobe will be able to provide any form of technical support for them. Boy, I'm getting harsh in my old age. . . .

To install the plug-ins, drag them from the Adobe Exclusives folder on your *Illustrator 7 Bible* CD-ROM into your Plug-ins folder. To remove them take them out of the Plug-Ins folder. The two tools will appear in the toolbox (under the Blend tool and Graph tool), while the Clock functions will appear in the Object menu.

The Analog Clock

This is the amazing plug-in that manages to show some of the incredible power of Adobe Illustrator's API. The clock was developed by Joe Holt of Adobe Systems, the chief engineer for Illustrator 6.0's suite-based API.

To install the plug-in, drag it out of the SDK folder on the Illustrator 7 CD-ROM and place it in your Illustrator 7 application's plug-ins folder. Launch Illustrator. The Object menu (see Figure 15-52) will contain two new items: Create Clock and Pause Clock.

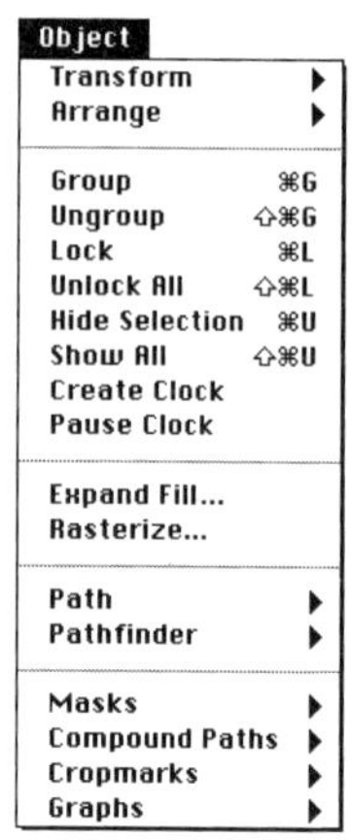

Figure 15-52: The Object menu when the Clock is installed

Choose Create Clock from the Object menu. A gray clock appears in the center of your document, with a ticking second hand (see Figure 15-53). When I first saw this, I thought, "Cool. Now I can see the time in Illustrator." I didn't grasp what was happening: the clock was made of Illustrator paths. The plug-in actually creates animated Illustrator paths, in this case a set of paths that keep the time (based on your Mac's time setting).

Figure 15-53: The clock when you first create it (the time shown will reflect the time on your system when you create the clock)

A few cool things you can do with the clock:

- Save the document and close it. Open it again a few hours, days or months later, and you'll see that it's been keeping time correctly.
- Select the second hand and change the fill color . . . while the second hand ticks its way around the center of the clock.
- Pause the clock (using the command in the Object menu) and Option[Alt]-copy it several times. Change the position of the hour hands by rotating them around the center of each clock slightly. When you Resume the clock running, you'll have a virtual (and accurate) set of clocks displaying the time in multiple time zones (see Figure 15-54).
- Pause the clock and use any of Illustrator's tools to distort the paths, then Resume the clock (see Figure 15-55).
- Finally, use the clock as a time stamp by shrinking it down and placing it in the corner of each Illustrator document.

Figure 15-54: Time zones in the U.S.

Figure 15-55: It keeps on ticking!

These are just the possibilities from a user's standpoint. From a developer's point of view, this opens up a whole new area of plug-in development.

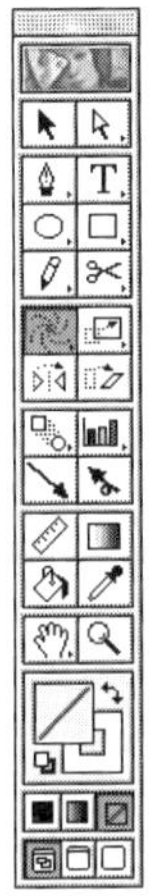

Figure 15-56: The Arrow tool in the toolbox

The Arrow Tool

This handy tool draws arrows. That's it. You don't even get to choose how the arrow looks. All you get to do is drag from the end of the arrow to the tip of the arrow. The Arrow tool is located in the toolbox under the Blend tool.

The arrow consists of a single closed path, so it doesn't look quite right with just a fill or just a stroke. Instead, give it a fill and stroke that are the same color, then change the stroke to match how thick you'd like the "tail" portion of the arrow to be. The tip of the arrow will increase in size as you do this, of course, so don't get carried away (see Figure 15-57).

Point and Delete

The Point and delete tool (see Figure 15-58) is rather simple, yet I've found it extremely powerful. To use it, simply click on any single path you wish to delete. The Point and delete tool doesn't care if the object is part of a group or a compound path, it just deletes that single path.

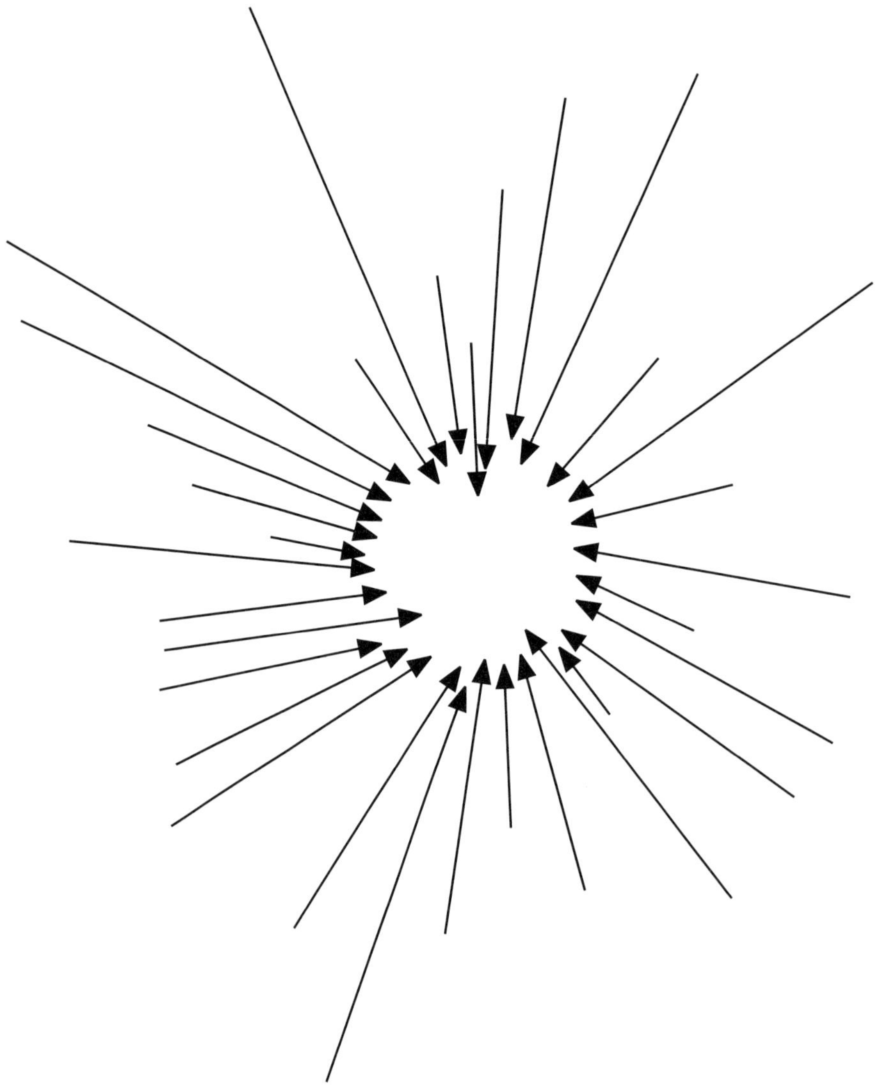

Figure 15-57: A bunch of arrows drawn with the Arrow tool

Figure 15-58: The Point and delete tool

Summary

- Third-party filters for Illustrator are created by companies and individuals outside Adobe.
- BeInfinite's InfiniteFX provides more than 50 distortion filters with a common interface.
- The CSI Socket Set 1 filter set includes several filters for color adjusting and selecting, as well as Plug-Ins and startup-document capabilities.
- The CSI Socket Set 2 filter set includes several object-oriented filters, including ones for aligning and repeating.
- KPT Vector Effects contains a baker's dozen of various filters, many for producing unique special effects with Illustrator.
- Several filters can be found on the CD-ROM included with this book; copy them to your Illustrator Plug-Ins folder and restart Illustrator to use them.

Mastering Illustrator

IV

There are many concepts in Illustrator that don't fall under one of the Illustrator menus, tools, or palettes. There are also several software packages (besides plug-ins) that work with Illustrator, adding features not found in the main program.

Part IV discusses a wide variety of Illustrator features that help round out your knowledge of Illustrator. The concepts presented in this part are unique and useful; in fact, even Illustrator experts will find information in here that they didn't know before.

Illustrator and the Web

16 CHAPTER

In This Chapter

- How vector graphics work with the World Wide Web
- How to export images in JPEG format
- How to export images in GIF format
- How to assign URLs to objects
- How to create an Image Map

Vector Graphics and the World Wide Web

As the century turns, the denizens of the Web don't appear to be overly concerned that the only real supported format for graphics is pixel-based. With the exception of the Acrobat PDF format, graphics on the Web are limited to images consisting of pixels.

Before Illustrator 7, Illustrator had little to offer in the way of Web graphics. Sure, people would use it to set type because Photoshop 1 through 4 had such terrible type capabilities (unless you used the PhotoType component of Extensis PhotoTools), but overall Illustrator was mostly left out in the cold.

Oddly enough, that didn't seem to stop Illustrator users from using Illustrator to create Web graphics.

But now, Illustrator is truly Web-ready, including the following Web-specific features:

- RGB color support
- GIF89A export capabilities
- JPEG export capabilities
- PNG export capabilities
- URL assignment to objects
- Image Map creation
- PDF 3.0 support
- Web-specific Swatches palette

The most significant new feature is Illustrator 7's RGB support, which enables you to create JPEG and PNG images with much more accuracy than ever before possible with Illustrator. Creating RGB images is discussed in Chapter 2.

The one thing to keep in mind if you're creating graphics for the Web is that the resulting image will be made of pixels, not vectors. This may or may not affect the way you design your image, but its a good thing to keep in mind.

The rest of this chapter provides guidelines for using Illustrator's Web features, and some handy tips on Web page creation as well. If you're new to Web page design, get yourself a copy of Adobe PageMill, which makes Web page creation a much more simple matter than ever before.

Exporting to JPEG Format

The JPEG format has been the most popular lossy compression standard for pixel-based images by far, allowing images to be compressed down to as little as 1 percent of their original size. Of course, this extreme compression comes at a price, and that price is loss of detail. Using the higher compression settings also can create blotches on images that look pretty terrible. Figure 16-1 shows an original image, and the image after having the different JPEG settings applied to it.

As when exporting to any bitmapped format, make sure you don't give the file being exported the same name as the Illustrator file; doing this overwrites the Illustrator file, making it uneditable.

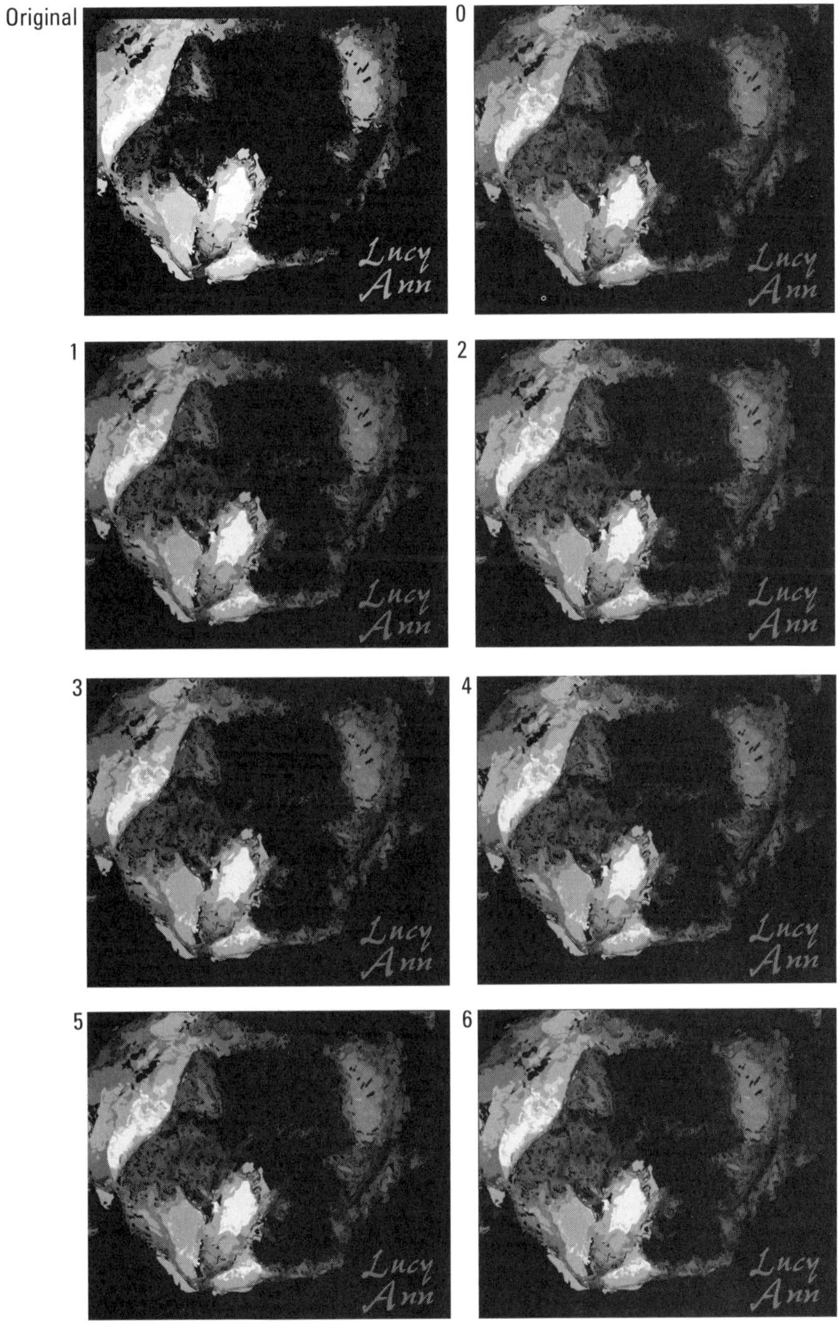

Figure 16-1: The original image (top) and the resulting JPEG images, each saved at a different compression setting

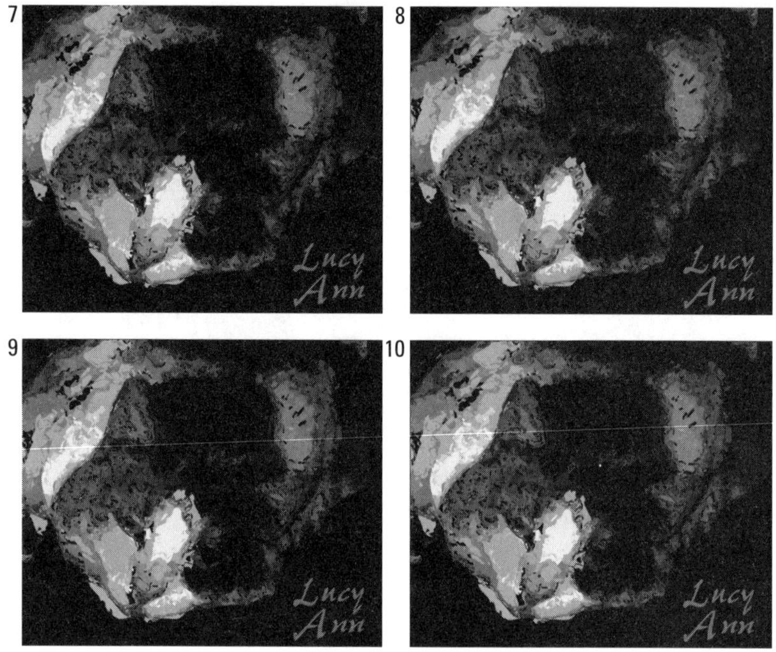

The main benefits to using JPEG images are that they enable you to use millions of colors (24-bit color) for Web pages, and that all browsers support JPEG. The JPEG export dialog box is shown in Figure 16-2.

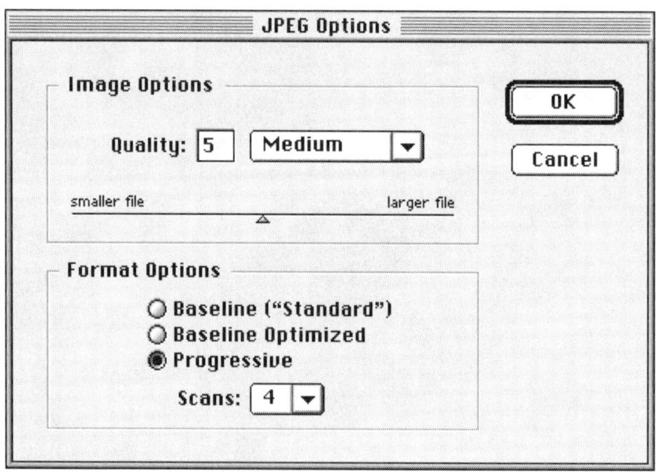

Figure 16-2: The JPEG Export dialog box

Exporting to PNG Format

The latest format, PNG, seems primed to take over for JPEG and many GIF uses, as it keeps file sizes small without losing any data. Files can be saved in up to 48-bit color for maximum quality. As of this writing, no currently shipping browsers support this technology without an additional plug-in.

Exporting to GIF Format

The GIF format is the closest to a standard that the World Wide Web has. One of the best things about GIF files is their flexibility. GIF files are used as plain images, images with transparency, image maps, and even as animations. Their biggest drawback — the limited number of colors — is also a giant strength. The GIF89A export option is the one you'll probably use most when creating Web graphics with Illustrator.

The GIF export dialog box (see Figure 16-3) in Illustrator provides you with all the options you'll need to create the exact type of GIF file you want.

Figure 16-3: The GIF export dialog box

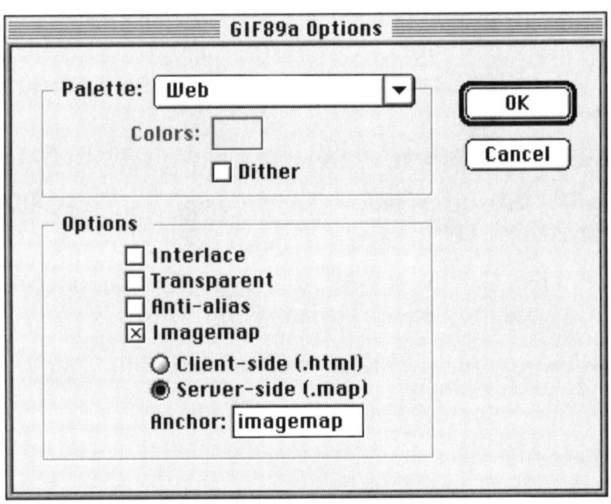

The Web-Ready Swatches Palette

Illustrator has a special Swatches palette that contains Web-specific colors. Using this palette, you can create illustrations that only use the 216 cross-platform colors commonly used for GIF images on the Web. You can access this palette (shown in Figure 16-4) by choosing Window⇨Swatch Libraries⇨Web.

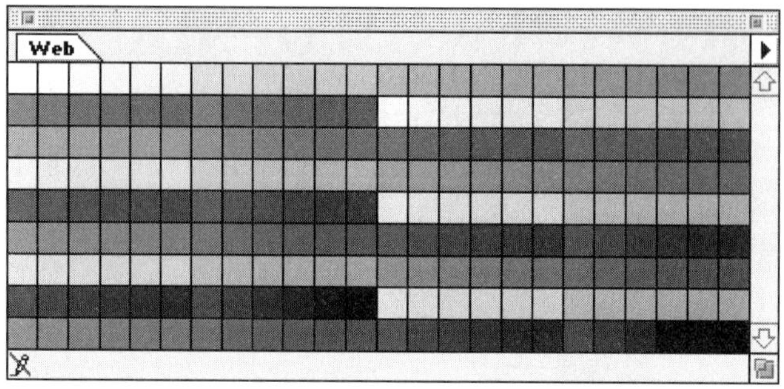

Figure 16-4: The Web colors Swatches palette

If you'll be using the Web swatches palette, be aware that using blends, gradients, color filters and the Pathfinder functions can dramatically change the colors in your document, creating potential dithering situations. If at all possible, stick to solid colors you find within the palette.

Assigning URLs to Objects

Objects in Illustrator can have URL (Uniform Resource Locators, like `http://` and `ftp://` addresses) attached to them via the Attributes palette.

STEPS: Applying a URL to a Path or a Group of Objects

Step 1. Select the path or group of objects you wish to attach the URL to.

Step 2. Display the Attributes palette by choosing Window⇨Show Attributes, or by pressing F11.

Step 3. Choose Show All from the Attributes pop-up menu. The Attributes palette should look like the one in Figure 16-5.

Step 4. Type in the complete URL for the selected object, such as

```
http://www.bezier.com/vectorville
```

Step 5. Press Return.

The object now has that URL assigned to it.

POWER TIP: Each time you type in a new URL in the attributes field, it is added to the URL pop-up menu (accessed by clicking to the right of the URL field). The Palette Options menu item (in the Attributes pop-up menu) lets you set the maximum number of URLs in the pop-up menu — up to 30 of them.

Figure 16-5: The Attributes palette

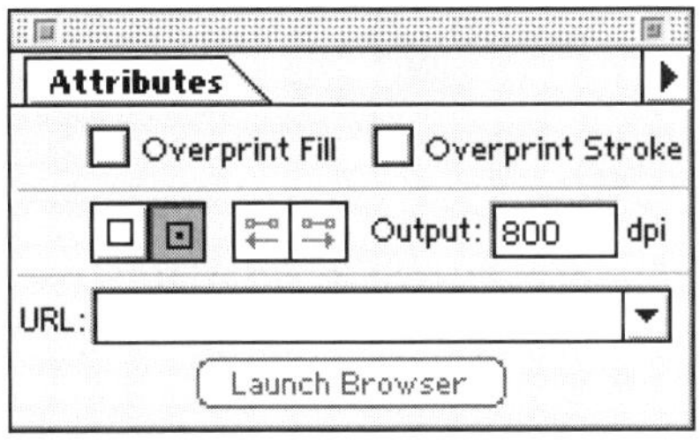

Creating Image Maps

The number one reason for assigning URLs to portions of an image is to generate GIF-based Image maps from your Illustrator documents.

STEPS: Creating an Image Map

Step 1. Assign pieces of artwork in your document to appropriate URLs.

Step 2. Choose File⇨Export.

Step 3. In the Export dialog box, choose GIF89A and name the file.

Step 4. In the GIF89A dialog box, choose the Image Map option. (Keep reading for an explanation of Client Side and Server Side image maps.)

Step 5. Click OK.

Client Side creates an HTML file with the appropriate HTML code in it for use with the GIF image that is being created. By using the HTML code, you can use the Image map easily.

Server Side creates a .map file that CGI Image map scripts use to determine the borders of your objects.

Illustrator 7 shipped with an Image map exporter that only supported the RECT command (rectangles). Polygon support is planned, but several issues (interface, the Image map limit of 100 sides per object, compound paths, curves) have yet to be satisfactorily resolved.

Creating Web Page Headings with Illustrator

This section originally appeared in a slightly different format in adobe.mag.

The number one strength of the GIF89A format is its capability to provide transparency. Illustrator is a perfect tool for creating partially *transparent images* — images without a rectangular background. In addition, the GIF89A format can be set up to use a minimum number of colors, keeping file sizes amazingly small.

However, what the GIF89A format is ideal for is creating headlines for Web pages. To get a page to look really good, fonts are needed. Unfortunately, specifying a font via HTML only works in certain browsers and then only if the specified font is installed on the system that is viewing the Web page. Of course (as always), the best alternative is the PDF format, but if you want a font on an HTML page, you'll probably end up creating a GIF file, which Illustrator really excels at. And then instead of just using a font, you can do all sorts of other things that HTML coders can only dream of.

Why use Illustrator instead of Photoshop for creating Web headings? The great thing about using Illustrator to create Web headings is that you can use the full power of Illustrator's type and distortion capabilities so that your headings look exactly the way you want them to. Many of Illustrator's type features — such as tracking, kerning, horizontal scaling, multiple fonts in one line, pattern and gradient fills, easy drop shadows, type on a curve, and more — are either impossible in Photoshop or cause undue strain on Photoshop's limited type capabilities.

STEPS: Creating a Web Heading

Step 1. Type your heading in Illustrator.

Step 2. Choose the Character attributes (font, tracking, and so forth) for the heading.

Step 3. Change the size of the heading to the size you want the text to appear on your Web site. It's usually best to view the document at 100%.

Step 4. Choose the Paint Style for the type. If you wish to use a gradient or pattern instead of a solid color fill, select the type and choose Type⇨Create Outlines (⌘-Shift-O) [Ctrl+Shift+O] first. One of the advantages of using Illustrator for Web headings is that you can go back to the original Illustrator document and make changes, and then re-export the document for the Web.

Step 5. To create a drop shadow (which can really make your text stand out), copy the text, Paste in Back (⌘-B) [Ctrl+B] and then Fill the pasted copy with Black. Use the arrow keys to move the shadow down and to the right. If you've used text that is thin and you can see white space between the original text and the shadow, put a black stroke on the drop shadow that is thick enough to cover the gap.

Step 6. Save the document as an Illustrator file (`Heading.ai7`).

Step 7. Export the document with a different name as a GIF89A file (`Heading.GIF`) in the same folder as your HTML page. In the GIF89A Options dialog box, choose Interlaced (which allows the heading to increase in resolution as it is downloaded to the browser), Exact (which uses *only* the colors in the heading), and check the Transparent checkbox. Checking the Transparent checkbox lets you place the heading on *any* background, even a tiled pattern.

Tips for Heading Design in Illustrator

- Take advantage of Illustrator's powerful kerning and tracking capabilities. You can quickly kern between two letters by placing your cursor between the two letters and then press ⌘-Shift-[[Ctrl+Shift+[ ] to remove space or ⌘-Shift-] [Ctrl+Shift+]] to add space between the letters. For tracking, select the range of characters to track and use the same key commands.
- If you have fonts in Adobe's Expert collection (such as Adobe Garamond), you can use really small caps in your heading, which always look classy.
- If you are using a gradient or a pattern as a fill, try to use a heavy sans serif font.
- Only check the anti-aliased option in the GIF89A box if you'll be using the same background color on your Web page as the one in your document. Two things happen when this box is checked: The file size (due to the increased number of colors) increases dramatically, and the edges along the transparency border look "dissolved."
- If horizontally scaling, try to avoid using fonts with big serifs, as they can often be stretched out of proportion.

Using the Heading in a Web Page (Text-Based Editors)

Here are the steps to using your new Web heading:

1. Where you would like the Heading to be, type

```
<IMG SRC="Heading.GIF">
```

2. Save your page and view it in your Web browser. If you rename or move the image, you'll need to type the correct path/file name into the IMG SRC code.

One of the benefits for creating a heading in Illustrator is that you can update it any time by opening the Illustrator file that contains the heading, then editing the text (if it isn't outlines), and then doing an Export to replace the GIF file with an updated version.

The GIF file shown in Figure 16-6 is only 3,072 bytes, which means it should download to a 28.8 Kbps modem in one or two seconds. You can help make Web pages that contain GIF file headings load faster by specifying the image size in the source code. For instance, the image created in this example is 519 x 39 pixels, so I'll put this code in:

```
<IMG SRC="Heading.GIF" Width=519 Height=39>
```

Now the rest of the page loads, and the heading will fill in afterward.

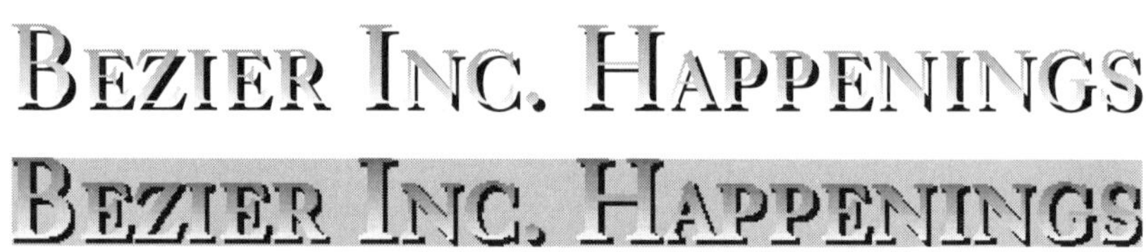

Figure 16-6: The original Illustrator image (top) and the GIF version of the image (bottom)

Heading Effects

Of course, using Illustrator to create such basic headings seems like a waste of all the great typographical power in Illustrator, so here's a few ideas to really spruce up those headings.

Path Type on Curved Paths. Why using straight, boring type when you could use funky curved type? Why indeed. Create a wavy line and click on it with the Path Type tool. Of course, path type is still completely editable.

3D Type with VectorEffects. Use MetaTools VectorEffects with Illustrator to create 3D type for headings. You must turn text into outlines before doing this, so you'll lose the future editability.

Place an Image in the Text. Use the Type as a mask and mask a placed image. The image can be a photograph, a pattern, or anything else you want to mask with the text.

The PDF Situation

When Adobe Illustrator 7 shipped, it did not provide URL-embedding support for PDF documents. Adobe hopes to release a fix/update for this, but if you have Version 7, chances are exporting a PDF from Illustrator does *not* retain assigned URLs. Once it does, however, Illustrator will become a valuable tool for creating PDF-based Web pages.

Summary

- The Web doesn't support vector-based graphics without specialized plug-ins, so Illustrator documents must be rasterized in order to be used on the Web.
- JPEG format is valuable because it supports an unlimited number of colors in any image.
- GIF89A images, while limted to 256 colors, provide transparency, Image-map capabilities, and interlacing.
- Assign URLs to objects (or several objects at once) by selecting them and using the Attributes palette.
- PDF exporting (in Version 7) does *not* support URL embedding.

Working with Strokes

17 CHAPTER

In This Chapter

- Understanding what you can do with Strokes
- How Outline Stroke works
- Stroke effects for letters
- Blends and Strokes
- Rough and feathered edges
- Creating designs on a Stroke
- Path type and Strokes

The ability to Stroke a path in Illustrator is greatly underrated. Strokes can do more than just outline shapes and vary thicknesses and patterns.

In the first part of this chapter, I explain some of the greatest mysteries and unlock some of the deepest secrets that surround Strokes. If that sounds at all boring, take a look at the figures in this chapter. I created most of them by using Strokes, not Filled paths. Amazin', ain't it?

Windows Update

Strokes work exactly the way they did in Version 4.1, except that now you use the Stroke palette instead of the Paint Style dialog box. The only significant new addition to working with strokes is the Outline Path function.

What's Missing	What's Replaces It
Paint Style palette	The Stroke palette (F10)

What's New

Object⇨Path⇨Outline Path for creating filled paths from Strokes.

The Secret Magic of Strokes

You create most effects with Strokes by overlaying several Strokes on top of one another. By copying and choosing Edit⇨Paste in Front (⌘-F) [Ctrl+F], you place an exact duplicate of the original path on top of itself.

Changing the weight and color of the top Stroke gives the appearance of a path that is a designer, or custom, Stroke. You can add Strokes on top of or under the original Stroke to make the pattern more complex or to add more colors or shapes.

Figure 17-1 and the following steps show you how to create a specialty Stroke that looks like parallel Strokes.

Figure 17-1: Creating parallel strokes

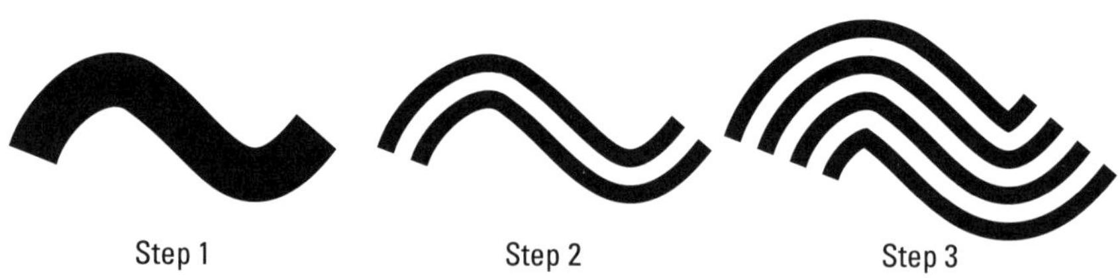

Stroke Essentials

Strokes, which were introduced in Chapter 2, act and work differently than Fills. Keep the following basics and rules (no pun intended) in mind when using Strokes:

- The most important thing to remember when using Strokes is that Stroke weight width is evenly distributed on both sides of a path. In other words, on a Stroke with a 6-point weight, there are 3 points of the Stroke on both sides of the Stroke's path.
- Patterns can be put into Strokes, but patterns cannot be viewed in Preview mode when they are on Strokes.
- Gradients may *not* be used to color Strokes.
- Using Outline Path (Object⇨Path⇨Outline Path) creates path outlines around the width of the Stroke. When a Stroke has been converted into an outline, it is really an outlined path object and can be Filled with patterns and gradients (both of which appear when previewing and printing).
- Stroke weight *never* varies on the same path.
- A Stroke with a color of None has no Stroke weight.
- Strokes are, for the most part, ignored when combining, splitting, or modifying paths with the Pathfinder functions. Strokes are never taken into account when the Pathfinder functions search for the lo-cations of the paths.

STEPS: Creating "Parallel Strokes"

Step 1. Use the Pencil tool to draw a short line. I usually set the Curve Fitting Tolerance (choose File⇨General Preferences or press ⌘-K) [Ctrl+K] to 10 for a very smooth path. Change the Fill to None and Stroke the path with 18-point Black.

(continued)

Selecting Hidden Strokes

Ann: I just can't seem to select some Strokes.

Toulouse: Are they locked?

Ann: No, if I Select All or drag a marquee around them, they're selected then.

Toulouse: So, what's the problem?

Ann: Well, they're directly under other Strokes. I can't seem to select those Strokes without selecting the ones on top.

Toulouse: The easiest thing to do is to lock the paths on top and then the other Strokes will be easier to select.

STEPS: *(continued)*

Step 2. Copy the Stroke and paste the copy in front (⌘-F) [Ctrl+F]. Change the copied (pasted in front) Stroke to 6-point White. Select both paths, copy them (⌘-C) [Ctrl+C], and lock them (⌘-L) [Ctrl+L]. The 6-point Stroke looks as if it has been subtracted from the 18-point Stroke. The result appears to be two separate 6-point black Strokes.

Step 3. Choose Edit⇨Paste In Back (⌘-B) [Ctrl+B]. Deselect All (⌘-Shift-A) [Ctrl+Shift+A] and click the top path. Change the weight of the Stroke to 30 points. Lock the path and select the remaining path. Change the Stroke on this path to 42. The 30 points is 12 points more than the 18 points of the black Stroke, or 6 points on each side. The 42 points is 12 more than the white 30 points.

When you are creating parallel Strokes, determine how thick each of the visible Strokes should be, multiply that number times the black *and* white visible Strokes that you want for the base Stroke, and work up from there. For example, if you want 10-point Strokes, and there are four white Strokes and five black strokes, the first Stroke would be 90-points thick and Black. The next Stroke would be 70-point White, and then 50-points Black, 30-point White, and 10-point Black.

This example is just the tip of the iceberg in creating custom Strokes. Not only can you have paths that overlap, but you also can give the Stroke on each path different dash patterns, joins, and caps. You can even add Fills to certain paths to make the

Stroke different on both sides of the path. And if all of that isn't enough, you can use Outline Path to outline Strokes.

Knowing the secrets doesn't let you in on the really good stuff, though. Read on to learn how to apply these to achieve truly amazing effects with Strokes.

Using the Stroke Charts

The stroke charts in Figures 17-2 through 17-5 show how some of the basic Stroke-dash patterns look with various options checked, at different weights, and in different combinations.

All the paths in the charts were taken from an original shape that included a straight segment, a corner, and a curve. The charts should help you determine when to use certain types of Stroke patterns because, as you can see, some patterns work better than others with curves and corners.

The first chart (Figure 17-2) consists of thirty-two 3-point Stroke paths that have a variety of dash patterns and end and join attributes. The second chart (Figure 17-3) shows eighteen 10-point Stroke paths with similar attributes. These two charts show Stroke effects with only one path. The area in the middle of each path in the chart describes the path.

The third chart (Figure 17-4) and fourth chart (Figure 17-5) contain paths that have been copied on top of the original by using the Paste in Front command. The paths are listed in the order that they were created. The first path is described at the top of the list. The first path is copied, pasted in front (⌘-F) [Ctrl+F], and given the Paint Style attributes of the second item in the list. The changes progress from the top left of each chart to the bottom left and then from the top right to the bottom right.

In some cases, paths are blended from one to another. To be able to select an end point on each Stroke (usually they will overlap), offset one of the paths by .1 point. When blending, use a number that is less than 100 for the number of blend steps, dividing the suggested number by 2 until it is small enough.

When you're creating the various Stroke patterns, frequently the original path is selected, copied, and then pasted in front or back (⌘-F [Ctrl+F] or ⌘-B [Ctrl+B]) several times. There is usually no need to recopy the original path after it has been copied. You can continue to paste it again and again on top of or under the original path.

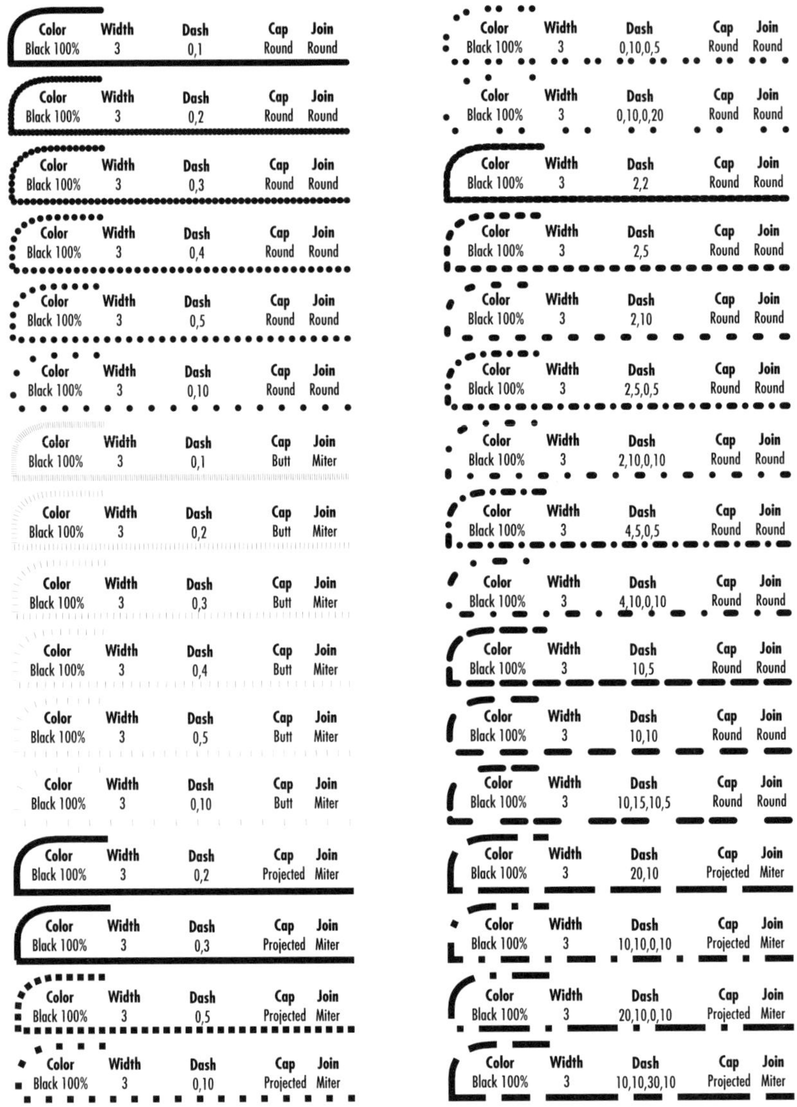

Figure 17-2: Thirty-two 3-point Stroke paths

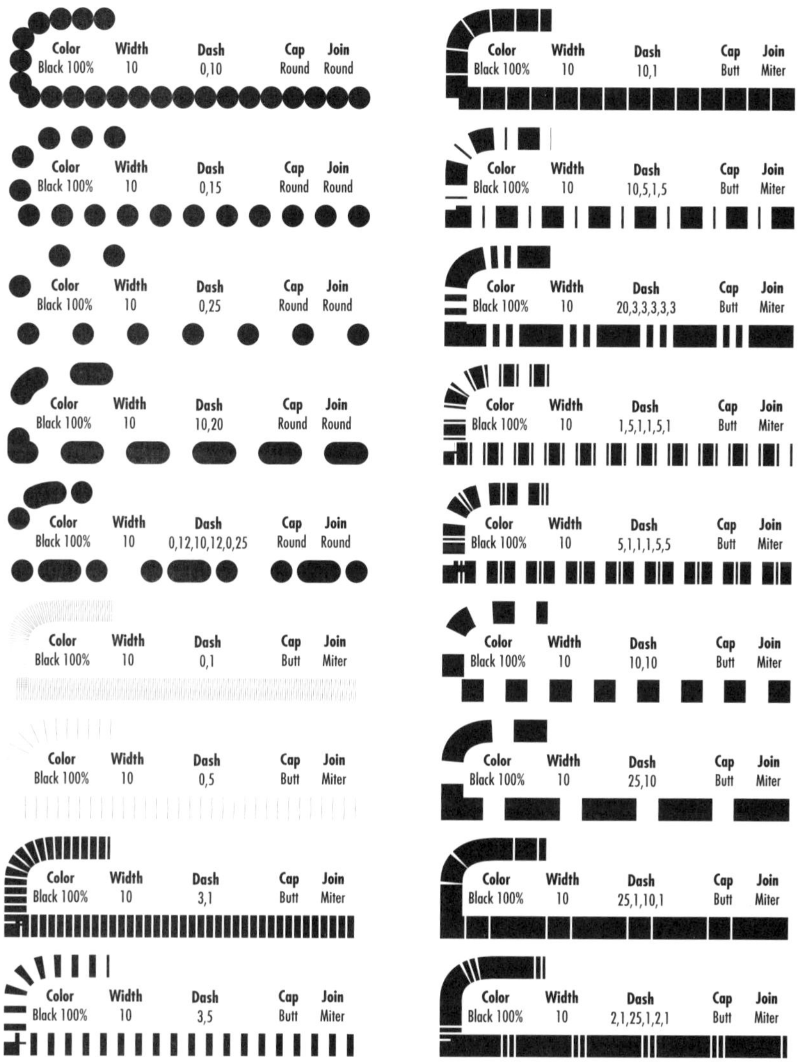

Figure 17-3: Eighteen 10-point Stroke paths

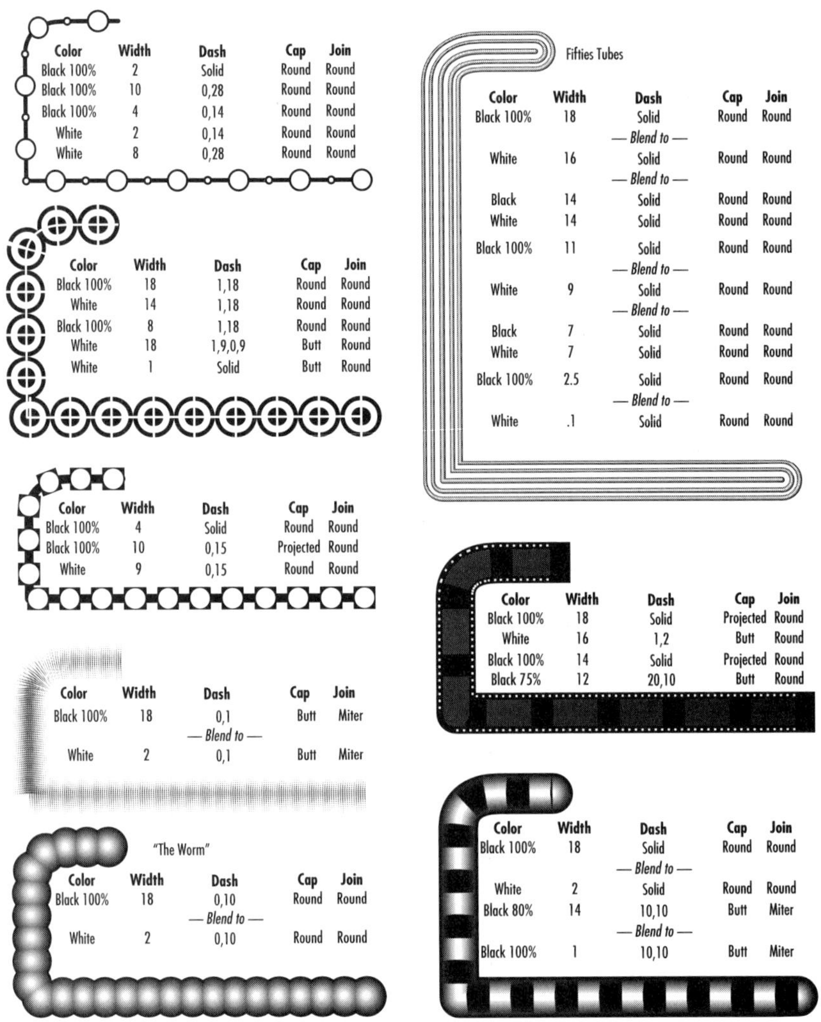

Figure 17-4: Paths that have been copied on top of the original paths

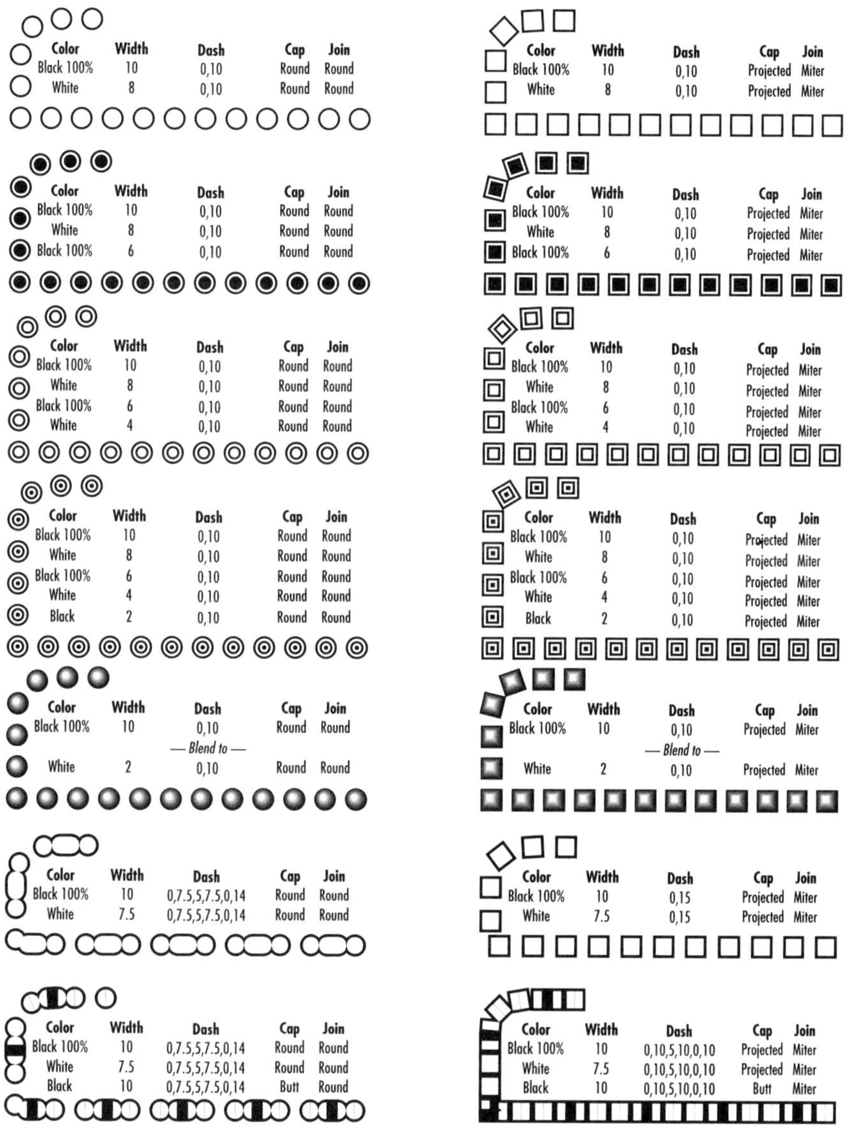

Figure 17-5: Another example of paths that have been copied on top of the original paths

In the middle of the right-hand column in the fourth stroke chart (Figure 17-5) is a Stroke that looks like a strip of film. The following steps describe how to create this film Stroke, which is a basic Stroke that produces a stunning effect.

STEPS: Creating a Film Stroke

Step 1. Draw a wavy path with the Pencil tool.

Step 2. Change the stroke of the path to Black, 18 points, and the Fill to None.

Step 3. Copy (⌘-C) [Ctrl+C] the path and choose Edit⇨Paste In Front (⌘-F) [Ctrl+F]. Change the Stroke to White, 16 points, and use a Dash Pattern of Dash 1, Gap 2.

Step 4. Choose Edit⇨Paste in Front (⌘-F) [Ctrl+F] again and change the Stroke to Black, 14 points, Solid.

Step 5. Choose Edit⇨Paste in Front (⌘-F) [Ctrl+F] one last time and change the Stroke to 75% Black, 12 points, with a Dash Pattern of Dash 20, Gap 10.

Figure 17-6 shows these steps. You can use this procedure to create any of the Strokes in the fourth Stroke chart (Figure 17-5) by substituting the values that are listed in the chart for the Stroke that you want.

Stroking Type

You can use Strokes to enhance type in a number of ways. The first example (shown in Figure 17-7) is based on Stroke blends. For more information on Stroke blends, see Chapter 10; for more information on type, see Chapter 8.

STEPS: Creating Ghosted Type with Strokes

Step 1. Type a few words in a heavily weighted font, like Helvetica Black, Futura Extra Bold, or Kabel Ultra.

Step 2. Select the type with the Selection tool. Choose Type⇨Create Outlines (⌘-Shift-O [Ctrl+Shift+O]) and change the Fill to None and the Stroke to Black or a light shade of gray. Change the weight of the Stroke to .1 point.

(continued)

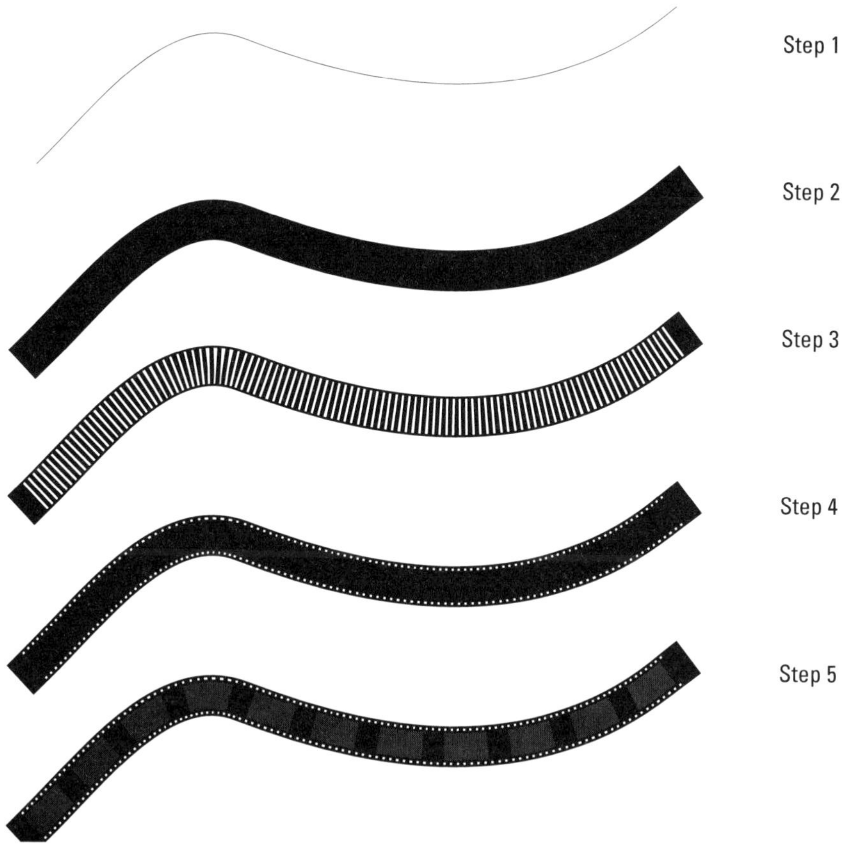

Figure 17-6: The steps for creating the film Stroke from Figure 17-5

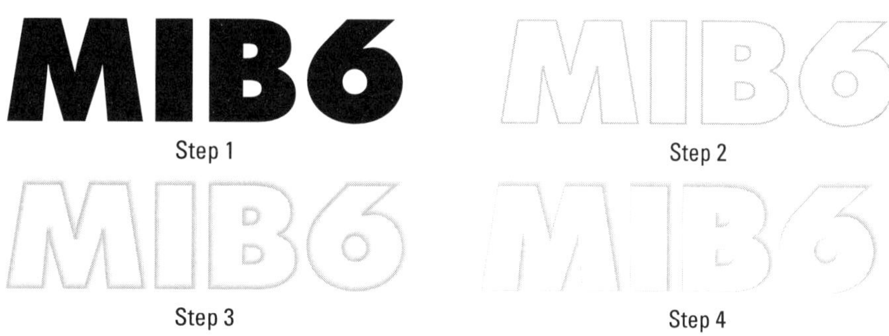

Figure 17-7: Steps for creating ghosted type

STEPS: *(continued)*

Step 3. Copy (⌘-C) [Ctrl+C] the words and choose Edit➪Paste in Back (⌘-B) [Ctrl+B]. Move the copy a few points up and to the right. Change the Stroke on the copy to 4-point White and blend each set of paths together with the Blend tool.

Step 4. Choose Edit➪Paste in Front (⌘-F) [Ctrl+F] and change the Fill to White and the Stroke to None.

Another popular effect (okay, it was popular in the '70s) for type is produced by creating several Strokes for each stroke of a letter, as described in the following steps and shown in Figure 17-8.

STEPS: Creating Type That Has Multiple Strokes

Step 1. Create a word or words in a lightweight typeface.

Step 2. Use the Pen tool to re-create the letters in the typeface. In Figure 17-8, I colored the letters in the original word light red and then locked those letters in place so that I could trace the letters more easily.

Step 3. Group all the paths that you have drawn and give them a heavy Stroke. (I used 18 points.) Change the join and cap style in the Stroke palette to rounded.

Step 4. Copy (⌘-C) [Ctrl+C] and paste in front (⌘-F) [Ctrl+F] in gradually decreasing Stroke weights. Change between white and a darker color as the weight decreases.

Creating Rough Edges

You can create some of the most interesting Stroke effects by using the Roughen filter in combination with a heavily weighted Stroke. Even with a Roughen filter setting of 1% or 2%, a heavily weighted Stroke can have many sharp, long points, as described in the following steps.

Figure 17-8: Making type that has multiple Strokes

STEPS: Using Strokes to Create Multiple Jagged Edges

Step 1. Create an object to which you want to add jagged or explosive edges. I used text that was converted to outlines in the example (see Figure 17-9). Copy the object off to the side before continuing.

Step 2. Use Offset Path to create a path that is offset by 20 points or more. Select all the paths and choose Object⇨Pathfinder⇨Unite.

(continued)

STEPS: ***(continued)***

Step 4. Paste in front one last time and roughen as before, but give the Stroke a lesser weight and Fill the path with the same color as the Stroke. Place the original art (which you copied off to the side in Step 1) on top of the roughened paths.

Using Fills to Create Half-Stroked Paths

One technique that I don't think is used enough is hiding one side of the Stroke as the path layers are built up. To hide half of the Stroke at any level, paste in front as you normally do and then press ⌘-Option-L [Ctrl+Alt+L]. This command locks everything that isn't selected; in other words, only the path that you just pasted (and which is currently selected) will not be locked.

Using the Pen tool, connect the ends of the just-pasted path and Fill it with the background color and a Stroke of None. This action obliterates one side of the Stroke because the file of the path covers the "inside" part of the Stroked path. Any Strokes that you place on top of this object will be visible on both sides of the path.

Workin' on the Railroad

Several effects that you can create with paths have a traveling theme, mainly because a path starts somewhere and finishes somewhere else. Railroad tracks, roads, highways, trails, and rivers all have a tendency to conform very nicely to Stroke effects with paths.

One of the trickiest traveling paths to create is railroad tracks. To get the real railroad-track look, some advanced cheating is necessary, as described in the following steps.

Figure 17-9: Creating roughened paths with Strokes

Just the Outside Edge?

Julie: I don't want to see the outside edge of my Stroke, only the inside.

Toulouse: There are a couple things you can do.

Julie: The easiest, please.

Toulouse: You know the path you can make on the inside of an object that knocks out the inside of a Stroke?

Julie: Yes, but I want to knock out the outside of the Stroke.

Toulouse: Select the overlapping inner path and the Stroked path, and choose Object⇨Mask⇨Make (⌘-7) [Ctrl+7]. The inside will be the only part that shows.

STEPS: Creating Railroad Tracks

Step 1. Draw a path to represent the railroad. Create a background shape and Fill the background with a color. In the example (see Figure 17-10), I used dark green.

Step 2. Copy the path. Give the path a Stroke weight of 30 points. Choose Edit⇨Paste In Front (⌘-F) [Ctrl+F] and give this path a Stroke weight of 20 points.

Step 3. Select both paths. Choose Object⇨Path⇨Outline Path to change the paths into outlined paths because Strokes cannot contain gradients. Fill the paths with a metallic gradient.

Step 4. Select both paths and choose Object⇨Pathfinder⇨Exclude. This command subtracts the inner section of the track from the two outer sections.

Step 5. Check the ends of the path and delete any excess paths that are not part of the tracks. In the example, I also joined the ends on each individual track.

Step 6. Paste in back (⌘-B) [Ctrl+B] and give the new path a Stroke weight of 40 points. Choose Object⇨Path⇨Outline Stroke and Fill this path with a gradient consisting of several woodlike browns. This path is the wood that underlies the tracks.

Step 7. The last thing to do is split the pieces of wood into individual railroad ties. Select the wood path and choose Edit⇨Paste in Front (⌘-F) [Ctrl+F]. This command pastes a path right on top of the wooden area. Give this Stroke the same color as the background and give it a Dash Pattern of Dash 20, Gap 10. The gaps will be the see-through areas, showing the wood-filled path below them.

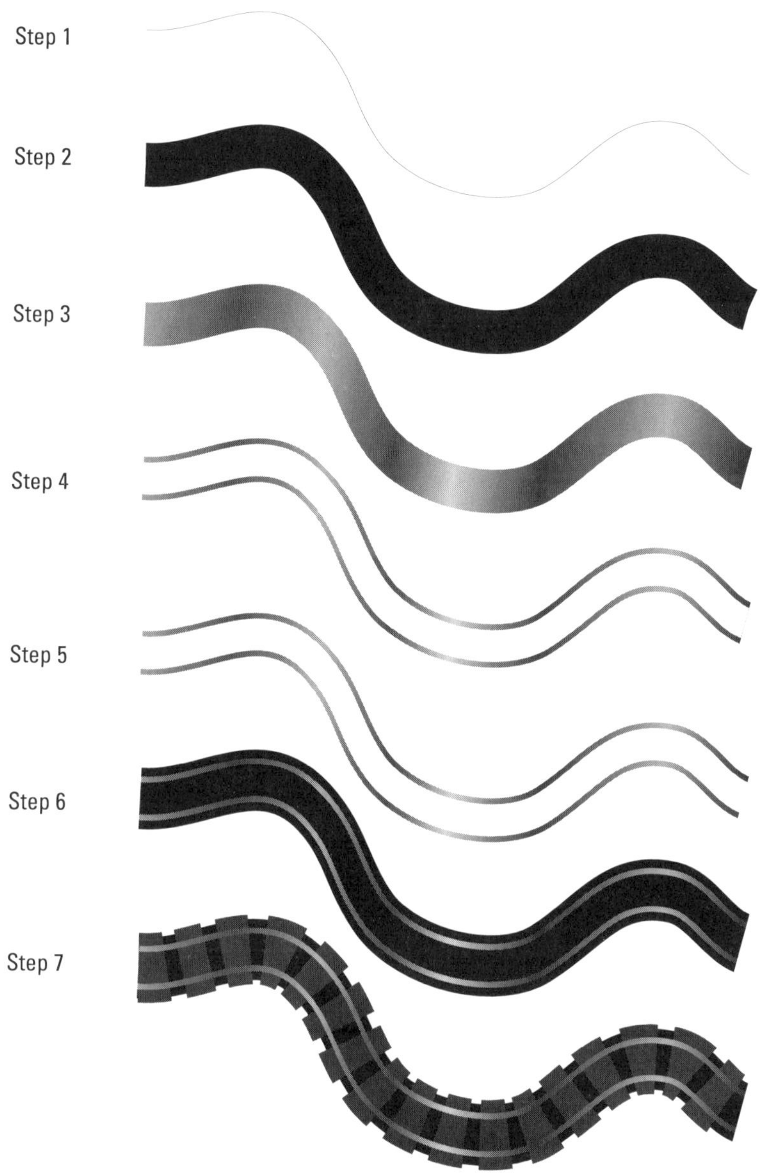

Figure 17-10: Steps for creating railroad tracks

To change the color of the new path in Step 7 easily, select the new path, choose the Eyedropper tool, and click the background.

Outline Path is often used on this type of Stroke design because Strokes can't have gradient Fills. The reason that the railroad ties were not given a dash pattern before Outline Path was applied is that Outline Path doesn't work with dash patterns.

The Wild River

A wild river is another path that you can create easily by using Strokes. One problem in getting rivers to look good is that creating the rough, in-out texture of a river's bank is difficult. Also, because different parts of rivers are different weights, connecting the parts smoothly is difficult. The following steps describe how to create a river.

STEPS: Creating a River

Step 1. Draw the paths for the river. In the example (see Figure 17-11), I created a Y at one end of the river and an island. For these features, I used the Pen tool to draw additional paths next to the river.

Step 2. Give the river a Stroke weight and color. In the example, I gave the main part of the river a Stroke of 18 points and the two additional parts 14-point Strokes. Copy all the paths, paste in front, and color the copy a little darker than the original river Stroke color. Make the Strokes on the copy a few points less wide than on the original.

Step 3. Blend the two Strokes together, using three blend steps.

Step 4. Select all of the Strokes and choose Object⇨Path⇨Outline Path. Select one of the new paths and choose Edit⇨Select⇨Same Fill Color. Choose Object⇨Pathfinder⇨Unite. Repeat this process for each of the five different colors.

Step 5. Select all of the paths and choose Filter⇨Distort⇨Roughen. In the Roughen dialog box, enter **.3** and **40** segments per inch and then click OK. The edges of the river are now a little ragged, and they appear to have ripples, or waves, in them.

The Highway

Figures 17-12 and 17-13 show a Stroke design that I discovered a few years back while I was playing around with Illustrator. It has the makings of a cute parlor magic trick that you can use to impress your friends. Back when you had to work in Artwork mode, before Illustrator 5.0, creating designs with Strokes was much more difficult. Artists couldn't see what they were drawing on-screen, so they had to envision it in their minds. Editing dashes and weights is almost a pleasure now that you can use the Stroke palette and undo multiple changes.

After creating the Railroad Tracks Stroke design, which I thought was pretty clever, I yearned for a similar effect — turning one path into some form of artwork. I especially liked the effect of doing several paths and several Stroke attributes in Artwork mode and then switching to Preview mode when I was finished.

Figures 17-12 and 17-13 show the steps that you take to create a four-lane highway by drawing just one path. These steps are described after the figures.

Figure 17-11: Steps for making a river

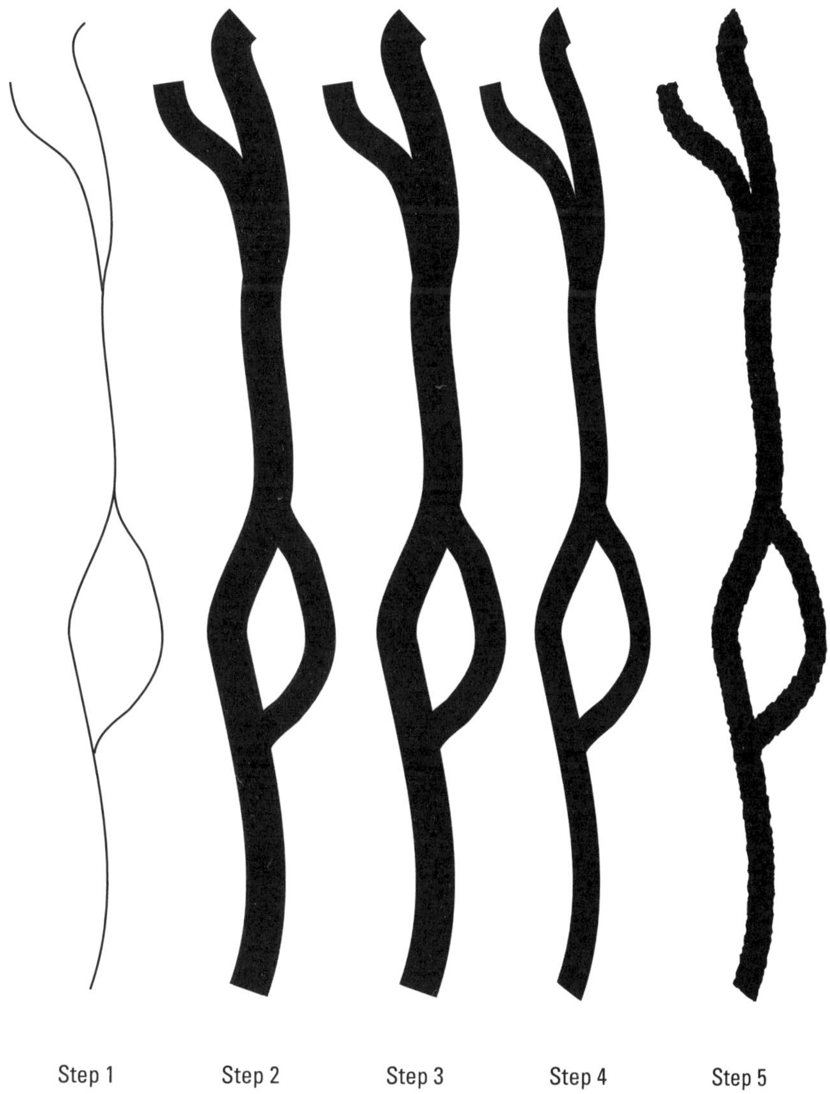

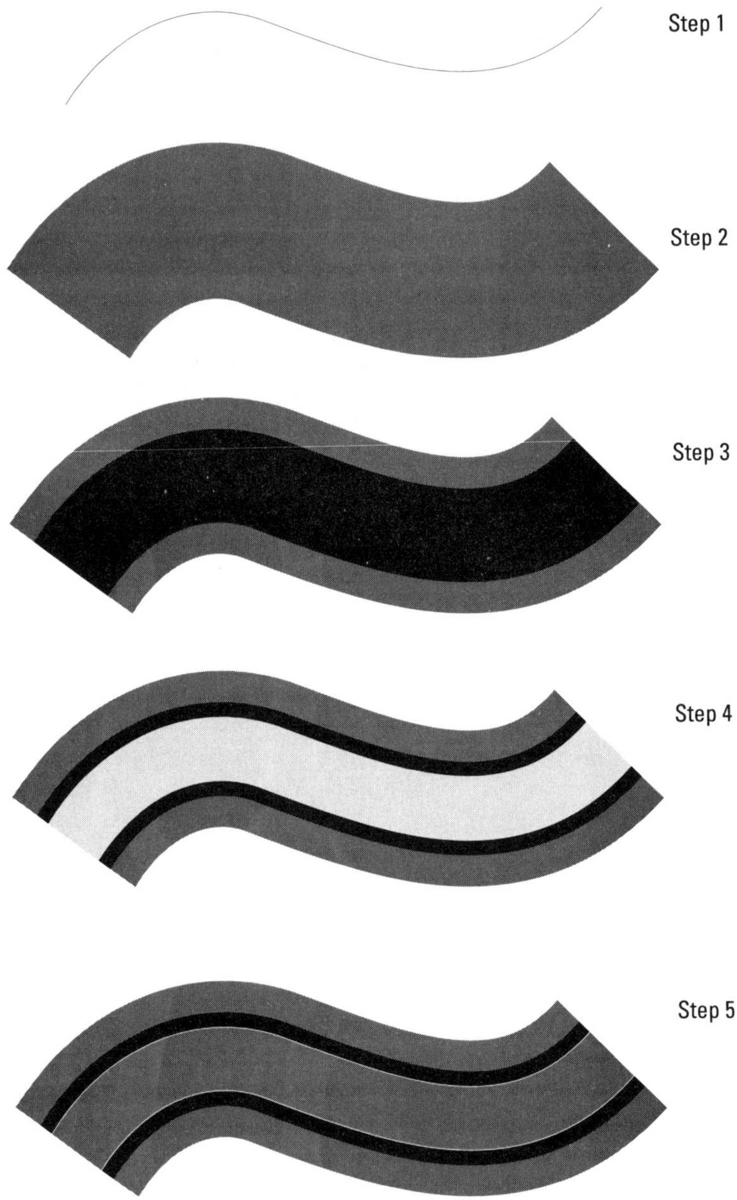

Figure 17-12: The first five steps in creating a highway

Figure 17-13: The last four steps in creating a highway

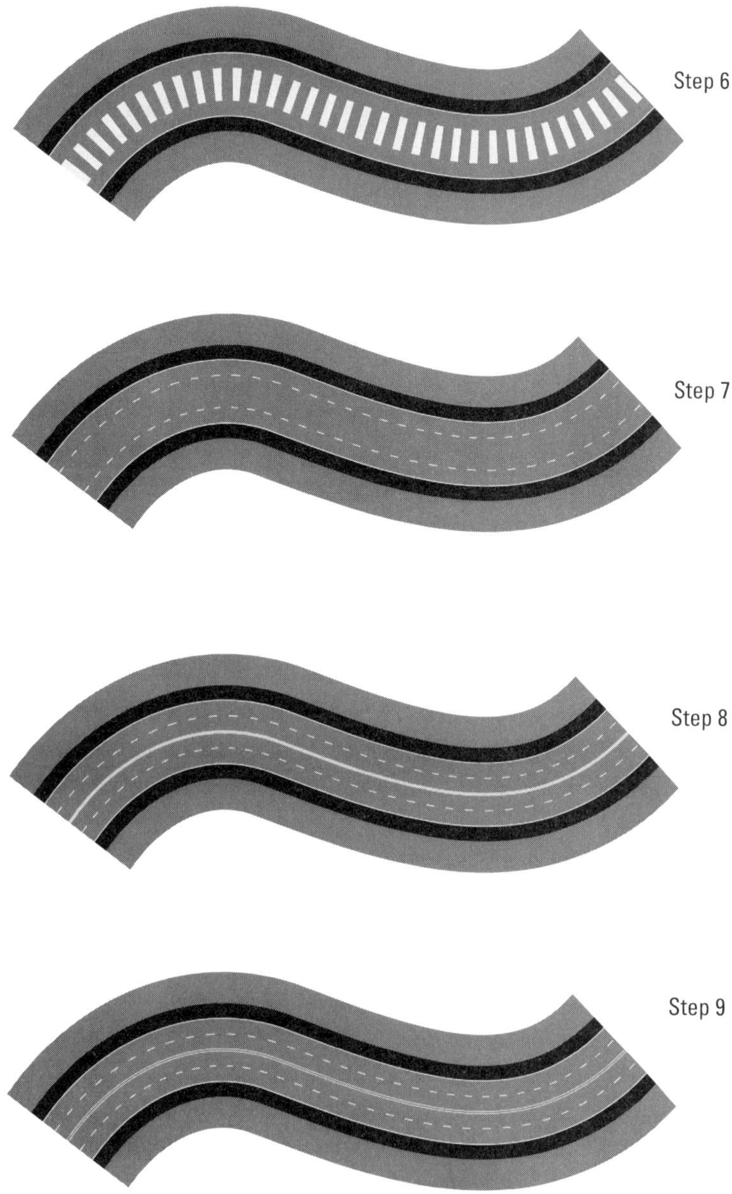

STEPS: Creating a Highway

Step 1. Use the Pencil tool to draw a slightly wavy path from the left side of the Artboard to the right side and then group the path.

Step 2. Change the Path to a Fill of None and create a 400-point Stroke that is colored as follows: Cyan 100, Magenta 25, and Yellow 100. This path is the grass next to the highway.

Step 3. Copy the path and paste in front. Change the paint style of the stroke to Cyan 25, Yellow 25, and Black 85, with a weight of 240 points. This path is the shoulder of the highway.

Step 4. Paste in front and change the paint style to Cyan 5 and Black 10, with a weight of 165 points. This path is the white line at the edge of the highway.

Step 5. Paste in front and change the paint style to Cyan 15, Yellow 10, and Black 50, with a weight of 160 points. This path is the highway's road surface.

Step 6. To create the dashed white lines for passing, paste in front and change the paint style to Cyan 5 and Black 10, with a weight of 85 points, a dash of 20, and a gap of 20.

Step 7. Paste in front and change the paint style to Cyan 15, Yellow 10, and Black 50, with a weight of 80 points. This path is the inner part of the highway's road surface.

Step 8. To create the double yellow line, paste in front and change the paint style to Cyan 15, Magenta 20, and Yellow 100, with a weight of 8 points.

Step 9. Paste in front and change the paint style to Cyan 15, Yellow 10, and Black 50, with a weight of 3 points. This path is the piece of highway that divides the double yellow line.

With Outline Path, I've taken the highway concept a step or two further by adding a passing zone to the highway. Use the following steps and the illustration in Figure 17-14 to create the passing zone.

STEPS: Adding a Passing Zone to the Highway

Step 1. Delete the top two paths of the original highway. Select all the paths and choose Arrange⇨Hide Selection (⌘-U) to hide the base of the road temporarily. You don't need to change anything about these parts of the highway to create the passing zone effect.

Step 2. Paste in front and change the paint style to Cyan 15, Magenta 20, and Yellow 100, with a weight of 8 points. This path is the same double yellow line as the one in Step 8 of the preceding instructions, but it is not yet split.

Step 3. Copy and paste in front. Keep the paint style at Cyan 15, Magenta 20, and Yellow 100 but change the weight to 3 points. This line is the same width as the road from Step 9 in the preceding instructions, but the color is the double-yellow-line color.

Step 4. Choose All (⌘-A) [Ctrl+A]. This command selects the last two paths that you placed on the illustration. Choose Object⇨Path⇨Outline Stroke. This command creates outlines around the edges of the Stroke so that it results in two Filled objects instead of two overlapping Stroked paths.

Step 5. Choose Object⇨Pathfinder⇨Exclude. This command subtracts the top object (the 3-point path) from the bottom one, resulting in two Filled objects that are grouped together. Ungroup the two objects by choosing Object⇨Ungroup (⌘-Shift-G).

Step 6. Deselect one of the two paths by Shift-clicking it once and deleting the selected object.

Step 7. Paste in front to put the line with the double yellow-line Stroke in front of the remaining Filled object. Change the paint style to Dash 20, Gap 20.

Step 8. Paste in front and change the paint style to Cyan 15, Yellow 10, and Black 50, with a weight of 3 points. These settings create a gray line that divides the dashed section from the solid section of line. The dashed section is actually on both sides of the 3-point gray divider line, but you cannot see the part that overlays the solid line because it is the same color and size as the solid line.

Step 9. Choose Object⇨Show All. The highway now has a dashed/solid yellow line.

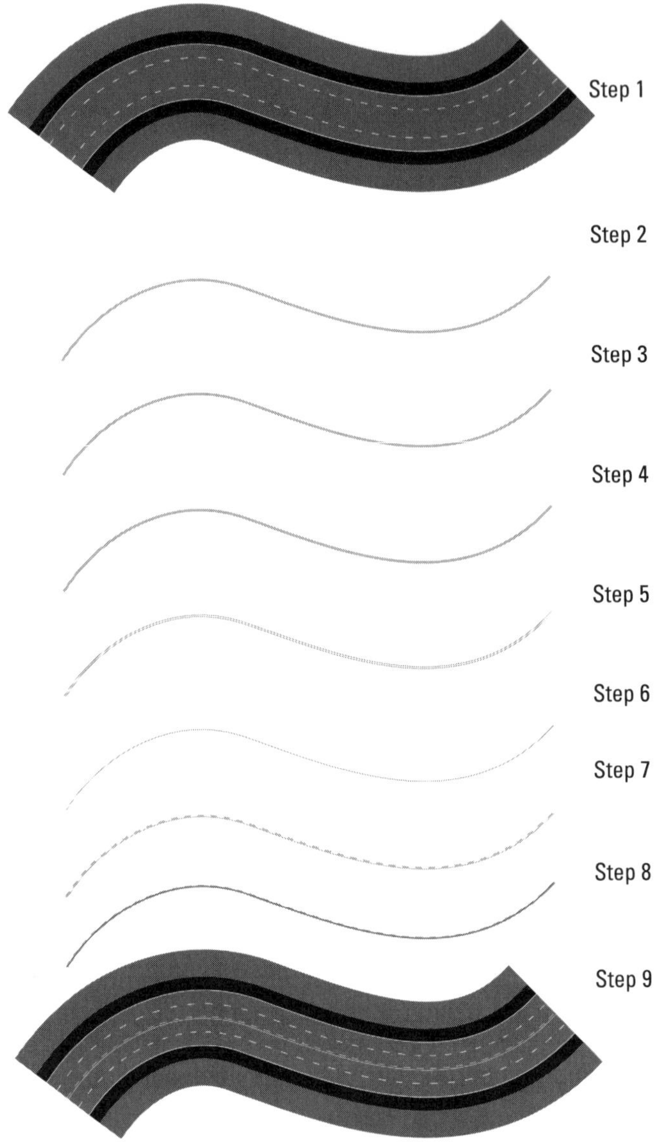

Figure 17-14: Steps for creating a passing zone for the highway

Putting Type into Strokes

You can put type into Strokes by creating Path type and giving the path a heavy enough Stroke weight to surround the type, as described in the following steps. Using symbols and special typefaces, you can create almost any pattern when you put type inside Strokes. (For more information on creating Path type, see Chapter 8.)

STEPS:	Making Type into a Stroke Pattern
Step 1.	Draw the path upon which you want the type to appear.
Step 2.	Click the path with the Path Type tool. Type the letters, numbers, or symbols that will make up the pattern.
Step 3.	Select the characters, copy, and paste. Paste until the path is full of characters.
Step 4.	Using the Type tool, change the Fill on the characters; using the Group Selection tool, change the Stroke of the path.

If you are blessed to own font-creation software, such as Macromedia Fontographer, you can achieve even better results. Simply incorporate any artwork that you create in Illustrator into a font and then use that artwork as Path type by using that font when you type.

Incredibly Intricate Strokes

Unfortunately, what you can do with Strokes is limited to the Stroke palette's options. Sometimes you'll wish you could do just a little bit more with strokes. That's where Path Patterns come in. Path Patterns is a filter that enables you to place patterns on Strokes. These patterns increase in proportions as the Stroke changes shape. Path patterns are discussed in Chapter 11.

Stroked Type in Strokes?

Barbara: Can I put Stroked type on a Stroke?

Toulouse: Sure. In fact, if you do it right, you can put Stroked type on Stroked type that's on a stroke.

Barbara: Really?

Toulouse: And so on....

Summary

- The most attractive aspect of Strokes is that they can be used together, on top of one another.
- The Stroke charts provided in this chapter show some of the possibilities of what can be done with Strokes.
- When you Stroke type, be sure to put another copy of the Filled text on top of the Stroked type.
- Use Outline Path to create Filled paths out of Strokes.
- Use Fills to create half-Stroked paths.

Printing, Separations, and Traps

CHAPTER 18

In This Chapter

- Understanding the difference between composites and separations
- Determining when to use process versus spot color separations
- Printing separations out of Illustrator
- Understanding line screens
- Printing separations from other programs
- Understanding trapping
- Using Pathfinder Trap
- Trapping after you create an image in Illustrator

You can print Illustrator documents in two ways: as a composite, which is a single printout containing all the colors and tints used; and as a series of color separations, a printout for each color. Color separations are necessary for illustrations that will be printed on a printing press.

Prior to Printing

Before you start the printing process, there are a number of things that might need to be changed or adjusted. For instance, you might need to change the page size and orientation, or set how certain colors will separate. This section deals with the issues you should be aware of *before* you go ahead and press ⌘-P [Ctrl+P] and send your file to the printer.

Windows Update

Printing has come a long way in a few years, with the most obvious change being in the Separation Setup box, which allows for printing separations from within Illustrator (Version 4 required a separate application — Adobe Separator — for printing separations of Illustrator documents).

What's Missing	What Replaces It
Adobe Separator	File⇨Separation Setup
Overprint option in Paint Style dialog box	Overprint option in Attributes palette

What's New

Object⇨Pathfinder⇨Trap for manually trapping between objects

Document Setup

Choosing File⇨Document Setup (⌘-Shift-D) [Ctrl+Shift+D] enables you to set the initial page size of an illustration via the Artboard. Bringing up the Document Setup dialog box (shown in Figure 18-1) displays a wealth of options that assist in printing. If the Use Page Setup box is checked, then the Artboard size is relative to the size of the page that is selected in the Page Setup dialog box. If the Artboard is smaller than the printable page, then anything entirely outside the edges of the Artboard will be cropped off when you print the illustration through Illustrator. Any objects that are partially on the Artboard will print. Anything outside the Artboard will print when you print the illustration through another application.

Another option in the Document Setup dialog box enables you to choose whether patterns will preview and print. Unchecking this box prevents patterns from printing when you print the illustration from Illustrator.

The Page Tiling options also affect the way that pages appear when a document is printed from Illustrator:

- If you choose Tile imageable areas, a grid appears on the Artboard. Any block of the grid that has a piece of the illustration will print. When this option is chosen, you can specify in the Print dialog box that only certain pages should be printed.

Figure 18-1: The Document Setup dialog box

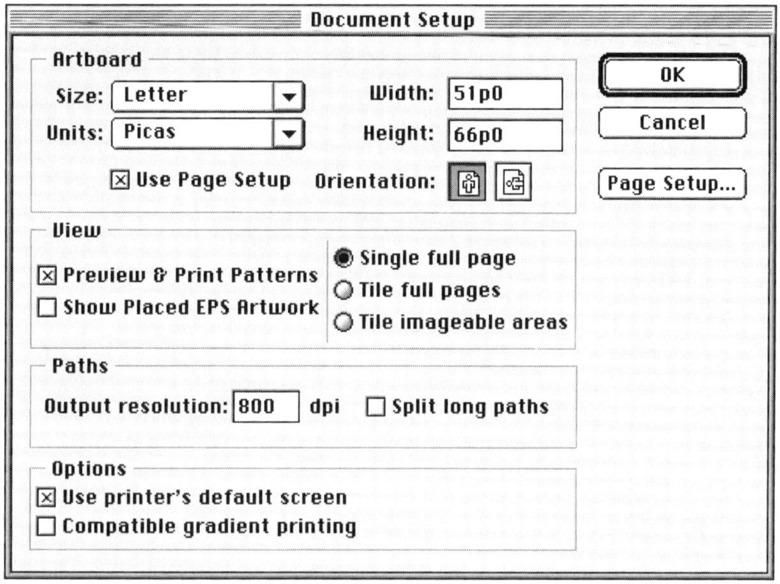

- If you choose Tile full pages, only full pages (as defined in the Page Setup dialog box) that appear on the Artboard will print. If no full pages can fit in the Artboard, everything in the Artboard will print.
- If you choose Single full page, only one page will print.

Page Setup (Macintosh)

The Page Setup dialog box (accessed through the Page Setup button in the Document Setup dialog box), shown in Figure 18-2, is used for specifying printing options when printing out a composite image.

Figure 18-2: The Page Setup dialog box

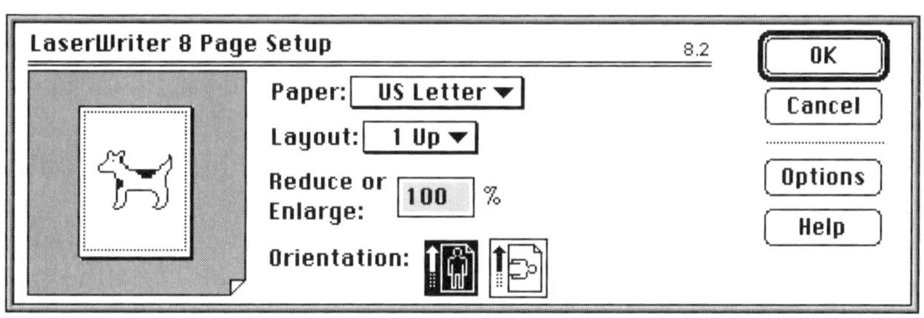

The printing options on this dialog box are:

- **Paper:** You can choose any paper size, even one that your printer does not have the capacity to use. The Tabloid option is the first option in a set of choices in a pop-up menu that also lists envelope sizes and positions. The size that you choose shows up on the document as a dotted-line boundary when the Tile full pages or Single full pages options are selected in the Document Setup dialog box. Another dotted-line boundary, inside the page-size boundary, is the printable area. The printable area is also displayed when the Tile imagable areas option is selected in the Document Setup dialog box.
- **Layout:** The Layout pop-up menu displays options of how many pages from the document can fit on the printed page. If you choose any option other than 1-Up (other options are only available with LaserWriter 8 and higher), the printed pages are scaled and reoriented so that the pages are printed at the largest possible size.
- **Reduce or Enlarge:** This option affects how much the page that the illustration is on is scaled when it's printed. Reducing or enlarging affects the way that the dotted-line page boundaries and imageable-areas dotted lines appear in the document. A value above 100% will make the page smaller, while a value less than 100% will make the page and its boundaries larger. This feature is helpful when you want to print everything that's on a large Artboard. If you select a reduced size in the Page Setup dialog box, the dotted lines in the document reflect the reduced size.
- **Orientation.** This option controls how the image is printed on the printed page — whether it is printed in portrait orientation (longest side vertical) or landscape orientation (longest side horizontal).

If you click the Options button, the Page Setup Options dialog box appears, as shown in Figure 18-3.

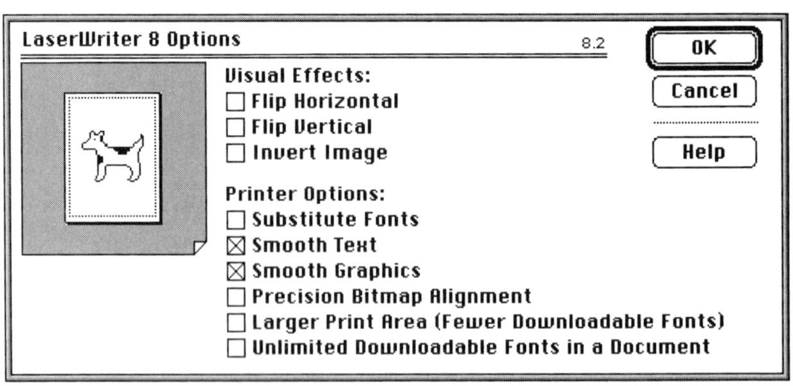

Figure 18-3: The Page Setup Options dialog box

The options on the dialog box are as follows:

- **Flip Horizontal:** This option causes the document to print as a mirror image of itself, flipped horizontally. You can use it in combination with the Invert Image option to print negatives from Illustrator.
- **Flip Vertical:** This option causes the document to print as a mirror image of itself, flipped vertically. You can also use this option in combination with the Invert Image option to print negatives from Illustrator. Using the Flip Horizontal and Flip Vertical options together causes the document to rotate 180°.
- **Invert Image:** This option prints a negative image of the illustration, where all white areas are black and all black areas are white.
- **Substitute Fonts:** Illustrator has built-in workarounds for font problems, and supposedly this check box may be irrelevant to Illustrator users. For other programs, this option replaces any bitmapped fonts with corresponding fonts that are installed on the printer, which usually means that if you have Geneva, New York, and Monaco installed in bitmapped format only, Helvetica, Times, and Courier will take their places. Any other bitmapped font will usually be replaced with Courier. In general, if you don't have the PostScript printer font or the font in TrueType format, you shouldn't use that font with Adobe Illustrator, and you shouldn't check this box.
- **Smooth Text:** When Substitute Fonts is not checked and an illustration has a bitmapped font in it, Smooth Text will make the bitmapped font look slightly better. It will still look bad, but it will look better than just the plain bitmapped font.

Color to Black and White?

Charles: Is there an easy way to make my color documents black and white *before* I print them?

Toulouse: Yes. It's quite simple.

Charles: It's something I do all the time.

Toulouse: Okay. Removing the color (cyan, magenta, or yellow) doesn't even come close to working, of course.

Charles: So what can I do?

Toulouse: The easiest thing to do is to choose Filter⇨Color⇨Convert to Gray-scale.

Charles: How does it work?

Toulouse: You select the art you want the color sucked out of, and then choose the filter, and Boom!, it's done.

Charles: Wow.

Toulouse: If you need more control, KPT ColorTweak, which is part of KPT Vector Effects, lets you specify the amount of gray.

- **Smooth Graphics:** Smooth Graphics does about the same thing that Smooth Text does, but it does it to graphics. Because this feature works only with PICT and Paint images, which you cannot print in Illustrator, you should not check this option.
- **Precision Bitmap Alignment:** This option resamples bitmapped graphics so that they print better at the resolution of your printer.
- **Larger Print Area (Fewer Downloadable Fonts):** This option increases the print area of the document so that it prints closer to the edge of the page. On a standard 8.5" x 11" Apple LaserWriter, not having this box checked results in margins that are approximately 1/2" on each edge. Checking this box changes the margins to 1/4" on the 11" edges and about 1/8" on the 8.5" edges. Of course, this extra printing area takes up a significant amount of printer RAM, so you may have trouble printing complex documents when this option is checked.
- **Unlimited Downloadable Fonts in a Document:** Checking this box interferes with Illustrator's own downloading mechanism. You shouldn't check it when printing from Illustrator. When printing from other programs, this option does more than enable you to use lots of fonts. Checking Unlimited Downloadable Fonts in programs *other* than Illustrator makes the RAM in the laser printer adjustable. As part of the document comes in and is processed, the information that was used to process that part of the document and the fonts that were needed to print it are flushed out of memory. The next section and its needed fonts are then loaded. This method takes longer than loading all of the fonts in the entire document at one time and then processing the document, but it prevents out-of-memory printing errors when printing from programs like QuarkXPress.

Print Setup (Windows)

The Print Setup box (accessed by clicking the Print Setup button in the Document Setup dialog box) contains Print Setup options that are specific to your printer. The Print Setup dialog box is shown in Figure 18-4. Clicking the Properties button displays a plethora of options for customizing page size and other print properties.

Printing Composites

A composite printout looks very much like the image that appears on the screen when you preview the document (choose View⇨Preview or press ⌘-Y [Ctrl+Y]). If you have a color printer, the image appears in color; otherwise, the colors are replaced by gray tints (see the next section, "Gray Colors").

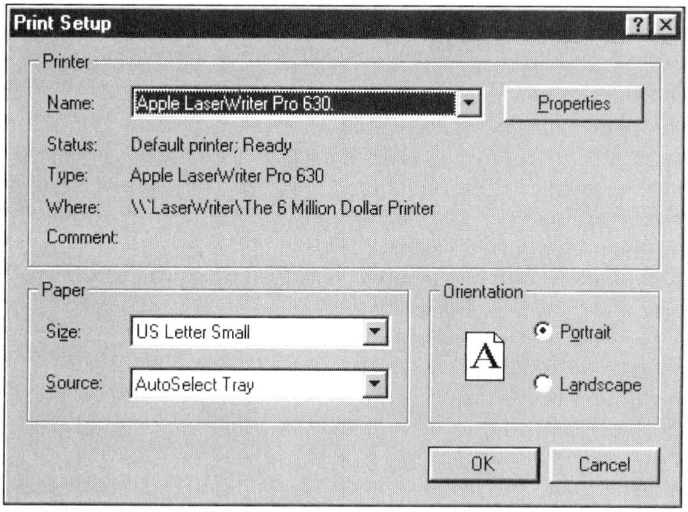

Figure 18-4: The Windows Print Setup dialog box

Objects that are hidden or that exist on layers that are currently hidden will not print, and neither will objects that exist on layers that have the printing option unchecked in the Layers Option dialog box.

The final printing step is to choose File⇨Print (⌘-P) [Ctrl+P]. This action opens the Print dialog box (the Mac version is shown in Figure 18-5: the Windows version in Figure 18-6), in which you may choose which pages to print, how many of each to print, and a few other options. If you click the Cancel button (⌘-period [Ctrl+ period]), the dialog box disappears, and no pages are printed. To Print, click the Print button or press Return or Enter.

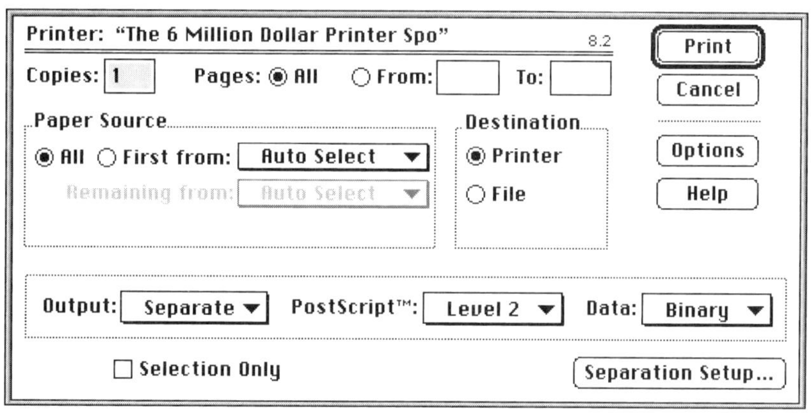

Figure 18-5: The Macintosh Print dialog box

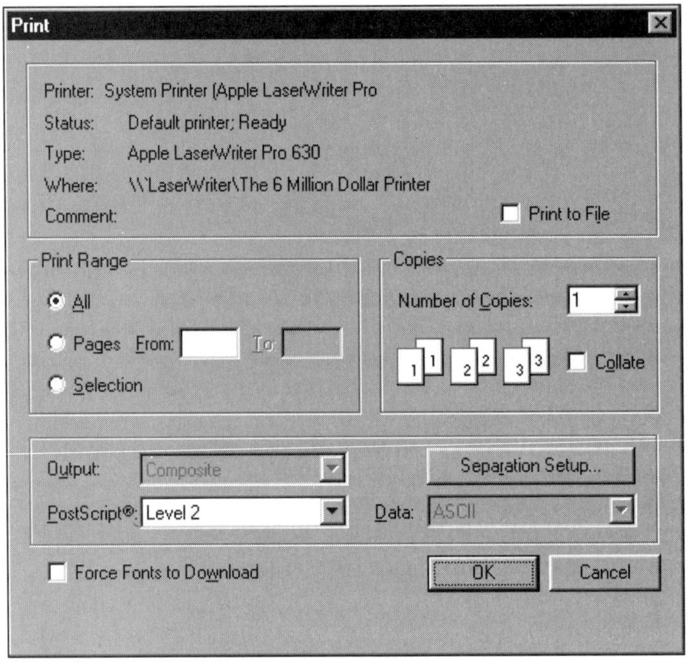

Figure 18-6: The Windows Print dialog box

The Print dialog box contains the following options:

- **Copies:** The number that you enter here determines how many copies of each page will print. All copies of a single page are printed at one time, so if you enter **4** when you are printing a four-page document, you get four copies of page 1, then four copies of page 2, and so on.
- **Pages:** If you check the All button, all the pages that have art on them will print. If you enter numbers in the From and To fields, only the pages that those numbers refer to will print. (Print Range in Windows)
- **Paper Source:** If Paper cassette (the default) is selected, all pages will print on paper from the printer's cassette. If Manual Feed is selected, then the pages will print on paper from the manual feed tray. (Mac only)
- **Destination:** Choosing Printer prints the document to the laser printer as usual. Choosing File prints the document to a PostScript file on the hard disk that you can download to a laser printer at a future time by using a utility such as Font Downloader or LaserWriter Font Utility. A PostScript file can also be used with Acrobat Distiller or Adobe ScreenReady. (Mac only)
- **Output:** This option determines if the illustration is printed as a composite or divided up into individual color separations.

- **PostScript:** This pop-up menu enables you to specify the PostScript interpreter (Level 1 or Level 2) that is included in your Laser Printer.

  Selecting Level 1 may eliminate various PostScript errors when printing to an older printer.

- **Data:** Keep this option on Binary, unless you have a really really old printer that only understands PostScript data in ASCII format.
- **Selection Only:** This handy little option allows for printing just the selected objects instead of the entire document. (Mac only)
- **Separation Setup:** This button opens the Separation Setup dialog box, discussed in detail later in this chapter.

If you click the Options button, the Print Options dialog box appears, as shown in Figure 18-7.

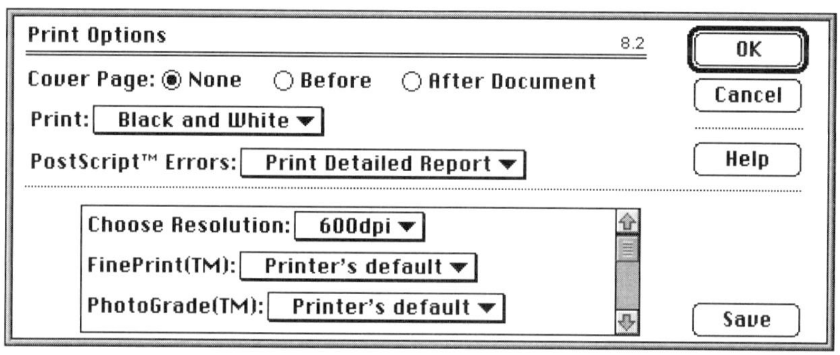

Figure 18-7: The Print Options dialog box

The options in this dialog box are as follows:

- **Cover Page:** If you choose First Page or Last Page, a separate sheet, which contains information about the name of the computer, the name of the file, the number of pages, and the dates, will print. This feature is useful for making each print job easily identifiable when several people share a laser printer.
- **Print:** This option has no effect when printing from Illustrator. From other programs, this option determines the way that documents will print to color or grayscale printers. If Black and White is chosen, no gray or color pixels will print, just patterns of black-and-white pixels. Illustrator writes its own PostScript and overrides this option, regardless of what is checked.
- **PostScript Errors:** This option allows for a detailed report to be printed when a PostScript error of some sort occurs.

  Always select Print Detailed Report. When an illustration will not print, a sheet of paper will come out of the printer with the error message on it.

- **Other Options:** The options in the lower section are specific to your printer. For instance, the printer information shown in the dialog box in Figure 18-7 is for an Apple LaserWriter Pro 630. Some of the other possible options are the resolution (300 or 600), and whether FinePrint and Photograde are turned on.

CAUTION

Always do a save before you print. Severe problems, when they happen, usually occur when you are printing. Don't let your unsaved document fall victim to one of those severe problems.

Gray Colors

When you are printing a full-color illustration to a black-and-white printer, Illustrator substitutes gray values for colors. In this way, the program creates the illusion that each color has a separate, distinct gray value.

Of course, each color can't have its own unique gray value, so the colors have to overlap at some point. Illustrator converts each of the process colors into specific gray values when it prints to a black-and-white printer.

Magenta is the darkest process color, ranging from 0% to 73% gray. Therefore, at 100% magenta, it prints at 73% gray. Cyan is second darkest, ranging from 0% to 57% gray. Yellow is extremely light, ranging from 0% to only 11% gray. Figure 18-8 shows a comparison of the four process colors at various settings and their printed results. The four bars show different values for each process color, as indicated above the bars. Within each bar is the percent of black that prints when you are printing that color at that percentage to a black-and-white printer.

Figure 18-8: How colors appear when printed on a black-and-white laser printer

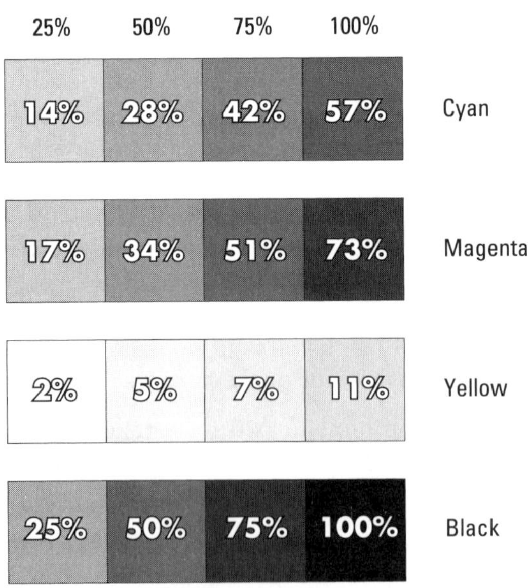

Different printers may produce different tints of gray. Lower-resolution printers, such as 300-dpi laser printers, do not create an accurate gray tint because they use dots that are too large to create accurate tint patterns.

Printing Color Separations

Color separations are necessary for printing a color version of an illustration on most printing presses. Each separation creates a plate that is affixed to a round drum on a printing press. Ink that is the same color as that separation is applied to the plate, which is pressed against a sheet of paper. Because the ink adheres only to the printing areas of the plate, an image is produced on paper. Some printing presses have many different drums and can print a four-color job in one run. Other printing presses have only one or two drums, so the paper has to pass through the press four or two times, respectively, to print a four-color job.

The two types of color separation are process color separation and spot color separation. Each type has its own advantages and drawbacks, and you can use either type or a combination of both types for any print job.

POWER TIP

You should always determine which type of separation you want *before* you begin to create a job electronically.

Spot Color Separation

Jobs that are printed with spot colors are often referred to as two-color or three-color jobs when two or three colors are used. Although you can use any number of colors, most spot color jobs contain only a few colors.

Spot color printing is most useful when you are using two or three distinct colors in a job. For example, if I needed only black and green to create a certain illustration, I would use only black and a green custom color for all of the objects in the illustration.

Learning Printing from the Experts

If you have never visited a printing company, make a point to visit one and take a tour. Most printing companies have staff members who are more than willing to explain their equipment and various printing processes. In a 30-minute tour with a knowledgeable guide, you can learn enough to save yourself hours of work, money, and misunderstandings.

When you are talking to a printing rep, find out what type of media they want your work on. Printing companies commonly have imagesetters that can output the job for you, and some companies even perform this service at no charge or for a significant discount if you have the job printed there.

Imagesetters are similar to laser printers, except that they produce images with a very high dpi, from 1,273 to 3,600, and sometimes higher. Imagesetters can print directly to RC (resin-coated) paper or to film negatives (or positives). The paper or film runs through the imagesetter and then must run through a developing process for the images and text to appear.

Most printing company salespeople are fluent to a minor degree in desktop publishing–speak, though few will know the difference between a TIFF and an EPS. They can tell you when to give them negs (film negatives) and paper and which service bureau to use if they don't have an imagesetter in-house. Many of them can tell you which software their clients prefer and which software packages create problems, and they can give you tips that can help you get your project through smoothly.

A service bureau is a company that has on its premises an imagesetter, and whose function is to provide the general community of desktop publishers with imagesetter output for a cost between $7 and $40 per page. Service bureaus often have color output capabilities, offer disk-conversion services, and other services that are sometimes needed by desktop publishers.

Better yet, do what I did: work at a printing company for a short period of time. The first job I had out of college, working in the prepress department of a four-color commercial printer, taught me more than I learned in four years of school. The experience instilled in me some of the most important basic skills for graphics design that I still use and need every day. Ever wonder why your printer gets so grumpy when you say your negs won't be available until two days past the promised date? Working at a printing company can give you an understanding of job scheduling, an art of prophecy and voodoo that givers ulcers to printing company managers and supervisors.

The more you know about printing and your printer, the better your print job will turn out, and the fewer hassles you will have to deal with.

There are three main reasons for using spot color separation, rather than process color separation:

- It's cheaper. Spot color printing requires a smaller press with fewer drums. For process color separation, you usually need to use a press with four drums or run the job through a smaller press a number of times.
- Spot colors are cleaner, brighter, and smoother than the same colors that you create as process colors. To get a green process color, for example, you need to mix both cyan and yellow on paper. Using one spot color will result in a perfectly solid area of color.
- You cannot duplicate certain spot colors, especially fluorescent and metallic colors, with process colors.

Illustrator creates spot colors whenever you specify a spot color in a swatch. If you use six different spot colors and Black, you could print out seven different spot color separations.

Spot colors also have their limitations and disadvantages, however. The primary limitation of using only spot colors is that the number of colors is restricted to the number of color separations that you want to produce. Remember that the cost of a print job is directly related to the number of different colored inks in the job.

The cutoff point for using spot colors is usually three colors. When you use four spot colors, you limit yourself to four distinct colors and use as many colors as a process color job that can have an almost infinite number of colors. Spot color jobs of six colors are not unusual, however. Sometimes people use more than three spot colors to keep colors distinct and clear. Each of the six colors will be bright, vibrant, and distinct from its neighbors, whereas different process colors seem to fade into one another.

Spot colors are often incorrectly referred to as Pantone colors. Pantone is a brand name for a color matching system. You can select Pantone colors as custom colors and use them in Illustrator, and you can print them as either spot colors or as process colors.

Process Color Separation

Process color separation, also known as four-color separation, creates almost any color by combining cyan, magenta, yellow, and black inks. By using various combinations of different tints of each of these colors, you can reproduce many of the colors (more than 16 million of them) that the human eye can see.

Process printing uses a *subtractive* process. You start with bright white paper, and darken the paper with various inks. Cyan, magenta, and yellow are the subtractive primaries, and black is added to create true black printing, which the primaries together don't do very well.

The use of process color separation is advisable when

- The illustration includes color photographs
- The illustration contains more than three different colors

How Many Colors?

Everyone always says that you can create as many colors as you could ever want when you are using process colors. Maybe.

In Illustrator, you can specify colors up to $^1/_{100}$ percent accuracy. As a result, 10,000 different shades are available for each of the four process colors. So, theoretically, $10{,}000^4$, or 10,000,000,000,000,000, different colors should be available, which is 10 quadrillion, or ten million billion. Any way you look at it, you have a heck of a lot of color possibilities.

Unfortunately, most imagesetters and laser printers can produce only 256 different shades for each color. This limitation of the equipment (not PostScript) drops the number of available colors to 256^4, or 4,294,967,296, which is about 4.3 billion colors — only 1 billionth of the colors that Illustrator can create.

This limitation is fortunate for us humans, however, because the estimate is that we can detect a maximum of 100 different levels of gray, probably less. As a result, we can view only 100^4, or 100,000,000, different colors.

We can run into a problem when we preview illustrations, however. An RGB monitor (used on computers) can display up to 16.7 million colors, theoretically, if each Red, Green, and Blue pixel can be varied by 256 different intensities. Most low-end Macintoshes can create only 32,768 colors with their on-board video, and some are limited to 256 colors (or, gasp, grayscale). You need to add special video cards or additional VRAM (Video RAM) to those Macs to display the 16.7 million colors that monitors can produce.

Another problem is that about 30 percent of the colors that you can view on an RGB monitor can't be reproduced by using cyan, magenta, yellow, and black inks on white paper. You can't create these unprintable colors in Illustrator, but you can create them in most other drawing and graphics software packages. These colors are for on-screen viewing pleasure only.

The secret to process color separation is that the four colors that make up all the different colors are themselves not visible. Each color is printed as a pattern of tiny dots, angled differently from the other three colors. The angles of each color are very important. If the angles are off even slightly, a noticeable pattern that is commonly known as a *moiré* will emerge.

The colors are printed in a specific order — usually cyan, magenta, yellow, and black. Although the debate continues about the best order in which to print the four colors, black is always printed last.

To see the dots for each color, use a magnifying device to look closely at something that is preprinted and in full color. Even easier, look at the Sunday comics, which have bigger dots than most other printed pieces. The different color dots in the Sunday comics are quite visible, and their only colors are magenta, cyan, yellow, and black.

The size of the dots that produce each of these separations is also important. The smaller the dots, the smoother the colors appear. Large dots (such as those in the Sunday comics) can actually take away from the illusion of a certain unified color because the the different color dots are visible.

For more information on the common dot sizes and on the relation of dot size to the quality of the illustration, see the section "Setting Up the Halftone Screen," later in this chapter.

Figure 18-9 shows how process colors are combined to create new colors. In the figure, the first four rows show very large dots. The top three rows are cyan, magenta, and yellow. The fourth row is all four process colors combined, and the bottom row shows how the illustration looks when you print it.

Process color printing is best for photographs because photographs originate from a continuous tone that is made on photographic paper from film, instead of dots on a printing press.

In Illustrator, you can convert custom colors to process colors either before or during printing. To convert custom colors to process colors *before* printing, select any objects that have a specific custom color and tint and click the process color icon. The color will be converted to its process color counterpart, and all selected objects will be filled with the new process color combination.

Figure 18-9: The top three rows display cyan, magenta and yellow; the fourth row displays their combination, and the fifth row displays them as they will print

After you click the Process Color icon, if the selected objects become filled with White and the triangles for each process color are at 0%, you have selected objects that contain different colors or tints. Undo the change immediately.

To make sure that you select only objects that have the same color, select one of the objects and choose Edit⇨Select⇨Same Paint Style. Objects that have different strokes or objects with different tints of the same color will not be selected.

You can convert custom colors to process colors in the Separation dialog box (see the "Working with Different Colors" section, later in this chapter) and in many page layout programs.

Combining Both Spot and Process Color Separations

You can couple spot colors with process colors in Illustrator simply by creating both process and named spot colors in a document.

Usually, you add spot colors to process colors for the following reasons:

- You are using a company logo that has a specific color. By printing that color as a spot color, you make it stand out from the other coloring. In addition, color is more accurate when it comes from a specific ink rather than from a process color combination. Often, the logo is a Pantone color that doesn't reproduce true to form when you use process color separation.
- You need a color that you can't create by using process colors. Such colors are most often metallic or fluorescent, but they can be any number of Pantone colors or other colors that you can't match with process colors.
- You need a varnish for certain areas of an illustration. A varnish is a glazed type of ink that results in a shiny area wherever you use the varnish. You commonly use varnishes on titles and logos and over photographs.
- You need a light color over a large area. The dots that make up process colors are most noticeable in light colors, but by using a spot color to cover the area with a solid sheet of ink that has no dots, you can make the area smoother and enhance it visually.

In some circumstances, you need to use a spot color as a spot color and also use it as a process color. Normally, you can't do both, but the following steps describe one way to get around this problem:

Can I Use Separator for Anything?

Mary: Can I use Separator (the one that came with Illustrator 5) for anything?

Toulouse: Sure, you can still print Illustrator 5.x and older EPS documents.

Mary: Is there any reason, ever so little, to keep Separator?

Toulouse: The Transfer Function feature of Separator is nice, but it appears that no one at Adobe thought it was worth keepng.

Mary: There's no Transfer function in Separation Setup?

Toulouse: No, oddly enough.

STEPS: Using a Spot Color as Both a Spot Color and a Process Color

Step 1. If the color doesn't exist as a swatch, create a swatch for the color.

Step 2. In the Swatch Options (double-click on the swatch), set the pop-up menu to Spot Color and click OK.

Step 3. Duplicate the Swatch by dragging it on top of the New Swatch icon (the little piece of paper).

Step 4. In the Swatch Options for the duplicated swatch, set the pop-up menu to Process Color and click OK.

You can tell which swatch is which by looking at the lower right corner of the swatches; the spot color swatch will have a white triangle with a "spot" in it, the process swatch will be solid.

The End of Adobe Separator

One of the biggest disappointments I've ever experienced was seeing Adobe Separator in the Adobe Illustrator 5.0 and 5.5 folders on my hard drive after I installed those versions. You can imagine my joy when I heard whispers, rumors, and finally read the press release for Illustrator 6, where it states something grandiose like, "You can even print your separations directly out of Illustrator 6!" I'll tell you, I'd like to meet the guy who writes those things and give him a piece of my mind. But that's old news, thank goodness.

Printing out separations is easier and more intuitive with Illustrator 7's Separation Setup dialog box than it was with Separator, though you'll notice some obvious similarities.

Using Separation Setup

After you choose File⇨Separation Setup, the Separation Setup dialog box appears (shown in Figure 18-10). The left side shows how the illustration is aligned on the page and which elements will print with the illustration. The right side contains all the options for how the illustration is to print on the page.

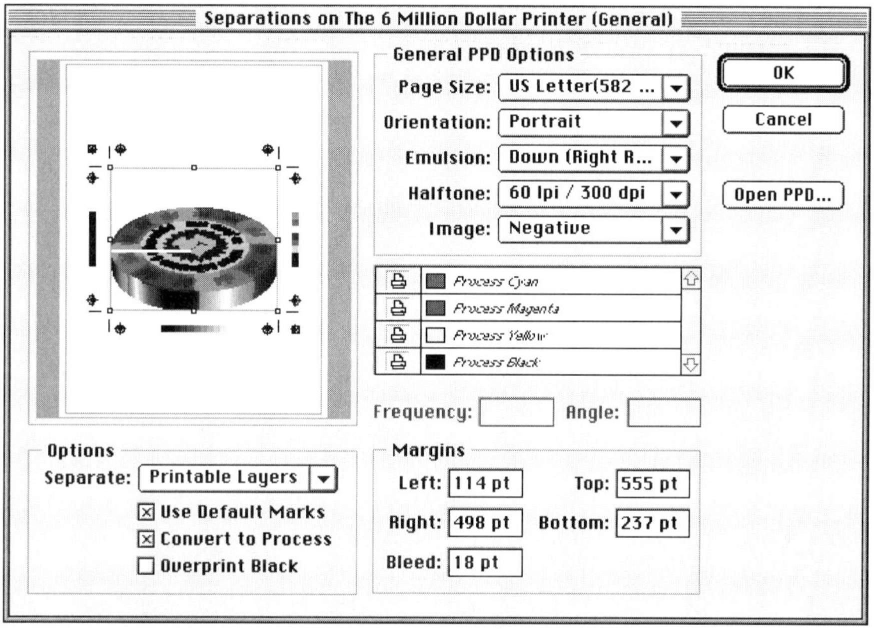

Figure 18-10: The Seperations Setup dialog box

The picture on the left side initially shows the illustration on a portrait-oriented page, even if landscape was selected in Illustrator. The various marks shown on the page are the defaults. You can move or rearrange them simply by clicking and dragging them.

The Bounding Box and Bleed

The illustration is surrounded by a bounding box, and only the parts of the illustration that are within this bounding box will print. Anything outside of the bounding box will be cropped off. When you first open the Separation Setup dialog box, the bounding box is the size of the illustration. The bounding box is as wide and as tall as necessary to include all the printable objects in the illustration.

When you resize the bounding box manually (by clicking on the edges or corners and dragging), the numbers in the Bounding Box text fields (at the very bottom of the dialog box) change because the four text fields correspond to the location of each of the edges of the bounding box. You also can resize the bounding box by typing new values in the Bounding Box text fields. The bounding box instantly reflects changes that you make in these text fields.

You can move the illustration within the bounding box by placing the cursor within the bounding box and clicking and dragging. As you move the illustration out of the bounding box, the illustration is cropped off at its edges.

The Bleed text field in the lower right of the Separation Setup dialog box defines how much of the illustration can be outside of the bounding box and still print. The default for bleed is 18 points, regardless of the size of the bounding box. To change the bleed, enter a distance in points in the Bleed text field. As you type the numbers, the bleed will change dynamically.

Bleed is useful when you want an illustration to go right up to the edge of the page. You need to account for bleed when you create an illustration in Illustrator so that the illustration is the correct size with *X* amount of bleed.

Changing Printer Information

To change the PPD, click the Open PPD button in the upper right of the dialog box. The Open a PostScript Printer Description (PPD) file window appears, as shown in Figure 18-11.

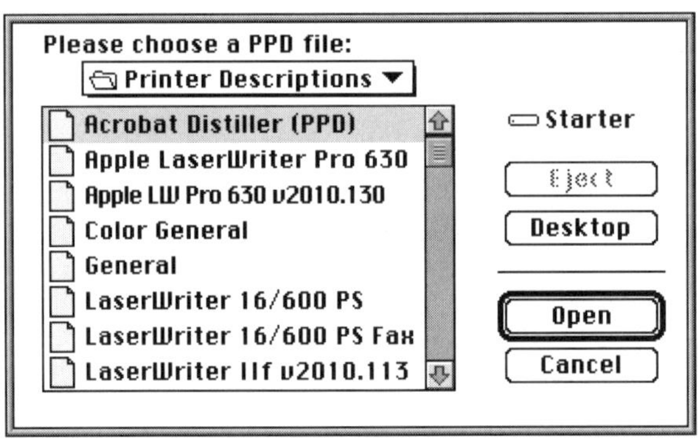

Figure 18-11: The Open a PostScript Printer Description file window

Select the PPD file that is compatible with your printer and click the Open button. The PPD folder is placed in the Utilities folder by the Adobe Illustrator Installer automatically.

PPDs were created with specific printers in mind. Unpredictable and undesirable results can occur when you use a PPD for a different printer than it is intended for. If you don't have a PPD for your printer and must use a substitute, always test the substitute PPD before relying on it to perform correctly.

If your printer's PPD is not included with Illustrator, contact the dealer from whom you purchased the printer and ask for it. If you bought the printer by mail order or from a retail store, the dealer will probably not have a PPD for you and may not even know what a PPD is, for that matter. In this case, contact the printer manufacturer directly. Another place to find PPDs from manufacturers is on online services such as America Online. Adobe does *not* have PPDs for printers other than the ones supplied with the software.

If you have two or more printers in your workplace, chances are that you will be changing the PPD file in the Separation Setup dialog box from time to time. To make this task easier, open the PPD folder on the hard drive, select all the PPD files that you don't use, and drag them to the trash. Having a shorter list to choose from makes finding the right PPD much easier and frees up space on the hard drive. If you get a new printer at a later date and need a different PPD, you can get it from the Illustrator floppy disk or CD-ROM.

When you choose a different PPD file, the information in the main panel changes to reflect the new selection. Certain default settings in the pop-up menus will be activated at this time. You can change the settings at any time, but most of them will revert to the defaults if you choose a new PPD.

Changing Page Size

The Page Size pop-up menu lists the available page sizes for the printer whose PPD is selected, *not* the printer selected in the Chooser. For laser printers, few page and envelope sizes are supported. For imagesetters, many sizes are supported, and an Other option enables you to specify the size of the page that you want to print on.

Wrong Printer

Laura: I used to be able to see what printer I was printing to in Separator, and be able to go directly to the Chooser from there.

Toulouse: You got your sight back?

Laura: Actually, I'm asking you this from season two.

Toulouse: Okay. You *can* see what printer is selected in the Chooser with Separation Setup.

Laura: So I could feasibly have the wrong printer selected when I go to the Separation Setup dialog box, have to close the dialog box, go to the Chooser, and change the printer then?

Toulouse: Not just feasibly. I do it all the time.

Laura: Is there a workaround?

Toulouse: Well, it is faster to check in the Print dialog box than the Separation dialog box (because the Separation preview takes a few seconds to show up), but you can't change the printer in the Print dialog box either.

When you choose Other in the Page Size pop-up menu, you see the Other dialog box. The default measurements in the box are the smallest size area that the current illustration can fit within. Enter the width and height of the desired page in their respective boxes. You can use the Offset option to move the illustration a certain distance from the right edge of the page, and you can save media by using the Transverse option to turn the image sideways on the paper or film that it is printing on.

Imagesetters print on rolls of paper or film. Depending on the width of the roll, you may want to print the image sideways. For example, on a Linotronic 180 or 230 imagesetter, paper and film rolls are commonly 12 inches wide. For letter-size pages, you should check the Transverse option to print the letter-size page with the short end along the length of the roll. For a tabloid page (11 x 17 inches), do not check the Transverse option because you want the long edge (17 inches) of the page to be printed along the length of the roll. If you check Transverse for a tabloid-size document, 5 of the 17 inches will be cropped off because the roll is not wide enough. As always when trying something new with printing, run a test or two before sending a large job.

The page size that you select in the Page Size pop-up menu determines the size of the page on the left side of the main panel. The measurements next to the name of the page size are not the page measurements; instead, they are the measurements of the imageable area for that page size. The imageable-area dimensions are always less than the dimensions of the page so that the margin marks can fit on the page with the illustration.

Changing the Orientation

The Orientation setting controls how the illustration is placed on the page. You have two choices from the pop-up menu: Portrait and Landscape.

Selecting Portrait causes the illustration to print with the sides of the illustration along the longest sides of the page. Selecting Landscape causes the illustration to print with the top and bottom of the illustration along the longest sides of the page.

Usually, the orientation reflects the general shape of the illustration. If the illustration is taller than it is wide, you usually choose Portrait orientation. If the illustration is wider than it is tall, you usually choose Landscape orientation.

It doesn't matter to Illustrator whether the illustration fits on the page in one or both of these orientations. If you can't see all four edges of the bounding box, chances are the illustration will be cropped.

Orientation is quite different from Transverse in the Other Page Size dialog box. Orientation changes the orientation of the illustration on the page, but Transverse changes the way that the page is put onto the paper. A seemingly small difference, but a distinct and important one to understand.

Figure 18-12 shows an illustration that is placed onto a page in both Portrait and Landscape orientations, with and without the Transverse option selected.

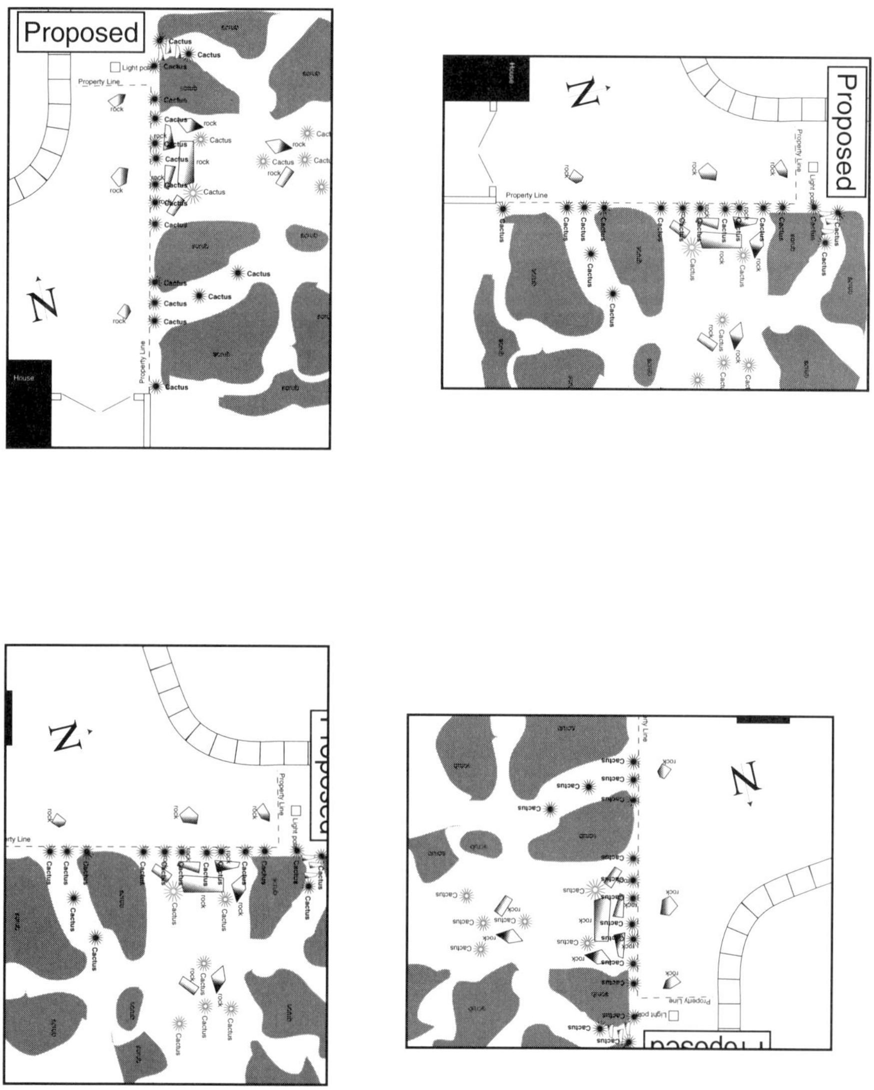

Figure 18-12: An Illustration placed onto a page in Portrait orientation (upper left), Landscape orientation (lower left), Portrait with Transverse checked (upper right), and Landscape with Transverse checked (lower right)

Understanding Emulsion

Hang out around strippers (at a commercial printing company . . . get your mind out of the gutter), and you will hear them constantly talking about "emulsion up" and "emulsion down." What they are referring to is the black stuff on film. If you have a piece of film from a printer lying around, look at it near a light. One of its two sides is shinier than the other. That side is the side without emulsion. When you are burning plates for presses, the emulsion side (dull side) should always be toward the plate.

In the Separation Setup dialog box, you use the Emulsion option to control which side the emulsion goes on. If you are printing negatives on film, choose Down (right reading) from the Emulsion pop-up menu. For printing on paper, just to see what the separations look like, choose Up (right reading). Always consult with your printer for the correct way to output film.

Although "wrong reading" isn't an option in the Separation Setup dialog box, you can reverse an illustration by choosing the opposite emulsion setting. In other words, Down (right reading) is also Up (wrong reading), and Up (right reading) is also Down (wrong reading).

Reversing text creates the kind of secret code illustrations that you can send to your friends. The only way to understand the illustrations is by viewing them in a mirror. This technique works best with text, of course, and I wouldn't expect to fool really smart people with this type of code.

Thinking of the emulsion as the toner in a laser printer may help you understand this concept better. If the toner is on the top of the paper, you can read it fine, as always (Up emulsion, right reading). If the toner is on the bottom of the paper, and you can read the illustration only when you place the paper in front of a light, the emulsion is Down, right reading. Thinking along these lines helped me back when I was new to the printing industry, and it should help you as well.

Setting Up the Halftone Screen

The halftone screen setting is one of the great mysteries of life to the graphic designer who has not been informed about it. A too-low halftone screen setting will render an illustration terribly, making text and pictures unclear and fuzzy, sometimes even showing the dots that create the tints in the illustration. But if the halftone screen setting is too high, blends and gradations will show banding, and some areas or the entire illustration may look posterized. The halftone setting can be too high for a particular press, resulting in smeary, terrible-looking results. Blends, gradations, and how to avoid banding are discussed in Chapter 10.

Understanding Halftone Line Screens

The most common mistake that graphic designers make is confusing dots per inch (dpi) with lines per inch (lpi). Lines per inch is another way of saying line screen or halftone line screen.

The number of dots per inch of the output device controls what the potential lines-per-inch settings are. The higher the dpi, the higher the lpi can be, but the higher the lpi, the lower the possible number of grays.

In bitmap graphics software, such as Photoshop, the dpi of the image is also important. In Illustrator, objects that you create are based on locations of points rather than on dots per inch. Trust me, dealing with an image's dots per inch is no picnic, and the fact that Illustrator can bypass this specification entirely is a great boon. Of course, if you have placed or imported pixel-based images in your file, you haven't learned anything. . . .

Line screens are made up of a combination of halftone cells. Each halftone cell has a certain number of dots within it that can be turned on and off. Usually the dots are turned on and off in a round pattern to create a halftone dot.

As an example, consider a common dpi/lpi ratio, that of a 300-dpi laser printer with a 60-line screen. Each halftone dot is made up of a 5 x 5 halftone cell (300/60 = 5). The number of pixels within each cell is 25. Figure 18-13 shows 5 x 5 halftone cells at different percentages.

Figure 18-13: 5x5 halftone cells at different percentages

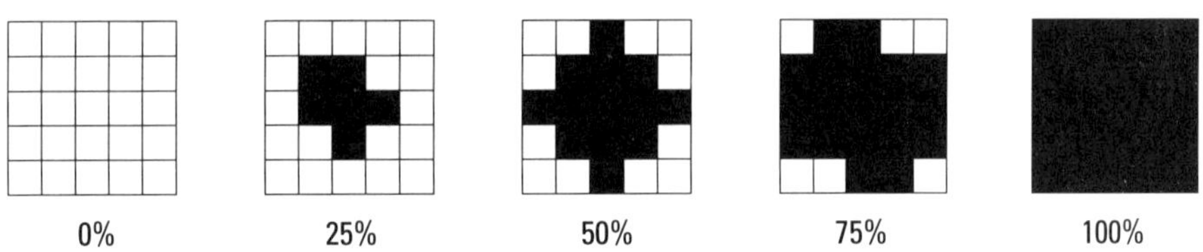

At a 25% tint, 25 percent of the dots are black. In a halftone cell of 25 dots, 6.25 dots would be black. Because you cannot print a quarter of a dot with this method, 6 dots are black.

Because the halftone cell has 25 pixels, only 26 different levels of gray are available when you are using a 300-dpi laser printer with a 60-lpi screen (1 level for each of the 25 pixels, plus 1 level for no pixels on at all, yields a total of 26). To get more grays, you need to lower the line screen.

Lower line screens seem rougher than higher line screens. The cutoff point for line screens is about 105; anything higher is considered a fine line screen, and anything lower is a coarse line screen.

A 300-dpi laser printer prints 90,000 dots for every square inch ($300 \times 300 = 90,000$). Figure 18-14 shows one square inch blown up 500% so you can see the different dot patterns in a small gradient.

Figure 18-14: Halftone gradients

In deciding on a halftone screen, you need to consider many things, the most important of which are the type of paper or other media that the image will eventually be printed on, and the press that it will be printed on.

Common settings for different types of print jobs are as follows: newsprint and photocopiers, 85 lpi; standard magazines, 133 lpi; better quality magazines, 150 lpi; and high-quality book images, 150 or 175 lpi.

Adding Custom Line Screens

In the Separation Setup dialog box, you can specify the line screen only by selecting one of the choices in the Halftone pop-up menu. This restriction can be very limiting, but you can get around it by doing a serious amount of tinkering, as described in the follwing steps.

STEPS: Adding New Halftone Screens to PPD Files

Step 1. Make a copy of the PPD file that you want to add halftone screens to and add a suffix, such as *new,* to its name (for example, Laserwriter.new). Open the copy with SimpleText or another word processor.

Step 2. Scroll down to a section that looks very similar to what you see in Figure 18-15. The halftone screen numbers may be different from the ones shown in the figure, depending on the PPD chosen. Select the entire section and copy it. Press the left arrow once and paste.

Step 3. In the copy, change the numbers highlighted in Figure 18-15 to whatever line screen you choose. Paste the copy and repeat this step for every new halftone screen that you want to include in the PPD file.

Step 4. Save the changes.

Step 5. Open the new PPD in the Separation Setup dialog box. If all went well, new pop-up menu items will reflect your recent changes.

```
*% For 60 lpi / 300 dpi ===============================

*ColorSepScreenAngle ProcessBlack.60lpi.300dpi/60 lpi / 300 dpi: "45"
*ColorSepScreenAngle CustomColor.60lpi.300dpi/60 lpi / 300 dpi: "45"
*ColorSepScreenAngle ProcessCyan.60lpi.300dpi/60 lpi / 300 dpi: "15"
*ColorSepScreenAngle ProcessMagenta.60lpi.300dpi/60 lpi / 300 dpi: "75"
*ColorSepScreenAngle ProcessYellow.60lpi.300dpi/60 lpi / 300 dpi: "0"

*ColorSepScreenFreq ProcessBlack.60lpi.300dpi/60 lpi / 300 dpi: "60"
*ColorSepScreenFreq CustomColor.60lpi.300dpi/60 lpi / 300 dpi: "60"
*ColorSepScreenFreq ProcessCyan.60lpi.300dpi/60 lpi / 300 dpi: "60"
*ColorSepScreenFreq ProcessMagenta.60lpi.300dpi/60 lpi / 300 dpi: "60"
*ColorSepScreenFreq ProcessYellow.60lpi.300dpi/60 lpi / 300 dpi: "60"
```

Figure 18-15: The line screen values that can be changed in a text editor

The final thing to think about when you are choosing a halftone screen is the type of media that the illustration will be output on from an imagesetter. If the output will be on paper, the halftone screen needs to be lower than if the output will be on film.

The Printing Process and Saving $$ with Your Computer

The following brief rundown of the process that a printer goes through when taking a job from start to finish can help you understand some of the choices that you need to make when you are printing out of Separator. Of course, the following is a generalization, and all printers do things a little differently.

First, the printer gathers all of the materials for the print job. These materials may include artwork, logos, photos, and copy. The materials may go to different places, depending on what equipment the printer has. A typical commercial printer has limited prepress equipment in-house.

Color artwork and color photos are sent to a color separation house that specializes in creating film separations from full-color originals. The cost for each piece of artwork can range from $50 to $1,000, depending on the quality desired and the quantity.

Black-and-white artwork is shot with a camera (usually in-house) and resized to fit. Text is sent to a typesetting firm and set.

Black-and-white artwork and text are pasted up onto pasteboards, proofed, and then shot with a camera. A stripper takes the resulting film to a light table, where any seams in the film are opaqued out.

Film from the separation houses is stripped into the film from the artwork and type. This particular process is the most time-consuming and adds substantially to the prepress portion of the labor bill.

At this point, proofs are created. Printers may use many different proofing methods, but the least expensive and most basic is the *blueline,* so called for the blue color of the text and artwork that appears on the sheets.

After the blueline is approved (or *if,* to be more exact), each piece of film is used to create a printing press plate for each color.

The plates are applied to presses, and the number of copies specified by the customer is run, plus several more copies to account for errors in printing and cutting.

After the ink on the printed paper dries, the copies are cut along crop marks, bound, and folded along fold marks. Depending on the type of product, the printed pieces may be bound, folded, and cut in any order.

The final piece is boxed and shipped to the client.

If you do everything you can with your system, you can save substantial amounts of money in all of the prepress areas. Do as many of the following as possible to save money and avoid problems:

- Do as much as you can electronically. This rule is one you should live by.
- Have someone else proof your work *before* you output it to film. Objectivity for your own work decreases geometrically in relationship to the time you spend working on it. Your subconscious doesn't want to find mistakes.
- Get a separation house to scan photos and traditionally created artwork and then provide you with the files on disk. Sure, you can buy a flatbed desktop scanner inexpensively, but color pictures from them can look like mush next to scans from a drum scanner at a separation house.
- Assemble all your artwork, type, and photos in QuarkXPress, FrameMaker, or PageMaker.
- Have all film negatives output by a reputable service bureau. If your job contains a large amount of color artwork or photos, or if you need the artwork and color photos to be of the best possible quality, take everything back to the color separation house, where your job will be output at a better quality than most imagesetters can produce.

Changing from Positive to Negative to Positive

You use the Image pop-up menu to switch between printing positive and negative images. Usually, you use a negative image for printing film negatives and a positive image for printing on paper. The default for this setting, regardless of the printer chosen or PPD selected, is Negative.

Working with Different Colors

At the lower right of the Separation Setup dialog box, a color list window displays where you can select different colors and set them to print or not print, and set Custom Colors to process separately.

The list of colors contains only the colors that are used in that particular illustration. At the top of the list of separation colors are the four process colors in italic, if they or spot colors that contain those process colors are used in the illustration. Below the process colors is a list of all the spot colors in the document.

CAUTION

If the illustration has any guides in it, their colors are reflected in the color list window. From looking at the preview of the illustration in the Separation Setup dialog box, you can't easily determine that these blank separations will print. The best thing to do is release all guides and delete them.

By default, all process colors are set to print, and all spot colors are set to convert to process colors. Clicking the Convert To Process checkbox at the bottom of the Separation Setup dialog box toggles between converting everything (checked) and spot colors (unchecked).

Each color in the list has its own frequency and angle. Don't change the angle or frequency for process colors because Separator has automatically created the best values for the process colors at the halftone screen you've specified. Instead, make sure that any spot colors that may be printing have different angles from each other so that no patterns develop from them.

As soon as you type new values or check different options using the color list, the changes are applied.

Printing Separations

To print with the settings you've selected, click OK in the Separation Setup dialog box and then choose File➪Print (or press ⌘-P [Ctrl+P]). This displays the Print dialog box. Change the Output option to Separations, and the separations you've specified will print.

Printing Separations from Other Applications

Many other software programs, particularly page layout software programs, incorporate color-separation capabilities. These programs usually enable you to import Illustrator files that have been saved as Illustrator EPS files.

When you produce color separations from other software, make sure that any custom colors that are in the Illustrator illustration are present and accessible in the document that the illustration is placed within. Usually, you can set the custom colors to process separately or to spot separately.

CAUTION You cannot change the colors of an imported Illustrator EPS document in a page layout program, so be sure that the colors are correct for the illustration while it is in Illustrator.

Trapping

Trapping is one of the most important but least understood issues in all of printing. In the past, desktop publishing has been noted for its inefficiency in trapping, but QuarkXPress and a few after-the-fact trapping software packages, such as Luminus TrapWise and Island Trapper, have gradually bettered the trapping capabilities of electronic publishing.

CAUTION Illustrator, while it does incorporate a trapping filter, is not a trap-happy piece of software. For detailed illustrations, it usually isn't worth your time to set the trapping inside Illustrator; instead, you'll want to have your printer do the work for you.

Understanding What Trapping Does

Traps solve alignment problems when color separations are produced. The most common problem that occurs from misalignment is the appearance of white space between different colors.

BY THE WAY The thought of trapping scares many graphic designers — not just because they don't know how to do it, but also because they aren't sure what trapping is and what purpose it serves. Understanding the concept of trapping is the hard part; trapping objects is easy (though somewhat tedious in Illustrator).

Figure 18-16 shows a spot color illustration with four colors. The top row shows each of the individual colors. The first illustration in the second row shows how the illustration prints if all the separations are aligned perfectly. The second illustration in the second row shows what happens when the colors become misaligned. The third illustration in the second row shows how the illustration looks when trapped, with black indicating where two colors overprint each other.

This example shows extreme misalignment and excessive trapping; I designed it just as a black-and-white illustration for this book. Ordinarily, the overprinting colors may appear a tiny bit darker, but they do not show as black. I used black so that you can see what parts of the illustration overlap when trapping is used. The trapping in this case is more than sufficient to cover any of the white gaps in the second illustration.

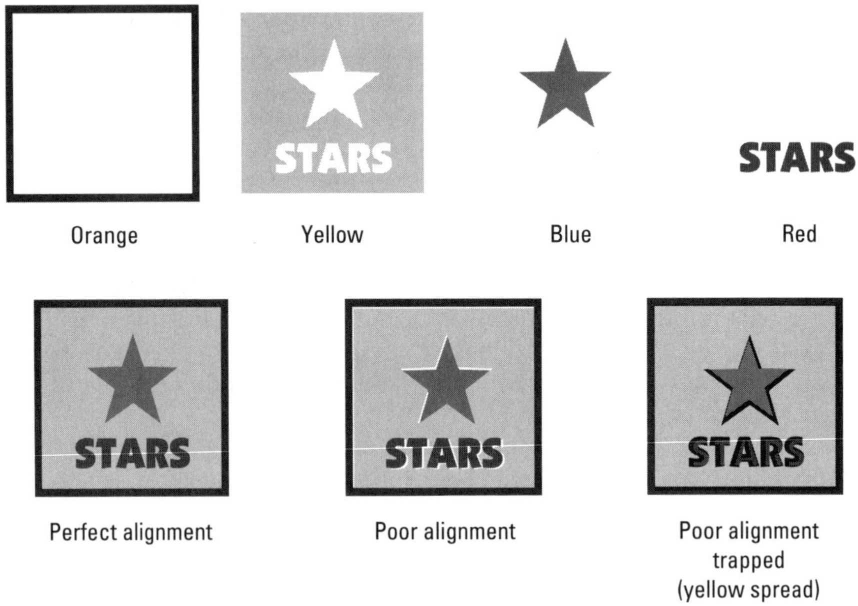

Figure 18-16: A Spot Color illustration that shows individual colors (top) and aligned misaligned, and trapped composites

Trapping is created by spreading or choking certain colors that touch each other in an illustration. To spread a color, enlarge an object's color so that it takes up more space around the edges of the background area. To choke a color, expand the color of the background until it overlaps the edges of an object.

The major difference between a spread and a choke has to do with which object is considered the background and which object is the foreground. The foreground object is the object that traps. If the foreground object is spread, the color of the foreground object is spread until it overlaps the background by a certain amount. If the foreground object is choked, the color of the background around the foreground object is expanded until it overlaps the foreground object by a certain amount.

To determine whether to use a choke or a spread on an object, compare the lightness and darkness of the foreground and background objects. The general rule of thumb is that lighter colors expand or contract into darker colors.

Figure 18-17 shows the original misaligned illustration and two ways of fixing it with trapping. The middle star has been spread by 1 point, and the third star has been choked by 1 point.

Figure 18-17: The original illustration (left), fixing the star by spreading it 1 point (middle), and fixing the star by choking it 1 point (right)

Why You Need Trapping

Trapping is a solution for covering gaps that occur when color separations do not properly align. Maybe this section should have been called, "Why Color Separations Do Not Properly Align," but now the book has been printed and it can't be changed.

The three reasons why color separations don't align properly are that the negatives are not the same size, the plates on the press are not aligned perfectly when printing, or the gods have decided that a piece is too perfect and needs gaps between butting colors.

Negatives can be different sizes for a number of reasons. When the film was output to an imagesetter, the film may have been too near the beginning or the end of a roll, or separations in the same job may have been printed from different rolls. The pull on the rollers, while fairly precise on all but top-of-the-line imagesetters — where it should be perfect — can pull more film through when there is less resistance (at the end of a roll of film), or less film when there is more resistance (at the beginning of a roll of film). The temperature of the film may be different if a new roll is put on in the middle of a job, causing the film to shrink (if it is cold) or expand (if it is warm).

The temperature of the processor may have risen or fallen a degree or two while the film was being processed. Once again, cooler temperatures in the chemical bays and in the air dryer as the film exits the process have an impact on the size of the film.

Film negatives usually don't change drastically in size, but they can vary up to a few points on an 11-inch page. That distance is huge when a page has several butting colors throughout it. The change in a roll of film is almost always along the length of the roll, not along the width. The quality of the film is another factor that determines how much the film will stretch or shrink.

Trapping with Quark?

Jenny: What's the difference between trapping with Illustrator and trapping with Quark?

Toulouse: Trapping Illustrator objects to multiple backgrounds *can't* be done in Quark.

Jenny: But what if I need something to trap to an Illustrator object within Quark?

Toulouse: The best thing to do is to create both objects in Illustrator, trap them, and *then* take them to Quark.

Most strippers are quite aware of how temperature affects the size of negatives. A common stripper trick is to walk outside with a freshly processed negative during the colder months to shrink a negative that may have enlarged slightly during processing.

Check with your service bureau staff to see how long they warm up the processor before sending jobs through it. If the answer is less than an hour, the chemicals will not be at a consistent temperature, and negatives that are sent through too early will certainly change in size throughout the length of the job. Another question to ask is how often they change their chemicals and check the density from their imagesetter. Once a week is acceptable for a good-quality service bureau, but the best ones will change chemicals and check density once a day.

The plates on a press can be misaligned by either an inexperienced press operator or a faulty press. An experienced press operator knows the press and what to do to get color plates to align properly. A faulty press is one where plates move during printing or are not positioned correctly. An experienced press operator can determine how to compensate for a faulty press.

No press is perfect, but some of the high-end presses are pretty darn close. Even on those presses, the likelihood that a job with colors that butt up against one another can print perfectly is not very great.

If a job doesn't have some sort of trapping in it, it probably will not print perfectly, no matter how good the negatives, press, and press operator are.

How Much Trap?

The amount of trap that you need in an illustration depends on many things, but the deciding factor is what your commercial printer tells you is the right amount.

The most important thing to consider is the quality of the press that the printer will use. Of course, only the printer knows which press your job will run on, so talking to the printer about trapping is imperative.

Other factors to consider include the colors of ink and types of stock used in the job. Certain inks soak into different stocks differently.

Traps range from $^{2}/_{1,000}$ inch to $^{6}/_{1,000}$ inch. Most traditional printers refer to traps in thousandths of inches, but Illustrator likes values in points for this sort of thing. Figure 18-18 shows a chart with traps in increments of $^{1}/_{1,000}$, from $^{1}/_{1,000}$ of an inch to $^{10}/_{1,000}$ of an inch, and gives their point measurements. The trapped area is represented by black to be more visible in this example.

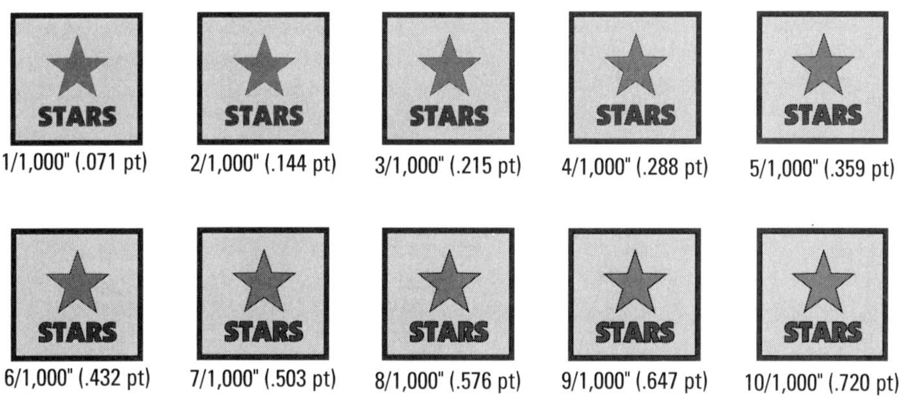

Figure 18-18: Different trap amounts

Remember, the greater the trap, the less chance that any white gaps will appear, but the trap may actually be visible. Visible traps of certain color pairs can look almost as bad as white space.

Trapping Illustrator Files Manually

In Illustrator, you accomplish manual (nonfilter) trapping by selecting a path's Stroke or Fill and setting it to overprint another path's Stroke or Fill. The amount that the two paths' Fills or Strokes overlap and overprint is the amount of trap that is used.

The most basic way to create a trap on an object is by giving it a Stroke that is either the Fill color of the object (to create a spread) or the Fill color of the background (to create a choke).

CAUTION

Be sure to make the width of any Stroke that you use for trapping twice as wide as the intended trap, because only half of the Stroke (one side of the path) actually overprints a different color. In some circumstances, fixing a Stroke that is not wide enough initially can be difficult.

STEPS: Manually Trapping between Two Paths

Step 1. Select one path of a pair of overlapping or abutting paths. If possible, select the lighter of the two paths.

Step 2. Give the Selected path a Stroke of the same color that the Fill is. Change the weight to the amount of trap you'd like to use. For this example, so it could be seen easily in this book, I've used a 3-point trap.

Step 3. Set the overlapping Stroke to overprint. These steps are shown in Figure 18-19.

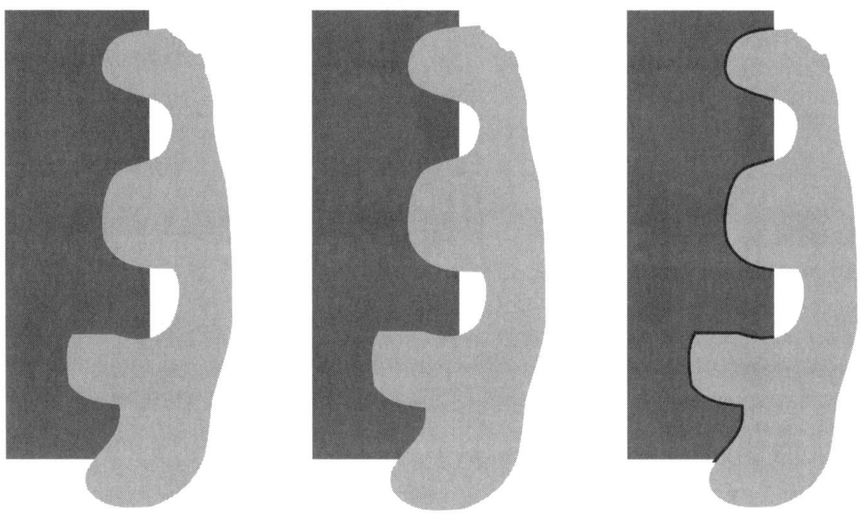

Figure 18-19: Steps for manual trapping

Trapping with Trap

For this example, I'll use the same paths from Figure 18-19 to show how Trap works.

STEPS: Trapping with Trap

Step 1. Select all pieces of art that are overlapping or abutting.

Step 2. Choose Object⇨Pathfinder⇨Trap, and enter the width into the Width text field (see Figure 18-20).

Step 3. Click OK and the object has trapping applied instantly (well, if the artwork is complex it won't be instant. . .).

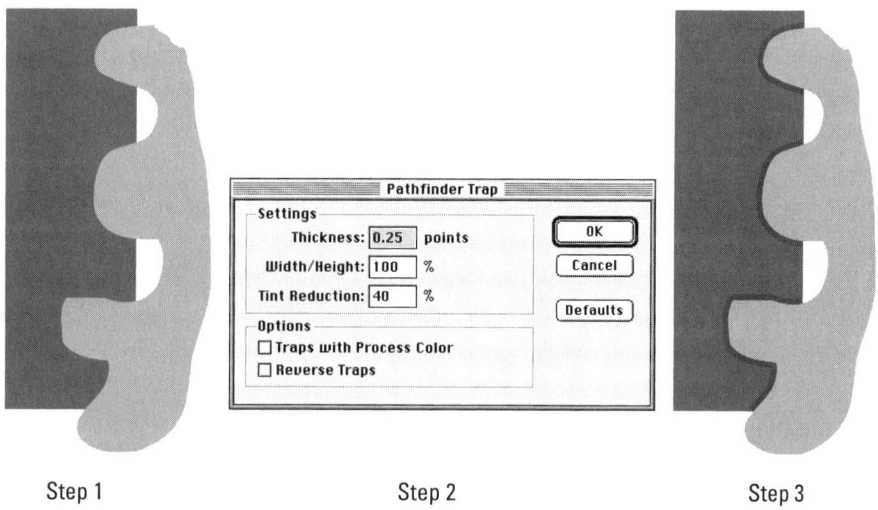

Figure 18-20: Steps for trapping with Trap

Complex Trapping Techniques in Illustrator

The preceding trap illustrations are extremely simplified examples of trapping methods in Illustrator. In reality, objects never seem to be a solid color, and if they are, they are never on a solid background. In addition, most illustrations contain multiple overlapping objects that have their own special trapping needs.

I consider trapping to be complex when I can't just go around selecting paths and applying trap quickly. Complex trapping involves several different techniques, which are described in the following list:

- **Create a separate layer for trapping objects.** By keeping trapping on its own layer, you make myriad options available that are not available if the trapping is intermixed with the rest of the artwork. Place the new layer above the other layers. Lock all the layers but the trapping layer so that the original artwork is not modified. You can turn trapping on and off by hiding the entire layer or turning off the Print option in the Layers Options dialog box.
- **Use the round joins and ends options in the Stroke portion of the Paint Style palette for all trapping Strokes.** Round joins and ends are much less conspicuous than the harsh corners and 90° angles of other joins and ends, and they blend smoothly into other objects.
- **Trap gradations by Stroking them with paths that are Filled with overprinting gradients.** You cannot Fill Strokes with gradients, but you can Fill paths with gradients. You can make any Stroke into a path by selecting it and choosing Object Path⇨Outline Path. After you have transformed the Stroke into a path, Fill it with the gradient and check the Overprint Fill box (in the Attributes palette) for that path.

Whenever I start a heavy-duty trapping project, I always work on a copy of the original illustration. Wrecking the original artwork is just too easy when you add trapping.

When Trapping Yourself Just Isn't Worth It

Before you spend the long amounts of time that complex trapping entails and modify your illustration beyond recognition (at least in Artwork mode), you may want to reconsider whether you should do the trapping yourself.

If you estimate that trapping your job will require several hours of work, the chances of doing it correctly dwindle significantly. If the illustration includes many crisscrossing blends and gradations or multiple placed images, you may not have the patience to get through the entire process with your sanity intact.

If you determine that you cannot do the trapping yourself, you can have it done after the fact with Liminus TrapWise or Island Trapper, or you can have a service bureau with special output devices create trapping automatically. These services will undoubtedly cost more than doing the trapping yourself, but it will get done right, which is the important thing.

Summary

- Illustrator can print separations right from within the program.
- Choose whether to print a composite or separations from the Print dialog box.
- Determine separation information in the Separation Setup dialog box.
- Trapping prevents potential white strips that can appear when a printer isn't perfectly aligned.
- Separation Setup lets you specify which colors print, and what angle and frequency they print at.

Using Streamline 4 and Dimensions 3 with Illustrator

CHAPTER 19

In This Chapter

- Understanding Streamline
- Streamline versus Illustrator's Auto Trace tool
- The tools and commands in Streamline
- Creating objects in three dimensions with Dimensions
- Extruding and revolving
- Going from Dimensions back to Illustrator
- Converting bitmapped art into Illustrator paths

Illustrator is not an island. (An island, you'll recall, is a small mass of land completely surrounded by water, while Illustrator is a software program.) Illustrator's capabilities are enhanced by additional programs, like Photoshop, Dimensions, and Streamline. Photoshop is more like a cousin, while Dimensions is a brother and Streamline is a sister.

Smoothing the Path

Esther: I really like the Smooth Paths option in Streamline.

Toulouse: Yep, it's one of the best features of Streamline, dramatically reducing the number of Anchor Points on a path.

Esther: Why isn't that an option in Illustrator?

Toulouse: I believe Streamline was developed outside of Adobe, and they don't have the rights to the code.

Esther: They should buy it. It would significantly increase Illustrator's worth.

Dimensions is worth the couple hundred dollars Adobe charges for it. And Streamline is well worth the paltry amount of money it costs, for using it just once will save you enough time that you'll be able to take your whole family island-hopping in the Caribbean.

Adobe Streamline

Imagine Illustrator's Auto Trace tool on steroids. That's the Streamline package: a super-powerful bitmap tracing tool. The options for converting images are staggering, and the results can be dramatically better than the results that you can achieve with the Auto Trace tool. A demo version of Adobe Streamline is included on the *Illustrator 7 Bible* CD-ROM.

The Auto Trace tool in Illustrator traces one solid part of a Placed Image. Sure, you can adjust the Curve Fitting Tolerance to make the created path stay closer to the image or be drawn a little less constrained, but the options end there.

The biggest advantage to using the Auto Trace tool instead of Streamline is that the Auto Trace tool is free, while Streamline costs about $100. (The Auto Trace tool and tracing within Illustrator are discussed in Chapter 4.)

On the other hand, Streamline can perform all of the following tasks:

- Trace bitmapped artwork that has been saved in the PICT, TIFF, TIFF Compressed, MacPaint, PCX, and Photoshop formats
- Convert artwork into EPS format, creating editable paths that you can manipulate in Illustrator
- Edit bitmapped artwork before converting it into paths

- Adjust paths that were created by converting bitmaps
- Support Adobe PostScript on the Clipboard for instant copy and paste capabilities between Illustrator, Photoshop, and Dimensions
- Provide complex control over how images are traced
- Convert line art and grayscale and color artwork to editable Illustrator paths

The Streamline Toolbox and Menu Items

The following pages contain an overview of the functions of the Streamline toolbox and some of the more significant menu items. Although Streamline is a fairly small program, I can't possibly cover all the facets of the software in one chapter, so I'll focus on information that isn't quite so obvious.

Streamline Tools

The toolbox in Streamline (see Figure 19-1) is a Photoshop/Illustrator hybrid; you use it to edit both bitmapped and path-based portions of images.

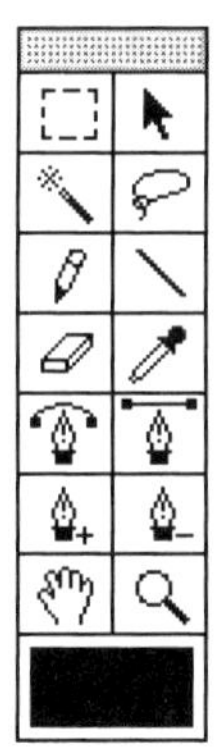

Figure 19-1: The Streamline toolbox

The toolbox contains the folowing tools:

- **The Marquee tool:** You use the Marquee tool to select an area in a bitmapped image. You can move, delete, copy, or cut the selected area. You also can convert the selected area into paths. You use the tool by clicking and dragging — just as you do with Illustrator's Rectangle tool. The Shift and Option keys have no effect on the Marquee tool. You can use the Marquee tool only when you are editing bitmapped images.

- **The Magic Wand tool:** You use the Magic Wand tool to select areas in a bitmapped image that are similar in color. The color at the point where you click with the Magic Wand tool determines which areas are selected. Double-clicking the Magic Wand tool displays the Magic Wand dialog box, where the "spread" of the wand is determined by a setting of Tight (little spread; only colors very closely related to the original are selected) or Loose (colors even loosely related to the original are selected). You can use the Magic Wand tool only when you are editing bitmapped images.
- **The Pencil tool:** You use the Pencil tool to draw on bitmapped images. It is most useful for touching up small areas that were problematic when you scanned an image. Double-clicking the Pencil tool displays the Pencil dialog box, where you can specify the width of the Pencil. You choose the color that the Pencil draws from the Paint Style palette (choose Options⇨Paint Style or press ⌘-I [Ctrl+I]). You can use the Pencil tool only when you are editing bitmapped images.
- **The Line tool:** The Line tool creates lines in the same way that the Pencil tool creates individual points. Double-clicking the Line tool enables you to specify the width of the line. The color that the Line tool draws is determined by the color in the Paint Style palette. You can use the Line tool only when you are editing bitmapped images.
- **The Eraser tool:** The Eraser tool erases bitmapped images by painting them with white. Double-clicking the Eraser tool displays a dialog box in which you can specify the width of the Eraser. You can use the Eraser tool only when you are editing bitmapped images.
- **The Delete Anchor Point tool:** The Delete Anchor Point tool deletes individual Anchor Points that are created in the conversion process. You can use the Delete Anchor Point tool only for editing converted images.
- **The Swatch:** The Swatch at the bottom of the toolbox isn't a tool. Instead, it's a color indicator. Clicking the Swatch displays the Paint Style palette.
- **The Selection tool:** You use the Selection tool to select points and paths that have been converted. You can use the Selection tool only when you are editing converted images.
- **The Lasso tool:** You use the Lasso tool to select either a group of pixels or a set of paths and points. You drag the tool around the objects or pixels that you want to select.
- **The Zoom In tool:** The Zoom In tool magnifies both bitmapped and converted images.

POWER TIP

Unlike in Illustrator, Dimensions, and Photoshop, you can use the Zoom In tool in Streamline to enlarge an image to *any* percentage.

- **The Zoom Out tool:** You use the Zoom Out tool to zoom out from an image.
- **The Hand tool:** You use the Hand tool to scroll around the document window.
- **The Eyedropper tool:** You use the Eyedropper tool to sample color from pixels or paths in both bitmapped and path-based images. Pressing the Control key accesses the Eyedropper. To use the tool, drag a marquee around the desired area.

POWER TIP

You can access the Selection, Zoom In, Zoom Out, and Hand tools by using the same shortcuts that you use in Illustrator. Press ⌘ [Ctrl] for the Selection tool, ⌘-Spacebar [Ctrl+Spacebar] for the Zoom In tool, ⌘-Spacebar-Option [Ctrl+Spacebar+Alt] for the Zoom Out tool, and the Spacebar for the Hand tool.

If you cannot use a tool on the type of image that you are currently editing, the tool is grayed out.

Using Streamline

The three basic steps in using Streamline are opening and editing a pixel bitmapped image, converting the pixel image into a vectored path drawing, and editing and saving the resulting Illustrator paths. Use the following steps to convert a bitmapped image into paths.

STEPS: Converting Bitmapped Art to Paths

Step 1. Open the bitmap image file (choose File⇨Open or press ⌘-O) [Ctrl+O] or use the TWAIN Acquire command to scan in the artwork.

Step 2. Use any of the bitmap editing tools to clean up stray pixels. If the area that you want to convert is only part of an image, use the Marquee tool to select that portion.

Step 3. Choose Options⇨Settings (⌘-T) [Ctrl+T] and choose the type of bitmapped image that you are converting. The list that you choose from contains the best generalized settings for each type of bitmapped image.

If none of the settings seem to fit your bitmapped image, choose Options⇨Conversion Setup (⌘-J) [Ctrl+J] and adjust the settings within the Conversion Setup dialog box.

(continued)

STEPS: *(continued)*

Step 4. Choose File⇨Convert (⌘-R) [Ctrl+R] to have Streamline begin to do its magic.

CAUTION

Macintosh only: Streamline can outline any size bitmapped artwork; it is limited only by the amount of RAM you allocate to the software. Streamline will, however, stop converting artwork before it finishes if it does not have sufficient memory. If the bitmapped artwork is overly complex (lots of colors or a big file), increase the RAM that is allocated to Streamline.

To increase the RAM allocated to Streamline, quit Streamline, select the Streamline icon from the Desktop, choose File⇨Get Info (⌘-I), and change the bottom box (called Preferred Size in System 7.5) to the amount of memory that you want to allocate to Streamline. If you aren't sure how much memory you can spare, choose Apple⇨About This Macintosh from the Apple menu to display the amount of RAM installed and the amount that the system and other software are using.

Step 5. Edit the new paths with the path-editing tools.

Step 6. If you have Illustrator running at the same time as Streamline, you can copy converted paths in Streamline, go to Illustrator, and Paste (⌘-V) [Ctrl+V] in Illustrator. The copied paths will be pasted in the Illustrator document.

If you want to save the converted file that you have just created, choose File⇨Save Art (⌘-S) [Ctrl+S].

Figures 19-2, 19-3, and 19-4 show images in bitmap form, and their respective Streamlined paths.

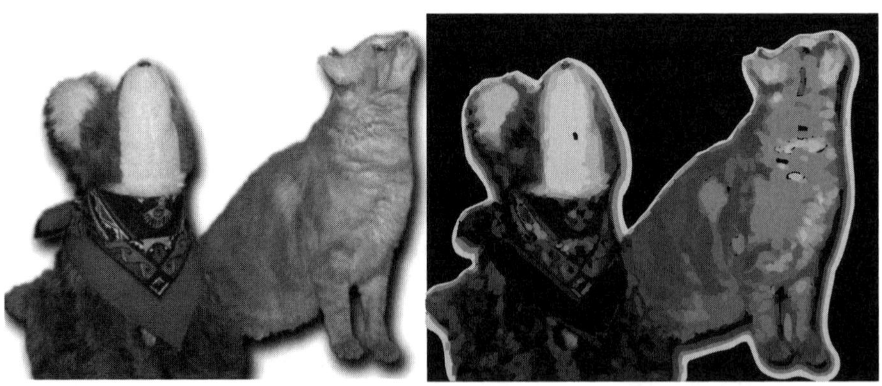

Figure 19-2: A pixel-based image (left) and after being Streamlined into paths

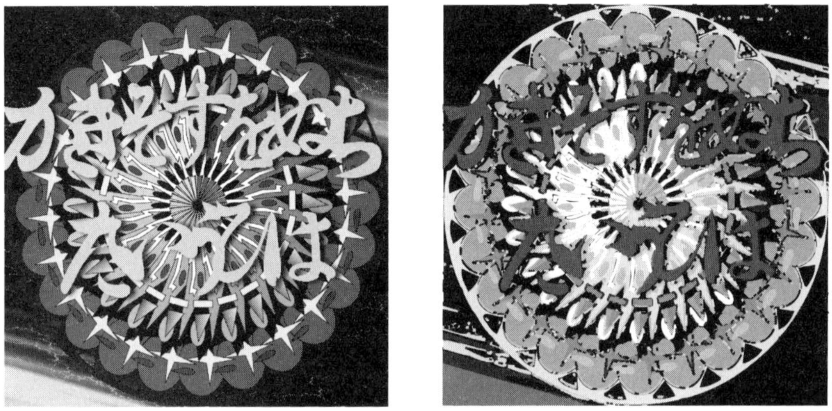

Figure 19-3: A pixel-based image (left) and after being Streamlined into paths

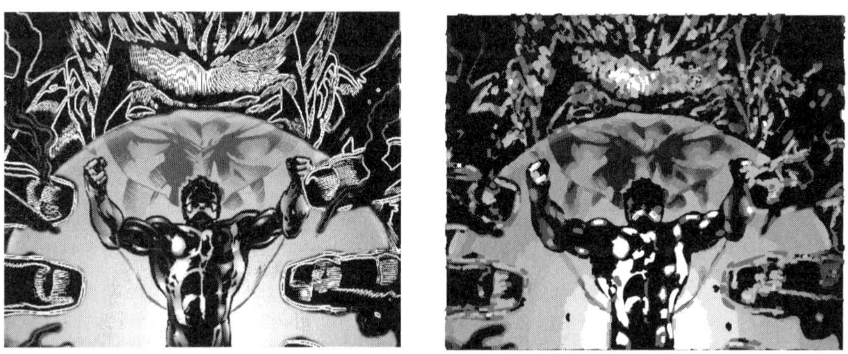

Figure 19-4: A pixel-based image (left) and after being Streamlined into paths

Streamline can be used as an econo-roughen filter. Rasterize your Illustrator artwork, export it as a TIFF, and then Streamline it. Play with the tolerance setting for a looser "feel" to the illustration.

Introducing Dimensions

Adobe Dimensions is PostScript-based software for creating artwork that looks three-dimensional. The great thing about Dimensions is that it was created expressly with Illustrator in mind.

Dimensions automatically creates four basic primitive shapes that have depth. It extrudes and revolves existing PostScript paths, and it can apply *surface* maps (artwork that is mapped onto the surface of 3D objects) of PostScript artwork to three-dimensional artwork. Finally, Dimensions can export three-dimensional artwork to Adobe Illustrator for inclusion in an Illustrator document.

A Brief History

Adobe released the first version of Dimensions, Version 1.0, at the end of 1992 and the next version (2.0) in the middle of 1994. The current version (3.0) just shipped with Illustrator. The three versions do basically the same thing.

This section discusses the features and capabilities of Dimensions and provides examples and techniques for using Dimensions with Illustrator. Although Dimensions is a huge program, this section gives you the lowdown on all of the great features of the software.

Be Frightened, Be Afraid, Be Intimidated

The speed of the computer's processor determines the speed of Dimensions. To a lesser degree, the amount of RAM that is allocated to Dimensions is also important, but processor speed is paramount.

If you have a 680 x 0 or 486 processor, you could be in for some frustration. Sure, even a Mac IIci with 8MB of RAM can do most things that Dimensions has to offer, but as they say, bring along a good book. You can expect to spend most of your time waiting for the computer to perform tasks.

I use a 200 MHz 604E Mac, and many times I get frustrated because things are taking too long. Most of the artwork that I create in Dimensions is similar to the samples in this chapter.

Extremely complex artwork requires time to create and to render, so be prepared for delays when you use Dimensions.

If you are the proud owner of a Power Mac or Pentium, this software makes your purchase of that system seem as if it were worth it. Even rendering will fly because of the way that the processors crank out numbers for Dimensions.

What Other 3D Software Has That Dimensions Doesn't Have

Three-dimensional software has always been around for the computer, but until Dimensions (and now Add Depth), no PostScript 3D software packages were available. Most of the three-dimensional software that is available at this time is used for creating either bitmapped images or QuickTime movies.

Other 3D software packages have many capabilities that Dimensions does not have. Most of these features are of the "gee-whiz" variety, but if you have been using other 3D packages for a while, these capabilities can seem important.

Don't waste your time looking for the following capabilities or features in Dimensions:

- **Lighting options:** The lighting options in Dimensions are nice, but most of the other 3D software packages enable you to create colored lights, spotlights versus omnidirectional lights, and light gels. Light gels are objects that you place in front of lights to make the lights appear in patterns on objects that are lit.
- **Reflective surfaces:** Shiny objects in most other 3D packages reflect nearby objects.
- **Object-cast shadows:** Objects in Dimensions do not cast shadows onto other objects.
- **Texture mapping:** You cannot place textures from bitmapped graphics onto three-dimensional objects in Dimensions.
- **Skinning:** Skinning is a three-dimensional technique that creates a flexible "skin" over structured ribs. This technique can produce incredibly complex three-dimensional objects.
- **Sweeps:** Sweeps are three-dimensional objects created by running a two-dimensional object along another two-dimensional path. Tube-like effects are the result.
- **Transparency:** Objects in Illustrator and Dimensions are opaque or transparent. Dimensions does have a way of simulating partial transparency, though.

(continued)

(continued)

The limitations of Dimensions may seem numerous, but in reality, you can create many of the features that it lacks by using different "cheating" methods in Dimensions and Illustrator. For example, you can simulate light gels, spotlights, and shadows by using the Mix Soft filter, and you can simulate transparency by using the Overprint feature.

Even if you are sure that you can't do something, relax. Adobe will continue to plug away at Dimensions until most of these features are incorporated. By the time that Version 4 of Dimensions appears (at about the turn of the century by my guess), all of these capabilities will probably be part of Dimensions, even on your antiquated 2,000 MHz processor.

Why Dimensions Is the Best 3D Software for Printing

Dimensions is the best 3D software for printing because of the following reasons:

- It produces PostScript output, which means that artwork that you create in Dimensions will look good at any size, just as Illustrator's artwork does.
- Unlike most 3D software, Dimensions enables you to create colors that are based only on four-color process printing. Most other 3D software packages create colors based on RGB, which doesn't usually translate well to CMYK and darkens most colors in the process.
- Dimensions can print proofs right out of the software. In Version 1.0, you had to export art to other software before you could print it.

In spite of the advantages that Dimensions offers, remember that you can accomplish very little entirely in Dimensions. For the best results, you need to export artwork from Dimensions to Illustrator.

Understanding the Three-Dimensional World

The concept of three dimensions should be simple for us to understand, for we are three-dimensional creatures who live in a three-dimensional world. But because most of what we see is two-dimensional (reading, watching television, working at a computer), adjusting to a three-dimensional world can be confusing and frustrating.

Changing from Two Dimensions to Three Dimensions

Television is a two-dimensional medium. The picture tube has height and width. Computer screens are two-dimensional. The pages of books are two-dimensional. Even driving is two-dimensional (drivers rarely consider up or down). Maps are two-dimensional, even though the world is round. Most people think in two dimensions.

Most of the two-dimensional objects that we deal with may very well be replaced with three-dimensional objects. Three-dimensional life will become a reality as soon as technology makes it so. Holograms have been around for a while, and technology is making them more accurate and lifelike. Video games and virtual-reality glasses already simulate three dimensions through the use of holograms and computer-generated imagery. Maybe sometime in the future we will have to look up and down when we are driving . . . although I doubt that we will be driving one of Apple's famed helocars.

Animation

MaryEllen: Can animation be done with Dimensions?

Toulouse: Yes, Dimensions has special controls just for that.

MaryEllen: How does it work?

Toulouse: Well, first you position your art the way it should appear in the first frame. Set that as a keyframe, and then position the art as you'd like it to end. Make that a keyframe as well. Then you can export a specific number of steps as the illustration transforms between the two keyframes.

MaryEllen: What if I want more than two positions?

Toulouse: You can blend between as many keyframes as you'd like.

Three-Dimensional Positioning

When you are trying to understand the concept of three dimensions on a computer screen, the most difficult aspect to grasp is depth. Left, right, up, and down are all simple concepts, but what about things that are closer or farther away?

You already are thinking in three dimensions in some ways if you have been using Illustrator long enough to grasp Send to Back and Bring to Front. If you feel comfortable with stacking order and layers, then you are one step further.

You use three different indicators to position objects in Dimensions:

- *X* is the horizontal location of the object. A value greater than 0 means that the object is positioned to the right of center (0). A value less than 0 (any negative number) represents an object to the left of center.
- An object's *Y* value defines its vertical position. A *Y* value that is greater than 0 means that the object is above center. A *Y* value that is less than 0 means that the object is below center.
- The third positioning variable is the depth of the object. *Z* represents how far forward or backward the object is from the center. A value greater than 0 means that the object is behind 0, or farther away. A value less than 0 means that the object is in front of 0, or closer to you.

Figure 19-5 shows the *X*, *Y*, and *Z* values as you would see them initially in Dimensions. In the status bar at the top of the screen, Dimensions shows the relative X, Y, and Z positions of selected objects. At a direct, straight-from-the-front view, you cannot determine an object's Z position. From the default position, which is a view of the objects from above and to the right of the front, you can determine all three positions visually.

Dimensions helps you manipulate objects by enabling you to move objects manually with a Selection tool or move them with the Move command (choose Operations➪Transform➪Move or double-click the Selection Tool). The Move palette for Dimensions, which is shown in Figure 19-6, is similar to the Illustrator Move dialog box, but Dimensions does not provide the option of moving an object by an angle. Instead, the Dimensions Move palette has a *Z* option that enables you to move an object forward or backward. Absolute and Relative options determine the starting point of the move.

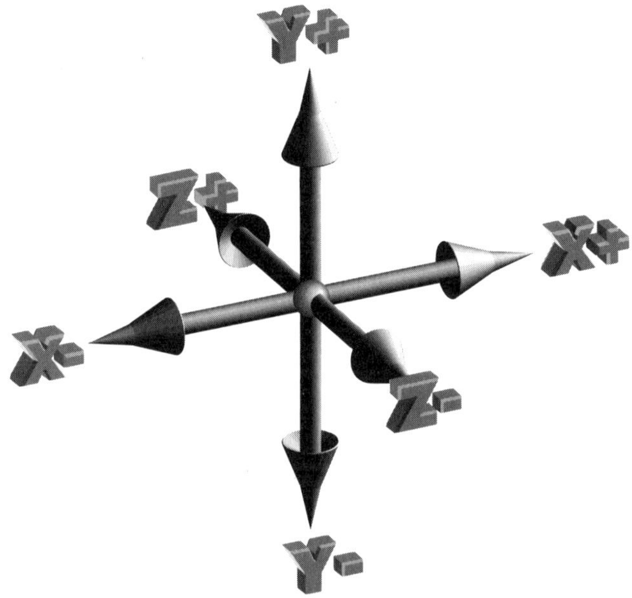

Figure 19-5: *X*, *Y*, and *Z* positioning of objects in Dimensions

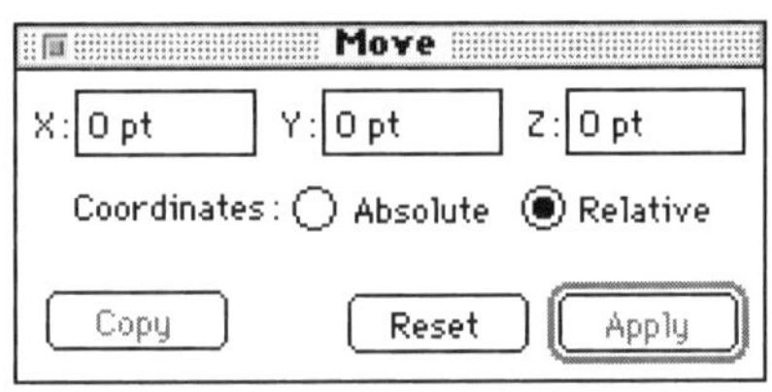

Figure 19-6: The Move palette in Dimensions

An Overview of Dimensions

The two main parts of Dimensions are a 2D drawing component and a 3D modeling component. Understanding their similarities and differences is key to understanding Dimensions. Each part uses a different toolbox and different menu options. Both parts also share several palettes, menu items, and tools.

Tools

The two toolboxes in Dimensions are shown and labeled in Figure 19-7. The 3D Toolbox is available when you are working with three-dimensional objects, and the 2D Toolbox appears when either the Artwork or Map windows is displayed. Most of the tools in the 2D Toolbox work the same way as their counterparts in the Illustrator toolbox.

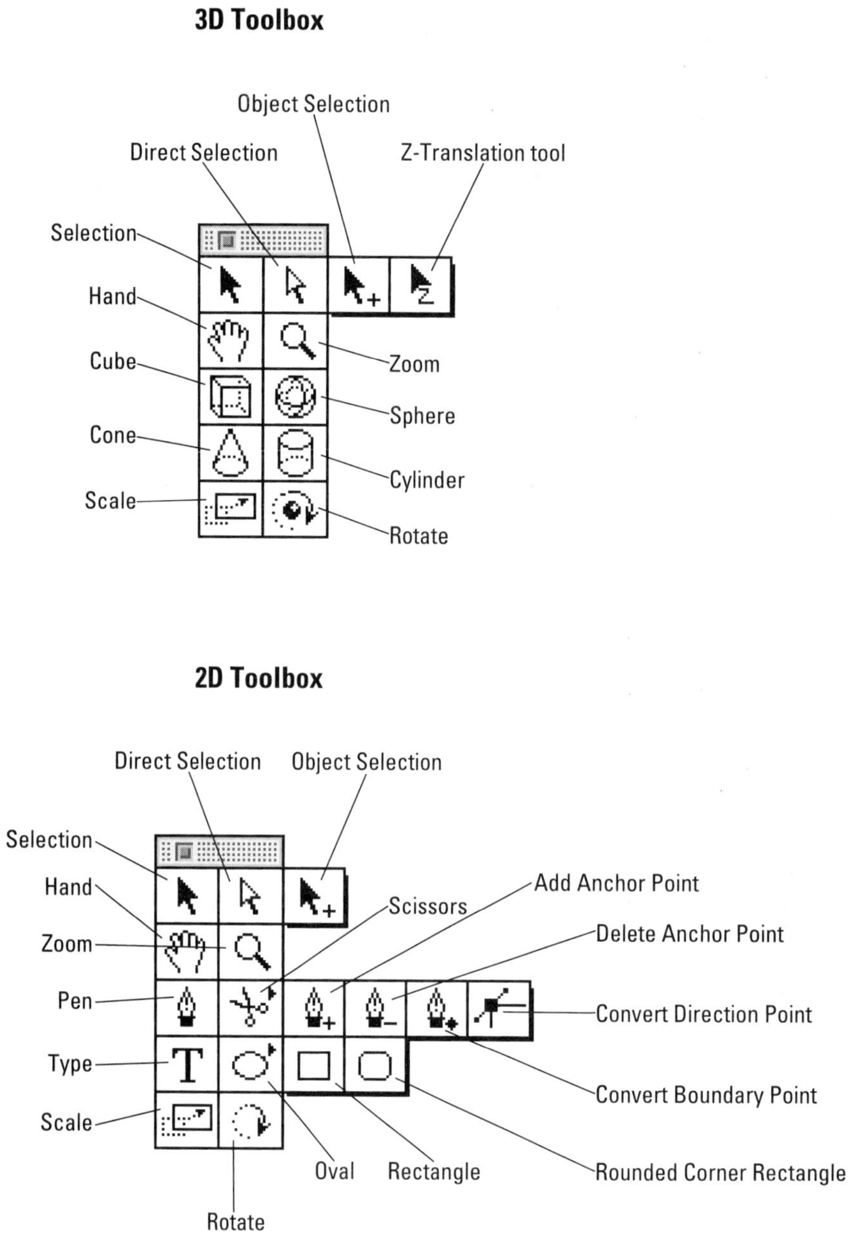

Figure 19-7: The toolboxes in Dimensions

The 3D Toolbox

The 3D Toolbox contains the following tools:

- **The Selection tool:** You use the Selection tool (⌘) [Ctrl] to select individual and grouped objects and to move them across the screen.
- **The Direct Selection tool:** The Direct Selection tool (⌘-Tab) [Ctrl+Tab] enables you to select individual faces of three-dimensional objects.
- **The Object Selection tool:** You use the Object Selection tool (⌘-Option) [Ctrl+Alt] to select an entire path that is part of a group of paths.
- **The Z-Translation tool:** The Z-Translation tool moves selected objects along the other axis. If you are viewing an object from the front, the Z-Translation tool moves the object forward and backward. If you are viewing the object from the bottom, the Z-Translation tool moves the object up and down.
- **The Hand tool:** The Hand tool (Spacebar) moves the entire Pasteboard within the screen area.
- **The Zoom tool:** The Zoom tool increases (⌘-Spacebar) [Ctrl+Spacebar] or decreases (⌘-Option-Spacebar) [Ctrl+Alt+Spacebar] the magnification level. If you drag a marquee with the Zoom tool, the area within the marquee will be zoomed up to fit within the document window.
- **The Cube tool:** The Cube tool creates cubical primitives. Dragging with the tool produces a cube the size of the drag, and clicking it brings up the Cube Size dialog box.
- **The Sphere tool:** The Sphere tool creates spherical primitives. Dragging with the tool produces a sphere the size of the drag, and clicking it brings up the Sphere Size dialog box.
- **The Cone tool:** The Cone tool creates conical primitives. Dragging with the tool produces a cone the size of the drag, and clicking it brings up the Cone Size dialog box.

Dimensions versus Vector Effects

Jim-Bob: I'm torn between buying Dimensions or KPT Vector Effects.

Toulouse: Yikes! You shouldn't be torn between them. They're totally different.

Jim-Bob: But don't they both extrude Illustrator art?

Toulouse: That's the only thing that both of them do. And they do that quite differently.

Jim-Bob: So how do I pick one?

Toulouse: From a standpoint of extruding, take note of the differences.

Jim-Bob: Which are...?

Toulouse: Vector Effects KPT 3D Transform is much faster, has almost instant previews, the capability to save presets, and a "metallic" setting. Also, Vector Effects creates paths that aren't masked, while Dimensions has to mask most things.

Jim-Bob: Wow. I bet Dimensions can't measure up to Vector Effects, then.

(continued)

(continued)

Toulouse: Well, in the area of extrusion, Dimensions lets you use custom bevels (VE only has a straight edge bevel, which you can change the size and angle of), more than one light source, and the capability to cast shadows. And, you can map 2D artwork to extruded art in Dimensions.

Jim-Bob: Gee, I had no idea. What other things do the packages differ in?

Toulouse: Vector Effects has 12 other filters (see Chapter 18 for more info on Vector Effects), while Dimensions can do basic animation and revolving, and it can create 3D Primitives. I need both packages; there's very little overlap between the two.

- **The Cylinder tool:** The Cylinder tool creates cylindrical primitives. Dragging with the tool produces a cylinder the size of the drag, and clicking it brings up the Cylinder Size dialog box.
- **The Scale tool:** The Scale tool enlarges or reduces the size of an object in much the same way that Illustrator's Scale tool changes an object's size.
- **The Rotate tool:** The Rotate tool enlarges or reduces the size of an object in much the same way that Illustrator's Rotate tool rotates objects, except that you can rotate objects in another dimension.

The 2D Toolbox

The 2D Toolbox contains the following tools:

- **The Selection tool:** This tool works the same way as the Selection tool in the 3D Toolbox works, but you use it for paths instead of for objects.
- **The Direct Selection tool:** You used this tool for selecting individual points, direction points, and line segments.
- **The Object Selection tool:** You use the Object Selection tool for selecting objects within groups.
- **The Hand and Zoom tools:** These tools work the same way that the Hand and Zoom tools in the 3D Toolbox work.
- **The Pen tool:** You use the Pen tool to create paths in the Artwork and Map windows. Its functionality is the same as that of the Pen tool in Illustrator.
- **The Scissors tool:** You use this tool to split an open path into two separated paths and to change a closed path into an open path.
- **The Add Anchor Point tool:** The Add Anchor Point tool adds Anchor Points to a path in the 2D window.

- **The Delete Anchor Point tool:** The Delete Anchor Point tool deletes an Anchor Point from a path.
- **The Convert Direction Point tool:** (⌘-Control) [Ctrl+Alt+Shift] The Convert Direction Point converts a direction point from a smooth point to a corner point.
- **The Type tool:** The Type tool enters a line of type into the 2D window.
- **The Oval, Rectangle, and Rounded Corner Rectangle tools:** These tools create the shapes they are named for, and they work the way their Illustrator equivalents work.
- **The Scale and Rotate tools:** These tools work the same way that their 3D counterparts work.

Creating Primitives

The most basic function in Dimensions is creating a primitive shape by using one of the four Primitive creation tools. The tools are the Cube tool, the Sphere tool, the Cone tool, and the Cylinder tool. They are called Primitive tools because you create other objects from the shapes that these tools create. As with all other sorts of drawings in Dimensions, you can create primitive shapes only in Artwork mode.

Figure 19-8 and the following steps show you how to create a basic primitive cone.

STEPS: Creating a Basic Primitive

Step 1. Select the Cone Primitive drawing tool.

Step 2. Click and drag with the tool. As you drag, a cube in wireframe form appears. You are still creating a cone, but when you drag with any of the primitive tools, you see a cube that holds the "space." Holding down the Shift key constrains the cube to have equal dimensions on all sides. Pressing Option [Alt] draws the cube from the center instead of from a corner.

Dimensions automatically constrains the depth of the cube to the width of the cube. By pressing Control as you drag, you constrain the depth of the cube to the height of the cube.

(continued)

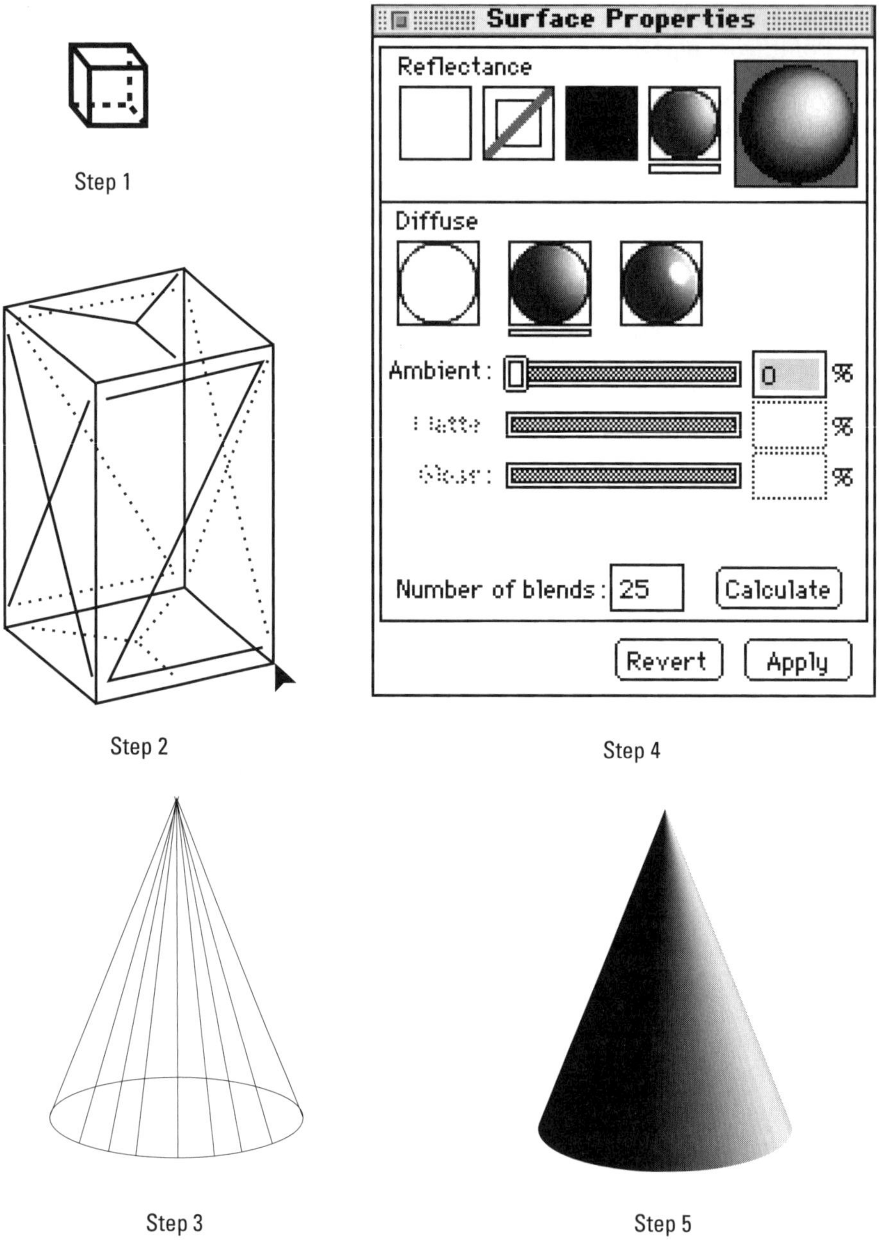

Figure 19-8: Steps for creating a basic primitive cone

STEPS: ***(continued)***

Step 3. When you release the mouse button, the cone appears as a wireframe version of the final cone.

The cone that you have drawn may look out of proportion or inexact because you are looking at it from the upper-left of the front of the cone. See the "Views and Perspectives" section, later in this chapter, for more information.

Step 4. After you draw a primitive, it is automatically selected. Choose Appearance⇨Surface Properties (⌘-I) [Ctrl+I] to display the Surface Properties dialog box. Change the Fill (the first box) to White, the Stroke (the second box) to None, the Shade (the third box) to Black, and the Reflectance (the fourth box) to Diffuse, and set Ambient to 0%.

After you draw the primitive, you can change its size. Double-click the primitive to display the Size dialog box for that particular primitive (see Figure 19-9) and then enter the exact dimensions.

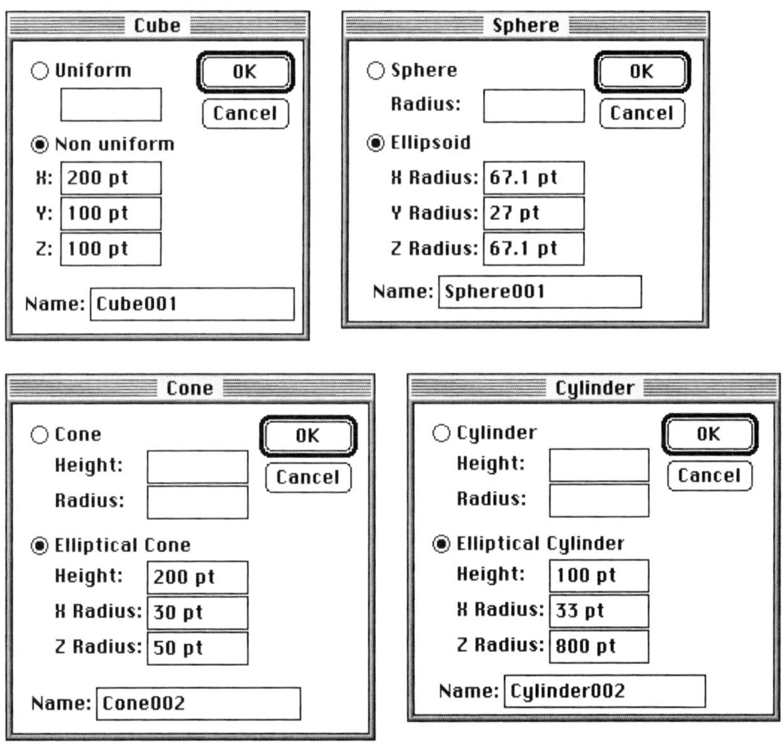

Figure 19-9: Size dialog boxes for each primitive

(continued)

STEPS: *(continued)*

Step 5. To see the final rendering, choose View➪Shaded Render (⌘-Shift-Y) [Ctrl+Shift+Y].

Another way to create primitives is by selecting a Primitive tool and just clicking without dragging. The primitive's Size dialog box appears. Enter the exact dimensions of the new primitive, and Dimensions creates it.

BY THE WAY: When the Size dialog box appears, it contains the values that were used the last time that Dimensions drew that shape.

Rendering Artwork

Before you can use artwork in other software or print it, you have to render it. Rendering is the process of turning the basic lines that make up a shape into a solid form.

Dimensions offers three different ways of rendering objects. The most basic way is wireframe rendering. Wireframe rendering (choose View➪Wireframe Render or press ⌘-Shift-W) [Ctrl+Shift+W] produces objects that look similar to the artwork representation of the three-dimensional objects.

The next step up in rendering is the Draft Render. To create a Draft Render, choose View➪Draft Render (⌘-Y) [Ctrl+Y]. Draft rendering creates surfaces with a minimum of shading for all objects, and mapped artwork is never shaded. Draft rendering is usually much faster than shaded rendering.

The best way to render in Dimensions is by choosing View➪Shaded Render (⌘-Shift-Y) [Ctrl+Shift+Y]. Shaded rendering produces smooth blends from light to dark areas of an object, as well as shading for mapped artwork. Shaded rendering can take a long time. The time required is directly related to the power of the host computer and the amount of RAM allocated to Dimensions.

Figure 19-10 shows a basic Dimensions document in the three different rendering styles. Note the differences between the draft rendering and the shaded renderings.

CAUTION: Extremely complex drawings can take hours to render, even on Quadra and PowerPC systems. To decrease rendering times, don't use bevels, mapped art, or curved objects, and use no more than one light.

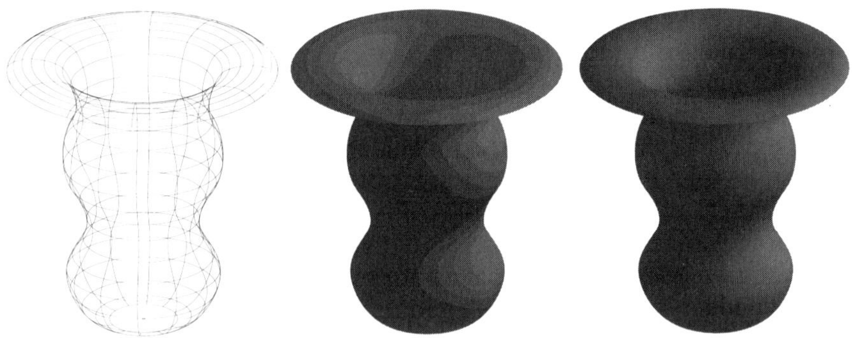

Figure 19-10: A comparison of the three types of rendering

Changing How Three-Dimensional Objects Look

Objects in Dimensions are not only colored, as in Illustrator, but are also lit. With lighting comes two additional specifications that are not present in Illustrator: Shading and Reflectance.

Two palettes, the Surface Properties palette and the Lighting palette, control how objects in Dimension look. Figure 19-11 shows both of these palettes.

The Surface Properties Palette

The Surface Properties palette is composed of four major parts: fill color, stroke color, shade color, and reflectance. The combination of all the parts is shown at the upper right of the palette on a sphere.

The different palette parts work as follows:

- **Fill color:** The Fill color box works very similarly to the one in Illustrator. The major difference is that you cannot choose patterns and gradients for Fills. You can select custom colors, and you can create them by choosing Appearance⇨Custom Colors. The Fill color is the color of the object at the point where a light source at 100% is shining on it.

Figure 19-11: The Surface Properties and Lighting palettes

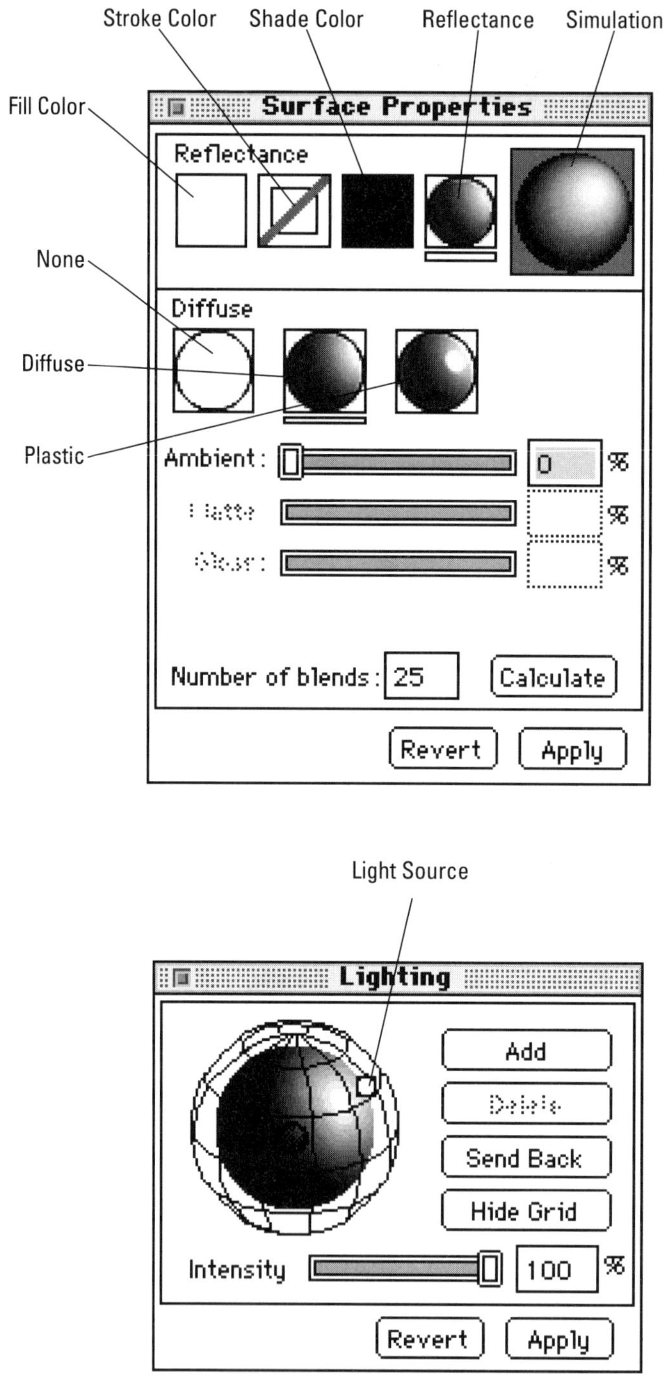

- **Stroke color:** The Stroke color box determines the color of the Stroke of the selected object. It works very similarly to the Stroke box in the Paint Style palette of Illustrator. A Stroke on a Dimensions object appears around the visible outline of an object. Strokes also show up on corners of objects, such as the rim of a cylinder.
- **Shade color:** The Shade color box is specific to Dimensions and is new in Version 2. The color in this box is the color that the object will be at its very darkest, in areas where no light source reaches it. A common technique for creating a shade color is to add black to a custom or process color. The following steps describe how to add black to a custom color.

STEPS: Adding Black to Custom Colors for Shading

Step 1. Select the object to be shaded and give a custom color Fill to the object in the Surface Properties palette (choose Appearance⇨Surface Properties or press ⌘-I) [Ctrl+I].

Step 2. Click the Shade color box. Select the custom color that was used for the Fill of the object. At this point, the object appears flat, with no change from light areas to dark areas.

Step 3. Click the Process square (it has four triangles on it). The custom color is converted to its process color attributes.

Step 4. Increase the black slider to a higher percentage, keeping in mind that this color will be the color of the shade at its darkest.

POWER TIP: I usually set the shading to the color of the Fill plus 75% black or more. This setting gives the best results for being able to see the color even in the darkest portions of the object.

Reflectance

The Reflectance box determines how light is reflected off the object. (See the "The Lighting Palette" section, later in this chapter, for more information on how objects are lit.)

Light can be reflected off three-dimensional objects in three ways, as shown in the boxes in the second row of the Surface Properties palette (shown previously in Figure 19-11). The first option is None, which more than anything else Fills the entire object with the Fill color and no shading at all. If the light source is behind the object, the object is still Filled with 100% of the selected Fill color. The None option is useful for quickly determining which objects are in front of others.

The second option is Diffuse, which diffuses light equally from where the light source hits the object to the edges of the object, where the light is its least bright. When Diffuse is selected, the Ambient control bar becomes selectable (as shown previously in Figure 19-11). The less Ambient light, the darker the shaded area. When Ambient is at 100%, no shading will appear. Figure 19-12 shows the effects of different ambient settings on the same three-dimensional object.

0% 20% 60%

Figure 19-12: Objects at different Ambient settings. Nothing is shown for 100%, because the object is completely white (the Fill color) at that setting.

The last box in the Reflectance section of the Surface Properties palette is the plastic box. When plastic is selected, you can manipulate the Matte and Gloss slider controls.

The Matte setting controls how plastic the object looks. An object appears more plastic when a highlight is present. The more obvious the highlight, the more plastic the object appears. A setting of 0%, which is the highest plasticity possible, makes the highlight very distinct. Figure 19-13 shows objects at a Matte setting of 0%.

The Gloss setting controls the size of the highlight. The higher the Gloss setting, the smaller the highlight. A Gloss setting of 0% creates a huge highlight. Highlights appear only on curved surfaces.

Figure 19-14 shows an object at different Gloss settings. Each object has an Ambient setting of 20% and a Matte setting of 40%.

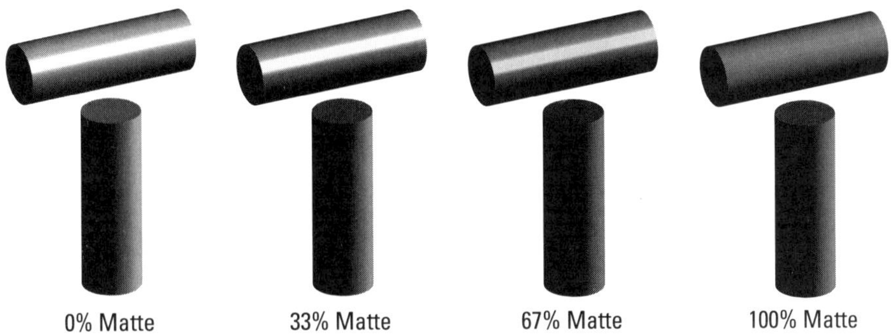

Figure 19-13: These objects are at the Matte setting shown under each object, with an Ambient setting of 0% and a Gloss setting of 50%

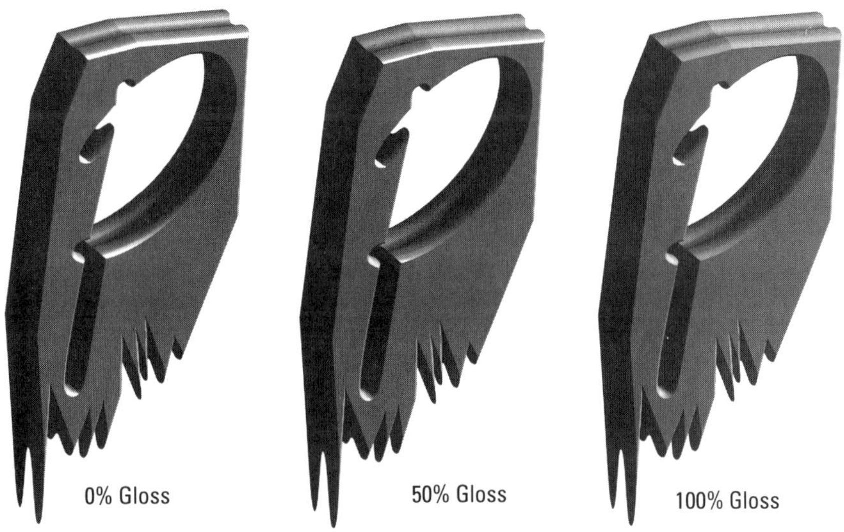

Figure 19-14: An object at three Gloss settings

In the Number of blends text box, you enter the number of blend steps. Clicking the Calculate button brings up the Calculate dialog box, where you can customize the number of blend steps for the output device by entering the resolution of the output device and the desired line screen.

Clicking the Apply button applies changes that you have made in the Surface Properties palette. Revert returns the settings to the what they were the last time you clicked Apply.

The Lighting Palette

You access the Lighting palette (refer to Figure 19-11) by choosing Appearance⇨Lighting (⌘-Shift-L) [Ctrl+Shift+L]. The Lighting palette controls the amount and direction of light sources. You always need to use at least one light, but you can use an unlimited number of lights.

The default light is always in the upper-right position, in front of objects in the document. Lights always shine into the document from outside it. To move a light around, click it and drag. Placing a light in the center of the sphere in the palette causes light to shine directly on the object from the front.

Understanding Lighting

Lighting can be a little confusing in a 3D program. The information in this sidebar can help you better understand the use of lighting.

Because lights in Dimensions are positioned an infinite distance from objects, shading for different objects is the same, no matter what the position of the objects. For example, if the lights are in the upper left, objects on the far left will have the same lighting as object on the far right. If the lights were positioned closer (they can't be in Dimensions), the shading on each object would appear differently.

A good way to think of the lights that you create in Dimensions is that they resemble sunlight to us earth-bound creatures. Light from the sun shines on an object in New York City almost exactly the same way that it shines on an object in neighboring Boston. Because the sun is so far away, the differences in the position of the sun relative to the two cities are minute. If the sun were an infinite distance away and the earth were flat (as everyone thought it was a few hundred years ago), the two cities would have exactly the same sunlight.

Because there are no shadows in Dimensions, objects that are between the light source and another object let light pass through them so that the light can reach the "hidden" object. This feature of Dimensions causes a problem when you are trying to make an image realistic, but creative use of the Soft filter can resolve the problem easily. Shadow creation in bitmapped 3D programs is one of the most time-consuming and power-consuming activities of using those software packages.

The most annoying thing about lights in 3D programs is where the highlights show up. The highlights are reflections of the lights, so your position relative to the objects and their position relative to the lights are the basis for where a highlight appears. The following figure shows that you perceive a highlight on a reflective surface at the point where the reflection of a light source meets your eye.

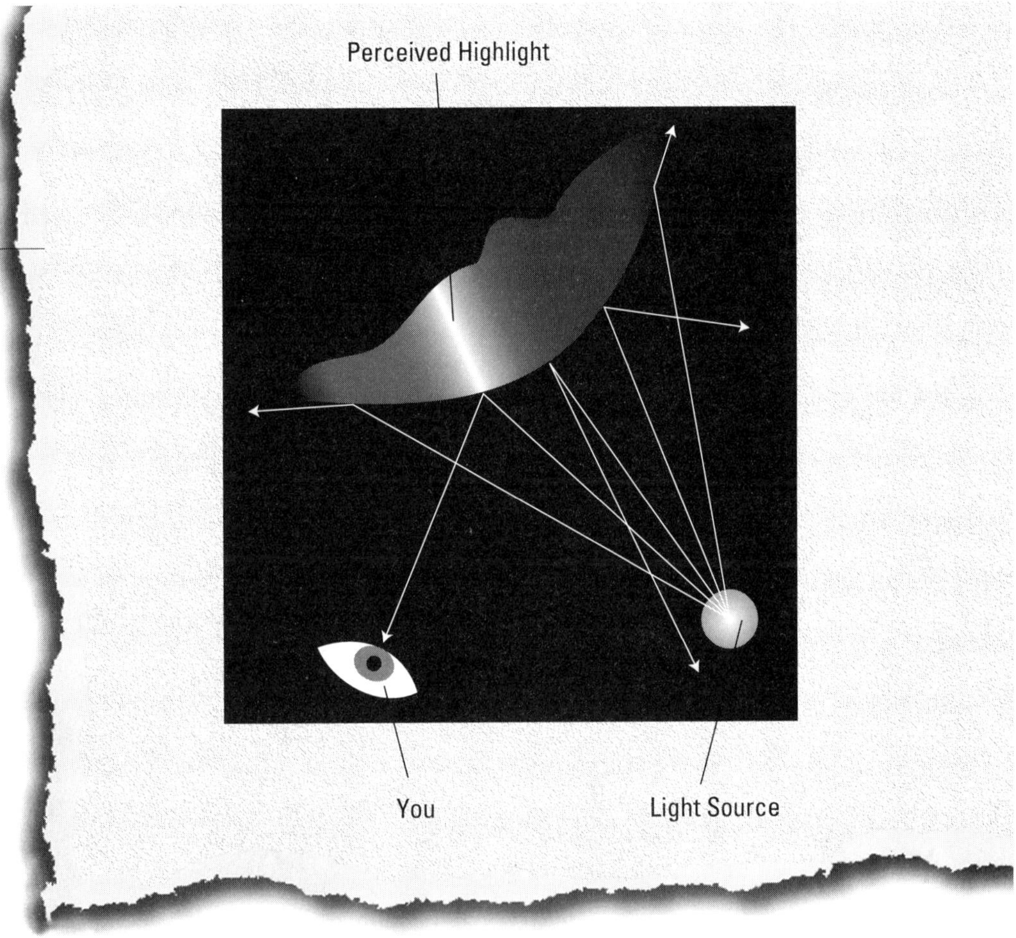

You can position lights on the other side of the objects in a document by clicking the Send Back button. When a light source is behind the sphere, you can bring it forward by clicking the Bring Forward button, which takes the place of the Send Back button.

The Intensity slider at the bottom of the Lighting palette controls how bright each light is. To change a light's intensity, select it and drag the Intensity slider to the correct position.

Add additional light sources by clicking the Add button. Delete selected light sources by clicking the Delete button. You cannot delete the only light, but you can change its intensity to 0%, which colors everything the same shade.

Points

Olivia: Why are the points bigger in Dimensions?

Toulouse: There is no good answer to this, unfortunately. They just are.

Olivia: It makes the 2D drawing portion of Dimensions feel clunky...like FreeHand on a good day.

Toulouse: Tell Adobe your dissatisfaction. That's the surest way to get them to make a needed change.

Creating Two-Dimensional Artwork

You can create two-dimensional artwork in Dimensions 2.0. Previously, all 2D artwork had to be imported or pasted into the software. Although this is a nice touch to Dimensions, it really has little bearing if you have Illustrator. The toolset is limited in comparison to Illustrator, and drawing in Dimensions is more frustrating than useful.

Instead of learning the nuances of drawing in Dimensions, do your drawing and editing in Illustrator. After all, art can be copied and pasted between the two programs rather easily.

Using Illustrator Artwork

You can use artwork from Illustrator in Dimensions by bringing it into the program in two ways. The first way is to choose File➪Import (⌘-Control-I) [Ctrl+Alt+Shift+I] and select the Adobe Illustrator file. If a 2D window is present, the artwork will appear in the 2D window; otherwise, the artwork will be in an artwork box in the 3D window.

The second method is to copy artwork in Illustrator and paste it into Dimensions. The artwork will appear in the active window.

Modifying 2D Artwork

You can use any of the tools in the 2D Toolbox to modify artwork. After you finish modifying the artwork, click the Update button in the Artwork window or simply close the window. If you close the window, a dialog box appears, asking whether you want to update with the artwork from the closing 2D window. Click Update to have the artwork in the 3D window reflect the changes that you made in the 2D window.

Saving 2D Artwork

Artwork that you create in the 2D windows of Dimensions isn't saved; instead, the artwork is exported in an Illustrator format. To export artwork that you create in the 2D window of Dimensions, make sure that the 2D artwork is active, and then choose File➪Export (⌘-Option-E) [Ctrl+Alt+E].

Previewing 2D Artwork

To preview artwork in the 2D windows, choose either View➪Preview (⌘-Y) [Ctrl+Y] or View➪Preview Selection (⌘-Option-Y) [Ctrl+Alt+Y]. You cannot manipulate artwork that you are previewing in Dimensions. Previewing 2D artwork does not preview the objects in the 3D window.

Using the Tile and Stack Options

Dimensions can automatically tile windows. When you choose Window➪Tile Windows, the 3D window is sized to take up the left half of the monitor, and the 2D window is sized to take up the right half of the monitor. Additional 2D windows are tiled on the right side.

If you have two or more monitors, choosing the Tile Windows option automatically tiles any Artwork windows to additional monitors; the main monitor (the one with the menu bar) then contains only the 3D window.

Extruding and Revolving 2D Artwork

You create two-dimensional artwork in Illustrator to use as mapped art on a three-dimensional object, as a bevel, or as a base object to extrude or revolve.

Before you extrude or revolve artwork, you can edit it by selecting the artwork and choosing Operations➪Edit Artwork (⌘-Option-A) [Ctrl+Alt+A]. However, extruding and revolving 2D artwork creates a three-dimensional object from the two-dimensional base object, and you cannot subsequently edit the three-dimensional object in the 2D window.

Extruding Flat Art

Extruding is the process of giving flat art depth that is equal on every part of the artwork. Figure 19-15 shows flat art and the same art after it has been extruded.

Figure 19-15: The same art, shown flat and extruded

The following steps describe how to create extruded 2D artwork:

STEPS: Extruding 2D Artwork

Step 1. Select the 2D artwork in the 3D window.

Step 2. Choose Operations⇨Extrude (⌘-Shift-E) [Ctrl+Shift+E]. The Extrude palette appears, as shown in Figure 19-16.

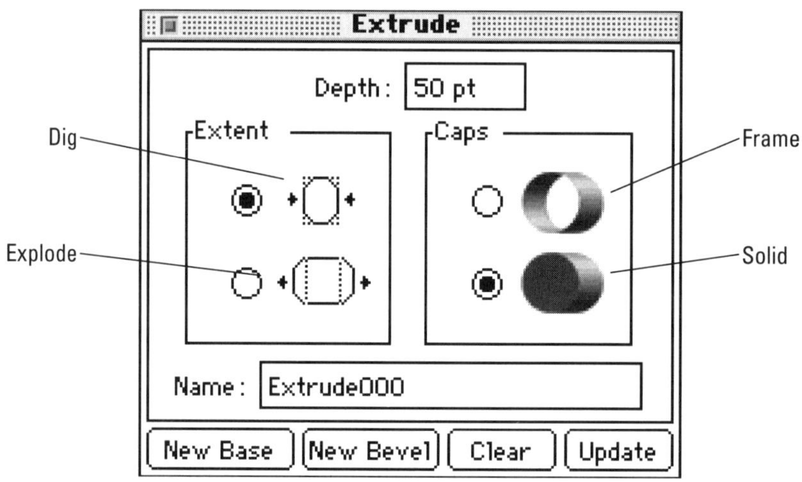

Figure 19-16: The Extrude palette

Step 3. Enter the depth that you want the object to be extruded along its *Z* axis. This setting determines the "thickness" of the artwork.

Step 4. In the Caps area, select the type of extrusion that you want. Choosing the solid extrusion button creates a solid object, and choosing the frame extrusion button creates a framed object.

Step 5. If you are going to bevel the surface of the 2D artwork, select the type of bevel to use by choosing a button in the Extent area of the Extrude palette. A Dig bevel digs into the extruded object along the *Z*-axis, and a Grow bevel grows out from the *Z*-axis.

Step 6. Choose the type of bevel to use by selecting the New Bevel button. Adobe Dimensions comes with a Bevel Library that contains several bevels. The New Bevel button opens an Open dialog box, in which you need to choose a bevel file.

A bevel file is a very basic Illustrator document that has an open path in it.

Step 7. Click the Update button to change the selected 2D artwork into an extruded three-dimensional object.

Understanding Bevels

The use of bevels can make or break your artwork (and yes, complex bevels will more often break than make it). Figure 19-17 shows samples of bevels, and the following steps describe how to create and apply a bevel.

STEPS: Creating and Applying a Bevel

Step 1. Create an object that you want to extrude and apply a bevel to. Choose Operations⇨Extrude (⌘-Shift-E) [Ctrl+Shift+E] to access the Extrude palette, and enter the depth of the extrusion.

Step 2. Click the New Bevel button. Click the Cancel button in the Open dialog box (⌘-period) [Ctrl+period] to see a new window in which you can create a bevel.

Step 3. Use the Pen tool to create a bevel that is a single open path.

Step 4. Click the Update button in the Extrude palette.

Step 5. Render the artwork as you desire.

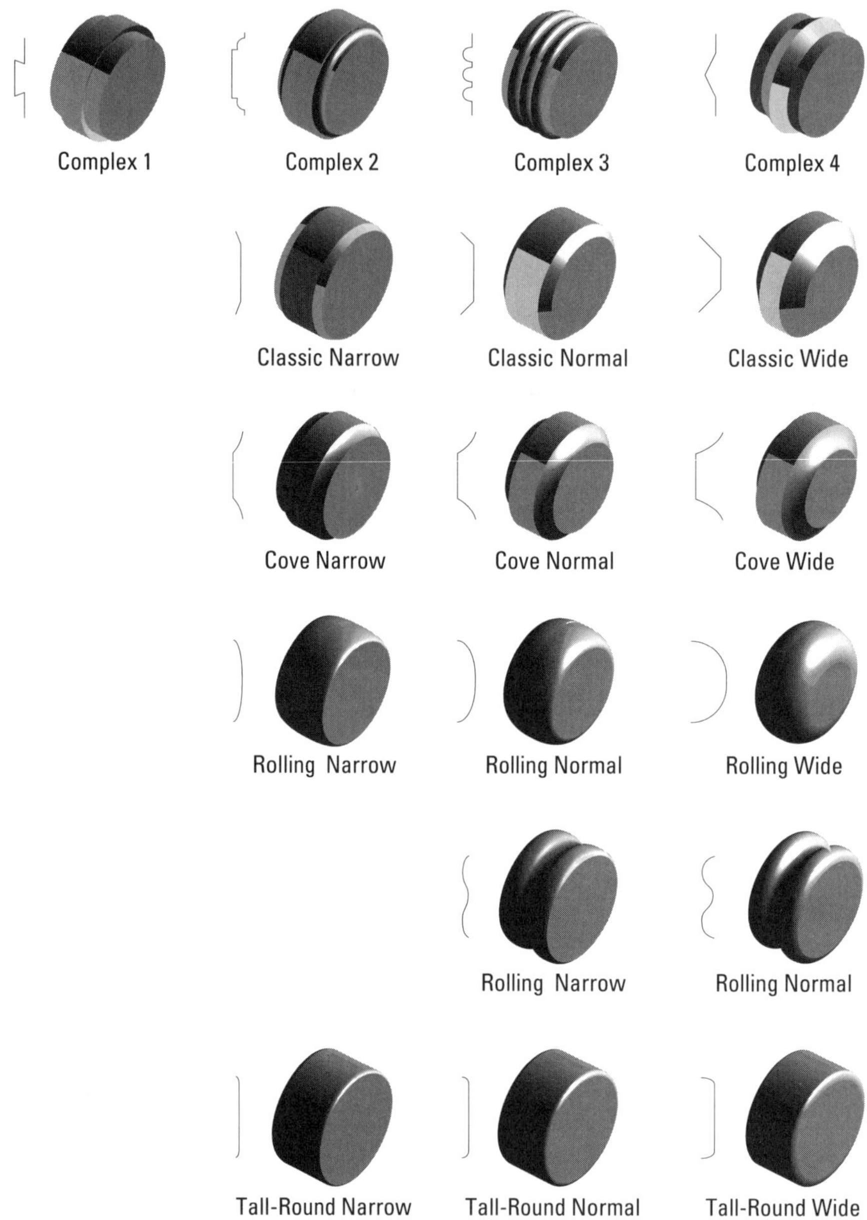

Figure 19-17: Bevels and the results of using them on extruded artwork

CAUTION

Bevels that have curves take a great deal of time when you are rendering an object. Using a few straight lines is better than using a curve. A good rule of thumb is that if the object doesn't redraw as art in the 3D window when you update it to the new bevel, you shouldn't try to render it. The rendering process could tie up your computer for long periods of time.

Often, when you select a wide format bevel, the Dig Extent option forces a bevel to self-intersect. Although self-intersection sounds like something you wouldn't want to read about in a family-oriented book, it is actually almost that bad. Intersecting bevels can produce, as the dialog box says, "unpredictable geometry," and the rendered result will probably turn out to be unusable.

Revolving Artwork

Revolving is what Adobe calls *lathing*. It is the process of spinning a two-dimensional object around an axis so many degrees in order to create a three-dimensional object. The following steps describe how to revolve 2D artwork into 3D artwork.

STEPS: Revolving 2D Artwork into 3D Artwork

Step 1. Create 2D artwork in the 2D window or in Adobe Illustrator. In the sample (Figure 19-18), I created separate paths for one side of a lamp and a lampshade.

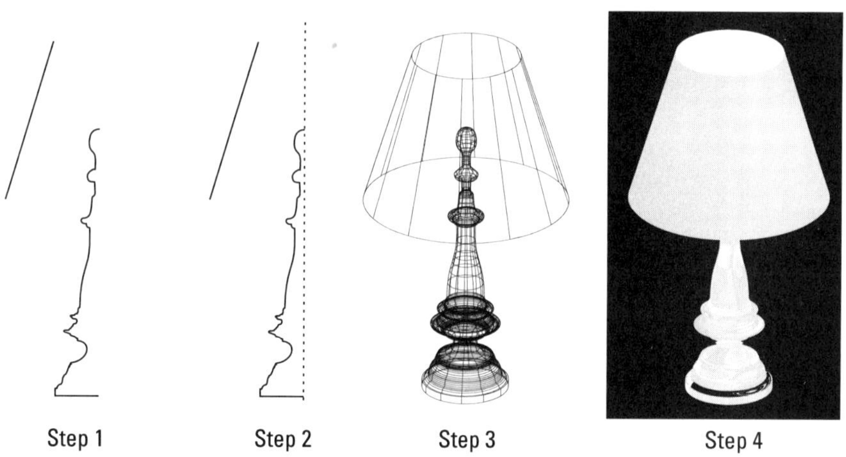

Figure 19-18: Steps for revolving artwork

(continued)

STEPS: *(continued)*

Step 2. Create a straight line with the Pen tool by clicking in one location and then in another. Position the newly created line so that it runs across the axis that you want to rotate the artwork around. After the line is in position, choose Draw⇨Make Guide.

If you do not create a guide, artwork will naturally revolve around its leftmost edge.

Step 3. Choose Operations⇨Revolve (⌘-Shift-R) [Ctrl+Shift+R] to display the Revolve palette that is shown in Figure 19-19. Enter **360** in the Angle text box to have the artwork make a complete revolution around the guide.

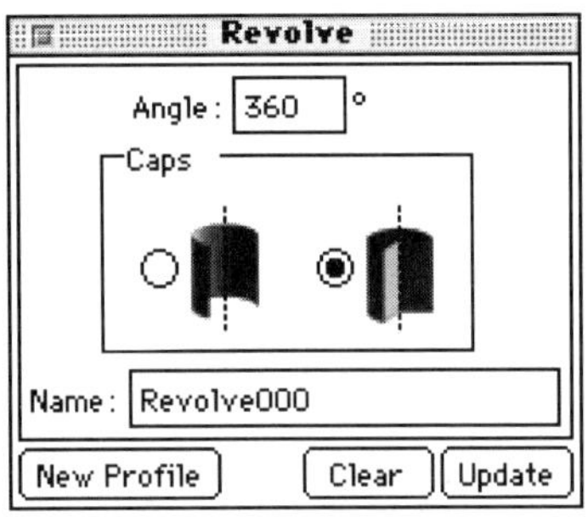

Figure 19-19: The Revolve palette

Step 4. Give the revolved object surface properties and render it. Use the Direct Selection tool to select individual portions of the object, such as the lamp base.

You can create many things by revolving different objects around different axes. Figure 19-20 shows the results of revolving the same three two-dimensional objects on different axes.

Remember that you don't have to revolve objects the entire 360° to achieve different effects. In fact, you can achieve some effects only by revolving the objects at less than 360°, as in the following steps.

STEPS: Extruding by Revolving

Step 1. In the 2D window, create the 2D artwork that you want to extrude.

Step 2. Far from the actual artwork, draw a path to use as the guide. Zooming out when you create this guide may be helpful.

Step 3. Choose Operations⇨Revolve and enter **5** for the revolve angle.

Step 4. Render the artwork. The result is an extrusion that is extruded more on one side (the side farthest from the guide axis) than on the other.

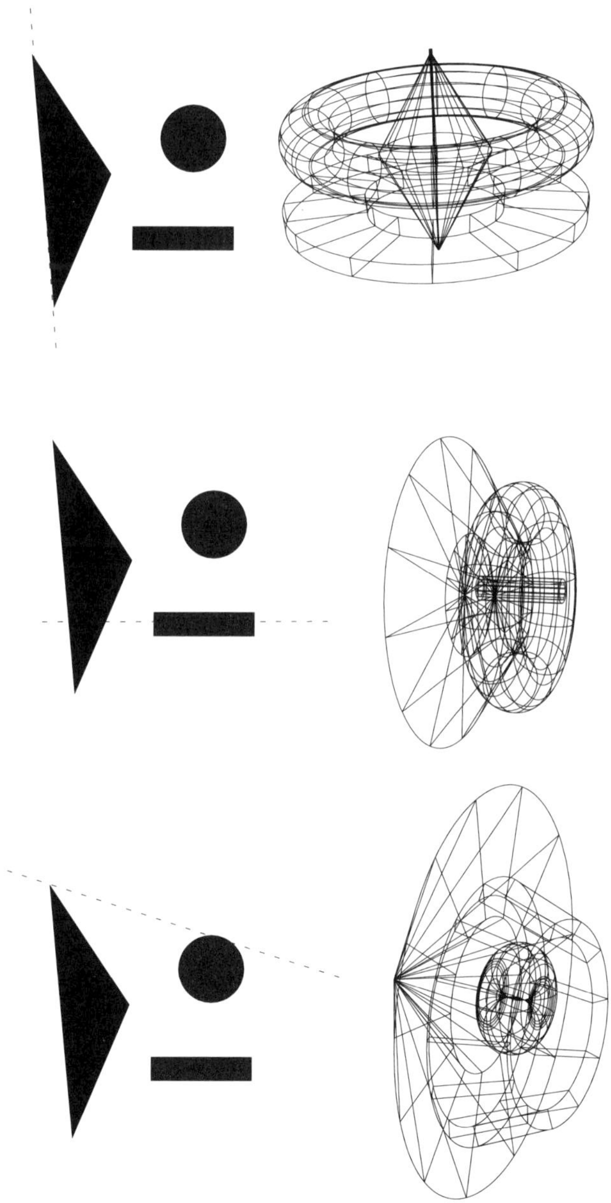

Figure 19-20: The same objects were revolved in each of these drawings, but they were revolved on a different axis in each example. The dotted lines show the axes that were used.

Rendering

Zeb: Some of the time, Dimensions artwork won't render at all.

Toulouse: There's several reasons for this. Are you using bevels?

Zeb: Yes. Is that a problem?

Toulouse: Bevels, especially ones with curved path segments, take up a lot of processing power.

Zeb: Anything else that causes problems?

Toulouse: The other major slowdowns are using complex art for mapping and too many light sources.

Manipulating 3D Artwork

You can manipulate artwork in Dimensions in three different ways. The most obvious way is by selecting various objects and moving them around the screen. A less-obvious method is to move the same objects forward and backward. Rather than simply using the Send to Back or Bring to Front commands, or even using the minor complexity of layers, you can change the location of each object in Dimensions along the *Z* axis.

The other two ways to manipulate objects in the 3D window of Dimensions are by scaling and rotating these objects. Although scaling and rotation sound simple, because by now you are undoubtedly a master of rotation and sizing in Illustrator, Dimensions presents a new challenge. The Rotate tool rotates objects in all three dimensions. The Scale tool reduces and enlarges objects in all three dimensions. And you cannot ignore that extra dimension.

Moving Objects in Three Dimensions

You can move objects in two dimensions, just as in Illustrator, by dragging them around the screen with the Selection tool. To drag an object back and forth along the *Z* axis, you have to use the Z-Translation tool.

All references to the Z-Translation tool assume that the reader is viewing artwork in Off-Axis Front or Front views. Using the Z-Translation tool in other views moves objects along other axes.

You select the Z-Translation tool by clicking the Direct Selection tool and dragging over to the arrow with a *Z* under it. For instant access to the Z-Translation tool at any time, press ⌘-Control (Mac only).

Dragging an object with the Z-Translation tool moves the object diagonally on the screen, but it is actually moving the object closer or farther from you, along the *Z* axis.

You cannot move objects along the depth axis (*Z* when in a Front view) with any tool but the Z-Translation tool. Dragging an object diagonally does not move it forward or backward.

When you are dragging an object down and to the right, it is getting closer to you, moving in front of other objects, and decreasing the *Z* value along the *Z* axis.

When you are dragging an object up and to the left, it is going farther away from you, moving behind other objects, and increasing the *Z* value along the *Z* axis.

All objects can be copied by pressing Option [Alt] when the mouse button is released, and are constrained to a movement of 45° when the Shift key is pressed before the mouse button is released — just as in Illustrator. The Option [Alt]-copy and Shift-constrain work this way in Photoshop as well.

Using the Move palette (refer to Figure 19-6) may be easier than moving objects manually. To access the Move palette, choose Operations⇨Move (⌘-Shift-M) [Ctrl+Shift+M]. By entering values in the *X*, *Y*, and *Z* text boxes, you can move objects along these axes.

When the Relative button is checked, objects are moved relative to their current location. If an object is at an absolute location relative to the center of the document of 10 *X*, –20 *Y*, and 100 *Z*, entering 10 in each of the three text boxes moves the object 10 points in each of those directions, leaving the object at 20 *X*, –10 *Y*, and 110 *Z*.

When the Absolute button is checked, the location of the object relative to the center of the document is displayed in the text boxes. If the object is at 10 *X*, –20 *Y*, and 100 *Z*, entering 10 in each of the text fields when the Absolute button is checked moves the object along all three axes to 10 *X*, 10 *Y*, and 10 *Z*.

The Absolute button stands for the relation of the object to the center of the document at 0 *X*, 0 *Y*, and 0 *Z*.

The Copy button in the Move palette creates a copy of the object at the coordinates specified.

Scaling in Three Dimensions

When you scale objects in two dimensions, you modify the width and height. The only difference when you are working in three dimensions is that you scale the depth as well as the width and height.

You can scale objects by using either the Scale tool or the Scale palette.

STEPS: Scaling in 3D with the Scale Tool

Step 1. To scale an object with the Scale tool, use any of the Selection tools to select the object.

Step 2. Select the Scale tool in the 3D Toolbox.

Step 3. Click to set the origin. As in Illustrator, I usually set the origin of the scale in either the center of the object or in a corner or edge that I don't want to move.

Step 4. Click far from the origin (usually on a far corner of the object) and drag. The depth of the scaling is changed relative to the change in the width of the object. Pressing the Control key provides for changes in the depth of only the object.

After you scale width and height, be sure to release the mouse button before you change the depth, and vice versa. Failing to release the mouse button causes the scaling that you have just done to be wiped out when you press or release the Control key.

Step 5. To make a proportional scaled copy, press Option [Alt] before releasing the mouse button.

To use the Scale palette (see Figure 19-21) to scale an object, choose Operations⇨Scale (⌘-Option-S) [Ctrl+Alt+S]. To quickly display the Scale palette, double-click on the Scale tool in the 3D Toolbox.

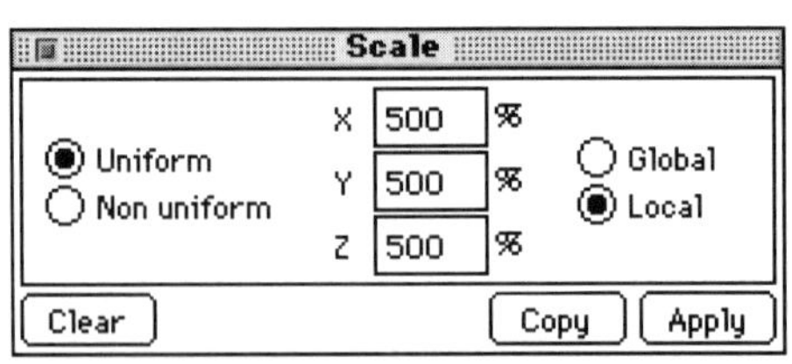

Figure 19-21: The Scale palette

In the *X, Y,* and *Z* text boxes, specify the amount that you want to scale the selected objects. If you check the Uniform button, all values for all three fields will be the same. If you check the Non uniform button, then you can change each field independently of every other field.

Rotating Objects in Three Dimensions

The easiest way to understand the concept of three-dimensional rotation is to imagine each axis as a pivot for objects. Figure 19-22 illustrates this concept.

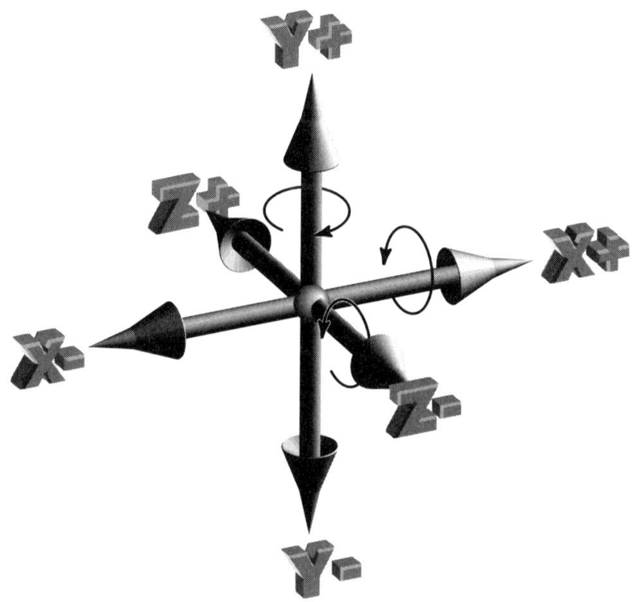

Figure 19-22: The circular arrows show the direction of rotating objects with positive values around each of the axes

In comparison with rotating, scaling isn't difficult to understand, because you scale objects in Illustrator in two dimensions. But rotation is another story. In Illustrator, you can rotate objects only around the *Z* axis. In Dimensions, you have to deal with the *Y* and *X* axes as well.

Actually, you can use Illustrator's Reflection tool to rotate objects around the *X* and *Y* axes in a twisted way. If you are comfortable with using the Reflection tool in Illustrator, rotating around *X* and *Y* axes shouldn't be much of a challenge.

I think that the hardest part about three-dimensional rotation is the difficulty in remembering which axis is which and how objects rotate around those axes. Since the beginning of time (circa 1990), I have used the memory tricks described in this section to help myself remember which axis to rotate around.

The *Z* axis, as stated previously, rotates objects in the same way that Illustrator (and every other graphics package in the western world) rotates objects. If you can remember that, great. If not, read on.

You use the *Z* axis to rotate objects the same way that a propeller on a plane spins. So remember Zis: Zee Axis powers in World War II flew propeller-equipped planes. Zimple.

Going along with the flying theme, remember the whirlybird things that you played with as a kid? You held a stick with a whirlybird shooting up and out of it at an angle and moved your hands back and forth to make the whirlybird fly. It looked like a *Y* in flight. The Y axis spins things the same way that a whirlybird spins.

X is the comin' at ya axis. Objects spinning around the *X* axis include such things as tires on a car racing at you. You being the target, and *X* marking the spot (you), makes this memory trick a no-brainer.

If these little tidbits don't help you, you always have Figure 19-22.

The best way to do controlled rotation is by using the Rotate palette (see Figure 19-23), which you access by choosing Operations⇨Rotate (⌘-Option-R) [Ctrl+Alt+R]. Or access the Rotate palette quickly by double-clicking the Rotate tool.

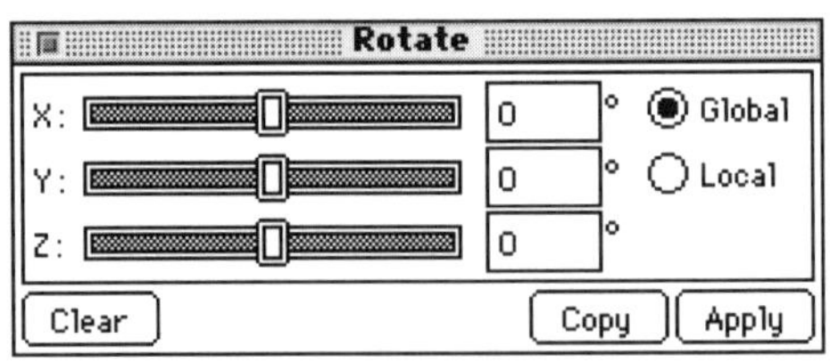

Figure 19-23: The Rotate palette

If the Local button is selected, objects rotate relative to the most recent rotation of the selected object. If the Global button is selected, objects rotate relative to 0° *X*, *Y*, and *Z*. Local rotates the object relative to its current *XYZ* axis. Global rotates the object relative to the page (0/0) *XYZ* axis. Also, when multiple objects are selected, the axis is always global.

Using the Rotate tool is a little more tricky. You have no clues to help you determine which way objects are being rotated. To rotate objects, you can either click to set an origin point or click and drag all at once. I have found that clicking and dragging all at once is easier (though by no means simple).

CAUTION Most objects (with the exception of text) can look the same at 180° rotations around all the axes. If you are unsure of the direction of the objects that you have rotated, do a draft render or a render selection to determine which way an object is facing.

Views and Perspectives

Possibly the most important aspect of any program for drawing three-dimensional objects is the capability to view any drawing from any angle. Some programs call this angle the *camera position*. Dimensions has 13 different ways of looking at objects.

Using different perspectives is another way to view objects differently as a sort of special camera effect.

Different Viewing Options

The viewing options in Dimensions fall into two categories: on-axis and off-axis. Within each of these categories are six different directional views. An isometric view, which is similar to an off-axis view, is also available.

Figure 19-24 shows how an object is viewed from each of the 13 different views available in Dimensions. The original object was lit from the default light in the upper-right corner. A basic Classic Normal bevel was applied to the extruded letters.

POWER TIP The views are most useful when you need to arrange different objects relative to each other. For Figure 19-24, I used off-axis front, front, back, top, and left views to position the objects before rendering each of them at different views.

Viewing objects from different locations does not move or rotate the objects. It just changes your viewing position relative to the objects. The light source and the objects are not modified at all.

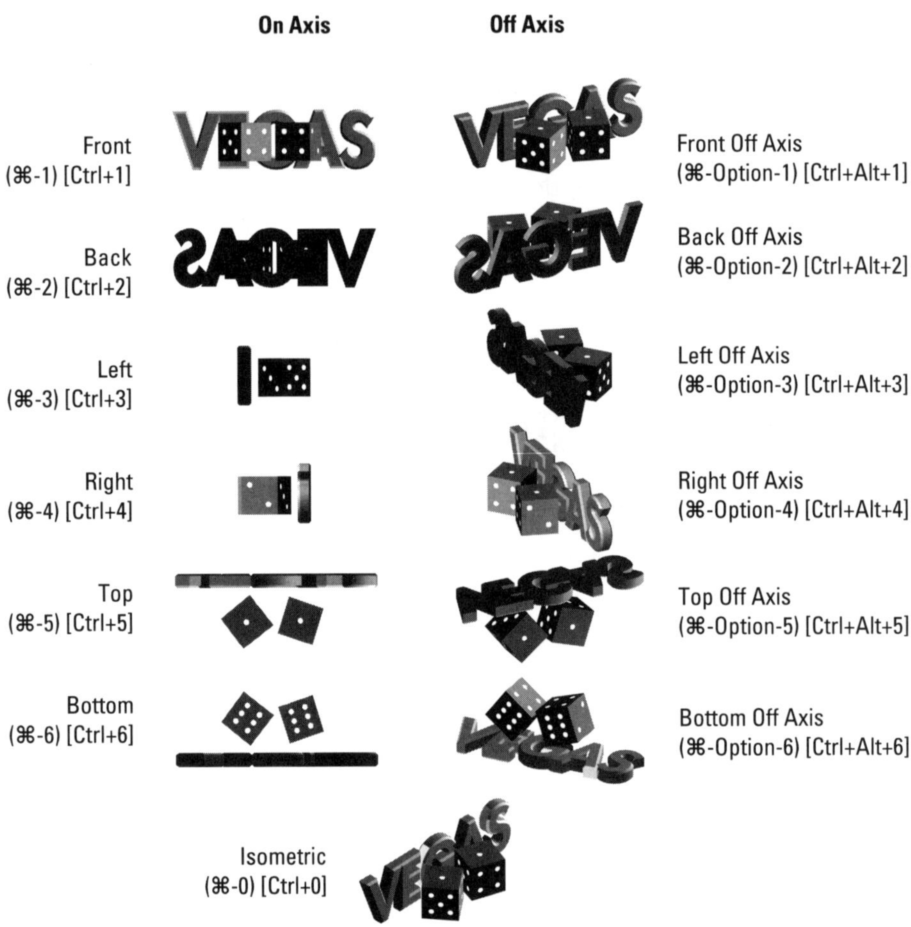

Figure 19-24: Viewing the same object from each of the 13 different views in Dimensions

Getting a Better Perspective

In addition to different viewing locations, you can choose several different perspectives. Perspective, though it doesn't look like it, is actually a simulated distance from the objects in the Dimensions document.

To change the perspective quickly, select an option from the Perspective pop-up menu at the top of the Dimensions window. You also can change the perspective by choosing View⇨Perspective and selecting one of the perspectives that is listed. For complete control of viewing objects, choose View⇨Custom Perspective (⌘-Control-P) [Ctrl+Alt+Shift+P] to display the Custom Perspective palette.

For complete control of viewing objects, choose View⇨Custom Perspective (⌘-Control-P) [Ctrl+Alt+Shift+P] to display the Custom Perspective palette. This palette, which is shown in Figure 19-25, enables you to view an object at a specific distance. Strangely enough, the perspective is measured in degrees rather than in centimeters, inches, or picas.

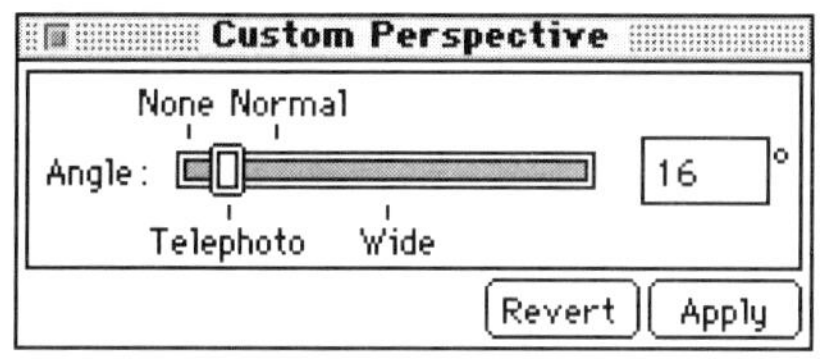

Figure 19-25: The Custom Perspective palette

The most common custom perspective values are shown in Figure 19-26.

The preset values are as follows:

- **None:** None views objects at an infinite distance, providing no perspective at all. Objects to the right and left appear to have similar depths. On-axis views create a flat appearance for objects. The Custom Perspective palette setting is 0° for None.
- **Telephoto:** Telephoto is similar to looking at the object from 2,000 points, or 28 inches, away. The Custom Perspective palette setting is 18° for None, because the field of vision is 18°.
- **Normal:** The field of vision for Normal is 35°, which is similar to looking at the object from 1,028 points, or 14 inches, away.
- **Wide:** When you choose the Wide perspective, the field of vision expands to 80°. This setting is comparable to standing at a distance of 450 points, or 6.25 inches, from the objects.
- **110°:** At a field of vision 110°, the distance is about 272 points, or 3.75 inches.
- **130°:** At a field of vision 130°, the distance from objects is down to 220 points, or 3 inches.
- **140°:** At a field of vision 140°, the distance from objects is only 200 points, or 2.75 inches.
- **150°:** At a field of vision of 150°, the distance from objects is 180 points, or 2.5 inches.
- **160°:** (not pictured). At 160°, objects start to become stretched rather bizarrely. Objects look as if they are at a distance of about 108 points, or 1.5 inches.

At 180°, you are smack up against the objects, and they take up your entire field of vision.

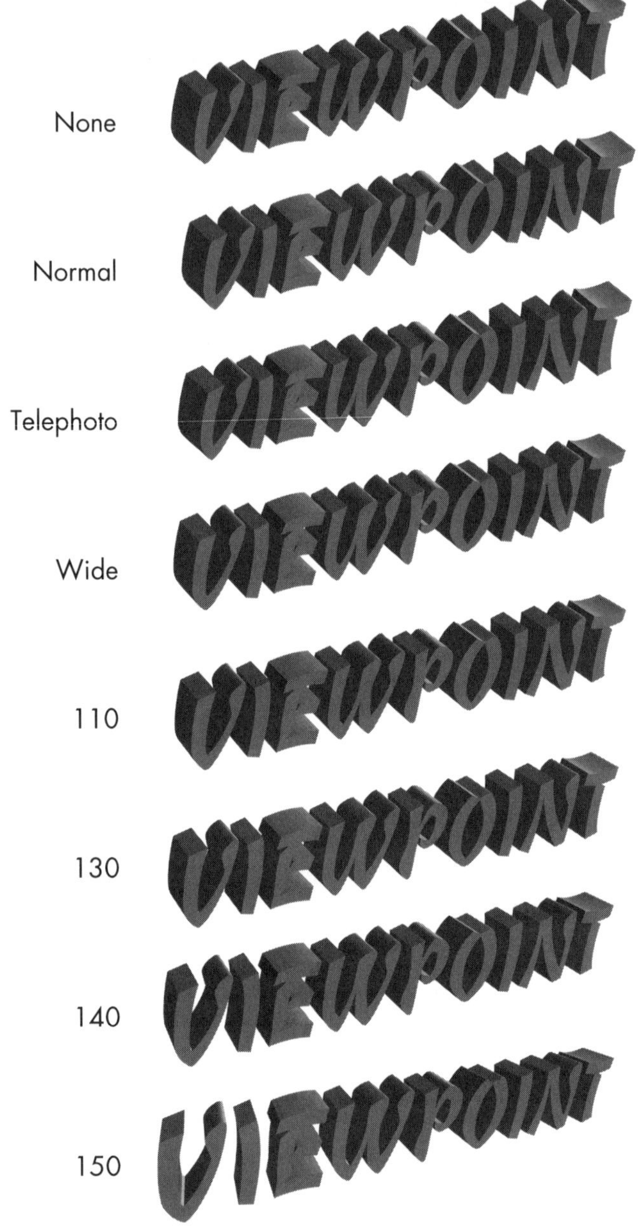

Figure 19-26: Different viewing perspectives available in Dimensions

Mapping 2D Artwork onto Three-Dimensional Surfaces

One of the most powerful features of Dimensions is its capability to wrap two-dimensional objects around three-dimensional surfaces. This feature alone makes the program worth every cent you paid for it.

The most important concept to understand when you are mapping artwork is that each three-dimensional object usually has several different surfaces, and each of those surfaces can have separate mapped artwork.

Use the following steps to map 2D artwork onto a three-dimensional surface.

STEPS: Mapping 2D Artwork onto a Three-Dimensional Surface

Step 1. Create the three-dimensional object that you want to map artwork onto. You can map artwork onto any object, including primitives, extruded 2D artwork, and revolved 2D artwork. I used a can that I often use as a three-dimensional base for "canned artwork." Figure 19-27 shows the steps that I took.

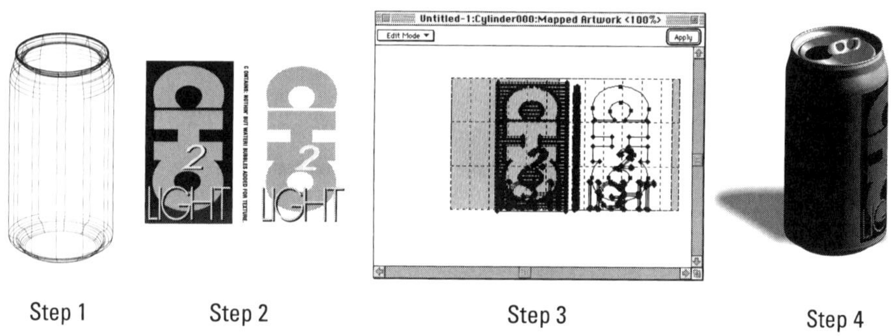

Figure 19-27: Steps for mapping 2D artwork onto a three-dimensional object

Step 2. In Illustrator or in a 2D Artwork window, create the 2D artwork that will appear on the surface of the object. You can skip this step by creating the artwork directly in the Map window.

Step 3. Select the surface of the three-dimensional object that you want to apply 2D artwork to by clicking it with the Direct Selection tool. The Tab key selects successive surfaces, and Shift-Tab selects the previous surface.

(continued)

STEPS: ***(continued)***

Choose Operations⇨Map Artwork (⌘-Option-M) [Ctrl+Alt+M] to bring up the Map window. Paste or import the 2D artwork into the window.

Position the artwork so that it will fit onto the surface of the objects as well as possible. Shaded areas in the Map window are surfaces that are not visible from the current view.

Step 4. Click the Update button (⌘-S) [Ctrl+S] or close the Map window. The three-dimensional object now shows (in wireframe artwork) the mapped artwork applied to it. Choose View⇨Shaded Render (⌘-Shift-Y) [Ctrl+Shift+Y] to view the finished objects.

Other 3D Techniques

Using Adobe Dimensions isn't the only way to create depth in illustrations. Software called AddDepth, available from Ray Dream, is similar in function to Dimensions in that it creates PostScript artwork. At this point, its feature set is quite limited, and although there was an interesting choice between AddDepth and Dimensions 1.0, there really is little to decide between Dimensions 2.0 and AddDepth. Dimensions 2.0 far outclasses AddDepth in almost every respect.

You can do many things in Illustrator to create the illusion of depth. Drop shadows and blended shadows help to define depth, but the most useful thing that you can do is to think about how a light source would hit an object and reflect back at the viewer.

Figure 19-28 shows several objects created in Illustrator.

Creating a Three-Dimensional Object in Illustrator

The most basic three-dimensional shapes in Dimensions are called Primitives, and these are the shapes that are easiest to create right in Illustrator. In fact, artwork in Illustrator can be more three-dimensional than similar artwork in Dimensions, through proper use of gradients. As examples, the following sets of steps describe how to create a cube and a basic metal tube.

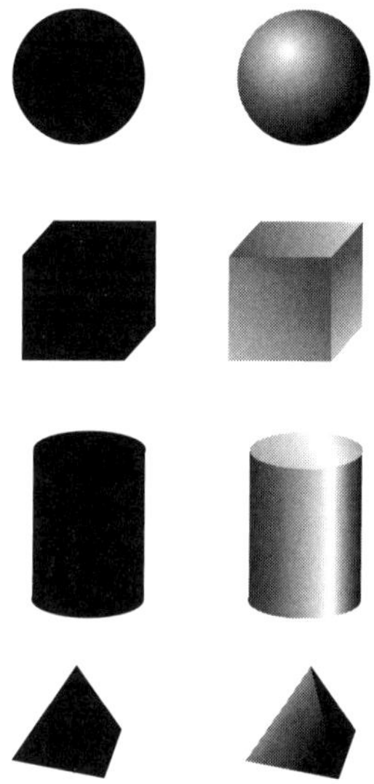

Figure 19-28: The objects on the left appear flat. The objects on the right appear to have depth. The difference is a result of the shading that was applied to each object by using various black-and-white gradients at different angles.

STEPS: Creating a Cube

Step 1. In Artwork mode, draw a square (use the Rectangle tool to draw while pressing Shift to constrain the width to the height).

Step 2. Option[Alt]-copy the square above the original square by clicking the lower, left corner and dragging upward with both the Shift and Option [Alt] keys pressed. When the arrow pointer is hollow, the copy is positioned directly above the original square. Release the mouse button, then the Option [Alt] and Shift keys.

Step 3. Select the Direct Selection tool, click the top segment of the copied square, and drag down. Press the Shift key while you drag to constrain the movement of the line to vertical movement only.

Step 4. With the Direct Selection tool, click the top line again and drag it to the right slightly.

You can perform Steps 3 and 4 at one time by dragging the topmost segment and not pressing Shift.

Step 5. Option[Alt]-copy the original square to the right of it. Use the technique in Step 2 to ensure that the copy is flush against the right edge of the original.

(continued)

STEPS: *(continued)*

Step 6. Use the Direct Selection tool to Shift-drag the rightmost line segment of the second duplicate to the right until it is even with the rightmost point of the top copy.

Draw a vertical guide at the rightmost point of the top square to ensure that the point lines up with the right edge of the second copy.

Step 7. Select the Shear tool and set the origin at the lower-left corner of the second copy. Click the upper-right point of the second copy and Shift-drag up until the cursor becomes hollow.

Step 8. Apply different gradients to each side to make the finished cube look three-dimensional. In the example in Figure 19-29, I used the standard black-and-white gradients and dragged different angles and starting and ending spots for each side to achieve the effect I wanted.

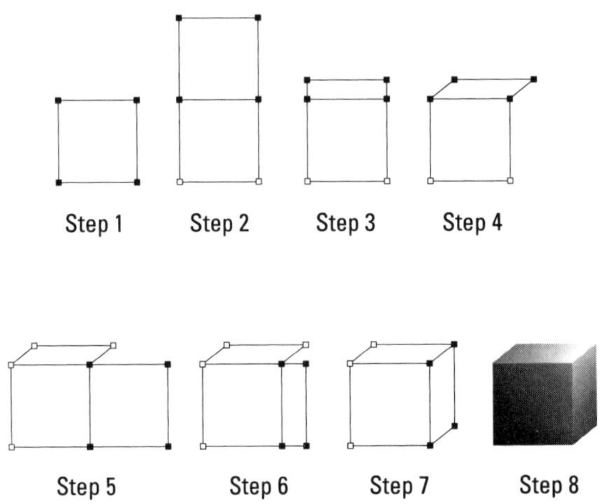

Figure 19-29: Steps for creating a basic cube in Illustrator

STEPS: Creating a Basic Metal Tube

Step 1. Draw an oval that will be the top of the cylinder. The oval should be flat and wide.

Step 2. Draw a rectangle by clicking with the Rectangle tool on the leftmost point of the oval and dragging right and down. Make the rectangle the exact width of the oval.

Step 3. Lock the rectangle and click the leftmost point of the oval. Press Shift and Option[Alt]-copy down until the cursor turns hollow. Release the mouse button and the Option [Alt] and Shift keys.

Step 4. Unlock the rectangle. Select both the rectangle and the bottom oval and choose Object⇨Pathfinder⇨Unite. Fill the new object with the Steel Bar gradient.

Step 5. Select the top oval and choose Arrange⇨Bring to Front (⌘-Ctrl+=).

Step 6. Fill the oval with the Steel Bar gradient, but change the angle of the gradient to 180° in the text box below the list of gradients.

Step 7. Double-click the Steel Bar gradient to open the Gradient palette. Click the Duplicate button and name the gradient **Inside Tube**. Change the white triangle on the Gradient slider to about 25% black and change the black triangles on the slider to 80% black.

You should have a metallic tube like the one in Figure 19-30.

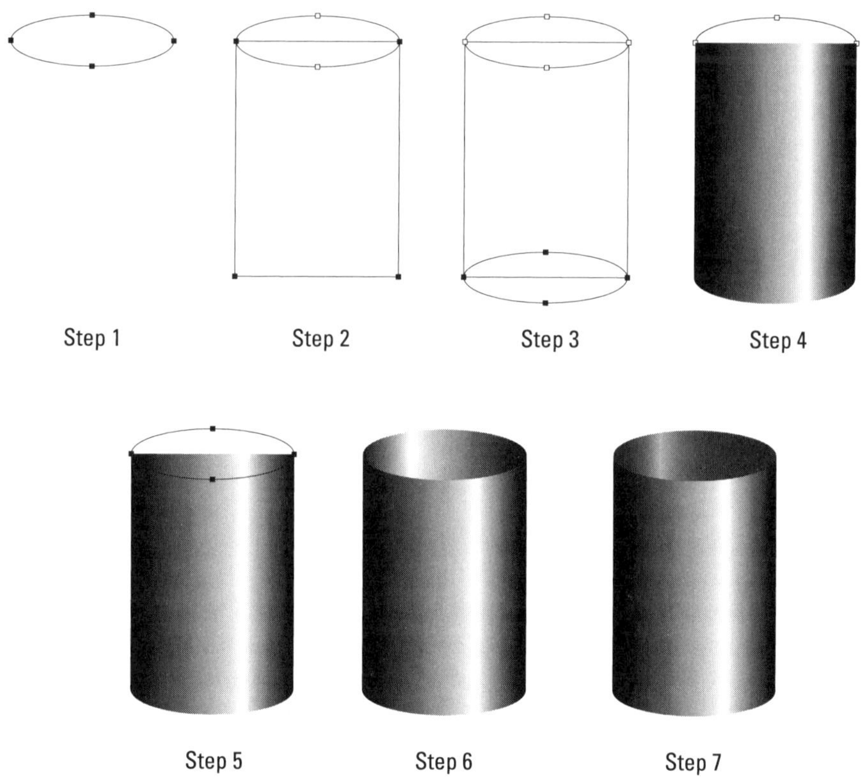

Figure 19-30: Steps for creating a metal tube. The last step was achieved by duplicating the Steel Bar gradient and adjusting the colors of the triangles on the Gradient slider. The darker highlight gives the appearance of darker areas.

Using Gradients to Make Bumps and Dents

When you place gradients on themselves and one gradient has a different direction from another, three-dimensional effects appear. If you remember that highlights reflect off surfaces that bounce light to your eye, that principle should help you determine the direction of the gradients.

Of course, whether an object is coming at you or going away from you should be obvious, shouldn't it? Figure 19-31 shows six different buttons. See whether you can determine which buttons are "innies" and which buttons are "outies." To assist you further, each button is on a standard background and has a button ring. The ring makes the direction of several of the buttons quite obvious. The answers are at the end of the chapter, after the Summary.

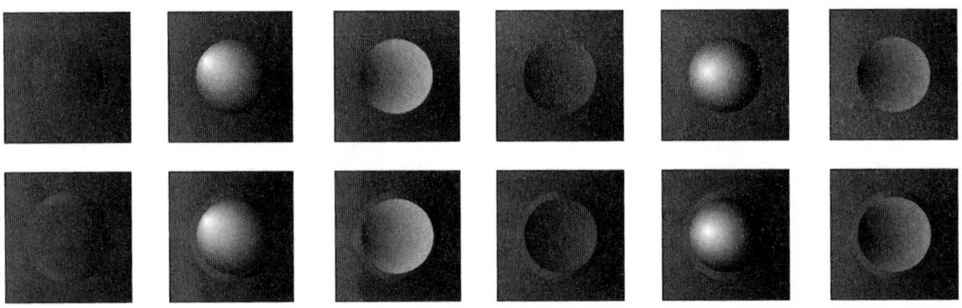

A B C D E F

Figure 19-31: Different in and out buttons created with black-and-white gradients, both linear and radial

Combining Dimensions Artwork with Illustrator

You can achieve the best three-dimensional effects by combining 3D artwork that you create in Dimensions with 2D artwork in Illustrator. Artwork that you create in Dimensions can look sort of flat because of the lack of texture maps in the software (3D images that wrap around other 3D images, like craters on the moon), so after you create something in Dimensions, take it into Illustrator and try to liven it up.

Dimensions is not a standalone product. Without Illustrator, Dimensions is just a fun toy. With Illustrator, the results can be stunning.

Figure 19-32 shows artwork that I created in Illustrator (the words *GILA MONSTERS*), took into Dimensions, extruded, viewed at an extreme perspective (135°), and shade-rendered. I then exported the artwork to Illustrator, where I added the little gila monster. I created the word *ARIZONA* as type on a circle and placed it into position. After seeing that the flat letters looked out of place, I took the letters into Dimensions, extruded them with a bevel, and exported them back into Illustrator. Little finishing touches were made to the artwork, and then it was color separated and printed. What part took the longest? Waiting for a shaded render in Dimensions.

Figure 19-32: Illustrator and Dimensions were used to produce the GILA MONSTERS logo

Perspective Drawing

John-Boy: Is there a way to easily give drawings perspective without Dimensions?

Toulouse: No...the best thing to do is to set up a perspective grid.

John-Boy: That sounds like a lot of work.

Toulouse: Just create a grid, select the top points in the grid, and average them. Instant perspective grid.

John-Boy: That's too easy. Thanks. And good-night.

Toulouse: However tempting, I'm not going to say it....

Summary

- Adobe Dimensions 3 is a unique, three-dimensional rendering software because it outputs editable PostScript outlines.
- Dimensions is power hungry and RAM hungry. Use a 100 MHz or higher processor.
- In addition to height and width, Dimensions also deals with depth.
- You can create Primitive shapes (cubes, spheres, cones, and cylinders) within the Dimensions 3D window.
- Not only can you color the Fills and Strokes of objects in Dimensions, but you also can specify the shade color and the amount of light reflectance.
- Use the Lighting palette (choose Appearance➪Lighting or press ⌘-Shift-L) [Ctrl+Shift+L] to add an unlimited number of infinite light sources.
- You can extrude or revolve two-dimensional objects to create three-dimensional objects.
- You can create two-dimensional artwork inside Dimensions' little Illustrator-like program, the 2D window. You can give extruded 2D artwork bevels to enhance the corners of the objects.
- To move objects along the *Z* axis (or the depth axis at different views), you use the Z-Translation selection tool.
- To scale objects in all three dimensions, use the Scale tool or the Scale palette (choose Operations➪Scale or press ⌘-Option-S [Ctrl+Alt+S]). You can rotate objects in all three dimensions by using the Rotation tool or the Rotate palette (choose Operations➪Rotate or press ⌘-Option-R [Ctrl+Alt+R]).
- From the keyboard, you can access all 13 positions from which you can view artwork. Changing perspective draws you closer to or farther from the objects in the Dimensions 3D window, distorting them as you get nearer.
- You map two-dimensional artwork onto the surface of three-dimensional artwork by selecting a three-dimensional surface, choosing Operations➪Map Artwork (⌘-Option-M [Ctrl+Alt+M]), and placing artwork into the resulting Map window.

- With a little ingenuity and the help of a few friendly gradients, you can create three-dimensional looking objects in 2D with Illustrator. Determining the light source can help you create accurate-looking and realistic three-dimensional artwork right in Illustrator.
- Using the Dimensions artwork in tandem with Illustrator provides greater flexibility and incredible results.

Answers to the Puzzle in Figure 19-31

A, out; B, out; C, in; D, in; E, out; and F, in. The light source is to the left, as established by both the ring and the background. Therefore, the buttons that are lighter on the left side are raised, and the buttons that are lighter on the right side are lowered.

Getting the Most out of Illustrator

CHAPTER 20

In This Chapter

- Looking at how art pieces are designed and assembled
- Copyrighting artwork
- How the artwork in this book was created
- Techniques for creating backgrounds
- Discovering new techniques and practices

Along with using Illustrator to do all types of incredible artwork is the practical, real-world side of Illustrator, where deadlines have to be met and there's little or no time for play. This chapter focuses on real-world applications of Illustrator, and on how to get the most out of the software.

What You Can Learn from Existing Artwork

Examples are a wonderful teacher for Illustrator. In light of this, we've included several figures from the color insert of *Illustrator 7 Bible* on the accompanying CD-ROM, so when you see a figure, you'll know exactly how it was created. But just looking at art doesn't tell you too much except that maybe a blend was used where you thought a gradient would be, and hey, that isn't pattern, it's really individual paths.

You can learn how to create better artwork by dissecting existing artwork and trying to modify it.

Taking Apart Artwork

Artwork created in Illustrator usually consists of hundreds of paths. Some of those paths are Filled, some are Stroked, others may be Filled and Stroked.

The best way to get started is by looking at the illustration in Artwork mode. This shows the basic framework of the art, and is the best first step in understanding how it was created.

Unfortunately, Artwork mode doesn't show you when paths are perfectly overlapping. For that, you'll need to switch between Artwork and Preview modes, or even delve into Preview Selection mode.

Making Your Art Easy to Understand

Possibly the most frustrating thing about editing artwork occurs when there was a different author of the original work. People have their own way of doing things, and while one way isn't necessarily better than another, there are a few things you can do to make your artwork more editable in the future. After all, it may be you opening up your art in a few months or years, and you'll never remember what screwy grouping methods you used that might have made sense back then.

One thing you can do that will make your art easier to interpret is to use common groupings. Blends should be joined to their end paths, and masks to the paths they mask. Text converted to outlines should be grouped together. The paths in objects should be grouped together. Related objects can be grouped to each other.

But more important than grouping is to use layers. Proper use of layers will let your artwork be compartmentalized quickly and easily, providing not only easy access for selecting and modifying sets of paths, but also a means for controlling printing of the Illustration.

Copyrighting Your Electronic Artwork

This is the opposite of the previous section. Often, you'll have done artwork that you'd rather not have anyone mess with. Unfortunately, there's no foolproof way of doing this, but you can put your "stamp" on any illustration and make it difficult for a would-be art thief to abscond with your artwork.

The most basic way of doing this is to put a copyright notice on each object in the document, using the Attributes dialog box as shown in Figure 20-1.

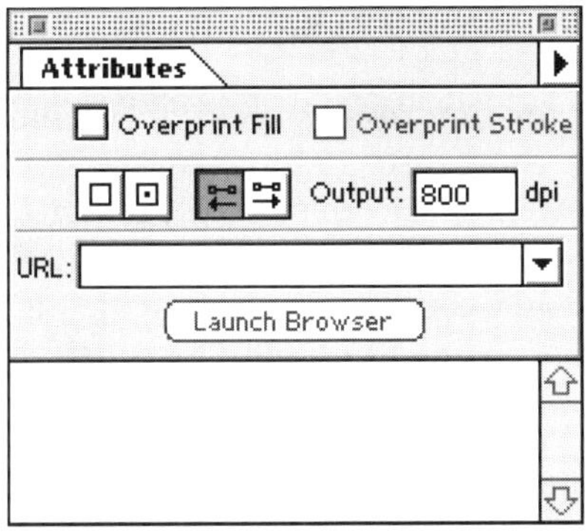

Figure 20-1: Attributes dialog box

STEPS: Quickly Copyrighting Your Artwork

Step 1. Select the artwork you wish to copyright.

Step 2. Choose Window⇨Show Attributes (F11), which displays the Attributes Palette.

Step 3. Type your copyright notice in the Notes section.

At this point, all the art in the document you selected will have this note attached.

To make the art more secure, create a white box somewhere outside the Illustration (which can't be selected or deleted easily). You can also lock your artwork. Another thing to do is to create a text box with your copyright notice in it and change the text color to None or White.

You could also use layers to secure copyrighted pieces of art by locking or hiding layers with objects that have the copyright in them.

The Art in the Illustrator 7 Bible

The art in this book was done entirely with Illustrator and Photoshop. The only thing I used Photoshop for was for quickly touching up screen shots. The following sections describe how particular figure types were created.

File Types

Because this book was written before most people had Illustrator 7, I decided early on to keep the file types for the figures in Illustrator 6. Each of the figures was saved as EPS, with an 8-bit preview, so they could be placed into the layout application.

Screen shots that stood alone were saved as grayscale PICTs. Screen shots and images that needed to appear with labels were saved as TIFFS so Illustrator 7 could import them easily.

The naming scheme for the files is structured *Book ChapterNumber-FigureNumber Description.FileType*, where the *Book* is an indicator based on the ISDN number (4027), *ChapterNumber-FigureNumber* is the four-digit number consisting of the chapter and number of the figure, *Description* is as accurate a description of the file as I could get in a few characters, and *FileType* was the format (PICT or AI). So the file name for Figure 13-1, which shows how to turn artwork of a clock into pixels, would be "4027 13-01 Clock to raster.ai7."

Paths

One distinction you'll find in the *Illustrator 7 Bible* that you won't find in any other Illustrator book is the way I've shown paths in the figures. The easy thing to do would be to take screen shots of paths and just use those. Unfortunately, while paths look fine on-screen, they look absolutely hideous on the printed page. So I re-created each path for the artwork views needed in figures, especially those at the front of the book.

Each path is a .3-point Stroked Black path; each selected Anchor Point is a 2-point x 2-point Black square with a .3 black Stroke (unselected Anchor Points have a White Fill); and each Control Handle is a 2-point x 2-point Black circle, with no Stroke. This made the printed paths look the way they do on-screen, but without the jaggies.

STEPS: Drawing Illustrator Paths and Points with Illustrator

Step 1. First draw the path in Illustrator that you want to appear as a path. Change the Stroke to .3-point Black.

Step 2. To draw the first point, create one 2-point x 2-point square, Filled with Black, and Stroked with .3-point Black.

Step 3. Zoom in to 1600%, and switch to Artwork mode. Drag the center of the square over a point on the path.

Step 4. Option[Alt]-copy the Anchor Point until all the points are properly on the path.

Step 5. Change any Anchor Points to "unselected" Anchor Points by selecting them and Filling them with White.

Step 6. To show Control Handles, first draw a 2-point x 2-point circle, and then change the Fill to Black and the Stroke to None.

Step 7. Position the Control Handles over the handles of the original path.

Step 8. Draw lines from the Control Handles to their corresponding Anchor Points.

Of course, for most of my examples (Steps), I had to Option[Alt]-copy the objects to the next position and then continue. I often used the Transform palette to accurately control spacing between steps.

Labeled Palettes

To label items within palettes (like the one shown in Figure 20-2), toolboxes, and dialog boxes, I placed a raster image and positioned it on the page. Then I drew one line from the area I wanted to label out of the image, painting the line with a .3 point Black Stroke and a Fill of None. I created a label with Point Type, usually using 10-point Futura Book.

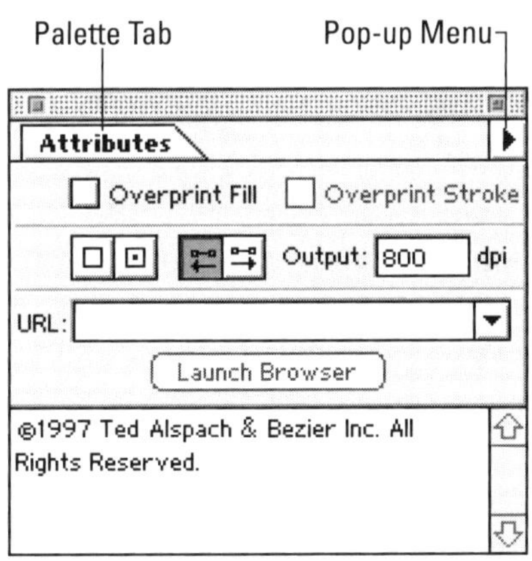

Figure 20-2: Labeled palette

After centering or positioning the type correctly, I Option[Alt]-copied both the label and line, placing the end of the line at the new location on the image. Then I selected the type and the other end of the path with the Direct Selection tool and positioned it accordingly. I repeated that process for each of the labels in a figure.

Color Section Artwork

The artwork in the color section is Illustrator based. To generate the backgrounds, I would often select a portion of the original artwork and scale it up, and then lighten it with Extensis VectorColor.

Where the background had to be lighter or darker for text, I copied the entire background, placed a path a little larger than the text area on top and masked it, and then lightened or darkened that portion with VectorColor again.

Using Art as Outlines for a Transparency

Use the following steps to create the outlines of the artwork for a transparency. (These steps are similar to the procedure I would use to show the Artwork mode of an Illustration.)

STEPS: Changing Full-Color Art into Outlines

Step 1. Change the Paint Style of the original artwork to a Fill of White and a Stroke of .25-point 100% Black.

Step 2. Release all the masks in the artwork by choosing Edit⇨Select All (⌘-A) [Ctrl+A] and then choosing Object⇨Mask⇨Release (⌘-Option-7) [Ctrl+Alt+7]. Check to see whether all the masks were released by choosing Object⇨Mask. If Release is still an option not grayed out, not all the masks have been released. Click Release until the Release option is no longer available.

Step 3. Delete all blend-generated paths by using the Group Selection tool. Click any blend-generated path twice to select all the paths generated by the blend. Repeat this process for each blend.

Step 4. Make any necessary adjustments. After checking the original to determine the weight of the Strokes, change the outline of those paths to that weight and then choose Object⇨Path⇨Outline⇨Path.

If an illustration includes a photograph or imagery created in Photoshop, you'll need to posterize it and outline it in Streamline to produce the outlining you need for a transparency.

Scanning Artwork at the Proper Resolution

By scanning at a high resolution and saving at a lower resolution without changing the file size, you produce an image that you can reduce in Illustrator to much smaller than its blown-up size. You can then use this image for zooming in to high levels of magnification without sacrificing clarity.

The Proper Image Size for Tracing

To produce the best possible image to trace in Illustrator, you have to save the file at the correct size and number of dots per inch. As a result, you need to know the original image's size and at what resolution (dpi) it was scanned.

To figure out what dpi to scan at, you first need to decide how much detail you want to be able to see in Illustrator. By *detail*, I am referring to the level at which you want to zoom in and still be able to see the scan clearly. Table 20-1 shows the zoom level as a percentage and the required dpi for scanning to achieve detail at that zoom level. The table also shows how much you need to reduce the image with the Scale tool to return it to the original size.

If you will be using the image at less than 100%, scanning at 72 dpi is still a good idea.

After you have scanned the image at the proper resolution, open it in Photoshop and select ImageÍImage Size. In the Image Size dialog box, make sure that the File Size and Proportions check boxes are checked. Use a setting of 72 in the dpi text field and press OK. Save the file as a raster image format.

In Illustrator, import or place the image and double-click the Scale tool. Enter the reduction amount from the third column of the list in the Uniform text field. You can now trace the image up to and including the zoom specified.

Keep in mind that the size of a pixel-based file may make an Illustrator file unmanageable. A 75MB image requires an enormous amount of time for redrawing and also uses a healthy chunk of the hard drive.

Table 20-1
Zoom Level Percentages and the DPI for Scanning That's Required to Achieve Detail at a Specified Zoom Level

Zoom	*Scan dpi*	*Scale image*	*Size (3" x 5" CMYK Color)*
100%	72 dpi	100.00%	.30MB
150%	108 dpi	66.67%	.68MB
200%	144 dpi	50.00%	1.19MB
300%	216 dpi	33.33%	2.67MB
400%	288 dpi	25.00%	4.75MB
600%	432 dpi	16.67%	10.70MB
800%	576 dpi	12.50%	19.00MB
1200%	864 dpi	8.33%	42.70MB
1600%	1,152 dpi	6.25%	75.90MB

Backgrounds for Illustrations

This section contains examples of backgrounds (see Figure 20-3) and suggestions for creating backgrounds for illustrations. You can create backgrounds in a number of ways. For example, you can use gradients, raster images, blends, and patterns. When you are deciding what type of background to use, remember that you need to consider how well a background will interact with the front artwork.

Using Gradients for Backgrounds

Gradients can be very effective backgrounds all by themselves, providing that they don't detract from the front artwork.

In the following example, I combined linear and radial gradients for an impressive effect.

STEPS: Using Gradients to Create a Sunset

Step 1. Draw a rectangle to serve as the background area. Create a bottom edge (I used mountains) that will sit in front of the background. For sunsets and other sky-related backgrounds, try to avoid a flat, horizontal base. Color the mountains or bottom edge with a solid Fill color and then select the background for the rectangle.

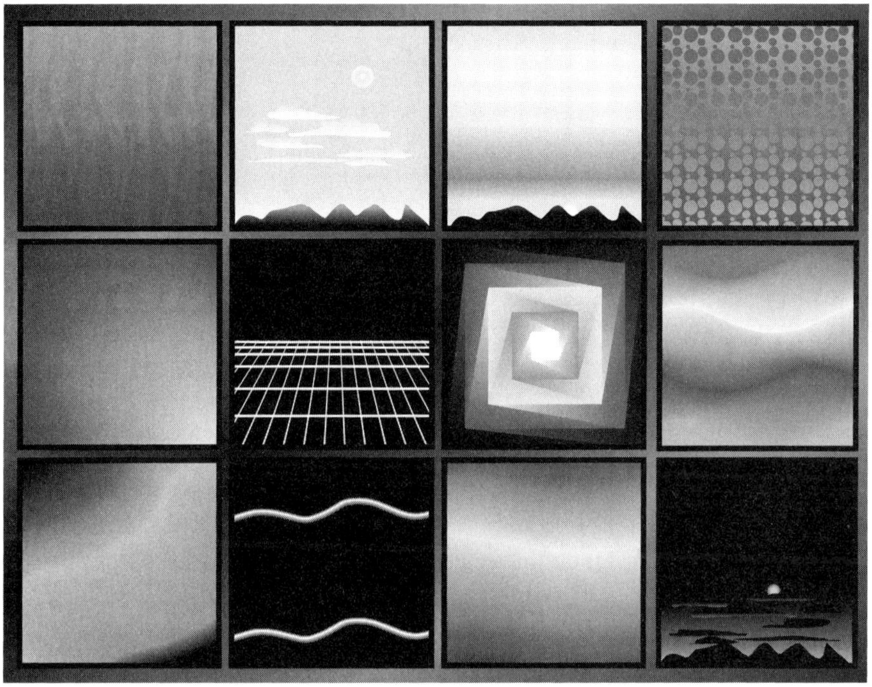

Figure 20-3: Different backgrounds created in Illustrator

You create the gradient after you create the object that it will Fill so that you can instantly see how the gradient will appear in that object in the illustration.

Step 2. Double-click the Gradient tool to display the Gradient palette (or press F9).

Step 3. In the Gradient palette, make the following color stops: at 0%, White; at 5%, Yellow 100%; at 15%, Yellow 100%; at 25%, Yellow 100% and Magenta 50%; at 35%, Magenta 50%; at 50%, Cyan 15% and Magenta 10%; at 80%, Cyan 25%; and at 100%, Cyan 50%.

The first two 100% Yellow color stops create a solid area of Yellow within the gradient.

Step 4. Draw a circle in the solid yellow area of the gradient. In the Gradient palette, create a new radial gradient called "Sunset Sun" with the following color stops: at 0%, White; at 5%, Yellow 30%; at 80%, Yellow 60%; at 100%, Yellow 100%. Because the sun blends into the color of the solid band in the sunset gradient, it appears to blend very nicely. In the example, I partially hid the sun behind some of the clouds.

Using the same technique, I created the sun for a blue sky. In the sun gradient, the last color stop is the same color as the sky.

By themselves, gradients can be effective backgrounds. When you combine gradients with patterns, blends, or other objects, they can form a complex, sometimes realistic, backdrop.

Using Blends and Blend Effects for Backgrounds

You can use a number of different methods to create backgrounds by using blends:

- One method is to blend two shapes together, one larger and one smaller. You can achieve different effects by choosing different shapes.
- By blending from a large circle to a small circle, you can create a very smooth blend that produces better results than using a radial gradient.
- One of the best ways to get a smooth, unobtrusive background when you are using gradients is to blend smoothly curved lines together and mask them in the shape of the background rectangle.
- You can achieve interesting highlights between two blend shapes by blending to different points on objects.

Using Textures for Backgrounds

There are a variety of ways to create textures in Illustrator, and with Version 7, the Ink Pen filter is undoubtedly the most efficient and productive method. With the Ink Pen Effects dialog box, you can quickly change a solid- or gradient-Filled background into a textured background.

STEPS: Creating a Textured Background from a Basic Gradient Fill

Step 1. Create the background object (typically a rectangle, although you can use any shape) with a gradient Fill. Make sure this object is behind all the other objects.

When using the Ink Pen filter to create textures, I usually lock all other objects in the document, and place the background object on a separate layer. This keeps the typically hundreds or thousands of paths that are generated separate from the rest of the illustration.

Step 2. Select the background object and choose Filter⇨Ink Pen⇨Effects. In the dialog box, change the hatch color to Selection, which makes the texture the same shades as the gradient. Adjust any of the other settings in the Ink Pen dialog box.

Step 3. Click OK. The texture is generated.

If the background is only showing around the edges of your artwork, or takes up less than 50% of the total background area, you might want to ungroup the Fill created with Ink Pen Effects and select and delete the objects that aren't visible. This is much easier if the other objects are locked away on a separate layer.

Another useful texture can be created by modifying a blend somewhat, so that it appears to be textured. With this method of creating a background, you *can't* delete unseen portions of the artwork.

The following steps show one common method of texturizing a blend.

STEPS: Texturizing a Blend

Step 1. Create a blend, either manually or by using the Expand command on an existing gradient-Filled object.

Step 2. Select the Blend steps (you might want to choose View⇨Hide Edges (⌘-H) [Ctrl+H] so the mass of selected paths doesn't obscure your view) and choose Filter⇨Distort⇨Roughen.

Discovering New Features on Your Own

This book contains many really neat tips and techniques. I discovered most of them by doing some really hard playing with Illustrator.

If you are excited and enthusiastic about Illustrator, you will undoubtedly discover things that I didn't include in this book because of a lack of space or a lack of time — or possibly, because I didn't know anything about them.

I have stuffed within these pages all of the best things about Illustrator that other graphic artists who contributed to this book and I could come up with, but I know that in the short time between writing the chapters and having the book appear on bookshelves, I will discover many more things that I could have included.

Illustrator is one of the, if not *the,* most versatile software packages around. There are limits to what you can do with it, but those limits are being pushed further and further each time an upgrade appears and every time computer systems become more powerful, faster, and cheaper. New technologies will continue to enhance Illustrator's capabilities, but the core of the product will always be the same.

Finding New Features

My observation in the area of finding "new" things that Illustrator can do is that any time I say to myself, "Golly! This sure does take a long time to do!" there is probably a shorter way to do it that I haven't figured out yet.

BY THE WAY: Very rarely do I exclaim "Golly!" but when I do, I take note. Others hearing this outburst take note as well, and yes, they have recommended counseling.

Like everyone else, I can't just sit and play with Illustrator all day in order to come up with techniques and tips that no one else has yet discovered. But when I do use Illustrator, I make the best use of my time, and I try to use key commands for everything. If I have to pull down a menu because I don't know a key command, it is a sad day in my life.

As I am using Illustrator, I try different ways of doing ordinary things. For example, I often select almost everything in an illustration and lock it. The first method that I used for this procedure was to select everything by selecting All, which selected all the objects in the illustration. I then deselected particular objects by Shift-clicking them and choosing Object⇨Lock (⌘-L) [Ctrl+L]. This method wasn't too productive because I usually had the other items selected (the ones that I didn't want locked), and I had to deselect all of them before I could lock the others.

The second method that I tried was a little better, but I knew that somehow there had to be a better way. Because all the things that I didn't want locked were selected, I chose View⇨Fit In Window (⌘-0) [Ctrl+0], pressed the Shift key, and dragged a marquee around everything. This action selected all the unselected objects and deselected all the selected objects. I then locked the selected objects.

The third method was the best up to that time. Because everything that I wanted to select and lock wasn't selected, I chose Edit⇨Select⇨Inverse, which selected everything that wasn't selected and deselected the selected objects. That way I didn't have to select the other objects with the mouse, which always slows me down. Then I locked the selected objects.

Have you noticed that these paragraphs are getting shorter? The method I now use is almost too easy. The objects that I want locked are the only things not selected, so I press Option [Alt] and choose Object⇨Lock (⌘-Option-L) [Ctrl+Alt+L], which locks everything that isn't selected.

Back when I was Shift-clicking, if I had known that ⌘-Option-L [Ctrl+Alt+L] locked everything that wasn't selected, I could have avoided a great deal of wasted time and frustration. But because I tried to do this operation so many different ways, I *know* that command, and I use it more than ever.

Knowing versus Memorizing

If you memorize all the key commands in this book and then take the time to memorize all the tips and techniques listed in these pages, you will still not be able to use Illustrator as well as the pros.

To get the most out of Illustrator, you need to use the software until the commands and techniques become intuitive. Memorizing the menus may help you find menu items faster, but knowing what each menu item does in depth will score that information into your subconscious and enable you to use Illustrator better than otherwise possible.

Very few people in the graphic arts industry know Illustrator inside and out; yet the ones who do are producing the best-quality illustrations. What does it take to know Illustrator? If you can see in your mind how to create an entire illustration, step by step, you know the software. On the other hand, if you make a mistake in real life and type a mental ⌘-Z [Ctrl+Z], it's time for therapy.

What You Can Do to Learn More

Read this book inside and out and think to yourself, "Gee, I can do that better *and* faster," and sit down and figure it out. Strangely enough, the first time you discover that you can do something faster than before, doing it will take twice as long as it used to take.

Look at the last set of steps in Chapter 17 and figure out how you can reduce the number of steps from 21 to 10. Before I came up with the printed version of the steps for creating a rounded rectangle with reversed corners, I must have thought of five other ways to create it. The method that appears in this book is the fastest, most accurate way to do it. Now if only I could come up with a better, tighter *name* for the darned things.

If you have to Option[Alt]-copy (duplicate a selected object, drag with the Option [Alt] key, and then release the mouse button before the Option [Alt] key) a hundred things, decide whether it would be better to choose Object⇨Transform⇨Transform Again (⌘-D) [Ctrl+D] 99 times or to select all the objects 10 times, Option[Alt]-copy *them,* and select Transform Again only 8 more times. Which method is faster for your job? Why?

Is it better to create an object and change the Paint Style information after it is selected or to deselect all (⌘-Shift-A) [Ctrl+Shift+A], change the Paint Style, and then create an object? Or maybe an object on the page already exists, so you can create the object and use the Eyedropper and/or Paintbucket tools to copy the color from one to the other. Or, if an object with that color exists, you can select the object, which changes the Paint Style to that color, and then create the new object.

If you think about all these things as you are drawing, your illustration time will decrease, the quality of your drawings will increase, and you will have more time for using Illustrator to design a solar-powered hang glider, or whatever you do when you aren't using Illustrator for real work.

Getting Answers and Information from Adobe

When you can't find an answer to a problem or want to know whether a way exists to do some tedious task faster, call the Adobe Tech Support line.

The main problem with most software company support these days is the "not our fault" answer. (Whatever problem or question you have, it isn't the software company's fault.) You don't find this attitude at Adobe. Most of the support staff are polite, and they will help even the most befuddled user along, as well as give additional tips and techniques. The main problem with Adobe Tech Support is the difficulty in reaching a human being. When you call, you get routed through a series of questions ("If you are having trouble designing a hang glider with Adobe Illustrator, press 465") that hardly ever seems to pertain to your particular problem. After a grueling mechanical question-and-answer session, you are put on hold while some tech people argue about who has to answer the call (and other tech people place bets on how long it will be before you hang up). Actually, I'm kidding about the tech support staff's behavior while you are on hold, and I'm sure they jump from one call to the next without pausing to catch a breath. Adobe now has a special support line that you pay a premium for, which the tech people are the first to answer, and most of them pick up within the first movement of the classical music you're forced to listen to.

If you don't need an answer right away, you can fax Adobe. (Check the Adobe Web site for correct phone number or your Illustrator documentation.) You should get a response within one business day, by either phone or return fax. Faxing is great because you can send along your illustration so the tech people can actually look at it.

In addition, Adobe has a free Bulletin Board Service (BBS) running at 28.8 Kbps that anyone can call. Adobe tech people regularly answer posted questions, and you can send your Illustrator file along with your questions.

Summary

- Taking apart existing artwork is one of the best ways to learn how to create that type of artwork.
- In order to make your art usable and modifiable in the future, create it logically and in an orderly manner; use layers when possible.
- Use gradients, textures, blends, and lightened artwork for quick, effective backgrounds.
- Focus on *knowing* Illustrator rather than memorizing commands and shortcuts.
- Talk to other Illustrator users to learn different techniques and to help solve technical snafus.

Part V

Appendixes

One of the best ways to begin using this book is to take a quick skim through the following appendixes. This is especially true if you have just upgraded your Illustrator software to Version 7 — Appendixes C and D list the features that are new to the Macintosh and Windows versions of the products, respectively.

Using the CD-ROM

APPENDIX A

The CD-ROM that's included with this book is packed full of surprises:

- An interactive PDF document with QuickTime tutorials
- An exclusive plug-in from Extensis, VectorFrame SE (Mac only)
- An exclusive plug-in from Cytopia, Doodle Jr. (Mac only)
- Most of the Illustrator artwork that appears in the color section of this book in vector format
- LeftyCasual and RansomNote fonts (Mac only)
- PDF files containing chapters and appendixes we couldn't fit into the printed version, and the Adobe Acrobat Reader (3.0) software
- Filter Charts from Sandee Cohen (Mac only)
- Demo software and filters

Installing Acrobat 3.0 Reader

If you already have Acrobat 3 Reader (or the full product) installed, skip to the next section, "Using the Illustrator Bible PDF and Tutorials."

Open the Acrobat 3.0 Reader folder/directory. Double-click the Acrobat Installer/Setup file. Restart your computer. You are now ready to begin using the tutorial PDF (next section).

Using the Illustrator Bible Tutorial PDF

Double-click the I7Bible.pdf file. The main screen appears (see Figure A-1).

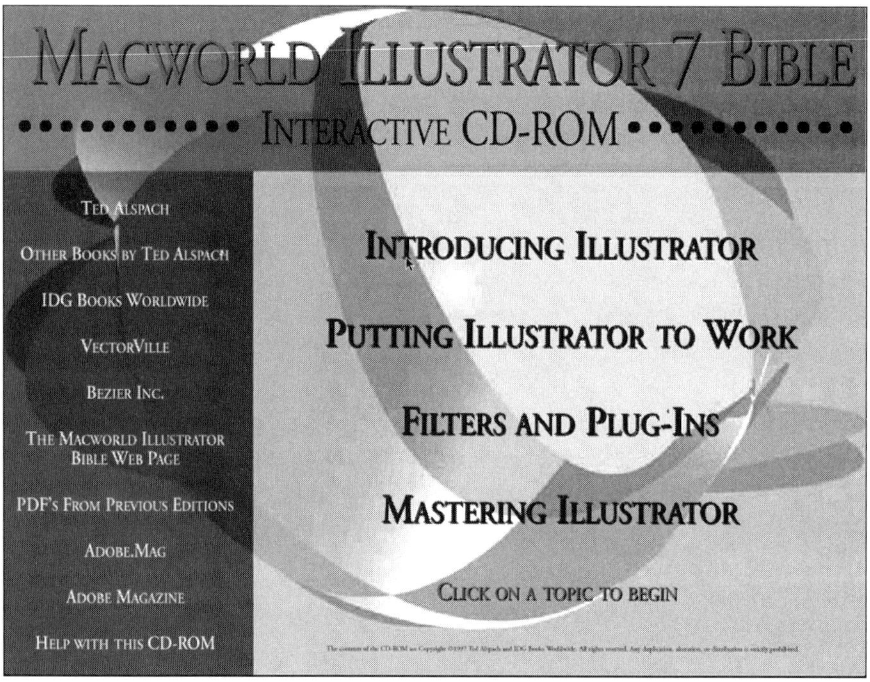

Figure A-1: The main menu of the tutorial PDF

Click any of the topics to view the page with that topic. Several options along the left column are Web destinations (you can tell they are; your cursor changes to a W when it passes over Web links). Figure A-2 shows one of the tutorial menu screens, this one for the Introducing Illustrator section.

Figure A-2: The Introducing Illustrator section of the PDF file

To play a movie, click the title of that movie. Press Esc to exit the movie early; it closes automatically once it is done playing. Figure A-3 shows a tutorial in progress.

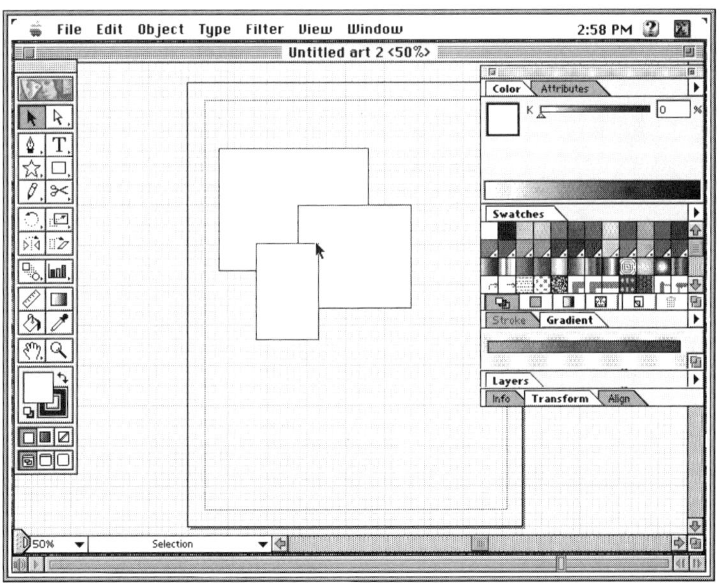

Figure A-3: A tutorial in progress

Quit the tutorial program by pressing ⌘-Q [Ctrl+Q].

Installing and Using VectorFrame SE (Mac only)

A fully functional trial version of VectorTools is included on your CD-ROM, but it will only work for 30 days before expiring. The VectorFrame SE plug-in we've included on the CD-ROM, on the other hand, is completely self-sufficient, and won't expire. Ever. If you're planning on buying VectorTools, or already have it, then you can ignore the instructions in this section and use VectorFrame with the free trial or as a fully functional package. The only difference is that with the SE plug-in (on this CD), it is chosen from the Windows menu. However, you might want to install VectorFrame SE to take advantage of the five additional presets you'll get for VectorFrame SE in addition to the five in VectorFrame.

To install VectorFrame SE, locate it inside the VectorFrame SE folder on the *Illustrator 7 Bible* CD-ROM. Drag it into your Adobe Illustrator Plug-Ins folder. Restart Illustrator; VectorFrame SE is now accessible from the Windows menu. To display the VectorFrame SE palette, select it from the Windows menu.

Installing and Using Doodle Jr. (Mac Only)

To install Doodle Jr., locate it inside the Doodle Jr. folder on the *Illustrator 7 Bible* CD-ROM. Drag it into your Adobe Illustrator Plug-Ins folder. Restart Illustrator. Doodle Jr. is now accessible in the Filter menu's Fun submenu. To display the Doodle Jr. dialog box, select it from the Fun submenu in the Filter menu.

Installing Illustrator

B APPENDIX

The installation of Illustrator is pretty straightforward. If you've installed any software recently on your Macintosh or Windows system, you're already familiar with the installation process. This appendix provides some additional information you might find helpful when installing Illustrator. The first section deals with installing Illustrator for Macintosh, while the second section addresses installing Illustrator for Windows.

System Requirements for Macintosh

To run Adobe Illustrator 7 on a Macintosh, there are certain requirements you need to fulfill with your computer system. Of these, the CPU and RAM are the most important.

Macintosh Computer Requirements

The following is a list of the Macintosh computers you *can't* use to run Illustrator 7. Don't attempt to load Adobe Illustrator 7 on any of the following systems:

- Macintosh 128 (the original Mac)
- Macintosh 512K or 512KE
- Macintosh Plus
- Macintosh SE
- Macintosh Portable

- Macintosh Classic
- Macintosh PowerBook 100
- Macintosh II
- Macintosh LC

Fortunately, Illustrator can run on all of the Macs sold today, including all members of the following classes (or families):

- Macintosh Performa (68030 models)
- Macintosh PowerBook, including Duos (except PowerBook 100)
- Macintosh Centris
- Macintosh Quadra
- Macintosh SE/30, Classic II, Color Classic
- All Power Macintoshes and Mac clones

The rule here is that your system must have a 68030 or greater processor or a PowerPC 6xx processor. The systems that don't make the cut are 68000-based.

RAM

Illustrator 7 needs a minimum of 10MB of memory to run efficiently. What this means is that your system should have *at the very least* 16MB of RAM total. The system software usually takes up between 3 and 4MB of RAM, and more for Mac OS 7 than for System 7.5.

A good way to check how much RAM you have available for Illustrator is to restart your system. After the desktop appears, go to the Apple in the upper-left corner and pull down About This Computer. The number in the Largest Unused Block box needs to be 8,000K or larger. If not, then you need to buy some RAM.

Other Attachments

You also need a hard drive with about 25MB of free space on it, a 640 x 480 (or larger) color monitor, a keyboard, and a mouse.

Macintosh System Recommendations

If you have the minimum system that Adobe recommends, Illustrator will work — kind of. If you have armloads of patience and plenty to do between certain operations, this minimum setup may work for you.

CPU and FPU

Although a 68030 is fast compared to a 68000, it crawls compared to a 68040, and it stops compared to a PPC 601, 603, or 604. To do color work, investigate your options regarding a 68040 or better. Systems with 68040s include Centris, Quadra, LCIV, and some of the latest PowerBooks and Performas.

There is a catch, however. If you are using KPT Vector Effects or Adobe Dimensions, make sure that your computer has a math coprocessor (also called a floating point unit, or FPU). Dimensions will run, though slowly, without an FPU, while Vector Effects won't run at all. Most computers have an FPU, but some don't. Here is a list of systems with a 68020 or greater processor that do *not* have a math coprocessor:

- Macintosh IIsi (FPU comes on the NuBUS adapter card), IIvi
- Macintosh, LCII, LCIII (optional)
- Macintosh Classic II, Color Classic (optional)
- PowerBook 140, 145, 145B, 150, 160
- PowerBook Duo 200 series (available on Duo Dock)
- Performa 200, 400, 600 (optional), 405, 430, 450 (optional)
- Centris 610
- Quadra 605
- Quadra 610 (base 8/160 model; all others have it)

Power PC computers have FPU functions integrated into their chip. Illustrator, Vector Effects, and Dimensions understand this, and regard PPC systems as having an FPU.

A way to get around this limitation if your computer does not have an FPU is to get Software FPU (available on most online services and many FTP sites), a shareware utility that fools KPT Vector Effects into thinking that there is an FPU installed. Unfortunately, this utility only serves to slow down the FPU version of Dimensions.

Too Much RAM Is Never Enough

Through the Get Info box (in the Finder, select the Illustrator 7 icon and then choose File⇨Get Info or press ⌘-I), you can allocate as much RAM to Illustrator as you like. If you don't have much RAM available, Illustrator uses as much RAM as it can.

A good setting for the Preferred Memory size of RAM (on the Get Info box) is at least 16,000K. This is more RAM than Adobe recommends, but this amount lets you work with medium-sized documents at a pretty fast clip.

No matter how much RAM you add to your system and allocate to Illustrator, there will surely be times when you get various types of out-of-memory errors. One of the most common of these errors is the "Not enough memory for Undo/Redo" error, which occurs when the computer doesn't have enough memory to keep some of the oldest undos in your system. Because different operations take up different amounts of memory and more complex drawings take up more memory than simpler ones, the amount of RAM you need at any one time can vary.

Other areas that need lots of RAM are patterns (especially transparent ones), blends, multicolor gradients, complex masks, compound paths, and the use of some filters (Object Mosaic and Roughen are notorious for RAM usage).

If you are installing additional filter sets, a good rule of thumb is to allocate about 1MB of RAM for every additional third-party filter set.

CAUTION: Certain KPT Vector Effects filters will generate large numbers of additional paths, which can quickly use up the available RAM. The filters to watch out for are KPT 3D Transform, KPT ShadowLand, and KPT ShatterBox.

Installing Illustrator 7 for Macintosh

Remove all extensions but the ones needed to run your CD-ROM drive (use a start-up manager to facilitate this quickly).

Double-click the Install Me icon. Click the Easy Install button, and Illustrator will install itself in a matter of minutes. It's actually faster and easier to install Illustrator this way and then remove items you don't want than to go through and do a Custom Install of Illustrator.

Illustrator will install ATM 4 into your System Folder, requiring you to restart after installation.

After restarting, run Illustrator and enter your serial number at the prompt.

System Requirements for Windows

To run Illustrator 7 on a PC, there are certain requirements that need to be met. Of these, the CPU, installed RAM, and operating system are the most important.

Windows System

The minimum system requirements for Illustrator 7 for Windows are:

- Intel 486 processor
- Windows 95, Windows NT 4.0 Workstation, or Windows NT 4.0 Server operating system
- VGA display card
- CD-ROM drive (a 3.5" disk set is available for purchase; however, it doesn't contain all the CD's "goodies")
- 16MB of RAM installed
- 25MB of free hard disk space for installation

However, Adobe recommends the following:

- Pentium or greater processor
- High-resolution (24-bit or greater Super VGA) video display card
- 32MB or more of RAM installed

Personally, I recommend a Pentium or better at 133 MHz. Anything slower (even a 90 MHz) starts to slow Illustrator down. Also, if you are using lots of placed bitmap images (or rasterizing at high resolution within Illustrator), you want to have more RAM on hand.

Installing Illustrator for Windows

Insert the Adobe Illustrator 7 CD-ROM. Double-click the Setup icon. The Install Wizard will prepare the installation (this takes a while on slower systems). When the Installation screen appears, choose Typical from the list of options, and press the Next button. Enter your name, title and serial number, and continue pressing Next until Illustrator has installed.

After installation, Illustrator provides a method for you to register at that time. This is a good thing to do, as it provides Adobe with your contact information regarding special deals, upgrades, and so on.

After the installation is complete, double-click the Illustrator 7 icon (or choose Illustrator 7 from the Start menu) to run Illustrator.

C

APPENDIX

What's New in Illustrator 7 for Macintosh

From its appearance at first, Illustrator 7 seems to have a wealth of new features. However, what it really has is a wealth of changes — most of which have made the software better, and some of which . . . well, some of which I'm not too fond — and scattered new features. This is, undoubtedly, the one full-version-number Illustrator upgrade with the least new stuff ever, but at the same time, the most changes ever (closely rivaled by the changes from Version 3.2 to Version 5.0, although that had multitudes of new features to boot).

This appendix is organized into three sections. First, the features that are really new are listed. Second, the more dramatic of the changes are listed. Finally, the last section lists the Top Ten Things to Know when starting to use Illustrator 7. One of the most dramatic changes to Illustrator is the remapping of keyboard commands; Appendix E, "Shortcuts for Illustrator 7 for Macintosh" lists all the Illustrator 7 commands, noting which ones have been changed or added.

New Features

Reshape Tool: This tool (located in the Scale tool slot) is used to bend and distort paths without destroying their basic shape. *Chapter 7.*

Figure C-1:
The new Reshape tool

Grids: Grids (turned on and off from the View menu) provide adjustable, customizable grids used for both alignment and to see transparency. Grid controls are in the Grids & Guides preferences (located in the Preference submenu of the File menu). *Chapter 4.*

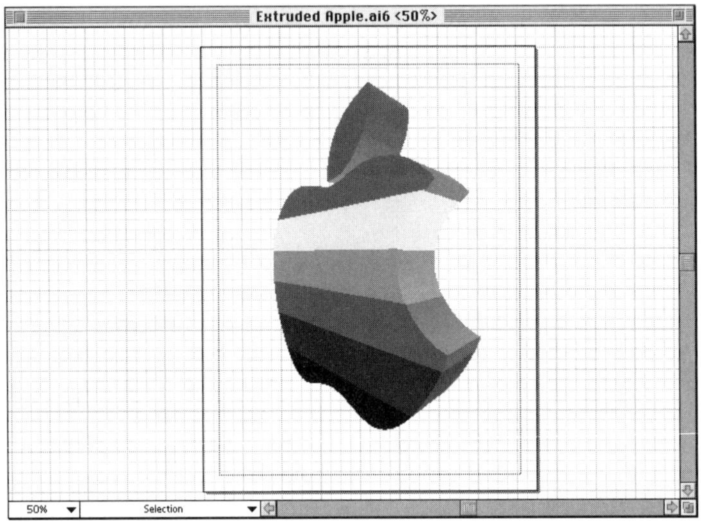

Figure C-2: The new grid function

RGB Color: Objects can now have RGB colors applied to them via the Color palette's RGB pop-up menu option. *Chapter 2.*

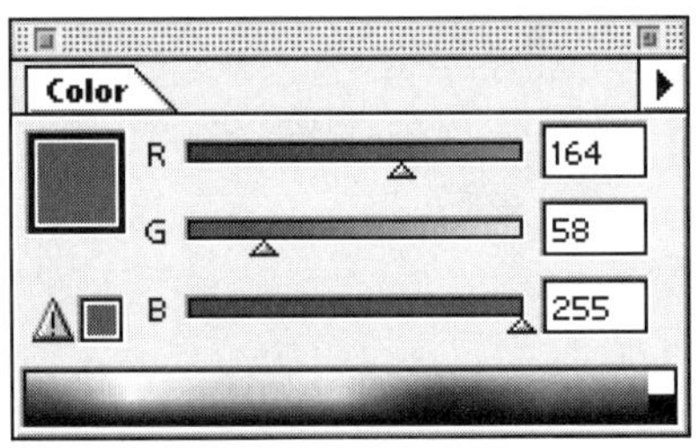

Figure C-3: The Color palette with RGB color settings

URL embedding: Objects can be assigned URLs via the Attributes palette. *Chapter 16.*

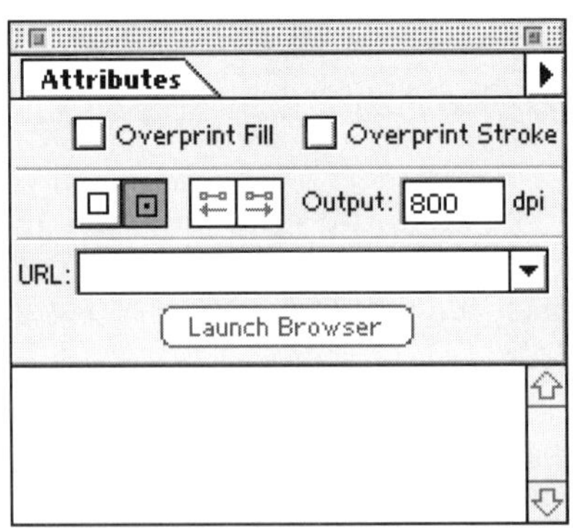

Figure C-4: The new Attributes palette is used to assign URLs to objects

Full Screen Mode: By clicking icons at the bottom of the toolbox, you can view documents without window borders, with or without the menu bar (pressing F toggles the shortcut). *Chapter 1.*

New Graph Type: The Radar Graph type has been added to the various graph types. *Chapter 11.*

Vertical Type: Using the new Vertical Type tools, type can be set up vertically instead of in the normal horizontal arrangement. *Chapter 8.*

Figure C-5: Vertical Type on a Path

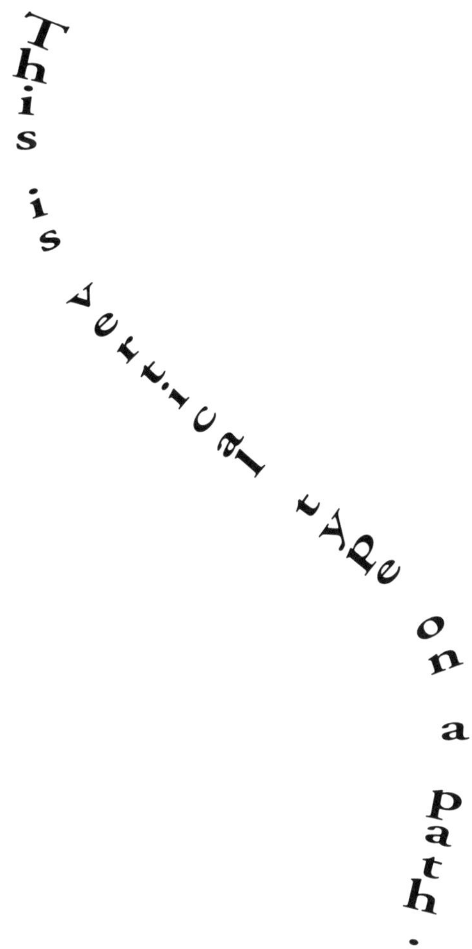

Convert To ColorSpace X Filters: The Color submenu of the Filter menu now contains three filters that switch the selected objects' colorspace from their current colorspace to RGB, CMYK, or Grayscale. *Chapter 12.*

Send Backwards/Bring Forwards: These functions (in the Arrange submenu of the Object menu) move selected objects through the stacking order one object layer at a time. *Chapter 7.*

Multiple Master Palette: This palette provides controls for manipulating Multiple Master typefaces. *Chapter 8.*

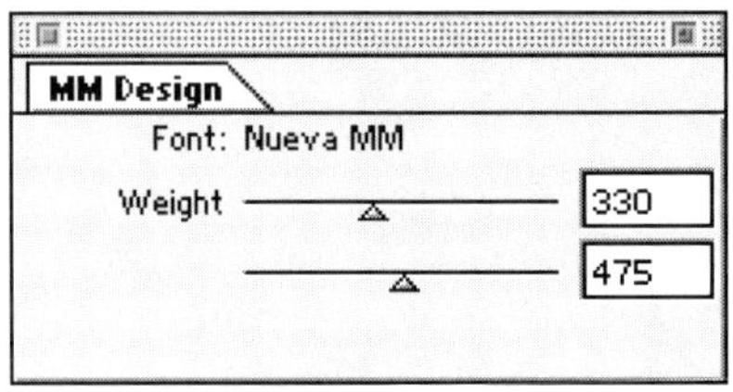

Figure C-6: The new Multiple Master palette

Context Sensitive Menus: These menus, which appear when you Control-click, contain typical and handy menu commands culled from all the Illustrator menus, specific to your selection. *Appendix I.*

Changes

Menu Changes

Page Setup: Now accessed by clicking a button (Page Setup) in the Document Setup dialog box. *Chapter 18.*

File⇨Save A Copy: Added to the File menu (⌘-Option-S). *Chapter 5.*

File⇨Place: Takes the place of Import for all graphics and text. *Chapter 5.*

File⇨Export: Used for exporting to all non-Illustrator graphics formats as well as text formats. *Chapter 5.*

File⇨Preferences: Instead of just General Preferences, this is broken down into six different items: General, Keyboard Increments, Units & Undo, Guides & Grid, Hyphenation Options, and Plug-ins and Scratch Disks. *Chapter 6.*

File⇨Color Settings: No longer in the Preference submenu; directly in the File menu. *Chapter 6.*

Edit⇨Paste in Front/Back: In the Edit menu. *Chapter 7.*

Edit⇨Define Pattern: In the Edit menu; instead of bringing up the Pattern dialog box (which no longer exists), a new swatch is created in the Swatch palette. *Chapter 11.*

Edit⇨Select: All the Select filters are now in the Select submenu of the Edit menu. *Chapter 3.*

Object⇨Transform: This Object menu submenu contains Transform Again, Move, Scale, Rotate, Reflect and Shear (just like their tool dialog boxes), and Transform Each. *Chapter 7.*

Object⇨Path: This Object menu submenu contains path-related functions, including Join, Average, Offset Path, Outline Path, Cleanup, Slice (previously Make Knife), and Add Anchor Points. *Chapter 7.*

Object⇨Pathfinder: This Object menu submenu contains all of the old Pathfinder filters. Now they're functions, not filters. *Chapter 7.*

Object⇨Pathfinder⇨Repeat Last Pathfinder: This option (⌘-4) repeats the last Pathfinder used. *Chapter 7.*

Object⇨Arrange: This Object menu submenu (which was a separate menu in 6.0 and older versions) contains Send to Back and Bring to Front, as well as the new Send Backwards and Bring Forwards. *Chapter 7.*

Type⇨MM Design: This floating palette provides controls for manipulating Multiple Master typefaces. *Chapter 8.*

Type⇨Type Orientation: This submenu controls the orientation of type (horizontal or vertical). *Chapter 8.*

Filter Menu: The filter menu has been reorganized so that native Illustrator filters are grouped at the top, Photoshop filters are grouped in the middle, and third-party filters are grouped at the bottom. *Chapter 12.*

Filter⇨Apply Last Filter: Applies the filter using the same settings as before. *Chapter 12.*

View⇨Preview/View⇨Artwork: Formerly two separate commands, this menu option (⌘-Y) changes dynamically depending on the current view. *Chapter 1.*

View⇨Make Guides: Now in the View menu. *Chapter 4.*

View⇨Release Guides: Now in the View menu. *Chapter 4.*

View⇨Lock Guides: Now in the View menu. *Chapter 4.*

View⇨Show Grid: Shows (or hides) the new Grid feature. *Chapter 4.*

View⇨Snap to Grid: Turns on (or off) snapping to the new Grid. *Chapter 4.*

Window⇨Show Transform: Shows (and hides) the new Transform palette (originally the Control palette). *Chapter 7.*

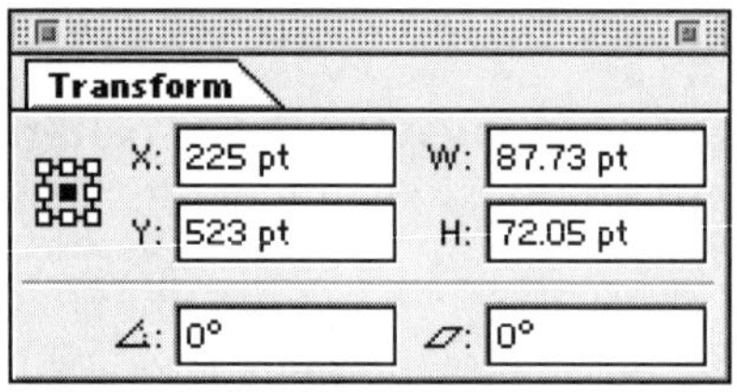

Figure C-7: The new Transform palette

Window⇨Show Color: Shows (and hides) the new Color palette, which replaces the right portion of the old Paint Style palette. *Chapter 2.*

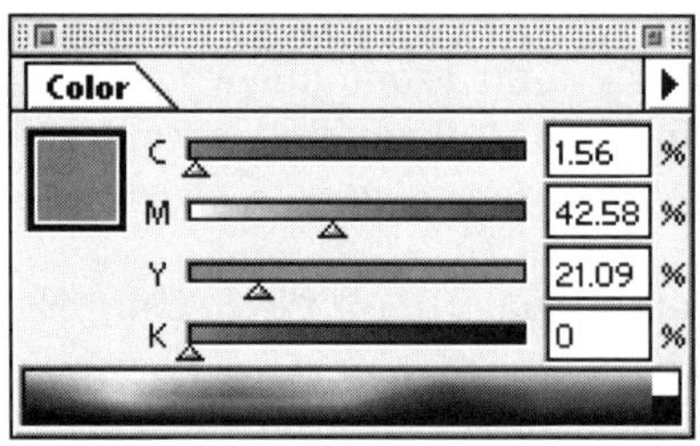

Figure C-8: The new Color Palette

Window⇨Show Stroke: Shows (and hides) the Stroke palette, which replaces the Stroke section of the old Paint Style palette.

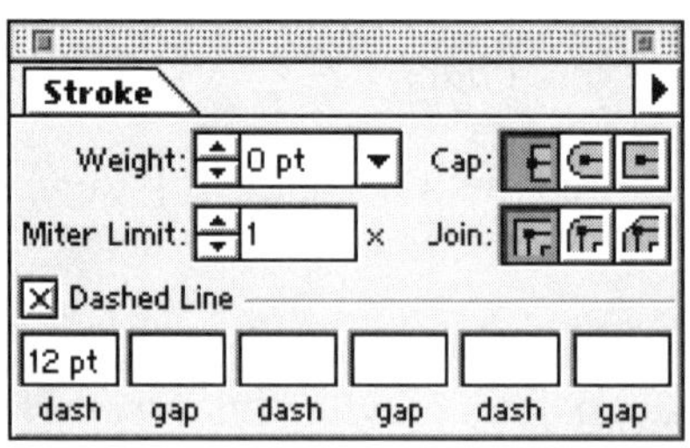

Figure C-9: The new Stroke palette

Window⇨Show Swatches: Shows (and hides) the new Swatches palette, which replaces the left panel of the old Paint Style palette. *Chapter 2.*

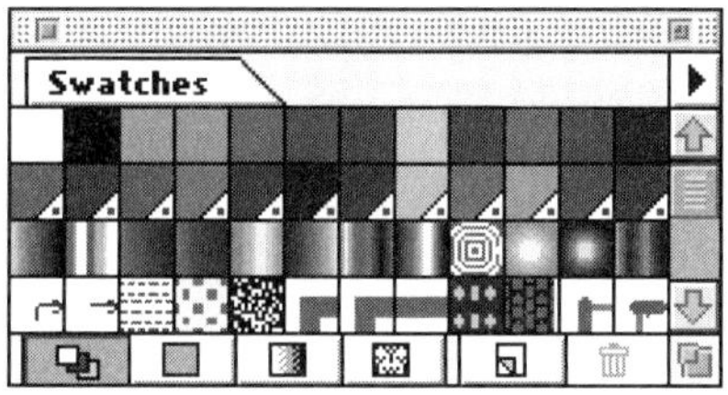

Figure C-10: The new Swatches palette

Window⇨Swatch Libraries: This submenu lets you pick from several swatch libraries, including Pantone, Focoltone, and Trumatch color sets. In addition, Illustrator documents can be opened as swatch libraries using the Window⇨Swatch Libraries⇨Other Library command. *Chapter 2.*

Window⇨Show Attributes: Shows (and hides) the new Attributes palette, which contains all the functionality of the old Object Attributes dialog box. *Chapter 7.*

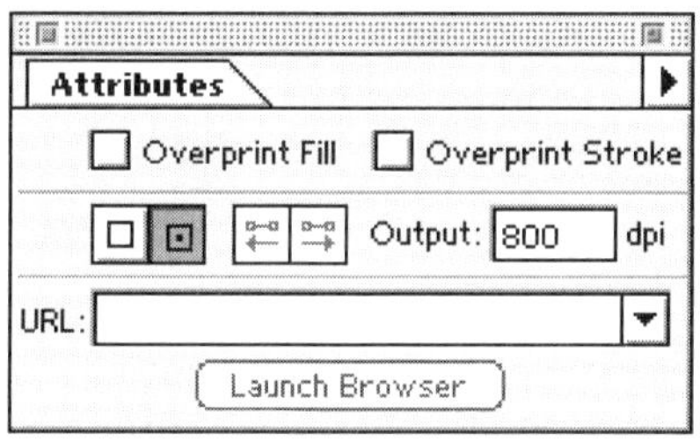

Figure C-11: The new Attributes palette

Tools

The toolbox has been dramatically reorganized (see Figure C-12). While most tool positions are evident in the toolbox, hidden tools within each slot are not. Also, the old FreeHand tool is now the Pencil tool. *Chapter 1.*

All the tools can be accessed by pressing an appropriate key; these keys appear when you rest your cursor over any tool (make sure "Show Tool Tips" is checked in General preferences). *Chapter 1.*

Fill and Stroke icons are on the toolbox. The frontmost icon is the active one. *Chapter 2.*

You choose the Fill/Stroke type right below the Fill/Stroke icons. Choose from Solid, Gradient, and None. *Chapter 2.*

The View mode settings (Normal, Full Screen with Menu, Full Screen without Menu) are chosen from the toolbox. *Chapter 1.*

The new Reshape tool is in the Scale tool slot. *Chapter 7.*

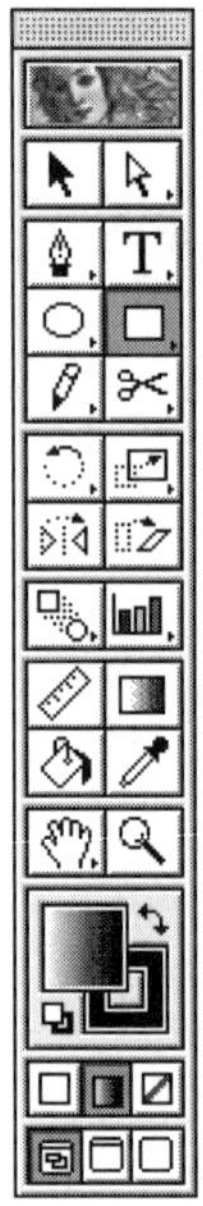

Figure C-12: The new Illustrator Toolbox

Palettes

The Paint Style palette is gone, replaced with the Fill/Stroke icons on the toolbox, the Color Palette, the Swatches palette, and the Stroke palette. *Chapter 2.*

Palettes can now be tabbed or docked together by dragging them inside or to the bottom of another palette, respectively. *Chapter 1.*

The Color Palette: For mixing, creating, and editing colors, with sliders and % values. *Chapter 2.*

The Stroke palette: For adjusting Stroke attributes. *Chapter 2.*

The Swatches palette: For selecting and storing colors, patterns and gradients. *Chapter 2.*

The Attributes palette: Path direction, Show/Hide Centerpoint, Notes, and URL. *Chapter 7.*

The Gradient palette: Color mixing has been removed (instead, click the color stop and make modifications in the Color palette). *Chapter 10.*

The Transform palette: Used to be the Control palette. *Chapter 7.*

The Align palette: Different look, same functionality. *Chapter 7.*

Figure C-13: All the Illustrator Palettes, tabbed and docked together

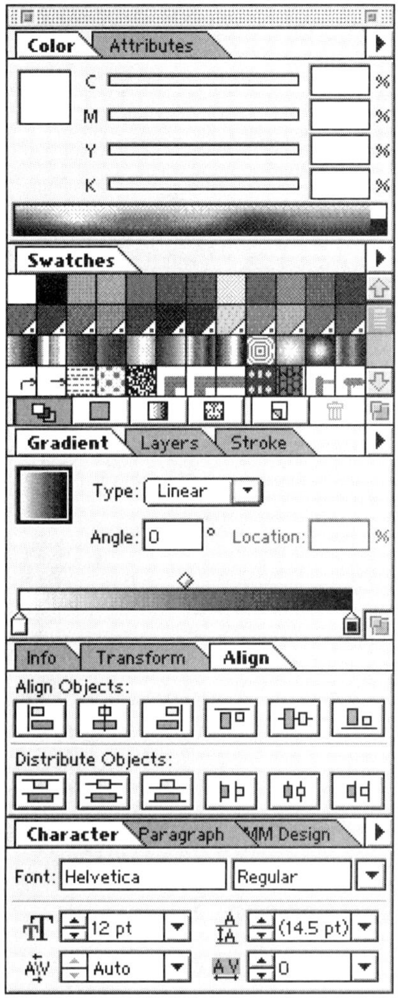

The Layers palette: Different look, with a few added features (Merge Layers and New/Delete icons). *Chapter 7.*

Figure C-14: The Layers palette

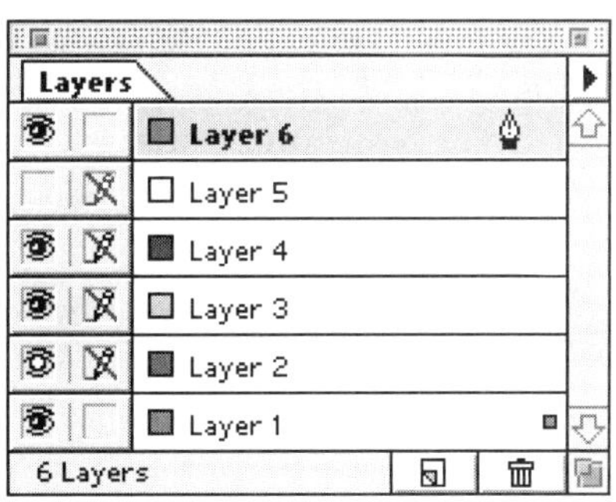

The Character palette: New Vertical Type/Kanji features added. Now only accessed from the Type menu (removed from the Window menu). *Chapter 8.*

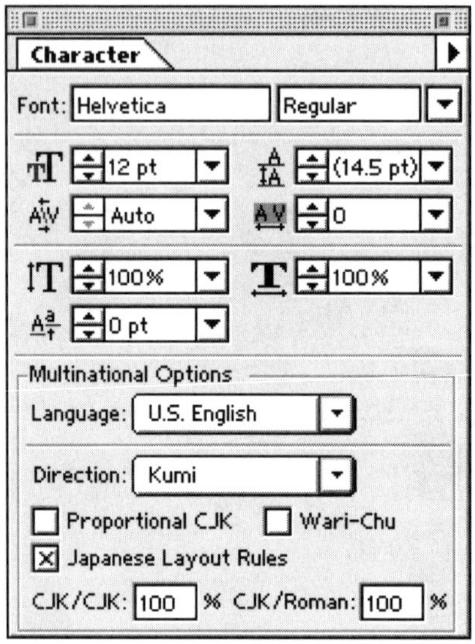

Figure C-15: The Character palette

The Paragraph palette: Same functionality as in previous versions. Now only accessed from the Type menu (removed from the Window menu). *Chapter 8.*

The Multiple Master Design palette: Accessed from the Type menu, allows changes to Multiple Master typefaces. *Chapter 8.*

Other Changes

Patterns: Now created by dragging art to be in the pattern to the Swatches palette, or by selecting the art and choosing Define Pattern from the Edit menu. *Chapter 11.*

Templates: No such thing in Illustrator 7. Instead, choose the Dim Placed Images option in a layer where bitmapped imported images reside. *Chapter 5.*

Disable Warnings: Choose this option in the General Preferences dialog box so you don't get the "You missed the point, you klutz" messages when using the Scissors, Add Anchor Point, Delete Anchor Point, and Convert Direction Point tools. *Chapter 6.*

The Top Ten List of Things You Need to Know When Using Illustrator 7 the First Time

This only applies to Illustrator 5 and 6 users. If you've never used Illustrator before, I'd have to make up a list of the top 500 things or so for you to know. Heh.

10. Adobe is not out to get you.

Okay, it may not seem like it at first, but all these changes were done to make you, the user, feel more comfortable using Illustrator. The idea is that Photoshop and Illustrator should work more alike (notice the sweeping changes in Photoshop 4). It's a good thing, and because your only other choice is FreakHand, just pretend to like it. It grows on you after a while. Like a mutant fungus. *Introduction.*

9. The Swatch palette is the epicenter of the Illustrator universe.

Spot colors, Process colors, Gradients, and patterns are all stored here. You even make patterns by dragging artwork into the Swatch palette. Keep this palette open and available all the time. *Chapter 2.*

8. Commit X and / to memory this very second.

X swaps the focus between Fill and Stroke. So once you've changed the Fill, press X and then work on the Stroke. You could click the appropriate icon, but then you'd have to move your cursor (usually across the screen). *Chapter 2.*

/ changes the Fill or Stroke (whichever is in focus) to None. The only other way to do this is by clicking that teeny tiny icon in the toolbox. *Chapter 2.*

7. Templates? I don't know what you're talking about.

Templates are now part of Illustrator history. You can simulate a template by creating a new layer, renaming the old (first, bottommost) layer Template, placing an image on the Template layer, and checking the Dim Images option in the Layer Options box of the Template layer. Oh, and the Auto Trace tool will trace any placed image, and it recognizes color, too. *Chapter 4.*

Although . . .

6. The Auto Trace tool still sucks.

Technically, the Eyedropper tool sucks, but the Auto Trace tool uses an alternate "suck" definition. Although it now works on any placed image, recognizes color, and is hidden behind the Blend tool (what's with *that?*), it still performs marginally worse than a sugared-up three-year-old with a new box of crayons and freshly painted drywall. *Chapter 4.*

5. You need VectorTools to be really happy with Illustrator 7.

I used to think I was happy with Illustrator. Now I have Extensis VectorTools, and I realize my former happiness was mere contentment. With VectorLibrary, ObjectStyles, VectorNavigator, VectorBars, and the rest, I'm finally directly in touch with my Vector side. *Chapter 14.*

4. Fix your Startup document right away.

Open up your Adobe Illustrator Startup document and set it up so that all new documents are correct in viewing percentage, window size, custom colors, gradients, patterns, and so forth. *Chapter 6.*

And while you're there,

3. Turn on grids and leave them on.

You might want to tone down the color/intensity a wee bit, but keep 'em on. Doing so will result in better-looking, more consistent images, while showing you transparent areas. The snap feature is handy as well. *Chapter 4.*

2. Use the toolbox keys to select tools.

Learn them now, thank me later. Save yourself gobs of time by pressing I for Eyedropper, B for Blend. Of course, some of the more goofy keyboard tool shortcuts may be harder to remember (who was the brainiac who thought that the Rectangle tool should be selected with an M?). *Chapter 1.*

And finally:

1. FreeHand, ShmeeHand.

What's an eight-letter word for Inadequate Drawing Software? While Illustrator 7 and FreeHand 7 share the same version number, we all know that Illustrator is still eons better than its rival. So don't mock FreeHand users; instead try to show them the light and help them to a better understanding of the vector world. And, in a related note, don't use the F—H— word around diehard Illustrator users — if not for them, for your own safety, as they might bludgeon you with that huge box of stuff that's packed with the product so that someone, anyone, might buy it.

Of course, the above is said in good fun. Macromedia FreeHand is an excellent graphics product, and actually does have more features than Adobe Illustrator if you're counting...they're just implemented a little differently. If you're a FreeHand user who is experimenting with Illustrator, be sure to check out the PDF on the *Illustrator 7 Bible* CD-ROM that deals with learning Illustrator from a FreeHand background.

If you *are* a diehard Illustrator user, don't hope that FreeHand goes away. The innovativeness and "we're number two: we'll do anything" mentality of the good folks at Macromedia insures that FreeHand will be breaking new barriers in the graphics field for some time to come in the future. Why is this good for Illustrator users? You don't think Adobe will sit around and get crushed by the competition do you?

Now that Illustrator is finally cross-platform and the groundwork has been laid for smooth cross-platform upgrades, be looking for all sorts of amazing features from the next few versions of Illustrator. And don't be surprised if some "FreeHand" features are part of Versions 8.0 or 9.0.

APPENDIX

D

What's New in Illustrator 7 for Windows

What a difference half a decade makes. An eternity of time in the computer world, that's how long it's been since Illustrator for Windows has been upgraded. So long that the version number has jumped from 4.1 to 7.0. So long that the list of new features is longer than the list of retained features.

To help all of you no-longer-frustrated Windows users cope with the massive changes from Version 4.1 to Version 7 of Illustrator, each chapter in this book contains a sidebar that details some of the more important changes for that topic since the 1992 version of Adobe Illustrator for Windows. This appendix is merely a summary of the new and different ways that Illustrator 7 for Windows works.

New Features

Gradients: A singe vector object can contain a linear or radial gradient, defined within the Gradient palette. The direction/location/angle/size of the gradient can be adjusted with the Gradient tool. *Chapter 10.*

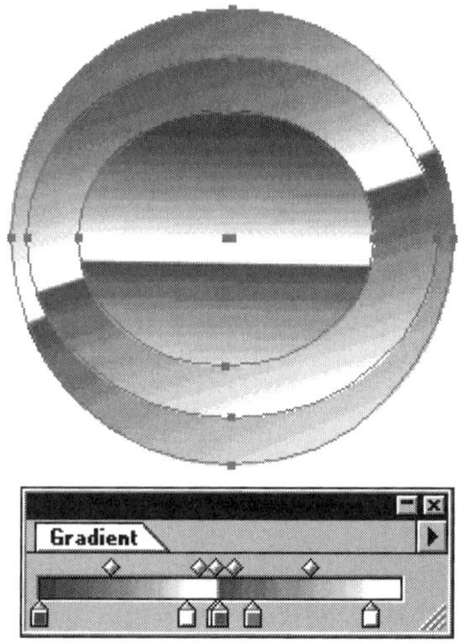

Figure D-1: The Gradient palette and gradient-filled objects

Layers: Objects within Illustrator can be organized into layers. Each layer can be shown, locked, and printed individually through options on the Layers palette. *Chapter 7.*

PostScript on the Clipboard: When Illustrator objects are copied or pasted, they temporarily reside in a special clipboard that other Adobe products can access (such as Photoshop, Dimensions, and Streamline). *Chapter 5.*

Custom Views: Any number of custom views can be saved and recalled via Illustrator's View menu. *Chapter 1.*

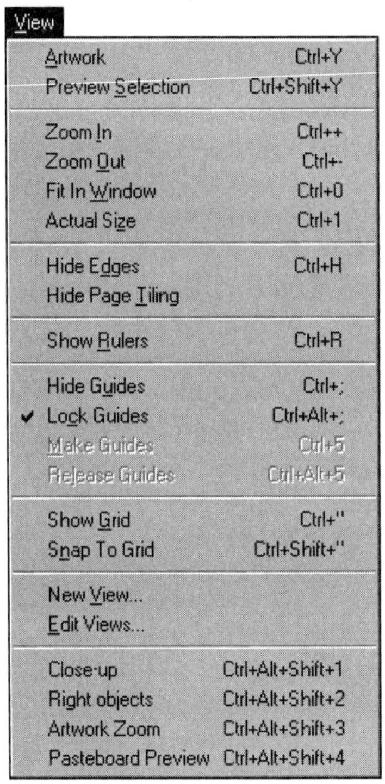

Figure D-2: Custom views at the bottom of the View menu

Plug-ins: Adobe and third-party developers can contribute to the functionality of Illustrator through plug-ins that add features and capabilities. *Chapter 15.*

Illustrator Filters: The top half of the filter menu contains all sorts of filters — from color modification to distortion filters — that modify selected vector artwork. *Chapter 12.*

Photoshop Filters: The bottom half of the Filter menu contains Photoshop filters that modify bitmap images within Illustrator. *Chapter 13.*

Pathfinder functions: Special Pathfinder functions (located in the Object menu) provide automatic means for combining and editing paths. *Chapter 7.*

Expand: Gradients can be expanded into blends, while patterns can be expanded into masked paths. *Chapters 10 and 11.*

Rasterize: Vector artwork can be pixelized into bitmap images by rasterizing them. *Chapter 5.*

Built-in Separations: Illustrator 7 can print separations directly. *Chapter 18.*

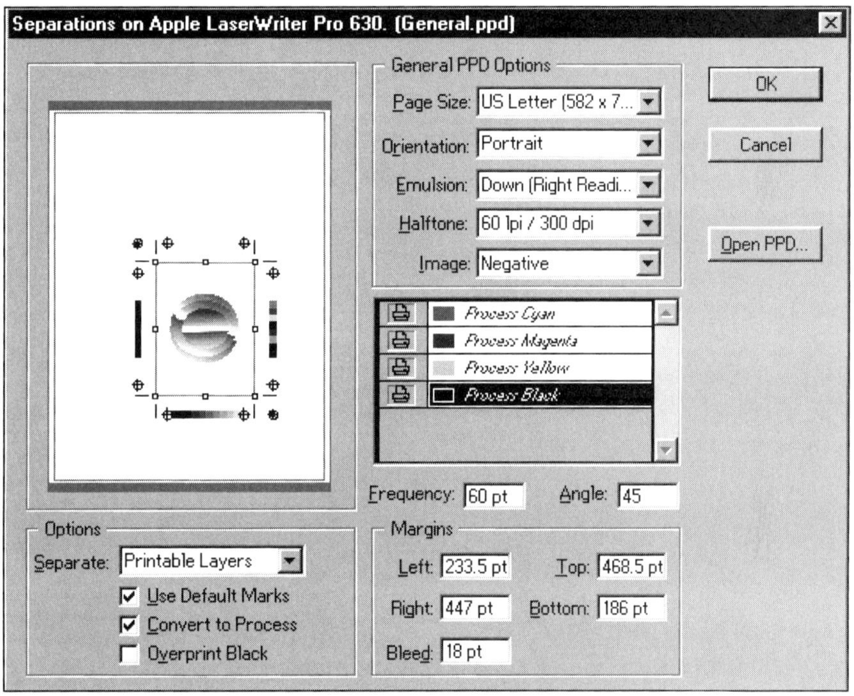

Figure D-3: The Separations dialog box

Make Knife: Any vector path can be turned into a cutting path that will slice through all paths below it. *Chapter 7.*

Bitmap File support: Raster (pixel-based) images can be combined with vector artwork in various ways. *Chapter 7.*

Advanced Path functions: Paths can be manipulated on a low level using path functions, such as Offset Path, Add Anchor Points, and Outline Path. *Chapter 7.*

Type functions: Word processor-like functions, including spell checking, find and replace, and rows and columns. *Chapter 8.*

Multiple Undos and Redos: Ctrl+Z continuously to undo again and again, and Ctrl+Shift+Z to redo anything you've undone. *Chapter 1.*

Transform Each: Multiple selected objects can be transformed at the same time, yet independently. *Chapter 7.*

Figure D-4: A path before (left) and after (right) Adding Anchor Points several times

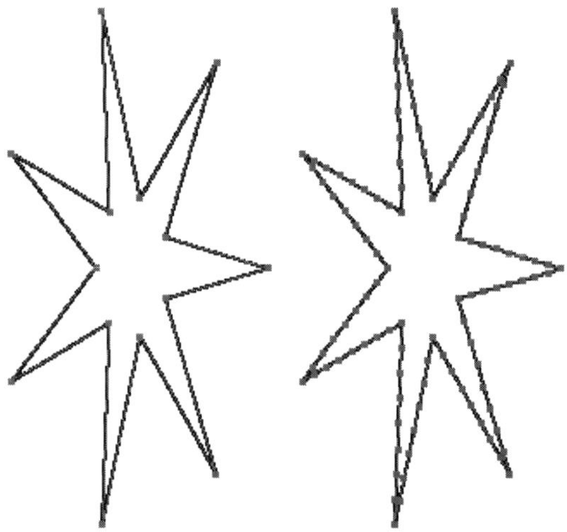

Figure D-5: The Transform Each dialog box

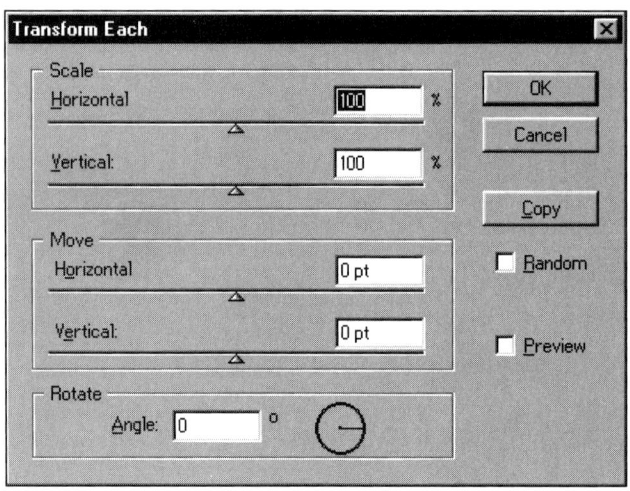

Tabs: Tab stops can be customized and set for any text area. *Chapter 8.*

Fit Headline: Text on one line can be automatically stretched to fill the line. *Chapter 8.*

Hide Edges: Selected paths can have their paths, points, and handles. *Chapter 7.*

Document Info: Various information about Illustrator documents can be viewed here. *Chapter 5.*

HSB Color: Objects can now be defined using HSB (Hue, Saturation, Brightness) values. *Chapter 2.*

RGB Color: Objects can now have RGB colors applied to them via the color palette's RGB pop-up menu option. *Chapter 2.*

URL embedding: Objects can be assigned URLs via the Attributes palette. *Chapter 16.*

Full Screen Mode: By clicking on icons at the bottom of the toolbox, you can view documents without window borders, with or without the menu bar (pressing F toggles the shortcut). *Chapter 1.*

Figure D-6a: The standard Illustrator screen

Figure D-6b: Illustrator's Menu mode

Figure D-6c: Illustrator's Full Screen mode

New Graph Type: The Radar Graph type has been added to the various graph types. *Chapter 11.*

Vertical Type: Using the new Vertical Type tools, type can be set up vertically instead of the normal horizontal appearance. *Chapter 8.*

Convert To ColorSpace X Filters: The Color submenu of the Filter menu now contains three filters that switch the selected objects' colorspace from their current colorspace to RGB, CMYK, or Grayscale. *Chapter 12.*

Context-Sensitive Menus: These menus appear when you right-click and contain typical and handy menu commands culled from all the Illustrator menus, specific to your selection. *Appendix H.*

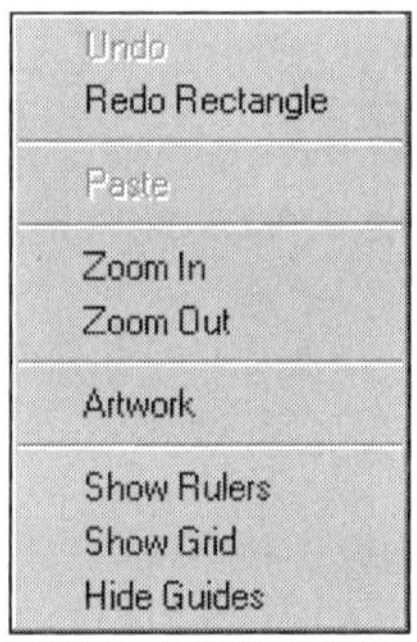

Figure D-7: A context-sensitive menu

Send Backward/Bring Forward: These functions (in the Arrange submenu of the Object menu) move selected objects through the stacking order one object layer at a time. *Chapter 7.*

Palettes

Palettes can be tabbed together or docked above and below each other to suit the way you work. *Chapter 1.*

Color Palette: The Color palette replaces the Paint Style dialog box's color mixing functions. *Chapter 2.*

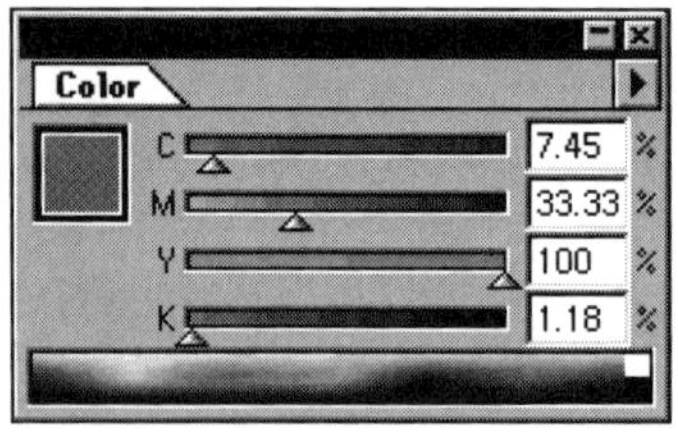

Figure D-8: The Color palette

Swatch Palette: The Swatch palette replaces the Paint Style dialog box's color list, adding several new capabilities. *Chapter 2.*

Figure D-9: The Swatches palette

Stroke Palette: The Stroke palette replaces the Paint Style dialog box's Stroke Attributes section. *Chapter 2.*

Attributes Palette: The Attributes palette provides a place to change path direction, to show or hide the selected path's center point, and to add notes and URLs to objects. *Chapter 7.*

Gradient Palette: The Gradient palette provides a method for adjusting and modifying gradients. *Chapter 2.*

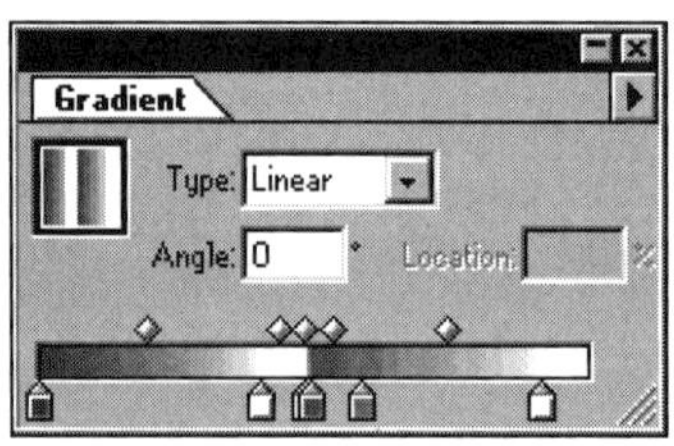

Figure D-10: The Gradient palette

Info Palette: The Info palette supplies real-time feedback about cursor location and selected object attributes and location. *Chapter 7.*

Transform Palette: The Transform palette provides a compact floating palette to transform (Move, Scale, Rotate, and Shear) objects from nine different origin points. *Chapter 3.*

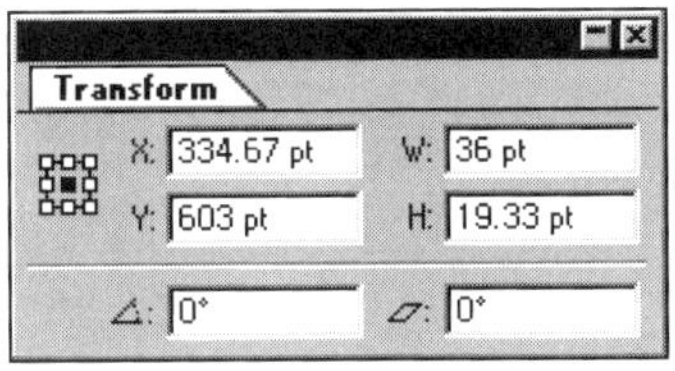

Figure D-11: The Transform palette

Align Palette: The Align palette contains several buttons for instant aligning and distributing of selected objects. *Chapter 7.*

Layers Palette: The Layers palette allows you to organize your artwork into easily manageable layers. *Chapter 7.*

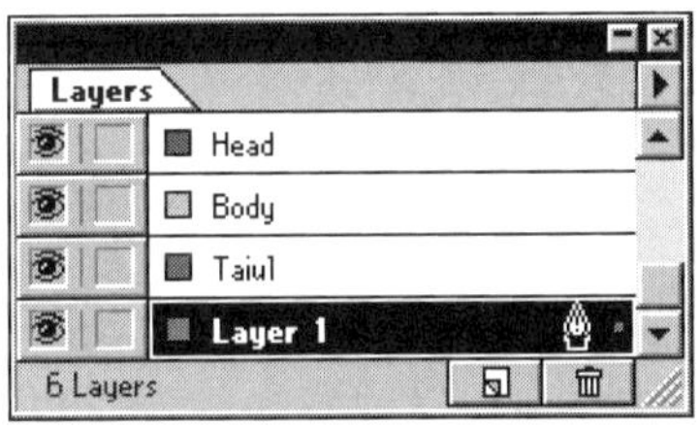

Figure D-12: The Layers palette

Character Palette: The Character palette replaces the Type dialog box's character functions. *Chapter 2.*

Paragraph Palette: The Paragraph palette replaces the Type dialog box's paragraph-specific functions. *Chapter 2.*

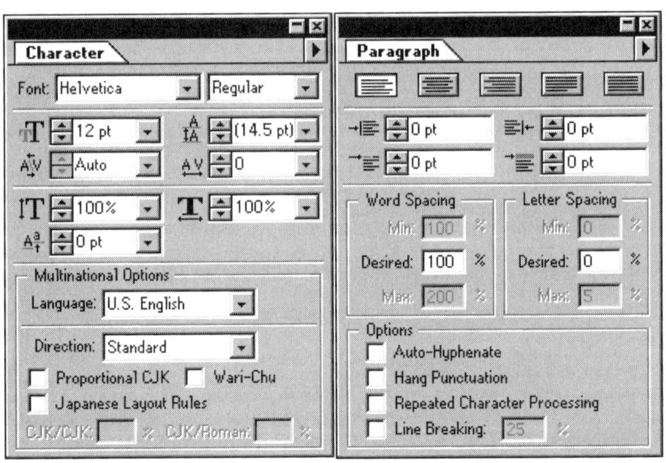

Figure D-13: The Character and Paragraph palettes

Multiple Master Palette: This palette provides controls for manipulating Multiple Master typefaces. *Chapter 8.*

New Tools

All of Illustrator's tools can now be accessed by pressing a specific key on the keyboard. *Chapter 1.*

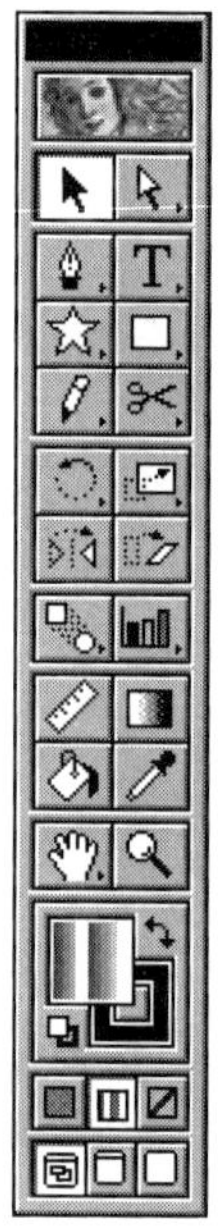

Figure D-14: The Illustrator 7 toolbox

Vertical Type Tools: The vertical type tools are used for creating type oriented vertically instead of horizontally. They are hidden in the Type tool slot. *Chapter 8.*

Gradient Tool: This tool is used for setting the location, angle, and size of gradients. *Chapter 10.*

Knife Tool: This tool is used for slicing paths (selected or not). It is hidden in the Scissors tool slot. *Chapter 7.*

Paintbrush Tool: The Paintbrush tool is used to create free-flowing filled paths that resemble brushstrokes. In conjunction with a pressure-sensitive tablet, the paths can vary in width as they're being drawn. This tool is hidden in the Pencil tool slot. *Chapter 2.*

Twirl Tool: This tool is used to spin objects proportionately around their center points. It is hidden in the Rotate tool slot. *Chapter 3.*

Radar Graph Tool: This tool is used to create Radar graphs, a new graph type in Illustrator 7. It is hidden in the (Column) Graph tool slot. *Chapter 11.*

Polygon Tool: The Polygon tool is used to create equilateral polygons. It is hidden in the Ellipse tool slot. *Chapter 2.*

Spiral Tool: This tool is used to create spirals. It is hidden in the Ellipse tool slot. *Chapter 2.*

Star Tool: The Star tool is used for creating a variety of star shapes. It is hidden in the Ellipse tool slot. *Chapter 2.*

Paint Bucket Tool: This tool is used to apply the current paint style to unselected paths. *Chapter 2.*

Eyedropper Tool: This tool is used to change the Paint Style to any path that is clicked on. *Chapter 2.*

Reshape Tool: This tool (located in the Scale tool slot) is used to bend and distort paths without destroying their basic shape. *Chapter 7.*

Changes

Menu Changes

The menu changes from Version 4.1 to Version 7 have been rather drastic. The menu items below are only the menu options from 4.0 that have been moved or deleted. New menu items are not covered here.

File⇨Place Template has been removed. Templates are no longer needed in Illustrator 7; instead, place art and choose Dim Placed Image from the Layer Options dialog box. *Chapter 4.*

File⇨Place Art is now File⇨Place. *Chapter 5.*

File⇨Import has been removed. Use File⇨Place in its place. *Chapter 5.*

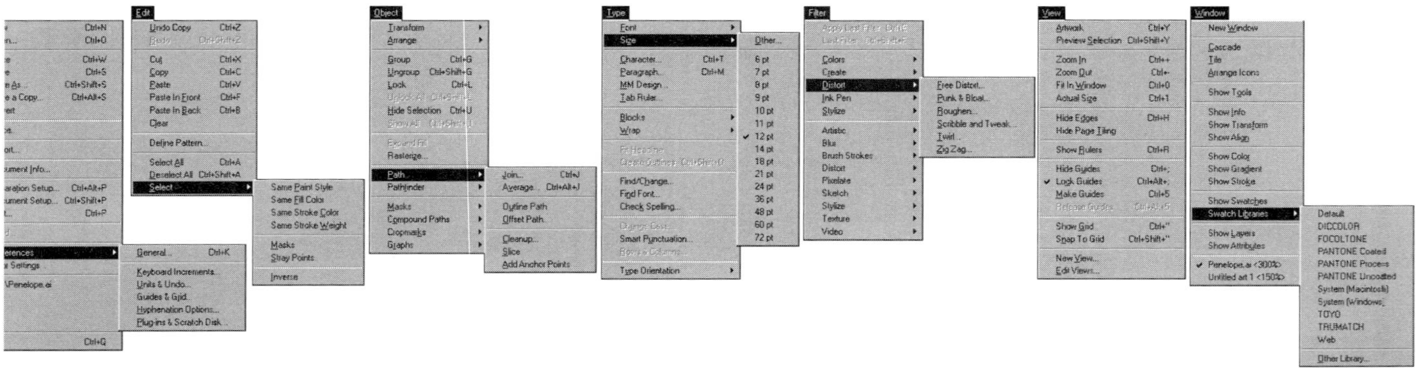

Figure D-15: Illustrator's Menu mode

File⇨Export Art is now File⇨Export. *Chapter 5.*

File⇨Print Setup is now accessed by choosing File⇨Document Setup and then clicking on the Print Setup button. *Chapter 18.*

Edit⇨Bring to Front is now accessed by choosing Object⇨Arrange⇨Bring to Front. *Chapter 3.*

Edit⇨Send to Back is now accessed by choosing Object⇨Arrange⇨Send to Back. *Chapter 3.*

Edit⇨Move is now accessed by choosing Object⇨Transform⇨Move.

Edit⇨Preferences is now accessed by choosing File⇨Preferences⇨General.

Arrange⇨Transform Again is now accessed by choosing Object⇨Transform⇨Transform Again. *Chapter 3.*

Arrange⇨Group is now accessed by choosing Object⇨Group. *Chapter 3.*

Arrange⇨Ungroup is now accessed by choosing Object⇨Ungroup. *Chapter 3.*

Arrange⇨Join is now accessed by choosing Object⇨Path⇨Join. *Chapter 7.*

Arrange⇨Average is now accessed by choosing Object⇨Path⇨Average. *Chapter 7.*

Arrange⇨Lock is now accessed by choosing Object⇨Lock. *Chapter 3.*

Arrange⇨Unlock All is now accessed by choosing Object⇨Unlock All. *Chapter 3.*

Arrange⇨Hide is now accessed by choosing Object⇨Hide. *Chapter 3.*

Arrange⇨Hide All is now accessed by choosing Object⇨Hide All. *Chapter 3.*

Arrange⇨Make Guide is now accessed by choosing View⇨Make Guide. *Chapter 4.*

Arrange⇨Release All Guides is now accessed by choosing View⇨Release Guides. *Chapter 4.*

Arrange⇨Set Cropmarks is now accessed by choosing Object⇨Cropmarks⇨Make. *Chapter 7.*

Arrange⇨Release Cropmarks is now accessed by choosing Object⇨Cropmarks⇨Release. *Chapter 7.*

View⇨Preview Illustration is now accessed by choosing View⇨Preview. *Chapter 1.*

View⇨Artwork & Template has been removed, as templates are no longer used with Illustrator 7. *Chapter 4.*

View⇨Artwork Only is now accessed by choosing View⇨Artwork. *Chapter 1.*

View⇨Template Only has been removed. *Chapter 4.*

View⇨Preview Illustration is now accessed by choosing View⇨Preview. *Chapter 1.*

View⇨Fit Artwork in Window has been removed. View⇨Fit In Window does a similar function, but is not the same. *Chapter 1.*

View⇨Fit Page in Window is now accessed by choosing View⇨Fit In Window. *Chapter 1.*

View⇨Fit Page Width in Window has been removed. View⇨Fit In Window does a similar function, but is not the same. *Chapter 1.*

View⇨Toolbox Options has been removed. *Chapter 1.*

View⇨Grid has been removed. However, choosing File⇨Preferences⇨Guides & Grid allows you to set up your grid. *Chapter 4.*

View⇨Show Guides in Preview has been removed. View⇨Show Guides does a similar function, but is not the same. *Chapter 4.*

View⇨Show Status Line has been removed. A status bar appears along the bottom left of the document window, and the Info palette displays much of the information from the old Status Line. *Chapter 1.*

View⇨Show Toolbox is now accessed by choosing Window⇨Show Tools. *Chapter 1.*

View⇨Show Unpainted Objects has been removed. *Chapter 1.*

Type⇨Type Style is now accessed by choosing Type⇨Character (displaying the Character palette). *Chapter 8.*

Type⇨Leading is now accessed by choosing Type⇨Character (displaying the Character palette) and then adjusting the leading value. *Chapter 8.*

Type⇨Alignment is now accessed by choosing Type⇨Paragraph (displaying the Paragraph palette) and then choosing one of five Alignments. *Chapter 8.*

Type➪Spacing Options is now accessed by choosing Type➪Paragraph (displaying the Paragraph palette) and then adjusting the Spacing options. *Chapter 8.*

Type➪Tracking/Kerning is now accessed by choosing Type➪Character (displaying the Character palette) and then adjusting the Tracking/Kerning values. *Chapter 8.*

Type➪Link is now accessed by choosing Type➪Blocks➪Link. *Chapter 8.*

Type➪Unlink is now accessed by choosing Type➪Blocks➪Unlink. *Chapter 8.*

Type➪Make Text Wrap is now accessed by choosing Type➪Wrap➪Make. *Chapter 8.*

Type➪Release Text Wrap is now accessed by choosing Type➪Wrap➪Release. *Chapter 8.*

Object➪Paint Style has been removed, replaced by the Stroke/Fill section of the toolbox, the Color palette, the Stroke palette, and the Swatches palette. *Chapter 2.*

Object➪Pattern is now accessed by choosing Edit➪Define Pattern. *Chapter 11.*

Object➪Custom Color has been removed, replaced by the Swatches palette. *Chapter 2.*

Object➪Make Compound is now accessed by choosing Object➪Compound Paths➪Make. *Chapter 9.*

Object➪Release Compound is now accessed by choosing Object➪Compound Paths➪Release. *Chapter 9.*

Graph➪Graph Style is now accessed by choosing Object➪Graphs➪Type. *Chapter 11.*

Graph➪Graph Data is now accessed by choosing Object➪Graphs➪Data. *Chapter 11.*

Graph➪Use Column Design is now accessed by choosing Object➪Graphs➪Column. *Chapter 11.*

Graph➪Use Marker Design is now accessed by choosing Object➪Graphs➪Marker. *Chapter 11.*

Graph➪Define Graph Design is now accessed by choosing Object➪Graphs➪ Design. *Chapter 11.*

Tools

The toolbox has been dramatically reorganized from the single column design of Version 4.1. While most tool positions are evident in the toolbox, hidden tools within each slot are not. *Chapter 1.*

Figure D-16: The Illustrator 7 toolbox

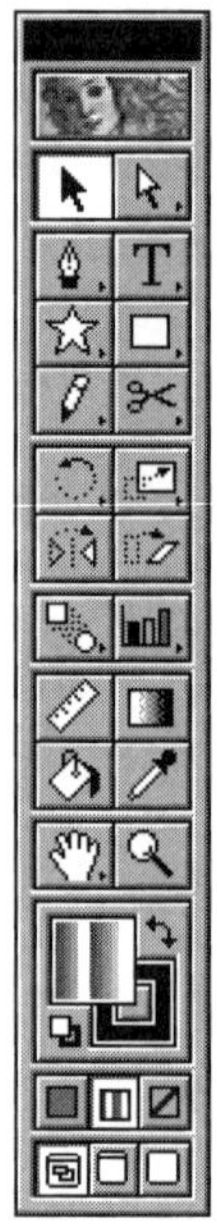

All the tools can be accessed by pressing an appropriate key; these keys appear when you rest your cursor over any tool (make sure Show Tool Tips is checked in General preferences). *Chapter 1.*

Fill and Stroke icons are on the toolbox. The frontmost icon is the active one. *Chapter 2.*

The fill/stroke type is chosen right below the Fill/Stroke icons. Choose from Solid/Pattern, Gradient, and None. *Chapter 2.*

The View mode settings (Normal, Full Screen with Menu, Full Screen without menu) are chosen from the Toolbox. *Chapter 1.*

The new Reshape tool is in the Scale tool slot. *Chapter 7.*

Palettes

Palettes have been added to Illustrator to replace most of the dialog boxes that were used in Version 4.1.

The Color palette: For mixing, creating, and editing colors, with sliders and percent values. *Chapter 2.*

The Stroke palette: For adjusting Stroke attributes. *Chapter 2.*

The Swatches palette: For selecting and storing colors, patterns and gradients. *Chapter 2.*

Figure D-17: The Swatches palette

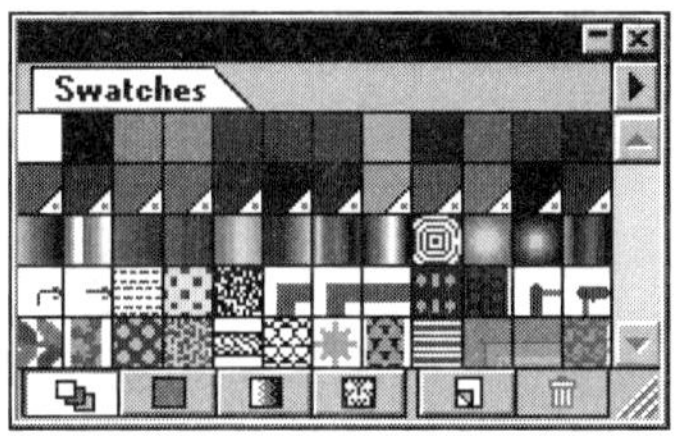

The Attributes palette: Path direction, Show/Hide Centerpoint, Notes, and URL. *Chapter 7.*

Figure D-18: The Attributes palette

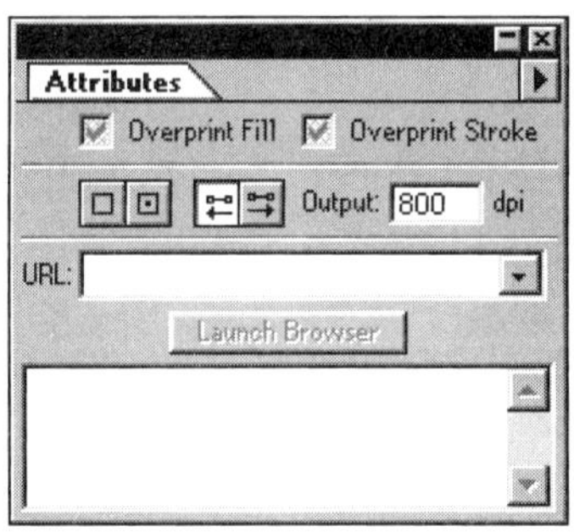

The Gradient palette: Color mixing has been removed (instead, click on the color stop and make modifications in the Color palette). *Chapter 10.*

The Transform palette: Used to be the Control palette. *Chapter 7.*

The Align palette: Different look, same functionality. *Chapter 7.*

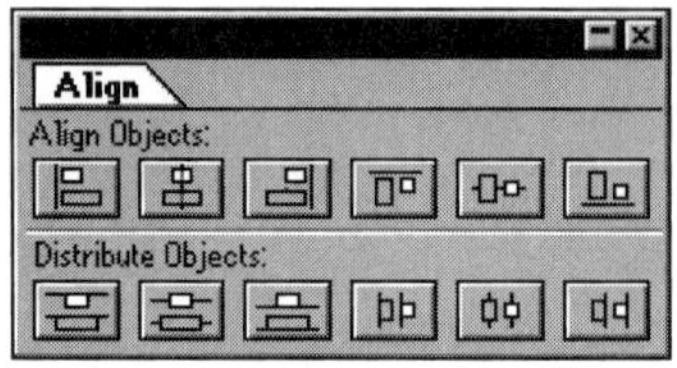

Figure D-19: The Align palette

The Layers palette: Different look, with a few added features (Merge Layers and New/Delete icons). *Chapter 7.*

The Character palette: New Vertical Type/Kanji features added. Now only accessed from the Type menu (removed from the Window menu). *Chapter 8.*

The Paragraph palette: Same functionality as in previous versions. Now only accessed from the Type menu (removed from the Window menu). *Chapter 8.*

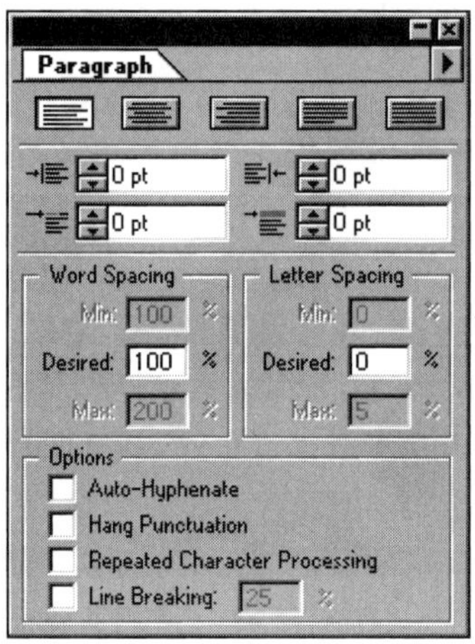

Figure D-20: The Paragraph palette

The Multiple Master Design palette: Accessed from the Type menu, allows changes to Multiple Master typefaces. *Chapter 8.*

Other Changes

Patterns: Now created by dragging art to be in the pattern to the Swatches palette, or by selecting the art and choosing Define Pattern from the Edit menu. *Chapter 11.*

Templates: There is no such thing in Illustrator 7. Instead, choose the Dim Placed Images option in a layer where bitmapped imported images reside. *Chapter 5.*

Figure D-21: An image placed in Illustrator and dimmed via the Layer Options dialog box

Disable Warnings: Choose this option in the General Preferences dialog box so you don't get the "You missed the point, you klutz" messages when using the Blend, Add Anchor Point, Delete Anchor Point, and Convert Direction Point tools. *Chapter 6.*

The Top Ten List of Things You Need to Know When Using Illustrator 7 for Windows for the First Time

This only applies to Illustrator 4 for Windows users. Actually, I had a list of 50 things, because the version change is so great, but I've pared the list down to the 10 of the most important issues.

10. Palettes are not Satan's Handiwork.

If you've been using Illustrator 4 for a long time, you're used to punching a key command like Ctrl+I, and then tabbing to enter values and whacking the Enter key when you're finished. All that is over. Now you can show or hide the Color palette with Ctrl+I, but because it's usually on your screen, instead of making it active, you zip it away. When you bring it back you have to click in or next to the text field to make a text field active. Properly used, however, the plethora of palettes in Illustrator 7 make your Illustrator work incredibly productive.

9. Just because Illustrator can do almost anything doesn't mean it can do almost anything.

With path-generating functions like the Pathfinder functions, Expand, and Ink Pen, you can create thousands and thousands of paths in relatively no time at all. That's bad. Illustrator gets rrreeeaaaallllyyyy sssssslllloooowwww when it has more than 25,000 paths or so, and gets exponentially slower after that. Use Document Info to check the number of paths, and try to keep it below 10,000 if you can.

8. Adobe doesn't hate Windows Users.

There was supposed to be a Windows version of 5.0, 5.5, and 6.0. All sorts of things happened in Adobe that prevented this, from engineers defecting to the enemy to political infighting to the cancellation of Hercules. Hercules was the code name for Illustrator 6.0, and then 7.0 when Popeye (Illustrator 6.0) came around. The version of Illustrator 7 you're using, however, was code-named Simba. The slight was not intentional, by any means. The bright side is that as a Windows user, you can upgrade to Illustrator 7.0 from 4.1 (three versions' worth) rather inexpensively.

7. The Swatch palette is magical.

Keep the Swatch palette up all the time. With it, you can apply colors, gradients, and patterns instantly, create patterns by dragging Illustrator paths into a swatch, and quickly change gradient stops.

POWER TIP: You can quickly select any named swatch by Ctrl+Alt+Clicking in the Swatches area, and then typing the first few letters of the swatch's name. When you Ctrl+Alt+Click in the Swatch area, a dark border will appear around the swatches in the Swatch palette.

6. Drag and Drop Illustrator Objects.

If you use Photoshop, Streamline, Dimensions, or PageMaker, you can drag any Illustrator item from Illustrator and right into any of these programs. You can also drag many items from these programs into Illustrator. Just make sure the "to" program has a window showing, and drag from the "from" program to the "to" program.

5. Use the extension .ai for Windows Illustrator files.

You actually can get away without doing this in some cases, but to be safe, always put a .ai after your file name.

4. Highlight most text fields by clicking to the side of them.

This works in palettes and dialog boxes. You can quickly highlight any field by clicking *once* next to a text field.

3. Grab a copy of VectorTools for Windows.

As I write this, just before Illustrator 7 is shipping, VectorTools for Windows has not been announced. Extensis has plans to release it before the end of the year, however, and as soon as they do, get yourself a copy and take advantage of all the great features VectorTools has to offer, such as toolbars, color management, and libraries.

2. Don't mix RGB and CMYK.

Doing so may result in your system just plain blowing up. Okay, maybe that won't happen, but no good will come of it. In any one document, pick a color model and stick to it.

1. Try not to make fun of your associates who use CorelDRAW!

Sure, they have an ugly behemoth of a program. Sure, it clogs printers with its unmanageable files. Sure, creating the most basic of illustrations is an exercise in stress management. But if you're nice to them, maybe they'll start using Illustrator 7 instead, making their lives and yours that much more enriched.

Shortcuts for Illustrator 7 for Macintosh

E APPENDIX

There are more shortcuts and keyboard commands in Illustrator than ever before.

Menu Commands

The File Menu

Command	Shortcut
New Document	⌘-N
Open Document	⌘-O
Close Document	⌘-W
Save Document	⌘-S
Save As	⌘-Shift-S
Save a Copy	⌘-Option-S
Revert	F12
Separation Setup	⌘-Option-P
Document Setup	⌘-Shift-P
Print Document	⌘-P
General Preferences	⌘-K
Quit Illustrator	⌘-Q

The Edit Menu

Command	Shortcut
Undo	⌘-Z F1
Redo	⌘-Shift-Z
Cut	⌘-X F2

(continued)

(continued)

Command	Shortcut
Copy	⌘-C F3
Paste	⌘-V F4
Paste In Front	⌘-F
Paste In Back	⌘-B
Clear	Delete
Select All	⌘-A
Deselect All	⌘-Shift-A

The Object Menu

Command	Shortcut
Transform Again	⌘-D
Move	Double-click Selection tool
Bring to Front	⌘-Shift-]
Bring Forwards	⌘-]
Send Backwards	⌘-[
Send to Back	⌘-Shift-[
Group	⌘-G
Ungroup	⌘-Shift-G
Lock	⌘-L
Lock Unselected	⌘-Option-L
Unlock All	⌘-Shift-L
Hide Selection	⌘-U
Hide Unselected	⌘-Option-U
Show All	⌘-Shift-U
Join	⌘-J
Average	⌘-Option-J
Join and Average	⌘-Option-Shift-J
Repeat Pathfinder	⌘-4
Make Mask	⌘-7
Release Mask	⌘-Option-7

Command	Shortcut
Make Compound Path	⌘-8
Release Compound Path	⌘-Option-8

The Type Menu

Command	Shortcut
Font	⌘-Option-Shift-M
Show/Hide Character palette	⌘-T (toggle)
Show/Hide Paragraph palette	⌘-M (toggle)
Create Outlines	⌘-Shift-O

The Filter Menu

Command	Shortcut
Apply Last Filter	⌘-E
Last Filter Dialog Box	⌘-Option-E

The View Menu

Command	Shortcut
Artwork/Preview	⌘-Y (toggle)
Preview Selection	⌘-Option-Y
Zoom In	⌘-+
Zoom Out	⌘-–
Fit In Window	⌘-0 Double-click Hand tool
Actual Size (100%)	⌘-1 Double-click Zoom tool
Hide Edges	⌘-H (toggle)
Show/Hide Rulers	⌘-R (toggle)
Show/Hide Guides	⌘-; (toggle)
Lock Guides	⌘-Option-;
Make Guides	⌘-5
Release Guides	⌘-Option-5

(continued)

(continued)

Command	*Shortcut*
Show/Hide Grid	⌘-' (toggle)
Snap to Grid	⌘-Shift-'
New View 1	⌘-Option-Shift-1
New View 2	⌘-Option-Shift-2
New View 3	⌘-Option-Shift-3
New View 4	⌘-Option-Shift-4
New View 5	⌘-Option-Shift-5
New View 6	⌘-Option-Shift-6
New View 7	⌘-Option-Shift-7
New View 8	⌘-Option-Shift-8
New View 9	⌘-Option-Shift-9
New View 10	⌘-Option-Shift-0

The Window Menu

Command	*Shortcut*
Show/Hide All Palettes	Tab (toggle)
Show/Hide Tools	none
Show/Hide Info Palette	F8 (toggle)
Show/Hide Transform Palette	none
Show/Hide Align Palette	none
Show/Hide Color Palette	F6 (toggle) ⌘-I (toggle)
Show/Hide Gradient Palette	F9 (toggle)
Show/Hide Stroke Palette	F10 (toggle)
Show/Hide Swatches Palette	F5 (toggle)
Show/Hide Layers Palette	F7 (toggle)
Show/Hide Attributes Palette	F11 (toggle) ⌘-Shift-I (toggle)

Tool Shortcuts

Many of the one-key tool shortcuts may require pressing the key more than once if that tool is hidden within a Tool slot. For instance, to access the Auto Trace tool, press B if the Auto Trace tool is showing in the Blend tool slot, or B B if it is not showing. All one-key tool shortcuts are shown, assuming the Tool slots contain the default tools; therefore, the shortcut for the Auto Trace tool is B B.

Toolbox Commands

Tool	*Shortcut*
Hide/Show toolbox & other palettes	Tab
Hide/Show all palettes except toolbox	Shift-Tab
Reset all tool slots to their default tools by . . .	⌘-Shift-Double-clicking any Tool

Selection Tools

Tool	*Shortcut*
Selection tool	V ⌘-Tab with Direct Selection tool, then hold ⌘ ⌘ with all other tools if Selection tool was the last tool used
Direct Selection Tool A	(toggles with Group Selection tool) ⌘-Tab with Selection tool, then hold ⌘ Option with Group Selection tool ⌘ with all other tools if Direct Selection tool was the last tool used
Group Selection tool	A A (if default Direct Selection tool is in slot; toggles with Direct Selection tool) Option with Direct Selection tool ⌘-Option with all other tools if Direct Selection tool was the last tool used

Function	*Procedure*
Select One Point	Click with Direct Selection tool
Select One Segment	Click with Direct Selection tool
Select One Path	Click with Group Selection tool
Select Next Group Up	Click again on selected path with Group Selection tool
Select Top Level Group	Click with Selection tool
Select Additional	Shift-click
Select Specific Points	Drag with Direct Selection tool

(continued)

(continued)

Function	*Procedure*
Select Specific Paths	Drag with Selection tool
Deselect Selected	Shift-click on Selected
Move Selection	Drag
Duplicate Selection	Option-drag
Constrain to 45° Movement	Shift-drag
Duplicate and Constrain	Option-Shift-drag
Select All	⌘-A
Deselect All	⌘-Shift-A

Path Tools

Tool	*Shortcut*
Pen tool	P (toggles with Add Anchor Point tool, Delete Anchor Point tool, and Convert Direction Point tool)
Add Anchor Point tool	P P (if default Pen tool is in slot; toggles with Pen tool, Delete Anchor Point tool, and Convert Direction Point tool) Option-Delete Anchor Point tool Option-Scissors tool
Delete Anchor Point tool	P P P (if default Pen tool is in slot; toggles with Pen tool, Add Anchor Point tool, and Convert Direction Point tool) Option-Add Anchor Point tool
Convert Direction Point tool	P P P P (if default Pen tool is in slot; toggles with Pen tool, Add Anchor Point tool, and Delete Anchor Point tool) Option-Pen tool ⌘-Option with Direct Selection tool ⌘-Option if Direct Selection tool was the last selection tool used
Pencil tool	Y (toggles with Paintbrush tool)
Paintbrush tool	Y Y (if default Pencil tool is in slot; toggles with Paintbrush tool)
Scissors tool	C (toggles with Knife tool)
Knife tool	C C (if default Scissors tool is in slot; toggles with Scissors tool)

Function	***Procedure***
Create a Straight Corner Point	Click with Pen tool
Create a Smooth Point	Drag with Pen tool
Continue Existing Open Path	Click/Drag with Pen tool on Endpoint of Existing Path
Close Open Path	While Drawing, Click/Drag with Pen tool on the Initial Endpoint Click/Drag with Pen tool on each Endpoint in succession
	Select Path and Join (⌘-J)
Constrain New Point to 45° from Last Point	Shift-click/Drag with Pen tool
Constrain Control Handles to 45°	Shift while Dragging with Pen tool
Create a Path	Click/Drag a succession of Points with Pen tool
Add Anchor Points to Existing Path	Click with Add Anchor Point tool on Path
Delete Anchor Points from Existing Path	Click with Delete Anchor Point tool on Path
Convert Anchor Point to Smooth Point	Drag with Convert Direction Point tool on Existing Point
Convert Smooth Point to Corner Point	Click with Convert Direction Point tool on Smooth Point
Convert Smooth to Combination Corner	Drag one handle with Direct Selection tool back into the Anchor Point
Convert Smooth to Curved Corner	Drag one handle with Convert Direction Point tool
Draw Freestyle paths	Drag with Pencil tool
Erase Pencil tool path while drawing	⌘-drag with Pencil tool over area to be erased
View Paintbrush Options	Double-click on Paintbrush tool (in Toolbox)
Split Path	Click with Scissors tool
Slice Multiple Paths	Drag with Knife tool
Constrain Knife Slice to 45°	Shift-drag with Knife tool
Duplicate Section of Paths	Option-drag with Knife tool
Use Selected Path to slice	Choose Object⇨Path⇨Slice

Type Tools

Tool	Shortcut
Type tool	T (toggles with all other type tools) Shift-Vertical Type tool
Area Type tool	T T (if default Type tool is in slot; toggles with all other type tools)
Option-Path Type tool	Shift-Vertical Area Type tool Option-Shift Vertical Path Type tool
Path Type tool	T T T (if default Type tool is in slot; toggles with all other type tools) Option-Area Type tool Shift-Vertical Path Type tool Option-Shift-Vertical Area Type tool
Vertical Type tool	T T T T (if default Type tool is in slot; toggles with all other type tools) Shift-Type tool
Vertical Area Type tool	T T T T T (if default Type tool is in slot; toggles with all other type tools) Option-Vertical Path Type tool Shift-Area Type tool Option-Shift-Area Type tool
Vertical Path Type tool	T T T T T T (if default Type tool is in slot; toggles with all other type tools) Option-Vertical Area Type tool Shift-Path Type tool Option-Shift -Area Type tool

Function	Procedure
Create Point Type	Click with Type tool
Create Rectangle Type	Drag with Type tool
Place Path Type on a Closed Path	Click on path with Path Type tool Option-click on path with Type tool Option-click on path with Area Type tool
Place Path Type on an Open Path	Click on path with Path Type tool Click on path with Type tool Option-click on path with Area Type tool
Place Area Type on a Closed Path	Click on path with Area Type tool Click on path with Type tool Option-click on path with Path Type tool

Function	Procedure
Place Area Type on an Open Path	Click on path with Area Type tool Option-click on path with Type tool Option-click on path with Path Type tool
Change Vertical Type to Horizontal Type	Choose Type⇨Orientation⇨Horizontal
Change Horizontal Type to Vertical entire Type	Choose Type⇨Orientation⇨Vertical Select Text Block; click on Text Block with Selection tool
Select one character	Drag across character with any Type tool
Select one word	Double-click on word with any Type tool
Select one paragraph	Triple-click on paragraph with any Type tool
Select all text in Text Block	Click in Text Block with any Type tool, and then press ⌘-A
Flip Type on a Path	Double-click the I-bar with any selection tool or just drag it to the opposite side

Shape Tools

Tool	Shortcut
Ellipse tool	N (toggles with Centered Ellipse tool, Polygon tool, Star tool, and Spiral tool) Option-Centered Ellipse tool
Centered Ellipse tool	N N (if default Ellipse tool is in slot; toggles with Ellipse tool, Polygon tool, Star tool, and Spiral tool) Option-Ellipse tool
Polygon tool	N N N (if default Ellipse tool is in slot; toggles with Ellipse tool, Centered Ellipse tool, Star tool, and Spiral tool)
Star tool	N N N N (if default Ellipse tool is in slot; toggles with Ellipse tool, Centered Ellipse tool, Polygon tool, and Spiral tool)
Spiral tool	N N N N N (if default Ellipse tool is in slot; toggles with Ellipse tool, Centered Ellipse tool, Polygon tool, and Star tool)
Rectangle tool	M (toggles with Rounded Rectangle tool, Centered Rectangle Tool, and Centered Rounded Rectangle tool) Option-Centered Rectangle tool

(continued)

(continued)

Tool	Shortcut
Rounded Rectangle tool	M M (if default Rectangle tool is in slot; toggles with Rectangle tool, Centered Rectangle Tool, and Centered Rounded Rectangle tool) Option-Centered Rounded Rectangle tool
Centered Rectangle tool	M M M (if default Rectangle tool is in slot; toggles with Rectangle tool, Rounded Rectangle tool, and Centered Rounded Rectangle tool) Option-Rectangle tool
Centered Rounded Rectangle tool	M M M M (if default Rectangle tool is in slot; toggles with Rectangle tool, Rounded Rectangle tool, and Centered Rectangle Tool) Option-Rounded Rectangle tool

Function	Procedure
Create Ellipse using Numbers	Click with Ellipse tool
Draw Ellipse	Drag with Ellipse tool
Draw Circle	Shift-drag with Ellipse tool
Create Centered Ellipse using Numbers	Click with Centered Ellipse tool
Draw Centered Ellipse	Drag with Centered Ellipse tool
Create Polygon using Numbers	Click with Polygon tool
Draw Polygon	Drag with Polygon tool
Constrain Polygon Angle	Shift-Drag with Polygon tool
Move Polygon while drawing	Spacebar-Drag with Polygon tool
Create Multiple Polygons	~-Drag with Polygon tool
Increase Polygon Sides	Up Arrow-Drag with Polygon tool
Decrease Polygon Sides	Down Arrow-Drag with Polygon tool
Create Star using Numbers	Click with Star tool
Draw Star	Drag with Star tool
Constrain Star Angle	Shift-Drag with Star tool
Move Star while drawing	Spacebar-Drag with Star tool
Create Multiple Stars	~-Drag with Star tool
Draw Even-Shouldered Star	Option-Drag with Star tool
Move Outer Points Only	⌘-Drag with Star tool
Increase Star Points	Up Arrow-Drag with Star tool
Decrease Star Points	Down Arrow-Drag with Star tool

Function	Procedure
Create Spiral using Numbers	Click with Spiral tool
Draw Spiral	Drag with Spiral tool
Constrain Spiral Angle	Shift-Drag with Spiral tool
Move Spiral while drawing	Spacebar-Drag with Spiral tool
Create Multiple Spirals	~-Drag with Spiral tool
Decrease Spiral Decay	⌘-Drag with Spiral tool
Increase Spiral Length/Size	Option-Drag with Spiral tool (toggle)
Increase Spiral Length	Up Arrow-Drag with Spiral tool
Decrease Spiral Length	Down Arrow-Drag with Spiral tool
Create Rectangle using Numbers	Click with Rectangle tool or Rounded Rectangle tool
Draw Rectangle	Drag with Rectangle tool
Draw Square	Shift-Drag with Rectangle tool
Create Rounded Rectangle using Numbers	Click with Rectangle tool or Rounded Rectangle tool
Draw Rounded Rectangle	Drag with Rounded Rectangle tool
Create Centered Rectangle using Numbers	Click with Centered Rectangle tool or Centered Rounded Rectangle tool
Draw Centered Rectangle	Drag with Centered Rectangle tool
Create Centered Rounded Rectangle w/Numbers	Click with Centered Rectangle tool or Centered Rounded Rectangle tool
Draw Centered Rounded Rectangle	Drag with Centered Rounded Rectangle tool

Transformation Tools

Tool	Shortcut
Rotate tool	R (toggles with Twirl tool)
Twirl tool	R R (if default Rotate tool is in slot; toggles with Rotate tool)
Scale tool	S (toggles with Reshape tool)
Reshape tool	S S (if default Scale tool is in slot; toggles with Scale tool)
Reflect tool	O
Skew tool	W

Function	Procedure
Rotate using Numbers	Option-click with Rotate tool
Rotate from Center of Selection w/ Numbers	Double-click with Rotate tool
Free Rotate (live)	Click with Rotate to set Origin, and then Drag with Rotate tool
Free Rotate around Selection center	Drag with Rotate tool
Constrain Rotation to 45°	Shift-drag with Rotate tool
Rotate a Copy	Option-drag with Rotate tool
Rotate Pattern only	~-drag with Rotate tool
Twirl using Numbers	Option-click with Rotate tool
Free Twirl (live)	Drag with Twirl tool
Scale using Numbers	Option-click with Scale tool
Scale from Center of Selection w/ Numbers	Double-click with Scale tool
Free Scale (live)	Click with Scale to set Origin, and then Drag with Scale tool
Free Scale around Selection center	Drag with Scale tool
Constrain Scaling to 45°	Shift-drag with Scale tool
Scale a Copy	Option-drag with Scale tool
Scale Pattern only	~-drag with Scale tool
Reshape a Path	Select points with Direct Selection, then Drag with Reshape
Reflect using Numbers	Option-click with Reflect tool
Reflect from Center of Selection w/ Numbers	Double-click with Reflect tool
Free Reflect (live)	Click with Reflect to set Origin, and then Drag with Reflect tool
Free Reflect around Selection center	Drag with Reflect tool
Constrain Reflecting to 45°	Shift-drag with Reflect tool
Reflect a Copy	Option-drag with Reflect tool
Reflect Pattern only	~-drag with Reflect tool
Skew using Numbers	Option-click with Skew tool
Skew from Center of Selection w/ Numbers	Double-click with Skew tool
Free Skew (live)	Click with Skew to set Origin, and then Drag with Skew

Function	Procedure
Free Skew around Selection center	Drag with Skew
Constrain Skewing to 45°	Shift-drag with Skew tool
Skew a Copy	Option-drag with Skew tool
Skew Pattern only	~-drag with Skew tool

Blend/Auto Trace/Graph Tools

Tool	Shortcut
Blend tool	B (toggles with Auto Trace tool)
Auto Trace tool	B B (if default Blend tool is in slot; toggles with Blend tool)
Column Graph tool	J (toggles with all other graph tools)
Stacked Column Graph tool	J J (if default Column Graph tool is in slot; toggles with all other graph tools)
Bar Graph Tool	J J J (if default Column Graph tool is in slot; toggles with all other graph tools)
Stacked Bar Graph tool	J J J J (if default Column Graph tool is in slot; toggles with all other graph tools)
Line Graph tool	J J J J J (if default Column Graph tool is in slot; toggles with all other graph tools)
Area Graph tool	J J J J J J (if default Column Graph tool is in slot; toggles with all other graph tools)
Scatter Graph tool	J J J J J J J (if default Column Graph tool is in slot; toggles with all other graph tools)
Pie Graph tool	J J J J J J J J (if default Column Graph tool is in slot; toggles with all other graph tools)
Radar Graph tool	J J J J J J J J J (if default Column Graph tool is in slot; toggles with all other graph tools)

Function	Procedure
Blend between two paths	Click on corresponding selected points on each path with Blend tool
Auto Trace Images	Click on area to be traced with Auto Trace tool
Create a Graph sized by numbers	Click with any Graph tool
Create a Graph Sized by dragging	Drag with any Graph tool

Measure/Paint Tools

Tool	Shortcut
Measure tool	U
Gradient tool	G
Paintbucket tool	K Option-Eyedropper tool
Eyedropper tool	I Option-Paintbucket tool

Function	Procedure
Measure a distance	Click on the start and end location with the Measure tool
Measure a distance by 45° angles	Shift-click on the start and end location with the Measure tool
Change Linear Gradient Direction/ Length	Drag with Gradient tool
Constrain Gradient Direction to 45° angles	Shift-drag with Gradient tool
Change Radial Gradient Size/Location	Drag with Gradient tool
Change Radial Gradient Origin Point	Click with Gradient tool
Sample color to Color palette	Click with Eyedropper tool
Sample Screen color to Color Palette	Shift-click with Eyedropper tool
Change Paint Style of selected objects	Double-click with Eyedropper tool on an object with the desired style
Paint unselected objects	Click on objects with the Paintbucket tool

Viewing Tools

Tool	Shortcut
Hand tool	H (toggles with Page tool) Spacebar (when not entering text)
Page tool	H H (if default Hand tool is in slot; toggles with Hand tool)
Zoom tool	Z ⌘-Spacebar
Zoom Out tool	Option-Zoom tool

Function	Procedure
Zoom In	Click with the Zoom tool ⌘-+
Zoom Out	Option-click with the Zoom tool ⌘- –
Zoom In to a specific area	Drag with the Zoom tool
Move the Zoom Marquee while drawing	Spacebar while Dragging with the Zoom tool
Draw the Zoom Marquee from its center	Control-drag with the Zoom tool

Viewing Shortcuts

Action	Shortcut
Zoom in Click with Zoom tool	⌘-+
Zoom Out	⌘- – Option-click with Zoom tool
Fit Document In Window	⌘-0 Double-click on Hand tool
View at Actual Size (100%)	⌘-1 Double-click on Zoom tool
Artwork/Preview Mode	⌘-Y (toggle)
Preview Selection Mode	⌘-P-Option-Y
Custom View Recall	⌘-Option-Shift-1 through ⌘-Option-Shift-0
Show/Hide Edges	⌘-H (toggle)
Show/Hide Guides	⌘-;
Show/Hide Grid	⌘-'
Show/Hide Rulers	⌘-R
Hide Selected Objects	⌘-U
Hide Unselected Objects	⌘-Option-U
Show All Hidden Objects	⌘-Shift-U
Window Mode (normal)	F (when in Full Screen mode)
Full Screen Mode w/Menu	F (when in Window mode)
Full Screen Mode (no menus)	F (when in Full Screen mode w/ menu)

Type Shortcuts

Action	*Shortcut*
Copy Type on a Path	Option-drag the I-bar using any selection tool. This shortcut actually creates two paths as well as two text stories.
Flip Type on a Path	Double-click the I-bar with any selection tool or just drag it to the opposite side of the path.
Move Insertion Point to next character	Right Arrow
Move Insertion Point to previous character	Left Arrow
Move Insertion Point to next line	Down Arrow
Move Insertion Point to previous line	Up Arrow
Move Insertion Point to next word	⌘-Right Arrow
Move Insertion Point to previous word	⌘-Left Arrow
Move Insertion Point to next paragraph	⌘-Down Arrow
Move Insertion Point to previous paragraph	⌘-Up Arrow
Select (by highlighting) all type in story	⌘-A when the Insertion Point is in the story
Select All type in document selected	⌘-A when any tool but the Type tools are
Select next character	Shift-Right Arrow
Select previous character	Shift-Left Arrow
Select next line	Shift-Down Arrow
Select previous line	Shift-Up Arrow
Select next word	⌘-Shift-Right Arrow
Select previous word	⌘-Shift-Left Arrow
Select next paragraph	⌘-Shift-Down Arrow
Select previous paragraph	⌘-Shift-Up Arrow
Select word	Double-click on word
Select Paragraph	Triple-click on Paragraph
Deselect All type	⌘-Shift-A
Duplicate column outline and flow text	Option-drag column outline with Direct Selection tool
Insert discretionary hyphen	⌘-Shift-hyphen
Insert Line Break	Enter (keypad)

Paragraph Formatting

Action	*Shortcut*
Display Paragraph palette	⌘-Shift-M
Align Paragraph Flush Left	⌘-Shift-L
Align Paragraph Flush Right	⌘-Shift-R
Align Paragraph Flush Center	⌘-Shift-C
Align Paragraph Justified	⌘-Shift-J
Align Paragraph Force Justified	⌘-Shift-F
Display Tab palette	none
Align Tab palette to selected paragraph	Click on Tab palette size box
Cycle through Tab Stops	Option-click on tab stop
Move Multiple Tab Stops	Shift-drag Tab stops
Cycle Tab measurements	Click

Character Formatting

Action	*Shortcut*
Display Character Palette	⌘-T
Highlight Font	⌘-Option-Shift-M
Increase Type size*	⌘-Shift->
Decrease Type size*	⌘-Shift-<
Increase Type to next size on Menu	⌘-Option->
Decrease Type to next size on Menu	⌘-Option-<
Highlight Size	none
Set Leading to Solid (same as pt. size)	Double-click Leading symbol (Character palette)
Highlight Leading	none
Increase Baseline Shift (Raise)*	Option-Shift-Up Arrow
Decrease Baseline Shift (Lower)*	Option-Shift-Down Arrow
Increase Baseline Shift (Raise) x5*	⌘-Option-Shift-Up Arrow
Decrease Baseline Shift (Lower) x5*	⌘-Option-Shift-Down Arrow
Reset Baseline Shift to 0	none
Highlight Baseline Shift	none
Kern/Track closer*	Option-Left Arrow

(continued)

(continued)

Action	Shortcut
Kern/Track apart*	Option-Right Arrow
Kern/Track closer x5*	⌘-Option-Left Arrow
Kern/Track apart x5*	⌘-Option-Right Arrow
Reset Kerning/Tracking to 0	⌘-Shift-Q
Highlight Kerning/Tracking	⌘-Option-K
Reset Horizontal Scale to 100%	⌘-Shift-X

Color Commands

Color Palette

Action	Shortcut
Show/Hide Color Palette	F6 (toggle)
	⌘-I (toggle)
Revert to default colors	D (White fill, Black stroke)
Toggle focus between fill and stroke	X
Choose current color in Color Palette	, (comma)
Change paint to none	/
Apply to inactive fill/stroke (fill when stroke is active, stroke when fill is active)	Option-click in color ramp on Color palette
Apply color to unselected object	Drag color swatch from Color palette to object
Apply color to selected object	Click on swatch in Color palette
Copy Paint Style to unselected objects	Click on unselected objects with Paintbucket
Copy Paint Style from any (source) object to all selected objects	Click on source object with Eyedropper
Tint process color	Shift-drag any Color palette slider
Cycle through Color Modes (Grayscale, CMYK, RGB)	Shift-click on Color Ramp

Swatches Palette

Action	*Shortcut*
Show/Hide Swatches Palette	F5 (toggle)
Toggle focus between fill and stroke	X
Add Swatch	Click the New Swatch icon Drag from Color or Gradient palette into swatches
Replace Swatch	Option-drag from Color or Gradient palette into swatches
Duplicate Swatch	Option-drag swatch onto New Swatch icon in Swatches palette
Delete Swatch	Drag to Trash icon in Swatches palette Click on Trash icon with swatches selected
Select Contiguous Swatches	Shift-click on first and last swatches
Select Discontiguous Swatches	⌘-click on each swatch
Switch keyboard focus to Swatches palette (for selecting swatches by name as they are typed)	⌘-Option-click in Swatches palette
Apply color to unselected object	Drag color swatch from Swatches palette to object
Apply color to selected object	Click on swatch in Swatches palette

Gradient Palette

Action	*Shortcut*
Choose current gradient in Gradient palette	. (period)
Show/Hide Gradient Palette	F9 (toggle)
Apply swatch to selected Color stop on gradient palette	Option-click on Swatch
Add new color stop	Click below gradient ramp
Duplicate Color Stop	Option-drag color stop
Swap Color stops	Option-drag color stop on top of another
"Suck" color for Color stop with Eyedropper	Shift-click with Eyedropper
Reset Gradient to default Black, White	⌘-click in Gradient swatch

(continued)

(continued)

Action	Shortcut
Apply color to unselected object	Drag color swatch from Gradient palette to object
Apply color to selected object	Click on swatch in Gradient palette

Stroke Palette

Action	Shortcut
Show/Hide Stroke Palette	F10 (toggle)
Increase/decrease Stroke weight	Highlight Stroke field, use Up/down arrows, press Enter when finished
Increase/decrease Miter amount	Highlight Miter field, use Up/down arrows, press Enter when finished

Other Palettes

Miscellaneous Palette Commands

Action	Shortcut
Collapse/display Palette	Click box in upper right
Cycle through Palette views	Double-click palette tab
Apply settings	Enter
Apply settings while keeping last text field highlighted	Shift-Enter
Highlight next text field	Tab
Highlight Previous Text field	Shift-Tab
Highlight any text field	Click on label or double-click current value
Increase value by base increment	Highlight field, up arrow
Decrease value by base increment	Highlight field, down arrow
Increase value by big increment	Highlight field, Shift-up arrow
Decrease value by big increment	Highlight field, Shift-down arrow
Combine palettes	Drag palette tab within other palette
Dock palette	Drag palette tab to bottom of other palette
Separate palette	Drag palette tab from current palette

Transform Palette

Action	*Shortcut*
Show/Hide Transform Palette	none
Copy object while transforming	Option-Enter
Scale Proportionately	⌘-Enter
Copy object while scaling proportionately	⌘-Option-Enter

Layers Palette

Action	*Shortcut*
Show/Hide Layers Palette	F7
New Layer	Click on New Layer icon
New Layer w/Options dialog box	Option-click on New Layer icon
New Layer Above Active Layer	⌘-Option-click on New Layer icon
New Layer Below Active Layer	⌘-click on New Layer icon
Duplicate Layer(s)	Drag layer(s) to New Layer icon
Change Layer order	Drag Layers up or down within Layer list
Select all objects on a layer	Option-click on that layer
Select all objects on several layers	Shift-Option-click on each layer
Select Contiguous Layers	Shift-click on layers
Select Discontiguous Layers	⌘-Click on Layers
Move objects to a different layer	Drag colored square to a different layer
Copy objects to a different layer	Option-drag color square to a different layer
Hide/Show Layer	Click on Eyeball icon
View Layer while hiding others	Option-click on Eyeball icon
View Layer in Artwork mode	⌘-click on Eyeball icon
View Layer in Preview while others are artwork	⌘-Option-click on eyeball
Lock/Unlock Layer	Click on Pencil icon
Unlock Layer while Locking others	Option-click on Pencil icon
Delete Layer	Drag layer to trash icon Select layer and click on trash icon
Delete Layer without warning	Option-drag layer to trash icon Select layer and Option-click on trash icon

Miscellaneous Commands

Action	Shortcut
Nudge Selection*	Arrow keys
See special Status Line categories	Option-click status bar (lower left)
Cycle through units	⌘-Control-U
Display Illustrator debug screen—dangerous	⌘-Option-Control-0 (zero)
View Anagrams of credits	Option-click Illustrator chick on toolbox
Speed up credits in About box	Option
Display Context-sensitive menus	Control-click
Highlight last active text field	⌘-~ (tilde)

Generic Dialog Box Commands

Action	Shortcut
Cancel	esc
OK (or dark bordered button)	Enter
Highlight next text field	Tab
Highlight Previous Text field	Shift-Tab
Highlight any text field	Click on label or double-click current value

*Value/amount set in Preferences

Shortcuts for Illustrator 7 for Windows

APPENDIX F

There are more shortcuts and keyboard commands in Illustrator than ever before, as you can see from this appendix.

Menu Commands

The File Menu

Command	*Shortcut*
New Document	Ctrl+N
Open Document	Ctrl+O
Close Document	Ctrl+W
Save Document	Ctrl+S
Save As	Ctrl+Shift+S
Save a Copy	Ctrl+Alt+S
Revert	F12
Separation Setup	Ctrl+Alt+P
Document Setup	Ctrl+Shift+P
Print Document	Ctrl+P
General Preferences	Ctrl+K
Quit Illustrator	Ctrl+Q

The Edit Menu

Command	Shortcut
Undo	Ctrl+Z F1
Redo	Ctrl+Shift+Z
Cut	Ctrl+X F2
Copy	Ctrl+C F3
Paste	Ctrl+V F4
Paste In Front	Ctrl+F
Paste In Back	Ctrl+B
Clear	Delete
Select All	Ctrl+A
Deselect All	Ctrl+Shift+A

The Object Menu

Command	Shortcut
Transform Again	Ctrl+D
Move	Double-click Selection tool
Bring to Front	Ctrl+Shift+]
Bring Forward	Ctrl+]
Send Backward	Ctrl+[
Send to Back	Ctrl+Shift+[
Group	Ctrl+G
Ungroup	Ctrl+Shift+G
Lock	Ctrl+L
Lock Unselected	Ctrl+Alt+L
Unlock All	Ctrl+Shift+L
Hide Selection	Ctrl+U
Hide Unselected	Ctrl+Alt+U
Show All	Ctrl+Shift+U
Join	Ctrl+J

Command	Shortcut
Average	Ctrl+Alt+J
Join and Average	Ctrl+Alt+Shift+J
Repeat Pathfinder	Ctrl+4
Make Mask	Ctrl+7
Release Mask	Ctrl+Alt+7
Make Compound Path	Ctrl+8
Release Compound Path	Ctrl+Alt+8

The Type Menu

Command	Shortcut
Font	Ctrl+Alt+Shift+M
Show/Hide Character palette	Ctrl+T (toggle)
Show/Hide Paragraph palette	Ctrl+M (toggle)
Create Outlines	Ctrl+Shift+O

The Filter Menu

Command	Shortcut
Apply Last Filter	Ctrl+E
Last Filter Dialog Box	Ctrl+Alt+E

The View Menu

Command	Shortcut
Artwork/Preview	Ctrl+Y (toggle)
Preview Selection	Ctrl+Alt+Y
Zoom In	Ctrl++
Zoom Out	Ctrl+–
Fit In Window	Ctrl+0 Double-click Hand tool
Actual Size (100%)	Ctrl+1 Double-click Zoom tool
Hide Edges	Ctrl+H (toggle)

(continued)

(continued)

Command	*Shortcut*
Show/Hide Rulers	Ctrl+R (toggle)
Show/Hide Guides	Ctrl+; (toggle)
Lock Guides	Ctrl+Alt+;
Make Guides	Ctrl+5
Release Guides	Ctrl+Alt+5
Show/Hide Grid	Ctrl+' (toggle)
Snap to Grid	Ctrl+Shift+'
New View 1	Ctrl+Alt+Shift+1
New View 2	Ctrl+Alt+Shift+2
New View 3	Ctrl+Alt+Shift+3
New View 4	Ctrl+Alt+Shift+4
New View 5	Ctrl+Alt+Shift+5
New View 6	Ctrl+Alt+Shift+6
New View 7	Ctrl+Alt+Shift+7
New View 8	Ctrl+Alt+Shift+8
New View 9	Ctrl+Alt+Shift+9
New View 10	Ctrl+Alt+Shift+0

The Window Menu

Command	*Shortcut*
Show/Hide All Palettes	Tab (toggle)
Show/Hide Tools	none
Show/Hide Info Palette	F8 (toggle)
Show/Hide Transform Palette	none
Show/Hide Align Palette	none
Show/Hide Color Palette	F6 (toggle) Ctrl+I (toggle)
Show/Hide Gradient Palette	F9 (toggle)
Show/Hide Stroke Palette	F10 (toggle)
Show/Hide Swatches Palette	F5 (toggle)
Show/Hide Layers Palette	F7 (toggle)
Show/Hide Attributes Palette	F11 (toggle) Ctrl+Shift+I (toggle)

Tool Shortcuts

Many of the one-key tool shortcuts may require pressing the key more than once if that tool is hidden within a tool slot. For instance, to access the Auto Trace tool, you would press B if the Auto Trace tool is showing in the Blend tool slot, or B B if it is not showing. All one-key tool shortcuts are shown assuming the tool slots contain the default tools; therefore, the shortcut for the Auto Trace tool is B B.

Toolbox Commands

Tool	*Shortcut*
Hide/Show toolbox & other palettes	Tab
Hide/Show all palettes except toolbox	Shift+Tab
Reset all tool slots to their default tools	by Ctrl+Shift+Double-clicking any Tool

Selection Tools

Tool	*Shortcut*
Selection tool	V Ctrl+Tab with Direct Selection tool, then hold Ctrl Ctrl with all other tools if Selection tool was the last tool used
Direct Selection tool	A (toggles with Group Selection tool) Ctrl+Tab with Selection tool, and then hold Ctrl
Alt with Group Selection tool	Ctrl with all other tools if Direct Selection tool was the last tool used
Group Selection tool	A A (if default Direct Selection tool is in slot; toggles with Direct Selection tool)
Alt with Direct Selection tool	Ctrl+Alt with all other tools if Direct Selection tool was the last tool used

Function	*Procedure*
Select One Point	Click with Direct Selection tool
Select One Segment	Click with Direct Selection tool
Select One Path	Click with Group Selection tool
Select Next Group Up	Click again on selected path with Group Selection tool
Select Top Level Group	Click with Selection tool

(continued)

(continued)

Function	***Procedure***
Select Additional	Shift+click
Select Specific Points	Drag with Direct Selection tool
Select Specific Paths	Drag with Selection tool
Deselect Selected	Shift+click on Selected
Move Selection	Drag
Duplicate Selection	Alt+drag
Constrain to 45° Movement	Shift+drag
Duplicate and Constrain	Alt+Shift+drag
Select All	Ctrl+A
Deselect All	Ctrl+Shift+A

Path Tools

Tool	***Shortcut***
Pen tool	P (toggles with Add Anchor Point tool, Delete Anchor Point tool, and Convert Direction Point tool)
Add Anchor Point tool	P P (if default Pen tool is in slot; toggles with Pen tool, Delete Anchor Point tool, and Convert Direction Point tool) Alt+Delete Anchor Point tool Alt+Scissors tool
Delete Anchor Point tool	P P P (if default Pen tool is in slot; toggles with Pen tool, Add Anchor Point tool, and Convert Direction Point tool) Alt+Add Anchor Point tool
Convert Direction Point tool	P P P P (if default Pen tool is in slot; toggles with Pen tool, Add Anchor Point tool, and Delete Anchor Point tool) Alt+Pen tool Ctrl+Alt with Direct Selection tool Ctrl+Alt if Direct Selection tool was the last selection tool used
Pencil tool	Y (toggles with Paintbrush tool)
Paintbrush tool	Y Y (if default Pencil tool is in slot; toggles with Paintbrush tool)
Scissors tool	C (toggles with Knife tool)
Knife tool	C C (if default Scissors tool is in slot; toggles with Scissors tool)

Function	Procedure
Create a Straight Corner Point	Click with Pen tool
Create a Smooth Point	Drag with Pen tool
Continue Existing Open Path	Click/Drag with Pen tool on Endpoint of Existing Path
Close Open Path	While Drawing, Click/Drag with Pen tool on the Initial Endpoint Click/Drag with Pen tool on Each end point in Succession Select Path and Join (Ctrl+J)
Constrain New Point to 45° from Last Point	Shift+Click/Drag with Pen tool
Constrain Control Handles to 45°	Shift while dragging with Pen tool
Create a Path	Click/Drag a succession of Points with Pen tool
Add Anchor Points to Existing Path	Click with Add Anchor Point tool on Path
Delete Anchor Points from Existing Path	Click with Delete Anchor Point tool on Path
Convert Anchor Point to Smooth Point	Drag with Convert Direction Point tool on Existing Point
Convert Smooth Point to Corner Point	Click with Convert Direction Point tool on Smooth Point
Convert Smooth to Combination Corner	Drag one handle with Direct Selection tool back into the anchor point
Convert Smooth to Curved Corner	Drag one handle with Convert Direction Point tool
Draw Freestyle paths	Drag with Pencil tool
Erase Pencil tool path while drawing	Ctrl+drag with Pencil tool over area to be erased
View Paintbrush Options	Double-click on Paintbrush tool (in toolbox)
Split Path	Click with Scissors tool
Slice Multiple Paths	Drag with Knife tool
Constrain Knife Slice to 45°	Shift+drag with Knife tool
Duplicate Section of Paths	Alt+drag with Knife tool
Use Selected Path to slice	Choose Object⇨Path⇨Slice

Type Tools

Tool	*Shortcut*
Type tool	T (toggles with all other type tools) Shift+Vertical Type tool
Area Type tool	T T (if default Type tool is in slot; toggles with all other type tools) Alt+Path Type tool Shift+Vertical Area Type tool Alt+Shift Vertical Path Type tool
Path Type tool	T T T (if default Type tool is in slot; toggles with all other type tools) Alt+Area Type tool Shift+Vertical Path Type tool Alt+Shift+Vertical Area Type tool
Vertical Type tool	T T T T (if default Type tool is in slot; toggles with all other type tools) Shift+Type tool
Vertical Area Type tool	T T T T T (if default Type tool is in slot; toggles with all other type tools) Alt+Vertical Path Type tool Shift+Area Type tool Alt+Shift+Area Type tool
Vertical Path Type tool	T T T T T T (if default Type tool is in slot; toggles with all other type tools) Alt+Vertical Area Type tool Shift+Path Type tool Alt+Shift -Area Type tool

Function	*Procedure*
Create Point Type	Click with Type tool
Create Rectangle Type	Drag with Type tool
Place Path Type on a Closed Path	Click on path with Path Type tool Alt+click on path with Type tool Alt+click on path with Area Type tool
Place Path Type on an Open Path	Click on path with Path Type tool Click on path with Type tool Alt+click on path with Area Type tool
Place Area Type on a Closed Path	Click on path with Area Type tool Click on path with Type tool Alt+click on path with Path Type tool
Place Area Type on an Open Path	Click on path with Area Type tool Alt+click on path with Type tool Alt+click on path with Path Type tool

Function	Procedure
Change Vertical Type to Horizontal Type	Choose Type⇨Orientation⇨Horizontal
Change Horizontal Type to Vertical Type	Choose Type⇨Orientation⇨Vertical Click on Text Block with Selection tool Select entire Text Block
Select one character	Drag across character with any Type tool
Select one word	Double-click on word with any Type tool
Select one paragraph	Triple-click on paragraph with any Type tool
Select all text in Text Block	Click in Text Block with any Type tool, and then press Ctrl+A.
Flip Type on a Path	Double-click the I-bar with any selection tool or just drag it to the opposite side

Shape Tools

Tool	Shortcut
Ellipse tool	N (toggles with Centered Ellipse tool, Polygon tool, Star tool, and Spiral tool) Alt+Centered Ellipse tool
Centered Ellipse tool	N N (if default Ellipse tool is in slot; toggles with Ellipse tool, Polygon tool, Star tool, and Spiral tool) Alt+Ellipse tool
Polygon tool	N N N (if default Ellipse tool is in slot; toggles with Ellipse tool, Centered Ellipse tool, Star tool, and Spiral tool)
Star tool	N N N N (if default Ellipse tool is in slot; toggles with Ellipse tool, Centered Ellipse tool, Polygon tool, and Spiral tool)
Spiral tool	N N N N N (if default Ellipse tool is in slot; toggles with Ellipse tool, Centered Ellipse tool, Polygon tool, and Star tool)
Rectangle tool	M (toggles with Rounded Rectangle tool, Centered Rectangle Tool, and Centered Rounded Rectangle tool) Alt+Centered Rectangle tool
Rounded Rectangle tool	M M (if default Rectangle tool is in slot; toggles with Rectangle tool, Centered Rectangle Tool, and Centered Rounded Rectangle tool) Alt+Centered Rounded Rectangle tool

(continued)

Tool	Shortcut
Centered Rectangle tool	M M M (if default Rectangle tool is in slot; toggles with Rectangle tool, Rounded Rectangle tool, and Centered Rounded Rectangle tool) Alt+Rectangle tool
Centered Rounded Rectangle tool	M M M M (if default Rectangle tool is in slot; toggles with Rectangle tool, Rounded Rectangle tool, and Centered Rectangle Tool) Alt+Rounded Rectangle tool

Function	Procedure
Create Ellipse using Numbers	Click with Ellipse tool
Draw Ellipse	Drag with Ellipse tool
Draw Circle	Shift+Drag with Ellipse tool
Create Centered Ellipse using Numbers	Click with Centered Ellipse tool
Draw Centered Ellipse	Drag with Centered Ellipse tool
Create Polygon using Numbers	Click with Polygon tool
Draw Polygon	Drag with Polygon tool
Constrain Polygon Angle	Shift+drag with Polygon tool
Move Polygon while drawing	Spacebar+drag with Polygon tool
Create Multiple Polygons	~+Drag with Polygon tool
Increase Polygon Sides	Up Arrow+drag with Polygon tool
Decrease Polygon Sides	Down Arrow+drag with Polygon tool
Create Star using Numbers	Click with Star tool
Draw Star	Drag with Star tool
Constrain Star Angle	Shift+drag with Star tool
Move Star while drawing	Spacebar+drag with Star tool
Create Multiple Stars	~+Drag with Star tool
Draw Even-Shouldered Star	Alt+drag with Star tool
Move Outer Points Only	Ctrl+drag with Star tool
Increase Star Points	Up Arrow+drag with Star tool
Decrease Star Points	Down Arrow+drag with Star tool
Create Spiral using Numbers	Click with Spiral tool
Draw Spiral	Drag with Spiral tool
Constrain Spiral Angle	Shift+drag with Spiral tool

Function	*Procedure*
Move Spiral while drawing	Spacebar+drag with Spiral tool
Create Multiple Spirals	~+Drag with Spiral tool
Decrease Spiral Decay	Ctrl+drag with Spiral tool
Increase Spiral Length/Size	Alt+drag with Spiral tool (toggle)
Increase Spiral Length	Up Arrow+drag with Spiral tool
Decrease Spiral Length	Down Arrow+drag with Spiral tool
Create Rectangle using Numbers	Click with Rectangle tool or Rounded Rectangle tool
Draw Rectangle	Drag with Rectangle tool
Draw Square	Shift+drag with Rectangle tool
Create Rounded Rectangle using Numbers	Click with Rectangle tool or Rounded Rectangle tool
Draw Rounded Rectangle	Drag with Rounded Rectangle tool
Create Centered Rectangle using Numbers	Click with Centered Rectangle tool or Centered Rounded Rectangle tool
Draw Centered Rectangle	Drag with Centered Rectangle tool
Create Centered Rounded Rect w/Numbers	Click with Centered Rectangle tool or Centered Rounded Rectangle tool
Draw Centered Rounded Rectangle	Drag with Centered Rounded Rectangle tool

Transformation Tools

Tool	*Shortcut*
Rotate tool	R (toggles with Twirl tool)
Twirl tool	R R (if default Rotate tool is in slot; toggles with Rotate tool)
Scale tool	S (toggles with Reshape tool)
Reshape tool	S S (if default Scale tool is in slot; toggles with Scale tool)
Reflect tool	O
Skew tool	W

Function	Procedure
Rotate using Numbers	Alt+click with Rotate tool
Rotate from Center of Selection w/Numbers	Double-click with Rotate tool
Free Rotate (live)	Click with Rotate to set Origin, and then Drag with Rotate tool
Free Rotate around Selection center	Drag with Rotate tool
Constrain Rotation to 45°	Shift+drag with Rotate tool
Rotate a Copy	Alt+drag with Rotate tool
Rotate Pattern only	~+drag with Rotate tool
Twirl using Numbers	Alt+click with Rotate tool
Free Twirl (live)	Drag with Twirl tool
Scale using Numbers	Alt+click with Scale tool
Scale from Center of Selection w/Numbers	Double-click with Scale tool
Free Scale (live)	Click with Scale to set Origin, and then Drag with Scale tool
Free Scale around Selection center	Drag with Scale tool
Constrain Scaling to 45°	Shift+drag with Scale tool
Scale a Copy	Alt+drag with Scale tool
Scale Pattern only	~+drag with Scale tool
Reshape a path	Select points with Direct Selection, and then Drag with Reshape
Reflect using Numbers	Alt+click with Reflect tool
Reflect from Center of Selection w/Numbers	Double-click with Reflect tool
Free Reflect (live)	Click with Reflect to set Origin, and then Drag with Reflect tool
Free Reflect around Selection center	Drag with Reflect tool
Constrain Reflecting to 45°	Shift+drag with Reflect tool
Reflect a Copy	Alt+drag with Reflect tool
Reflect Pattern only	~+drag with Reflect tool
Skew using Numbers	Alt+click with Skew tool
Skew from Center of Selection w/Numbers	Double-click with Skew tool
Free Skew (live)	Click with Skew to set Origin, and then Drag with Skew

Function	***Procedure***
Free Skew around Selection center	Drag with Skew
Constrain Skewing to 45°	Shift+drag with Skew tool
Skew a Copy	Alt+drag with Skew tool
Skew Pattern only	~+drag with Skew tool

Blend/Auto Trace/Graph Tools

Tool	***Shortcut***
Blend tool	B (toggles with Auto Trace tool)
Auto Trace tool	B B (if default Blend tool is in slot; toggles with Blend tool)
Column Graph tool	J (toggles with all other graph tools)
Stacked Column Graph tool	J J (if default Column Graph tool is in slot; toggles with all other graph tools)
Bar Graph tool	J J J (if default Column Graph tool is in slot; toggles with all other graph tools)
Stacked Bar Graph tool	J J J J (if default Column Graph tool is in slot; toggles with all other graph tools)
Line Graph tool	J J J J J (if default Column Graph tool is in slot; toggles with all other graph tools)
Area Graph tool	J J J J J J (if default Column Graph tool is in slot; toggles with all other graph tools)
Scatter Graph tool	J J J J J J J (if default Column Graph tool is in slot; toggles with all other graph tools)
Pie Graph tool	J J J J J J J J (if default Column Graph tool is in slot; toggles with all other graph tools)
Radar Graph tool	J J J J J J J J J (if default Column Graph tool is in slot; toggles with all other graph tools)

Function	***Procedure***
Blend between two paths	Click on corresponding selected points on each path with Blend tool
Auto Trace Images	Click on area to be traced with Auto Trace tool
Create a Graph sized by numbers	Click with any Graph tool
Create a Graph Sized by dragging	Drag with any Graph tool

Measure/Paint Tools

Tool	***Shortcut***
Measure tool	U
Gradient tool	G
Paint Bucket tool	K Alt+Eyedropper tool
Eyedropper tool	I Alt+Paint Bucket tool

Function	***Procedure***
Measure a distance	Click on the start and end location with the Measure tool
Measure a distance by 45° angles	Shift+click on the start and end location with the Measure tool
Change Linear Gradient Direction/ Length	Drag with Gradient tool
Constrain Gradient Direction to 45° angles	Shift+drag with Gradient tool
Change Radial Gradient Size/Location	Drag with Gradient tool
Change Radial Gradient Origin Point	Click with Gradient tool
Sample color to Color palette	Click with Eyedropper tool
Sample Screen color to Color Palette	Shift+click with Eyedropper tool
Change Paint Style of selected objects	Double-click with Eyedropper tool on an object with the desired style
Paint unselected objects	Click on objects with the Paintbucket tool

Viewing Tools

Tool	***Shortcut***
Hand tool	H (toggles with Page tool) Spacebar (when not entering text)
Page tool	H H (if default Hand tool is in slot; toggles with Hand tool)
Zoom tool	Z Ctrl+Spacebar
Zoom Out tool	Alt+Zoom tool

Function	Procedure
Zoom In	Click with the Zoom tool Ctrl++
Zoom Out	Alt+click with the Zoom tool Ctrl+–
Zoom In to a specific area	Drag with the Zoom tool
Move the Zoom Marquee while drawing	Spacebar while Dragging with the Zoom tool
Draw the Zoom Marquee from its center	Ctrl+drag with the Zoom tool

Viewing Shortcuts

Action	Shortcut
Zoom in	Ctrl++ Click with Zoom tool
Zoom Out	Ctrl+– Alt+click with Zoom tool
Fit Document In Window	Ctrl+0 Double-click on Hand tool
View at Actual Size (100%)	Ctrl+1 Double-click on Zoom tool
Artwork/Preview Mode	Ctrl+Y (toggle)
Preview Selection Mode	Ctrl+P+Alt+Y
Custom View Recall	Ctrl+Alt+Shift+1 through Ctrl+Alt+Shift+0
Show/Hide Edges	Ctrl+H (toggle)
Show/Hide Guides	Ctrl+;
Show/Hide Grid	Ctrl+'
Show/Hide Rulers	Ctrl+R
Hide Selected Objects	Ctrl+U
Hide Unselected Objects	Ctrl+Alt+U
Show All Hidden Objects	Ctrl+Shift+U
Window Mode (normal)	F (when in Full Screen mode)
Full Screen Mode w/Menu	F (when in Window mode)
Full Screen Mode (no menus)	F (when in Full Screen mode w/menu)

Type Shortcuts	
Action	***Shortcut***
Copy type on a path	Alt+drag the I-bar using any selection tool. This shortcut actually creates two paths as well as two text stories
Flip type on a path	Double-click the I-bar with any selection tool or just drag it to the opposite side of the path
Move insertion point to next character	Right Arrow
Move insertion Point to previous character	Left Arrow
Move insertion point to next line	Down Arrow
Move insertion point to previous line	Up Arrow
Move insertion point to next word	Ctrl+Right Arrow
Move insertion point to previous word	Ctrl+Left Arrow
Move insertion point to next paragraph	Ctrl+Down Arrow
Move insertion point to previous paragraph	Ctrl+Up Arrow
Select (by highlighting) all type in story	Ctrl+A when the insertion point is in the story
Select all type in document	Ctrl+A when any tool but the Type tools are selected
Select next character	Shift+Right Arrow
Select previous character	Shift+Left Arrow
Select next line	Shift+Down Arrow
Select previous line	Shift+Up Arrow
Select next word	Ctrl+Shift+Right Arrow
Select previous word	Ctrl+Shift+Left Arrow
Select next paragraph	Ctrl+Shift+Down Arrow
Select previous paragraph	Ctrl+Shift+Up Arrow
Select word	Double-click on word
Select paragraph	Triple-click on paragraph
Deselect all type	Ctrl+Shift+A
Duplicate column outline and flow text	Alt+drag column outline with Direct Selection tool
Insert discretionary hyphen	Ctrl+Shift+hyphen
Insert line break	Enter (keypad)

Paragraph Formatting

Action	*Shortcut*
Display Paragraph palette	Ctrl+Shift+M
Align Paragraph Flush Left	Ctrl+Shift+L
Align Paragraph Flush Right	Ctrl+Shift+R
Align Paragraph Flush Center	Ctrl+Shift+C
Align Paragraph Justified	Ctrl+Shift+J
Align Paragraph Force Justified	Ctrl+Shift+F
Display Tab palette	none
Align Tab palette to selected paragragh	Click on Tab palette size box
Cycle through Tab Stops	Alt+click on tab stop
Move Multiple Tab Stops	Shift+drag tab stops
Cycle Tab measurements	Click

Character Formatting

Action	*Shortcut*
Display Character Palette	Ctrl+T
Highlight Font	Ctrl+Alt+Shift+M
Increase Type size*	Ctrl+Shift+>
Decrease Type size*	Ctrl+Shift+<
Increase Type to next size on Menu	Ctrl+Alt+>
Decrease Type to next size on Menu	Ctrl+Alt+<
Highlight Size	none
Increase Leading*	Alt+Down Arrow
Decrease Leading*	Alt+Up Arrow
Set Leading to Solid (same as pt. size)	Double-click Leading symbol (Character palette)
Highlight Leading	none
Increase Baseline Shift (Raise)*	Alt+Shift+Up Arrow
Decrease Baseline Shift (Lower)*	Alt+Shift+Down Arrow
Increase Baseline Shift (Raise) x5*	Ctrl+Alt+Shift+Up Arrow
Decrease Baseline Shift (Lower) x5*	Ctrl+Alt+Shift+Down Arrow

(continued)

Action	Shortcut
Reset Baseline Shift to 0	none
Highlight Baseline Shift	none
Kern/Track closer*	Alt+Left Arrow
Kern/Track apart*	Alt+Right Arrow
Kern/Track closer x5*	Ctrl+Alt+Left Arrow
Kern/Track apart x5*	Ctrl+Alt+Right Arrow
Reset Kerning/Tracking to 0	Ctrl+Shift+Q
Highlight Kerning/Tracking	Ctrl+Alt+K
Reset Horizontal Scale to 100%	Ctrl+Shift+X

Color Commands

Color Palette	
Action	**Shortcut**
Show/Hide Color Palette	F6 (toggle) Ctrl+I (toggle)
Revert to default colors (White fill, Black stroke)	D
Toggle focus between fill and stroke	X
Choose current color in Color Palette	, (comma)
Change paint to none	/
Apply to inactive fill/stroke (fill when stroke is active, stroke when fill is active)	Alt+click in color ramp on Color palette
Apply color to unselected object	Drag color swatch from Color palette to object
Apply color to selected object	Click on swatch in Color palette
Copy Paint Style to unselected objects	Click on unselected objects with Paintbucket
Copy Paint Style from any (source) object to all selected objects	Click on source object with Eyedropper
Tint process color	Shift+drag any Color palette slider
Cycle through Color Modes (Grayscale, CMYK, RGB)	Shift+click on Color Ramp

Swatches Palette

Action	Shortcut
Show/Hide Swatches Palette	F5 (toggle)
Toggle focus between fill and stroke	X
Add Swatch	Click the New Swatch icon Drag from Color or Gradient palette into swatches
Replace Swatch	Alt+drag from Color or Gradient palette into swatches
Duplicate Swatch	Alt+drag swatch onto New Swatch icon in Swatches palette
Delete Swatch	Drag to Trash icon in Swatches palette Click on Trash icon with swatches selected
Select Contiguous Swatches	Shift+click on first and last swatches
Select Discontiguous Swatches	Ctrl+click on each swatch
Switch keyboard focus to Swatches palette (for selecting swatches by name as they are typed)	Ctrl+Alt+click in Swatches palette
Apply color to unselected object	Drag color swatch from Swatches palette to object
Apply color to selected object	Click on swatch in Swatches palette

Gradient Palette

Action	Shortcut
Choose current gradient in Gradient palette	. (period)
Show/Hide Gradient Palette	F9 (toggle)
Apply swatch to selected Color stop on gradient palette	Alt+click on Swatch
Add new color stop	Click below gradient ramp
Duplicate color stop	Alt+drag color stop
Swap color stops	Alt+drag color stop on top of another
"Suck" color for color stop with Eyedropper	Shift+click with Eyedropper
Reset Gradient to default Black, White	Ctrl+click in Gradient swatch
Apply color to unselected object	Drag color swatch from Gradient palette to object
Apply color to selected object	Click on swatch in Gradient palette

Stroke Palette	
Action	***Shortcut***
Show/Hide Stroke Palette	F10 (toggle)
Increase/decrease Stroke weight	Highlight Stroke field, use Up/Down arrows, press Enter when finished
Increase/decrease Miter amount	Highlight Miter field, use Up/Down arrows, press Enter when finished

Other Palettes

Miscellaneous Palette Commands	
Action	***Shortcut***
Collapse/display Palette	Click box in upper right
Cycle through Palette views	Double-click palette tab
Apply settings	Enter
Apply settings while keeping last text field highlighted	Shift+Enter
Highlight next text field	Tab
Highlight Previous Text field	Shift+Tab
Highlight any text field	Click on label or double-click current value
Increase value by base increment	Highlight field, Up arrow
Decrease value by base increment	Highlight field, Down arrow
Increase value by big increment	Highlight field, Shift+Up arrow
Decrease value by big increment	Highlight field, Shift+Down arrow
Combine palettes	Drag palette tab within other palette
Dock palette	Drag palette tab to bottom of other palette
Separate palette	Drag palette tab from current palette

Transform Palette

Action	Shortcut
Show/Hide Transform Palette	none
Copy object while transforming	Alt+Enter
Scale Proportionately	Ctrl+Enter
Copy object while scaling proportionately	Ctrl+Alt+Enter

Layers Palette

Action	Shortcut
Show/Hide Layers Palette	F7
New Layer	Click on New Layer icon
New Layer w/ Options dialog box	Alt+click on New Layer icon
New Layer Above Active Layer	Ctrl+Alt+click on New Layer icon
New Layer Below Active Layer	Ctrl+click on New Layer icon
Duplicate Layer(s)	Drag layer(s) to New Layer icon
Change Layer order	Drag Layers up or down within Layer list
Select all objects on a layer	Alt+click on that layer
Select all objects on several layers	Shift+Alt+click on each layer
Select contiguous Layers	Shift+click on layers
Select discontiguous Layers	Ctrl+Click on layers
Move objects to a different layer	Drag colored square to a different layer
Copy objects to a different layer	Alt+drag color square to a different layer
Hide/Show Layer	Click on Eyeball icon
View Layer while hiding others	Alt+click on Eyeball icon
View Layer in Artwork mode	Ctrl+click on Eyeball icon
View Layer in Preview while others are artwork	Ctrl+Alt+click on Eyeball icon
Lock/Unlock Layer	Click on Pencil icon
Unlock Layer while Locking others	Alt+click on Pencil icon
Delete Layer	Drag layer to Trash icon Select layer and click on Trash icon
Delete Layer without warning	Alt+drag layer to Trash icon Select layer and Alt+click on Trash icon

Miscellaneous Commands

Action	*Shortcut*
Nudge Selection*	Arrow keys
See special Status Line categories	Alt+click status bar (lower left)
View Anagrams of credits	Alt+click Illustrator click on toolbox
Speed up credits in About box	Alt
Display Context-sensitive menus	Right-click
Highlight last active text field	Ctrl+~ (tilde)

Generic Dialog Box Commands

Action	*Shortcut*
Cancel	Esc
OK (or dark bordered button)	Enter
Highlight next text field	Tab
Highlight Previous Text field	Shift+tab
Highlight any text field	Click on label or double-click current value

*Value/amount set in Preferences

Appendix G

Trouble-shooting

If you have questions about Illustrator, chances are that other users have been asking those same questions. I've compiled this appendix by talking to many Illustrator users and to Adobe's Technical Support Department.

Is it possible to create a gradient Fill that goes from a process tint to transparent, rather than to white?
No, because the in-between steps can never be partially transparent. But with some careful overprint manipulating you could simulate transparency for separations.

I'm trying to blend text, but I keep getting error messages.
Change your type to outlines before blending them.

Is it possible to open a PageMaker file in Illustrator?
Yes, create an Acrobat PDF file from Pagemaker. Illustrator can open Acrobat files. Or just save it as EPS and open it.

I keep getting the message "Can't open the hyphenation file 'US English Hyphenation.' Text will not be hyphenated."
Choose File⇨Preferences⇨Plug-Ins and Scratch Disk, and reselect the Plug-Ins folder in your Illustrator folder.

Is there a way to add a custom arrowhead to the Add Arrowhead filter?
Yes, about only on the Macintosh. Follow these steps:

STEPS: Adding an Arrowhead to the Add Arrowheads Box

Step 1. Create the artwork you wish to use as an arrowhead in Illustrator.

Step 2. Copy the artwork.

Step 3. Open the Add Arrowhead filter in ResEdit or Resourcer.

Step 4. Paste the artwork.

Step 5. Number the arrowhead by adding 3 to the last arrowhead (the last standard arrowhead is ID 17078).

Step 6. Save and relaunch Illustrator. The arrowhead now appears as a black box in the Filter dialog box (you can change this in ResEdit if you have the time and the inclination).

Can you view "invisibles" in Illustrator?

No. I use the following technique: Press ⌘-A [Ctrl+A], ⌘-C [Ctrl+C], and then go to Word and press ⌘-V [Ctrl+V], ⌘-8 [Ctrl+8]. This shows me spaces, tabs, soft returns, and more.

Why is Curve Fitting Tolerance limited to 10?

The number in Tolerance isn't really a limit, considering the number is an arbitrary number. The engineers who created Illustrator could have incorporated a slider from Nothing to Maximum tolerance, and there would be no difference.

Is there a limit on the number of points on a path? Will too many points cause printing problems?

There's no real limit per se. The number of Anchor Points on a path has nothing to do with the number of points interpreted by a PostScript interpreter. What the number of points means when printing is this: Curves are converted to lots of little straight-line segments at an interpreter level. Long, continuous paths use the Curve to command in PostScript and are converted down to line-to path segments. Each line-to is two PostScript points. It takes a lot more PostScript points (line-tos) to draw a smooth curve at high resolution (imagesetter) than low resolution (laser printer). This is why the file will print on your laser printer and not your imagesetter.

To prevent overly long or complex paths: First, change the output resolution to match the dpi of the imagesetter. Second, select the Split long paths option in Document Setup (you may want to do this on a copy of the original document, especially if you have to edit it later).

Streamline counts points, but Illustrator doesn't. You *can* count paths by choosing File Document Info (⌘-Shift-P) [Ctrl+Shift+P] filter from the Filter⇨Other submenu, however.

Why does type converted to outlines look so heavy?

Primarily due to type hinting, which is present in PostScript type at small type sizes. Also, type usually has a preset bitmapped version at small point sizes that looks thinner than outlines, where the pixels are generated on-the-fly.

I can't arc type. Is there a way to do this?

The best thing to do is to pick up a copy of KPT Vector Effects. The Warp Frame filter in the set is perfect for that sort of reshaping.

Drag-and-drop into Photoshop doesn't work.

You need Photoshop 3.0.4 or later to use drag-and-drop.

Why is it that when I try to export files with Pantone gradients into Quark for separations, they convert to process?

Make sure you don't convert the gradients to blends (saving as Illustrator 3 will do this). You also need to add the Pantone colors you are going to print out of Quark to its color list (see Quark's documentation). QuarkXPress 3.2 or later tries to do this automatically.

I get the message "Can't save preview but all other information was saved successfully" when I save images that have large dimensions.

EPS files need to have a certain size preview, and this preview gets built when you save an EPS file. If you are running low on memory, the preview might not be able to be created. Allocate more memory to Illustrator, or reduce the number of undos.

What is Adobe's technical support number?

(206) 628-3953.

Why doesn't Illustrator always save colors I've created with the document they were created in?

Illustrator will save only those colors that have been used in an object in the document in swatches, or originally created in that document. The same is true for gradients and patterns.

Sometimes my gradients drop out when printing on a QMS printer.

QMS uses a PostScript clone instead of real Adobe PostScript. Change the PostScript option in the Print dialog box to Level 1.

What's a good way to get complex illustrations to print faster?

Select all the paths and give them a high flatness setting by increasing the Output Resolution value in the Attributes palette. Actually, you want to decrease the number in the Output Resolution field. The Formula Printer resolution (2,540) divided by the Output Resolution number (800) equals the flatness (3.175). Don't get this confused with Output Resolution in Document setup, which is for Split Long Paths. In that case, you want a higher number for more splitting.

How can I import my FreeHand documents into Illustrator?

Illustrator can open Freehand 7 documents via File⇨Open (⌘-O) [Ctrl+O].

How can I get certain Pantone colors to appear in every document I create?

Save the colors in the Adobe Illustrator Startup file (which is in your Plug-Ins folder). Simply open the existing Startup file, and then open the file that contains the colors you want to add. Draw objects that you want to contain the new default colors. Then paint the new objects with these colors. When you're finished, resave the Startup file.

When I open up certain documents, my measurement units change. Why?

I used to always change my measurements in General Preferences until 5.0. Then a weird thing happened. Situations like you described started to happen. At the time I was ruler-happy, so I noticed the changes as soon as the documents were opened.

The secret is that there are *two* areas where you can change the measurement system: Units & Undo, which changes the way you currently see the document you're working with and all future documents that are created; and Document Setup, which changes the current document but keeps the settings in units and undo what they were originally, so new documents aren't affected by changes you make in Document Setup.

What I do, because I work predominantly in picas, is to keep my measurement settings at Picas in Units & Undo, and change the settings (usually to points or inches — I haven't used millimeters in a long time) in Document Setup. That way, only that document is affected.

I added color swatches to my Adobe Illustrator Startup file, but they don't appear in new documents.

Make sure the Adobe Illustrator Startup file is in the active plug-ins folder, or it won't work.

Not all of my Photoshop filters work in Illustrator.

Some of them may not if they don't follow Adobe's plug-in guidelines completely. Ask the third-party filter manufacturer for an update.

How can I keep from running out of memory?

Lower the number of undos down to 1 or 2.

How can you color text differently from the box it is inside of?

Select the box with the Direct Selection tool, and then change the Fill color. Select text with the text tool to change the color of just the text.

I can't select a path.

The path is either locked, or it is on a locked layer.

What am I missing out on by not having QuickDraw GX installed on my Mac?

Nothing. Illustrator doesn't take advantage of QuickDraw GX.

I keep getting this error message:

```
Opened the artwork up to the following condition: The illustra-
tion contains an illegal operand. Offending operator: 'TZ'
Context: 195/radical 197/approxequal 198/Delta 214/divide/
lozenge 240/apple/_symbol_/Symbol 0 0  0 TZ
```

In earlier versions of Illustrator, this problem is caused by using special characters (such as Option-8) in a font alphabetically below Symbol. There is nothing wrong with the file. It is a bug in Illustrator's reading mechanism. Here's the scoop on how to fix the problem.

The bad line is "/_symbol_/Symbol 0 0 0 TZ." To fix the file, open it in a text processor. Find the above line and add a "[" to the beginning of the line so it reads

"[/_symbol_/Symbol 0 0 0 TZ." Save the file (as text only), launch Illustrator, choose File➪Open, locate the fixed Illustrator file, and open it. After you have the file open, apply a font that is alphabetically above Symbol (such as Helvetica). Just apply it to a space or something. Now resave the file and it will be okay from that point on.

Note: This problem is fixed in Illustrator 7.

Several blank pages print when I print out of Illustrator.

If a Tiled option is on in Document Setup, and a portion of the illustration extends onto any of the "other" pages, additional pages will print that include Control Handles.

I've had a problem on my Macintosh that seems like a virus. It's a strange musical sound that happens occasionally when I use the Shift key.

Remove the Easy Access control panel from your Control Panels folder, and all will be quiet.

Sometimes when I zoom in, I zoom all the way to really close in. Other times, it's just in the preset increments. What gives?

The Zoom tool works in two ways:

- Click once and the image zooms to the next increment (100 to 150, 1200 to 1600, and so on.)
- Drag a marquee around the area you wish to zoom in to. Surrounding it with a Zoom Marquee enables you to zoom in to a specific area quickly.

What's probably happening is that instead of clicking, you're drawing a teeny tiny little box and Illustrator, loyal drawing program that it is, is zooming to 1600% right at that spot. Try not to drag while you're clicking with the Zoom tool to prevent this.

It used to be in previous versions of Illustrator that if you saved a file as black and white, it printed in black and white, whether it was a composite or as a separate plate. Now, if you save as 1-bit, it prints out with screens to approximate the color. Why?

That option *only* affects the preview. It was useful for all those computers with black-and-white screens, and because it cut down on file size dramatically. If it *didn't* print in color, then you weren't linked to the file anymore, and just the preview printed.

I tried to open an Illustrator 5.5 document and got an error message saying the following:

```
Opened the artwork to the following error condition: The
illustration contains an incomplete or garbled object descrip-
tion.
Offending operator: 'Bg'
Context:
% 4 Gr GX
```

```
% 1 0 0 1 0 4 4312 4295 1 Gm
% 0 0 Gx 0 Gr GX
% 1 1 4 3 0 Gf
% Bd
% 2 () -4013 4715 1 0 1 0 0 1 0 0 Bg
```

Bg is "begin gradient."

Compare this line to a file that opens and modify it accordingly:

```
% 2 ( ) -4013 4715 1 0 1 0 0 1 0 0 Bg
```

This won't happen in anything but Version 5 documents.

Why does my Illustrator program have the generic icon on my Macintosh?
Rebuild your desktop (press ⌘-Option [Ctrl+space] during startup) [Ctrl+space] and it will look normal again.

Why does ⌘-space not always work? Shouldn't it always access the Zoom In tool?
There are two potential conflicts with this key command on the Macintosh.

1) SCSI Probe, a control panel for mounting SCSI devices, uses ⌘-space as the default command for mounting drives. Change this command in the SCSI Probe control panel.

2) System 7.5 uses ⌘-space to change keyboard layouts. Remove any other keyboard layouts from your System file, and you won't run into this problem.

What happened with Illustrator 6.0.1 and 6.0.2?
Illustrator 6.0.1 was a free upgrade from Adobe, though you had to pay $9.95 for shipping. It included four new import/export plug-ins, as well as numerous bug fixes. Version 6.0.2 fixed a problem with the Color Matching dialog box in Version 6.0.1, and was downloadable as a patch for 6.0.1 users only.

When I press (whatever), nothing happens. It worked fine in Illustrator 6.
Many keyboard commands were changed or removed entirely from Illustrator 6. See Appendixes E and F for a list of all the changed and new shortcuts.

A few keyboard combinations were removed and not replaced. The following combinations don't work anymore:

⌘-Shift-M for move

⌘-Shift-[and ⌘-Shift-] to change tracking

All of the ⌘-Control shortcuts

Resources

APPENDIX H

This Appendix contains resources for related products, services, and other information that Illustrator users may find useful. All phone numbers, addresses, and version numbers are subject to change without notice, of course.

People and Companies

Jennifer Alspach

jen@bezier.com

Jennifer is a nationally known artist and writer, with clients all over the United States. Her work has appeared in several books, including *The Illustrator WOW! Book.* She has authored or coauthored two Illustrator books: *Illustrator Filter Finesse* and *Illustrator 7 Complete.* Many of the figures throughout the *Illustrator 7 Bible* (and its previous editions) were created by Jennifer.

Joe Jones

DujaVe@aol.com

Joe Jones has been a professional graphic artist in the Denver area since 1983, and vice president and art director of his own production screen printing shop, Cotton Grafix. There, Joe had his multicolor, hand-separated preprint work sold at the retail level over the entire Mountain region of the United States. He has created artwork for almost every conceivable application and requirement. Joe's other passions include his wife, Carmen, and his two beautiful daughters, Layla and Cyanne. Joe's work has been featured in other texts such as *KPT Studio Secrets* and *Illustrator Complete.* Joe's full-color image "High Prairie" is displayed in the color section of the *Illustrator 7 Bible.*

Robert Burger

BurgerBobz@aol.com

Robert is an award-winning illustrator whose work can be seen in many magazines and books, on magazine and book covers, on album covers, in advertising, and on Web pages. His work has been honored by the Society of Illustrators of Los Angeles, the Society of Illustrators of New York, Graphics Design Annual, Print's Regional Design Annual, The Art Directors Club of Philadelphia, and the Art Directors Club of New Jersey. Robert's Illustration, "Anatomy of Wonder," appears in the color section of the *Illustrator 7 Bible.* This is Robert's second straight appearance in editions of the *Illustrator Bible,* a first for any artist (his "Future Music" Illustration appeared in the color section of the last edition).

Teeple Graphics

rob@teeple.com
(717) 944-2034
Middletown, Pennsylvania

Teeple Graphics is a Macintosh VAR and World Wide Web service provider specializing in desktop publishing and high-end graphic systems integration. Their expertise is unparalleled.

Thomas-Bradley Illustration and Design

tkn@gridley.org
bradneal@gridley.org
(309) 747-3266
Gridley, Illinois

Tom Neal and Brad Neal are partners in the Illinois-based Thomas-Bradley Illustration and Design firm, considered to be the premier house of vector realism. Established in 1987, the firm has had articles on their work appear in *The Illustrator WOW! Book*, *MacWEEK* magazine, *Computer Artist* magazine, *Adobe Spotlight,* and several technical journals, and 13 published books. Their photo-realistic Avia sneaker was featured in the last edition of the *Illustrator Bible*. Their recent clients include Pepsi-Cola, Anheuser-Busch, Nike, State Farm Insurance Company, Deere & Company, Caterpillar Tractor Company, and six major automobile manufacturers. They have also been featured speakers at several conferences and seminars across the country. The incredible cover illustration on the front of this edition of the *Illustrator 7 Bible* was created by Brad Neal.

Adobe Systems, Inc.
1585 Charleston Road
P.O. Box 7900
Mountain View, CA 94039-7900
Customer Service: (800) 833-6687
Technical Support (available to registered users with a valid serial number only): (206) 628-3953
BBS (First Class software): (206) 623-6984

Publisher of Adobe Illustrator, Adobe Photoshop, Adobe PageMaker, Adobe Streamline, Adobe Premiere, Adobe Dimensions, and several other products. Demo versions of Illustrator, Streamline, and Dimensions are included on this book's CD-ROM.

BeInfinite
BeInfinite@aol.com

Publisher of InfiniteFX1 filters for Adobe Illustrator and FreeHand. A demo version of IFX is included on the CD-ROM at the back of this book.

Cytopia Software, Inc.
1735 E. Bayshore Road, Suite 30b
Redwood City, CA 94063
(415) 364-4594
Fax: (415) 364-4592
http://www.cytopia.com

Publisher of CSI Socket Set 1 & 2 for Adobe Illustrator, and CSI PhotoLab filters for Adobe Photoshop. Demo versions of Cytopia products are on the CD-ROM included with this book.

Extensis Corporation
1800 SW First, Suite 500
Portland, OR 97201
(503) 274-2020
Fax: (503) 274-0530
http://www.extensis.com

Publisher of Extensis VectorTools, Plug-Ins for Adobe Illustrator, and Micromedia FreeHand. A demo version is available on the CD-ROM that comes with this book.

hot door
40 Nieto Avenue, Suite #17
Long Beach, CA 90803
(888) 236-9540
www.hotdoor.com/cadtools/

hot door is the publisher of CADtools, plug-ins for Adobe Illustrator 7. A demo of CADtools is found on the *Illustrator 7 Bible* CD-ROM.

MetaCreations, Inc.
6303 Carpinteria Avenue
Carpinteria, CA 93013
Customer service: (805) 566-6200
Fax: (805) 566-6385
kptsupport@aol.com

Publisher of KPT Vector Effects for Illustrator and FreeHand, Kai's Power Tools, KPT Convolver, KPT Bryce, and more. A demo version of KPT Vector Effects is included on the CD-ROM that comes with this book.

Other Illustrator Books

Several books are available on Adobe Illustrator and related topics, but the following books are especially good and come highly recommended. They are books that I have in my Illustrator library, and all are fantastic supplements to the *Illustrator 7 Bible.* Of course, some of these books I've written (I'm certainly not above blatant self-promotion), so naturally I'm going to recommend them.

Illustrator 7 Studio Secrets

By Ted Alspach

This full-color book contains all the good stuff about not just Adobe Illustrator, but about Macromedia FreeHand, Extensis VectorTools, Adobe Dimensions, and other vector products too. Featuring the world's most talented vector artists. IDG Books Worldwide, Inc.

Illustrator 7 Complete

By Jennifer Alspach and Steven Frank

Yet another giant entry in Hayden Books' Complete series (which also features a delightful Photoshop volume coauthored by yours truly), *Illustrator Complete* leaves no stone unturned in its exploration of every feature in Illustrator. Graphics gurus Jennifer and Steve provide a unique perspective and "Complete" coverage of Adobe Illustrator. Hayden Books.

The Illustrator 7 Book

By Deke McClelland

Written by *Macworld* magazine's contributing editor on graphics, this book takes a markedly different approach from that of the *Illustrator 7 Bible* to explain Illustrator's functionality. Deke's enjoyable writing style and comprehensive coverage of areas such as graphs make this book a must-have. Peachpit Press.

Illustrator Filter Finesse

By Ted Alspach and Jennifer Alspach

The best (and only) book devoted to Illustrator and FreeHand plug-ins. Complete coverage of all the native filters, Vector Effects, Socket Sets, and more, combined with an outstanding how-to portion, make this book invaluable for all plug-in users. Random House Electronic Publishing.

The Illustrator WOW! Book

By Sharon Steuer

A fantastic full-color collection of Adobe Illustrator artwork and techniques from the industry's leading artists. Peachpit Press.

Design Essentials
Imaging Essentials

By Luanne Cohen, et al.

These full-color books provide step-by-step examples and techniques for using Adobe Illustrator with Photoshop and Dimensions to produce the cornerstone elements of design. Luanne's wonderful art makes the examples come alive on each page. Adobe Press.

Illustrator Effects Magic

By Ted Alspach

Have you always pondered amazing-looking Illustrator drawings, wondering how they were done? Illustrator Effects Magic takes you step-by-step through dozens of examples from start to finish, featuring incredibly complex-looking artwork broken down into digestible steps. Full color. Hayden Books.

FreeHand Books

Huh? What? Well, if you must succumb to using *that other program* because you can't convince your boss and/or spouse to use Illustrator 100 percent of the time, you'll find the following books quite handy:

FreeHand 7 Visual QuickStart

By Sandee Cohen

This is the best way to learn FreeHand. Written by an Illustrator expert, it makes FreeHand's quirkiness understandable and almost usable (hey, it's still FreeHand, after all). Peachpit Press.

The Macworld FreeHand 7 Bible

By Deke McClelland

The antithesis to the book you're holding (although they do look awful nice sitting on a shelf together), Deke's *FreeHand Bible* has long been the most comprehensive guide to the Dark Side of vector graphics. IDG Books Worldwide Inc..

Real World FreeHand

By Olav Martin Kvern

Written by FreeHand and PageMaker know-it-all (I'm not kidding, he knows everything there is to know about both programs, and even wrote the FreeHand tips for Extensis VectorTools) Ole Kvern, this book explores FreeHand in depth, with all sorts of incredible insights and lengthy explanations you won't find elsewhere. Peachpit Press.

Context-Sensitive Menus

APPENDIX I

As a Macintosh user, have you ever jealously coveted your Windows-using buddies' right mouse button? Okay, neither have I. And likewise, I doubt that many Windows users have lusted after the Mac's extra modifier key (Windows has Shift, Ctrl, and Alt; Macs have Shift, Control, Command, and Option).

To compensate Macintosh users for the loss of several keyboard commands associated with the Control key (which wouldn't be available on Windows systems), the Control key now works as a "mouse button switcher" between the right mouse button and left of Windows users. And what does the right mouse button do for Windows users? It gives them context-sensitive menus, an up-and-coming standard for most Windows software.

What's a Context-Sensitive Menu?

Glad you asked, or this whole appendix wouldn't be necessary. A context-sensitive menu is a menu that pops up at your cursor when you press Control and click. The menu typically contains several standard options, such as Undo, and other selection-specific ones. For instance, if type is selected, you'll often see the Font and Size submenus in the context-sensitive menu.

The idea behind this is that there's no need to travel up to the menu bar each time you want to select a menu item; chances are many menu items will be available right at your cursor. This can often be faster than pressing a keyboard shortcut. Even so, I'm a bit perplexed as to why Adobe does not list the shortcuts next to each of the pop-up menu's commands; to see the shortcuts, you'll need to look in the real menu or refer to the comprehensive list in Appendix D of the *Illustrator 7 Bible*.

The Context-Sensitive Menus

There are six main context-sensitive menus you'll find in Illustrator 7. Each of them is shown below next to explanations for when they appear.

No Selection

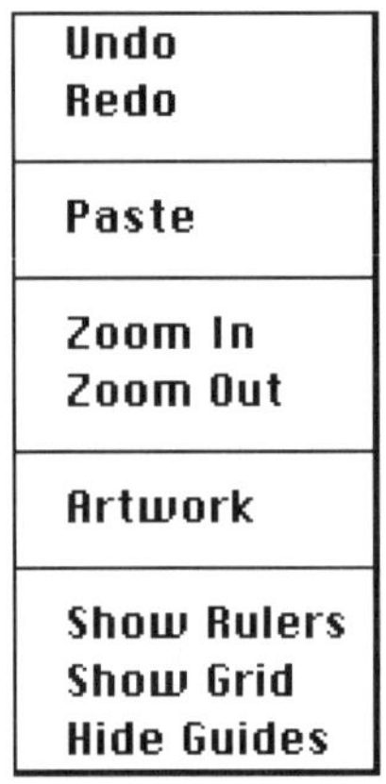

Figure I-1: The context-sensitive menu that appears when no items are selected

Standard Path Selection

Figure I-2: The context-sensitive menu that appears when regular paths are selected

Group, Mask, or Compound Path Selection

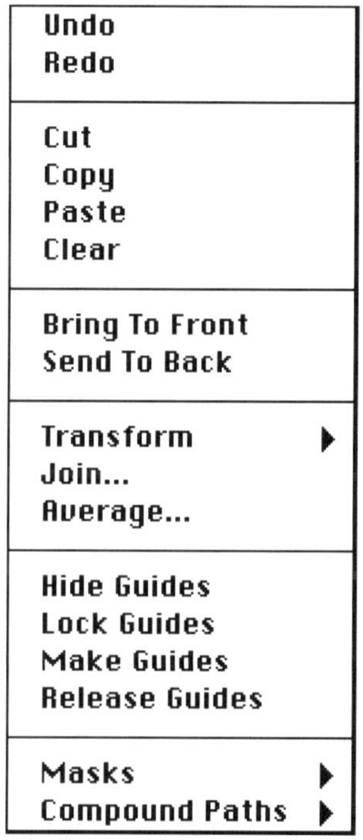

Figure I-3: The context-sensitive menu that appears when a group, a mask, or a compound path is selected

Placed Image Selection

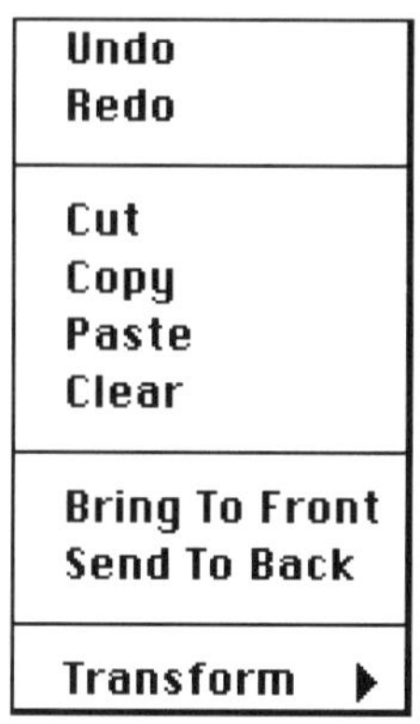

Figure I-4: The context-sensitive menu that appears when a placed image is selected

Type Selection

Figure I-5: The context-sensitive menu that appears when type is selected

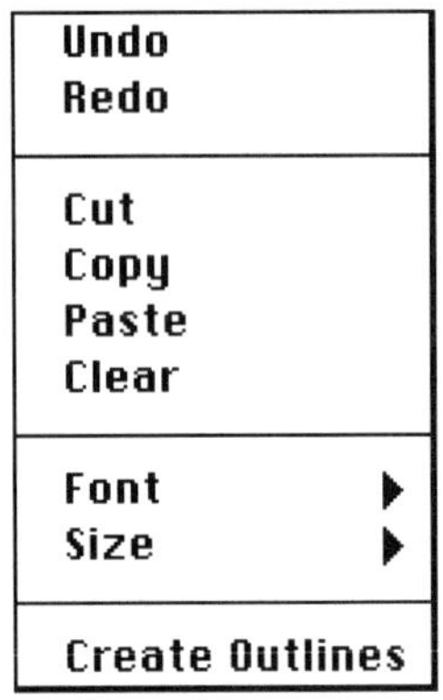

Graph Selection

Figure I-6: The context-sensitive menu that appears when a graph is selected

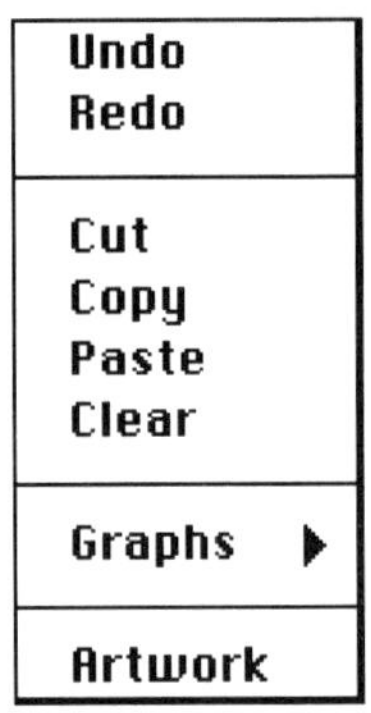

Index

Note: Page numbers in **bold** indicate definition of term or primary discussion of topic.

~ (tilde) key
duplicating spirals with, 72 | Spaz function and, 66, 67
transforming patterns with, 273, 293

• A •

About Illustrator command, 211
About Plug-Ins command, 211
About this Computer command (Macintosh), 211
Acrobat Reader, 204, 813–816
Add Anchor Point tool, **237**, 240
Add Anchor Points filter
editing and, 240
Roughen filter and, 536
Add Arrowheads dialog box, 543, 544
Add Arrowheads filter, 542–546
Adjust Colors dialog box, 508
Adjust Colors filter, 507–508, 511–512
Adjust Colors filter (CSI), 603–604
Adjust Stroke filter (CSI), 604
Adobe Acrobat Reader, 204, 813–816
Adobe Dimensions, 747–750
adjusting shading and reflectance, 761–769
Lighting palette, 766–767
Reflectance (Surface Properties palette), 763–765
Surface Properties palette, 761–763
combining with Illustrator, 790–791
creating primitive shapes, 757–760
features of, 747–748
FPU and, 819
history of development, 748
Illustrator shadows in, 458–459
other 3D applications and, 749–750
printing with, 750
processing speed and, 748
rendering artwork, 760–761
3D artwork, 776–781, 786–790
creating in Illustrator, 786–789
moving objects, 776–777
rotating objects, 779–781
scaling, 778–779
using gradients for bumps and dents, 790
tools, 753–757
3D toolbox, 754, 755–756
2D toolbox, 754, 756–757
2D artwork, 769–775
creating and modifying, 768
extruding flat art, 770–771
mapping on 3D surfaces, 785–786
previewing, 769
revolving artwork, 773–775
saving, 769
understanding bevels, 771–773
using Illustrator artwork, 768
views and perspectives, 781–784
changing perspectives, 782–784
viewing options, 781–782
Adobe Illustrator
Application Program Interface (API), 646–647
applying Photoshop filters in, **564–572**
basics of, 3–45
about paths, **20–23**
Anchor Points, **23–24**
the artboard, **42**
Artwork and Preview modes, **35–37**
Bézier curves, **25–26**
clear, cut, copy, and paste, **30–33**
Control Handles and Control Handle Lines, **27–30**
cursors, **9**
fonts, **11–16**
keyboard commands, **9–10**
learning tips, 6–8
menus, **37–39**
mouse functions, **8–9**
Page tool, **42–43**
palettes, **39–40**
the pasteboard, **41**
PostScript printing, **16–20**
summary of new features, 4
terminology, 10
toolbox, **43–45**
undo and redo, **33–34**

Adobe Illustrator *(continued)*
built-in filters, 502–504
combining Adobe Dimensions with, 790–791
compatibility of file formats, 201–202
creating plug-ins, 646–650
Illustrator API and SDK, 646–647
plug-in types, 648
suites, 648
wishlist for plug-ins, 649–650
creating 3D objects in, 786–789
default type and styles for text, 343
dragging artwork between Photoshop and, 32, 563–564, 904
generic icon for, 908
learning, 805–809
Adobe Technical Support, 808–809, 905
by playing, 6–7
how to learn more, 808
Illustrator Conferences, 7
mastering Illustrator technique, 807
Pen tool techniques, 117–120
tips for, 806–807
mastering, 795–809
Photoshop filters and raster images in, 559–573
Streamline and Dimensions with, 741–793
support for Web graphics, 663–664
system requirements
for Macintosh, 817–818
for Windows, 821
terminology, 10
user feedback on, 282
VectorFrame SE plug-in, 579
working with files, 175–209
Artwork mode vs. Preview mode, 189–193
changing document setup, 178–183
custom views, **194–195**
Document Info dialog box, 207–208
hiding and showing parts of illustrations, 193–194
managing files, 196–197
navigating in documents, 183–189
opening and closing files, 204–205
placing art, 205–206
Publish and Subscribe options (Macintosh), 206–207
saving files, **197–204**
setting up documents, **175–178**
Window menu, 195–196
See also features
Adobe Illustrator Startup file
about, 834
adding swatches to, 906
modifying, 213–214
Adobe Photoshop, 559–573
drag-and-drop, 904
filters, **564–572**
comparison of built-in Photoshop and Illustrator, 504–505
limitations of, 566
Photoshop plug-ins in Illustrator, 566–572
third-party, 566
Magic Wand tool and VectorMagicWand, 585–586
raster images
colorizing one-bit TIFF images, 563–564
masking, 401
moving artwork between pixels and, 32
Adobe picas, 168–169
Adobe Streamline
about, 742–743
cleaning up paths and, 246
Smooth Paths option, 742
toolbox and menu items for, 743–745
tracing with, 155–156
using, 745–747
zooming in, 744
Adobe Technical Support, 231, 808–809, 905
Adobe Type Manager (ATM), **14–15**
AI Plug-In Manager (CSI), 602–603
AI Startup Manager (CSI), 603
AI User Dictionary file, 332
airbrushed shadows, 446–447
Alien Skin Stylist, 597, 641–642
Align and Distribute filter (CSI), 608, 609
Align Edges filter (CSI), 608, 609
Align palette, 253
new features in Macintosh, 830

new features in Windows, 845, 853–854
Align to Guide filter (CSI), 609–610
aligning
and distributing objects, 252
paragraphs, 373–374
type in rows and columns, 335–338
vertical type, 383–384
alphabet commands, 11
Alspach, Ted, 653
Alt key (Windows), **10**
Ambient settings (Surface Properties palette), 764–765
America Online Illustrator Special Interest Group, 7
Analog Clock plug-in, 654–656
Anchor Points
adding, 238–239, 240, 436, 536, 539
adjusting, 269
averaging and joining, 248–252
basics of, **23–24**
Bézier curves and, 25
blending and, 425
blending with unequal selection of, 434
Control Handle Lines and, **27–29**
converting, 253–257
Combination Corner Points, 253, 255–257
Curved Corner Points, 253, 255–257
Smooth Points, 253–254
Straight Corner Points, 253, 254–255
defining paths with, 20
Direct Selection tool and, 137–138
drawing, 798–799
infinity shape, 130, 132
with Pencil tool and, 110
straight lines and, 121–122
end points, 251, 416, 417
moving, 279–280
paths between, 21
printing, 24
Punk and Bloat filter and, 527
removing, **237**, 238, 241–242, 436
reshaping curved points, 269–270
Roughen filter and, 240, 535–536
Round Corners filter and, 548
Scribble and Tweak dialog box and, 539
selecting, 298–299
types of, **119–120**, 253
using Pen tool and, 119–120, 128–129
See also Control Handles; paths
angled rows and columns, 337–338
angles
aligning objects and, **216–217**
changing for straight lines, 432–433
animation, 751
ANSI codes for hidden special characters (Windows platform), 381
anti-aliased type, 361
API (Application Program Interface), 646–647
Software Developer Kit and, 646–647
suites, 648
arc type
with KPT Vector Effects, 904
words and phrases, 325–326
arced illustrations, 532–533
area graphs, 487
Area Selection option (General Preferences dialog box), 221–222
Area type, 345–352
changing area of, 350–351
choosing shapes for, 346
creative uses for, 351–352
justification and, 374
outlining areas for, 346–348
using transformation tools with, 348–349
Area Type tool, 340, 341
arrow buttons, 363
Arrow tool, 657, 658
arrowheads
adding custom, 542–546, 903
available styles for, 546
arrows for Selection tools, 134
art filters (third-party Photoshop), 567
Artboard
basics of, **42**
changing setup options, 179–180

artwork
- changing graphs to, 487
- converting bitmapped art to paths, 745–746
- copying, 795–797
  - copyrighting artwork, **796–797**
  - taking it apart, 796
  - tracing images, 801
  - using layers effectively, 796
- creative uses for Area type, 351–352
- duplicating before trapping, 738
- editing
  - adding Anchor Points, 238–239, 240, 436, 536, 539
  - fine-tuning techniques for paths, 235–237
  - hiding and showing parts of, 193–194
  - moving in bounding box, 720
  - removing Anchor Points, 241–242, 436
  - splitting paths, 181–183, 242–243
  - tools for, 237–238
- locating with VectorNavigator, 41
- printing composites, 706–710
- rasterizing, 560–561
- showing parts of, 193–194
- in this book, 797–802
  - art as outlines for transparency, 800
  - in color section, 800
  - file types of, 798
  - labeling items in palettes, 799
  - paths and, 798–799
  - scanning art, 801–802
- 3D, 776–781, 786–790
  - adjusting shading and reflectance, 761–769
  - applying effects with VectorShape, 590–591
  - creating in Illustrator, 786–789
  - moving objects in 3D, 776–777
  - rotating objects, 779–781
  - scaling, 778–779
  - setting lighting for, 766–767
  - using gradients for bumps and dents, 790
- 2D, 768, 769–775
  - extruding flat art, 770–771
  - mapping on 3D surfaces, 785–786
  - modifying, 768
  - revolving artwork, 773–775
  - saving, 769
  - understanding bevels, 771–773
  - using Illustrator artwork, 768
  - using tile and stack options, 769
- views and perspectives, 781–784
  - changing perspectives, 782–784
  - viewing options, 781–782

Artwork mode, 189–193
- basics of, **35–36**
- changing to, 189–190
- combining with Preview mode, 192–193
- illustrated, 5
- overlapping holes in, 393
- paths visible in, 21
- placed art in, 190
- speeding up, 35
- switching views, 50
- viewing Fill in, 22, 74–75

Artwork Speedup Plug-In, 190
ascenders and descenders for type, 365
ATM (Adobe Type Manager), **14–15**
Attributes palette, 397–398
- illustrated, 829
- new features
  - in Macintosh, 830
  - in Windows, 844, 853
- setting information on, 144

Auto Hyphenate option (Paragraph palette), 313
Auto tab stops, 315
Auto Trace Gap option (General Preferences dialog box), 218
Auto Trace tool, 834
- Curve Fitting Tolerance and, 116
- shortcuts for, 871, 893
- tracing placed images, 155

automatic tracing, 155
averaging points and joining, 248–252
- aligning and distributing objects, 252
- joining, 250–252
- types of averaging, 249

axis of reflection, 276–277

• B •

background color, 439
backgrounds, 802–805

and boundaries of patterns, 467–468
creating bounding box for pattern tile with, 468
using blends and blend effects, 804
using gradients, 802–804
using textures in, 804–805
backlighting, 451
banding, 428–429
baseline shift
adjusting for vertical type, 383–384
adjusting type above and below path with, 357
Baseline Shift option (Character palette), 313, 362
Baseline Shift option (Units and Undo Preferences dialog box), 225
basics of Adobe Illustrator, 3–45
about paths, **20–23**
Anchor Points, **23–24**
the artboard, **42**
Artwork and Preview modes, **35–37**
Bézier curves, **25–26**
control handles and control handle lines, **27–30**
BeInfinite Infinite FX, 596, 599–601
IFX filter theory, 600
IFX filters, 600–601
BeInfinite Smart Remove Points filter, 652
beveled joins, 95
bevels
software for creating, 756
understanding, 771–773
Bézier, Pierre, 25, 26
Bézier curves, **25–26**
bitmap file support, 839
bitmap fonts, **12**
screen fonts as, **12–13**
TrueType fonts and, 14
bitmap images
converting to paths, 745–746
enlarging, 18
black
adding to custom colors for shading, 763
overprinting, 509–510
reversing with white, 705
bleed, 719–720
Blend Front To Back filter, 508, 513
Blend Horizontally filter, 508
Blend tool, 415
Blend Vertically filter, 508
Blend/Auto Trace/Graph tools, shortcuts, 871, 893
blends and gradients, 411–460
blends
avoiding banding, 428–429
basic, **415–416**
blend steps, 415
blending colors with filters, 508
compound paths and, 391, 392
defined, 411
difficulties clicking on, 448
linear, 416–431
masking, 421–424
shape, 431–443
Stroke, 443–451
texturizing, 804–805
trimming, 265
troubleshooting errors, 903
using in backgrounds, 804
gradients, 452–459
converting to blends, 458–459
embossing, 456–457
Expand Fill command, 459
ghosting, 455
Gradient tool, 452
shadows, 458
using Gradient palette, 453–454
using preset, 453
understanding, **412–415**
blur filters (third-party Photoshop), 567
books
on FreeHand, 914
on Illustrator, 912–914
bounding box, 335
creating for pattern tile with backgrounds, 468
defined, **467**
determining pattern tile size with, 467
previewing image size in, 722
Scribble option and, 539, 542
setting bleed in, 719–720
viewing, 468
Bring Forward command, 826, 843
brush stroke filters (third-party Photoshop), 568
built-in filters, **502–504**
color, 507–514
comparison with Photoshop filters, 504–505
create, 514–523

(continued)

built-in filters *(continued)*
  distort and stylize, 524–534
  random mangle, 535–542
  stylize, 542–557
bump curves, 122–123
butt cap, **76**
buttons for menu commands, 39

• C •

CADtools, 597
Calligraphy filter
  Calligraphic option and, 107
  using, 550–551
camera position, 781
cap styles
  defined, **75**
  illustrated, 76
  setting for Paintbrush tool, 108
CD-ROM (included), 650–658, 813–816
  contents of, 813
    Analog Clock, 654–656
    Arrow tool, 657, 658
    BeInfinite Smart Remove Points filter, 652
    Doodle Jr., 597, 653
    KPT Gradients/Patterns to Paths, 651
    Melt & Drip filters, 651–652
    Point and delete tool, 657, 658
    VectorTools trial software on, 575
  installing
    Acrobat 3.0 Reader, 813–816
    VectorFrame SE, 579, 816
  locating artwork on, 7
  using the tutorial PDF file, 8, 814–816
Center option (Paragraph palette), 313
Change Case dialog box, 333
changing
  area of Area type, 350–351
  direction of type, 384–386
  document setup, 178–183
  measurement units, 159–160
  path directions, 398
  View options, 180–181
  See also editing
character attributes, 362–370
  adjusting for vertical type, 383–384
  Character palette, 362–363
  font and style changes, 363–364
  kerning and tracking, 367–369
  Language and multinational options, 370
  leading, 366–367
  measuring, 365
  size changes, 364–365
  vertical and horizontal scale, 370
Character command, 312
Character palette, 362–363
  illustrated, 40, 313
  new features
    in Macintosh, 832
    in Windows, 845, 854
Character Palette Options menu, 313
Check Spelling dialog box, 331
checking
  punctuation, 333–335
  spelling, 330–332
choke, 732, 733
Chooser, reselecting printers from, 721
circles
  arcing type and, 326
  blending to star, 433–435
  creating, 58–64
  type on, 354–356
cleaning up
  paths, 242, 245
  using Trim command for, 265
Cleanup dialog box, 245
Clear command
  basics of, **30–31**
  Delete key and, 30–31
clicking
  control- and double-clicking, **8**
  difficulties clicking on blends, 448
  scrolling and, 188
Clipboard
  about the, **32–33**
  copying, cutting, and pasting objects with, 31
  new features, in Windows, 838
clipping path (Photoshop), 401
close box, illustrated, 40
closed paths, 20
  creating with Pen tool, 122, 129–130
  defined, **112**
  Fill for, 22, 74
  illustrated, 113
  Paintbrush tool and, 103
  wrapping text and, 320
closing
  curved paths with Pen tool, 129–130
  files, 204–205
  paths, 122
CMYK colors
  changing to spot color, 92
  Convert to CMYK filter, 509, 825, 843

inverting colors for, 509
setting with Color palette, 88
See also process colors; RGB colors

color
adjusting
monitor for, 228–229
with sliders, 89
applying to text, 92, 906
black, 509–510, 705, 763
blending with filters, 508
changing
for hatch style, 493
for patterns, 469–470
choosing and mixing for Fill and Stroke, 87–89
Eyedropper tool and, 97–98, 453, 691
of grids, 163–164
Hide/Show Color command, 195
HSB, 88, 841
indicators for swatches and colorspace, 84–85
inverting, 509
layering and, 306
multiple-color linear blends, 419–421
for one-bit TIFF images, 563–564
options for Stroke, 75
Paintbucket tool, 97–98
purple, 78
randomizing, 589
recoloring images, 588
reversing black and white, 229
RGB, 509, 824, 841
saving, 905
selecting
multiple, 295
paths by, 294–295, 296, 297
from Swatches palette, 82–83
with X key, 90
spot, **91–92**
of Stroke icon, 81
for type anchored to paths, 349
of type vs. type color, 350–351
using X key to select, 90
See also color filters; process colors; spot colors

Color command shortcuts
Macintosh, 876–878
Windows, 898–900

color controls (VectorColor), 587–589

color filters, 507–514
Adjust Colors filter, 507–508, 511–512
for blending colors, 508
Convert to CMYK filter, **509**, 825, 843
Convert to Grayscale filter, **509**, 705, 826, 843
creating
extruded multiple path objects, 512–513
negatives with, 513–514
shadows and highlights with, 511–512
Invert Colors filter, 509
Overprint Black Plug-In, 509–510
Saturate filter, 510–511
VectorColor, 507

Color icon, **81**

color linear blends, 425–426

Color Matching dialog box, 229

color models
changing with color filters, **509**, 803, 825
converting for paths, 508
HSB, **88**, 841
RGB, 87–88, 509
See also CMYK colors

Color palette, 80
choosing and mixing color, 87–89
Color Ramps, 90–91
illustrated, 828
new features
in Macintosh, 830
in Windows, 843–844, 853
Out of Gamut indicator, 91
setting
grayscale with, 87
HSB colors and tints with, 88
RGB colors with, 87–88
shortcuts, 876, 898

color plates, 800

Color Ramps
adjusting color with, 90–91
cycling through color spaces, 89

color sets, 523

Color Settings dialog box, 228–229

color wheels, 421–424

colorspace
converting spot to process, 92
indicators for, 84–85

ColorTweak filter (KPT Vector Effects), 619–621

columns
aligning type in, 335–338
designing in custom graphs, 490–491
grouped-column graphs, 483–484

(continued)

columns *(continued)*
stacked-column graphs, 484
Combination Corner Points, **24**
changing existing points to, 132
converting, 253, 255–257
using Pen tool for, 120, 132
See also Corner Points
Command key shortcuts, **9**
commands
keyboard, **9–10**
shortcuts
for generic dialog box, 880, 902
for miscellaneous palettes, 878, 900–901
for toolbox, 863, 885
of Window menu, 195–196
compatible gradient printing, 183
complex shape blends, 435–438
complex trapping, 737–738
composites, 706–710
compound blending (KPT ShadowLand filter), 392
compound paths, 21, 389–395, 405–409
about, 391
blends and, 391, 392
context-sensitive menu when selecting, 917
creating, **390–391**
complex, 406–408
holes in, 392–393
from separate paths, 394
with Unite command, 398–399
faking, 399
masks, 327, 405
in illustrations, 406–409
stroking and filling, 402–404
overlapping holes in, 393–394
path directions, 395–398
determining, 395–396
reversing, 397–398
winding numbers rule, 396–397
releasing, 392
selecting, 37
typeface and, 394–395
using Unite command to create compound paths, 398–399
See also paths
cone, 758
Cone dialog box (Dimensions), 759
Constrain Angle option (General Preferences dialog box), 216–217
constrain angles
aligning objects and, **216–217**
drawing and, 73
setting, 77
Shift key and, 121
constraining movement of measuring line, 158
context-sensitive menus, 826, 843, 915–918
about, **915**
for graph selection, 918
for group, mask, or compound path selection, 917
with no selection, 916
for placed image selection, 917
for standard path selection, 916
for type selection, 918
Control Handles
Bézier curves and, 25
Control Handle Lines, **27–29**
controlling shape of curve with, 125
using Pen tool and, 126–128
dragging, **27–30**, 527
drawing with Pencil tool and, 110
points and, 24
Control key (Macintosh), **10**
Convert Direction Point tool, **237**
Convert to CMYK filter, 509, 825, 843
Convert to Grayscale filter, 509, 705, 825, 843
Convert to RGB filter, 509, 825, 843
converting bitmapped art to paths, 745–746
Copy command, **31–32**
copying artwork
copyrighting and, **796–797**
taking it apart, 796
tracing images, 801
using layers effectively, 796
copyrighting artwork, **796–797**
Corner Points, **24**
effect of Roughen filter on, 535–536
Round Corners filter and, 548
types of, 119–120
See also Combination Corner Points; Curved Corner Points; Straight Corner Points
corner radius, **55–56**
Corner Radius option (General Preferences dialog box), 217

corners
  Calligraphy filter and, 550
  creating for Path Patterns, 555–556
create filters, 514–523
  Fill & Stroke for Mask, 514–515
  Object Mosaic, 515–523
    color sets design, 523
    creating object mosaics, 515–518
    for overlapping tiles with no white space, 522–523
    for Seurat-like illustrations, 519, 520
    for tiled roof, 519–522
Create Outlines command, 320–321
creating
  complex shape blends, 435–436
  compound paths, **390–391**
    holes in, 392–393
    from separate paths, 394
    with Unite command, 398–399
  cone, 758
  cropmarks, 169–171
  cube, 786–788
  ellipses and circles, 58–64
  graphs, **479–481**
  guides, 166
  highway design, 692–693, 694–698
  Illustrator plug-ins
    suites, 648
    wishlist for plug-ins, 649–650
  layers, 301–302
  masks, 400–401
  moving shapes, 47, 49–50
  parallel strokes, 676–679
  polygons, 65–66
  radial blends, 430–431
  railroad-track look, 688, 690–691
  rectangles, 50–54
  a river, 692, 693
  rough edges for Stroke, 686–688, 689
  rounded rectangles and squares, 54–57
  rounding corners backward, 57–58
  shadows, 286–287
  shape blends, 431–443
  shapes at an angle, 73
  spirals, 71–73
  squares, 54
  stars, 66–71
  a strip of film, 684–685
  sunsets, 802–804
  a tear in a path, 537–538
  using Round Corners filter, 57
Crop command, 266
cropmarks
  creating, 169–171
  enabling Japanese, 223
  Japanese cropmarks and trim marks, 171–172
  setting imageable area and, 179–180
cropping vs. masking, 404
CSI Socket Set 1, **597**, 601–607
  CSI Adjust Colors filter, 603–604
  CSI Adjust Stroke filter, 604
  CSI AI Plug-in Manager, 602–603
  CSI AI Startup Manager, 603
  CSI Process to Grayscale filter, 607
  CSI Select Colors filter, 605
  CSI Select Placed Art filter, 606
  CSI Select Similar filter, 606–607
  CSI Select Strokes filter, 606
  CSI Select Text filter, 606
CSI Socket Set 2, **597**, 607–614
  CSI Align and Distribute filter, 608, 609
  CSI Align Edges filter, 608, 609
  CSI Align to Guide filter, 609–610
  CSI Patterns to Paths filter, 610
  CSI Reflect Each filter, 610, 611
  CSI Scale to Dimension filter, 610–612
  CSI Scale to Fit Page filter, 612
  CSI Step and Repeat filter, 612–614
  stepping and, 168–169, 170
Ctrl key (Windows), **10**
cube, 786–788
Cube dialog box (Dimensions), 759
Cursor Key option (Units and Undo Preferences dialog box), 225
cursors
  basics of, **9**
  hot point of type, 359
  setting
    controls for, 225
    preferences for crosshair, 112
  toggling between standard and precise, 220
  types of, **220**
  using precise, 219–220

Curve Fitting Tolerance
  limits of, 904
  smoothing paths with, 114–116
  tracing images and, 155
Curve Fitting Tolerance option (General Preferences dialog box), 217
Curved Corner Points, **24**
  changing to Combination Corner Points, 132
  converting, 253, 255–257
  Smooth Points and, 130, 254
  using Pen tool for, 120, 130–131
  See also Corner Points
curved paths, 129–130
curved points, 269–270
curves
  adjusting without moving Control Handles, 30
  correcting misdrawn, 129
  creating basic, 122–123
  drawing
    the infinity shape, 130, 132
    with Pen tool, 122–126
    S curves, 124–125
custom line screens, 727
Custom Paint Style Selections command, 297
Custom Perspective palette (Dimensions), 783
custom views, 194–195, 838
customizing Illustrator, 211–231
  arrowheads, 542–546, 903
  changing General Preferences dialog box, 215–224
  Color Settings dialog box, 228–229
  features not customized, 231
  fonts, 381–382
  gradients, 453–454
  graphs, 488–491
  Guides & Grid Preferences dialog box, 227
  Hyphenation Options dialog box, 227
  modifying the Startup file, 213–214
  new layers, 301–302
  patterns, 465–467
  placement of palettes and toolbox, 229
  Plug-Ins and Scratch Disk preferences, 227
  preferences, 212–213
  toolbars, 582–585
  tools, 216–218
  Units and Undo Preferences dialog box, 224–227
    Baseline Shift option, 225
    Cursor Key option, 225
    Greek Text Limit option, 226–227
    Size/Leading option, 225
    Tracking option, 226
    Undo Settings option, 227
  See also General Preferences dialog box
Cut command, **31–32**
Cylinder dialog box (Dimensions), 759

• D •

Dash patterns
  Outline Path feature and, 248
  for Stroke, **76**, 95–96
default fill patterns, 463–465
Delete Anchor Point tool, **237**, 238
Delete Empty Text Paths option (Cleanup dialog box), 245
Delete key, 30–31
Delete Stray Points option (Cleanup dialog box), 245
Delete Unpainted Objects option (Cleanup dialog box), 245
deleting
  Anchor Points, **237**, 238, 241–242, 436
  entire paths, 139–140
  items from Startup file, 213–214
  portions of paths, 141–142
  swatches, 83–84
density
  setting for Ink Pen, 493, 494
  setting for textures, 493
deselecting paths, 136, 138–139
diagonal-line patterns, 476
dialog boxes
  generic shortcuts
    for Macintosh, 880
    for Windows, 902
dictionary, 331–332
dimmed images for templates, 153–154
Direct Selection tool, 137–138
direction of type, 384–386
Disable Warnings option (General Preferences dialog box), 223–224, 239, 243, 832, 855
discretionary hyphens, 377
disk space requirements, 197–198
dispersion patterns, setting for textures, 493–495

distort and stylize filters, 524–534
  Free Distort filter, 524–527
  Punk and Bloat filter, 527–529
  Twirl filter, 530–533
  Zig Zag filter, 533–534
distort filters (third-party Photoshop), 569
Divide command, 262–264
dividing and duplicating paths, 243–248
  cleaning up paths, 245
  with Knife Tool, 244
  offsetting path, 246–247
  outlining Stroke of path, 247–248
  slicing paths, 245
docking palettes, 40
Document Info command, 841
Document Info dialog box, 207–208
Document option (Document Info dialog box), 207
Document Setup command, 42, 702–703
Document Setup dialog box, **178–183**, 703
document window, 41–42
documents, 175–209
  about new, **175–178**
  Adobe Illustrator Startup, 213–214
  Artwork mode vs. Preview mode, 189–193
  changing
    Artboard options, 179–180
    document setup, 178–183
    path splitting options, 181–183, 242–243
    View options, 180–181
  compatible gradient printing, 183
  custom views, **194–195**
  Document Info dialog box, 207–208
  hiding and showing parts of illustrations, 193–194
  managing files, 196–197
  multiple pages in, 180–181
  navigating in, 183–189
  opening and closing files, 204–205
  placing art, 205–206
  Preview and Print Patterns option, 465
  Publish and Subscribe options (Macintosh), 206–207
  saving files, 197–204
  setting up, **175–178**
  Use Printer Default Screens checkbox, 183
  Window menu, 195–196
Doodle Jr., 597, 653
double-clicking, **8**
dpi (dots per inch)
  laser printer technology and, 16–17
  scanning art and, 801–802
dragging, **8**
  Control Handles, 27–30, 527
  and dropping art between Illustrator and Photoshop, 32, 563–564, 904
  tools off edge of window, 105
drawing
  constrain angles and, 73
  the infinity shape, 130, 132
  moving marquees while, 185
  with Paintbrush tool, 105–107
  with Pen tool, 121–126
  with Pencil tool, 112–114
  points, 798–799
  rectangles, 50–54
  rounded rectangles, 55
  S curves, 124–125
  squares, 54
  tools for creating paths, 101–102
Drop Shadow dialog box, 547
Drop Shadow filter, 547–548
drop shadows, 53, 547–548
duplicating
  art before trapping, 738
  objects with Option [Alt] key, 354
  paths, 243–248
  spirals, 72

• E •

edges
  creating rough edges for Stroke, 686–688, 689
  CSI Align Edges filter, 608, 609
  hiding, 194, 377–378
  masking for Stroke, 690
  Path Patterns and, 557
  softening for Stroke, 449
Edit Curves button (VectorColor), 590
Edit menu
  Select submenu, 293–294
  shortcuts, 859–860, 882
editing
  Add Anchor Points command, 240
  adding Anchor Points, 238–239, 240, 436, 536, 539

(continued)

editing *(continued)*
clear, cut, copy, and paste, **30–33**
removing Anchor Points, **237**, 238, 241–242, 436
splitting paths, 181–183, 242–243
tools for, 237–238
type, 360–361
See also changing
elevator box, 43
Ellipse tool, 117
Ellipse tool slot, illustrated, 64
ellipses
adjusting, 334–335
creating, **58–64**
ellipsis (. . .), on menus, 38
Embedded Images option (Document Info dialog box), 208
Emboss filter (KPT Vector Effects), 621–622
embossed art, 622
embossing gradients, 456–457
emulsions, 724
en and em dashes, 334
Encapsulated PostScript. *See* EPS
end paths
defined, 415
for linear blends, 426–427
end points
joining, 251
selecting opposite points of, 416, 417
EPS (Encapsulated PostScript) files
preview options for, 203–204
saving, 203
saving previews as, 905
as standard, 17
tracing images, 60
See also PostScript
EPS Format dialog box, 203
erasing with Pencil tool, 114
errors and error messages, 906–908
errors with insertion point, 334
opening files with Illegal Operand 'TZ', 197–198
selecting report for printing errors, 709
Exclude and Intersect commands, 261
Expand command
converting patterns to paths, 476
as new feature in Windows, 839
Expand Fill command, 459
Expand Fill dialog box, 459
Export command, 382
exporting
files, 204
files with Pantone gradients to Quark, 904–905
to GIF format, 667
JPEG format, 664–666
to PNG format, 667
text, 382
Extensis VectorTools, 597
extruding and revolving
extruded multiple path objects, 512–513
software for, 755–756
2D artwork, 769–775
extruding flat art, 770–771
understanding bevels, 771–773
Eyedropper tool
changing color of path with, 691
icon for, 97
options for, **97–98**
sampling color to Gradient palette, 453

• F •

Fade pop-up controls, 497
Fade to White option (Hatch pop-up menu), 497–498
features
of Adobe Dimensions, 747–748
new to Illustrator 7
changing color models with color filters, **509**, 803, 825
creating shapes (Windows), 48
for files (Windows), 176
of Filter menu, 503
for fine-tuning artwork (Windows), 236
location of tools, 45
in Macintosh, 823–835
organization of tools, 65
for Paintbrush tool (Windows), 102
for patterns, 467
summary of, 4
for type controls and tools (Windows platform), 310, 843
in Windows, 837–857
not customized, 231
tips for discovery, 806–807
Unite command, 261
of VectorNavigator, 593–594
See also Macintosh platform; Windows platform
file formats
compatibility of Illustrator, 201–202
exporting
to GIF, 667
to JPEG, 664–666
to PNG, 667
TeachText, 208

files
  AI User Dictionary, 332
  for artwork in this book, 798
  document info, 208
  exporting, 204
  file types and saving, 201
  format compatibility of Illustrator, 201–202
  managing, 196–197
  naming, 198–199
  new features (Windows), 176
  opening
    and closing, 204–205
    with Illegal Operand 'TZ' errors, 197–198
    PageMaker, 903
  reverting to last saved version, 201
  saving
    with Save a Copy command, 200–201
    with Save As command, 200
    with Save command, 197–200
Files menu, shortcuts, 859, 881
Fill
  adding
    black for shading, 763
    to shapes, **74–75**
  applying
    to paths in Preview mode, 21
    patterns in Preview mode, 465
    to shapes, 78–79, 81
  color
    choosing and mixing, 87–89
    selecting for paths, 92
  creating
    half-stroked paths with, 688
    textured backgrounds, 804–805
  Fill & Stroke for Mask filter, 298, 514–515
  for open paths, 22
  selecting paths by, 294–295, 297
  shortcut keys for swapping with Stroke, 833
  Stroke
    combining with, 77
    compared with, 677
    knocking out, 77
  See also paths; Stroke
Fill & Stroke for Mask filter, 298, 514–515
Fill icon, 80
  color of, 81
  selecting, 78–79
Filter menu
  illustrated, 504
  new features of, 503
  shortcuts, 861, 883
filters, 501–557
  about, **504**
  built-in, **502–504**
    color, 507–514
    comparison with Photoshop filters, 504–505
    create, 514–523
    distort and stylize, 524–534
    random mangle, 535–542
    stylize, 542–557
  new features, in Windows, 838
  Photoshop filters
    in Illustrator, **564–572**
    third-party, 566
  plug-ins
    Artwork View Speedup, 35–36, 190
    creating for Illustrator, 646–650
    CSI Socket Sets, 168, 597, 601–614
    Overprint Black, 509–510
    Photoshop, 566–572
    placement on menus, 503
  reapplying last, 507
  relocating Plug-Ins folder, 506
  third-party, 506, 595–669
  vectors vs. pixel-based images, 559–564
  See also plug-ins; third-party filters
Find Font dialog box, 330
Find/Change dialog box, 329
finding and changing, 329–330
  case, 333
  with Find Font dialog box, 330
  text, 328–330
First line indent option (Paragraph palette), 313
Fit Headline command, 320, 840
Fit in Window view, 187
fixed stars, **68**
Flare filter (KPT Vector Effects), 622–624
floating palettes, 648
floating point unit (FPU), 819
Flush left option (Paragraph palette), 313

Flush right option (Paragraph palette), 313
folders. *See* Plug-Ins folder
Font command, 311
Font option (Character palette), 313, 362
Font pop-up menu, 362
Font/Style menu (Character palette), 313
fonts, **11–16**
  Adobe Type Manager (ATM), **14–15**
  bitmap, **12**
  changing
    font and style, 363–364
    size, 364–365
  choosing type for Illustrator, 14
  customizing, 381–382
  displaying type in Clipboard, 32
  finding and changing, 330
  hinting and Type 1, 328
  Kara Fonts, 597, 643–645
  kerning and tracking, 367–369, 383–384
  Multiple Master fonts, **15–16**
  PostScript, **12–13**
  TrueType, **14**, 15, 320
  vertical and horizontal placement of, 370
Foster, Matt, 651–652
FPU (floating point unit), 819
fractions, 334–335
framing placed images, 580–582
Free Distort dialog box, 524
Free Distort filter, 524–527, 532–533
FreeHand
  books on, 914
  opening documents in Illustrator, 905
Freehand tool. *See* Pencil tool
full screen mode
  new feature
    in Macintosh, 825
    in Windows, 841–842

• G •

General Preferences dialog box, 215–224
  Area Selection option, 221–222
  Disable Warnings option, 223–224, 239, 243
  Japanese Cropmarks option, 223
  New Tool Shortcuts option, 221
  Paste Remembers Layers option, 221
  Scale Line Weight option, 222
  setting cursor preferences, 112
  Show Tool Tips option, 222
  Snap to Point option, 219
  Tool Behavior options, 216–218
    Auto Trace Gap option, 218
    Constrain Angle option, 216–217
    Corner Radius option, 217
    Curve Fitting Tolerance option, 217
  Transform Pattern Tiles option, 219
  Use Precise Cursors option, 219–220
generic icon for Adobe Illustrator, 908
ghosted type, 684–686
ghosting gradients, 455
GIF format, 667
Gloss settings (Surface Properties palette), 765
glows, 448–449
gradient Fill
  creating textured background from, 804–805
  troubleshooting errors, 903
Gradient icon, using, **81**
Gradient palette, 453–454
  new features
    in Macintosh, 830
    in Windows, 837, 844, 853
  shortcuts, 877–878, 899
Gradient tool, 452
gradients, 452–459
  converting to blends, **458–459**
  customizing with Gradient palette, 453–454
  embossing, 456–457
  Expand Fill command, 459
  ghosting, 455
  Gradient tool, 452
  for halftones, 726
  printing with QMS printer, 905
  putting into patterns, 477–478
  shadows, 458
  transforming, 287–288
  understanding blends and, **412–415**
  using
    in backgrounds, 802–804
    preset, 453
    Stroke with, 677
    for 3D bumps and dents, 790
  See also blends and gradients

Gradients/Patterns to Paths (KPT filter), 476, 651
Graph Data dialog box, 489–490
Graph tools, 479
Graph Type dialog box, 480
graphs, 479–491
  combining types of, 489
  context-sensitive menu for selecting, 918
  creating, **479–481**
  customizing, 488–491
    with Graph Data dialog box, 489–490
    using marker and column designs, 490–491
  grouping and, 489
  types of, 483–488
    area graphs, 487
    grouped-column graphs, 483–484
    line graphs, 484–486
    pie graphs, 487, 488
    radar, 825, 843
    scatter graphs, 487
    stacked-column graphs, 484
  when to use, 481–483
grayscale
  Convert to Grayscale filter, 509, 705, 826, 843
  CSI Process to Grayscale filter, 607
  setting with Color palette, 87
Greek Text Limit option (Units and Undo Preferences dialog box), 226–227
greeking, **15**, 226–227
grid patterns, 476
gridline spacing, 476
grids and guides, 151–173
  grids, 162–165
    about, **162–163**
    color, style, and spacing of, 163–164
    creating for patterns, 474–476
    creating with CSI Step and Repeat, 612–614
    making precision adjustments with, 257
    as new Macintosh feature, 823–824
    rotating, 164, 476
    as transparency indicator, 164–165
    turning on, 834
  guides, 165–168
    about, **165–166**
    creating, 166
    moving, 166–167
    selecting and releasing, 167
    setting Guide Preferences, 167–168
  measuring distances, 156–162
    changing measurement units, 159–160
    Measure tool, 157–158
    measuring with objects, 161
    methods of, 156
    using Offset Path, 161–162
    using rulers, 160
    using Transform palette, 158–159
  printing and, 168–172
    creating cropmarks, 169–171
    creating stepped artwork, 168–169, 170
    Japanese cropmarks and trim marks, 171–172
  templates, 152–154
    dimming images for, 153–154
    new features for, 152–153
  See also measurements; tracing
group selecting, 135
Group Selection tool, 138–139, 149
grouped-column graphs, 483–484
grouping
  creating compound paths and, 391
  graphs and, 489
  masks and, 401
  menus while, 917
  objects on paths, **147–149**
  Stroke and Fill to mask, 514–515
Guide Preferences, 167–168
guides, 165–168
  about, **165–166**
  creating, 166
  moving, 166–167
  selecting and releasing, 167
  setting Guide Preferences, 167–168
  showing and hiding, 194
  See also grids and guides
Guides & Grid Preferences dialog box, 164, 227
gutter, 335–336

• H •

H option (Transform palette), 281
halftone line screens, 725–726
halftone screens, 724
Hand tool, scrolling with, 188–189

hang punctuation
  about, **375–376**
  adjusting for vertical type, 383–384
Hang Punctuation option (Paragraph palette), 313
Hard and Soft commands, 266–267
hard returns and Point type, 343
Hatch pop-up menu, 497
hatch style
  changing color for, 493
  scaling for textures, 497
  selecting for Ink Pen tool, 492
Hide Clipboard command, 33
Hide Edges command, 194
  new features in Windows, 840
  selecting type and, 377–378
Hide/Show Align command, 195
Hide/Show Attributes command, 196
Hide/Show Color command, 195
Hide/Show Gradient command, 195
Hide/Show Info command, 195
Hide/Show Layers command, 196
Hide/Show Stroke command, 196
Hide/Show Swatches command, 196
Hide/Show Tools command, 195
Hide/Show Transform command, 195
hiding
  copyright layer, 797
  edges, 194, 377–378, 840
  objects on paths, 143–144
  page tiling, 194
  parts of illustrations, 193–194
  paths after checking for colors, 514
  rulers, 193–194
highlights, 511–512
highway design, 692–693, 694–698
hinting, 328
Hodge, Bruce, 80
holes in compound paths, 392–393
Holt, Joe, 654
horizontal percentages, 542
Horizontal scale option (Character palette), 313, 370
horizontal type, 342
hot point of type cursor, 359
HotDoor CADtools 1.0, 634–638
HSB colors
  new feature in Windows, 841
  setting with Color palette, 88
hyphenating
  discretionary hyphens, 377
  paragraphs, 376–377
  troubleshooting errors, 903
Hyphenation Options dialog box, 227, 314

• I •

icons
  cursor, 9
  for Eyedropper and Paintbucket tools, 97
  Fill and Stroke, 78–79, 80, 81
  Reshape tool, 270
  toolbox, 44
IFX filters, 600–601
Illegal Operand 'TZ' errors, 197–198
Illom Development plug-ins, 597
illustrations. *See* artwork
Illustrator Conferences, 7
image maps, 669
images
  altering with masks, 409
  bitmap, 18, 745–746
  dimmed for templates, 153–154
  framing placed, 580–582
  masking raster, 401
  pixel-based, 559–564, 745–747
  recoloring, 588
  resolution of PostScript, 17–19
  sunken, 456
  tracing, 60, 155, 801
  trapping, 269
  See also artwork; raster images
indenting
  adjusting for vertical type, 383–384
  paragraphs, 374
Infinite FX dialog box, 599
infinity shape, drawing, 130, 132
Info palette, 844
Ink Pen Effects dialog box, 492
Ink Pen filter
  creating textures with, 491–492
  setting density for hatch style, 493, 494
  in Windows platform, 462
  See also Pen tool
Ink Pen Hatches dialog box, 492

changing colors, 493
insertion point
errors with, 334
Point type and, 343
pressing Shift key while moving, 360
Inset filter (KPT Vector Effects), 624, 625
installing
Acrobat 3.0 Reader, 813–816
Illustrator for Macintosh, **820–821**
recommendations for memory and processor, 819–820
system requirements for, 817–818
Illustrator for Windows, **822**
system requirements, 821
third-party filters, 598–599
VectorFrame SE, **816**, 579
interface
characteristics of KPT Vector Effects, 615–616
Illustrator program, 646–647
InterGroup selections, 136
InterPath selections, 134
interruptable redraw, 37
Intersect and Exclude commands, 261
Invert Colors filter, 509
invisibles, 904

• J •

Japanese cropmarks and trim marks, 171–172, 223
joins
averaging points and joining, 248–252
changing open to closed paths, 112
illustrated, 76
for paths of different groups, 250
setting for Paintbrush tool, 108
types of, **75**, 94–95
Joins pop-up menu, 246
JPEG Export dialog box, 666
JPEG format, 664–666
Justify all lines option (Paragraph palette), 313
Justify full lines option (Paragraph palette), 313

• K •

kaleidoscopes, 292
Kara Fonts, 597, 643–645
kerning and tracking, 367–369, 383–384
Kerning option (Character palette), 313, 362
key commands, **38**
keyboard
adjusting
arrow buttons from, 363
type from, 365
choosing Selection tools from, 137
keys for symbol typefaces (Macintosh), 379
keyboard commands, **9–10**
Keyboard Increments dialog box, 362
keyboard shortcuts. *See* shortcuts
keys
changing
colors with X, 90
Stroke with X, 79
Command, **9–10**
Control (Macintosh), **10**
Ctrl (Windows), **10**
for symbol typefaces (Macintosh), 379
using with Spiral tool, 72
for Zapf Dingbats (Windows), 379
See also Option [Alt] key; Shift key
Knife tool
about, **237**
dividing and duplicating paths with, 244
vs. Slicing function, 245
KPT Vector Effects, 597, 614–634
arc type, 904
ColorTweak filter, 619–621
compound blending with ShadowLand filter, 392
Emboss filter, 621–622
extruding and revolving artwork, 755–756
Flare filter, 622–624
FPU and, 819
Inset filter, 624, 625
interface characteristics of, 615–616
KPT 3D Transform filter, 617–619
KPT Warp Frame filter, 326
Neon filter, 624–625
Point Editor filter, 626
RAM for filters, 820
Resize and Reposition filter, 626
ShadowLand filter, 627–628
creating extruded multiple path objects, 513

(continued)

KPT Vector Effects (continued)
RAM required for filters, 820
ShatterBox filter, 628–630
Sketch filter, 630–631
Vector Distort filter, 631–633
Warp Frame filter, 633–634
Kumi Character Direction, 386

• L •

labeling items in palettes, 799
Landscape orientation (Separations Setup dialog box), 723
Landscape with Transverse checked orientation (Separations Setup dialog box), 723
language and multinational options, 370
Layer Options dialog box
bypassing, 302
opening, 305
layering, 299–306
about, **299–300**
creating
and customizing new layers, 301–302
multiple, 300
Traps layer, 268
grids as transparency indicator, 164–165
Layers palette icons, 304
Layers palette pop-up menu, 304–305
locking and selecting layers, 298
locking or hiding copyright layer, 797
moving objects between layers, 303–304
Paste Remembers Layers option and, 147
printing and hidden, 707
3D positioning and, 752–753
tips for, 306
tracing, 156
turning printing off for template, 152
using the Layers palette, 302–303
Layers palette
Merge Layers option, 305
new features
in Macintosh, 831
in Windows, 838, 845, 854
Paste Remembers Layers option, 147
shortcuts, 879, 901
using, 302–303
Layers palette icons, 304
Layers palette pop-up menu, 304–305
leading, 366–367
adjusting for vertical type, 383–384
decreasing and increasing, 225
Leading option (Character palette), 313
learning Illustrator
by playing, 6–7
getting to know Illustrator, 807
how to learn more, 808
Illustrator Conferences, 7
mastering Illustrator technique, 807
Pen tool techniques, 117–120
technique, 807
tips for, 806–807
Left indent option (Paragraph palette), 313
Letraset Envelopes, 597, 642–643
letter spacing
adjusting ligatures, 334
setting, 313, 375
Letter Spacing options (Paragraph palette), 313
lighting
setting in 3D programs, 766–767
setting reflectance, 763–765
Lighting palette (Dimensions), 762, 766–767
Line Breaking % option (Paragraph palette), 313, 377
line graphs, 484–486
line screens
adding custom, 727
halftone, 725–726
linear blends, 416–431
airbrushed shadows with, 446–447
basic, 416–419
calculating number of printing steps, 427, 429–430
color, 425–426
creating radial blends, 430–431
end paths for, 426–427
multiple colors, 419–421
nonlinear, 421
pseudolinear, 424–425
lines
changing angle of straight, 432–433
measuring with, 161
straight, 121–122
Links Blocks command, 316–318
locking
layers, 298
objects, **142–144**

Logo Corrector, 242
logos, 324–325

• M •

Macintosh platform
About this Computer command, 211
Control key, **10**
installing illustrator, **820–821**
recommendations for memory and processor, 819–820
system requirements for, 817–818
new features, 823–835
menu changes, 826–829
palettes, 830–832
patterns, templates, and disable warnings option, 832
rearrangements to toolbox, 829–830
tips for using, 833–835
tools and functions, 823–826
Page Setup command, 703–706
Publish and Subscribe options, 206–207
selecting menu items, 38
shortcuts, 859–880
special characters, 377–379
toggling measurement units, 224
using Command key for, **9–10**
Magic Wand tool (Photoshop), 585–586
Make Knife command (Windows), 839
Make Wrap command, 318–320
managing files, 196–197
manual tracing, 155
manual trapping, 735–736
mapping 2D artwork on 3D surfaces, 785–786
MAPublisher 2.0, 597, 643
marquees
moving while drawing, 185
selecting paths using, 191
Zoom Out tool and, 184–185
masks
about, 399–400
altering images with, 409
blends, 402, 421–424
compound paths, 405
context-sensitive menus when selecting, 917
creating, 400–401
Crop command and, 266
Fill & Stroke for Mask filter, 298, 514–515
in illustrations, 406–409
masking vs. cropping, 404
outside edge of Stroke, 690
patterns as masked Type 3 fonts, 478
printing and, 404–405
raster images and, 401, 561
releasing, 403–404, 478
selecting
before making changes, 515
paths by, 298
stroking and filling, 402–404
for type outlines, 326–327
math coprocessor, 819
Matte settings (Surface Properties palette), 765
Measure tool, 157–158
Measure/Paint tools, 872, 894
measurements, 156–162
adjusting, 280
changing units for, 159–160, 905–906
Measure tool, 157–158
measuring with objects, 161
methods of, 156
in Rows & Columns dialog box, 335
rulers and, 160
setting preferences for, 52
for type, 365
types of, 224
using
Offset Path, 161–162
Transform palette, 158–159
Melt & Drip filters, 651–652
memory
designating scratch disks, 227
layering and, 306
requirements
for Macintosh, 818, 819–820
for Object Mosaic filter, 517
for Vector Effects filters, 820
for Windows, 821
running out of, 906
undoing and, 34
Menu command shortcuts
Macintosh, 859–862
Windows, 881–884
menus
basics of, **37–39**
changes
in Macintosh, 826–829
in Windows, 847–851
context-sensitive, 826, 843, 915–918

(continued)

menus *(continued)*
effective use of, 38–39
ellipsis (. . .) on, 38
illustrated for Windows, 848
selecting items from, 37–38
for Streamline, 743–745
for VectorTools, 580
See also specific menus listed individually
Merge command, 265–266, 458
MetaCreations Vector Effects. *See* KPT Vector Effects
metrics, 159–160
Minus Front and Minus Back commands, 262
miscellaneous shortcuts, 880, 902
miter limit, **75**, 76
Miter Limit option (Offset Path dialog box), 246
mitered joins, 95
MM design command, 314
MM Design palette. *See* Multiple Master Design palette
modal dialogs, 648
modifying
patterns, 477
2D artwork, 768
monitor settings, 228–229
mouse
activating context-sensitive menus, 915
alternatives for Paint-brush tool, 105
basics of, **8–9**
clicking
control- and double-clicking, **8**
difficulties with blends, 448
scrolling and, 188
dragging, **8**
artwork between Photoshop and Illustrator, 32, 563–564, 904
Control Handles, 27–30, 527
tools off edge of window, 105
right mouse button (Windows), 10
scrolling
with Hand tool, 188–189
using scroll bars, **43**, 187–188
Move dialog box, 157, 279
Move palette (Dimensions), 753
moving
entire paths, 139–140
guides, 166–167
objects, 279–280
objects between layers, 302–304
portions of paths, 141–142
shapes, 47, 49–50
templates, 153
with Transform Each dialog box, 283
Multinational option (Character palette), 313, 370
Multiple Master Design palette, 314
in Macintosh, 826, 832
in Windows, 846, 854
Multiple Master fonts, **15–16**
multiple pages, 180–181
musical sounds, 907
muted reflections, 439–441

• N •

Name viewing mode (Swatches palette), 85, 95
naming files, 198–199
navigating in documents, 183–189
scrolling, **43**
with Hand tool, 188–189
using scroll bars, 187–188
with VectorNavigator, 189
zooming
techniques for, 186–187
Zoom tools, 184–185
See also zooming
negatives, 513–514
neon effects, 450–451
Neon filter (KPT Vector Effects), 624–625
New Document command, 175–178
new document window, 176
New Tool Shortcuts option (General Preferences dialog box), 221
New Window command, 195
None icon, **81**
nonlinear blends, 421

• O •

Object menu
Pathfinder submenu, 258
shortcuts, 860–861, 882–883
Transformation submenu, 274
Object Mosaic dialog box, 516

Object Mosaic filter, 515–523
  color sets design, 523
  creating object mosaics, 515–518
  for overlapping tiles with no white space, 522–523
  for Seurat-like illustrations, 519, 520
  for tiled roof, 519–522
objects
  aligning and distributing, 252
  bounding box and, 335
  creating rows and columns for nonrectangular, 336–337
  graphical tabs and, 316
  grouping and ungrouping, 147–149
  inverse selection of, 297–298
  locking and hiding, 142–144
  measuring with, 161
  moving, 279–280
  pasting, 146–147
  printing and hidden, 707
  punked and bloated, 528
  rotating into a path, 288–289
  scaling, 275–276
  setting URLs for, 144, 668–669
  storing in VectorLibrary, 586–587
  transforming, 272–280
  transforming on portion of paths, 290–291
Objects option (Document Info dialog box), 208
Offset Path dialog box, 162, 246
offsetting paths
  creating, 246–247
  measuring distances and, 161–162
  outlining areas for Area type, 346–348
Open a PostScript Printer Description file window, 720–721
open paths, 20
  defined, **112**
  Fill for, 22, 74
  illustrated, 113
opening
  files, 204–205
  Layer Options dialog box, 305
  PageMaker files, 903
  PPD files, 720–721
optimizing performance
  decreasing rendering times, 760
  printing, 905
  speeding up Artwork mode, 35
  turning off Preview checkbox for Zig Zag filter, 534
Option [Alt] key
  adjusting
    reflection axis and, 277
    spirals with, 72
  with Color Ramp, 90–91
  creating Curved Corner Points with, 131
  drawing
    rectangles and, 53–54
    rounded rectangles and, 55
    squares and, 54
  duplicating objects, 354
  rotating guides with, 166
  scaling objects and, 276
  shearing objects and, 278
origin point
  for circles, 59
  defined, **51**
  illustrated, 273
  with rounded corners, 55
  transformation tools and, 273
  twirling objects around, 270–271
origins for rulers, 160, 161, 194
Out of Gamut indicator, 91
Outline command, 264–265
Outline Path command, 459, 677
outlining
  areas for Area type, 346–348
  artwork for transparency, 800
  converting typefaces to, 328
  searching and replacing words converted to, 330
  type, 320–328, 371–372
    adding Stroke to, 371–372
    masking and filling, 326–327
overlapping holes in compound paths, 393–394
overlapping paths, 265
overlapping points, 251
Overprint Black dialog box, 510
Overprint Black Plug-In, 509–510
  viewing overprinting, 37

• P •

page
  changing size of separation, 721–722

(continued)

page *(continued)*
  orienting for separations, 722–723
Page Setup command (Macintosh), 703–706
Page Setup dialog box (Macintosh), **703**, 179
Page Setup Options dialog box (Macintosh), 704–706
Page Size pop-up menu (Open a PostScript Printer Description file window), 721–722
page tiling, 194
Page tool, **42–43**
PageMaker files, 903
Paint Style palette, 80
Paint Style section (toolbox), 78
paint styles
  selecting paths by, 295–296
  selecting with VectorMagic Wand, 296
Paintbrush tool, 103–109
  Calligraphy filter and, 550
  drawing paths with corners, 105–106
  drawing with, 106–107
  keyboard shortcuts for, 101
  paintbrush strokes, 104, 106
  setting calligraphic angle for, 107
  specifying joins and caps, 108
  using pressure-sensitive tablets to draw, 109
Paintbucket tool, **97–98**
Palette Tab, illustrated, 40
palettes
  basics of, **39–40**
  components of, 40
  demise of Paint Style, 80
  docking, 40
  floating, 648
  labeling items in, 799
  new features
    in Macintosh, 830–832
    in Windows, 843–846, 853–854
  placing, 229
  shortcuts
    for Macintosh, 878–879
    for Windows, 900–901
  tabbing and docking, 40, 830, 831
Pantone colors, 904–905
Paragraph command, 312, 314
Paragraph palette
  illustrated, 313, 372
  new features in Macintosh, 832
  new features in Windows, 845, 854
paragraphs, **310**, 370–377
  aligning, 373–374
  formatting shortcuts, 875, 897
  hang punctuation, 375–376
  hyphenating, 376–377
  indenting, 374
  outlining type, 371–372
  space before, 374
  spacing within, 375
parallel strokes, 676–679
Paste command, **31–32**
Paste dialog box, 563
Paste Remembers Layers option (General Preferences dialog box), 221
Paste Remembers Layers option (Layers palette), 147
Pasteboard, **41**
Path Pattern dialog box, 553
Path Patterns, 551–557
  creating
    corner tiles for, 556
    corners for, 555–556
    patterns for, 553–554
    tube patterns for, 553–554
  edges and, 557
  using, 551–553
path selections, 135
Path tools, shortcuts, 864–865, 886–887
Path Type tool, 340, 341
Pathfinder Crop filter, 404
Pathfinder menu items, **257–269**
  about, 257–258
  Crop command, 266
  Divide command, 262–264
  examples of, 263
  Hard and Soft commands, 266–267
  Intersect and Exclude commands, 261
  Merge command, 265–266
  Minus Front and Minus Back commands, 262
  new features, in Windows, 839
  Outline command, 264–265
  Pathfinder Options dialog box, 259
  Trap command, 267–269
  Trim command, 265
  Unite command, 259–260
Pathfinder Options dialog box, 259
paths, 101–150, 235–237
  between Anchor Points, 21
  applying Strokes to, 22–23

Area Select feature
and, 222
for artwork in this book,
798–799
averaging points and
joining, 248–252
aligning and distributing
objects, 252
averaging points, 249
joining, 250–252
specifying joins and
caps, 108
basics of, **20–23**
blending and, 425, 679
cleaning up with
Streamline, 246
closed, 543
closing, 122
curved paths with Pen
tool, 129–130
coloring type anchored
to, 349
Combination Corner
Points, 132
compound, 389–410
creating, **390–391**, 394,
398–399
faking, 399
holes in, 392–393
overlapping holes in,
393–394
path directions, 395–398
releasing, 392
selecting, 37
typeface and, 394–395
context-sensitive menus
when selecting, 916
converting
Anchor Points, 253–257
bitmapped art to,
745–746
color model for, 508
converting patterns
to, 476
copying, 32
Curved Corner Points,
130–131
deselecting, 136, 138–139
directions, 395–398
changing, 398
determining, 395–396
reversing, 397–398
rotating objects into
paths, 288–299
winding numbers rule,
396–397
dividing and duplicating,
243–248
cleaning up paths,
245, 246
creating offset paths,
246–247
with Knife Tool, 244
outlining existing Stroke
path, 247–248
slicing paths, 245
splitting, 181–183,
242–243
drawing
curves, 122–126
open and closed paths,
112–113
on pressure-sensitive
tablets, 109
semistraight segments,
113–114
straight lines, 121–122
techniques
for Pen tool, 117–120,
126–129, 133
for Pencil tool, 110–112
tools for, 101–102
editing
adding Anchor Points,
238–239, 240, 436,
536, 539
erasing, 114
layering, 299–306
locking and hiding
objects, 142–144
moving and deleting,
139–142
removing Anchor Points,
237, 238, 241–242, 436
tools for, 237–238
end paths
defined, 415
for linear blends,
426–427
grouping and ungrouping
objects, 147–149
limits of points on, 904
masking
blends and other
masks, 402
compound paths, 327
in illustrations, 406–409
raster images, 401
stroking and filling
masking objects,
402–404
moving, 279–280
new features in
Windows, 839
open, adding to, 116–117
pasting
in front of or behind
selected objects,
146–147
in Photoshop as pixels,
562–563
Pathfinder menu items,
257–269
placing type in, 345–352
selecting, 190–191,
293–299
about, 293–294
by Fill and Stroke, 297
by Fill color, 294–295
by paint style, 295–296
by Stroke color, 296
(continued)

paths *(continued)*
by Stroke weight, 296
colors for, 92
in group, 149
masks, 298
objects not selected, 297–298
in Preview mode, 37
stray points, 298–299
Stroke on blended, 679
selection tools, 133–139
smoothing paths, 114–116, 435
spinning, 438
stacking order, 144–146
Stroke
charts of, 679–684
outlining, 247–248
tips for checking, 514
transforming
objects on, 272–280
a part of, 290–291
Twirl filter and, 530
type on, 353–358
creating reversed type, 357–358
spacing for, 356–357
type on a circle, 354–356
using
KPT Flare on selected, 623
Reshape tool with, 269
Transform Again command, 286
Transform Each dialog box, 283–285
Transform palette, 280–282
wrapping, 318, 320
See also compound paths; Fill; Paintbrush tool; Pen tool; Pencil tool; Stroke
Pattern dialog box. *See* Swatches palette
pattern tile, 465–467
creating bounding box for, 468
creating equi-distance, 472
determining size with bounding box, 467
patterns, 461–479
about, **461–462**
backgrounds and boundaries of, 467–468
changing color of, 469–470
converting to paths, 476
creating
custom, 465–467
for Path Patterns, 553–554
default fill, 463–465
diagonal-line and grid patterns, 476
line patterns and grids, 474–476
modifying, 477
new features, 467
in Macintosh, 832
in Windows, 854
putting patterns and gradients into, 477–478
seamless, 468–472
symmetrical, 472–474
transforming, 293, 478–479
transparent, 462, 477
Patterns to Paths filter (CSI), 610
PDF documents, 673
PDF format, 204
Pen tool, 117–133
about the, 103
closing paths with, 122, 129–130
Combination Corner Points, 132
Curved Corner Points, 130–131
drawing
curves, 122–126
straight lines, 121–122
keyboard shortcuts for, 101
preventing curved tips, 125–126
techniques for, 117–120, 126–129, 133
using with Straight Corner Points, 119
See also Ink Pen filter
pen width, 550
Pencil tool, 109–117
adding to open paths, 116–117
advantages of, 109–110
drawing
open and closed paths with, 112–113
semistraight segments, 113–114
erasing, 114
keyboard shortcuts for, 101
smoothing paths, 114–116
techniques for, 110–112
Photoshop filters and plug-ins
comparison with Illustrator filters, 504–505
new in Windows, 838
troubleshooting, 906
using in Illustrator, 566–572
picas
as default unit of measure, 224
measuring, 159–160
traditional vs. Adobe, 168–169
PICT file previews, 203–204
pie graphs, 487, 488
pixelate filters (third-party Photoshop), 569–570

pixel-based images
converting to paths, 745–747
vs. vectors, 559–564
pixels
changing Illustrator art to, 560–561
comparison with tiled images, 518
Curve Fitting Tolerance and variation in, 218
device, 21
pasting paths in Photoshop as, 562–563
preventing jagged illustrations, 17–19
placed images, 205–206
in Artwork mode, 190
context-sensitive menu when selecting, 917
framing, 580–582
templates and, 152, 154
tracing with Auto Trace tool, 155
trapping, 269
plug-ins
Artwork View Speedup Plug-In, 35–36, 190
creating for Illustrator, 646–650
Illustrator program interface and software tools, 646–647
types for Illustrator, 648
CSI Socket Sets, 168, 597, 601–614
new features (Windows), 838
Overprint Black, 509–510
Photoshop, 566–572
placement on menus, 503
See also filters; third-party filters
Plug-Ins and Scratch Disk preferences, 227
Plug-Ins folder
about folders in, 573
caution for AI User Dictionary file, 332
preferences for location of, 227
relocating, 506
PNG format, 667
Point and delete tool, 657, 658
Point Editor filter (KPT Vector Effects), 626
point sizes, 12
Point type, 343
pointing, **8**
points. *See* Anchor Points
points (pt)
as default unit of measure, 224
as unit of measure, 159–160
Polygon dialog box, 65
Polygon tool, illustrated, **65**
polygons, 65–66
pop-out menus, 40
pop-up menus
for palettes, 40
selecting, 38
pop-up tools, 44–45
Portrait orientation (Separations Setup dialog box), 723
Portrait with Transverse checked orientation (Separations Setup dialog box), 723
PostScript
EPS files
preview options for, 203–204
saving, 203
saving previews as, 905
fonts, **12–13**
measurements in, 158
opening PPD files, 720–721
outlines, 17–18
printing, **16–20**
advantages of, 19–20
development of, 16–17
problems printing long paths, 181–183
tracing images, 60
PPD (PostScript Printer Description) files
adding halftone screens to, 727
opening, 720–721
preferences
customizing, 212–213
for guides & grids, 227
for Plug-Ins folder and scratch disk location, 227
setting for guides, 167–168
setting with General Preferences dialog box, 215–224
for tool behavior, 216–218
for units of measurement and Undos, 224–227
prepress work
preparing for printing, 701–706
savings using Illustrator, 728–729
preset gradients, 453
pressure-sensitive tablets, **109**
preventing curved tips, 125–126
Preview & Print Patterns option (Document Setup dialog box), 180, 465
Preview checkbox (Zig Zag dialog box), 534
Preview mode, 189–193
applying Fill in, 21
applying patterns to Fill and Stroke, 465

(continued)

Preview mode *(continued)*
basics of, **36–37**
choosing, 191
combining Artwork and, 192–193
overlapping holes in, 393
paths visible in, 21
selecting paths in, 37
switching views, 50
viewing Fill in, 22, 74–75
preview options for Illustrator EPS files, 203–204
Preview Selection mode, 192
primitive shapes, 757–760
Print Detailed Report option (Print Options dialog box), 709
Print dialog box (Macintosh), 707
Print dialog box (Windows), 708
Print Options dialog box, 709
Print Setup command (Windows), 706–711
Print Setup dialog box (Windows), 707
Print Setup (Windows), 706–711
printing color images on black-and-white printers, 710–711
printing composites, 706–710
printer output, 427–430
printers
avoiding patterns used as Stroke, 465
compatible gradient printing and, 183
fonts for, **12**
printing color images on black-and-white, 710–711
resolution
advantages of PostScript images, 17–19
maintaining quality and scaling objects, 19–20
selecting for separations, 720–721
printing, 168–172, 701–739
advantages with Dimensions, 750
Anchor Points and Control Handles, 24
avoiding banding, 428–429
basics of PostScript, **16–20**
blank pages, 907
calculating steps for blends, 427, 429–430, 445
composites, 706–710
creating
cropmarks, 169–171
Japanese cropmarks and trim marks, 171–172
stepped artwork, 168–169, 170
device pixels, 21
documents with gradient, 183
image area of Artboard and, 42
layering
hidden, 707
turning off for, 152
masks, 404–405
multiple pages, 180–181
overprinting, 37, 509–510
patterns, 478
preparing for printing, 701–706
Document Setup command, 702–703
Page Setup command (Macintosh), 703–706
Print Setup command (Windows), 706–711
problems with long paths, 181–183
saving before, 710
separations, 730
combining spot and process color, 717–718
from other applications, 730–731
for process color, 713–716
Separation Setup command, 718–730
for spot color, 711, 713
touring print shops and service bureaus, 712
trapping, 731–738
about, 731–732
complex, 737–738
manual, 735–736
setting values for, 734–735
with Trap command, 736–737
uses for, 733–734
troubleshooting, 905
printing separations, 730
process colors
indicators for, 84–85
selecting for separations, 729–730
separations
about, **713–716**
combining spot and process colors, 717–718
of, 713–714
tint control and, 79
See also CMYK colors; spot color
Process to Grayscale filter (CSI), 607
projected cap, **76**

pseudolinear blends, 424–425
Publish and Subscribe options (Macintosh), 206–207
punctuation, 333–335
Punk and Bloat dialog box, 529
Punk and Bloat filter, 527–529

• Q •

QuarkXpress
- Artboard drawing area and, 179
- converting tracking and kerning values to, 369
- trapping with, 734

QuickDraw GX, 906
quotation marks, 334

• R •

radar graph
- new feature, in Windows, 843
- as new Macintosh feature, 825

radial blends, 430–431
railroad-track look, 688, 690–691
RAM. *See* memory
random mangle filters, 535–542
- Roughen filter, 535–539
- Scribble and Tweak filter, 539–542

randomizing
- color with VectorColorRandomize filter, 589
- with Roughen filter, 535

raster images, 559–573
- changing Illustrator pixel art to, 560–561
- colorizing one-bit TIFF images, 563–564
- creating with Rasterize command (Windows), 839
- masking, 401
- rasterizing Object Mosaic objects, 517

Rasterize command, as new feature in Windows, 839
realistic effects
- for glows, 448
- with shape blends, 438–443

reapplying last filter, 507
Rectangle dialog box, 52, 57
Rectangle type, 344–345
rectangles
- creating basic drop shadow box, 53
- drawing, 50–54
- measuring with, 161
- rounded, 54–57
- rounding corners backward, 57–58
- transforming into cropmarks, 171
- using Round Corners filter with, 57

Redo command
- basics of, **33–34**
- new features in Windows, 840

redrawing in Preview mode, 191
Reflect Each filter (CSI), 610, 611
Reflect tool
- making tile with, 289–290
- rotating objects with, 779
- transforming objects with, 276–277

reflectance. *See* shading and reflectance
Reflectance settings (Surface Properties palette), 763–765
reflections
- blending shapes for surface, 442–443
- creating muted, 439–441
- reusing blends for, 440

Release Wrap command, 320
releasing
- compound paths, 392
- cropmarks, 171
- guides, 167
- masks, 403–404
- text wraps, 320

rendering artwork (Dimensions), 760–761
Repeat Pathfinder function, 258
Repeated Character Processing option (Paragraph palette), 313, 377
resetting
- horizontal scale, 370
- tools in toolbox, 45

Reshape tool
- icon for, 270
- refining artwork with, 269

reshaping curved points, 269–270
Resize and Reposition filter (KPT Vector Effects), 626
resolution
- maintaining quality and scaling objects, 19–20
- of PostScript images, 17–19
- scanning art and, 801–802

resources
  books on FreeHand, 914
  books on Illustrator, 912–914
  people and companies, 909–912
reversed type on path, 357–358
reversing path directions, 397–398
Revert command, 201
revolving artwork, 773–775
RGB colors
  inverting colors for, 509
  new feature
    in Macintosh, 824
    in Windows, 841
  setting with Color palette, 87–88
Right indent option (Paragraph palette), 313
right mouse button (Windows), 10
Rotate dialog box, 275
Rotate palette (Dimensions), 780
Rotate tool
  spinning paths with, 438
  transforming objects with, 274–275
rotating
  direction of type, 384–386
  grids, 164
  guides, 166
  objects
    into a path, 288–289
    into kaleidoscopes, 292
  textures, 495
  with Transform Each dialog box, 283
Rotation option (Transform palette), 281
Roughen dialog box, 69–70, 536, 537
Roughen filter, 535–539
  about, 504
  Add Anchor Points filter and, 536
  adding Anchor Points with, 238–239, 240, 436, 536, 539
Round Corners dialog box, 549
Round Corners filter, 57, 548–549
rounded cap, **76**, 108
rounded joins, 95, 108
rounded rectangles, 548
rows, aligning type in, 335–338
Rows & Columns dialog box, 335
rows and columns
  angled, 337–338
  creating for nonrectangular, 336–337
rulers
  changing origins for, 160, 161, 194
  measuring with, 160
  shortcuts for, 157–158
  showing and hiding, 193–194

• S •

S curves, 124–125
Same Fill Color command, 294–295
Same Paint Style command, 295–296
Same Stroke Color command, 296
Same Stroke Weight command, 296
Saturate dialog box, 511
Saturate filter, 510–511
Save a Copy command, 200–201
Save As command, 200
Save command, 197–200
saving
  files, **197–204**
    compatibility of Illustrator file formats, 201–202
    exporting files, 204
    file types and, 201
    as Illustrator EPS, 203
    Illustrator EPS preview options, 203–204
    reverting to last saved version, 201
    with Save a Copy command, 200–201
    with Save As command, 200
    with Save command, 197–200
    when to save, 199–200
  money on prepress work, 728–729
  printing and, 710
  2D artwork, 769
  Undo command and, 34
Scale dialog box, 276
Scale Line Weight option (General Preferences dialog box), 222
Scale palette, 778
Scale to Dimension filter (CSI), 610–612
Scale to Fit Page filter (CSI), 612
Scale tool
  transforming objects with, 275–276
  vs. Offset Path feature, 248
scaling
  hatch style for textures, 497
  objects, 19–20

Stroke weight and, 222
with Transform Each dialog box, 283
vs. offsetting, 248
scanning art, 801–802
scatter graphs, 487
Scissors tool
about, **237**
splitting paths and, 242–243
scratch disks, 227
screen fonts, **12–13**
Scribble and Tweak dialog box, 541
Scribble and Tweak filter, 539–542
scrolling
with Hand tool, 188–189
using scroll bars, **43**, 187–188
with VectorNavigator, 189
SDK (Software Developer's Kit), 646–647
segments
drawing semistraight, 113–114
moving, 279–280
verifying selection of, 142
Select Colors filter (CSI), 605
Select commands, 293–299
about, 293–294
Custom Paint Style Selections command, 297
Same Fill Color command, 294–295
Same Paint Style, 295–296
Same Stroke Color command, 296
Same Stroke Weight command, 296
Select Inverse command, 297–298
Select Masks command, 298
Select Stray Points command, 298–299
Select Placed Art filter (CSI), 606
Select Similar filter (CSI), 606–607
Select Strokes filter (CSI), 606
Select submenu, 293–294
Select Text filter (CSI), 606
selecting
all guides, 167
Anchor Points, 298–299
color, 82–83, 92, 294–295, 297
for Fill and Stroke, 87–89
compound paths, 37
Fill and Stroke icons, 78–79
fonts, 14
hatch style, 492
hidden Strokes, 678
layers, 298
opposite points of end points, 416, 417
paths, 190–191, 293–299
adding points and, 239
by colors, 92
by Fill and Stroke, 297
by Fill color, 294–295
by paint style, 295–296
by Stroke color, 296
by Stroke weight, 296
entire, 139–140
with Intersect and Exclude commands, 261
masks, 298
minus front or back paths, 262
moving, and deleting, 139–142
multiple paths with Shift key, 140
objects not selected, 297–298
portions of, 141–142
in Preview mode, 37
stray points, 298–299
pop-up menus, 38
positive or negative images, 729
Preview mode, 191
shapes for Area type, 346
spot and process colors for separation, 729–730
Stroke, 93
Stroke on blended paths, 679
tools, 44
type, 358–360
Selection tools, 133–139
choosing from keyboard, 137
Direct Selection tool, 137–138
Group Selection tool, 138–139
Selection tool, 137
shortcuts, 137, 863–864, 885–886
types of selections, 134–136
group, 135
InterGroup, 136
InterPath, 134
path, 135
Send Backwards command, 826, 843
Separation Setup command, 718–730
adding custom line screens, 727
bounding box and bleed, 719–720

(continued)

Separation Setup command (continued)
changing
orientation settings, 722–723
page size, 721–722
printer information, 720–721
choosing positive or negative images, 729
printing separations, 730
saving money on prepress work, 728–729
selecting process and spot colors, 729–730
setting up
halftone line screens, 725–726
halftone screen, 724
understanding emulsion, 724
separations, 711–718
about process color, **713–716**
choosing positive or negative images, 729
combining spot and process separations, 717–718
cropmarks and, 170–172
printing, 730
from other applications, 730–731
process color, 713–714
saving money on, 728–729
spot color, 711, 713
understanding emulsion, 724
Separations dialog box (Windows), 839
Separations Setup dialog box, 719
Separator (Illustrator 5.0)
demise of, 718
uses for, 717
service bureaus
services offered by, 712
trapping and, 738
Seurat-like illustrations, 519, 520
shading and reflectance, 761–769
Lighting palette, 766–767
Reflectance (Surface Properties palette), 763–765
Surface Properties palette, 761–763
ShadowLand filter (KPT Vector Effects), 627–628
compound blending with, 392
creating extruded multiple path objects, 513
RAM required for filters, 820
shadows
airbrushed, 446–447
creating, **286–287**
drop shadows, 53, 547–548
with gradients, 458
highlights and, 511–512
effects with KPT ShadowLand, 627–628
Illustrator shadows in Dimensions, 458–459
shape blends, 431–443
blending circle to star, 433–435
changing angle of straight lines and, 432–433
complex, 435–436
creating complex shape blends by cheating, 436–438
creating realism with, 438–443
muted reflective surfaces in type, 439–441
surface blending, 442–443
Shape tools, shortcuts, 867–869, 889–891
shapes, 47–99
choosing for Area type, 346
creating
at an angle, 73
bump curves, 122–123
ellipses and circles, 58–64
moving shapes, 47, 49–50
polygons, 65–66
rectangles, 50–53
rectangles from their centers, 53–54
rounded rectangles and squares, 54–57
rounding corners backward, 57–58
spirals, 71–73
squares, 54
stars, 66–71
using Round Corners filter, 57
drawing
infinity shape, 130, 132
S curves, 124–125
Eyedropper and Paintbucket tools, 97–98
Fill and Stroke
adding Fills, **74–75**
adding Strokes, **75–76**
applying, 78–79, 81
caps, 94
choosing and mixing colors, 87–89
Color Ramps, 90–91
combining Strokes and Fills, 77
dashes, **95–96**
joins, 94–95
Out of Gamut indicator, 91

selecting colors for paths, 92
selecting Strokes, 93
spot colors, 91–92
Stroke weight, 75, 93
swatch and colorspace indicators, 84–85
Swatch Libraries submenu, 85–86
using Swatches palette, 81–84
ShatterBox filter (KPT Vector Effects), 628–630, 820
Shear dialog box, 278
Shear option (Transform palette), 281
Shear tool, 277–278
Shift key
aligning spirals with, 72
constrain angles and, 121
deselecting paths with, 138–139
selecting
characters with insertion point and, 360
multiple paths with, 140
for Windows platform, **10**
shortcuts, 859–880, 881–902
accessing Pencil, Paintbrush, and Pen tools, 101
adjusting arrow buttons from keyboard, 363
for Adobe Dimension, 745
for baseline shift, 357
Blend/Auto Trace/Graph tools, 871, 893
changing point size, 312
character formatting, 875–876, 897–898
Color palette, 876, 898
for Edit menu, 859–860, 882
enabling version 7, 221
for Files menu, 859, 881
Filter menu, 861, 883
generic dialog box commands, 880, 902
Gradient palette, 877–878, 899
for Group Selection tool, 149
key commands as, **38**
for KPT Vector Distort filter, 632–633
Layers palette, 879, 901
Measure/Paint tools, 872, 894
miscellaneous, 880, 902
for Object menu, 860–861, 882–883
for palette commands, 878, 900–901
paragraph formatting, 875, 897
Path tools, 864–865, 886–887
resetting horizontal scale, 370
for rulers, 157–158
for Selection tools, 137, 863–864, 885–886
Shape tools, 867–869, 889–891
Stroke palette, 900
Swatches palette, 877, 899
toolbox commands, 863, 885
for tools, 83, 862–876, 885–898
Transform palette, 879, 901
Transformation tools, 869–871, 891–893
troubleshooting, 908
for Type menu, 861, 883
Type shortcuts, 874, 896
Type tools, 866–867, 888–889
using, 38
using Command key for, **9**
for VectorTools, 580
View menu, 861–862, 883–884
viewing shortcuts, 873, 895
viewing tools, 873, 894–895
Window menu, 861–862, 884
Show Attributes command, 397–398
Show Clipboard command, 32–33
Show Guides command, 194
Show Page Tiling command, 194
Show Placed EPS Artwork option (Document Setup dialog box), 181
Show Rulers command, 193–194
Show Tool Tips option (General Preferences dialog box), 222
Single full page option (Document Setup dialog box), 181
size
changing for primitives, 759, 760
changing type, 364–365
creating type of any, 311
Size command, 311–312
Size dialog box (Dimensions), 760
Size option (Character palette), 313, 362
Size/Leading option (Units and Undo Preferences dialog box), 225
Sketch filter (KPT Vector Effects), 630–631
sketch filters (third-party Photoshop), 571

Slicing function vs. Knife tool, 245
Smart Punctuation dialog box, 334
Smart Punctuation filter, 333–335
Smooth Paths option (Streamline), 742
Smooth Points, 24
  changing to Combination Corner Points, 132, 253
  converting, 253–254
  Curved Corner Points and, 130, 254
  effect of Roughen filter on, 535–536
  Round Corners filter and, 548
  using Pen tool with, 119
smoothing paths, 114–116, 435
Snap to Point option (General Preferences dialog box), 219
Soft and Hard commands, 266–267
softening edges of Stroke blends, 449
software applications
  development of third-party filters, 596
  for extruding and revolving, 755–756
  other 3D applications and Adobe Dimensions, 749–750
  See also plug-ins; third-party filters; *and applications listed individually*
Software FPU, 819
Space before paragraph option (Paragraph palette), 313
spacebar, 72
spacing
  before paragraphs, 374
  of grids, 163–164
  for Path type, 356–357
  Smart Punctuation filter and, 334–335
  within paragraphs, 375
Spaz function, 66, 67
special characters
  for Macintosh platform, 377–379
  for Windows, 379–381
speeding up Artwork mode, 35
spelling
  checking, 330–332
  Create Outlines command and, 321
Sphere dialog box (Dimensions), 759
spin controls, illustrated, 40
Spiral dialog box, 73
spirals, 71–73
spirographs, 291
Split long paths option (Document Setup dialog box), 181–183
splitting paths, 181–183, 242–243
spot colors, **91–92**
  combining in separations with process color, 717–718
  indicators for, 84–85
  selecting for separations, 729–730
  separation of, 711, 713
  trapping with, 732
  troubleshooting Pantone colors, 904–905
  See also process colors
spread, 732, 733
spring-tube blends, 445–446
squares
  creating, 54
  measuring with, 161
  pattern tiles and, 472
  rounded, 54–57
  rounding corners backward, 57–58
stacked-column graphs, 484
stacking order for paths, 144–146
stars
  blending circle to, 433–435
  creating, 66–71
Startup file. *See* Adobe Illustrator Startup file
status bar, 43
Step and Repeat filter (CSI), 612–614
stepped artwork
  creating grid with CSI Socket Set 2, 612–614
  in Illustrator, 168–169, 170
stories, **310**
Straight Corner Points, **24**
  converting, 253, 254–255
  using Pen tool with, 119
  See also Corner Points
straight joins, 108
Streamline. *See* Adobe Streamline
Stroke, 675–700
  adding
    to shapes, **75–76**
    to Type 3 fonts, 13
  applying
    to paths, 22–23
    to paths in Preview mode, 21
    patterns in Preview mode, 465
    to shapes, 78–79, 81
  cap style, 94
  changing weight for, 75, 93

choosing and mixing
colors for, 87–89
combining with Fill, 77
compared with Fills, 677
creating
parallel strokes, 676–679
a river, 692, 693
rough edges,
686–688, 689
a strip of film, 684–685
dash patterns for, **76**
Divide and Outline
commands with
color, 265
and Fill
to create half-stroked
paths, 688
with gradient, 459
masking objects with,
402–404
Fill & Stroke for Mask
filter, 298, 514–515
highway design, 692–693,
694–698
masking outside edge
of, 690
outlining
areas for Area type,
346–348
paths, 247–248
paintbrush strokes
and, 104
Path Patterns filter
and, 699
railroad-track look, 688,
690–691
scaling and weight of, 222
selecting, 93
colors for paths, 92
hidden, 678
paths by color of, 296
paths by weight of, 296
setting for trapping, 736
shortcut keys for swap-
ping with Fill, 833
Stroke charts, 679–684
type, 684–686
type as Stroke pattern,
698–699
using Pathfinders options
with, 268
wrapping text and, 318
See also Fill; paths
Stroke blends, 443–451
airbrushed shadows,
446–447
backlighting, 451
calculating number of
printing steps, 445
creating
spring-tube blends,
445–446
tubular blends, 443–445
glows, 448–449
neon effects, 450–451
softening edges of, 449
Stroke charts, 679–684
Stroke icon, 80
color of, 81
selecting, 78–79
Stroke palette, 80
illustrated, **93**, 828
new features
in Macintosh, 830
in Windows, 844, 853
shortcuts, 900
Style option (Character
palette), 313
style sheets (VectorObject
Styles), 592
stylize filters, 542–557
Add Arrowheads filter,
542–546
Calligraphy filter, 550–551
Drop Shadow filter,
547–548
Path Patterns with,
551–557
creating corners for,
555–556
creating tube patterns
for, 553–554
using, 551–553
Round Corners filter,
548–549
suites, 648
sunken images, 456
sunsets, 802–804
Surface Properties palette
(Dimensions), 761–763
surface reflections, 442–443
Swatch Libraries com-
mand, 196
Swatch Libraries submenu,
85–86
Swatch Options dialog box,
82, 83
swatches
about the Swatches
palette, 81–84
adding to Adobe Illustra-
tor Startup file, 906
deleting, 83–84
indicators for, 84–85
Name view mode for,
82, 95
Swatches palette, 80
about, 833
illustrated, **82**, 829
Name view mode for,
82, 95
new features
in Macintosh, 830
in Windows, 844
selecting patterns on,
466, 467
shortcuts, 877, 899
using, 81–84
Web colors on, 667–668
Swatches palette pop-up
menu, 84
symmetrical patterns,
472–474
symmetrical textures, 496

system requirements
for Macintosh, 817–818
processors, 819
RAM, 820
processors, Adobe Dimensions and, 748
virtual memory disk space requirements, 198
for Windows, 821

• T •

Tab Ruler palette, 314–316
graphical tabs, 316
tabbing and docking palettes, 40
tabs
adjusting Tab Ruler for vertical type, 383–384
graphical, 316
new features in Windows, 840
setting, 314–316
TeachText file format, 208
techniques
for Pen tool, 117–120, 126–129, 133
for Pencil tool, 110–112
for zooming, 184–187
templates, 152–154, 833
dimming images for, 153–154
new features, 152–153
in Macintosh, 832
in Windows, 854–855
turning printing off for, 152
See also tracing
text
adding tabs to, 314–316
adjusting leading, 366–367
applying color to, 92, 906
blank fields in palettes, 359
Calligraphy filter and, 550
copying, cutting, and pasting, 32
default type and styles for, 343
embossing, 456
exporting, 382
finding and changing, 328–330
fitting headlines, 320
greeking options, 226–227
kerning and tracking, 367–369, 383–384
linking, 316–318
scaling vs. offsetting, 248
setting
baseline shift options, 225
hyphenation preferences for, 227
tracking options, 226
unlinking, 318
upside-down, 77
using with Free Distort filter, 525
Vertigo 3D Words with, 638–641
wrapping and unwrapping, 318–320
text fields
adjusting, 89
in Character palette, 363
entering information in, 364
illustrated, 40
in Transform palette, 281
texture filters (third-party Photoshop), 572
textures, 491–498
Fade to White option for, 497–498
rotation controls for, 495
scaling hatch style for, 497
setting
density for Ink Pen, 493, 494
dispersion patterns, 493–495
thickness for, 495
using
in backgrounds, 804–805
Ink Pen, 491–492
texturizing blends, 804–805
thickness settings for textures, 495
third-party filters, 506, 596–659
Alien Skin Stylist, 597, 641–642
BeInfinite Infinite FX, 596, 599–601
IFX filter theory, 600
IFX filters, 600–601
creating plug-ins for Illustrator, 646–650
Illustrator API and SDK, 646–647
plug-in types, 648
suites, 648
wishlist for plug-ins, 649–650
CSI Socket Set 1, 601–607
CSI Adjust Colors filter, 603–604
CSI Adjust Stroke filter, 604
CSI AI Plug-In Manager, 602–603
CSI AI Startup Manager, 603
CSI Process to Grayscale filter, 607
CSI Select Colors filter, 605
CSI Select Placed Art filter, 606
CSI Select Similar filter, 606–607
CSI Select Strokes filter, 606
CSI Select Text filter, 606

CSI Socket Set 2, 607–614
CSI Align and Distribute filter, 608, 609
CSI Align Edges filter, 608, 609
CSI Align to Guide filter, 609–610
CSI Patterns to Paths filter, 610
CSI Reflect Each filter, 610, 611
CSI Scale to Dimension filter, 610–612
CSI Scale to Fit Page filter, 612
CSI Step and Repeat filter, 612–614
development of, 596
fun plug-ins on CD-ROM, 650–658
Analog Clock, 654–656
Arrow tool, 657, 658
BeInfinite Smart Remove Points filter, 652
Doodle Jr., 597, 653
KPT Gradients/Patterns to Paths, 651
Melt & Drip filters, 651–652
Point and delete tool, 657, 658
HotDoor CADtools 1.0, 634–638
installing and using, 598–599
Kara Fonts, 643–645
KPT Vector Effects, 614–634
ColorTweak filter, 619–621
Emboss filter, 621–622
Flare filter, 622–624
Inset filter, 624, 625
interface characteristics of, 615–616
KPT 3D Transform filter, 617–619
Neon filter, 624–625
Point Editor filter, 626
Resize and Reposition filter, 626
ShadowLand filter, 392, 513, 627–628, 820
ShatterBox, 628–630
Sketch filter, 630–631
Vector Distort filter, 631–633
Warp Frame filter, 633–634
LetraSet Envelopes, 642–643
MAPublisher 2.0, 643
overview of, 596–598
for Photoshop, 566
art filters, 567
blur filters, 567
brush stroke filters, 568
distort filters, 569
pixelate filters, 569–570
sketch filters, 571
texture filters, 572
Vertigo 3D Words, 638–641
3D artwork, 776–781
Adobe Dimensions, 747–750
adjusting shading and reflectance, 761–769
advantages with printing, 750
creating primitive shapes, 757–760
features of, 747–748
history of development, 748
other 3D applications and, 749–750
processing speed and, 748
rendering artwork, 760–761
2D and 3D tools, 753–757
applying 3D effects (VectorShape), 590–591
concepts, 751–753
changing from 2D to 3D, 751
3D positioning, 752–753
moving objects in, 776–777
rotating objects, 779–781
scaling, 778–779
3D techniques, 786–790
creating 3D object in Illustrator, 786–789
using gradients for bumps and dents, 790
3D toolbox (Dimensions), 754, 755–756
3D Transform filter (KPT Vector Effects), 617–619
using gradients for bumps and dents, 790
views and perspectives, 781–784
Thunder Lizard Productions, 7
TIFF formats, 206
TIFF images, 563–564
tilde (~) key
duplicating spirals with, 72
Spaz function and, 66, 67
transforming patterns with, 273, 293
Tile full pages option (Document Setup dialog box), 181
Tile Imageable areas option (Document Setup dialog box), **181**, 180
tile patterns, 462

tiling
  comparison with images in pixels, 518
  creating
    corner tiles for Path Patterns, 556
    tiled roof, 519–522
  defined, **42**
  making tile with Reflect tool, 289–290
  memory requirements for, 517
  overlapping tiles with no white space, 522–523
  printing
    blank pages, 907
    documents and, 702–703
  showing and hiding page, 194
  using tile and stack options for 2D artwork, 769
tinting
  process colors, 79
  setting with Color palette, 88
tips
  for customizing toolbars, 584–585
  for discovering new features, 806–807
  for layering, 306
  for learning Adobe Illustrator, 6–8
  for using new features
    Macintosh, 833–835
    Windows, 855–857
  for using type, 386–387
  for Web page heading design, 671
  when to save files, 199–200
title bars, 43
toolbox
  basics of, **43–45**
  Dimensions 2D, 754, 756–757
  Dimensions 3D, 754, 755–756
  illustrated, 44
  Paint Style section of, 78
  placing, 229
  reorganizing
    in Macintosh, 829–830
    in Windows, 852
  resetting tools in, 45
  shortcuts for commands, 863, 885
  for Streamline, 743–745
tools
  Adobe Dimensions, 753–757
  arrows for Selection, 134
  creating for plug-ins, 648
  customizing, 216–218
    Auto Trace Gap option, 218
    Constrain Angle option, 216–217
    Corner Radius option, 217
    Curve Fitting Tolerance option, 217
    toolbars with VectorBars, 582–585
  dragging off edge of window, 105
  for drawing paths, 101–102
  for editing, 237–238
  keyboard shortcuts for, 834
  new features in Windows, 846–847
  organization of in Version 7, 65
  shortcuts
    Macintosh, 862–876
    Windows, 885–898
  transformation, 272–274
  type controls (Windows platform), 310
  See also shortcuts
tracing, 154–155
  about, **154**, 154
  automatic and manual, 155
  EPS images, 60
  images, 801
  layering and, 156
  with Streamline, 155–156
  as Windows feature, 152
  See also grids and guides
trackballs, 105
tracking
  about kerning and, **367–369**
  setting increments for, 226
Tracking option (Character palette), 313, 362
Tracking option (Units and Undo Preferences dialog box), 226
Transform Again command, 286
Transform Each dialog box new features in Windows, 840
  refining artwork and, 283–285
Transform Each filter, 438
Transform palette
  illustrated, 828
  measuring distances and, **158–159**
  new features
    in Macintosh, 830
    in Windows, 844–845, 853
  refining artwork with, 280–282
  shortcuts, 879, 901
Transform Pattern Tiles option (General Preferences dialog box), 219

Transformation
submenu, 274
Transformation tools
shortcuts, 869–871,
891–893
using with Area type,
348–349
transforming
objects, 272–280
about transformation
tools, 272–274
creating shadows,
286–287
gradients, 287–288
making tile with Reflect
tool, 289–290
moving points, seg-
ments, and paths,
279–280
patterns, 293
on portion of paths,
290–291
Reflect tool, 276–277
Rotate tool, 274–275
rotating
objects into a path,
288–289
objects into kaleido-
scopes, 292
Scale tool, 275–276
Shear tool, 277–278
patterns, 293, 478–479
with tilde (~) key,
273, 293
transparent fill and
stroke, 23
transparent patterns,
462, 477
Trap command, 267–269,
736–737
trapping, 731–738
about, **731–732**
complex, 737–738
duplicating artwork
before, 738
manual, 735–736
setting values for,
734–735
with Trap command,
736–737
uses for, 267–269, 733–734
triangles, 38
Trim command, 265
trim marks, 171–172
trimming blends, 265
troubleshooting, 903–908
TrueType fonts, **14**
Adobe Type Manager
and, 15
Create Outlines command
and, 320
tubes
blends for, 443–445
blends for spring-tube,
445–446
creating in Illustrator,
788–789
neon, 450–451
tips for realistic
colors, 445
tubular blends, 443–445
tutorial
on CD-ROM, 8
using PDF files, 814–816
Twirl filter, 530–533
creating arced illustra-
tions with Free Distort
filter and, 532–533
using, 531–532
Twirl tool, using, 270–271
2D artwork, 768
changing to 3D, 751
revolving artwork,
773–775
extruding, 769–775
by revolving, 774–775
extruding flat art,
770–771
understanding bevels,
771–773
mapping on 3D surfaces,
785–786
modifying, 768
previewing, 769
saving, 769
using
Illustrator artwork, 768
tile and stack
options, 769
2D toolbox (Dimensions),
754, 756–757
type, 309–388
aligning in rows and
columns, 335–338
anti-aliased, 361
Area type, 345–352
changing area of,
350–351
choosing shapes for, 346
creative uses for,
351–352
outlining areas for,
346–348
using transformation
tools with, 348–349
areas of, 338–339
changing direction of,
384–386
checking
punctuation, 333–335
spelling, 330–332
context-sensitive menus
when selecting, 918
customizing fonts,
381–382
defining type areas,
338–339
editing, 360–361
finding and changing,
328–330, 333
case, 333
Find Font dialog
box, 330
text, 329–330
ghosted, 684–686

(continued)

type (continued)
hinting and Type 1 fonts, 328
making into Stroke pattern, 698–699
new features in Windows, 839
paragraphs, 370–377
aligning, 373–374
hang punctuation for, 375–376
hyphenating, 376–377
indenting, 374
outlining type, 371–372
space before, 374
spacing within, 375
Path, 353–358
avoiding spacing problems for, 356–357
creating reversed, 357–358
type on a circle, 354–356
placing Stroked type on, 699
Point, 343
Rectangle, 344–345
selecting, 358–360
setting character attributes for, 362–370
Character palette, 362–363
font and style changes, 363–364
kerning and tracking, 367–369, 383–384
Language and multinational options, 370
leading, 366–367
measuring, 365
size changes, 364–365
vertical and horizontal scale, 370
size, decreasing and increasing, 225
special characters
Macintosh, 377–379
Windows, 379–381
tips for using, 386–387
Type menu items, 310–321
Character command, 312
Create Outlines command, 320–321
Fit Headline command, 320
Font command, 311
graphical tabs, 316
Links Blocks command, 316–318
Make Wrap command, 318–320
MM design command, 314
Paragraph command, 312, 314
Release Wrap command, 320
Size command, 311–312
Tab Ruler palette, 314–316
Unlink Blocks command, 318
type outlines, 322–328
avoiding font conflicts with, 327–328
creating logos from, 324–325
distorting words and phrases, 325–326
hinting and, 328
masking and filling, 326–327
using type tools, 339–342
about, 339–340
Area Type tool, 341
Path Type tool, 341
the Type tool, 340–341
Vertical Type tool, 341–342
vertical, as new feature, 825, 843
working with Stroke, 684–686
Type 1 fonts, 13
Create Outlines command and, 320
hinting and, 328
Type 3 fonts, 13
patterns as masked, 478
type color vs. color of type, 350–351
type cursor, 359
Type menu
illustrated, 311
items, 310–321
Character command, 312
Create Outlines command, 320–321
Fit Headline command, 320
Font command, 311
graphical tabs, 316
Links Blocks command, 316–318
Make Wrap command, 318–320
MM design command, 314
Paragraph command, 312, 314
Release Wrap command, 320
Size command, 311–312
Tab Ruler palette, 314–316
Unlink Blocks command, 318
shortcuts, 861, 883
type outlines, 322–328
avoiding font conflicts with, 327–328
creating logos from, 324–325

distorting words and phrases, 325–326
hinting and, 328
masking and filling, 326–327
Type shortcuts, 874, 896
type size, 225
Type tools, 339–342
about, 339–340
Area Type tool, 340, 341
changing case and, 333
Path Type tool, 340, 341
shortcuts, 866–867, 888–889
the Type tool, 340–341
Vertical Type tool, 340, 341–342
typefaces
compound paths and, 394–395
converting to outlines, 328
symbol (Macintosh), 379
types
ascenders and descenders, 365
converted to outlines, 904
of graphs, 483–488
paragraph formatting, shortcuts, 875, 897

• U •

Undo Settings option (Units and Undo Preferences dialog box), 227
Undos
basics of Undo command, **33–34**
of filters in Illustrator, 564
new features in Windows, 840
with Punk and Bloat filter, 527
Revert command and, 201
saving and, 34
scrolling and, 188
setting number of, 227
Ungroup command, joining paths of different groups, 250
ungrouping objects, **148**
unit of measure. *See* measurements
Unite command, 259–260
creating compound paths with, 398–399
features of, 261
using with type, 323
Unite filter, adjusting overlapping paths, 105–106
Units and Undo Preferences dialog box, 224–227
Baseline Shift option, 225
Cursor Key option, 225
Greek Text Limit option, 226–227
Size/Leading option, 225
Tracking option, 226
Undo Settings option, 227
Unlink Blocks command, 318
unlocking guides, 166–167
Untitled Art command, 196
URLs
assigning to objects, **668–669**, 144
embedding
in Macintosh, 824
support for in PDF documents, 673
in Windows, 841
Use Precise Cursors options (General Preferences dialog box), 219–220
Use Printer Default Screens checkbox (Document Setup dialog box), 183
user feedback, 282

• V •

Vector Distort filter (KPT Vector Effects), 631–633
Vector Effects. *See* KPT Vector Effects
VectorBars (VectorTools)
about, **577**
creating buttons for menu commands, 39
customizing toolbars with, 582–585
illustrated, 583
VectorColor palette (VectorTools), 588
VectorColor (VectorTools)
about, **578**
adding color controls with, 587–589
advantages of, 507
using Edit Curves button in, 590
VectorFrame palette (VectorTools), 580
VectorFrame SE, installing and using, **816**, 579
VectorFrame (VectorTools)
about, **578**
framing several placed images, 580–582
Illustrator API and, 647
installing and using VectorFrame SE, **816**, 579
viewing bounding box with, 468
VectorLibrary palette (VectorTools), 587

VectorLibrary
  about, **577**
  Illustrator API and, 647
  storing objects in, 586–587
VectorMagicWand palette, **586**
VectorMagicWand
  about, **577**
  adding tolerance to attributes, 585–586
  adjusting attributes with, 585–586
  Illustrator API and, 647
  selecting paint styles with, 296
VectorNavigator palette, 593
VectorNavigator
  about, **578**
  features of, 593–594
  Illustrator API and, 647
  locating art with, 41
  scrolling with, 189
VectorObjectStyles palette, 592
VectorObjectStyles
  about, **577**
  adding style sheets with, 592
  Illustrator API and, 647
vectors vs. pixel-based images, 559–564
  advantages of vectors, 562
  changing Illustrator art to pixels, **560–561**
  colorizing one-bit TIFF images, 563–564
  pasting paths in Photoshop as pixels, 562–563
VectorShape palette, 590
VectorShape
  about, **578**
  applying 3D effects to art, 590–591
  Free Distort filter and, 525
VectorTips (VectorTools)
  about, **578**
  illustrated, 594
VectorTools, 575–594, 597, 834
  on CD-ROM, 575
  components of, **577–578**
  Illustrator API and, 647
  using, 579–580
  VectorBars
    about, 577
    creating buttons for menu commands, 39
    customizing toolbars with, 582–585
  VectorColor
    about, 578
    adding color controls with, 587–589
    using Edit Curves button in, 590
  VectorFrame
    about, 578
    framing several placed images, 580–582
  VectorFrame SE, installing and using, 579, 816
  VectorLibrary
    about, 577
    storing objects in, 586–587
  VectorMagicWand
    about, 577
    adding tolerance to attributes, 585–586
    selecting paint styles with, 296
  VectorNavigator
    about, 578
    features of, 593–594
    locating art with, 41
    scrolling with, 189
  VectorObjectStyles
    about, 577
    adding style sheets with, 592
  VectorShape
    about, 578
    applying 3D effects to art, 590–591
  VectorTips
    about, 578
    illustrated, 594
Vectorville Web site, 7
vertical percentages, 542
Vertical scale option (Character palette), 313
vertical type, 340, 370
  adjusting character attributes for, 383–384
  new feature, in Windows, 843
  as new Macintosh feature, 825
Vertical Type tool, 340, 341–342
Vertigo 3D Words, 597, 638–641
View command, 50
View menu shortcuts, 861–862, 883–884
View options (Document Setup dialog box), changing settings for, 180–181
views
  custom, **194–195**
  shortcuts for, 873, 895
  switching, 50
  switching to Fit in Window view, 187
  tool shortcuts for, 873, 894–895
virtual memory requirements, 198

• W •

W option (Transform palette), 281
warnings, disabling, 223–224, 239, 243
Warp Frame filter (KPT Vector Effects), 326, 633–634
Web graphics, 663–673
  assigning URLs to objects, **668–669**, 144
  creating
    image maps, 669
    Web page headings, 670–671
  exporting
    to GIF format, 667
    JPEG format, 664–666
    to PNG format, 667
  Illustrator support for, **663–664**
  using headings in Web pages, 672–673
  Web colors Swatches palette, 667–668
Web page headings
  creating, 670–671
  effects for, 672–673
  URL-embedding support for PDF documents, 673
  using in Web pages, 672
weight
  changing for Stroke, 75, 93
  scaling and Stroke, 222
  selecting paths by Stroke, 296
  of Stroke, 677
width
  pen, 550
  setting stroke of Paint-brush tool, 104, 106
winding numbers rule, 396–397
Window menu, 195–196
  shortcuts for, 861–862, 884
windows
  dragging tools off edge of, 105
  new document, 176
  palettes as, 40
  showing Artwork and Preview modes in separate, 193
Windows platform
  clicking for, **8**
  creating shapes with, 48
  Ctrl, Alt, and Shift keys, **10**
  customizing Illustrator, 212
  file management in, 176
  filters for, 502
  gradients, 412
  installing Illustrator, **822**
  new features, 837–857
    for fine-tuning artwork, 236
    functions and features, 837–843
    menu changes, 847–851
    in Paintbrush tool, 102
    palettes, 843–846, 853–854
    patterns, templates, and disable warnings option, 832
    printing, 702
    tips for using, 855–857
    tools, 846–847, 852
  patterns and Ink Pen filter in, 462
  Print Setup command, 706–711
  raster images on, 560
  right mouse button for, 10
  selecting menu items, 38
  shortcuts, 881–902
  special characters
    ANSI codes for hidden, 381
    keys for Zapf Dingbats, 379
  system requirements, 821
  third-party filters for, 598
  tracing, 152
  type controls and tools on, 310
  updates for Strokes, 676
  using Command key for, **9**
  VectorTools software for, 576
wishlist for plug-ins, 649–650
Word Spacing options (Paragraph palette), 313, 375
words
  distorting shape of, 325–326
  setting spacing for, 313, 375
WYSIWYG (what you see is what you get), 16–17

• X •

X key
  changing Stroke with, 79
  selecting colors with, 90
X option (Transform palette), 281

• Y •

Y option (Transform palette), 281

• Z •

Zapf Dingbats (Windows), 379
Zig Zag dialog box, 534
Zig Zag filter, 533–534
Zoom In tool, 184–185

Zoom Out tool, 185
zooming
  about, **184**
  creating custom
    views vs., 195
  shortcuts for, 873, 895
  in Streamline, 744
  techniques for, 184–187
  tools for, 184–185
  troubleshooting, 907
  Undo command and, 35
Z-translation tool (Dimensions), 776–777

IDG BOOKS WORLDWIDE LICENSE AGREEMENT

Important — read carefully before opening the software packet. This is a legal agreement between you (either an individual or an entity) and IDG Books Worldwide, Inc. (IDG). By opening the accompanying sealed packet containing the software disc, you acknowledge that you have read and accept the following IDG License Agreement. If you do not agree and do not want to be bound by the terms of this Agreement, promptly return the book and the unopened software packet(s) to the place you obtained them for a full refund.

1. License. This License Agreement (Agreement) permits you to use one copy of the enclosed Software program(s) on a single computer. The Software is in "use" on a computer when it is loaded into temporary memory (i.e., RAM) or installed into permanent memory (e.g., hard disk, CD-ROM, or other storage device) of that computer.

2. Copyright. The entire contents of this disc and the compilation of the Software are copyrighted and protected by both United States copyright laws and international treaty provisions. You may only (a) make one copy of the Software for backup or archival purposes, or (b) transfer the Software to a single hard disk, provided that you keep the original for backup or archival purposes. The individual programs on the disc are copyrighted by the authors of each program respectively. Each program has its own use permissions and limitations. To use each program, you must follow the individual requirements and restrictions detailed for each in Appendix A of this Book. Do not use a program if you do not want to follow its Licensing Agreement. None of the material on this disc or listed in this Book may ever be distributed, in original or modified form, for commercial purposes.

3. Other Restrictions. You may not rent or lease the Software. You may transfer the Software and user documentation on a permanent basis provided you retain no copies and the recipient agrees to the terms of this Agreement. You may not reverse engineer, decompile, or disassemble the Software except to the extent that the foregoing restriction is expressly prohibited by applicable law. If the Software is an update or has been updated, any transfer must include the most recent update and all prior versions. Each shareware program has its own use permissions and limitations. These limitations are contained in the individual license agreements that are on the software discs. The restrictions include a requirement that after using the program for a period of time specified in its text, the user must pay a registration fee or discontinue use. By opening the package which contains the software disc, you will be agreeing to abide by the licenses and restrictions for these programs. Do not open the software package unless you agree to be bound by the license agreements.

4. **Limited Warranty**. IDG Warrants that the Software and disc are free from defects in materials and workmanship for a period of sixty (60) days from the date of purchase of this Book. If IDG receives notification within the warranty period of defects in material or workmanship, IDG will replace the defective disc. IDG's entire liability and your exclusive remedy shall be limited to replacement of the Software, which is returned to IDG with a copy of your receipt. This Limited Warranty is void if failure of the Software has resulted from accident, abuse, or misapplication. Any replacement Software will be warranted for the remainder of the original warranty period or thirty (30) days, whichever is longer.

5. **No Other Warranties**. To the maximum extent permitted by applicable law, IDG and the author disclaim all other warranties, express or implied, including but not limited to implied warranties of merchantability and fitness for a particular purpose, with respect to the Software, the programs, the source code contained therein and/or the techniques described in this Book. This limited warranty gives you specific legal rights. You may have others which vary from state/jurisdiction to state/jurisdiction.

6. **No Liability For Consequential Damages**. To the extent permitted by applicable law, in no event shall IDG or the author be liable for any damages whatsoever (including without limitation, damages for loss of business profits, business interruption, loss of business information, or any other pecuniary loss) arising out of the use of or inability to use the Book or the Software, even if IDG has been advised of the possibility of such damages. Because some states/jurisdictions do not allow the exclusion or limitation of liability for consequential or incidental damages, the above limitation may not apply to you.

7. **U.S.Government Restricted Rights**. Use, duplication, or disclosure of the Software by the U.S. Government is subject to restrictions stated in paragraph (c) (1) (ii) of the Rights in Technical Data and Computer Software clause of DFARS 252.227-7013, and in subparagraphs (a) through (d) of the Commercial Computer — Restricted Rights clause at FAR 52.227-19, and in similar clauses in the NASA FAR supplement, when applicable.

CD-ROM Installation Instructions

The CD-ROM located inside the back cover of the book can be used on both Macintosh and Windows 95/NT systems. The CD-ROM includes an Acrobat PDF with QuickTime tutorials, product demos, and artwork featured in the color section of the book. Some files are available only for Macintosh, and some, only for Windows.

Mac-only Items

Most third-party filter demos and free plug-ins

All fonts

Windows-only Items

CADtools demo plug-in set

To Install Acrobat Reader

Macintosh: Open the Acrobat Reader folder. Double-click on the Acrobat Reader Installer icon, and follow the prompts through the installation.

Windows: Open the Acrobat Reader directory. Double-click on the Setup icon, and follow the prompts through the installation.

To Install QuickTime

Macintosh: Open the QuickTime and Helpers folder. Double-click on the QuickTime Installer icon, and follow the prompts through the installation.

Windows: Open the QuickTime directory. Double-click on the Setup icon, and follow the prompts through the installation.

To Run Tutorials

Open the tutorials folder/directory. Double-click on the IB7.pdf document. On the main tutorial screen, click on a category which corresponds to a section in the *Illustrator 7 Bible*. Click on any of the listed movies in that category. Both Acrobat Reader 3.0 and QuickTime 2.1 or later *must* be installed in order to view the CD-ROM tutorials.

To Install Fonts

Macintosh only: Open the fonts folder. Drag the folders from the CD-ROM to your System Folder. When prompted to allow your Mac to place the fonts in the Font folder, click OK. In order to see your fonts in any application, it must be started up *after* the fonts are installed.

To Install Product Demos

Macintosh: Open the product demos folder. Double-click on the folder of the product you want to install. Double-click on the Installer icon in that window. Follow the prompts during installation. After installation, double-click on the program icon to run the demo.

Windows: Open the product demos directory. Double-click on the directory of the product you want to install. Double-click on the Setup icon in that window. Follow the prompts during installation. After installation, choose that product from the Start menu.

Updates

Check the Vectorville Web site for updates to the files included on the CD-ROM: www.bezier.com/vectorville

IDG BOOKS WORLDWIDE REGISTRATION CARD

RETURN THIS REGISTRATION CARD FOR FREE CATALOG

Title of this book: Illustrator 7 Bible

My overall rating of this book: ❑ Very good [1] ❑ Good [2] ❑ Satisfactory [3] ❑ Fair [4] ❑ Poor [5]

How I first heard about this book:

❑ Found in bookstore; name: [6] ________

❑ Book review: [7] ________

❑ Advertisement: [8] ________

❑ Catalog: [9] ________

❑ Word of mouth; heard about book from friend, co-worker, etc.: [10] ________

❑ Other: [11] ________

What I liked most about this book: ________

What I would change, add, delete, etc., in future editions of this book: ________

Other comments: ________

Number of computer books I purchase in a year: ❑ 1 [12] ❑ 2-5 [13] ❑ 6-10 [14] ❑ More than 10 [15]

I would characterize my computer skills as: ❑ Beginner [16] ❑ Intermediate [17] ❑ Advanced [18] ❑ Professional [19]

I use ❑ DOS [20] ❑ Windows [21] ❑ OS/2 [22] ❑ Unix [23] ❑ Macintosh [24] ❑ Other: [25] ________ (please specify)

I would be interested in new books on the following subjects:
(please check all that apply, and use the spaces provided to identify specific software)

❑ Word processing: [26] ________

❑ Spreadsheets: [27] ________

❑ Data bases: [28] ________

❑ Desktop publishing: [29] ________

❑ File Utilities: [30] ________

❑ Money management: [31] ________

❑ Networking: [32] ________

❑ Programming languages: [33] ________

❑ Other: [34] ________

I use a PC at (please check all that apply): ❑ home [35] ❑ work [36] ❑ school [37] ❑ other: [38] ________

The disks I prefer to use are ❑ 5.25 [39] ❑ 3.5 [40] ❑ other: [41] ________

I have a CD ROM: ❑ yes [42] ❑ no [43]

I plan to buy or upgrade computer hardware this year: ❑ yes [44] ❑ no [45]

I plan to buy or upgrade computer software this year: ❑ yes [46] ❑ no [47]

Name: ________ Business title: [48] ________ Type of Business: [49] ________

Address (❑ home [50] ❑ work [51]/Company name: ________)

Street/Suite# ________

City [52]/State [53]/Zipcode [54]: ________ Country [55] ________

❑ **I liked this book!** You may quote me by name in future IDG Books Worldwide promotional materials.

My daytime phone number is ________

IDG BOOKS®
THE WORLD OF COMPUTER KNOWLEDGE

❑ YES!

Please keep me informed about IDG's World of Computer Knowledge. Send me the latest IDG Books catalog.

SECRETS™

...FOR DUMMIES™ COMPUTER BOOK SERIES FROM IDG

MACWORLD MW AUTHORIZED EDITION

AUTHORIZED PC WORLD EDITION

NO POSTAGE NECESSARY IF MAILED IN THE UNITED STATES

BUSINESS REPLY MAIL

FIRST CLASS MAIL PERMIT NO. 2605 FOSTER CITY, CALIFORNIA

IDG Books Worldwide
919 E Hillsdale Blvd, STE 400
Foster City, CA 94404-9691